AMERICA: CHANGING TIMES

GENERAL EDITOR
Charles M. Dollar

CONTRIBUTORS
Joan Rezner Gundersen
Ronald N. Satz
H. Viscount Nelson, Jr.
Gary Reichard

Assistant Editor
Reid A. Holland

Writers
Edmund White
John Hammond Moore

John Wiley & Sons

New York
Chichester
Brisbane
Toronto

AMERICA: CHANGING TIMES

Photo Research: Marjorie Graham
Rosemary Eakins, Research Reports
Photo Editor: Stella Kupferberg

This book designed by Joseph Gillians
Cover illustration by Joseph Gillians
Maps by John V. Morris
Production supervised by Janet Sessa

Library of Congress Cataloging in Publication Data:

Main entry under title:
America, changing times.

Includes index.
1. United States—History. I. Gundersen, Joan R.
II. Dollar, Charles M. III. Holland, Reid A.
E178.1.A489 973 78-12242

ISBN 0-471-05029-6
ISBN 0-471-21767-0 pbk. (v. 1)
ISBN 0-471-04769-4 pbk. (v. 2)

Printed in the United States of America

10 9 8 7 6 5 4 3

Note: *America: Changing Times* is available in a one-volume clothbound edition and in a two-volume paperbound edition. The contents of both editions are the same with the exception of separate indexes. Volume One of the two-volume edition ends with Chapter 15, "Restoring the Union," providing coverage up to 1877. This same chapter is repeated as the first chapter in Volume Two, providing coverage beginning at 1865. The *Instructor's Manual* that accompanies the one-volume edition applies equally to the two-volume edition.

Publisher's Foreword

Any new text should be both different from and better than its predecessors in the same field. This was the challenge faced in preparing *America: Changing Times,* a challenge quickly translated into very specific goals: a readable, exciting presentation using the latest research to reveal history as the interpretation of movements of people and issues through time, a fully developed story brimming with social, cultural, economic, and political aspects of America's rich past, and, perhaps most important of all, proof in words and pictures that our nation's development has been affected in a very profound way by *all* of its people.

This undertaking, like most, began as an idea. At a meeting of historians held in Denver, Colorado, early in 1974, I sought out Charles Dollar, a quantitative historian then teaching at Oklahoma State University. I wanted his views on how to create a better and different basic American history text and his help in determining the preferences of other professors. Dollar, with the assistance of Reid Holland, solicited ideas from over 300 classroom instructors. This survey, refined and adapted, produced our working model. At that point, Dollar became General Editor with Holland as his Assistant Editor.

To be certain that this text would meet the day-to-day needs of students, we began an extensive search for four very unique people: specialists in various realms of American history with close classroom ties who had publishing experience of their own and who gave their students (and thus could give others) an effective blend of social, cultural, economic, and political history. In short, we sought historians who had a firm grasp of their subject, utilized the most effective teaching techniques, and clearly understood student needs. Our specialists and their fields of interest are: Joan Gundersen, colonial and eighteenth century America and the history of women; Ronald Satz, nineteenth century America and Indian history; H. V. (Berky) Nelson, Jr., late nineteenth and twentieth century America and Afro-American history; and Gary Reichard, modern America and politics.

These four very able individuals were assisted by two professional writers, Edmund White and John Hammond Moore, who translated their ideas and desires into meaningful prose; yet, though a team effort throughout of editors, writers, and reviewers, this text is essentially the creation of classroom instructors who know college and university life firsthand and are intimately involved in teaching and interpreting America's past to undergraduate students. They have been committed to preparing a text designed to help both students and teachers understand the complexity, diversity, continuity, and change that has affected our nation and *all* of its people. That commitment is evident on every page that follows.

Wayne Anderson, Editor
John Wiley & Sons, Publishers

Chapter Opening Picture Credits

Chapter 1	Library of Congress.
Chapter 2	Courtesy Essex Institute, Salem, Mass.
Chapter 3	New York State Historical Association, Cooperstown.
Chapter 4	New York Public Library Prints Division.
Chapter 5	Abby Aldrich Rockefeller Folk Art Center, Wiliamsburg, Virginia.
Chapter 6	Library of Congress.
Chapter 7	Courtesy New York Historical Society, New York.
Chapter 8	Worcester Art Museum, Worcester, Massachusetts.
Chapter 9	Philbrook Art Center, Tulsa, Oklahoma.
Chapter 10	Library of Congress.
Chapter 11	The St. Louis Art Museum.
Chapter 12	Library of Congress.
Chapter 13	Courtesy New York Historical Society, New York.
Chapter 14	Library of Congress.
Chapter 15	Library of Congress.
Chapter 16	Smithsonian Institution.
Chapter 17	George Eastman House International Museum of Photography.
Chapter 18	Library of Congress.
Chapter 19	Library of Congress.
Chapter 20	Library of Congress.
Chapter 21	Culver Pictures.
Chapter 22	National Archives.
Chapter 23	Brown Brothers.
Chapter 24	Oliver B. James Collection of American Art, University Art Collection, Arizona State University, Tempe.
Chapter 25	Bettmann Archive.
Chapter 26	U.S. Coast Guard Photo.
Chapter 27	Joe Clark.
Chapter 28	J. P. Laffont/Sygma.
Chapter 29	Yves Billy/Sygma.
Chapter 30	Sygma.

Preface

America: Changing Times, a blend of political and economic history, foreign and domestic affairs, and new insights into America's social development, reflects the concerns our nation faces as it begins its third century. Throughout the book you will read about ethnic minorities and women as well as about long-established institutions and processes: the family, business, technology, urbanization, and globalization. As the title indicates, the emphasis is on change and continuity—on how past, present, and future generations contend with those forces that give American life its zest and vitality. Where appropriate, the subject is treated both chronologically and topically, with a synoptic timeline providing a chronological framework at the beginning of each chapter.

Each chapter, which is a distinct unit but also a unifying part in a total fabric, contains several biographical sketches to highlight the personal facets of daily life often obscured by the broad sweep of history. Each chapter ends with a brief essay. Offering a wide range of subject matter—from civil rights and political dissent to publishing and health care—each essay is firmly rooted within a chapter. But it also moves through time to develop the full scope of the subject under scrutiny and, at the same time, to relate it to other eras and to other chapters. Each chapter includes a list of selected readings, arranged under topical headings, to offer easy access to some of the best booklength studies available. Color inserts, organized thematically, provide additional understanding of key events and issues that have shaped America's past and present and that are determining its future.

America: Changing Times is about people—great and small, haves and have-nots, heroes and villains, movers and moved, shakers and shaken. Issues, ideas, confrontations, and disputes that changed the way our forefathers lived and worked and created our own late twentieth-century milieu are also in these pages, but wherever possible—from the first meeting between Europeans and Indians to the landings on the moon—all of these aspects are treated as parts of the human situation.

Every effort has been made to insure that this book reflects the most recent historical scholarship. This does not mean that American history, and especially this book, is a finished subject in which all questions have been answered and the last word written. Indeed, the diversity of interpretations of historians mentioned in these pages underscores this.

America: Changing Times is the result of a collaborative effort in which each of the four contributors prepared chapter material in which he or she is a specialist. Joan Gundersen contributed the material for Chapters 1 through 7; Ronald Satz for Chapters 8 through 15; H. V. Nelson, Jr., for Chapters 16 through 22; and Gary Reichard for Chapters 23 through 30. And, each contributor exchanged ideas and concepts for every chapter.

In addition to the contributors and writers, many other people helped to produce this book. John Wiley's History Editor, Wayne Anderson, was a continual source of encouragement at every point and invariably reduced seemingly insurmountable obstacles to mere difficulties. Stella Kupferberg, Senior Photo Editor at John Wiley, assembled an outstanding collection of photographs and illustrations as well as the color folios.

Special thanks must go to our outside readers: Allen

Yarnell of the University of California at Los Angeles has helped us from the inception of this project, pointing out problems and suggesting refinements at every stage of development. James Henderson of Oklahoma State University, Mary Young of the University of Rochester, and Morton Keller of Brandeis University provided insightful comments and advice on the material covering their respective fields of specialization. We further benefitted from the opinions of Joan Huffman (Macon Junior College), Robert Becker (Louisiana State University), and Magne Olson (Chicago State University) who reviewed the first volume and from the opinions of William Reynolds (Mercer County Community College), John Monfross (American River College), and Larry Hill (Texas A&M University) who reviewed the second.

To my wife, Martha, a special note of acknowledgment is due. She spent long hours typing the manuscript several times and deciphering numerous handwritten comments. For these and other reasons, I could not have completed my part of this project without her help.

This collaborative effort has benefitted from the contributions of many people, but I have made the judgments on its final form and content.

Charles M. Dollar
General Editor

JOAN REZNER GUNDERSEN grew up in the suburbs of Chicago. After graduating from Monmouth College, Illinois, she received an M.A. in history at the College of William and Mary in 1969. In 1972 she received a Ph.D. from the University of Notre Dame and has since completed postgraduate work at the Newberry Library. She has previously published in the fields of colonial and southern history and has taught at the University of Notre Dame, Indiana University-South Bend, and Vanderbilt University. She is currently an Assistant Professor of History at St. Olaf College in Minnesota.

RONALD N. SATZ, a native of Chicago, received an M.A. in history from Illinois State University in 1967 and a Ph.D. in history from the University of Maryland in 1972. He is the author of books and articles in the fields of Native American history and Indian-white relations. He has taught since 1971 at the University of Tennessee at Martin and is currently the Dean of Graduate Studies and Research.

H. VISCOUNT (BERKY) NELSON, JR. was born and reared in Oxford, Pennsylvania. After receiving his Ph.D. in history from the University of Pennsylvania in 1969, he taught at UCLA. Since 1971 he has taught at Dartmouth College specializing in Afro-American, urban, and social history. His previous publications have been in the fields of Afro-American and urban history.

GARY REICHARD grew up in Newark, Delaware, and was educated at the College of Wooster, Vanderbilt University, and received his Ph.D. in history from Cornell University in 1971. He has taught at the College of Wooster and, since 1971, at the Ohio State University, where he is presently Chairman of the History Department. He has published in the fields of recent American history and American political history.

CHARLES M. DOLLAR grew up in Memphis, Tennessee. He completed graduate work at the University of Kentucky, receiving a Ph.D. in history in 1966. He has previously published in the fields of quantitative history and the history of the South. After teaching several years at Oklahoma State University, he is now the Director, Machine Readable Archives Division, National Archives, Washington, D.C.

REID A. HOLLAND was born in Fort Bragg, North Carolina. He completed his graduate work at Oklahoma State University, receiving a Ph.D. in history in 1972. His previous publications are in the fields of Native American history and instructional techniques in the teaching of history. He has taught at Oklahoma State University, Oklahoma City Junior College, College IV, and is currently Assistant Dean, College IV, Grand Valley State Colleges in Allendale, Michigan.

EDMUND WHITE was born in Cincinnati, Ohio, and educated at the University of Michigan. From 1962–1970 he was a staff writer for Time-Life Books. Subsequently he worked as an editor for *Saturday Review* and *Horizon.* In 1976–1977 he taught writing at Yale University and now teaches writing at Johns Hopkins University. He is the author of two novels, *Forgetting Elena* and *Nocturnes For The King of Naples,* and the coauthor of an anthropological study, *The First Men.* He resides in New York City.

JOHN HAMMOND MOORE received his Ph.D. in history from the University of Virginia in 1961. As reporter, editor, writer, and researcher, he has over ten years of varied experience in publishing and journalism, and as a history teacher, ten years of classroom experience. In addition to feature writing and news experience, he has edited and prepared for publication nine books and over sixty articles in various magazines and journals. His latest books are: *Albemarle: Jefferson's County, 1727–1976* (1976), which received the 1977 "Award of Merit" from the Association of State and Local History, *Australians in America, 1876–1976* (1977), and *The Faustball Tunnel: German POWs in America and Their Great Escape* (1978). He resides in Washington, D.C.

List of Maps

Contents

18 Response to the Urban-Industrial Order 620

19 The Emergence of Modern Politics 654

20 Our American Empire Takes Shape 688

21 Progressivism at Home 726

22 Progressivism Abroad 764

23 War and Peace 798

Chapter 1

Americans and European Newcomers

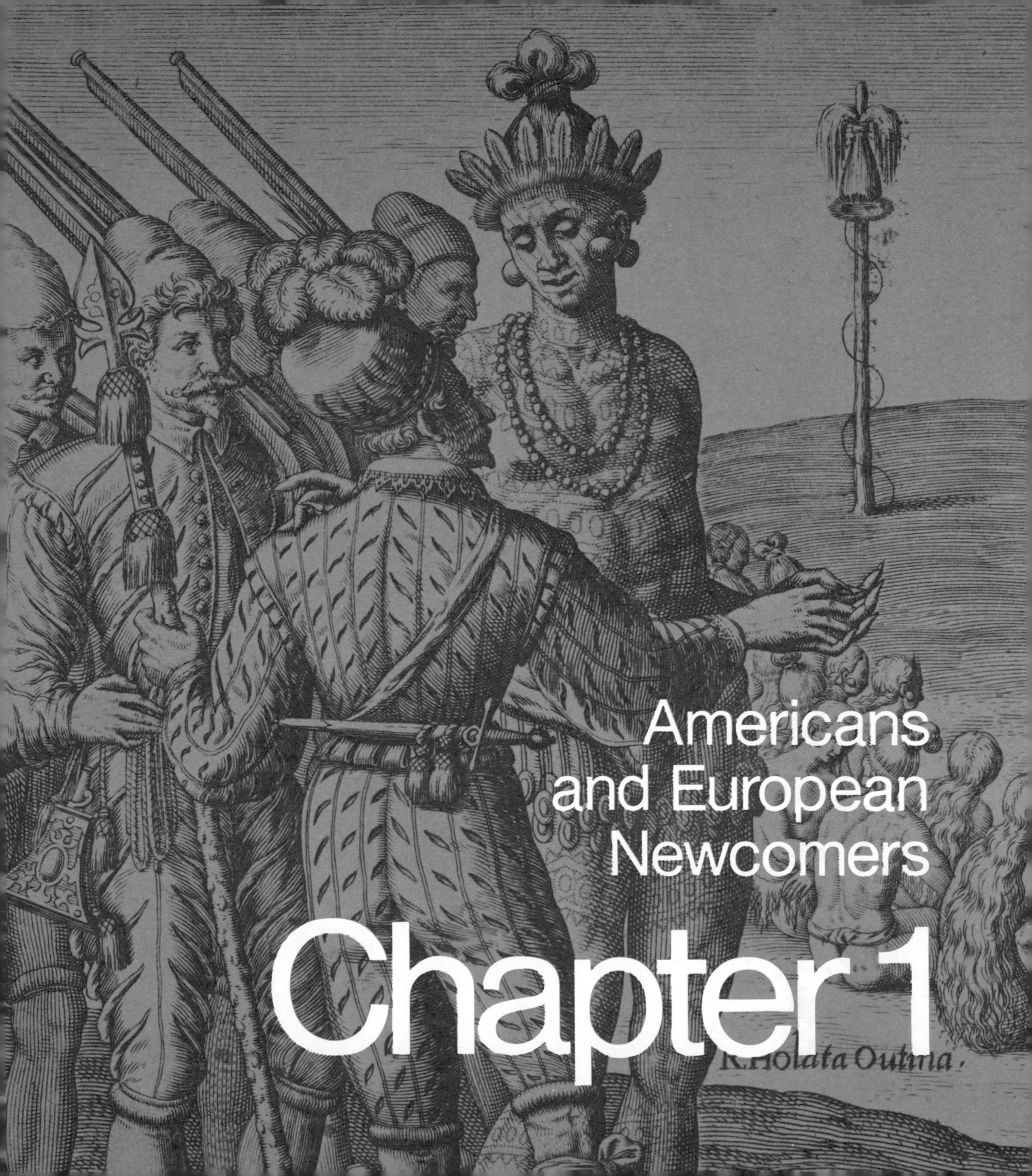

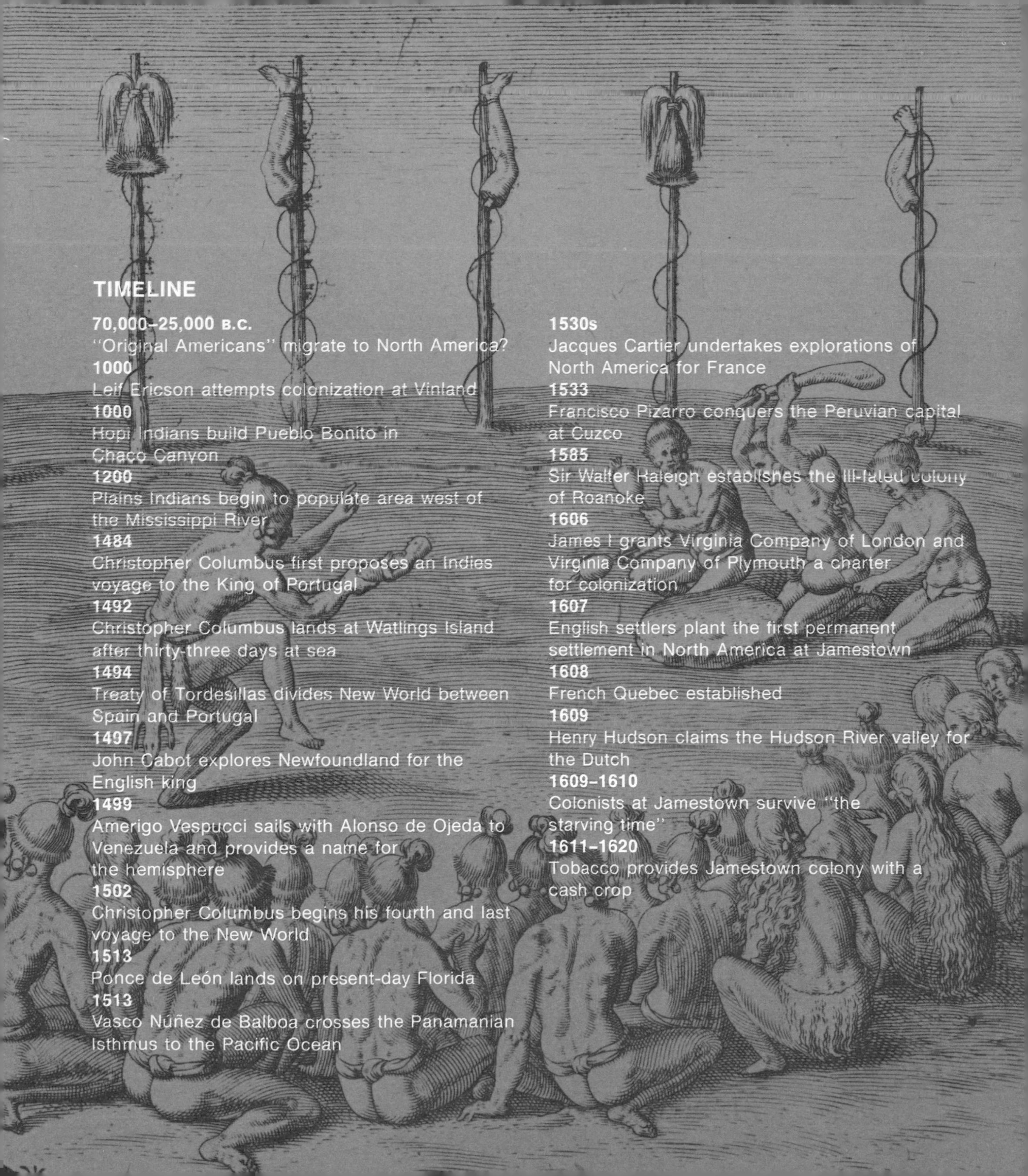

TIMELINE

70,000–25,000 B.C.
"Original Americans" migrate to North America?

1000
Leif Ericson attempts colonization at Vinland

1000
Hopi Indians build Pueblo Bonito in Chaco Canyon

1200
Plains Indians begin to populate area west of the Mississippi River

1484
Christopher Columbus first proposes an Indies voyage to the King of Portugal

1492
Christopher Columbus lands at Watlings Island after thirty-three days at sea

1494
Treaty of Tordesillas divides New World between Spain and Portugal

1497
John Cabot explores Newfoundland for the English king

1499
Amerigo Vespucci sails with Alonso de Ojeda to Venezuela and provides a name for the hemisphere

1502
Christopher Columbus begins his fourth and last voyage to the New World

1513
Ponce de León lands on present-day Florida

1513
Vasco Núñez de Balboa crosses the Panamanian Isthmus to the Pacific Ocean

1530s
Jacques Cartier undertakes explorations of North America for France

1533
Francisco Pizarro conquers the Peruvian capital at Cuzco

1585
Sir Walter Raleigh establishes the ill-fated colony of Roanoke

1606
James I grants Virginia Company of London and Virginia Company of Plymouth a charter for colonization

1607
English settlers plant the first permanent settlement in North America at Jamestown

1608
French Quebec established

1609
Henry Hudson claims the Hudson River valley for the Dutch

1609–1610
Colonists at Jamestown survive "the starving time"

1611–1620
Tobacco provides Jamestown colony with a cash crop

CHAPTER OUTLINE

When a sailor, Rodrigo de Triana, spied land at 2:00 A.M. on October 12, 1492, the curtain went up on an astounding human drama. Triana, the lookout on one of Columbus's three ships, thought (as did his captain) that he was about to see the fabled riches of Asia. He had no way of knowing that the world he was entering was far stranger and less comprehensible than anything Marco Polo had seen on his extensive travels.

Columbus, who thought he had found an island just south of Japan, was in fact in the Bahamas, on a small island that he christened San Salvador, that the local inhabitants called Guanahani, and that the British later renamed Watlings Island. As soon as Columbus encountered the inhabitants, he was struck by their physical beauty, generosity, and peaceful ways. As he wrote, "They invite you to share anything that they possess, and show as much love as if their hearts went into it." Their nudity, kindliness, and lack of money led Columbus to think they were in the state of innocence that Adam and Eve enjoyed before the expulsion from Paradise.

These naive impressions of the first Americans encountered by Columbus and his men have been perpetuated in one form or another over the centuries, and a figure labeled "the Indian" has emerged in white American folklore. Depending upon whether one feels sympathetic or antagonistic toward "the Indian," he is either good—a being in tune with nature, democratic, proud, and ecologically minded—or he is bad—a creature warlike when not lazy, set against change and "betterment," and instinctively cruel. *The* Indian never existed, of course. What did exist were a range of cultures as varied as those in Europe, if not more so, and a diversity of language groups as different from one another as Finnish is from Spanish. The Indians of Mexico and Peru lived in empires as hierarchical as that of ancient Egypt. The Natchez and Pueblo Indians of North America may well be related to the highly developed corn-growing empires of Mexico. Other North American Indians were seminomadic hunters, living on a simple level of technology but extraordinarily knowledgeable about the forests they inhabited and the game they pursued. Some moved in small bands with virtually no leadership; others formed large confederacies with well-defined borders. Some figured descent through mothers; others through fathers. Some were shockingly sadistic toward prisoners taken in battle; others never waged war. In short, the differences among them were far greater than the similarities.

This amazing variety of cultures was not perceived by Europeans in their first contact with the New World. It became evident only after prolonged exploration and increasing familiarity. Nevertheless, the differences among the Indians created widely divergent responses to the first white settlers—who themselves, of course, belonged to different nationalities and held different values.

2 Americans and European Newcomers

Origins of the Indians

It is safe to say that the Indians preceded the Europeans to the Americas by thousands of years—but their exact origins and the time of their various migrations remain shrouded in mystery. Today, militant Indians insist their ancestors never immigrated to the New World at all but always lived here. However appealing this theory may be in strengthening the claims long advanced by Indians that they are the only true "natives" of the New World, there is little evidence to support it. True, recent excavations have unearthed Indian remains dating from a much earlier period than anyone had previously thought possible. All the same, no human traces in the New World are so old as those found in Java, India, and Africa.

The biological makeup of the first Americans indicates that they inhabited this hemisphere long enough to develop distinctive genetic characteristics. For instance, few American Indians have such traits as red-green color blindness, and few become bald or have gray hair. Even their fingerprints conform to a distinctive pattern (arches rather than whorls). Although these traits may not sound significant if taken singly, they are impressive enough in combination to lead some anthropologists to classify the Indians as a separate race.

When the first Indians arrived in the Americas is not known. Geologically the conditions for overland travel from Asia to Alaska seem to have been favorable about 70,000 years ago. Rough estimates obtained from carbon-14 dating of wood artifacts buried with human remains suggest a period perhaps only about one-third as long, some 25,000 years at the most.

In any case, the Indians probably came to the New World across a land bridge that during the last Ice Age connected the Chukchi Peninsula of Siberia with the Seward Peninsula of Alaska. Today only twenty-three miles of water separate the tip of Siberia from Big Diomede Island, and from there it is only another twenty-five miles to the tip of Alaska. During the Ice Age, much of the world's water supply was locked up in great masses of ice, which lowered the level of the ocean considerably and exposed land connecting Asia and North America. If the sea level dropped by as much as 300 feet—as some geologists suggest did happen—the land bridge would have been 1,000 miles wide, certainly an adequate bridge for a substantial migration.

Equally controversial is the question of how many Indians were in the Americas in 1492. One of the traditional European rationalizations for wresting these two continents from the Indians is that the hemisphere was sparsely populated. This rather specious line of reasoning holds that if the Indians were not fully exploiting the land and resources of the New World, then Europeans had an open invitation, even an obligation to do so. Exact population figures can never be established for certain since neither the Indians before Columbus nor the Europeans afterwards took an accurate census. In the Caribbean, contact with the first Spanish explorers decimated whole islands of their Indian populations. The Spanish impressed the Indians into work gangs and killed thousands through exhaustion and privation. Far more devastating was the effect of European diseases upon Indians who had never been exposed to them and therefore had never built up immunities against them. In Mexico alone, smallpox and other unidentified diseases caused an estimated two million deaths. The first Indian tribes Columbus encountered were soon extinct. The native population of Haiti, for example, declined from about 200,000 in 1492 to an estimated 30,000 in 1514.

For many years historians thought the pre-Columbian population of the Western hemisphere was perhaps eight to fourteen million, only one million of these individuals living in North America. This estimate was obtained by starting with the population of Indians in this century, calculating backwards to 1492, and taking into account the effects of exploitation and disease. More recent interpretations boost this total from 50 to 100 million and set the figure for North American at perhaps ten to thirteen million. These higher figures are inferred from estimates of thirty million Indians in Mexico at the time of the Spanish conquest. There is obviously no way to reconcile these different sets of statistics nor to arrive at more reliable ones. What is not questioned is that European diseases, especially smallpox and measles, drastically reduced the number of Indians in the Americas.

The Americans before Columbus

From the beginning, Europeans were curious about the origins of the Americans. Were they one of the lost tribes of Israel? Or were they people who had escaped from the mythical island of Atlantis? Were they savages in need of the moral guidance of Christianity? Or were they innocents closer to an original state of purity than any European could hope to be?

Almost all of these speculations were irrelevant, culture-bound, and shrouded in arrogance and ignorance. As we have indicated, the civilization of the American Indians was even more diversified than that found in Europe. Some 2,200 languages were spoken in North and South America. From the Eskimo in Alaska to the Alacaluf and the Yahgan at Cape Horn, virtually every kind of social organization and level of technological expertise was represented.

South and Central American Indians

Indian cultures ranged from highly sophisticated agricultural societies to smaller, more vulnerable tribes of seminomadic hunters and gatherers. In Mexico, the highly evolved civilization that Hernando Cortés (1485-1547) encountered was the Aztec. The Aztecs had established their empire on the ruins of an older civilization, the Toltecs, who in turn had subdued the Mayan empire.

Courtesy of the American Museum of Natural History.

This Indian painting shows Cortez marching to Mexico City. The Aztecs first thought the Spaniards were Gods. The eagle on the cactus was the Aztec national symbol.

Perhaps the Mayans were the most remarkable of these societies. More than 800 sites of Mayan cities and towns have been discovered in the Yucatan Peninsula and in Guatemala. They worked out a solar calendar more accurate than that in use in Europe until the eighteenth century. Between A.D. 250 and 600, the Mayan capital of Teotihuacán contained a population of about 100,000 people who lived in apartment-like buildings covering some eight square miles. Society was divided into classes of artisans and ruled by administrators and priests who lived in sumptuous palaces. Although the Aztecs never rose to such heights of sophistication, they did impress the Spanish with their well-defined class structure, hieroglyphics, and carefully organized economy.

The Incas of Peru lacked a written language, but in every other way their empire rivaled the world's most advanced civilizations. They ruled a territory some 3,000 miles long and as vast as the states that now line our Atlantic seacoast, an area tied together by a well-maintained road system and populated by sixteen million inhabitants who used a system of arithmetic based on units of tens. Like the society of the ancient Egyptians, that of the Incas was divided into a rigid caste system; only members of the nobility could act as priests in the official cult of the sun. Peasants were confined to working the fields, which were laid out and administered with dictatorial precision.

North American Indians

North of Mexico, some 600 different tribes lived on the deserts and plains and in the forests and mountains. Although each developed in its own way and at its own pace, often making unique adjustments to environmental factors, similarities also existed since all possessed a common ancestry.

Northeastern Woodland Indians The only North American Indians politically organized to a degree even remotely resembling that of the Aztec and Inca empires belonged to the Iroquois Confederacy in the northeastern section of what is today the United States. This league, probably established in the early sixteenth century, included five tribes (Mohawk, Cayuga, Onondaga, Oneida, and Seneca); in 1715 a sixth tribe, the Tuscarora joined.

Unlike the Indians pictured so often in novels and films, the Iroquois tribes were sedentary and agricultural. Farming was performed exclusively by women, the three

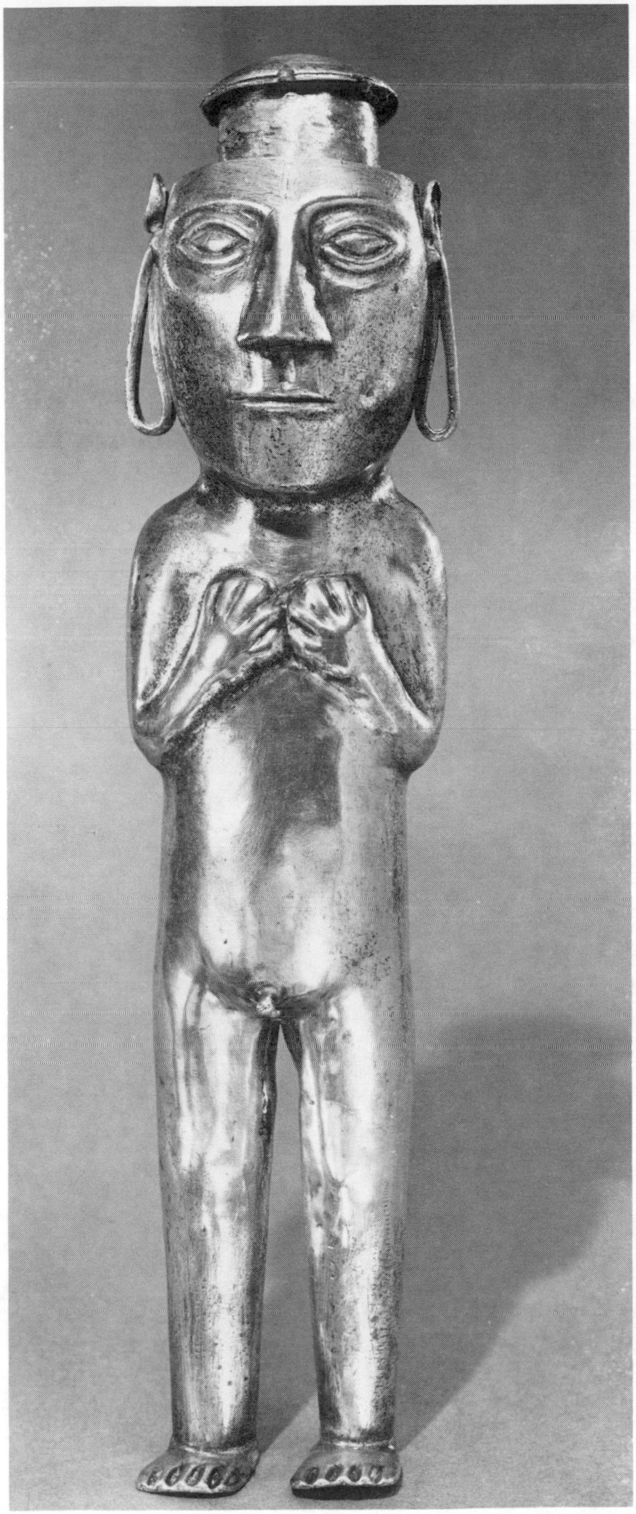

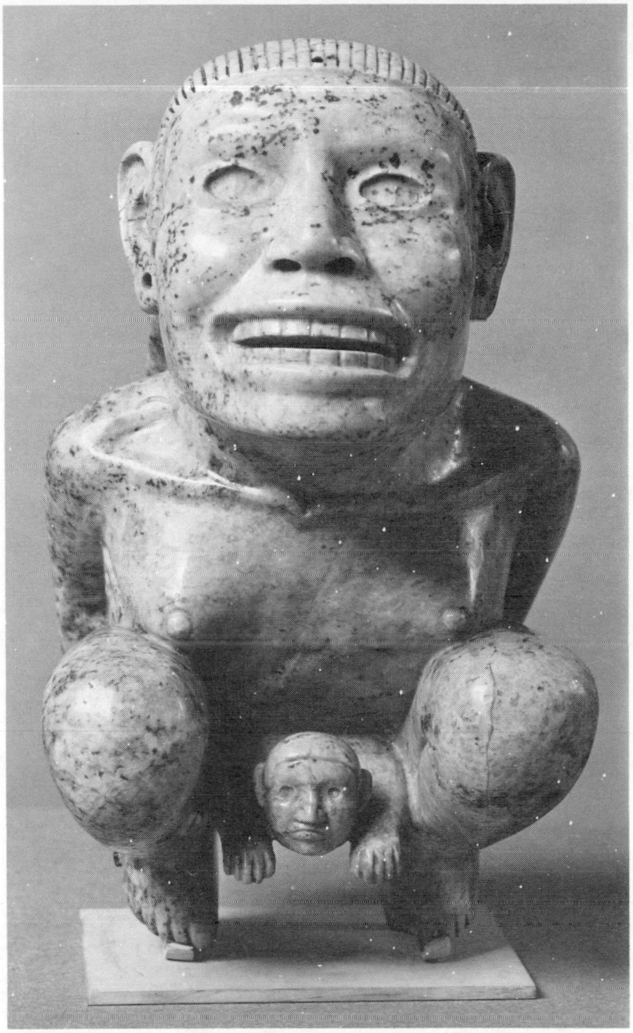

Dumbarton Oaks, Washington, D.C.

Two examples of pre-Columbian art. An Inca artisan hammered in silver the figure of the standing man. The Aztec statue shows a woman in childbirth. Note the highly stylized features on both figures.

most important crops being corn, beans, and squash. The men helped to clear the land but spent most of their time waging war, hunting, and traveling. In winter they hunted deer, beaver, and small game with bows and arrows; in the summer they made long trips in their canoes in order to trade excess corn to other tribes for tobacco and other commodities. The Iroquois lived in villages protected by stockades of upright logs driven into the ground. Each village included as many as fifty huts, some of which were 100 feet long and sheltered eight to ten families.

Of all the North American Indians that the Europeans encountered, the Iroquois had the most orderly government, complete with rules determining property inheritance (the women owned the fields), marriage, burial, and even the playing of games (dice and lacrosse were favored pastimes). Because the Iroquois were members of a league, strong by virtue of their numbers, and because they had a developed economy based on farming, hunting, fishing, and trade, they were the most potent force the first white settlers had to deal with. Indeed, the Iroquois cleverly played off the French against the English for more than 100 years, and until the time of the American Revolution, they remained an important and sometimes even a decisive element in the balance of power in colonial America.

Surrounding the Iroquois nation were the Algonkian tribes from whose languages we have derived the names of such New England states as Massachusetts and Connecticut. These northern hunters, who had little organized leadership, moved in small bands during the winter, pursuing moose, caribou, small game, and birds as well as deer and beaver. In the summers most of the Algonkian Indians raised corn and fished. Before the coming of the white man, the seacoast was well stocked with lobsters, clams, and even whales and seals. They lived in wigwams, which were constructed out of a circle of saplings whose tops were bent and tied together in order to form arches. Over this basic frame work (usually no more than six slender poles) woven mats or sheets of

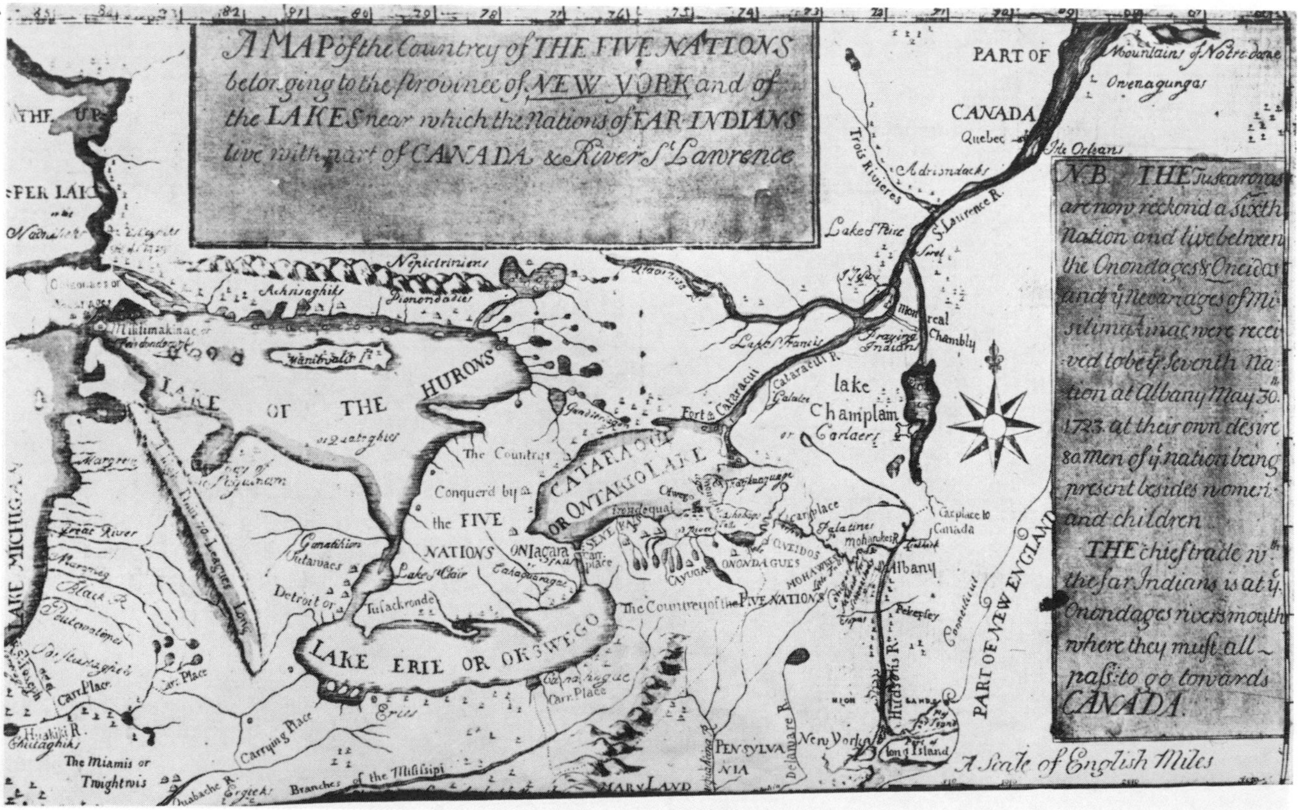

By the time this map of the Iroquois country was drawn in 1739, white settlement extended north along the Hudson but had hardly penetrated the Iroquois heartland despite its nearness to both English and French settlements.

Courtesy of the New York Historical Society.

birch bark were placed. One of the northernmost tribes, the Penobscot, built tipis, or conical bark shelters stretched over an inner framework of poles and reinforced by an outer, matching set of poles.

Indians who spoke one or another of the Algonkian languages lived not only in the Northeast but also further south along the Atlantic seaboard. One of the Algonkian tribes, the Powhatan of Virginia, was the first to contend with permanent English settlements.

Plains and Mississippi Woodland Indians Although Algonkian Indians could also be found in the Midwest around the Great Lakes and along the Mississippi Valley, the Midwest was a great melting pot of many tribes—the Ottawa, the Ojibwa, the Menomini, the Winnebago, and countless others. Beyond the Mississippi were the Plains Indians. Until 1600 this vast area was sparsely populated by Indians who raised corn. Only after 1600 did enough Indians have horses—animals captured from wild herds or confiscated from Spanish settlements—so that a new nonagricultural way of life could develop. A heterogeneous mixture of Indian tribes from all parts of North America poured into the plains beyond the Mississippi and, mounted on mustangs, hunted herds of buffalo. Among the many tribes who became horseborne hunters of the buffalo were the Blackfoot, Arapaho, Cheyenne, Crow, Comanche, and Sioux. These fierce tribes played a major role in the story of white settlement of the West, especially after the Civil War. At the time of Columbus, however, their distinctive lifestyle, since it depended on the horse, had not evolved.

The year before this sketch of an Indian was made in Virginia in 1645, the colony there won the last major war against native tribes. Europeans, such as this artist, saw the Indian as a noble savage, however, not a foe.

Southeastern Indians The southeastern Indians, unlike many of those to the north, did not ordinarily don feather headdresses. Rather, the men of the Southeast wore nothing but loin cloths in the summer and cloaks in the winter; they pulled out with tweezers the hair on one side of their heads and covered their bodies with elaborate tattoos, signifying success in warfare. The women wore simple deerskin skirts and occasionally shell necklaces.

Until white settlers began to disinherit the Indians of this region, numerous tribes, all pursuing a sedentary and rather luxurious way of life, inhabited the Southeast. The Creek Indians, whose name derived from the fact that they were found along creekbeds by Indian traders, lived in inland Georgia and Alabama. One subdivision of the Creek, called the Seminole, inhabited the swamps of Florida where they hunted and practiced agriculture. The Chickasaw, located along the Mississippi River, were related linguistically to the Creek, as were the Choctaw and the Natchez.

One of the highly organized tribes flourishing at the time of Columbus, the Natchez, who lived in what is now the state of Mississippi, had little in common with other North American tribes. They resembled much more closely the settled, hierarchical societies of Central and South America. For instance, the Natchez had a well-defined social structure composed of four different classes. Their pottery and engravings suggest techniques and motifs derived from Mexico. Their ruler, known as the Sun, was an absolute monarch treated as though he were a god—at the time of his death his entire retinue and wife were killed and buried with him. The Natchez, who probably were the last survivors of a Moundbuilders culture, developed skill in building large mounds: on one, they would erect a temple to enshrine an eternal fire; on another nearby, they would construct the residence of their Sun. The Natchez religion had a "heaven" in which brave warriors feasted and were honored with continual festivals, dances, and obliging women. By contrast, "hell" was a place that, according to an early French observer, was "unfruitful and entirely covered with water." The damned "will not have any kind of corn, but will be exposed entirely naked to the sharp bites of mosquitoes . . . and have no nourishment but the flesh of crocodiles, spoiled fish and shell-fish."

At the time of first contact with whites, the Cherokee Indians claimed as their homeland the beautiful mountain areas of the Appalachians from present-day West Virginia to Georgia. A tribe apparently driven southward sometime before Columbus arrived in the New World, they represented a blend of Iroquois and southern Indian cultures. The Cherokee had well-established villages and built substantial log or stick dwellings; the largest, a seven-sided structure used for meetings, stood near the center of each community. Farmers as well as hunters, their basic crops included corn, peas, squash, pumpkin, beans, and strawberries.

Their social and political customs resembled those of the Iroquois, although they had no strong alliances with other tribes and few formal relationships between one Cherokee settlement and another. Cherokee towns recognized no single chief; instead, they had two leaders: one for peace and another for war. Women took an important part in town and tribal matters, and war councils might include a group of women who advised on strategy. Although towns chose men as chiefs, family ties were reckoned through maternal lines. Membership in one of the seven clans of the tribe was determined by the mother's bloodline and an individual's membership in a clan provided a link of sorts to residents of other towns. Each clan usually had a "mother" town, although members actually lived in many other places.

The Cherokees had no formal law, but numerous customs. Clan retaliation or "law of blood" often settled problems created by crime. The only escape for an accused criminal was to reach a specially designated town earmarked as a place of refuge. Once a year at a ceremony of "new beginnings," old wrongs except murder were forgiven and tribal members could return home safely. The Cherokee religious year revolved around the planting seasons, but religious leaders did not play a significant role in community life.

Except for possibly brief contact in the early 1540s with the expedition led by Hernando de Soto and for occasional raids on Spanish territory, the Cherokees and whites saw very little of each other until 1700. In the eighteenth century this tribe, which became crucial to the British trade in deerskins, blocked settlement westward into the area now known as Tennessee. Then, new associations with whites brought continuous warfare (usually as an ally of Britain) and modification of customs and dress.

Southwestern Indians In vivid contrast to the warlike peoples of the Southeast were the peaceful agriculturalists of the Southwest: the Mogollon, Honokam, Pueblo, and Pima. These various tribes scarcely can be discussed as a unit, since their cultures differed in many important ways. Nevertheless, one characteristic of the region was its peacefulness. When forced to wage war, the southwestern Indians did so reluctantly and never rejoiced in victory. Similarly, there was little competition for positions of leadership.

The Hopi (a word that means "peaceable") are the most famous branch of a larger group known as the Pueblo Indians ("pueblo" being the Spanish word for "village"). They lived in terraced apartment-like houses that sometimes were many stories high; an entire village dwelled within a single building. Construction consisted of piling large stones on top of one another and then plastering them with a mixture of clay, straw, and water, which dried in the sun to resemble brick. Large underground rooms were reserved for religious ceremonies, and the whole complex was serviced by an intricate system of stone drains. Sometimes these buildings were fitted into large openings on high cliffs. One of the largest of these, Pueblo Bonito in Chaco Canyon, New Mexico was built about A.D. 1000. Containing about 800 rooms, it was five stories high and 700 feet long. Many of these impressive Pueblo villages were constructed long before Europeans began to settle in the Americas.

Unlike most of the other North American Indians, the Pueblos were primarily agriculturalists. While other tribes, such as the Algonkian group, supplemented

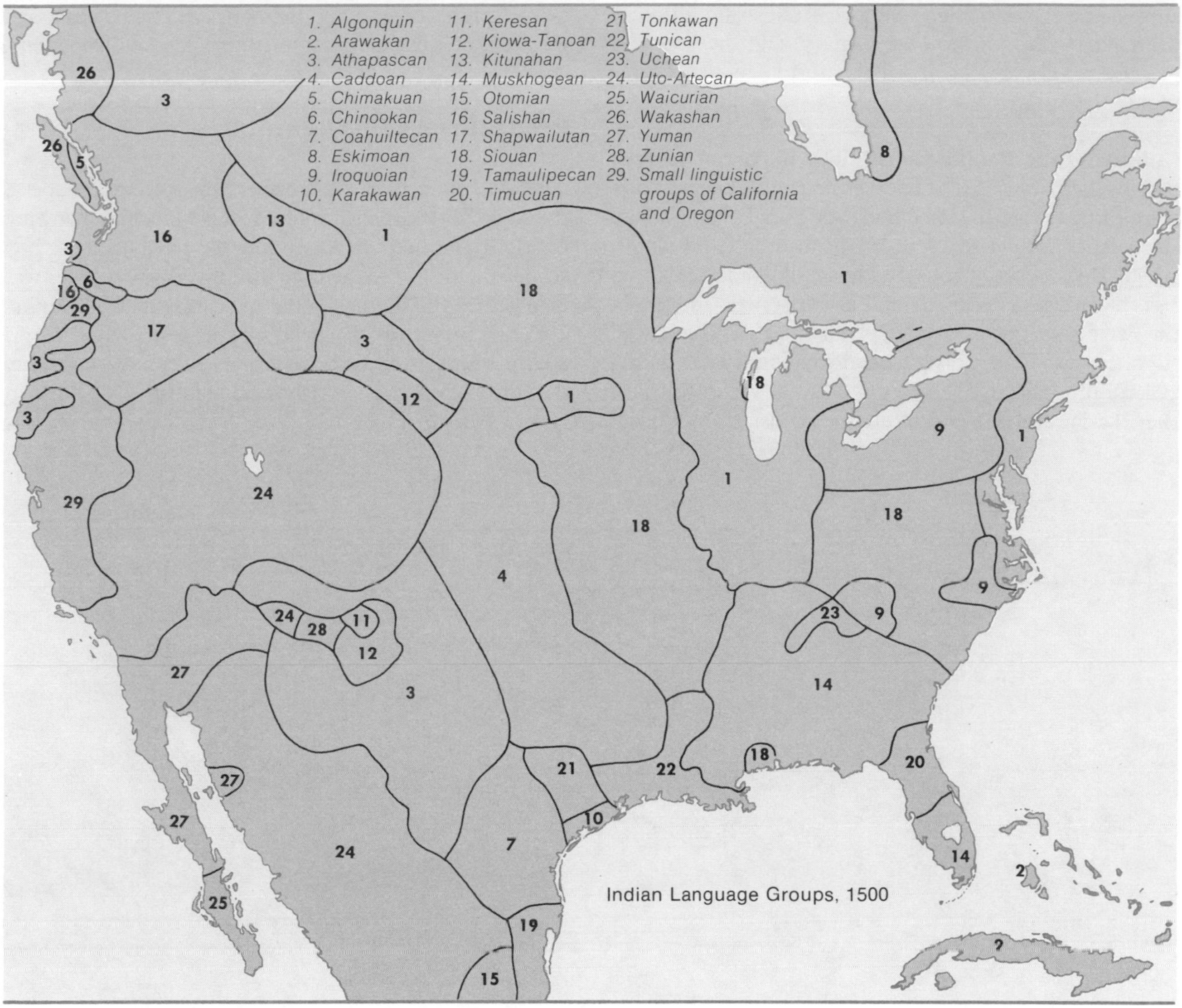

their food supply with farming done by women, the Pueblos of New Mexico and Arizona were farmers first, hunters second. Moreover, the men played an active part in the actual tilling of the fields. The Pueblo men also spun and wove cotton—a domestic activity that most other Indian males would have regarded as contemptible. Pueblo women were expert potters and their polished wares were finer than those produced elsewhere in North America. Since the Indians did not have pottery wheels, bowls were formed out of coils of clay, one laid upon the other; while the clay was still fresh, it was smoothed, painted with a black and white design, fired, and sometimes decorated with an additional layer of paint.

With few exceptions, the Pueblo were peace-loving, settled agrarians, and they created a distinctive culture strongly influenced by Mexican tribes. They were ingenious engineers, capable of executing large-scale irrigation systems and erecting impressive apartment-like complexes. As craftsmen, they were unusually gifted in producing pottery, turquoise jewelry, and the beautiful painted wooden masks and dolls used in religious ceremonies.

Indians of the Pacific Coast The Indians of California dwelled in small, stable settlements. Their homes were earth-covered, domed huts, and they lived on a bare subsistence diet of seeds, acorns, and other wild plants, which they supplemented with small game and even insects such as caterpillars and grasshoppers. Indians of the Pacific Northwest lived in plank houses and were well supplied with food by fishing and whaling. Just as Mexican culture influenced the art and life of the Pueblos, so the Siberian and Eskimo cultures had considerable impact on the tribes living along the northern Pacific coast and inspired their extraordinary carvings in wood and stone.

Predecessors of Columbus

Theories about pre-Columbian voyages from Europe to the New World are manifold. Most are fanciful, many are politically inspired, and very few are widely accepted by scholars. One of the earliest politically inspired tales was invented by the English in the sixteenth century. Seeking a pretext to buttress England's rights to the New World and to discredit Spain's, historians elaborated a fantasy that Prince Madoc, a Welshman, established a colony in North America in 1170. By 1580 Madoc's journey was

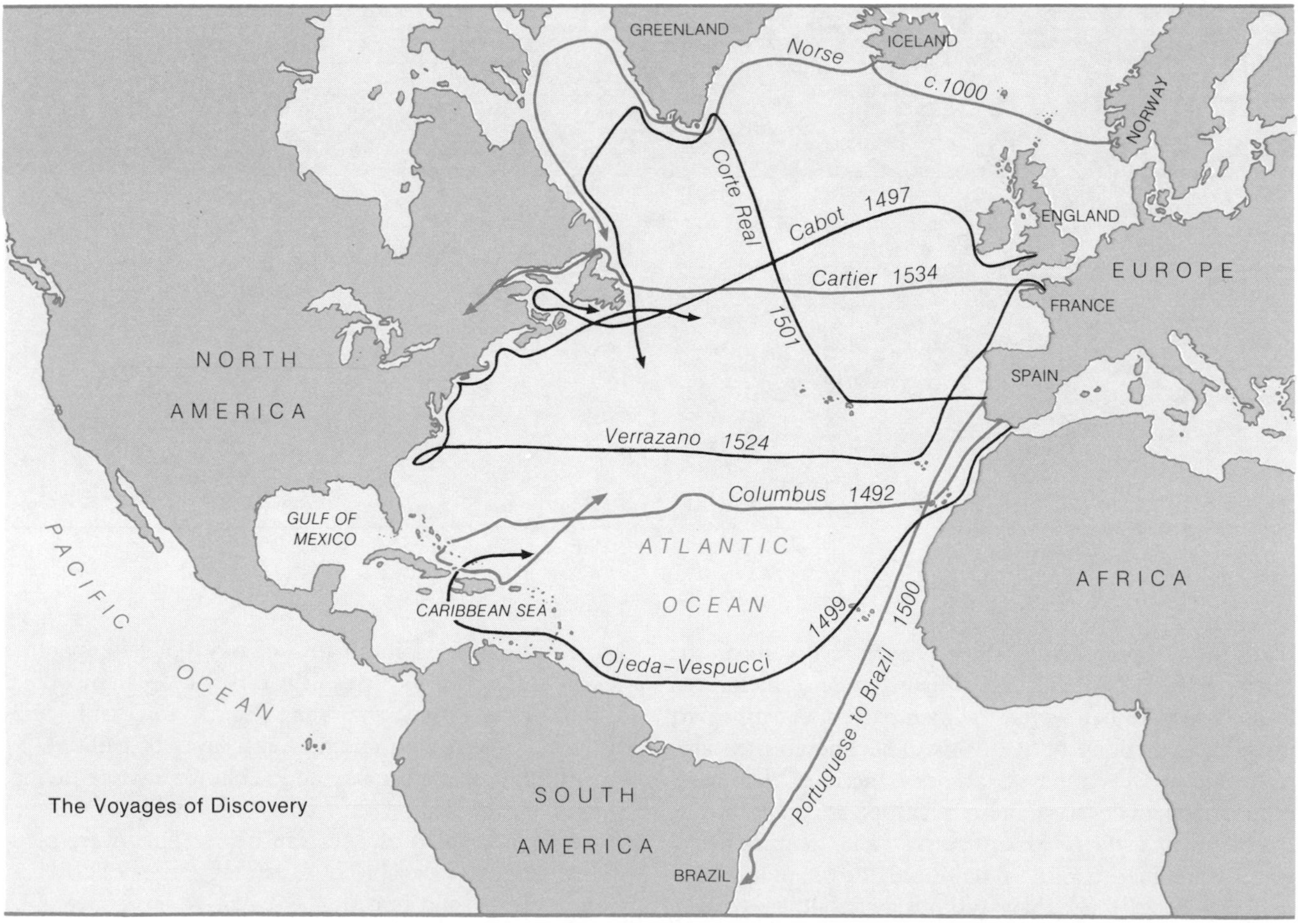

The Voyages of Discovery

pictured on English maps; in 1583 an account of his travels was printed; and, a hundred years later, a Welsh cleric claimed to have found an Indian tribe in the Carolinas who, since they were the descendants of the Indians who had learned the language from Prince Madoc, understood Welsh perfectly. Only in the eighteenth century was the legend of Welsh-speaking, blue-eyed Indians laid to rest.

The Norse Voyages

A Scottish prince, an Irish monk, a Phoenician king—all of these figures and more have been championed as the first Europeans to come to North America. The only pre-Columbian voyages that most scholars regard as having taken place are Norse expeditions, one of them led by Leif Ericson to Newfoundland about A.D. 1000. Between A.D. 800 and 1000, the Norse were leaving their homes in great numbers to settle in France, England, the Mediterranean, and Greenland. The gradual destruction of the Carolingian Empire in the West and the Roman Empire controlled by Byzantium in the East disrupted long-established trade routes. And these hardy northern seafarers set out in search of merchants, markets, land, and plunder. Those who colonized Greenland were outlaws from Iceland. On Greenland their small settlement survived for almost five hundred years but then died out mysteriously. During these centuries, however, the Norse maintained a trade with the European mainland based on New World products.

Surveys begun in 1960 by the Norwegian archaeologist, Helge Ingstad, unearthed several large dwellings in Newfoundland that resemble those built by the Norse in Greenland. In the ruins of the largest house, Ingstad found a late Viking-type spindle whorl used to spin thread from wool. He also discovered four boat sheds along the shorelines. The site, named after a nearby village called L'Anse aux Meadows, is on the northernmost tip of Newfoundland.

Ingstad is certain Newfoundland is the "Vinland" of two ancient sagas. These Icelandic sagas recount the tale of Leif the Lucky who was ordered by the King of Norway to Christianize Greenland. Leif set out to perform this task, but his ship was carried in a storm to a land where wild grapes grew, which he named Vinland or "Wine Land." One saga describes huts and a large house Leif built. After spending one winter in Vinland, Leif sailed back to Greenland. A few years later, a trader from Greenland attempted unsuccessfully to establish a colony there.

Dr. Helge Ingstad, Norway.

The spindle whorls shown here provided early clues to the Norse occupation of Newfoundland. They also indicated the presence of women, who did the spinning.

Ingstad has several good reasons for thinking L'Anse aux Meadows may be Leif's settlement. For years historians have had difficulty envisioning Newfoundland as Vinland since grapes do not grow that far north. Ingstad suggests that Vinland may be derived from an obsolete term that means "pasturage" and that the wine of the sagas may have been juice from local red berries. Carbon dating of the timbers of the excavated huts supports the date of A.D. 1000. All other claims for pre-Columbian voyages still seem questionable, and even Ingstad's evidence is at best circumstantial.

Despite the romance of these explorations, their lasting effect, other than in sagas and folklore, is minimal. No one found riches in sufficient quantity to attract others across the broad Atlantic in their wake. No individual representing a European state or nation capable of fostering and supporting such far-flung colonies appeared because, for nearly a thousand years (A.D. 500–1500), the influence of that continent was shrinking, not increasing.

Europe was divided into a patchwork of fiefdoms and principalities warring among themselves and vainly trying to thwart waves of invaders from the north, east, and south.

Gradually, however, a few nobles gained regional power, often by leading successful campaigns against such diverse groups as the Vikings or Moors, and isolated city-states such as Venice waxed rich on trade with the eastern half of the old Roman Empire which, although only a pale imitation of its once-great splendor, remained impressive compared to the chaos of a fragmented Europe. In time, nobles who were able to assert their rule over substantial areas became kings and, through alliances with other powerful elements of the society such as the Catholic Church and well-to-do merchants, curtailed the activities of lesser nobles in their midst. In short, they created modern nation-states ready to expand through colonization, trade, and the export of goods, but they were prepared also to do battle with anyone who opposed them.

Portugal, a compact little country somewhat removed from the hurly-burly of Europe yet superbly positioned for exploration, and Spain, a larger, more complex realm whose rulers soon developed strong dynastic ties throughout the Continent, were the first of these so-called nation-states. And, being the first to consolidate, the Portuguese and Spanish were the first in the Americas as well. This made them rivals for land and gold, not only in the New World, but in Africa, India, and Asia.

The Spanish Voyages

Even though Columbus had a very peculiar notion of the world's true size, he deserves full credit for his first voyage. Born in the Italian city of Genoa in 1451, Columbus was brought up as the son of an unsuccessful clothier. In his twenties he became a sailor and traveled on one voyage as far north as Iceland where he may have heard tales of Vinland. Later, while sailing for the Portuguese on a trading expedition down the coast of west Africa, Columbus learned a great deal about seamanship from the skilled Portuguese pilots. By 1484 he was ready to propose to the king of Portugal his great "Enterprise of the Indies."

This project, first submitted to the king of Portugal and later to the rulers of Spain, outlined a scheme for sailing west to the Orient. The Portuguese and Spanish monarchies were skeptical—and with good reason. They and their court scholars did not, as fairy tales would have it, believe that the world was flat. They knew it was a

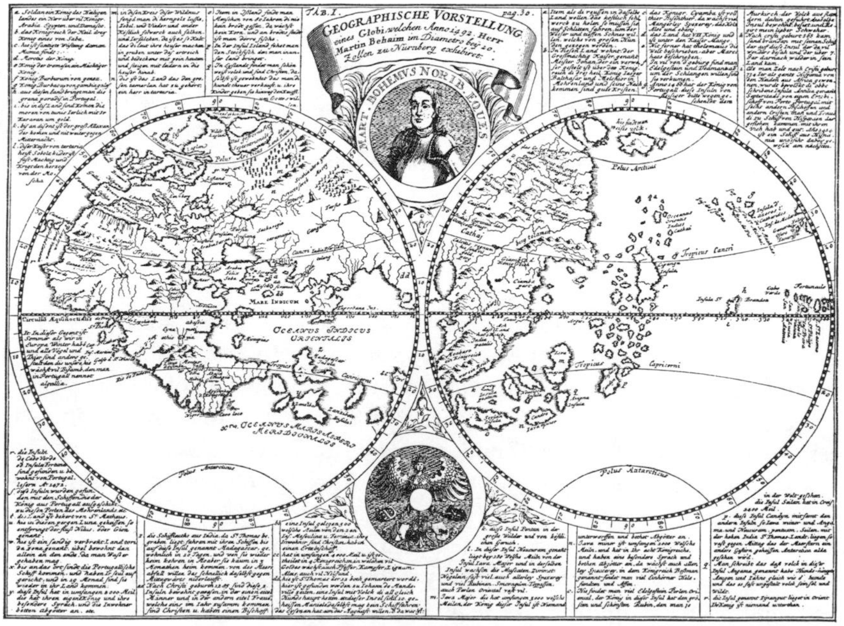

The New York Public Library, Map Room.

Martin Behaim's globe of 1492 comes close to describing Christopher Columbus's version of the world. Note the extended size of Japan (in the middle of the right hemisphere), the small circumference, and the Azores where Hawaii ought to be.

Library of Congress.

Isabella I
(1451–1504)

Isabella the Catholic, Queen of Castile from 1474–1504, became the bride of the future Ferdinand II of Aragon at the age of eighteen. Both were strong rulers and not only restored order to their respective kingdoms but after 1481 ruled jointly, thus laying the groundwork for the unification of Spain. At the time, however, their marriage merely united two dynasties, not two countries.

Isabella, devoutly religious and severe, but a just queen, possessed political vision, although her zealous persecution of Jews was a crippling mistake. A campaign for religious purity forced many able, energetic businessmen to leave the realm and made it necessary for her heirs to borrow from German and Italian bankers who exploited Spain.

This ambitious queen first met Columbus in 1486 and, after listening to his proposals for exploration, she and her husband set up a commission to study his vague and often secretive ideas. Four years later the commission said no, but the two monarchs still were intrigued with the possibilities of what this Italian seaman hoped to do. They summoned him to court and asked what the venture would cost. His price, they thought, was much too high, and he was dismissed. But several royal advisers remained convinced that Columbus should sail with Spanish backing and arranged yet another audience; this time the dreamer from Genoa prevailed.

Although both Isabella and Ferdinand were eager for power, religious motives were usually uppermost in the queen's mind while politics were her husband's main concern. This combination of royal interest and intuition, plus lobbying by courtiers and considerable luck, finally sent Christopher Columbus sailing westward into the unknown. ■

---

sphere and actually, as it turned out, a much larger sphere than Columbus estimated. Columbus miscalculated the distance from the Canary Islands (which are off the coast of Spain) to Japan by 8,200 miles. A fantastic juggling of figures, acceptance of an ancient Greek estimate of the earth's size, a theory that the proportion of land to sea was exactly the opposite of what it actually is, an overestimation of the size of Asia—all of these mistakes supported Columbus's fallacious reasoning.

Despite the fact that a royal Spanish commission decided (after years of deliberation) that Columbus's scheme seemed "impossible to any educated person," the Queen, Isabella of Castile, finally endorsed his project. A woman of more than ordinary political vision, Isabella saw the potential of this proposal for providing Spain with an alternate route to Asia since Portugal controlled the route around Africa. She was also influenced by the fact that Luis de Santangel, keeper of the privy purse to

Ferdinand, her husband, had become a firm backer of Columbus, willing to raise funds in his behalf. Soon Columbus was fitted out with a fleet of three ships, the flagship *Santa María,* and two smaller caravels named the *Pinta* and the *Niña.* (A caravel, originally designed by the Portuguese, has several aftermasts with triangular sails that, unlike the completely square rigging of conventional ships of the period, allow the craft to be sailed more directly into the wind.) The entire crew of the three ships numbered about ninety men and boys.

The Four Voyages of Columbus

The first voyage went surprisingly well. Twice the crew threatened mutiny, the food was monotonous, there were no bunks except for the captains—but despite these problems, Columbus's determination and favorable sailing conditions made the crossing relatively easy. On one day winds were so strong that the fleet traveled 182 miles; on five other days it averaged 142 miles. The entire voyage lasted little more than a month (from September 9 to October 12), though that perhaps was considerably longer than any other Europeans had ever been out of sight of land.

Columbus made four voyages to the New World. On the first he explored the Bahamas and the island of Hispaniola, which today has Haiti on its western half and the Dominican Republic on the eastern. In the following year, 1493, he returned to Hispaniola with a much larger fleet and established the first settlement there. On the third voyage, in 1498, Columbus investigated Trinidad and a section of the South American coast—his first contact with the mainland. Since Columbus refused to accept the fact that he had not reached Asia, he did not know how to account for South America. No traveler to the Orient had ever mentioned this large continent to the South. Columbus's ingenious way of dealing with the continent was to declare that it was Paradise, which he named Gracia, the Spanish word for God's "Grace."

Although Columbus intended to return to South America, in 1502 on his fourth and last voyage he only cruised past Honduras, Nicaragua, Costa Rica, and Panama. Then he was marooned for many months on Jamaica when his ships sank—the hulls had been honeycombed by shipworms. In 1503 he and his party were rescued. Ill with malaria, disgruntled by Spain's failure to honor its original contract with him (Columbus claimed for himself and his heirs a third of the value of all trade between Spain and the Indies), the great navigator returned disconsolate to Spain. He died on May 19, 1506.

Later Voyages

Other Spanish fleets made frequent crossings of the Atlantic even while Columbus was still alive. One of the most colorful and unpleasant personalities was Alonso de Ojeda (ca. 1468–1514), who led an expedition in 1499. It was he who first saw an Indian village built on pilings above water which he named "little Venice"—Venezuela. The greedy Ojeda attacked other Spanish ships in order to seize weapons and provisions for his own fleet; worse, he treated the Indians he met with intense cruelty and returned to Spain with buckets of valuable pearls he obtained from native Americans at gun or sword point. With him sailed Amerigo Vespucci, a Florentine banker and supplier of ship's stores, whose name was given to the "Americas" in the early 1500s. As Samuel Eliot Morison, the best biographer of Columbus, once wrote: "America was discovered accidentally by a great seaman who was looking for something else; when discovered it was not wanted; and most of the exploration for the next fifty years was done in the hope of getting through it or around it. America was named after a man who discovered no part of the New World. History is like that, very chancy."

The Conquests

During their first thirty years in the New World, the Spanish were primarily intent upon establishing a colony on the island of Hispaniola. Although ships returned home with gold, cotton, and Indian slaves, this booty fell far short of the Oriental riches they had hoped to obtain. This disappointment ushered in a new era of exploration, during which the Spanish conquistadores ranged throughout much of the Americas. One Spaniard, Juan Ponce de León (ca. 1460–1521), subjugated Puerto Rico and on April 2, 1513, landed just north of what is now Indian River inlet in the state of Florida, which he thought was an island. In the same year, Vasco Núñez de Balboa (ca. 1475–1519) led an expedition across present day Panama to the Pacific Ocean.

The great treasures so long sought finally were found in Peru and Mexico. In 1533 Francisco Pizarro (ca. 1471–1541) and his troops overwhelmed the Peruvian capital of Cuzco, where they immediately began to melt down the city's vast stores of gold into portable

Library of Congress.

Amerigo Vespucci
(ca. 1451–1512)

Born in Florence, this Italian merchant and navigator whose name was given to the New World entered the employ of the powerful Medici family as a young man and in 1491 was sent to Seville where they had business interests. Giannoto Berardi, who managed the Medici outlet in that city, outfitted Columbus for his first voyage and Vespucci probably was among those greeting the famed explorer upon his return. When Berardi died in the mid-1490s, Vespucci succeeded to his position.

Between 1497 and 1504, Amerigo Vespucci made several voyages across the Atlantic, just how many is not known, but at least two, during which he became convinced that the land in the Western hemisphere was not Asia. In 1505 he was summoned to the Spanish court and given a post with the Commercial House of the West Indies; three years later he became that organization's chief navigator, a position of great importance since he had to prepare maps and charts for the Spanish government.

Meanwhile, Vespucci published several letters describing his travels which soon were circulated and reprinted. In 1507, M. Waldseemüller of Lorraine produced a pamphlet that included Vespucci's words, as well as some of his own. More importantly, Waldseemüller suggested that the new southern lands be called "America" in honor of Amerigo Vespucci. This proposal won acceptance and the name quickly spread to the northern region, too. Although the full details of Vespucci's life remain somewhat obscure, he was obviously a man of considerable ability, scrupulously honest, and thoroughly trustworthy; otherwise, as a foreigner, he would not have been given such a sensitive position in the emerging Spanish imperial structure. ■

blocks. Soon the lure of so much gold drew thousands of conquistadores to Peru. The earlier conquest of Mexico and the subsequent taking of Chibcha (in modern Colombia) placed the three wealthiest empires in the New World in the hands of Spanish explorers. Columbus and the first explorers met only the simpler (and poorer) civilizations of the Caribbean, but the Spanish now had not one but three Eldorados at their disposal. One-fifth of all the gold taken in the New World went to the Spanish monarch; the rest was divided among the conquistadores.

The Spanish Empire

Spanish claims in the New World were based upon Columbus's voyages and a treaty signed with Portugal in 1494. The Treaty of Tordesillas, which had the approval of the Pope, divided the new territory between the two nations. Land west of a line drawn north and south between the present forty-sixth and forty-seventh meridians (a straight line from Newfoundland in the north to present-day Brazil in the south) belonged to Spain. Everything east of it, including Africa and the rich trade routes to India and the Orient, belonged to Portugal. The Pope's approval was contingent upon these "heathen lands" being converted to Christianity. Although Portugal maintained its claim to Brazil, it was not an active competitor with Spain in the New World; the Portuguese were too busy developing an exclusive sea trade route with Asia and defending their possessions against the newly independent Dutch.

The Spanish empire, a possession of the throne, was directly administered by the monarch. A Council of the Indies in Spain managed bureaucratic details, but had no independent will of its own. The only restraint on the Spanish king's power was the rebelliousness of the proud colonists themselves; for instance, when the king attempted to put into effect radical reforms in Peru, the conquistadores threatened revolt—and the king was forced to back down.

What enticed the conquistadores to the Americas were dreams of limitless gold; what lured the friars were dreams of countless souls to be saved. Both succeeded in their quests to a spectacular degree. The friars were able to present Catholicism in terms the Indians often understood and accepted, and native religions, mingled with Catholicism, underwent many accommodations. Thus the Spanish friars came to believe that the Aztec deity, Quetzalcohuatl, was the apostle Thomas, who somehow strayed to the New World to win souls for Christ. Similarly, the Mexicans equated some Catholic saints with the local gods; one of the most celebrated substitutions occurred when the Mexican "Our Lady Spirit" became the patron saint of Mexico—the Virgin of Guadalupe. Much of the success of the Spanish friars was due to their undogmatic outlook in stressing the importance of sincere conviction and faith rather than the formalities of church ritual. This intellectual orientation made the Spanish friars flexible in their assimilation of native American religious attitudes and practices. This outlook also is evident in their efforts to change the Spanish labor policy that forced Indians into peonage. Eventually, through the work of missionaries such as Bartolome de las Casas, the church began to oppose Spanish mistreatment of native Americans.

The very year Columbus arrived at Watlings Island marked another historic event in the fate of Spain, one that was to shape the character of Spanish America. That

Aqui comiença vn vocabulario enla lengua Castellana y Mexicana, Compuesto por el muy reuerendo padre fray Alonso de Molina: Guardia del coueto de sant Antonio de Tetzcuco dla orde delos frayles Menores.

Signasti domine seruum tuum Franciscum signis redemptionis nostre.

dorum nimia te fecit prole parentem.
qui genuit moriens, quos pater alme foues.
Confixus viuis, langues: cum mente reuolus.
vulnera, cum speceas, stigmata carne geris.

John Carter Brown Library, Brown University.

In their eagerness to learn enough about the natives to aid in converting them, Spanish missionaries became recorders of Indian culture. This is the title page of the earliest Spanish-Indian dictionary.

Library of Congress.

Bartolomé de las Casas (1474–1566)

A Dominican priest, Bartolomé de las Casas was a Spanish missionary who became the first outstanding European defender of the Indians against the conquistadores. The son of a merchant who sailed on Columbus's second voyage, Las Casas settled in Hispaniola in 1502. And in accordance with the practice of the conquistadores, he worked Indian slaves on his estate until sometime around 1515. In that year, as a result of a crisis of conscience, he decided to champion the Indians against his own countrymen. What he particularly condemned was a labor system that forced the Indians to work to the point of death on farms and in mines. For the *encomienda* system, which at first was a form of tenancy, quickly became peonage and, in effect, turned into slavery.

To make the plight of the Indians better known, Las Casas wrote a massive *History of the Indies* that told the tale of Spanish conquest in three volumes up to the year 1520. Fortunately, for later historians, he also copied out Columbus's log of his first voyage; it is the only copy that has survived. In another original work, Las Casas refuted the charge that the Indians were "savages" in need of the civilizing presence of Spain. He described Aztec and Inca cities, agricultural methods, industries, religion, government, and laws. He concluded that the Indians "equaled many nations of this world that are renowned and considered civilized, and they surpassed many others, and to none were they inferior."

Unfortunately, the concern Las Casas felt for the Indians led him to advocate the use of black slaves to replace Indian slaves. In 1518 he proposed that the Spanish crown prohibit Indian slavery and suppress, in gradual degrees, the forced-service *encomiendas*. Indian slaves and laborers were to be replaced with blacks purchased in North Africa. Las Casas himself apparently owned slaves in Hispaniola as late as 1544. It is ironic that in his zeal to improve the life of the Indians, the "Protector of the Indians," as Las Casas was known, contributed to the introduction and establishment of black slavery in the Western Hemisphere. ■

event was the Spanish conquest of the Moors. In 1492 the last Moorish populations on the Iberian peninsula were subdued by the Spanish monarchs. This conquest had a profound effect on Spanish politics. Knights and aristocrats no longer had peninsular lands to conquer and plunder. Without a source of wealth from warfare, the old feudal Spanish aristocracy (and the king) might have faded into relative obscurity as power passed into the hands of a small, rising merchant class. Suddenly the vast American nations of the Aztecs, the Chibchas, and the Incas were new empires to exploit and plunder, and the feudal values of knightly valor against the heathen were reinvigorated by translation to the New World.

This turn of events was as much a curse as a blessing. Although Spain brought hundreds of shiploads of American gold back to the Old World, the bullion was spent largely to finance European wars. These conflicts were so costly that eventually most of Spain's wealth passed into the hands of foreign bankers, in the form of interest on huge loans. Worse, Spain was slow to develop a sizable merchant class, local industries, and a modern economy. In one very important sense, the wealth of the New World permitted Spain to remain a bastion of conservatism.

This "curse," however, became evident only much later. Throughout the sixteenth century, the Americas appeared to be nothing but a godsend for Spain and its king. Initially the New World was divided into several viceroyalties, each independent and answerable only to the crown. Periodically investigators were sent from Spain to review the accounts and actions of administrators, all of whom had to be Spanish-born and of "pure" Spanish stock.

The original conquistadores were given vast *encomiendas,* but upon their deaths those lands reverted to the throne—and the king issued no new land grants. By the middle of the sixteenth century the throne had established a highly centralized administration over South and Central America. By the time England and France could begin to plant their first miserable and starving colonies in North America, the Spanish empire in the New World boasted impressive cities, a far-flung network of missions, several major universities—and even a high literary and artistic culture of its own. Of course this empire was, from a humane point of view, cruelly oppressive. It was first maintained by Indian labor and then, after the Indians were decimated by disease and exhaustion, by black slaves imported from Africa.

William L. Clements Library, University of Michigan.

This watercolor, done for a French edition of *A Very Brief Account of the Destruction of the Indies* by de las Casas shows Spaniards sacking an Indian village.

Exploiting and Settling North America

Since Spain had such a secure hold on the Caribbean and on Central and South America, the French, Dutch, and English turned their attention to unoccupied areas in North America. To be sure, Spanish conquistadores explored the southern section of the United States from modern day South Carolina to California, but they were looking for gold. Not finding it in sufficient quantities, they withdrew; as a consequence, California was not settled by the Spanish until the seventeenth century, and then only sparsely.

England, France, and Holland did not expand into the New World in the early sixteenth century because all three countries were too fragmented politically and too preoccupied with internal affairs to organize and finance a major expedition. In 1500 England was a minor power still attempting to recover from 100 years of dynastic war. To be sure, Henry VII of England sent John Cabot (1450–ca. 1498) to the New World in 1497. In June of that year Cabot landed in Newfoundland, saw not one native but was nevertheless convinced he had discovered a land in the north of Asia. The following year he set out for Japan—and never returned. The English, discouraged at finding only codfish, an eagle, and various strange fauna, did not send out new expeditions. After Henry VIII came to the throne, his desire to divorce his first wife to marry another (who might bear him a male heir) led him into conflict with the Pope, who refused to annul Henry's marriage. This conflict culminated in England's break with the Catholic Church. Thus, throughout most of the sixteenth century, Catholic Spain attempted to force England to rejoin Christendom.

Domestic stability returned to England only with the ascension of Elizabeth I to the throne, but throughout most of her reign, the nation continued to be threatened by a hostile Spain—and, much closer at hand, by the separate kingdom of Scotland and a rebellious Ireland. Planting a colony required more money than either the crown or private English merchants were willing to invest. In addition, reports from voyagers to the New World made it sound like an uninviting place. Much better, easier, more patriotic, and more immediately profitable were English piratical raids on gold-laden Spanish ships in the Caribbean.

Colonial Williamsburg Photograph.

Queen Elizabeth I of England. Her reign made England prosperous enough to attempt colonization.

Early English Settlements

Only one small group of courtiers in England was interested in colonizing. In 1583 Sir Humphrey Gilbert attempted to establish a colony in Newfoundland but was lost at sea on the return voyage. His younger half brother, Sir Walter Raleigh (ca. 1552–1618), next took up the challenge and in 1584 he sent a party of explorers to reconnoiter the coast of present-day North Carolina. These Englishmen claimed the land for the queen, who on their return named the entire Atlantic seaboard Vir-

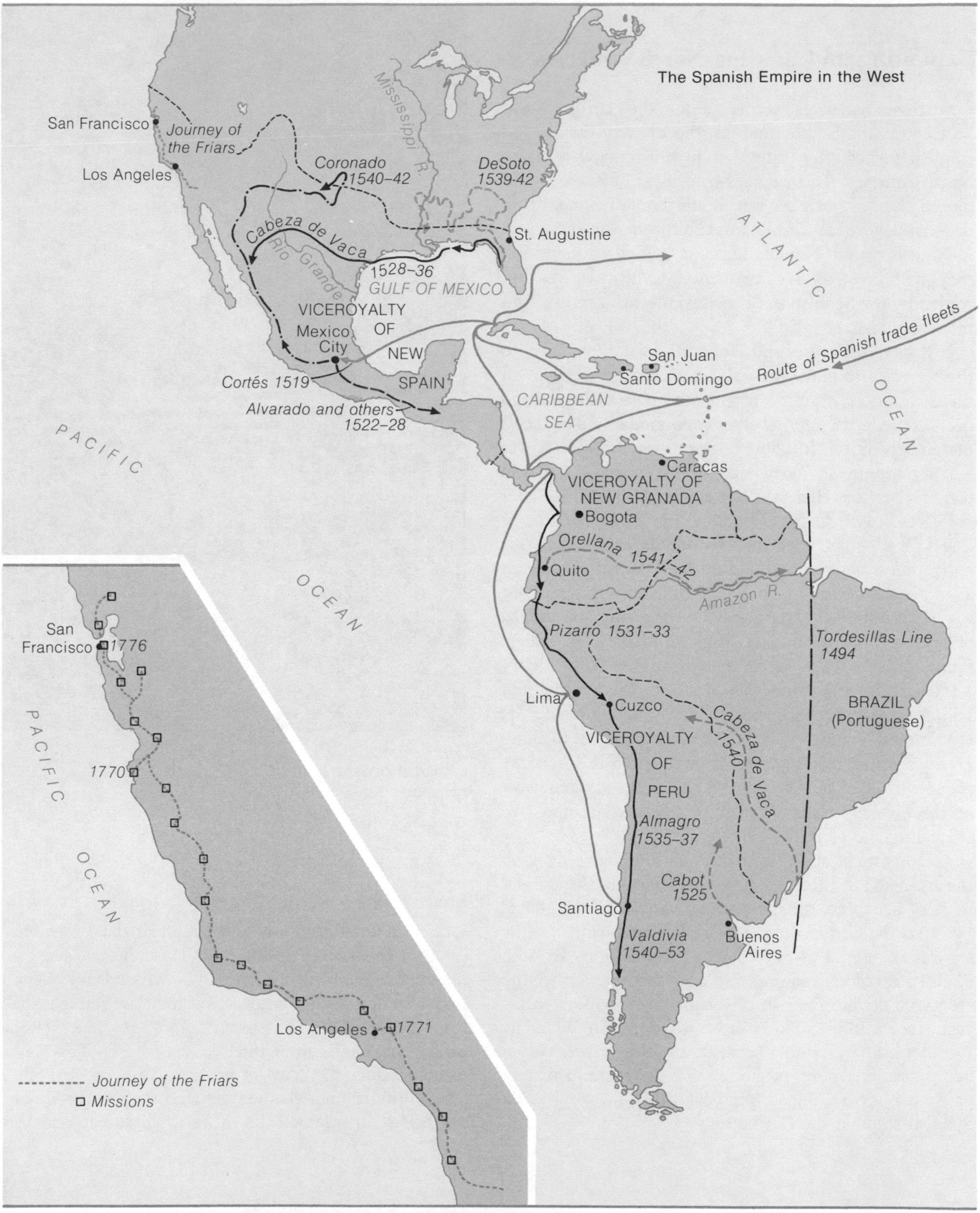

The Spanish Empire in the West
San Francisco
Journey of the Friars
Los Angeles
Coronado 1540–42
DeSoto 1539-42
Mississippi R.
Cabeza de Vaca 1528–36
Rio Grande
St. Augustine
GULF OF MEXICO
ATLANTIC OCEAN
VICEROYALTY OF NEW SPAIN
Mexico City
Cortés 1519
Alvarado and others 1522–28
San Juan
Santo Domingo
Route of Spanish trade fleets
CARIBBEAN SEA
PACIFIC OCEAN
Caracas
VICEROYALTY OF NEW GRANADA
Bogota
Orellana 1541–42
Quito
Amazon R.
Pizarro 1531–33
Tordesillas Line 1494
Lima
Cuzco
VICEROYALTY OF PERU
Cabeza de Vaca 1540
BRAZIL (Portuguese)
Almagro 1535–37
Cabot 1525
Santiago
Valdivia 1540–53
Buenos Aires
San Francisco
1776
1770
Los Angeles
1771
Journey of the Friars
Missions

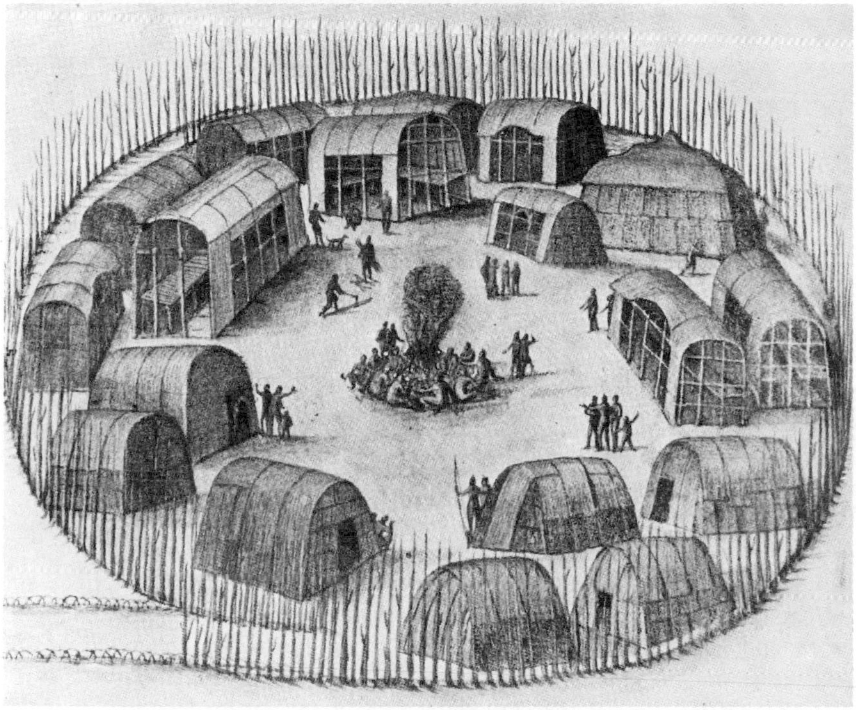

This watercolor by John White is one of the best pieces of evidence about the life style of American Indians before extensive contact with Europeans.

ginia, an allusion to her unmarried state. (The name may have been suggested by the ever courtly Sir Walter Raleigh.)

Encouraged by the reports of these men, Raleigh decided in 1585 to establish a colony, and 108 male settlers eventually landed on Roanoke Island. This group included John White, an artist who brought back invaluable paintings of the strange plants and animals of North America as well as handsome portraits of the Indians. When these paintings were engraved in 1590, they were widely circulated in England, and for a century or so they determined the view the English held of the Indians and of America as well. Although the colonists built a fort and cottages, they soon were on very bad terms with the Indians. During the winter, when food became scarce, they declared war on the Indians, and by the summer of 1586 conditions had so deteriorated that the colonists returned to England.

Raleigh's last attempt to plant a permanent colony on Roanoke occurred a year later. Unlike earlier expeditions, this one included women and children, and it was at this time that the first child of English parents was born in the New World: Virginia Dare. But this party met with even less good luck. When the crew of a relief ship bringing supplies, which was delayed for several years by the Spanish armada, tried to find the colonists in 1590, they had disappeared, leaving behind only the mysterious inscription "Croatoan," a way of suggesting perhaps they had gone to live among the nearby Croatan Indians.

Jamestown

Conditions had not been right for English settlement in the New World in the sixteenth century. But at the beginning of the seventeenth century a Scottish ruler became James I of England, thereby uniting the two thrones. Moreover, James achieved a new peace with Spain. These stabilizing circumstances encouraged Englishmen to invest in colonies in North America. (Speculation of this sort today would be called expending "venture capital.")

The English pattern of colonization differed from the Spanish in many important respects. The Spanish king directly controlled his New World empire, using its vast resources to bolster his position among a restive nobility and usually sending only citizens of high social position and unquestionable piety to the New World. England, on the other hand, set up private companies to

New York Public Library, Rare Book Division

John White
(dates unknown)

Except for a decade or so, the career of John White was as obscure as that of his famous granddaughter, Virginia Dare. Between 1585 and 1590 this English artist and cartographer made at least three trips to the New World, but his fame rests on his watercolors of the natives and of the flora and fauna he saw near the ill-fated colony of Roanoke. White also apparently made sketches in Florida, Greenland, and the Caucasus during his lifetime, or he copied the work of others who visited those regions.

In 1585, Sir Walter Raleigh asked White to join the original Roanoke colony on the outer banks of North Carolina and make drawings of the area. He sailed from Plymouth on April 9th of that year, one of a group of men who, at their own request, accompanied Sir Francis Drake back to England fourteen months later. In July 1587, White went forth a second time, on this occasion as governor. He was accompanied by several relatives, including his daughter Ellinor, mother of Virginia Dare. About six weeks later he was persuaded, against his better judgment it seems, to return to England for provisions.

The following year he set out for Roanoke, but the sailors on his vessel were more interested in Spanish prizes than colonies and tangled (unsuccessfully) with enemy ships and had to return to port. In 1590 White finally got to Roanoke Island, found it deserted, and, denied the opportunity for an effective search, had to put to sea and sail for home. That same year about one-third of the drawings he had made earlier were published in Thomas Harriot's *Brief and True Report of . . . Virginia.* These illustrations, soon copied and adapted, long formed the basis of what much of the Old World knew of the New. Seventy-five of White's original watercolors can be seen at the British Museum in London. ■

settle along the Atlantic coast of North America and regarded the colonies as a proper dumping ground for paupers, vagabonds, criminals, and religious dissidents. The practice of including families and women in these colonizing groups helped to stabilize the settlements. England also gained some stability at home since the relocation of dissenting religious sects helped to relax religious tensions.

In 1606 James granted a charter shared by the Virginia Company of London, which was to settle what now are the southeastern states, and the Virginia Company of Plymouth, which lay claim to the northeastern areas. In 1607 both branches of the Virginia Company attempted colonization. The Plymouth branch failed; the colony planted in Maine returned after a year, discouraged by a terrible winter.

Jamestown's early homes, as shown in these restorations, were half-frame thatched buildings much like those the settlers left in England. The chimneys were wood and it is no wonder Jamestown burned several times.

But the London branch succeeded—if anything as painful, disorganized, and profitless as the first years of the Jamestown settlement can be called "success." The purpose of this foothold in the Chesapeake Bay area was to create a permanent colony that would convert the Indians to Christianity, seek gold and silver, challenge the power of the Spanish in Florida, develop natural resources, and achieve a host of other minor goals.

The 1607 expedition was made up of 104 people. During the voyage, no one knew who among them would be their leaders, since the identity of their councilors was kept secret until the ship reached its destination. Upon arrival in April, the men selected by the company back in London assumed office—and soon began quarreling with one another. Disputes between Edward Wingfield and John Smith (1580–1631) were particularly bitter. Smith, who led the sort of life young men dream of, was a soldier, explorer, author, and, of course, one of the founders of permanent English settlement in North America. As a youth he fought in the Netherlands, then Hungary where he deluded the enemy with fireworks. Left for dead on a battlefield, he became a prisoner of the Asiatic Turks, escaped to Russia, and returned to his native England three years before setting out for America. In the New World he explored the rivers of coastal Virginia, and perhaps was saved by young Pocahontas (ca. 1595–1617), only to be threatened upon his return to Jamestown with yet another execution for losing several men during his travels. Spared by the arrival of Captain Christopher Newport from England, Smith soon became president of the little colony's council—in fact, a dictator of sorts since all of the other council members had died or returned to England.

Drastic measures of some sort were certainly demanded, since malaria and other diseases had reduced the original number of settlers to thirty-eight people. Unwisely, the settlers ignored company instructions to build the colony on a high and healthy site and instead chose Jamestown, a peninsula lying between malarial swamps. The Powhatan Indians who lived nearby were alternately friendly and hostile. The parent company added to the burdens of the settlement by sending a new supply of colonists at a time when food was scarce. Fire leveled the first fort and feeble attempts to set up a glassmaking industry failed.

Heeding the advice of Smith, who returned to England in 1609 for treatment of gunpowder burns and never returned, the company obtained a new charter from King James. This document, not officially approved until three years later, allowed the company to claim much of North America, to enhance their appeals to investors, and to offer stock and land to each settler over ten years of age. More important, perhaps, Virginia would be ruled henceforth by a single individual, not by a cumbersome council.

Despite the good intentions of Smith and of the company's governors, the winter of 1609–1610—"the starving time,"—almost wiped out Jamestown. The supply of corn was consumed by rats and 440 of the 500 colonists died. When Sir Thomas Gates, the colony's new governor, who was shipwrecked on Bermuda en route from London, arrived the following May, he saw nothing but devastation. To him Jamestown seemed "rather as the ruins of some ancient fortification than that any people might now inhabit it; the pallisades torn down, the ports open, the gates from the hinges, the church ruined and unfrequented, empty houses (whose owners' untimely death had taken newly from them) rent up and burnt, the living not able, as they pretended, to step into the woods to gather other firewood; and, it is true, the Indian as fast killing without as the famine and pestilence within."

The survivors had decided to leave with Gates and return to England when they learned that fresh supplies and 150 new settlers were arriving with Lord De La Warr, the new governor who was to replace Gates, their provisional leader. His auspicious entry on the scene along with a new charter granted in 1609 marked the beginning of success. Slowly the colony began to prosper. Sir Thomas Dale, successor to De La Warr and a ruthless administrator, imposed militarylike discipline on the settlers. He forced laggards to work the fields, he made peace with the Indians, and under provisions of the new charter, he eventually granted three-acre plots to individuals. Up to this point, the settlers were shareholders working the land jointly. Best of all, in 1611, the colony finally found a cash crop: tobacco. Eight years later Jamestown was shipping 40,000 pounds of tobacco to England and the foundations of economic well-being were emerging.

The French Colonies

Like the English, the French did not begin their first tentative movements into the New World until the second half of the sixteenth century, nor did they plant their first permanent settlement until the early seventeenth century. And like the English, the French were forced by the Spanish hegemony over Latin America to confine their interests to North America.

There most of the resemblances end. For the French, unlike the English, were eventually more adept in fashioning a workable Indian policy, but less successful in building an agricultural economy. Perhaps their success in establishing relatively amicable relations with the Indians stemmed in part from their failure to appropriate Indian land for substantial farms and for widespread settlement. Also, unlike the English, the French did not encourage Nonconformists to populate the New World; rather, they resembled the Spanish in this regard, eventually permitting only faithful adherents to Catholicism and solid citizens to emigrate.

In the 1530s Jacques Cartier (1491–1557) led several expeditions to the coast of Newfoundland, Nova Scotia, and the Saint Lawrence River. He also spent two winters in Canada, the second time with the intention of establishing a colony. The neighboring Indians dropped hints that were either deliberately misleading (or simply misunderstood) of a great civilization to be found in the interior of Canada. Cartier eagerly set out for this fabled realm where gold, silver, and rare spices must abound. He did find something that looked like gold, but he was forced to return since the colonists were threatened by hostile Indians and winter weather began to claim many victims. When his "gold" was assayed, it proved worthless.

Quebec, the first permanent French settlement, was founded in 1608, only a year after Jamestown. The French colony was essentially little more than a trading post where the French exchanged European goods for Indian furs, especially beaver pelts, which were used in the new French fashion of felt hats. But the fur trade was

McCord Museum, McGill University, Montreal.

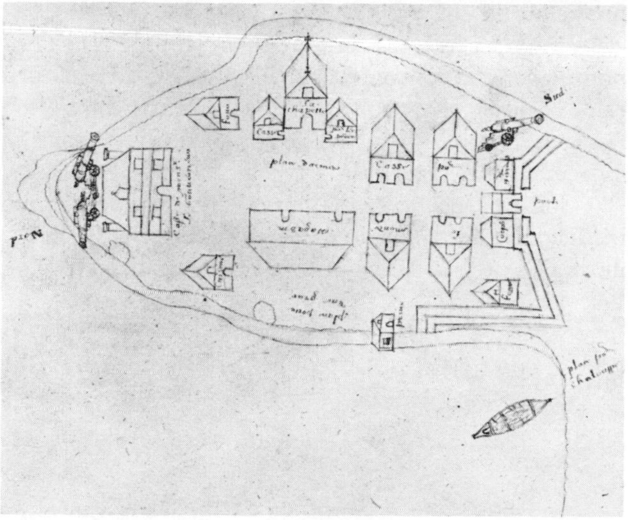

The church, houses, and fortifications of Montreal all are clear in this 1642 map sketch. Montreal's position as an outpost of the French empire is clearly reflected in its structures.

seen only as a means of supporting the colony until two greater goals were realized: the discovery of a Northwest Passage to the Orient and the development of profitable gold mines. As it turned out, neither ambition was to be realized, but for decades the French pursued these impossible dreams of great wealth.

Like Jamestown, the French colony was backed by a private stock company with a charter from the king. The settlement, indeed the entire French enterprise in North America for the first three decades of the seventeenth century, owed much to Samuel de Champlain (ca. 1567–1635), a sailor, soldier, and administrator, who charted maps of the new territory, established peaceful relations with several Indian tribes, and explored the interior.

As in Jamestown, the toll of living in the wilderness was heavy. After the first year in Quebec, only eight of the original twenty-eight men survived, the rest having died of dysentery or scurvy. The next summer Champlain joined three Indian tribes (the Algonkians, the Montagnais, and the Hurons) in attacking and defeating the Mohawks. This alliance earned the French trading rights with the Huron Confederacy, which collected furs from the more northern tribes and exchanged them for French goods. But these attacks on the Mohawks incurred the wrath of the Iroquois, an enmity that the English and the Dutch exploited to the fullest. Indeed, this affront to the Iroquois Confederacy explains why the French experienced difficulty when later they tried to expand to the south. During this period, it is also apparent that, for their part, the Indians were using both the Europeans and their firearms against rival tribes.

In its early years, Quebec and other French colonies in Canada had a precarious lease on life. They depended on France for much of their food and goods to trade with the Indians. Although the king insisted that the colonists farm, agriculture was slow to start and even slower to expand.

Still more serious were threats from the English over disputed territory. Although treaties might be signed in Europe designating lines of demarcation, the actual outcome of colonial rivalries on the frontier in North America depended on the force of arms available on this side of the ocean. England made good its claim to Newfoundland, though France held the areas just to the south; further south, English settlements appeared along the Atlantic seaboard. The English envied French control over the rich fur trade that flowed through the Saint Lawrence River—and in 1621 a Scot, after obtaining a grant from James I, seized Nova Scotia from the French and pushed up the Saint Lawrence to Quebec, which surrendered. But a new treaty signed in Europe returned Quebec to the French. This competition between England and France in the late seventeenth and eighteenth centuries for trade and political power eventually erupted into a series of wars fought in Europe and in America. These wars finally led to the defeat of France and to her expulsion from most of the New World.

Dutch Holdings

The French dominated the Saint Lawrence River, one of the two broad avenues to the fur-rich interior of North America; the Dutch controlled the Hudson River, the other great waterway. In 1609 Henry Hudson, an Englishman working for the Dutch, sailed up the river that now bears his name in search of a passage to the Indies. He stopped his fruitless pursuit at Albany, having laid claim to the entire Hudson River valley, Long Island, and the Delaware Bay for the Dutch. In this vast area the Dutch established their colony of New Netherlands.

Within a few years they had developed two strongholds: Albany and the island of Manhattan.

The primary Dutch colony in the New World was in Brazil. This rich prize they attempted to wrest from the Portuguese, but were finally expelled by the middle of the seventeenth century. Enterprising and exulting in their recent independence from Spanish rule, the Dutch were more intent on making money than on establishing settlements. They actually had too small a population to send forth colonists; and their primacy in international trade (especially in the Far East) was too rewarding to encourage them to waste much time or effort on the North American holdings. Fur trade with the Iroquois and Algonkian tribes did, however, prove profitable—as did trade with other European colonists. The Dutch introduced slaves from Africa into French and English islands in the Caribbean, bought the sugar these slaves grew, and throughout much of the seventeenth century traded freely with other English and French outposts.

The Three Empires

Despite the contributions of the Dutch and the Portuguese to the New World, the three most important European powers in the hemisphere were Spain, England, and France.

Each of these three empires took on a distinctive character. Spanish America was administered directly by the king; all important decisions were made in Spain. A static, rigidly stratified social system was grafted onto areas where—at least in Mexico, Peru, and Colombia—such a system already had long existed under native rule. The government was appointed and no local assemblies existed. Few Spanish men migrated to the colonies, and even fewer Spanish women. Consequently, intermarriages existed among whites, Indians, and black slaves. Spanish slave codes even permitted slaves to marry and own property. The resulting gradations of race mixture were officially sanctioned and recognized by the government. But if Spanish America was coherent politically, it was geographically fragmented. Deserts, mountains, and impassable jungles separated one section of the empire from another.

The French settlement in New France (Canada) was originally under the auspices of several private stock companies chartered by the king. By the middle of the seventeenth century, however, the stock companies were bankrupt and the crown assumed control. Conducting the fur trade and converting the Indians to Catholicism became the chief activities of the French. If the French had prevailed, Canada would have been as hierarchical and rigid a society as Spanish America. But there were too few settlers spread over too large a territory to make an autocratic system feasible.

Some French settlers came to Canada to engage in the lucrative fur trade; they were thus constantly on the move in search of Indian tribes from whom they could

Canadiens en Raquette allant en guerre sur la nege

The New York Public Library, Rare Book Division.

The French-Canadian soldier in 1697—as sketched here, on snowshoes, ready for winter warfare—has a romantic and unrealistic appearance. Note the way he holds the gun.

buy furs. The majority of French settlers became farmers and were prosperous since the relatively small population consumed most of the agricultural products. Subsistence farming, along with the long winter season that made export trade precarious, meant that farmers did not have a large cash crop. Under these conditions, slavery could serve no economic purpose, hence it played almost no role in New France, though it did on French islands in the Caribbean.

Most of the English settlers, unlike the Spanish and French, were Protestants. Though they had some interest in Christianizing Indians, they did not exercise this talent with the same zeal as their European rivals. Like the early French colonies, the first English settlements were financed by private stock companies chartered by the king; and, in similar fashion, when these companies experienced financial difficulties, the colonies were taken over by the crown. Yet English settlements possessed at least one striking difference; they contained the seeds of parliamentary government. For example, the House of Burgesses, which first gathered in 1619 to discuss company regulations and community affairs, continued to meet after Virginia became a royal colony in 1624. In time, since the king permitted similar assemblies to develop in other colonies, Americans began to view their colonial legislatures as miniature parliaments. This raised basic, fundamental questions concerning the role of Parliament. How much control did it have over the colonies? What was the relationship of these assemblies to Parliament or, for that matter, to the king and his ministers? Here, of course, lie not only the seeds of parliamentary, representative government, but of the American Revolution, too.

In America, the English generally became prosperous farmers because they came in far greater numbers, brought their families with them, and settled in a climate that permitted the development of successful cash-crop farming. They learned to raise Indian corn—and they discovered a cash crop, tobacco. This success in agriculture eventually would make slavery an economically feasible institution in Virginia and other Southern colonies under English control.

If the English outshone the French as farmers, they were, by comparison, dismal failures in working out a practical Indian policy. While the French fur trade depended on friendly relations with the Indians, the English colonial system failed to draw the Indians into its economic sphere. Moreover, the English tended to cling to their farms along the Atlantic seaboard for many decades and made little effort to penetrate into the interior.

Library of Congress.

Settlers in the New World built their homes on Old World models. The Adam Thoroughgood House in Virginia is a perfect example of an Old World style adapted to the New.

Essay

Life on Board Columbus's Ships and the Technology of Sailing

The ninety men and boys who sailed west across the uncharted Atlantic with Columbus on his first voyage must have been anxious about unknown aspects of the voyage. Although the trip lasted only thirty-three days, less time than required to sail from Italy to England—no member of the crew had any way of knowing that in advance. When Columbus was not stern he reassured his men with "soft words" as one contemporary put it—but could he be trusted? The trade winds that blew Columbus's three small ships westward were so favorable that soon the crew began to fear they would never find a wind to bear them back home. For days on end the weather was perfect—but even that aroused misgivings. This mad foreigner, the men muttered, this maniac from Genoa, will order us to continue sailing westward until our water runs out. And under a sky that never rains, how will we replenish our supplies?

Other odd phenomena troubled the sailors. On September 16 (the voyage began on September 9, 1492), the fleet entered the Sargasso Sea, a vast, calm pond in the Atlantic covered with green gulfweed. The men were afraid to sail through it lest their ships become enmeshed and becalmed. Columbus, with all the courage of his convictions (or obsessions), ordered them to head on—and his decision turned out to be right, for the gulfweed forms only a slight blanket over the water and could be easily sliced by the prow of a ship. Then a new problem beset the mariners. At night the compass no longer pointed directly towards the North Star. Until then, sailors had always assumed the North Star marked True North; in fact, its position relative to the earth shifts daily, and observably so in western latitudes. This peculiar behavior of an old and reliable friend disturbed the sailors.

Sailing conditions during the first voyage were, by and large, so auspicious that the crew had idle time to joke, to troll for fish—and to grumble. To say the sailors were "idle" is, of course, something of an oversimplification, since life aboard a fifteenth century ship followed a highly regulated schedule. At dawn the men on watch scrubbed down the deck with salt water and twig brooms. The new watch coming on duty were awakened. Arising was a simple affair, since the men slept in their clothes on the

Theodore De Bry's imaginative version of Columbus claiming Hispaniola shows little knowledge of the landscape or native possessions (note the jewels) but a better understanding of ships. Note the rigging of the ship on the left.

planks of the deck or, if it was raining, down below on top of the equally uncomfortable casks of water and wine. (Not until much later did sailors sleep in hammocks, which were invented by Indians in the New World.) Grouchy and aching, the men ate a cold breakfast—cheese, pickled sardines, garlic cloves, dried peas and beans, and hardtack, a tasteless but easily preserved bread. (Dried fruit was a luxury reserved for officers.)

Since all wooden ships draw water, the caulker and a few hands pumped the vessel dry every morning. The caulker had the responsibility for keeping the ship watertight—by sealing shut (or caulking) seams, by coating the hull with tallow, and by operating and maintaining the pump, a hollow log outfitted with a piston and leather valves at the bottom of the ship.

Up on deck two watches were posted, one in the front (fore), the other at the back (aft). They were on the lookout for brewing storms, for enemy vessels—and, on the first voyage, for land or any hint that land might be near (birds, for instance). The Spanish sovereigns had offered an extra award of money to the first man who spotted land, and a lookout on the *Pinta,* Rodrigo de Triana, collected the prize.

What were the majority of the crew doing? Most of the men were setting sail or taking it in according to the captain's orders. Others were repairing frayed ropes or torn or damaged sails under the direction of the boatswain. The steward might be checking out the provisions, making certain they were not being ruined by water or rats, or training ships' boys in their duties.

The only hot meal of the day was served at noon, though who cooked it remains a mystery (records of the time never list the position of cook). Food was prepared in an open firebox—that is, an iron tray lined with sand and fed with logs (it was probably in the front of the ship, in the forecastle). Though not sumptuous, the food was no worse than what the average peasant ate on land during the winter: pickled beef or pork, hardtack, sardines, and anchovies. No fresh fruit or vegetables were served, and this lack of vitamins caused a horrible disease—scurvy. Fortunately Columbus's first voyage was so brief that the disease did not afflict his crew.

Just before the meal was served, a boy chanted: "Table, table, sir captain and master and good company, table ready; meat ready; water as usual for sir captain and master and good company. Long live the King of Castile by land and sea! Who says to him war, off with his head; who won't say amen, gets nothing to drink. Table is set, who don't come won't eat."

In the evening, if the winds dropped, the crew would sit around and tell stories. Then evening prayers would begin. Columbus's men and boys were intensely religious—as were most of the Spanish of that day. The cross was painted on sails, and every change of watch was marked with prayers and pious songs. But the evening ceremony was most impressive. The gathered mariners recited an "Our Father" and a "Hail, Mary." They then said the Credo and sang an old chant, the "Salve, Regina," addressed to the Virgin Mary, patron saint of sailors.

Interest in life aboard Columbus's fleet should not stop short of curiosity about the ships themselves, for innovations in ship design that occurred during the fifteenth century in Portugal and Spain made the voyage possible—and eventually enabled Europe to master the world. Columbus sailed with three ships. One was a cargo ship called a *nao* (this was Columbus's flagship, named the *Santa María*). The other two vessels (nicknamed *Niña* and *Pinta*) were caravels. The *nao* and the caravels were the most successful ships for long open-sea voyages, and their design resulted from the blending of various elements from several different sources. Caravels had square sails but they also had at least one or more lateen sails. These are triangular sails suspended from a single mast and running from the front to the back of the ship. This design was a departure from traditional European rigging which, since the days of the Roman Empire, had consisted of square sails spread across the width of the ship, from one side to the other. A square sail was fine when the wind was blowing from behind the ship. But the lateen sail, which originated in India was introduced to Europeans by Arabs, and was far more flexible. It could be tilted at many different angles, which greatly increased maneuverability and allowed ships to take advantage of winds blowing from several different directions.

If the lateen sail was a contribution from India, two elements of ship construction came from northern Europe. One was a new design for square sails. Square sails on early Mediterranean ships were clumsy, being controlled by very few ropes. Northern square sails were far more flexible since the ropes used to raise each sail were separate from the ropes used to position it. When this more sophisticated rigging was introduced to Portugal and further refined, the square sail became a much more useful device for long voyages under varying wind conditions. The other major contribution of northern ship design was the rudder operated from within the ship. Before the fifteen century, Mediterranean ships used rudders that protruded from the sides of the ship toward the back (quarter-rudders). The new rudder imported from the north, placed dead center at the back of the boat (the axial rudder) was much more efficient.

Northern ships, however, had their drawbacks. Normally they only had one mast and their hulls were tubby. By combining the slender hull and the lateen sail of the Mediterranean with the unusually efficient square sails and the axial rudder of the North, the Portuguese were able to create a new and effective kind of ship. It had, ordinarily, three masts outfitted with two square sails and one lateen sail. The lateen sail was particularly good for maneuverability along the coastline and for sudden changes of direction; the square sails were ideal for smooth passage across the ocean when the wind was coming from behind the ship. Columbus's flagship, the *Santa María,* was rigged in precisely this way: a huge square sail in the center, a much shorter mast in the front with another square sail, and at the back of the ship, a lateen sail.

Skills in navigation also were much improved in the late fifteenth century. This improvement, like the new ship design, resulted from a blend of northern and southern European experience. The navigators who made the first trans-Atlantic crossings were indebted to their Mediterranean ancestors for a tradition of careful navigational records and charts and especially for the compass, an instrument invented by the Chinese centuries before but adopted belatedly by Mediterranean sailors. Southern navigators also had learned how to estimate, even on a cloudy night when stars were not visible, where their ship was. Called dead reckoning, this method involves plotting a course on a chart by correlating direction, time, and speed. Time was measured by small hourglasses. Speed only was guessed at

This engraving illustrated Columbus's letter of 1493. The ship is not a likeness of one of his three ships, but a stylized version of a carrack from that period.

The New York Public Library.

in the fifteenth century, and Columbus consistently overestimated the speed of his ships. Further errors in dead reckoning crept in because early navigators did not know how to evaluate the force of ocean currents. Nevertheless, dead reckoning was an intuitive skill raised to the level of an art in the late fifteenth century.

Another valuable navigational instrument was the quadrant. It was a simple apparatus for measuring how far one had moved north or south from an original starting point (latitude). By looking through two pinhole sights at the North Star when the quadrant was held in an absolutely upright position (determined by a dangling plumb line), a navigator could determine the altitude of the North Star—and from that information figure out his own latitude.

From the northern European tradition, navigators inherited far simpler skills, but one proved invaluable—dropping a weighted line overboard in order to measure the ocean's depth. Since Columbus was sailing through uncharted waters and, once he arrived in the New World, piloting his ships from one island to another in the Caribbean, he needed constant measurements of how deep the water was. Without such measurements, he easily could have wrecked his ships on hidden reefs or shallows.

Technological innovations in European ship design in the late fifteenth century can be seen as part of technological innovations in transportation that have given rise to the Modern World. As larger and more efficient sailing vessels were developed, they made possible the movement of large numbers of people and goods between America and Europe. The development of steamships between 1850 and 1920 permitted the emigration of millions of Europeans to America to settle in cities and on farms. During this same century a network of railroads gradually came into existence that contributed to the settlement of the West and promoted the exchange of goods between East and West and North and South. Introduction of the streetcar in the 1880s began to give a definite shape to America's cities. Then in the 1920s the automobile helped to create suburban America and gave Americans what appeared to be unlimited geographic mobility. Limitations of time and space were even more greatly reduced with the rise of air transportation after World War II. While none of these technological innovations in transportation has been an unmixed blessing, they have cumulatively helped to shape both land and people from the time of Columbus to the present.

The New York Public Library, Picture Collection.

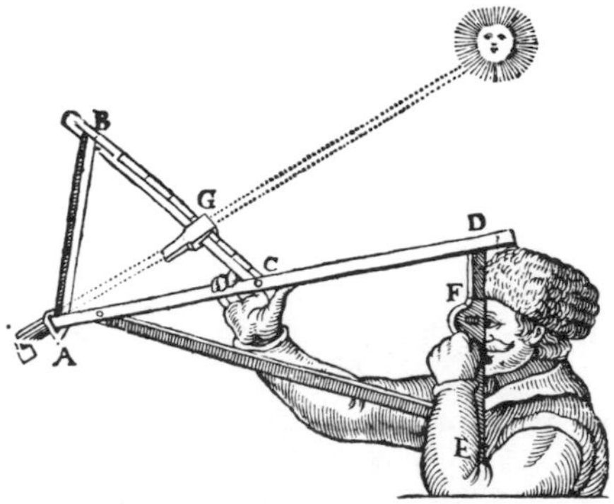

The Davis quadrant, developed in the late seventeenth century, was a major navigational advance that allowed sailors to use the sun's position to determine latitude.

General and Exploration Studies

Helge Ingstad, *Westward to Vinland: The Discovery of Pre-Columbian Norse House-Sites in North America* (1969)

J. H. Parry, *The Age of Reconnaissance* (1963)

Samuel Eliot Morison, *Admiral of the Ocean Sea* (2 vols., 1942)

David B. Quinn, *Raleigh and the British Empire* (1949)

C. R. Boxer, *Dutch Seaborne Empire, 1600–1800* (1965)

American Indians

Alfred Crosby, Jr., *The Columbian Exchange: Biological and Cultural Consequences of 1492* (1972)

Frances Jennings, *The Invasion of America: Indians, Colonialism, and the Cant of Conquest* (1975)

Wilcomb Washburn, *The Indian in America* (1975)

Grace Woodward, *Pocohantas* (1969)

Origins of British Settlement

Wallace Notestein, *The English People on the Eve of Colonization* (1954)

Alden Vaughan, *American Genesis: Captain John Smith and the Founding of Virginia* (1975)

Wesley F. Craven, *Dissolution of the Virginia Company: the Failure of a Colonial Experiment* (1932)

Comparative and General Colonial Studies

Clarence Ver Steeg, *The Formative Years, 1607–1763* (1964)

W. C. Eccles, *France in America* (1972)

Van Cleaf Bachman, *Pelteries or Plantations: Economic Policies of the Dutch West India Company in New Netherland, 1623–1639* (1970)

Charles Gibson, *Spain in America* (1966)

Carl Sauer, *The Early Spanish Main* (1966)

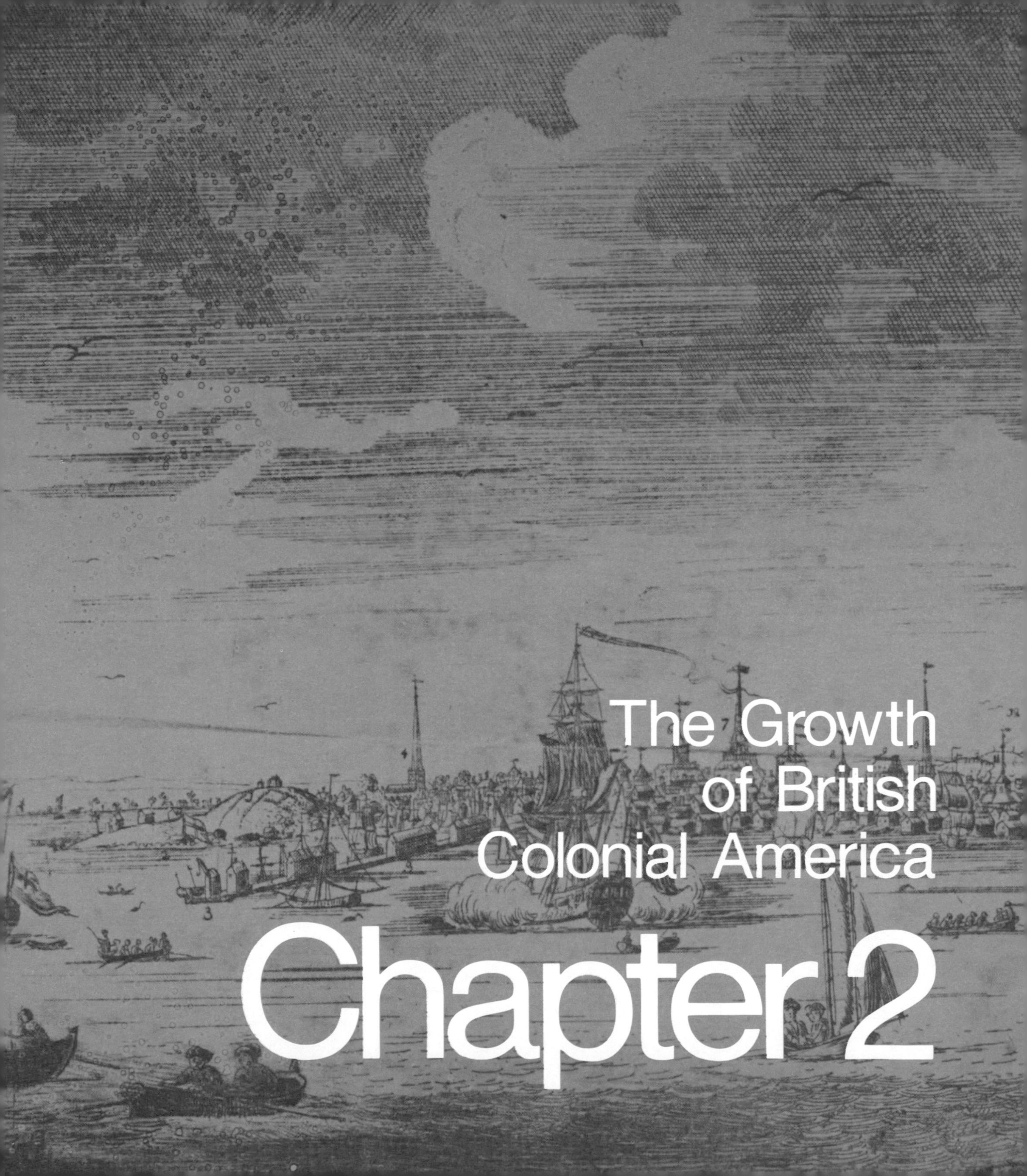

Chapter 2

The Growth of British Colonial America

TIMELINE

1620
Separatist Pilgrims settle Plymouth Colony
1622
First major Indian uprising against the colonists
1624
Jamestown becomes a royal colony directly responsible to the king
1629
Puritans emigrate to Massachusetts Bay
1637
Pequot War in New England
1638
Anne Hutchinson banished from Massachusetts Bay
1649
Maryland Assembly passes the Act of Toleration to protect Catholics
1659
Richard Cromwell, Oliver Cromwell's son, resigns as Lord Protector
1660
The Stuart monarchy under Charles II is restored
1664
Charles II gives the Duke of York a proprietary grant to a large tract between Maryland and New England
1669
Slavery is incorporated into Carolina constitution
1675
Bacon's Rebellion in Virginia
1676
King Philip's War ends the Indian threat to settlement in New England
1681
William Penn receives a grant from the king to settle Pennsylvania
1685
France revokes the Edict of Nantes
1689
William and Mary promulgate the Act of Toleration
1705
Virginia unifies its various laws on slavery
1732
James Oglethorpe establishes a settlement of debtors in Georgia

CHAPTER OUTLINE

"They say there's bread and work for all," went the line of a popular song English immigrants to North America liked to sing, "and the sun shines always there." To be sure, the promise of improved economic opportunity, if not a brighter climate, was a chief attraction enticing settlers to leave England and come to the original colonies in the seventeenth century. Before 1700, the lure to North America worked most strongly in England itself and Wales; after 1700, it was felt most steadily in Scotland, Ireland, and Germany. And throughout the eighteenth century, the number of black slaves increased to an ever larger portion of the annual arrivals.

Immigrants and Their Origins

Apart from a scattering of Dutch, Swiss, Swedish, Finnish, and French settlers who reached North America in the seventeenth century, the majority of settlers were English, parted from their homeland because of deliberate religious persecution and pervasive economic hardship. Although leaders of English society lacked the techniques of taking an accurate census of the population, many of them sincerely believed that the British Isles were perilously close to being overpopulated. What made this conclusion plausible was the growing number of vagrants caused by the transformation of an agricultural to an industrial society. During much of the seventeenth century, many tenant farmers either suffered crushing rises in rent or were dispossessed of their lands. Many of the landless drifted to the towns and cities and there formed a large, restless mass of actual or potential troublemakers. It was understandable for the government to treat the colonies as safe and productive places to siphon off these unemployed.

Yet the desperately poor did not find their way to the American colonies. Although fear of vagrants was one reason for the government's cultivation of new colonies, the emigrants who did leave for North America were mostly young men and women of modest but respectable backgrounds. Among the men were former yeomen (small farmers who once cultivated their own land) or husbandmen (workers whom we would now call "farmhands"). Of the 10,000 indentured servants who sailed from the port of Bristol between 1654 and 1685, for example, about thirty-six percent of them were farmers and farm workers; twenty-two percent were skilled nonfarm workers; and ten percent were unskilled nonfarm workers. Skilled workers and farmers outnumbered common laborers by about five to one. What we can conclude is that the lowest recognized rank of English society, the unskilled laborer, seldom entered the New World, although farmers and skilled workers did come in large numbers—usually in search of land.

The Lust for Land

Tradesmen as well as farmers wanted land in America. To Englishmen of the seventeenth century, land meant security and social position. Tradesmen, moreover, were often the sons of farmers. If they were not working the land, that was generally because there was no land to be had. According to English law and custom, a father's farm went intact to his oldest son, and younger sons were apprenticed to various trades. But they accepted their landless positions only by default. They still wanted real property of their own, a desire that was increasingly thwarted because land was becoming ever scarcer and more expensive. In the semifeudal English tradition of property, many small farmers did not actually own their land but leased it for a long term (usually ninety-nine years) from their local lord. During the seventeenth century, many of these leases were expiring. To renew them, farmers had to agree to prohibitively high rents. Some large landholders would not renew leases because they were consolidating small plots of farmland into pastures for sheep. Wool and mutton were far more profitable products than barley or wheat.

Deprived of land, yet convinced that owning land was the only sure way of winning security and independence, the yeomen and husbandmen of England listened eagerly to tales of vast, free acreage available in America.

Few of these land-hungry farmers had the means to pay for their own passage to the New World. More than half of the colonial settlers from England came as indentured servants. Indenture usually required a settler to agree to serve a master in North America for four years in return for free passage across the Atlantic. At the end of his or her term of service, at least during the early seventeenth century, the indentured worker would be rewarded with "freedom dues." More often than not, one of these rewards would be a plot of land, although other freedom dues might include a fixed sum of money, specified tools, clothes, or even food. After 1650, this practice of granting liberal freedom dues fell into disuse.

The terms and conditions of indenture varied considerably, depending upon the age and ability of the servant. Although four years was the usual period of service, indenture could last as long as seven, or even nine, years. Once the worker arrived, he or she generally received no wages, only food, shelter, and clothing, although in some cases skilled artisans also earned small annual wages. The indenture was a legal contract and could be written in many ways. For instance, children frequently were indentured with the understanding they would be given an elementary education or taught a trade.

NOVA BRITANNIA.
OFFERING MOST
Excellent fruites by Planting in
VIRGINIA.
Exciting all ſuch as be well affected
to further the ſame.

LONDON
Printed for SAMVEL MACHAM, and are to be ſold at
his Shop in Pauls Church-yard, at the
Signe of the Bul-head.
1609.

The New York Public Library, Rare Book Division.

The authors of this pamphlet hoped to attract settlers to Virginia by stressing economic gain. Its stress on "Excellent fruites" is ironic considering the starving condition of the colony in 1609.

Today, this system of servitude may strike us as harsh, undemocratic, and unfair, but to a person without property in seventeenth century England, it seemed both fair and normal. The tradition of apprenticeship was an ancient practice, and for hundreds of years apprentices had entered into legal agreements to exchange their services to master craftsmen in return for instruction in one trade or another.

Few farmers in North America could afford to travel to England to select their own workers. As a result, enterprising English merchants filled up ships sailing to the colonies with cargoes of indentured servants. A merchant could turn a profit by selling the servants at a price above the cost of contracting and transporting them. For their part, colonial planters found the procedure profitable, since by buying the labor of many farmhands, they could quickly go beyond merely supplying their own needs to producing large surplus crops. Finally, the English government was pleased with the system since it assured a peopling of the colonies with little or no expense to the state.

In order to attract indentured servants to the New World, colorful and not quite truthful accounts of the "paradise" beyond the Atlantic were circulated in England. Unmarried girls frequently came in search of husbands. Single young men without property or prospects came in search of both. Sometimes the government arranged for convicted criminals to be indentured and deported as a form of punishment and rehabilitation.

Whether they came as indentured servants or paid their own passage, nearly every immigrant wanted land, which could be acquired by many different methods. In their early years, all colonies handed out free land to newcomers. The Southern colonies distributed land according to a "headright system" whereby a particular number of acres (usually fifty) was given to each person (or "head"). Thus a family of four, two parents and two children, could collect the rights to 200 acres upon arrival. All the family was required to do was to survey and register a claim for land that was available on the frontier; and at this period the frontier was usually only a few miles inland from the Atlantic coast. As for indentured male servants, they frequently had, as noted earlier, contracts specifying land as a due at the end of their periods of service.

By the eighteenth century, land speculators, who now held most of the unoccupied land in the original colonies, were selling it to new arrivals. The price per acre, however, was still very low since cheap land along the frontier was abundantly available, and was to remain so for many decades even after the prices of property in the built-up coastal areas became relatively high.

Still other settlers passed through two stages in their search for land. First they were tenants, renting small farms from large landowners, who offered them tools, seed, and homes. After a number of years spent in renting, tenants often accumulated enough money to purchase their own land.

After 1700, England was no longer the main source of immigrants. By then, numerous social changes favored stability in Great Britain and made the New World less appealing. The rampant unrest, which had afflicted English life throughout much of the seventeenth century, had subsided, and the great religious questions seemed resolved. Even though the Church of England enjoyed a preferred status after 1689, a general tolerance of Protestant sects decreased the outward flow of immigrants. As forests dwindled, coal mining became a vast growth industry that drew more and more workers into the pits as coal became the major fuel. Other industries that prospered in seventeenth and eighteenth century England were shipbuilding, glass manufacturing, iron mining, and salt processing. As a result, policymakers in government became concerned about the loss of skilled workers and even passed laws to prevent them from going to America.

The new source of immigrants was Scotland and Ireland. Although Scotland and England had the same king after 1603, Scotland did not officially become a part of Britain until 1707. Before then, Scots were regarded as aliens and had to submit to unfavorable arrangements to emigrate to the English colonies. After 1707, however, the New World was easily accessible to the Scots, and they poured into North America. Among them were many Highlanders defeated in various uprisings against the English, and many crofters (or cottagers) deprived of their leaseholds. Others were representatives, so-called "factors," of Edinburgh firms eager to do business with the new tobacco wealth of Maryland and Virginia, a trade the Scots nearly monopolized by the 1750s.

Meanwhile, a large number of Scots migrated, not to America, but to Ireland, especially the northern part. These Scots-Irish began to find life in Ireland increasingly uncongenial as they got caught up in the long-standing feud between the colonizing English and the native Irish. The English Parliament passed laws forbidding Irish cloth traders to export fabrics to any area where such products would compete with English cloth—and these laws eventually destroyed the Irish cloth trade. Most Scots-Irish farmers tried to establish themselves as tenants, but rising rents in Ireland soon made emigration again attractive. Finally, although the Scots were Presbyterians, they had to pay a sizable part of their incomes to support the so-called "Church of Ireland," a local branch of the Church of England. This

Library of Congress.

Samuel Vetch
(1668–1732)

Soldier, trader, and the first man to formulate an adequate plan for the expulsion of the French from North America, Vetch was born in Edinburgh, Scotland. He spent an uneasy boyhood in northern England where his father preached the outlawed Presbyterian faith and conspired against the crown. As a teen-ager, Vetch received some higher education in the Netherlands and, when William and Mary assumed power, gained a commission in a Scottish regiment.

In 1698 he joined an ill-fated venture in Central America, and a year later when most of the colonists fled to New York, Vetch went with them. There, his handsome and commanding presence won him a bride, Margaret Livingston, daughter of the secretary of Indian affairs, and soon Vetch was deeply involved in the Albany Indian trade and its illegal connections with the French at Montreal. A few years later he moved to Boston, purchased boats, and expanded the growing trade in arms and ammunition with the enemy. Public opinion became so aroused that in 1706 he and his associates were convicted and fined by the General Court of Massachusetts for these activities, but Vetch fled to England, demanded a new trial, and eventually escaped punishment.

While there he concocted a scheme for ousting the French from Canada, which included an attack on Montreal by way of Lake Champlain and seizure of Quebec by land and sea. After those bastions were taken, he believed that other French outposts and perhaps even some Spanish colonies would fall easily into English hands. In March 1709, Vetch won the approval of the Whig government in London for his plan and set out for Boston. Within a few months he had three well-trained regiments in the field and the enthusiastic backing of New England and New York, although Quaker Pennsylvania and New Jersey expressed little interest in this undertaking. Then, as a result of the British decision to use its support troops elsewhere and poor execution of Vetch's ideas, the plan faltered. In 1710 colonial forces were able to seize Nova Scotia where Vetch became military governor.

Four years later, at odds with civil authorities, he fled to England once more where he spent the rest of his life in a futile search for a government job. Tempted by the promises of various ministries, he lingered on and died there in 1732, a prisoner for debts he had accumulated. ■

---

combination of pressures set off the first mass emigration from Ireland.

The Beginnings of Slavery

After 1700, another large group of immigrants came to North America, but these individuals came against their will and in chains. The eighteenth century saw the full development of slavery in Britain's New World colonies as thousands of blacks were forcefully relocated under brutal conditions from their native Africa, a horrifying experience that left dark scars upon that era and has embittered race relations ever since. In 1700 no colony had more than 5,000 slaves; but by 1770 New England had about 13,000 slaves, and Virginia had about 170,000 slaves, who constituted half of the population of the colony. Expressed in other terms, in 1760 twenty-three percent of the entire population were slaves; four-fifths of the slaves, however, lived in the South, generally near the Atlantic coast. Black population growth was only partially due to importation. For instance, between 1710 and 1769 only 55,000 slaves were brought from Africa to Virginia, although, as noted, by 1770 the Old Dominion had some 170,000 blacks, many of whom were obviously second-, third-, or even fourth-generation Virginians.

Although slavery flourished in the eighteenth century, it was an institution that evolved gradually during the preceding century. During the seventeenth century the English prided themselves on the high degree of personal liberty they enjoyed. The entire political and judicial thrust of English society was toward greater personal freedom. That the colonists, who invariably regarded themselves as English, should have created and accepted an extensive system of slavery demands a close investigation of the seventeenth century colonial environment. During the Middle Ages the English had a feudal social structure within which serfs were bound to the lord of the manor, but this practice died out by the time the English came to the New World. Within the confines of English society, there was no precedent for slavery. In order to devise the institution of slavery, the English had to pass through a series of complex and subtle shifts of attitude.

The concept of slavery as it developed in North America implies the complete loss of personal freedom. Because it is a lifelong condition and is hereditary, it can be contrasted with indentured servitude. The indentured servant traded his services in return for free passage across the Atlantic, and this bargain was carefully regulated by the law of contracts. The servant sold his services, not his body, and only for a fixed period of time. The children of an indentured servant in no sense became the property of that servant's master. In all these ways, slavery and servitude differed.

What was it that made the enslavement of blacks acceptable to English colonists? For English people of the sixteenth and seventeenth centuries, the color black had deep psychological associations with evil which are difficult to analyze with precision. Black was not only the color of physical defilement, of the tortured ways of the human heart, of the Devil, of negation and nothingness, but also the palpable sign of the loss of God's grace, of extreme spiritual deprivation and of utter unworthiness.

Virginia Gazette.

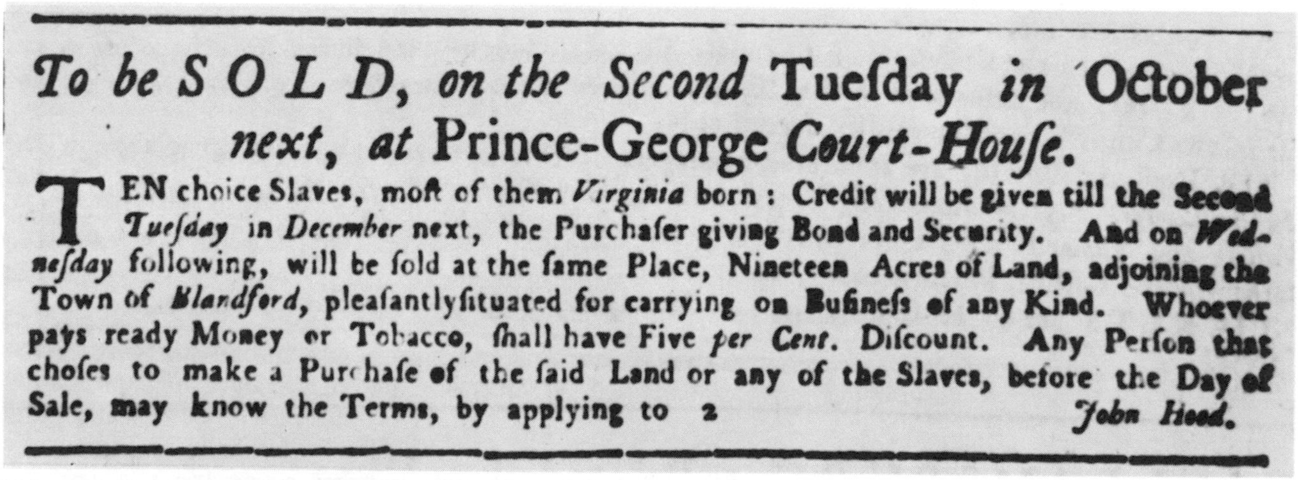
To be SOLD, on the Second Tueſday in October next, at Prince-George Court-Houſe.

TEN choice Slaves, moſt of them Virginia born: Credit will be given till the Second Tueſday in December next, the Purchaſer giving Bond and Security. And on Wedneſday following, will be ſold at the ſame Place, Nineteen Acres of Land, adjoining the Town of Blandford, pleaſantly ſituated for carrying on Buſineſs of any Kind. Whoever pays ready Money or Tobacco, ſhall have Five per Cent. Diſcount. Any Perſon that choſes to make a Purchaſe of the ſaid Land or any of the Slaves, before the Day of Sale, may know the Terms, by applying to 2 John Hood.

This advertisement, which appeared in the September 19, 1755 issue of The Virginia Gazette, makes clear the slave's status as property. Land and slaves are sold on the same terms.

White, on the other hand, was the color of virginal purity, the emblem of high moral rectitude beyond all reproach, of unblemished integrity fused with consuming intensity.

Also it was easier on the seventeenth century conscience to enslave black Africans because seldom were they Christians. True, the English had an aversion to enslaving their fellow Christians, but this scruple did not extend to "heathens." African religions, customs, clothing (or lack of it)—all seemed so strange to the English that they could scarcely regard blacks as fellow human beings. In an effort to rationalize their bias against black skin color, the English resorted to the Bible and traced the descent of Africans to Cham, the wicked and disobedient son of Noah. By this reasoning, blacks were by their very nature evil and deserving of punishment.

Other ingredients also must be examined in order to understand how the English evolved the concept of slavery. At least in theory, English writers on jurisprudence recognized that enslavement of an enemy taken in battle could be an alternative to death. Slavery and captivity were equated, and both were seen as one possible destiny for the defeated. On the level of more practical experience, the English were able to observe the enslavement of black Africans as a familiar aspect of Spanish settlements in the New World. For centuries the Portuguese and Spanish had enslaved Moors captured in religious wars, and in the fifteenth century the Portuguese began to carry thousands of blacks back from Africa to Europe. After 1500, Portuguese traders transported black slaves to Spanish and Portuguese colonies in America. That the English tended to regard blacks through the eyes of the Spanish can be deduced from the fact that in the mid-sixteenth century, *negro,* the Spanish word for black was incorporated into English. Indeed, "Negro" was used far more commonly than the perfectly adequate English word "black."

This brief sketch of the development of slavery in North America should not gloss over the fact that the primary reasons for slavery were economic, not ideological. Throughout the English colonies in the seventeenth and eighteenth centuries, there was a severe labor shortage. To some extent, indentured servitude helped to reduce this problem, but black slavery was the ultimate solution. Tobacco-growing colonies such as Virginia and Maryland needed a form of labor cheaper, more abundant, and more easily managed and identified than freed indentured servants. The first blacks in Virginia clearly were indentured servants and were freed at the end of a term of service. After 1640, however, there is evidence that some of them were regarded as lifetime slaves. For in that year three indentured servants, Victor, a Dutchman, James Gregory, a Scot, and John Punch, a black, escaped and were captured in Maryland. Victor and James Gregory were forced to serve an additional year of indenture, but John Punch was sentenced to serve "for the time of his natural life."

After 1660, slave codes began to be written into law, and by 1705 Virginia had set down a unified compilation of its various laws on slavery. Although slavery developed gradually in Virginia and Maryland, it was written into the very constitution of Carolina in 1669 by settlers who came from Barbados where slave codes already existed. According to this document, each freeman of the colony would have "absolute power and authority over his Negro slaves, of what opinion or religion soever."

In New England and other Northern colonies, farming usually had little use for whole regiments of African slaves, yet slaves were found in some sections of New York, Rhode Island, and Connecticut well into the eighteenth century. By the end of the colonial period, Rhode Island had the largest number of slaves per capita in New England. All the same, throughout the colonial period, New England was deeply involved in the economy of the developing slave trade. Merchants from that region often carried blacks from Africa to islands held by the English in the West Indies. And again, at the close of the colonial era, it was Rhode Island that had the greatest stake in the slave trade. Although slaves were not used extensively in New England to raise cash crops, they were in a certain sense—as an institution—fundamental in shaping the early prosperity of that region. As one of the governors of Massachusetts put it, "It pleased the Lord to open to us a trade with Barbados and other Islands in the West Indies."

Political and Religious Influences

Many emigrants from England were drawn to America by a hunger for land and the hope of economic opportunity. Another large group came to practice their religion free from English interference, but this freedom proved to be selfish and parochial since each group of colonists denied, with the one notable exception of Rhode Island, the right to others to worship differently in its midst.

Library of Congress.

All of the phases of tobacco production are compressed into one scene for an English readership in 1750.

Throughout much of Europe, church and local government were closely linked for centuries. Yet the Roman Catholic Church, whose claims were transnational and supratemporal, had to contend with competing dogmas within and conflicting political interests without. The rise of nation-states in the fifteenth and sixteenth centuries precipitated a clash of allegiances that eventually took northern Europe—and, in time, England as well—into the Protestant fold, while southern Europe, France, south Germany, and Ireland remained predominantly Catholic.

As it evolved under Elizabeth I (1533–1603), the Church of England was sort of a halfway house between Protestantism and Catholicism. This new official state church was supported by tax monies that once were sent to Rome, the English sovereign replaced the Pope as head of the church, and bishops sat in the House of Lords—in short, church and state were closely bound together. Debate over the spiritual value of what had occurred created three distinct groups in opposition to each other but all eager to overturn or to modify the Church of England and, failing that, to emigrate. These included disgruntled Catholics, Puritans (those who wanted to "purify" the new church and to make it more Protestant in form and outlook), and Separatists such as Pilgrims, Presbyterians, Quakers, and Baptists, who, as the term implies, wanted to establish their own congregations free of all state interference—or, perhaps, to set up their *own* state.

As these various groups struggled for supremacy, England experienced constant turmoil throughout the 1600s. For the most part, the confrontation was three-sided: Catholics who wished to reestablish the old ties with Rome; Anglicans who wished to strengthen the state church under the headship of the English monarch; and dissenters, some who wished to cleanse the Church of England of popish ritual and others to allow each isolated congregation to have Christ for its immediate head.

Between 1641 and 1660 England was torn by civil war as Puritans battled monarchists pledged to uphold the new faith. Puritan forces, led by Oliver Cromwell (1599–1658) emerged victorious in 1649 and beheaded Charles I; however, in 1660 his son, Charles II, was restored to the throne. In 1688 his brother, James II, was ousted after a brief reign during which he tried to insure that his male heir (born in 1688) would be Catholic. James was banished and replaced by his Protestant daughter, Mary and her Dutch husband, William.

Ruling jointly, William and Mary promulgated an Act of Toleration (1689); yet for a century or more dissenters were still viewed with hostility. Toleration did not mean complete religious freedom, only that the sovereign would "tolerate" reluctantly the existence of those who dissented from the Church of England, which remained as the established state faith supported by the taxes paid by all, regardless of belief. In addition, those who chose to retain their status as Nonconformists were barred from full civil rights.

Needless to say, such turmoil provided a powerful impetus for migration. Over 20,000 Puritans arrived in Massachusetts Bay, for example, in the early 1630s. Yet one should be aware that in such a fluid situation by no means all of those who left England came to the New World. Many, especially Catholics during the time of Cromwell, went instead to the Continent. Even the small band of Pilgrims who settled in Plymouth in 1620 lived for a time in Holland.

While Puritans undoubtedly were the most numerous of the dissenting groups to come to America from England in the seventeenth century, immigrants of those decades also included Quakers, by far the most radical of the Separatists, so much so that several Quaker missionaries who ventured into Puritan Massachusetts were hanged. However, between 1680 and 1710 larger groups of Quakers appeared in New Jersey, Pennsylvania, and Delaware.

Although the fanatical fires of religious faith and their attendant stifling of individual conscience in England may be difficult to comprehend in our age, the English were, in fact, more liberal about religious choice than most other European countries. As a result, English colonies soon became a refuge for religious minorities from France and Germany. During the 1580s and 1590s, like England of a few decades later, France was torn by religious strife. In 1598, when Henry of Navarre had become King of France, he issued the Edict of Nantes assuring Protestants, the followers of John Calvin (1509–1564)—called Huguenots in France—that the state would "tolerate" their faith. However, these Protestants were viewed as an irksome minority in a Catholic realm, and in 1685 the Edict was revoked. The borders of France were sealed and Huguenots were avidly hunted down; nevertheless, thousands managed to escape and flee to Protestant nations in Europe. Some of them settled in the Netherlands, where they fought on the side of the Dutch ruler, William of Orange (1650–1702), against France. When William married Mary, the daughter of England's King James II, and they acceded jointly to the

Historical Society of Pennsylvania.

Quakers at first considered portraits too worldly and vain; but as the group prospered, the wealthy succumbed to the desire for memorials and compromised on silhouettes such as this one of merchant John Reynell.

throne of England in 1689, he was in a position to reward the Huguenot refugees who had fought in his behalf. He granted them land in the English colonies and helped pay their transportation costs. Many of them settled in South Carolina, where they established rice plantations along the coast; others took up residence in Virginia and New York.

German religious groups also began to seek refuge in the colonies. Germany at that time was not a single

Courtesy Henry Ravelnel Dwight, Jr.

The parents of Catherine Le Serrurier Le Noble were Huguenot refugees to the colonies. Her family prospered in the New World as reflected in this portrait.

country but rather a mosaic of many small kingdoms, principalities, duchies, bishoprics, and independent cities—each with its own particular religion that forbade the toleration of all other sects. Some of these states were Catholic, others Lutheran or Calvinist. Each of these major branches of Christianity persecuted the others, and they all hounded small sects such as the Mennonites, the Moravians, and the Amish. Since these sects had much in common with English Quakers, they found a home in the Quaker-dominated colony of Pennsylvania.

Not only religious differences but also the terrors of war drove Germans to the New World. Throughout the seventeenth and eighteenth centuries, the German states were the scene of prolonged dynastic strife fused with contending religious factions. When German princelings were not forcing their subjects to fight their own wars, they were renting them out as mercenary troops to other European powers, or putting them in coalitions for or against the Swedes, the French, the Prussians, and the Austrians. The ravages of war and the tribulations of religious persecution motivated many Germans to emigrate and settle in the English colonies of North America.

Two other religious groups also sought refuge in the colonies: Catholics and Jews. The province of Maryland was designed by George Calvert, Lord Baltimore (ca. 1580–1632), an English Catholic, who ruled a large domain in Ireland which was a haven for members of his faith. In 1649 the Maryland Assembly passed an Act of Toleration. This famous document reads in part:

“Whereas the enforcing of the conscience in matters of religions hath frequently fallen out to be of dangerous consequence in those commonwealths where it hath been practised, and for the more quiet and peaceable government of this province and the better to preserve mutual love and amity amongst the inhabitants thereof: Be it therefore . . . enacted . . . that no person or persons whatsoever within this province . . . professing to believe in Jesus Christ shall from henceforth be any ways troubled, molested, or discountenanced for, or in respect of, his or her religion, nor in the free exercise thereof within this province.”

The Act of Toleration did not endure for long since a Puritan majority gained control over Maryland in 1654 and repealed it. Reinstated four years later, the act was gradually modified to the disadvantage of Catholics by the end of the seventeenth century. With the ouster of James II and the so-called “Glorious Revolution” of 1688, the Anglican Church in a few years became the official faith in Maryland and received tax support. Roman Catholics were tolerated but could not hold governmental office. In short, events in the Maryland colony mirrored at a distance the fluctuating fortunes of religious factions in England.

The first Jews arrived in the colonies in the 1650s. At its best, toleration in the seventeenth and eighteenth centuries extended only to other Christians. Settling in New Amsterdam, Rhode Island, and Philadelphia, the Jews attempted to remain as inconspicuous as possible in every community without sacrificing their heritage. Yet, as late as 1762, the Superior Court denied fifteen families of Jews in Newport, Rhode Island, the right to be naturalized as citizens.

Courtesy Society of Friends of Touro Synagogue. Photo by John Hopf.

Even Jewish synagogues reflected colonial architectural styles. Touro Synagogue in Newport, Rhode Island was designed by Peter Harrison for the prosperous community there.

Patterns of Settlement

As communities began to take form along the Atlantic seaboard in the seventeenth century, a few distinct patterns of settlement emerged. Immigrants brought to America against their will—slaves, convicts, and many of the indentured servants—had no choice, of course, where they were to be settled. Families were often split apart and all sense of their original communal life destroyed. By contrast, voluntary immigrants transplanted their past into the present, the Old World into the New. They moved with families and relatives, often to locations where their former neighbors had already established towns or farms. Members of the same generation frequently migrated together. For instance, when Anne Hutchinson arrived in Massachusetts, she came with her husband and children and was soon followed by her sister and brother-in-law. Similarly, the Reverend Archibald Campbell (an Anglican minister who may have been George Washington's teacher) was one of four brothers who settled in Virginia.

The joint migration of relatives and neighbors to America helped to preserve Old World customs. The German settlers of eastern Pennsylvania retained their native language, styles of dress, and religious beliefs. In New England the system of landholding in each town was based on the particular practices of the majority of the first settlers. Thus a study of Sudbury, Massachusetts, reveals that, although people came to Sudbury from many parts of England, most of the original settlers were from a section of England where fields were not fenced in and the land was farmed communally, the identical pattern upon which Sudbury was modeled.

The Early Years, 1607–1660

During the decades from the establishment of Jamestown in 1607 to the Restoration in England in 1660, several permanent and eventually successful colonies appeared. The most important of them were Virginia (1607), Massachusetts Bay (1629), and Maryland (1632). Virginia and Massachusetts Bay were joint-stock ventures governed under a charter granted by the king; Maryland, a proprietary grant of land given to the first Baron Baltimore by his sovereign. While settlers at Jamestown and Massachusetts Bay had considerable control over their own affairs, the Baltimore family (or their resident agents) tended to exercise almost feudal power.

The little band of Pilgrim Separatists that settled at Plymouth in 1620, although celebrated in legend, fiction, and Thanksgiving, existed without a charter, grew slowly, and, in time, was swallowed up by the nearby and more prosperous Massachusetts Bay Colony of the Puri-

Culver Pictures.

William Bradford
(ca. 1590–1657)

Brought up by his uncles and grandfather after the death of his father, the future Pilgrim leader William Bradford was a sturdy Yorkshire yeoman who at an early age began to read the Bible and take an unusual interest in Nonconformist beliefs. Braving the scorn of relatives and neighbors, he continued this association and in 1609 joined a congregation that was emigrating to Leyden. Two years later, as Bradford relates, he came into "a comfortable inheritance left him by his honest parents."

During the decade that the Pilgrims were in Holland, Bradford worked as a weaver, and by the time they decided to sail for America, he obviously was one of the group's leaders. That the little Plymouth colony survived at all is a tribute to his stamina, zeal, dedication, and basic good sense. Although he urged rotation in office, he was governor for much of the first quarter of the century (1620–1645) and he also exerted great authority as principal judge and treasurer until 1637. Neither in the colony's records nor in Bradford's famous *History of Plimouth Plantation,* does one see much democracy at work in this government—that is something woven into the Plymouth story later by historians. In 1623 Bradford declared that the colonists would be allowed to share in the government "only in some weighty matters, when we think good." Two decades later only one-third of the men required to bear arms were freemen.

Bradford's first wife, whom he married in Leyden, drowned in 1620 while the *Mayflower* was anchored off Cape Cod. He subsequently courted by mail and then married in 1623 Alice Carpenter Southworth, widow of a former member of the Leyden congregation. They had a daughter and two sons whose descendants now number in the thousands. About 1630 Bradford began to write his *History,* a work probably intended only for family and friends as a memorial to high enterprise. It was finally printed in full in 1856 and is responsible, both directly and indirectly, for the large role the Plymouth colony plays in American history. Distressed by secular trends he saw on every hand, this undertaking undoubtedly consoled Bradford in his old age as he reflected upon the glory of Plymouth's early years. Lest anyone think him dour and drab, it should be noted that his estate included a red waistcoat, silver buttons, a colored hat, a violet cloak, a great silver "beer bowle," two silver wine cups, four Venice glasses, ninety-seven pounds of pewter dishes, and, not surprisingly, one of the largest libraries in Plymouth. ■

tans. Stern believers in congregational self-government, this band first settled in Holland for a decade (1609–1619), but about 100 members eventually set out for the New World aboard the *Mayflower.* They secured a land patent from the Virginia Company of London, but then settled outside of the area specified when they made first landfall at Cape Cod in midwinter. After the death of their first leader, Deacon John Carver, William Bradford became governor. Another New World outpost settled by the English during these years was Bermuda (1609), where some of the colonists bound for Jamestown found refuge for a time.

In 1624, after two devastating Indian raids and considerable financial and political turmoil, the weakened Virginia settlement at Jamestown surrendered its company charter and became a royal colony, a trend that was to be increasingly common throughout colonial history. These three settlements—Massachusetts, Maryland, and Jamestown—represent the three types of colonies that evolved in British North America: the charter or joint-stock company, the proprietary grant, and the royal colony with resident officials appointed by the crown. Each, in turn, reflected political conditions in England. A sovereign beset by civil strife often had little money to expend on colonial expeditions; hence, stock ventures and proprietary grants then suited his purposes well enough. But, at the same time, he and his advisors fretted over the absence of state control and usually asserted royal authority whenever able to do so; nevertheless, each colony eventually developed a local representative assembly, a miniature "parliament" of sorts.

Expanding the Colonies, 1660–1700

When King Charles II of England assumed power in 1660, he found himself deeply indebted to numerous individuals and consequently canceled these obligations with lavish gifts of real estate in the New World. In 1664 he gave his brother, the Duke of York, a huge proprietary grant covering all of present-day New York, Vermont, Pennsylvania, and New Jersey, half of Connecticut, Massachusetts, and Maine, and various offshore lands such as Long Island, Nantucket, and Martha's Vineyard. The duke had to oust the Dutch from New Amsterdam in order to claim his gift and name it "New York."

The Duke of York, later James II, subsequently gave the provinces of East and West Jersey to two of his friends, Sir George Carteret and Lord John Berkeley, who sold out to other groups which included a number of Quakers. Although proprietors enjoyed absolute power in theory, most permitted some form of representative government in practice in order to attract immigrants. West Jersey, which was settled mainly by Quakers, had, for example, an assembly and enjoyed religious toleration. In 1704 the crown united the two Jerseys into a single royal colony of New Jersey.

In 1681, William Penn (1644–1718), a Quaker, received the proprietary province of Pennsylvania as settlement for a loan his father had made to the Duke of York. Penn also ruled the Swedish and Dutch settlements in Delaware until 1700 when he created the separate colony of Delaware over which he and his heirs continued to exert some authority. Pennsylvania, well situated and blest with farsighted leadership, became within a few years one of the most prosperous of the English outposts.

Meanwhile, far to the South, the nucleus of another stable colony was evolving in the Carolinas. Between 1629 and 1670, several attempts, all ill fated, were made to settle that region. In 1663, a group of distinguished noblemen, led by the Earl of Shaftsbury, received a proprietary charter, but it was not until seven years later that a small band of 140 people from Barbados agreed with the Carolina proprietors to found the city of Charlestown. Aided by social philosopher John Locke, the earl and his friends tried to set up a strange hereditary aristocracy complete with feudal dues, manors, restrictive trade policies, which were never fully implemented as settlers succeeded in negotiating changes. Unfortunately, the proprietors proved unwilling or unable to protect their farmers and traders from incursions by the French, Spanish, and Indians. All the same, thanks to rice, indigo, and a flourishing trade with the West Indies, South Carolina, like Pennsylvania, became in time an important colonial settlement.

After 1680 the crown, which had until then granted North American lands so liberally to private business and to royal favorites, reversed its policy and tried to assert direct control, a reversal that had its counterpart at home where attempts were made to curb the special privileges of English cities. In 1685 a short-lived Dominion of New England was established encompassing all of present-day New England, New York, and New Jersey. With the "Glorious Revolution" and the overthrow of James II, however, William's ministers, who were busy at home

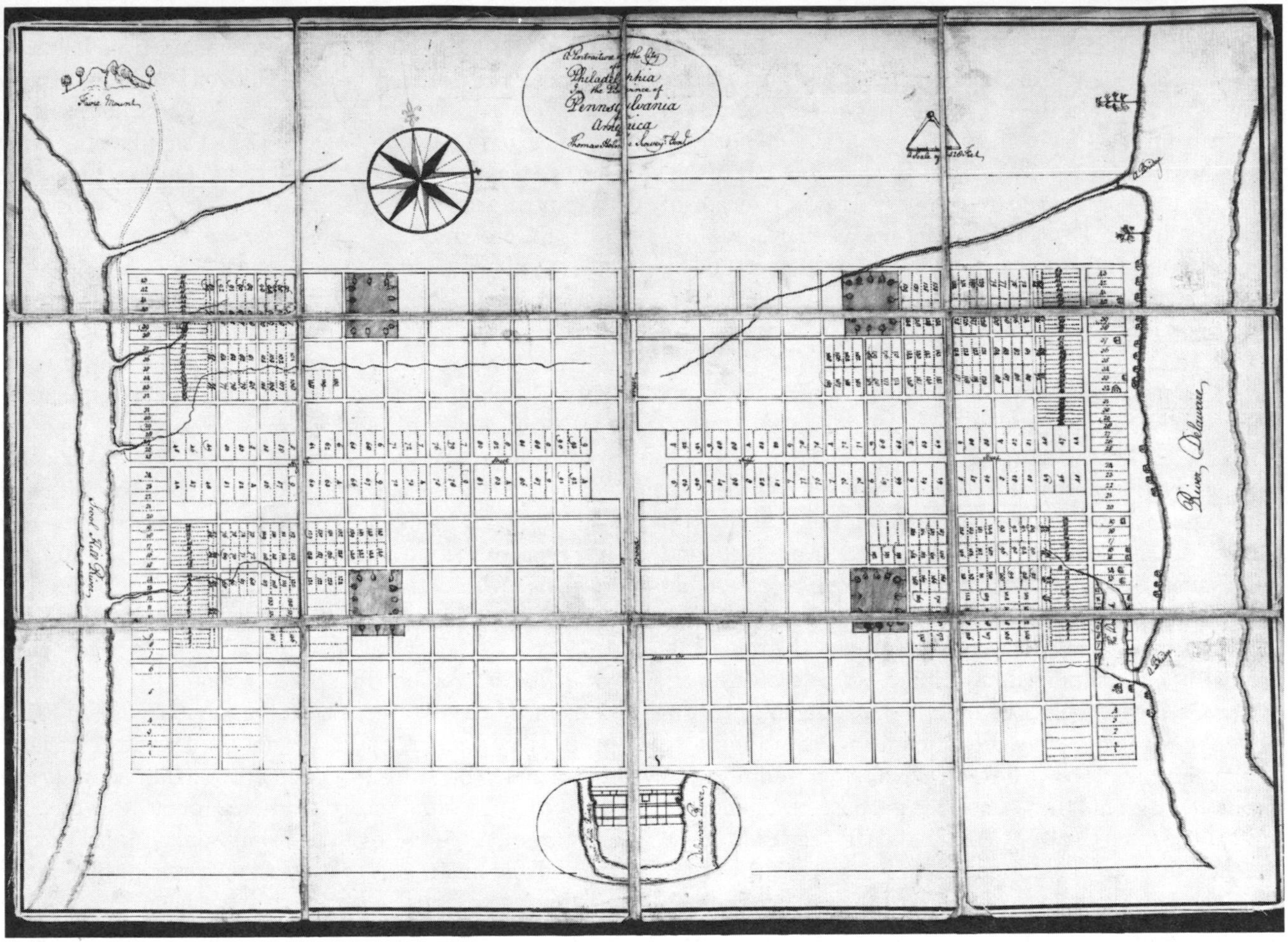

Historical Society of Pennsylvania.

The city plan for Philadelphia represented the growing ideal for order. Its neat squares and numbered streets left their imprint on cities across the United States.

and unfamiliar with colonial matters, permitted the Dominion to dissolve. Connecticut and Rhode Island resumed their old charters. Massachusetts became a royal colony that included Massachusetts Bay, Plymouth, and surrounding territories. And New York and New Hampshire each became royal colonies. Indeed, the latter had been—prior to the Dominion fiasco (1685–89)—a royal colony for about a decade. But the Jerseys, unlike New York, were returned to their original proprietors, at least temporarily.

The steady encroachments by royal authority are clear; by the mid-eighteenth century only five of the thirteen colonies that were destined to create a new independent nation were *not* ruled as royal colonies. Pennsylvania, Delaware, and Maryland, which were proprietary colonies, were still the personal domains of the Penn and Baltimore families; Connecticut and Rhode Island, which were relics of the past, continued to exist under charters. Yet even in these colonies the crown had managed to exert considerable power. In 1696, for example, a revision of the Navigation Acts required all governors to take an oath to enforce its provisions, and a customs service run by the English Treasury appeared in each colony. These agents of the crown could prosecute alleged vio-

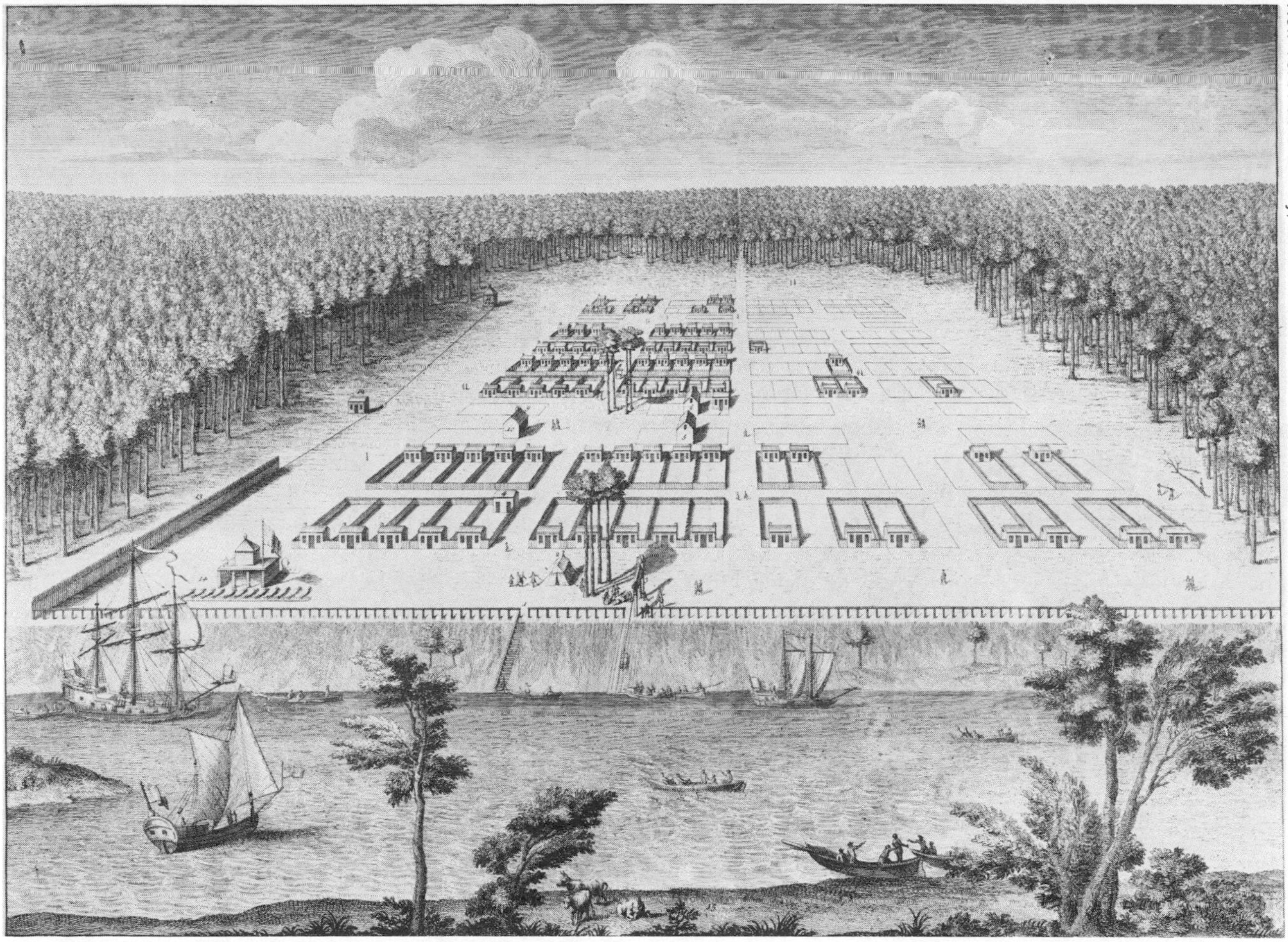

New York Public Library, Prints Division.

Savannah was a busy port before it had more than a handful of homes. Georgia's status as frontier colony is clear in this 1734 view of Savannah.

lators of the law in Admiralty courts set up by the Privy Council (a group of advisors to the sovereign), courts in which the deliberations of juries played no part.

Rounding Out the Colonies, 1700–1750

During the first half of the eighteenth century, the southernmost of the British settlements along the Atlantic coast assumed more recognizable form. In 1719, when the Carolina proprietors summoned the local militia to stem an Indian attack, the colonists used their arms against their rulers instead. Rather than quell the rebellion, the government in London used the opportunity to buy out the proprietors and to establish not one but two royal colonies, North and South Carolina.

The last of the thirteen colonies, Georgia, was somewhat of an anomaly. In 1732 a group of philanthropists led by James Oglethorpe and Thomas Coram set up a proprietary colony for debtors at Savannah, long after the crown had decided such colonial proprietorships were unworkable. The reason for this exception to royal policy was the desire of the government to create a buffer zone between the Carolinas and Spanish Florida and, at the same time, to rid England of debtors. Like the Earl of Shaftsbury before him, but with far different goals in mind, Oglethorpe tried to create an ideal society. And like Shaftsbury, his efforts also proved a dismal failure. By mid-century, Georgia was a royal colony.

Religious and Ethnic Tensions

Religious dissension, especially in seventeenth century New England, was one reason for the expansion of colonial settlement. The Massachusetts Bay Colony was not founded in order to create religious freedom for every sect but only to preserve the rights of Puritans to practice their own religion. In fact, dissenters who might have found common cause against the Church of England became hostile toward one another once they arrived in the New World. As various religious groups came to disagree with the established order in Massachusetts, they sought freedom in unsettled sections of New England not under the direct control of the Bay Colony. Sometimes these "heretics" withdrew from Massachusetts voluntarily; at other times they were banished.

One of the most famous "heretics" in early Puritan society was Anne Hutchinson. Extremely well-versed in the subtleties of religious doctrine, Anne Hutchinson became an important citizen of Boston soon after she arrived from England in 1634. Wealthy and the mother of fourteen children, she had followed her spiritual leader, the Reverend John Cotton, to the New World. She quickly met many people in Boston by serving as a midwife and soon began to invite her new friends to her home to discuss the Reverend Cotton's sermons. In time, these discussions constituted a challenge to local authority, and early in 1638, following a trial and excommunication, she, her husband and family, along with a few friends, fled to Rhode Island.

The events of Anne Hutchinson's life are crucial in understanding the early history of the Massachusetts Bay Colony. Her civil trial for "dangerous" beliefs discloses how seriously the Puritans viewed religious doctrine and her fate demonstrates to what extent the Puritans felt called upon to create a society in harmony with their religious beliefs—a harmony that had to be protected forcefully against the slightest threat of disruption.

The Flow of Migration

The simplest pattern of growth and expansion was natural drift; settlers in search of free or cheap land moved away from the older colonies and populated, for example the hinterlands of North Carolina, New Hampshire, and Connecticut. This expansion almost always flowed along natural "highways" such as rivers and bays. Springfield in Massachusetts on the Connecticut River was settled long before the land between the town and the coast. Because Virginia has such a convoluted coastline—hundreds of small inlets on the Chesapeake Bay—settlers had little reason for moving inland; for generations they could find farms immediately adjacent to a waterway. As a result, land no farther from the Virginia coast than fifteen miles often remained unsettled. Indeed, as late as 1700, settlement everywhere in North America was limited to a string of occupied areas along the coasts and rivers.

After 1700, immigrants began to move inland slowly. By that time some Indian tribes, decimated by disease and defeated in wars, had retreated so that Europeans could extend their frontiers at least to the eastern foothills of the Appalachians. On arrival, new settlers often found the coastal harbors and river towns heavily populated, with the only free land available to be found inland. Throughout the eighteenth century, immigrants from the European Continent, Ireland, and Scotland outnumbered those coming from England. These "ethnic" groups settled along the western frontier, frequently producing social tensions. In general, the eastern segments of the colonies were settled by the older, English immigrants, whereas the interior was filled by new arrivals, ethnic minorities.

William Penn's Colony

In Pennsylvania, for instance, the Scots-Irish moved to the frontier and there formed a geographically distinct and religiously separate group. These feisty frontiersmen, exposed to the rigors of the wild, frequently were attacked by the Indians. Back in sedate Philadelphia, the Quakers were preaching pacifism—a philosophy that won little sympathy from the embattled Scots-Irish. The Quakers refused to vote funds for military protection against the Indians; indeed, they forbade the formation of a militia. When the enraged Scots-Irish marched on Philadelphia, some Quakers (who were expelled subsequently from their church) took up arms to protect their city against them. A visiting Lutheran clergyman, unsympathetic to the Quakers, jotted down these notes in his journal for February 5, 1764:

Brown Bros.

Anne Hutchinson
(1591–1643)

Born into the family of a Lincolnshire minister with Puritan leanings, Anne Hutchinson absorbed much of her father's philosophy and religious outlook. In 1612 she married William Hutchinson, a merchant, and in 1634 moved to Massachusetts Bay where this large family—fourteen children—joined the congregation of John Cotton.

Known as "a woman of ready wit and bold spirit," Anne Hutchinson organized discussion groups at her home at which she began to elaborate upon religious ideas that led to her downfall. In essence, she came to believe that the Holy Spirit could dwell in all "justified" persons. The result was a belief in direct revelation which Puritans rejected.

She and her followers confidently, perhaps arrogantly, took it upon themselves to proclaim which fellow citizens were of the Elect (slated for salvation) and which were already damned. They denounced all of the ministers in Massachusetts except two, one of them being Anne's brother-in-law; the rest they accused of preaching the false idea that salvation could be won by performing good works.

Soon the colony was split between admirers and enemies, and when John Winthrop was re-elected governor in 1637 he decided to stamp out this heresy. He convened the ministers who condemned Anne for her beliefs and then summoned her before the General Court. Records reveal she performed brilliantly but also indicate the verdict had been decided even before she appeared.

Following excommunication and banishment, early in 1638, Anne Hutchinson, her husband and children, and a few friends emigrated to the island of Aquidneck in Rhode Island. Later they moved on to Long Island and then back to the mainland. In the summer of 1643 she and all but her youngest daughter were killed by Indians. ■

"Toward evening the rumor sprang up that a corps of backwoods settlers . . . were on the march toward Philadelphia. . . . Some reported that they numbered 700, others said 1500, etc. The Friends, or so-called Quakers, and the Moravians ran furiously back and forth to the barracks, and there was a great to-do over constructing several small fortresses or ramparts near the barracks. Cannons were also set up. Some remarked . . . that it seemed strange that such preparations should be made against one's own fellow citizens and Christians, whereas no one ever took so much trouble to protect from the Indians His Majesty's subjects and citizens on the frontier."

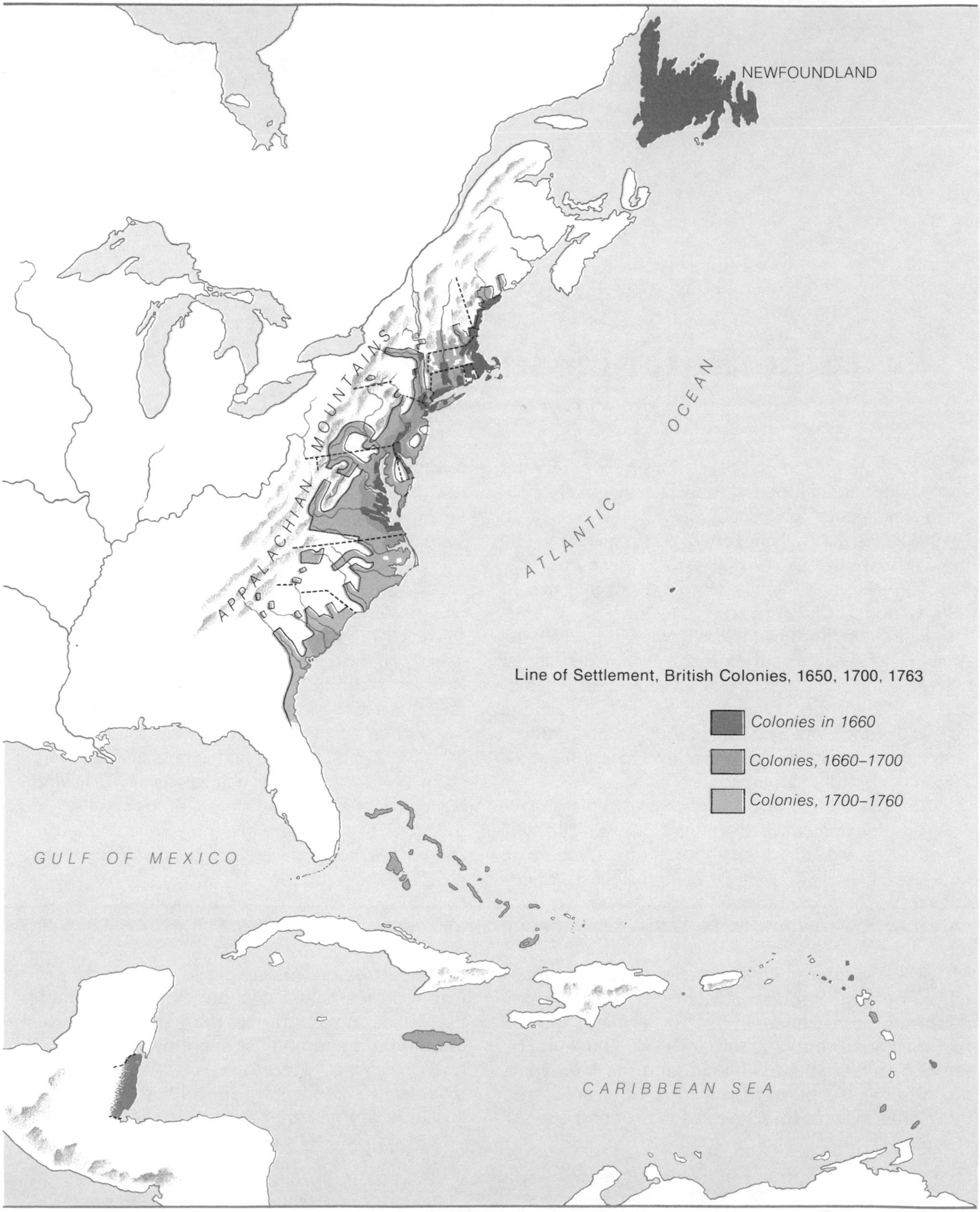
NEWFOUNDLAND
APPALACHIAN MOUNTAINS
ATLANTIC OCEAN
GULF OF MEXICO
CARIBBEAN SEA
Line of Settlement, British Colonies, 1650, 1700, 1763
Colonies in 1660
Colonies, 1660–1700
Colonies, 1700–1760

Settlement in the South

After 1730 the interior or back country of the South began to fill up with various ethnic groups. Again, the most numerous were the Scots-Irish; the next largest elements of the population were made up of Germans, Scots, Welsh, and a number of English Quakers. Many of these people originally settled in Pennsylvania or other Middle colonies, but were drawn to the backwoods of Maryland, Virginia, and the Carolinas by cheap land. For many, the Shenandoah and other valleys formed a natural pathway to new and less costly tracts. The average farm in Pennsylvania was expensive and consisted of only about 128 acres. In Maryland a plan was devised to attract newcomers by offering 200 acres to heads of families—and this property was free and exempt from taxation for the first three years.

These tough frontiersmen lived on a bare subsistence level. They built log cabins, grew corn and other vegetables, and fashioned their own wooden furniture, cloth, soap, and candles; the only commodities they bought were salt and iron. Isolated and exposed to dangers, often poorly educated, these backwoods settlers disliked those well-to-do colonists living along the coast, especially those professing a different faith. When an Anglican clergyman, Charles Woodmason, traveled through the Carolina frontier in the 1760s, "ornery" farmers misdirected him, refused to sell him food or lodging, and insulted him wherever he went. In one village they disrupted the Anglican service by releasing fifty-seven dogs in the church. But Woodmason had his revenge.

"What I could not effect by Force—or Reason—I have done by Sarcasm—for at the Time when they sent the fellows with their Dogs, one of the Dogs followed me down here—which I carried to the House of one of the principals—and told Him that I had 57 Presbyterians came that Day to Service, and that I had converted one of them, and brought Him home—I left the Dog with Him—This Joke has made them so extremely angry that they could cut my throat—But I've gained my Aim, having had no disturbance from them since—for if a Presbyterian now shews his face at Service, our People ask him if he is come to be *Converted*. So shame has driven them away."

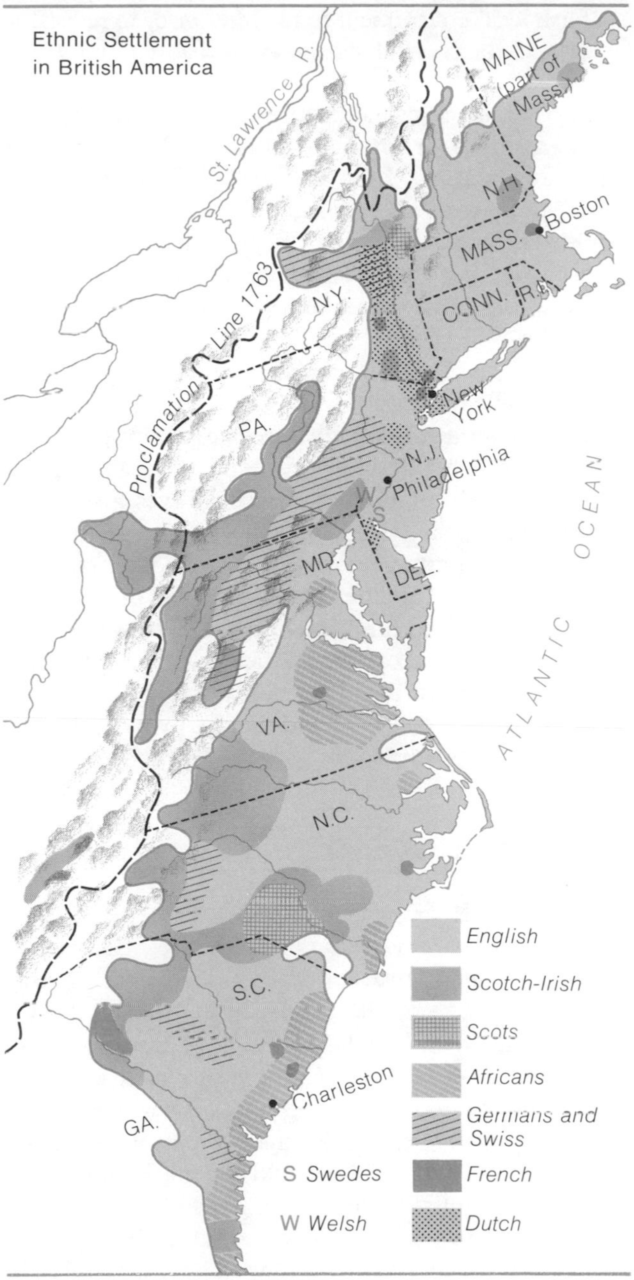

Settlement of the frontier led to political problems in the Southern colonies such as North and South Carolina, though for somewhat different reasons. South Carolina, like other expanding settlements, was reluctant to establish local government in the interior or to redistribute seats in the colonial legislature so that the backwoods would be adequately represented. Because settlers were expected to travel several hundred miles in order to vote, to find a sheriff, or to appear in court, they became so embittered against "Low Country" officials that they staged an open rebellion against the government in the 1760s. The South Carolina "Regulators" sought more government, not less, and under pressure Charleston agreed to set up new counties. London, however, disallowed these decisions.

In North Carolina, another group of frontiersmen who also called themselves "Regulators," was incited to violence by disgust at what was seen as a corrupt coastal elite—judges, sheriffs, attorneys, and other officers almost exclusively of English descent. Taxes, payoffs to county officials, a system of collecting tithes for the established Anglican Church—all of these infringements on the freedom of frontier settlers aroused the wrath of the Regulators. And for a brief time, they drove out the legal authorities and conducted their own court. Finally, however, Governor Tryon put down the rebellion at the Battle of Alamance in 1771 and summarily hanged some of the men who led this outburst.

Indian-White Relations

Throughout the seventeenth century, the expansion of English colonies resulted in friction between Europeans and Indians—and in several wars. Initially, the English were impressed by the hospitality of the Indians. Given the advantage of hindsight, we think of the English as having *conquered* North America, yet in many cases the Indians actually received the first colonists with generosity, even pity for their inadequate supply of food. In some cases, an Indian tribe would see the Europeans as potentially useful allies in defeating their rivals. In Virginia, for instance, Powhatan helped the Jamestown settlers survive because he wanted European weapons in his campaign to subdue neighboring tribes. Between 1607 and 1609, Indians and colonists enjoyed an uneasy alliance, as Powhatan increased his supply of armaments and metal and the English relied on the Indians to teach them how to farm in the New World. Similarly, in New England the Pilgrims survived the first two winters because they received food from two friendly Indians, Squanto and Samoset. The Indians taught early colonists how to grow such American plants as corn, squash, and pumpkin.

But there was distrust, misunderstanding, and even contempt on each side from the very beginning. As early as 1607, Captain John Smith, while exploring the James River, observed that the Indians "are naturally given to treachery, howbeit we could not finde it in o'r travell up the river, but rather a most kind and loving people."

The lack of mutual comprehension was heightened by religious difference. Indian "paganism" distressed the English. Since the Indians were polytheistic, some tribes

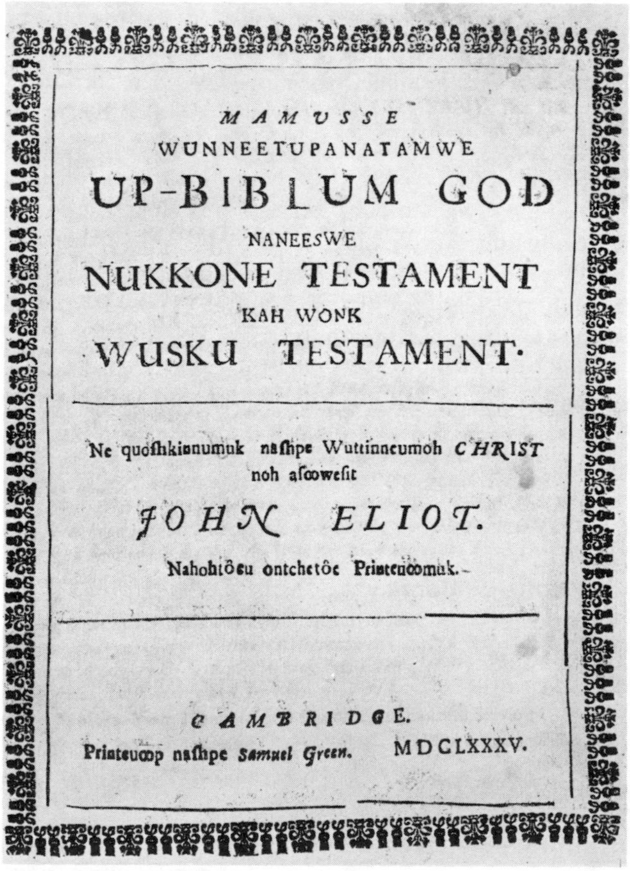
MAMUSSE
WUNNEETUPANATAMWE
UP-BIBLUM GOD
NANEESWE
NUKKONE TESTAMENT
KAH WONK
WUSKU TESTAMENT.

Ne quoshkinnumuk nashpe Wuttinneumoh CHRIST
noh asoowesit
JOHN ELIOT.
Nahohtôeu ontchetôe Printeuoomuk.

CAMBRIDGE.
Printeuoop nashpe Samuel Green. MDCLXXXV.

John Carter Brown Library, Brown University.

In order to translate the Bible into Algonquian, John Eliot had to devise a system of writing for the language as well as learn it himself. He had his first work printed in New England in 1661.

New York Public Library—Prints Division.

Plans for a college to educate Virginia's Indians were finally effected when the Brafferton Foundation supported an Indian School at William and Mary College. The Brafferton is the building on the left in this early engraving.

regarded the Christian God as merely another deity. When the chief of one tribe asked an Englishman to pray to his God for rain, since the Indian deities had failed to provide it, the Englishman was confused. Why could this chief not be persuaded to "forsake his false Gods?" Throughout the seventeenth century the Puritans attempted to convert the Indians, but of the 15,000 or so natives scattered throughout New England, only 2,500 were turned into "praying Indians." Granted, the problems of conversion were made especially difficult in New England because the Puritans insisted that every believer be sufficiently literate to read the Bible. As a result, the Puritans built an Indian College at Harvard and established schools in many Indian villages. But acceptance of the white man's God proved hazardous. It meant exposure to European diseases and thus a higher mortality rate among Christian Indians. It also meant that Indians who became Christians aroused the enmity of non-Christian Indians.

Many barriers, of course, continued to separate Europeans and Indians: technology, religion, language, and customs. One of the biggest sources of misunderstanding was the difference in European and Indian concepts of property. Who owned the lands of North America? Even the English were confused over this point. The Indians had some sort of "natural right" to the territories they had long occupied, and yet the English king also had a right to grant patents to colonists in America. Roger Williams—the Separatist who was forced out of Massachusetts and founded Providence, Rhode Island—was one of the few English thinkers to face up to this contradiction. He declared that the king had no right over the American lands at all.

The Puritans attempted to justify their seizure of Indian territory with a tangle of self-serving arguments: God intended Christians to conquer and convert pagans; the king had the political right to grant patents in the lands he claimed; America was vacant and stood as an open invitation to further settlement. But none of these arguments seemed quite sufficient, and the Puritans prudently took the further precaution of buying land from the Indians. All too often, however, the Indians did not comprehend the full meaning of such sales.

The English also failed to understand the political structure of Indian tribes. Colonists often called an Indian leader the "king," unaware that few chiefs could make important decisions without consulting a council of tribal elders. The muddle in English thought is well illustrated by the varying reactions of the Virginia colonists to the marriage of John Rolfe to Pocahontas, daughter of the Indian chief Powhatan. Some English people dismissed the baptism of Pocahontas as a Christian and objected to the marriage on the grounds that Rolfe was marrying a savage, someone of a different race. Other colonists objected that Rolfe had no right to marry her, since Pocahontas was a "princess" and Rolfe a mere commoner.

Hostility developed openly between Indians and Europeans, especially when colonists found their food supplies dwindling and turned to pillaging Indian grana-

MATOAKA ALS REBECKA FILIA POTENTISS. PRINC: POWHATANI IMP: VIRGINIAE
Ætatis suæ 21. A°. 1616.
Matoaks als Rebecka daughter to the mighty Prince
Powhatan Emperour of Attanoughkomouck als Virginia
converted and baptized in the Christian faith, and
Wife to the wor.ll Mr Tho: Rolff.

National Portrait Gallery, Smithsonian Institution, Washington, D. C.

Pocahontas, at age 21.

ries. And, as the Indians became more familiar with European firearms and acquired some of their own, they feared white military superiority less and less. Thus, as the colonists penetrated deeper and deeper into Indian territories, the situation grew more and more inflammatory, ready to explode with the first small spark.

Wars in the South

In the South the struggle for land resulted in the first major Indian uprising in 1622. Powhatan's successor, his brother Opechancanough, convinced the Virginia tribes, the so-called "Powhatan Confederacy," that the colonists were devastating their traditional sources of food—berries and game—by planting more and more tobacco fields. Indian warriors of the confederacy descended on the English colonists and nearly succeeded in wiping them out. The attack came as a complete surprise to the English; it resulted in the death of more than 300 settlers and the destruction of almost all outlying farms. In reprisal, the English conducted a war against the Indians that lasted several years. As the English governor succinctly put it, "Either we must clere them or they us out of the Country." The English forces ruined the Indian corn fields, starving their enemies into submission. The Virginia Company used the uprising as a pretext for driving Indians off their cleared fields and for enslaving their prisoners. The English even put poison in the cup of wine they offered the Indians after the signing of a peace treaty in 1623. On another occasion in the same year, the English came to an Indian village on a peace expedition, obtained white hostages the Indians were holding, and then opened fire on the village, killing some forty Indians.

In 1644, after two decades of peace, Opechancanough led a second uprising. By now, he was so feeble that his braves carried him onto the battlefield to make a last-ditch attempt to exterminate the colonists. But the uprising failed, Opechancanough was captured, and horrible reprisals were again enacted against the Powhatan Indians. With the peace treaty of 1646, a new era of relations seemed about to begin since a line was drawn between Indian and colonial lands and for the first time Indians were put on a "reservation." For their part, the Indians promised to warn the colonists of imminent attacks from other tribes and to pay a yearly tribute to the colony.

Bacon's Rebellion in 1675, however, spelled the end of Virginia's coastal tribes. There were various causes for Bacon's Rebellion. The high-spirited settlers along the frontier had many grievances against the royal governor, William Berkeley (1606–1677), and the English government he represented. In an effort to protect its own merchants against foreign—and especially Dutch—competition, the English Parliament passed a number of Navigation Acts restricting the sale of Virginia tobacco. Only English ships could carry it, and it could be sold only to England. As a result of this restricted market, the price of tobacco dropped severely, and economic depression followed. To force prices back up, the Virginians attempted to forbid the growth of all tobacco in their own colony and in Maryland and North Carolina as well. Lord Baltimore, the proprietor of Maryland, refused to cooperate, and prices continued to sink.

But economic discontent was only a general cause of the rebellion; a more immediate cause was tension between frontier settlers and the Indians. Traditionally, historians have portrayed Nathaniel Bacon (1647–1676), the young leader of the rebellion, as the defender of the poor frontiersmen against the rich grandees of Jamestown. Governor Berkeley has been shown as a tyrant and Bacon as a freedom fighter. Berkeley was charged with refusing to protect the frontier settlers against murderous Indians. As the story went, the fiery rebel Bacon was forced to form a militia that would perform two functions: drive back the Indians and force Berkeley to pass laws that would alleviate the suffering of poor white Virginians.

Virginia State Library.

Governor Berkeley of Virginia was deeply involved in Indian trade.

The facts are simple, even if the interpretation of them is elusive. Some Indians stole hogs from Bacon's frontier farm and killed his overseer. A company of militiamen pursued and murdered many Indians, both friends and foes, which touched off in turn widespread Indian raids along the frontier. Governor Berkeley refused to march against the Indians; instead he offered to build a chain of forts to protect the frontier. Bacon openly rebelled. He temporarily seized control of the government and forced it to pass laws that would limit tobacco production. He continued hostilities against the Indians until he died of fever and the rebellion dwindled away.

A close examination of documents shows that, although the rebellion was fought over many issues, the central point of disagreement was over Indian policy. For years Berkeley struggled to control English expansion into Indian territory. When the Virginia assembly stripped him of this power, the governor still tried unsuccessfully to enforce an English law that forbade Indians to sell lands to settlers. As one contemporary wrote, the law was necessary: "Whilest the Indians had liberty to sell theire lands the english would ordinaryly either frighten or delude them into a bargaine and for a trifle get away the grownd they should live on, then he comes and settles himselfe there and with his cattle and hoggs destroyes all the corne of the other Indians of the towne. . . ."

Berkeley's efforts to bridle English greed for Indian lands was what made him so hated. The frontiersmen despised him, not because he refused to defend the colony against Indians but because he would not kill and dispossess *all* Indians, both friendly and hostile tribes.

Although the rebellion was quelled, Bacon's men managed to kill off almost all of Virginia's coastal tribes: the Susquehanna, the Algonkians, the Pamunkey—the Indians of the tidelands. By the end of the seventeenth century an English clergyman observed: "This is very certain that the Indian inhabitants of Virginia are now very inconsiderable as to their numbers and seem insensibly to decay though they live under the English protection and have no violence offered them."

Conflict in New Netherlands

In New Netherlands a similar tale of European-Indian relations can be told. Between 1614 and 1639 the Dutch, who depended on the Indians for the lucrative fur trade, were on good terms with the local tribes. But a new Dutch governor, Willem Kieft, was determined to humble the Indians, an act that he felt would open up the Hudson River valley to Dutch expansion. When a group of Raritan Indians sought refuge from another Indian tribe, Kieft received the refugees—and then slaughtered them. This outrage stirred the Indians to revenge—Kieft's War lasted for several years.

Wars in New England

In New England, relations with the Indians also were peaceful at first. But in 1637 the Puritans of Massachusetts and Connecticut attacked the Pequots, a warlike tribe that had recently moved into the area and posed a threat both to the English and to local tribes. The war was brief and ruthless. The Pequots, who were disbanded as a tribe, were either killed or sold into slavery in the West Indies, or they were handed over as "wards" to tribes friendly to the Puritans.

After the Pequot War, the four Puritan colonies—Massachusetts, Plymouth, Connecticut, and New Haven—formed a military pact called the New England Confederation (1643). Indian policy in New England consisted of pitting one tribe against another and of favoring peaceful allies. And, to assure themselves of immediate protection, most colonies required every English male citizen between the ages of sixteen and sixty to serve in militia units organized town by town.

In 1675 a new Indian conflict broke out, King Philip's War. The new leader of the Wampanoag tribe that had once been so friendly to the Pilgrims, Philip (Metacomet), came to loathe the increasing domination of the English over his people. When three of his braves were hanged by the English for having murdered a Christian Indian who was also an informer for the whites, Philip decided to take up arms. His strategy was to organize several tribes into a league.

The Wampanoags and other northeastern tribes were driven to war by several factors. They resented the erosion of tribal authority and custom by colonial justice; for Puritan authorities, rather than tribal councils were trying Indian offenders. The introduction of alcoholic drink was further disorganizing tribal life. English farmers and Indian farmers found living side by side fraught with difficulties. For instance, many English farmers refused to fence in their property; as a result, their livestock wandered into Indian fields and ate the crops. All of these contacts with white settlers threatened Indian culture and created considerable uneasiness. The Atlantic seaboard tribes might have migrated further west, but that alternative was closed to them, for there the powerful Iroquois Confederacy ruled supreme.

Hemmed in and frustrated, the Wampanoags attacked settlers before King Philip had thoroughly worked out a master plan for routing the enemy, and the war spread in a disorganized fashion from tribe to tribe. It quickly became the most ferocious Indian onslaught of the seventeenth century. Colonial villages throughout Massachusetts were sacked and burned one after another. Brookfield was reduced to ashes, Northfield had to be evacuated, Deerfield was taken, and the war spread as far north as Maine, where the town of Saco on the seacoast was assaulted. Lancaster, Medfield, and Groton were burned; in Rhode Island, Providence and Warwick were abandoned; in Connecticut, Simsbury was evacuated. Many other towns throughout New England were raided.

In August 1676, King Philip was trapped and killed, and soon the war died out, but the losses on both sides were great. New England's frontier was pushed back some forty miles, almost a thousand colonists lost their lives, and a dozen frontier villages were obliterated. But if the war had frightful consequences for the colonists, it also served to unite them into a tighter confederacy; henceforth the Puritans felt no moral pangs in grabbing Indian lands.

With the breakup of Indian resistance, the tribal life of the Indians began to disintegrate completely. Although the Narragansett tribe of Rhode Island at first maintained an uneasy neutrality, the Puritan leaders waged a "preventive" war against them and trapped their mighty forces in a village that was put to the torch. Of those Indians captured, many were executed, but others were sold as slaves and exported to the West Indies, Spain, and the Mediterranean. Even tribes that supported the English were punished since they were herded into reservations. Just as Bacon's Rebellion spelled the end of Indian autonomy in Tidewater Virginia, so King Philip's War, which occurred at about the same time, reduced the New England tribes to pitiful remnants of their former glory.

Colonial Wars

During the first half of the eighteenth century, English involvement in continental affairs precipitated a series of

Public Archives of Canada.

The French fortress at Louisbourg fell to a colonial force led by Britishers Jeffrey Amherst and James Wolfe in 1758. Louisbourg had been a center for French preying on colonial shipping.

conflicts that sometimes had reverberations on the North American continent as English, French, and Spanish partisans bribed Indian allies to attack outposts of their European foes. These included Queen Anne's War (1702–1713) and the War of Jenkin's Ear (1739–1742), which merged into the War of Austrian Succession (1740–1748), a general melée of conflicting dynastic ambitions. The first of these, Queen Anne's War, enabled the English to push the Spanish southward into Florida, to assert limited control over what is now Georgia, and thus to lay the foundations of the colony launched by Oglethorpe in 1732.

Jenkins, an English master mariner, reported in 1731 that Spanish sailors boarded his vessel and cut or tore off his ear. Seven years later he told a committee of the House of Commons of this indignity and even exhibited what he claimed to be his severed ear. A public outcry for revenge, fed by other alleged Spanish outrages, led to war. The conflict over the Austrian succession was justified from the English point of view by the need to protect the balance of power in Europe. The outcome of this dynastic squabble settled nothing and had little immediate impact upon affairs in North America. In the following decade, however, the bad blood of the 1740s erupted into yet another general war that altered drastically the course of colonial history.

A Firm Beginning

By 1750 the English foothold along the Atlantic coast of North America was secure. Even the broad outlines of possible control of much of the entire continent could be discerned as the chain of settlements grew stronger and as native tribes withered to insignificance. Unlike the French, whose outposts were weak, isolated, and scattered, and unlike the Spanish, whose interests focused on South America, Mexico, and the Caribbean isles (some of which London merchants certainly coveted), the English had created in hit-or-miss fashion a necklace of economically sound, prosperous towns, villages, and farms.

Viewed from Mother England, the most important and most valuable possessions in the New World were none of the thirteen colonies destined to rebel but the tiny sugar islands of the sun-soaked Caribbean, often pawns in wars with Spain. The Southern colonies (Maryland, Virginia, and the Carolinas), rich with tobacco, rice, indigo, and with turpentine, pitch, and timber ranked next in importance, followed by the Middle colonies (New York, Pennsylvania, New Jersey, and Delaware). New England, a mix of marginal farming, trade, and seafaring, was less valuable in English eyes. Nevertheless, ships from innumerable little northeastern ports were beginning to play a key role in the emerging colonial-imperial economy, messengers of commerce tying diverse parts of the huge Atlantic basin together.

Yet in growth lay seeds of discord. As England began to construct the first British empire, it held to the basic tenets of *mercantilism.* As an imperial policy, mercantilism asserted that an empire should be self-sufficient and its colonies should provide raw materials and crops not available in the mother country. These, then, would be processed or turned into manufactured goods and sold throughout the empire. If rigorously applied, a policy of mercantilism would allegedly result in a strong navy, provide a favorable cash flow to the homeland, and concentrate manufacturing there as well.

To make mercantilism work there were rules known as Navigation Acts that aimed to regulate trade in favor of England and, in many instances, to the detriment of colonials. What impact these various acts had upon seventeenth and eighteenth century commerce is debatable since smuggling clearly became big business. Although the effect of wars, inflation, and overproduction was probably much greater, these regulations often seemed to hurt more than they helped colonial farmers, merchants, and sea captains, and thus they became a disruptive rather than a unifying factor in trans-Atlantic relations.

As the colonists from New Hampshire to Georgia prospered, grew in population, and began to feel their strength, opposition to these trade restrictions became keener and more open. Mingled with this resentment was the age-old suspicion of authority and even abhorrence of *English* authority, an authority that had forced thousands to cross the Atlantic Ocean because of its repressive policies toward dissident believers, marginal farmers, and minor offenders. By 1750, a vibrant, diverse society was emerging along the eastern coast of North America, one that was no longer willing to be tied to the center of empire by mere rules and regulations and made to dance to their tugs and twists like a marionette. For thousands of American colonists, England had ceased to be—if it ever had been—a distant but beloved homeland.

Essay

Tobacco: The Gift and The Curse of the Indians

In recent years, cigarette smoking has been denounced as a major health hazard. Every pack of cigarettes sold in the United States must bear the words: "Warning: The Surgeon General Has Determined That Cigarette Smoking Is Dangerous to Your Health." A detailed study by the United States Department of Health, Education and Welfare has documented that cigarette smoking (but not pipe and cigar smoking) is directly related to lung cancer, circulatory and heart diseases, and to chronic bronchitis and emphysema. The death rate from smoking can be related to such factors as the age at which one begins to smoke and the number of cigarettes one consumes a day. For instance, males who smoke fewer than ten cigarettes a day have a death rate about 40 percent higher than male nonsmokers; those who smoke more than 20 cigarettes a day have a death rate that is 90 percent higher; and those who smoke 40 cigarettes or more, have a rate that is 120 percent higher. The statistics for females are not yet so complete.

Oddly enough, Europeans originally regarded tobacco as a medicine. One of its first great promoters, Jean Nicot—from whose name the word *nicotine* was derived—thought so highly of the plant's medicinal properties that he sent seeds of the plant from Portugal back to the Queen Mother of France to cure her migraine headaches. Nicotine therapy was soon the rage throughout Europe. For a time, only druggists were allowed to dispense the valuable leaf, which was prescribed as a cure for hundreds of ills.

During the sixteenth and seventeenth centuries, tobacco conquered the whole world, becoming even more popular than another New World product—coffee. It was slow to catch on in Europe, but once it became a medical and social fad, it quickly swept the Old World. In 1558 the plant was first cultivated in Spain. By 1565 the French and English were smoking it. By the end of the first decade of the seventeenth century, its production and consumption had circled the globe, and it was to be found in Russia, the Philippines, Virginia, Java, India, and Ceylon. Almost everywhere it was taken in all three ways—snuffed, smoked, and chewed. At first, smokers used pipes, then switched to cigars, and at the beginning of the nineteenth century turned to cigarettes.

Tobacco at first was used as medicine, but the habit of "drinking smoke" soon became the European rage. By the time that Virginia discovered tobacco as a cash crop, there was a market for it in Europe as this 1595 print illustrates.

LONDON,
Printed for William Barlow,and are
to be ſold at his ſhop in Gracious-
ſtreet. 1595.

New York Public Library—Arents Collection.

Sir Walter Raleigh enjoyed a great vogue in London when he puffed on his pipe before Queen Elizabeth. So intriguing was this strange practice of inhaling smoke that two Indians were brought from Virginia to London in 1584 to demonstrate it. Dealers soon varied the product by adding other ingredients such as musk, amber, and orange blossom. Dandies were soon entertaining ladies by puffing smoke rings and performing other tricks; learned doctors were recommending a decoction of tobacco leaves, boiled and applied to the face as a lotion, to clear up pimples and blotches.

Not everyone liked the new "medicine." King James I was so irritated by smoking that he published anonymously his *Counterblaste to Tobacco* in which he stated that smoking is a "custome lothsome to the eye, hatefull to the nose, harmefull to the braine, dangerous to the Lungs and in the blacke stinking fume thereof, nearest resembling the horrible Stigian smoke of the pit that is bottomelesse." On this point the Puritans agreed with him and attempted to ban smoking in New England, but with little success.

Who invented this strange custom of inhaling burning smoke? Tobacco is a purely American plant; before Columbus it had not been heard of in Europe, Africa, or Asia. The oldest known evidence of smoking is a Mexican wall sculpture, carved in the seventh or eighth century and portraying a Mayan priest blowing smoke through a long tube. Indeed, tobacco smoking was a religious ritual, or at least a ceremonial act, throughout the New World. Where tobacco was first raised experts have yet to determine; some say in Peru, others in Argentina, and still others that the Mayans of Mexico were the first to cultivate it.

Columbus was puzzled when friendly Indians offered him "some dry leaves" as a present soon after landing at San Salvador. The mystery was solved a few weeks later when members of his crew saw natives of Cuba who "drank smoke." Chewing and smoking tobacco at first struck the Spanish as a distasteful practice, as it still must seem to anyone who tries smoking for the first time. By the middle of the sixteenth century, however, Europeans not only were smoking but also had recognized the economic advantages of growing and selling tobacco. For hundreds of years tobacco had been a form of currency among Indian tribes, and in the sixteenth century it became a valuable commercial crop for Europeans as well. Because it was scarce, tobacco at first was worth its weight in silver: in 1600 a pound of tobacco sold in London for a pound of silver.

In the English colony of Virginia, the cultivation of tobacco proved a godsend. Between 1607, when Jamestown was settled, and 1614, the settlers failed to discover an industry or a cash crop that would support the colony. But in 1610 an Englishman named John Rolfe arrived at Jamestown and soon began to experiment with tobacco. The type of tobacco that the Virginia Indians grew was not acceptable to English smokers. Rolfe introduced some seeds of the more attractive variety, *Nicotiana tabacum,* from the Caribbean and raised and cured it successfully. When Rolfe heard that tobacco buyers in London liked his Virginia brand, he felt so jubilant that he immediately informed the other settlers. They abandoned their other efforts and devoted themselves to raising tobacco. By 1627, England was importing half a million pounds of tobacco every year, much of it from Virginia; by 1770, this figure had risen to an astounding 100 million pounds. The future of Jamestown—in fact, of all Virginia and Maryland—was secure. The colonies flourished, some planters became extremely wealthy—and the economy of early Virginians became exclusively bound up with the production of tobacco. This single-crop economy put Virginia at the mercy of fluctuating tobacco prices. When overproduction and English laws restricting tobacco commerce caused the price to drop drastically in the second half of the seventeenth century, Virginia suffered a major depression.

More tragically, tobacco eventually wedded Virginia to the slave system of labor. The cultivation of tobacco requires an extraordinary amount of care. In colonial times tobacco seed was sown in December in small plant beds. In the spring, after the tobacco plants had begun to sprout, the tender shoots were transplanted to fields thoroughly worked with hoes. Transplanting was a delicate operation. After the transplanted tobacco began to grow, most of its leaves were pinched off so that the remaining leaves would be larger. Insects and particularly worms had to be picked off the plants continually. Harvesting the plants was equally arduous, since they could be cut only at the moment they became ripe and since a whole field never ripened at one time. Drying and curing tobacco was yet another complicated process, the last of several intricate but easily learned steps. All this backbreaking labor required small groups of field hands, and slavery became the most economical means of providing the necessary labor. If cancer has turned out to be one of the curses of tobacco, then slavery must surely be counted as the other.

In the late nineteenth century, cigarette smoking began to be promoted by vigorous advertising and soon emerged as a vast American industry. It came to be monopolized by two brothers, Benjamin and James Duke. In 1883 the Duke brothers replaced the handrolling of cigarettes with a new machine invented by James Bonsack. By the end of the following year, this machine was producing 120,000 cigarettes a day, a rate fifty

Early tobacco advertising bore slogans such as "Best under the Sun." They were more concerned with presenting an image of refinement than an accurate picture of the tobacco South.

Petum optimum fubter Solem.
Le meilleur Tabac desous le Soliel.
The Best Tobacco under the Sun.

New York Public Library—Picture Collection.

Library of Congress.

Cigarette girls continued to handroll cigarettes in this Richmond factory in 1887. Production was slow compared to that of a cigarette machine since the best cigarette girl could roll only four or five cigarettes per minute.

times faster than that of the handrollers. Mechanization allowed the Duke brothers to cut their prices in half and to sell a box of ten cigarettes for five cents. Joining with several other outflanked corporations to form the American Tobacco Company in 1890, the Dukes became the czars of the industry. In fact, Benjamin Duke was able to invest his enormous profits in many southern industries and thereby became a leader in the South's economic revival after the Civil War.

The success of the Duke brothers must be attributed to two features that long distinguished American industry: advertising and mechanization. Before the Duke brothers adopted the Bonsack machine, it had been turned down by several leading companies on the grounds that it was not reliable and the public would never accept machinemade cigarettes. The Dukes perfected the machine and even boasted of it in their advertisements: "These cigarettes are manufactured on the Bonsack Cigarette Machines." The Dukes spent $800,000 in 1889 on advertising. They tirelessly thought up new gimmicks for their cigarettes, such as sending a Polo team on roller skates across the country to advertise one brand and putting the picture of a favorite French actress on another.

Although temperance workers who were fighting alcoholism also condemned smoking, their efforts were futile when confronted by the aggressive business tactics of the Duke brothers and the growing popularity of cigarettes. Religious groups, who abhorred smoking as a vice, and many physicians, who regarded it as a health hazard, attempted unsuccessfully to quell the growing fad of cigarette smoking. For decades "respectable" women thought that smoking was unattractive, but in the 1920s this prejudice was overcome and flappers proudly puffed on cigarettes. Only after the 1950s did the general public become aware of the dreadful damage to health that smoking represents.

Selected Readings

General

Clarence Ver Steeg, *The Formative Years* (1964)

Wesley F. Craven, *The Colonies in Transition* (1968)

M. Eugene Sirmans, *Colonial South Carolina: Political History, 1663–1763* (1966)

Wilcomb Washburne, *The Governor and the Rebel: Bacon's Rebellion* (1957)

Richard M. Brown, *The South Carolina Regulators* (1963)

Immigration and Ethnic Patterns

Carl Bridenbaugh, *Vexed and Troubled Englishmen, 1590–1642* (1967)

George Willison, *Saints and Strangers: Pilgrim Fathers* (1945)

William Bradford, *Of Plymouth Plantation,* ed. Samuel Eliot Morison (1952)

R. J. Dickson, *Ulster Emigration to Colonial America* (1966)

James Lemon, *The Best Poor Man's Country* (1972)

Colonial Frontier

Douglas Leach, *Arms for Empire* (1974)

Douglas Leach, *Flintlock and Tomahawk* (1958)

Verner Crane, *The Southern Frontier, 1670–1732* (1928)

Labor and Race

Winthrop Jordan, *White Over Black* (1968)

Gary B. Nash, *Red, White and Black* (1974)

Edmund Morgan, *American Slavery, American Freedom: the Ordeal of Colonial Virginia* (1975)

Peter Wood, *Black Majority: Negroes in Colonial South Carolina from 1670 through the Stono Rebellion* (1974)

Abbot Smith, *Colonists in Bondage: White Servitude and Convict Labor in America 1607–1776* (1947)

Puritan Settlements

Emery Battis, *Saints and Sectaries: Anne Hutchinson and the Antinomian Controversy* (1962)

Francis J. Bremer, *The Puritan Experiment* (1976)

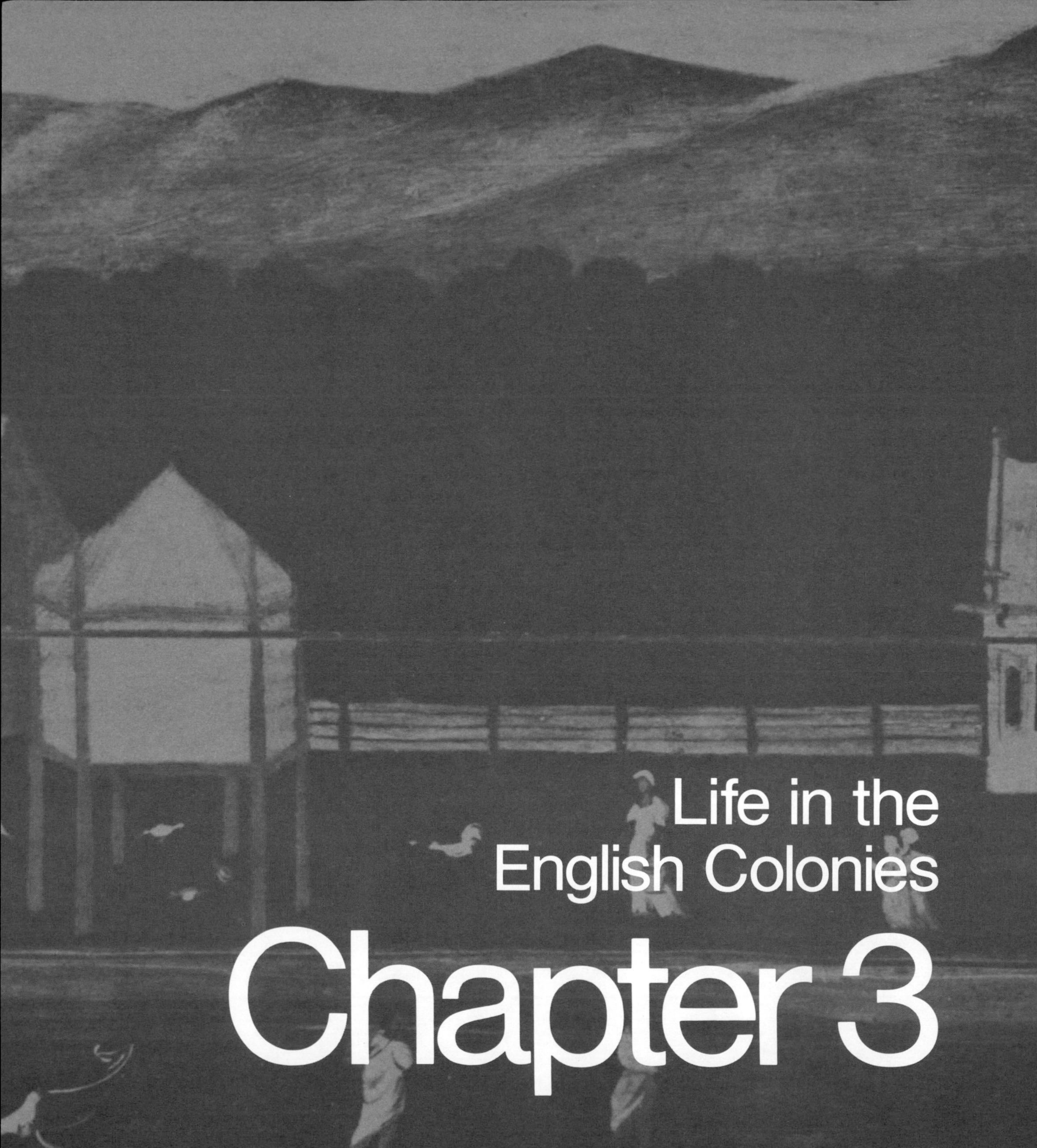

Chapter 3

Life in the English Colonies

TIMELINE

1619
The first blacks arrive in British North America

1637
Harvard College opens

1640
The Whole Books of Psalms published

1650
Beginning of English regulation of colonial trade

1662
The Halfway Covenant established to allow wider Puritan church membership

1692
Salem Village holds witchcraft trials

1699
Wool Act forbids export of colonial textiles

1704
Anglican Church established in New Jersey

1739–40
George Whitefield, an Anglican priest, tours the colonies

1776
Philadelphia population reaches 40,000 citizens

CHAPTER OUTLINE

Life in colonial America was marked by startling diversity. In the seventeenth century Virginia seemed as foreign to most members of the Massachusetts Bay Colony as England itself—possibly more so, since Massachusetts was full of recent arrivals from England. No single style of life prevailed throughout the colonies, so single religion or political structure or economy—not even a unified system of weights, measures, and money. As late as 1724, when young Ben Franklin returned for a visit to his native Boston from his adopted city of Philadelphia, the men who worked in his brother's printing house quizzed him about Philadelphia as though it were a distant land. "The journeymen were inquisitive where I had been," Franklin wrote, "what sort of a country it was, and how I liked it. I praised it much and the happy life I led in it, expressing strongly my intention of returning to it; and one of them asking what kind of money we had there, I produced a handful of silver and spread it before them, which was a kind of raree they had not been used to, paper being the money of Boston."

Geography isolated the colonies one from another. Roads were few and inadequate, and even travel by water could be perilous and slow (Franklin's voyage from Philadelphia to Boston took fourteen days). Various economic systems could be just as isolating. A small subsistence farmer in the backcountry of Virginia had little reason to deal with the outside world at all. If he were Presbyterian and Scottish, he probably was distrustful of or openly antagonistic towards most of the wealthy commercial planters, who were generally both English and Anglican and lived in the Tidewater, the term for those lands served by rivers influenced by ocean tides. And if such enmities could spring up between members from different regions of the same colony, what would a Virginia small farmer have made of a Puritan merchant in Boston?

Even the leaders of different colonies pursued different lives. For instance, one eighteenth century Virginia farmer, Robert Carter of Corotoman, owned 300,000 acres, sent his sons to school in England, read Latin and Greek classics from his well-stocked library, but devoted most of his time to managing his estates, selling the tobacco they produced, and speculating in still more land. John Hull of Boston came to Massachusetts from England with his family. As a boy he helped his father on the family farm, but at eighteen he apprenticed himself to a goldsmith. Through perseverance and business acumen, Hull eventually became the owner of a large fleet of merchant ships, built a fine house, but continued working at his trade as a goldsmith. Worldly success and religious piety, far from being at odds with one another, seemed to Hull to be inextricably bound together, and he ordered his captains to be "careful to see to the worship of God

Valentine Museum, Richmond, Virginia.

Shirley Plantation passed into the hands of the Carter family in the eighteenth century. Charles Carter, grandson of "King" Carter, built this home overlooking the James River. Carters still own and occupy this working plantation.

Courtesy Museum of Fine Arts, Boston.

The Isaac Winslow family's status as prosperous colonials was reflected in their dress and in having this family portrait done by Josiah Blackburn.

every day on the vessel and to the sanctification of the Lord's Day and suppression of all profaneness that the Lord may delight to be with you and his blessing upon you." Both men, Virginian and Bostonian, were ceaselessly industrious, both spoke English, both were extremely pious, both made money—but there the resemblances stopped. The commercial farmer of Virginia was a representative of the landed gentry. He ruled over a small kingdom of his own and there raised tobacco, operated a gristmill and a sawmill, employed a score of trained craftsmen on his estates, and maintained daily contacts with his black slaves. The merchant of Boston, no matter how wealthy, considered himself to be little more than a successful small tradesman.

The Colonial Economy

For most of its history America has been predominantly an agricultural land, and never was this more true than during the colonial period, when ninety-five percent of the people were farmers.

The Southern Colonies

For Virginia, Maryland, and part of North Carolina, tobacco was the leading cash crop. In the seventeenth century the large planters acted as merchants in England for their own crops, but by the end of the century more and more Virginians were relying on a few large English merchant houses to do the marketing for them. Tobacco was so valuable that in the colonies around the Chesapeake Bay it was a medium of exchange. Salaries were paid in tobacco, taxes were collected in tobacco, rents were figured in tobacco.

In South Carolina the search for a cash crop took longer. At first the Indian trade provided tens of thousands of deerskin hides every year, but no farming surplus was produced until it was learned, after some experimentation, that the hot, wet coastal lands were suitable for growing rice. A young woman, Eliza Lucas (1722-1793) introduced a second cash crop from the West Indies that could be grown in the same coastal areas—indigo, a plant from which a valuable blue dye is extracted. Rice and indigo, then, became the exportable crops of the coast, but the backcountry failed to find a comparable product and remained on a level of subsistence farming.

The varying economy of these regions has led to a theory that there were three distinct colonial Souths, each with its own interests to protect: the tobacco-growing Chesapeake Bay area; the rice-growing coastal lands of South Carolina; and the backcountry throughout the South. This picture of a tripartite South may be oversimplified, but it is a useful scheme for recognizing the various patterns of life. The coastal and Piedmont commercial farmers used slaves, congregated periodically in such cities as Williamsburg and Charleston, and had frequent business dealings with England and the backcountry. Along the frontier, farmers kept fewer slaves or perhaps none, visited the coast seldom if at all, and had few surplus crops to sell. Pioneers in different colonies along the frontier often had more contact with one another than with residents of the older sections of their own colony. Travel between western and eastern regions was extremely difficult. Few roads existed, the mountains acted as a barrier, and even the rivers could not be used as waterways, since they were broken by rapids at the fall line. North and south travel, by contrast, was somewhat easier, and a north-south trade grew up between Philadelphia and the entire backcountry as far as the Carolinas.

The Middle Colonies

The Middle colonies were the breadbasket of America. Wheat was the principal crop, though other important cash crops such as lumber often were exported. The agricultural wealth of the Middle colonies was increased by trade and industry. Philadelphia was the commercial capital of British North America and of the Middle colonies as well. In 1776 Philadelphia counted 40,000 citizens, which made it the second largest city in the empire, second only to London. New York, Philadelphia's most serious rival, had about 25,000 inhabitants, though it would soon surge ahead. At that date Boston, which grew imperceptibly during the years from 1760 to 1775, had 16,000 citizens.

The chief problem that Philadelphia merchants faced was that the Middle colonies did not produce anything that could be sold in England. Aside from furs, the natural products of the region—and of New York—simply had no market in the homeland. Most of the farms of the region were family-size holdings, not vast estates such as those found in the Virginia Tidewater or Low Country South Carolina. As a result, Philadelphia

South Caroliniana Library, University of South Carolina.

Indigo became an important second crop for South Carolina slave owners. Here the dye-producing plant is being harvested.

merchants were obliged to devise more complex and less obvious trade routes. Shipments of provisions (grain, flour, bread, pork, and beef) and lumber (barrel staves, hoops, and shingles) to the West Indies became the backbone of their commerce. Similar products and fish from New England were also shipped from Philadelphia to Portugal. From there Philadelphia ships often carried cargoes of sugar, molasses, rum, or wine to British ports. On the voyage home to Philadelphia the ships brought back British dry goods and hardware and sometimes stopped in the West Indies to pick slaves as well.

But Philadelphia also was active in intercolonial trade. Iron goods manufactured in Philadelphia were sold to other colonies; furniture from Philadelphia graced the best Southern homes. The vast hinterland along the frontier looked to Philadelphia as its supply center as did Delaware and New Jersey.

The New England Colonies

This region was basically a patchwork of subsistence farms, producing little that could be exported and not unlike those found along the southern frontier. This meant that each year hundreds of able young men turned to the sea or towns such as Boston, Providence, and Newport for their livelihood.

Boston, like Philadelphia, became a commercial center dealing in products from many sources. Molasses

Library Company of Philadelphia.

Philadelphia was well on the way to becoming the second city of the British empire when Peter Cooper sketched its busy port in 1720.

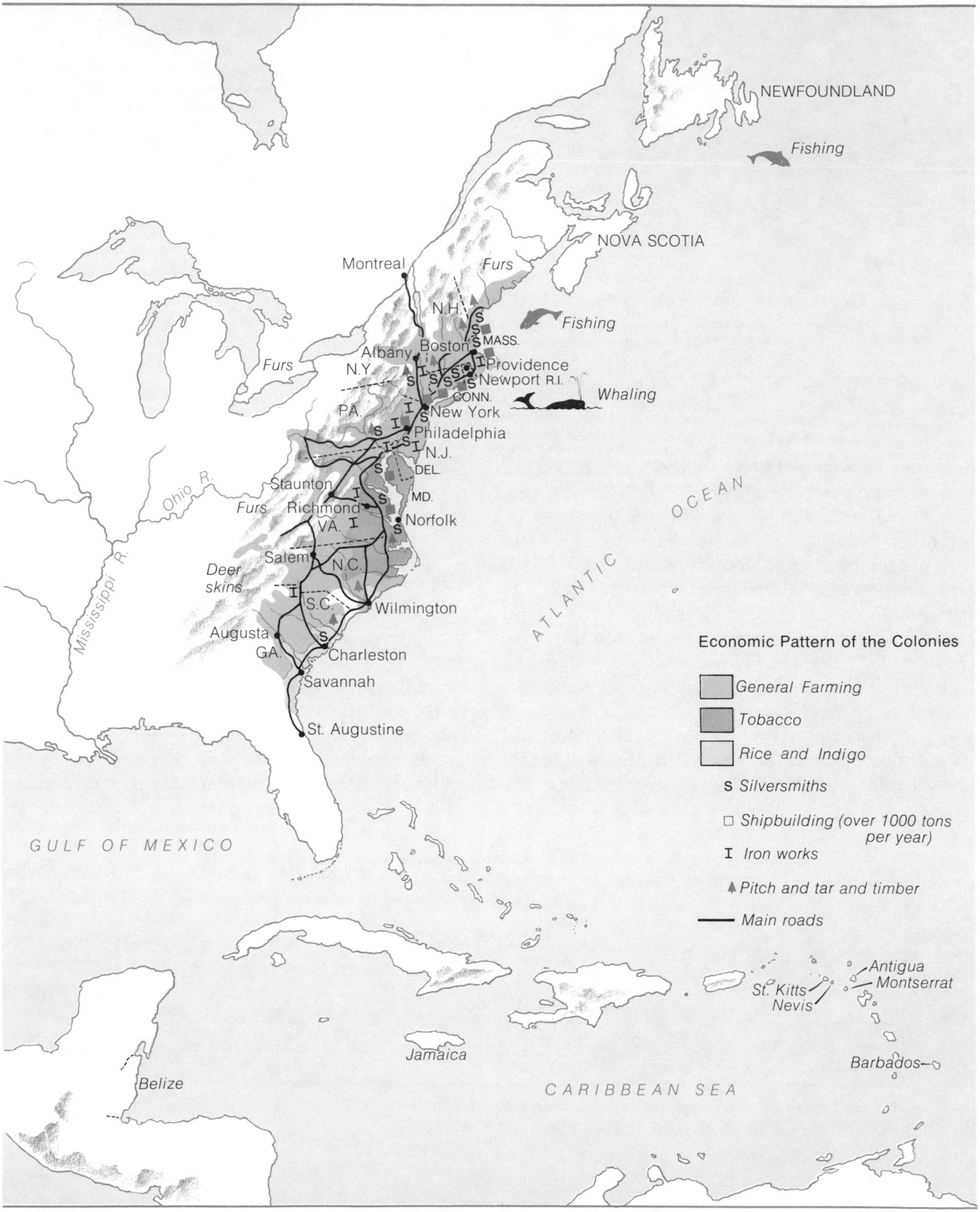

NEWFOUNDLAND
Fishing
NOVA SCOTIA
Montreal
Furs
N.H.
Fishing
MASS.
Boston
Albany
Furs
N.Y.
Providence
Newport R.I.
CONN.
Whaling
PA.
New York
Philadelphia
N.J.
DEL.
Staunton
Ohio R.
MD.
Furs
Richmond
Norfolk
VA.
ATLANTIC OCEAN
Salem
N.C.
Deer skins
Mississippi R.
S.C.
Wilmington
Augusta
GA.
Charleston
Savannah
St. Augustine
Economic Pattern of the Colonies
General Farming
Tobacco
Rice and Indigo
S Silversmiths
Shipbuilding (over 1000 tons per year)
I Iron works
Pitch and tar and timber
Main roads
GULF OF MEXICO
Antigua
Montserrat
St. Kitts
Nevis
Jamaica
Barbados
Belize
CARIBBEAN SEA

(made from sugar) was carried from the West Indies to Boston where it was converted into rum that was then transported back to the Caribbean. Often a rum ship would also carry salted fish, which was fed to slaves in the West Indies, and manufactured items. And in their trade with the Old World, Boston merchants carried fish to the Mediterranean and parts of Africa. In fact, fish was the chief cash crop that Massachusetts could export, though barrels, lumber, and whale oil were other native products that Bostonians sold abroad at a profit. Ships from Massachusetts also engaged in the slave trade. As the vessels worked their way north from the West Indies, they would stop off at southern ports and sell African slaves bought in the Caribbean. The pattern of trade practiced by ships from Boston, Providence, Newport, and other New England coastal centers cannot be reduced to the simple diagram so well known to school children—the "triangular trade" of rum, slaves, and molasses. Though slaves were sometimes brought directly from Africa to America, more often than not they were purchased in the West Indies. Rum, rather than being sold to Africans in exchange for slaves, was usually shipped to the West Indies.

In the second half of the seventeenth century, a pattern emerged that prevailed throughout the colonial period: agricultural products flowed into Boston from the farms of the colony; and English imports moved in the opposite direction, from Boston into the towns and villages of the hinterland. Rather than sea trade competing with agriculture, the two pursuits complemented one another perfectly. Boston merchants shipped Massachusetts grain, beef, bread, and fish to the West Indies, where, according to John Winthrop, the islanders were "so intent upon planting sugar that they had rather buy foode at very deare rates than produce it by labour." Agricultural produce also was conveyed across the Atlantic. Moreover, cheap Massachusetts foodstuffs were purchased in Boston by foreign vessels; outfitting ships with provisions became a major Boston industry. The entire region profited from this trade—ship chandlers who fitted and loaded ships, butchers who packed and salted beef, coopers who built casks to hold it, millers and bakers who transformed wheat into bread and hardtack, even doctors who sometimes treated injured sailors.

Economic Regulation

The British began to regulate colonial trade in 1650; the regulations were called Navigation Acts. In successive decades more and more such acts were added, growing up through small accretions like the precedents in common law. The Navigation Acts were not aspects of a well-conceived strategy imposed on the colonies all at once, nor were they, as is often claimed, originally part of an economic master plan called mercantilism, an economic system and theory which contended that an empire grows wealthy only if it functions as a self-contained system, buying little or nothing from outside.

The first Navigation Acts required that all trade with the colonies be carried only by British ships, that is, by ships that were staffed with crews at least half English and that were owned either by colonials or Englishmen. The intention of this act was to encourage the growth of the British merchant marine and to prohibit Dutch vessels from trade within the empire.

Not only did trade have to be confined to British ships, it also had to be conducted with English merchants exclusively if the transaction involved specified goods. The first such enumeration of specific items was issued in the seventeenth century; but as new colonial crops and manufactured goods became profitable, they, too, were added to the list. As the eighteenth century wore on, the list of restricted items grew quite long.

Careful statistical studies have not yet determined the exact influence the Navigation Acts had on the flow of commerce, though certain generalizations can be safely made. The restrictions inhibited certain colonial industries (finished iron production and hatmaking, for example) and encouraged other activities (growing indigo and making pig iron, for instance). And the Navigation Acts undoubtedly contributed to the widespread depression that occurred throughout the colonies in the second half of the seventeenth century. When a 1673 law placed a duty on tobacco transported from one colony to another, the added cost hurt both the Southern colonies and tobacco retail agents in New York. And certainly the Navigation Acts distorted the colonial economy, making it one-sided. The Iron Act of 1750, for example, prohibited the construction of new colonial iron mills. Similarly, the Wool Act of 1699 forbade the exportation of specified textiles manufactured in the colonies, just as the Hat Act of 1732 made it illegal for colonials to export manufactured hats. All of these laws were designed to: (1) prevent colonial industries from competing with favored English industries; (2) build up the British merchant marine; and (3) keep the colonies as a source of raw materials for

British manufacturing and as a market for finished British products. To the degree that they were successful in achieving these goals, the laws maintained the colonies as a dependent aspect of the British economy, but understandably they also created a vast army of lawbreakers, colonials who resented such restrictions upon their economic, even their personal freedom.

Farms, Towns, and Cities

Most colonial Americans were, as noted earlier, farmers—so much so that ninety-five percent of all residents of the English colonies earned their living directly from agriculture. But farms, like farmers themselves, came in various sizes and types. Most small farms undoubtedly were hardscrabble, subsistence affairs, their owners eking out a meager livelihood from season to season. Yet a small plot near an urban center such as Philadelphia or Boston might prove highly profitable and be more efficiently organized than some sprawling commercial enterprise teeming with slave or tenant labor.

Farm Life

Today the tenant farmer is generally regarded as an oppressed and exploited agricultural worker, deprived of the fruits of his labor by a greedy landlord. But during the colonial period, tenant farmers were not necessarily poor and in debt, nor were they denied the right to vote. Although suffrage usually was restricted to adult white males who owned a certain amount of property, a twenty-one-year lease of land met the property requirement in most colonies.

When there was so much free land to be had for the asking, why did anyone become a tenant farmer? Because the system had some advantages, especially for the farmer without capital. The landlord provided housing and seed; tenantry enabled recent immigrants to begin supporting themselves immediately while earning money needed for purchasing their own land and basic supplies.

Although there were tenant farmers in every colony, they were more common in New York, Pennsylvania, and other Middle colonies than they were elsewhere. In New York, for instance, vast tracts of land were claimed by landlords. The largest, an old Dutch estate, named Rensselaerswyck, comprised a million acres; another estate, the Philipse Highland Patent, was 205,000 acres; and there were a dozen others several hundred thousand acres large—much of the best land in the colony. Since most of these immense holdings were sparsely settled or empty (as late as 1720 Rensselaerswyck had only eighty-one families living on it), landlords had difficulty defending their titles. The British government did not look kindly on vacant estates and, when possible, attempted to break them up. There were many opportunities to contest ownership, since Massachusetts and Connecticut claimed territory along their western borders that New York regarded as its own. Moreover, on many occasions these New York landlords had been grossly high-handed in land dealings with the Indians. By lavishly entertaining a few chiefs and obtaining their approval of a deed, they claimed control of the land in question although a tribal council had to approve the document for it to be legal. Thus, New York landlords seized Indian territory through fraud, and by keeping descriptions of property deliberately vague, the landlords further infringed on Indian rights.

These weak or shaky claims to land, however, could be strengthened if landlords could settle their estates. To do so, they made tenantry as attractive as possible. Some landlords collected a mere token rent from their tenants ("three peppercorns" a year, for instance); others charged a rent equal to a tenth of the annual produce of a farm. Thus the yearly rent for a seventy-two-acre farm amounted to four fat hens, the fruit of ten choice apple trees, and twenty-five sheaves of wheat. Often even these reasonable rents were not collected with much care or regularity. Landlords frequently offered their land rent-free to new settlers for the first three to five years, a not surprising practice where land was cheap, labor dear. And in almost every case, landlords assisted lessees by giving them dwellings, livestock, wagons, and tools—surely unexpected blessings for penniless immigrants. Such generous terms were dictated by the real fears of landlords that unless they settled and farmed their estates, they would lose title to them.

This system had drawbacks, however. When a lease expired, the lessee or his heir had to pay a fee to the landlord that was equal to one-quarter or one-third of the price of the farm in order to renew it. Tenants had to agree to grind their wheat at the landlord's mill and to pay him part of the meal for this service. In many cases tenants could not sell crops to the highest bidder but had to offer them first to the landlord. Generally, tenants also

Valentine Museum, Richmond, Virginia.

Eighteenth century Virginia parishes were required by law to furnish ministers with a glebe house of four rooms and outlying kitchen. This is one of the few surviving glebes and illustrates the middle-class standards of the gentry.

were required to pay rents on their farms. And leasing land was not the same as owning it. Even if the terms of a lease were secure and generous, there was an appreciable psychological difference between owning land and renting it; as one New Yorker put it in the mid-eighteenth century, tenantry was suspect since "the hopes of having land of their own & becoming independent of Landlords is what chiefly induces people into America."

The small landowner lived in much the same style as the tenant farmer. Every member of the family did chores—the wife, children, and, if the farmer prospered, a servant or slave. If the farm was on the frontier, the farmer's first concern was clearing the land; since digging up tree stumps consumed too much time and effort, crops were usually planted around them. If the land was already cleared and had been functioning for a number of years, then the farmer struggled to maintain its fertility. In the South soil was quickly exhausted by tobacco crops; in New England land often was rocky and inhospitable from the start. Knowledge about crop rotation, fertilization, and erosion prevention was meager and uncertain.

Crops were supplemented by poultry, pigs, and vegetables or fruit raised by the farmer's wife, but the diet was monotonous since there was no method of preserving food other than salting and drying. The wife not only kept a garden, prepared the food, cared for the young children, and tended the livestock but she also clothed the family. To do so she had to start from scratch: first by carding, combing, and spinning wool or cotton thread; then by weaving fabric; and finally by cutting it and sewing garments. Although nearly every household had at least a spinning wheel, looms for weaving were less common, and that process might be done at the home of a more affluent neighbor, for a fee or an exchange of some service or produce.

Few small landowners were able to rise beyond subsistence farming, though in the South they grew tobacco for sale and in the Middle colonies raised surplus wheat. The size of farms also varied with the location. In the South 200 acres was considered a smaller than average holding; in New England the same size farm would be regarded as splendid. Indeed, by the eighteenth century the successive divisions of property through inheritance often had reduced New England farms to thirty or forty acres.

Large-scale commercial farming was a big business pursued for high profits in several of the colonies. It depended, of course, on hired or enslaved field hands. By the middle of the eighteenth century, Virginia—the stronghold of commercial tobacco farming—had a total population of 293,472, of which 120,156 were black, most of whom were slaves concentrated in the Tidewater area, where large farms often resembled independent villages. On the next page is the description of one estate made in a letter written in 1686 by its owner, William Fitzhugh.

"The plantation where I now live contains a thousand acres, at least 700 acres of it being rich thicket, the remainder good hearty plantable land, without any waste either by marshes or great swamps. The commodiousness, conveniency, and pleasantness yourself [*sic*] well knows. Upon it there is [*sic*] three quarters well furnished with all necessary houses, grounds and fencing, together with a choice crew of negroes at each plantation, most of them this country born, the remainder as likely as most in Virginia, there being twenty-nine in all, with stocks of cattle and hogs at each quarter. Upon the same land is my own dwelling house furnished with all accommodations for a comfortable and genteel living, as a very good dwelling house with rooms in it, four of the best of them hung [with tapestry] and nine of them plentifully furnished with all things necessary and convenient, and all houses for use furnished with brick chimneys; four good cellars, a dairy, dovecote, stable, barn, henhouse, kitchen, and all other conveniences and all in a manner new; a large orchard of about 2500 apple trees, most grafted, well fenced. . .; a garden a hundred foot square, well paled in. . .; together with a good stock of cattle, hogs, horses, mares, sheep, etc., and necessary servants belonging to it for the supply and support thereof."

Colonial Williamsburg Photograph.

William Byrd II was one of Virginia's outstanding political and literary figures. He rose before five to read Greek, after which he pursued his plantation and governmental duties.

The highly colored notion of the southern planter as a gentleman of leisure is quite misleading. According to this fiction, the planter was an "aristocrat," above demeaning work and trade, who devoted himself to gaming, drinking, hunting, and courting. Actually, the large-scale commercial farmer worked hard, long hours and was often an industrious merchant peddling his own produce. William Byrd II, for instance, was one of the most prominent eighteenth century Virginians, but he rose at three in the morning, read till breakfast, then began his round of chores. He supervised the planting of trees, gardens, and crops; he acted as the doctor for his household and servants; he bought the tobacco of neighbors and merchandised it and his own; he operated a gristmill and a sawmill; he arranged for shipments of tobacco to England from Richmond, the Virginia town he built at the first falls of the James River; and in the evenings he usually settled in with a good sermon, though on special occasions he gambled heavily with friends and flirted with their wives. As he confesses in his diary, he kissed a Mrs. Chiswell "on the bed till she was angry and my wife also was uneasy about it and cried as soon as the company was gone."

The revised picture of the southern commercial farmer that emerges is of a man who was cultivated but not idle. He may have imitated the manners of the English gentry; William Fitzhugh, for instance, though the son of an English woolen draper, researched his family coat of arms and crest, which a servant hired especially for that purpose engraved on all his silver plate. And when his sister announced she would come from England to visit the colony, Fitzhugh anxiously expressed his desire that "she come out handsomely and genteel and well-clothed, with a maid to wait on her." These pretensions, however, did not lead the big Virginia farmers to look down upon trade; Fitzhugh grew wealthy as much by bartering the commodities he picked up from visiting ship captains as by raising tobacco. And the first William Byrd made money by trading pots, pans, guns, and rum as well as Indian and black slaves. Nor was the wife of a planter a pampered socialite; she generally supervised such household activities as the weaving and dyeing of cloth and the smoking of meats.

The New England Town

Farmers in the South often lived isolated lives, but in New England they tended to gather in towns. In many ways the American town resembled—and was an adaptation of—the English parish. In England a parish was defined as the community served by a single church, but it was a unit of government as well as of religion. For the ten or twenty vestrymen (officers in charge of the practical affairs of the church) also acted as local administrators. In modifying this pattern to meet the conditions of New England life, the first settlers of Massachusetts established towns or corporations that were governed by a small number of selectmen, or elected officials.

There were important differences between the New England town and the English parish, however. Puritans believed in separation of church and state, and their New England towns reflected this belief. The church had its elders, but their jurisdiction did not extend into civil matters. Conforming to Puritan ideals, the church was a spiritual assembly of believers and not an imposing building maintained by taxation. In fact, the seventeenth century New England towns had nothing but a plain meeting house where church services and assemblies of any sort could be conducted.

What of the government of the town? The town meeting was the basic political unit. Most adult men in the town could take part in town meetings and vote, providing they were church members. Before 1691 a townsman in Massachusetts had to have at least eighty pounds sterling worth of taxable property and be a church member in order to vote in local meetings; after 1691, however, the General Court (the highest governing body in Massachusetts) lowered the local value of taxable property from eighty to twenty pounds and dropped the church membership requirement.

When a new town was being organized, a number of families gathered together and asked the General Court for permission to occupy previously unsettled territory, usually a tract of thirty-six square miles constituted a township. If the permission was granted, these farmers, who were called the *proprietors* of the town, then built a meeting house and sometimes a school and distributed land to various families. Land distribution was not egalitarian; families received smaller or larger parcels of land according to their wealth, social status, and number of children. When possible, each farmer received a parcel of tillable acreage, including pasturage together with some wooded land. A large portion of the land was kept in reserve for future settlers; this land, owned jointly by the proprietors, was called the *commons*.

Society for the Preservation of New England Antiquities.

The New England Meeting House was both town hall and religious center. The architecture reflected this social and theological fact. The absence of towers, bells, and crosses at the Rocky Hill Meeting House was a statement of belief.

In analyzing the evolution of a New England town, a distinct difference can be detected between the community's earlier years in the seventeenth century and its later development in the eighteenth century. During the first fifty years of a town's existence, farming was virtually the only occupation of its inhabitants. It should be recalled that the Puritan settlement in New England was a utopian experiment, an attempt to create a pure and simple Christian life in the isolation of the wilderness. To some extent this ideal was realized in the beginning. The economy of each town was extremely simple. Typically, the townsman was a subsistence farmer who raised only a few surplus crops for trade. The townspeople lived close to one another, a practice designed to facilitate the moral surveillance of the citizens by their elected officials, the selectmen, and the minister. Ministers, in fact, were frankly called "*Watchmen,* because they should Watch the Actions of all Men, and with an Aim of Religious Curiosity spy out, how every one liveth, with his Household in his House." And as a study of Dedham, Massachusetts, has shown, the people in a town during its first generation were passive politically, inclined to choose good town officials and let them handle public affairs.

During this early period, towns were remarkably homogeneous. Most of the adult men were proprietors of the town, and most of them could vote in the town meeting. Virtually every citizen was a white Anglo-Saxon Protestant; Massachusetts was hostile to the Germans, Scots, Irish, Scots-Irish, and blacks. The New England town was unified racially, religiously, and culturally. When a farmer wanted to move to a town, he had to apply for permission from the proprietors. This screening assured the town of continuing harmony and kept out all "such whose dispositions do not suit us, whose society will be hurtful to us."

One Massachusetts community, chiefly Salem Village (now Danvers) gained widespread notoriety in the early 1690s when it was swept by a wave of witchcraft hysteria. Between June and September 1692, nineteen people were convicted and hanged, largely on the testimony of three young girls. After a summer of madness and frenzy, the clergy discouraged the conduct of the court which had tried fifty-five others. A new court using stricter rules of evidence ended the trials. Years later the colony tacitly admitted error by paying indemnities to families of victims.

Why the citizens felt compelled to search out and destroy persons who were "witches" remains something of a mystery. Their reaction may have been triggered in part because Salem Town was becoming a commercial center of importance leaving the village area a commercial backwater. The most enduring and popular explanation sees the Puritans as religious bigots—people so narrow-minded and superstitious that they were easy prey for such mass hysteria. And because the citizens of Puritan towns had little privacy and were encouraged to spy upon one another and to report any signs of irregular behavior, how vulnerable they must have been to an invasion of witches. Recent historians have tried to trace elements of sexual repression and envy in the Salem trials since most of the accusers were young, single women between the ages of thirteen and twenty-six and the accused middle-aged, married women. Other historians have documented long-standing family feuds between the accusers and the accused. And it is quite possible that the "witches" were indeed unpleasant, quarrelsome, antisocial persons. Overall, the soundest explanations are probably to be found in the political turmoil of the times, a sense of failure as Puritanism declined, all of which led people to search for witches rather than try to find a cure for the bewitched.

In the eighteenth century the character of the New England town changed subtly as the old homogeneity disappeared. It remained a preserve of white Anglo-Saxon Protestants, but an increasing number of newcomers created two groups of people; recent arrivals and descendants of the original proprietors who often tried to retain their political dominance by denying certain rights to newcomers. Town meetings appear to have become more contentious; no longer were townspeople willing to let the selectmen make decisions for them. The society, which had been paternal and static in the seventeenth century, became more democratic and dynamic in the eighteenth century.

The town itself became more dispersed. In the early days, most of the inhabitants lived close to one another, sometimes along a single street, but as the community became more populous, some farmers found it both more convenient and safe to live out of town on their property. Typically, a father might give his son twenty acres a few miles outside of town, or a newcomer might be granted a distant parcel of property. Eventually the settlers in

Courtesy Massachusetts Historical Society.

Samuel Sewall (1652–1730)

Sewall was born in England and moved with his family to Boston in 1661 when he was nine years old. After graduating from Harvard College in 1671, he vacillated between entering the ministry and a mercantile career. Eventually, he settled on the latter and about 1675 married Hannah Hull, the first of his three wives, and by whom he had fourteen children.

Although Sewall held many public offices during a long career, he is best remembered as a special commissioner at the Salem witchcraft trials which sent nineteen people to their deaths. Subsequently, Sewall became convinced that he had decided incorrectly in these cases and publicly confessed his wrongdoing. He was the only judge to repent of his decision. His contemporaries apparently did not condemn his error, since he was appointed chief justice of the superior court of judicature in 1718, a position he held for ten years. Today he also is known for his diaries, which were published late in the nineteenth century by the Massachusetts Historical Society. In three long volumes, the diaries give a vivid picture of the mind of a Puritan. Sewall combines a zest for money with a morbid preoccupation with death, a harsh moral scrupulosity with a gentle compassion for Indians and black slaves. Hannah died in 1717 and two years later Sewall married a twice-widowed lady who died within a few months. He subsequently courted Madam Kathrine Winthrop with gifts of sermons, gingerbread, and sugar almonds, but she insisted on his keeping a coach and wearing a wig and in 1722 Sewall married a Miss Gibbs instead. He died eight years later. ■

these outlying districts might become sufficiently numerous to start a new town with a church and a school of its own. Sometimes the establishment of a new town was a painful, strife-ridden bit of surgery and left painful scars.

Although the New England town remained basically rural in the eighteenth century, it did begin to acquire some commercial importance as more and more citizens took up a trade, if only on a part-time basis. Crafts and commerce became necessary means of supplementing wealth since after three generations a New England town that prospered would have less land to bestow on its young citizens. Families did not follow the ordinary English practice of primogeniture (making the eldest son sole heir), but rather divided their property among all the children, including daughters. As a family proliferated, portions of land became smaller and smaller. And, as long as the parents lived, the children had little or no legal control of their land. As a result, families began to provide for their children in other ways—setting them up in trades, acquiring land for them in other locations, or giving them their inheritance early in the form of a cash settlement or perhaps a gift of funds when they married. In a country as vast as America, relocation was the obvious solution to this problem, but people with ties to a village were reluctant to leave. A study of Andover, Massachusetts, has revealed that not until that community's fourth generation did young people move away from it in large numbers.

Cities

Very few Americans lived in cities, but by the 1760s several important urban centers had emerged, chief among them Philadelphia (30,000 people). Boston and New York City were perhaps half as large, and Charlestown, Newport, Albany, and Providence somewhat smaller still. Aside from these major cities, there were a number of secondary centers—such as Wilmington, North Carolina, New Haven, Connecticut, and Williamsburg, Virginia—that played a larger role in the colony's cultural life than population size might suggest. Williamsburg, for instance, was by modern standards a small town; at the time of the Revolution it had about 1,400 people, half of them black slaves. But despite its size, Williamsburg was the cultural center of Virginia, a place where the wealthiest farmers came to socialize, attend balls, and conduct business.

During the colonial period, cities were not industrial but rather commercial centers and, accordingly, many urban workers were concerned either directly or indirectly with the transportation of goods. Of course some manufacturing did take place in cities; Boston, for instance, was the biggest producer of shoes and furniture in the colonies. But these products were manufactured not in factories but in small shops, and such shops could also be found scattered throughout the countryside.

Unlike the homogeneous New England town, the colonial city was a mixture of many social classes. Single women who had to support themselves congregated in cities, where they earned a living sewing, running shops and businesses (even taverns), washing, and cooking. Among the men, a class of day laborers sprang up who represented the beginnings of a free urban proletariat without property. During the eighteenth century there was a growing scarcity of immigrants who came to America as indentured servants. In Boston, for instance, only 250 of the 2,380 people who moved there between 1764 and 1768 were indentured servants. A labor shortage resulted, and as a consequence, poor men without property could earn a living wage by renting out their labor by the day.

This increase of urban life, although infinitesimal by modern standards, nevertheless gave birth to modern urban problems: sanitation, sewerage, fire control, hospitals, libraries, higher education facilities—and crime. For the most part, at least in colonial decades, volunteer organizations and charity institutions tried to meet such needs, not local governments. Cities had their volunteer fire companies, night watches kept an eye on thieves and prostitutes, and the well-to-do gave money to support orphanages, schools, and hospitals.

One of the commonplaces about pre-Revolutionary America holds that it was basically democratic, composed of a huge middle class and devoid of extremes in wealth and poverty. This democratic experience, the theory contends, prepared the way for the Revolution with its assertion of the principles of equality. A statistical analysis of colonial Boston, perhaps the most significant city before the Revolution, tends to challenge this theory. Comparison of the tax lists of 1687 with those of 1771, shows that the distribution of wealth became increasingly unequal. Small property owners—the middle class—became less numerous proportionally, whereas merchant princes at the top and day laborers at the bottom of the social scale became more numerous. In 1687, for instance, the richest five percent of the Boston population had held only 26.8 percent of the city's wealth; by 1771, the richest five percent held 44.1 percent. In some ways, however, Boston may not be a good test case since it was experiencing hard times. Its population grew by only a few hundred souls between 1760 and 1775, and this lengthy economic depression created both widespread poverty and fertile soil for revolutionary ideas.

Social fragmentation in the cities was furthered by two other aspects of the urban experience: the increasing diversity of Protestant sects and the deepening animosity of city politics, which frequently degenerated into demogoguery. The resident in a New England town saw few strangers and pursued the simple and timeless occupation of farming; the city dweller could observe foreign sailors in the port, meet a German Lutheran or French Huguenot or English Quaker at a neighborhood store, and hear a wide spectrum of political opinions.

Each city, of course, had its own character. New York was a free and easy port, careless about promoting the arts, religion, and education but avid in its pursuit of pleasure; thirteen years after Manhattan was settled, one-quarter of the houses were taverns or tobacco shops. Philadelphia, by contrast, was a quiet, Quaker city of compulsive readers and ardent gardeners. As the Quaker merchants became increasingly wealthy, they began to build fine houses and buy handsome coaches, but every display of worldly splendor aroused some disapproval. Quaker grandees, despite guilty consciences, seemed incapable of resisting conspicuous consumption; in that regard they were just like the rich of other denominations. In looking back on the evolution of Philadelphia life since the beginning of the century, an elderly Quaker recalled in 1764 what those early days were like.

"Friends were a plain lowly minded people and that there was much tenderness and Contrition in their meetings and That at the end of twenty years from that time the society increasing in wealth and in some degree conforming to the fashions of the World, true Humility decreased and their meetings in general were not so lively and Edifying That at the end of Forty years many of the Society were grown rich, that wearing of fine costly Garments and with fashionable furniture, silver watches became customary with many and with their sons and daughters."

In every city, no matter what its peculiar character, there was a social ladder composed of many rungs. At the bottom were slaves and servants. Working alongside the servants were apprentices bound to a master for a period of time in order to learn a trade or business. Above these servants, slaves, apprentices, and a growing horde of day laborers were the "mechanics"—men who had a trade (printing, say) and practiced it on the free labor market. If the mechanic owned his own shop and was successful, he moved up the social ladder still higher.

A self-employed mechanic or small businessman usually kept his entire family busy working in his shop. The wife often would help out as bookkeeper and the children would perform errands and small tasks. Some women learned trades from their husbands and carried on the business after their husbands died.

At the top of the economic ladder were prosperous tradesmen, merchants, and professionals. In England, "trade" was considered respectable but distinctly and irrevocably appropriate only for the middle classes, low or high. In America, it did not prevent people who engaged in it from rising to the heights of social distinction. For instance, William Pepperrell, born in 1696 in Maine, joined his father in the family business—selling fish, lumber, and ship's stores. Soon the business was so successful that Pepperrell was able to invest excess profits in real estate and in a fleet of merchant ships that carried products to the West Indies and Europe. In 1730 Pepperrell was appointed chief justice of Massachusetts, though the position preceded his competence; only after he became a justice did he bother to send to London for a set of law books. By leading a military expedition in 1745 against the French, Pepperrell was rewarded by the king: he became the first American-born baronet. When Sir William visited London in 1749, he was feted by the entire city. In England the "taint of trade" would have made such a rise in social position next to impossible; in America many of the families of greatest power and prestige were founded by merchants or tradesmen.

Success, however, did not lead to idleness. Just as the Virginia commercial farmers, despite their wealth, were constantly busy, in the same way the urban merchant princes worked hard for their preeminence. And their women were equally busy. Servants might relieve the upper class wife of the necessity of performing the drudgery of keeping house, but much of her time was devoted to supervisory tasks. What free time she had was spent in the arduous social whirl of cities—paying formal calls on other families, attending parties and musical evenings, and going to balls and formal receptions.

What characterizes modern cities, of course, is that they are industrial centers. But industrialization, or "manufacturing," was thought undesirable by many colonial Americans eager for a piece of land and the independence it presumably bestowed upon them. In addition, the Navigation Acts frequently made industrial activity illegal. In 1755 Ben Franklin expressed the point of view held by leaders throughout the colonies on industrial development.

Museum of the City of New York.

American homes were graced by beautiful pieces of home-made art such as this sampler done about 1800. Young girls learned sewing skills by working on complicated pieces of decorative stitching.

“England might quiet her fears that the Colonies should take to manufacturing. Manufactures are founded in poverty. It is the multitude of poor without land in a country, and who must work for others at low wages or starve, that enables undertakers to carry on a manufacture and afford it cheap enough to prevent the importation of the same kind from abroad and to bear the expense of its own exportation. But no man who can have a piece of land of his own sufficient by his labor to subsist his family in plenty is poor enough to be a manufacturer and work for a master. Hence, while there is land enough in America for our people, there can never be manufactures to any amount or value.”

The Human Perspective

Until recently the traditional view of colonial life was that of a rather grim existence. Women were seen as marrying soon after puberty, being constantly pregnant, and dying of exhaustion at an early age. Although men presumably lived somewhat longer, they, too, were seen as having a brief life. If a man reached fifty, he was thought by traditionalists to be old.

This set of assumptions has been seriously challenged in recent years by historians who have analyzed colonial population statistics. Most of these studies have concentrated on settlements in New England. Additional research suggests that the South had a heavy mortality rate in the first generation, but life expectancy rose for the native born.

First, it appears that the average age of marriage was quite close to the present-day average. In colonial times women were usually twenty-one when they married and men were twenty-three. (In 1970 the average marrying age for women was 20–21 years and for men 23–24 years.) Second, families were neither so large nor pregnancies so frequent as formerly believed. Children were usually born two years apart from one another, and births occurred less frequently the older the mother became. This incidence of childbirth can be explained biologically, since infants usually were breastfed during the first year and breastfeeding inhibits fertility. The average colonial family had a total of five to seven children. Analyzing seventy households in colonial Bristol, Rhode Island, one historian discovered that almost half were comprised of four, five, and six persons.

Death rates were high by modern standards, though infant mortality accounted for the biggest losses. If someone reached age twenty-one, then the chances were quite good that he or she would live to be sixty. In an era with only the most primitive notions of diet and hygiene and no medicines to prevent or cure infection, ordinary childhood diseases were all too often fatal. Similarly, an epidemic of a virulent disease could wipe out a large portion of a town's population.

Epidemics could have long-term influences on the development of a community. For instance, if a smallpox epidemic struck a town and killed half its children, as it did in 1700, then thirty years later there would be few young adults, though these few would have rosier prospects. They would inherit larger plots of land, not needing to divide their property with many siblings. A decent inheritance would enable these young adults to marry earlier—and thereby bear more children. Conversely, if a village was spared, an upcoming generation would be more numerous, inheritances smaller, and the age of marriage correspondingly later. An example of a community that was healthy and long-lived is Andover, Massachusetts. Following settlement in 1645, few deaths were recorded during Andover's first forty years of existence. The longevity of the first generation delayed second-generation marriages, especially for young men. The average marrying age for second-generation women was 22.8 years, for second-generation men it was 27.1 years—a high figure indeed. The second generation of Andover had to wait until middle age before it gained control of land and town politics.

Geographical and Social Mobility

As a land of immigrants, America was, of course, founded on geographical mobility. Indeed, as late as 1775, on the eve of the Revolution, about twenty percent of the population in the colonies was born in England or Europe. Upon their arrival most immigrants did not settle permanently. In fact, a handful did not settle at all, but instead moved on to other parts of the expanding British Empire or foreign lands, or even back to their homelands. About forty percent of those who stayed changed their places of residence every few years. A few of these people in flux were habitual drifters, but in most cases the move was made in order to acquire a farm of one's own. Thus geographical mobility was generally an aspect of social mobility; a family moved in order to improve its chances in the world.

The movement usually was westward, towards the cheap and previously unfarmed lands along the frontier. But this overall pattern should not disguise exceptions to the rule; in Connecticut, for instance, the eastern part of the state near the Rhode Island border was not settled until the eighteenth century. Settlement remained sparse, both far to the south and far to the north; for neither Georgia nor Maine attracted many newcomers. Though most of the mobility was prompted by the search for cheap land, in some cases urban centers attracted landless young men apprenticed to trades and runaway slaves. Even as small a town as Williamsburg provided protection for an escaped slave, who was often concealed by other slaves. And there have always been Americans who preferred the excitement of city life to the conservative, static existence of the farmer.

The colonies witnessed a few examples of a dramatic rise in social position and many cases of a less remarkable advance. From the point of view of social mobility, the colonies offered something of a contradiction, for society was definitely hierarchical but just as surely fluid. That is, social position was strictly defined, but a person had opportunities to change the position of his or her birth. Virginia law dictated that only gentlemen could race horses, and throughout the seventeenth century numerous colonies attempted to regulate dress so that no one would be garbed in clothes too fine for his or her station. People could change status, but at any given moment everyone knew quite precisely how far up or how far down he or she stood in the social order.

The colonists made up what has been called by historians a "deferential" society—that is, one in which people deferred to those they regarded as their betters. This view of colonial society is useful, since it explains some startling facts. For instance, although small farmers in Virginia greatly outnumbered the large landowners, nevertheless they consistently voted for these "aristocrats." In traditional England the big landowner had been the local lord, and in America the habit of deferring to the big commercial farmer (no matter how low his original status might have been) persisted despite social differences. But this theory of a deferential society may be only partially true; certainly there are indications that by the 1770s prerogatives of class were breaking down. Just why is not entirely clear, but answers may lie in rising expectations of middle and lower classes, competition among the elite for wider support of their political views, and, of course, the turmoil created by revolution itself. Certainly a tradesman, whatever his class, is not going to defer to a nabob whose views on imperial policy differ greatly from his own.

The Maryland Historical Society, Baltimore.

Indentured servants seldom left records behind or rose to prominence. A notable exception was Daniel Dulany who became a noted lawyer in Maryland.

New World settlers did not start out with an equal degree of wealth. Some came from well-to-do English backgrounds. Others, such as the large number of indentured servants, brought little wealth or prestige with them. Once they were in America, upward mobility could and did occur. Daniel Dulany, to cite an unusually fortunate man, arrived in Maryland in 1703 as an indentured servant from Ireland. Dulany had the good fortune to be sold to a lawyer who needed a clerk. Within ten years Dulany was a lawyer in his own right as well as a landowner. His law practice, his speculation in land and his marriage to a daughter of a well-to-do family enabled him to accumulate a sizable fortune.

Most social mobility was upwards, but there were cases of people who lost status. None of the families active in Virginia politics before 1660 is important in the later colonial period. In New England, the descendants of a prosperous farmer could be reduced by the successive division of lands through inheritance to the level of mere subsistence.

Wealth and prestige are not precisely the same thing, not even in a new land like colonial America. Whereas wealth is comparatively easy to estimate, prestige is harder to define, since it depends on the opinion of contemporaries which is often irrecoverable. Moreover, there are indications that colonial Americans experienced a degree of confusion about which occupations were the most prestigious, a confusion further complicated by the fact that few well-to-do citizens had a single profession. A man was a farmer, land speculator, politician, doctor, lawyer, everything but an Indian chief. Yet it was his role as farmer that he often prized most highly, and farmers thought of themselves as the most eminent element in colonial society. Other segments of the agrarian economy usually paid lip service to their high rank, especially if they had substantial land holdings. Thomas Jefferson was expressing a common sentiment when he wrote in 1787: "I know no condition happier than that of a Virginia farmer might be. . . . His estate supplies a good table, clothes itself and his family with their ordinary apparel, furnishes a small surplus to buy salt, sugar, coffee, and a little finery for his wife and daughter, enables him to receive and visit his friends, and furnishes him pleasing and healthy occupation."

But despite this supposedly high status, when American voters (most of whom were farmers) came to elect their leaders, they favored merchants and professional men, who, again, often were farmers of a sort as well. Attitudes towards families that had grown wealthy in commerce were contradictory; the same ambiguity colored opinions about successful lawyers and other professionals, as is suggested by this statement by William Bradford: "As gain is the sole pursuit of the merchant he is much more likely to contract an inordinate desire of wealth than the lawyers, whose pursuit is as much after fame as Wealth; indeed they are both improper pursuits, yet generosity and Benevolence are the product of the one Extortion and Selfishness of the other."

Slaves and indentured servants were at the bottom of society in terms not only of wealth but also of prestige. Free blacks also suffered from low social status. "There still exists too great an interval between them and the Whites, especially in the public opinion," wrote Brissot de Warville (1754–1793) about free blacks in the North. "This humiliating difference prevents those efforts which they might make to raise themselves." This gentleman, who died on the guillotine, visited America in 1788.

Artisans, or mechanics, were ranked slightly higher, though not so high that most artisans were not eager to exchange their role for the more prestigious one of landowner or shopkeeper. The professions—doctor, lawyer and clergyman—ranked higher than the mechanics, but the highest position of all was reserved for wealthy farmers and prosperous merchants.

The Law

Curiously enough, colonial laws varied more from English laws in the seventeenth than in the eighteenth century. While a modern observer would expect the colonies to take an independent course later rather than earlier, the reverse was actually true. In the seventeenth century the colonies were in less frequent contact with England than in the eighteenth century, and this isolation allowed immigrants to drift inadvertently from English standards or steer purposefully away from what were considered corrupt English practices. In Massachusetts, for example, the Puritans deliberately enacted new laws in order to foster their utopian social experiment. Similarly, in Philadelphia the Quakers enacted legislation consistent with their religious views (their strong pacifism, for instance). As one Quaker put it, "There is no distinction in Christianity between civil and religious matters; we are to be pure, holy, undefiled in all manner of conversation."

In the eighteenth century, closer English supervision and weakening of high, religious resolve caused colonial laws to conform more closely to English standards. Moreover, eighteenth century colonial lawyers were more knowledgeable about the English legal system than their counterparts of the previous century, a time when lawyers were amateurs. In some cases, Parliament passed laws that applied to the whole empire, which, of course, included the colonies; in other situations, the king instructed the colonial assemblies to pass laws that duplicated English legislation. By the close of the eighteenth century, the laws of the various colonies had come to resemble those of both fellow colonies and the homeland on the most important matters.

There were some appreciable differences between colonial laws and English laws, however. In England the long accumulation of tradition made more than two hundred crimes subject to capital punishment; the colonies reduced the number (depending on the particular colony) to fewer than twenty. English inheritance laws also were usually modified by the colonists. In England primogeniture meant that a father must leave all of his property to his eldest son, and the related law of entail prohibited the heir from selling or parceling out the property he received. Since land was not so precious in the New World, these laws were disregarded. In New England, for instance, children (including daughters) divided the property of their parents equally among themselves. If a widow outlived her husband, she, too, inherited a proportion of the estate by law. In Virginia primogeniture prevailed unless a man wrote a will; as a result, many Virginians made specific provisions for their children. During the first decades of settlement in Georgia, women were not allowed to inherit, since Georgia's original proprietors thought only fighting men should own land. But soon angry landowners with daughters as their only heirs changed that ruling—and many others that did not suit their interests.

Family Life

Some aspects of family relationships were regulated by law in all colonies. Children were expected to obey their parents, and they were occasionally punished by courts for not doing so. Marriage was not regarded as one of the sacraments but rather as a strictly civil ceremony, and the duties of the marriage partners were spelled out. Divorce in the seventeenth century was possible on the grounds of desertion, adultery, or absence from home. A marriage could be annulled if the husband was impotent. Neither husband nor wife could abuse the other. Laws forbade married partners from striking each other, and even verbal abuse was punished. Although the wife was expected to obey her husband, she was not his slave or servant. When one man told his wife that "shee was none of his wife, shee was but his Servantt," eavesdropping neighbors reported the remark to the authorities. The husband was fined forty shillings, despite the fact that his wife protested "that I have nothinge Agenst my husband to Charge him with."

Despite these provisions on behalf of women, the law definitely favored men. The man was considered the head of the household and had custody of the children. When men and women were guilty of the same crime, women usually received more severe punishment; for instance, adulterous men were usually only fined whereas adulterous women were physically punished—perhaps because they had no money of their own with which to pay fines. Under the law, a man gained the control and ownership of his wife's entire personal estate at the time of marriage, and he received all the money she earned. The crime for which women were arraigned more often than any other was bastardy—giving birth out of wedlock. Since paternity in such cases was difficult to prove, men were seldom convicted of fornication or begetting a bastard. The usual punishment for an unwed mother was a fine or a public whipping. If the woman was an indentured servant, she was obliged to compensate her master for the loss of service he suffered during her pregnancy by working for him for an additional time beyond the terms of her indenture.

The next most common crime for which women were punished was slander, and the usual punishment was ducking. A letter written in Virginia in 1634 gives a vivid account of this ordeal:

> "The day afore yesterday at two of ye clock in ye afternoon I saw this punishment given to one Betsey wife of John Tucker, who by ye violence of her tongue had made his house and ye neighborhood uncomfortable. She was taken to ye pond where I was sojourning by ye officer. . . . They had a machine for ye purpose yt belongs to ye Parish, and which I was told had been so used three times this Summer. It is a platform with 4 small rollers or wheels and two upright posts between which works a Lever by a Rope fastened to its shorter or heavier end. At the end of ye longer arm is fixed a stool upon which sd Betsey was fastened by cords, her gown tied fast around her feete. The Machine was then moved up to ye edge of ye pond, ye Rope was slackened by ye officer and ye woman was allowed to go down under ye water for ye space of half a minute. Betsey had a stout stomach, and would not yield until she had allowed herself to be ducked 5 severall times. At length she cried piteously Let me go Let me go, by Gods help I'll sin no more. Then they drew back ye machine untied ye Ropes and let her walk home in her wetted clotes a hopefully penitent woman."

Blacks and Indentured Servants

Blacks had a special—and inferior—place under the law. Not all blacks were slaves, but all were barred from certain privileges, such as the right to bear arms or to testify against whites in court. (An exception, however, was New England where the testimony of blacks was permitted.) Worse, blacks were not allowed to vote. Slaves, of course, had very few legal rights. In fact, the slave had a peculiar position in the eyes of the law. In one sense the slave was regarded as property, much like a piece of real estate; a slave could be owned and sold. But in another sense, the slave's humanity was minimally recognized; laws attempted to protect a slave from flagrant abuse by his or her master. Yet, the real estate designation prevailed, as was stated explicitly in 1705 by the Virginia assembly in its statute that "all negro, mulatto, and Indian slaves in all courts of jurdicature, and other places, within this dominion, shall be held, taken, and adjudged to be real estate. . . ."

When the first twenty blacks arrived in Virginia in 1619, their status as slaves was unclear. In the first few decades after 1619, some blacks, treated as though they were indentured servants, gained their freedom and bought property. They may have even voted, and at least one possessed one or more slaves of his own. Those blacks who converted to Christianity were often freed, since the original justification for enslaving blacks was that they were heathens. Yet from the first blacks were treated by whites as inferiors, and by the 1640s slavery was the common lot for the blacks in America, though the legal terms of perpetual and inheritable servitude were not clearly defined until 1661.

Servants also had a special and lesser place in colonial laws. The law protected the property rights of owners in the labor of indentured servants. Accordingly, runaways were punished when apprehended by tacking extra time onto their terms of service to make up for periods of absence. But laws also protected servants by spelling out their "freedom dues"—the amount of money, clothes, land, or other property they would receive when the contract expired. Legal remedies were also provided for servants who had been detained in service too long or had been physically abused.

Voting Rights

Voting rights were established through legislation, though they differed from colony to colony and from decade to decade. Women were denied the vote, though they may have taken part in elections in the seventeenth century; for example, Virginia did not specifically bar women until 1696, and New Jersey forbade female suffrage only in 1807. Even when women were barred from colonywide elections, they may have voted in town affairs or as members of a religious congregation. Similarly free blacks may have voted until later legislation specifically denied them this right.

White adult males were the voters in the colonies, and the vast majority of men qualified to vote sometime during their lifetime. Qualifications were elaborate and designed to restrict suffrage to the property-owning segment of the population. In the South the voting requirement was the ownership of between 50 and 100 acres of land. Elsewhere the most common requirement was possession of a forty-shilling freehold, that is, land with an annual income of forty shillings. This was not a very high demand, since in the 1760s an income of ten shillings a day was necessary to maintain a Boston family, for instance, in moderate circumstances. Farmland, however, was not the only possession that qualified a man to vote. Men who paid taxes of a stipulated amount, who owned a developed town lot, or who were master craftsmen qualified under special clauses in many colonies were also eligible to register as voters.

The colonial voter usually stepped up to a registrar and announced his choice orally. Since such a declaration was a public act, the voter's choice was known by everyone; accordingly, the voter could be pressured by the community or by wealthy local candidates into selecting one name rather than another. Moreover, candidates thought nothing of lavishly entertaining voters just before an election. When George Washington ran for office in 1758, his agent in Frederick County, Virginia, supplied 160 gallons of liquor to 391 voters—a quart and a half a voter! And candidates often kept open house for voters on their way to an election, and at least one bold candidate had a cart of liquor drawn up to the very door of the courthouse on election day.

Despite such flagrant abuses, the overwhelming testimony of colonial candidates and political observers holds that the American voter was a tough, independent character and not easily swayed. For example, the freeholders of Williamsburg, Virginia, declared in 1775 that they were "greatly scandalized at the Practice which has too much prevailed throughout the Country of entertaining the Electors, a Practice which even its Antiquity cannot sanctify." These townspeople asked Peyton Randolph, who was then a candidate for reelection to the House of Burgesses, "not to think of incurring any Expense or Trouble at the approaching Election . . . but that you will do us the Honour to partake of an Entertainment which we shall direct to be provided for the occasion."

Religion

Religion, as an integral part of colonial life, also was regulated by law. Legislation established a given denomination as the legal church of the colony. Such legal establishment meant that the government was empowered to draw boundaries between congregations, set clerical salaries, and collect taxes for the support of the church. In the Southern colonies (Maryland, Virginia, the Carolinas, and Georgia), the Anglican Church was the established faith, though in North Carolina it received no tax support and scant respect until nearly the end of the colonial period. In Virginia the Anglican parish handled the welfare duties of the state by caring for the old, the infirm, and the orphaned; the Church even built roads. Governors, who saw the church as a legitimate arm of government, had the right to send clergy of their choice to parishes.

In New England (except Rhode Island) the established faith was Congregationalism, but in the Middle colonies no single church was legally established. In New York the Anglican Church had a semilegal status, but individual towns were free to make other sects official. When New Jersey passed from the hands of its Quaker proprietors to the crown in 1704, the Anglican Church was partially established there. Pennsylvania, in keeping with Quaker views of toleration, had no legally established church, though in the seventeenth century Quakers were sufficiently influential to legislate such Quaker beliefs as pacifism.

In 1689 England passed the Acts of Toleration, which permitted dissenters from the established church in any colony to choose their own ministers, build meeting places, and worship in peace. The regulations did not, however, relieve dissenters from paying the taxes due the established church, and this inequity led to much political agitation against the collection of church taxes or tithes. And toleration did not extend to non-Protestants. Even Rhode Island, the most liberal of the colonies, denied citizenship and voting rights to Jews and Catholics. Atheists and free thinkers also were banned from holding office, since to qualify one had to profess a belief in the Trinity.

Anglicanism

The Church of England, or Anglicanism or Episcopalianism as it is variously known, was an outgrowth of the Protestant Reformation. When Henry VIII broke with the Roman Catholic Church in 1534, he did little more than reject the Pope's authority. Queen Elizabeth I, however, shifted Anglicanism farther towards Protestanism, though the Church of England remained the most moderate of the Protestant sects. Such Protestant beliefs as the supremacy of the Bible over later church teachings were embraced, but Anglicanism retained many of the old Catholic rituals and traditions (the use of vestments and sacraments, for instance). This emphasis upon ritual

Virginia State Library.

Christ Church in Virginia is a good example of colonial Anglican architecture. The cross-shaped church and the churchyard reflect both the Georgian influence on building and the colonial simplicity of ritual.

and the sacraments, upon the use of the Book of Common Prayer rather than preaching and sermons, clearly distinguished the Anglican faith from others in the Protestant fold. When Jamestown was settled in 1607, Anglicanism was the only faith legally recognized in England.

In the colonies, the Anglican Church enjoyed more independence than it did in England. For instance, there was no Anglican bishop in America during the colonial period, and the distance from episcopal authority allowed parishioners to exercise considerable control over their own churches, even to choose their own ministers without interference from London. In the New World, Anglicanism also lost much of its pomp and ceremony. As one Virginian put it, "the high-flown up-top notions and great stress that is laid upon ceremonies, any farther than decency and conformity, are what I cannot come into the reason of. Practical godliness is the substance—these are but the shell."

Methodism, an offshoot of the Anglican faith, has its roots in the work of John Wesley (1703–1791), who stressed piety and the power of sermons, not ritual and sacraments performed strictly to rule. Since Wesley was a chaplain in the new colony of Georgia for only a short time, his views were spread in the colonies by others who worked mostly in Philadelphia and Virginia and other seacoast areas. Methodists, merely a reform group at first, did not become a separate church until after the Revolution.

Congregationalism

Opposition to anything that smacked of Roman Catholicism was carried to much greater extremes in New England than elsewhere. It was settled largely by Puritans and Separatists—that is those who hoped to reform the Church of England from within and those who gave up and withdrew from it completely. English Puritans wanted to eliminate bishops, restore control of ordination to the local congregation, do away with the Book of Common Prayer, and eliminate any symbols of the old religion. When Puritans and Separatists reached the New World, distinctions between them began to blur, since both groups had literally separated themselves from England as well.

The new faith created in Massachusetts Bay was called Congregationalism because of its stress on the individual congregation as the basic unit of church structure. Each congregation was (at least in theory) independent of all the others. The congregation chose and ordained its ministers.

Membership in a congregation was difficult to obtain. Only those people who were deemed among the elect (that is, those whom God had predestined for salvation) could become members; all the others, though not members, still had to attend services. Members, who believed they were saved and gave signs of salvation in the saintly conduct of their lives, belonged to what the Puritans called the Church Covenant (a covenant, in this case, was the agreement with God that He would protect the faithful so long as they obeyed His commandments and remained true to Him). In the early days of the colony, voting was restricted to full members of the Church Covenant, but in the second generation so few people seemed eligible for membership that the ministers in 1662 worked out a new concept—the Halfway Covenant. According to this rule, children of members who wished to belong to the church and who embraced Christian principles could vote on church matters, though they were barred from communion and other privileges of full membership.

Although some conservatives opposed this compromise (the term "Halfway Covenant" was derisive), most congregations had accepted it by 1700. By that time another, still more liberal notion was being propounded by Solomon Stoddard (1643–1729), who taught that communion should be administered to all of "good life and conversation." The ideal of the independence of each congregation also was modified in time. Too much dissension, "heresies" such as those of Anne Hutchinson and Roger Williams, led various congregations to band together; their ministers worked out a more uniform body of church doctrine.

Baptist congregations formed both outside of and within the Puritan system but shared the congregational form of organization. Firmly opposed to all established churches, the Baptists emphasized adult conversion and personal religion. More than the members of any other religious denomination in colonial America, the Baptists championed religious liberty. From their traditional center in Rhode Island, they had developed by 1740 more than 150 congregations in America, largely in the Middle colonies. They added converts as their preachers went south after 1740, but the greatest growth came after the Revolution and then at the expense of the former established faiths, Anglicanism and Congregationalism.

Courtesy Essex Institute, Salem, Massachusetts.

Roger Williams
(1603–1683)

Son of a well-to-do London merchant tailor with a shop on Cow Lane, Roger Williams was descended from new landed gentry who numbered among their relatives a high sheriff of Hertfordshire and a lord mayor of London. With the aid of jurist Edward Coke, he was able to attend Cambridge, graduating in January 1627. During the next two years he studied for holy orders, became chaplain to a wealthy Puritan family living in Essex, fell madly in love with a young lady whose aunt thought Williams an unsuitable suitor, and married eventually another local girl.

Even before taking a wife, Williams became interested in New England, and in December 1630 he and his wife sailed on the *Lyon* for Boston where he had secured a pulpit. However, he rejected that post and became increasingly critical of the church-state alliance developing in the New World.

He preached for a time in Salem and Plymouth, but because of his avowed Separatist views, he was soon in deep trouble. Williams, a sweet but stubborn man, enraged authorities by contending that the king of England had no authority to grant land to the Massachusetts Bay Company. He also expressed the inflammatory view that the Anglican Church was anti-Christian. Even the government in Boston came under his attack, since he believed civil government had no authority in religious matters and could not even require people to go to church. On every point, Williams was a stickler for an exact interpretation of the Bible, but his reading of the Scriptures threatened the very foundations of New England society and ran the risk of arousing the anger of the throne.

In October of 1635 the General Court of Massachusetts Bay banished him from the colony, but because of illness and the birth of a second child, he was permitted to remain until spring. Nevertheless, Williams continued to speak his mind and the magistrates decided to exile him to England before he could organize a rival colony.

Williams learned of this plan and in January 1636

set out on foot for Narragansett Bay, an inlet of the Atlantic Ocean southeast of Massachusetts Bay. Here he worked as a missionary among the Narragansett Indians for several months and then purchased land from them and founded the village of Providence. Soon his family and friends from Salem who believed as he did joined him at Providence. He founded what was probably the first Baptist church in North America and established freedom of religion, although his policy of freedom did not include citizenship and voting rights for Jews and Catholics. The Puritan clergy in Boston referred to Providence as "that sewer" in which the "Lord's debris" had collected.

This freedom of religion soon attracted other religious dissidents to what became Rhode Island. Like Providence, these outposts were squatter settlements until a royal charter was obtained in 1644, largely through the personal efforts of Williams himself. However, this document never was fully implemented because of bickering among the settlements. Finally, in 1663 after a second trip to England, Williams secured a new charter from Charles II.

One of the great disappointments in Williams's life was the failure to maintain peace with the Narragansett Indians. Almost from the beginning he enjoyed warm, friendly relations with these Indians and endeavored to protect their property rights at all times. Despite this concern, during King Philip's War the Narragansett Indians joined forces with other Indian tribes against the British. Williams, one of two commanders of local forces, saw Providence burned to the ground and the Narragansett tribe, once his friends, virtually wiped out. ■

Quakerism

The Society of Friends held beliefs that made them suspect in the eyes of all other Christians. Catholics stressed the authority of the Pope and church tradition; Protestants dismissed most of these sources and relied on the authority of the Bible alone; the Quakers took a third position. For the Friends, the soul or spirit residing within each believer was the ultimate guide and arbiter in religious matters. Quakers regarded the Scriptures as "a Declaration of the Fountain, and not the Fountain itself." Consequently, the sacred texts "are not to be esteemed the principal Ground of all Truth and Knowledge, nor yet the Adequate Primary rule of Faith and Manners," but rather "a secondary Rule, subordinate to the Spirit, from which they have all their Excellency and Certainty."

This belief in the primacy of the Inner Light over the Bible led Quakers to reject the ministry altogether. No longer was there a need for ministers to interpret the Bible to a congregation. Another corollary to the conviction that there is a bit of God in every person was tolerance of all groups—American Indians, Jews, Catholics, blacks, and so on. This universalist ethic also fostered pacifism—for how could one fight with and kill a person inhabited by divinity?

Early Quakers were persecuted for these unconventional beliefs in England and were hanged in Massachusetts and arrested or banished in other colonies. Finally, William Penn established his proprietary colony of Pennsylvania in 1681 as a refuge for all oppressed people but especially for his fellow Quakers. Many German pietist sects, hounded out of their own country for beliefs similar to those of the Quakers, emigrated to Pennsylvania; the Dunkers (German Baptist Brethren) and the Mennonites were two of the better-known groups.

Despite their respect for individual testimony, Quakers were capable of exerting strong moral sanctions against those of whom they disapproved—through social pressure if not direct coercion. At all levels, compliance with group decisions and mores was urged through reason, and people who could not conform eventually were driven out. Moreover, local meetings did not function in isolation. They sent representatives to larger quarterly and yearly meetings, where policies were hammered out. Although Quakers had no ordained ministers, certain "elders" considered wise or eloquent or particularly spiritual carried more weight than other members during meetings. Thus the original vision of Quakerism became transformed into a church structure that resembled those of other sects. Even more significantly, the outstanding financial successes of Quaker merchants led to the gradual secularization of life in Pennsylvania. Nevertheless, Quakers were able to build a distinct social order that forbade the taking of oaths and that stood for pacifism and the avoidance of such frivolous and worldly activities as attending the theater.

The Quaker Collection, Haverford College Library.

Quaker meetings puzzled worshipers of other denominations because of their lack of form. This painting of an English meeting shows a combination of silent meditation and spontaneous preaching.

Presbyterianism

Except for two brief periods during the seventeenth century, Presbyterianism was the established Church of Scotland. Like Puritanism, the Presbyterian Church embraced the Calvinist doctrine of predestination—that God has already decided who shall be saved and who shall be damned and that a person's deeds cannot modify this decision—but, unlike the Puritans, the Presbyterians favored a strict form of church organization. Congregations were under the control of larger, supervisory presbyteries. Moreover, a doctrinal decision of the church as a whole was binding on all members; private conscience was not the final source of authority among the Presbyterians.

When Presbyterianism was introduced into America at the end of the seventeenth century by the mass influx of Scots-Irish, the newcomers brought with them a deep hatred of the Anglican Church and the English government, which had repeatedly attempted to make them join the Church of England. Since the Scots-Irish settled along the frontier in the Middle and Southern colonies, this pattern meant that the western border sometimes harbored deep-seated animosities against all governmental authorities—a factor that later played a part in the Revolution.

Other Religious Sects

The Dutch of New Netherland had their own form of Calvinsim, the Dutch Reformed Church. While the Dutch still retained control of the Hudson River valley, they made their faith the exclusive religion of the region; after the British takeover, those of Dutch descent often remained adherents to the Reformed Church, though some of the young drifted into the Church of England. As one observer reported in the mid-eighteenth century, "The younger generation scarcely ever spoke anything but English, and there were too many who became offended if they were taken for Dutch because they preferred to pass for English. Therefore it also happened that the majority of the young people attended the English church, although their parents remained loyal to the Dutch."

The influx of Germans in the eighteenth century made Lutheranism a significant sect in America. Lutherans had a close affinity to Anglican theology and like the Anglicans were organized under the authority of bishops.

Roman Catholics and Jews were present in the colonies but had little influence on religious affairs. Both groups tried to remain inconspicuous, although in Maryland Catholic missionaries bought up lands for their church. Both groups were viewed with suspicion and suffered political disabilities, the Jews because they were non-Christians and the Catholics because they were considered agents of a foreign power (the Pope) and therefore a threat to the Protestant English throne.

The Religious Climate

Colonial America was characterized by its remarkable diversity of religious groups, but there was one intellectual trend in the eighteenth century that challenged the role of all religions. That movement was rationalism. Many thinkers in America and Europe, made skeptical of the claims of religion by the advances of science, began by doubting specific doctrines (such as the literal truth of the story of Creation in the Book of Genesis) and ended up by rejecting broader beliefs (such as the idea that God responds to an individual's prayer). In America the very diversity of religions made the claims of each appear somewhat arbitrary. Some educated Americans, such as Benjamin Franklin (1706–1790) and Thomas Jefferson (1743–1826), came to regard the church not so much as a source of absolute truth as a school for the improvement of public morals. Franklin went so far as to draw up a scheme for the creation of a new, interdominational sect called The Society of the Free and Easy. Its creed he distilled from a survey of the various sects into a few principles such as the statement "that the most acceptable service of God is doing good to man." Within the traditional sects rationalist ministers appeared; Jonathan Mayhew (1720–1766) and Charles Chauncy (1705–1787) were both Congregationalists who attempted to accommodate rationalism with the beliefs of their religion. Eventually this rationalist branch of Congregationalism split off to form a new church, the Unitarians.

But there was also an equal but opposite force towards what a twentieth century reader might label "fundamentalism." The first rumblings came from Northampton, Massachusetts, where Jonathan Edwards (1703–1758) began to preach a direct, intuitive apprehension of God in all of His glory. He blamed New England's moral ills upon its assumption of religious and moral self-sufficiency. This force grew into a dramatic rush of evangelical fervor that swept the land and was called the Great Awakening.

The movement was aided by George Whitefield (1714–1770), an Anglican priest with unorthodox views who toured the colonies in 1739–1740, preaching as he went. Although the evangelist was not of a commanding presence, his voice was so huge, melodious, and dramatic that some who heard him said it could melt the most hardened sinner. In complete contrast to the rationalists, Whitefield (pronounced "Wit-field") invoked an angry personal God who saw through every person's sham piety

National Portrait Gallery, London.

Anglican minister George Whitefield's powerful voice and message made audiences on both sides of the Atlantic forget his physical appearance and instead concentrate on a Calvinist message of damnation and salvation.

into the inner depravity. Even the cool and normally skeptical Franklin was impressed.

"In 1739 arrived among us from Ireland the Reverend Mr. Whitefield who had made himself remarkable there as an itinerant preacher. He was at first permitted to preach in some of our churches; but the clergy, taking a dislike to him, soon refused him their pulpits, and he was obliged to preach in the fields. The multitudes of all sects and denominations that attended his sermons were enormous, and it was matter of speculation to me, who was one of the number, to observe the extraordinary influence of his oratory on his hearers and how much they admired and respected him, notwithstanding his common abuse of them by assuring them they were naturally *half beasts and half devils.* It was wonderful to see the change soon made in the manners of our inhabitants. From being thoughtless or indifferent about religion, it seemed as if all the world were growing religious, so that one could not walk through the town on an evening without hearing psalms sung in different families of every street."

Franklin helped Whitefield build a church in Philadelphia and later visited him in England.

When Whitefield descended on Boston, he turned the city into a tumult. His visit had been carefully heralded by organized advance publicity, and his preaching caused in that city a paroxysm of confession and conversion. Nearly two decades later one man recalled the time when "multitudes were seriously, soberly and solemnly out of their wits."

In Whitefield's footsteps came many other itinerant preachers galvanizing the countryside, winning converts, and criticizing local ministers who did not join in the revival. The result was a period of intense religious strife. Congregational and Presbyterian churches split into "Old Light" (traditional) and "New Light" (revivalist) factions. In New England, the congregations that separated from the traditional religion formed a new sect, the Separate Baptists. In the South, Anglican clergymen were bewildered by fervent missionaries who attacked the established church. Government officials of the Anglican faith fought back by arresting lay preachers (many of the itinerants had not been ordained) and by restricting the number of places where meetings could be held.

Within a few years the Awakening was over. What had the entire movement meant? Some historians ascribe it to an upsurge of democracy among the general run of humanity intent upon enforcing religious toleration on the established church because the Awakening was indeed interdenominational. Other historians suggest that the movement was a conservative backlash marked by its own forms of intolerance (an anti-intellectual disdain for the educated clergy, for instance). Certainly the Awakening struck at the foundations of the two religions in America, Anglicanism and Congregationalism, which had arrived with the first colonists and grown to be the strongest. Also, the mood of this upheaval clearly created

Dress

Worcester Art Museum, Worcester, Massachusetts.

Elizabeth Freake and her daughter Mary wore their best clothes for this rare portrait done about 1674 in New England. Adult women would not appear in public without some covering on their heads. Note the colors and bulky silhouette. Aprons were also a standard item of dress, with specially embroidered ones for fine occasions.

Courtesy of the New-York Historical Society.

This group portrait of the children of Garret Rapalje illustrates the common attitude that colonial children were miniature adults. The boys' clothes are exact miniatures of their fathers' items of dress. The major difference for the young girl is that her hair is done in a child's style.

Connecticut Historical Society.

Eighteenth century westerners had a fascination for things from the orient and middle east. The portrait of Jonathan and Faith Trumbull by John Trumbull shows how that fascination affected the at-home attire of the wealthier colonials about the time of the American Revolution.

CAPTAIN SAMUEL CHANDLER
Winthrop Chandler
National Gallery of Art, Washington
Gift of Edgar William and Bernice Chrysler Garbisch.

MRS. SAMUEL CHANDLER
Winthrop Chandler
National Gallery of Art, Washington
Gift of Edgar William and Bernice Chrysler Garbisch.

Captain Samuel Chandler and his wife had these portraits done about 1780. By that time American fashion had rejected powdered wigs and most men and women "wore their own hair." Fashions did not really change during the summer, but those who could afford it wore fine muslin rather than wool and brocades of the winter. Mrs. Chandler's gloves and fan and the Captain's sword were for formal occasions.

Abby Aldrich Rockefeller Folk Art Center, Williamsburg, Virginia.

By 1800 fashion was changing greatly. This painting done about 1815 shows the old and the new. The school master is dressed in the old style knee pants and long coat. The young scholars wear the new shorter coats and long pants. Notice also that the boys have short hair.

Courtesy of the Fogg Art Museum, Harvard University Gift—Estate of Harriet Anna Niel.

Like many young women around 1800, Harriet Leavens adopted the lightweight, low-cut Empire fashions. Made from muslin and worn without voluminous petticoats, the style was certainly more comfortable in summer heat, but no protection in the winter chill.

Footwear was personally fitted in the age before mass production. This sign advertising the shop of bootmaker Josiah Turner illustrates two styles favored about 1800. The hussar boot and the flat heeled slipper were both worn by either sex.

The Museums at Stony Brook, Gift of Frederick Sturges, Jr., 1954.

William Sidney Mount caught the everyday dress of Americans in this 1836 painting "Farmers Nooning." Note the simple smock style shirts which had been a standard item of dress for laborers for over one hundred years.

Abby Aldrich Rockefeller Folk Art Center, Williamsburg, Virginia.

This painting of the Tilton family in 1837 reflects the new middle class. Mrs. Tilton wears an apron as did her colonial ancestors, but the full sleeves help emphasize her fragile hands. The child's clothes mimic fashion but are shorter and are worn with pantaloons that are suitable for play. The father is somberly dressed with little ornamentation, except for a print vest, as became a serious citizen of the new republic.

Collection of the Newark Museum.

When Mr. and Mrs. Tilton left the comfort of their home they dressed much as these customers at a butcher shop in 1837. A bonnet shielded the woman's face from the elements. The butchers are dressed formally for their work, aprons tied over their suits. Note that the man in the rear is wearing a top hat while he works.

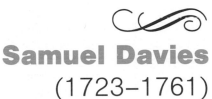

Princeton University Library.

Samuel Davies
(1723–1761)

Despite the brevity of his life, Davies was the most admired preacher of his generation, and his sermons remained popular reading till the end of the eighteenth century. He was a Presbyterian evangelist, one of the powerful figures who arose in the aftermath of the Great Awakening. By preaching with fire and tireless energy throughout Virginia, he built up a strong Presbyterian following in that Anglican stronghold. Born of Welsh parents in New Castle, Delaware, Davies was educated in Pennsylvania, ordained, and began in 1747 a Virginia crusade. A year later, his first wife having died, he married Jean Holt, daughter of a Hanover County (Virginia) resident. In time, Davies led the battle on behalf of all dissenters in Virginia and North Carolina, and his fame spread far afield when he was sent to England and Scotland to raise funds for the College of New Jersey, a venture that proved to be extremely successful. In 1759 he became president of that college, which was later and better known as Princeton. And, although he lived for only two more years before succumbing to pneumonia, he left behind an enviable record: degree standards raised, admission requirements strengthened, and plans laid for the construction of a more suitable library. ■

some disrespect for all forms of authority, often made a sham of that deferential bow to the local gentry who were pillars of the established faith, and perhaps paved the way for revolution a few decades later.

Culture and Learning

The earliest American colleges were religious and were founded to train clergymen. Harvard College opened in 1637, and by 1650 it had forty undergraduates and ten graduate students. Education always had been crucial to the Puritans, since they saw reading the Bible as the primary act of acquiring the word of God. Although Harvard attempted to be a college for all the colonies, its Puritanism made it unattractive to Southerners; in its first seventy years, not one student came from anywhere in the South, or even from as nearby as the Hudson River valley.

The College of William and Mary, established in 1693, was an Anglican stronghold in Williamsburg, Virginia. It, too, trained ministers, though for the first decade it was little more than a grammar school and had only a handful of students. Throughout the colonial period one of the deepest fears of the settlers was that their children would not obtain the graces of civilization but would grow as wild as the land beyond the frontier. A student orator at William and Mary on May Day, 1699, justified the school's importance by pointing out that "it is a common complaint that in many counties there are not men enough to be found to fill the bench and to administer justice between man and man, and we insensibly decline to a state of ignorance and abjectness of spirit." Another student remarked that the previous lack of education in Virginia has led to a situation in which many people "can neither write good sense nor true English" because "the comeliness of our mother tongue is most intolerably corrupted." The college did succeed in turning out some well-trained minds during the colonial period, notably Thomas Jefferson.

Yale was founded in 1701 by conservative Congregationalists who feared that Harvard had grown too lax in its morality and discipline. By the mid-eighteenth century the Great Awakening and rationalism combined their effects to produce a number of other colleges. The New Light Presbyterians sponsored Princeton (earlier the College of New Jersey); the Dutch Reform Church founded Rutgers (then called Queen's College); the Baptists created Brown (orginally Rhode Island College); and the Anglicans and Presbyterians joined forces to found the University of Pennsylvania (then the College of Philadelphia). King's College (now Columbia) became interdenominational by default; ministers of various religions quarrelled with one another until finally it was decided that the president should be Anglican but that the board of governors should represent many different faiths and the school should not exclude any student "on account of his particular tenets in matters of religion." Until a few years before the Revolution, there were no law or medical schools in the colonies, and students had to go to England or Scotland for professional training of any sort.

Most of these colleges, which were in fact simply high schools or academies throughout the colonial era, developed a unique form of administration consisting of an outside board of directors and a strong president. This tended to limit somewhat faculty control of collegiate affairs. By the eighteenth century many clergy, merchants, and some professional men as well were being educated at these colleges, not in England, thus increasing the "Americanization" of colonial life.

Education during colonial times was not, however, primarily gained in schools. The most important training of the day was vocational, and skills were learned through apprenticeships or from parents at home. Even the professions usually were learned on the job by law clerks and medical assistants attending men of established reputation. Tutors also were hired to educate children at home—a system much used by wealthy Virginians who lived too far apart from one another to send their children to a single school.

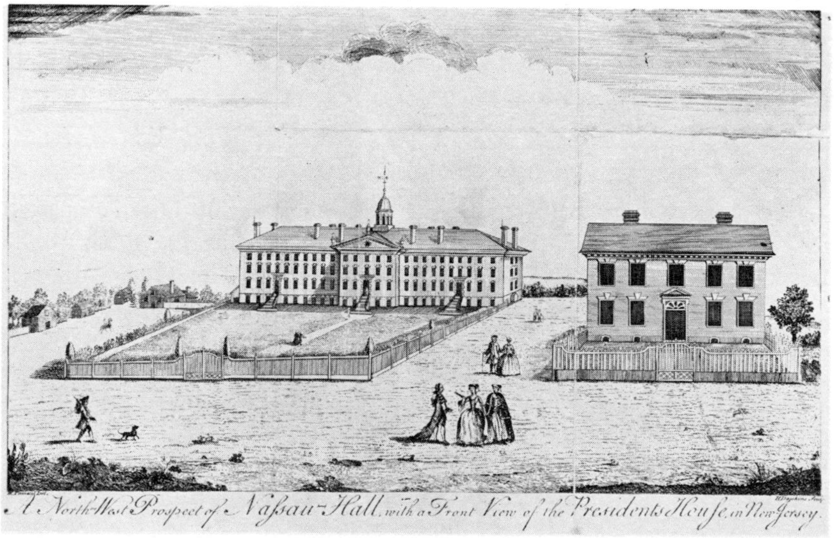

A North-West Prospect of Nassau-Hall, with a Front View of the Presidents House, in New Jersey.

Princeton University Library.

By 1763 when this engraving was made the College of New Jersey (Princeton) had served for seventeen years as the educator for New Light Presbyterians and others who came because of its strong program.

The New England colonies followed the lead of Massachusetts in legislating public schools. Every town of fifty householders was required to hire a schoolmaster "to teach all such children as shall resort to him to write and read"; every town of 100 householders had to build a Latin grammar school that would prepare students for college. In the other colonies education depended on more haphazard arrangements. Churches or ministers sometimes ran schools. Private individuals sometimes endowed a school, or paid for scholarships to be awarded deserving but poor students. Women were educated much less frequently than men: about half of the adult men in the colonies could read; only about a third of the adult women were literate. In Massachusetts these figures were higher, but even there men remained the better educated segment of the population.

Science

Colonial America did not produce any significant scientist or any vital body of scientific knowledge; nevertheless, some individuals began the arduous task of understanding in a *scientific* fashion their new world. Natural science, the collection and description of previously unclassified plants and animals, was one area of scientific endeavor that cried out for the effort of gifted Americans. In the eighteenth century a busy network of correspondence between colonials and scientists in Europe was established. Alexander Garden (1730–1791) of South Carolina was in regular contact with Peter Collinson in England and other naturalists in Pennsylvania, Virginia, and New York. John Bartram (1699–1777), a Quaker botanist of Philadelphia, classified hundreds of plants and also assembled information about Indians and their culture. Through correspondence Americans provided specimens to the great Dutch scientist Linneaus, who was classifying all known genera and species.

The chief medical contribution made by the colonies was the first testing of mass immunization against smallpox. Cotton Mather (1663–1728), a Congregational minister, read about the procedure and inoculated his family and a number of volunteers during an epidemic in 1721. He did so against the advice of most of Boston's doctors, who argued that too little was known about the vaccine and its properties. But the experiment was successful and Mather described the results in a paper that helped to promote the adoption of the technique.

In 1769 American astronomers participated in an event of international importance—observing the transit of Venus across the sun on June 3. Exact observation of the transit (which differed from a lunar eclipse only in that Venus was a mere spot against the sun) was useful in determining the precise distance of the earth from the sun. Until then, all of the distances within the solar system were known only relatively. Proportions and ratios were clear and could be expressed in formulas. But no single value within any formula could be expressed in absolute terms (number of miles). Once the distance between the sun and the earth was figured out in miles, all the other dimensions of the solar system could be computed. David Rittenhouse (a self-taught clockmaker who lived from 1732 to 1796) and others made the necessary observations in America.

Electricity was another field of American scientific experimentation. A Scotish doctor, Archibald Spencer, toured the colonies lecturing about the topic; when he spoke in Philadelphia he awakened the curiosity of Benjamin Franklin. Through his famous experiment with a key on a kite string, Franklin established the link between lightning and electricity. He also described electrical current in terms still used today. His published results and his practical invention, the lightning rod, made him an international scientific hero.

The Arts

In the secular twentieth century, Americans find it hard to imagine the interest that their colonial antecedents lavished on religion. The arts, like every other aspect of colonial America, were deeply religious. Sermons were the favorite form of entertainment, instruction, and literary effort. Educated men and women read sermons at home for pleasure, and the public became connoisseurs in the best style of sermon delivery. The *History of Plimouth Plantation,* a historical chronicle written by the early Pilgrim leader William Bradford, is a highly readable and highly religious account of that settlement. A later work by the minister Cotton Mather is frankly titled the *Ecclesiastical History of New England.* Even a seventeenth century book about Indian life written by the Puritan Daniel Gookin concentrated on the small Indian population that was Christian; it was titled *An Historical Account of the Doings and Sufferings of the Christian Indians of New England.* The first printed "poetry" in America was *The Whole Book of Psalms* published at

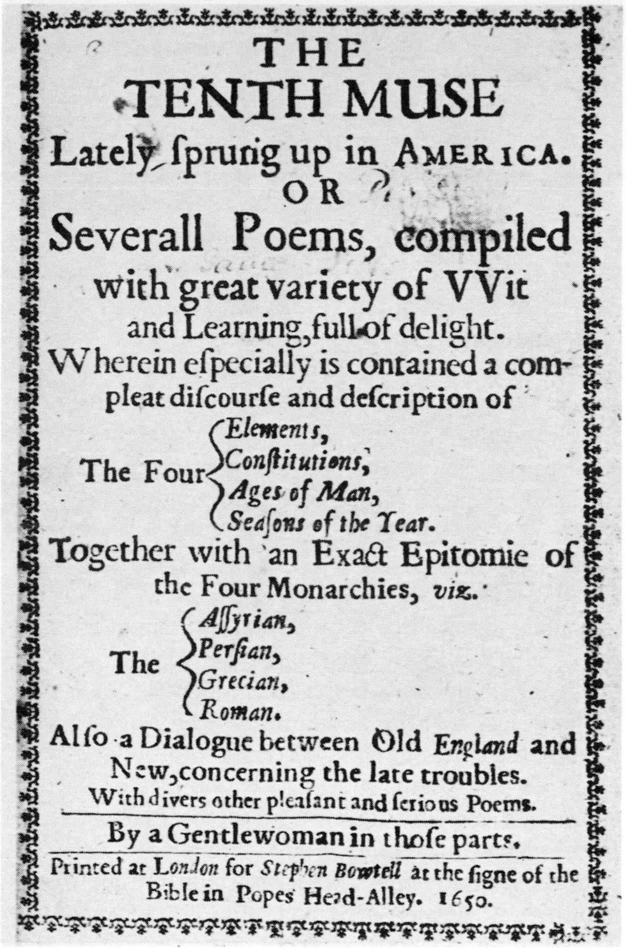

THE
TENTH MUSE
Lately ſprung up in AMERICA.
OR
Severall Poems, compiled
with great variety of VVit
and Learning, full of delight.
Wherein eſpecially is contained a compleat diſcourſe and deſcription of
The Four *Elements, Conſtitutions, Ages of Man, Seaſons of the Year.*
Together with an Exact Epitomie of
the Four Monarchies, *viz.*
The *Aſſyrian, Perſian, Grecian, Roman.*
Alſo a Dialogue between Old England and
New, concerning the late troubles.
With divers other pleaſant and ſerious Poems.
By a Gentlewoman in thoſe parts.
Printed at *London* for *Stephen Bowtell* at the ſigne of the
Bible in Popes Head-Alley. 1650.

New York Public Library.

Anne Dudley Bradstreet

(1612–1672)

Shall I then praise the heavens, the trees, the earth
Because their beauty and their strength last longer
Shall I wish there, or never to had birth,
Because they're bigger, and their bodyes stronger?
Nay, they shall darken, perish, fade and dye,
And when unmade, so ever shall they lye,
But man was made for endless immortality.

America's most celebrated poet of the seventeenth century was born and raised in England as the daughter of a wealthy steward to the Earl of Lincoln. In 1628 she married Simon Bradstreet, who two years later immigrated with her and her parents to Boston. Her father became the first deputy governor of the Massachusetts Bay Company. In the new Puritan society, Anne Bradstreet occupied a high social position. But despite the demands of her public and private life (she was the mother of eight children), she found time to write a book of poems, *The Tenth Muse Lately Sprung Up in America,* that was published without her knowledge in London in 1650. Though well-written, these early poems scarcely reflect her exotic environment. A posthumous book, *Several Poems Compiled with Great Variety of Wit and Learning,* published in Boston in 1678, does show originality. These poems deal with the New England landscape and with her children and husband; all of them are infused with her profound but flexible religious intuitions. ■

Cambridge in 1640. And the best-known colonial poet, Anne Bradstreet, made religious themes the subjects of her meditative works.

Two other nonfiction writers of note were William Byrd II, a diarist, and Mary Rowlandson, who began a new genre of literature—the captivity narrative—with a description of her experiences among Indians during King Philip's War. Bradstreet's first poems were published in England, as were most other colonial works of literature and history. In seventeenth century America there was only one printing press, at Harvard. The first newspaper to endure beyond a few issues appeared only in 1704, again in Massachusetts. But in the eighteenth century, printing developed quickly and by the time of the Revolution all the colonies (except North Carolina, Delaware, and New Hampshire) had their own newspapers. Philadelphia was the printing capital of the colonies and even had several houses that published works in foreign languages.

Colonial poetry and fiction were generally dismal, and no plays of any interest were written until the 1760s. But Americans were accomplished writers of nonfictional prose. Benjamin Franklin's *Autobiography* is a classic, and he delighted his readers with such humorous essays as *Advice to a Young Man on Choosing a Mistress* (1745).

In the crafts colonial Americans achieved results that strike the modern observer more and more as the true "art" of the period. For generations scholars attempted to discover examples of early American triumphs in traditional categories of high art (drama, poetry, painting). Now art historians have come to appreciate the beautiful and vigorous products of artisans working in silver, wood, and glass. Colonial furniture, houses, home utensils, and rifles, quilts—these are the "masterpieces" of a practical people.

The key to understanding and appreciating colonial life is adaptation. Separated from Europe and each other by great distances and by huge expanses of water, forests, and mountains, these first generations in the New World had to adapt their heritage—be it English, Scottish, Irish, Welsh, German, French, Dutch, Scandinavian, Spanish, Portuguese, Italian, or African—to existing conditions. What they realized only after the fact perhaps was that adaptation in the midst of diversity and challenge was creating a new being: the American.

Yale University Art Gallery,
Mabel Brady Garwan Collection.

National Gallery of Art,
Washington Index of American Design.

American artisans combined practical uses with design to produce such varied pieces as Josiah Dummer's silver dinner bowl and the carved Hadley chest, both done in the seventeenth century.

Essay

"Repent, Sinner, Repent"

During the past three centuries four great waves of the revival spirit have stirred the American public. Lasting about a generation or so, each one has been national in scope. According to William G. McLoughlin, Jr.'s *Modern Revivalism,* the first extended from 1725 to 1750; the second, from 1795 to 1835; the third, from 1875 to 1915; and the fourth, from 1945 to perhaps 1970. "In each of these periods," he writes, "a theological and social reorientation coincided with an intellectual and social reorientation in such a way as to awaken a new interest in the Christian ethos which underlies American civilization." Each time, McLoughlin adds, this experience altered both the definition of that ethos and its relationship to our society.

The Great Awakening, which occurred during the second quarter of the eighteenth century resulted from multiple causes, yet it carried, like all revival movements in its wake, the same basic message: organized religion is failing to do its job properly and, as a result, social ills are multiplying on every hand. The Great Awakening clearly knew no distinct bounds and was at home in Europe and America and in both Protestant and Catholic congregations. Theologians saw this phenomenon as a reaction against attempts by the Age of Reason to explain the wonders of Christianity in simplistic, rational terms. Many colonial Americans were disturbed by clergymen who rattled off formal ritual each Sabbath, neglected their pastoral duties, and perhaps even led riotous, debauched lives. This scorn increased if a colonial governor forced them against their will to support with hard-earned money or crops an "established" faith alien to their personal convictions.

Prime spokesmen for a "New Birth" of religious life included Theodorus Frelinghuysen of New Jersey; Gilbert Tennent, an Irish-born Presbyterian who preached in the Philadelphia area; Samuel Davies, the most eloquent Presbyterian voice in Virginia; and, of course, New England's Jonathan Edwards and the noted English clergyman, George Whitefield, who toured the colonies, 1739–1740. Although these men and their disciples were accused of displaying too much enthusiasm, stirring up the faithful in parishes where they had not been invited to preach, fostering turmoil and then quickly moving on (all of which was more or less true and, interestingly, constituted the same charges leveled at any revivalist in any age), they set in motion, perhaps unwittingly, a democratizing force that pervaded all realms of colonial life.

In a sense the Great Awakening was a natural outgrowth of the Act of Toleration promulgated in England in the 1680s and tended to loosen denominational bonds still further; but, more importantly, it encouraged political independence as well. Had established colonial churches remained strong, it is quite possible that powerful voices thundering down from scores of pulpits would have snuffed out the seed of separation from Britain long before it took root.

But such was not the case, and the two Protestant groups that profited most by the Revolutionary War, Baptists and Methodists, have never ceased their periodic tilts with Satan. Their cry in mounting tumultous campaigns is the same heard in the 1730s: much of organized religion is not true to its goals, and sin is rampant in our midst. What distinguished these initial waves of revivalism, however, was true spontaneity. A revival preacher could suddenly ignite an audience and whip to a frenzy those eager to repent their alleged transgressions. Although this aspect of revival meetings persists to the present day in some parts of our nation, as Baptists, Methodists, and Presbyterians gained respectability and numbers their exhortations to the ungodly became quieter and more subdued, and their crusades much more organized.

In August 8, 1801, some 25,000 people thronged into Cane Ridge near Paris, Kentucky, bringing with them children, food, a love of God, and a thirst for social companionship only the loneliness of frontier existence could nurture. Barton W. Stone, a Presbyterian worthy, and his assistants had been working for nearly a month to publicize this gathering and clearly did their job well. Since one man could not possibly address such a mob, according to Daniel Cohen's *The Spirit of the Lord,* eighteen Presbyterian clergymen and a handful of uninvited Baptists and Methodists preached simultaneously.

For three days and three nights the woods and hillsides echoed to the sonorous tones of these men of God, their voices often overwhelmed by the shrieks, uncontrolled laughter, and singing of those possessed by the Holy Spirit. If one listened carefully he also could learn where to buy a pint of liquor or meet a damsel eager for a romp in the woods, for drink and sex were fully as much a part of the nineteenth century camp meeting scene as prayer.

Although camp meetings that lasted from several days to several weeks remained a vital part of rural America almost to the present day, the true pulse of revivalism was elsewhere in the growing cities. There one could exert more influence, confront more blatant sin, organize bigger campaigns, and attract larger crowds.

Eve Arnold/Magnum.

The intense faith experience of the revival has often produced physical reactions. At this tent meeting a woman receives the laying on of hands for healing.

During the last century and a half, four men have dominated revivalism: Charles Grandison Finney (1792–1875), Dwight Lyman Moody (1837–1899), William Ashley Sunday (1862–1935), and William Franklin Graham (1918–).

Charles Finney, a tall, handsome man with piercing eyes and hypnotic stare, rose to power in central New York state in the 1820s at gatherings not unlike that held at Cane Ridge; but, in 1830 he moved on to Rochester, a growing center of 10,000 crammed with new rich created by the Erie Canal who were not about to shriek, cry, or roll on the ground. Speaking as a liberal Presbyterian, he lectured the anxious and even urged solid church members to look deep into their souls. What this man did, writes Cohen, was "regularize" revivalism. He no longer sought miracles and noisy, on-the-spot conversions to Christ; instead he depended upon efficient organization and more subtle techniques to achieve in a quiet, urbane (and urban) manner the goals desired.

Later Finney spoke in Boston and New York, but with much less success. The fault was not entirely his. Abolition, the consuming issue of the day, was writing an end to the second "Great Awakening" as reform-minded folk pondered how to end slavery, not how to win eternal salvation and sit by the throne of God. In 1835, Finney became president of Oberlin College in Ohio; and, although he continued to preach, his true revival days were over.

Dwight Moody, cast in the Horatio Alger mold, fled from his rural Massachusetts home at the age of seventeen and went to work in Boston where he became a zealous shoe salesman. Unlike most revivalists, Moody apparently experienced no tortured, mystical rebirth, nor was he tied closely to any faith, although nominally a Congregationalist. Moody brought to the selling of salvation the same enthusiasm and zeal he had once lavished on shoes. For him, conversion was a business just like any other. In 1856 he went to Chicago, became involved in YMCA work, taught Sunday school (despite very bad grammar and sketchy knowledge of the Bible), and in time organized a successful interdenominational church.

When the Chicago fire of 1871 destroyed his church and school, this energy-charged man decided to go to England to conduct revival meetings. With him went Ira D. Sankey, a portly federal tax collector and Christian worker, who played a small cabinet organ and sang beautifully. Moody himself was tone deaf but could appreciate the effect of music and song upon an audience. The English tour started out slowly, but in Edinburgh, home of conservative, moss-covered Presbyterianism, the two

Americans were a stunning success. As crowds grew, so did their reputation in both Britain and America, and throughout the rest of the 1870s the Moody-Sankey team thrilled thousands with their simple, no-nonsense approach: come forward and accept Christ as your savior. But by 1880 this brand of evangelism began to pale. Moody never gave up preaching entirely, but turned more to organizational work, devoting much time to the Moody Bible Institute in Chicago. He died suddenly of a heart attack, probably as he wanted to, while leading a revival in Kansas City in 1899.

Billy Sunday, an Iowa farm boy who ran away from home at the age of fifteen and in 1883 became a professional baseball player with the Chicago White Stockings, is a most unusual candidate for the shoes of Jonathan Edwards. His personal habits, until he heard a rescue mission group rendering Gospel hymns his mother once sang, gave no hint that his future lay in religious work. But Billy followed that little band back to the mission, went forward, got down on his knees, and accepted Christ as his savior. He gave up drinking and gambling, continued to play baseball for a time (no longer on Sundays, however), but eventually quit to work for the YMCA.

In 1895, after several years as advance man for an evangelist, Sunday decided to conduct revival campaigns alone. The result was like nothing seen before or since. This man was a

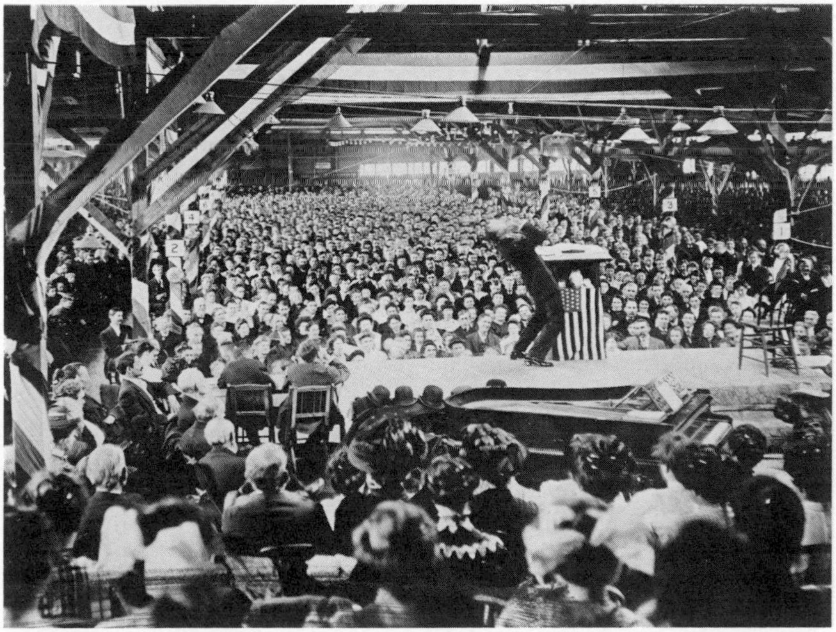

Brown Brothers.

Billy Sunday, like many revivalists, could draw large crowds for his services. Here he is acting out a story standing on a flag-draped platform in a sea of people.

consummate athlete and, not satisfied with merely telling Bible stories, he acted them out. Using sports vernacular, body English, and blazing, near blasphemous invective, he made audiences applaud, laugh, gasp—and repent, too, although his call often was phrased in a jocular manner: "Come on down and take my hand against booze, for Jesus Christ, and for your flag." Sunday brooked no competition as he went through his acrobatics for the glory of God. No one shrieked, rolled, or even uttered an "amen." He had all the lines, it was his show, and it was pure theater, Billy Sunday's theater.

Sunday reached the heighth of his power during the World War I era. The roaring Twenties, radio, and moving pictures killed him. Of course, they killed vaudeville, too, which is what Billy Sunday really was. He continued to preach and act in small cities and towns, becoming more and more convinced that the world would end in 1935. For him, it did.

Culver Pictures.

Aimee Semple McPherson was one of the first evangelists to realize the power of radio. Her career in Hollywood was notably theatrical.

Although several individuals tried to take Billy Sunday's place—Sister Aimee Semple McPherson, Bob Jones, Oral Roberts, and Rex Humbard among them, his mantle clearly has fallen upon the shoulders of another Billy—Billy Graham. Born in 1918 in Charlotte, North Carolina, Graham attended several fundamentalist colleges and in 1943 accepted a pastorate in a Chicago suburb. His first break came as a radio preacher; his second, as field organizer for a Youth for Christ movement.

In 1949, while conducting a businessmen's revival in Los Angeles, this young man attracted the attention of the aging newspaper tycoon, William Randolph Hearst, who told his editors to "puff Graham." This publicity, plus Graham's use of radio, movies, and television, have produced larger and larger audiences, many thousands that sometimes fill huge football stadiums. No revivalist ever has presented mass meetings so carefully staged, so expertly managed, so appealing to the eye.

Whether one felt Finney's hypnotic gaze, watched the Moody-Sankey team in action, laughed at Billy Sunday's antics, or has marveled at the klieg light showmanship of Billy Graham, some basic questions remain unanswered. In winning converts, does a successful revivalist, an individual who is often only loosely associated with some established religion, merely reinforce the faith of the faithful for a time, or does he perhaps exert no significant influence at all? Few evangelists care to speculate about such matters since by claiming huge numbers of converts, a revivalist could exacerbate his or her tenuous relations with local clergy and make future meetings in the same city unlikely. The best evidence indicates that all of these men and women, from Jonathan Edwards to Billy Graham, have been speaking to those solidly within the fold, not to erring sinners.

This is not to say that revivalism has failed to achieve some of its goals, yet the recurring waves of exhortations over three centuries lead one to believe that achievement can be neither permanent nor even very significant.

Actually, the greatest and most enduring impact of the sawdust trail has been in the realm of education, not in that of religion per se. Throughout these decades since the early 1700s, the fervent desire to train young ministers in the true faith, or to be certain that one's children drink from the proper spring, has led to the establishment of scores of American preparatory schools, academies, colleges, and universities. Any institution of learning with religious roots at one time or another was the bastion of an old faith or the beacon for a new, upstart rival. Revivalism clearly is a recurring phenomenon given to mounting excess, to gathering momentum, and then to losing it; education, by contrast, is a quiet, ongoing process. Yet, strangely, the classroom owes much to the pulpit-thumping evangelist whose words through the years undoubtedly have built many more schools than churches.

Selected Readings

Intellectual and Cultural History

Louis B. Wright, *The Cultural Life of the American Colonies* (1957)

Lawrence Cremin, *American Education: the Colonial Experience 1607–1783* (1970)

Samuel Eliot Morison, *Intellectual Life of Colonial New England* (1960), earlier title *Puritan Proanos* (1936)

Louis Wright, *First Gentlemen of Virginia: Intellectual Qualities of the Early Colonial Ruling Class* (1940)

Brooke Hindle, *The Pursuit of Science in Revolutionary America, 1735–1789* (1956)

Society and the Family

Carl Bridenbaugh, *Cities in the Wilderness* (1938)

Edmund Morgan, *The Puritan Family: Religion and Domestic Relations in Seventeenth Century New England* (1944)

John Demos, *A Little Commonwealth: Family Life in Plymouth Colony* (1970)

Philip Greven, *Four Generations: Population, Land, and Family in Colonial Andover, Massachusetts* (1970)

Michael Zuckerman, *Peaceable Kingdoms: New England Towns in the Eighteenth Century* (1970)

Politics

Patricia Bonomi, *A Factious People: Politics and Society in Colonial New York* (1971)

Jack Greene, *The Quest for Power: the Lower Houses of Assembly in the Southern Royal Colonies 1689–1776* (1963)

Charles Sydnor, *Gentlemen Freeholders* (1952) also published as *American Revolutionaries in the Making* (1965)

Religion

Richard Bushman, *From Puritan to Yankee: Character and the Social Order in Connecticut, 1690–1765* (1967)

William G. McLoughlin, *Isaac Backus and the American Pietistic Tradition* (1967)

William Sweet, *Religion in Colonial America* (1942)

Frederick B. Tolles, *Meeting House and Counting House: Quaker Merchants of Colonial Philadelphia* (1948)

Economics and Labor

James Henretta, *The Evolution of American Society, 1700–1815* (1973)

Gerald Mullins, *Flight and Rebellion: Slave Resistance in Eighteenth Century Virginia* (1972)

Richard Pares, *Yankees and Creoles: Trade between North America and the West Indies* (1956)

John Rainbolt, *From Prescription to Persuasion* (1974)

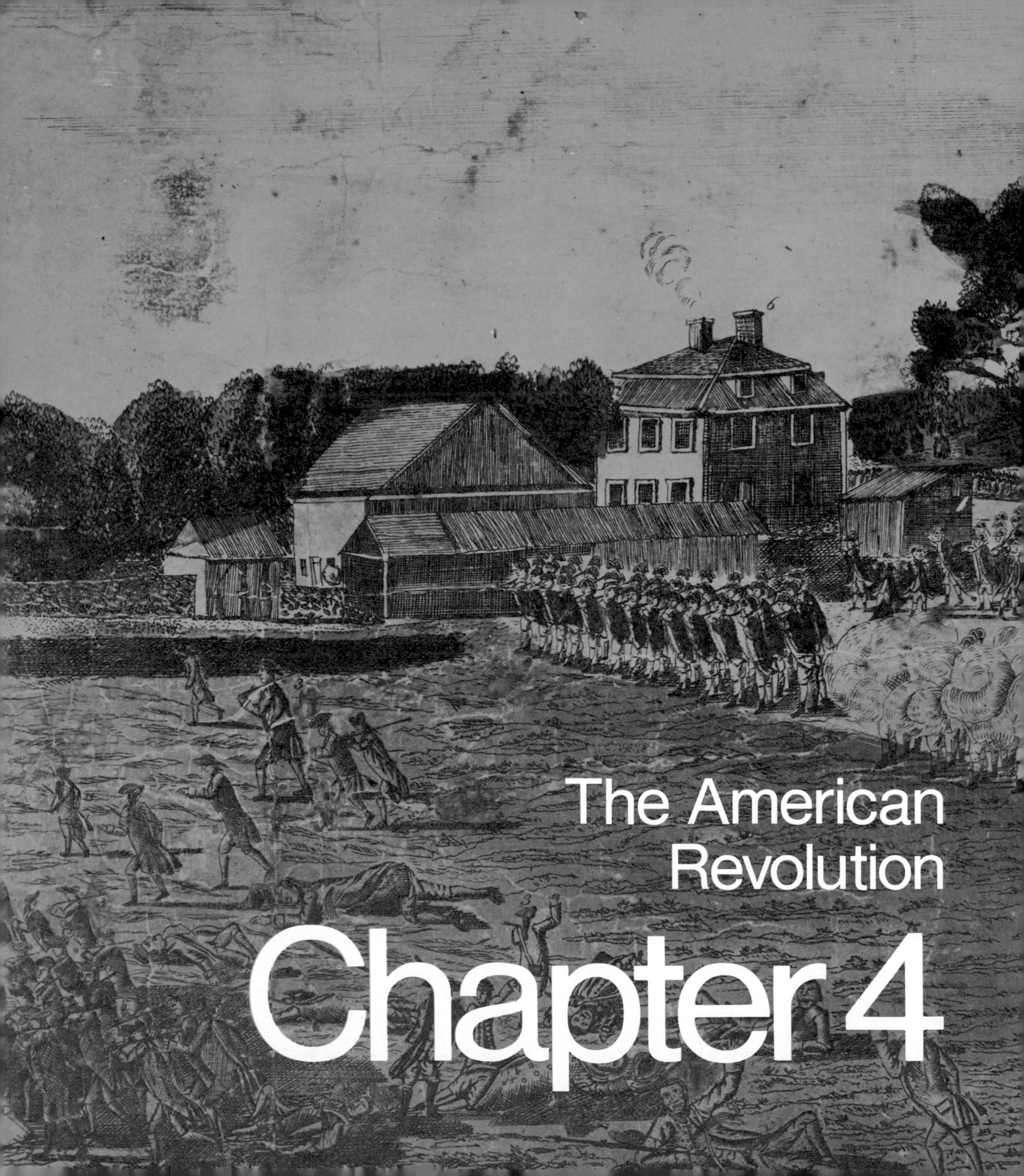

The American Revolution

Chapter 4

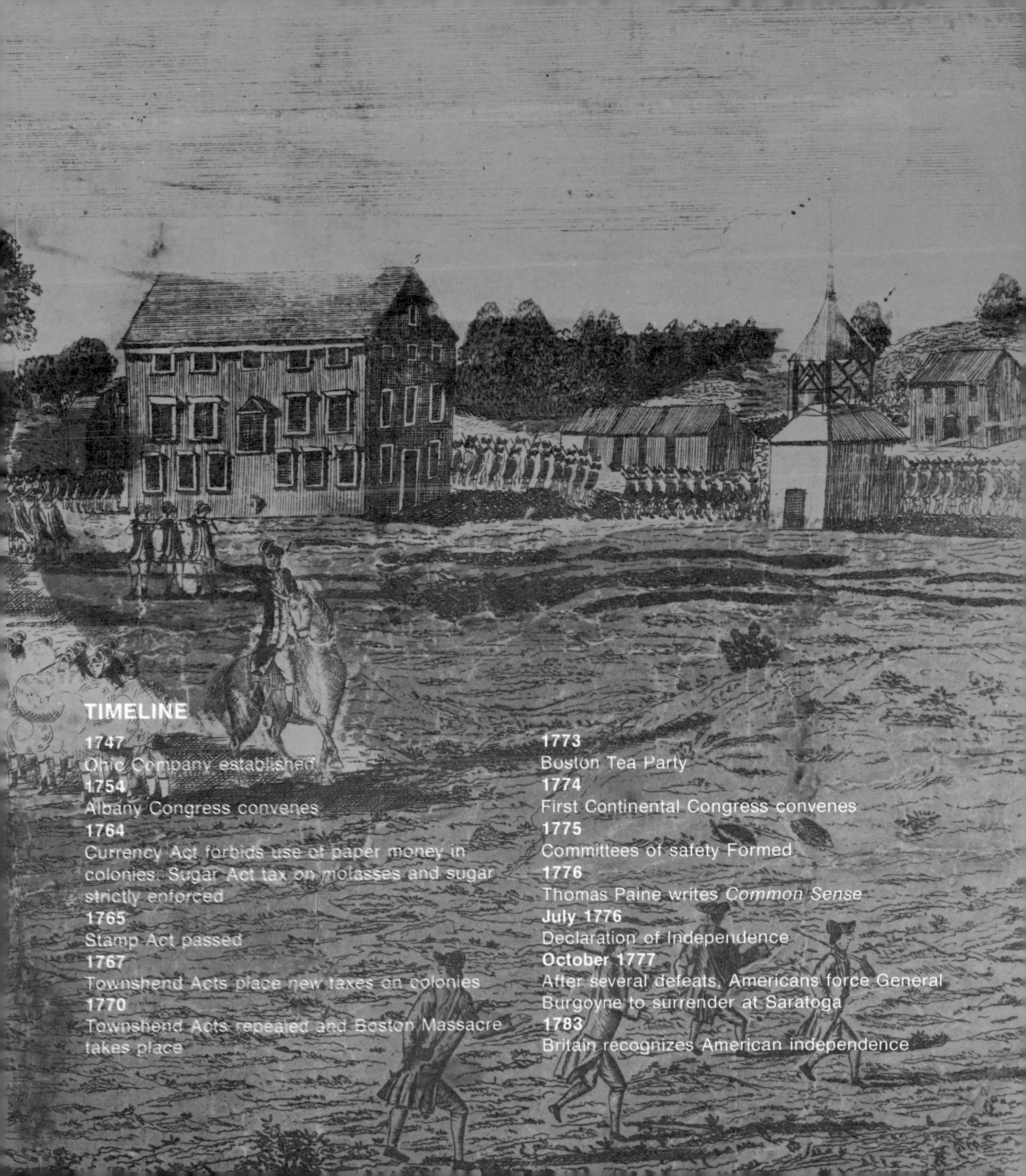

TIMELINE

1747
Ohio Company established

1754
Albany Congress convenes

1764
Currency Act forbids use of paper money in colonies. Sugar Act tax on molasses and sugar strictly enforced

1765
Stamp Act passed

1767
Townshend Acts place new taxes on colonies

1770
Townshend Acts repealed and Boston Massacre takes place

1773
Boston Tea Party

1774
First Continental Congress convenes

1775
Committees of safety Formed

1776
Thomas Paine writes *Common Sense*

July 1776
Declaration of Independence

October 1777
After several defeats, Americans force General Burgoyne to surrender at Saratoga

1783
Britain recognizes American independence

CHAPTER OUTLINE

The War for Independence broke out because the colonies and Britain held different interpretations as to what role America should play in the empire. These differences had deep roots in economic interests and divergent historical experiences; the war was not fought over idle intellectual quibbling. But, on the other hand, blind forces did not impel the combatants to a struggle they could not understand; in the years preceding the Revolution the inflammatory issues had been widely and articulately debated.

War was not inevitable. There is always the beguiling temptation to read all the events leading up to a major rupture as signposts pointing towards disaster. Throughout the seventeenth and early eighteenth centuries, however, Britain and her colonies coexisted in relative peace, harmony, and mutual benefit. The divisive differences began to appear only towards the middle of the eighteenth century.

The French and Indian War

Between 1689 and 1763 England and France engaged in four wars, each of them fought as a contest over disputed colonial territory. The French and Indian War (called the Seven Years' War in Europe) lasted, despite its European name, from 1754 to 1763 and was the most bitter of the conflicts. In a study of the origins of the Revolution, the French and Indian War is of interest because it pointed up how disunited the colonies were at that time. More importantly, as a result of the war Britain incurred new financial obligations that it attempted to force the colonies to share; this attempt was one of the causes of the Revolution.

The Albany Congress

In June 1754, twenty-three representatives from Pennsylvania, Maryland, New York, and the New England colonies, at the suggestion of the British government, met in Albany, New York, with Iroquois chieftains; their goal was to win the allegiance of the Iroquois in the upcoming war against France. The conference with the Indians proved fruitless, but the colonial representatives used the opportunity to discuss an intercolonial defense league against Indian incursions. Benjamin Franklin proposed a plan whereby Parliament would establish a central council composed of elected representatives from each colony and a president-general appointed by the king and responsible for handling all relations with Indians.

When the Congress submitted this Albany Plan to the colonial legislatures for their consideration, it was ignored or vetoed. Two features of the proposal made it unattractive to various legislatures. First, the council would have the right to levy taxes in order to build forts and maintain troops, and colonial legislatures were loathe to surrender their control over taxation to any other agency. Secondly, the colonies were competing sharply with one another over Indian territories in the interior; a united council might promote the claims of one colony at the expense of a rival.

While the British government viewed the plan as granting too much independence to the colonies, failure of the Albany Congress gave many administrators in England a false impression that the colonies could never act in concert and thus could never present a united front against the mother country.

British Victory

The Seven Years' War was the costliest and bloodiest conflict the modern world had ever witnessed. It was waged in Europe, India, and America, and on each continent France, despite the aid of its allies, Spain and Austria, was roundly defeated by England and Prussia. In the New World the contest was between England and France alone, and the object of dispute was New France—an area comprising modern-day Canada and the interior of the United States. The immediate source of friction was ownership of the Ohio River valley. Based on a 1609 charter Virginians claimed all land west and northwest of their territory. In 1747 a group of Virginia planters, including the brothers of George Washington, established the Ohio Company to trade with Indians and to speculate in western lands. Two years later a grant of 200,000 acres between the Monongahela and Kanawha rivers was made to the land company. Thus in 1754, when the French began to move into that region, Governor Robert Dinwiddie of Virginia, himself an investor in the Ohio Company, instructed twenty-two-year-old George Washington to construct a fort where the Monongahela and Allegheny rivers join to form the Ohio. By the time the expedition arrived French forces controlled the juncture and had begun construction of Fort Duquesne. Washington built a crude stockade, which he called Fort Necessity, about fifty miles south of the French fort. However, on July 3, 1754, he was compelled to surrender to a superior enemy force whose commander permitted Washington and his men to return to Virginia.

This defeat was the first of several that England and the colonies suffered during the next three years. Since England was concentrating its might against France in European battles, the war in America, to the degree it was thought about at all, was regarded by London as an unimportant side issue. But in 1757 England acquired a new leader, William Pitt, obsessed with the future of England as a great imperial power. Through Pitt's intervention, the major thrust of the British war effort was shifted to America. It was Pitt's ambition to drive the French out of North America altogether and to annex the entire continent to the British Empire.

At the close of the war a triumphant Britain occupied the French territories of Canada and the West Indies as well as the Spanish territories of Florida. Despite Spain's efforts to wrest Gibraltar away from the English, they still held that promontory guarding the western entrance to the Mediterranean. In Asia, England had driven France out of India.

At the peace table England returned to France its holdings in the West Indies but retained control over Florida and Canada. Now the entire eastern half of North America was British. As a result of this astounding victory, Britain became the most powerful nation in the world.

But the very moment of victory foreshadowed Britain's eventual defeat in the Revolution. The French and Indian War, fought in America to secure and expand British frontiers, brought the colonies to the forefront of British consciousness. No longer would the colonies be allowed to enjoy the benign neglect that had characterized earlier British administrations. Now the colonies would be ruled with a tighter hand—and this increased intervention in colonial affairs would bring into sharp focus fundamental differences that were developing between the colonies and Britain.

Evidence of closer supervision of American life is seen in a proclamation designed to simplify relations with Indians and foster orderly colonial growth. The Proclamation of 1763 promised Indian tribes that lands west of the Appalachians would not be handed over to white settlers without their consent. In theory, colonists were not allowed to travel beyond these mountains; anyone looking for new land was encouraged to go to Florida and Canada, newly acquired possessions that could be held only if they were populated by English families. Closing the Western frontier riled colonists who had been looking avidly toward the rich lands of the Ohio River valley for years. The belated vigor with which the British government suddenly began to regulate Indian affairs, even appointing special agents responsible to the crown alone, not to colonial legislatures, increased this widespread anger.

New York Public Library, Prints Division.

The capital city of New France reflected the city's role in ecclesiastical, governmental, and military affairs. It was a walled fortress set high above the St. Lawrence River. The engraving was made just before the British captured the city.

The war served to remind the British of the need for tighter colonial supervision as well. Disloyal colonial merchants had smuggled food and other goods to the French throughout the war, thereby aiding the French military and naval effort. Lord Loudoun, the commander-in-chief of British forces in America, wrote William Pitt that colonial traders were "a lawless set of smugglers, who continually supply the Enemy with What Provisions they want, and bring back their goods in Barter for them."

In another way, equally bad, colonists had undermined the British war effort by quibbling over their financial support for troops. Colonial legislatures begrudged every cent they handed over to the royal army and navy, and only after the British government promised to reimburse the colonies did they produce adequate

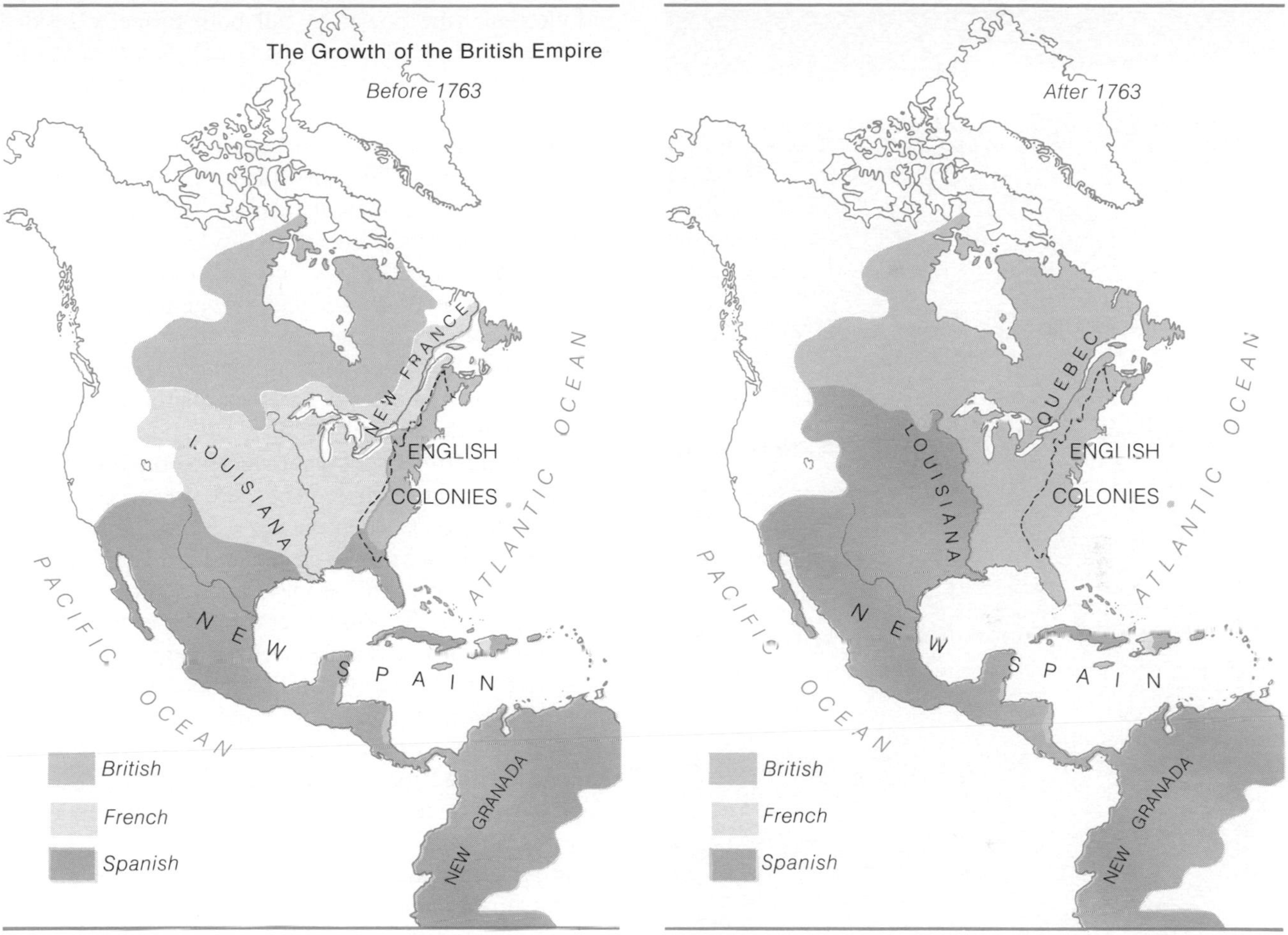

military funds. This lackluster participation in a war that had been, after all, fought to protect and extend colonial territory quite naturally irritated English officials; and, when the war was over, they were determined to remedy the situation by reorganizing colonial administration.

The Constitutional Debate

Important as finances, smuggling, Indian affairs, and other issues might have been, they all worked only to throw into relief deeper trans-Atlantic differences based on divergent interpretations of the British constitution. Unlike the later American Constitution, the British constitution did not exist as a single set of resolutions that had at one time been framed by a group of legislators and signed by them into law. Rather, the "constitution" was nothing more than an accumulation of traditions and documents setting forth the separation of powers between Parliament and the throne.

For more than a hundred years preceding the outbreak of this dispute with the colonies, British governmental life was dominated by the slow rise to power of Parliament as the more or less absolute sovereignty of the monarch was eroded by wars and frequent changes of rulers and even ruling families. The ouster of James II in 1688 clearly established the power of Parliament over the throne. When the crown passed in 1714 to a German

Colonial Williamsburg Photograph.

Americans hailed George III when he ascended to the throne, but their delight with the young king turned to disenchantment within ten years as he insisted on Parliament's right to legislate for the colonies.

family, the Hanoverians, Parliament further increased its dominance; the new monarch was assisted by a group of cabinet ministers, who, with the Parliament, effectively ran the government.

The Supremacy of Parliament

Parliamentary supremacy was spelled out at the time of the Glorious Revolution. William and Mary made formal agreements that Parliament could hold regular meetings and elections (the power to call both formerly resided with the king, and Charles I had once dissolved Parliament for eleven years). And the new monarchs also agreed that dissenters would be tolerated and that several other important liberties would be vested in the people or their Parliament. This settlement of 1689–1690, the strongest guarantee of parliamentary rights, came to be interpreted differently on the two sides of the Atlantic.

A philosophical, legal, and political question that was much debated in England throughout the seventeenth and eighteenth centuries was the location of sovereignty—that is, who has the ultimate authority to rule. Most theorists on both sides of the Atlantic at least paid lip service to the idea of popular sovereignty—the idea that the people retain the final right to rule themselves. Beyond that point of agreement there was no consensus. The relationship between the people and the king was, according to liberal thinkers such as John Locke (1632–1704), fairly simple: the people agreed to do homage to the king, but if the king overstepped his powers too grievously, then the people's elected representatives in the House of Commons could remove him from his throne. There were conservative politicians in England, however, called Tories, who challenged this interpretation and believed the king should not be subject to the people's will under any conditions. But the opposing party, the Whigs, were much more vocal, both in England and in America, and it was they who stood for the supremacy of Parliament. According to their formula, the location of sovereignty lay with the king-in-Parliament; that is, the king ruled only with the cooperation of Parliament.

Exactly how did Parliament represent the people? The British system of representation was complex. Individual chartered cities (called "boroughs") had the right to elect a stipulated number of delegates, no matter what their current size. Old, chartered cities that had lost most or all of their population retained their right to send representatives to Parliament; new, unchartered cities had no representation at all. Universities sent special representatives and each of the forty shires (or counties) elected a representative. Scotland, united with England in 1707, had its own allotted number of delegates. The upper house of Parliament, the House of Lords, represented the privileged classes; any lord of a certain rank and the bishops of the Church of England had a right to sit in that house.

The House of Commons, though it was governed by elected representatives, did not directly represent specific shires or boroughs. Each member of the House of Commons was supposed to vote for the entire empire, including the colonies in America. No member was immediately responsible to his particular constituents, and indeed such a notion of representation would have seemed strange to the English. Representatives were insulted, in fact, if their constituents told them how to vote. Since each representative supposedly had the good of the entire empire in mind whenever he voted, he thought of himself as *virtually* (if not literally) representing every British subject. Because of this idea of virtual representation, members of Parliament argued that they were legislating on behalf of the colonies, even though colonists did not elect anyone to Parliament. As the delegates would have put it, colonials did not vote for members of Parliament but then neither did many Englishmen.

The concept of "virtual representation" did not make sense to the colonists. A higher percentage of men voted in the colonies than in England, and in America a representative to a colonial legislature had, by law, close ties to the particular district that had put him in office (to be eligible for office one usually had to own land in his home district). Moreover, delegates, at least in New England, were quite used to receiving specific instructions from their constituents on how to vote. Accordingly, the whole theory of virtual representation seemed mere sophistry to Americans. As an editorial in the *Providence Gazette* of May 11, 1765, expressed it: "How trifling then is the supposition, that we in America virtually have such share in the national councils, by those members whom we never chose? If we are not their constituents, they are not our representatives. . . . It is really a piece of mockery to tell us that a country, detached from Britain, by an ocean of immense breadth, and which is so extensive and populous, should be represented by the British members, or that we can have any interest in the house of commons."

But there was another aspect of the constitutional crisis that was seized on as a bone of contention—the supremacy of Parliament. In the eighteenth century no English or American thinker had the sophistication to imagine that different areas of public life could be the province of *multiple* legislatures with *coordinate* powers. Today we readily recognize that the city council, state legislature, and national Congress have as their jurisdictions separate domains of political decision, and few people waste much time arguing about which body is *superior* to the others, nor does the question often come up even when two federal bodies such as the Senate and the House of Representatives are concerned. In the eighteenth century, however, the concept of multiple legislatures acting cooperatively was not a familiar one, and the constitutional crisis was made more violent because of this confusion. Parliament insisted on its superiority to the colonial legislatures. Soon the argument degenerated into an either-or stalemate: *either* colonial legislatures were superior to Parliament in determining colonial affairs *or* Parliament was superior to them. Since the Whigs felt that parliamentary supremacy was the only guarantee of the commonwealth against the tyranny of the king, the English Whigs viewed the colonists as Tories, reactionaries who favored royal rule over representative government.

The Authority of Colonial Assemblies

Americans, of course, interpreted their own behavior quite differently. They saw a resemblance between Parliament and their own legislatures. Throughout the colonial period the assemblies had striven for such rights and privileges as choice of their own speaker, the decision on when to adjourn, the initiation of laws, the immunity of members from prosecution during debates, and the right to settle contested elections. Throughout these colonial struggles both to obtain and retain specific rights, the opponents of the assemblies were the governors. Just as Parliament gained ascendancy over the king by withholding appropriations, in the same way the assemblies brought the governors to heel through fiscal pressure. Thus the colonists would have contended that their efforts to wrest power from the governors (who represented the will of the monarch) was similar to Parliament's struggle to gain dominance over the king.

The Whig warning that the sovereign was a threat to representative government was no idle fear. The king was by no means a mere figurehead in the eighteenth century. The crown had a separate income, independent of Parliament's appropriations. Furthermore, the king wielded a great deal of influence within Parliament since he controlled a number of seats in Parliament through his patronage. The king could choose his ministers and they were responsible to him alone; through his ministers the king could attempt to gain a majority in the Parliament. And the king's relationship with the colonies was direct and personal, for the crown's administrative powers included governing the colonies (as well as handling all foreign affairs). Despite this royal prerogative, Parliament never doubted it had the right to interfere in colonial matters; it regarded itself as the supreme protector of all British rights and liberties.

The central ideological issue of the Revolution can be seen as the conflict between Parliament and colonial legislatures over sovereignty. Both colonial and British representatives were eager to restrict royal prerogative; the insistence upon the primacy of colonial assemblies in America was as much a Whig characteristic as was the insistence upon the primacy of Parliament in England. The ironic truth of the Revolution is that in one sense it was a war in which both sides believed in the same principles. Both the colonists and the members of Parliament claimed to be protecting their Whig heritage.

At no point were these issues startlingly clear to either side. Only as the battle grew more fierce did the colonists and the delegates in Parliament hone their arguments and follow to bitter conclusion the full implications of their different interpretations of the constitutional crisis.

The Events Leading to the War

The constitutional debate emerged between 1763 and 1765 when the British initiated a number of measures designed to bring the empire more fully under the aegis of Parliament. These measures only raised the hackles of colonists resolved to preserve what they regarded as the status quo, and their hereditary rights.

The Currency Act

In 1764 Parliament created the Currency Act, which forbade the use of paper money in the colonies as legal tender. The colonies, which mined no precious metals, always had been bedeviled by the lack of hard money, or specie. An unfavorable balance of trade with England drained the colonies of whatever specie they might have, much of it derived from trade with the Spanish and French West Indies.

To solve this problem colonial land banks issued paper money in the form of loans to individuals, who put up their property as mortgage. In addition, colonial legislatures printed paper money during war time to pay for extraordinary expenses. Thus governments met expenses by issuing a paper medium, whether currency or certificates, which could be used to pay taxes and make other payments. This paper could not, however, be exchanged for coin or specie.

In 1764 this system was severely curtailed by a currency act. Parliament always had been suspicious of the inflationary nature of paper money issued by the colonies; thus, after the French and Indian War, acting through its Board of Trade, Parliament responded favorably to pressure exerted by English merchants, who were complaining of inflated colonial currencies. Franklin later cited British restrictions against colonial paper money as one of the main reasons for the alienation of the American provinces.

The Sugar Act

Another act passed in 1764 was far more obnoxious to the colonies—the Sugar Act. At first glance one might fail to understand why this act should have aroused such a storm, since it *reduced* the duty imposed on molasses and sugar from unrealistically high levels set by the Molasses Act of 1733. But the Molasses Act had been flagrantly abused or ignored by American smugglers. The new Sugar Act was to be strictly enforced. British warships would patrol American waters, and customs officials and naval officers had the right to inspect any cargo on demand. Not only was commerce with other nations so regulated, but intercolonial trade also was affected. A farmer or merchant shipping produce from one colony to another had to report to the nearest custom house, post bond for his cargo, and file a detailed invoice describing his shipment—even when the "nearest" customs house was thirty or forty miles from his home.

If restrictions on intercolonial trade were annoying and time-consuming and served to impede commerce, regulations on foreign trade cut into colonial profits. A heavy duty was levied on wine imported from the islands off Spain to America. New duties were placed on foreign coffee, indigo, and sugar. American lumber destined for European ports had to pass through England. Importation of foreign rum to the colonies was totally forbidden.

Americans in their first objections to the Sugar Act

stressed economic hardships it would impose on them. And indeed, the new restrictions on paper money and currency did deepen a depression triggered by the end of the French and Indian War. One businessman writing from Rhode Island observed that "all business seems to wear a gloom not before seen in America," and another, writing from New York City, said, "Business in this town is very much stagnated, Cash excessive scarce. . . . The Prospect is really very discouraging, the Sound of Terror every Day encreasing [*sic*]."

There were more fundamental reasons, however, for this discontent. Americans were angered because the express purpose of the new acts was to raise revenue to pay part of the expenses of maintaining 10,000 British troops in America. These troops were supposed to defend the frontier against Indian attacks, but as they demonstrated during Pontiac's Rebellion of 1763 near Detroit, they were quite unsuited for Indian fighting. The colonists began to suspect that the real reason for the large standing force in America was to force compliance with new rules and regulations and to put an end to profitable smuggling. As one correspondent from Connecticut wrote home from London, the British government "seems determined to fix upon us a large Number of regular Troops under pretence for our Defence; but rather designed as a rod and Check over us." Equally irritating was the fact that not a single colonist was chosen to serve as an officer in this army.

Worse, violators of the Sugar Act were to be tried not in ordinary common-law courts, where they would be judged by a jury of peers and fellow Americans, but by admiralty courts, which handed down judgments without the use of juries. Traditionally, these courts tried cases involving crimes committed on the high seas. In practice, common-law courts assumed the accused was innocent until proved guilty, while admiralty courts proceeded under the assumption that the defendant was guilty until he could demonstrate his innocence. Admiralty courts also were unpopular for less high-minded reasons; they usually convicted smugglers, whereas jury trials almost always let those accused go free. In a long petition sent on October 18, 1764, from the New York Assembly to the House of Commons, colonial legislators, politely but firmly objected to the admiralty courts "who proceed not according to the old wholesome Laws of the Land, nor are always filled with Judges of approved Knowledge and Integrity."

The Stamp Act

The strongest objection of principle to the Sugar Act was that it was a parliamentary law designed to raise revenue. One of the deepest convictions entertained by the colonists was that as Englishmen they could not be taxed except by their own representatives. Though members of Parliament might argue they represented the colonists "virtually," this position, as noted, seemed like arrant nonsense to Americans. Their anger at indirect taxes on merchandise was only a fit of pique when compared to the fury which erupted when they learned of direct taxation to be enforced by the Stamp Act, a law signed by young King George III on March 22, 1765.

This new act stipulated that a tax could be collected on every legal document (or, as the text of the act itself put it, "every skin or piece of vellum or parchment, or sheet or piece of paper"). Every time one American sued another or put up bail or wrote a will or received a college degree or cleared merchandise through customs or surveyed property or sold liquor or performed any other public or legal act, he or she was taxed; a stamp showing that the tax had been paid would be affixed to the document in question. The act also arranged for the taxation of newspapers, almanacs, playing cards, and dice.

To complete the insult, in May 1765 Parliament put through the Quartering Act, which made the government of any colony where British troops were stationed responsible for providing the soldiers with living accommodations, drink, bedding, and basic supplies.

To the English these arrangements, passed through the House of Commons with scarcely any debate, seemed perfectly reasonable. The Seven Years' War, the costliest military venture in British history, left the mother country saddled with an enormous debt. To pay this debt, the government had to invent new sources of tax money both at home and in the colonies. Cider, the drink of the average Englishman, was taxed for the first time, an innovation that set off violent riots in apple-growing districts of Britain. That costly war, in the view of Parliament, the king, and his ministers, had been fought to extend American boundaries, and now that a standing force was required to defend those new lands, it seemed only just that the colonists should pay some of the expenses (no English leader suggested the colonies should shoulder the whole burden). England itself had a stamp

The·TIMES are
Dreadful,
Dismal
Doleful
Dolorous, and
DOLLAR-LESS.

An Emblem of the Effects of the STAMP
O! the fatal Stamp

Thursday, October 31, 1765. THE NUMB. 1195.

PENNSYLVANIA JOURNAL;
AND
WEEKLY ADVERTISER.

EXPIRING: In Hopes of a Resurrection to LIFE again.

Courtesy of the New York Historical Society, New York City.

The Pennsylvania Journal expressed its dissatisfaction with the Stamp Act by announcing that it would die rather than use stamped paper. The motto in the upper left reminds readers of another unpopular act restricting colonial currency.

act that taxed all printed materials and legal documents; the new colonial stamp act was in no way more severe.

The author of the Stamp Act was George Grenville, William Pitt's brother-in-law. Pitt had stepped down from office in 1761 and was succeeded by Lord Bute, who in turn left office after two years to make room for Grenville. Trained as a lawyer, Grenville served in the House of Commons until he was appointed to the Admiralty Board. He later worked as a member of the Treasury Board and as treasurer of the navy. The king turned to him largely because of his reputation as a financial expert acquired while serving as first lord of the Treasury. This reputation rested on his concern about an enormous national debt and a determination to reduce that debt by increasing revenue and decreasing expenditures.

Grenville's Stamp Act alarmed Americans for many reasons. It was a revenue measure not imposed on the colonies by their own legislature but by Parliament. The money raised by the Stamp Act was slated to support British soldiers in the colonies, and some alarmists in America felt that the law could be used to censor or suppress newspapers by denying them the requisite stamped paper. Finally, the act increased the price of everyday legal transactions, including the transfer of land. Since infractions of the Stamp Act were to be tried by admiralty courts, accused colonists would be denied trial by jury.

What most Englishmen in positions of power did not realize was that the American colonists were probably the most politically sophisticated people in the world during the eighteenth century. The franchise was not nearly so limited as it was in England; most adult men voted at one time or another during their lives. Complex questions of constitutional rights were discussed openly and intelligently by colonists and, at least in New England, ordinary citizens actively participated in local government. Even as early as 1761 New Englanders were strenuously objecting to Parliament's high-handedness. The fiery James Otis (1725–1783) denied the validity of parliamentary acts that contradicted the British constitution and the natural rights of man. As John Adams later recalled, Otis "asserted that every man, merely natural, was an independent sovereign, subject to no law, but the law written on his heart, and revealed to him by his Maker, in the constitution of his nature, and the inspiration of his understanding and his conscience. His right to his life, his liberty, no created being could rightfully contest. Nor was his right to his property less incontestable."

Few responsible Americans were willing to take such a strong stand against established authority as did Otis; like Adams, they feared the consequences of unbridled liberty. The Stamp Act aroused a furor of protest in the colonies. The Virginia House of Burgesses approved a petition protesting the act and sent it on to London. Most of the other colonies soon followed this example, and Parliament was deluged with resolutions from the various assemblies.

Riots broke out in many cities, and wealthy merchants and colonists in high positions, men who once dreaded mob rule, now directed the assaults on crown officers. The stamp masters were maligned and mistreated wherever they went. And by appointing Americans to fill such positions, George Grenville made the stamp masters all the more hated. "A Foreigner we could more cheerfully endure," said one colonist, "because he might be supposed not to feel our Distresses; but for one of our Fellow Slaves, who equally shares in our Pains, to rise up and beg the favor of inflicting them—is not that intolerable?" Clubs of patriots named "Sons of Liberty" sprang up, and these radical societies became the first effective means for uniting the disparate colonies behind a common cause. The Sons of Liberty soon set up committees of correspondence that relayed news of the latest British "tyrannies" and created plans for thwarting the machinations of Parliament.

James Otis conceived a strategy of his own. He proposed an intercolonial congress that would send a joint petition to Parliament opposing the Stamp Act. The Stamp Act Congress met in New York in October 1765 and drew up three documents—a petition to the king, one to the House of Lords, and another to the House of Commons. In the petition to the House of Commons, the Stamp Act Congress stated in unambiguous terms the doctrine of no taxation without representation.

The revolution might well have begun in 1765 had the Stamp Act not been repealed. On the first of November, the day the act went into effect, there were many demonstrations. An effigy of Liberty was buried, many Americans wore black, and thousands of New Yorkers rioted. In resistance to both the Sugar Act and the Stamp Act, Americans mounted a thorough boycott of British manufactured goods. So effective was the colonial boycott that British merchants, already afflicted by the depression that had followed the Seven Years' War, pressured Parliament to withdraw the new legislation. George Grenville was replaced by a new ministry more kindly disposed toward the colonies. The venerable William Pitt supported the new ministry, headed by the young Marquis of Rockingham. Moreover, Pennsylvania's agent residing in London, Benjamin Franklin, launched a cam-

The Metropolitan Museum of Art, Bequest of Charles Allen Munn, 1924.

An early American history written in 1829 remembered the role of mobs in colonial protest with this version of Massachusetts patriots burning the stamp collector in effigy.

paign to convince British lawmakers of the necessity for repeal. A heated and prolonged debate broke out in Parliament. On one side, in favor of repeal, were such men as Rockingham and Pitt, aided and assisted by Franklin and most of England's merchant class. On the other were those staunch defenders of Parliament's right to rule the colonies. In the middle was a bewildered and indecisive George III. Finally the crisis was resolved when Parliament decided that repeal was essential for maintaining the health of British commerce. Repeal, rather than being construed as submission to colonial demands, was presented as an act of benevolence to British business interests. To drive this point home, Parliament—at the same time it revoked the Stamp Act—passed a Declaratory Act reasserting parliamentary authority over the empire. While the colonies considered the Declaratory Act as a mere face-saving gesture and rejoiced over their triumph, Parliament viewed it as a reassertion of its own authority. This conflict illustrates the growing degree of difference in American and British views on the place and rights of the colonies in the British Empire.

The Townshend Acts

During debate over repeal of the Stamp Act, members of Parliament closely questioned Benjamin Franklin, who made an elegant distinction between internal and external taxes. According to Franklin, the colonists objected only to internal taxes such as those included in the Stamp Act. He asserted that external taxes (duties on imports and exports) did not strike Americans as unjust. As he put it in his testimony, "I know that whenever this subject has occurred in conversation where I have been present, it has appeared to be the opinion of everyone, that we could not be taxed by a Parliament where we were not represented. But the payment of duties laid by act of Parliament, as regulations of commerce, was never disputed."

Unfortunately, Franklin was misrepresenting colonial opinion. Most Americans had never given a thought to the distinction he drew. If anyone had bothered about the issue at all, it was only to distinguish between raising emergency funds in wartime, say, and regular peacetime taxation. Any sustained program of taxation, whether it was internal or external, was anathema to the colonists. Nevertheless, in 1767 the British ministry decided to impose upon the Americans a new set of duties that would conform to the distinction Franklin had made.

These duties are known as the Townshend Acts. After the repeal of the Stamp Act, the shaky regime of the Marquis of Rockingham collapsed, and George III summoned William Pitt out of retirement and named him first minister once again. Pitt, however, was unable to take an active part in government owing to gout and encroaching madness. The most important man in the realm, therefore, became the Chancellor of the Exchequer, Charles Townshend. Known as "Champagne Charley" for the vivacious figure he cut in society and his ability to rattle off a dazzling speech even when drunk, Townshend was ill-suited for his new job. His speeches were as clever as his judgment was faulty and, according to one contemporary, he often argued "most inimitably on both sides of the question" in the House of Commons.

Townshend persuaded Parliament to levy duties on tea, paint, glass, and several other luxury items that the colonists imported; this act was inaugurated in 1767. The colonists reacted by erecting a new economic boycott of English goods. Americans did not respond to the Townshend Acts with the instantaneous fury that the Stamp Act had evoked, perhaps because this legislation touched only specific commodities and was not an immediate irritant to lawyers, businessmen, and editors. But within a year almost all of the colonies implemented Nonimportation Agreements. This boycott of luxuries led well-to-do American women to doff feathered hats and their husbands to stop wearing powdered wigs. Doctors announced that imported English punch was unhealthy. The graduating classes at Harvard and Princeton refused to wear English silks and woolens and donned native homespun instead. Tea was planted in New England, and the southern colonies attempted to cultivate the silkworm.

The Townshend duties provided the British Exchequer with very little money and further embittered the American colonists. The preamble of the law specifically stated that the purpose of the duties was to raise money to be used "for defraying the charge of the administration of justice, and the support of civil government" in America. In other words, some of the revenue was handed over to colonial governors and judges formerly dependent on colonial assemblies for their salaries. The Townshend Acts served further to reduce the financial control exerted by colonial legislators over their

The John Hill Morgan Collection, Yale University Art Gallery.

The day after the Boston massacre, Paul Revere had the first copies of this engraving circulating on the streets. Instead of a colonial mob harassing British troops, the engraving shows innocent citizens being murdered by an aggressive military.

administrators. The new British ministry vexed the Americans still more by establishing additional admiralty courts and a new board of customs officials. Both the courts and the officials had the responsibility for stopping all smuggling and rigidly enforcing the Townshend duties.

The dissent that Townshend's measures touched off was heightened by widespread belief among Americans that Parliament was taking only the first steps in a long-range, well-designed course of oppression. If each new infraction of colonial rights was not contested, where would the "tyranny" end?

Boycotts and a shower of petitions led Parliament to lift all the Townshend duties except the one imposed on tea. This colonial victory, which was accomplished by 1770, reduced American opposition to the British government. However, the political climate remained stormy. Frequent changes in policy, accompanied by the rise and fall of several ministries ousted because of events at home and not those in America, tended to undermine British authority on this side of the Atlantic. For instance, London, alarmed by colonial rebelliousness, dispatched four regiments of soldiers to Boston in 1768, but then, unaccountably, withdrew two of them a year later. The remaining force was large enough to continue to draw the wrath of the Bostonians, yet it was too small to quell unruly mobs. Formerly, the duties enacted by Parliament angered only wealthy merchants and politicians; now the masses themselves developed a hatred of the mother country. The constant presence of English sol-

Historical Society of Pennsylvania.

John Dickinson (1732–1808)

Although he was a peaceful Quaker who held out for reconciliation between the colonies and Britain until the eve of the Revolution, Dickinson wrote in 1768 a pamphlet that spelled out colonial grievances with great clarity. This pamphlet was called *Letters from a Farmer in Pennsylvania to the Inhabitants of the British Colonies.* Dickinson, intensely conservative and a political rival of Benjamin Franklin, was attacked by many patriots for his reluctance to approve violence, but he served as a member of the Continental Congress and wrote two petitions for Congress to the king. Since he feared the colonies could only lose a war against Britain, Dickinson cast his vote against the Declaration of Independence. But once the decision for war was made, Dickinson took up arms and fought gallantly in a conflict he had hoped could be avoided.

In 1787 he was a delegate from Delaware to the convention that wrote the federal Constitution; he also worked hard to assure its ratification by the states. In the last years of his long life he refused to hold public office, but he did see into print two volumes of his collected writings.

This thoughtful, intelligent man, educated in the law at London's Middle Temple, represents a strange paradox among the leaders of the Revolutionary period. In the forefront of penetrating criticism of British imperial policy during the turbulent decade that preceded the outbreak of hostilities, he recoiled at the mere mention of violence.

Bedeviled by a mixture of revolutionary-conservative ideas, John Dickinson clearly disliked injustice, but he loved peace more. ■

diers enflamed popular imagination, as did untrue accounts of atrocities perpetrated by the redcoats on harmless citizens. On the night of March 5, 1770, a mob of Bostonians gathered at the custom house and began to heckle soldiers guarding the customs revenue. "Come on you Rascals," they shouted, "you bloody-backs, you

Lobster Scoundrels. . ." When the mob advanced, throwing snowballs filled with rocks, the redcoats panicked and fired. Five Bostonians were killed and a new wave of violence inundated the city. Americans quickly dubbed this event the "Boston Massacre."

An incident involving the *Gaspee,* an armed schooner designed to hunt down American smugglers, demonstrates a continuing enmity towards British authority. When it ran aground off the coast of Rhode Island in 1772, a mob from Providence boarded the helpless vessel, looted it, and put the captain out to sea in a small boat before setting the *Gaspee* afire. When royal commissioners investigated this "attrocious offence" not a single Rhode Islander came up with useful information. The British were unable to find any witnesses.

Soon afterwards two patriots, James Otis and Sam Adams (1722–1803), used the anniversary of the Boston Massacre as an occasion to call for permanent committees of correspondence. Within three months eighty Massachusetts towns set up such committees, and by the middle of 1773 a network of committees covered all of New England, Virginia, and South Carolina. By 1744, town, county, and regional committees had been formed in nearly all of the colonies, although they were less common in Pennsylvania, North Carolina, and Georgia. The function of these committees was to draw up statements of American rights and lists of American grievances against Britain and to publicize this information throughout the colonies. Although the various colonies had failed to cooperate in any appreciable way in previous decades, British opposition now was uniting them. The committees were the first step that would soon lead to an American government.

The Tea Act

Charles Townshend died in 1767, still believing that his solutions to the problem of raising colonial revenue were working splendidly. His successor as Chancellor of the Exchequer was Lord North. North recognized that the Townshend Acts constituted an unnecessary irritation to the colonies and a serious threat to the British economy. The chief reason for possessing colonies was so they could supply the mother country with raw materials and buy its finished products. Townshend's duties—and the boycott they incited—negated this whole concept by encouraging Americans to forego English goods and manufacture their own. It was North who suggested that the duties be repealed, with only the tax on tea being retained. Tea could not be grown in the colonies, yet the colonists were inverterate tea drinkers. More importantly, the duty on tea was the only one yielding substantial revenue. London was careful to point out to colonial assemblies that the reason for repealing the Townshend Acts had nothing to do with their boycotts. Parliament was merely working in the interests of English industry. Lord North went on to announce that he would not be satisfied until he saw America at the feet of Great Britain. An easygoing aristocrat, known for his sense of humor and distaste for contention, North was an unlikely man to have been chosen to serve during such troubled times. Yet for the next twelve years he was George III's chief spokesman to the colonies.

In 1773 Lord North turned his attention once again to tea. The East India Company, a leading British firm, was on the verge of bankruptcy. It was a huge company and the agency by which England maintained its hold over India. Since duties on the company's imported goods also were a major source of British revenue, North recognized that Britain's role in Asia and the company's solvency were intertwined. One of the main products the company depended upon was tea grown in India and sold throughout the empire. Much of the company's financial distress started at the time of Townshend's original tea duty since Americans ceased buying English tea and began drinking smuggled Dutch tea instead.

North set about to recover the colonial market for the East India Company and, incidentally, to save the company as well. By the Tea Act of 1773, the British government permitted the East India Company to market tea directly in the colonies through agents who were granted a monopoly. Since the company got a rebate on duties paid on tea shipped to America via England, this enabled those agents to undercut competitors. Previously the company was required by law to put tea up for auction in England; British merchants then resold the tea at a higher price. Both by eliminating British and American middlemen and by reducing other costs to the company, Lord North hoped to win back American customers. But North insisted upon retaining the tea duty in order to demonstrate that Parliament still had the right to tax the colonies. Since English tea was now cheaper, even with the duty, than Dutch tea, North hoped the colonists would ignore their principles and pay the tax without complaint.

American leaders, once they learned of the plan, recognized that Lord North's scheme might work—if ordinary citizens in the colonies were given the chance to buy English tea. Accordingly, patriots decided to make sure that the tea was never unloaded from British vessels. This measure seemed necessary; a simple boycott apparently would not be effective, since the company had set up a ready means of distribution and sale. The newly formed committees of correspondence went into action, urging patriots everywhere to prevent the tea from being unloaded.

The resistence was remarkably successful. Consignees in American ports were coerced into refusing acceptance of shipments; tea-bearing vessels were turned around before they had a chance to drop anchor. In some cases the tea was unloaded, but merchants who received it were pressured into not paying the necessary duty; as a result, the produce was impounded. Only in Boston did resistance escalate into open violence.

The Boston Tea Party

The royally appointed governor of Massachusetts was Thomas Hutchinson. A man who enjoyed a brilliant political career by staunchly defending British policies, Hutchinson seized upon a legal technicality whereby he hoped to outwit the radicals. He unearthed a seventy-year-old law stating that any vessel remaining in Boston harbor longer than twenty days without unloading, could be seized and the cargo impounded until duties were paid. To make sure the three East India Company ships did not sail out of Boston, Hutchinson ordered the Royal Navy to block the entrance of the harbor. The period of grace was coming to an end on December 16, 1773. The ships were still in harbor and the law required their cargo be unloaded.

But Boston radicals, led by Samuel Adams, concocted a scheme of their own. On the night of the sixteenth, several of them, their faces painted or blackened with soot, their bodies draped in old blankets, boarded the three ships and dumped 342 chests of tea into the harbor. John Adams recorded in his diary the next day, "This is the most magnificent Movement of all. There is a Dignity, a Majesty, a Sublimity in this last Effort of the Patriots that I greatly admire. . . . This Destruction of the Tea is so bold, so daring, so firm, intrepid & inflexible, and it must have so important Consequences and so lasting, that I cannot but consider it an Epocha [*sic*] in History."

Parliament's Revenge

The immediate consequences were indeed important—and disastrous. The English were outraged by this anarchical destruction of property. Lord North won overwhelming majorities in Parliament as he pushed through several bills—called by the colonists "The Intolerable Acts"—designed to punish Boston and serve as a warning to all of the colonies. First, the port of Boston was closed to all traffic until the East India Company was reim-

Courtesy of New-York Historical Society.

This engraving shows the American point of view. A brutal British ministry forces tea down the throat of an American Liberty while Justice weeps. The British navy bombards Boston in the background.

bursed for its losses. The policy of coercion against Boston was justified on the grounds that the city was a center of rebellion. One witness before Parliament testified that the Bostonians were "not only the worst Subjects, but the most truly immoral Men" he ever had to deal with—and that seemed to be the general opinion in England. The Boston Port bill further stipulated that the capital of Massachusetts Bay would be transferred to Salem. The law created a panic in Boston. Not only would it destroy the economy but it also would make shipment of food to the city almost impossible. Help from the other colonies began to pour in; this first Coercive (or "Intolerable") Act won Boston widespread sympathy on this side of the Atlantic.

The second act was the Massachusetts Government bill, which vastly increased the powers of the royal governor. He now could appoint members to the governor's council; previously they were elected every year by the legislature. The governor also could appoint judges to inferior courts. Worst of all was the provision that limited town meetings to once a year and forbade any business other than electing officers and passing rules for local administration. This last provision threatened the whole New England system of government.

Another stipulation, the Administration of Justice Act, which the colonials dubbed the "Murder Act," decreed that English officials charged with a crime committed in the course of their official activities were given the right to trial in Britain. Not only did this mean few officials would be convicted (how many colonial witnesses could afford to travel to England to testify?), but it also implied that colonial courts were prejudiced against English officials. This supposition was manifestly unfair, since Boston courts acquitted several British soldiers involved in the Boston Massacre and pardoned the rest.

As a final bit of tidying up the colonies, Parliament revised the Quartering Act so that it permitted British commanders to seize housing for their troops in town. Under this act troops were stationed in Boston. The sign (if any was needed) that Boston was regarded as a rebellious city that must be punished was the fact that Massachusetts now received a military governor, General Thomas Gage.

Reaction to the Intolerable Acts

The colonists were outraged by Parliament's latest measures. Soon they were able to add yet another "tyrannical" act in what was becoming a long list. Ever since England acquired Canada in 1763, that colony had been under the temporary rule of a military government. Now Parliament, by the Quebec Act, devised a permanent form of government for Canada. The former French colony was to have no legislature, it was to retain the French system of law, and the Catholic Church would keep its privileged position. In fact, the Quebec Act made specific provisions for a Catholic bishop. As though to rile the colonists further, Parliament gave territorial control of the Illinois heartland to Canada, thereby ignoring the claim of other colonies to that land. In every regard the Quebec Act incensed the colonists, who looked upon it as Britain's plot to suppress representative government, favor popery, and limit settlement to the eastern seaboard. British and Canadians thought it an act of statemanship. Colonists lumped the Quebec Act with the Intolerable Acts. Amidst colonial calls for a Continental Congress, Virginia's House of Burgesses met illegally after Governor Dunmore dissolved the assembly. They issued a call for a Congress and a new boycott of British goods.

Library of Congress.

Joseph Galloway failed in his efforts to head off independence following the first Continental Congress and reluctantly joined the British side.

Colonial Williamsburg Photograph.

The news that American women in North Carolina had signed their own agreement not to import from Britain brought this satirical response in England. Note the mannish features on the woman with the gavel.

The first Continental Congress met in Philadephia from September 5 to October 26, 1774. During that time the delegates discussed a plan for union, submitted by Joseph Galloway, that proposed establishment of an intercolonial legislature endowed with the right to tax all colonies and to control the appointment of all officials. The Congress rejected the plan on the grounds that it took away too much power from the individual colonies. Had this plan passed, the colonies would have been saddled with a weak, ineffectual government. Fortunately, the Massachusetts committee of correspondence seized this opportunity to press for much more radical measures. Paul Revere was sent to Philadelphia with a set of resolutions called the Suffolk Resolves. These resolves, adopted by the Suffolk County Convention (created hastily after Massachusetts town meetings were banned), called for total resistance to the Intolerable Acts. According to the resolves, taxes should be collected but not handed over to the royal government until the traditional government of Massachusetts was restored. In a more inflammatory tone, the resolves invited military resistance to British troops stationed in Boston and recommended that citizens be empowered to arrest and imprison British officials if a single patriot leader were taken by the British authorities.

The Continental Congress approved the Suffolk Resolves, although Massachusetts was warned that it must behave peaceably toward General Gage. A declaration of rights set forth the injustices committed by Parliament against the colonies, stated the colonists' view of the constitutional crisis, and denounced the Intolerable Acts. The Congress also petitioned the king to intercede on behalf of the colonies and declared a new Nonimportation Agreement against Britain if the Intolerable Acts were not repealed. When the delegates recessed, they had not been able to agree on a plan to curtail exports but resolved to meet again in May of 1775.

The new Nonimportation Agreements set up local committees of safety to enforce the boycott. These committees functioned as revolutionary cells in each town. They began to gather gunpowder and store it secretly in places unknown to British officials. In Massachusetts local units of revolutionary militia, called minutemen, were organized; they were pledged to defend the colony against British encroachments. By now the colonies formed a powder keg that was ready to blow sky-high. Although General Gage recognized that any military move might lead to shooting, nevertheless upon an order from London, on April 19, 1775, he set out to seize a supply of weapons stored in Concord outside Boston. He also hoped to capture leaders of the resistance.

What Gage failed to judge accurately was the extent of local indignation and organization. The people of Massachusetts still remembered vividly the Boston Massacre, which in retelling became more gory every year. For their part, the British military leaders misjudged the will of the colonists in Massachusetts: "I am satisfied, " an officer concluded, "that one active campaign, a smart action and burning two or three of their towns, will set everything to rights."

Every move the British troops made in search of patriot weapons and leaders was reported to the people of Massachusetts by messengers on horseback. The most famous of these, of course, was Paul Revere, although others, not immortalized in legend and poetry, finished their rides that night and completed their assigned tasks. Revere did not. When 700 British soldiers arrived in the village of Lexington on their way to Concord on the morning of April 19, they found patriot militiamen standing in ranks on the village green. No one knows for certain who shot first, but according to patriot accounts a British officer ordered his men to disarm and disperse the gathering militia. In the following confusion, shots were fired on both sides as the militia fled. The British quickly moved on to Concord where the militia made a stand. Very few supplies were found and as the British marched back to Boston, they were fired upon by patriots behind walls and trees. Lexington and Concord may not have been in all respects glorious rebel victories, but these encounters provided the revolutionaries with martyrs. Inflamed accounts soon circulated throughout the colonies, tales that told of "women in child-bed" who were "driven by the soldiery naked into the street; old men, peaceably in their house, were shot dead." The redcoats behaved in such a manner that would make even the Iroquois "blush at such horrid murder," it was said. And the war was on.

Organizing a Rebellion

Of course, the colonists did not react in unison to British incursions. One of the first duties of the Revolutionary leaders was to whip up enthusiasm for their cause through propaganda. In the year immediately preceding the bloodshed at Lexington, Americans produced several very able pamphleteers—James Otis, Daniel Dulany, Thomas Jefferson, and John Dickinson. Colonial literature perhaps reached its highest point in these political tracts; certainly they are better written than all of the poetry of that era. Once the war was under way, the pamphleteering continued. Indeed, in January 1776, Congress actually requested one member to write a pamphlet that would prepare people for independence. This effort, however, was made unnecessary after Thomas Paine wrote a spirited defense of American liberty entitled *Common Sense.* About half a million copies of this pamphlet were sold during the war. So successful was Paine in articulating American ideas and sentiments that Congress hired him as a regular paid propagandist and he continued to turn out tracts throughout the Revolution. The rebels, with their healthy respect for the power of the printed word, rushed their highly partisan versions of Concord and Lexington into print before British apologists could give their versions of the incidents.

During the course of the Revolution the rebels relied upon newspaper stories, pamphlets, ballads, and broadsides (printed, posterlike sheets) to win popular support. Mercy Warren, the sister of the Revolutionary leader James Otis, wrote many poems and several plays on behalf of the cause. Rebel preachers thundered forth sermons from the pulpit that stressed natural law, the right to rebellion, and patriotic duty. Tory preachers countered with urgent pleas for loyalty to the king, stating that passive obedience of the monarch was the only

John Singleton Copley. Courtesy Museum of Fine Arts, Boston. Gift of Joseph W., William B., and Edward H. R. Revere.

Paul Revere
(1735–1818)

Renowned as the night rider who warned the patriots of the British advance on Concord, Paul Revere was a Boston silversmith. He was an early convert to the concept of an independent America; and through the strength of his convictions, he helped to draw Boston's tradesmen and mechanics to the side of patriotism. Funded with inexhaustible energy, Revere issued political cartoons lampooning the English, took part in the Boston Tea Party, carried the Suffolk Resolves to Philadelphia on horseback, and helped the patriots win the day at Lexington and Concord.

During the Revolution, Revere designed and printed the first continental dollars and created the first official seal for the colonies and for the new state of Massachusetts, a state seal that is still in use. After the war he was instrumental in bringing about the ratification of the Constitution, but he also found time to cast bells, make cannon, and furnish Robert Fulton with the copper plates and boilers for his steam ferryboat. Until the end of his long life, Revere continued to wear the clothes of the Revolutionary era through the streets of Boston. His beautifully designed and executed silver pieces, both flatware and hollow ware, are still highly prized by collectors and conoisseurs. ■

---

moral course to be pursued. When the Tory minister Jonathan Boucher (1738–1804) gave vent to such opinions from a pulpit in Annapolis, he had two loaded pistols at his side so as to ward off interruptions from the congregation.

The committees of safety, which had been set up by the Continental Congress in 1775 to enforce the boycotts against the British, now began to exert pressure on American Tories. Their tactics were embarrassing to a people who claimed they were fighting a war to secure liberty. The committees searched out disloyal books, punished merchants who attempted to break the boycott, and forced out of office Americans who did not subscribe to patriot goals. The Reverend Thomas Johnson, for example, had to compose a written apology to a committee of safety in Virginia after he wished the British army success in a toast he made in a local tavern. Johnson's first apology was rejected and a second demanded. All decisions made by local and congressional leaders were carried out by these committees of safety.

John Singleton Copley. Courtesy Museum of Fine Arts, Boston. Bequest of Winslow Warren.

Mercy Otis Warren
(1728–1814)

Perhaps the most eloquent female intellectual of the period was Mercy Otis Warren. An early and able patriotic writer, Warren turned her hand to satiric plays beginning in 1772. These plays, meant to be read rather than performed, attacked Tory Officials in her native state of Massachusetts. These enemies of liberty she disguised under such caustic names as Judge Meagre, Brigadeer Hate All, and Hum Humbug. Her first play was named *The Adulateur* and it depicted the despised royal governor of Massachusetts, Thomas Hutchinson, as a tyrant. In 1775 she published *The Group,* a play that again pilloried Massachusetts Tories.

After the revolution she brought out a collection of poems that included two dramas in verse, *The Sack of Rome* and *The Ladies of Castile,* both embodying a message on behalf of human liberty. But her greatest effort was a three-volume *History of the Rise, Progress and Termination of the American Revolution,* published in 1805. That she was to turn out such a massive study while married to James Warren, a merchant and farmer, and looking after her five sons and household chores is a testimony to her vitality and determination. In this work she made such biting remarks about John Adams, whose politics she regarded as too conservative, that Adams (a former friend of the Warrens) was moved to complain, "History is not the province of Ladies."

Until her death at the age of 86, she continued to live in Plymouth, Massachusetts, and to correspond actively with her many friends in public life. At every point in her writing career, Mercy Warren revealed a strong commitment to democracy. In fact, her fight with John Adams broke out when she detected in him a new leaning toward monarchy and a "pride of talents and much ambition," unsuitable qualities in a democratic leader. ■

Who Were the Tories?

Traditionally, historians have stated that the Tories (persons who remained loyal to England and opposed the Revolution) were wealthy members of the upper class. This conclusion was supported by examinations of the records of those who submitted claims for compensation for property loss at the end of the war; most of the claimants were indeed rich. The equation of the wealthy with the Tories was further strengthened by the fact that many outspoken Tories—Jonathan Boucher, Joseph Galloway, and Thomas Hutchinson, for instance—were wealthy men.

But today the general view of historians is changing. First, simple statistics make it impossible that all Tories belonged to the elite. Some 55,000 Americans enlisted in the British army and about 100,000 Tories emigrated from America, some to settle in Nova Scotia, New Brunswick, and the Bahamas, others to live out their lives in Britain. Not all of these people could have been rich.

When Massachusetts banished 300 Tories in 1778, about one-fifth were merchants, members of a profession, or gentlemen who did not work for a living; about a third were farmers; and the remainder were craftsmen, laborers, or small shopkeepers. Other lists of Tories reveal that working-class people always outnumbered the rich.

Divided loyalties turned the Revolution into a civil war in many frontier areas. Tories fought alongside the Iroquois Indians in the north while raiding their former homes. A sizeable number of Tories could be found in the region along the seacoast in the Middle Colonies, including Long Island, the Lower Hudson Valley, the counties around Philadelphia, and the peninsula that separates the Delaware Bay from the Chesapeake. While some frontier areas seem to have chosen sides in a way designed to continue land quarrels (notably in New York and Pennsylvania), other disputes that had divided lowland and upland areas, such as the Regulator movement, disappeared in general support for the war. While it is true that Tories fled west during the war, it also was the refuge for patriot partisan groups in South Carolina and Georgia.

Clearly, not all Tories had English backgrounds. Some were British-born diehards, of course, but many others were Scottish, Dutch, German, and French. Indeed, among Tory ranks could be counted many members of religious and national minorities who had one thing in common: they felt threatened. This sense of insecurity and uneasiness in the midst of impending change, a characteristic of Tory leaders, was equally evident among the rank and file.

The Tories made up, it seems, about one-fifth of the American population, which was then between two and one-half and three millions. Two-fifths were actively rebel, and the rest either vacillated or remained essentially neutral. Tories were most numerous in the Middle colonies, less so in the South and in New England.

Most of the 100,000 Tories who emigrated from America were forced out. By the end of the war the states, urged on by Congress, passed laws declaring the Tories to be traitors and began confiscating their lands and exiling them. Even before declaring independence, Congress had passed a resolution forbidding its opponents to congregate in large groups or to publish their objections. And, during the war, Tories suspected of aiding the British were jailed, driven inland away from all contact with the enemy, or forced to sign loyalty oaths. Mobs tarred and feathered Tories, and the term "Lynch law" was coined to describe behavior similar to that of Judge William Lynch (1742–1820) in the backcountry of Virginia, who handed down during the Revolution one decision after another against Tories.

The New Government

Throughout the Revolutionary period, as colonies became states there was a transfer of power from royal to rebel hands. Starting in 1774, few of the colonies experienced untroubled meetings of their legislatures since royal governors invariably dissolved these assemblies as hotbeds of rebellion. While the governors were curtailing legislative meetings for insufficient loyalty to the crown, committees of safety were forcing the resignations of Tory sheriffs, judges, ministers, and other local officials. Sometimes, depending upon local sentiments, the path to statehood was relatively smooth; on other occasions, extremely rocky and rough.

In some colonies the royal governor was removed from office by rebels. William Franklin, Benjamin Franklin's illegitimate son and the governor of New Jersey, was arrested by rebels. Other royal appointees simply fled in the face of mounting violence. John Murray, Earl of Dunmore and the Governor of Virginia, fearing for his safety, retreated to the security of a British ship anchored in Chesapeake Bay and eventually sailed away. For all practical purposes, his departure ended royal rule after 169 years.

Committees of safety, really interim agencies of local administration, arranged for new elections in their districts, generally retaining pre-Revolutionary voting requirements. The legislators elected served in quasi-legal state assemblies that declared themselves to be the legitimate government of the state and set about writing constitutions. Framing a constitution, however, usually requires considerable time, and in states such as New Hampshire and Massachusetts that submitted their constitutions to the voters for ratification, the whole process of establishing a new system of rule could be delayed for years. Interestingly, those colonies that first led this parade to statehood wrote quite liberal documents; those that debated and delayed produced constitutions markedly more conservative in tone and outlook. This transition to independent status sometimes produced bizarre anomalies. For instance, in Pennsylvania the old colonial assembly was so conservative that the patriots created one of their own. The two assemblies both sat in Philadelphia, and some men were members of both. Pennsylvania remained a stronghold of Tories or neutrals, since the Quakers there feared the religious intolerance of other Americans. Moreover, the Quakers were pacifists and had no wish to engage in a war for any cause. In order to keep Quakers from voting, the Revolutionary charter in Pennsylvania required voters to take an oath—a practice that was contrary to the religious convictions professed by the Society of Friends.

The Declaration of Independence

Between January and July of 1776, state governments, with or without finished constitutions, came firmly under the control of the revolutionary leaders. The creation of state governments that opposed continued union with Britain went hand in glove with establishment of an independent federal government.

As a result, when the Declaration of Independence was finally signed, it did not engineer America's freedom but rather acknowledged officially the independence that already existed. The pressures of waging a war had already turned the Congress into a functioning government, and the various states had already given approval to the idea of independence. In fact, the reason Congress delayed signing the Declaration was its desire to wait until American approval of the document would be unanimous.

A committee to draft a Declaration of Independence was set up in June of 1776 by Congress. Richard Henry Lee had previously introduced a resolution calling for full independence that mandated a declaration, a statement of foreign policy, and a constitution. On July 1 the Lee resolution was submitted to a general vote; it passed, although three states (Pennsylvania, New Jersey, and South Carolina) opposed it and one state abstained (New York). Since this scarcely constituted a united front, the resolution was submitted to a vote again the next day. Private conversations among representatives during the night produced a unanimous vote (New York still abstained since its delegates, though favoring independence, felt they must wait for instructions from the new rebel government just forming in their state). Strictly speaking, it was this resolution penned by Richard Henry Lee and passed on July 2 that officially severed all connections between the thirteen colonies and Britain.

The Declaration itself was prepared by a committee of five delegates appointed by Congress on June 11. Its members were Thomas Jefferson, John Adams, Benjamin Franklin, Roger Sherman, and Robert R. Livingston. Jefferson wrote a rough draft that was corrected by both Adams and Franklin. This corrected version was submitted to the committee on June 28. On July 3, the day after virtually unanimous approval of Lee's resolution, members began discussion of the committee's report. The following day, July 4, the text was approved and put into final form. The actual signing, however, did not occur until some weeks later as delegates, fully empowered to do so by their state legislatures, appended their signatures to the Declaration of Independence, thus assuring that their new nation would henceforth chart its own course and that they would win immortality as its founding fathers.

The document is divided into two parts. In the first part the Declaration furnishes the reader with the moral and legal justification for rebellion on the basis of natural rights. No longer were Americans invoking their rights as British subjects—a useless argument since they wanted to withdraw from the British Empire. Rather, they were invoking "the laws of nature and of nature's God." Reiterating a belief long held by British political philosophers, Jefferson stated that all governments derive "their just powers from the consent of the governed" and that "whenever any government becomes destructive of these ends, it is the right of the people to alter or to abolish it." In the second part, Jefferson listed the American grievances against the king. Before now, of course, the colonists had seen Parliament as the enemy. But in the Declaration, Parliament was never named, and it was the king who was singled out as the tyrant. Taking this stand was not only a good strategy for eliciting the

Attr. John Trumbull. Maryland Historical Society, Baltimore.

Thomas Jefferson (1743–1826)

One of the most important American leaders to emerge during the Revolutionary War was Thomas Jefferson. A rather shy, loose-limbed, redheaded youth, Jefferson was the son of a well-to-do frontier planter whose wife, Jane Randolph, was related to the most distinguished families in colonial Virginia. Young Jefferson first lived near Richmond, but at the age of nine, shortly before his father's death, the family moved west to Albemarle County. After being tutored in the classics, he entered the College of William and Mary in 1760, graduated two years later, began to practice law, and in 1769 was elected to the House of Burgesses. There Jefferson immediately joined the strong anti-British faction and helped to create the Virginia Committee of Correspondence.

In 1772 he married a twenty-four-year-old widow, Martha Wayles Skelton, who bore him six children before her death ten years later; however, only two daughters, Martha and Mary, lived to maturity. In 1774 he penned a set of resolutions titled *A Summary View of the Rights of British America,* a document that spelled out many of the legal and political doctrines that Americans would use to justify their rebellion. Just as the Saxons conquered England, Jefferson reasoned, in the same way British colonists seized the American mainland—and this immigration in no way indebted the colonists to England. Rather, it was a "natural" right of conquest. Jefferson also denied Parliament's authority over the colonies and insisted that the only link between America and England was the colonists' voluntary submission to the king. However, the most widely read composition Thomas Jefferson ever wrote was the Declaration of Independence, in which he expressed his belief that a government ruled only by popular consent, a notion he had derived from the English philosopher John Locke.

In 1779 Jefferson was elected governor of Virginia, a job he performed reasonably well until the British invaded his state in the spring of 1781. This military action, coming at the very end of his term, inspired political rivals to level charges of unpreparedness, accusations that were renewed when he emerged as a presidential candidate in 1800.

The most versatile of the founding fathers, Thomas Jefferson built a stunning mansion on a hilltop near Charlottesville, his beloved "Monticello," where he experimented with fruit and vegetable culture, tinkered with scientific pursuits, played the violin, and accumulated probably the best private library in America, which later became the nucleus of the famed Library of Congress. After his White House years (1801–1809), Jefferson returned to Monticello where he conceived, designed, and brought into being the University of Virginia, the last of many achievements to flow from a truly brilliant mind. ■

sympathy of Europeans, who were more likely to sympathize with a revolt against a cruel king than one against an elected assembly, but the omission of all mention of Parliament also was the final slap in the face against that institution. The colonists were implicitly denying, once and for all, the legal connection between Parliament and America. Parliament had no authority to rule the colonies; only the king had that right, and he had abused it.

The Logistics of War

In 1775, even as the colonies were creating new state governments, a war was in progress. By July 3, 1775, George Washington had taken command of the Massachusetts militia near Boston—and not until eight years later was peace finally secured.

America and its new governing body, the Continental Congress, were peculiarly unsuited for the strenuous tasks of fighting a war. Congress had no power to tax citizens or to draft soldiers. There were no organized armies beyond the groups of local militia. There were few arms and munitions, almost no cash, no military manuals—nothing. And America had no allies.

Financing the war was a challenge that Congress could meet only by issuing paper money in larger and larger amounts until the currency lost virtually all its value. By the end of 1775 Congress already had printed \$6 million; by the end of 1776, \$25 million; and by the end of 1779, \$263 million. Inflation reached such ridiculous levels that at one point 170 continental dollars were worth about only one gold dollar. As one congressman put it, "A Revolution, a war, the dissolution of government, the creating of it anew, cruelty, rapine and devastation in the midst of our very bowels. These, sir, are circumstances by no means favorable to finance." The problem was only compounded by the fact that the states also were issuing paper money.

The other principal means of raising money was through loans from foreign governments, but until 1780 such aid was limited. France provided the most help—in the form of money, supplies, and material. Total French aid amounted to more than \$2 million; Spain contributed about \$70,000 and Holland came up with \$32,000.

Financial matters were made worse by the corruption and avarice found in all wartime situations. The Quartermaster General, Nathaniel Greene, thought nothing of handing out the best war contracts to his own private firm. Congressmen speculated by investing in privateer ships that preyed on British shipping and turned over the spoils to the investors. No matter that these pirate vessels used up supplies desperately needed by the American navy. Silas Deane, sent to France by Congress to secure supplies, worked so many deals on his own behalf that he was recalled in disgrace. Besides outright corruption, American merchants were using the war as an opportunity to boost prices and profits, and the war boom nearly kept pace with the rate of inflation. New York merchants, for example, were supplying both the British and the patriots.

No less disheartening was the struggle to raise troops. Militiamen, as one would expect, remained attached to their own states, and, though they might take up arms to drive the enemy away from their homes, they would not travel elsewhere nor would they sustain any prolonged campaign. Nathaniel Greene, for instance, knowing that his Southern militia would not stay in the field through a bloody battle, put them in the front lines, where they might shoot at least once before running.

The only real troops were the "continentals," those who served long-term enlistments and were recruited from each of the state governments. By 1777 the states were unable to fill these quotas through volunteers and were forced to draft men. Unfortunately, the Continental army and the state militias competed for supplies and failed to act together. However, this picture of inflation, corruption, wartime profits, and the scramble for manpower should not overshadow considerable sacrifice, heroism, and devotion to a cause that thousands obviously thought just, worth fighting for, and even worth dying for. The patriot death rate was about 12 percent (the American death rate in World War II was about 2 percent.) The enemy grappled with precisely the same problems and admittedly demonstrated the same valor, the same sense of duty. One of the biggest dilemmas facing rebel leaders was how to sustain interest in a struggle that waxed and waned as it drifted southward from Boston, eventually touching every former colony in one way or another and even involving Canada and various regions not in revolt.

Black Soldiers

When Congress in July 1775 called for volunteers to join state militia units, blacks stepped forward and served, especially in New England. Ten months after Lexington and Concord, however, blacks began to be excluded from the various armed forces; whites were afraid that if free blacks were armed they would stage insurrections and liberate slaves. The British were not plagued with such fears. Their own difficulties in raising soldiers were formidable. About one-third of the British soldiers were hired mercenaries, mostly Germans; another third were American Tories; and only the remaining third actually British. To keep up manpower, the royal governor of Virginia created what he called his Ethiopian Regiment and issued a proclamation inviting blacks to join. Eventually about 800 slaves joined the British, although the *Virginia Gazette* warned that slaves would be worse off under the British than under their American masters "who pity their conditions, who wish in general to make it as easy and comfortable as possible, and who would willingly, were it in their power, or were they permitted, not only prevent any more negroes from losing their freedom, but restore it to such as have already unhappily lost it."

In the end, the patriots were forced to rely on black soldiers and sailors. Whites were permitted to send blacks to the army in their stead if called upon to serve, and by the summer of 1778 the Continental army was regularly enlisting blacks for three-year stints, most of whom came from New England states. All of the states from North Carolina and farther north made provisions for enlisting blacks. Blacks and whites served together in racially mixed units, although blacks generally did not bear arms. Nearly all of these blacks were free or won instantaneous freedom once seized with patriotic zeal.

What is important here is that a revolutionary spirit seemed to hold the promise of freedom for all blacks, a better life for all oppressed classes, regardless of color or status. Ominously, the Continental Congress fleetingly considered a ban on the slave trade while discussing the Declaration of Independence, but then dropped the idea. This decision, portent of much serious debate in the future, demonstrates the ambivalent attitude of the founding fathers toward freedom, a "blind spot" the British exploited to the fullest throughout the war.

Winning the War

Until the end of 1776, most of the fighting was concentrated in New England, where the first conflicts had broken out. After 1776, the war generally drifted southwards, though there were many exceptions to this rule. The former colonies were threatened from all sides—at sea by the British navy—the greatest in the world—on land by Indians in the West, and everywhere by redcoats.

Following the minor British defeat at Lexington and Concord, the royal troops retreated to Boston. The Massachusetts militia leaders decided to fortify one of the several hills overlooking the city, Bunker Hill (though in fact the men selected Breed's Hill). On the afternoon of June 17, 1775, the British marched up the hill in orderly columns—and when the smoke cleared, it was evident that the Americans had dealt a stunning blow. Of the 2,400 British soldiers, half were hit and 226 were dead, including a sixth of all the English officers who would be killed or wounded in the Revolution. The Americans actually had been greatly outnumbered (there were only 1,600 patriots on Breed's Hill), and of those about 100 were killed and 267 wounded. Despite such losses, the patriots were jubilant. As one officer said, "I wish we could sell them another hill at the same price."

Technically, Bunker Hill was a British victory, for the redcoats drove the patriots off the promontory. Shortly after the battle, Washington arrived to take command and to create the Continental army. Of course, the selection of this man was no accident. He had military experience, an imposing presence, was well-to-do, and was living proof of cooperation between Virginia and Massachusetts, two of the most important states in the new nation. What he found were 16,000 badly organized Massachusetts militiamen, milling about and utterly lacking in discipline. Slowly Washington assembled a true army, though throughout the war he was plagued with desertions, mutinies, and rebellions. Not the least of his annoyances were foreign officers wanting to build up their service record during a period of peace in Europe. Many of these officers could not speak English. Only a handful were useful, such as Gilbert du Motier, the Marquis de Lafayette, a rich and brave young Frenchman. Other foreigners who helped Washington were Thaddeus Kosciusko and Casimir Pulaski from Poland, Johann de Kalb, and, most of all, a Prussian captain who pretended he was a baron. This man, named Steube, changed his name to Baron von Steuben. He was a crack military man and lent discipline to the ragtag American troops.

In the early months of the war, the Americans scored several successes. Ethan Allen, assisted by Benedict Arnold, took Fort Ticonderoga on Lake Champlain in May 1775. The victory, not especially impressive since

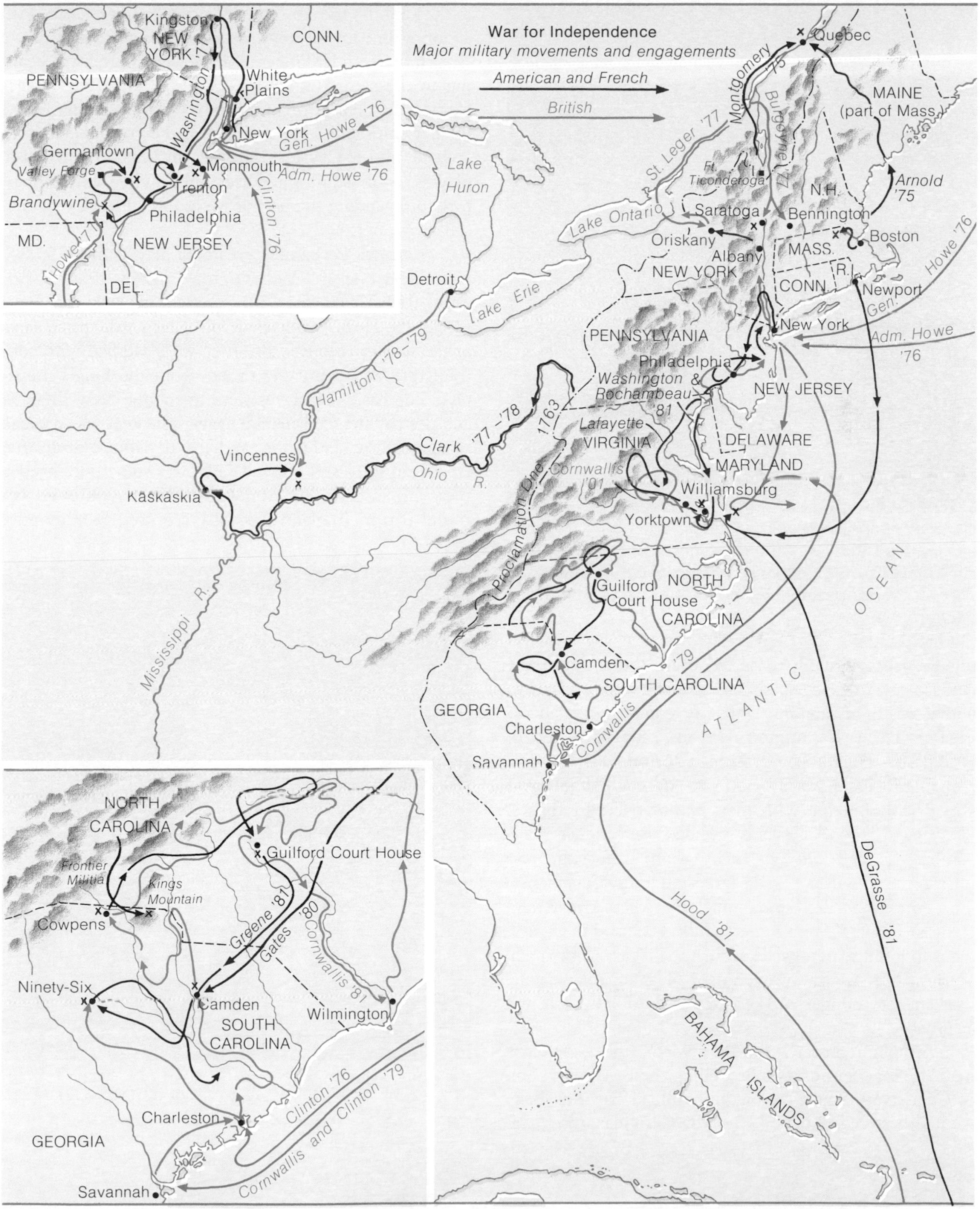

War for Independence
Major military movements and engagements
American and French
British
Kingston
NEW YORK
CONN.
PENNSYLVANIA
White Plains
Washington '77
New York
Gen. Howe '76
Germantown
Valley Forge
Monmouth
Adm. Howe '76
Trenton
Brandywine
Philadelphia
Clinton '76
MD.
NEW JERSEY
Howe '77
DEL.
Quebec
Montgomery '75
Burgoyne '77
MAINE (part of Mass.)
St. Leger '77
Lake Huron
Ft. Ticonderoga
Arnold '75
N.H.
Lake Ontario
Saratoga
Bennington
Oriskany
Boston
Albany
MASS.
NEW YORK
R.I.
Detroit
CONN.
Newport
Gen. Howe '76
Lake Erie
New York
PENNSYLVANIA
Adm. Howe '76
Hamilton '78–'79
Philadelphia
Washington & Rochambeau '81
NEW JERSEY
Proclamation Line 1763
Lafayette
VIRGINIA
DELAWARE
Clark '77–'78
Vincennes
MARYLAND
Ohio R.
Cornwallis '01
Williamsburg
Kaskaskia
Yorktown
Guilford Court House
NORTH CAROLINA
OCEAN
Mississippi R.
Camden
'79
SOUTH CAROLINA
GEORGIA
ATLANTIC
Charleston
Cornwallis
Savannah
NORTH CAROLINA
Guilford Court House
Frontier Militia
Kings Mountain
Cowpens
Greene '81
Gates '80
Cornwallis '81
Ninety-Six
Camden
Wilmington
SOUTH CAROLINA
Clinton '76
Cornwallis and Clinton '79
Charleston
GEORGIA
Savannah
Hood '81
DeGrasse '81
BAHAMA ISLANDS

Courtesy Museum of Fine Arts, Boston. Deposited by City of Boston.

General Henry Knox was painted standing in uniform by Charles Stuart. Knox had helped to force the British from Boston by hauling cannon from upstate New York in the winter of 1776, hence the cannon in the background.

the fort was virtually deserted, nevertheless gave the Americans clear access to Canada and provided them with a wealth of cannons, which were hauled overland to Boston. There Washington used the cannons to fortify Dorchester Heights overlooking Boston. The British, realizing their hold on Boston was slipping, withdrew to Nova Scotia, taking with them the first Tory refugees.

Elated, the Americans decided to conquer Canada—if, as the cautious instruction from Congress phrased it, "it will not be disagreeable to the Canadians." The Americans, led by Colonel Benedict Arnold and General Richard Montgomery, fully expected the Canadians to join them in battle against the tyrannical British. Nothing of the sort, however, happened, and the patriots, weakened by hunger and disease, were roundly defeated at Quebec.

Although defeated in the North, the Americans made up for their losses by repelling the British invasion of Charleston, South Carolina, in June 1776. The British had been led to believe that the Carolinas were loyal to the king. As the American Major General Charles Lee, a sloppy but jovial man, rushed to defend the South, a British force under General Sir Henry Clinton was heading to the same destination by water. The two armies clashed at Charleston, Clinton's force was augmented by fifty ships and 3,000 men that had come directly from Ireland under Charles Lord Cornwallis. The British, plagued by mosquitos and heat and heavily shelled by the fort commanding the harbor, were forced to give up and sail away, defeated.

Alarmed, Parliament created a new army of 55,000 men under General William Howe and his brother, Admiral Richard Howe. As the leaders of such enormous forces, the Howe brothers should have made quick work of the former colonies. But they were saddled with contradictory and confusing orders from the king's ministers. The basic objectives were to subdue New England and destroy the Continental army. The fleet was ordered to support the land troops and also to capture or destroy American ships and ports. The Howes sometimes heeded these instructions, sometimes ignored them (after all, the round trip to England normally required four months,

Victoria and Albert Museum.

Sir Henry Clinton was eager to lead the British forces in America, but when given a chance he proved indecisive.

much too long to wait for guidance in fighting a war). The real reason the Howes hung fire and hesitated in their prosecution of the war, however, was their hope that Americans sooner or later would recognize rebellion was hopeless and would come back into the British fold. The Howes feared that if they hit the Americans too hard, reconciliation would become impossible. If the Howes had been more ruthless, they might well have defeated the Americans conclusively in 1776. Lord Howe arrived in America a few days after America declared independence, but he hoped to achieve a peaceful settlement of the issue almost immediately. He sent one letter addressed to "Mr. Washington." When this letter was refused, Howe sent another addressed "George Washington Esq., etc. etc." The etceteras were supposed to be a tacit reference to Washington's rank and title as Major General of the Continental Army—an allusion to but not an acceptance of the position the rebels had created. Again, Washington refused the letter.

The first encounter between Washington and Howe was a disaster for Washington. When Howe and his men landed on Long Island on August 22, 1776, Washington attempted to stop them with only about 9,000 troops and no navy—and failed miserably. The Battle of Long Island was Washington's first major battle, and he revealed his lack of experience at that encounter when he permitted the enemy to get behind him and nearly cut off any escape route from his island stronghold. And in September Howe easily pushed Washington off the nearby island of Manhattan. New York, the second largest city in the colonies, was surrendered to the enemy.

As winter set in, the prospect was bleak for the new country. Washington was hounded out of the New York area into New Jersey. There he hatched a plan for boosting morale. On Christmas Eve 1776, he made his famous crossing of the Delaware River and staged a surprise attack on Trenton. The town, an encampment for German mercenaries, was taken with little struggle. Washington captured 909 men, whom he led across to Pennsylvania amidst general cheers. While this was a very minor victory, it did wonders for rebel morale.

In the spring of 1777, General Howe, dismayed by Washington's continued resistance, decided to capture the rebel capital of Philadelphia. In July he sailed with 15,000 men from New York to the head of Chesapeake Bay. Congress fled in panic. Washington attempted to stop Howe at Brandywine Creek on September 11, but his defeat at Long Island was repeated, for once again Howe outflanked the Americans. During the winter Howe remained in Philadelphia; there he was so comfortable that he remained "snug as a flea," as a later song put it. Washington moved his headquarters to Valley Forge, where ragged rebel troops suffered unbearably from the unusually cold weather and shortages of food and clothes. Of Washington's troops, nearly three thousand men were unfit for duty because they were barefoot and scantily clothed (one unit was called "The Naked Regiment"). Congress was equally dispirited. It met in exile in Lancaster, Pennsylvania, but only a few members bothered to attend, and those present quarreled bitterly with one another.

Meanwhile, the British developed a brilliant (on paper), two-pronged plan to split the colonies and end this troublesome rebellion. Howe was to contain the rebel army at Philadelphia while another British force, made up in part of Iroquois Indians and led by General John Burgoyne, was to advance southward from Canada, and a second army, comprised of Tory troops and Iroquois Indians, commanded by Colonel St. Leger, was to cut eastward across New York state from Lake Ontario and join up with Burgoyne and Howe. Burgoyne, after spending an idle year in Canada, descended upon Fort Ticonderoga, which he easily took. Buoyed up by this victory, Burgoyne pursued the Americans across an overland route. For the British, this trip was slow and arduous, since Burgoyne's personal baggage alone requirred thirty ponderous carts, and the company included a straggling retinue of officers' families and servants. Despite these handicaps, Burgoyne felt certain of success, since he knew that the entire Continental army was with Washington in Pennsylvania. Obviously it would be impossible for the Americans to raise another force.

But the impossible happened. Within six weeks after a new call to arms went out, the American general Horatio Gates was in command of 20,000 men, most of them New York and New England militia. Meanwhile, St. Leger was routed and turned back. Ironically, Howe never received precise instructions from England and remained in Philadelphia. Burgoyne, perplexed and outnumbered three to one, withdrew to Saratoga, his retreat constantly harassed by rebel raids. There he refused to act and indulged himself in riotous living. As a German baroness who was with him recalled, Burgoyne "liked having a jolly time and spending half the night singing

Courtesy New-York Historical Society, New York City.

The diary of Baroness von Riedesel recounts her experiences while accompanying her husband on the ill-fated Burgoyne expedition. Her strong will and intelligence stood her well while a prisoner of the Americans.

and drinking and amusing himself in the company of the wife of a commissary, who was his mistress and, like him, loved champaigne." On October 17, 1777, Burgoyne was forced to surrender. Saratoga was a major American victory and it had extremely important consequences; for it convinced European powers that the rebels did indeed have a chance of victory. The French, stinging from the results of the Seven Years' War and fearful that the British might now offer the Americans enough concessions to end the war, soon signed a treaty of commerce and a defensive alliance with the United States. The latter would take effect if Great Britain should go to war with France.

During this same period George Rogers Clark, with the backing of Virginia authorities, embarked upon an expedition against the British and the Shawnee Indians, and the Loyalists who were raiding settlements in the Ohio River valley, the so-called "Old Northwest." On July 4, 1778, he occupied Kaskaskia, on December 17, took Vincennes, and early in 1779 overwhelmed a British force from Detroit. While the campaign had little effect upon events along the eastern seaboard, it gave rebel forces a secure claim to a vast region beyond the Appalachians.

In the spring of 1778 the British, realizing the war now threatened their far-flung empire, deserted Philadelphia and returned to New York, somewhat easier to defend than Philadelphia. By moving there, the British were able to dispatch troops to the West Indies where the French were threatening to seize British possessions. Washington pursued the British army as it made its way to New York, but he was unable to score a victory. The British settled in at New York as Washington kept a wary watch.

Although the British kept New York as their chief base, they conducted raids on the South during the rest of the war. Until now the South had not been the scene of much conflict. In May 1780 Sir Henry Clinton (who replaced General Howe as supreme commander the preceding spring) conquered Charleston, South Carolina. Horatio Gates was sent south to defend the Carolinas against the British, but he received a thorough drubbing there. Nathaniel Greene replaced Gates and devised a new strategy. Rather than meeting the enemy head on, Greene tried to divide and conquer various army units on sites of his own choice. Week after week the British under Lord Cornwallis lost so many men that, in despair, Cornwallis at last admitted defeat and turned his attention to the conquest of Virginia. Cornwallis settled at Portsmouth in July 1781 and then, soon afterwards, moved to Yorktown.

The Decisive Victory

At this point the long-awaited French fleet arrived, and with its aid the United States was able to win the war. Washington and Clinton were still locked in a stalemate in New York. But when Washington learned that twenty French warships were sailing toward the Chesapeake Bay he decided to swoop down on Yorktown, thereby crushing the town between American land forces and French naval might. The plan worked perfectly. British naval squadrons stationed in New York rushed down to the Chesapeake Bay to head off the French, but were badly battered in the encounter and had to limp home for repairs. Washington, leading an army of American and French soldiers, laid siege to Yorktown, which quickly capitulated. The defeated Cornwallis sent word of his surrender to Washington, whom he addressed as "His Excellency Gen. Washington." At last the British were willing to acknowledge Washington's status.

Fireworks went off in Philadelphia, and the bells in Boston churches rang all day. When the young James Madison heard the good news, he observed, "If these severe doses of ill fortune do not cool the phrenzy [*sic*] and relax the pride of Britain, it would seem Heaven had in reality abandoned her to her folly & her fate."

Diplomatic efforts of Benjamin Franklin and John Jay in Europe helped in no small way to make this astounding battlefield victory possible. Despite clumsy instructions from Congress, they effectively isolated Britain and won, in addition to invaluable French aid, financial loans and considerable good will for a weak, struggling, little republic as it grappled with a giant empire.

The Peace Treaty

Britain's pride had finally been "relaxed" and peace negotiations were opened soon after Yorktown. When the official treaty, called the Peace of Paris, was signed in 1783, the British recognized America's independence. The western border of the new country was to be the Mississippi, the northern border would follow the natural line of rivers and lakes near the fortieth parallel (almost exactly where it is today); but in the South the United States would stop short at the border of Florida which England returned to Spain. The Americans promised to help British creditors collect prewar debts and to cease confiscating Tory property, promises that were not kept for the most part. The British agreed to remove their troops with all deliberate speed.

The treaty was supposed to have been worked out by an American peace commission made up of Benjamin Franklin, John Adams, Thomas Jefferson, John Jay, and Henry Laurens. But Laurens was captured by the British and Jefferson stayed home. Franklin handled the preliminaries by himself when Lord North fell from power and was replaced by a new administration in Britain committed to peace. John Jay and John Adams arrived in time to work out the final terms of the treaty. Something momentous had happened. The world's greatest power had been defeated militarily by the collaborative efforts of a handful of its own colonies, and those colonies were now embarking on a great political experiment—independence and self-government.

Courtesy The Henry Francis duPont Winterthur Museum.

Benjamin West began this portrait of the peace negotiators in 1783, but never finished it when British-American relations cooled. The missing figures are the British delegates.

Essay

Dissent in Time of War

Dissent is as American as apple pie, perhaps even more so because the thirteen colonies and the nation formed from them were born in dissent. To be truly effective, dissent involves action connoting clear disagreement with the avowed policies of a church, government officials, or a government structure, some agency or organization to which one ostensibly should give support. Balloting is a form of dissent, and all governments (even the sternest of dictatorships) recognize that some citizens inevitably will disagree with those in power. The First Amendment to the Constitution acknowledges the right of protest, the right to dissent and present publicly divergent views: "Congress shall make no law respecting an establishment of religion, or prohibiting the free exercise thereof; or abridging the freedom of speech, or of the press; of the right of the people peaceably to assemble, and to petition the Government for a redress of grievances."

Dissent in time of war, however, creates special problems for the combatants. It matters little whether they are engaged in a revolution, a formally declared state of hostilities resplendent with parchment, ribbons, and signatures, a guerrilla operation, or a "police action." The basic question is the same: to what extent can any government that is locked in what may be a life-or-death struggle permit its citizens to question fixed, ordained policies? Open, defiant criticism may convert others to their point of view, encourage the enemy to press on, and make it impossible for an established state—or a revolutionary force that hopes to supplant it—to defend itself. The rebels of the American Revolution soon uttered the same cry heard during every such upheaval: "All who are not with us are against us!"

But every American war, with the possible exception of World War II, has elicited considerable protest on the home front. American citizens have held scores of mass meetings, burned tons of effigies, thought up countless slogans, and uttered a torrent of angry words. The so-called "little" wars such as the War of 1812, The Mexican War, The Spanish-American War, and the wars fought in Korea and Vietnam present the clearest examples of organized, highly vocal dissent. In each instance the fighting commenced with high resolves and general (if not totally enthusiastic) approval. Since these undertakings had the backing of a majority of the elected officials sitting in the United States Congress, one is forced to conclude that at the outset they enjoyed the support of the electorate as well.

Library of Congress.

Jonathan Boucher, an Anglican minister who had taught Washington's stepson, was among the loyalists who fled to British lines for protection. Boucher went into exile in England.

But initial conditions have a way of changing drastically. In the second war with Britain, for example, New Englanders saw the diabolical hand of Napoleon and soon talked of secession at the Hartford Convention. Only Andrew Jackson's after-the-fact victory at New Orleans and the Ghent Treaty ended a savage threat to disunion. In the 1840s, many Americans questioned the morality of seizing land from Mexico, especially if they were abolitionists who thought they discerned a scheme to create still more slave states. Henry Thoreau went to jail rather than pay taxes to support that war. His essay on "Civil Disobedience" grew out of these experiences. A government of majority rule, he cautioned, cannot be based on justice since the majority, at times, will consider only the expediency of the moment, not conscience. "A minority is powerless while it conforms to the majority; it is not even a minority then; but it is irresistible when it clogs by its whole weight. Under a government which imprisons any unjustly, the true place for a just man is also in prison."

The Spanish-American War, as it was very brief, aroused little outcry until it was over and the United States decided to keep the Philippines. Then a wave of anti-imperialism swept the nation as Mark Twain and other well-known voices railed in protest, one spokesman noting that all wars of conquest evoke the phrase, "My country, right or wrong!" "That spirit," he thundered, "ridicules morality, cows religious teaching and is the forerunner of national decay."

The Korean and Vietnamese experiences began quite differently but soon developed marked similarities. The Korean affair in 1950 burst like a thunderclap for all to hear; the quagmire in Vietnam started quietly in the early 1960s and gradually engulfed more and more of our national resources until it brought down a president and fractured American society. By the time a peace of sorts came in Korea, it was seen as a "no-win" war, a precursor of what happened in Vietnam a decade later.

What is striking about these five confrontations is that those who dissent strike two very familiar chords, one sounded by those on the left, the other by those on the right. The first group says the conflict is immoral and unjust; the second, that it is being carried on in a stupid manner. Those who protest are not allied with the enemy nor are they (for the most part) conscientious objectors opposed to war in principle. They apparently would fight in a moral war, if one could be found without too much trouble, or they might even join in the current sacrifice of money and blood if it were only conducted in a fashion more to their liking. These "little" wars clearly delineated the "ins" from the "outs." The established government was pursuing policies that the Hartford Convention, the sage of Walden Pond, Samuel

Library of Congress.

Henry David Thoreau was jailed for refusing to pay taxes in protest of the Mexican-American War. While in jail he wrote *Civil Disobedience.*

Clemens, those opposed to "limited" war in Korea, and millions perplexed by the agony of Vietnam (and America) did not like.

The two world wars present somewhat different aspects of dissent, as do the American Revolution and the Civil War. In each of the twentieth-century conflicts there was widespread conscription of manpower that met with some resistance, just as a rather capricious draft during Korea and Vietnam fed the fires of protest. Deferring college students, for example, permitted those who could afford college to buy their way out of serving their country. However, not hearing the request of the state to bear arms is a very old, rather personal game, even a semirespectable maneuver during an unpopular war; and, unless resistance to the draft becomes a highly organized, active force encouraging general disregard for the law within the nation itself, it cannot be classified as true dissent.

During World War I, Woodrow Wilson's government passed two sedition laws signaling that active opposition to wartime programs would be tantamount to treason. The American minister to the Netherlands even suggested that all dissenters be hanged. Under the terms of this legislation, some 1,500 citizens were arrested and many of them ended up behind bars. Ironically, in 1918 the producer of a movie, *The Spirit of '76,* about the American Revolution received a ten-year sentence for stirring up anti-British feeling!

The best-known of these World War I dissidents was Eugene V. Debs (1855–1926), five times Socialist candidate for president. In June 1918, Debs spoke in Canton, Ohio, where he stressed the deeply engrained opposition of all Socialists to war. Since men of draft age heard his words, under the terms of Wilson's new laws he was charged with sedition, convicted, and sentenced to ten years in prison. While there, he campaigned for the White House and got an astounding 920,000 votes. On Christmas Day, 1921, the man who won, Warren G. Harding, granted him a pardon.

Dissent during the American Revolution and the Civil War was a complex phenomenon, for both conflicts were, in fact, revolutions. The problem is, from a practical standpoint, as long as hostilities are underway, to whom does one actually owe allegiance? A Tory living in rebel-dominated Virginia might refuse to swear allegiance to the new regime. One of his grandsons living in the same state perhaps viewed the Confederacy with equal disdain, while another residing in Maryland gave it his wholehearted support and scorned federal rule. Of course, once peace came this dilemma was solved. The Tory had either to move elsewhere or to stay and accept a new way of things, and both of his descendants found themselves under firm federal authority once more. But during the war years, the Tory, the Confederate

Culver Pictures.

The antiwar leaders of the North are satirized in this cartoon, which suggests that the Confederates found them equally distasteful.

sympathizer, and the Unionist could maintain—and with considerable justification—that the governments about them, not they themselves, were in dissent.

If these individuals expressed their strongly held views within the confines of their own homes and made no effort to organize resistance to the rule of such men as Patrick Henry, Thomas Jefferson, Abraham Lincoln, and Jefferson Davis, then their antiregime stance should have concerned very few, except perhaps some overpatriotic neighbors. But this was not always the case. The state governments of Revolutionary War days and the Confederacy were new, unsure of themselves, and eager for the aura of respectability, and Lincoln's wartime administration was extremely sensitive to the threat posed by disloyalty. As a result, nonbelievers often had a rough time of it.

Even before the Declaration of Independence—in January 1776—the Continental Congress encouraged suppression of dissent by passing a resolution urging every state to act vigorously against those favorable to England and critical of the patriot cause. Six months later the Congress suggested that the states consider opposition to the war as treason, and some states declared that those suspected of British sympathies should forfeit their property without a hearing.

The Revolutionary War editor, as Arthur M. Schlesinger has tartly observed, enjoyed little "liberty of speech" unless he spoke "the speech of liberty." Ministers whose sermons did not please rebel leaders had to seek out new pulpits. Loyalty oaths were commonplace in hundreds of colonial communities, and governors often used the state militia to maintain order (as they interpreted the word), seize dangerous Tories, and rout any groups suspected of aiding the enemy. Yet some prominent Tories—Ralph Wormley of Virginia and Daniel Dulany of Maryland among them—lived unmolested throughout the war. Apparently they posed no direct threat to the rebel cause. Editors and ministers, being more active and able to influence public opinion, clearly did.

During the Civil War, Lincoln's government arrested 13,000 citizens for antienlistment activity or aiding the enemy. Twenty-one newspapers were shut down. Early in July 1863, at the time that the crucial Battle of Gettysburg was running its course, an antidraft riot with racial overtones left hundreds dead in Manhattan. In Ohio, Indiana, and Illinois, Lincoln also harassed the "Copperheads," groups of disgruntled Democrats who wanted to preserve the Union by negotiation, not through open conflict. Although much maligned by their Republican critics, these dissident Democrats forcefully proved they were not rebel sympathizers by joining in battle against Confederate forces that invaded their homelands. Nonetheless, like the citizens who later on were opposed to our involvement in Korea and Vietnam, the Copperheads urged that peace be reached through give-and-take at the bargaining table, not through blood-and-death on the battlefield.

When eleven states seceded from the Union in 1861, they took with them a hard core of pro-Unionists who soon became openly critical of the Confederate cause, especially as the tide of war began to turn. One state, Virginia, was split asunder by secession, and another, Tennessee, almost went down the same road. Within a year or so "peace societies" began to appear in Arkansas, Texas, Alabama, Georgia, and North Carolina, complete with secret grips, passwords, and special oaths. Unlike Lincoln's federal government, which grew stronger, the Confederacy became steadily weaker, so much so that during the last two years of the war the manpower and resources of entire sections such as northern Alabama and the mountain counties in several other states were denied to the southern cause.

It is obvious that (1) the United States Constitution recognizes the right of dissent, (2) a nation cannot defend itself in time of war if dissent becomes too pervasive, and (3) conflicts that drag on and become unpopular inevitably foment more and more protest. They may even reach a point at which some individuals become firmly convinced that righteousness actually lies in the cause of the enemy, not in that of their own nation. This occurred in the Revolutionary War, in the Civil War, in

Vietnam, and perhaps in other conflicts as well. As Abe Fortas, a former U.S. Supreme Court justice, wrote at the height of the Vietnam holocaust, "Wars tend to create danger or the fear of danger to the state, and the state is always apt to respond to fear by taking measures which its officials consider necessary for its defense, and which sometimes are far more drastic than justified."

This, then, is the basic dilemma posed by dissent in time of war, especially in a republic that prides itself on free speech, a free press, and the right of peaceful protest. To stifle criticism a government may resort to controls that transform the state into a replica of the enemy. At that juncture citizens may well ask: "Why fight?" Although Fortas does not say so, what is essential to a republic engaged in war—if it is to remain a republic—is *not* to respond to dissent in so unjustified a manner that it changes itself into a dictatorship. For, if it shelves basic freedoms "for the duration of the emergency," a government may discover it, too, is put aside by its citizens because they value those freedoms highly. When a citizenry can no longer tell the difference between its own government and that of its adversary, then a war is effectively lost, regardless of what the enemy may do.

Selected Readings

Background to the War

Oliver M. Dickerson, *Navigation Acts and the American Revolution* (1951)
John Shy, *Toward Lexington: the British Army in the Coming of the American Revolution* (1965)
Pauline Maier, *From Resistance to Revolution* (1972)
Edmund Morgan, *The Stamp Act Crisis: Prologue to Revolution,* rev. ed. (1962)
Benjamin Labaree, *The Boston Tea Party* (1964)
David Ammerman, *In the Common Cause: American Response to the Coercive Acts of 1774* (1974)

Participants in the War

Ira D. Gruber, *The Howe Brothers and the American Revolution* (1972)
Benjamin Quarles, *The Negro in the American Revolution* (1961)
Jack Sosin, *Revolutionary Frontier* (1967)
Paul Smith, *Loyalists and Redcoats: a Study in British Revolutionary Policy* (1964)
William Nelson, *The American Tory* (1961)
Robert Gross, *The Minutemen and their World* (1976)
James H. O'Donnoll, III, *Southern Indians and the American Revolution* (1973)

Conduct of the War

Marshall Smelser, *The Winning of Independence* (1972)
Eric Robson, *The American Revolution in its Political and Military Aspects* (1966)
Howard Peckham, *The War for Independence* (1958)

Growth of Constitutional Thought

Bernard Bailyn, *The Ideological Origins of the American Revolution* (1967)
Carl Becker, *The Declaration of Independence* (1922)
David Hawke, *Transaction of Free Men: Declaration of Independence* (1964)
Merrill Jensen, *The Articles of Confederation* (1940)

Diplomacy

Samuel Flagg Bemis, *The Diplomacy of the American Revolution* (1935)
Richard B. Morris, *The Peacemakers: Great Powers and American Independence* (1965)
Richard Van Alstyne, *Empire and Independence: American Revolution* (1965)

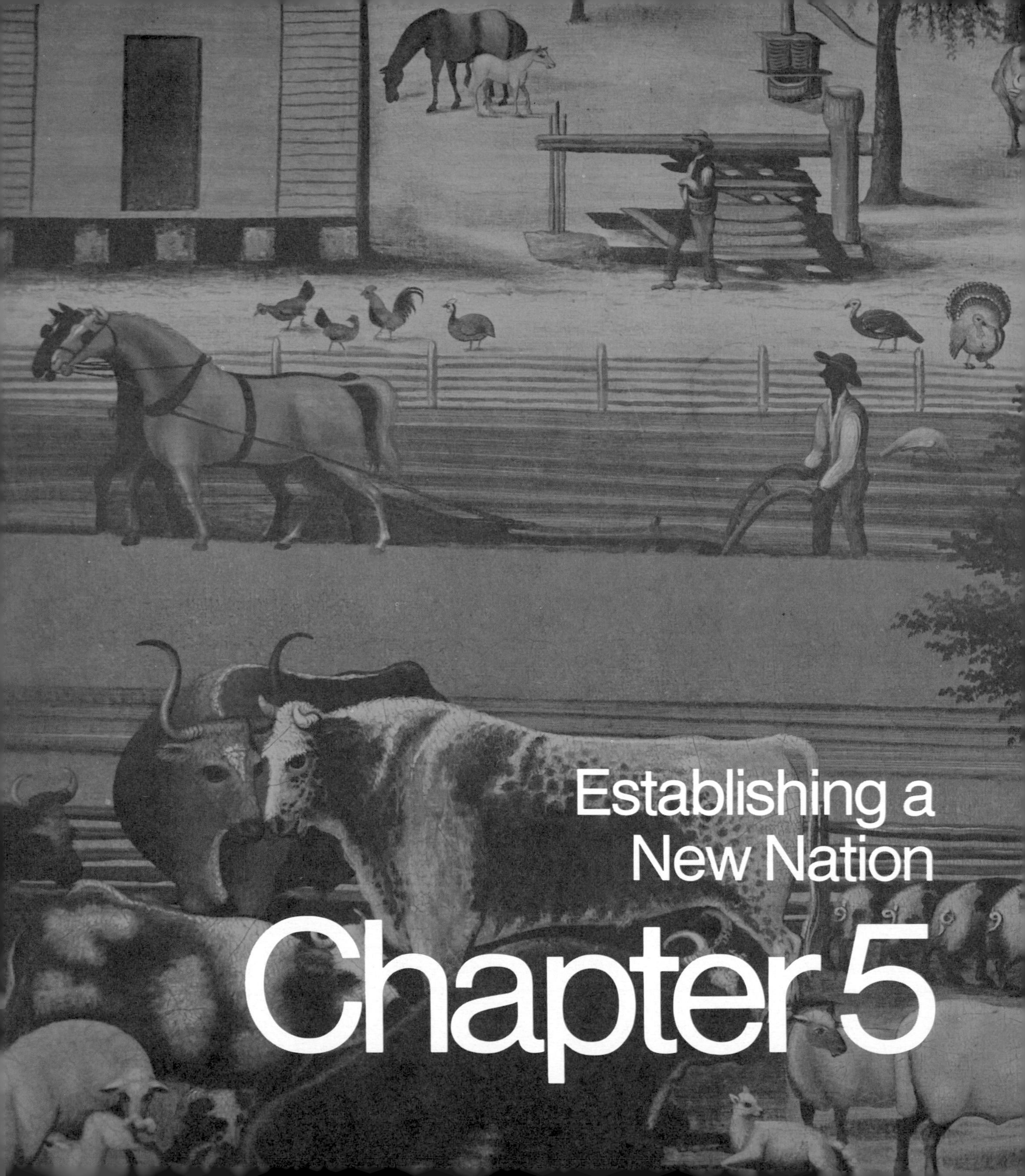

Chapter 5
Establishing a New Nation

TIMELINE

1775
Settlement of Kentucky
1776
Declaration of Independence
1777
Articles of Confederation drafted
1781
Ratification of Articles of Confederation
1783
Treaty of Paris
1784
Ordinance of 1784
1785
Land Ordinance of 1785
1786
Shays' Rebellion
1786
First American publication of Phillis Wheatley's poetry
1786
Annapolis Convention
1787
Northwest Ordinance
1787
Constitutional Convention
1789
Constitution takes effect with George Washington as President
1791
Philip Freneau establishes *National Gazette*
1791
Bill of Rights
1791
Establishment of the Bank of the United States
1792
Washington reelected President
1794
Whiskey Rebellion
1794
Jay's Treaty
1795
Treaty of San Lorenzo or Pinckney's Treaty
1796
John Adams elected President, and Thomas Jefferson elected Vice President
1797
XYZ Affair
1798
The Alien and Sedition Acts
1800
Jefferson defeats Adams in presidential election.

CHAPTER OUTLINE

In the years following the Revolution, American leaders were deluged with problems. The solutions they came up with have influenced all subsequent national history. The travail of those exciting years contributed to the settling of the Old Northwest, establishing a strong central government under George Washington, developing a two-party system, creating of a foreign policy, and making something we now call our "national character."

"The American war is over," Dr. Benjamin Rush (ca. 1745–1813), a well-known Philadelphia physician, wrote in 1787, "but this is far from being the case with the American Revolution. On the contrary, nothing but the first act of the great drama is closed. It remains yet to establish and perfect our new forms of government; and to prepare the principles, morals, and manners of our citizens for these forms of government after they are established and brought to affection."

Courtesy of the University of Pennsylvania.

Dr. Benjamin Rush of Philadelphia wanted to shape the new nation. He urged the education of women and an end to slavery as two reforms needed to create a virtuous republic.

Western Expansion

During the Revolutionary era the states functioned as nearly autonomous powers and nowhere was this more evident than in territory some of them claimed beyond the Appalachians. From 1781 to 1789, the United States was (or rather *were*) governed under the Articles of Confederation, a document that placed virtually no restraints upon the states. In fact, the Articles were designed specifically to protect states' rights against those of a central government.

The first settlers moved into Kentucky in 1775, and throughout the Revolution westward expansion continued. At every point conflicting state claims led to squabbles and even bloodshed. In several cases original settlers who held claims from one state were violently dispossessed by those who held claims granted by another.

The boundaries between various claims were nebulous to say the least. For instance, both Virginia and Pennsylvania claimed the area around Fort Pitt. Pennsylvania and Connecticut had conflicts since Connecticut insisted it owned lands in western Pennsylvania. The borders of New Hampshire, Massachusetts, and New York were disputed, and all three claimed Vermont. Competing states handed out the same land to different settlers and each tried to exercise its sovereignty by appointing local officials and collecting taxes.

The dissolution of ties with England did not resolve any of these disputes, for the states based their claims on long-established royal charters. These charters had created an inequity from the very beginning, since Georgia, the Carolinas, Virginia, Connecticut, and Massachusetts all received the right to lands west of their own boundaries—sometimes all the way to the Pacific Ocean; the other colonies had few territorial claims beyond their borders.

These disputes became acute since the population in the West was growing steadily throughout the Revolutionary era. By 1790 there were more than 100,000 settlers in the territory beyond the Appalachians. The frontier needed protection, government, and a legal system. It especially needed to be defended against Indian tribes who resented this usurpation of their traditional lands.

Since the national government was too weak to aid the settlers, they frequently took matters into their own hands. Kentucky pioneers created their own legislature in 1776 but petitioned for statehood to no avail. Virginia offered the area the status of a county and maintained Kentucky as a private possession until 1792. Settlers in eastern Tennessee set up an independent government, but North Carolina refused to recognize the independence of the area and made it a county as well. At one time North Carolina ceded Tennessee to the Continental Congress, then withdrew the offer. The settlers of Vermont, although active as patriots in the early years of the Revolution, eventually entered into secret talks with the British government in hopes of gaining recognition as an independent state or country.

Land disputes figured so prominently in American politics that they delayed ratification of the Articles of Confederation until 1781. Maryland refused to sign until Virginia ceded her western lands to the national government. In 1781 New York abandoned her western claims in hope of winning the legislative support of the "landless" states in her fight over Vermont. Virginia followed suit in the same year by ceding to Congress all land north of Kentucky.

This complex political maneuvering over the fate of western lands was intimately connected with the war itself. In 1779 the British invaded the South. Only a renewed national government could prevent possible defeat—and yet that government was powerless and penniless. The first step toward achieving ratification of the Articles of Confederation and thereby promoting a national government of sorts depended upon solving the problem of the western lands. By making Congress sole owner of most of those lands, the states not only reduced

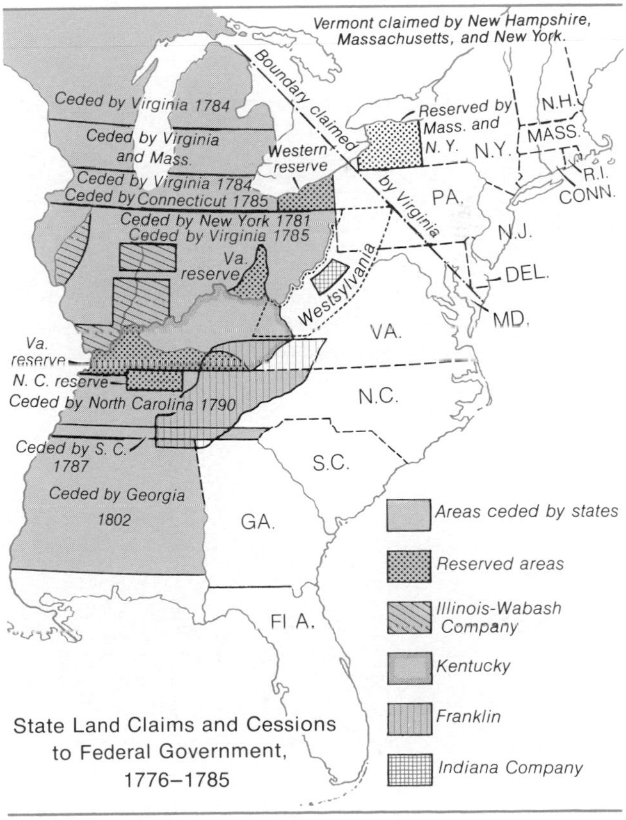

State Land Claims and Cessions to Federal Government, 1776–1785

their own rivalries but also provided the national government with a source of income. The Continental Congress was not allowed to tax Americans; but by selling off western lands, it could raise badly needed funds. And, perhaps most importantly, the cessions constituted a strong move toward nationalization.

Although the Articles of Confederation provided for some sort of central authority, this government had little power. Only with actual implementation of a new constitution in 1789 did the nation in general and the West in particular have a strong hand at the helm. Nevertheless, under the Articles, Congress did begin to work out a national land policy. The Ordinance of 1784 divided lands north of the Ohio River (the Old Northwest region) into sixteen districts, established a pattern of limited self-government, and arranged for a logical process leading to statehood when the population of each reached 20,000. Although later repealed, this legislation drafted by Thomas Jefferson is important because it introduced the fundamental concept of territorial government. The Ordinance of 1785 set up a plan for surveying western lands so they could be sold more readily. Each entire region was divided into ranges, sections, and townships, all divisions being made in square units. A township, for instance, was six square miles and was broken up into thirty-six units, each one square mile. Every sixteenth section of a town was set aside for the maintenance of a school. This plan has imposed a grid pattern on most of the American landscape.

Finally, the Northwest Ordinance (1787) revised the earlier 1784 Ordinance in order to give Congress greater control over the frontier and to delay statehood until each area was more adequately settled. It decreed that no less than three nor more than five states could be carved out of the Northwest. During the initial years of settlement a territory would be ruled by a governor, a secretary, and three judges, all appointed by Congress. When the area had 5,000 free adult male citizens, it could send a representative to Congress, but that representative would not have the right to vote. The territory also could elect a legislature and begin the process of self-government, but that body had to submit all of its proposals to the gover-

NASA

The imprint of the Northwest Ordinances is still obvious throughout the Midwest. Roads and farm fields follow the old section and range lines.

nor. Only when the territory had a population of 60,000 could it become a full-fledged state. Slavery, although at first permitted, was forbidden throughout the Northwest Territory after 1787 and religious freedom was guaranteed.

These three ordinances embody an orderly process by which new states, once they have sufficient population, can join the republic on a par with the old. This means that, instead of creating a centralized empire with a galaxy of dependent and politically inferior colonies, the United States of America became a constantly expanding republic. Also, these acts gave Congress complete control over frontier growth and helped to unify a young, struggling nation.

Creating a Government

To a large extent the American Revolution was fought over the constitutional question of the power of the British Parliament. The American colonies argued that their own legislatures should be supreme in deciding internal affairs. Each colonial legislature was regarded as a parliament in its own right. When the states attempted to form a national government they were wary of yielding their hard-won authority to a central congress. As early as 1774 a Continental Congress convened, but it merely passed resolutions, not laws. With the outbreak of war Congress took on more power and created a Continental army and navy, although it had not been authorized by the states to do so. When Congress drew up the Declaration of Independence in 1776 it also decided to write a framework for central government. A year later that document, known as the Articles of Confederation, was completed, and Congress began to act under its provisions even though it was not ratified by all the states until 1781.

The Articles provided for a very weak central government. The state legislatures jealously guarded their right to tax, and Congress received funds only through state appropriations. Moreover, Congress was not given any means to force its decisions on the states. There was no chief executive, although the President of Congress could act as a ceremonial head of state, and there was no judiciary. The sovereignty of the states was underlined by the fact that each state, no matter what its size or population cast only one vote in Congress.

The Articles did concede to Congress a number of specific powers that later would be incorporated into the Constitution. Congress controlled foreign affairs and the army and could issue currency and borrow money. The legislators themselves were granted immunities similar to those enjoyed by the members of Parliament in Britain. They were guaranteed freedom of debate, the right to decide on the length, place, and dates of their own meetings, the right to choose their own officers, and the right to be free from arrest except for major crimes.

The two chief powers that the Articles denied the national government were the power to tax and the power to regulate commerce. Nevertheless, Congress was not totally impotent. It conducted a successful war against the British, worked out a viable foreign policy whereby the United States formed military and political alliances with other countries and received large foreign loans, and wrote the various ordinances that regulated western expansion.

The shortcomings of the Articles, however, were manifest. The legislators formed many small committees through which all important business was conducted. The committee system became so tangled that soon Congress decided to reorganize itself; in 1781 the plethora of committees was reduced to a few executive departments. But no amount of reorganization could combat the problem of absenteeism. Toward the end of the rule of the Congress, there were several months during which it could not get a quorum.

Since Congress relied upon appropriations from the states for its funds, it was unable to deal with the huge national and foreign debt. To meet interest payments on foreign loans, Congress was forced to borrow money from Dutch bankers—which, of course, only increased the deficit. In 1786 the United States defaulted on interest payments due French citizens. The money owed to Americans, on the other hand, was paid after each state assumed the responsibility for paying its own citizens.

Four years earlier, Robert Morris (1734–1806), then Superintendent of Finance, had urged the states to accept a five percent duty on imports payable to Congress. General Washington himself wrote a circular pleading with the states to endorse this proposal, since the Continental army was going unpaid and threatening to disperse. When the states said no, young Alexander Hamilton (1755–1804) was so discouraged that he wrote a friend: "There is so little disposition either in or out of

Congress to give solidity to our national system that there is no motive to a man to lose his time in the public service . . . Experience must convince us that our present establishments are Utopian before we shall be ready to part with them for better."

The Critical Period

Historians have long debated over the period from 1781 to 1789, during which the national government functioned under the Articles of Confederation. These years were first called the "Critical Period" by John Fiske (1842–1901), who wrote a book by that title in the 1880s. Fiske argued that the difficulties of this period led the Founding Fathers to write the Constitution in order to insure a much stronger form of government. According to Fiske the Constitution saved America from civil and financial disorder and crowned the Revolution with a strong national government.

Later historians, led by Charles A. Beard, challenged Fiske's interpretation. In particular, Beard's follower, Merrill Jensen, stressed the positive aspects of the Articles of Confederation and suggested that they were more democratic than the Constitution. According to this thesis, the so-called "critical period" was not truly critical. The states were beginning to pay off the national debt, and Congress was about to receive independent income from the sale of western lands granted to it by the states. Lack of a strong central government actually was a blessing, since the powerful state governments were more responsive to the electorate than any national congress could have been.

Jensen identified the creators of the Articles of Confederation as the same radicals who initiated the Revolution; the drafters of the Constitution, by contrast, were those who supported the Revolution reluctantly and, once the war was over, were eager to found a strong central government. Those who gave birth to the Constitution were men with vested interests in raising the value of their personal property and in seeing the inflated national currency returned to its face value. Only if a national government was imposed upon the states could their financial ambitions be realized.

Recently a more subtly shaded interpretation of the period has emerged. Today historians recognize that the Articles of Confederation functioned reasonably well, especially during the late 1780s. And there were many Americans, independent small farmers, for example, who suffered little during this period. Nevertheless, in the opinion of these present-day historians, the nation faced grave problems that Congress under the Articles could not solve. The federal government was so weak that it was unable to redress wrongs perpetrated by foreign powers. When the British refused to abandon some of their forts around the Great Lakes under terms of the 1783 peace treaty, Congress had no way of driving them out. Merchants who dreamed of a flourishing interstate commerce were frustrated by lack of cooperation among the states in building roads and abolishing local duties. This chaos was partially due to absence of a strong executive to administer federal policy and a judiciary to punish infringements of federal law.

Cumbersome procedures further impeded the daily business of Congress. To make up a quorum, two delegates from at least seven states had to be present. If fewer than seven states were present, every decision had to be approved unanimously. Certain bills, especially those appropriating money and approving treaties, had to be approved by at least nine states. For Congress to collect a duty on imports, the proposal would have had to be approved by all thirteen states. Twice, in 1781 and in 1783, a single state blocked this measure. Delegates were elected only for a single year and could not serve for more than three out of every six years. As a consequence, representatives frequently left office as soon as they became familiar with congressional business. This system obviously was far from efficient.

The Constitutional Convention

The convention that wrote the Constitution began its meetings in May 1787, but it was far from a formal, full-dress affair. In fact, the gathering happened almost by accident, and deliberation of the Constitution was well underway before most of the delegates completely understood and accepted what they were doing.

In September 1786 five states sent delegates to a convention in Annapolis called by the Virginia legislature to discuss trade regulations among the states. This meeting clearly was illegal since only Congress had the power to convene such a meeting. Nothing was accomplished—except Alexander Hamilton recommended that the states should send delegates to Philadelphia the following May "to devise such further provisions as shall appear to them necessary to render the Constitution of

New York Public Library, Picture Collection.

A scene from "Shays' Rebellion."

Daniel Shays
(ca. 1747–1825)

A humble Massachusetts farmer, Daniel Shays, led an insurrection in western Massachusetts that is known to history as "Shays' Rebellion." This uprising of the poor was so distressing to propertied Americans that it strengthened their resolve to draw up a Constitution that would ensure orderly, stable government.

The date of birth and early life of Shays remain obscure, but it is known that he served gallantly during the Revolution and was commissioned a captain in 1777. After the war, a depression aroused widespread unrest among the poor farmers along the frontier. In 1786 the people of western Massachusetts met in several local conventions and lodged objections to the high level of their land taxes. A band of insurgents prevented the court of common pleas from meeting and handing down decisions against debtors. Shays, commanding 800 men, finally agreed to let the court sit if it would agree not to convict farmers unable to pay their mortgages.

During the winter of 1786–1787, Shays and his men realized their grievances would not be settled peaceably. He attacked the arsenal at Springfield and was defeated by the Massachusetts militia, which finally routed his troops at Petersham. Shays was captured and condemned to death by the state's supreme court, but he was soon pardoned.

After this brief moment of notoriety, Shays moved to New York, where he spent the rest of his days as a farmer. Although he had little education, Shays proved he possessed leadership qualities and was capable of arousing loyalty among the discontented. ■

---

the Foederal [*sic*] Government adequate to the exigencies of the Union." The purpose of the Philadelphia convention, therefore, was to revise the Articles of Confederation, not to write a new Constitution. Congress specifically limited the upcoming convention to "the sole purpose of revising the Articles of Confederation."

The first meeting of the Federal Convention was held on May 14 in Philadelphia at Independence Hall (then known as the State House)—but only two states, Virginia and Pennsylvania, were fully represented. Those assembled had to wait eleven days to begin serious deliberations. Even when the convention was in full swing, no delegates from New Hampshire appeared since that state had no funds for representatives. Rhode Island never named or sent delegates. Some states chose as their delegates to the convention men who were members of Congress, which met in New York.

Nevertheless, once the convention began to function, it was quite obviously a collection of the most distinguished men in the country. Nine signers of the Declaration of Independence were among the company. George Washington, who at fifty-five was universally revered as the hero of the Revolution, presided over the session.

Almost as famous as Washington was Benjamin Franklin who, at eighty-one, could look back on almost sixty years of accomplishment. He was a seasoned negotiator, having helped to draft the Declaration of Independence and draw up the peace treaty with Britain. Missing, however, were four well-known Revolutionary figures. Patrick Henry refused to attend and later led the antiratification forces in Virginia. Thomas Jefferson, minister to France, followed the proceedings with avid interest and, unlike Henry, strongly favored the new document. John Hancock, at first opposed to the Constitution, at length gave it his support as presiding officer of the Massachusetts ratifying convention. Samuel Adams, also a member of that body, followed the lead of Hancock, his political rival. Assured that a bill of rights would be added, he eventually backed ratification.

Almost all of the delegates who did attend had served at one time or another as congressmen—and this experience gave most of them a nationalistic outlook. New York had as one of its delegates the thirty-year-old Alexander Hamilton, the supreme advocate of a strong federal government. At one time Hamilton even recommended the dissolution of state governments and at all times held that "American liberty and happiness had much more to fear from the encroachments of the great states, than from those of the general government."

The other members of the assembly included ministers, doctors, and the governors of several states. They were a highly educated, relatively young group (average age forty-three), and for the most part represented the propertied interests of the new nation. This was the rising class of state and national leaders who, thanks to the departure of royal government and royal appointees, had moved into positions of power. And with this new prominence came money, land, and a somewhat more conservative outlook than that evident of a dozen or so years earlier when these men were rebels against King George III. Virginia undoubtedly had the most distinguished representatives, and outstanding among them was James Madison (1751–1836). He spoke frequently and kept careful notes on the debates, which many years later were published. Madison, instrumental in arranging the Annapolis convention, arrived at Philadelphia with very firm ideas concerning how to reform the Articles of Confederation. Even before the sessions got underway, he wrote to Washington and others describing his scheme for a strong central authority, the so-called "Virginia Plan," which actually went beyond mere reform and created a new governmental structure.

Constitutional Compromises

The convention almost immediately decided to keep its sessions totally secret—ostensibly, according to George Mason of Virginia, because secrecy was "a necessary precaution to prevent misrepresentation or mistakes," but in part because secrecy allowed the delegates to consider

Virginia State Library.

George Mason of Virginia considered the Virginia Bill of Rights one of his most important contributions to law. He opposed the federal Constitution for not including a similar grant.

far more extensive governmental changes than any state would have permitted them to make. Secrecy also permitted freewheeling discussion and compromise. At the same time, the body could present a unified front to the public. From the outset members agreed that each state would vote as a unit.

Throughout the convention one of the main subjects of debate was Madison's Virginia plan, a sweeping call for constitutional change. This plan divided the government into three branches: executive, legislative, and judicial. A national, two-house legislature would choose a chief executive for a single seven-year term. Each state would be represented in that body by a number of delegates proportional to its population. While adult male citizens with the franchise would elect the lower house, that body would choose the upper from among candidates proposed by the state assemblies. The executive branch would have the right to veto bills passed by the legislature. The most striking feature, other than proportional representation, was that the legislature could veto state laws which it thought prejudicial to the national interest.

All of these changes (still called "amendments" to the Articles of Confederation) would be ratified by state conventions elected by the people specifically for that purpose, not the state legislatures. This provision had both ideological and practical repercussions. It effectively bypassed the state legislatures, seen only as agents to carry out powers delegated by the electorate. The Virginia plan was based firmly on the will of the people themselves.

The plan was discussed, revised, and attacked during the Convention, but the states that favored the plan consistently outvoted those that disapproved of it. The one aspect of the plan that drew the most wrath from the smaller states (led by New Jersey and Connecticut) was the decision to base representation on population. States with small populations and little chance of growth feared that their interests never would be adequately represented in such a Congress.

William Patterson of New Jersey introduced an alternative proposal. According to this plan, basically a mere revision of the Articles of Confederation, the national legislature would represent the states and not the people. Each state would have only one vote, no matter how large or small it might be. Only Northern states supported Patterson's "small-state" scheme. The bigger Southern states objected on the grounds that, since the new Congress would have the power to tax, it was unfair for a few people to decide what the majority must pay. As Benjamin Franklin neatly summarized the conflict, "The diversity of opinions turns on two points. If a proportional representation takes place, the small States contend that their liberties will be in danger. If an equality of votes is to be put in its place, the large States say their money will be in danger. . . . Both sides must part with some of their demands, in order that they both join in some accomodating proposition."

After careful discussion the problem was turned over to a committee, which worked out a compromise. The lower house would be left proportional, but in the upper house states would have equal representation. This arrangement aroused the anxiety of Madison, among others, who believed that once states were recognized as independent entities, the whole concept of a strong federal government would collapse. But these fears were somewhat misplaced since the delegates agreed that the members of the upper house (the Senate) would vote as individuals, thus emphasizing they were accountable to the people they represented, not to their state.

At this point, the end of July, the convention adjourned for ten days to give the Committee of Detail time to write a draft of the new Constitution. It was in this draft that the elements of government received names now in common usage. The legislature became "Congress," the lower house became "The House of Representatives," the upper house became "The Senate," and the "supreme tribunal" became "The Supreme Court." The executive was now known as "The President of the United States of America."

But once the draft was prepared, debate broke out anew. The conflicts were now clearly sectional. Southern states feared that the congressional power to regulate commerce might be used against them and in the interest of merchants in the North. The South wanted the passage of bills regulating duties to be decided in Congress by a two-thirds majority. Many Northerners were interested in banning the slave trade, not only for humanitarian reasons but also because northern farmers did not want to compete with slave labor, especially in the western territories. But more immediately a dispute arose over two questions: should slaves be counted as population in determining a state's representation in the House? Should the value of slaves be included in computing taxable property?

The solution to this dispute required two trade-offs. Duties, like all other bills, would be passed in Congress by a simple majority, not by a two-thirds majority (a victory for the North). In return, the slave trade could not be abolished until after 1807 (a victory for the South). Slaves would be counted for purposes of taxation (a point for the North), but also for determining representation (a point for the South). However, slaves would not be counted in the same way as free white citizens. Each slave would be the equivalent of three-fifths of an ordinary white citizen. This ratio was not pulled out of thin air. Under the Articles of Confederation, Congress had long been using that ratio (3:5) to determine the amount of money each state had to contribute to the federal government.

The final issue to be settled was the presidency. Many people were wary of the seven-year term proposed by the Virginia plan (a term that could not be renewed through reelection). Since the President was to be given impressive powers, infrequent elections would allow him to assume the authority of a monarch. Alexander Hamilton was almost alone in not being adverse to a powerful executive. In fact, he wanted the President elected for life, as well as the members of the Senate, And, according to Hamilton, the states themselves should be under the rule of the federal government, which would appoint the various governors.

During August and September, the convention discussed the powers and duties of the President and finally agreed that his term of office would be not seven years but four and that he could be reelected. The method of election was a complex matter that generated an even more complex solution. The first draft of the Constitution, as prepared by the Committee of Detail, stipulated that the President be elected by Congress. But this plan, some of the delegates objected, would make the executive branch dependent on the legislature. If various state legislatures were allowed to elect the President, that method would make the federal government dependent on the states—and neutralize the centralizing trend of the Constitution. Theoretically the best solution would be for the people to elect their leaders directly, but the members of the convention by and large distrusted the judgment of the people, who they feared would choose a rabble-rouser. Finally, the convention decided that a special electoral college composed of the same number of men as each state had representatives in Congress would elect the President. The electors would meet in each state and cast their ballots by mail for a President. The runner-up would be Vice President. The House of Representatives would count the ballots. If two candidates tied, the House would decide the election, but each state would have only one vote in the matter. This plan had two advantages: it placed the decision in the hands of the people's representatives; but it gave an equal voice to each state, regardless of its size.

Ratification

The Constitution, then, far from being a mere revision of the Articles of Confederation, forged a vigorous central government, one that embraced a strong executive, a legislature more representative of the people than of the states, and a Supreme Court. The proposed government had the right to tax Americans, sign treaties with foreign powers, issue money, conduct wars, and regulate domestic and foreign commerce.

For the Constitution to go into effect, only nine states had to ratify it. The Constitution now appears such a solid, inevitable, and "respectable" document that it is difficult to conceive how it was regarded otherwise in the 1780s. A body of men ("demi-gods," as Jefferson considered them) instructed to amend the Articles had ignored their orders and fashioned something entirely new, which they now intended to put into effect by appealing, not to the states nor to the already existing Congress, but to the people. The whole strategy was a high-handed maneuver; had it not been backed by men such as Washington and Franklin and were the country not in such need of reform, the document might well have been dismissed as mere arrogance.

In fact, a pitched battle was fought between those who supported ratification and those who opposed it. Supporters were called Federalists, although logically they should have been termed Nationalists or Centralists since they favored a strong national government. Opponents, known as anti-Federalists, actually favored a true federalism in which the states wielded great power. Of the two camps, the Federalists were far better organized. They knew how to publicize their position (most notably in a series of brilliantly argued papers by Alexander Hamilton, James Madison, and John Jay, *The Federalist*), how to change the minds of delegates, and when to push and when to back off. They were able to create a ground swell by securing four quick ratifications, three of which

Yale University Art Gallery.

John Jay served the new nation as diplomat, first Chief Justice of the Supreme Court and member of Congress. John Trumbull, who chose patriotic themes, thus felt at home doing this Founding Father's portrait.

were unanimous (Delaware, New Jersey, and Georgia). In Pennsylvania the Federalists were not above resorting to bullying. The Pennsylvania legislature was predominantly in favor of ratification and was prepared to call an election for choosing delegates to the special ratifying convention. But the opposition boycotted the meeting of the legislature, thereby preventing a quorum and passage of the call. To achieve a quorum, a Federalist mob hunted up two of the missing anti-Federalists and dragged them to the legislature, forcibly retaining them until the motion passed. When the Pennsylvania convention met, it ratified the Constitution after some debate.

Connecticut easily ratified the Constitution by a vote of 128 to 40. But in Massachusetts passage was more difficult. Skillful lobbying and reasoned argument finally ensured passage by the narrow margin of 187 to 168. Here as in other states promise of amendments, especially a bill of rights spelling out basic civil liberties, carried the day. Maryland was the seventh state to ratify, by a six-to-one majority. South Carolina followed suit, and New Hampshire became the necessary ninth state in June 1778.

New York and Virginia, however, had not acted and they were among the most populous and wealthy states in the country. In Virginia Patrick Henry vehemently opposed the Constitution on many grounds. He felt that a republican form of government was suitable for only a very small, homogeneous territory. No other large country, he insisted, ever had successfully attempted the republican form of government. Henry, like many other Americans, was alarmed by the fact that there was no bill of rights. As he declaimed in his fiery style before the state convention: "The rights of conscience, trial by jury,

Courtesy Massachusetts Historical Society.

The conversion of wealthy John Hancock to the cause of the U.S. Constitution helped to ensure ratification in Massachusetts. John Singleton Copely's portrait catches the spirit of this wealthy merchant leader of the rebellion.

liberty of the press, all your communities and franchises, all pretentions to human rights and privileges, are rendered insecure, if not lost, by this change. . . . Liberty, greatest of all earthly blessings—give us that precious jewel, and you may take everything else!"

Henry's speeches filled up nearly 500 pages in the transcript of the meetings, which ran only to a total of 600. But it was Madison's quiet, reasoned argument that won the day—that and the support of John Marshall and Governor Edmund Randolph, once the latter agreed to work for a bill of rights.

New York state distrusted the Constitution, but New York City was so in favor of it that the city threatened to secede from the state unless ratification won out. Although Hamilton, Madison, and Jay were publishing *The Federalist* in New York, it was too subtle to influence popular support. The governor, knowing that the Constitution would not permit the use of import duties as a source of state income, opposed the Constitution. But while the New York convention was debating the question, news of Virginia's approval reached the delegates. Ratification in New York passed by the narrow margin of thirty to twenty-seven.

North Carolina did not ratify until November 21, 1789, after the new government already had been formed and a bill of rights was under discussion. Rhode Island, vexed by economic problems of its own, did not approve ratification until the following May, and even then it acceded only because the new Congress was threatening to levy a tariff on trade with the "foreign" domain of Rhode Island.

Anti-Federalist Fears

Arguments against the Constitution reflected fear that the proposed new government would reinstate a tyrannical rule similar to the one Britain had imposed on America. After all, the new government would possess four great powers: the right to wage war; the right to regulate commerce; the right to tax; and the right to decide the fate of the western territories. At the same time, the Constitution enforced economic restrictions on the states.

How could the states be certain that the federal government would not abrogate all their rights? Nor was there a bill of rights to protect such traditional English liberties as the right to trial by jury or freedom of speech. Was this not suspicious? To many Americans, who had witnessed their autonomy dwindle as the British government in London made more and more administrative decisions for the colonies, centralized power meant increased intolerance.

The problem of centralization seemed particularly acute in a republic. The people would feel out of touch with a distant central government where they were inadequately represented. Their lack of interest might lead to the emergence of tyranny. "From the moment we become one great Republic," one anti-Federalist essayist

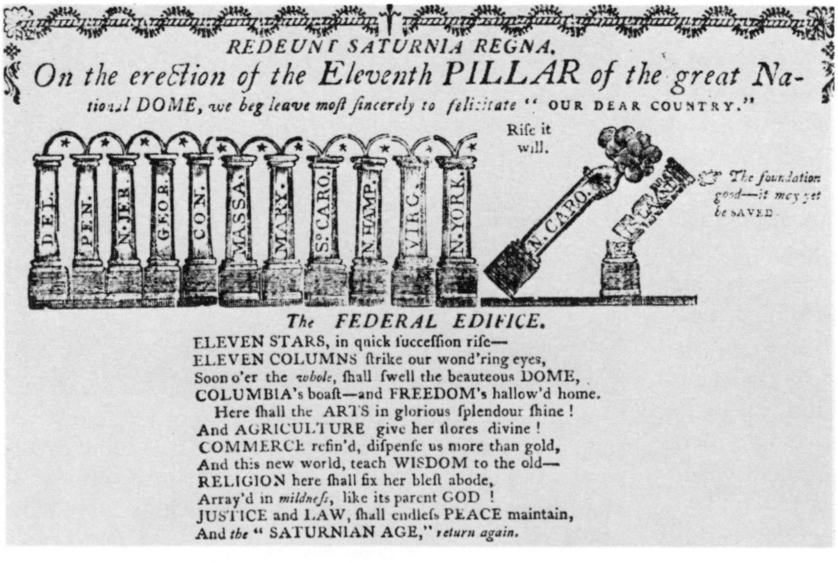

Courtesy New-York Historical Society, New York City.

This cartoon celebrates the ratification of the Constitution by the eleventh state (New York). The symbolism of the classical columns reminds readers of an earlier republic.

wrote, "either in form or substance, the period is very shortly removed, when we shall sink first into monarchy, and then into despotism." Sure signs of the coming despotism were the government's powers to levy national taxes and to maintain a national standing army. And in the shadowy "elastic" clause of the Constitution (Article I, Section 8) lay seeds of future federal tyranny—the clause granting the government the right "To make all Laws which shall be necessary and proper for carrying into Execution the foregoing Powers, and all other Powers vested by this Constitution in the Government of the United States, or in any Department or Officer thereof."

Finally, the anti-Federalists believed the Constitution would promote an aristocratic (or even a monarchical) form of government. Some of those who held this view pointed to the upper-class background of the men who framed the Constitution. Others argued their case from the contents of the document itself. Elections, instead of taking place once a year as under the Articles, would be held every two years for representatives and every six for senators. These long terms of office would separate Congress from the people: "In proportion to the duration of power, the aristocratic exercise of it, and attempts to extend it, are invariably observed to increase," wrote one anti-Federalist. Behind many of these objections was a conviction that human nature is basically selfish and consumed with a lust for power. Only rigorous checks and balances can hold this lust within bounds, and as Patrick Henry declared, "There will be no checks, no real balances, in this government. What can avail your specious, imaginary balances, your rope-dancing, chain-rattling, ridiculous ideal checks and contrivances?" The anti-Federalists were particularly alarmed by failure of the Constitution to insist on a limited number of terms for any congressman.

Historians have offered two basic theories to explain the split between Federalists and anti-Federalists. One theory focuses on social and economic backgrounds of the two groups. The anti-Federalist bloc was made up basically of small inland farmers; the Federalists were merchants who lived in the cities and were generally better educated. The other theory highlights ideological differences. For instance, some historians believe that Federalists had a national outlook, while anti-Federalists were more narrow and parochial in their views. The Federalists may well have been businessmen and "aristocrats" with a more cosmopolitan outlook based on broader experience. Many anti-Federalists were small farmers with limited incomes who feared a federal government that would have the power to tax. Suspicious of "foreigners" from other sections of the country, these untraveled anti-Federalists had little vision of the possible future greatness of a united country.

Using the Constitution

Elections for the new government were held in 1788 and Congress met for the first time in 1789. The first few months of activity were devoted to organizational matters. The House chose its Speaker and counted the electoral votes, and George Washington, as everyone had expected, was the unanimous choice for President. John Adams had the second highest number of votes and accordingly became the Vice President. In the new Congress the Federalists had won the day. There were only eight anti-Federalists in the House and only two anti-Federalists in the Senate (both elected by Virginia). These election returns clearly demonstrated the people's confidence in the great experiment.

At first this confidence might have seemed misplaced, since Congress devoted much time to arguing about how to address the President. A committee, after considerable deliberation, decided that the chief executive should be called "His Highness the President of the United States and Protector of the Rights of the Same." The Senate devoted so much time to the question of a title that John Adams, the official most eager for pomp and circumstance, was dubbed "His Rotundity." Congress finally decided on this simple title: "The President of the United States."

The Bill of Rights

Lack of articles guaranteeing specific freedoms and rights had been one of the chief objections to the Constitution. Following the ratification vote, six states suggested that a bill of rights should be added by the first Congress. The ten amendments, passed by Congress and eventually ratified by the states, protected such freedoms as the right to trial by jury; freedom of religion, speech, and the press; the right to assembly; and the right to petition the government. As safeguards against the sort of actions that precipitated the Revolution, the Bill of Rights forbade quartering of troops in private residences. Cruel and

New York Public Library-Prints Division.

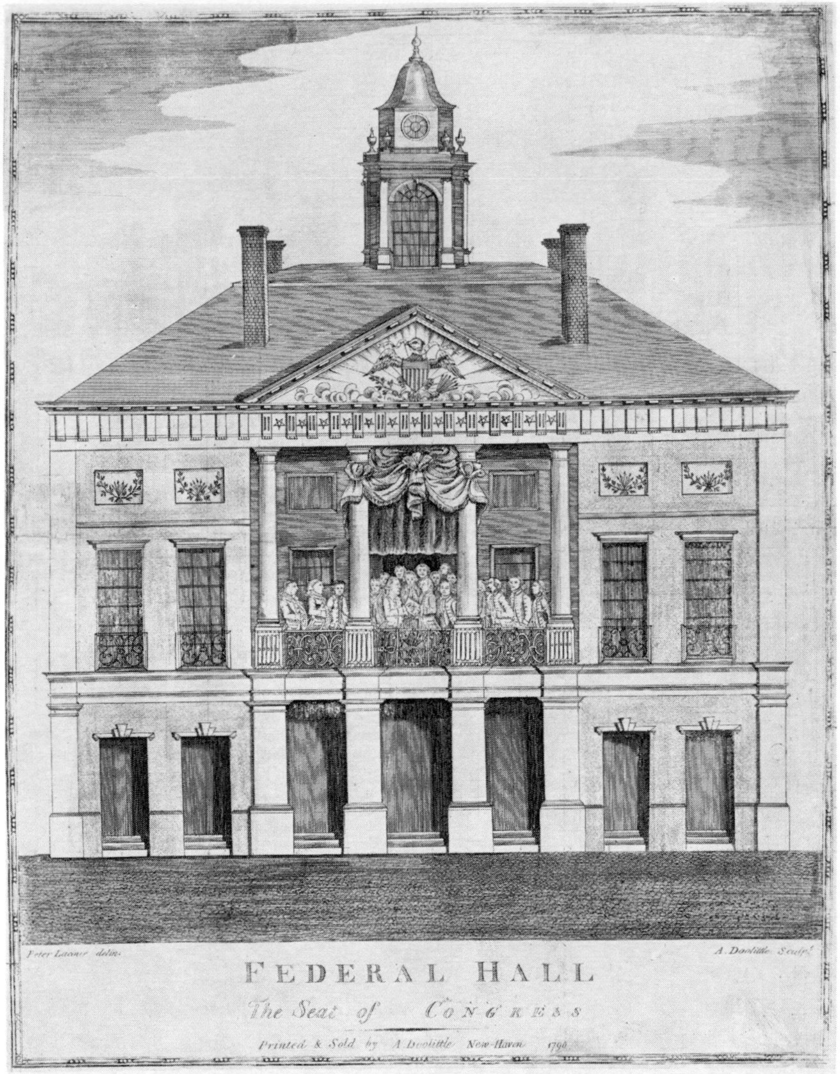

FEDERAL HALL
The Seat of CONGRESS
Printed & Sold by A Doolittle New-Haven 1790

This 1790 engraving purports to show Washington taking the oath of office. The capital at that time was in New York City.

unusual punishments, excessive bail, and general warrants also were forbidden. The Tenth Amendment, drawn up to mollify defenders of states' rights, reserved powers to the states which were not specifically given to the federal government.

While the process of ratifying the Bill of Rights was going on, three new states joined the union (North Carolina, Rhode Island, and Vermont). Had they not become states, the Bill of Rights would not have been ratified, since three states (Massachusetts, Connecticut, and Georgia) failed to approve the amendments.

The Presidency

Article II of the Constitution states that all executive power is vested in the President. It says he will command the army, navy, and any state militia called to national service, may grant reprieves and pardons, carry on foreign relations, appoint numerous officials (including Supreme Court judges), veto laws passed by the Congress, convene either or both houses of that body, and should they disagree with respect to adjournment "he may adjourn them to such time as he shall think proper." He also is required "from time to time" to report to the

Congress on the "State of the Union" and "recommend to their Consideration and Measures as he shall judge necessary and expedient," words most presidents have interpreted as an invitation to submit proposals for new legislation. It is very doubtful if the Founding Fathers would have endowed this office with so much power if it had not been assumed that Washington—wise, impartial, widely respected—would be the first President.

Although the Constitution named only a Treasury Department, other "executive departments" were mentioned. The President was granted the right to appoint "Heads of Departments" and other officials with the Senate's approval. Washington created the positions and filled them with old friends. Alexander Hamilton, the young Federalist, became the Secretary of Treasury. Thomas Jefferson was recalled from France and made Secretary of State. Edmund Randolph became Attorney General and Henry Knox, Secretary of War. The most pressing problems facing the executive branch were finances, foreign policy, and westward expansion. In all three areas, of course, the President could act only in conjunction with Congress.

Financial Policy

During the Revolution the federal government as well as the state governments contracted enormous foreign and domestic debts. The new central government was determined to settle these debts, but most members of Congress wanted to pay back only a percentage of the money borrowed. After all, they reasoned, the domestic debt was owed to only a few citizens, many of them speculators. Why should the population as a whole pay taxes to enrich the few?

No one questioned that the foreign lenders (France, Spain, and Holland) should be repaid in full; repayment in this case was considered a sacred responsibility. But of the entire national debt of $50 million, some $40 million was owed to American citizens. During the war many soldiers were paid with paper certificates, but in the years after the Revolution, many veterans sold their certificates to speculators for a pittance of their face value. Why should these financiers get rich at public expense?

Alexander Hamilton took an entirely different approach that drew upon recommendations of Robert Morris, Superintendent of Finance under the Articles of Confederation, and upon precedents set by the Bank of England. He proposed in his "Report on Public Credit" that the federal government pay back all debts in full, both foreign and domestic (called "funding"). Moreover, the federal government also should assume all state debts incurred in waging the Revolution (called "assumption"). By repaying these debts at full face value, Hamilton was making the national debt as large as it possibly could be. Although it might enrich speculators, payment in full would also set the highest standards of financial reliability for the new government. Equally important, assumption of state debts would exert a strong centralizing influence on the country since many more people would have the new government's interests at heart.

Both of Hamilton's proposals—to pay all debts at face value and to assume state debts—met with stiff opposition. The opponents were led by James Madison, who objected to the first proposal on the grounds that full

Independence National Historical Park Collection.

Alexander Hamilton's drive and energy are obvious in this portrait by Charles Willson Peale. Hamilton was the single greatest influence on the Washington administration.

repayment would enrich the few and to the second on the grounds that some states, including Madison's own Virginia, had already paid off their war debts. Under Hamilton's plan debt-free states would share the cost of repaying the debts of states less prompt in meeting their responsibilities.

Despite vehement attacks on the scheme, Hamilton prevailed and Congress passed his plan, which raised the national debt from $50 to $100 million. While it did enrich both American and many foreign speculators (some of whom were Hamilton's friends), it also restored American credit. By 1792 the United States was well on the way to repaying its debts, and the price of government securities soared to something close to face value. Washington said that he had seen "our affairs desperate & our credit lost, and that this was in a sudden & extraordinary degree raised to the highest pitch."

Hamilton next turned his attention to chartering a national bank. The bank would draw on federal funds, but most of its capital would come from private investors. The bank would print bills and lend money, thus providing the nation with capital for industrial and commercial development and a much-needed currency for its daily business. Madison and Jefferson both opposed the idea by pointing out that nowhere in the Constitution was such an institution mentioned. Hamilton said the bank could be justified by referring to the clause that gave Congress the right "To make all Laws which shall be necessary and proper for carrying into Execution the foregoing Powers, and all other Powers vested by this Constitution in the Government of the United States, or in any Department or Officer thereof." Since a bank was "necessary" for collecting taxes and regulating commerce, it was clearly constitutional. Furthermore, the Constitution did not specifically prohibit such a bank, a matter of some consequence in the Supreme Court's affirmation of the constitutionality of the Bank in 1819. Hamilton's position was the first instance of the "broad construction" of the Constitution; Jefferson and Madison, by contrast, at least on this occasion, stuck to a "strict interpretation."

Hamilton finally won the day, though the victory cost him the support of his former friends, Jefferson and Madison. Many American leaders began to see in Hamilton, who was born in the West Indies, the very personification of the monarchical Federalist that so many anti-Federalists feared would develop.

Traditionally historians have written that during the dispute over the assumption of state debts, Hamilton struck a secret bargain with his opponents from the South. Hamilton reputedly agreed to the removal of the national capital from New York, where it was originally located, to the South in return for support of his fiscal policies. Recent research has shed doubt on this story. The permanent location of the capital, however, was undoubtedly a matter of concern. The Constitution provided that the permanent seat of government would be a district (not more than ten miles square) where Congress, not the states, would "exercise exclusive Legislation." Eventually that body worked out a compromise that appeased various sections of the country. The capital would remain in New York for a while, then move to Philadelphia. The permanent site would be land deeded to the government by Virginia and Maryland. If this new city (present-day Washington, District of Columbia) were never built, the government would remain in Philadelphia.

Indians and the Frontier

Although the Northwest Ordinance of 1787 set up procedures for the settlement of the western territories and their admission to statehood, it did nothing to solve the difficulties with Indians. Indian tribes still held on to the land, and sporadic but bitter fighting continued between Indians and settlers in Kentucky and Tennessee. Most settlers were convinced that these outbreaks were inspired by the British, who still illegally held forts on American territory (such as the one at Detroit). The Northwest was economically depressed because the Spanish closed their port of New Orleans to American produce, and settlers, unable to ship down the Mississippi, were forced to haul their produce over the Appalachians, a costly, slow, and perilous undertaking.

Indian resistance also met white expansion in the Southwest. Creek Indians blocked the growth of Georgia and threatened sparse, exposed settlements in Tennessee. When the United States met these Indians in battle, the results were dismal defeats. In the Old Northwest, Indians under the leadership of Miami Chief Little Turtle defeated General Josiah Harmar in 1790; in the following year they completely routed a much larger force under the command of Arthur St. Clair. When Congress investigated, it discovered St. Clair's troops were not properly supplied and quickly dwindled to half their number through starvation and desertion. Their Indian foes, by contrast, had been well supplied by the British with guns and even additional soldiers.

The government's failure to defend the frontier prompted many settlers to consider seceding from the Union. Only some successes through arms and diplomacy stemmed this drift toward anarchy. In 1794 "Mad" Anthony Wayne bested the Northwest Indians at Fallen Timbers, and one year later the Indians ceded most of the present state of Ohio to the United States by the Treaty of Greenville. At last the West was truly opened to intensive settlement, though subduing the Indians had cost the country $5 million between 1790 and 1796—one-sixth of the total federal budget.

The Whiskey Rebellion

One outbreak of violence in the West was launched by frontiersmen not against the Indians, the British, or the Spanish but against the United States government. In order to raise federal revenue, Hamilton instituted, among other taxes, an excise tax on whiskey. This levy aroused a rebellious spirit in four of the western counties of Pennsylvania beyond the Alleghenies. Along the frontier, whiskey circulated in place of currency, and more than one minister received his salary in flasks of distilled spirits. More importantly, whiskey was the most common product derived from corn. It did not spoil and it could be easily transported.

By 1794 open resistance to the tax erupted. Mobs pursued federal tax collectors and a federal marshal who tried to summon offenders to court met with violence. Washington, relying on Hamilton's advice, viewed the incident as an opportunity to demonstrate the new government's authority. He and Hamilton rode out at the head of 15,000 troops—but found not a single rebel. Washington pardoned the leaders of the rebellion and the incident was soon forgotten. As Washington told Congress, the event "has demonstrated that our prosperity rests on solid foundations, by furnishing an additional proof that my fellow-citizens understand the true principles of Government and liberty; that they feel their inseparable union; that, notwithstanding all the devices which have been used to sway them from their interest and duty, they are now as ready to maintain the authority of the laws against licentious invasions, as they were to defend their rights against usurpation."

Foreign Affairs

Although President Washington relied upon the counsel of his Secretary of State, Thomas Jefferson, he also solicited the advice of Alexander Hamilton and other national leaders. Differences between Jefferson and Hamilton engendered by fiscal matters deepened during the Whiskey Rebellion (Hamilton took a much harsher approach towards the rebels than Jefferson). Now, in the conduct of foreign affairs, the rift between them became still more serious.

Jefferson was pro-French and Hamilton was pro-British, though neither man's allegiance was as straightforward as historians have sometimes asserted. Jefferson, who had lived in Paris, was very sympathetic to the French Revolution, which broke out in 1789, even welcoming its excesses for a time. Hamilton, on the other hand, felt American trade and commerce needed British connections in order to prosper. He did not see these ties as permanent or subservient; but, for the moment, he believed they were necessary. The success of his funding plan depended on duties on British imports, which supplied nine-tenths of all U.S. tariff revenues. To offend Britain, Hamilton thought, would invite economic disaster.

When Britain and France became embroiled in war in 1793, these sympathies clashed head on. Hamilton, Washington, and Jefferson all agreed that the United States should remain neutral. But beyond that single point of agreement, radical differences arose. Hamilton advocated a much stricter neutrality than Jefferson proposed. According to Hamilton, Washington should not receive the minister Edmond Genêt, whom the French revolutionary government sent to America. Moreover, Hamilton wanted Washington to revoke the treaties of alliance that the United States had signed with France in 1778; since the royal French government had been overthrown, Hamilton believed the treaty was no longer binding.

Jefferson offered very different advice. He wanted Washington to recognize Genêt as a legitimate minister and not to declare publicly America's neutrality until the best diplomatic terms were wrested from both France and England. As long as those two countries remained uncertain about American sympathies, the United States would be in a better bargaining position, Jefferson argued.

Hamilton had Washington's ear, and the President followed his advice, though he tempered it with Jefferson's suggestions. Genêt was formally recognized and treaties with France were not revoked, but Washington revealed America's neutral stance (without actually using the word). Genêt, showing deplorable judgment, complicated these diplomatic maneuvers. He did not go directly to New York to report to Washington but instead made a triumphant tour of the South, telling wildly cheering crowds about the French Revolution. At Charleston he commissioned American ships to sail under the French flag and raid British vessels. When the captured vessels were brought back to America, Genêt set up impromptu courts to try the crews. Genêt even organized an American force and ordered it to attack Spanish New Orleans. Washington was forced to demand Genêt's recall; but, as it turned out, Genêt was terrified he would be guillotined if he returned to France. Washington reluctantly granted him asylum. A gratified Genêt settled down in New York and married New York Governor George Clinton's daughter.

Jay's Treaty

Many Americans sympathized with the French Revolution, which they saw as similar to their own, and this sympathy was increased by new conflicts with Britain on the high seas. The British stood behind their so-called "Rule of 1756," which held that if, during peace time, any power (France in this case) refused to let another power (America in this case) trade with its colonies, then, during wartime, the same restrictions must prevail. But, now, the French had opened their islands in the West Indies to American vessels, and it was this trade that the British denounced. Americans, by contrast, held that neutrals could trade nonmilitary goods with any nation on earth. The English, accordingly, began to seize American ships in December 1793. This action infuriated the American public, as did allegations of British encouragement of Indian raids along the American frontier. Jefferson resigned as Secretary of State in December 1793; shortly before doing so, he recommended restrictions on trade with Britain.

Hamilton did not resign his post until a year later (his salary as Secretary of Treasury was too small to meet his family's needs), but before he left the government, he convinced Washington to avert war with Britain by sending John Jay on a special mission to England. Jay, unaware that Hamilton had secretly disclosed the American position to the British, found the negotiations very difficult since the British would make no concessions. Consequently, he came back with a treaty that Washington signed with great trepidation, that the public denounced, and that Congress almost revoked.

Indeed, Jay did make extraordinary concessions in this much maligned treaty. He renounced the American principle of the freedom of the seas and subscribed to the Rule of 1756. America would not sell provisions to the enemy (France) nor trade in naval stores. And American ports would not welcome privateers threatening the British navy. In exchange, very small American vessels (scarcely larger than fishing smacks) could trade with the British West Indies, though not in certain key commodities (sugar, molasses, coffee, or cotton). British possessions in India also were partially open to American trade. Although these concessions sounded minor at the time, they eventually brought great wealth to the United States. Between 1795 and 1800, American exports to Britain and its colonies increased by 300 percent.

The remaining terms were equally distressing. The British promised to withdraw their troops from American soil if British merchants could continue to trade with the Indians (the troops did not leave). Americans whose ships had been seized in the West Indies would be compensated for their losses only if the American government reciprocally compensated British creditors for debts owed them from the period before the Revolution. No guarantees were given that the British would cease impressing American sailors into the English navy.

Jay's Treaty was the most unpopular act of Washington's administration, and Jay, who was then Chief Justice of the Supreme Court, was threatened with impeachment. Rather than face this indignity, he resigned. Yet, Jay probably quit for other reasons as well: he was convinced that the Supreme Court was powerless, especially since Congress had just passed the 11th Amendment which overturned a recent court decision, and was eager to run for the governorship of New York, a campaign that proved successful. Also, the House of Representatives insisted that some of the terms (the list of excluded commodities) be modified before it appropriated funds necessary to pay the pre-Revolutionary debts owed British creditors. In addition, members of the House of Representatives asked to inspect the documents concerning the negotiations, but Washington refused, invoking

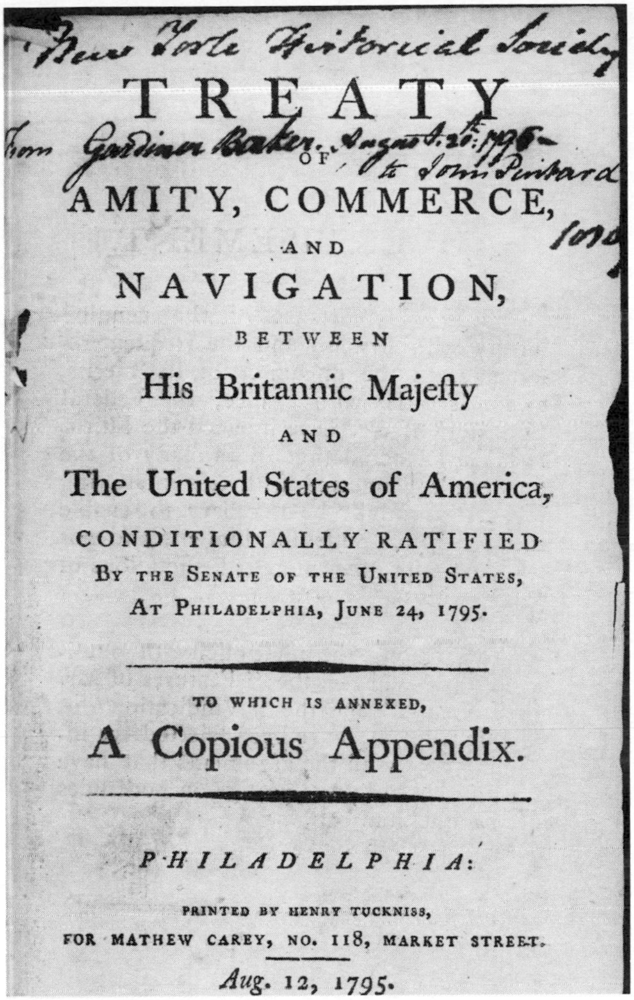
TREATY

OF

AMITY, COMMERCE,

AND

NAVIGATION,

BETWEEN

His Britannic Majesty

AND

The United States of America,

CONDITIONALLY RATIFIED

BY THE SENATE OF THE UNITED STATES,

AT PHILADELPHIA, JUNE 24, 1795.

TO WHICH IS ANNEXED,

A Copious Appendix.

PHILADELPHIA:

PRINTED BY HENRY TUCKNISS,

FOR MATHEW CAREY, NO. 118, MARKET STREET.

Aug. 12, 1795.

Courtesy New-York Historical Society, New York City.

Printer Mathew Carey lent his support to the debate over Jay's Treaty by printing this copy of the terms along with a series of comments in the appendix.

executive privilege, a kind of presidential step the Founding Fathers had probably not anticipated and proof they had created a stronger presidency than they envisioned.

As Samuel Flagg Bemis has noted, in the face of British might, the United States abrogated its 1778 treaty with France, but this decision was a "necessary evil," later justified by history. Jay's Treaty was the price the Federalists paid for peace and financial stability at a time when the young nation needed both desperately.

Luckily for the Washington administration, in 1795 a much better treaty, the Pinckney Treaty (or the Treaty of San Lorenzo) was worked out with Spain. This treaty was inspired by Spanish fears that Britain and the United States might join arms and seize the Spanish possession of Louisiana. Thomas Pinckney was thus able to open the Mississippi to American navigation and win for Americans the right to deposit goods in New Orleans until cargo could be reshipped to ports throughout the world. The Spanish agreed that America's western boundary would be the Mississippi and its southern boundary the thirty-first parallel, leaving only Florida and a slim crescent of the Gulf Coast to the Spanish. This boundary settlement was remarkable, since Spanish colonists already were living north of the line.

The First Party System Is Born

Most of the framers of the Constitution envisioned a government devoid of factionalism and united in patriotism. But soon after Washington's inauguration two parties began to grow. Significantly, they appeared first among the people's representatives in Congress. These factions developed in reaction to programs and events initiated by Washington's administration.

Federalists and Republicans

One group, the Federalists, was led by the Secretary of the Treasury, Alexander Hamilton, and it was his plan for fully funding state and federal debts incurred during the Revolution that first aroused opposition. Most Americans were dismayed and disturbed as these legislative divisions grew into political organizations. Washington tried to remain aloof, but was unable to do so because his administration, which was made up almost entirely of Federalists, had firm control of federal offices and the flow of information. The opposition, lacking tradition, was in a difficult position. Congress represented the will of the people and attempts to thwart that will were, in the eyes of many Americans, tantamount to treason. Nevertheless, as congressmen took stands on Hamilton's policies, treaties, and other issues, they discovered that these political factions were coalescing into definable groups. Since the Federalists were in power and excluded the opposition from federal offices, these divisions soon became obvious to all. Those aligning themselves with Madison and Jefferson could not use government posts to

AMERICAN POLITICAL PARTIES SINCE 1789

The dates given in this chart indicate the years parties either ran presidential candidates or held national conventions. The lifespan for many political parties can only be approximated because parties existed at the state or local level before they ran candidates in presidential elections; and parties continued to exist at local levels long after they ceased running presidential candidates.

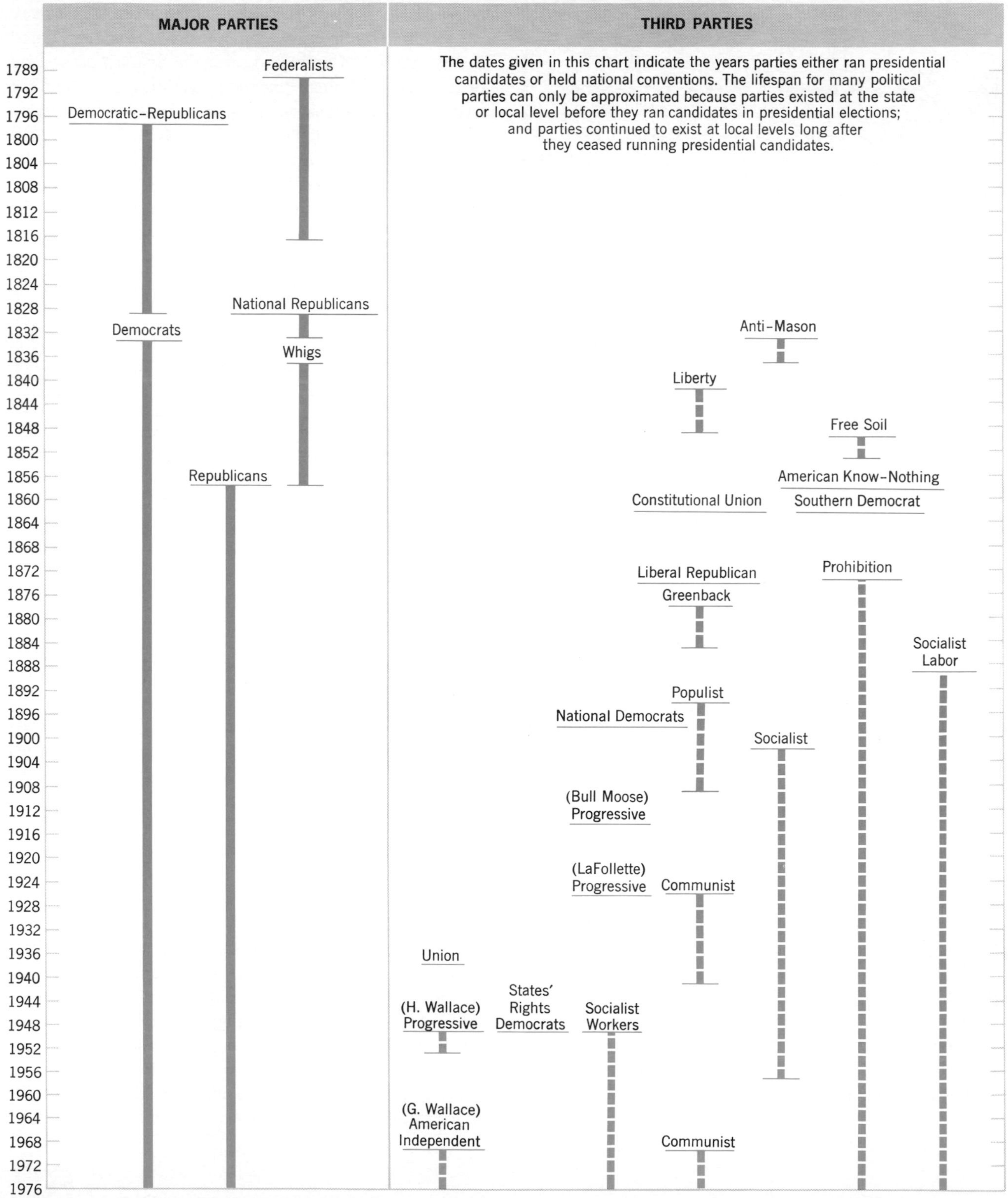

create a party structure, so they reached out to voters with promises to dispense future rewards once they had gained power.

Library Company of Philadelphia.

The anti-Jefferson propaganda is summed up in this cartoon, which shows the American eagle preventing Jefferson from burning the Constitution on an altar to French despotism.

The second party was not yet established as a clear entity in 1792 and Washington and Adams were returned easily to office. But in 1793 foreign affairs became stormy, and disagreements about America's position vis-à-vis France and England deepened the domestic rift. The second party, headed by Jefferson in the cabinet and Madison in Congress, came to be known as the Democratic-Republicans or Jeffersonian Republicans.

Differences between the two parties were founded on personalities, ideologies, policies, and tastes for invective. Though both Hamilton and Jefferson were well educated and well-to-do, Hamilton represented the interests of Northeastern merchants and financiers, and Jefferson identified himself with the cause of farmers and the "common man." Hamilton was articulate and quick-witted; Jefferson was far more retiring, and ruminative. Hamilton was a declared foe of local government and an ardent Federalist; Jefferson distrusted centralization and advocated minimal government intervention. Hamilton saw the American future as depending upon trade and industrialization; Jefferson saw the American future as bound to agrarian pursuits and their encouragement. Hamilton was pro-British because he felt that England was America's best commercial ally: Jefferson was pro-French because he felt that only Revolutionary France shared America's republican ideals. In fact, he and Madison built upon the grass-roots support of some forty Democratic societies formed in imitation of Jacobin societies in France.

The contrast between the two men has sometimes been overdrawn, and certainly they both responded to the exigencies of practical politics. Nevertheless, beneath their divergent political stands lay different views of human nature. Hamilton distrusted people in general; Jefferson believed thay would make wise decisions, at least in the long run, and took a much more benign view of the populace, especially the majority tilling the soil: "Those who labour in the earth are the chosen people of God, if ever he had a chosen people, whose breasts he has made His peculiar deposit for substantial and genuine virtue."

Competing newspapers soon fueled this growing controversy. Before 1791, the *Gazette of the United States,* published in Philadelphia by John Fenno, was the only journal that reported political events extensively. It was solidly Federalist, as Hamilton intended it to be. The arch-Federalist Fisher Ames said of the editor, "No printer was ever so *correct* in his politics." Jefferson and Madison quickly founded a rival voice, the *National Gazette,* edited by the poet, Philip Freneau. Hamilton, writing under a pseudonym, attacked Jefferson in the *Gazette of the United States,* and Jefferson's allies counterattacked in the *National Gazette* with verbal darts at Hamilton.

After Jefferson left the cabinet in 1794, Edmund Randolph, former Attorney General, became Secretary of State. But Randolph was the only Republican in Washington's circle; all of the others were Federalists dominated by Hamilton. And before long Randolph was forced to resign when the British produced papers sug-

Historical Society of Pennsylvania.

Philip Freneau
(1752–1832)

An ardent Jeffersonian, Philip Freneau was the editor of the Democratic-Republican newspaper, the *National Gazette.* In its lively pages Freneau subjected Jefferson's enemy, Alexander Hamilton, to the most biting vilification. Hamilton was so incensed that he personally penned an attack on Jefferson and his "hireling."

Freneau was clearly in Jefferson's employ. In his characteristically subtle manner, Jefferson hired Freneau to translate documents for the State Department at a salary of $250 a year. Jefferson assured Freneau the work was so minimal that the translator would have time to pursue "any other calling." The unspecified "calling" Jefferson had in mind was publishing a Republican newspaper. When a Philadelphia printer put up the money for the endeavor, Freneau obliged his patron and in 1791 established the *National Gazette.* In its pages he not only cut Hamilton to ribbons but also praised Jefferson as "that illustrious Patriot, Statesman and Philosopher." Hamilton became so angry that he begged President Washington to choose between him and Jefferson. Washington persuaded the two cabinet ministers to remain in office—but the newspaper war continued at full force until 1793, when a yellow fever epidemic drove Freneau out of Philadelphia and forced the *National Gazette* to close its doors.

Although his work as a newspaper editor had the greatest effect on his fellow Americans, Freneau had the reputation of being "the poet of the American Revolution." Indeed, as early as 1771 he wrote a poem entitled "The Rising Glory of America" prophesying American independence. And after a ghastly period as a political prisoner aboard a British vessel during the war, Freneau published *The British Prison-Ship: A Poem in Four Cantoes* (1781). In still other lyrics he celebrated American military victories against the British.

Yet it was as a journalist that he promoted most effectively his highly emotional version of Jeffersonian democracy. In fact, Jefferson himself said that Freneau's editorials "saved our Constitution, which was galloping fast into monarchy." ■

gesting he might have been involved in questionable dealings with the French.

The British gave the incriminating papers to Washington in order to turn the administration against France and ensure endorsement of Jay's Treaty. During the congressional investigation of the treaty, Hamilton insinuated that Madison launched this review of the administration to embarrass Washington. Hamilton's followers flooded Congress with petitions supporting the President. So exalted was Washington's reputation that Madison lost considerable Republican support in Congress. Washington was so distressed by the fighting that he dismissed his entire cabinet—but he could not find replacements not aligned with a party. Instead, his new cabinet was dominated by supporters of Hamilton who consulted their out-of-position but not out-of-power leader.

The Adams Administration

In the election of 1796, John Adams became the second President of the United States and Jefferson, as the runner-up, Vice President. The campaign brought factionalism out into the open, both between and within parties. Adams refused to campaign openly and was the choice of most Federalists, some of whom did not like Hamilton. Meanwhile, Hamilton backed Thomas Pinckney of South Carolina who, he thought, might undercut Jefferson's support in the Electoral College; however, this maneuver failed.

Party spirit of the times should not obscure more important signs of harmony. In September 1796, Washington framed his famous "Farewell Address," a valedictory statement explaining why he would not seek a third term and counseling all Americans on steps to be taken in the future. He cautioned against the dangers of the party system, stressed all citizens must obey the Constitution, and warned against permenent alliances with foreign powers, especially European states, which had "a set of primary interests" and are "engaged in frequent controversies, the causes of which are essentially foreign to our concerns." With these words, later frequently quoted by isolationists to support their views, Washington charted a foreign policy course adhered to for a century and a half. He also bequeathed to his successor an adequate bureaucratic system.

Nevertheless, Adams inherited a far from peaceful situation. His Vice President was captain of the opposi-

Courtesy Massachusetts Historical Society.

Courtesy Massachusetts Historical Society.

John and Abigail Adams, whose portraits were done early in their married life by Benjamin Blythe, found themselves caught in a torrent of partisanship while presiding over the nation. It alienated them from old friends such as Mercy Warren and Thomas Jefferson.

tion party and his cabinet, dominated by friends of Alexander Hamilton, wasted little affection on Adams. And the world situation was even more perilous. The French government was far from satisfied with the American policy of neutrality, having expected the United States to grant it the status of most-favored nation. Instead, the Americans signed the pro-British Jay's Treaty. In retaliation, France began to seize American ships bound for British ports. Moreover, the French began to treat Americans serving on British ships as pirates.

This turn of events of course delighted Hamilton and his allies, the High Federalists, who hoped the United States would declare war on France—a step that would place America firmly in the British camp, where Hamilton believed his country's material interests would be best served. Adams, however, opted for a more moderate policy. The new President sent three men to France, though the trio he chose seemed unlikely to secure a peaceful settlement. John Marshall was a well-known Federalists and an enemy of Jefferson and Madison. Charles Cotesworth Pinckney was a leading South Carolina Federalist and older brother of Thomas Pinckney. The third member of the delegation, Elbridge Gerry, was a nominal Federalist but acceptable to Jefferson.

At the same time, Adams announced that he intended to prepare for war by strengthening coastal defenses, arming merchant vessels, and building a provisional navy. The Jeffersonians suspected, and quite correctly, that the Hamiltonian wing of the Federalist party wanted war with France, not only to cement the English alliance but also to use as a pretext for suppressing the Democratic-Republican Party. If war broke out, the Federalists could denounce the Republicans for their French leanings and invoke patriotism as an excuse for outlawing the rival party.

The American mission to France ended in disaster. Talleyrand, the French Minister of Foreign Affairs, devised a clever way of lining his pockets—extortion. He routinely required foreigners to bribe him in order to receive an appointment. To the Americans he sent three of his agents (later referred to by Adams in a report to Congress as X, Y, and Z); the agents said they could arrange for a meeting with Talleyrand if the United States would pay him $250,000 under the counter and lend the French government $12 million. "Not a sixpence," Pinckney declared. He and Marshall returned to America, leaving behind Gerry, whose passport Talleyrand withheld. Because Gerry stayed in France other Federalists shunned him when he finally returned to America in 1798, though he was able to supply Adams with useful information that helped to avert war.

Library of Congress.

The building of the frigate *Philadelphia* was part of the United States's efforts to protect the nation's honor at sea during the troubled 1790s.

The Alien and Sedition Acts

The XYZ Affair seemed to make war with France inevitable and opened the way to suppress the opposition to government policy as treasonous. President Adams suddenly became a national hero, and the most popular songs were "Adams and Liberty" and "The President's March." Indignation against the French—and the pro-French Republicans—was so strong that Federalist leaders were able to persuade Congress to appropriate money to build up the army and the navy and to pass legislation designed to crush all opposition.

These measures, known as the Alien and Sedition Acts, were defended as necessary wartime laws. Two of the alien acts hit hard at part of Jefferson's growing constituency—newly arrived Americans. The time for naturalization (and therefore for voting) was increased from five to fourteen years and the President was empowered to imprison or deport foreigners in time of war. Adams signed the bill, but did not like its provisions and made no concerted attempt to enforce them.

More serious was the Sedition Act of 1798, which curtailed freedom of the press. The law defined sedition as uttering or writing or printing any false, scandalous, or malicious opinions about the government or the President. The government indicted fifteen offenders under the Sedition Act and convicted and punished ten of them. All four of the leading Republican newspapers were attacked and the three most influential Republican editors were convicted of wrongdoing.

Prosecutions under the act were highly selective. The

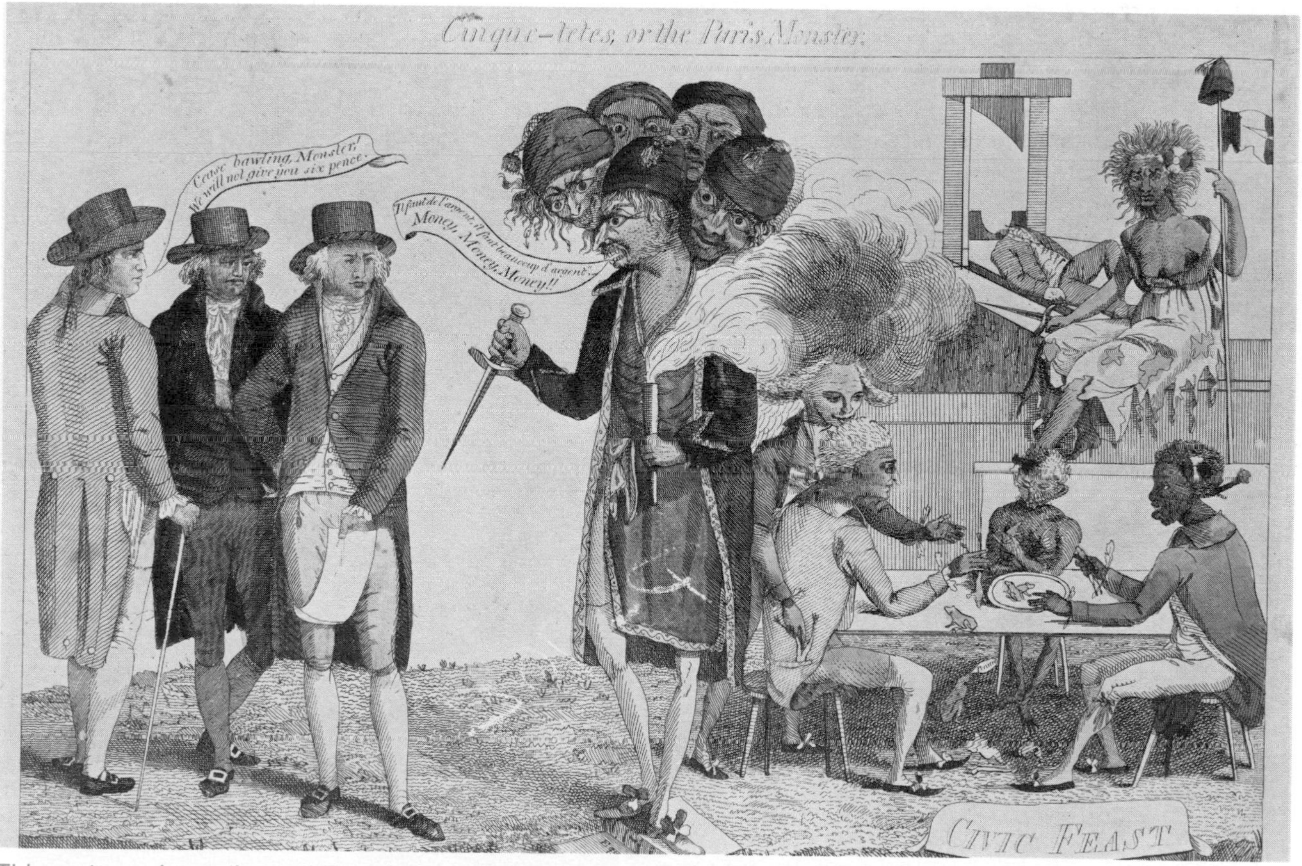

This cartoon shows the anti-French feeling following the XYZ Affair. The three American ministers reject the French demand for money. The black at the table is to remind people of the rebellion on Haiti.

Henry E. Huntington Library and Art Gallery.

first victim was Mathew Lyon, a Vermont congressman, charged with having questioned the government's French policies. Lyon was convicted, assessed a fine of $1,000, and sentenced to four months in jail. Despite the conviction, his constituents reelected him.

The courts, with Federalist judges presiding, willingly went along with the trials. The Democratic-Republicans reacted with outrage. Jefferson and Madison persuaded the legislatures of Virginia and Kentucky to pass resolutions stressing that states had the right to oppose clearly unconstitutional federal laws. The Republicans resorted to the state legislatures because the Supreme Court had not yet established its practice of declaring laws unconstitutional—not that the Federalist court of the time would have judged the laws unconstitutional in any event. Although the Virginia and Kentucky resolutions dramatized Jefferson's alarm, the acts endangered the whole federal system by investing the states with extraordinary power. Fortunately for the health of the central government, no other states followed suit.

Washington reluctantly agreed to come out of retirement to command the army, but only if a true emergency arose. Many officers asked for commissions but few privates enlisted, and popular opinion gradually turned against the war. Jefferson and his followers, certain that the troops raised were being trained to attack his Virginia supporters, began to arm and drill an army of their own to repel a Federalist invasion.

When Gerry returned in 1798, he informed Adams that the French did not want to fight and would negotiate a treaty. Adam's son, John Quincy Adams, sent the same news home from Europe, as did the American minister to England, Rufus King. Adams, sensing that Americans did not favor war and growing more suspicious of Hamilton's motives for promoting hostilities, sent a new minister, William Murray, to France.

The High Federalists exploded with fury, certain that by removing the threat of war Adams had destroyed his party's chances of winning the election of 1800, although rank-and-file Federalists supported him strongly. Jeffersonians, of course, were delighted. As for the President, he said simply, "The end of war is peace—and peace was offered me." Murray and two other Americans worked out an agreement with the French (the Convention of 1801), but Adams had stirred up discord within his own party. Hamilton's wing of the Federalists denounced this shift of policy to no avail. War had been avoided, and Adams was once again immensely popular with the people.

An Exciting Generation

Anyone born in America in the 1770s had, by 1800, witnessed momentous events: war, victory, development of a struggling little republic (first under the Articles of Confederation, then under the Constitution), and a dramatic turnover of political parties. But, as interesting as independence from Britain and creation of a functioning new government might be for the average American, social changes of that era undoubtedly were of much greater importance.

The Revolution improved the lot of the common man in some measure. Independence opened up the West for settlement and created new opportunities in business, the army, and government. In a practical sense, the right to vote had little immediate impact, but in time men such as Thomas Jefferson would lead political upheavals that demonstrated the true worth of the ballot. What impact independence had upon the status of specific groups

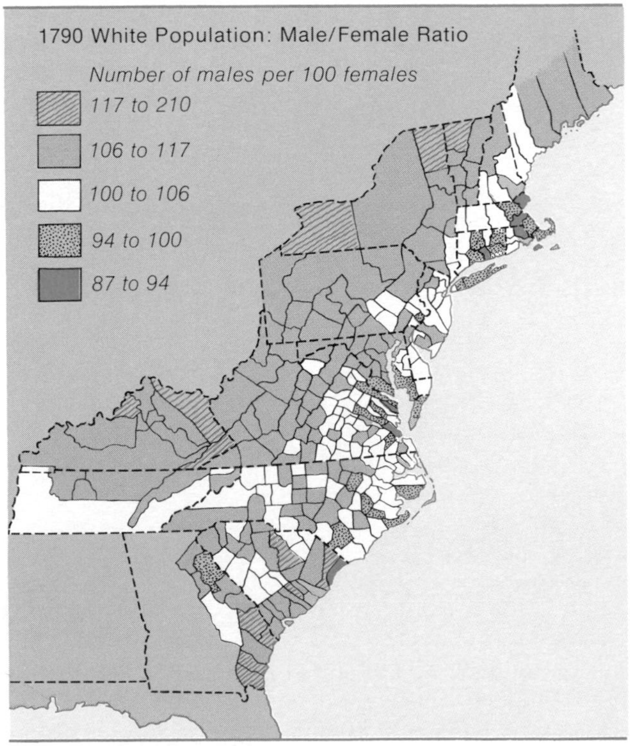

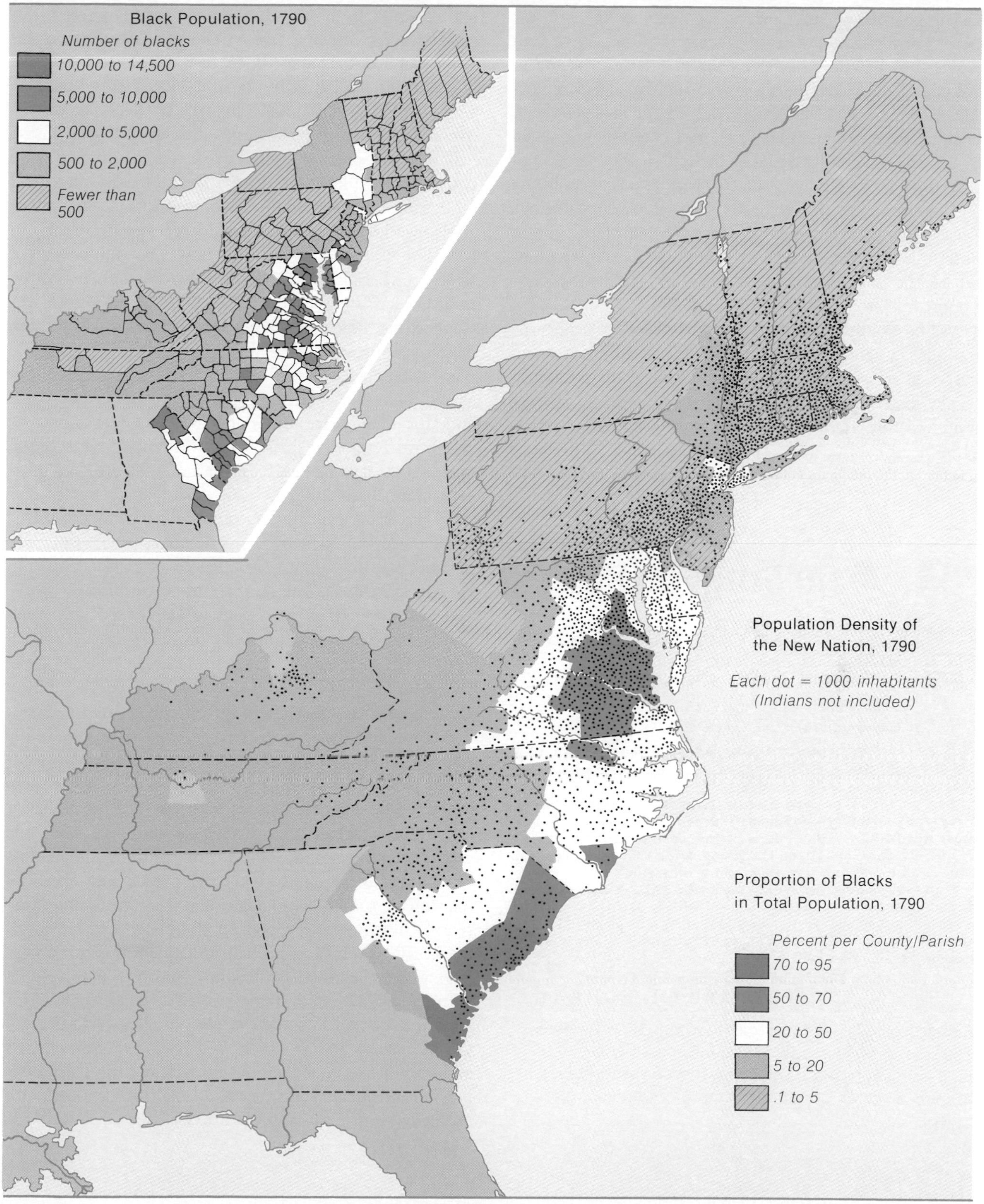

Black Population, 1790
Number of blacks
10,000 to 14,500
5,000 to 10,000
2,000 to 5,000
500 to 2,000
Fewer than 500
Population Density of the New Nation, 1790
Each dot = 1000 inhabitants
(Indians not included)
Proportion of Blacks in Total Population, 1790
Percent per County/Parish
70 to 95
50 to 70
20 to 50
5 to 20
.1 to 5

within colonial society such as women and slaves is less clear. During much of the eighteenth century, American women worked hard on farms and in small shops, and in colonial days they were not specifically barred from voting. However, as the colonies matured, the role of women became more ornamental. True, more academies opened to "educate" young women of the well-to-do classes, but there they learned how to sew, to speak and write politely, and to appreciate the decorative arts. State constitutions denied them the suffrage (the last women of this era to vote in New Jersey did so in 1806), and as shops moved out of the home and became factories, women had less opportunity to learn meaningful trades.

The Founding Fathers had mixed feelings concerning slavery since they believed in class differences and harbored racist views. Nevertheless, all of them thought legal equality a prerequisite for the preservation of freedom and thus found themselves on the horns of a troublesome dilemma. Slavery, in short, made them very uncomfortable. Pennsylvania approved a system of gradual abolition in 1780: adult slaves were not freed, but their children became free at the age of twenty-eight. Soon Connecticut and Rhode Island followed suit, the latter deciding all children born to slaves after March 1, 1784, would automatically be free. A year earlier the Massachusetts Supreme Court, noting that the phrase "all men are created equal" appeared in the new state constitution, ruled that slavery did not exist there. All other states, except South Carolina and Georgia, either abolished the institution or considered steps to modify it.

The trend of the times, however, did not favor widespread abolition. Owners of blacks were convinced they needed their labor, a view that became more entrenched as the Cotton Kingdom expanded, after 1800. Moreover, no one came forward to propose a feasible plan of compensation if slaves were set free. Also, ex-slaves themselves showed no wish to migrate to Africa and, for their part, few states welcomed ex-slaves or runaways with open arms. What was to become the great question of the nineteenth century only festered and grew ever more threatening.

The American Revolution, strangely enough, seems to have isolated women on a pedestal and sown the seeds of more, not less slavery for American blacks. Growing economic wealth created a male-oriented business world and westward expansion, a demand for cheap labor which half of the nation thought only unfree blacks could satisfy.

Economic problems fostered by that conflict at first seemed insurmountable. No longer could American captains trade legally with the British empire, especially the rich islands of the West Indies. Other European nations either prohibited numerous U.S. exports or taxed them heavily. These regulations hit tobacco, long the mainstay of Southern agriculture, extremely hard. In 1783 the young republic had some four million inhabitants (700,000 of them slaves) widely dispersed and served by inadequate roads, few banks, and an unworkable currency. Only a decade or so later conditions had improved markedly. Several factors help to explain this turnabout, among them shrewd leadership, Europe's involvement with its own affairs, and unexpected wartime demand for American goods. As some citizens plunged westward into the wilderness and as others began to develop factories and mills to serve a growing population, the nation expanded and grew strong. It was an exciting age beset with problems, but it was also a time rich with promise.

Library of Congress.

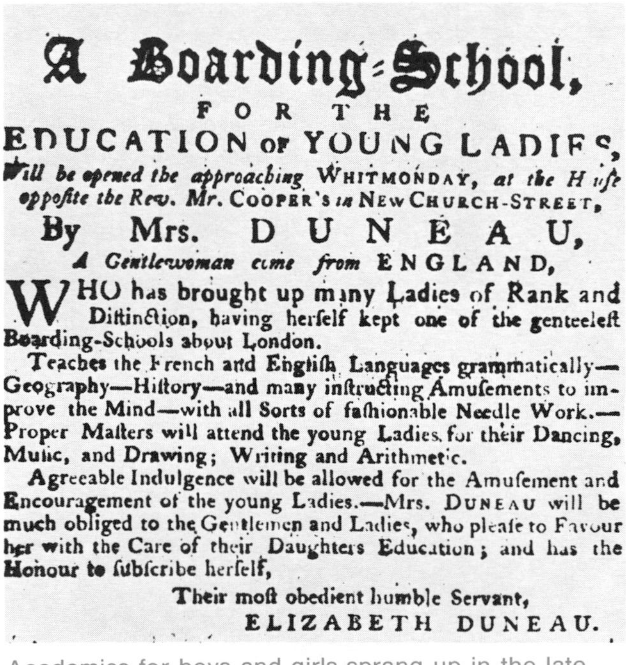

A Boarding-School,
FOR THE
EDUCATION OF YOUNG LADIES,
Will be opened the approaching WHITMONDAY, at the House opposite the Rev. Mr. COOPER'S in NEW CHURCH-STREET,
By Mrs. DUNEAU,
A Gentlewoman come from ENGLAND,

WHO has brought up many Ladies of Rank and Diſtinction, having herſelf kept one of the genteeleſt Boarding-Schools about London.

Teaches the French and Engliſh Languages grammatically—Geography—Hiſtory—and many inſtructing Amuſements to improve the Mind—with all Sorts of faſhionable Needle Work.—Proper Maſters will attend the young Ladies for their Dancing, Muſic, and Drawing; Writing and Arithmetic.

Agreeable Indulgence will be allowed for the Amuſement and Encouragement of the young Ladies.—Mrs. DUNEAU will be much obliged to the Gentlemen and Ladies, who pleaſe to Favour her with the Care of their Daughters Education; and has the Honour to ſubſcribe herſelf,

Their moſt obedient humble Servant,
ELIZABETH DUNEAU.

Academies for boys and girls sprang up in the late 18th century. This advertisement makes clear that girls of middle and upper class figures were being trained more as ornaments than as practical helpmeets.

Courtesy New-York Historical Society, New York City.

Phillis Wheatley
(1753–1784)

The first black woman poet in America, Phillis Wheatley was born in Africa but brought to the United States as a little girl. In Boston she was bought as a slave by John Wheatley, who raised her with his other children as a virtual equal. At least Wheatley, his wife, and family taught the girl to read and write with such diligence that after sixteen months of instruction Phillis was able to compose verses. She ate with the family and was admitted as a member of their church. In a period when many Americans considered blacks to be inherently inferior intellectually, Phillis attracted much curiosity. Her conversation was brilliant, her writing skillful, her personality charming.

In 1773 she traveled to England, where she was a guest of the Countess of Huntington, who arranged for the publication of a volume of Phillis's writing, *Poems on Various Subjects, Religious and Moral.* But the young poet's triumph was brief. She was recalled to America to attend the dying Mrs. Wheatley. When John Wheatley also died soon afterwards, the young woman was left destitute and friendless. She married a free black to whom she bore three children, but the husband periodically deserted her, and two of the three children died in infancy.

Phillis Wheatley and her remaining child died in Boston on December 5, 1784, where she had worked in a boardinghouse. Two years after her death the first American edition of her poems was published. ■

Essay

Banking—Money, Confidence, Boom, and Bust.

Americans of every generation have often viewed banking as a mysterious, secretive enterprise, especially when bank doors have failed to open and savings, diligently accumulated, have disappeared. Banks deal in money—other people's money—and this naturally arouses suspicions and fears; yet, the basic commodities in which every successful bank must deal are not really money and financial services but confidence and trust. Metallic money (coins of specie) has intrinsic value: it contains so much gold, copper, or silver. Paper money is, for all practical purposes, virtually worthless; nevertheless, paper notes and bills come in much higher denominations and are more highly prized because of the confidence that bankers, merchants, and customers have in them.

With the beginning of centralized government in 1789, some Americans realized the need for a national bank. According to the Constitution, the Congress, and not the states, now had the sole power to produce coins and to regulate their value. The worth of state bank notes, bits of paper promising to pay a certain amount upon demand, would be influenced directly by two factors: the value of federal coins (since presumably one could exchange a note for hard money) and the faith of the general public in those state-run institutions. In 1791, Alexander Hamilton engineered the establishment of the First Bank of the United States with a twenty-year charter. At that time four other banks were operating in the nation: in Baltimore, Philadelphia, New York, and Boston. Public institutions in which the state might be a major stockholder and wield considerable influence, they had come into being because mercantile houses needed credit to carry on their operations. Unlike their European counterparts, American businessmen lacked capital. Short-term loans at so much interest took the place of capital, made profits for the bank and its stockholders, and oiled the wheels of commerce—and so long as customers who received goods paid their bills on time, merchants could meet their obligations to bankers.

Hamilton's bank, a mix of public and private interests like others of its day and modeled after the prestigious Bank of England, was an extremely successful financial enterprise. During its lifetime it loaned the national government $13.5 million, and the United States of America realized a profit of

Library of Congress.

The First Bank of the United States was an imposing structure when this engraving appeared in 1799. Its pre-eminence in American finance was as notable as its overshadowing of nearby buildings.

$700,000 when the stock it held was sold. The First Bank of the United States opened eight branches in coastal cities, but it was primarily a commercial undertaking that was unable (or unwilling) to meet the needs of the agricultural frontier. People living there required long-term credit extending over several seasons, not fast, thirty-day loans. To satisfy local needs such as these, scores of little banks appeared, especially in new states and territories, which granted loans so freely that the central bank would not back up their notes when a bad crop created pressures that often ruined both customers and bankers.

These failures aroused the enmity of the Jeffersonians who concentrated their wrath on Hamilton's bank; and, in 1811 they refused to extend its life, although the Senate vote was so close that the Vice President had to vote to break a tie. However, five years later, sobered by the sudden growth of numerous wildcat banks and wartime inflation, Congress chartered the Second Bank of the United States, another twenty-year institution. It was located in Philadelphia and quickly had sixteen branches, eleven of them south or west of the central office.

This bank, like its predecessor, soon got into trouble. At first it followed a loose, liberal policy, which was favored by the western expansionists and led to disaster; then, under Nicholas Biddle (1786–1844), the bank charted a much more conservative course, which pleased the East and also brought on disaster. To Andrew Jackson of Tennessee, the bank was a monopoly using

"I leave this great people prosperous and happy" — Manager's last kick
Roman Firmness
6 CENTS
"Better Currency"
Hickory Leaf.
HUMBUG GLORY BANK
SIX CENTS in mint drops or Glory at cost
Cunning Reuben Cash'r
Honest Amos Pres't
"In seven months from this time bank rags shall be abolished—Globe of 1834.
6
6

Courtesy New-York Historical Society, New York City.

This fake bill is actually poking fun at the attempts of Jackson to destroy the Second National Bank and rely instead on state banks. Note the use of the donkey and the hickory leaf.

the people's money to make a few rich men richer and the common man poorer. This question got entangled in the election of 1832. President Jackson handily won reelection that year, and the Second Bank of the United States was doomed. To extend its charter was politically impossible, no matter how well the bank might have been functioning. After 1836, that institution continued to operate as a state bank until it folded in 1841.

During these same years (1837–1842), the nation experienced a major financial panic, its worst depression up to that time. This downturn was fed by crop failures, unpaid loans, dizzy state debts created to build roads, canals, and railroads—up from $13 million in 1820 to $200 million in 1840—and unprecedented sales of public lands that rose from $2 million in 1830 to $30 million in 1836. These land sales so alarmed Jackson that he issued the specie circular in July 1836, requiring all payments to be made in gold and silver coin. This action eroded confidence in paper money and merely added to the nation's economic woes.

To replace the second national bank, Martin Van Buren, Jackson's handpicked successor, set up a network of subtreasuries designed to collect revenues, disburse government funds, promote the circulation of hard currency in various regions of the country, and discourage state banks from issuing excessive amounts of paper money. Although discontinued for a few years, this scheme functioned reasonably well, especially if

Courtesy New-York Historical Society, New York City.

Jackson's supporters also used cartoons. Here Jackson destroys the bank while his political foes run to save themselves and moan the loss of bribes and fees from the bank.

times were good, from 1846 to 1913 when it became part of the Federal Reserve System.

During the 1850s some states began to exert more control over banks, requiring them to keep a certain amount of specie on hand or prohibiting them from issuing small notes of $5 or less. More important was the development of clearinghouses in financial centers such as Boston and New York. Every business day each bank in the city would present drafts or checks drawn on money deposited in other local banks and receive credit for the total amount. If all checks drawn on the Bank of New York, for example, exceeded the amount it presented in checks, then it had to pay the difference to the clearinghouse; if not, it got the balance in cash. The obvious advantage was to reduce substantially the amount of currency changing hands from bank to bank.

It should be noted that many other business transactions were carried on in much the same way. Merchants and customers frequently maintained long-standing accounts that included debits and credits, goods supplied by the merchant and produce delivered as payment by customers. Money was used only to settle up such accounts. The best example of this sort of exchange would be a rural storekeeper who, although he issued no notes and was not a banker in the true sense of the word, often functioned as one in communities lacking financial institutions. His store was a sort of primitive clearinghouse where—since money, notes, and checks were unknown to many of his customers—a local commerce was carried on, and perhaps even flourished, by bargain and barter.

Despite centralized operations in the East and the subtreasury scheme, banking continued to be a scoundrel's dream and a merchant's nightmare beyond the Appalachians. Some Indiana "banks" had no capital, no office, no deposits, no assets, and no liabilities—only the plates needed to print paper money. The owner of those plates might never set foot in the state of Indiana—and perhaps that was just as well since those stuck with his currency probably would not have been too hospitable. Wisconsin for a time boasted of "George Smith's money." Smith headed an insurance company that had no right to issue notes, but did. That money, highly prized and easily converted to coin, traded at par value and for years was the best currency in that region. Most bank notes, however, were discounted somewhat, the percentage often related directly to the distance from point of issue. New bills without holes were especially suspect, but old tattered bits of paper, soiled and riddled with the imprint of scores of filing pins, usually were treated with considerable respect.

More sophisticated services such as the New York clearinghouse, state banks, commercial transactions arranged by the local storekeeper, and even "George Smith's money" fitted well the divergent needs of an expanding nation as long as times were good. But when times turned bad or conditions in the marketplace were made chaotic by war or threats of war, this financial system—if one can call it that—functioned poorly indeed.

The United States entered the Civil War with some 1,600 banks and nearly 7,000 different kinds and denominations of notes. Since state laws were far from uniform and no central place of redemption existed, most of these notes were discounted by varying amounts whenever they were used in financial transactions. Both the North and the South chose to finance the war largely by loans, and the federal government quickly faced a series of crises that brought about major changes in both money and banking. Late in 1861, the U.S. Treasury discovered that hard money (especially gold coins) was in such short supply that it suspended payment in that medium.

This caused considerable hardship, and for a time postage stamps doubled as small change. Then, in 1862 and again in 1863, the federal government issued "greenback" notes, so-called because of green ink used on the reverse side. Unlike all previous federal issues, these bits of paper, which circulated as currency, bore no interest, could not be redeemed in coin, and appeared only in small denominations.

In an effort to sell bonds to finance the war, the government took other giant steps. A national bank act granted federal charters to private banks so long as they held enough government bonds to back up whatever notes were issued. These notes, underwritten by federal authority, circulated at a uniform exchange rate. At the same time, a federal tax of ten percent was imposed on state bank notes, killing them in effect. These measures did not eliminate state banks, which could be organized more cheaply than national banks. They continued to serve as loan agencies, centers for deposit, and clearinghouses for checks and other commercial paper. In short, after seven decades of discount disarray, Civil War legislation brought uniform currency regulations, although banks operating under both state and national charters continued to function side by side. By 1890, state banks even outnumbered national banks since checking account operations, which they could easily handle, nearly doubled during the last half of the nineteenth century.

During those years, especially from 1870 to 1900, money moved to the forefront as a political issue, largely because of a steady downward trend in prices favoring creditors and squeezing those contracting loans to be repaid at fixed sums. A farmer who got a ten-year bank loan for $1,000 at six percent discovered that, as what he received for his crops dwindled, he had to sell perhaps twice as much wheat and corn to repay the banker. To a large extent the creditors of the nation lived in the industrial East, the debtors in the agricultural West. Money panics in 1873, 1893, and 1907, augmented by William Jennings Bryan's famous "Free Silver" campaign of 1896, underscored one vital fact: money was not well distributed throughout the country. The currency supply was not elastic and did not flow automatically to areas where it was needed.

In an effort to solve such problems, in 1913 the Federal Reserve Act divided the nation into twelve districts, setting up a branch bank in each one, the whole apparatus presided over by a board of governors in Washington. This system is composed of all national banks and those state banks that wish to join. These branches are, of course, "bankers' banks" and do not deal directly with the public. Only about half of the banks in America are associated with the Federal Reserve System, but they control the bulk of all deposits. In an effort to avert panics, each one must maintain certain reserves with the branch facility in its district. Presumably, in time of crisis, these funds can be loaned to member banks in need of support.

However, the Great Depression that began in 1929 proved too great a burden. During 1932 some 1,400 banks failed, and in 1933 various states declared "bank holidays," that is, a closing down of all banks for a few days. Shortly after becoming President, Franklin D. Roosevelt made this holiday nationwide in scope. Within ten days about half of the banks reopened under new regulations; soon others followed suit under the watchful eyes of "conservators." About one thousand banks, roughly five percent, shut their doors for good.

Within the next few months several reform measures appeared. Most notable among them was the Federal Deposit Insurance Corporation (FDIC) created by the Banking Act of 1933, which insured individual deposits in all Federal Reserve member banks and in non member banks that qualified. Originally each deposit was insured for up to $5,000, but that figure has now been increased to $40,000. Today very few banks are not under FDIC regulations, and nearly all accounts are completely covered.

Yet federal supervision and an expanding economy such as America has enjoyed for most of the years since World War II are no guarantees against failure. Banks, after all, are competing business ventures that happen to deal in money and financial services. They are run by men and women who sometimes make mistakes such as overexpanding, extending loans to poor risks, or investing in projects that flounder. Sins of this sort caught up with New York's Franklin National Bank in October 1974. But, unlike 1933, there was no loss to depositors and no panic.

At its prime, the Franklin National Bank had assets totaling $5 billion, making it the twentieth largest of some 14,000 institutions insured by FDIC. When the Franklin informed the Federal Reserve Board that it was throwing in the towel, the FDIC immediately approved a take-over by another bank. The European-American Bank & Trust Company, which bid successfully for Franklin's assets and liabilities and agreed to invest $125 million into it, opened all branches for business the day after the Franklin closed. Hastily printed window cards were the only indication of change seen by depositors, their funds fully protected by the FDIC.

There is, of course, one common theme throughout the history of banking in America, in good times and bad, and that is the need to maintain the confidence of the customer. "George Smith's money" from Wisconsin was sounder, so long as people believed in it, than the $1.6 billion in assets that the Franklin had as it went under (its liabilities totaled \$1.7 billion). Huge foreign losses and a declining record of profits since 1970 finally put the Franklin on the rocks. Even rumors of financial difficulty, true or not, can be fatal. A banker deals in money, but if a customer does not believe he knows how to handle it well, or is doing a poor job, the customer and his money go elsewhere—and eventually so does the banker.

Selected Readings

Confederation Period

Forest McDonald, *We the People: Economic Origins of the Constitution* (1958)
Merrill Jensen, *The New Nation: a History of the United States during the Confederation* (1959)
Jackson T. Main, *Political Parties before the Constitution* (1973)
James Ferguson, *The Power of the Purse* (1961)
Curtis Nettles, *Emergence of a National Economy, 1775–1815* (1962)

Constitution Making

Leonard Levy, ed., *Essays on the Making of the Constitution* (1969)
Gordon Wood, *The Creation of the American Republic* (1969)
Max Farrand, *The Framing of the Constitution of the United States* (1913)
Jackson T. Main, *The Anti-Federalists* (1961)
Linda De Pauw, *Eleventh Pillar: New York and the Federal Constitution* (1966)
Robert Rutland, *The Birth of the Bill of Rights* (1955)

Federalists in Power

John C. Miller, *The Federalist Era, 1789–1801* (1960)
Richard B. Morris, *John Jay, the Nation and the Court* (1967)
Leonard White, *The Federalists* (1948)
Stephen Kurtz, *The Presidency of John Adams: the Collapse of Federalism, 1795–1800* (1957)
James M. Smith, *Freedom's Fetters: Alien and Sedition Laws* (1956)
Reginald Horsman, *Expansion and American Indian Policy* (1967)

Diplomacy

Samuel Bemis, *Pinckney's Treaty,* rev. ed. (1960)
Alexander De Conde, *Entangling Alliance: Politics and Diplomacy under Washington* (1958)
Bradford Perkins, *First Rapprochment: England and the United States 1795–1805* (1955)

Adolescent America

Chapter 6

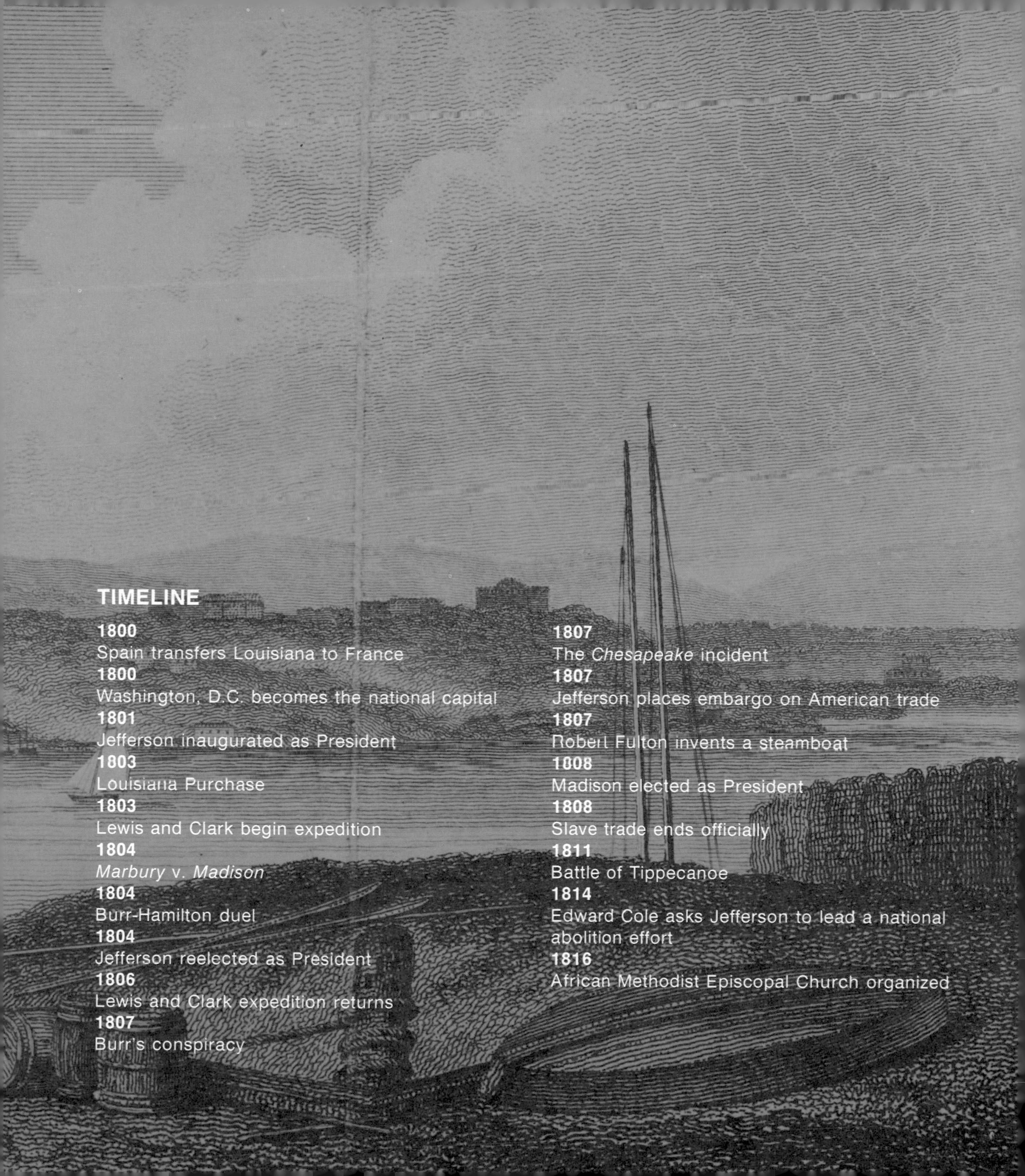

TIMELINE

1800
Spain transfers Louisiana to France
1800
Washington, D.C. becomes the national capital
1801
Jefferson inaugurated as President
1803
Louisiana Purchase
1803
Lewis and Clark begin expedition
1804
Marbury v. *Madison*
1804
Burr-Hamilton duel
1804
Jefferson reelected as President
1806
Lewis and Clark expedition returns
1807
Burr's conspiracy
1807
The *Chesapeake* incident
1807
Jefferson places embargo on American trade
1807
Robert Fulton invents a steamboat
1808
Madison elected as President
1808
Slave trade ends officially
1811
Battle of Tippecanoe
1814
Edward Cole asks Jefferson to lead a national abolition effort
1816
African Methodist Episcopal Church organized

CHAPTER OUTLINE

The years from 1800–1812 were among the most difficult and exhilarating our nation has experienced. The Revolution was now history, and the problems of the United States were those of adolescence and youth. The republic was, in fact, a gangling youngster, brash, boastful, secretly unsure, but brimming with outward confidence, bright dreams, and high hopes. At home there was an unexpected turnover in political leadership, the first time that "the rascals were thrown out," a development which those who framed the Constitution had not anticipated and one which raised hard, serious questions. Would Jefferson and his followers try to reshape the national government? Could they change policies and programs set into motion by the revered Washington and his successor, Adams? Might they, for example, gain control of the courts by removing judges from the bench? How many jobs could they fill—or, to put it another way, how many Federalists could they toss out?

The international scene presented considerable danger. A general European war spilled over into the Americas from time to time, resulting in heated words, bloodshed, and seizure of numerous American ships and many seamen. The British, who seemed bent upon reversing the decision at Yorktown and the Peace of Paris (1783), treated the former colonies like wayward children, not as an independent nation. France, England's chief rival, and Spain as well regarded the young republic with almost equal disdain, using their influence in North America and on the high seas to enhance their power at home at the expense of various enemies.

Key problems faced by Jefferson and Madison were how to keep the United States both neutral and prosperous (international commerce was a prerequisite for general prosperity even though the man from Monticello sometimes tried to ignore this fact), how to thwart disunion fomented by various European powers with designs on territories in the Mississippi and Ohio River basins, and how to convince the disgruntled Federalist opposition that they were not madmen incapable of running a government. How both of these Virginians reacted to these crises was of utmost importance. Like Washington and Adams before them, they were pathfinders who were setting vital precedents. Their decisions and what they did might well determine whether the adolescent ever would attain maturity.

A New Party Takes Over

"Let us then fellow citizens unite with one heart and mind, let us restore to social intercourse that harmony and affection without which liberty, and even life itself are but dreary things. . . . But every difference of opinion is not a difference of principle. We have called by different names brethern of the same principle. We are all republicans; we are all federalists." This call to reconciliation in Thomas Jefferson's first inaugural address was in response to the bitter partisan battle of 1800, an election which reminded Americans that they truly had embarked on an amazing experiment in government. That campaign was disturbing to many Americans not only because it whipped up partisan furies and dire predictions of doom should candidates of the opposing side prevail, but also because it demonstrated an unpalatable truth. The leaders of competing political organizations are most likely to make decisions based on the needs of their party, not on those of the nation as a whole.

Both Thomas Jefferson and his opponent, John Adams were nominated by a congressional caucus, the first procedure devised for placing presidential candidates before the public. In 1796, once Washington announced he would not seek a third term, the Federalists in Congress met secretly and agreed to support John Adams and Thomas Pinckney for President and Vice President. The Jeffersonian Republicans then convened and named Thomas Jefferson and Aaron Burr as a rival slate. Four years later members of the two parties who held seats in Congress met openly, not in secret, and pledged their support to Adams and Charles Cotesworth Pinckney and, once more, to Jefferson and Burr. Jefferson, of course, was then Vice President, having defeated Thomas Pinckney for that office in 1796. During the next two decades, the congressional caucus system controlled by two political parties faced mounting criticism; many thought it was virtually unconstitutional—or at best undemocratic—for representatives and senators to nominate presidential candidates without consulting the electorate. In 1824 only about a fourth of the members of Congress attended a caucus that nominated William H. Crawford as the Republican candidate for President. This was the last such meeting ever held. During the succeeding decade, the more familiar national convention system developed.

Adams campaigned for reelection by being President and carrying out established Federalist programs. Jefferson, who lacked oratorical talents, disclosed his political views in letters to friends, who then dispersed them to an eager populace that came to see him as the spokesman for the common people and Adams as the representative of men of property, portraits that are much too simplified. Although both John Adams and Thomas Jefferson believed fervently in an independent United States of America under a constitution that promoted liberty and preserved order, disagreement over the means to such goals interrupted a long friendship, which was renewed only when both were very elderly statesmen.

There are numerous reasons for the defeat of Adams, a proud, doughty patriot. Among them were Federalist moves that alienated large blocks of voters (Hamilton's fiscal measures, the Whiskey Rebellion fracas, the Alien and Sedition Acts, and the alleged schemes to declare war on France) and among some of Hamilton's followers, there was strong opposition to Adams for his alleged weakness in dealing with France. In addition, the fractured Federalists failed to build up support among voters who had newly gained the franchise, especially among those lower-class and middle-class elements living outside of the Northeast. In short, they ignored changing conditions, and virtually committed political suicide.

This head-in-the-clouds (or sand) attitude not only caused a political turnabout with profound reverberations but it also produced something the men meeting at Philadelphia in 1787 had not anticipated: a tie in the Electoral College, where, according to the Constitution, the top votegetter would be President and whoever came in second, Vice President. An equal number of ballots (seventy-three) for Jefferson and Aaron Burr, ostensibly candidates for the presidency and the vice presidency on the Democratic-Republican ticket, threw the election into a lame-duck House where the Federalist opposition still wielded considerable power. Some of these disgruntled congressmen considered installing Burr as a puppet president, but after thirty-six ballots Jefferson won. Ironically, Jefferson's victory owed much to the efforts of Alexander Hamilton, who, as Burr's keenest rival in New York state, had told his followers to support Jefferson.

Although he disliked both men, who for long were his political foes, Hamilton respected his Virginia adversary much more than he did the unscrupulous, handsome Burr. Yet all this uproar and Burr's tragic downfall a few years later should not disguise a crucial fact: the winners had hit upon a political partnership that has demonstrated considerable power ever since—Southern agrarians hand-in-hand with urban politicians of the Northeast.

Having experienced two confusing national elections that put a President and Vice President of rival parties in office for four years and nearly turned a vice-presidential candidate into a President, the Congress decided something must be done. Before the next election the Twelfth Amendment to the Constitution was ratified; it was now clear that the electors must vote separately for the two offices and specify which position they were voting for. This amendment contains the intriguing provision that at least one of the men named on an elector's ballots "shall not be an inhabitant of the same state with themselves," an obvious rebuff to Virginia.

Benjamin Henry Latrobe (1764–1820)

Although the architect and engineer Benjamin Latrobe is most famous for his work on government buildings in Washington, D.C., he distinguished himself in many different fields of endeavor, including designs for private homes, urban waterworks, and state buildings, to say nothing of contributions to the development of waterways and steamboats.

After a classical education in Germany, Latrobe returned to his native England where he studied architecture under the Greek revival pioneer Samuel Pepys Cockerell and engineering under the equally well-known John Smeaton who had rebuilt the Eddystone Lighthouse. After the death of his wife in 1793, he emigrated to America, arriving in Norfolk in March 1796.

His first serious assignments in America were improvements in the navigational potential of the river near Richmond and improvements on the canals in the Dismal Swamp. After designing the Richmond penitentiary and completing the exterior of Thomas Jefferson's Virginia state capitol, he designed and supervised the construction of the Bank of Philadelphia. The bank, with its porticos of Ionic columns and templelike circular room topped with a dome and lantern, was the first Greek revival monument in the New World.

Latrobe's early work for the federal government included designs for a military academy and a dry dock for twelve sea-readied frigates. The office of Surveyor of the Public Buildings was created for him by Thomas Jefferson. His first task in that capacity was completion of the south wing of the Capitol. Latrobe raised substantial objections to William Thornton's plans; but, through a series of compromises, the two architects finished the wing.

Latrobe was responsible for the colonnaded terraces, the semicircular portico and the northern portico of the President's House; he remodeled the Patent Office and designed the Marine Hospital in Washington. Latrobe was commissioned to oversee the reconstruction of the Capitol and the President's House after their destruction by the British in 1814. After three years of work on these projects, a disagreement with the commissioner, Samuel Lane, caused Latrobe to resign.

The prolific Latrobe was responsible for countless private homes, churches, and monuments in Virginia, New York, Pennsylvania, and Louisiana. He died in New Orleans in 1820 of yellow fever while attempting to complete a lighthouse started by his son, who also died of yellow fever. ■

Jeffersonian Triumphs

The inauguration of the lanky, red-haired Jefferson on March 4, 1801, was the first such ceremony held in the raw, unfinished capital city of Washington, which was really only a village of woods, two or three pretentious public structures, and magnificent vistas. The scene reflected the state of the new nation as well. Streets were mere paths, muddy or dusty depending upon the season. A few rudimentary boardinghouses clustered around the Capitol provided basic shelter for congressmen and bureaucrats, most of whom yearned to return to the pleasures of New York or Philadelphia. Shortly before the election of 1800, John and Abigail Adams moved into the presidential mansion, which would soon be known as the White House. Like much of the city, it was unfinished, but they tried to maintain the elegant style set by their predecessors, the Washingtons, amid these crude, almost frontier surroundings.

On March 4, 1801, Thomas Jefferson rose at sunrise, soaked his feet in cold water for five minutes, washed, shaved, selected a green outfit with gray stockings and gray waistcoat, and went downstairs to breakfast in a boardinghouse located about a half hour's walk from the Capitol. The other boarders quietly awaited his arrival and tried to seat him in a place of honor at the head of a large common table, but he declined, noting he was about to become the president of a republic, not the sovereign of a kingdom.

To their surprise this fifty-eight-year-old Virginian did not ride to the Capitol in a carriage; he walked and rubbed shoulders with his fellow citizens along the way. In the Senate chamber there was a brief ceremony, not especially impressive. Those present included a few close friends and two men who were not: Chief Justice John Marshall, whose duty it was to administer the oath of office and Aaron Burr, the new Vice President, a man Jefferson did not trust. Among the missing were John Adams and nearly all of the Federalist congressmen who had hurried out of town rather than witness what they were certain were the initial death throes of the American dream.

The Cabinet

Although the Republican victory in effect witnessed the birth of a long-lasting and successful political partnership between Southern agrarians and urban politicians of the Northeast, Jefferson and Burr themselves did not get along well. Aware that Burr was eager to reward his New York political machine with jobs, the President did not

Library of Congress.

The new capital was in the rough countryside, with mud roads and a few boarding houses nearby. This view of the capitol was painted in 1800.

consult with him concerning cabinet appointments, and the distance between himself and his Vice President increased daily. Both were extremely able, brave men, but Burr craved excitement, intrigue, action. Jefferson liked repose, books, pleasant conversation, and philosophy. Their personalities were so different that cooperation was virtually impossible.

James Madison, Jefferson's associate for over a quarter of a century, became Secretary of State and the most important member of the cabinet. Swiss-born Albert Gallatin (1761–1849) eventually was Secretary of the Treasury, but not until a new Senate took over since his confirmation by Federalist stalwarts was in doubt. Besides Madison and Gallatin, Jefferson's official family included General Henry Dearborn as Secretary of War, Levi Lincoln as Attorney-General, and Gideon Granger as Postmaster General (not a cabinet-level post until 1829). Dearborn, Lincoln, and Granger were New Englanders, proof that the new President was trying to give his cabinet a regional balance. Jefferson had so much difficulty getting someone to head up the Navy Department that he once jokingly remarked perhaps the position should be advertised in the newspapers. At length, Robert Smith, a Baltimore lawyer, accepted the office and did a creditable job. A harmonious group of men, the Cabinet was clearly dominated by the President, Madison, and Gallatin.

One of Jefferson's first decisions involved the hated Alien and Sedition Acts. Those jailed under the acts were set free and their fines returned and the two laws were allowed to lapse. The Naturalization Act, which set a fourteen-year residence requirement for citizenship, was repealed and the original five-year residence requirement restored. Jefferson, who was distressed by both the size and the existence of the national debt, told Gallatin to keep finances simple and reduce costs. Like any good farmer of his own day, he believed that the federal government should pay its own way. In two years Gallatin cut the debt by $5 million and outlined a scheme for eliminating it entirely within about a decade and a half. Most of this saving resulted from cuts in military spending, but some jobs created by the Federalists were also eliminated.

Patronage and Spoils

Despite his statesman's image, Jefferson was no stranger to patronage. Sudden expansion of various departments, one way to create jobs the party faithful thought they had earned, was obviously in direct opposition to his philosophy of strict economy and small government. After much deliberation Jefferson concluded that only those who had abused their powers, men who had enforced the Sedition Act, for example, would be ousted. Adherence to Federalist principles alone was no cause for dismissal. Vacancies, he said, would be filled by Democratic-Republicans until they held half the places, thus equalizing the number of officeholders. Yet by mid-1803 only 130 Federalists remained in 316 positions over which the President had appointive power. Since Jefferson was an adroit, consummate politician, "equalization," to no one's surprise, meant a 40–60 percent split, with his followers clearly in the majority.

Taming the Barbary Pirates

As minister to France in the 1780s, Thomas Jefferson had urged war on a number of small Moslem states along the southern coast of the Mediterranean. An assortment of pashas and beys who lived in that part of North Africa demanded, and usually got, payment from both small and large powers in return for letting their merchant ships pass unmolested. He subsequently tried without success to interest President Washington in an international blockade that would smash this crude protection racket. Federalist leaders however, felt that the annual costs of protection were not excessive, about $2 million during the 1790s, and cheaper than war, despite some humiliating experiences such as ransom payments for American seamen imprisoned for many years.

Shortly after Jefferson became President, the Pasha of Tripoli demanded an increase in his annual subsidy. When the United States turned him down, the Pasha declared war. Angered by this effrontery, Jefferson dispatched Commodore Richard Dale to protect the interests of the nation in that region. Dale and the local consul arranged a blockade of sorts along the coast of Tripoli. The so-called Tripolitan War, which dragged on until 1805, was marked by occasional exploits now celebrated in legend and song. The Navy got a handful of heroes, notably Stephen Decatur (1779–1820) who boldly sailed into Tripoli harbor on the night of February 16, 1804, destroyed the frigate *Philadelphia* (once his father's flagship) which had gone aground there several months earlier and despite heavy fire, managed to withdraw without suffering any losses. Congress gave him a sword and pro-

The American navy ended extortion against U.S. vessels after this attack on Tripoli in 1804. This colored engraving, done the next year, commemorated the new nation's first successful naval operation.

moted him to captain. And the Marines got the inspiration for their stirring march when seven of them and a few Greek civilians made a land assault in the same general area.

On June 4, 1805, fearing internal disorders and further American attacks on his city, the Pasha signed a treaty of peace with the United States. Although the terms were reasonable, they included $60,000 in ransom money for the release of American prisoners he held. (A decade later Decatur returned to North Africa once more, crushed a new outbreak of piracy, and ended for all time payment of tribute by the United States to these Barbary pirates). The importance of this episode is twofold. Though a costly affair, the war gained new respect for the young republic on the high seas and provided invaluable experience for the naval commanders who were soon destined to grapple with a much mightier foe.

The Frontier

Although Jefferson naturally was interested in the course of the Tripolitan War, he had to face a potentially much more dangerous enemy than the Pasha of Tripoli long before it ended. North America hardly figured in Napoleon Bonaparte's schemes for conquest and power, yet his influence upon Jefferson's administration and the development of the United States was profound indeed. For a brief moment it appeared that he might seize the heartland of the continent and end all dreams of expanding frontier growth.

The lands beyond the Appalachians, source of considerable Democratic-Republican support, were of special concern to Jefferson. New territories and states were appearing there almost every year. Kentucky became a state in 1792; Tennessee, four years later; and Ohio, in 1803. Meanwhile, territorial governments were being organized in Indiana, Illinois, and Michigan. By 1800 some 400,000 citizens, many of them from New England or eastern regions of the South, were carving out homesteads in the new territories. In 1796 the Federalists cut the minimum purchase to 640 acres, then in 1800 to 320, also reducing down payments to 25 percent with the balance due in four years, not one. The price of land, however, remained the same, $2 per acre. Four years later the Jeffersonians lowered the minimum purchase to 160 acres, with the down payment set at only $80.

New frontiers also were being carved out further south. Frequently, in these areas land speculation led to massive fraud. In the Mississippi-Alabama region, for example, the famed Yazoo Land Fraud resulted when Georgia officials granted property to rival claimants. Federal officials stepped in to organize territorial governments, but legal tangles delayed admission of that region to the nation for more than a decade.

These reduced requirements for land purchase aided small farmers who swarmed in, erected simple log structures in a day, cleared only partially eight or ten acres of their property, raised a few crops, let their stock run wild, and moved on, often within a few years. To be successful in the wilderness, or course, one needed money, land, seed, and basic tools. The frontier, therefore, never was a haven for the extremely poor. Such folk tended to remain in eastern cities where they became day laborers or factory workers or, if they somehow got beyond the mountains, became squatters who were subsequently displaced by those who acquired legal title to the land.

The Louisiana Purchase

Pinckney's Treaty (or the Treaty of San Lorenzo, 1795) gave Americans the right to use the broad Mississippi and to deposit goods on Spanish soil for reshipment to the rest of the world. The growing West, however, re-

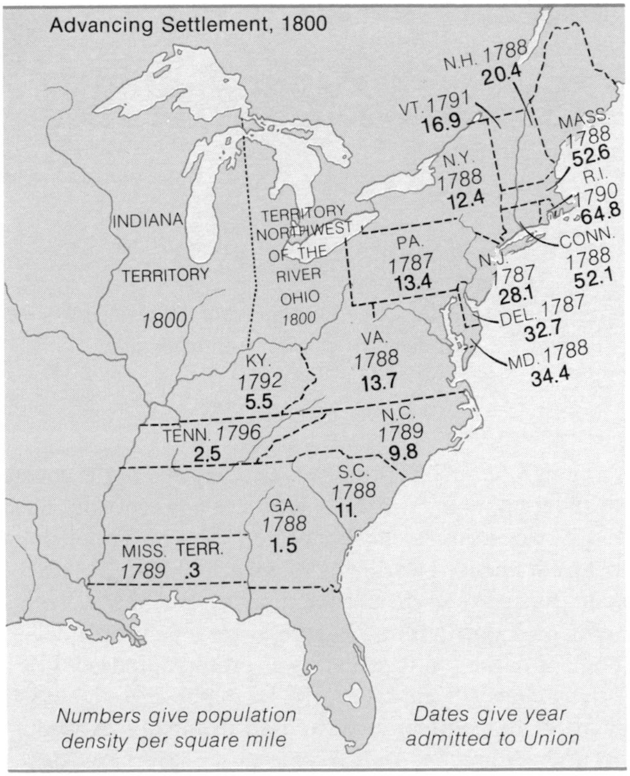

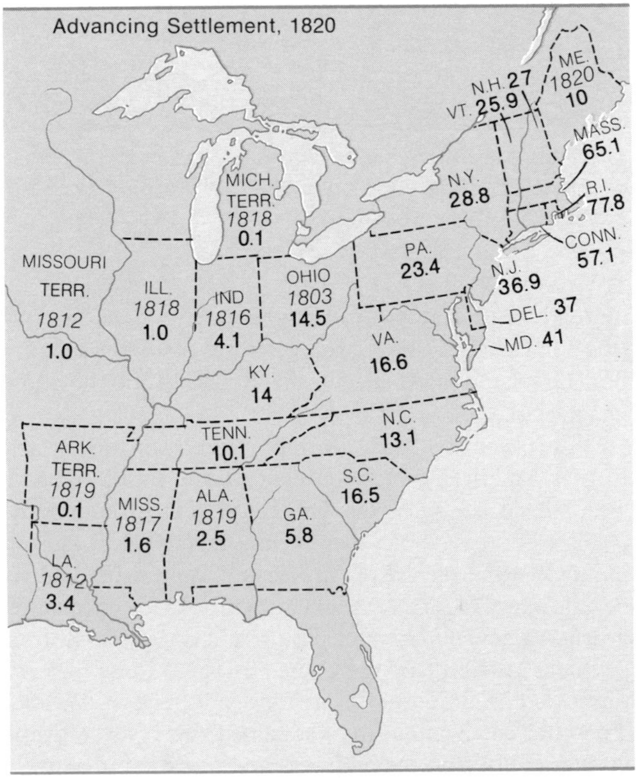

Public Library of Cincinnati and Hamilton County.

The Ohio River bustled with traffic. In the foreground is a flatboat floating downstream. The keel boat is propelled by men with poles. In the background another keel boat uses a sail to head upriver.

mained uncertain, nervous, wary. What would happen if the river were closed to them? How could they get their goods to market? So long as Spain held the port of New Orleans, President Jefferson did not share these western fears, at least not to the same degree. The Spanish empire seemed to be crumbling as American strength increased year by year.

Soon after taking office, however, Jefferson learned of a secret treaty transferring New Orleans and the vast Louisiana Territory to France. Spain and France were closely allied and, in return for this land, Napoleon promised to establish an Italian kingdom for the brother-in-law of the Spanish sovereign. The ambitious French emperor wanted Louisiana because, thanks to a momentary peace with Great Britain, he could turn his attention to the restoration of the New World empire France lost in 1763. Louisiana, he thought, could provide foodstuffs for Haiti and other tropical islands he planned to add to his realm.

Alarmed by this news, Jefferson asked Robert Livingston, minister to France, to find out what was going on. He told Livingston to discourage the transfer of Louisiana if it were not completed and to obtain West Florida for the United States if it were. The French, however, were unwilling to discuss these matters, and Jefferson clung to the hope that international complications would prevent Napoleon from actually taking possession of Louisiana. As it turned out, these hopes were realized, but not before Jefferson experienced some extremely anxious moments.

In October 1802 the acting Spanish intendant at New Orleans suddenly terminated the right of Americans to deposit goods there, duty free, for reshipment. Beset by angry frontiersmen from Kentucky and Tennessee crying for war and by political adversaries eager to embarrass the administration, Jefferson dispatched James Monroe as a special emissary to both France and Spain. Monroe had orders to determine the precise borders of Louisiana and was authorized to offer up to $2 million for control of New Orleans and as much of the Floridas as possible. If he had no success whatsoever, then he was free to approach the British concerning an alliance against France.

By the time Monroe arrived in Paris in April 1803, Napoleon had changed his plans completely. After some initial success, his West Indies armies were bogged down by disease and revolt. Spain refused to give up the Floridas, without which defense of Louisiana was difficult, and because of bad weather, the expedition outfitted to set up French administration in Louisiana never departed from a Dutch port. Of greater importance, Napoleon did not want a rupture with the United States since he was planning to resume his war with England. The British navy, he fully realized, could seize Louisiana easily enough once hostilities began.

For all of these reasons, Napoleon decided to sell,

and even before Monroe got to France he offered Livingston the entire territory of Louisiana, although no one was quite certain how much land actually was involved. The territory's true boundaries, especially along the Canadian frontier in the north and in the west and southwest were unknown, and these details would have to be resolved later with the British, Spanish, and Mexicans by bickering, bluster, and bullets. Somewhat taken aback, the two Americans exceeded their original instructions and quickly agreed to pay France $11.25 million and to assume claims totaling $3.75 million by U.S. citizens against France.

At a cost of about $15 per square mile Livingston and Monroe more than doubled the size of their nation and struck a death blow to lingering European hopes of somehow containing the young republic along the Atlantic seaboard. Yet signing a bill of sale with Napoleon Bonaparte, a very sly negotiator, was only the first of several possible hurdles. The French legislature and Spain might not sanction this transaction since Napoleon had promised not to hand Louisiana over to a third power. Also, President Jefferson at first believed that acquisition of so much land might require a constitutional amendment. However, during the summer heat of 1803 all of these obstacles evaporated, and in October an enthusiastic Congress controlled by Jeffersonian Republicans gave its approval, notwithstanding the opposition of Federalists from New England. Two months later a special French commissioner dispatched to New Orleans handed Louisiana over to the United States.

Chicago Historical Society.

UNDER MY WINGS EVERY THING PROSPERS

New Orleans was already the main port for the growing Ohio valley of the United States when Louisiana was purchased in 1803.

Meanwhile, even before Napoleon offered to sell this vast territory, Jefferson had sent a combined scientific and military expedition westward to find out what lay beyond the Mississippi River. Alarm over Spain's decision to end the right of deposit at New Orleans prompted this move, and what the President probably had in mind was an alternate route for western produce, or at least to ascertain if such might exist. Heading this group of explorers was his former personal secretary, Meriwether Lewis (1774–1809), a young man who idolized him, and William Clark (1770–1838), the younger brother of George Rogers Clark who had won fame in the Revolutionary War.

This small, well-equipped expedition, secretly financed by Congress since its goal was to explore lands then owned by foreign powers, set out in 1803. All of the military men were required to keep journals of their daily observations, which added to the natural history notes recorded by trained observers who accompanied them. The party followed the Missouri River nearly to its headwaters and then crossed the Rockies, finally reaching the Pacific Ocean in November 1805. Part of the way, they had as guides a French Canadian trapper, Touissaint Charbonneau, and his Indian wife, Sacajawea. The Lewis and Clark expedition returned to St. Louis, now American soil, in September 1806, loaded with journals, samples of flora and fauna, and much valuable knowledge about the great Northwest.

During these same months another Army officer, Lt. Zebulon M. Pike, set out on two expeditions in the West. Like Lewis and Clark, Pike departed from the St. Louis area each time. In 1805 he went up the Mississippi into what is now Minnesota in an effort to find the headwaters of that great river. He collected a wealth of information but failed to achieve his goal. The following year Pike and a small party headed for the great Southwest and, by way of the Arkansas and Colorado rivers, reached a tributary to the Rio Grande, only to be captured by Spanish soldiers based at Santa Fe. Pike and his men eventually were escorted back to American soil by a circuitous route.

His narrative, published in 1810, described these adventures. Although Pike once more garnered considerable data, he is best remembered today for Pikes Peak (14,110 feet), a Colorado mountain he described but did not climb. There is a note of tragedy in this man's career. His exploits, overshadowed by those of Lewis and Clark, were marred by mistakes—not really finding the source of the Mississippi, getting captured by the Spanish, and not scaling the peak that bears his name, but his greatest mistake of all lay in his choice of patron and sponsor, General James Wilkinson, who was soon to be caught up in the Burr conspiracy. When that scandal broke, Pike protested his innocence, and his later conduct gave proof of patriotism, if not luck. In 1813, now a thirty-four-year old brigadier general, he led his men to victory at Toronto, only to be killed instantly when a powder magazine exploded.

John Marshall's Court

Alexander Hamilton remarked in 1788 that "the judiciary is beyond comparison the weakest of the three departments of power," and indeed the Supreme Court was of minor importance under the Federalists. It heard few cases and only a very small number were of any significance. The justices met in the basement of the Senate, the designers of the Capitol having forgotten to build special quarters for them. Shortly after the election of 1800, Chief Justice Oliver Ellsworth quit. His health was poor, but the Democratic-Republicans believed he stepped down so Adams could install a younger, healthier man to keep bright the flame of Federalism.

John Jay, who had been the first Chief Justice (1789–1794), refused to accept the position again, and Adams eventually appointed John Marshall, his Secretary of State, to head the court. Federalist stalwarts in the Senate were not impressed. Marshall was a Virginian, a simple, modestly-dressed, person, democratic in bearing and close to Adams, then much out of favor with the party regulars. Reluctantly they confirmed the man who would preside over the Supreme Court for the next thirty-four years.

Marshall wasted no time in organizing the court so as to produce maximum results. It was his aim to use it to strengthen the national government; to do so, the position of the court itself would have to be enhanced considerably. Marshall saw the future of the nation as being determined by the ability of the Constitution to accommodate to the changing forces of daily life and to harness those forces to the national purpose. He contended that the Supreme Court had the final power *and the responsibility* to interpret the Constitution, and he was determined to succeed in securing that authority for his court.

To project a strong, unified voice to the public,

State Historical Society of North Dakota.

Sacajawea
(ca. 1787–1812)

Born in a Shoshone village in present-day Idaho and daughter of a chief, Sacajawea was captured in 1800 by a war party of a rival tribe, the Hidatas. Along with another Shoshone girl, she was sold to Touissant Charbonneau, a Canadian trapper who lived with her captors. He subsequently married both of them according to local Indian rites. In the winter of 1804–1805, Lewis and Clark appeared in the region and hired Charbonneau as an interpreter and guide, with the understanding that both he and Sacajawea would accompany the famous explorers. In February 1805 she gave birth to a son and, less than two months later, with the papoose strapped to her back, set out for the Pacific.

Sacajawea proved her worth to the expedition in many ways. She was visible evidence to the various Indian tribes encountered on the journey of the peaceful nature of this expedition, and her knowledge of Indian dialects made her an invaluable aid to communication with those natives. She was instrumental in gaining the aid of her kinsmen in leading the expedition across the Continental Divide and without their help it is quite possible that Lewis and Clark never would have reached their objective.

William Clark later took Sacajawea's son into his care, and provided for his education. Clark also helped Charbonneau and Sacajawea to settle in St. Louis. However, both desired a less civilized life and returned to a life of fur trading.

The legend of Sacajawea as sole guide of the Lewis and Clark expedition arose from a novel based on the expedition. Few women have been honored by so many memorials, and her character and exploits have evoked great praise. She was an early heroine of the suffragettes, and the celebrations marking the centennial of the Lewis and Clark Expedition added to her fame. Lewis only mentions her once in his journal, rather disdainfully in fact, but Clark obviously thought very highly of her. He nicknamed her "Janey" and called Jean-Baptiste "Pomp," a name he also bestowed upon Pompey's Pillar on the Yellowstone River. ■

Missouri Historical Society.

St. Louis was a frontier Indian trading center for the French and Spanish when the United States bought Louisiana. Lewis and Clark passed through this area on their way west.

Marshall persuaded the justices to forgo traditional individual opinions and through private conferences to forge differing views into an official decision, usually penned and delivered by Marshall himself. In this way the pronouncement became the verdict of an institution rather than the random thoughts of a handful of men.

The opening round in Marshall's drive to increase the powers of his court began as soon as the Democratic-Republicans assumed control of the national government. The Judiciary Act of 1801, passed just six days before Jefferson took the oath of office, set up sixteen new circuit courts, thereby creating jobs for sixteen judges and a host of marshals, attorneys, and clerks. This act cut the number of Supreme Court justices from six to five, the actual reduction to occur upon the next vacancy. This meant two justices would have to retire before Jefferson could name anyone to the court. It also permitted Adams to appoint as many justices of the peace as he wanted to. Before his precipitious departure he managed to make forty-two such appointments, all of them, of course, solid, sturdy Federalists.

The Democratic-Republicans repealed this act and in April 1802 passed yet another judiciary measure, restoring membership on the high bench to six and reestablishing six circuit courts with one Supreme Court justice assigned to each one. This meant the justices would have to "ride" circuit as before and hold court throughout the nation. More significantly perhaps, the new law set up a system of annual (not semiannual) Supreme Court sessions. This eliminated the upcoming meeting and virtually closed the court for fourteen months. If one political party could restructure the highest court in the land, the Republicans believed the other party could do the same thing.

When James Madison became Secretary of State he found a stack of commissions signed, sealed, and ready to be handed over to new Federalist officeholders created by the Judiciary Act of 1801. These so-called "midnight appointments" (John Adams presumably stayed up late on the evening of March 3, 1801, to complete this task) were not delivered before the Democratic-Republicans

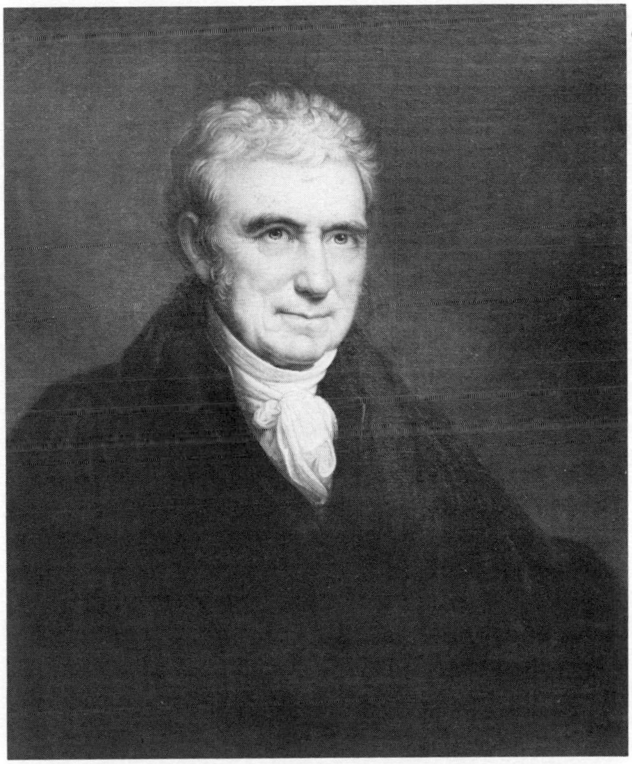

Virginia Museum of Fine Arts.

Chief Justice John Marshall used his personal charm and strong mind to shape the Supreme Court into a force for nationalism. Rembrandt Peale caught the gentle force in Marshall's eyes in this 1834 portrait.

took office, and Jefferson told Madison not to do so. William Marbury, finding himself unemployed, asked the Supreme Court to issue a writ forcing Madison to give him his commission. Madison ignored a preliminary order to do so, and in 1803 the court turned to the Marbury matter in earnest.

This famous case, *Marbury* v. *Madison*, presented the justices with a complex dilemma. If they ordered Madison to award the commission, might he not again refuse to comply and thus make the court lose face since it had no way to enforce its decisions. If the justices ruled in favor of Madison, then they would be helping their political foes. Marshall's way out was shrewd indeed. The court, he said, did not have the jurisdiction to issue the writ sought by Marbury since the provisions of the Judiciary Act of 1789 granting such powers were unconstitutional. Marshall then proceeded to lecture the administration on the *justice* of the case, informally urging James Madison to give William Marbury what he wanted. In short, Marbury should get his post as a justice of the peace; but, because a 1789 law was defective, the Supreme Court lacked the power to issue the desired writ.

For the first time the court had declared a federal law unconstitutional, and this decision suggested an answer to the sticky question of how to protect the people from unconstitutional acts by the executive and legislative branches of the national government. Virginia and Kentucky tried to assert, when the Alien and Sedition Acts were passed, that a state could rule on the constitutionality of federal laws. In his opinion, Marshall said, the Supreme Court was the final arbiter, a view that would keep the states out of national affairs. During the same session, the Marshall court ruled that Jefferson's Circuit Court Act of 1802 was constitutional, the Chief Justice thus winning public respect for what appeared to be impartiality, while actually reasserting the court's awesome power of judicial review.

Unmoved by the court's approval of the 1802 act, the Jeffersonians were firmly convinced that they must somehow restrict judicial power. At issue, in their opinion, was the ability of six Federalists to thwart the will of the majority of American voters. The only method of unseating federal judges was, according to the Constitution, impeaching them for "high crimes and misdemeanors." The first case sent to the Senate for trial involved Judge John Pickering of New Hampshire. Pickering was charged with malfeasance and general unfitness because of excessive drinking and loose morals. Although he was obviously unstable and a disgrace to the bench, it was not clear whether his "sins" fell within the constitutional definition of impeachable offenses.

But the administration won its case, and within an hour set out after still bigger game. Its target was Justice Samuel Chase of the United States Supreme Court. Chase, an arch-Federalist, had been less than impartial in the Alien and Sedition cases he had heard, and in 1803 criticized the administration before a Baltimore jury, charging that Congress was jeopardizing the independence of the judiciary. His trial, held in 1805, with Aaron Burr as a disgraced, lame-duck Vice President presiding, was a disaster for the Jeffersonians. The defense, ably conducted, held to a strict interpretation of impeachment; the administration argued for a loose construction of what the Constitution said. Although Jefferson's party enjoyed a substantial majority in the Senate, the leaders could not gain a conviction, which required a two-thirds vote. With Chase's precedent-setting acquittal, the administration abandoned this route and concentrated instead upon appointing the right men whenever and wherever vacancies occurred.

Burr, Hamilton, and the "Essex Junto"

Despite occasional setbacks, Jefferson's first term was a success. His inexperienced party grasped the reins of national government, provided generally constructive legislation, and proved it was not the demon Federalists had feared it would be. More importantly, the Jeffersonians demonstrated that the transfer of power in a republic was indeed possible without bloodshed. They had also "shown the flag" in North Africa and, incidentally, more than doubled the size of the nation with an unexpected and very successful real estate deal. Not surprisingly, Jefferson was reelected by a huge majority in 1804, carrying every state except Connecticut and Delaware. His running mate, however, was not Aaron Burr, but another New Yorker, George Clinton.

Burr's troubles began four years earlier when he was suspected of permitting the Federalists to use him in an electoral college scheme to supplant Jefferson as President. This crude ploy, which ruined him in the eyes of most Jeffersonians, seemed also to end his usefulness on the national scene. Aware that he would not be renominated on the ticket with Jefferson, Burr listened to the siren song of some disgruntled New England Federalists known as the "Essex Junto." This small band of malcontents, led by Senator Thomas Pickering of Massachusetts, viewed with alarm and dismay the admission of new Democratic-Republican strongholds such as Ohio to the United States and the national rule of southern aristocrats. They were certain their party was doomed. The solution, they thought, was to secede and form yet another republic.

These New Englanders first sounded out Alexander Hamilton as a leader, but were turned down. Burr, however, was interested and agreed to run for the governorship of New York, a position that would lend prestige to this disunion movement. It was a bruising campaign with Hamilton and other Federalists who feared Burr's intriguing mind solidly behind his Democratic-Republican opponent, Lewis Morgan. Morgan won, and angry words uttered during that fight led to a duel between Burr and Hamilton near Weehauken, New Jersey, on the morning of July 11, 1804.

The two took their positions thirty feet apart, Burr (the challenger) aimed and fired. So did Hamilton but his shot skittered off harmlessly into some tree branches as he tottered and fell, fatally wounded. The ensuing uproar stunned Burr. New Jersey and New York authorities issued murder warrants since dueling was illegal, and he agreed to surrender if they in turn would allow him to post bail. When no such arrangement proved possible, he fled to the South where dueling was a more respected pastime but returned to Washington to preside over the Chase trial.

This affair was a tragedy of epic proportions. Hamilton, a truly brilliant individual who neither understood the public mind nor cared to, died—as he had lived—amid controversy. Yet during the formative years of the 1780s and the early 1790s, he was the indispensable man. Burr, a handsome, engaging conniver, potentially Jefferson's only rival for national leadership, was now thoroughly discredited. Had there not been additional intrigues and conspiracies later on, Burr might have continued to play some role in national affairs.

Jeffersonian Troubles

The issues and personalities shaping Jefferson's first four years in the White House continued to dominate his second administration, but somehow the magic touch was gone. Nothing seemed to go well. Burr out of office was more of a problem than when in, escalation of hostilities between England and France created one incident after another on the high seas, and worse yet, the administration's policies breathed new life into the Federalist party. Like many of his successors who have been returned to office by huge landslides at the polls, Thomas Jefferson learned that public acclaim can be transitory and that sustained political success is a difficult feat.

The Wilkinson-Burr Conspiracy

The full dimensions of this scheme are not totally clear even today since Burr told different people different things at different times, but it apparently included a plan to attack Texas with volunteers raised in Kentucky and Tennessee and possibly an attempt to lure the West out of the Union. While still Vice President, Burr became closely associated with General James Wilkinson, governor of the Louisiana Territory, political opportunist, and Spanish intelligence agent. The two pored over maps of the Southwest, dreamed dreams, and began rallying sympathetic politicians to their cause. The Burr net, cast widely and loosely, touched the governor of Tennessee, the territorial governor of Indiana, and some Federalist senators. Even Andrew Jackson was taken in for a time, thinking that the Secretary of War, Henry Dearborn, was behind the plot; however, he soon relized his error and severed all ties with Burr.

As Aaron Burr sought funds from various foreign ambassadors and began organizing a fighting force, word of these maneuverings crept into the press. Harman Blennerhasset, an active conspirator, indiscreetly talked with editors and reporters, and before long Jefferson dispatched investigators westward to find out what was up. Meanwhile, one of Wilkinson's friends alerted the Spanish government to a scheme to liberate Mexico. Although the desired war with Spain seemed unlikely, Burr seized upon a military buildup along the Sabine River as an excuse for action and set out for that region. Wilkinson, who had decided to betray Burr in order to gain a more important post with the American government, notified both Jefferson and the Spanish of the impending attack, and early in 1807 Burr was arrested.

The original charge against Burr was merely the misdemeanor of organizing an assault against foreign territory, but a grand jury increased the offense to treason. Burr was brought to trial in Richmond in a

Courtesy New-York Historical Society, New York City.

Aaron Burr combined ambition and political maneuvering to both build and destroy his own political career.

circuit court presided over by John Marshall. From the moment the proceedings began this episode took on new importance, for the real battle now was not over Burr's alleged crimes but was between the President and the Chief Justice. Marshall, still smarting over presidential threats to the judiciary, was eager to embarrass Jefferson. In the process he abandoned impartiality and in effect became the leading lawyer for the defense. Jefferson offered pardons to anyone incriminated by evidence they gave to the prosecution, spoke openly of Burr's guilt even before the trial began, and allowed publication of material relevant to the proceedings.

Marshall issued a subpoena for Jefferson to testify, but he refused to comply, noting that to do so might make the executive branch of the federal government subservient to the judicial. Marshall's masterstroke of partisanship was his charge to the jury, defining treason in the strictest possible terms. This man, normally an advocate of broad construction, suddenly found it expedient to advocate the opposite approach. According to the Constitution, conviction required two witnesses to an overt act of war or an open confession by the accused. The prosecution could produce neither, and Marshall's charge assured Burr of acquittal.

The administration immediately sought a new trial outside of Marshall's jurisdiction on lesser charges, but Burr jumped bail and fled to Europe. Only one man in Burr's entourage was convicted of any crime and he paid a twenty-dollar fine and spent three hours in an Indiana jail. The final irony of this fiasco is that if Jefferson had not secured repeal of the Judiciary Act of 1801, Marshall would not have heard the case. No one involved—Burr, Wilkinson, Jefferson, or Marshall—emerged from this sordid mess with his reputation enhanced. And the Chief Justice defined treason so tightly that rarely has anyone since been accused of that crime. Instead the federal government has seen fit to press for conviction on the lesser charge of espionage.

Trouble on the High Seas

England and France resumed their war in 1803, and by 1805 England controlled the high seas while France was winning on land. America, her shipping industry caught between two world powers, found herself in a very uncomfortable position. Each nation resorted to economic pressures in an attempt to weaken the other. Neither could tolerate neutral trade with its adversary. To maintain control of the seas, England needed a massive number of able seamen and increased greatly the practice of impressment or forced enlistment. Under British law, any able-bodied subject of the king could be conscripted for emergency service in the navy. The British navy thus began to search American vessels for deserters and any other Englishmen who might be subject to impressment. American captains resented the delays involved, loss of some of their crewmen, and searches of their ships conducted by a foreign power.

Modern estimates of the number of illegal impressments are lower than claims made at the time, but they suggest that some 10,000 seamen were seized between 1793 and 1811. Although there were more than enough British deserters, British subjects, and Americans to keep ships properly manned, national pride was wounded. The British conducted so many searches close to American ports that in 1804 the resident British consul in New

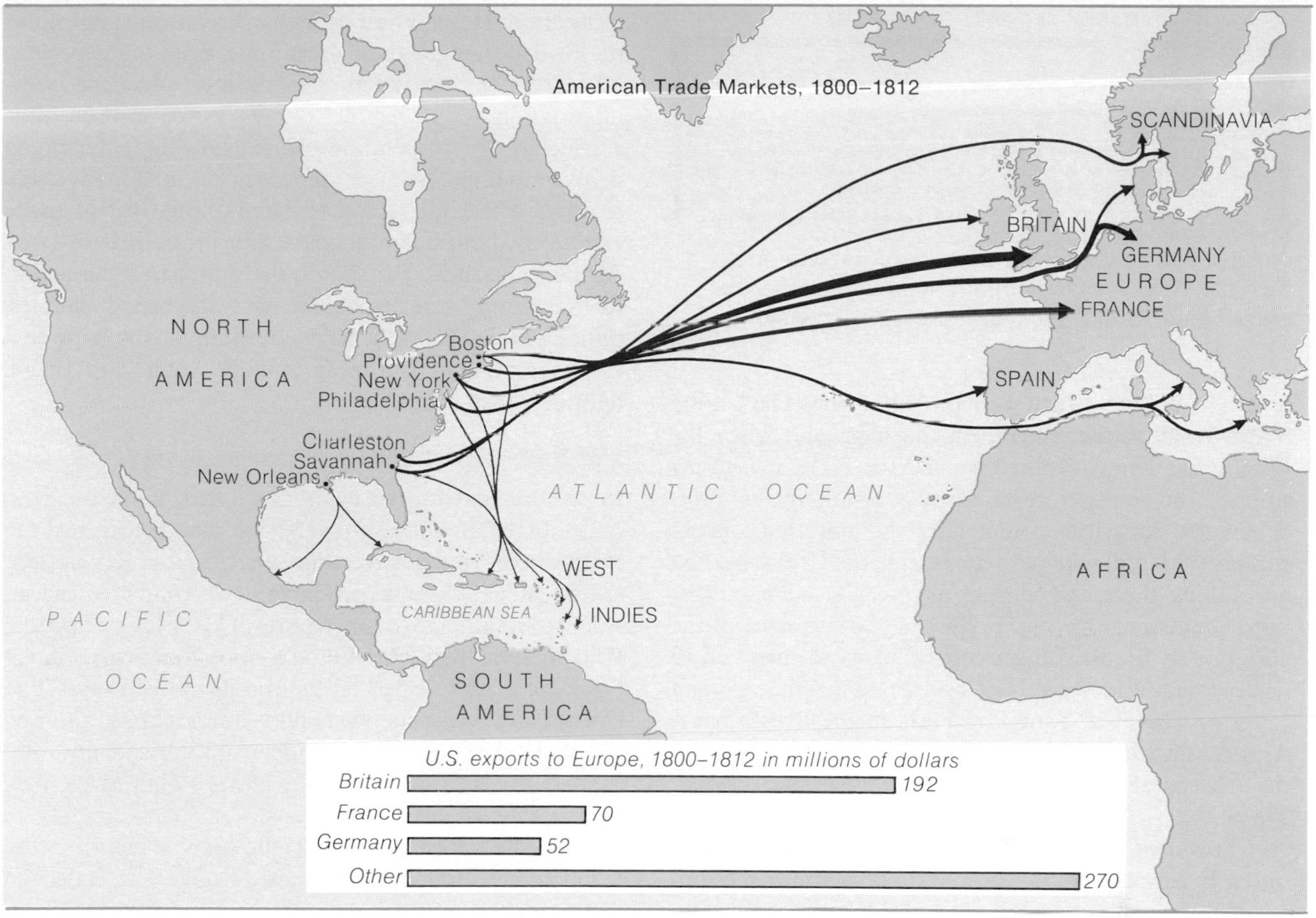

York City considered that port to be under "blockade."

For their part, the British resented the success of the American carrying trade, which was growing by leaps and bounds while their maritime strength was tied up in naval warfare. With the Americans taking over markets once theirs, the British began enforcing the Rule of 1756. Seizure of cargoes under this rule, an infuriating reminder of former colonial status, was extensive and damaged American commerce severely. In retaliation, Napoleon issued his Berlin Decree (1806), a paper blockade of the British Isles, and French privateers began taking possession of all ships loaded with goods bound for Britain. The British answered in kind by prohibiting neutrals to trade with ports from which their own ships were barred, unless such vessels first stopped in the British Isles and paid British duties. In his Milan Decree, Napoleon warned that any ship that did so would be considered denationalized, henceforth a British vessel, and subject to seizure as a prize of war.

Impressment, meanwhile, was becoming a much more troublesome issue. For months the *H.M.S. Leander* had been working the coastline just off New York, often detaining a dozen ships at a time pending search. In 1806 its seamen accidentally killed an American while firing a warning shot across the bow of a merchantman. Riots erupted in Manhattan, and Jefferson barred both the *Leander* and its sister ship, *H.M.S. Cambrian,* from port. Later that year the *H.M.S. Melampus* destroyed a French warship within the Virginia capes, clearly American waters.

The following year the British accused an American naval vessel, *U.S.S. Chesapeake,* of enlisting two British

Courtesy New-York Historical Society, New York City.

British Barbarity and Piracy!!

The Federalists say that Mr. Christopher Gore ought to be supported as Governor—for *his attachment to Britain.*—If British influence is to effect the suffrages of a free people, let them read the following melancholy and outrageous conduct of British Piracy, and judge for themselves.

The " LEOPARD OUTSPOTTED" or Chesapeak Outrage outdone.

This broadside linked the outrage of national pride over the Chesapeake-Leopard incident to other impressments, in this case an incident in Macao.

deserters, charges which were probably true. The United States Navy refused to return the men, and when the *Chesapeake* left Norfolk, Virginia, the *H.M.S. Leopard* stopped the ship before it was able to mount its guns. When the American commander did not immediately comply with orders to permit a search, the British opened fire, killing three and injuring eighteen seamen and severely damaging the ship. Following the surrender of the *Chesapeake,* the British seized four of its seamen said to be deserters. Widespread rioting greeted this outrage, and Jefferson closed all American ports to the British navy. As a result, the British established a virtual blockade of the Chesapeake Bay and began ravaging the coast of Maine.

President Jefferson clearly did not want to be drawn into a European war, but he could not permit American rights to be ignored. Sadly, the nation was in no position to fight: the economy-minded Jeffersonians had done little to build up defense installations or to increase naval strength. As relations with London worsened, the President tried to negotiate, using American trade as a bargaining tool. On the last day of 1806, the British agreed to a treaty allowing "broken voyages," that is, the reexportation of goods. In exchange the American negotiators said their nation would not place any restrictions on commerce for ten years, thus blunting their only true weapon in such talks. Americans were to ignore French decrees, and their country was granted "most-favored-nation" status and given a promise that the British no longer would stop unarmed U.S. ships within five miles of the American coast.

These provisions clearly put the United States in a very unneutral position, while actually imposing no restrictions on the British. Jefferson was so disgusted that he did not even present the document to the Senate for ratification. He said he was willing to continue talks, but the British thought they already had been too generous. The President reacted by putting into effect the Nonimportation Act passed by Congress earlier in 1806. This act included a suspending clause allowing Jefferson to invoke nonimportation whenever he deemed it advisable to do so. This ended importation of certain British goods and aroused considerable animosity in the British Isles. At the same time, Jefferson quietly prepared the nation for war. Forts were armed, the navy spruced up, and the militia readied for action. Yet he clung to the hope that the wide-ranging European conflict would end before fighting broke out.

The Embargo of 1807

In one last attempt to avoid hostilities, Jefferson, who remembered the success of economic coercion against the British in the decade preceding the American Revolution, asked Congress to enact an embargo to prohibit American ships from sailing to foreign ports. This measure hurt the British more than the French since the British naval blockade already sealed off the continent of Europe. The British, however, depended upon American food and raw materials. Although the President did not actually rally support for this measure, most citizens obeyed the new law, at least at the outset.

The full effects of what would become known as the "Obnoxious Embargo" are hard to assess. It ended an American shipping boom, and the American merchant marine lost its prominent role in world trade. There was widespread unemployment in many ports, but New England merchants soon became masters of evading the letter of the law, shipping goods to Canada and from there to Britain. Additional measures passed by Congress then barred overland export. The Federalists claimed these acts were unconstitutional, but the Marshall Court disagreed.

The British, of course, encouraged smuggling and opened their West Indian ports to American ships willing to go there. Some Yankee captains, once they learned of the embargo, never returned home and spent many months trading from one foreign port to another, piling up profits as they went. The embargo clearly failed as a weapon of foreign policy. Colonies of the great powers, caught in a general war, needed American goods much more than their mother countries; and, just as American ports were closing, the British found substitute com-

Courtesy New-York Historical Society, New York City.

In this satire of the Embargo of 1807, the embargo is represented by a snapping turtle called the "Ograb-me," which is embargo backwards.

merce in Spanish colonies throughout the New World. English manufacturers stockpiled some cotton, located a plentiful source in Asia, and got still more from American smugglers eager to make money. London was not even interested in an American offer to rescind the embargo in return for relief from British restrictions on U.S. trade.

Although New England merchants complained the loudest, the commercial farmers of the South actually suffered the most. What the embargo really did at home was to force American manufacturing out of its "swaddling clothes," but the transfer of investment capital to factories took time and, in the interim, thousands were out of work. Needless to point out, the embargo became a very hot political issue and revived the Federalist party in both New York and Maryland, giving that political organization a momentary reprieve. It also split the Republican party into warring factions. This controversial measure was repealed shortly before Jefferson left office and replaced by the Nonintercourse Act (1809), which opened trade with all nations except Britain and France and held out the possibility of removing those restrictions on either country agreeing to respect American rights.

The Election of 1808

Despite the furor over the embargo (something many Federalists were certain was designed in Paris) and bickering among the Jeffersonians, the President's handpicked candidate, James Madison, won easily in 1808. Yet it was no landslide. C. C. Pinckney, once more the Federalist standard-bearer, got nearly three times as many electoral votes as in 1804, and New England resumed its solid Federalist stance. George Clinton, Jefferson's Vice President, and James Monroe both were a bit miffed because Madison received the nomination instead. Although Madison, a founder of the Democratic-Republicans and an early foe of the Federalists, had certainly earned the nomination, he lacked the personal appeal of his mentor, Jefferson. The first choice of the congressional caucus, Madison did not enjoy similar support among state branches of his party, some of them badly split by Jefferson's policies and personal factionalism.

Nevertheless, the Democratic-Republicans retained a respectable, if diminished majority in the Congress, and Madison was elected. Despite his credentials as party leader, he was very much a creature of Congress, unable to exert the influence Jefferson had displayed. This dependence was unfortunate since his administration would face new crises on the world scene.

The last months of Jefferson's second term were among the most distressing in his long life. Even his own party refused to support the embargo and, as noted, it became a nonintercourse scheme. The triumphs against the Barbary pirates, the Louisiana Purchase, the Lewis and Clark expedition, and other earlier successes seemed insignificant in the light of the ill will generated by a policy designed to maintain peace. What Jefferson failed to realize was how interdependent the United States and Europe really were. This fact, more than any conscious desire on the part of the American public for peace or war, doomed any plan that interfered with this close, natural relationship.

Jeffersonian America: An Overview

Political infighting, foreign dilemmas, and domestic intrigue should not disguise the growth and development of the United States during the first decade of the nineteenth century. In 1800 the nation had a population of 5,308,483; a decade later, 7,239,881. Every state and region demonstrated substantial growth, although the Middle Atlantic states (especially New York), Kentucky, and Tennessee registered the most dramatic gains.

Despite agricultural practices often thought primitive by Old World standards, farm output had increased sufficiently by 1800 to permit very impressive wheat exports to overseas markets. The South was in the midst of the switch to cotton. This crop, seldom seen prior to the Revolution except on the Sea Islands of Georgia and in South Carolina, now was grown from Virginia southward into the growing frontier. Invention of the cotton gin by Eli Whitney in 1793 made it possible for a man to process as much as fifty pounds of the hardy upland variety in a single day. As cotton, almost a mania, became increasingly important in the new western territories of Alabama and Mississippi, even to the point of being accepted as currency, many planters abandoned traditional crops. Eight times as much cotton was produced in 1804 as in 1794, and by 1810 Georgia and South Carolina were growing enough of the staple to account for nearly one-fourth of all American exports.

Since those expanding fields demanded gang labor, pressure to revive the slave trade grew apace. South Carolina, which because of hard times had placed a ban on foreign slave trading in 1787, decided to discard its anti-importation law in 1803. While Congress prohibited the importation of slaves in 1808, some smuggling of human cargoes continued after that date. Between 1790 and 1810, influenced largely by cotton, the number of blacks in South Carolina alone rose from a fifth of the total population to a third.

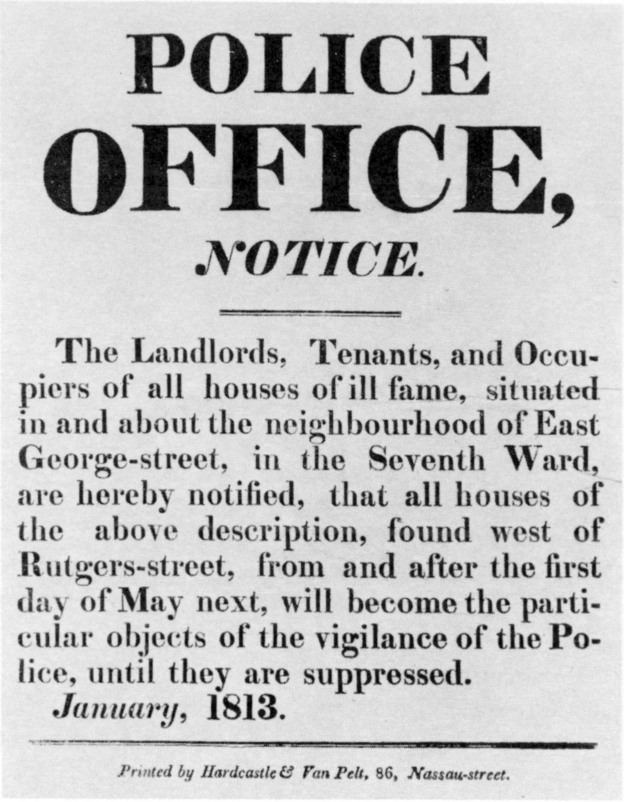
POLICE OFFICE,

NOTICE.

The Landlords, Tenants, and Occupiers of all houses of ill fame, situated in and about the neighbourhood of East George-street, in the Seventh Ward, are hereby notified, that all houses of the above description, found west of Rutgers-street, from and after the first day of May next, will become the particular objects of the vigilance of the Police, until they are suppressed.

January, 1813.

Printed by Hardcastle & Van Pelt, 86, *Nassau-street.*

Museum of the City of New York.

America's growth brought it the problems of cities and poverty, including prostitution, as noted in this warning from the New York police.

Other areas of American agriculture were expanding, too. Spanish sheep of the fine Merino strain appeared in 1802, and within eight years a strong wool-producing industry was evident in New York, Pennsylvania, and some parts of New England. The opening of new lands aided this agricultural upsurge. By 1810 more than a million Americans lived west of the Appalachians, many of them using rivers as their highways to spread settlement and transport supplies. At the same time, the beginnings of transportation revolution were apparent in the East. By 1810 some 200 turnpike companies had been chartered in New England, and many other areas were quick to follow this example. In an age when transportation was crucial, privately constructed roads, paid for by the collection of tolls, provided one way to fulfil obvious

Public Library of Cincinnati and Hamilton County.

The city of Cincinnati grew as a result of its strategic position on the Ohio where it could tap the agricultural wealth of the Midwest and South. This early photo from 1848 shows the relationship of the river to city growth.

needs. Several inventors were experimenting with steam-powered craft for inland travel. In 1807 Robert Fulton demonstrated that his steamboat could make its way upstream in the Hudson River, and soon afterwards he inaugurated commercial steamship service.

Speculation in lands, so common during Jefferson's administration, continued under Madison. Under constant pressure, Indian tribes made further cessions, especially north of the Ohio River where 100 million acres were ceded between 1801 and 1810. As they were pushed closer together and further west the Indians found themselves caught between the frontier and the hostile Sioux and Chippewa. Those living in the Old Northwest found a leader in the Shawnee chief Tecumseh (ca. 1768–1813), who warned Indiana's territorial governor, William Henry Harrison, that he intended to form a confederation of tribes to resist further incursions. In late 1811 Harrison marched on an Indian town on the Wabash River, but Tecumseh had departed for the South to find new allies. A battle ensued on Tippecanoe Creek, which Harrison won despite heavy losses. Tecumseh returned, mobilized the survivors, and sought out British help. When the War of 1812 erupted, he would seek his revenge.

Similar pressures existed in the Spanish Floridas where runaway slaves sometimes joined forces with hostile Indians. Nevertheless, Americans were flowing into West Florida (a coastal strip later apportioned among Mississippi, Alabama, and Louisiana), and in 1810 they staged a revolt against Spanish rule. Madison immediately announced the annexation of the region. Spain was too weak to do more than protest, but two years later the Spanish threatened war when Madison tried to seize East Florida. This time the Americans backed down.

There is in these experiences in the Floridas a theme

Courtesy Burton Historical Collection, Detroit Public Library.

The British gave up the fort of Detroit very reluctantly, despite its location on American soil. The reason is clear in this 1794 watercolor—Detroit was a major center of Indian trade.

frequently repeated during ensuing decades. Restless American settlers moved on to foreign soil—land that was distant from the capital of the ruling power, saddled with weak colonial administration, and lacking military and naval installations. Within a few years, a decade at the most, as their numbers increased so did pressure for annexation by the United States. Eventually the foreign power either bowed to the inevitable and negotiated the best deal possible or went to war.

If there is one word that epitomizes Thomas Jefferson's America, it is expansion. The Louisiana Purchase was merely emblematic of what was transpiring in agriculture, population trends, transportation, and, thanks to the "Obnoxious Embargo," even in manufacturing. This was not the path of development that the Squire of Monticello had in mind, nor was it precisely what Alexander Hamilton had anticipated.

It is often said that the United States of America has been a fortunate land isolated from Europe's woes and profiting from them. To a degree this observation has merit, but America in 1810 was still very much a part of Europe in spite of its independence, the wide Atlantic, and a republican government. Soon those bonds, twist and turn as Americans might, would lead to war, a struggle some of them entered with great relish, but one that all Americans were delighted to see end.

Library Company of Pennsylvania

Richard Allen (1760–1831)

Born in slavery in 1760, Richard Allen became the founder of the African Methodist Episcopal Church, an organization which by 1836 controlled property worth $125,000 and was a major force in the antislavery movement.

As a youth, Allen, the property of a farmer residing near Dover, Delaware, was converted by the Methodists. Because of this strong interest in religion, his master permitted him to hold prayer meetings in his home. As a result, the master also became a Methodist and a firm believer in emancipation, thus enabling Allen and his family to escape from slavery in an era of increasing toleration and religious freedom.

In an effort to educate himself, Allen labored at a variety of occupations, while continuing to preach the Gospel to blacks and white alike. He was accepted as a minister in the Methodist Church at a general conference held in Baltimore in 1784. After traveling with Bishop Asbury, he began to hold services for blacks in Philadelphia. His magnetic style attracted many blacks to the St. George Methodist Church in which he occasionally preached; but, after a particularly insulting racial incident when a white worshiper pulled blacks up from a kneeling position and banished them to the gallery, black church members organized a "Free African Society." That group soon split up, but Allen influenced one of the groups to establish an independent Methodist church. Eventually this church merged with sixteen similar black churches to become the African Methodist Episcopal Church, with Allen as bishop.

Although the church never had any influence in the South, it spread widely in the Northern states east of the Mississippi. By 1836 there were eighty-six churches, serving 7,594 members. Allen's influence made this organization a source of inspiration for many. Originally only a religious force, after his death in 1831 the church he founded became a major voice in the antislavery movement, an integral part of both the underground railroad and the battle for emancipation. ■

Essay

Explorers and Exploration: From Lewis and Clark to Neil Armstrong

At the turn of the nineteenth century the land beyond the Mississippi River comprised an intriguing unknown, a mysterious land in which some men thought even the most fantastic forms of fauna and flora might exist. Its inhabitants, geographical features, and mineral wealth were only rumor and speculation. Although the southern and eastern boundaries of the vast area known as Louisiana were defined, it was uncertain just how far north and west the unexplored wilderness extended. English and Scottish trappers and traders were operating in areas just south of the Great Lakes region, and the Russians and British had begun to explore sections of the Pacific coastline; but, except for the port city of New Orleans and a few Spanish military installations, white settlers and explorers had exerted little influence in the area.

The Mississippi River, eastern boundary of this region, was becoming the major artery for commerce in the rapidly expanding American frontier. The fur trade long had depended upon the Mississippi for access to the outside world, and the increasing importance of agriculture in the territories and new states west of the Appalachians increased the need for fast and easy transportation routes to the markets.

As the river trade became more important, control of the port of New Orleans became an issue of increasing significance. Clearly, whoever controlled the port controlled the river and easily could determine the economic destiny of families living in Kentucky, Ohio, and Tennessee, not to mention those in the mushrooming American territories as well. However, as long as Louisiana was held by the weak Spanish government, these Americans felt reasonably certain that the Mississippi would remain open.

Although well-known for his actions as a patriot and statesman, Thomas Jefferson deserves to be equally well-known for his serious interests in natural science and the unexplored western lands. While minister to France, he was approached by the enthusiastic John Leyard, an American who had attempted unsuccessfully to reach the western coast of North America by way of Siberia. Leyard wanted Jefferson to help him obtain aid in his efforts to explore the area between the Mississippi River and the Pacific Ocean. Jefferson agreed to do what he could, but

Leyard died before any plans were formulated. Later, while Secretary of State, Jefferson encouraged the French botanist André Michaux to organize an expedition to explore the wilderness. He suggested to Michaux the possibility of mammoths inhabiting the vast Louisiana Territory, since remnants of their bones had been discovered in Kentucky; he also expressed hope that the easily domesticated South American llama had migrated into the North American continent. Unfortunately, Michaux's political ambitions were greater than his scientific interests; and, before the venture got off the ground, he was discredited by his efforts to organize an independence movement in the transmountain territories.

Although he had no idea that the United States was about to purchase Louisiana and thereby double in size, President Jefferson continued his plans to explore the French-held western territory. In a "secret" message to Congress in January 1803, he requested a grant of $2,500 to finance an expedition staffed by members of the U.S. Army. Jefferson was careful to point out to representatives of the Spanish, French, and British governments that the venture was "literary" (that is, "informative") rather than military, the major task of the expedition would be to search out the "Northwest Passage"—the water route to the Pacific that had fascinated scientists, adventurers, and traders since the discovery of the continent.

Courtesy New-York Historical Society, New York City.

This fanciful painting of Captain Meriwether Lewis shows him dressed in the full regalia of an explorer.

Jefferson appointed Meriwether Lewis to act as leader of this expeditionary force. The Lewis family, neighbors of the Jeffersons in Virginia, moved to upper Georgia when Meriwether was young. Life as a planter's son afforded Lewis a great deal of time to spend in the wilds, where he became a fine hunter and skilled observer of natural scientific phenomena. Although he returned to Virginia to pursue a classical education, the death of his father cut short his academic career when he was eighteen and Lewis enlisted in the army. During the Indian wars in the Northwest Territory, he fought under William Clark. After several years of military service, Lewis became private secretary to President Jefferson, who listed Lewis's "knowledge of the Western country, of the Army and of all its interests and relations" among the reasons for his appointment.

It seems that the search for the Northwest Passage was a common topic of conversation for Jefferson and Lewis, and the two shared the enthusiasm that eventually set the expedition into motion. Lewis chose William Clark, with whom he served in the Indian wars, to assist him in the leadership of the expedition. Clark was the son of a Virginia planter who moved to Louisville in 1785. While his older brother, George Rogers Clark, was making a name for himself as a military patriot, William was learning about frontier life. Although he received little formal education, Clark became proficient in surveying and the drawing of maps, and developed a keen interest in the activities of animals. After seven years in the Army, Clark resigned, returning to private life until summoned by Lewis.

Although the two leaders had similar backgrounds, the success of the venture rested on the combined special talents of each. Lewis had higher military rank and actually was in command; he led his band of explorers with a sense of humane responsibility that echoes throughout the pages of his journals. Clark had more wilderness experience, and his resourcefulness was of incalculable value. He was both the illustrator of flora and fauna found enroute and the chief mapmaker.

In a detailed letter of instructions sent to Meriwether Lewis on June 20, 1803, Jefferson outlined the objectives of the expedition, itemizing provisions to be taken along and giving advice pertaining to the return trip. They were to make careful observations of all manner geological, botanical, and zoological phenomena and supply detailed reports of natives encountered, complete with as much anthropological detail as could be gathered.

Lewis went to Philadelphia for crash courses in celestial navigation, geology, and emergency techniques of surgery and medicine. Lewis already had set out for the West when news of the purchase of the entire Louisiana Territory reached him, negating any further need for secrecy.

After unexpected delays in the construction of the flatboat which was to be home base to the travelers for much of the venture, Lewis and his party shoved off from Pittsburgh on August 31, 1803. The delay made this first leg of the journey difficult; for the Ohio River was nearing its seasonal low-water mark, and the vessel, although designed by Lewis with this problem in mind, encountered shoals shallower and more numerous than expected. Heavy fogs further impeded progress. After several minor incidents, the party reached Louisville where Clark joined it on October 26.

During a winter spent encamped on the eastern bank of the Mississippi about eighteen miles from St. Louis, Lewis questioned traders passing through the area about minerals and other features to be encountered on their trip. On May 14, 1804, the party, now numbering about forty-five men and one Newfoundland dog set out up the Missouri.

Although the river provided the men with an abundant supply of fish, it was often treacherous, and even with both sails and poles, the party sometimes made only a few miles a day. There were disciplinary problems and a few accidents, but the Indians and trappers they met at the outset proved to be friendly, and the expedition proceeded much as planned. During

Library of Congress.

An American having struck a Bear but not killed him, escapes into a Tree.

This illustration appeared in the 1810 edition of Patrick Gass's account of the exploration. The explorers were thoroughly impressed by the strength of western bears after this incident.

these months they saw prairie dogs, grizzly bears, and thousands of buffalo.

The party wintered among the Mandan Indians at the junction of the Knife River and the Missouri in what is now North Dakota. Fort Mandan, their home until April 7, 1805, was of crude log and mud construction but had fieldstone fireplaces for heat and eight-foot walls for protection against possible Indian attacks. The explorers got along well with the Mandans, trading them the usual beads and trinkets, whiskey, and tobacco.

As the ice began to thaw after the severe winter, the flatboat went back down river with ten of the party and various specimens to be delivered to the President. These included live birds, squirrels, and plants, as well as samples of Indian clothing and the bones and skins of various animals.

The rest of the group pushed on in canoes and the larger keel boats, carrying with them an interpreter, Touissant Charbonneau, his Indian wife, Sacajawea, who was to prove very helpful before the journey ended, and their son, Jean-Baptiste, born at Fort Mandan in February. Although the going was rough because of ice in the river and bad weather, the trek proceeded without a hitch until the Missouri River forked and the leaders could not decide which branch to take. After several days of scouting and decision making, they correctly chose the southern branch and soon were within sight of the majestic Rockies. The discovery of the breathtaking falls of the Missouri was an exciting event, but it meant a sixteen-mile portage. Lewis decided to cache most of the heavy baggage, discard the keel boats, and continue in canoes.

As the terrain became progressively more rugged, game grew scarcer. Now Lewis and Clark were especially anxious to contact Indians, for they thought that the Shoshone (Sacajawea's original tribe) had horses, which the expedition badly needed. The explorers also were fearful of spending the winter in an unfamiliar wilderness. In August a lone Indian on a horse was encountered, but after a brief, frustrating meeting, he rode away. Several days later, after crossing the Great Divide and discovering the first westward-running river, the party made successful contact with a group of mounted Shoshone; one of the chiefs turned out to be Sacajawea's brother.

Lewis and Clark managed to get about thirty horses from the Shoshone, but no food. The Indians were close to starvation themselves and spent most of their days foraging for edible roots and whatever game could be found. They told Lewis that the small river he had discovered eventually flowed into the Columbia but that much of the intermediate waterway was impassable. Winter was arriving early (there was a heavy frost on August 19), and the expedition set out hurriedly to cross the mountain barrier. Now near starvation, they had to slaughter horses for food.

On September 19 a Nez Percé settlement was discovered. These hospitable Indians literally saved the explorer's lives. After recovering from near disaster, the leaders decided to continue by water, even if the going became difficult. They built canoes in the Indian fashion, left their remaining horses with the Nez Percé, and set off westward.

It took the shabby band another month to reach the Pacific. Their trail, the Kooskooskee River, consisted of a long series of rapids, and the Sanke, into which it emptied, was no easier to navigate. The Indians met along this leg of the journey were shrewd traders. As the expedition approached the mouth of the Columbia it encountered Indians who were familiar with the white man, according to D. B. Chidsey in his account of the expedition, and one was overheard to call another a "son of a pitch [*sic*]." Fleas, syphilis, and English vernacular expressions such as this gave evidence that these folk had been "blessed" by contact with the white man.

It rained incessantly during the first week that was spent near the Pacific. When the weather finally improved, the men set about building Fort Clatsop (named after the local Indians). There they spent the winter. The party became relatively friendly with the Clatsop, and much space was devoted to their customs in the journals of the explorers. There were only twelve days without rain during the four-and-a-half-month stay at the mouth of the Columiba, and the winter was bitter indeed.

Several descriptions of the expedition were distributed to

various Indian chieftans with instructions to give them to any traders or trappers they met; Lewis and Clark hoped some record of the expedition would reach civilization even if the party did not survive. The trip back was difficult, but not so arduous as the initial westward journey since the explorers had made friends with several tribes that could be counted upon for guidance, provisions, and assistance.

After crossing the Rockies, the expedition split into three groups in order to collect more data. In this fashion they were able to explore both the Yellowstone and Missouri rivers. The band led by Lewis had a frightening confrontation with hostile natives, and he was painfully injured in a hunting accident before the groups rendezvoused on the Missouri above Fort Mandan. The trip down river was basically uneventful, and the expedition arrived in St. Louis on September 23, 1806. Its return was celebrated in St. Louis, Louisville, and Washington with much pomp, and the explorers were the celebrities of the day, being awarded acclaim much like that given to twentieth-century aviators and space travelers. Lewis and Clark had explored territory that would become ten states. They had discovered twenty-five hitherto unknown varieties of fish (including the anchovy), six species of birds, five reptiles, and four amphibians. They had greatly expanded the body of scientific knowledge of the western lands as the Louisiana Purchase had expanded the physical limits of the United States.

This epic undertaking ended all speculation concerning a water route via the Louisiana Territory to the Pacific but provided Americans with some insight into what they had bought for $15 million. Both Lewis and Clard resigned from military service shortly after this famous expedition ended, and both subsequently became territorial governors. There the similarities end. Clark, twice married, was active in the War of 1812 as chief executive of the Missouri Territory and led an assault against allied British-Indian forces in Wisconsin. He spent his last years quietly in St. Louis where he was host to numerous Indian delegations and carried on a substantial correspondence with government officials in Washington on their behalf. His home became a museum of sorts, filled with many Indian and natural curiosities. This collection, bequeathed to the St. Louis Natural History Society when he died in 1838, has now virtually disappeared.

Jefferson's reward to Lewis was the governorship of all of the Louisiana Territory north of the state bearing that name. Lewis proved to be an able administrator, but in the fall of 1809 he decided to go to Washington to straighten out some tangled personal finances. Accompanied by two servants, a black and a half-breed Spaniard, on the evening of October 11 Lewis arrived

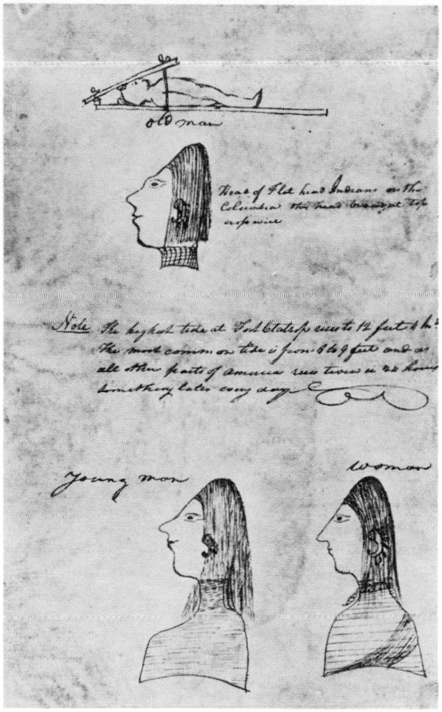

Missouri Historical Society.

William Clark's Journal of the trip included this careful diagram of the Indian custom of head-flattening.

at a crude inn located in central Tennessee. The next morning he was dead. Just what happened is not clear even today. Jefferson, who knew Lewis well, assumed he committed suicide. Others believed he was murdered. (No money was found on his body, and his watch later surfaced in New Orleans).

During the last century or so numerous monuments have been raised to Lewis and Clark, but none are necessary. Their exploits, their deeds, and their journals assure them of prominent places in the annals of American heroes.

Since 1900 a handful of explorers have stirred the admiration of their fellow Americans as they followed in the wake of Lewis and Clark, striking out into the unknown to battle incredible odds and conquer ice, air, and space. These include men such as Robert E. Peary, Richard E. Byrd, Charles A. Lindbergh, and the astronauts of the 1960s.

Peary (1856–1920), a Pennsylvania-born naval officer, made several trips to the Arctic between 1891 and 1906, each time learning more about that region and getting closer to the famed North Pole. On April 6, 1909, Peary, accompanied by four Eskimos, a long-time black companion named Matthew A. Henson, and forty dogs hauling five sleds, reached their goal. Seventeen years later, Richard E. Byrd (1888–1957), another naval officer, flew over the Pole, and then turned his attention to the exploration and conquest of Antarctic where he led five expeditions (1928–1956). During the first of these, he also flew over the South Pole.

The most celebrated American explorer of the early twentieth century was, however, Charles A. Lindbergh (1902–1974), a shy, handsome, twenty-five-year-old youth who flew the Atlantic from New York to Paris alone in a small plane in May 1927, the first man to do so. For a decade or so "Lindy" was the nation's shining hero, but his reputation suffered somewhat when the Lindbergh family fled to England for several years to escape incessant publicity following the kidnap-murder of their oldest son. His popularity waned even more when he became associated with neutrality activists in 1940. Denied a wartime commission, he nevertheless tested aircraft and even flew combat missions in the Pacific as a civilian. During his last years, Lindbergh became an active conservationist seeking aid for primitive tribes and endangered animal species throughout the world.

No astronaut of recent years has enjoyed such adulation as that which greeted young Lindbergh, but among the best-known of America's space veterans are John Glenn, Jr., a pioneer space explorer who is now a United States senator, and Neil Armstrong, Edwin Aldren, and Michael Collins, the first aerospace team to reach the moon. These men wrote no journals as they went, but their deeds alone spoke a special message to Americans. Sitting in the security of our homes, we watched their exploits and almost experienced the thrill of discovery and exploration at firsthand.

Selected Readings

Federalist Politics

David Fischer, *Revolution of American Conservatism: Federalist Party in Jeffersonian Democracy* (1965)

Linda Kerber, *Federalists in Dissent: Imagery and Ideology in Jeffersonian America* (1970)

Jeffersonian Politics

Noble Cunningham, *The Jeffersonian Republicans in Power: Party Operations, 1801–1809* (1963)

Marshall Smelser, *The Democratic Republic, 1801–1815* (1968)

Leonard White, *The Jeffersonians: Administrative History, 1801–1829* (1951)

M. J. Heale, *The Making of American Politics* (1977)

Leonard Levy, *Jefferson and Civil Liberties: the Darker Side* (1963)

Development of Law

Robert K. Faulkner, *Jurisprudence of John Marshall* (1968)

Kent Newmyer, *The Supreme Court under Marshall and Taney* (1969)

Richard Ellis, *The Jeffersonian Crisis: Courts and Politics in the New Republic* (1971)

Foreign Relations

Bradford Perkins, *Prologue to War: England and the United States, 1805–1812* (1961)

Louis Sears, *Jefferson and the Embargo* (1967)

Glen Tucker, *Dawn Like Thunder: Barbary Wars and the Birth of the U. S. Navy* (1963)

Special Incidents

John Bakeless, *Lewis and Clark, Partners in Discovery* (1947)

Thomas Abernethy, *Burr Conspiracy* (1954)

Francis Beirne, *Shout Treason: Trial of Aaron Burr* (1959)

War and Peace

Chapter 7

TIMELINE

1810
Macon's Bill No. 2 removes trade restrictions
1810
Napolean revokes Berlin and Milan Decrees
1812
Congress declares war against Great Britain
1812
Madison reelected as President
1813
Perry's naval victory on Lake Erie
1813
Chief Tecumseh killed
1814
Andrew Jackson defeats the Creek Indians at Horseshoe Bend
1814
British army captures and burns Washington
1814
"The Star-Spangled Banner"
1814
Treaty of Ghent ends war with Great Britain
1814
Hartford Convention
1815
Battle of New Orleans
1816
Second Bank of United States chartered
1816
James Monroe elected President
1819
Panic of 1819
1819
Tallmadge amendment opens slavery controversy
1819
McCulloch v. *Maryland* upholds constitutionality of the National Bank
1820
Missouri Compromise
1821
Florida acquired from Spain
1823
Monroe Doctrine promulgated
1824
House of Representatives elects John Quincy Adams President

CHAPTER OUTLINE

The War of 1812 spelled the end of the Revolutionary era. James Madison, who led the country through the war, was the last of the presidents to have played an active role in founding the nation. The next two presidents, James Monroe and John Quincy Adams, were the last prominent politicians to have served in government before the Constitution was written. After the War of 1812, the first political parties began to disintegrate and new ones came to the fore. Also following the War of 1812, the economy prospered and then entered a serious recession—thereby setting a pattern of boom-and-bust that would plague the American people into the twentieth century.

By 1820, sectionalism, which would burst forth within two generations into the great conflagration of the Civil War, had already begun to smolder. At the same time, hand-in-hand with sectionalism and not always inimical to it, went a sense of nationalism. Some viewed these rivalries of sectional pride as the building blocks that, as they were fitted together, were creating the nation; others saw them as the divisive forces that were destroying it.

The Path to War

During the twenty years preceding the War of 1812, the United States was caught between two superpowers at war, Britain and France. These two nations, engaged in an on-and-off contest for empire, had only minor regrets if in the process they trampled on the dignity or sovereignty of the United States. The key issue was the manner in which the combatants interfered with trade on the high seas. Both the French and the British forbade American captains to enter enemy ports, and the British seized seamen said to be British citizens and forced them to join the British navy. America was not willing to withdraw from the arena of conflict because it found trade with the belligerents far too profitable. Nevertheless, after 1800 British action brought the Jefferson administration to the brink of war. But the President decided to impose the Embargo of 1807 on his own country rather than fight. When James Madison became President in 1809, he partially resumed trade, replacing the unpopular Embargo with the Nonintercourse Act, which permitted American ships to trade with any nation except Britain and France.

Violation of American Neutrality

England controlled the seas and most of the incidents that provoked war were maritime. By 1812, the British had seized some 10,000 Americans from U.S. ships and impressed them into their service. Of course, as claimed, some undoubtedly were British citizens, but these acts still were tantamount to kidnapping and certainly constituted unwarranted interference with neutral commerce. Worse, Britain refused to recognize America's right as a neutral to trade with any nation. Although France under Napoleon seized 600 American ships between 1801 and 1813, by 1811 the British had virtually destroyed the

Courtesy New-York Historical Society, New York City.

Dolley Madison
(1768–1849)

On September 14, 1794, Dolley Payne Todd, a vivacious young Philadelphia widow of Quaker background, married James Madison, a forty-three-year-old Virginia bachelor. Perhaps it was inevitable that this lively lady who lived only one block from where Congress was meeting would marry one of its eligible members, but her choice of slender, stiff, five-and-a-half-foot Madison was something of a surprise.

Dolley (or Dolly, the spelling varies) was born in North Carolina, but her family later moved to a house once owned by Patrick Henry in Hanover County, Virginia. In 1782 her father, unhappy with slavery, freed all of his blacks and went to Philadelphia to open a starch business, an enterprise that collapsed seven years later. To keep the family going, her mother opened a genteel boardinghouse, which enabled Dolley to meet numerous eligible young men. She soon married a Quaker lawyer named Todd who died of yellow fever in 1793, leaving her with a son, John Payne Todd.

Dolley's subsequent marriage to Madison (a non-Quaker) resulted in her expulsion from the Society of Friends. However, the Paynes were not in especially good standing since she was the sixth member of that clan to be ousted in five years. Her marriage to James Madison turned out to be a very happy union as respect and affection blossomed into love.

The place in history of this "fine, portly, buxom dame," as Washington Irving described her, was assured by her long reign as White House hostess from 1801 to 1817. She served unofficially in that capacity for the widower Jefferson and then in her own right during her husband's administration. The key to Dolley Madison's popularity was not elegance or brilliance but an innate friendliness that sometimes won her husband the political support he badly needed.

From 1817 until James Madison's death in 1836, they lived at Montpelier in Orange County, Virginia, a lovely estate that her wayward son managed to ruin. Dolley Madison spent her last years in Washington, beset by financial problems, yet a gracious reminder of an earlier age and a living link to America's Revolutionary past. ■

French navy. As a result, provocations by France on the high seas became fewer and fewer, but high-handed British action continued unabated.

When the Nonintercourse Act proved unworkable, the United States government issued Macon's Bill No. 2 declaring that if either England or France would remove restrictions on American trade, then the United States would favor the complying nation and impose an embargo on the other major power. In 1810 Napoleon ordered his foreign minister to announce in an ambiguous letter that he would revoke his Berlin and Milan decrees and respect American neutral rights. Despite warnings by John Quincy Adams that Napoleon was not to be trusted, Madison announced that the French had complied with Macon's Bill No. 2. This apparent triumph of American policy led the President to ban trade with Britain. Yet when Madison sought concrete guarantees that France would honor American rights, Napoleon was evasive. In fact, he soon announced a new tariff that would make trade with France still more difficult and unprofitable for American merchants.

The British, unconvinced that Napoleon had complied with American demands, asked for proof—and obviously the Americans were unable to produce it. Despite the fact that Napoleon had duped them, the Americans decided to subject the British to commercial restrictions. Madison, unwilling to reverse policy, revived the Nonintercourse Act against Britain; that nation could neither ship goods to America nor import produce and products from there. No matter how untrustworthy Napoleon might be, American leaders still regarded Britain as their great enemy. The clear winner in this jockeying for position was Napoleon; for, when the smoke cleared, the United States was at war and for all practical purposes his ally against Britain.

Impressment and interference with American trade were not the only British crimes. The Americans suspected they were deliberately stirring up anti-American hostility among the Indians of the Old Northwest. And indeed the Shawnee leader Tecumseh and his brother, known as "The Prophet," received aid from British officers in Canada after 1807. Because of the Embargo (although they blamed the British navy instead), Americans in the West were suffering from an economic depression after 1808; their produce brought low prices and imported goods were expensive. To some, a war seemed an excellent way to cure these ills—and, in the process, to smash the British-Indian alliance in the Northwest. War might even provide an opportunity for seizing Florida from Britain's ally, Spain.

The War Hawks

Those most eager for a fight were known as the "War Hawks," politicians who wanted to end British meddling on American soil and defend the nation's honor as well. Men from New Hampshire, western New York state, Kentucky, Tennessee, South Carolina, and Georgia led this group, notably Henry Clay (1777–1852) of Kentucky, Felix Grundy (1777–1840) of Tennessee, and John C. Calhoun (1782–1850) of South Carolina. Young, patriotic to the point of being chauvinistic, they resented wrongs done by both Britain and France (occasionally talked of fighting both) and scorned efforts to accommo-

National Portrait Gallery, Smithsonian Institution, Washington D.C.

John C. Calhoun was a southern nationalist during the War of 1812. By the 1820s when this portrait was made his intense intellectualism had led him to a sectional stance.

Courtesy New-York Historical Society, New York City.

As a War Hawk and peace commissioner Henry Clay would help both to both begin and end the War of 1812.

date either power and maintain peace. In addition, almost without exception they possessed a vision of a great United States encompassing all of North America.

Declaration of War

In Madison's war message, issued on June 1, 1812, the President stressed impressment and violations of American neutrality rights as the principle causes for hostility:

> "Our commerce has been plundered in every sea, the great staples of our country have been cut off from their legitimate markets, and a destructive blow aimed at our agricultural and maritime interests. . . . Not content with these occasional expedients for laying waste our neutral trade, the cabinet of Britain resorted at length to the sweeping system of blockades, under the name of orders-in-council, which has been molded and managed as might best suit its political views, its commercial jealousies, or the avidity of British cruisers."

Despite these charges and a decade or more of provocation, Madison's call for action faced stiff opposition. Eighteen days later Congress declared war, but the vote was close—19 to 13 in the Senate, 79 to 49 in the House. New England, the last bastion of the dying Federalist party, and the Middle Atlantic states generally opposed the war. The South and West were for it. Coastal and mercantile folk were cool, even downright hostile to this campaign to protect trade on the high seas. Citizens in some New England towns and cities flew flags at half-

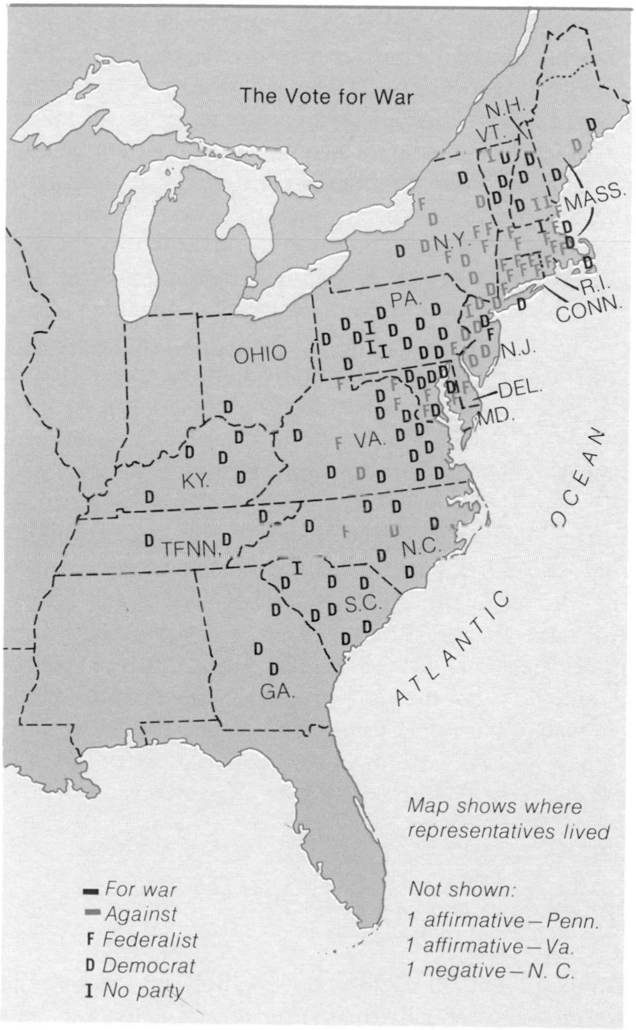

mast, while those living farthest from the Atlantic Ocean cheered loudest.

At the beginning of the twentieth century, historians dismissed some of Madison's motives as mere rhetorical camouflage for America's deeper lust for new land. They pointed out that if freedom of the seas had been the true cause of the war, then surely East coast merchants would have been the most bellicose element of the population. The South and the West, this interpretation said, longed to annex Canada and Florida to the United States, and these expansionist ambitions were the underlying reasons for war. The classic statement of this position is *The Expansionists of 1812* by Julius Pratt.

In the last fifteen years, historians have taken a new look at the War of 1812. One view is that Madison and Congress truly feared Britain might reduce the United States to colonial status once more. From 1807 to 1812 America tried to solve problems with Britain peacefully, but the British, underestimating the anger such acts engendered, continued to violate U.S. rights. Some Jeffersonian Republicans eventually concluded that, if America did not use force, Britain might reassert its dominion over the young republic. Another view is that the war was fought to ensure American economic freedom. The West and the South were suffering a real depression because of British interference with Atlantic commerce. American shipowners might be humiliated by British policies, but all the same they were making money by supplying British armies in Europe. American farmers, however, blamed their economic woes on Britain and saw that nation's arrogance as a threat to American independence. Shipowners of the Northeast were making a killing—ocean freight rates doubled in the ten years preceding the war, and Boston's harbor was never busier. Conversely, agricultural prices were sagging—farm prices had declined 15 percent since 1801. This undoubtedly is not the last word on the causes of this brief, confusing, but rather important conflict, for debate continues. Nevertheless, most historians agree that this war can be seen as "the completion of American independence."

The War of 1812

Although not all Democratic-Republicans backed the war, it was essentially their struggle, and as the war went on, more and more stood behind it despite a lingering apathy. The Federalists fell into an antiwar stance that lost them sympathy and badly damaged the party. In South Carolina and Georgia, Federalism died out completely. Many prominent Federalists, including John Adams and his son, defected to the Republican party. Even in New England, the Federalist stronghold, young people ignored their elders and enlisted in the federal army at a respectably patriotic rate.

New England in general, however, was so opposed that it flirted with treason. Taking a strong states' right approach and a narrow view of the Constitution, Federalist leaders obstructed Madison at every turn. The governors of Massachusetts and Connecticut refused to let their state militia serve in the war. Worse, New England actively traded with the enemy, selling supplies and exporting a million bushels of grain to Britain. The Federalists held that the Republicans were Napoleon's lackeys who were deliberately fighting in order to impoverish the Northeast and enrich the West.

Antiwar sentiment in New England found its strongest expression in the Hartford Convention of 1814. During the war Federalists gained so much strength in the Northeast that they felt confident enough to call a meeting of New England states to discuss the grave issues of the day. The state legislatures of Massachusetts, Connecticut, and Rhode Island appointed delegates, though New Hampshire and Vermont largely ignored the proceedings. John Quincy Adams accused the convention of planning to secede from the union, but the delegates were in fact more moderate and merely recommended several amendments to the Constitution. One would diminish the power of the prowar Republican South by basing representation and taxation on the number of free people alone (under the Constitution three-fifths of the slaves were counted for this purpose). A second amendment limited embargoes to no more than sixty days—clearly a way to avoid a repetition of Jefferson's Embargo of 1807, which had been so harmful to northeastern commerce. A third amendment barred naturalized citizens from holding federal offices; this resolution struck hard at the Democratic-Republican party, whose greatest strength was in the new states and among naturalized citizens everywhere. A fourth amendment required a two-thirds vote of both houses of Congress to admit new states, an obvious effort to restore the region's national political power.

The convention expected to meet again after Congress responded to these demands, but when the three-man delegation arrived in Washington early in 1815, the war was over. In the general jubilation of peace, Americans soon forgot the proposals forged at Hartford, but this action—bordering on treason in the eyes of some individuals—virtually ruined the Federalist party. Never again was it a factor in American politics.

Yet the Democratic-Republicans under Madison had problems, too. Political maneuvering within Madison's party forced him to accept a cabinet that did not please him. Robert Smith, Secretary of State until 1811, was most famous for having substituted bourbon whiskey for rum in the navy ration when he served as Jefferson's Secretary of Navy. The President wanted Albert Gallatin to head the State Department, but the Senate never would confirm the appointment because Gallatin had uncovered and publicized graft in the Senate. Gallatin remained as Secretary of the Treasury until 1813, when he resigned in disgust after learning that Madison, out of political expediency, had named an incompetent person as Secretary of War and other incompetents to lucrative posts as well. During the war years, Madison's only able cabinet member was James Monroe, who replaced Robert Smith in 1811 as Secretary of State.

Despite this confused state of affairs in both cabinet and Congress, the voters did not repudiate the Democratic-Republicans in the election of 1812, although Madison faced stiff opposition. A coalition of eastern antiwar Democratic-Republicans and Federalists supported DeWitt Clinton of New York who carried all of the northeastern states except Vermont and Pennsylvania. The Federalists even increased their strength in Congress momentarily.

Library of Congress.

Albert Gallatin, Secretary of the Treasury to both Jefferson and Madison, watched his frugal budgets destroyed by war. This sketch was made when he was part of the peace commission at Ghent.

Although constant disaster led to a major overhaul of both the army and navy as soon as peace returned, events in the economic and political realms (both before and during the war) probably had more impact on American life than those on the battlefield or high seas. Several factors help to explain an upsurge in manufacturing, especially in New England. Various machines such as the spinning jenny, improved casting techniques, steam engines, and both the assembly line and the use of interchangeable parts paved the way for rapid innovation. Jefferson's Embargo, plus nonintercourse schemes and war, cut European imports and created unprecedented demands for finished goods. Considerable capital flowed into new factories where quick profits were realized. Cotton mill spindles increased at least sixteenfold (1807–1815) and the value of factory-made woolens, nearly five times, from $4 to $19 million (1810–1815). The war clearly sparked an economic boom that soon burst, an all-too-familiar theme in U.S. history.

This conflict was the watershed of Jeffersonian democracy. It ruined the Federalists but also changed the outlook of their opponents. Embarrassed and sobered by bungling defeat and disaster, they realized that many basic Federalist tenets—higher taxes, a strong army and navy, a federal bureaucracy, factories, and industrial urban centers—were necessary for the total well-being of a growing nation. Agriculture alone was not enough. In short, the Democratic-Republicans ended up embracing many planks in the platform of their vanishing foe.

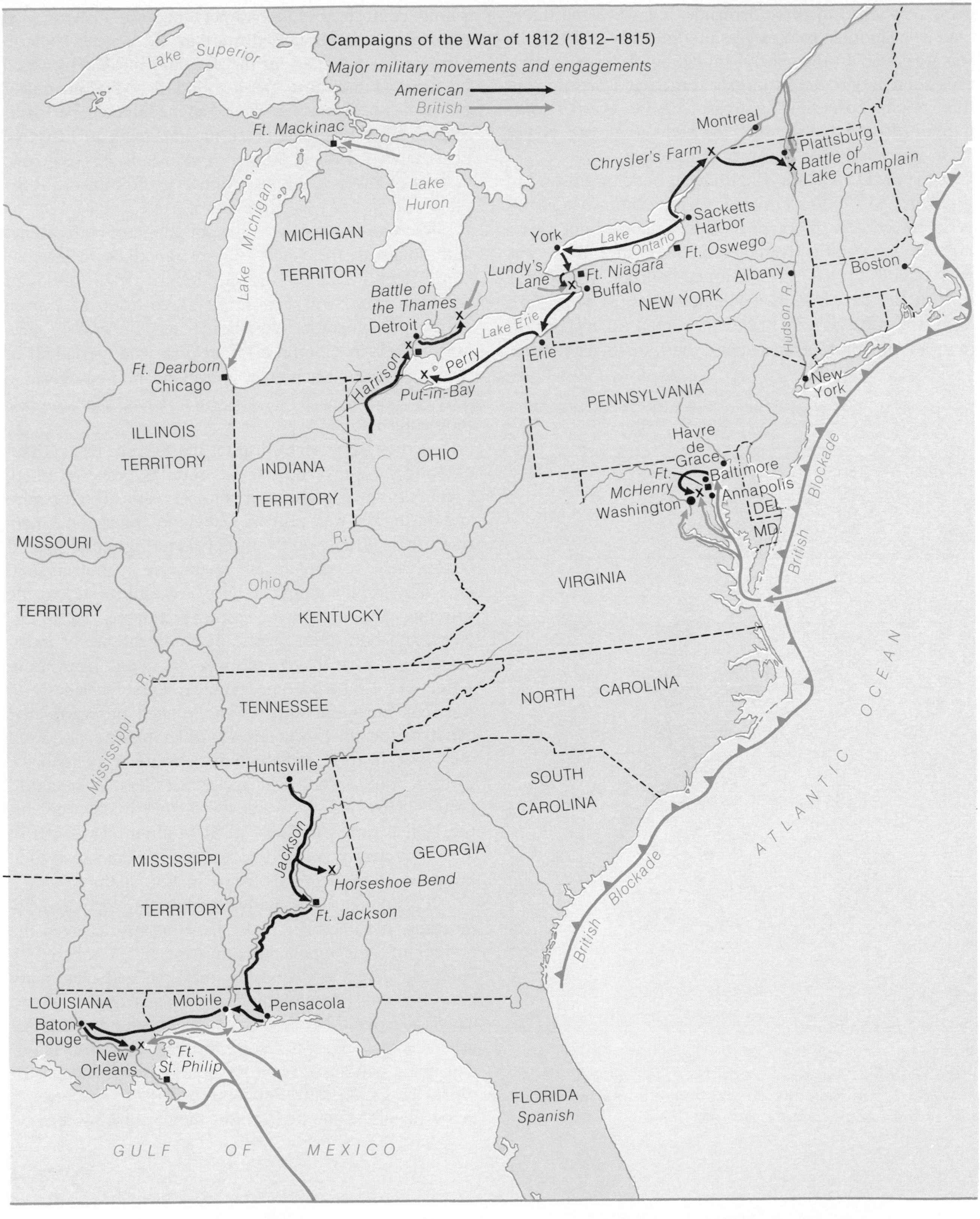

Campaigns of the War of 1812 (1812–1815)
Major military movements and engagements
American
British
Lake Superior
Ft. Mackinac
Lake Michigan
Lake Huron
MICHIGAN
TERRITORY
Montreal
Chrysler's Farm
Plattsburg
Battle of Lake Champlain
Sacketts Harbor
York
Lake Ontario
Ft. Oswego
Lundy's Lane
Ft. Niagara
Buffalo
Albany
Boston
Battle of the Thames
Detroit
Lake Erie
NEW YORK
Hudson R.
Erie
Harrison
Perry
Put-in-Bay
Ft. Dearborn
Chicago
New York
PENNSYLVANIA
ILLINOIS
TERRITORY
INDIANA
TERRITORY
OHIO
Havre de Grace
Baltimore
Ft. McHenry
Annapolis
Washington
DEL.
MD.
British Blockade
MISSOURI
TERRITORY
R.
Ohio
VIRGINIA
KENTUCKY
Mississippi R.
NORTH CAROLINA
TENNESSEE
Huntsville
SOUTH CAROLINA
ATLANTIC OCEAN
Jackson
MISSISSIPPI
TERRITORY
GEORGIA
Horseshoe Bend
Ft. Jackson
British Blockade
LOUISIANA
Mobile
Pensacola
Baton Rouge
New Orleans
Ft. St. Philip
FLORIDA
Spanish
GULF OF MEXICO

The Canadian Incursion

Once the Americans declared war, the only British soldiers they could easily attack were in Canada. For years Americans nurtured the fond if unfounded dream that Canadians wanted nothing so much as to join the United States. An attack on Canada had additional virtues. Canada had a much smaller population than the United States and was even less well prepared for war. There were only a few thousand British soldiers there, and England was unlikely to send more since the much larger struggle against Napoleon was entering its final stages.

Despite all these advantages, the American invasion of Canada proved to be a humiliating fiasco. A sorry set of bunglers led the American army, and various militia units refused to obey them. General William Hull, stationed in Detroit, advanced on Canada but turned back without firing a shot when he heard that Tecumseh had joined the Canadians. The Canadian general, Isaac Brock, pursued Hull, besieged Detroit, and forced the Americans to surrender without a fight. Loss of control of the Northwest meant that military campaigns could only be mounted in the East and that later in the war Americans would have to win back their own land.

The next major front of the war was the area around Niagara Falls. An American army decided to attack the capital of Upper Canada, York (modern Toronto), but once more the Canadians routed the invading force. Finally, a campaign up the Lake Champlain corridor to Montreal ended in similar chaos. When General Henry Dearborn tried to follow this route, his men refused to travel more than twenty miles.

The campaign against Canada would be remembered as pure farce were it not for the splendid victory of Captain Oliver Hazard Perry. Working feverishly, early in 1813 Perry began to construct a small navy on Lake Erie using supplies hauled across mountains and floated on barges upriver. But all the work paid off handsomely, for in September Perry smashed the British fleet at Put-in-Bay on Lake Erie. Elated, Perry reported: "We have met the enemy and they are ours." Perry's victory forced the British to abandon Detroit and surrender control of the Great Lakes. General William Harrison's defeat of the retreating British helped nail down this American triumph. During this encounter the Indian leader Tecumseh was killed, and with his death the Indian confederacy of the Northwest collapsed.

Pursuing their winning streak, the Americans advanced on York, seized it, and burned the houses of Parliament. Nevertheless, American leaders, convinced that they could not subdue Canada, retreated back to their own borders. By the end of 1813 the United States had a secure hold over its own territory, but it had made scarcely a dent in Canada. If anything, the American invasion served to stir patriotism among Canadians as they defended their homeland against foreign enemies.

The Sea Battles

Although Madison stressed maritime grievances in his war message, Americans had no hope at all of besting the British navy, the greatest in the world. At the beginning of the war, the entire American navy consisted of sixteen vessels; the British had more than 100 frigates (intermediate war ships) and about the same number of ships of the line (huge three-deckers, all of them mounted with at least seventy-four cannon). Yet, in the first year of the war, to the bewildered astonishment and the ecstatic delight of the Americans, their tiny navy held its own. Hundreds of merchant vessels became privateers (that is, they were armed and their captains authorized to seize enemy craft) and attacked British commercial ships sailing between London and the colonial ports in the New World. Some of them even raided British ships in the English Channel and off Ireland.

Far more troubling to British morale, however, was the contest between the American frigate, the *Constitution* ("Old Ironsides"), and a British ship, the *Guerrière.* The two ships sighted each other about 450 miles southeast of Halifax, Nova Scotia, on the afternoon of August 19, 1812. They were almost equally matched, though the *Constitution* had six more guns and nearly 200 more men. Like so many British vessels of the day, the *Guerrière* was seriously undermanned, a problem only exacerbated when ten impressed American sailors aboard her were allowed to go below rather than fight their countrymen.

After an hour of jockeying for position, the *Constitution* drew up to within 50 yards of the British vessel and fired heavily, one well-aimed cannon ball cracking a mast and toppling it. Soon the *Guerrière's* other two masts fell, debris covered its decks and the main guns dipped into the water. The British ship surrendered without further resistance. Fifteen crew members were dead and 63 wounded (the *Constitution* had seven dead and seven wounded).

Courtesy New-York Historical Society, New York City.

Oliver Hazard Perry
(1785–1819)

America's first naval hero was born in Rhode Island, where he began to study navigation at an early age in Newport. When he was fourteen, he became a midshipman aboard his father's ship, served in the West Indies, and took part in the war with Tripoli.

Handsome, polite, and extremely ambitious, Perry was eager for glory when the War of 1812 broke out. He traveled to Washington, D.C. to ask for a commission and was eventually put in command of the naval forces on Lake Erie. In the spring of 1813, he and his men built a small fleet of ten ships. Put-in-Bay, near the present city of Sandusky, Ohio, became his headquarters, and it was there that he fought his famous battle with the British commander, Robert H. Barclay.

The encounter took place between noon and 3 P.M. on September 10, 1813. The two navies were about equally matched. When Perry's flagship was so battered by enemy fire that he was forced to abandon it, he transferred to another vessel. Fifteen minutes later the entire enemy fleet surrendered. Barclay lost 41 sailors; Perry 27.

This was the first time that an American had ever captured a British fleet, and the feat made Perry a national hero. More importantly, it secured American control of Lake Erie for the rest of the war. After elaborate fetes in his honor in several American cities, Perry took command of a small force of seamen along the Potomac.

In May 1819 Perry was sent to South America. There he protested the piratical raids of ships from the republics of Venezuela and Buenos Aires on American vessels, but he died of yellow fever a few days after completing his negotiations. His body was buried first on Trinidad but was later transferred to Newport. ■

The *Constitution* scored another stunning victory in December when it destroyed the British frigate, the *Java,* off the coast of Brazil. Earlier a third frigate, the *Macedonian,* was lost to the Americans. *The Times* of London, dismayed by these defeats and news that American privateers had seized 500 smaller British vessels, asked,

Courtesy J. Ross Robertson Collection, Metropolitan Toronto Library Board.

Americans attacked the British in the most convenient location, Canada. The invasions were all defeats for Americans and helped to create Canadian nationalism. This shows the attack on York (Toronto), April 27, 1813.

The news of spectacular one-on-one victories at sea such as the Constitution's over the Guerriere helped to distract Americans from defeats on land.

Anne S.K. Brown Military Collection, Brown University Library.

"Can these statements be true; and can the English people hear them unmoved?"

Humiliated, the Royal Navy sent more and more ships to America, and early in 1813 British vessels succeeded in bottling up American ships in their home ports. A tight British blockade of the East coast proved effective in stopping the depredations of the American navy. American privateer vessels, however, continued to stage raids; by the end of the war they had captured more than 1,300 British ships valued with their cargoes at more than $40 million.

The Burning of Washington

In April 1814 Napoleon abdicated, and the war in Europe was over. Now the British could turn their attention to the United States. In August, 10,000 European veterans arrived on American shores. Their chief goal was to secure Canada and to win a new boundary that would give it the Great Lakes, Lake Champlain, and northern Maine, but the Battle of Plattsburg (September 11) dashed these hopes. An American naval captain, Thomas Macdonough, had ordered his men to fashion ships out of Vermont timber, an arduous task they were able to ac-

Library of Congress.

This aquatint was done shortly after the British burned the U.S. Capitol. People view the roofless building while debris still lies in the street.

complish in a few short weeks. Suddenly the Americans had a navy on Lake Champlain—four warships and ten gunboats confronting four British warships and twelve gunboats. In the ensuing conflict, Macdonough commanded with such brilliance (except when he was knocked unconscious for a moment by the flying head of a decapitated sailor) that all four British warships were destroyed. Sir George Prevost, commander of the British forces, retreated to Canada and gave up plans of encroaching on American territory.

Events elsewhere, however, cast a pall over this stunning triumph. President Madison had worried about the lack of defenses for the city of Washington, but Secretary of War Armstrong assured him there was no danger. The Secretary was wrong, for in August 1814, 4500 redcoats moved up the Chesapeake Bay and fought the ill-equipped, poorly trained, and cowardly militia of Maryland and the District of Columbia. The battle ended quickly as the Americans fled in panic, an encounter some wits dubbed "the Bladensburg Races." Madison departed in such haste that his dinner was still warm on the table of the White House when the British commanders sat down to eat it. After finishing Madison's meal, the redcoats set fire to the White House and the Capitol—retribution for the American sacking of York and Dover in Canada. "The capital and the Union lost by cowardice," read an anonymous scrawl on the wall of a building in Washington.

Courtesy New-York Historical Society, New York City.

This primitive engraving was sketched the morning of the bombardment of Fort McHenry. The bombs bursting above the fort attracted both this artist and poet Francis Scott Key.

Leaving a stunned, smoke-scarred Washington, the British marched on Baltimore. There they met a more resolute militia force, which turned back their assault, and a short time later these invaders departed. In the midst of this highly embarrassing episode, really a nuisance raid to teach the upstart Yankees "a lesson," America's national anthem was born. On the evening of September 13, Francis Scott Key (1779–1843), a young lawyer, went aboard a British warship to secure the release of a Maryland physician. Before they could depart, the bombardment of Baltimore began. Through the long night Key watched in agonized suspense; but, to his delight, at daybreak the Stars and Stripes still flew proudly over the ramparts of Fort McHenry, so he wrote the poem that was later set to the music of a British tavern song.

The Hero of New Orleans

Throughout the War of 1812, American forces in the South whittled away at Spanish Florida, a goal of young War Hawks from Georgia and South Carolina. In 1812, an American force gained control of part of West Florida, the section that rimmed the Gulf Coast from New Orleans east to the present state of Florida, thus annexing the important outpost of Mobile.

These moves alarmed the Indians of the Southeast. Traditionally they played off one nation against another and precariously maintained hegemony over their lands, but now the French had pulled out of the area, the Spanish were powerless, and the British were concentrating their interests in Canada and along the eastern coast of the United States. White American settlements were pressing in around the Creek, Cherokee, Choctaw and Chickasaw Indians—and more and more bloody incidents occurred. When Creeks friendly to Tecumseh staged a raid on Fort Mims (near Mobile) in August 1813 that left over 200 whites dead, white Americans had a pretext for a massive reprisal. In March 1814, Andrew Jackson (1767–1845) defeated hostile Creeks at Horseshoe Bend on the Tallapoosa River, killing over 800 and forcing them to cede two-thirds of their lands.

The American militia was in firm control of the Southeast when rumors began to circulate that the British were planning an attack on Louisiana. On his way to defend New Orleans, Jackson burned Pensacola in West Florida on November 7 so that the British could not use it as a base. The British then had to launch their attack from Jamaica.

In the first move of the Battle of New Orleans, the British won a point by marching through the bayous

Courtesy New Orleans Museum of Art.

This painting of the Battle of New Orleans was done by a participant. Note the heavy guns in the front of the American lines. These produced the most casualties among the British.

rather than taking the easier river route to the city—the one Jackson planned to defend. But then the British waited too long for reinforcements, and Jackson had time to reorganize his defenses. Commanding a motley army of bedraggled Tennessee militia, free blacks, former French pirates, and New Orleans citizens, Jackson seemed an easy mark.

But when the British troops, led by Sir Edward Pakenham, advanced in a rigid frontal attack, the slaughter was terrifying. In five crucial minutes Jackson's twenty cannon killed 2,036 redcoats, Pakenham, and another general. Only 8 Americans were killed. The massacre was so total that the British hastily withdrew.

This dazzling victory quickly made Jackson a national hero and launched him on the path to the White House. It also helped Americans to forget many months of inglorious defeats. Although serious negotiations were underway long before Pakenham and Jackson met, news traveled so slowly that neither was aware that a peace treaty had been signed. Perhaps of greater importance than the outcome of this belated triumph itself was the strategic advantage it gave Americans. The British, weary of war, had no heart to renew this faraway contest and any hopes of wresting the Louisiana Purchase from the United States (perhaps by giving it to Spain at the Congress of Vienna) were dashed once and for all.

Library of Congress.

This cartoon shows Britain (John Bull) dictating trade terms to the Americans. Bull asks for everything except Porter and Perry, two American naval heroes of the War of 1812.

The Harry T. Peters Collection, Museum of the City of New York.

Andrew Jackson's defense of New Orleans became the crowning triumph remembered by Americans. This engraving, done while Jackson was president shows his appeal as a military hero.

Peace Negotiations

Even during the first months of the war, peace talks were already under way between Britain and the United States. In fact, in the first week of the conflict Russia, England's ally against Napoleon, offered to act as an intermediary. John Quincy Adams, the urbane, intellectual son of John Adams, then serving as the American minister in Russia, encouraged these overtures. President Madison, willing to consider this route to peace, sent two more American representatives to Russia—James A. Bayard and Treasury Secretary Albert Gallatin.

When Russian mediations failed to interest Britain, Bayard and Gallatin went directly to London for negotiations. Early in 1814 the British decided to begin peace talks and Madison added the fiery, hard-drinking Henry Clay and Jonathan Russell, the American chargé d'affaires in London, to the official delegation. The peace talks, which at length opened at Ghent in Belgium, started off on an inauspicious note when the Americans insisted that the British promise to abandon the practice of impressment. The British balked—and a stalemate seemed inevitable over the old question of American rights on the high seas. But fortunately Madison, recognizing that now that the European war was over the British would have no need to continue impressing American sailors into their navy, sent new instructions to his delegates: they need no longer discuss the issue at all.

The British demands were ominous because they revealed that the British, unable to face the reality of American independence, clearly intended to undo the treaty of 1783. England wanted to create a buffer state for the Indians of the Old Northwest, a scheme that would take a large bite out of America's northern boundary since the proposed territory would lie north of the Ohio River. By so doing, England planned to protect Canada from future invasions, reward its Indian allies with an independent state of their own, and exclude Americans from the profitable fur trade. When the Americans flatly refused this demand for an Indian state, the British pressed for a new, more southern Canadian boundary that would include much of Maine and the Great Lakes.

The treaty talks easily could have broken down at this point and war continued. But external events suddenly made the British more reasonable. News of Macdonough's victory and failure of the British invasion of the Northeast arrived. Then the Duke of Wellington, the English military genius who defeated Napoleon, shrewdly observed that no victory was possible in America unless the Royal Navy could gain control of the Great Lakes. Finally, the simultaneous Congress of Vienna that was settling the fate of Europe in the wake of Napoleon's abdication was experiencing some uneasy moments. Renewed war in Europe seemed possible, and Britain had no heart for a continuation of hostilities in two hemispheres. Her war debt already was staggering, and another year of military operations in America surely would be opposed by the British public and the House of Commons.

As a result, the British softened their hard line and on December 24, 1814, signed the Treaty of Ghent. Impressment and neutral rights, though these were the stated reasons for Madison's declaration of war, were not even mentioned. Neither were questions of fishing rights, trade regulations, or indemnities. Americans were neither granted nor denied the right to trade with British India; the British did not gain specific permission to navigate the Mississippi (one of their fondest hopes). All of these unsolved problems were referred to joint commissions for future discussion, and the Treaty of Ghent is as notable for what it did not spell out as for the terms it did.

The treaty simply returned everything to where it had been before the war, the status quo ante bellum. As Adams put it, "Nothing was adjusted, nothing was settled—nothing in substance but an indefinite suspension of hostilities was agreed to." Some Americans (Henry Clay most vociferously) considered the treaty worthless, but the majority rejoiced in the fact that the new nation had held its own against mighty Britannia.

And, as history has demonstrated, the treaty was a remarkably good one. Never again have the United States and England gone to war with each other. The joint commissions that handled the unsolved problems won many advantages for America, and established a precedent for settling Anglo-American disputes in the future. The Canadian boundary, as far west as the Rockies, was established along the forty-ninth parallel. Another agreement arranged for both Americans and Canadians to settle in what are now the states of Oregon and Washington. A commercial treaty opened the entire British empire (except the West Indies) to unrestricted American trade—a complete reversal of England's long-held mercantilistic policy of maintaining the mother country and her colonies as a closed economic system. A pact limiting both Britain and the United States to only four armed ships each on the Great Lakes defused any threat of renewed hostilities in that region.

Postwar Developments

During the next decade (1815–1825), momentous but subtle, far-reaching changes occurred in American life. Various statesmen, for the best of reasons, charted a course that, while it did not make civil strife inevitable, certainly heightened sectional tensions. Although Madison and the Democratic-Republicans were committed spiritually to the Jeffersonian ideal of America as an agrarian paradise, they were realistic enough to recognize the importance of the nation's infant industries. In effect, they began to pursue Hamilton's dream of an industrial nation, not that of their aged mentor at Monticello. In 1816 Congress passed a mild protectionist tariff to guard American industry against British competition—the first U.S. tariff not designed simply to raise revenue. At the time, this action won widespread support because even men like the aging Jefferson, who ostensibly abhorred factories and cities, realized the young republic must have some industry. However, England, fast becoming the world's leading industrial power, was alarmed. Its mills had to have American customers. Although the English might remain contemptuous of their transatlantic cousins, whom they considered uncouth bumpkins, they wanted their dollars. To dissuade America from pursuing a protectionist course, England passed a series of trade laws making America's business dealings with England more profitable. Though John Quincy Adams, Secretary of State, acknowledged these favors with a few gracious nods, America actually was unimpressed and went on to pass a still stiffer tariff bill in 1824.

Although these measures tended in time to divide more settled parts of the United States into a factory North and a plantation South, intense national feeling created by the outcome of the war with Britain muted these experiences. And no national voice boomed louder than that of Chief Justice John Marshall as he and his fellow justices handed down decisions strengthening federal power. The disarray of the Federalists as they faded into oblivion accentuated this national mood, political party lines becoming so blurred and indistinct that some historians call these years "The Era of Good Feelings." However, this supposedly euphoric mood did not extend to voters in the listless national election of 1816, when three-fourths of the congressmen lost their seats. Since few Federalists were extant, the electorate that elected James Monroe as Madison's successor, simply replaced one set of Democratic-Republicans with another. The reason? The lawmakers had just passed a bill raising their own salaries, an unpardonable sin in the eyes of tight-fisted Americans of those days.

Monroe's two campaigns for the White House cannot be termed stirring or dramatic. In 1816, despite a general lack of enthusiasm for Monroe in the congressional caucus, Jefferson's protégé and one-time neighbor received the nomination; yet, except for some incredible bungling by admirers of Georgia's William H. Crawford, it might have gone to him. Crawford, an engaging, popular figure, was Madison's Secretary of War and the only obstacle between Monroe and the presidency. He reportedly said he would not oppose Monroe, so about two dozen of his supporters failed to attend the caucus, thereby giving Monroe an eleven vote margin and the support of less than half of his party's congressmen. Monroe went on to win 183 electoral votes to 34 for Rufus King, the candidate of the discredited Federalists, who carried only Massachusetts, Connecticut, and Delaware. Four years later Monroe got all of the electoral votes except that of a New Hampshire man who cast his ballot for John Quincy Adams.

Acquisition of the Floridas, 1815–1821

Although the United States invaded West Florida during the War of 1812 and Jackson temporarily seized the Spanish fortress at Pensacola, Spain and the United States were not officially at war. Therefore the question of the two Floridas could not come up at the peace talks at Ghent, and they remained Spanish. In the postwar years, however, the clever John Quincy Adams was able to secure the territory for the United States. Although his efforts to purchase that peninsula were aided immeasurably by the high-handed tactics of Andrew Jackson.

After the Battle of Horseshoe Bend, the defeated Creeks fled into Florida where they found a safe haven from which they could dart across the Georgia border and harass American settlers. Skirmishes and reprisals occurred constantly. When the American commander in Georgia burned a Seminole village, the Seminoles retaliated in 1817 and seized an American hospital ship and killed thirty-six soldiers, six women, and four children.

The American reaction was outrage. Early in 1818, acting on vague instructions from Washington, Andrew Jackson decided to track down the Creeks in East Florida. He put two Indian chiefs to death on the grounds that he *suspected* they might have encouraged raids.

Next, Jackson made Fort St. Marks his base of operations, sending the Spanish garrison fleeing to Pensacola. In his march through Florida he arrested two British subjects, tried them, and convicted one for writing letters to European and American governments on the Indians' behalf and the other for aiding and comforting the Indians in their war on the United States. The first man was hanged; the second, shot. Now Jackson returned to Pensacola, the scene of his earlier triumph, and seized it. By late May he had wiped out all Spanish and Indian opposition and captured the Spanish governor, Don José Masot.

When the news of Jackson's actions reached Washington, the President and the Cabinet panicked and were in favor of disowning General Jackson. Clearly Jackson had violated international law by putting two British subjects to death in Spanish territory. Worse, negotiations with the Spanish minister to Washington concerning boundaries in both Texas and East Florida might break down.

Only John Quincy Adams saw the diplomatic hay to be made out of Jackson's antics. Instead of apologizing profusely, Adams went so far as to suggest coolly that the Spanish government ought to pay the United States for the expense of policing its unruly colony. Adams cleared Jackson of all blame, shook a disapproving finger at Spanish incompetence, and announced that the two British subjects Jackson killed had been plotting "a creeping and insidious war, both against Spain and the United States . . . to plunder Spain of her province, and to spread massacre and devestation along the borders of the United States." All of these charges Adams knew to be untrue.

But this strategy worked. The Spanish, weakened by European wars and revolts in many parts of their empire, accepted the inevitable, and in 1819 a treaty, the Adams-Onís Treaty, was drawn up, though Spain did not approve it until 1821. Spain agreed to turn the Floridas over to the United States in return for $5 million, which the American government would pay to its own citizens with claims against Spain. The Spanish were willing to make such a drastic settlement in order to gain firm title to Texas. The original terms of the Louisiana Purchase had been vague, and Adams was willing to give up Texas (temporarily at least) if Spain would cede to the United States all claim to the Oregon country. The bargain was struck, and it was so favorable to the United States that Adams recorded in his diary: "The acquisition of the Floridas has long been an object of earnest desire to this country. The acknowledgement of a definite line of boundary to the South Sea forms a great epoch in our history. The first proposal of it in this negotiation was my own."

The Monroe Doctrine

Turmoil in Spain's dominions in Central and South America and belated British recognition of the true role of the United States gave birth to a document that meant little when issued but eventually became a cornerstone of American diplomatic policy.

As early as 1811, Simón Bolívar led a revolution that freed Venezuela from Spain. In the following years the vast Spanish empire in Latin America began to dissolve with great rapidity as a series of republics appeared.

In 1815 at the Congress of Vienna, the victors over Napoleon—Great Britain, Russia, Prussia and Austria—pledged to combat republicanism and preserve monarchical rights. Spain's loss of her South American colonies concerned them greatly and the Quadruple Alliance theoretically was duty bound to restore those lands to their former king. The sovereigns of Russia, Prussia, and Austria, while not willing to go to war to subdue the South American republics, did support the Spanish cause. England, however, was less interested in protecting royal prerogatives than in capturing new markets—and South America, freed from the closed mercantilistic system of the Spanish empire, was a very tempting market indeed.

As a result, Britain wanted to keep South America independent, free of Spanish control, and this concern increased in 1823 when a French army marched into Spain with the ostensible purpose of protecting King Ferdinand VII from his own rebellious people. If the French gained control over Spain, might they not take the next step and attempt to recapture former Spanish colonies?

Britain offered to announce, in conjunction with the United States, a statement saying that neither nation could stand idly by and watch French interference in Latin America. John Quincy Adams, however, thought joint action would make America a mere instrument of Britain's will. There were other disadvantages, too. Any pledge of noninterference might stand in the way of eventual acquisition of Cuba, an island Adams thought should belong to the United States. Finally, in Adams' opinion, America's true rival for control of the New World was not France but Britain.

Adams convinced James Monroe, the new President, to issue a unilateral policy; after some hesitation (Monroe was always slow to make up his mind), the President did so in a speech to Congress delivered in December 1823. The Monroe Doctrine, written by Adams, stated two basic principles: European powers could not create new colonies in the New World; and European powers could not intervene in the affairs of the Americas, nor should the New World attempt to intervene in those of the Old. As Monroe put it: "The occasion has been judged proper, for asserting a principle in which the rights and interests of the United States are involved, that the American Continents, by the free and independent condition which they have assumed and maintain, are henceforth not to be considered as subjects for future colonization by any European Power." Nor could citizens of the United States, as they looked at the new Latin American republics, "view any interposition for the purpose of oppressing them, or controlling in any other manner, their destiny, by any European power, in any other light, than as the manifestation of an unfriendly disposition towards the United States." This doctrine was aimed as much at Britain as at the other European powers. At the time, the Monroe Doctrine scarcely interested, and certainly failed to intimidate, any European nation, since the United States was a third-rate power incapable of backing up its strong words, and it was actually the British fleet, not this doctrine, which stymied European meddling. After the middle of the nineteenth century, however, it was frequently invoked with decided effect.

The Bank of the United States

In the years following the War of 1812, the United States scored important successes: Britain now recognized that the United States would never be a colony again and must be courted as a market. Jackson and Adams secured the Floridas for America. American industry, aided by the British wartime blockade, was growing and the entire economy was flourishing.

This happy turn of events made the Democratic-Republicans supreme; after 1816 the moribund Federalists did not even attempt to run a presidential candidate. To win the support of commerce and business, the Democratic-Republicans talked less about agriculture and small government. To be sure, some party faithful remained distrustful of nationalism.

On December 5, 1815, Madison submitted his seventh state of the Union message to Congress. It was not a ringing document, but clearly reflected change both present and future. The President called for a "uniform national currency" administered by a national bank if state banks could not do the job, a tariff to protect infant industries from foreign competition, and a program to create roads and canals "which can best be executed under national authority . . . requiring national jurisdiction and national means." Had he not been in his grave for over a decade, Alexander Hamilton could have written these words himself.

Especially representative of the changing views of the Democratic-Republicans was their attitude towards a national bank. Under Jefferson the Democratic-Republicans opposed Hamilton's first Bank of the United States as unconstitutional and as an undemocratic ally of merchants and financiers in the Northeast. Indeed, the party allowed the bank's charter to expire in 1811—even though its financial help obviously would be needed to pay for the upcoming war. In 1816, however, the party reversed its position and, as Madison suggested, chartered a second National Bank. The government would deposit all of its revenues in the bank, and that institution, in turn, would provide a stable currency for the country. Legally, the bank was a semiprivate corporation managed by a board of directors, a few appointed by the government, though the majority would be elected by private stockholders (only American stockholders could vote; foreign investors could not directly influence bank policies). The bank's charter would expire after twenty years. Establishment of such an institution required a great deal of tenuous justification from a party that had denounced the first bank as illegal and dangerous. Unfortunately, the new bank, poorly administered, helped to bring on several financial panics by overextending credit.

The newly chartered bank would pay out a substantial part of its dividends to the federal government, and some congressmen suggested that these funds be invested in improving or building roads and canals. Kentucky's Henry Clay led this drive for a federal transportation system, since farmers of the interior found it costly and difficult to ship produce to the East. President Madison, despite his call for such internal improvements, thought the project an invasion of states' rights and an unconstitutional enlargement of federal prerogative. The constitutional issue was indeed shadowy. Could the administration appropriate money for roads? Could it supervise their construction? Could it operate finished roads and canals? When Congress finally sent a modified federal improvements bill to the White House, Madison vetoed it. He did so strictly on principle. He was an advocate of better transportation, but he believed that before the federal government could build it a constitutional amendment would have to delegate that specific power to Washington. This position denied the United States the network of roads and canals it so desperately needed. In the end, Congress merely passed appropriations for transportation projects carried out by states and communities—which doomed the venture to the corruption and inefficiency of local politics dominated by special-interest groups.

The Panic of 1819

The postwar boom, inflated by events in Europe and peacetime expansion at home, collapsed into a depression within five years. Crop failures in a Europe already ravaged by war brought a demand for American produce, and English mills once again were free to buy American cotton. Since the price of crops was high, Americans wildly bought up farmland in the West. State banks, which increased in number from 89 to 250 between 1811 and 1816, tried to take up the slack between the demise of the first National Bank and creation of the second. Far from curbing reckless speculation in crops and lands, they encouraged it by issuing their own notes, even if they lacked assets to back up the paper. As long as American farmers enjoyed the prosperity of a world market, they were riding high. As long as customers had faith in the value of these notes, they were accepted as money in commercial transactions, although such paper usually was discounted somewhat if traded far from the state where issued. In theory, valuable assets such as gold and silver backed up all of the paper money issued by banks, but few state banks, often called "wildcat" banks, had such reserves. Hence people often refused to accept the paper notes they issued (unless discounted considerably from face value); instead, they demanded coins that possessed true intrinsic value. Such coins at least contained some precious metal; paper might prove worthless.

In 1819 the mirage of boundless and endless national prosperity evaporated. The most profound cause of the Panic of 1819 was worldwide and beyond the power of the United States to temper—a shortage of hard money. The gold and silver mines of Mexico and Peru, the chief sources of the world's specie, were scarcely functioning during the revolutions in those countries against Spain. More significantly, national treasuries were hoarding the world's stock of precious metals as governments everywhere became fearful of economic collapse and the sudden devaluation of paper money.

But there were two other important reasons for America's depression. One was that the demand for American farm produce, especially for American cotton, was slacking off as Europe returned to normal agricultural production. The other factor, however, was nothing less than incredible fiscal mismanagement within the United States, especially in the booming West. Irresponsible banking practices and feverish land speculation created an irridescent bubble that could only burst. To some extent this oncoming financial disaster was a sectional phenomenon. The Northeast, with more established banks and conservative management, was demanding fiscal responsibility; the South and West, scornful of such mossback attitudes, were plunging forward with abandon, confident that the boom fed by expansion on every hand was endless. What was lacking, of course, was any sort of central banking policy, a problem that would plague Americans until the first decades of the twentieth century.

The second Bank of the United States made the situation all the more precarious by permitting state banks to trade their paper money for hard federal coin. But instead of retaining these metal coins to back up the paper being issued, they continued to issue more and more paper to fuel the boom. When the new National Bank belatedly got around to calling in its loans, ending its liberal credit policies and submitting state bank notes for settlement with those who issued them, boom turned to bust. As one man said: "The Bank was saved and the people were ruined." Although that sentence neatly expressed the sentiment of most angry Americans, it ignored the fact that speculation and depressed cotton prices were the most immediate causes of the panic. That the crisis was severe cannot be doubted. In Baltimore rents dropped to half their previous rate; in Virginia land was almost worthless; in Pennsylvania some 14,000 cases of debt were heard; in Pittsburgh almost a third of the population, finding no livelihood, deserted the city for the country; and in Cincinnati the city government was forced to repossess everything from stores to stables. Everyone caught in this downward spiral called the bank "the Monster." The majority of Americans were farmers, more used to barter than banking, and they were especially resentful of an institution controlled largely by Philadelphia financiers.

The Marshall Court and Centralized Power

The panic prompted a major Supreme Court decision. Several of the states had concurred with popular hatred of the National Bank by levying taxes on the bank's branches or on notes they issued. The Baltimore branch was one of the most poorly run in the country, and on February 11, 1818, the state government passed a law requiring all federal notes issued in Maryland to be printed on stamped paper bought from the state. The Baltimore branch of the National Bank ignored the law, whereupon Maryland sued a federal cashier, James McCulloch. The case quickly worked its way up the judicial ladder to the Supreme Court.

In *McCulloch* v. *Maryland* John Marshall, the Chief Justice, wrote a decision that greatly strengthened the authority of the federal government. He declared that the National Bank was constitutional since it was necessary for the fulfillment of the government's stated power "to lay and collect taxes; to borrow money; to regulate commerce; to declare and conduct a war, and to raise and support armies and navies." This broad construction of the Constitution clearly validated the most general interpretation of the federal government's implied powers. More startlingly, Marshall and the other justices, went on to announce that, though a state could legally tax an individual or organization, the federal government could exempt itself from state taxation. Marshall relied upon the supremacy clause of the Constitution, arguing that a supreme national government's will could not be thwarted by state taxation.

In other court decisions, Marshall and his associates strengthened this nationalistic outlook. When states attempted by legislation to relieve citizens from debts, Marshall ruled that a state law could not erase personal obligations contracted *before* such laws were passed. In the crucial decision, *Sturges* v. *Crowninshield* (1819), the Supreme Court said a New York bankruptcy law was invalid since it applied to contracts signed prior to its enactment.

In another case, *Dartmouth College* v. *Woodward* (1819), the court ruled that a charter granted by the King of England in 1769 to the college was a contract between the state government and the institution—the state could not violate the terms of the original agreement. This decision gave great powers to any chartered institution or business and freed it from state control. From the politi-

Library of Congress.

Fulton's successful run of the Clermont meant that Americans would be able to tap their extensive network of rivers. The early boats still depended on sails and gave little shelter to passengers, as is illustrated in this artist's reconstruction of the first ship.

cal point of view, any loss of states' rights was a gain in federal authority. Still other cases asserted the right of the Supreme Court to reverse the decisions of state courts.

Among the most important rulings of these years was *Gibbons* v. *Ogden* (1824). Ogden, who held a monopoly license granted by the state of New York to operate steamboats to New Jersey, tried to force Gibbons, a man with a federal but no state license, out of business. If Ogden prevailed, then states, not the national government, would have the power to regulate such operations. Marshall and the court interpreted the constitutional provisions relative to commerce broadly to include not only buying, selling, and bartering but also navigation and other forms of intercourse as well. They seized on a federal licensing statute for regulating sea going vessels as a means of ruling that the state law conflicted with the national law. So, Ogden lost.

Emerging Sectionalism

While Marshall was strengthening the Union, a controversy erupted that foreshadowed decades of turmoil ahead. Indeed, the farsighted John Quincy Adams wrote, "I take it for granted that the present question is a mere preamble—a title-page to a great tragic volume."

Apart from Louisiana itself, Missouri was the first

territory within the Louisiana Purchase to petition for statehood. Missouri first applied for statehood just after the Congress agreed to admit Alabama. Transformation of Alabama from territory to state (a formality not complete until December 1819) meant the number of slave and free states would then be equal. Missouri obviously would be yet another slave state (there were 10,000 slaves in Missouri in 1820). This fact troubled Northerners, but the full problem surfaced only when James Tallmadge of Poughkeepsie, New York, affixed an amendment to the Missouri statehood bill. The Tallmadge amendment, introduced in the House of Representatives on February 13, 1819, prohibited the importation of any new slaves into Missouri and stipulated that all children born of slave parents automatically would be free at the age of twenty-five. Although the House passed the amendment by a narrow vote after violent debate, the Senate struck it down. Voting in both the House and Senate followed strict North-South sectional lines.

Late in 1819 the possibility of a compromise emerged when Maine applied for statehood (it was then part of Massachusetts). Southern Congressmen made the admission of Missouri as a slave state a necessary condition for the admission of Maine as a free state. That proposal might have seemed attractive—except it did not settle the greater question of whether slavery would be permitted in the rest of the Louisiana Purchase. Fights raged back and forth in 1820 over this question and the other issues to which it was linked.

The problem was still further complicated by acquisition of the Floridas, which would surely enter the Union someday as slave states. Texas, although Spanish, also might become an American territory in the future. Would it be yet another slave state? And could the so-called "free" state of Illinois, recently admitted, be truly considered free? Both Illinois and Indiana at this time were settled primarily by Southerners, and the constitution of Illinois permitted permanent indentured servitude, but not slavery per se. When applying for statehood in 1818, state leaders feared that they would be rebuffed if they spelled out slavery too clearly. Six years later, voters narrowly rejected a call for a constitutional convention designed to legalize slavery there.

During the prolonged debate in Congress, the most violent insults were hurled by Northerners against Southerners and vice versa. "The words civil war and disunion," Henry Clay confessed wearily, "are uttered almost without emotion." Although a few Northerners at this time were genuinely opposed to slavery on moral grounds, the animosity of most was less idealistic. Northern politicians feared that soon slave states would outnumber free and thereby control Congress. The constitutional arrangement whereby three-fifths of a slave would count as a single free citizen in determining representation in Congress had always angered Northerners. The issue of states' rights also was germane. The Virginian John Taylor was not alone in fearing that if the Supreme Court could establish the legality of a national bank, it also could order the emancipation of slaves. Taylor declared that slaves were private property not subject to government jurisdiction of any sort.

The agonizing deadlock was finally broken when Henry Clay proposed a compromise. The Kentucky statesman linked the admission of free Maine to slave Missouri but prohibited slavery in the future in the Louisiana Purchase north of 36°30'N, Missouri's southern border. Since the struggle over Missouri was threatening to disrupt the unity of the Democratic-Republicans, the Missouri Compromise came as a welcome expedient to some congressmen who formerly had insisted on banning slavery from the entire Louisiana Purchase. Even so, Clay, Speaker of the House and a wily tactician, had his plan voted on in two sections and thereby drummed up differently composed majorities to pass each section.

Few Northern representatives changed their minds. The crucial votes came almost entirely from dubiously "free" areas of Indiana and Illinois. Monroe almost toppled the entire delicate structure by threatening to veto the Missouri Compromise on constitutional grounds, but he was talked out of his objections by pleas of party unity. He even wrote a veto message in which he asserted that "the proposed restriction to territories which are to be admitted to the Union, if not in direct violation of the Constitution, is repugnant to it." But, after consulting with his Cabinet, he signed the bill, thus establishing the precedent that Congress indeed could exclude slavery from lands acquired after 1789. But the controversy still was not over. When Missouri presented its constitution to Congress for approval, the document prohibited the entry of free blacks into that state. Northerners once again were up in arms, this time arguing that the clause violated that part of the federal constitution granting

Chicago Historical Society.

Edward Coles
(1786–1868)

A neighbor of Thomas Jefferson and private secretary to President James Madison, Edward Coles was a well-to-do young man who at the age of twenty-one inherited a farm in Albemarle County, Virginia, and twenty blacks. Fresh from lectures at the College of William and Mary where he began to question the morality of slavery, Edward (the youngest of nine children) shocked his family by announcing plans to free his slaves. To evade the letter of Virginia law which said emancipated blacks had to leave the state within a year or face possible reenslavement, he planned to retain these workers as hired hands and grant them final freedom at the time of his death. He soon realized, however, that his family and friends would not tolerate such a scheme.

As Coles wrestled with this dilemma, an older brother, Isaac, private secretary to Jefferson, suggested he take a similar post with the incoming chief executive. Edward Coles, a second cousin to Dolley Madison, knew the Madisons well and eventually agreed to take the job, thus deferring any emancipation plans for a time. In 1814 he wrote Jefferson urging him to lead a manumission movement and "put into practice those hallowed principles contained in that renowned Declaration, of which you were the immortal author." Jefferson replied he was much too old; this was work for younger men, he added, such as Coles himself. Keenly disappointed by these excuses, Coles told Jefferson he should consider the notable example of Benjamin Franklin who was very active and "usefully employed after he had passed your age." Jefferson, then seventy-one, subsequently asked several younger men in the neighborhood to form a "phalanx" to eradicate slavery. But no "phalanx" appeared, and Edward Coles realized that if he wanted to be a pioneer abolitionist he must act alone.

After two visits to Illinois, in 1819 he secured a post as Register of the Land Office in Edwardsville and soon took his blacks to Pittsburgh and from there down the Ohio River. En route he gathered the slaves around him and told them they were free—free to leave, go where they wished, or remain with him. Some of them were shocked. How would they live? Where would they go? As the hubbub subsided, Coles said he was willing to hire them as free laborers and would give the head of each family or any male over twenty-one 160 acres of land. A few days later, Coles took up his duties at the Land Office, and his ex-slaves began working on their own property about three miles from Edwardsville.

In 1822, Edward Coles became governor of Illinois and used his powers to thwart all attempts to revise the state constitution so as to permit slavery. It was a savage fight, but the antislavery forces won. This was a key victory in a very important state and undoubtedly had profound effect upon the slave-free debate throughout the upper Mississippi Valley. A few years later Coles lost a bid to become a member of Congress and, still a bachelor, moved to Philadelphia. At forty-seven he married, raised a family, and occasionally visited relatives in Virginia; but, as the abolition fury increased, it was obvious he could not live there. However, Robert, his eldest son and the apple of his father's eye, succumbed to the charms of the South, moved to Albemarle County in 1860, and became master of slaves. In February 1862, as a Confederate officer, he died in action at Roanoke Island defending the institution his father fought to abolish. ■

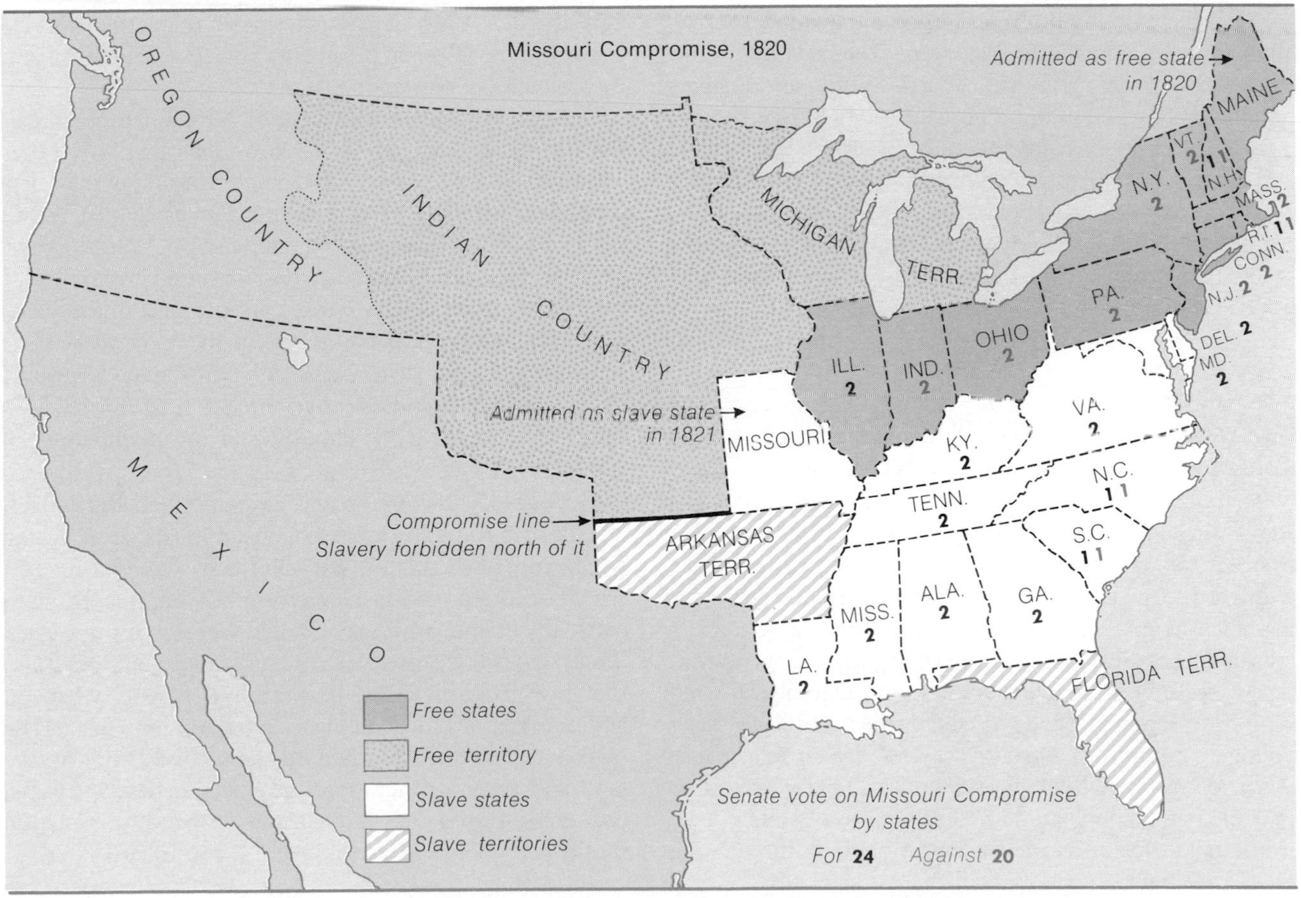

citizens of one state all privileges and immunities bestowed by another.

Charles Pinckney of South Carolina, who claimed authorship of that provision, insisted that it never was intended to cover free blacks. Southerners chose this moment, naturally enough, to point out that free blacks in the North did not enjoy true equality with whites. Finally, Clay came forward with yet another compromise, this one still more circuitous than the earlier one and a great deal more ridiculous. He argued that the state constitution should be accepted as written but with the proviso that the state legislature would promise not to enforce it. According to this Alice-in-Wonderland reasoning, the Missouri constitution could forbid the entry of free blacks. In 1825 the legislature of that state effectively repudiated this agreement by excluding all blacks and mulattos without naturalization papers, documents none of these individuals could get since states where they were regarded as citizens had not naturalized them.

All the painful and heated issues that would eventually result in the Civil War were touched on in the controversy over Missouri. North-South sectionalism became more rigid, as did regional East-West differences. The North roundly condemned the Southern way of life, and formerly moderate Southerners, who conceded the evil of slavery, began to defend and justify the institution. An active abolitionist movement emerged in the North, made up largely of ex-Federalists of the middle and upper classes.

The 1824 Election

Many communities in the upper Mississippi Valley, populated by families from both the North and the South, were unsure of their loyalties. At the same time, new states were granting suffrage quite freely to white males in order to attract population; older states, fearful as the westward surge gained momentum, in turn, lowered ballot-box barriers. The decade of the 1820s was a crucial, confusing era. Solid issues were emerging which laid raw sectional differences. Older regions, accustomed to running the republic, had to share that privilege with younger, bumptious upstarts west of the Appalachians. And, to make matters worse, political party structure provided no guideposts. "The Era of Good Feelings," an ironic name for a decade that gave birth to the fury of abolition and charted a course to war, had destroyed the original two-party system.

The voters of 1824, all of them ostensibly Democratic-Republicans of one shade or another, clearly were looking for both a leader and a platform. Many candidates tried to capture their attention. William Crawford, though seriously ill, was nominated by the "Old Republicans" at a legislative caucus in Washington, the last time this method would be used. John Quincy Adams had the blessing of James Monroe; Adams had served as Secretary of State, and that position had become a stepping stone to the presidency. Andrew Jackson and Henry Clay both had followings in the West, but only Clay worked out a clear program, his "American System" that called for internal improvements and encouragement of business. John C. Calhoun had presidential ambitions but he recognized they were futile and announced for the position of Vice President; many Northerners who found this brilliant South Carolinian repugnant might well have agreed with a New Jersey newspaper that called for the exclusion "of all slave presidents and slave cabinets from the councils of the nation."

Andrew Jackson, the hero of New Orleans and of the Florida campaigns, won more votes than any other candidate, but no one received an electoral vote majority. The choice therefore went to the House, which would elect one of the three leading candidates (Adams, Crawford, or Jackson). Clay, the most influential member of the House, feared Jackson as a political rival in the West; and, although he and Adams had many differences, Clay himself and the delegations of Ohio and Kentucky switched their support to his camp. Yet, despite Clay's efforts, the whole game almost went up in smoke when the large New York delegation in the House was deadlocked, 17–17. The tie breaker, Stephen Van Rensselaer, an elderly Federalist, bowed his head in prayer as voting began and, he said later, saw an Adams ballot at his feet which he interpreted as a sign from heaven. According to some historians, however, Daniel Webster produced an omen somewhat earlier when he informed Van Rensselaer that if Adams prevailed he promised to end a ban on appointment of old Federalists to federal jobs. Had New York voted differently, then on the second ballot Maryland and several other states planned to desert Adams, and many feared that if balloting dragged on Calhoun might yet emerge as a compromise president.

Whether Clay, Webster, or a ballot carefully dropped at the feet of a wavering old politico decided this strange election, Adams won. When the new President named Clay as Secretary of State (and thus seemingly heir apparent to the presidency), Jackson accused Adams and Clay of corruption. But the real lesson to emerge from the election was that the Democratic-Republican Party could no longer contain the competing ambitions of so many political figures who espoused divergent views. The old order was ending.

Courtesy New-York Historical Society, New York City.

John Quincy Adams began his diplomatic experience as secretary to his father during the Revolution. He used that experience to good advantage as Monroe's Secretary of State.

Essay

Mr. Monroe's Elastic Doctrine

On December 2, 1823, President James Monroe delivered his annual message to the first session of the Eighteenth Congress. Very early in his communication he alluded to negotiations with Russia and Great Britain concerning their rights and interests on the Pacific coast, noting that these discussions had seemed a

Library of Congress.

James Monroe announced the idea of an American sphere of influence removed from European intervention in his annual message to Congress. The doctrine bears his name although John Quincy Adams created the policy.

proper forum "for asserting as a principle in which the rights and interests of the United States are involved, that the American Continents, by the free and independent condition which they have assumed and maintain, are henceforth not to be considered as subjects for future colonization by any European Power." Monroe then digressed to report on the army, navy, West Point, Indian affairs, piracy in Cuba and Puerto Rico, and various other matters (including an estimated treasury surplus of $9 million) before returning to the rest of what has become known as the Monroe Doctrine, words that could be and have been interpreted in many ways.

"In the wars of the European Powers, in matters relating to themselves, we have never taken part, nor does it comport with our policy, so to do. It is only when our rights are invaded, or seriously menaced, that we resent injuries and make preparation for our defense. With the movements in this Hemisphere we are of necessity more immediately connected, and by causes which must be obvious to all enlightened and impartial observers. The political system of the allied powers, is essentially different in this respect, from that of America. This difference proceeds from that, which exists in their respective Governments, and to the defence (sic) of our own, which has been achieved by the loss of so much blood and treasure, and matured by the wisdom of their most enlightened citizens, and under which we have enjoyed unexampled felicity, this whole nation is devoted. We owe it therefore to candor, and to the amicable relations existing between the United States and those powers, to declare that we should consider any attempt on their part to extend their system to any portion of this Hemisphere, as dangerous to our peace and safety. With the existing Colonies or dependencies of any European power, we have not interfered, and shall not interfere. But with the Governments who have declared their Independence, and maintained it, and whose Independence we have, on great consideration, and on just principles, acknowledged, we could not view any interposition for the purpose of oppressing them or controuling (sic) in any other manner, their destiny, by any European power, in any other light than as a manifestation of an unfriendly disposition towards the United States."

In essence, Monroe was dealing with two specific, immediate problems that troubled him and little realized he was promulgating a sacred "doctrine," a word not linked to his name until three decades later. He was telling the Russians that they should not establish colonies on the Pacific coast of North America, and the Holy Alliance that the United States was opposed to plans designed to return the newly independent Latin American republics to Spanish rule. This was basically a transatlantic warning from the United States to Europe, which dealt only incidentally with Central and South America. It contained the proposition that the United States will remain isolated from European strife (under certain circumstances) and a somewhat more categorical promise not to interfere with existing European colonies in the New World—and that is about all.

To succeeding generations, who probably know nothing else about Monroe (perhaps not even his first name), this doctrine has become a sacrosanct cornerstone of American liberty. It is not quite equal to the Constitution and the Bill of Rights, but may rank in the opinion of some on a par with the Declaration of Independence. It has been used to justify practically every territorial change since 1823 and twisted to explain why American boys fought twice in the Philippines and France and even in such faraway places as Korea and Vietnam. Those who assert such a broad stand argue that waging war thousands of miles from the Americas will keep war from the Western hemisphere.

The Latin Americans, presumably the benefactors of a policy designed to guarantee their continued independence and freedom, sometimes have expressed their gratitude in strange ways. Culturally and emotionally much more attuned to southern Europe than to the United States, they soon interpreted the emerging doctrine to mean "America for the United States," not "America for the Americans." And throughout the nineteenth century, they realized full well that the British fleet, not actions by the U.S., kept them free from outside meddling. "Inside" meddling, they learned from sad experience, was much harder to deal with.

Until the 1840s, when the United States tried to annex Texas and got embroiled with Great Britain in Oregon, the Monroe Doctrine lay dormant and forgotten. On December 2, 1845, in another annual message to Congress, President James Polk breathed new life into Monroe's words. At the same time he made two major alterations. Polk (who had Texas foremost in his mind) spoke only of North America as he warned European powers not to experiment with colonization in this hemisphere and cautioned against diplomatic as well as armed intervention in the affairs of the New World.

In the last half of the nineteenth century, the Monroe Doctrine was transformed into hallowed dogma (at least north of the Rio Grande) and simultaneously met its stiffest challenges and realized its greatest triumphs. During the Civil War, Spain reasserted control over the Dominican Republic and Louis

Napoleon of France set up a short-lived empire in Mexico. After Appomattox there were tense moments, but by the close of 1865 both powers had withdrawn their forces. While urging annexation of Santo Domingo in 1870, President Ulysses S. Grant added another dimension to the Monroe Doctrine, that European powers could not trade lands in the New World among themselves like so many pieces or real estate. This view had been implied earlier but never was enunciated clearly until that time.

In the 1870s and 1880s congressmen and would-be congressmen often cited the Monroe Doctrine as forbidding construction of any canal across Panama, implying that, if one was dug, the United States must control it. President Grover Cleveland, in a particularly brash move, cited Monroe in 1895 when he asserted that either Great Britain would settle a border dispute between British Guiana and Venezuela or he would name a commission to do the job. When this matter finally was resolved, the British got much of the land they had claimed; nevertheless, in the process of these negotiations, a British spokesman specifically rejected any claims that the Monroe Doctrine had the force of international law.

Shortly after the turn of the century, another crisis erupted when Great Britain, Germany, and Italy blockaded Venezuela, not to seize territory, but to collect debts due their citizens. The U.S. State Department originally took a mild view of this affair, but the American public, certain that this trio planned to invade Venezuela and especially distressed by Germany's high-handed attitude, thought otherwise. President Theodore Roosevelt, who

Culver Pictures.

Theodore Roosevelt used the Monroe Doctrine vigorously. This 1901 cartoon shows Uncle Sam as a mother hen watching over its Latin American chicks.

experienced some nervous moments before the Venezuelan adventure ended, soon proclaimed his renowned corollary. He said, in effect, that the United States would apply the Monroe Doctrine and intervene to assure stable rule in any country in the Western hemisphere whenever "chronic wrong-doing, or an impotence which results in the general loosening of the ties of civilized society" became apparent. In short, Uncle Sam was no longer the benevolent, distant protector, he was a mix of policeman on the block, evangelical reformer, and moral crusader. In this guise and for a variety of reasons, U.S. customs officials, warships, and marines appeared in the Dominican Republic, Nicaragua, and Haiti between 1904 and 1916. Although each U.S. chief executive used the Monroe Doctrine to justify whatever was done, the reaction throughout Central and South America was extremely hostile, for this was the using of brute force to protect American interests.

In the mid-1920s the United States began to pull its troops out of Caribbean countries, and in 1930 officially repudiated the Roosevelt corollary. This decision and subsequent overtures by both Herbert Hoover and Franklin D. Roosevelt laid the foundations of the "Good Neighbor Policy," a conscious effort to foster friendly relations to the south. These steps paid huge dividends during World War II when the Americas presented a generally unified front against the Axis powers. At the same time, the Monroe Doctrine was stretched to cover both Greenland and Iceland, islands not always considered part of the Western hemisphere.

In 1960, as Fidel Castro began to develop his brand of Cuban Communism almost within sight of Florida, the doctrine was evoked once more against a nation that had inspired Monroe to speak out in 1823. At one point, Nikita Khrushchev offered support to the Cuban people, coupling that promise of aid with a denunciation of the "dead" Monroe Doctrine. The U.S. State Department reacted with a stern rebuke, and two years later the missile crisis prompted several senators to quote profusely from James Monroe's message on the floor of the U.S. Senate. Not surprisingly, these gentlemen discovered that his words fitted precisely the space age dilemma confronting them. Officially, however, the U.S. government chose not to cite the doctrine, suggesting instead action by the United Nations or the Organization of American States. Nevertheless, newspaper headlines featured Monroe's name prominently, and Richard M. Nixon, then an ex-Vice President, called for a quarantine of Cuba "in the name of the Monroe Doctrine."

Despite the careless manner in which the term "Monroe Doctrine" has been tossed about and the many uses to which it has been adapted, for all practical purposes it has applied only to Mexico, Central America, and lands in or bordering on the Caribbean. Its popularity has waxed and waned from time to time as the United States and various neighbors to the south have evoked its presumed concepts when it was in their interests to do so. Although Mr. Monroe's message of 1823 dealt with two very specific threats that soon evaporated, his ideas were firmly grounded in a basic principle long understood by residents of the New World: having turned their back upon the troubles of Europe, they did not want to become involved in them once more, nor did they want Europeans to meddle in their affairs.

Selected Readings

General Studies

Marshall Smelser, *The Democratic Republic, 1801–1815* (1968)
Charles Wiltse, *The New Nation* (1961)
George Dangerfield, *The Awakening of American Nationalism, 1815–1828* (1965)
George Dangerfield, *The Era of Good Feelings* (1963)

War of 1812

Roger Brown, *Republic in Peril* (1964)
Reginald Horseman, *The Causes of the War of 1812* (1962)
Harry Coles, *The War of 1812* (1965)
Charles Borkks, *Seige of New Orleans* (1961)
H. S. Halbert and T. H. Ball, *Creek War of 1813 and 1814* (1970)
C. S. Forester, *The Age of Fighting Sail* (1956)

Politics

Philip Klein, *Pennsylvania Politics, 1817–1832: a Game Without Rules* (1940)
Shaw Livermore, Jr., *Twilight of Federalism: Federalist Party, 1815–1830* (1962)
James Kehl, *Ill Feeling in the Era of Good Feeling* (1956)
Murray Rothbad, *The Panic of 1819* (1962)
Ronald Banks, *Maine Becomes a State: Movement to Separate Maine from Massachusetts, 1785–1820* (1970)
Glover Moore, *The Missouri Controversy* (1953)

Foreign Policy

Bradford Perkins, *Castlereagh and Adams: England and the United States 1812–1823* (1964)
Dexter Perkins, *A History of the Monroe Doctrine*, rev. ed. (1963)
Samuel F. Bemis, *John Quincy Adams and the Foundations of American Foreign Policy* (1949)

The Genesis of Industrial America

Chapter 8

TIMELINE

1807
Robert Fulton develops first practical steamboat

1808
Albert Gallatin calls for federal road system

1811
Construction of Cumberland Road begins

1815
Cotton boom in Lower South

1817
Construction of Erie Canal begins

1819
Dartmouth College v. *Woodward*

1825
Erie Canal opens

1827
Mechanics Union of Trade Associations organized

1828
Steampower replaces waterpower in factories

1830
Tom Thumb steam locomotive

1835
Samuel Colt mass-produces revolving pistol

1837
Charles River Bridge v. *Warren Bridge*

1839
Charles Goodyear vulcanizes rubber

1844
Samuel F. B. Morse demonstrates telegraph

1845
Elias Howe perfects sewing machine

CHAPTER OUTLINE

The first four decades of the nineteenth century witnessed the beginnings of industrial growth in the United States, a phenomenon that was part of a general development of machines, factories, and working classes which was common to many parts of the North Atlantic basin. After 1815, both Europe and America enjoyed two generations or more of peace during which barriers to international trade relaxed somewhat and the movement of goods was encouraged. In this milieu, favorable to the growth of both domestic and international commerce, the young republic had several factors in its favor: a steady flow of inward migration that provided workers and, in turn, lured European investment capital; a series of bumper crops of grain and cotton; and a willingness—even a dynamic Yankee eagerness—to tinker, to experiment, to improve, and somehow to produce more, faster. Those uppity Europeans had to be shown what could be done.

The Transportation Revolution

In these years, more so than after mid-century when the United States had become somewhat self-sufficient, the economic health of the country depended upon trade, which in turn was linked to transportation. Although "transportation" may sound like a specialized and rather abstract topic, it was in fact vitally associated with almost every facet of American life—the migrating of whole populations into new regions, the choosing of sites for cities to be built, the developing of manufacturing and agriculture, and the improving of the standard of living of citizens everywhere.

Roads

Before and after the War of 1812, farsighted leaders sought to link the larger centers in the Northeast with each other and with the growing settlements in the West. As early as 1808, Secretary of the Treasury Albert Gallatin called for a comprehensive system of federal roads. After much controversy about the constitutionality of such a federally sponsored project, the government began to build a highway (known as the "Cumberland Road") from Cumberland, Maryland, to Wheeling, Virginia, a town located on the Ohio River, now a major city in West Virginia. Construction took place between 1811 and 1818; later the road was extended to Vandalia, Illinois. The original road cost $1.7 million at the rate of about $13,000 a mile. The Cumberland Road (also called the National Road) was raised in the center for drainage and had a ditch on each side. Most early dirt roads were rutted in dry weather and a sea of mud in wet weather. The rock roadbed of the National Road permitted year-round travel at relatively high speeds.

Westerners, not satisfied with only one overland link to the East, persistently called for more East-West highways. The lack of such roads meant that few commodities could be transported between the two areas, and those carried overland were extremely expensive. For instance, in 1813 it cost $9 to move 100 pounds of goods overland from Philadelphia to Pittsburgh. The nation's inferior roads slowed trade considerably and prevented one region from using the natural resources of another. Indeed, the early factories of the Northeast had easier access to the raw materials of Europe than to those of the American interior, since transatlantic transportation was cheaper than communication between New England, say, and the Great Lakes area. When transportation in ships along the Atlantic coast was closed by the British blockade during the War of 1812, shipment of goods into New England became quite costly and difficult; a barrel of flour cost $5.03 more in Boston than it did in New York, and this difference in price was attributable to overland transport.

Despite the obvious advantages of building more and better roads, several sectors of the nation objected. Many of the eastern states feared that improved East-West transportation would enable factories in the West to compete with those in the East. New, improved roads also threatened to lure more and more eastern workmen and their families to western settlements. Southerners had their own fears about federal roadbuilding. They were apprehensive that an expensive federal transportation project would lead to high tariffs, which would impede the flow of trade between the South and Europe. Finally, national leaders frequently were troubled by the constitutionality of federal roadbuilding.

This question was almost as old as the republic itself and goes back at least to Alexander Hamilton's plans for internal improvements at federal expense. At issue was whether national funds could be used for the direct benefit of a region or of a class, such as businessmen, when those outlays might, at best, only be for the very indirect aid of the total population. This point was one of fundamental disagreement between some Federalists and Democratic-Republicans; and many Jeffersonians still viewed such undertakings with considerable skepticism.

As a consequence, the government did not build roads on a full-fledged scale. The job was left to private turnpike companies, which were especially active between 1789 and 1830. These turnpikes (or toll roads) did not constitute a lengthy system of roads; most of them could be found only in the older, more settled parts of the country. Among the best-known were those linking Philadelphia and Lancaster in Pennsylvania and the Old Post Road between New York and Boston.

Water Transportation

From the earliest times of white occupation of North America, water transport was the most common way to convey goods. The cost of transporting goods 100 miles overland (an average of $10 a ton) was not much less than shipping them from America to Europe. Water transport was considerably less expensive, though it, too, had disadvantages. Most river freighting ran with the current,

Toll gate on the Baltimore-Reisterstown Road.

The Metropolitan Museum of Art, Gift of Mrs. John Sylvester, 1936.

usually from north to south in the United States; up-country freighting, by contrast, relied on wagons and packtrains or, along the coasts, on sloops and schooners.

The trouble with transport by water was that it restricted trade to the patterns prescribed by the natural system of rivers and bays, and even these networks were often not navigable in winter. In good weather a trip upstream could be very long; on the Ohio-Mississippi river route, for instance, the journey downstream from Pittsburgh to New Orleans took six weeks; the same journey upstream required nearly three times as long. High river banks made sailboats ineffective, and much slower barges, flatboats, and rafts, all poled or paddled, had to be used.

Two innovations completely changed the nature of water transportation shortly after the War of 1812: steamboats and canals. As early as 1807, Robert Fulton constructed the first practical steamboat, the *Clermont,* a vessel 133 feet long and 7 feet deep equipped with a steam engine, a twenty-foot boiler, and two side paddle wheels, each fifteen feet in diameter. On its first voyage up the Hudson River to Albany, New York, the *Clermont* rushed along against the current at the astounding speed of about five miles an hour! After the war, Fulton established a regular service of steamboats between New York City and Albany. Although ingenious men had been working out the details of steam navigation since 1790, Fulton deserves credit for bringing the various mechanical features—engine, boiler, paddle wheels, and hull—into the proper functioning balance.

Soon steam vessels were plying the Mississippi, and New Orleans, the port near the mouth of the river, became one of the world's major trading centers. By 1852 steamboats had transformed the commerce along the Mississippi River valley into a business worth more than $650 million annually. Along the eastern seaboard,

Denver Public Library Western Collection, by Karl Bodmer.

Water transportation on the Ohio River in the 1830s. Steam power and muscle power at work. Before the coming of the railroads, water transportation was predominant on America's expanding frontier.

steamboats facilitated rapid passenger transportation; Cornelius Vanderbilt operated numerous coastal vessels after 1829 and made a fortune doing so—within seven years he was worth half a million dollars.

The most dramatic effect of the steamboat was on the Mississippi, Ohio, and other rivers of the Old Northwest (Illinois, Ohio, Indiana, Michigan, and Wisconsin). By 1830, these craft were traveling all of the main rivers of that region and many of the principal tributaries as well. The resulting commercial traffic made the West an integral and very vital part of the national economy.

While steamboats were improving the flow of commerce in the West, the construction of canals was providing a direct link between the Northeast and the West. The Erie Canal was the first and by far most important of these projects; in fact, it continues to carry a substantial amount of freight even today. A massive undertaking, the canal covered a distance of 364 miles and connected Albany on the Hudson River with Buffalo on Lake Erie. Begun in 1817, the canal was finished in 1825 at a cost of $7 million to the state of New York. The first voyage was taken by New York's governor, DeWitt Clinton, who traversed the canal from Buffalo to Albany and then went down the Hudson on a steamboat to New York City, where he poured a keg of water from Lake Erie into the Atlantic, symbolizing the marriage of the Great Lakes to the ocean. The marriage turned out to be a highly profitable one; New York became the country's major city, outstripping Philadelphia, Boston, and New Orleans. Western lumber, flour, whiskey, and some manufactured items, such as pig iron, were conveyed to New York; the trade from the east to the West, however, was still larger. Moreover, the canal carried thousands of settlers to the West and greatly increased the value of western land.

Museum of the City of New York.

The opening of the Erie Canal as a toll waterway connecting the Hudson River with Lake Erie was a joyous occasion in 1825. It set off a nationwide craze for canal-building.

Courtesy of New-York Historical Society, New York City.

Cooper's Tom Thumb, the first efficient steam engine locomotive built in the United States, races against a horse-drawn car on the Baltimore and Ohio Railroad on August 28, 1830, and wins.

Traveling along the canal was slow. The ordinary speed was only about three miles an hour. The brightly painted canal boats were dragged along by one or more mules or horses, which walked beside the canal on tow paths. The cost, however, was low; the rate on a small boat that did not offer sleeping accommodations or food was one cent a mile, which was much less than the cost of travel by stagecoach; the rate for larger packet boats with bunks and food was about five cents a mile. The cost of stage travel varied greatly depending on competition, but it could be as much as ten cents a mile or even higher. Of greater importance was the movement of crops and freight. Thanks to the Erie Canal, much of the Great Lakes region now had easy access to the Atlantic Ocean. Freight charges between Buffalo and New York dipped 85 percent and shipping time shrank from eight to less than four days. Two years after the Erie opened, a Georgia governor complained that wheat grown in New York state sold for less in Savannah than that produced only 100 miles away in inland counties of his own state.

Philadelphia, recognizing that the Erie Canal was diverting western business to New York, sought to compete by building its own canals. The terrain of Pennsylvania, however, was much hillier, and the Pennsylvania system of dams, locks, stagecoaches, and horse-drawn railroad cars may have been ingenious but proved to be impractical. Other East coast canals were similarly costly and unsuccessful; few ever reached their avowed goal, and most of them eventually gave way to railroads. The Chesapeake & Ohio Canal designed to lure commerce to the Washington, D.C. area and the James River and Kanawha Canal linking Richmond with the Virginia interior might be termed limited successes. Both carried considerable commerce in the mid-nineteenth century, but neither could compete successfully with rival modes of transport.

In the Old Northwest, "canal fever" seized the citizens, and many canals were started. The most ambitious and useful of these schemes was the Ohio Canal, a 308-mile undertaking that connected the Ohio River with Lake Erie. Western canals fostered urban growth and expanded the economy, but these waterways also led to the eviction of Indian tribes, such as the Miamis and Potawatomis, who blocked the path of the white man's "progress."

Railroads

Canals and the steamboat were only harbingers of a true transportation revolution ushered in by the steam-powered railroad. In addition to creating a huge demand for workers, materials, and supplies, railroads virtually eliminated the confining restraints of weather and topography. No longer did one have to be so concerned with snow, rain, and mountains. Seasonal layoffs because of icebound rivers and canals were a thing of the past, and both invested capital and labor could be used much of the year around. Railroads, although expensive and time consuming to build, were direct, relatively fast, and in continuous operation, factors that had a profound effect upon growing American industry in general.

Peter Cooper's steam engine, *Tom Thumb,* demonstrated as early as 1830 that steam locomotion was practical. In the following decade, railways assumed local and, after 1840, national importance. Nevertheless, until 1850 canals remained the country's main arteries of transportation. In the early years of steam locomotion, construction was hindered by the opposition of canal owners and other vested interests, who tried to persuade state governments to limit railroad traffic to passengers. Carrying freight, they claimed, should be permitted only in areas where canals did not exist.

Railroads, a combination of steampower and a system of carts and tracks used in British mines for a century or more, began to function in the United States in 1830. Among the pioneer companies were the Baltimore & Ohio and a line between Charleston, South Carolina, and the town of Hamburg near Augusta, Georgia. In 1833 the South Carolina railroad had 136 miles of track, the longest stretch in the entire world. By 1840 railroads were operating more than 2,800 miles of track in the United States, which was more than that found in all of Europe. For the most part, these were short lines of varying gauges designed to haul inland produce to the port that had promoted the railroad. Little or no thought was given to connecting up with rival centers; that would come later. At the same date, the nation had 3,326 miles of canals; but, unlike railroads, canal construction was ending, not beginning. Virtually no canals were dug after 1840, although for a decade or so their backers expended millions in a last ditch effort to thwart the rise of the "iron horse."

Construction of all kinds ceased for a time following an economic panic in 1837. But after the economy improved in the 1840s, the railroad-building pace picked up again and reached boom proportions in the 1850s.

Government and the Economy

Economic expansion and scientific improvements in America were promoted by both federal and state governments. In the past, many historians believed that during this period the federal government seldom intervened to determine economic policy or to plan and finance internal improvements. Now this view has been revised. It seems Americans of the period spent a great deal of time discussing whether the Constitution granted Washington officials the right to give government aid to local projects, but much of this debate centered on whether or not state or national authorities should act. Americans were not opposed to government aid; some simply wondered whether the Constitution permitted federal money to be given to specific projects

Government Intervention

Between 1816 and 1836, the federal Treasury showed a deficit in only three years; at all other times there were large surpluses. After 1832 this money was deposited in state banks—with so little care and in such large amounts that the practice led to unsound banking practices. In 1837 federal surpluses were distributed as grants to the states.

The federal government also affected economic life by passing tariffs designed to shelter young industries such as the manufacture of cotton and woolen goods from foreign competition. These regulations, which produced considerable revenue, began with a moderately protective tariff in 1816. This measure was revised upward in 1824 and again four years later, so much so that critics called the Tariff of 1828 "the Tariff of Abominations." These maneuverings, though they aided industries in the Northeast, angered Southerners, who were convinced that this protection hurt their trade with foreign markets; imported manufactured goods, they said, cost more, and foreign merchants were more reluctant to buy southern cotton and tobacco.

The national government intervened in the economy in several other ways. The United States Post Office was one of the biggest businesses in the country, and the federally built National Road was a giant enterprise. Until the government's Indian trading posts, or "factories," were abolished in 1822, they sold supplies to Indians and bought their furs and animal hides. By arranging for the removal of Indian tribes from states and territories, the government aided the economic activities of white citizens. Congressional legislation protected the merchant marine by excluding foreign vessels from domestic trade along the Atlantic and Gulf coasts, and often provided substantial sums for internal improvements, despite the debate such measures aroused. Washington stimulated

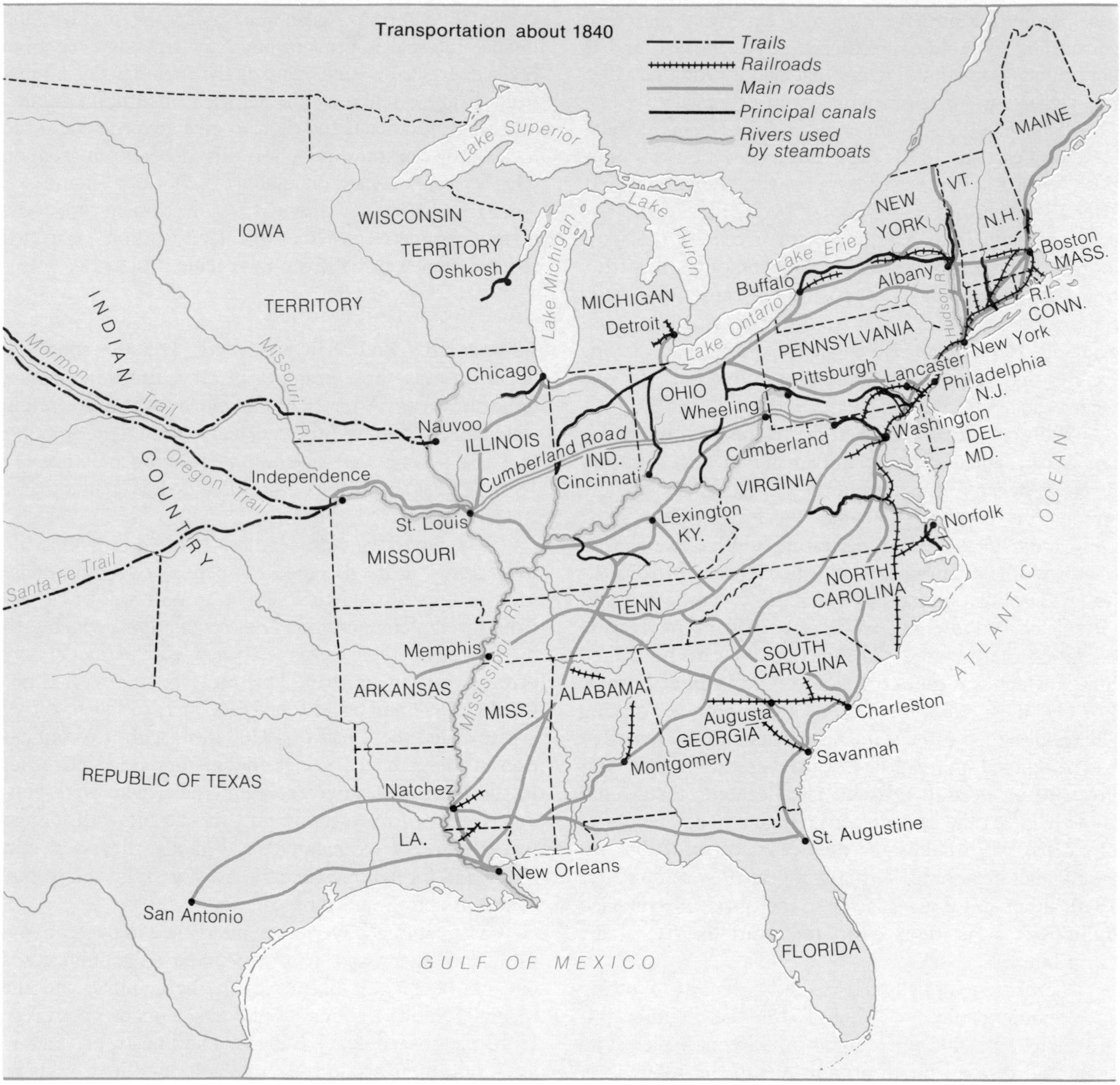
Transportation about 1840
Trails
Railroads
Main roads
Principal canals
Rivers used by steamboats
Lake Superior
Lake Michigan
Lake Huron
Lake Erie
Lake Ontario
MAINE
VT.
N.H.
NEW YORK
Boston
MASS.
R.I.
CONN.
Albany
Hudson R.
Buffalo
New York
PENNSYLVANIA
Philadelphia
N.J.
Lancaster
Pittsburgh
Washington
DEL.
MD.
Cumberland
Wheeling
OHIO
MICHIGAN
Detroit
WISCONSIN
TERRITORY
Oshkosh
IOWA
TERRITORY
INDIAN
COUNTRY
Mormon Trail
Oregon Trail
Santa Fe Trail
Missouri R.
Chicago
Nauvoo
ILLINOIS
Cumberland Road
IND.
Cincinnati
Independence
St. Louis
MISSOURI
Lexington
KY.
VIRGINIA
Norfolk
ATLANTIC OCEAN
NORTH CAROLINA
TENN
Memphis
Mississippi R.
ARKANSAS
MISS.
ALABAMA
SOUTH CAROLINA
Charleston
Augusta
GEORGIA
Savannah
Montgomery
REPUBLIC OF TEXAS
Natchez
LA.
New Orleans
St. Augustine
San Antonio
GULF OF MEXICO
FLORIDA

John Jacob Astor (1763–1848)

One of the wealthiest men in the days of the early republic was John Jacob Astor, a German who came to New York in 1784 with nothing but $25 and seven flutes. Within two years Astor had set up his own music shop in Manhattan, but his great ambition was to become a fur trader.

He soon began to realize this dream in a modest way, but after 1796, when Jay's Treaty led to the evacuation of British forts along the Canadian border, he expanded his fur-trading operations with aggressive vigor. And, as soon as the government lifted trade restrictions with Canada, Astor started dealing directly with fur merchants in Montreal.

The Louisiana Purchase opened up still more fur-rich territory to Astor, who in 1808 incorporated all of his far-flung little businesses into one giant enterprise, the American Fur Company. By 1811 Astor had worked out a complex and rewarding system. His traders collected furs in the new town of Astoria in the Oregon Country at the mouth of the Columbia River. From there they were shipped on Astor's vessels to China, a major market for furs. Chinese goods were then carried to Europe and sold. Finally, European products were bought and shipped to New York.

In the meantime, Astor was gaining wealth in other ways as well. He lent the government enormous sums at high interest rates during the War of 1812. And he kept acquiring more and more real estate in Manhattan. Eventually this land formed the major part of the Astor estate, which was conservatively estimated at $20 million at the time of the magnate's death. Astor had become the very image of the selfish capitalist; as one obituary put it, "He has exhibited at best but the ingenious powers of a self-invented money-making machine." ■

industries by handing out large government contracts—for instance, to the manufacturers of pistols and rifles.

The United States Patent Office encouraged and protected inventors by ensuring their rights to the profits earned by their discoveries. This vitally important bureau was organized in 1802 when a single individual in the

Department of State was designated as the superintendent in charge of patents. In 1849 it became part of the Department of Interior and in 1925 was transferred to the Department of Commerce. In addition, the federal government influenced the economy in a very real way by regulating the sale of public lands.

In the short run at least, whatever steps the national government took tended to aid one section or region at the expense of another. Sale of cheap public land encouraged westward movement and caused problems for the economies of some settled areas of the East. This could mean labor shortages and perhaps even diminished political power if population decline led to reduced representation in Congress. Federal aid for turnpikes, canals, and railroads bestowed few immediate benefits upon some coastal inhabitants or upon communities already blessed with functioning transportation systems. And, as noted, nonindustrial areas such as the South and West deeply resented tariffs designed to protect burgeoning factories of the Northeast.

The answer to sectional jealousies lay in a scheme of "trade offs" or compromises, each area getting something while none reaped all of the rewards. As a rising young politician, Henry Clay, spokesman for the new West, devised his "American System" to do just that. He proposed creation of a great domestic market by means of a protective tariff to stimulate industry, federally funded internal improvements to aid the commerce of all sections, and a national bank to regulate credit and the transfer of funds throughout the nation. Of course, the bank appeared (1816), and so did the tariffs (1816, 1824, 1828), but somehow the balance wheels of Clay's "American System" were missing. The result was constant competition among rival sections, bitterness when one region won what residents of another viewed as unfair advantages, and recurring efforts at compromise.

The Role of the Judiciary

Working hand in hand with Congress was another branch of the federal government, the Supreme Court. Alexis de Toqueville (1805–1859), that well-known French observer of American life, wrote in 1835: "Scarcely any political question arises in the United States that is not resolved, sooner or later, into a judicial question." To a degree Toqueville was right; the courts wielded enormous influence in deciding political questions, and in the first half of the nineteenth century, the Supreme Court determined policies that were largely economic in nature. Under Chief Justice John Marshall, who presided until he was succeeded by Roger B. Taney in 1836, the Court viewed the business community as an important agent of progress—and decided many cases in favor of private enterprise. The Marshall court's decisions in cases such as that involving the Dartmouth College Charter (1819) and *Gibbons* v. *Ogden* (1824) came down solidly in favor of private enterprise and the businessman. The Taney court continued to side with business, but it stressed the role of business as an agent for social change and growth.

One of Taney's most famous decisions was the *Charles River Bridge* case. In 1785 the Massachusetts legislature had granted a company a charter to build a toll bridge; when a competing company wished to build another bridge nearby, the first company took the second to court. Taney and four justices in 1837 decided in favor of the second company; they did not think that the Supreme Court should protect the exclusive claims of one enterprise when such protection would work against the interests of the public, which was obviously better served in this instance by having the use of more than one bridge. As Taney put it: "While the rights of private property are sacredly guarded, we must not forget that the community also have rights, and that the happiness and well-being of every citizen depends on their faithful preservation." Taney's modification of Marshall's earlier rulings defending the sanctity of contracts—notably in the Dartmouth College Case—was the Supreme Court's first pronouncement of the doctrine of the social responsibility of private property.

The Influence of State Governments

Between 1800 and 1850, neither the federal government nor the various state governments were as active in regulating the economy as they would become later. Nevertheless, both on the federal and state levels, government did have some economic impact.

The state governments appear to have played a larger role than Washington during the antebellum period. Conferring charters that allowed businesses to incorporate was one of the chief economic functions of state governments. In addition, states granted tax benefits to certain favored enterprises. Massachusetts, for example, granted a monopoly to a pioneer glass manufacturer. Maine subsidized wheat and corn producers to the tune of $150,000 in a single year (1839); other states aided silk culture, fisheries, and the production of naval stores. Some states exempted workers from militia and jury duty so as not to disrupt industries where they were employed. Pennsylvania set prices for some goods and services, and many states continued the colonial practice of inspecting goods such as tobacco bound for interstate commerce so as to assure quality.

Aside from granting corporate charters, providing tax benefits, and conducting regulatory activities, the states intervened in the economy by supporting internal improvements. A careful analysis of the railroads built before 1860 in the South, for instance, reveals that almost three-fourths of the financing came from public sources. Local and state governments had to pay for railroads, since only they could raise the necessary capital. The state of Pennsylvania invested more than $100 million in its public works system, especially in canals and railroads. Power to grant corporation charters gave states obvious influence over both banks and transportation companies; and, in many cases, the corporation itself was a "mixed" institution—that is, partially public and partially private. Pennsylvania's state government not only invested heavily in many corporations but also placed public directors at the head of these enterprises; by 1844 there were some 150 "mixed" corporations in that state.

The Factory System

"There are several factories in Lowell," the English novelist Charles Dickens wrote when he visited the United States in 1842, "each of which belongs to what we should term a Company of Proprietors, but what they call in America a Corporation. . . . I happened to arrive at the first factory just as the dinner hour was over, and the girls were returning to their work. . . . They were all well dressed, but not to my thinking above their condition. . . . They were healthy in appearance, many of them remarkably so, and had the manners and deportment of young women: not of degraded brutes of burden."

Dickens, a bitter foe of the evils of industrialization in England, was quite favorably impressed by what appeared to be much better working conditions in America. The factories in Lowell, Massachusetts, that he saw did indeed exemplify careful organization and farsighted planning, though they were not typical; and, had Dickens looked elsewhere, he would have found many factories all too reminiscent of what he deplored in his native England.

The factory system was by no means the predominant mode of American industry until mid-century. Small household manufacturing operations continued to play a major role, although by the 1840s factories were becoming more and more common, especially in the Northeast.

The first American factory was established by Samuel Slater in 1790 in Pawtucket, Rhode Island. Backed by a mercantile partnership in Providence, Slater (an English immigrant and a mechanical wizard) succeeded in setting up a cotton-spinning mill that was fully operative by 1793. Twenty years later there were many such mills throughout southern New England, almost all of them located along streams and rivers since their looms were driven by waterpower. A growing immigration of skilled English laborers aided these New England ventures; the newcomers were attracted by the high wages they could earn in the United States.

The factory can be distinguished by a few distinctive features that set it apart from the craftsman's shop. A factory turns out a substantial quantity of standardized items; instead of producing two pairs of custom-made shoes a day, for instance, it manufactures hundreds, or even thousands, of nearly identical pairs. Secondly, a factory is manned by an assembly of workers ruled by rigid discipline. A craftsman might be relatively free to set his own hours and working conditions; the factory laborer adheres to an unvarying schedule and usually performs only one step in a process of many stages. The factory worker is not self-employed and does not directly enjoy the full profits of his or her own labor. A single entrepreneur or a group of investors owns the physical plant, the machinery, and the tools. The owners reap most of the profits; the worker receives a fixed salary.

Before the War of 1812, the factory system grew slowly in the United States, hampered by a shortage of skilled machinists, an inadequate knowledge of factory management, and a lack of capital for buying the necessary equipment. What American capital was available was going into such areas as commerce and trade, real estate, and building. More significantly, new enterprises, particularly in textiles, faced both strong foreign competitors, especially the more efficient and well-developed

The Rhode Island Historical Society.

Pawtucket Falls in Rhode Island where Samuel Slater established the first cotton-spinning mill in 1790.

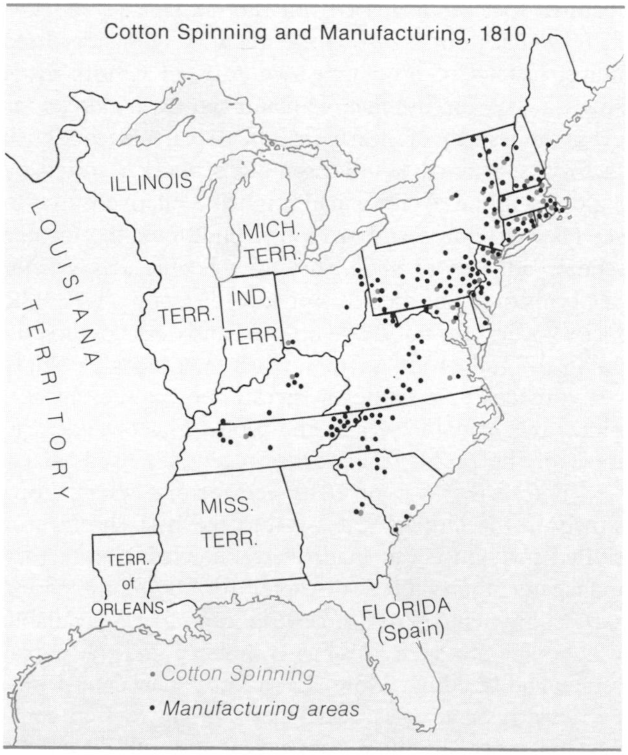

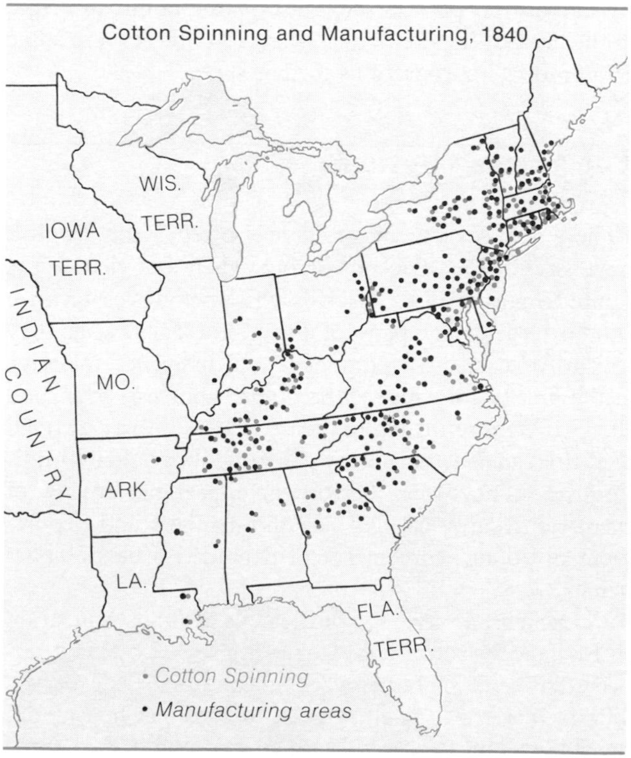

English factories that could undersell those in America, and marginal domestic manufacturers that were scattered in thousands of homes and still much more important than factory producers of the same items.

The years preceding and during the War of 1812 aided industrialization. The Embargo of 1807, the Non-intercourse Act, and the interruption of trade with England during the war itself all served to seal off British competition temporarily and to make Americans dependent on their own resources for manufactured goods. The enormous profits acquired by Yankee merchants of the period also provided New England with the capital necessary for building factories and buying machinery.

But the industrialization of the Northeast was not based on such transitory factors alone. Even when the war was over and British industrialists were free to compete for the American market once more, factories continued to spring up there because that region had decided advantages in this movement towards industrialization. One of these "advantages" was actually a shortcoming—the soil was so poor in New England and the average farm so small that many farmers needed to supplement their meager incomes by sending their wives, sons, and daughters to work in factories. Most of the young women Dickens saw at Lowell, for instance, were recruited from impoverished farms in communities where females outnumbered males by a substantial margin. In addition to having a ready labor force and capital, New England had numerous rivers gushing toward the sea rich with power easily harnessed to run looms and mills. Soon large brick and stone structures were dotting the banks of the Merrimack in northeastern Massachusetts; the Naugatuck, Quinnipiac, and Housatonic in Connecticut; the Blackstone in Rhode Island; and the Androscoggin in southern Maine.

Manufacturers in the Northeast were also blessed with easy access to raw materials. Pennsylvania had rich resources of iron and coal, essential to smelting. The chief manufactured goods were made of cotton which, though grown in the South, could be shipped inexpensively up the Atlantic coast to Boston, New York City, and other ports of the Northeast. For all of these reasons, factories spread in the Northeast, and manufacturing gradually replaced commerce after 1815 as the economic mainstay in urban communities throughout the region.

In 1810, Boston (38,746), New York (100,775), and Philadelphia (87,303) were the major urban centers. (These figures for New York and Philadelphia, now archrivals, include both the metropolis and the surrounding county). That same year Portsmouth had 6,934 inhabitants; New Haven, 5,772; Providence, 10,071; and Trenton, 3,002. Though some of these cities were insignificant by modern standards, they were growing rapidly, and an urban population provided factories with both workers and a ready market for manufactured goods. When poor immigrants from the British Isles, especially Ireland, began to flood into the United States, most of them went to the Northeast where they constituted a pool of cheap labor as well as customers. Boston's population grew and by 1850 35,000 Irish were living there, most of them refugees from the Irish potato famine.

Yankee Inventions

By 1840 only England was more highly industrialized than the United States. Considering that Americans had a late start, their success can be partially attributed to such factors as an everexpanding population, growing prosperity, and plentiful natural resources—but these factors should not obscure the importance of "Yankee ingenuity." American industry was aided greatly by American inventions. As Simeon De Witt, a New Yorker, wrote in 1813: "The Americans are an inventive people; perhaps more so than any other existing. Without arrogating to ourselves any superiority of intellect, the cause may be traced . . . to the facility with which a respectable education and comfortable subsistence may be procured, and which leaves leisure to the mind to wander through the mysterious, unfathomable repositories of possible things." De Witt's rhetoric is confirmed by one simple index—the number of patents registered by the federal government. Between 1790 and 1811, an average of only 77 patents was registered annually; from 1820 to 1830 the number rose to an average of 535 a year (as compared with a mere 145 a year in England).

De Witt's emphasis on education as a source of Yankee ingenuity, though difficult to establish as a direct cause, may have some validity. Certainly formal education was more common in New England than anywhere else in the world; one out of every four persons in New England was a student in 1850, for instance, as compared to one out of seven in Great Britain.

The number of major American inventions is too great to list, but a few milestones can be mentioned. In

1819 Jethro Wood perfected a cast-iron plow made of three replaceable parts; by 1825 this plow, despite unfounded fears on the part of some farmers that iron would "poison" the soil, came into general use. A plow, along with an axe, seed, a gun, and a few animals, accompanied practically every frontiersman as he moved westward. Wood's plow (later improved somewhat by a blacksmith named John Deere) literally was the cutting edge of settlement, and its iron—then later its steel—blade proved more than equal to the task of slicing through tough prairie grass and virgin soil tangled with roots. After 1820 food storage changed radically with the introduction of canning. At first seafoods and later, vegetables, and fruits were sealed in glass bottles or tin cans and preserved for future use. This process introduced seasonal variety into diets at low cost and made the foods of one region available in another.

In the 1830s Cyrus Hall McCormick and Obed Hussey, working independently of each other, perfected the reaping machine, a device that allowed one worker to cut about ten acres of grain a day. Soon McCormick, who built a plant in Chicago in the heart of the grain-raising part of the country, was manufacturing about 1,000 reapers a day. The innovative policy of selling to farmers on the installment plan, a strategy adopted earlier in the century by clock manufacturers in New England, increased his business substantially.

In 1835 Samuel Colt began to mass-produce the revolving pistol. In the following years Americans got their first glimpse of other new inventions and processes: rubber was "vulcanized" by Charles Goodyear (1800-1860) so that it would hold up under extremes of heat and cold; the telegraph of Samuel Morse (1791-1872) put every section of a vast nation in touch with every other region; and the sewing machine of Elias Howe (1819-1867) revolutionized the textile and clothing industries. Goodyear's feat actually resulted from an accident in 1839. While experimenting, he spilled rubber heated with sulphur on a hot stove and found, to his delight, that it retained its elasticity. However, fame and fortune eluded him and he died a poor man. In 1841 an English manufacturer told Parliament that scores of new inventions were coming from America and offered this explanation: "I should say that most of the American inventions have had their origin in this way: in America we know that labour has hitherto been dear. . . . Parties, not having access to the machine-makers of this country for the supply of their wants, have set themselves about to make a machine in the readiest mode to accomplish that which they required; they have been untrammelled by predilections in favor of a machine already in existence. . . ." In other words, a shortage of labor and a freedom from tradition and precedent created an environment conducive to inventiveness.

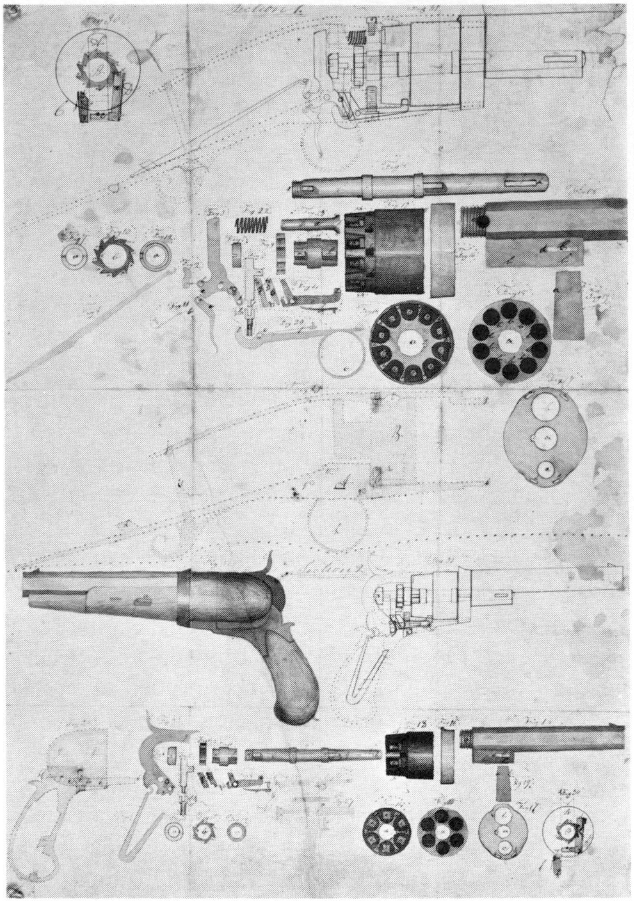

Colt Firearms Collection, Museum of Connecticut History, Hartford.

The 1835 patent drawing for Colt's repeating pistol using the system of interchangeable parts.

New inventions especially benefited the textile industry. In 1790 the various stages of producing fabric—the preparing and cleaning, spinning, weaving, and finishing—were all done by hand; by 1815 machines performed these tasks. The cotton gin mechanically separated seeds from fibers. Two other American inven-

Library of Congress.

Eli Whitney's cotton gin revolutionized the cotton industry and consequently increased the demand for black slaves.

tions, "pickers" and "willows," cleaned the raw fibers and pulled out burrs. After 1826 yet another American invention, the Goulding condenser, not only carded wool but also compressed the various fibers into a single strand ready to be spun into yarn. After the War of 1812, power-driven jennies did the spinning. The jenny consisted of a belted spinning wheel to one side of a horizontal loom with bobbins, which reproduced the work of hand spinners as waterpower or steampower turned the belt and wheel. The manufacture of textiles involved many small steps, some quite intricate, and at almost every point Americans either invented new devices to do the work or improved already existing techniques. As a result, factory-made cotton and woolen cloth soon became so cheap that household production of fabrics declined, undersold by industrial competition.

These improvements in the textile industry had far-reaching results. A secondary industry sprang up to produce textile machines and related equipment, and this industry in turn spawned a third—shops to make machine tools.

The Cotton Boom

The effects of the textile industry were not confined to the Northeast. Many parts of the Southeast greatly increased the cultivation of cotton. Indeed, when territories opened up along the Gulf of Mexico after the defeat of hostile Creek Indians during the War of 1812, most of these lands became cotton plantations. After 1815, cotton was king in much of the lower South, although states below the Mason-Dixon Line continued to produce other crops as well. Maryland and Virginia grew considerable wheat and corn. Tobacco also flourished in those states and in North Carolina. Kentucky and Missouri raised hemp; Louisiana, sugar; and small, subsistence farms could be found throughout the entire area. Yet, despite this diversity, those rich green bushes flecked with white balls were the South's most important crop for several decades and perhaps the nation's as well.

The regional supremacy of cotton had national, even international reprecussions. Since so many southern whites turned their fields over to cotton, they had to purchase some of their food from the West. Northern merchants profited from handling the transportation and insurance involved in shipping southern cotton to domestic and foreign markets. English fabric manufacturers looked to the South as a prime source of raw cotton. The three main regions of the country—the South, the Northeast, and the West—became increasingly specialized and interdependent.

In time, as a one-crop mentality gripped much of the Lower South—an arc of states stretching from South Carolina westward to Texas and Arkansas—and manufacturing loomed ever more important in the Northeast, the Mississippi Valley became the great breadbasket of the nation, a role once enjoyed by the Middle Atlantic region. It is no accident, for example, that although McCormick perfected his reaper in Virginia, he produced those machines in Chicago. It is easy to oversimplify this three-sided portrait of the American economy after the War of 1812, but by the 1830s cotton clearly was one of the foundation stones. The Northeast provided its manufactured goods and various services; the West, food; and, the Deep South, cotton, which became a basic ingredient in this interchange. Those heavy bales created fortunes for growers, manufacturers, and distributors of finished goods, money to be invested in still more lands and factories. They facilitated westward expansion, quickly accounting for over half of all American exports, and were a major force in developing patterns of both domestic and foreign trade.

During the years immediately after the War of 1812 and again in the 1830s cotton was a crucial factor in American economic expansion. By mid-century, however, the boom was over. An analysis of land sales, cotton prices, and cotton production between 1833 and 1843 reveals what was happening in the so-called "Cotton Kingdom." After 1836 the sale of lands dropped sharply and prices began a slow downward trend, while production generally continued to climb. One could make money in cotton, but no longer expect quick, spectacular returns. As a result, investment capital turned elsewhere—to California and its gold fields and to newer and bigger factories in the Northeast. The Far West, more industrialization, and the first big wave of immigrants (few of whom settled in the South) fueled the expansion fires of the 1850s, not cotton.

While it lasted the cotton boom had a dramatic impact indeed. Production rose by leaps and bounds. In 1820, the South was producing 335,000 bales, each weighing approximately 500 pounds; by 1840, the annual crop rose to 1,348,000 bales and would triple by 1860. Several unique factors frustrate efforts to estimate the profits of a cotton plantation: the soaring cost of new black workers, the birth of offspring to slaves already living on the plantation, and income derived from sources other than cotton. In the 1820s, for example, a prime Georgia field hand averaged about $700; in 1860, about $1,800. In 1817-1818 cotton reached a peak market price of nearly thirty cents a pound in New Orleans but cotton prices plunged rapidly to 14.3 cents per pound the next year as a result of the Panic of 1819.

More impressive than columns of annual prices are census statistics which reveal how many people were lured to the Deep South by cotton. Between 1790 and 1860 the population of the South rose from two to more than eleven millions. Alabama, for example, had 1,250 residents in 1800, 964,201 in 1860. During the last two decades before the Civil War, expanding American factories used up one-quarter of the cotton crop, yet that commodity still accounted for half of all U.S. exports and helped mightily to pay for imports and attract foreign investment across the Atlantic to America. Widespread cultivation led to increased demand for slave labor; picking cotton had to be performed by hand, and slaves, for the most part, did this work. As a result, slave trading within and between states became a flourishing enterprise.

Although Southerners made a few efforts to build textile factories, first in the 1790s and again after the War of 1812, these attempts were largely halfhearted. Several factors tended to discourage their growth. The Northeast, with its know-how, capital, labor resources, and waterpower, surged so far ahead in industrial capabilities that it usually was cheaper to buy whatever was produced than to emulate this development and compete. So much money could be made in cotton that many Southerners invested their capital in land and slaves, leaving little for factories. By tradition the South was a rural, agricultural region, not eager to welcome urban masses and the resultant problems found wherever workers congregated. In addition, as the abolition fury grew, any substantial influx of "nonbelievers" could cause considerable unrest. Perhaps the key factors militating against industrialization lay simply in habit and attitude. The South had labor, capital, raw materials, and waterpower. If it had wanted factories badly enough, as later decades demonstrated, it could have had them.

Improvements in Industry

American industry took an important step toward assembly-line mass production when goods with interchangeable parts appeared. This innovation first occurred in the firearms industry. Whether Eli Whitney (the inventor of the cotton gin) or the less well-known Simeon North (1765–1852) first came up with the concept of interchangeability of parts is not known, but the two men, working independently, both made major contributions to the method. Interchangeability requires another, equally important concept and practice—subdividing the production of a product into many small steps.

In 1813 Simeon North signed a government contract to make 20,000 pistols. In the contract North wrote this provision: "The component parts of pistols are to correspond so exactly that any limb or part of one Pistol may be fitted to any other Pistol of the twenty thousand." Each one cost $7. For a decade or more, North, Whitney, and other gun manufacturers in Connecticut had been turning out interchangeable parts. Working with these components, their laborers could assemble guns in a fraction of the time previously required. The assembly line later was introduced into other industries as well. By the 1850s items ranging from watches to locks were being mass-produced by scores of workers, each doing one simple task over and over.

In 1828 steampower replaced waterpower at the Slater cotton mills in Pawtucket. Soon steam was powering many other American industries, freeing them from the necessity of having to be located beside a stream or river.

America was slower than England to industrialize, primarily because it was a newer, developing land and because American entrepreneurs lacked the capital to purchase expensive machinery. Even after the War of 1812, despite the remarkable successes of the American factory system in the production of cotton textiles, local craftsmen and traveling artisans were still providing most of the nation's manufactured goods, items such as pianos, tin utensils, shoes, cigars, hats, clothes, and hundreds of other necessities and luxuries. Development of centralized production in what we now call factories was far from orderly or systematic. By their very nature, some commodities fitted quickly into such a scheme of things; others did not. Reacting to increased market demand created by an evergrowing population, a producer often went through three steps: enlarging his shop or handicraft output, spreading the growing workload among various households (the so-called domestic or putting-out system), and eventually constructing a much larger shop complete with laborsaving machinery perhaps powered by a water wheel or steam, in short, a factory. Of course, a specialization process accompanied these changes as a few men in each trade emerged as capitalists or manufacturers, some became managers or foremen, and many more, rank-and-file workers.

In the early days of industrialization, most factories catered strictly to local needs and did not produce goods for distant markets. Even in the most rural parts of the country, local entrepreneurs turned out flour, lumber, brick, ironwork, cheese, and liquor to satisfy community needs. If one of these operations reached a larger market, this increase in business did not necessarily entail a departure from domestic methods of production. For instance, the hatmakers of Danbury, Connecticut, sold their wares all over the country, but until the 1850s they continued work by old-fashioned handicraft techniques.

Yale University Art Gallery, Gift of George Hoadly.

Eli Whitney, inventor of the cotton gin and proponent of the concept of the production of goods with interchangeable parts.

Capital needed for mechanization was in short supply. The number of banks willing to extend credit to American businessmen increased from 300 to 1,000 between 1820 and 1840, but this proliferation did not stimulate industrialization as rapidly as one would expect. The public distrusted banks, and this distrust deepened when nearly half of the recently founded banks in the country failed by 1825; twenty years later a similar proportion of new banks founded between 1830 and 1840 collapsed. Even in the best of times, banks were unable to stabilize the value of the notes they issued. As a well-known economist has observed, "The country tended to divide between those who felt that banks could make everyone rich and those who feared they would make everyone poor, and neither side lacked for evidence to support its case."

Nevertheless, banks did play a significant role in financing American industrialization. Bank credit, for instance, helped Eli Whitney to set up his mass production of firearms, and banks helped to finance the business interests of Peter Cooper, who in 1828 established the Baltimore ironworks that produced America's first steam locomotive.

The corporation was another mode of financing industrialization after the War of 1812. A corporation is a legal entity that provides investors with the benefit of "limited liability." If two or more people enter into a partnership, each partner is fully responsible (or "liable") for debts incurred by the enterprise as a whole. But in a corporation, by contrast, each stockholder is legally responsible for the corporation's debts only to the extent of his or her own investment. This form of organization evolved through the centuries in Europe, and in America it had proved to be a convenient means of attracting large numbers of investors to such enterprises as building turnpikes, bridges, and other large and expensive types of internal improvement. Only after 1815, however, did the corporation begin to play a major role in industrial life.

Like banks, corporations were regarded with suspicion by the general public and even by many entrepreneurs. Since individual investors had limited liability and in many cases did not participate directly in running the company's affairs, the corporation was associated with corruption and the undermining of individual enterprise. The very success of corporations was seen as evil, since their size, wealth, and efficiency enabled them to drive out smaller businesses and create monopolies.

Before 1837 businessmen eager to incorporate their enterprises faced legal difficulties. Each group interested in forming a corporation had to petition a state legislature for a special act of incorporation. As a result, businessmen with money and political connections had an advantage over those lacking leverage with lawmakers. This inequitable situation awakened protest and led to a demand for the general enactment of revised laws of incorporation enabling any group, once it met certain minimum requirements, to obtain a charter. Connecticut passed the first such general act in 1837, and in the following years the chief manufacturing states revised their own statutes accordingly.

Extensions of Industrialization

By mid-century virtually every American household had been influenced in some measure by changes in transportation, business, and industry, and many U.S. wares were being sold overseas as well. These included, among other things, cotton and woolen goods, shoes, boots, clothing, rubber products, various machines and agricultural implements, and processed foods. Interestingly, one invention often spawned others. Preservation of meats, fruits, and vegetables by sterilization and enclosure in airtight receptacles (begun in the 1820s) led within two decades to a canning machine, a process for storing milk through evaporation, and the utilization of glass jars with screwtop lids.

The sewing machine of Elias Howe inspired Isaac Merrit Singer (1811–1875), a superb salesman, to build a foot-operated version for use in the home. The two men fought several court battles over patents, but eventually formed a "combination" that divided all the royalties. Howe actually was deeply indebted to Singer who understood merchandising techniques much better than he did. Singer's goal, one he almost achieved, was a sewing machine in every home. Singer's sewing machine and McCormick's reaper were two inventions that elicited considerable praise overseas. In 1851 the reaper gave a spectacular demonstration at a farm near London's Crystal Palace Exhibition and quickly attracted more attention than the fabulous Kohinoor diamond.

Technology in the Classroom

The mechanization of American industry made applied science a subject of great interest to the educated public.

The Metropolitan Museum of Art, Gift of I.N. Phelps Stokes, Edward S. Hawes, Alice Mary Hawes, Marion Augusta Hawes, 1937.

Elias Howe
(1819–1867)

The inventor of the sewing machine led a life that sounds as though it had been written by Horatio Alger—a truc rags-to-riches saga. Born in Massachusetts, the son of a poor farmer, Howe was hired out to a neighboring farmer when he was twelve because his family was too poor to fccd or clothe him. When he was sixteen, young Elias was apprenticed to the machinery shop at the cotton mills in Lowell, Massachusetts.

After a number of other small jobs, Howe ended up two years later as an apprentice to Ari Davis, a maker of precision instruments in nearby Cambridge. One day Howe overheard Davis say that the next important invention would be a machine that could sew automatically. Armed with the technical skill he had acquired in Davis's shop and inspired by this suggestion, Howe began to work on this invention. His first attempt was a total failure, but in 1844 he made a new stab at a sewing machine, incorporating principles he had observed in the power looms at Lowell. His father gave him and his wife free board while Howe worked on his invention, and a friend, George Fisher, donated $500 to buy equipment. By April 1845, Howc had perfected a sewing machine that operated swiftly and efficiently and could make 250 stitches a minute, faster than the speed of five people sewing by hand. This invention revolutionized the manufacturing of clothing.

Howe registered his invention with the United States Patent Office in 1846, but no one in America seemed interested in producing the machine. So, Howe traveled to England where he found a buyer—but he had to sell his British rights for a mere pittance.

Meanwhile, back in America, manufacturers started producing sewing machines without giving Howe credit or royalties. Only after a five-year battle in the courts did Howe win his case in 1854; every machine that had been turned out or that would be manufactured in the future was to earn him royalties. During the Civil War, Howe sometimes was earning as much as $4,000 a week. ■

Traditional education in the United States had devoted little attention to science of any sort, but in the early nineteenth century this neglect came to an end.

One of the leading crusaders on behalf of science education was Benjamin Silliman (1779–1864), a professor at Yale University for more than half a century. Beginning in 1808 Silliman occasionally opened his lectures to the public in New Haven. And in 1818 he founded the *American Journal of Science and Arts,* which became one of the world's great scientific journals, and served as its editor for many years. Later, in the 1830s he became a famous public speaker, addressing Boston and New York audiences on geology and chemistry. Each chemistry lecture in Boston typically drew crowds of 1,500, and most of the speeches had to be repeated for those who were turned away. Still later, Silliman toured the country to address throngs in New Orleans, St. Louis, and other major cities. At Yale University he founded the forerunner of the Scientific School which became by the 1850s the center of scientific inquiry.

In 1824 another school of technology was established. The Rensselaer Polytechnic Institute in Troy, New York, was dedicated to applying science to "the common purposes of life." This school pioneered the laboratory method of classroom instruction and, in 1835, became the first engineering school in the United States to grant degrees.

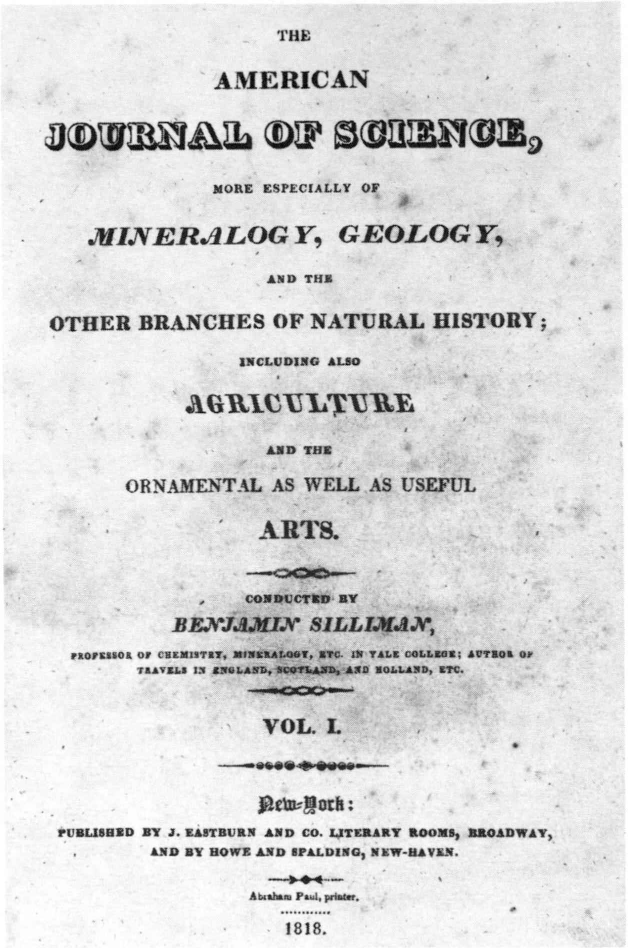

THE

AMERICAN

JOURNAL OF SCIENCE,

MORE ESPECIALLY OF

MINERALOGY, GEOLOGY,

AND THE

OTHER BRANCHES OF NATURAL HISTORY;

INCLUDING ALSO

AGRICULTURE

AND THE

ORNAMENTAL AS WELL AS USEFUL

ARTS.

CONDUCTED BY

BENJAMIN SILLIMAN,

PROFESSOR OF CHEMISTRY, MINERALOGY, ETC. IN YALE COLLEGE; AUTHOR OF TRAVELS IN ENGLAND, SCOTLAND, AND HOLLAND, ETC.

VOL. I.

New-York:

PUBLISHED BY J. EASTBURN AND CO. LITERARY ROOMS, BROADWAY, AND BY HOWE AND SPALDING, NEW-HAVEN.

Abraham Paul, printer.

1818.

Between 1818 and 1846, *The American Journal of Science and Arts,* popularly known as "Silliman's Journal," helped to promote interest in natural and physical science.

Industrial Workers

Government support of business was not accompanied by corresponding concern for the industrial workers. Although American workers usually were far better off than their European counterparts, nevertheless their situation was often grim—and the government did little to ameliorate it.

In colonial times and in the days of the early republic, the scarcity of labor meant relatively high wages. Laborers of those decades, often apprentices, worked at the side of their boss who usually owned the shop and perhaps had in his employ sons, daughters, nephews, and other assorted relatives. These factors tended to create good working conditions. Even in 1830 the American urban working class was still fairly small, since nearly three million of the country's four million laborers (including men, women, and children) worked on farms. Indeed, prior to 1830 the urban wage-earning class was going through a transitional period from an earlier era when jobs had been performed primarily by self-employed craftsmen to an era increasingly dominated by large factories. In this process the employer became separated from the individual worker, and personal bonds which once gave them common interests and common concerns disappeared.

Industrial Paternalism

Many European visitors were quite favorably impressed by the working conditions of American laborers. They were particularly delighted with the industrial paternalism practiced by the Boston Associates in what came to be known as the "Waltham System." The Associates, headed by Francis C. Lowell, Patrick Tracy Jackson, and Nathan Appleton, opened a complete, self-sufficient cotton mill in Waltham, Massachusetts, in 1813, the first such operation in the world. There, under one roof, workers and machines performed every step from preparing thread and weaving cloth to printing finished calico. Their so-called "system" involved the recruitment of hundreds of young women, a new, previously untapped source of labor that was plentiful since so many men had departed from scores of towns and villages to go West or to seek their fortunes in growing cities. The women lived in boardinghouses or dormitories under the careful supervision of matrons—a precaution against immorality. Most of these women were from rural families, and the textile mills offered them an excellent opportunity for earning an income and supplementing the often meager livelihood of their families. Nevertheless, the fathers of these young women had to be assured that their daughters were safe from moral or physical danger—and to provide this assurance the "Waltham System" was devised. This highly successful scheme soon expanded to other factories. In 1821 the Associates established a new plant in a community on the Merrimack River named Lowell in memory of their founder who had died four years earlier. A quarter of a century later at least one resident still had high praise for the Lowell plant. In 1845, Henry A. Miles, a Lowell minister, published a reassuring tract in which he said, "A more strictly and universally temperate class of persons cannot be found than the nine thousand operatives of this city; and the fact is as well known to all others living here as it is of some honest pride among themselves. In relation to other immoralities, it may be stated that the suspicion of criminal conduct, association with suspected persons, and general and habitual light behavior and conversation, are regarded as sufficient reasons for dismissions, and for which delinquent operatives are discharged."

Throughout the Northeast, factory employment provided the members of rural families the opportunity to earn cash badly needed in an area suffering from agricultural competition with the West. Many eastern farm sons and daughters helped their parents pay off farm mortgages by working in factories. For some farm offspring, moreover, the factory provided a means of escaping the loneliness and boredom of rural life. The youngsters were eagerly sought as employees since they could be paid lower wages than adults. Child labor, far from being viewed as an evil, was considered a chance for youngsters to learn good work habits and the virtue of thrift. In addition, the employment of minors eased the burden on community charity for the care of orphans and paupers.

Although mills following the Waltham or Lowell system employed women only, other New England factories hired whole families; in fact, in 1832 about half of the factory workers in New England were families. Newspapers frequently carried industrial advertisements seeking families of five or six children. Workers in the family-system mills were supposed to be of good moral character. "Those who are in the habit of profanity and Sabbath breaking and intend to continue these practices," one advertisement warned, "are invited not to make application." Each person in the family was put to work at a task deemed suitable for his or her strength and maturity, and all members lived together in company-constructed tenements.

Industrialization required a large pool of labor and a work force with specialized skills. European immigrants provided the country with both these necessities. Some 425,000 immigrants came to America between 1790 and 1830; most of them became farmers, but some stayed in seaboard cities to work as skilled laborers in textile mills, in machine shops and foundries, and in factories manufacturing shoes and boots. In the 1840s and 1850s, some four million immigrants crossed the Atlantic. Most of them were unskilled workers who were welcomed by American industrialists as a cheap source of labor. Before long, immigrants were settling in cities and towns and displacing white and free black workers in mills, factories, and other urban occupations.

Working and Living Conditions

Even in the supposedly idyllic environment of the Lowell factories, young women worked an average of seventy-five hours a week and earned only a dollar or two a week. In most American urban industries, working hours lasted from sunrise to sunset, with only a half hour off for meals, and wages varied from $1 to $6 a week.

Both living and working quarters were often cramped, stuffy, and noisy, and even skilled workers watched fearfully as larger and more complex machines appeared—mechanical monsters that they knew would soon take over their jobs. In one industry after another during the pre-Civil War period, mechanization put thousands of craftsmen out of work.

Competition within a single industry could have equally disastrous effects. At Lowell, for instance, competition from other textile plants led to a reduction in the price of fabrics, which resulted in an increase in the number of hours each Lowell woman was expected to work and in the number of machines she was required to operate. In 1834 and again in 1836, wages were cut by as much as 25 percent. These cuts inspired threats of strikes. One protestor in 1836 announced, "As our fathers resisted unto blood the lordly avarice of the British ministry, so we, their daughters, never will wear the yoke which has been prepared for us."

The hard life of factory workers was reflected in the crowded dwellings in drab factory towns. In Philadelphia, for instance, working families lived in tenements, one room for each family. Not only were laborers plagued by bad living conditions, they also were faced with other concerns. In 1829, for instance, a philanthropic organization announced that 75,000 Americans were jailed every year for indebtedness, though half of these people owed less than $20. In addition, most factory workers watched their children grow up ignorant, unable to read or write, for education cost money. Only in some New England communities or in towns located in states dominated by Yankee settlers (Ohio, for example) was basic primary education provided free of charge. Even where classrooms did exist, attendance often was poor. Agricultural demands and a family's need for factory pay frequently took precedence over the three Rs—reading, writing, and arithmetic.

The Early Labor Movement

Since colonial days American craftsmen had banded together to form benevolent associations. In these early workingmen's societies, factory workers played no part; these organizations were made up of craftsmen and artisans. Their goals were to keep wages on the same level with the prices of consumer goods, to fight for shorter working hours, to establish and maintain a "closed shop" (one that could not hire nonmembers), to regulate the training and selection of apprentices, and to promote fraternal unity. Until 1820 most of these workingmen's associations were weak and accomplished little. They were really local clubs, few of them lasting longer than a decade. Membership rose during periods of prosperity, but it fell during depressions because workers were more willing to accept wage cuts than risk being fired.

The modern labor movement in America began with the founding of the Mechanics' Union of Trade Associations in Philadelphia in 1827 (a "mechanic" was an artisan). This organization was an outgrowth of an abortive strike by Philadelphia carpenters for a ten-hour day; the failure led various craft unions to band together into a larger body. While unionization continued among skilled artisans in the urban Northeast, the growing number of unskilled factory workers there remained unorganized.

The number of unions representing skilled workers grew rapidly in the mid-1830s, largely in response to the pressures of inflation. Though wholesale prices nearly doubled during that period, wages advanced very little. Unions lost their old fraternal character and became fighting instruments intent on raising wages and reducing hours. More and more craftsmen were organized, including milliners, handloom weavers, and plasterers; and craft unions also sprang up in cities in the West and South.

Labor parties also appeared, though they were short-lived. Almost all of them attempted to secure free public education for children of workers and abolish imprisonment for debt. The most successful of these, the Workingmen's Party, sprang up in Philadelphia in 1828. It published the first labor newspaper, the *Mechanic's Free Press.* Soon more than fifty labor newspapers were being printed from Maine to Missouri. By 1832, however, most of these early labor parties ceased to exist.

The parties enjoyed brief, chaotic lives because most Americans of the times—including laborers themselves—did not perceive the working class as a distinct entity. In a sense, early labor parties failed for the same reason that labor unions experienced difficulties: they lacked an ideology and a program that appealed to a sufficient number of workers to sustain any sort of labor movement, whether it was a political organization or a class-structured association. Native-born or immigrant, the American worker of those decades did not see himself tied to a class, and the political issues that interested him often had little relevance to how he made his living. Most American workers had faith in their own abilities to rise economically without the aid of either parties or unions. At every point, unions faced opposition, not only from

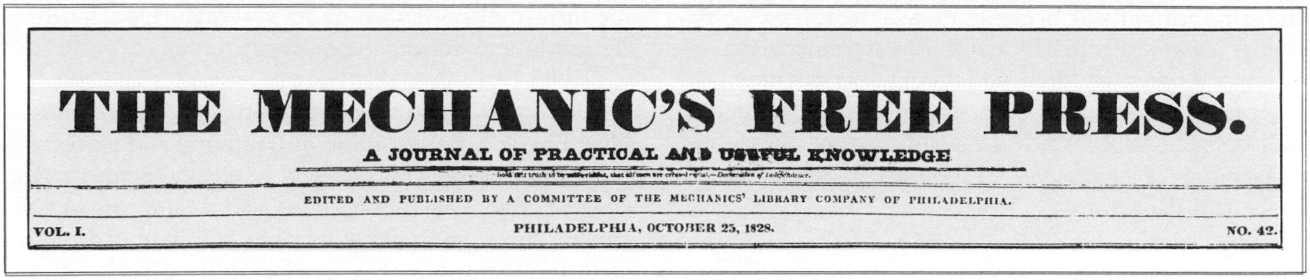
THE MECHANIC'S FREE PRESS.

A JOURNAL OF PRACTICAL AND USEFUL KNOWLEDGE

EDITED AND PUBLISHED BY A COMMITTEE OF THE MECHANICS' LIBRARY COMPANY OF PHILADELPHIA.

VOL. I. PHILADELPHIA, OCTOBER 25, 1828. NO. 42.

The goals of the Workingmen's Party were ably expressed in the pages of labor newspapers such as *The Mechanic's Free Press.*

the courts but also from employers, who blacklisted "troublemakers," hired recent immigrants to replace dissidents, and fired union members.

Nevertheless, some of the workingmen's party planks were built into the platforms of the major political parties. Goals such as the ten-hour day, public education, and abolition of debtor's prisons were achieved in some states by 1840, as were many of the other reforms urged by workers: universal male suffrage without property qualifications; laws to protect hired workers against default on the payment of wages by employers; restrictions on child labor; state regulation of all banks; reform of the tax system; and abolition of compulsory state militia service. The militia system, the workers argued, was unfair, since rich citizens, when punished for not serving, had only to pay a fine; poor workers, unable to pay the fine or take off from their jobs to serve in the militia, received jail sentences.

The workingmen's parties and unions of the 1820s and 1830s signalled a false dawn in the American labor movement. The main reason they failed to survive can be traced to the Panic of 1837; the depression forced rebellious workers to accept poor working conditions and low wages, which were preferable to unemployment. But the early movement also lacked cohesion and did not include the female work force. The rank-and-file members included not only mechanics and laborers but also merchants, lawyers, physicians, and other groups of professionals and businessmen.

To some extent, the early labor movement may have been undermined by the lure of the frontier. Historian Frederick Jackson Turner (1861–1932) propounded a theory, called the Frontier Thesis, which held that the abundance of cheap land in the West acted for generations as a "safety valve" for discontented factory workers from the East. Recently, historians have attacked Turner's thesis and pointed out that few Eastern workers had the money to move West. Nevertheless, cheap land in the West did at least attract some farmers from the East who, had they not moved, might have joined the labor pool in the Northeast. The frontier, in addition, did give some recent immigrants a place to go; had these newcomers not headed west they would have settled in the East, swelling the ranks of laborers and driving down wages still further. Even as an escapist fantasy, the frontier worked a powerful spell; thousands of factory workers, farm boys, tired apprentices, and overworked immigrants *thought* they could go to the West and start life anew. Although they might never actually pack up and go, that dream alone somehow made life more bearable.

Workingmen who remained in the East seldom moved up the economic or social ladder in a dramatic way. There were very few self-made wealthy men, and the gulf between the working class and the rich was widening. Although Andrew Jackson, in appealing to newly enfranchised voters from the working class, employed the rhetoric of equality, in fact his was not an egalitarian age. Wages did not keep pace with inflation in the period between 1827 and 1840, and John Quincy Adams expressed the opinion that although in the North there was "a great equality before the law . . . it ceases absolutely in the habits of life. There are upper classes and working classes."

Abject poverty may not have been the lot of most American workers, who were certainly better off than their European counterparts, but their hours were long, their salaries low, their lives tedious, their homes crowded and unhealthy, and their opportunities few.

Industrialization was bringing greater wealth to the nation as a whole after 1815, but it also engendered exploitation of women, children, and immigrants and meant the loss of independence for the artisan. As the New England philosopher Ralph Waldo Emerson warned the public: "Machinery is aggressive. All tools are in one sense edge tools, and dangerous."

The Rise of Cities

New modes of transportation, new factories, new inventions, new immigrants—even the new lands of the West to a surprising degree—all contributed directly to the growth of an urban America. Between 1820 and 1860 cities grew more rapidly than in any earlier period in our history, three times as fast as the rate of the nation as a whole, and by the eve of the Civil War 20 percent of Americans were living in communities of 2,500 or more. The shift to an industrial society—for that was what was happening during these decades—required considerable capital, managerial skills, a good supply of labor, a specialized work force, and an extensive transportation network. Four of these factors are found only in cities, and the fifth (transportation) by its very nature obviously is related to and depends upon them.

The basic ingredient in the rise of cities was the factory, but it could take many forms such as textiles in New England, flour milling in Baltimore and Rochester, New York, iron castings in New Jersey and Pennsylvania, clocks and guns in Connecticut, and steamboats in Cincinnati. Water and rail connections fed these behemoths, collecting whatever they needed from all parts of the nation and later distributing their products to eager customers. These networks, in turn, created cities at points where tracks converged and canal, river and oceangoing boats docked. The end of a line, "the jumping off place," often developed a momentum of its own for a time, especially in the West. There settlers departed for new farms and homesteads and returned with goods to be shipped to market. Although many of these communities were not large by modern standards, they exerted considerable influence.

This phenomenon of urban growth was not limited to any region. During these decades, the South, often thought of as rural, lagged only behind the North and Great Britain in urbanization. St. Louis, Memphis, Louisville, New Orleans, Mobile, Savannah, Richmond,

URBAN GROWTH, 1800–1840

City	1800	1810	1820	1830	1840
Baltimore, Md.	26,514	46,555	62,738	80,620	102,313
Boston, Mass.	24,937	38,746	54,027	85,568	118,857
Charleston, S.C.	18,824	24,711	24,780	30,289	29,261
Louisville, Ky.	—	—	4,012	10,341	21,210
Memphis, Tenn.	—	—	53	663	1,799
Mobile, Ala.	—	—	—	3,194	12,672
New Haven, Conn.	4,049	5,772	7,147	10,180	12,960
New Orleans, La.	—	17,242	27,176	46,082	102,193
New York, N.Y.	60,515	100,775	130,881	214,995	348,943
Norfolk, Va.	6,926	9,193	8,478	9,814	10,920
Philadelphia, Pa.	61,559	87,303	108,809	161,271	220,423
Portsmouth, N.H.	5,339	6,934	7,327	8,026	7,887
Providence, R.I.	7,614	10,071	11,767	16,833	23,171
Richmond, Va.	5,737	9,735	12,067	16,060	20,153
St. Louis, Mo.	—	—	—	4,977	16,469
Savannah, Ga.	5,146	5,215	7,523	7,303	11,214
Trenton, N.J.	—	3,002	3,942	3,925	4,035
Washington, D.C.	3,210	8,208	13,247	18,826	23,364

Washington, and Baltimore all registered impressive population gains, usually because of the influence of cotton or the success of rail lines funneling raw materials, manufactured goods, and people into their midst. The only traditional center that lagged behind was Charleston, stifled somewhat as the "Cotton Kingdom" moved ever westward and new rail lines leading to municipal rivals diverted business to their docks and warehouses.

One result of this urbanization surge was a quickening faith in the American future, a sincere belief in what the promoter of each "new Athens" had to say. Sometimes their blarney rang true. In 1835 William Ogden, a resident of upstate New York, moved to Chicago, a town of 3,200 residents. Two years later he became that community's first mayor. Convinced of Chicago's future greatness and aware of benefits railroads could bring, he wisely invested in land and made a fortune. By 1850 Chicago had 30,000 inhabitants, ten years later nearly four times that number, and Ogden was worth several million dollars.

Thomas Jefferson warned in 1800 that cities were "pestilential to the morals, the health, and the liberties of man." A half century later Horace Greeley observed that "we cannot all live in cities, yet nearly all seem determined to do so." Despite Jefferson's words, he spent considerable time in cities—Paris, New York, Richmond, Philadelphia, and Washington—although the nation's capital was little more than a strung-out village during his White House days. Editor Greeley, the man who told everyone "to go West" (he only went from New England to Manhattan himself), was nearly as far off the mark as Jefferson. America still was overwhelmingly rural at mid-century, but few could ignore the trends set into motion by industrialization. The city, regardless of what it did to morals, health, and liberty, was fast becoming an integral part of the American landscape. And so was the fortresslike factory surrounded by a sea of tenements filled with thousands of workers, many of them willing refugees from the boredom of villages and towns that had lost out in the struggle for turnpikes, canals, and railroads.

Library of Congress.

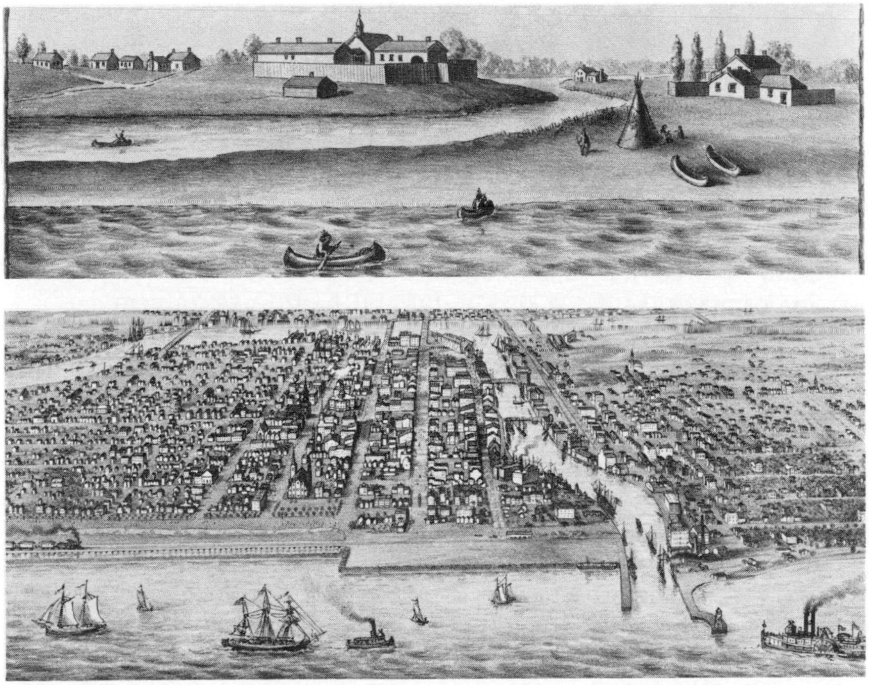

Chicago's history is the remarkable story of how profit-minded and public-minded boosters helped to transform a frontier outpost into a thriving city. In 1830 (top) its population was 50. By 1853 (bottom) it had grown to more than 60,000.

Essay

The Birth of Mass Production

The industrialization of America in the early nineteenth century was intimately connected with the accumulation of large supplies of capital. In the South, the leading citizens were planters who sank all ready cash into land and slaves; in the Northeast, the leading citizens were merchants who had accumulated, after years of speculation in commerce and trade, sufficient money to make the big initial outlays that industrial development required. Moreover, the business experience of successful New Englanders had conditioned them to wait years for full returns on their investments and to plot with care and imagination every step of the industrial process, from the building of plants to the merchandising of final products.

Development of world trade was, in the long run, another key to this success story. Cotton for textiles and hides for boots and shoes could be brought to New England from Georgia, Egypt, and South America. And the same ships that gathered raw materials could distribute finished products to customers in all parts of the world.

In a unique fashion, New England's disadvantages proved blessings in disguise. Lacking rich soil and abundant minerals, she was not tied to any tradition-bound enterprise and could experiment freely with new ways of doing things. Even the turmoil fostered by Jefferson's Embargo and the War of 1812 tended to aid the movement toward large scale production. Labor and capital which, temporarily at least, could not go to sea or move west quickly sought and found new outlets.

The most efficient and successful of the pioneer industries in the Northeast was founded by a rich Boston merchant, Francis C. Lowell. Lowell, a well-to-do young man, was banished from Harvard in 1789 for lighting a bonfire in the historic College Yard; however, he continued his studies under private tutors and graduated with his class in 1793. Lowell then worked in his family's import-export business until ill health caused him to travel to England in 1810. There he was deeply impressed by textile machinery he saw in Lancashire. When Lowell returned to the United States in 1812, he formed a corporation for the manufacturing of cotton textiles. Among the other members of the New Boston Manufacturing Company were Lowell's brother-in-law, Patrick Tracy Jackson, and Nathan Appleton, whose family's trading firm was dissolved on the eve of the war with England, since the conflict signalled an end to international

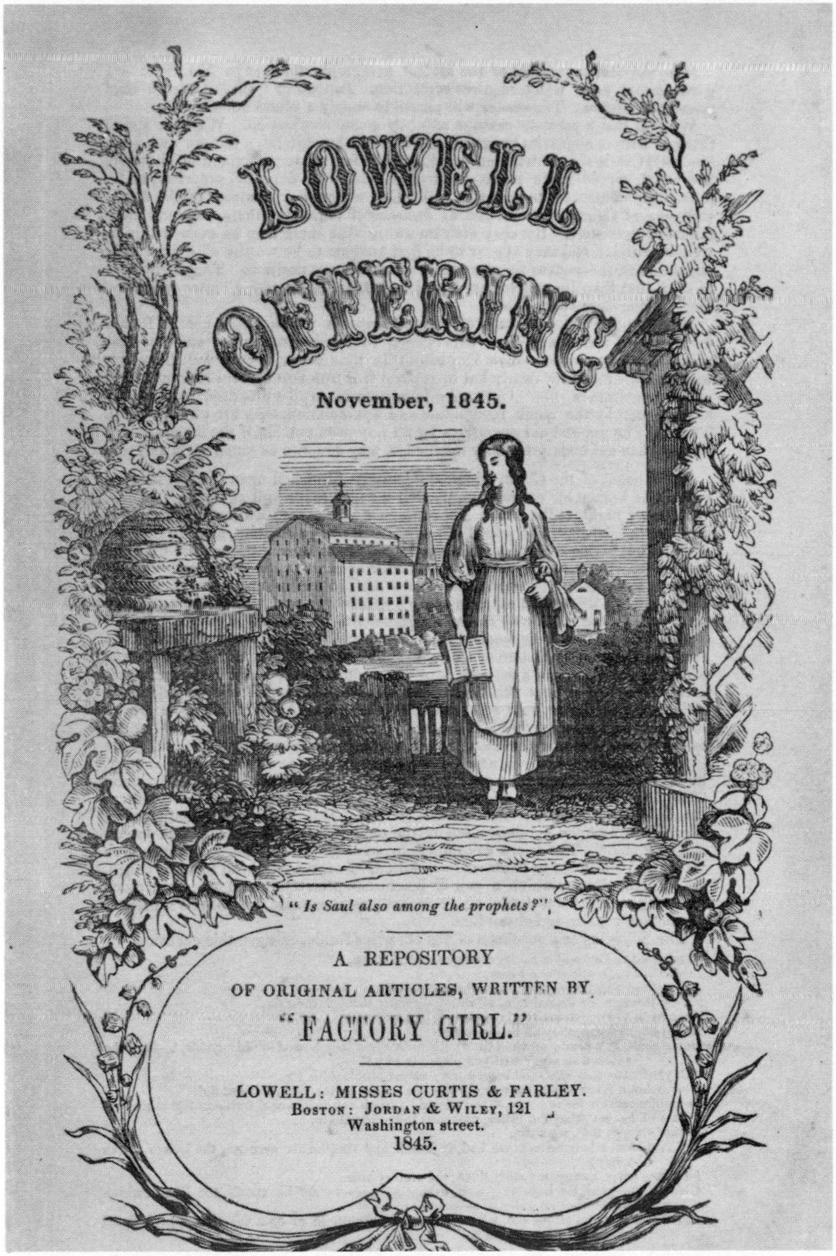

The female workers at the Lowell mills had their own literary magazine. The editors of the *Lowell Offering* published stories of moral uplift and left such matters as hours and wages in the hands of the directors of the company.

trade. Appleton invested $5,000 in 1813; by 1840 the company owned mills worth $12 million.

These men, the Boston Associates, quite literally were the fathers of American big business. In their petition to the Massachusetts legislature for an act of incorporation, the investors sounded much like modern businessmen: "Your petitioners believe that a great capital, always at the command of the manufacturer, is essential to his success.'' This capital, accumulated quite rapidly, amounting to the astounding sum of $300,000. In an astute move, the members of the corporation decided to invest only two-thirds of the money in mills and machinery and to reserve the remaining $100,000 for operating expenses.

Their innovation did not stop there. The Boston Manufacturing Company reorganized virtually all aspects of the factory system. They placed every step of the manufacturing process, from bleaching thread to printing calicos, under one roof. Based on rough sketches of equipment Lowell saw in England, a mechanical genius named Paul Moody was able to construct an efficient power loom (all other mills in New England still used handlooms).

In 1813 they built their mill on the Charles River at Waltham. It was the first completely self-sufficient cotton-manufacturing plant in the world. Although the Boston Associates spent some $600,000 on the project in the first six years of operation, nevertheless annual sales rose by the end of that period to $260,000. The corporation was able to survive the Panic of 1819, which ruined or crippled many other mills—to survive and even to flourish, probably because Waltham fabrics were unusually durable (''stout and thick,'' as salesmen described them). The Waltham factory also was protected by the Tariff of 1816, which placed a high duty on all imported power-loomed cotton fabrics.

Although the success of the Waltham enterprise can be attributed in part to its handsome capitalization and efficient plant organization, in addition, the owners tapped a new source

Courtesy of the Lowell Museum.

The Waltham Mill operated by the Boston Manufacturing Company was the first factory in the world to manufacture cotton cloth by power machinery enclosed in one building.

of labor. Rather than hiring poor families and employing children, as so many other mills did, young women formed the bulk of their labor force. These workers, usually the daughters of impoverished farmers, worked at Waltham for a year or two and then, after accumulating some small savings, returned to their homes. Though temporary, these laborers were hard-working and efficient—and their wages were low.

At the time, those who organized this ''boardinghouse'' system were convinced that America would never have a permanent factory class, and Waltham and similar communities became show places that drew hundreds of visitors each year. The well-groomed young ladies lived in spacious homes where they had ready access to religious life, learning, and lectures. Of course, New England soon had grubby factory towns where workers lived in squalor, but here was an ideal to which both labor and management could aspire.

The Boston Manufacturing Company also devised a new way to merchandise its goods. Instead of placing their fabrics on consignment with a large number of merchants scattered here and there, the company set up a separate sales organization and worked through agents who received a commission of only 1 percent but received in exchange the exclusive right to merchandise Waltham goods in a certain area.

The most astonishing thing about this undertaking, which goes far toward explaining many differences between American everyday life in the eighteenth and twentieth centuries, is that no one had done it before. Waltham produced nothing strange or exotic, only cotton cloth. This was little more than the successful

Library of Congress.

Alert and neat-looking young women at work in New England mills impressed foreign visitors and American dignitaries alike with the new world of the factory.

marriage of the experience of others, efficient machinery, good labor practices, and shrewd distribution techniques. And to the amazement of Old World visitors (and perhaps to Americans as well) the world's most advanced form of industrial organization had appeared unheralded in a "back water" area of civilization along the rocky streams of New England.

The postwar depression of 1819 destroyed many competitors, but the Boston Manufacturing Company prevailed—and in doing so set the pattern for later American enterprises. From the wreckage of bankrupt and shuttered firms, there arose a solid, new business form epitomized by the Boston Manufacturing Company. By 1820 the Associates were ready to expand. They bought land bordering the Merrimack River at East Chelmsford and dubbed the new community Lowell, in honor of the founder of the company, who had died in 1817. As business revived throughout the United States in 1821, the new factory at Lowell thrived.

In this enterprise and others that soon emulated its success, executive management, sales, and production functioned independently. Each segment — decision making, sales promotion, and work on the looms themselves — was organized so as to reap maximum benefits from mass production. In this manner the Boston Manufacturing Company was able to turn a country hamlet into the industrial city of Lowell. Also, in this new community Moody developed a machine works that was soon turning out new and improved cotton machinery to be used in Lowell, Waltham, and other cities that would try to duplicate their success.

In 1830 the expanding corporation solved yet another problem—transportation. The Middlesex Canal and turnpikes serving Lowell were inadequate, and Patrick Tracy Jackson, one of the original members of the corporation, suggested a railroad be built between Boston and Lowell. The company soon laid out a line of track—a big but ultimately rewarding investment.

In the 1840s an influx of cheap immigrant labor changed the paternalistic relationship between employer and employee; nevertheless, the early years at Waltham and Lowell served as a prototype for the modern corporation.

Two aspects of this pioneer enterprise are especially revealing: versatile management and specialized machines. The three men who started it—Lowell, Jackson, and Appleton—had virtually no experience with textiles or with manufacturing, but they knew how to organize a business venture and were not afraid to experiment with new techniques. Second, the machines developed for their factories and others that appeared throughout America became more and more specialized, not the workers.

Both management and labor were, in effect, interchangeable parts and could adapt quite easily to scores of enterprises, no matter how diverse their needs might be. This attitude has, of course, influenced American industrial life to the present day. One experienced in sales, advertising, or management can move quite easily from a job in the automotive industry to an allied or quite different field of endeavor. Much like the assembly line, this versatility of management and labor—a willingness and an ability to work almost anywhere and at anything—became an integral part of the emerging process known as mass production.

Selected Readings

General Accounts

Richard D. Brown, *Modernization: The Transformation of American Life, 1600–1865* (1976)

Stuart Bruchey, *The Roots of American Economic Growth, 1607–1861: An Essay in Social Causation* (1965)

Douglas T. Miller, *The Birth of Modern America, 1820–1850* (1970)

Douglass C. North, *The Economic Growth of the United States, 1790–1860* (1961)

Robert E. Riegel, *Young America, 1830–1840* (1949)

The Transportation Revolution

George Rogers Taylor, *The Transportation Revolution, 1815–1860* (1951)

Leland D. Baldwin, *Keelboat Age on Western Waters* (1941)

Louis C. Hunter, *Steamboats on the Western Rivers: An Economic and Technological History* (1949)

Ronald E. Shaw, *Erie Water West: A History of the Erie Canal, 1792–1854* (1966)

John F. Stover, *The Life and Decline of the American Railroad* (1970)

Government and the Economy

Carter Goodrich, ed., *The Government and the Economy, 1783–1861* (1967)

R. Kent Newmyer, *The Supreme Court under Marshall and Taney* (1968)

James Willard Hurst, *Law and the Conditions of Freedom in the Nineteenth-Century United States* (1956)

Malcolm J. Rohrbough, *The Land Office Business: The Settlement and Administration of American Public Lands, 1789–1837* (1968)

Louis Hartz, *Economic Policy and Democratic Thought: Pennsylvania, 1776–1860* (1948)

Oscar and Mary Handlin, *Commonwealth: A Study of the Role of Government in the American Economy: Massachusetts, 1774–1861* (rev. ed., 1969)

Industry, Technology, and Workers

Thomas C. Cochran and William Miller, *Age of Enterprise: A Social History of Industrial America* (2nd ed., 1961)

Nathan Rosenberg, *Technology and American Economic Growth* (1972)

Paul W. Gates, *The Farmer's Age: Agriculture, 1815–1860* (1960)

Constance McLaughlin Green, *Eli Whitney and the Birth of American Technology* (1956)

Herbert G. Gutman, *Work, Culture and Society in Industrializing America: Essays in America's Working Class and Social History* (1977)

Alan Dawley, *Class and Community: The Industrial Revolution in Lynn* (1976)

Hannah Josephson, *The Golden Threads: New England's Mill Girls and Magnates* (1949)

William A. Sullivan, *The Industrial Worker in Pennsylvania, 1800–1840* (1955)

Edward Pessen, *Most Uncommon Jacksonians: The Radical Leaders of the Early Labor Movement* (1967)

The Rise of Cities

Constance McLaughlin Green, *American Cities in the Growth of the Nation* (1957)

Richard C. Wade, *The Urban Frontier: The Rise of Western Cities, 1790–1830* (1959)

Samuel B. Warner, Jr., *The Urban Wilderness: A History of the American City* (1972)

Allan R. Pred, *Urban Growth and the Circulation of Information: The United States System of Cities, 1790–1840* (1973)

Robert G. Albion, *The Rise of New York Port, 1815–1860* (1939)

Stuart M. Blumin, *The Urban Threshold: Growth and Change in a Nineteenth-Century American Community* (1976)

Chapter 9

Race, Sex, and Nationality

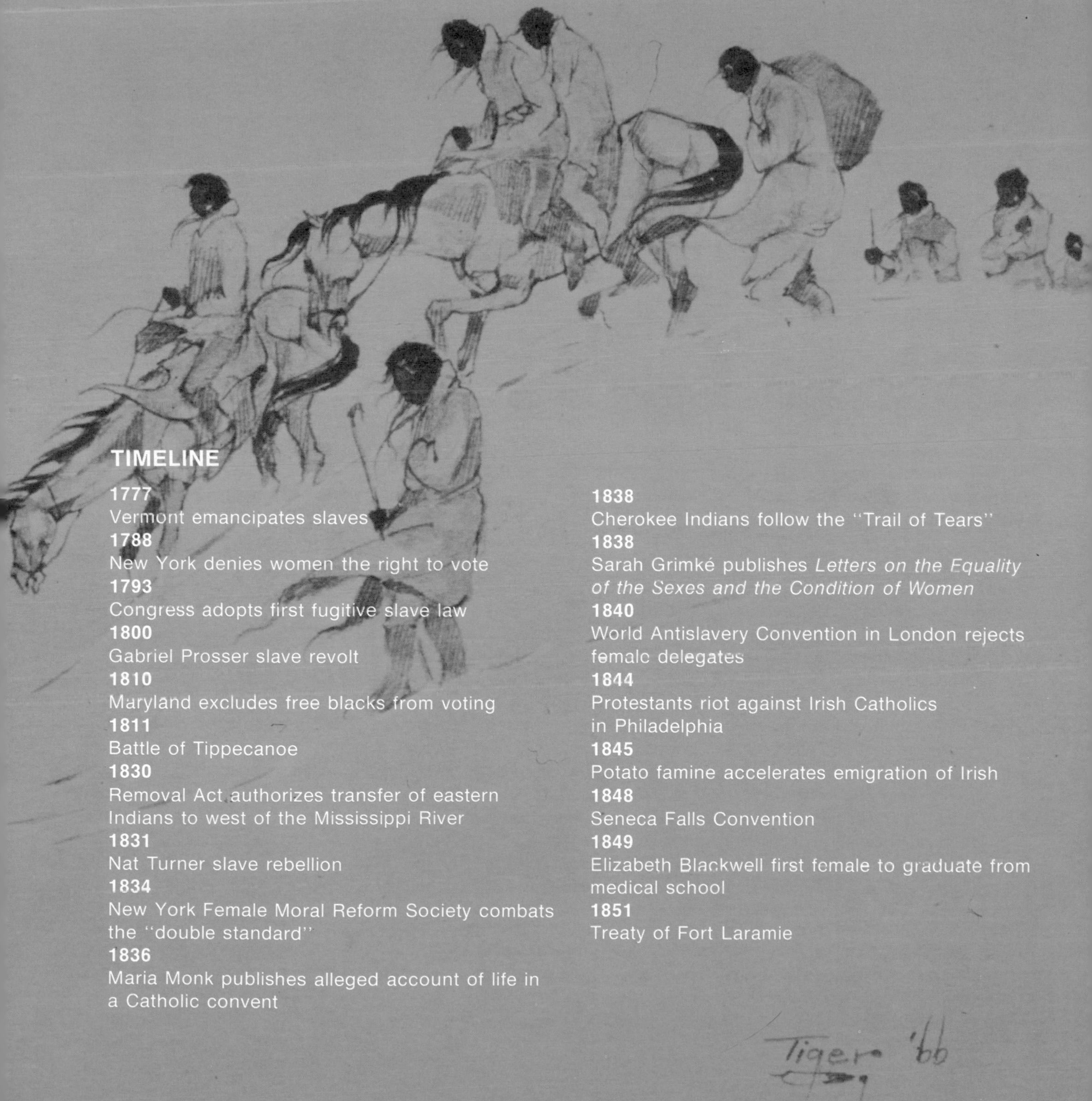

TIMELINE

1777
Vermont emancipates slaves
1788
New York denies women the right to vote
1793
Congress adopts first fugitive slave law
1800
Gabriel Prosser slave revolt
1810
Maryland excludes free blacks from voting
1811
Battle of Tippecanoe
1830
Removal Act authorizes transfer of eastern Indians to west of the Mississippi River
1831
Nat Turner slave rebellion
1834
New York Female Moral Reform Society combats the "double standard"
1836
Maria Monk publishes alleged account of life in a Catholic convent
1838
Cherokee Indians follow the "Trail of Tears"
1838
Sarah Grimké publishes *Letters on the Equality of the Sexes and the Condition of Women*
1840
World Antislavery Convention in London rejects female delegates
1844
Protestants riot against Irish Catholics in Philadelphia
1845
Potato famine accelerates emigration of Irish
1848
Seneca Falls Convention
1849
Elizabeth Blackwell first female to graduate from medical school
1851
Treaty of Fort Laramie

CHAPTER OUTLINE

The ideals of the American Revolution included the promise of equality, liberty, and happiness for all, yet in the first half of the nineteenth century the nation clearly denied legal and economic equality to blacks, Indians, women, and many recent immigrants. The factories of the Northeast, in their search for cheap labor, exploited women, children, and immigrants. As the textile industry called for more and more cotton, southern farmers turned increasingly toward cotton cultivation—and the use of slave labor. As the white population grew, valuable lands held by Indians in the South and the Old Northwest became increasingly attractive to settlers. Finally, the government removed most of the Indians living east of the Mississippi to land in the West so white settlers could get what they wanted.

Both competition and cooperation sprang up among the various oppressed groups in America. Women crusading for the abolition of slavery recognized that they, too, were denied basic civil rights. Poor Irish immigrants to the big cities of the Northeast took the jobs of free blacks and other whites—and thereby earned the hostility of longtime residents. The Irish, in turn, conceived a hatred of blacks. In almost every instance such antagonisms grew out of a blend of basic insecurity, economic competition, and group consciousness fed by differences that were religious, social, and ethnic in nature—and perhaps racial and linguistic as well. Yankee-bred New Englanders feared that the strange Irish Catholic peasants could not be assimilated into their society. The Irish scorned abolition because the end of slavery might increase competition for their jobs. At its best, this awareness of a common background produced a sense of belonging and an interest in one's heritage. At its worst, which was more often the case, it led to riots, mob violence, and bigotry; to the burning of churches, murder, and an upsurge of nativism (policies favoring native-born inhabitants). And strange as it may seem in a civilization descended from immigrants, it led to demands that foreign immigration cease, or at least be curtailed somewhat.

Black Americans

By the mid-eighteenth century, Americans began to develop a self-awareness and to become conscious of their growing, diverse society. They realized they were no longer really Englishmen and that, as a result of the introduction and expansion of slavery, they had a race problem in their midst. The first group to face up to this fact was the Quakers of Pennsylvania, who, in time, became the spearhead of an abolition movement led by men such as Benjamin Lay, John Woolman, and Anthony Benezet. Blacks were also active in efforts to gain freedom for their race. Such blacks as Benjamin Banneker and Thomas Fuller, both mathematical geniuses, Richard Allen and Absalom Jones, both very able ministers and writers, Prince Hall, the founder of the Black Masonic

Order, and James Derham, the pioneer physician, achieved fame, engendered admiration, and also aroused support for the cause of abolition by their impressive accomplishments.

With the drift toward revolution, aided and abetted by a strong humanitarian impulse stirred by religious revivals, the attack on slavery quickened. This onslaught provoked scattered proslavery tracts during the early 1770s. For the most part, however, white Americans pushed this issue to one side as they concentrated on war and independence. To some patriots, especially Virginians, slavery was an institution forced upon them by the British enemy, and victory might (in some unexplained way) solve the matter. Many Americans were embarrassed by their unfree black laborers, especially when both the British and Tories taunted them concerning highflown phrases such as "all men are created equal." Others thought some sort of gradual emancipation scheme would evolve. Some 5,000 free blacks served heroically in American forces during the Revolutionary War alongside white comrades, increasing abolition pressure.

Although slavery knew no sectional boundaries on the eve of the American Revolution, it was dying a slow death north of the Potomac River. The new state constitution of Vermont abolished slavery in 1777. Perhaps the high water mark of antislavery movement that began during the Revolutionary period was reached in 1787 when Congress banned slavery in the Old Northwest. By 1805 every northern state had abolished slavery or had made provisions for eventual emancipation.

Yet no national emancipation movement developed and hopes generated by the Revolutionary War began to fade. Why? The principal reason, the stumbling block frustrating all such efforts for the next few decades, was that no one could answer some hard questions: How would former masters be compensated for the loss of their slave property? Where would the ex-slaves live? How would they be cared for during the initial months and years of freedom? What would happen to the nation's social and economic life if one-eighth of its inhabitants—most of them uneducated and familiar with little except agricultural labor done under the direction of others—suddenly were free to do as they wanted?

From 1783 to 1800 the new, independent republic was struggling to stay afloat. The last thing needed was debate over an issue that obviously would exacerbate regional differences and perhaps lead to disunion. During those same years, several events occurred to strengthen slavery and to slow the momentum toward racial equality. These included the invention of the cotton gin, revulsion against the excesses of the French Revolution, a black uprising in Haiti, rumors of slave rebellions in the South, and a constant demand for cheap labor in the South.

Despite arguments to the contrary, slavery was highly profitable, even before the invention of the cotton gin; after much of the South converted to the cultivation of cotton, slave labor was basic to the economy. In time, many Americans began to consider blacks as inherently inferior, and this supposed inferiority was invoked to justify slavery. As William Harper of South Carolina put it, "The African negro is an inferior variety of the human race . . . , his distinguishing characteristics are such as peculiarly mark him out for the situation he occupies among us."

The Constitution prohibited Congress from stopping the importation of slaves for twenty years; in 1793 Congress passed the first laws enforcing the return of fugitive slaves to their owners. More importantly, one constitutional clause stipulated that each slave should be counted only as three-fifths of an ordinary white citizen in determining taxation and representation in Congress. These actions served to sanction slavery.

As the black population in the South increased, a growing fear of slave rebellions and the concurrent anxiety that freed blacks would seek revenge against former masters snuffed out an incipient abolition movement in that region. In the 1790s Southerners heard with alarm of a black uprising in Haiti against French rulers. In 1800 a young slave, Gabriel, convinced some 1,100 slaves to take an oath to fight for their freedom. The blacks planned to seize the arsenal in Richmond, Virginia and launch a general slaughter of their white oppressors. The plot was discovered at the last moment and put down, but it inspired hysteria in Southern whites everywhere. As a result of the Gabriel plot, some three dozen blacks were executed, though no whites had been killed. Caught between paranoia and economic pressure, Southern whites responded to the abolition movement by generating a copious literature defending slavery. Between 1800 and 1810, Southern legislatures tightened legal controls over slaves. In 1806, for instance, Virginia adopted a law making it more difficult for a white master to free his slaves. The humanitarian flood that had swept the coun-

Library of Congress.

Slave labor was basic to the cotton economy of the South.

try, even parts of the South, in the wake of the Revolution subsided.

In the period before the Civil War, as southern farmers moved into the Gulf states and started cotton plantations, the slave population followed this trend in settlement. Older Atlantic seaboard states in the upper South, such as Virginia and Maryland, which had considered abolition just after the Revolution, now supplied slaves to the cotton-growing areas in the Deep South.

Between 1790 and 1810, the number of slaves nearly doubled, increasing from 697,897 to 1,191,354, and during each succeeding decade another 550,000 or so would appear. By 1860 there were nearly four million slaves in the United States. The free black population kept pace, rising from 59,466 in 1790 to 488,070 in 1860. Although the number of whites grew even faster in those years (3,172,464 to 26,957,471) it is apparent that the institution of slavery was becoming ever more deeply enmeshed in American life.

State Laws

Congressional measures such as the fugitive slave law of 1793, the Compromise of 1820, which led to the admission of Missouri as a slave state and Maine as a free state, and the Compromise of 1850, which enacted stringent fugitive slave regulations and admitted New Mexico and Utah as territories without restrictions on slavery—all governed and gave legal sanction to slavery.

But it was the state laws in the South that spelled out the details of black servitude. Southern slave codes were designed to perpetuate a rigid system of social control. They relegated slaves to the status of chattel (that is, movable property). Slaves could not legally own anything themselves. They were compelled by law to submit completely to their masters. Although the codes prohibited brutal treatment, a master or an overseer usually was not held responsible for the death of a slave who was receiving or resisting "just" punishment. All slaves had to show respect to all whites, even to total strangers.

Percentage of Slaves in Total Population, 1800

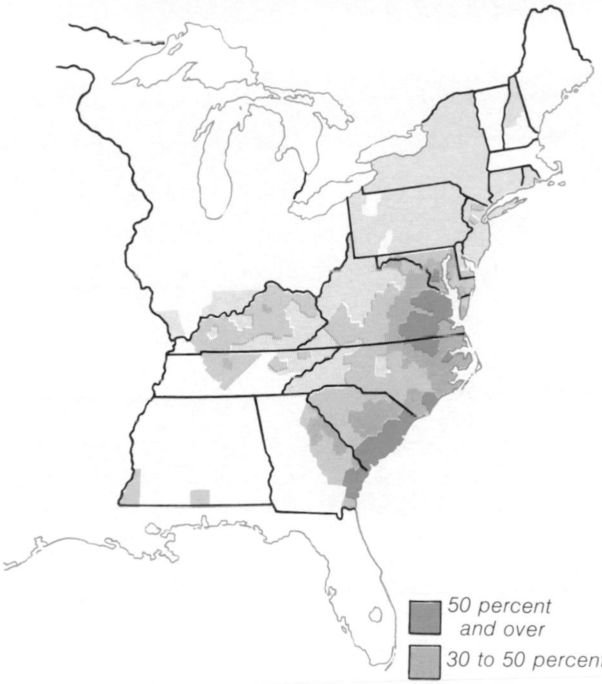

Patrols of white men frequently rode through the countryside checking passes to make sure that each slave was on his master's plantation or had permission to be elsewhere. Such patrols also sought to prevent slave uprisings and to capture runaways. Before the Civil War much of the South was like a prison in which all whites, regardless of their wealth, status, or social class, were jailers supervising black inmates.

The slave codes restricted the legal movement of blacks unless they could produce a pass authorizing their travel. A slave who traveled alone by train sometimes had to get two passes: one he deposited at the depot at his point of departure; the other he kept with him to produce if accosted. Contact with slaves from adjoining farms and plantations—and particularly with free blacks—was limited unless it took place under white supervision. Slaves were prohibited from owning books or printed matter of any sort, and no one was supposed to teach a slave to read, though this law was often ignored. Slaves could not testify against a white person in court. There was no legal recognition of slave marriages or divorces; marriage was regulated by whatever rules a master chose to devise. Some masters assigned mates to their slaves, though most permitted them to choose their own husbands or wives.

50 percent and over
30 to 50 percent
10 to 30 percent
Under 10 percent
Areas without slaves, or unsettled

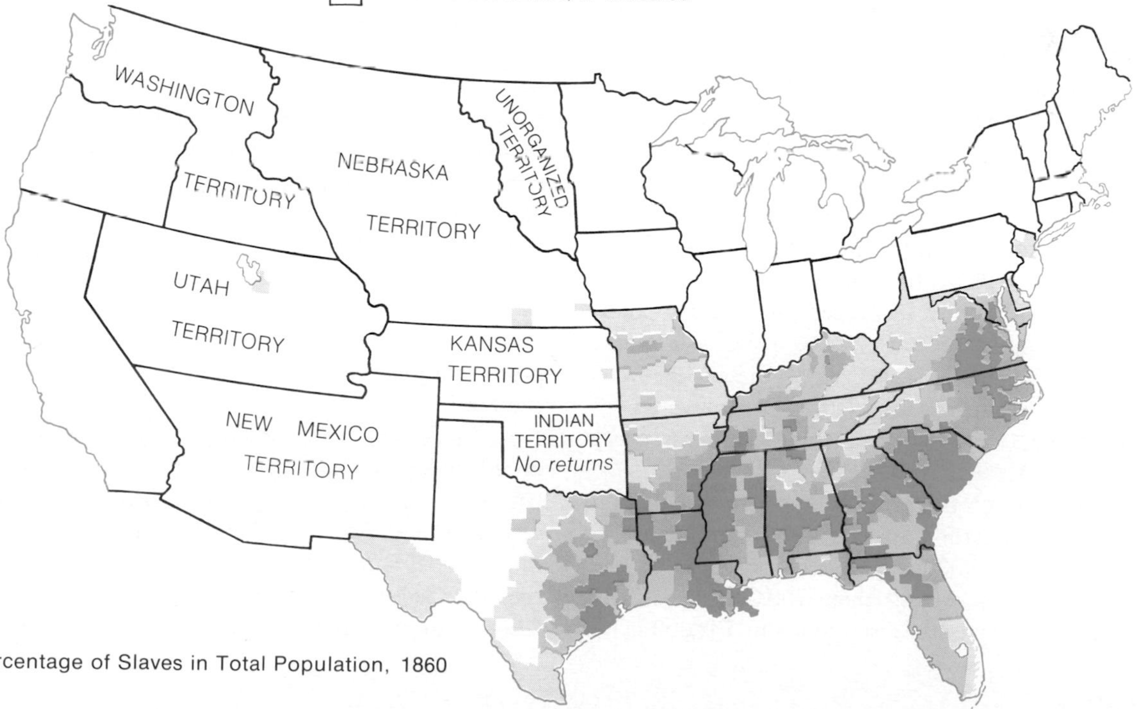

Percentage of Slaves in Total Population, 1860

Slave couples and families, however, usually were broken up when one member was sold; a slave preacher in Kentucky joined couples in wedlock "until death or *distance* do you part." As a result, the family did not provide slaves with the security afforded whites.

The system of social control embodied in the slave codes, of course, was not always observed. The individual master could treat his property more kindly or more harshly, depending on whim or temperament. Even southern judges and courts occasionally made decisions that contradicted the codes; for instance, a judge might rule that a slave could make contracts for the purchase of his or her own freedom, sometimes on the installment plan. One of the prime factors mitigating against extreme cruelty was simple economic self-interest; unless consumed by sadism, a master had no motive for destroying the spirit and health of his property. In fact, slave masters frequently employed hired labor, usually Irish or German immigrants, to perform the most dangerous tasks. Such an expedient avoided the risk of losing the year-in, year-out labor of a costly slave. A relatively humane policy toward slaves was evident on some plantations and was directly proportional to the numbers involved; once a master owned a substantial body of workers he often lost personal contact with them. Slaves who served as foremen were known to be extremely harsh in their discipline; as Frederick Douglass, an escaped slave, observed, "Everybody, in the South, wants the privilege of whipping somebody else." Worse, white overseers were paid according to the amount of labor they exacted from slaves, and this system was fully in force on larger plantations.

Library of Congress.

Although the slave trade was outlawed in 1808, slave ships continued to land cargoes of Africans in Southern ports during the antebellum period.

Slave Life

By 1850 there were 3,204,313 slaves in the United States (including southwestern territories that had not yet achieved statehood). Only 12 percent of the slave population lived in cities or towns. The remainder (some 2,800,000) worked in agriculture; of these, 1,815,000 lived on cotton plantations, and the rest cultivated tobacco, sugarcane, rice, and hemp. About one out of every eight people in America was a slave.

A comparison of the growth of cotton production with the slave population reveals close correlation. In 1790, for instance, 3,000 bales were produced in the South, and there were less than 700,000 slaves. By 1830 cotton production had risen to about 732,000 bales and slaves numbered about 2,009,043. By 1860 the South was turning out about 3,841,000 bales and there were nearly 4,000,000 slaves. These statistics are surprising since slave importation was outlawed after 1808. Although slaves were brought over illegally from Africa after 1808 (the number is estimated at between 54,000 and 270,000), the majority of nineteenth century slaves were American-born. This high birthrate can be explained in part by the fact that many masters encouraged slaves to reproduce. Slave women were offered rewards for giving birth to children, and little was done to reduce promiscuity among slaves or to preserve the sanctity of the family.

Slaves who were agricultural workers typically labored under the gang system on cotton, sugar, and tobacco plantations, that is, they worked in groups on a general project. Most field hands rose before dawn, cooked their meals, sometimes looked after the livestock, and then hurried to the fields before sunrise. There they labored till dusk, planting, hoeing weeds, picking worms

Culver Pictures.

Simon Gray
(?–?)

Although Simon Gray was not famous, he is of interest because his life as a slave suggests that regulations governing the lives of slaves involved in trade and commerce may have been much more lenient than those restricting plantation slaves. Simon Gray belonged to Andrew Donnan of Natchez, Mississippi, who rented him out to Andrew Brown at the rate of 75 cents a day. Brown, in turn, paid Gray a salary of $8 a month plus a bonus for each trip to New Orleans.

Gray's job was to convey lumber on flatboats down the Mississippi to New Orleans. He began his career in 1835 working in Brown's sawmill, but by 1838 he was directing a rafting crew, and by 1845 he had been promoted to the rank of flatboat captain. As a captain, Gray had authority over crews of ten to twenty men, some of whom were slaves, others hired whites. Gray himself employed the whites, paid their salaries and expenses, and kept their work records.

His responsibilities were numerous. On some occasions he would deliver lumber from the Natchez mill to the New Orleans lumberyard. At other times he would go on trips lasting two to three weeks and sell lumber to plantation owners. Gray solicited orders, quoted prices, and collected money. His business records reveal that he was literate and trained in simple mathematics.

In 1850 his employer bought Simon's wife and children for $500 and allowed Gray to live with them in a rented house in Natchez; Brown did not make use of the family and simply purchased them in order to please Gray. In 1853 Gray himself appears to have been freed by his old master, Andrew Donnan, informally if not legally. After this date, Simon Gray's monthly wages rose from $8 to $20, and he began to do jobs on the side for profit. On the eve of the Civil War, he was wealthy enough to be able to spend $1,000 at Hot Springs, Arkansas, where he took the cure for his rheumatism. Sometime in 1863, probably after the fall of Vicksburg, his name no longer was listed in business transactions of his employer. It is not known if he died or gained his freedom.

Simon Gray's life was so different from that of the plantation slave that he must be described as "quasi-free." He earned a salary, he knew how to read, made business trips, was a manager who employed whites, and was allowed to live apart from other slaves. Perhaps other nonagricultural slaves—those employed in construction, in factory work, in the mines, and on riverboats—enjoyed something of the same sort of relative freedom. ■

off plants, and finally harvesting. At night some slaves attended livestock again, cooked their meals, and performed other chores before retiring.

Discipline was maintained through physical punishment. As historian John W. Blassingame has asserted, "Floggings of 50 to 75 lashes were not uncommon. On numerous occasions, planters branded, stabbed, tarred and feathered, burned, shackled, tortured, maimed, crippled, mutilated, and castrated their slaves. Thousands of slaves were flogged so severely that they were permanently scarred." But most planters preferred to keep control by merely threatening corporal punishment or by withholding privileges and imposing such penalties as solitary confinement, additional work, public humiliation, and demotion from easier, more prestigious jobs to lower, more menial ones. Good behavior was rewarded with free time, better tasks, and other benefits. A system of rewards and nonphysical punishments, however, was more likely to exist on a plantation with fewer than ten slaves, where the master was personally in charge; once a plantation had more than 30 slaves, overseers were hired, and they all too often treated slaves inhumanely.

Aside from agriculture, slaves engaged in a host of tasks. Some were skilled artisans, mechanics, lumberjacks, mining and construction workers, and laborers in factories producing cotton textiles, turpentine, and iron or in factories processing tobacco. Still other slaves served as dockworkers, loading and unloading ships, or as deckhands. But the most important category of rural nonagricultural slaves were house servants. The butler, the cook, the maid, and the nurse were all slaves of rank and privilege in the eyes of the other slaves and of the white family. Through prolonged contact with whites, the domestic servants often learned to read and keep accounts; more subtly, the household staff absorbed white values to some extent and often became loyal to the family they served.

The house servants ate the leftover food of their masters and wore the hand-me-downs of the white family, but the life of a field hand was at a subsistence level. Living quarters were small, cramped, and crude, clothing was of poor quality, and the diet sometimes was so bad and deficient in protein that it failed to provide the workers with enough stamina for the manual labor demanded of them. As a result, slaves built up little resistance to disease and were more than normally susceptible to infection. The diet consisted mainly of salt pork, corn meal, and molasses—filling but not very nourishing food. Medical care usually was administered by the planter's wife.

On holidays and Sundays slaves amused themselves by dressing up in their best clothes and visiting with slave friends. Hunting and fishing were other favorite pastimes, as was producing such handicrafts as woven baskets,

Library of Congress.

Black house servants dressed in plain clothes serve their master's household. Note the elegant dining area, furniture, and clothing of the white family.

Virginia State Library.

Playing musical instruments and dancing provided entertainment for black slaves.

dolls, clothes, and other useful items, which slaves sometimes sold or bartered for profit. On some plantations slaves were allowed to have their own gardens. Saturday nights could be joyous occasions when slaves danced to a fiddle or a banjo or an improvised rhythm band. One white observer found it difficult to describe "all the contortions, and springs, and flings, and kicks, and capers" of a complex slave dance. Listening to folktales was another exciting entertainment, and storytellers invented for their audiences episodes in the lives of the deceitful Br'er (Brother) Rabbit, the bumbling Br'er Bear, and the shrewd Br'er Fox, who, despite his craftiness, always was outwitted by Br'er Rabbit.

Fiddling, dancing, and raucous merriment did little to mask the boredom, agony, and frustration of a barbarous system. These merely provided temporary release from a degrading, confining world. Even Br'er Rabbit was telling a moral tale. He was the personification of the smart slave shrewd enough to outwit his master, Br'er Fox.

While free blacks in the North had their own churches, slaves in the South were forced to attend services with whites or were preached to by white ministers at special services. Nevertheless, many of them held secret religious meetings. Whether these services were legal or illegal, religion was generally a matter of intense emotionality and fervor for the slaves, who found personal meanings directly applicable to their lives in Old Testament accounts of Israel's release from bondage and in the New Testament doctrine of release from suffering through belief in Christ. The haunting spirituals of the slaves ("Nobody knows the trouble I've seen") expressed the pain they felt and their longing for redemption. On some occasions religion was used by slave leaders to foment rebellion; apparently the rebel Gabriel, according to one contemporary, portrayed the Israelites as "a type of successful resistance to tyranny; and it was argued, that now, as then, God would stretch forth his arm to save, and would strengthen a hundred to overthrow a thousand." But Christianity had another impact on slavery. Although it may have strengthened the bonds of some slave communities and thereby provided a source of unrest and rebellion, the church, with its promise of reward in the afterlife, also may have reconciled some slaves to their present status.

Urban Slavery

The slave system was static, closed, and self-perpetuating on the plantation where the two main classes were black slaves and white owners. But in the city the institution of slavery soon began to decay.

Urban slaves sometimes traveled by day without close supervision, performing various errands. Owners often hired out their slaves as laborers in factories or shops; after working hours, slaves were free to do more or less what they pleased. Slaves in cities, accordingly, had many opportunities to mingle with free blacks and with whites, and the line between slavery and freedom became blurred. The urban master's dilemma was how to control his slave when the day was done or as he moved about the city doing various tasks. While busy on the job, he was no problem, but in the evenings city slaves would gather in homes, churches, grogshops, and around dock areas, regardless of ordinances to the contrary.

Another problem for the "peculiar institution" (as slavery was called) was fraternizing between whites and blacks, and between slaves and freemen. More than a third of the free blacks in the South lived in the larger cities; there were more than 10,000 in New Orleans alone in 1860. At that time the South had some 385,000 slaveholders who were owners of nearly 4,000,000 blacks. In their midst lived nearly 262,000 free blacks.

In an attempt to stamp out the social familiarity between whites and blacks, segregation was introduced in Southern cities and efforts made to reduce the black population, both slave and free. On the plantation discipline was the private domain of the owner or an overseer. But in the cities, where blacks were less clearly in subordination to whites, segregation separated whites from blacks by the 1830s in public means of transport, public facilities, churches, jails, parks, hospitals, cemeteries, and elsewhere. Blacks, both free and enslaved, sometimes were moved from the centers of cities and forced to find housing on the peripheries. On the job, free and enslaved southern blacks were pushed out of one line of employment after another in the last few decades before the Civil War; increasingly new immigrants, especially Irish and Germans, took over jobs formerly held by blacks. The exclusion of blacks from crafts, trades, and other positions requiring skill usually was enforced by city ordinances; even the less-skilled positions, such as those of household servants, were handed over to white immigrants.

Yet one should keep in mind that pre-Civil War segregation like that which would rise in the 1890s, was a mosaic of custom, ordinances, state laws, public pressure, and convenience. It was awash with absurd contradictions, and its rules and regulations interpreted in a capricious manner. The avowed goal was to keep the white and black races separate and to prevent what most people knew was happening. In fact, police blotters, bits of gossip in newspaper columns—even a short stroll down the streets of almost any city or town—revealed the failure of segregation, for miscegenation was a fact of southern life. Of course, racial mixing was occurring in the countryside as well, but there it was greeted with a veil of silence or a sly wink.

Slave Trading

Planters moving into the lower Mississippi Valley and Gulf states took their slaves with them. If they prospered, they quickly needed more manpower, and this need was fulfilled by the domestic slave traders. These businessmen drove slaves in chains overland or shipped them by river or ocean steamers or by train to the markets at New Orleans, Mobile, Natchez, or Galveston, where purchasers bid on them in exactly the same manner as they bid for livestock at auctions. During these auctions slave families often were split apart. Virginia farmers who generally were turning from tobacco to wheat and planters in the Carolinas now had an excess of blacks, many of whom were sold "down river." Some masters, however, refused to sell their slaves to men who planned to take them to Alabama, Mississippi, and the new lands of Arkansas and Texas.

The domestic slave trade was a vile business, but its horrors were exceeded by the foreign slave trade. Slaves were shackled together in dark, stuffy hulls for days, allowed little exercise and fed sparse, often rotten food. Before 1807 more than 20 percent of those who left Africa for America died en route. And, when that trade became illegal in 1808, the risk to these unwilling immigrants increased dramatically, for a captain pursued by federal authorities might jettison his cargo to get rid of the evidence. Nevertheless, some Africans continued to be smuggled into a few southern ports throughout the antebellum period. The domestic trade, however, was far more active.

Historians View Slavery

During recent decades historians have hotly debated the effect of slavery on antebellum blacks. Ulrich B. Phillips began modern research with the publication of his major works, *American Negro Slavery* (1918) and *Life and Labor in the Old South* (1929). Born in Georgia, Phillips took the position that the plantation actually had benefited blacks and provided a naturally backward and childlike race an opportunity for acquiring civilization. In his second book, Phillips wrote, "The white household taught perhaps less by precept than by example. It had

Courtesy Chicago Historical Society.

Following an auction, these slaves are being sent "down river" from Richmond. While the whites complete their business arrangements, the blacks say goodbye to relatives they may never see again.

much the effect of a 'social settlement' in a modern city slum, furnishing models of speech and conduct, along with advice on occasion, which the vicinage is invited to accept."

Herbert Aptheker, a Marxist historian, took a very different stand in *American Negro Slave Revolts,* published in 1943. Far from being the lazy and contented child that Phillips portrayed, the slave actually was rebellious and discontented—or so Aptheker asserted. In his preface to the 1969 edition of the book, Aptheker stated: "Contemporary evidence—newspapers, court records, journals, diaries, letters, speeches—make crystal clear to anyone who views black men and women as human beings that American Negro slavery was a monstrously cruel system of exploitation and that its victims despised it and sought in every possible way to oppose it."

In 1956 Kenneth Stampp published *The Peculiar Institution* in which he asserted that slavery was a thoroughly cruel and brutal system of social control. In contrast to Phillips, who assumed black inferiority, Stampp argued that "Negroes *are,* after all, only white, men with black skins, nothing more, nothing less." Blacks responded to slavery just as white people would have done if they were placed in the same situation—they resisted it.

Writing in 1959, Stanley Elkins (*Slavery: A Problem in American Institutional and Intellectual Life*) contended that the dominant black personality type under slavery had been docile and passive—the "Sambo" stereotype so pervasive in white Southern literature and folklore. But Elkins, unlike Phillips, did not attribute these qualities to innate traits of black slaves. Rather, Elkins argued, blacks became docile because of their environment, just as imprisonment in German concentration camps supposedly reduced inmates to a childlike, confused docility. Elkins claimed that the absolute power of the master made slaves into Sambos. Elkins emphasized that slaves had few contacts, except in cities, with free society; the master established himself as the all-knowing figure who determined every slave's activities—and his self-image as well. Elkins concluded that slaves came to accept their alleged inferiority to whites as a result of deliberate efforts on the part of slaveholders to encourage infantilism in blacks.

John Blassingame has contended in *The Slave Community: Plantation Life in the Antebellum South* (1973) that Stanley Elkins' concept of the slave personality type ignores entirely the accounts that slaves have left of their own lives. While conceding that it is impossible to know objectively how discontented the slave really was, nevertheless Blassingame points out that judicial records of the period show that "hundreds of slaves sued for their freedom, ran away from their masters, assaulted, robbed, poisoned, and murdered whites, burned their master's dwellings and committed suicide. Hundreds more fought whites in self-defense and were guilty of insubordination."

In 1974 Robert W. Fogel and Stanley L. Engerman published their highly controversial quantitative study, *Time on the Cross: The Economics of American Negro Slavery*. Using economic statistics (and a methodology that has been denounced from several quarters), the authors maintain that neither southern planters nor black slaves fit the concentration camp model depicted by Elkins. Indeed, Fogel and Engerman state that plantation slaves were not typically lazy or inefficient, nor were planters intent on maintaining perfect submission. The plantation was a business, and masters were interested primarily in making it pay. Since slaves provided a very productive working force, they generally achieved their goals. The authors believe that the Sambo myth may not only have been perpetuated by the racism of slaveowners but also by the unconscious prejudice of abolitionists. "With very few exceptions, both those in the anti- and in the proslavery camps shared the conviction that blacks were, for racial reasons, generally inferior to whites both as laborers and as human beings." This bias, Fogel and Engerman write, is belied by the fact that blacks, though working under great adversity, were able to make plantations economically successful concerns.

To Eugene Genovese, however, the slave society that developed in the United States was "first and foremost . . . a record of one of history's greatest crimes." His *Roll, Jordan, Roll: The World the Slaves Made* (1974) argues that plantation slavery and its inherent paternalism made white and black Southerners one people while actually making them two, binding them together in bitter confrontation and creating a relationship so complex, and so interdependent that neither could express his feelings without reference to the other.

Slaves and Slavery

Some slaves may have acted in a Sambo fashion in order to pacify their masters; house servants may have identified with their white masters; and still others may have become deeply frustrated with their status. (Many documents of the antebellum period mention stammering and stuttering in blacks—sometimes regarded by clinical psychologists as signs of frustration.)

A few reacted with individual acts of resistance. They murdered their masters, mutilated their own bodies, or sabotaged their masters' property. Resistance could take much more subtle forms. Slaves knew their labor benefited only the master, so they were often clumsy, inefficient, passive, and smiling. Such tactics possessed several innate advantages: the satisfaction of "hitting back" without fear of retribution; a record of minimal work output which they could not be expected to exceed; and the possibility a dissatisfied, cruel owner would sell them. The end result was, of course, a rather inefficient labor system.

And some slaves periodically banded together in rebellion. The most famous of these uprisings were those planned by Gabriel Prosser in 1800, Denmark Vesey in 1822, and Nat Turner in 1831. Turner, after allegedly hearing a voice from heaven commanding him to lead an

Culver Pictures.

An artist's conception of Nat Turner telling his four trusted co-conspirators that they will strike first at the home of his master.

uprising, joined with four other slaves in killing the white family he was serving. He and his comrades then moved from house to house in Southampton County, Virginia, killing whites and liberating other slaves. Turner's group swelled to seventy blacks; they killed sixty whites before they were captured. Over forty of them, including Turner, died as a result of the revolt.

Such bloody rebellions, however, were rare in the antebellum South. Most whites, however, feared the prospects of a slave revolt, but the lack of organized resistance may have encouraged whites to regard blacks as Sambos. Not only did this way of looking at blacks provide a convenient defense of slavery against northern abolitionists ("Our slaves are happy"), it also helped allay persistent white fears of a black revolution. Whether or not slavery converted blacks into Sambos, it did undermine their basic human dignity. Winthrop Jordan suggests in his definitive study, *White Over Black: American Attitudes Toward the Negro, 1550–1812* (1968), that white males invented the myth that black men wanted to rape white women as a coverup for their own erotic attraction to black women. Slavery also led most Southerners to regard manual labor, especially if performed by a hired hand, as a demeaning task unworthy of a white man; this attitude discouraged poor whites and any white immigrants who went South from working as field hands.

Free Blacks

By 1860 there were nearly half a million free blacks in the United States. Many had bought their freedom; others had been granted it, frequently at the death of their masters; still others had been born into free black families. Forty-six percent of the free blacks lived in the North, while the remainder lived south of the Mason-Dixon line. In the South the major concentrations of free blacks during the antebellum period could be found in the Tidewater counties of Virginia and Maryland, the Piedmont regions of Virginia and North Carolina, and in the cities of Baltimore, Washington, Charleston, Mobile, and New Orleans. In the North free blacks usually settled in the cities, including Boston, New York, Cincinnati, and Philadelphia. Occasionally they took up residence in isolated areas of the Old Northwest such as Cass County in Michigan, Hammond County in Indiana, and Wilberforce, Ohio. There also were communities in Massachusetts, North Carolina, and Florida where blacks mixed freely with Indians. In general, however, free blacks preferred to live in cities or towns where their unique status was well-known and recognized.

In the eighteenth century and the first two decades of the nineteenth, free blacks in the South could own property, retain their earnings, marry legally, and participate in their own churches and various mutual aid societies. But a growing fear of conspiracies among free blacks

Distribution of Free Blacks, 1810

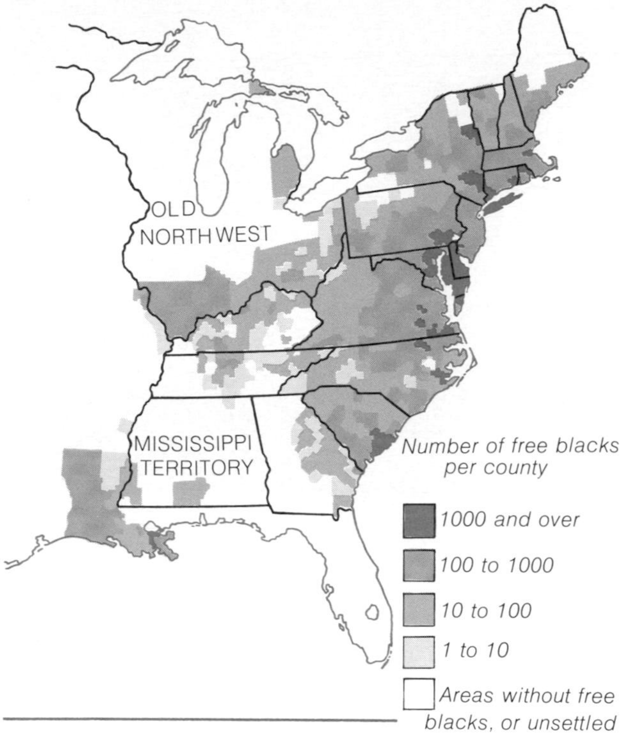

and slaves led southern whites to impose more and more restrictions on free blacks until they became only "quasi-free." By 1835 the right of assembly had been taken away from free blacks in most of the South; blacks were not able to hold church services unless a white minister was present. If blacks in Georgia violated this prohibition, each offender could be fined a hundred dollars—and if the individual could not pay the fine (often the case), he or she was sold back into slavery. Reenslavement was a constant threat for free blacks in the South. If a white person claimed, no matter how falsely, that a black was a runaway slave, the courts usually "returned" the black to the alleged master. Similarly, almost any infringement of the law might cause a free black to be reenslaved as punishment.

The free black's second-class status was ensured by any number of discriminatory measures. Free blacks could not enter most southern states—or leave and return for a period of more than ninety days. Whatever schools existed were segregated, not only in the South but in the North, as were most churches, transportation facilities, and public accommodations.

Although free blacks were subject to taxation, more and more of them were being barred from polling places

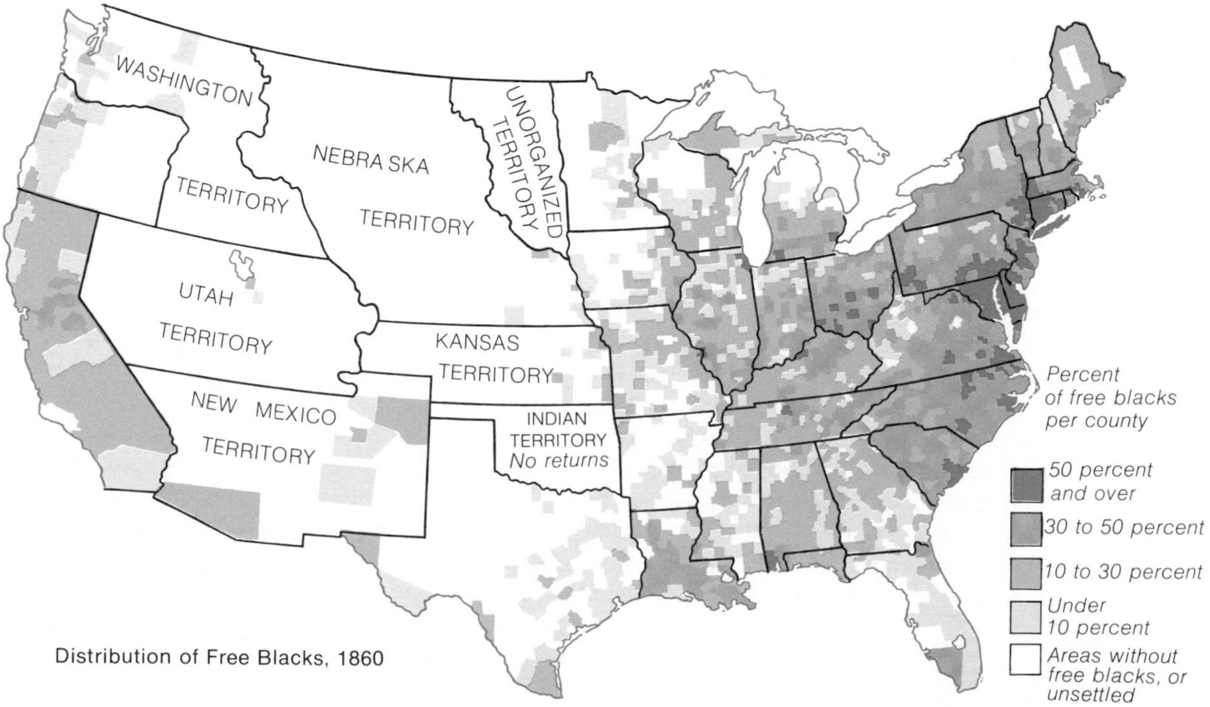

Distribution of Free Blacks, 1860

in all parts of the nation by the time of the Civil War. The movement to disenfranchise the free blacks gained ground throughout the early nineteenth century (in Maryland free blacks lost the vote in 1810, in Tennessee in 1834, in Pennsylvania in 1838, in Indiana in 1851). If a political party needed their help, free blacks might continue to cast ballots, regardless of what state legislatures decreed. This was true in Maryland and Ohio, and until 1860 free blacks of Rapides Parish, Louisiana, were mustered to the polls by various local factions.

The condition of free blacks was far from being ideal in the North. Not only were free northern blacks subject to a host of restrictions, but they also encountered mob violence. In 1834 whites in Philadelphia instigated a three-day reign of terror, during which they beat up blacks and burned their houses. In Cincinnati white hoodlums drove a thousand blacks out of the city. Similar outbreaks occurred in several northern cities, especially during times when blacks and poor whites were in competition for jobs. As Fanny Kemble, a foreign visitor, wrote about northern blacks: "They are not slaves indeed, but they are pariahs, debarred from every fellowship. . . . All tongues . . . have learned to turn the very name of their race into an insult and a reproach."

In response to oppression, free blacks in the North held conventions with increasing frequency between 1830 and 1860. At first, participants at these assemblies sought to encourage blacks to start their own businesses and to educate their children, but after 1840 the movement became more political. Some leaders even proposed black militancy and separatism as the only ways to combat the ruling white society. One of the first to speak out was David Walker, a Boston merchant. Walker, born in North Carolina in September 1785 to a free black woman and a slave father who had died a few months before, published his famous *Appeal* in 1829. In four, closely reasoned articles he examined the history of slave societies, cited profusely from the Declaration of Independence, and called upon white Americans to reflect upon the words "all men are created equal." "Compare your own language above, extracted from your Declaration of Independence, with your cruelties and murders inflicted by your cruel and unmerciful fathers on ourselves and our fathers and on us, men who have never given your fathers or you the least provocation!!!"

In 1843 the black leader, Henry Highland Garnet, called for southern slaves to rise up in rebellion: "Strike for your lives and liberties. . . . You cannot be more oppressed than you have been—you cannot suffer greater cruelties than you have already. *Rather die freemen than live to be slaves.* Remember that you are FOUR MILLIONS."

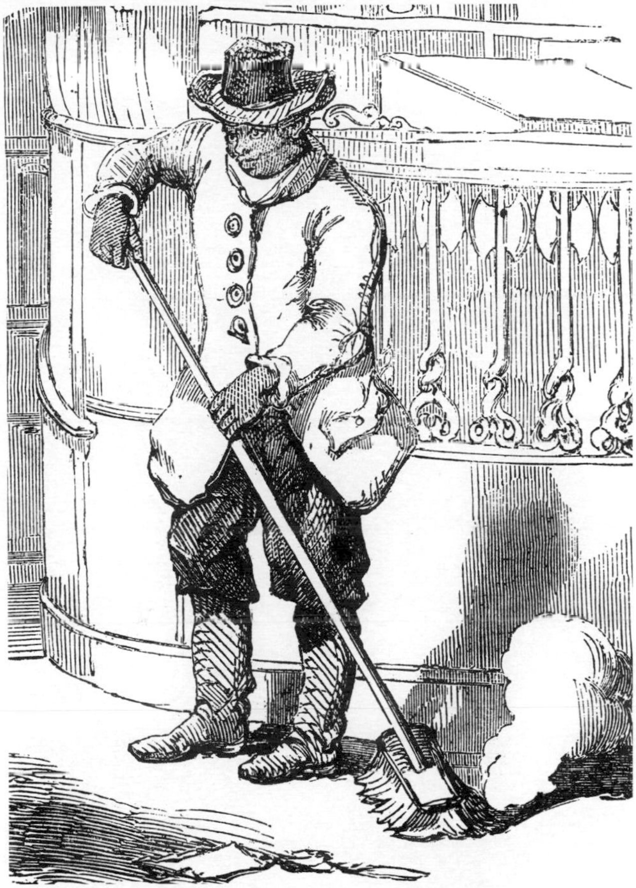
New York Public Library, Picture Collection.

Northern free blacks could generally only find employment doing menial labor such as sweeping up at the close of business on Wall Street in New York City.

Neither the convention movement nor the work of abolitionists could eradicate the deep prejudice evident everywhere in America. This bias assumed that blacks were either savages, ready to rape white women, or that they were children, incapable of managing their own lives.

This child/savage image of blacks came to represent to white Americans everything that their nation was not or should not become. It performed an identity function for white Americans, northern and southern, who were

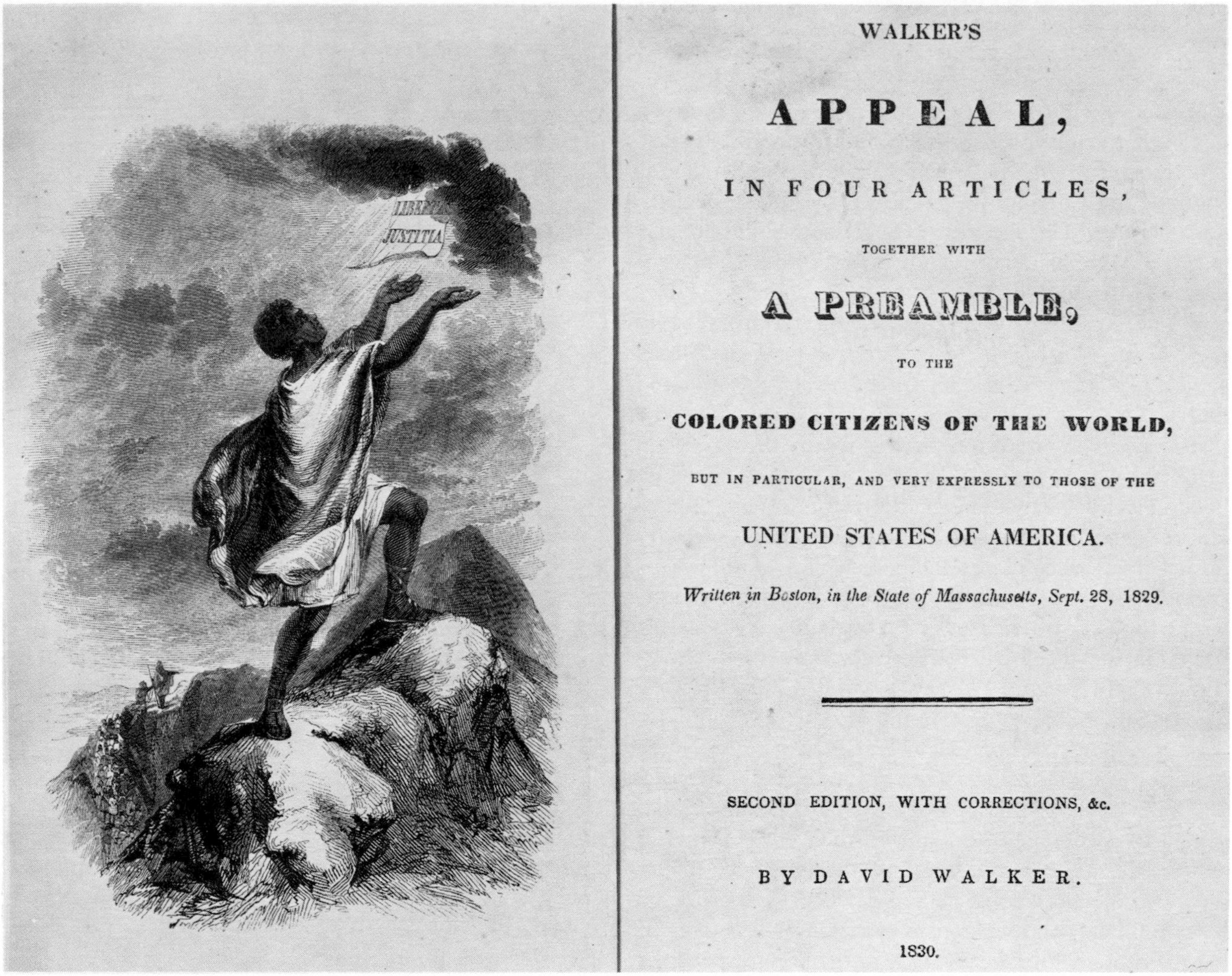
WALKER'S

APPEAL,

IN FOUR ARTICLES,

TOGETHER WITH

A PREAMBLE,

TO THE

COLORED CITIZENS OF THE WORLD,

BUT IN PARTICULAR, AND VERY EXPRESSLY TO THOSE OF THE

UNITED STATES OF AMERICA.

Written in Boston, in the State of Massachusetts, Sept. 28, 1829.

SECOND EDITION, WITH CORRECTIONS, &c.

BY DAVID WALKER.

1830.

Library of Congress.

David Walker's *Appeal* was an early expression of black nationalism. It called upon white Americans to remember the lofty words of the Declaration of Independence, "All men are created equal," and urged slaves to rise up against their masters.

groping for self-identification. They were civilized; the slave was not. In the age of Andrew Jackson, for example, a time of very rapid change, the slave helped to define the norms of white society. Yet that society—made up in part of rough frontiersmen, Indian fighters, slave traders, religious zealots, rapacious entrepreneurs, die-hard nativists, uncompromising abolitionists, and a great mass of uneducated and unschooled adults—often seemed bent upon breaking every rule in the book and discarding whatever pretensions to culture, refinement, and social mores the young republic had acquired.

Indians

During the Revolutionary War the Congress signed a treaty with the Delaware tribe (1778) recognizing Indians as foreign nationals, and this policy was continued and greatly expanded under the federal government.

President George Washington began the practice of providing friendly Indian tribes with clothes, agricultural tools, and teachers to instruct them in the various "arts of civilized life." Treaty commissioners inserted provisions for such items in the documents they negotiated, and Congress appropriated the money. In 1819 Congress established a separate Civilization Fund that remained in effect until 1873. With the aid of missionaries, the Bible, hoes, and trinkets, and ignoring the role of agriculture in many Indian societies, Washington officials hoped to convert hunters into farmers. The latter supposedly would need less land and thereby cause less trouble; however, that land could not be in areas where whites wanted to settle. In the early 1800s substantial numbers of Indians were still living in the Old Northwest and the South.

The cotton boom sealed the fate of the Indians in the South. Planters in that region were eager to appropriate the vast Indian holdings within their borders and convert these lands into cotton plantations. Moreover, southern whites disliked the presence of an alien people in their midst, especially since fugitive slaves could hide out in Indian country; as whites came to fear black uprisings more and more, their hostility toward Indians increased.

President Thomas Jefferson had instructed government agents to encourage Indians to purchase more goods at U.S. trading posts than they could pay for with furs or animal pelts. Jefferson hoped that Indians would run into debt—and, in order to pay the government, would be forced to sign land-cession treaties and move into the newly acquired Louisiana Purchase west of the Mississippi River. At the same time, he urged the "civilization" of the Indians. Ignoring the tribal traditions of Indian farmers in the South, Jefferson insisted that Indians would have to learn the white man's agricultural practices and give up the custom of communal ownership of the land in favor of private ownership. If the Indians made these changes, Jefferson believed, then they would not only become "civilized" but also would be more easily assimilated into American society. Even more important, assimilation presumably would lead Indians to take up trades and give up their surplus lands to white settlers. What actually happened, however, came as a complete surprise. The Cherokees in the South did in fact adopt many of the patterns of white society and thereby became "civilized," but they made these societal changes in order to preserve their tribal integrity and lands from further encroachments. The "civilization" program, from the white point of view, had misfired.

Old Northwest

The Indians of the Old Northwest also encountered persistent pressure from white Americans to give up their lands. In this region in the early nineteenth century two Indian leaders appeared who attempted to unite the Indians all the way from Canada to the Gulf of Mexico into a single confederacy that would stop the westward advance of the United States.

These men were Tecumseh, a man of Shawnee and Creek background, and his brother, the Prophet. They used the twin appeal of Indian nationalism and religious

Denver Public Library Western Collection.

Tecumseh, wearing an English uniform and medal. This Shawnee leader had a vision of uniting the Indians against the Americans. When the War of 1812 between the British and the Americans broke out, he joined the British and fought with his supporters against the Americans.

vision while preaching that the deteriorating condition of various tribes was caused by the white man's whiskey and ways and by the failure of Indians to maintain their own traditions. Tecumseh was particularly opposed to land-cession treaties. As he told an American officer, "The way, the only way to stop this evil is for all the red men to unite in claiming a common and equal right in the land, as it was at first, and should be now—for it never was divided, but belongs to all. No tribe has a right to sell, even to each other, much less to strangers, who demand all, and will take no less. . . . Sell a country! Why not sell the air, the clouds, and the great sea, as well as the earth? Did not the Great Spirit make them all for the use of his children?"

Tecumseh and his followers gathered at an old Indian town on Tippecanoe Creek in the Indiana Territory known as Prophetstown, which by 1811 housed about a thousand warriors from various tribes who had joined the cause. But when Tecumseh traveled south in the summer of 1811 to recruit tribesmen there, the Prophet disobeyed his brother's instructions and allowed some warriors to attack a nearby American military camp. General William Henry Harrison retaliated by attacking Prophetstown, burning it to the ground.

Nevertheless, Tecumseh seemed a force that could not be stopped. He eventually gathered under his banner braves from numerous tribes, though the allegiance of these particular warriors did not assure the support of their tribes. When the War of 1812 broke out, Tecumseh hoped that the Anglo-American conflict would end the westward migration of the whites. Instead, it spelled his downfall. During the Battle of the Thames in Canada in October 1813, American soldiers killed Tecumseh. Soon afterwards, on March 27, 1814, General Andrew Jackson subdued Tecumseh's Creek allies in the South by wiping out 800 of their finest warriors at the horseshoe bend of the Tallapoosa River in Alabama.

Jackson's victory helped to pave his way to the White House in 1828. Old Hickory was interested primarily in southern Indian removal, but events in the spring of 1832 precipitated action in the Old Northwest as well. A group of Sac and Fox Indians, under the leadership of a proud, old warrior named Black Hawk, left Iowa Territory in search of food and crossed the Mississippi into Illinois. Although this was no war party—for it included women and children—a short bloody confrontation provoked by white militia ensued. The Jackson Administration used this "invasion" as an excuse to seize Sac-Fox lands beyond the river and push other tribes westward, too. If the Indians failed to provide a motive for action, then soldiers simply used brute force.

The Period of Removal

The War of 1812 proved a disaster for Indians in the Old Northwest and in the South. Neither Tecumseh nor the British had been able to stop the westward migration of whites, and when the war was over, the United States continued to seize Indian lands. Even tribes such as the Cherokees and Choctaws who had fought on the side of the United States were forced to relinquish territory. Presidents James Madison, James Monroe, and John Quincy Adams advocated removing the Indians to locations west of the Mississippi, but the actual dispossession was accomplished largely through treaties secured by President Andrew Jackson under the Removal Act of 1830.

The fact that Jackson had long advocated Indian removal was one of the reasons he swept the South in the 1828 election. His Indian policy was in harmony with his belief in American expansion. Jackson was, curiously enough, both a nationalist and a champion of states' rights; his Indian policy suited both sympathies, since it made room for a growing nation and simultaneously asserted the supremacy of the state governments of Georgia, Alabama, Mississippi, North Carolina, and Tennessee and the government of the Florida Territory over the Cherokee, Choctaw, Chickasaw, Creek, and Seminole Indians within their boundaries. Although Jackson was opposed by powerful pro-Indian humanitarians, he won a majority of the Congress to his side by stressing that removal was itself a humanitarian measure "actuated by feelings of justice and a regard for our national honor."

During the years of Jackson's presidency, the United States acquired through removal of Indians about 100 million acres of land east of the Mississippi, in exchange for about $68 million and 32 million acres west of the Mississippi, which were given to the Indians. In order to secure this excellent bargain, the government removed some 46,000 Indians from their tribal lands in the South and the Old Northwest by 1837, while a little more than that number had treaty stipulations calling for their removal. Only a few scattered tribes, mostly in New York and the Great Lakes region, escaped without treaty stipulations requiring their removal.

The Ordeal of Removal

Typical of Indian dispossession, and in many ways a precedent for the emigration of other tribes, was the Choctaw removal from 1831 to 1833. Despite government promises to make the move as comfortable and orderly as possible, the first wave of Choctaws to depart in 1831 was handled by the War Department with total confusion and inefficiency. Washington did not send the necessary funds, which caused long delays that pushed the migration into the winter of 1831–32 and exposed the Indians to severe storms. A French visitor, Alexis de Toqueville, observed the presence of "the sick, newborn babies, and the old men on the point of death" among the emigrants. The picture of suffering was one, he said, that would "never fade from my memory." Subsequent Choctaw removals were planned better, but still were executed poorly and took place during unexpected attacks of cholera. Rations were poor, owing to the fact that the budget-minded administration appropriated about seven cents a day to feed each Indian. Some Choctaws took advantage of a treaty provision allowing them to stay behind in Mississippi and receive land allotments if they submitted to state laws, but they became victims of flagrant fraud, intimidation, and speculation. Hounded by avaricious land speculators, most of the Choctaws sold their land for fifty cents an acre. (By an act passed in 1820, the federal government was selling land for $1.25 an acre.) Among the beneficiaries of this swindle were politicians in Jackson's party, federal marshals, and friends and relatives of agents in the General Land Office.

Some of the worst crimes of Indian removal were committed against the Cherokees during the presidency of Martin Van Buren in 1838. The Cherokees, one of the largest tribes in the South, refused to abide by a removal treaty signed by a minority faction of their people in 1835. When the deadline for the evacuation arrived in 1838, they were rounded up by government troops and placed in temporary internment camps, where white militia raped and murdered some Indians in a manner so hair-raising that one Georgia soldier said years later, "I fought through the Civil War and have seen men shot to pieces and slaughtered by thousands, but the Cherokee removal was the cruelest work I ever knew." Under orders from President Van Buren, General Winfield Scott began the forcible ejection of the Cherokees in the summer of 1838. After about 3,000 captive Indians had departed under military escort, Scott agreed to suspend the operations until the hot summer season was over. Scott, a Whig favorite, rival of Jackson, and a man sympathetic to the condition of the Cherokees, worked out a compromise with John Ross, Cherokee chief. Between October 1838 and March 1839, Ross led the remaining Cherokees to the trans-Mississippi West. Some 17,000 Cherokees and their slaves traveled on a virtual Trail of Tears to present-day Oklahoma between the summer of 1838 and March of 1839. About 4,000 Indians died as a result of the circumstances surrounding their capture and detention before emigration began or as a result of the hardships on their trek to the West. Those who left the South under the guidance of Ross fared better than those who had embarked earlier under military escort.

Many Americans spoke out eloquently against Indian removal. Perhaps the ablest opponent was New Jersey Senator Theodore Frelinghuysen, who demanded that Indian treaty rights be respected. He accused President Jackson of using fraud, bribery, and force to remove the Indians. Jackson (and Van Buren, too) maintained that only removal would allow the Indians to practice self-government and receive the blessings of white civilization (religion, private property, and education) without the risk of contamination from evil, ne'er-do-well whites. In addition, only removal could end the political and legal anomaly of independent Indian nations residing within state boundaries but immune from their jurisdiction.

European visitors to the United States were unimpressed with such arguments. Frances Trollope, an English novelist, accused American whites of outright hypocrisy: "You will see them one hour lecturing their mob on the indefeasible [*sic*] rights of man, and the next driving from their homes the children of the soil, whom they have bound themselves to protect by the most solemn treaties."

Many Americans considered the Indian removal policy of the 1830s as morally wrong, but the evidence indicates that there was no official policy of racial extermination or genocide perpetrated against the Indians by the government. While Indian policy was not deliberately brutal, it was characterized by ethnocentricism, mismanagement, inept planning, and, too often, hypocrisy. Members of both major political parties condemned and

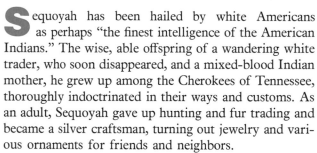

Library of Congress.

Sequoyah

c. 1770–1843

Sequoyah has been hailed by white Americans as perhaps "the finest intelligence of the American Indians." The wise, able offspring of a wandering white trader, who soon disappeared, and a mixed-blood Indian mother, he grew up among the Cherokees of Tennessee, thoroughly indoctrinated in their ways and customs. As an adult, Sequoyah gave up hunting and fur trading and became a silver craftsman, turning out jewelry and various ornaments for friends and neighbors.

Although he neither spoke nor wrote English, Sequoyah was intrigued by the white man's printed pages ("talking leaves") and about 1809 began to construct a syllabary—a set of characters that stand for syllables, unlike the letters of the alphabet, which stand for individual sounds. Despite considerable ridicule, within a dozen years he completed the work, and this system of writing quickly spread throughout the Cherokee Nation. The Cherokees thus became the first North American Indian tribe to develop their own written language.

This unique contribution gave great impetus to the spread of literacy among the Cherokees, and Sequoyah was much honored by his people. He then went to teach the syllabary to the Cherokees who had settled West of the Mississippi River. As a result, Cherokees in the East and the West were able to communicate in writing. In 1828 the western Cherokees sent him to Washington as a special envoy. Years later Sequoyah retired from active tribal political undertakings and began a search for a lost band of Cherokees that, according to legend, had crossed the Mississippi River in earlier times and wandered off somewhere in the West. He died in 1843, somewhere in Mexico, while pursuing this search.

This account of aboriginal genius recently has been challenged by an Indian who claims direct descent from the "true Sequoyah" and relates a quite different story. In *Tell Them They Lie: The Sequoyah Myth* (1971), Traveller Bird maintains that the existence of a Cherokee syllabary was known to whites as early as 1792 and certainly was not invented by Sequoyah. Bird writes that for a quarter of a century this rugged, full-blooded warrior, born in 1776, fought against white encroachment. As the only scribe remaining among the Cherokees, he taught his people their language in a vain effort to thwart alien influence; he also led several groups westward to Spanish soil.

According to Bird, in 1816 Sequoyah was captured by "progressive" Cherokees receptive to white ideas and, because of his activities, convicted of witchcraft and mutilated. Missionaries among the Cherokees, alarmed by this turn of events and unable to suppress the syllabary, fostered a legend that comported well with federal schemes to "civilize" the Cherokees. The man subsequently honored as Sequoyah, says Traveller Bird, was a white-created imposter named Thomas Maw. The real Sequoyah supposedly went West once more; he died in July 1839, cut down by soldiers' bullets while crossing the Brazos River.

Although Indian and white scholars have denounced Bird's book as a hoax, the emergence of a "new" Sequoyah raises the interesting possibility that, as American Indians delve into their own history, much of what whites have written about them could be revised. Yet the fame of the man known as Sequoyah in the early nineteenth century seems secure: Oklahoma has placed his statue in the Capitol in Washington, giant redwoods (Sequoias) honor his memory, and generations of Americans have been certain that the man whose picture is here is not one Thomas Maw, but Sequoyah. ■

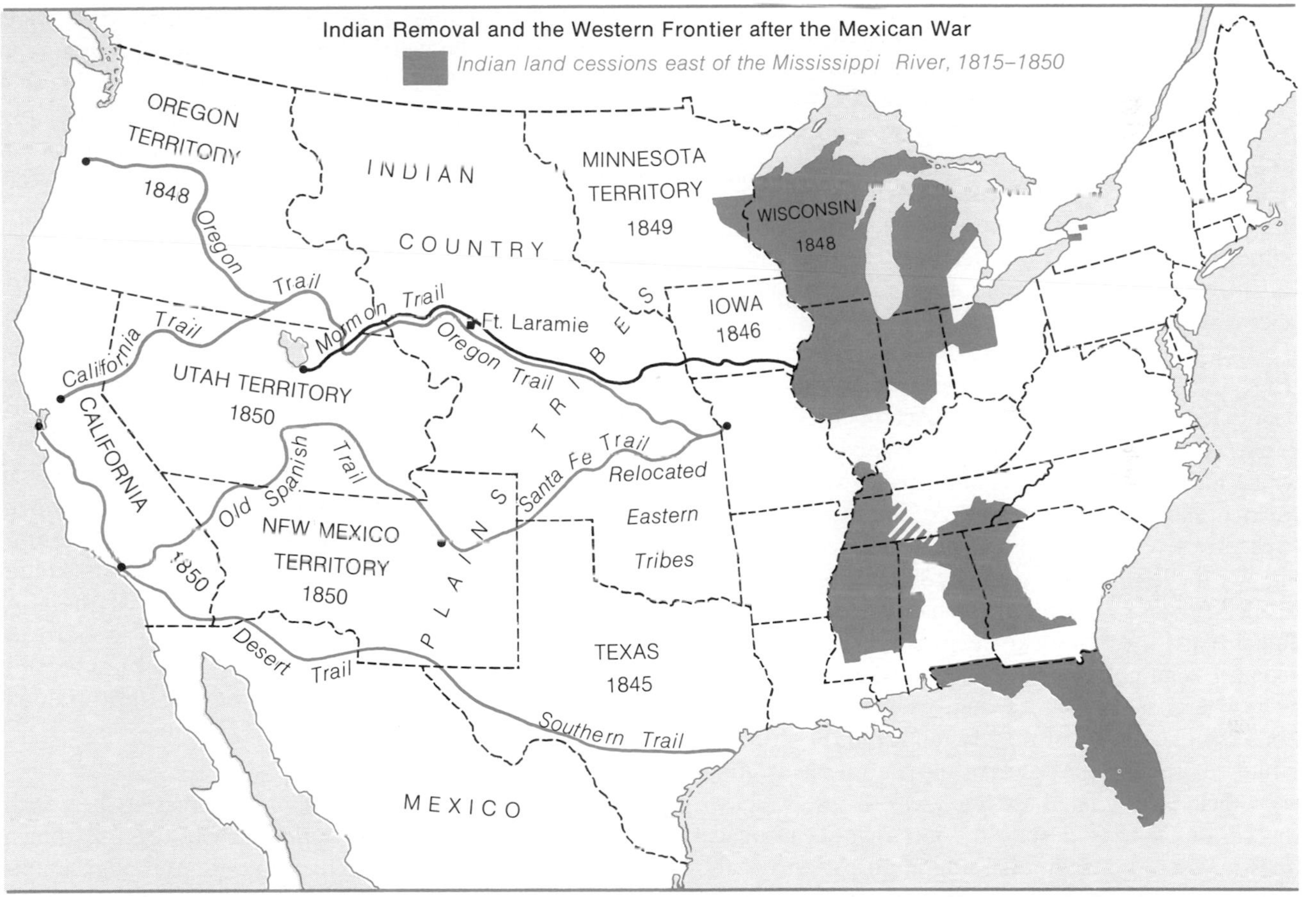

supported it, and some of the most outspoken critics—Daniel Webster, Edward Everett, Caleb Cushing, and Ralph Waldo Emerson—were among those who nevertheless speculated in what once had been Indian land. Since the 1790s the War Department had used economic coercion as a means of pressuring Indians to sign land cession treaties by only paying them the annual interest on money owed under treaty obligations. Thomas Jefferson established the precedent of withholding these annuities as a lever for social control, and during the administration of Jackson American officials found that withholding annuities was a very convenient means of inducing tribes to sign removal treaties and to emigrate westward. Jackson was no admirer of what he referred to as the "erratic" ways of native life, yet his actions were governed not so much by any personal animosity toward the Indians, but by his great concern for the growth, unity, and security of the nation. So long as Indian enclaves remained within the states, the potential for an explosive confrontation between armed militia and Indian warriors, or between state and federal authorities, clearly existed.

The American people in the Jacksonian era were a restless people accustomed to moving every generation or so. To these people there seemed no reason why a band of "savages" could not exist just as well on one plot of ground as another. Their wants were few and the supply of land in the West apparently inexhaustible. Between 1845 and 1848, the United States acquired nearly 1.5 million square miles of new territory. Instead of solving Indian-white relations, the removal policy greatly complicated those relations.

By 1850, the "permanent" homes granted to eastern tribes in areas west of the Mississippi River by treaties negotiated under the Removal Act of 1830 formed a barrier between white settlements and the new lands which included Texas and California as well as the New Mexico and Utah Territories. At the same time, these expansive acres were the home of still more Indian tribes.

By the late 1840s and early 1850s, American officials in the Office of Indian Affairs had determined that the Indian barrier to westward expansion created by Jacksonian Indian policy would have to be removed; Indians everywhere in the West would be placed on "reservations." In the Treaty of Fort Laramie (1851) between the United States and the tribes of the central plains, American officials designated specific areas as reservations for the various tribes—despite the fact that such boundary lines violated the traditional migration patterns of these peoples. In the future this arrangement would permit whites to force individual tribes onto more restricted areas without upsetting other nearby tribes. Henceforth "removals" might cover shorter distances, but the consequences were no less devastating.

Women and Women's Rights

Feminism as an American political movement had its beginnings in the 1830s and 1840s. It was not an isolated phenomenon, but rather integrated with other events of the era, in particular industrialization, abolitionism, and an upsurge of general interest in reform.

Industrialization affected women both directly and indirectly. Its direct effect was the fact that women formed a significant portion of the working population; as early as 1816 a congressional committee discovered that of 100,000 factory workers in the United States, nearly two-thirds were women and girls. But these individuals received less than men for the same work, were generally not allowed to join men's unions, and were kept from rising in the factory hierarchy. Worse, whole categories of industrial work (usually the better-paying jobs) were closed to women. One of the leading feminists of the era, Sarah Grimké, remarked in 1837 that American society's disdain for women

> "bears with tremendous effect on the laboring classes, and indeed on almost all who are obliged to earn a sustenance, whether it be by mental or physical exertion—I allude to the disproportionate value set on the time and labor of men and women. . . . As for example, in tailoring, a man has twice or three times as much for making a waistcoat or pantaloons as a woman, although the work done by each may be equally good. In those employments which are peculiar to women, their time is estimated at half the value of that of men. A woman who goes out to wash, works as hard in proportion as a wood sawyer, or a coal heaver, but she is not generally able to make more than half as much by a day's work."

Indirectly, industrialization, by increasing the wealth of the middle class, increased the leisure time of women in that social stratum. At the same time, foreign immigration to America made Irish and other European servants more plentiful, and thereby gave some middle class women considerably more time for outside interests and activities. From this emergent leisured group came many of the members of the early women's rights movement.

If the Industrial Revolution provided some women with the time to devote to feminism, it also increased the plight of most women. For, as the nineteenth century wore on, women were increasingly relegated to a minor role in society. During the colonial period and in the early years of the republic, most Americans were engaged in a hard struggle to survive; on a small subsistence farm a man's wife and daughters worked hard and, as a consequence, had considerable say in the conduct of family affairs. But in the city and among the middle classes as the decades passed, women no longer played an important economic role—and, correspondingly, their independence and authority diminished. This loss of status was disguised in a deceptive cult of "true womanhood." In the period before 1850, middle class women were taught that obedience to the husband and to male-dominated society was a positive feminine virtue; the qualities most admired in women were piety, purity, submissiveness, and domesticity. As one male writer of the period said, "Woman never looks lovelier than in her reverence for religion." The passivity and naiveté of the woman's role were sugarcoated and served up as moral superiority; women were supposed to "guide" men and "uplift" them, not in any practical way, of course, but in a shadowy spiritual realm.

The position of women in antebellum society was one of great inequality relative to men. Although women were not denied political rights during the early years of the Revolutionary period, one state after another soon began to take the vote away from them, starting with New York in 1778 and ending with New Jersey in 1807. Harriet Martineau, an English visitor to America, wrote in 1837 that in America women had a "political nonexistence."

Legally and economically, women also were at an extreme disadvantage. Every cent a married woman earned belonged to her husband. If a woman divorced her husband, he usually retained custody of the children. Married women were not allowed to write their own wills. In fact, in most states married women could not legally hold property in their own names. As Alexis de Toqueville wrote: "In America a woman loses her independence forever in the bonds of matrimony."

The "Double Standard"

The meager wages offered to lower class women as workers drove many of them into a better-paying, if more demeaning, occupation—prostitution. A statistical study of New York taken near the end of the antebellum period revealed that half of the city's prostitutes formerly worked as seamstresses or servants. Many young women, especially confused immigrants and farm girls, were kidnapped and forced into prostitution by unscrupulous people called "white slave traders." Brothelkeepers found ways of bribing local police departments to ignore their illicit activities. Women forced by economic necessity or by abductors into prostitution were victims of sexual mores that ignored male promiscuity but insisted on

ADVOCATE OF MORAL REFORM.

Vol. I. No. 9 — NEW-YORK, SEPTEMBER, 1835. — Whole No. 9.

Published by the New York Female Moral Reform Society.

For there is nothing covered that shall not be revealed: Neither hid, that shall not be made known.—Luke xii. 2.

A monthly periodical, price $1 per annum, in advance.

OFFICE OF THE ADVOCATE,
No. 149 Nassau-street, in the Basement.

TERMS: The ADVOCATE OF MORAL REFORM will be furnished to single subscribers for $1,00 per annum, *in advance*.

Any person sending us $5,00, *postage paid*, shall receive seven copies sent to one person.

Auxiliary societies, and persons wishing to distribute, and taking not less than twenty-five copies, shall receive them at 60 cents a copy, per annum, enclosed in one wrapper and sent to one person.

All the profits of this paper, together with the donations entrusted to our charge, will be *faithfully* expended in Missionary, and other labors to promote the cause of Moral Reform.

Communications for the Advocate, Reports of Auxiliary Societies, and letters enclosing donations for the cause of Moral Reform, may be addressed to the "Advocate of Moral Reform, care of GEORGE CRAGIN, Office agent and accountant, 149 Nassau-st."

AUXILIARIES.

This month we are enabled to add the following to the list of our auxiliaries, viz.:

The Young Men's Moral Reform Society in the Third Free Church in this city;

The Female Moral Reform Society in Verona, N. Y.; and

The Female Moral Reform Society in Upper Middletown, Conn.

We are glad to see that the Young Men's Society have become auxiliary to us, for the reasons we presented last month in our remarks respecting the auxiliary in the Oberlin Institute. We hope the example of these young men in coming up to this work, will be followed by others in other churches, and especially by those in our Literary and Theological Institutions. Young men should feel a special interest in this cause; they are now to become the principal actors upon the stage of human life, and it is for their interest to endeavor to effect a reformation in public morals. We publish below the Address of the Young Men's Society in the Third Free Church to their Christian brethren, together with the Preamble, and a part of the articles of their Constitution.

The thought has occurred to us, that the Constitution of a Moral Reform Society ought to include a pledge, aiming definitely at the exclusion of *licentious men* from the circles of the virtuous. *One class* of the licentious, i. e. women, are *now* effectually excluded, and obliged to associate only with the impure. The great object of Moral Reform is to shut out *also* the *men* who are licentious, and oblige them to have no society, male or female, but with birds of their own feather. The work of exclusion is *done* for the women; let Moral Reform do it for the men. Would not this object be better effected by aiming at a "*single point*," viz. *the exclusion of licentious men*, rather than "all classes," seeing that the women are already excluded?

ADDRESS,

Of the Young Men's Moral Reform Society, of the Third Free Presbyterian Church, New-York, to their Christian brethren.

BRETHREN,—In presenting to you our Constitution, and soliciting your co-operation in the cause of Moral Reform we esteem it our duty to make known to you our reasons for associating together.

We would acknowledge, with shame, our guilt, in so long remaining inactive on this important subject, whilst the tide of licentiousness has been sweeping through the land, bearing on its putrid bosom so much infamy, wretchedness, and guilt, and plunging such myriads of immortal souls in hopeless perdition. But light has at length broken upon us, with such power, that we have been compelled to look around, and view the desolations caused by this monster—vice.

From our situation in this vast metropolis, where the demon of licentiousness holds such unbounded sway, we have full opportunity to witness his operations. We have seen his guilty emissaries, not only prowling about our city, seeking to allure the unwary to the "chambers of death," but sallying forth to the towns and villages of the surrounding country, entering the abodes of happiness and peace, and dragging unsuspecting, helpless innocence, to be immolated on the altar of lust and hellish passion.

We have seen our young companions, associates in the business of life, drawn away, step by step, from the path of virtue, through the deceitful influence of the abandoned libertine; whilst others, casting off the fear of God, and rejecting parental admonitions, allured by the fascinations of the harlot, have given way to their unhallowed passions, and become the voluntary victims of degrading lust.

We have seen those who sat by *our* side at the table of the Lord, overcome in the hour of temptation; thus bringing reproach upon the cause of Christ, and causing the hearts of the children of God to bleed at every pore.

We have seen the perjured libertine assume the garb of sanctity, that under the cloak of a Christian profession, he might the more easily select his prey, and fasten his deadly fangs upon his confiding victim.

With facts like these before us, we feel that we can no longer with impunity, be indifferent to the cause of Moral Reform; and are resolved firmly to stand by those engaged in this noble work, and aid them by every means in our power, notwithstanding the sneers and contempt of the profligate, and the prudent cautions of many, who, rather than offend a corrupt public sentiment, can remain unmoved, whilst thousands by this soul-destroying vice, are annually hurried to an untimely grave, and a dismal eternity.

For our plan of operations, we refer you to our Constitution, and earnestly invite you to unite your influence and exertions with ours in the suppression of licentiousness. Do you say the vice is so extensively prevalent, and the opposition to reform so mighty, that our feeble efforts will be fruitless?—Whilst we fear not opposition, we admit the extent of the sin. But when a deadly pestilence is sweeping over the land, shall we not use every precautionary means for the safety of those as yet uninfected? Shall we not describe to them the forms of its approach, and entreat them to be on their guard, and use every possible preventive? Let the note of warning be sounded through the land* let the character and devices of the libertine be portrayed in their true light—let the united voice of the virtuous community be raised in indignation against the profligate of every description, and the debauchee and harlot will be compelled to herd with those of like character with themselves, nor dare again pollute the ranks of virtue with their presence.

Believing that young men may engage in this cause with peculiar appropriateness and effect, and that their interest is deeply involved in its advancement, we again ask your co-operation. We would appeal to your feelings of philanthropy and benevolence, and point you to the thousands of our city sunk in debauchery and lewdness—miserable in this world, with the prospect of eternal misery in the world to come. But a few years ago, and others occupied their places; others preceded them: thus, as one generation of these unhappy beings passes away, another of like character succeeds. Come up with us, then, to the work of reform, and those now on the stage may be the last actors in this melancholy drama.

We would urge you, as lovers of the well-being and interest of our country, to aid us in this work. From well authenticated facts, the result of careful investigation, it has been shown, on the most moderate calculations, that there are in this land, at least fifty thousand females abandoned to licentiousness, whose vices are supposed annually to cost the nation thirty millions of dollars. Shall we sit calmly by, and see the wealth of the community perverted to such base purposes? But more than this, our political interests are in jeopardy; in a government constructed like ours, the only safety of its free institutions is based on the moral purity of the people. Let licentiousness and libertinism gain the ascendancy, and our happy republic will soon be numbered among the things that were. In proof of this, we would point to Sodom, to ancient Greece and Rome, and especially to France, when infidelity and licentiousness reigned triumphant, when the only true God was banished from the sanctuary, and a vile harlot, styled the Goddess of Liberty, was worshipped in His stead. And is there no danger that we are approximating to a state like this?

Finally, we appeal to your Christian sympathies. When this giant-vice is making such inroads upon the sanctuary of God—when scarcely a church in our land is free from its infection—when the religion of Christ, in consequence of it, is brought in such contempt before the world when so many immortal souls are hurried down to endless death is this the time for the Christian to sleep? For the love you bear to the cause of Christ, and the deathless souls for which he died, we solicit your assistance, and the aid and prayers of all who love the cause of purity and righteousness.

PREAMBLE.

Whereas, we are conscious that the sin of licentiousness, in all its forms, and with all its horrors, exists to an alarming extent throughout the length and breadth of our beloved country—gnawing the vitals of our republic—poisoning the fountain-head of morality and virtue—sapping the life-blood of domestic happiness, and sweeping with its deadly wave hundreds from the bosom of our churches—destroying men's bodies, and drowning their souls in perdition;

And whereas, believing as we do, that it is the imperative duty of every man, whether he be a patriot, philanthropist, or Christian, to endeavor to roll back this tide of death;

And whereas, we have already witnessed the happy effects of combined influence for the suppression of vice:—Therefore, we have resolved to form ourselves into a society, to be governed by the following

CONSTITUTION.

ARTICLE I.

This association shall be called "The Young Men's Moral Reform Society, of the Third Free Presbyterian Church, New-York," auxiliary to the "New-York Female Moral Reform Society."

ARTICLE II.

The object of this Society shall be, using such means as are sanctioned by the word of God—to prevent the desolating progress of licentiousness,

* One of the most efficacious means of dispersing light on this subject, is through the press. We would confidently recommend, as a judicious and highly useful publication, the "*Advocate of Moral Reform*," hoping that all engaged in this cause will both personally patronize it, and endeavor by every means to promote its extensive circulation.

Courtesy New York Public Library.

The Advocate of Moral Reform supported the goals and programs of the New York Female *Moral* Reform Society. It was put into production and marketed by women.

chastity in "respectable" women—the double standard.

The New York Female Moral Reform Society, organized in May 1834 by a group of women who met at a Presbyterian Church in Manhattan, declared open war on the city's houses of ill fame and tried to convert prostitutes to Christianity. Despite a lack of success, the society's members were among the first women of this period to question the well-known double moral standard and to indict the sexual behavior of American men. The organization never embraced feminism overtly, but it did urge women to unite in denouncing male behavior and in proclaiming female moral superiority. The society's members, moreover, traveled everywhere without male chaperones, formed their own organization, and propagandized for their own causes in their publication, *The Advocate of Moral Reform.* By mid-century the society abandoned its attack on prostitution and instead took up the cause of working women in general, even urging them to join unions. And, to demonstrate what the female of the species could do, they took over all of the tasks necessary for the production of the *Advocate:* editing, typesetting, keeping accounts, folding, and mailing out the journal.

Courtesy New York Infirmary, New York City.

Elizabeth Blackwell, the first woman in America to receive a medical degree.

Pioneers in the Professions

Although most recognized professions were closed to women during the antebellum period, more and more women were becoming school teachers. Like women workers in the textile mills, however, female teachers received less money than their male counterparts. And teaching, never a high-status profession in America, had fallen a few notches farther in public esteem by the time women outnumbered men teachers in 1850.

The more prestigious professions, such as law and medicine, were closed to women. Indeed, when doctors formed the American Medical Association in 1846, they specifically excluded females. Some women, however, broke through these barriers. Elizabeth Blackwell (1821–1910) became the first woman to graduate in medicine. She received her degree on January 23, 1849, after finishing the course of study at a small medical school in New York where she was admitted as a prank. For the next seven years she found it difficult to establish her practice in New York, where she was barred from hospitals and attacked by anonymous letter writers. Nevertheless, in 1853 she opened a one-room clinic for the poor, and there she treated 200 indigent women in the first year alone. Soon she was joined by two other women doctors, one of whom was her sister. In 1868 she established a medical college of her own, although by that time there were also medical schools for women in Boston and Philadelphia.

Among other prominent women of the period were Sarah (1792–1873) and Angelina Grimké (1805–1879) who became active in abolitionist circles in the 1830s. The sisters were born into a wealthy Huguenot family in South Carolina (their father was equivalent to chief justice of the state), and they were accustomed to the services of slaves. But when they traveled to Philadelphia, the views of the Quakers and their strong abolitionist stand changed their lives. Both of the Grimké sisters moved north, became Quakers, and took up the antislavery cause.

Library of Congress.

Angelina Grimké was an active abolitionist who came to realize that women had to secure their own rights.

When Angelina addressed mixed audiences in New England in 1837, she created a scandal; the Congregational ministerial association of Massachusetts objected in a circular letter. Angelina quickly saw that they must secure their rights as women before they could fight slavery effectively. As she wrote at the time, "We are placed very unexpectedly in a very trying situation, in the forefront of an entirely new contest—a contest for the *rights* of *woman* as a moral, intelligent and responsible being." Sarah responded to attacks on their right to speak by publishing *Letters on the Equality of the Sexes and the Condition of Women* (1838) and by lashing out boldly in the columns of *The Advocate of Moral Reform.*

"We are so little accustomed *to think for ourselves* that we submit to the dictum or prejudice, and of usurped authority, almost without an effort to redeem ourselves from the unhallowed shackles which have so long bound us; almost without a desire to rise from that degradation and bondage to which we have been consigned by man, and by which the faculties of our minds, and the powers of our spiritual nature, have been prevented from expanding to their full growth, and are sometimes wholly crushed."

When, Sarah Grimké used *The Advocate* to attack the Protestant ministry and its standard interpretations of the Bible, both of which, in her opinion, denied woman's true role, the result was a wave of angry letters that convinced the editors never again to overtly assault traditional family structure or orthodox Christianity. Nevertheless, the Grimkés became leaders of both the abolitionist and the feminist movements. Their own rectitude of character and clearheaded grasp of the issues made them irreproachable and forceful champions of the two causes, as did their firsthand knowledge of slavery.

The abolitionist movement was the immediate vehicle for other women to recognize that their own rights were being denied. In the summer of 1840, the British held an international meeting of the World Antislavery Convention in London. When several women, delegates from antislavery groups in America, tried to be seated, the majority of the delegates, who were men, ruled that the women could not participate but would have to watch silently from the galleries. Lucretia Mott was one of the delegates shunted upstairs. Elizabeth Cady Stanton (1815–1902), whose husband was a delegate, also had to watch from the galleries. After their humiliation in London, Mrs. Mott and Mrs. Stanton both became active feminists.

The feminism these women embraced was not without precedent. One of the earliest and most prolific women to speak about feminism before American audiences of men and women was a Scottish writer, lecturer and reformer, Frances Wright (1795–1852). Originally Fanny Wright, as she was known, was caught up by a desire to bring about the emancipation of slaves, and she proposed a plan whereby slaves could work large tracts of public lands and, with the profits, buy their freedom. When she turned to feminism, perhaps Wright became far more radical than any other woman of her time. She aroused hostility and ridicule when she advocated free love, equal education for women, liberal divorce laws,

Sophia Smith Collection, Smith College.

Lucretia Coffin Mott
(1793–1880)

Outstanding reformer and Quaker preacher, this energetic, cheerful woman was born on Nantucket Island. Her mother, whose family had been staunch Tories, and her father, a somewhat more democratic sea captain, both were members of the Society of Friends. When she was eleven the family moved to Boston (her first trip to "the Continent," she later recalled) where her father became a businessman. She briefly attended local public schools, but at the age of thirteen was sent to boarding school near Poughkeepsie, New York. This was her home for four years as student and teacher.

In 1811 she rejoined her parents, now living in Philadelphia, but soon married James Mott (1788-1868), a fellow teacher at the Poughkeepsie school. Mott, later a distinguished abolitionist and unique in his early advocacy of women's rights, recently had joined Lucretia's father in the cut nail business.

Although a Quaker background developed Lucretia Mott's antislavery sympathies, several experiences sharpened this interest and also piqued her concern for women's rights. The death of an infant son in 1817 caused this highly intelligent woman to reflect seriously concerning religion; and, as she began to speak at meetings, she easily won recognition as an acknowledged minister. Her views supported those of Elias Hicks, and in time she and her husband became associated with the "Hicksite" branch of the Quakers, a group with Unitarian-like leanings.

As her reputation as a speaker increased, she directed her attention to temperance, peace, antislavery, and women's rights. Concern for the latter seems to have stemmed from her brief teaching career when for the same work she received half as much money as her male counterparts. When officials at a worldwide antislavery convention held in London in 1840 refused to recognize Lucretia Mott and several other American women as official delegates, her interest in the rights of women increased markedly. Eight years later, together with Elizabeth Cady Stanton, she helped organize the famous Seneca Falls meeting (held in a Methodist church) which launched the women's rights movement in America. Despite this step and the fame it bestowed upon her, Lucretia Mott's first devotion as a reformer was to abolition. After passage of a new fugitive slave law in 1850, her home became a stop on the underground railroad to freedom.

This lady was a sprightly, impulsive woman who displayed both firmness and courage in behalf of whatever causes she espoused. She is a good example of how Quaker upbringing and practical experience could convert an agile mind into a multipurpose reform spirit. Also, Lucretia Mott is an early example of a woman who gracefully managed a public career without sacrificing a private life. ■

Library of Congress.

Frances Wright was denounced in the press as a "bold blasphemer and voluptuous preacher of licentiousness" for her so-called radical views.

and birth control. Today her positions strike many people as rational, but in the 1820s they were shocking in the extreme, especially when coupled with her efforts to set up an interracial utopia in West Tennessee and her attacks on racially segregated schools, organized religion, and marriage.

Frances Wright's views alienated most American women, but she did stimulate other feminists to consider the merits of suffrage for women, equal educational opportunities, and liberal divorce laws. Margaret Fuller (1810–1850), a teacher and transcendentalist writer, never identified herself with the feminists but one of her books, *Women in the Nineteenth Century* (1845), argued for equality of opportunity. In speaking about women's careers, Fuller said: "If you ask me what offices they may fill, I reply—any. I do not care what case you put; let them be sea captains if you will."

Seneca Falls

The high watermark of early feminist agitation was the first feminist convention held at Seneca Falls, New York, in 1848. Led by Elizabeth Cady Stanton, nearly 300 reformers (including forty men) proclaimed that women were the equals of men and should be free to speak in public, write, teach, and participate equally "in the various trades, professions and commerce." Elizabeth Cady Stanton offered a resolution declaring: "It is the sacred duty of the women of this country to secure to themselves their sacred right to the elective franchise." Even among the enlightened people at Seneca Falls, the suffrage resolution seemed too extreme, and only with support from Frederick Douglass, an ex-slave and prominent abolitionist, did the measure pass. The Seneca Falls convention adopted a Declaration of Sentiments and Resolutions modeled after the Declaration of Independence, which stated that "all men and women are created equal" and listed the "injuries and usurpations" women had endured at the hands of men.

Although women did not obtain the right to vote or hold elective office in any state until the last decades of the nineteenth century, they did make some gains. In 1838, for instance, Kentucky granted widows and single women with taxable property the right to vote for district school officials. In 1839, Mississippi granted married women the right to control their own property. And by 1848, New York conceded that women had certain rights in controlling property. Other states followed the New York example. Meanwhile, some state legislatures made divorce laws less stringent. Yet the equality of women spelled out by the delegates at the Seneca Falls Convention remained an ideal rather than a statement of reality for women in antebellum America.

Immigrants

Industrialization, that great economic and cultural shift that was dramatically affecting the lives of women, drew half a million immigrants to American shores in the 1830s and a million and a half in the next decade. The need for labor, created by the Industrial Revolution, provided jobs for the newcomers whose reasons for leaving Europe were worsening economic and political conditions in their own countries.

Before 1830, most of the new arrivals in America were Protestant artisans and well-to-do farmers from England and the six northern counties of Ireland. After 1830, however, the number of improverished Catholic peasant immigrants from southern Ireland increased dramatically until, in the 1840s, most of the people moving to the United States were either Irish or German. Smaller groups of foreigners came from Scandinavia, France, England, Canada, Holland, Poland, Italy, Hungary, and China. The ethnic flavor of America also was enriched by the inclusion of large numbers of Mexican Catholics, who were incorporated into the United States after the Mexican War (1846–1848).

Antebellum immigration may have provided America with a new work force, but it led to increased social stratification. Each new wave of immigrants pushed some of the people who had been in the United States longer a rung up the social ladder. But greater wealth and prestige for the so-called "native" Americans was only one result of immigration; the influx of foreigners also lowered wages in some areas and hurt many "native" laborers. During the 1830s the daily wage of an unskilled laborer dropped from $1 to less than 75 cents. The weekly pay received by journeymen hatters fell from about $12 in 1835 to $8 in 1845. A newspaper lamented in 1844 concerning the effects of large-scale immigration: "Our labouring men, native and naturalized, are met at every turn and every avenue of employment, with recently imported workmen from the low wages countries of the world. Our public improvements, railroads, and canals are thronged with foreigners. They fill our large cities, reduce the wages of labor, and increase the hardships of the old settlers."

Full of resentment towards the new immigrants, those whose families had been in America longer began to call themselves "natives" and to champion "nativism." Many of these self-styled "natives" were Protestants caught in the midst of a strong evangelical movement, which will be discussed in Chapter 10. They were, therefore, alarmed both by the job threat posed by the new arrivals and by the Catholicism of the Irish and many of the German immigrants.

Irish and German Immigrants

Irish peasants came to America to escape from extreme poverty and misery. A potato blight began to destroy Ireland's primary subsistence crop in the 1820s, and the island experienced a severe famine in 1845 and 1846 when rot destroyed stored potatoes to be used as food and seed for the next crop. By 1845 almost a million Irish had moved to the United States; by 1860 there were more than 1,611,000 people born in Ireland living in America (almost 40 percent of all foreign-born residents).

Typical of the agony of the Irish peasantry during the famine which greatly increased this migration was this scene in southern Ireland that an Englishman witnessed in 1847: "Out of a population of 240 I found thirteen already dead from want. The survivors were like walking skeletons—the men gaunt and haggard, stamped with the livid mark of hunger—the children crying with pain—the women in some of the cabins too weak to stand." At a time when other countries were growing in population, Ireland lost almost one-fourth of its people through emigration and starvation.

Because they were unskilled and quite different from most Americans in their religious, social, and linguistic customs (many of the Irish peasants still spoke Gaelic or heavily accented English), they gathered in ethnic enclaves in ports such as Boston. Cities were not well suited to most of the Irish, who were rural people, but the

Courtesy New-York Historical Society, New York City.

Hard times in Ireland and the prospect of a new life in America brought a great influx of Irish to America in the antebellum period.

newcomers preferred staying close together in the shadow of the Catholic parish church rather than dispersing through the countryside and encountering hostility from other ethnic groups; moreover, the Irish seldom had enough money to buy a farm or farm equipment, livestock, and seed.

The Irish came to Boston because it was a major port for British ships. Many stayed there because they could not afford to move elsewhere. Before 1830 the total number of immigrants entering Boston never exceeded 2,000. But between 1840 and 1849 the number increased rapidly from 3,396 (1840) to 28,917 (1849) and most of these arrivals were Irish. By 1850, some 35,000 Irish lived in Boston, far outnumbering the next two most numerous minority ethnic groups—free blacks (2,085) and Germans (about 2,000).

Of course, the Irish clustered in large numbers in other cities besides Boston; among them, Lowell, Hartford, New York, Philadelphia, Brooklyn, Albany, Buffalo, Cleveland, Cincinnati, Chicago, and St. Louis. In general, they followed the canals and railroads (often helping to construct them) and also settled in southern ports such as Baltimore, Charleston, Savannah, and New Orleans. The Irish were, in fact, urban pioneers and their ghettolike enclaves gave them considerable political clout, which they quickly used. And the same muscles that helped lay railway ties, dig ditches, and keep the foes of their political boss patron away from the ballot box on election day soon were carrying arms in the local militia, fighting fires, and bringing the law (if not true order) to bustling city wards.

Unskilled Irish peasants, willing to work for low wages, provided Boston with the labor that helped to create a new industrial economy for the city. Because the men were paid such low wages, their wives were forced to seek employment as domestic servants. By the mid-1840s many Irish were seeking better jobs, but they often were met with prejudice. Newspaper advertisements offering employment often stipulated "None need apply but Americans."

Even the free blacks of Boston fared better than the Irish on the job market. Although it was difficult for blacks to acquire an education, skills, or capital, many did become traders, barbers, or seamen, and some even rose into the professional ranks. The Irish, by contrast, remained at the bottom of the occupational hierarchy.

The Boston Irish were hired by southern planters looking for cheap labor to perform jobs deemed too dangerous for expensive slaves. New railroad companies used them to lay miles and miles of track. In the late 1840s and well into the 1850s, Boston's Irish provided factory owners with labor so inexpensive that industrialists could reap enormous profits. After Elias Howe revolutionized the clothing industry by inventing the sewing machine in 1846, the Irish were employed in the mass production of garments. Many other industries, held back from expanding by high wages, could now grow as a result of the abundance of cheap Irish labor. For the Irish immigrant, the independence of a peasant's life had been exchanged for fifteen-hour working days and a ceaseless scramble for survival. In America the Irish were no longer haunted by starvation, perhaps, but they had become, to use George Fitzhugh's phrase, "white slaves." Fitzhugh (1806–1881), a Virginia lawyer and proslavery propagandist, became a confirmed defender of slavery after a visit to the North in the 1830s. He claimed that the conditions of plantation slaves were preferable to those of northern workers. Life was indeed bleak for Irish in the North. Nevertheless, they endured as free people.

Excluded from participation in the normal affairs of the white Boston community, the Irish responded by developing an ethnic consciousness. They sought to preserve their own cultural heritage in churches, parochial schools, Irish newspapers, and social organizations such as the Charitable Irish Society and the Shamrock Society.

During the 1840s and 1850s, another group of immigrants, who like the Irish had been coming to America for generations, suddenly increased their numbers dramatically. These were the Germans. In 1851, 72,482 Germans often called the "Forty-Eighters" because of the failure of liberal revolts of that year, arrived in American ports. For the most part they were a relatively well-to-do group who turned their back on Europe for political, not economic reasons. During the next two years another 288,000 of their countrymen came to America. Although many remained in cities, more so than the Irish these folk tended to become farmers in states such as Ohio, Wisconsin, Illinois, and Texas. Their arrival created a special religious problem. Since many were Catholic, they keenly resented Irish domination of church affairs. And Protestant Americans were equally critical of their Sabbath custom of a "Continental Sunday," that is, going directly from church to a beer garden

Library of Congress.

John Roebling's suspension bridge at Niagara Falls.

or saloon for an afternoon of pleasant sociability. Despite the middle class ideology of most German immigrants, many Americans viewed them as atheists or radicals.

In their midst were a considerable number of Jews, primarily an urban people who settled in the larger cities, especially New York. In 1840, there were only about 15,000 Jews in the United States out of a total population of more than 17,000,000. At that time about half of them lived in New York, Philadelphia, Milwaukee, and Richmond. By 1860 their numbers had increased to 150,000, largely because of the revolts of the late 1840s which shook not only Germany, but Austria, Italy, and France as well. Unlike Catholic immigrants, the Jews were such a tiny minority that attacks upon them as a group were rare.

Anti-Catholicism

Native Americans were alarmed by the clannishness of all these immigrants, but they were most frightened by the Catholicism of the Irish. Samuel F. B. Morse (who later invented the telegraph) was Professor of Sculpture and Painting at New York University in 1834 when he published a rabid anti-Catholic tract, *The Foreign Conspiracy Against the Liberties of United States.* Morse contended that America was about to witness an epic struggle between the Pope's followers and the Protestant defenders of liberty. According to Morse, the Catholics (that is, the Irish) intended to take over the government and destroy the separation of church and state. For many Americans—Morse's predictions seemed grimly plausible.

These fears were exacerbated by the Reverend Lyman Beecher, a prominent Boston Protestant clergyman who moved to the West in 1830 and later became president of Lane Theological Seminary in Cincinnati, Ohio. Beecher pictured for his numerous followers a contest between Catholics and Protestants that would decide the fate of the West. As he put it, the "competition now is for . . . the education of the rising generation, in which Catholics and infidels have got the start on us. . . . If we gain the West, all is safe; if we lose it, all is lost."

The bewildering social changes racking America after the War of 1812 gave focus to a general but totally unfounded fear of a Catholic conspiracy. These tensions found release in a series of mob actions. In 1831 rioting Protestants burned St. Mary's Church in New York. On August 10, 1834, a mob of forty or fifty Bostonians, excited by an anti-Catholic speech given by Lyman Beecher, burned the Ursuline Convent in Charlestown. In 1836 a sensationalist book, *The Awful Disclosures of the Hotel Dieu Nunnery of Montreal,* appeared. Written by Maria Monk (1816–1849), a Canadian adventuress, the book pretended to be the account of ordeals suffered by a nun forced to submit to the sexual advances of priests. Even after the public learned that the author actually was a Protestant imprisoned for picking the pocket of her companion in a house of prostitution, the book continued to sell well. In fact, more than 300,000 copies were sold before the Civil War and the book was widely circulated by anti-Catholics well into the twentieth century.

Some of the leading Protestants in the country had endorsed Maria Monk's book. When the controversy

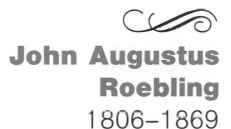

Library of Congress.

John Augustus Roebling
1806–1869

Born in Thuringia to a German family of limited means, John Roebling nevertheless got a good basic education and was able to attend the Royal Polytechnic Institute where the philosopher Hegel was one of his instructors. However, bridges and roads, not philosophy, interested this young man. For three years after graduating at the age of twenty, he worked for the Prussian government but felt hampered by red tape and official inertia.

In the spring of 1831, after analyzing carefully the possibilities of life in America, he and a brother, Karl, went to Bremen and later sailed from there to Philadelphia. A short time later, they bought 7,000 acres of land near Pittsburgh and settled down with a group of their fellow countrymen. However, the land they chose was not good for farming, and in 1837, the year after he married the daughter of another German immigrant, Roebling began working for the state government on the canal-railway project being constructed across Philadelphia.

In connection with this enterprise, he noticed the inefficient, clumsy cables of Kentucky hemp that were being used and began to experiment with rope made of twisted strands of wire. In 1841 his small factory at Saxonburg, the site of his ill-fated farm, began to turn out the first wire rope made in America. Demand for this product for tow lines and dredges led Roebling to move his operations to Trenton, New Jersey, in the late 1840s.

Although he was becoming a successful manufacturer, bridgebuilding continued to fascinate Roebling, and in 1846 he completed an eight-span suspension bridge over the Monongahela River at Pittsburgh, a structure that was used for thirty-five years. Although this design was new to Americans, it was similar to chain suspension bridges Roebling had studied as a youth.

As it turned out, this was the first of many bridges he would build, but this man is best known for the famous Brooklyn Bridge. In June 1857 he wrote to New York authorities suggesting the possibility of constructing a bridge over the East River between lower Manhattan and Brooklyn, then an independent city. His plan was to build the structure so high that it would not interfere with water traffic. Finally, nearly twelve years later he received orders to commence. On June 28, 1869, while inspecting the site, a ferry entering a slip on the Brooklyn side crushed several toes on one foot. It was a very painful but not serious injury, and Roebling was taken to his son's home where the toes were amputated. Everyone expected him to recover; he was robust, sixty-three years of age, and in good health, but tetanus developed and he died several weeks later.

Roebling, a punctual individual who never wasted a minute and scorned those who did, was a wealthy man and bequeathed to his eldest son, Washington Augustus Roebling (1837–1926) not only a huge wire rope factory but plans for the Brooklyn Bridge as well. In time, that structure crippled this man, too, although he lived to an advanced age. The younger Roebling, like scores of his workmen, suffered from the dreaded "bends," which attacked those who spent long hours in high-pressure caissons as the foundations were being built. By the spring of 1872 his health was so seriously impaired that he never visited the construction site again, instead he directed the work from his Brooklyn home until the bridge was completed eleven years later. Although this is a story of wealth, achievement, and success, the Roebling saga is tinged with sadness. The bridge which stands as a memorial to their genius killed the father who conceived it and permanently injured the son who finished it. ■

---

it aroused reached monumental proportions, several of them visited the Hotel Dieu in Montreal and discovered that, for one thing, it was nothing like the institution described in the book. One prominent Protestant newspaper editor, Colonel William L. Stone, reported after his visit to the convent that her "confession" was utterly false and "the priests and nuns are innocent in this matter." Maria Monk's advocates, however, refused to believe Stone and branded him a hireling of the Jesuits. Enough people continued to believe in her story to encourage publication of a second installment of her adventures, *Further Disclosures,* in 1837.

Between 1840 and 1844 the anti-Catholic movement took on a new form. At that time the Public School Society, dedicated to teaching students the "sublime truths of religion and morality contained in the Holy Scriptures" and endorsed by the Protestant groups, operated the "public" schools of New York City. Catholic parents did not want their children exposed to the King James version of the Scriptures, which was not in accord with Catholic dogma, nor did they approve of religious instruction, which openly mocked Catholicism. When Catholics, led by New York's Bishop John Hughes (1797–1864) attempted to obtain state tax funds to institute their own educational system, a great debate erupted. One Protestant newspaper indignantly exclaimed in an attack on Catholics, "They demand of Republicans to give them funds to train up their children to worship a ghostly monarchy of vicars, bishops, archbishops, cardinals, and Popes! They demand of us to take away our children's funds and bestow them on the subjects of Rome, the creatures of a foreign heirarchy!" When Bishop Hughes switched tactics and campaigned for nonsectarian public schools, from which religion of any sort would be excluded, he only aroused more Protestant ire. An increasing number of Protestants believed that the Pope was preparing to conquer America and that American Catholics were his agents.

The worst rioting of this period occurred in Philadelphia in 1844. When Catholics demanded that their children be allowed to read their own version of the Bible and not be forced to receive Protestant religious instruction, the American Protestant Association responded with fanatical antipathy. This group, organized in November 1842 by about 100 local ministers, was convinced that "Popery" was trying to gain control of the Mississippi Valley and cited letters of the reigning Pope supposedly attacking such freedoms as those of conscience, opinion, and the press and bewailing separation of church and state anywhere in the world. In May of 1844 clashes broke out in Philadelphia between Irish Catholic workers and militant Protestants; after three days of mob rule, several Catholic churches were burned, thirteen citizens killed, and many more wounded.

Rioting was only the most overt expression of anti-Catholicism. Beginning in the mid-1830s and continuing through the next decade, nativists organized politically and fought to limit the influence of immigrants, especially Catholics in every aspect of public life. In many states, ministers and local politicians, seeking instant public sympathy from their Protestant constituents, quickly embraced the banner of nativism. However, the Philadelphia riot cooled the ardor of many Americans, who thought the movement had gone beyond the bounds of reason; and in 1846 Congress rejected a major nativist objective, passage of stricter laws governing the naturalization of citizens.

Yet nativism did not die out. In the 1840s, when its adherents saw that open political action was ineffectual in combating immigrants, they formed secret societies such as The Native Sons of America, The United Daughters of America, and The Order of the "Star-Spangled" Banner.

The great influx of immigrants to America during the antebellum period certainly aroused strong tensions that still have not been entirely resolved. But the phenomenon was not without its more positive side. Before the controversy over religious instruction in the schools occurred, Protestant teachers had freely used the Bible as a textbook. The objections of Catholics to this practice led at first to a strong parochial school system and in the twentieth century to a secularization of education and a truer separation of church and state, and undoubtedly created widespread interest in true public education. If nothing else, this controversy awakened all Americans to the many problems immigration brings in its wake, and those who arrived quickly learned a basic lesson in democracy American style: how to use the ballot box to get what they wanted.

Library of Congress.

In May of 1848, Philadelphia was rocked by mob violence directed against the Irish. In this scene, militant Protestants wearing tall beaver hats battle the militia called in to stop the rioting.

Percentage of Foreign-Born, 1860

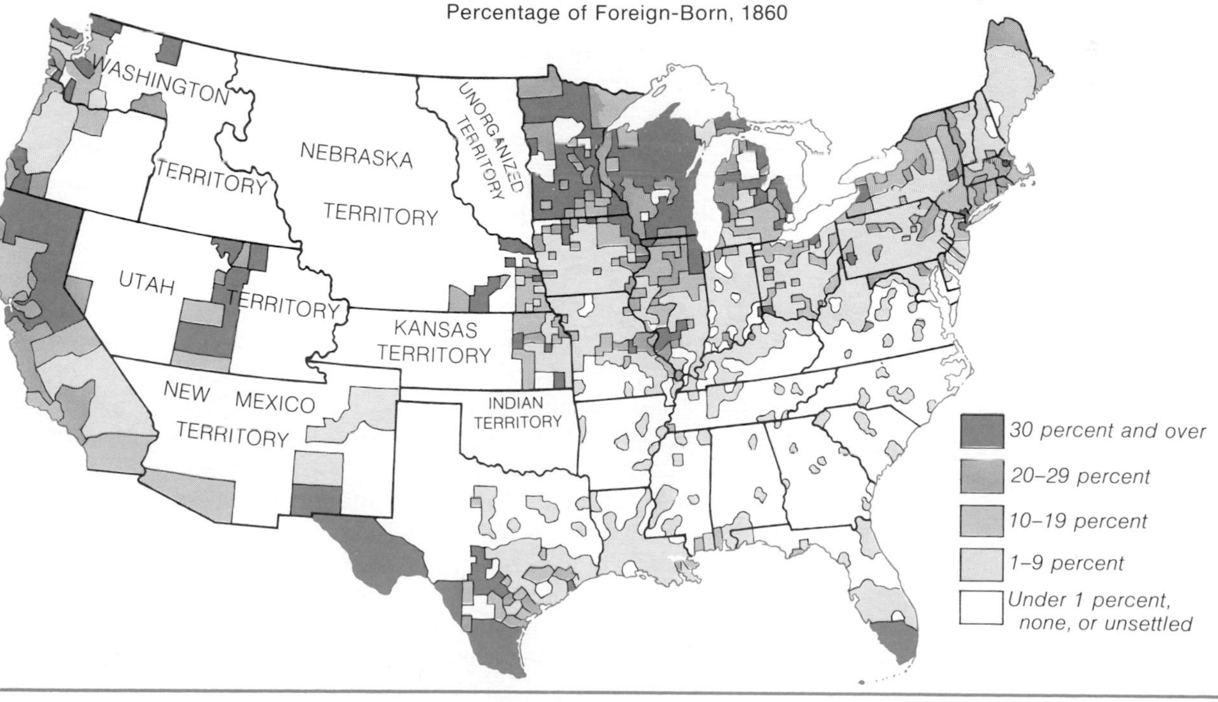

Essay

The Struggle for Full Citizenship

For all practical purposes, citizenship is much like good health and the ability to walk or talk. It is something most Americans take for granted, and rarely reflect on except when going to the polls or traveling abroad. The ballot, passport, and an occasional burst of pride during a Fourth of July parade or when some celebrity sings the national anthem at a sports event are the most common expressions of a rather intangible concept.

Citizenship is, in essence, the relationship between an individual and a state as prescribed by the laws of that state. It is a condition acquired at birth or by naturalization, that is, choosing to renounce one's native land for another. In the modern sense, citizenship is a by-product of the American and French revolutions, and represents an obvious attempt to discard the word "subject" with its connotations of feudal service and inequality.

The tempestuous 1770s created countless problems concerning just who was and who was not an American citizen. Throughout the middle decades of the eighteenth century, London had pursued a contradictory policy of encouraging immigration to the New World but had balked at naturalization of aliens by colonies themselves; instead, those running the empire wanted foreign immigrants to take an oath of allegiance to the Crown before they departed for America. Nevertheless, until 1773 the government generally permitted naturalization by colonial officials, providing still more evidence of "benign neglect." The decision of George III to change this practice led to one of the many "He has" phrases in the Declaration of Independence: "He has endeavoured to prevent the Population of these States; for that purpose obstructing the Laws of Naturalization of Foreigners."

That next great document, the Constitution, failed to define citizenship, either because those writing it assumed everyone knew what the word meant, or because this was an expedient means of sidestepping what could have been an explosive issue. In any case, the Founding Fathers implied that anyone who voted in national elections had to be white, male, and at least 21 years of age. They left the determination of citizenship to the individual states but gave federal authorities sole power of naturalization, thus creating a potentially awkward situation. In theory, any state could admit aliens to virtually all privileges of citizenship and, at the same time, refuse those rights to individuals properly naturalized by the central government.

In 1789, David Ramsay, a well-known South Carolina historian, published a carefully phrased, eight-page document entitled "A Dissertation on the Manner of Acquiring the Character and Privileges of a Citizen of the United States." In Ramsay's view, any person living in a state or country was an inhabitant or resident, not necessarily a citizen. Blacks, he observed in passing, clearly were not citizens; concerning women, he was silent.

There were, Ramsay emphasized, few paths to U.S. citizenship. Those party to the original compact clearly were citizens, that is, adults who were present in the new nation on July 4, 1776 and who gave active support to the break with Britain. Others who swore "an oath of fidelity" to one of the several states in the next dozen years or so also were citizens. And still others had acquired that status by tacit consent or acquiescence (such as coming of age after 1776), by birth and inheritance, and by "adoption" (naturalization).

Colonial Americans who on July 4, 1776 were orphans less than 21 years of age, Ramsay argued, still were British subjects unless they had subsequently taken an oath to a state or had been naturalized. Since no one could say whether their parents would have been Tory or Patriot, they could not claim citizenship merely by the fact of birth on what was now American soil. Pointing to little-noticed provisions in the Constitution, he stressed that U.S. citizenship did not exist before July 4, 1776. That document required members of the House of Representatives to have been citizens for seven years before their election and Senators to have been citizens for nine, but the President (only to be an individual who was a citizen at the time of the adoption of the Constitution or a natural-born citizen, not a naturalized citizen, a barrier which still exists) had to have been "a Resident within the United States" for 14 years.

It is readily apparent that any revolution gives rise to numerous dilemmas concerning citizenship, the most notable being: Where does one's allegiance lie? Citizenship is, after all, merely one of several obligations. An individual also has ties to family, church, locality, region, and the old regime, all of which may seem more important than the ones to an amorphus and perhaps ineffective, embryonic national entity. Yet the greatest impact on the nature of citizenship in our own revolutionary era was the failure of the Founding Fathers to define its scope, thus precipitating an on-going battle by disfranchised white males, blacks, women, and immigrants to achieve what they termed *full* citizenship.

Throughout the first six decades of the nineteenth century, these groups enjoyed varying success, most of their assaults being directed at state laws that restricted the right of suffrage.

The State of Mississippi Department of Archives and History.

Greenwood Leflore, mixed-blood leader of the Choctaws.

As older and newer states vied for population, regulations prohibiting white adult males from voting disappeared. Also, as territories changed into states, all white residents were welcomed as citizens *en masse,* but the status of women, blacks, Indians, and other ethnic minorities remained unclear. They sometimes were viewed as citizens, depending on treaty provisions, state laws, and local customs, but they were rarely given the vote. There were occasional exceptions to this. For example, Greenwood Leflore (1800–1865), a mixed-blood Choctaw chieftan who elected to remain in Mississippi when the rest of the tribe moved to the West beginning in 1831, became a U.S. citizen under the terms of the Treaty of Dancing Rabbit Creek. Eventually he became a wealthy planter and served as a member of the Mississippi Senate. Women generally were less fortunate, though by 1850 they had won the right to own property and to contract and sue in their own names. They now had a legal identity and no longer were viewed as wards of their father or husband.

In 1857, the Dred Scott decision shattered any hope for participatory citizenship for blacks. Scott, a slave born in Virginia about 1795, was taken by his owner to free territory and then to slave Missouri. Later Scott sought his freedom on the basis of his prolonged residence in Minnesota. A majority of Supreme Court justices ruled that a slave was not a citizen and could not bring suit in federal courts. They went on to state that even if Scott could have sued, he would not have won his freedom since the Missouri Compromise of 1820, which outlawed slavery in much of the Louisiana Purchase, was unconstitutional. Congress, they added, had no power to exclude slavery from the territories. Although this decision hardly caused the Civil War, it did little to calm rough waters and clearly made imperative a definition of citizenship by federal statute.

Actually, this decision of 1857 should not have come as a great surprise. The previous year the Department of State informed a New York City resident that his repeated requests for passports for "eleven colored persons" would not be honored since blacks were not citizens of the United States.

"The question whether free negroes are such citizens is not now presented for the first time, but has repeatedly arisen in the administration of both the National and State governments. In 1821 a controversy arose as to whether free persons of color were citizens of the United States within the intent and meaning of the acts of Congress regulating foreign and coasting trade, so as to be qualified to command vessels; and Mr. Wirt, Attorney-

General, decided that they were not, and he moreover held that the words 'Citizens of the United States' were used in the Acts of Congress in the same sense as in the Constitution. This view is also fully sustained in a recent opinion of the present Attorney-General."

Nevertheless, this State Department official said his superiors were willing to issue certificates stating that the eleven blacks were free, native-born, inhabitants of the United States, "and that the Government thereof would regard it to be its duty to protect them if wronged by a foreign Government, while within its jurisdiction for a legal and proper purpose."

Three years after Appomattox the Fourteenth Amendment was ratified recognizing "all persons born or naturalized in the United States, and subject to the jurisdiction thereof" as citizens of the United States and the state where they lived. Although this amendment implied that only males 21 years of age and older (except Indians not taxed) qualified for full citizenship, in 1871 suffrage pioneer Susan B. Anthony and several other women invoked its provisions to cast ballots in an election held in Rochester, N. Y. They subsequently were indicted by a federal grand jury for voting illegally and, with the aid of the judge, convicted. The judge, while addressing the jury, drew a strict distinction between citizenship and suffrage: all women now were citizens, true, but state law conferred the ballot only upon men. The women refused to pay the fines levied, and at that point the federal government abandoned the proceedings.

The Supreme Court ruled three times in the 1870s on matters relating to women's citizenship. A Missouri woman sued an election official for refusing to let her vote. When the case reached the Supreme Court, the judges ruled that women were not covered by the Fourteenth Amendment, at least for voting rights. A later test, brought by a woman claiming rights under the Fifteenth Amendment, also was disallowed. Although the Amendment did not mention gender, it was deemed to apply only to males. The Supreme Court in the same decade also ruled that married women had no legal existence, thus following common law. This decision was prompted by an audacious "she-lawyer" who sued the Illinois Bar for the right to practice law. Finally, the Nineteenth Amendment, ratified in 1919, gave women the right to vote.

Yet the citizenship status of a few women remained somewhat obscure for three more years. Until 1922 any American woman who married an alien assumed the nationality

Library of Congress.

Margaret Fuller, one of the most vivid intellectual personalities of antebellum America, sometimes referred to as the "Priestess of Transcendentalism," wrote an impressive feminist study in 1845 entitled *Women in the Nineteenth Century*.

of her husband. In fact, if he was ineligible for naturalization, this situation persisted until 1931. For the most part, these laws, while unfair, attracted little attention, until prospective voters discovered they actually were foreigners and no longer U.S. citizens.

Margaret Fuller (1810–1850), noted social reformer, journalist, and critic, lost her citizenship by marriage to an Italian nobleman. However, since they perished in a storm on the eve of their return to New York City, the issue of citizenship never arose. President Grant's daughter, Nellie, married an Englishman in 1874; and, when he died 22 years later, she returned to live in America. To clear up her legal status, she petitioned Congress to restore her citizenship, a request that was granted in 1898. Ruth Bryan Owen, daughter of William Jennings Bryan, ran into some difficulty as the result of her marriage to a British subject. She and her husband came to America at the close of World War I and the 1922 law clearly restored her U.S. citizenship; however, when she won a seat in the House of Representatives six years later, her defeated opponent charged she had not been a citizen for seven years before the election. This claim ultimately was rejected by Congress.

During these same decades all Indians became citizens. In 1901 Theodore Roosevelt claimed that 60,000 Indians living apart from their tribes already were U.S. citizens, and the Indian Citizenship Act of 1924 completed this process. However, unlike other minorities, most Indians were more anxious to retain tribal identity than gain the right to vote. Efforts of those Indians desiring to retain tribal identity were promoted by Indian Commissioner John Collier in the 1930s. Even Asiatics, despite the Chinese Exclusion Act of 1882, scored a few victories. Wong Kim Ark, a laborer born to Chinese parents who lived in San Francisco and enjoyed dual citizenship, made a trip to China in the early 1890s to visit relatives. On his return, federal officials barred his reentry. This case eventually reached the Supreme Court in 1898, the justices ruling in Wong's favor: he was a native-born U.S. citizen and could not be deported or excluded from his homeland.

Despite the struggle of disfranchised white males, blacks, and women to be recognized as full-fledged citizens, citizenship by naturalization remains a dramatic experience. In the late nineteenth and early twentieth centuries this process of Americanization reached its peak as millions of immigrants studied manuals designed to prepare them for citizenship. These volumes usually included a brief, simplistic overview of American history and government and a list of questions that were frequently asked before one could swear an oath of allegiance to

Referring to your letter of April 30, asking whether the daughter of a naturalized citizen of the United States who has married an alien may obtain a passport through her father's citizenship, you are informed that, inasmuch as a woman's citizenship follows that of her husband, she is not a citizen of the United States and can not, under the law, receive a passport.

The woman merges her nationality in that of her husband upon marriage to a foreigner. In case of legal separation, the practice places her in a position similar to that of a minor child, born of foreign parents, who has been adopted by a citizen of the United States, upon reaching majority. The wife may elect whether to preserve the foreign nationality acquired by her marriage, or reacquire her former American citizenship.

I have to acknowledge the receipt of your No. 506, of the 11th ultimo, reporting the application of Humper Nespar, or Wadded Moccasin, a Sioux Indian, for a passport.

In reply, I have to say that Indians are not citizens of the United States by reason of birth within its limits. Neither are our *general* naturalization laws applicable to them, but various Indian tribes have been naturalized by *special* acts of Congress.

These nineteenth-century statements demonstrate the attitude of government officials toward the citizenship status of women and Indians.

the United States of America: What is a republic? What is the meaning of citizenship? How are bills passed in Congress? Who is the lieutenant-governor of this state? What did John Cabot do? How do presidential electors vote? Who can become senator?

During World War I whole units of servicemen were naturalized, 1500 U.S. Navy men in one New York ceremony, for example. Two decades later, although immigration laws were more strict, thousands of aliens serving in the armed forces once more became American citizens.

Today, as far as the responsibility of the federal government is concerned, little difference exists between citizens and so-called "nationals." The Immigration and Nationality Act of July 27,1952, designates as "nationals" both citizens and those who owe permanent allegiance to the United States. Inhabitants of American Samoa are the only remaining noncitizen nationals.

They enjoy diplomatic protection and can enter the United States freely, but have no political rights.

Some efforts have been made in recent decades to cancel U.S. citizenship under certain conditions, especially the citizenship of naturalized persons who live overseas for extended periods. Anyone who votes in a foreign election, serves a foreign power, goes outside of the United States to avoid the draft, or commits treason or desertion runs considerable risk; however, for the most part, the Supreme Court has declined to approve congressional legislation depriving both native-born and naturalized individuals of their citizenship.

The cautious, restrained wording of the Constitution as written in 1787 is a far cry from the amendments of 1868, 1919, and 1971 extending the right of suffrage to blacks, women, and 18-year-olds. For some, it has been a long, hard struggle; for others, the right to vote, if that is what full citizenship means, came easily indeed. If the road had been harder, they perhaps would value this prize more highly.

Selected Readings

Black Americans (also see the studies mentioned in this chapter)

James H. Dormon and Robert Jones, *The Afro-American Experience: A Cultural History Through Emancipation* (1974)

Herbert G. Gutman, *The Black Family in Slavery and Freedom, 1750-1925* (1976)

Lawrence W. Levine, *Black Culture and Black Consciousness: Afro-American Folk Thought From Slavery to Freedom* (1977)

George P. Rawick, *From Sundown to Sunup: The Making of the Black Community* (1972)

Richard C. Wade, *Slavery in the Cities: The South, 1820-1860* (1964)

Ira Berlin, *Slaves without Masters: The Free Negro in the Antebellum South* (1975)

Leon F. Litwack, *North of Slavery: The Negro in the Free States, 1790-1860* (1961)

Indians and Indian Removal

Robert F. Berkhofer, Jr., *The White Man's Indian* (1978)

Dale Van Every, *Disinherited: The Lost Birthright of the American Indian* (1966)

Glen Tucker, *Tecumseh: Vision of Glory* (1956)

Gary E. Moulton, *John Ross: Cherokee Chief* (1978)

Ronald N. Satz, *American Indian Policy in the Jacksonian Era* (1975)

Grant Foreman, *Indian Removal: The Emigration of the Five Civilized Tribes of Indians* (new ed., 1953)

Robert A. Trennert, Jr., *Alternative to Extinction: Federal Indian Policy and the Beginnings of the Reservation System, 1846-1851* (1975)

Women and Women's Rights

Ann Douglas, *The Feminization of American Culture* (1977)

Nancy F. Cott, *The Bonds of Womanhood: "Woman's Sphere" in New England, 1780-1835* (1977)

Anne Firor Scott, *The Southern Lady: From Pedestal to Politics, 1830-1930* (1970)

Barbara Welter, *Dimity Convictions: The American Woman in the Nineteenth Century* (1976)

Katherine D. Lumpkin, *The Emancipation of Angelina Grimke* (1974)

Eleanor Flexner, *Century of Struggle: The Woman's Rights Movement in the United States* (rev. ed., 1975)

Miriam Gurko, *The Ladies of Seneca Falls: The Birth of the Women's Rights Movement* (1976)

Immigrants and Nativism

Marcus L. Hansen, *The Atlantic Migration, 1607-1860: A History of the Continuing Settlement of the United States* (1940)

Oscar Handlin, *Boston's Immigrants: A Study of Acculturation* (rev. and enlarged ed., 1959)

Kathleen N. Conzen, *Immigrant Milwaukee, 1836–1860: Accommodation and Community in a Frontier City* (1976)
Carl F. Wittke, *Refugees of Revolution: The German Forty-Eighters in America* (1952)
Leon A. Jick, *The Americanization of the Synagogue, 1820–1870* (1976)
Ray Allen Billington, *The Protestant Crusade, 1800–1860: A Study of the Origins of American Nativism* (1938)
Ira M. Leonard and Robert D. Parmet, *American Nativism, 1830–1860* (1971)
Michael Feldberg, *The Philadelphia Riots of 1844: A Study in Ethnic Conflict* (1975)

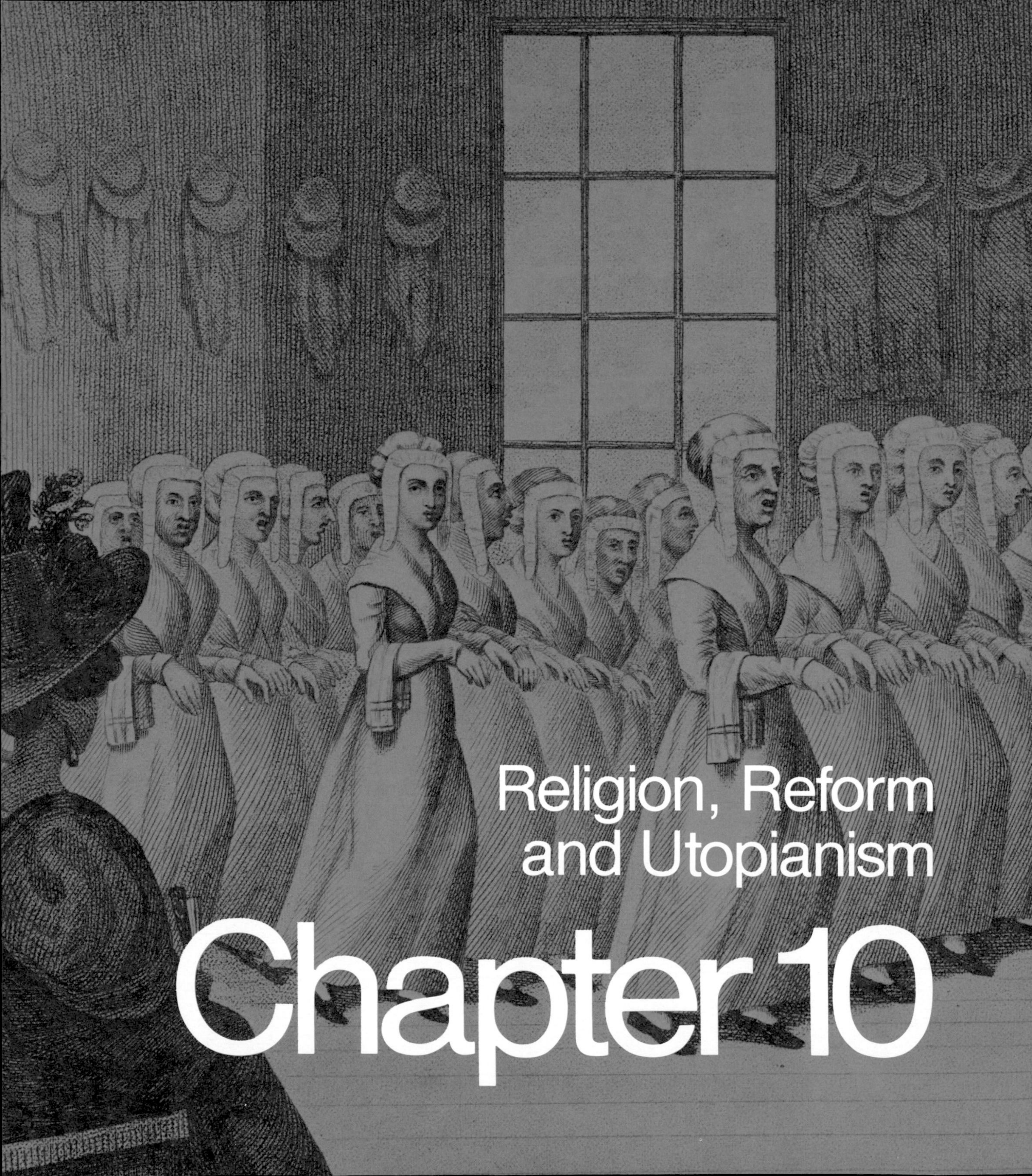

Chapter 10

Religion, Reform and Utopianism

TIMELINE

1817
Organization of American Colonization Society

1821
Kentucky outlaws imprisonment for debt

1825
New York establishes reform school for juvenile delinquents

1825
Robert Owen founds New Harmony

1826
American Society for Promotion of Temperance formed

1826
Charles G. Finney begins revival campaign in upstate New York

1828
American Peace Society established

1830
Joseph Smith founds the Mormon Church

1833
American Anti-Slavery Society founded

1836
John Humphrey Noyes founds Oneida Community

1836
Georgia Female College, the first woman's college, founded

1837
Elijah P. Lovejoy killed in Alton, Illinois

1837
Horace Mann becomes Secretary of the Massachusetts Board of Education

1841
Brook Farm organized

1843
Dorothea Dix exposes treatment of mentally ill

1843
Racial segregation on trains in Massachusetts ends

1846
Maine adopts prohibition

1847
Frederick Douglass begins publication of *The North Star*

CHAPTER OUTLINE

During the decades from 1820 to 1850, the United States was caught up in a frantic wave of reform inspired by the near universal conviction that on this continent, free from the decayed, restraining hand of Europe, Americans could create a perfect civilization, at least something more perfect than what they and their forefathers had known in the Old World. Political independence seemed assured and the inhabitants of the republic could now get on with "the great experiment." The preamble to the Constitution, before it digressed into a mundane catalog of facts detailing how the machinery of government would work, held out the hope of "a more perfect Union," justice, domestic tranquility, and "the Blessings of Liberty." Paramount among those blessings was the exhilarating opportunity to try to reshape society to fit one's special design. It was sort of like playing God, or perhaps carrying out what one *knew* the Almighty willed be done. Of course, God spoke to different people in different ways, and as a result different people dreamed different dreams. The result was a hodgepodge of contradictions that did anything but "insure domestic Tranquility." For example, hostility towards blacks, immigrants, Indians, and some women reformers was widespread because either their presence or programs conflicted with what many Americans thought a "perfect" society should be. At the same time, millions were susceptible to evangelical appeals that fed one of the greatest outbursts of humanitarian reform our nation has ever known.

Why America should have experienced a great wave of humanitarian concern at this time is far from clear, but surely one of the causes was the traumatic social change brought about by industrialization. Urbanization and the growth of factories and an industrial economy were generating very visible extremes in wealth and poverty, attracting hordes of immigrants not easily assimilated and separating people not only from the soil but also from one another. These departures from traditional American living patterns only served to point up contradictions between practices and ideals. While in the eighteenth century, America was predominantly a stronghold of English colonists defending English liberties, in the pre-Civil War years America was being inundated by immigrants from other nations, especially from Ireland and Germany. Despite the fact that the agrarian idealism of Thomas Jefferson was still widely accepted and the greater part of the population was still rural and self-employed, it was apparent that in the years preceding the Civil War that America was becoming an industrial power. Even though America did not become an industrial power until the late nineteenth century, the social strains and stresses resulting from immigration, urbanization, and industrialization were clearly visible from the 1830s on.

Rather than reacting to these social changes with their heads and seeking political and institutional solutions, Americans responded with their hearts. While Europe was witnessing the birth of socialist parties calling for radical reform or even revolution, the United States (which had already had its Revolution) was undergoing a religious revival. Even utopian experiments that disavowed traditional religion harbored a guiding philosophy that was unmistakably religious in that it depended upon awakening the individual conscience rather than on engineering large social movements.

Religion

That religion was able to enter into so many aspects of American life is at least partially attributable to a new twist in theology. Calvinism, the prevailing orientation of the New England Puritans and of many other Protestant sects in the seventeenth and eighteenth centuries, preached a stern, unrelenting determinism—or, more exactly, a fatalism. According to Puritan theology, God had predestined—even before people were born—who would be saved and who would be damned. To argue the possibility that God did not know the outcome of individual destinies would limit His limitless powers. Although most practicing Puritans were not eager to confront the full implications of this doctrine, the Puritan belief in predestination did suggest that any person's particular efforts to reform his or her ways were ineffectual in achieving heavenly salvation.

During the eighteenth century, Calvinism was challenged by beliefs more in keeping with the views and hopes of an optimistic people imbued with Enlightenment principles and encouraged by scientific progress. Benjamin Franklin, for instance, proposed as early as 1731 a United Party for Virtue that would contain "the essentials of every known religion" such as the idea that "the most acceptable service of God is doing good to men." Franklin espoused Deism, the belief that God created the universe as a rational, self-perpetuating system. Humanity was gifted with reason, and society, if it behaved in an enlightened fashion, would reward virtue.

The Deists rejected the notion of a personal God who answers prayers, watches over individuals, and intervenes in human affairs. Because the deity proposed by this philosophy seemed impersonal, deism did not attract many people besides intellectuals. More widespread was Arminian theology which stressed a person's ability to achieve salvation, which combined with Deism to rehabilitate the belief that performing good works was "the most acceptable service of God," a tenet that Protestants had long doubted since predestination, at least in its purest form, made good works useless.

Revivalism

Just as America had been seized in the 1730s by a revivalist spirit, in the same way the country experienced a Second Great Awakening that began in 1795 in a series of camp meetings (open-air religious convocations) held in Kentucky and Tennessee. The new wave of revivalism lasted until 1837, and before it ran its course exerted a mighty impact on antebellum life. The Methodist, Baptist, and Presbyterian preachers who participated in this religious awakening were for the most part uneducated and unpolished speakers, but a training in theological niceties was not necessary to their message emphasizing personal redemption rather than doctrinal purity.

At about the time this movement began, seven religious bodies dominated the American scene, all of them having been battered to some extent by disestablishment, war, and the fast pace of events since 1775. These were (in order of approximate numerical strength) the Congregationalists, Presbyterians, Episcopalians, Methodists, Baptists, Quakers, and Roman Catholics. The Congregationalists and Presbyterians were virtually one faith; the Methodists, a society within the Episcopal fold until 1784. The latter, stunned by disestablishment and loss of the Methodists, failed to set up churches in new areas. In 1820, for example, there was no Episcopal minister in Indiana, Tennessee, Illinois, or Missouri, and probably none in any territory either.

At the outset of the Second Great Awakening, the Congregationalists and Presbyterians were the leading religious bodies in the United States, but because of doctrine, internal disputes, and poor leadership, neither reaped substantial benefits from the fervor that ensued. The Congregationalists tended to sit self-satisfied in New England, and the Presbyterians, although they certainly tried to exploit the frontier, were hampered by their rejection of emotionalism, insistence upon an educated clergy, and general unwillingness to adapt to the needs of the backwoodsman and his family.

Quaker scorn of slavery meant the Friends had little following in the South, and, like the Congregationalists, they made only feeble efforts to follow the course of migration westward. The Roman Catholics, in addition to traditional bases of strength in Maryland and various port cities, developed surprising strength in Kentucky (nineteen churches with 10,000 faithful in 1815), picked up hundreds of French and Spanish believers with the purchase of Louisiana, and gained even more adherents

Library of Congress.

Outdoor camp revivals such as this one were emotional affairs led by preachers who emphasized personal redemption.

with the increasing flow of migration from Ireland and Germany.

Yet the two faiths that profited most from revivalism and grew by leaps and bounds in all parts of the country were the Methodists and Baptists. The key to the success of the methodist, the leading religious body at mid-century (1.2 million), was the circuit rider. Close behind (with 750,000) were the Baptists who, free of ecclesiastical machinery, could establish a church almost at will and present God and Christ in down-to-earth terms that the common man could understand and appreciate.

The most powerful revivalist of the Second Great Awakening was Charles Grandison Finney. Wherever he preached or spoke, whether from his pulpit in New York's Broadway Tabernacle or later from his office as president of Oberlin College in Ohio, he inspired religious enthusiasm. According to another evangelist, Lyman Beecher, some 100,000 Americans joined churches in 1831 alone, and Finney was the man who moved many of them to repent. The most intense area of religious zeal was upstate New York, especially during Finney's revival campaigns there in 1826 and 1831.

Finney, like other evangelists, stressed that redemption was possible for everyone. By repenting of past sins and believing in Jesus Christ, salvation could be secured. Finney rejected Calvinist determinism and advocated the idea that both sin and salvation are freely chosen behavior. By 1831, Finney had welded his evangelism to the

Allen Memorial Art Museum, Oberlin College.

Charles Grandison Finney was an immensely successful revivalist whose emphasis on benevolence was a factor in shaping the reform spirit in antebellum America.

general reform movement in America as he dwelt upon the sins of men in society rather than the specific sins of the men themselves. This concept of social responsibility or moral stewardship began to have a direct impact on the reform impulse of those decades.

Benevolent Societies

Since religion is part of the life of almost every element in society, it cannot be said to represent any one set of interests alone. Indeed, the religious impulse that eventually gave rise to reform initially manifested itself as a politically and socially conservative movement. Between the end of the War of 1812 and 1830, conservative moral reformers established a number of benevolent societies. In the eyes of these people—generally industrialists, merchants, bankers, or lawyers who were often disgruntled Federalists from the Northeast—the country was in serious trouble. The tide of immigrants, especially Catholics, the rise of new political parties and the corresponding decline of the Federalists, and the emergence of the West as the fastest-growing section of the nation—all of these factors dismayed such individuals. The country was, they thought, "going straight to Hell!" In an effort to defeat Catholicism; to ensure the continued rule of the wealthy, the educated, and the wellborn; and to control the supposedly lawless and godless West through evangelism, about a dozen great interdenominational societies appeared. The members were primarily Presbyterians, Congregationalists, and a smaller number of Methodists, Baptists, and Episcopalians.

Among these benevolent associations were the American Education Society, founded in Boston in 1815 to subsidize the education of future ministers, and the American Bible Society, which in 1816 began distributing millions of copies of the Bible throughout the nation. In 1824 the American Sunday School Union was established in Philadelphia to send missionaries to set up schools; between 1825 and 1860 the American Tract Society issued some 200 million religious books and pamphlets; and in 1826 the American Home Missionary Society began to subsidize poor congregations, giving them funds with which to pay their pastors.

The purpose of all these societies was to perpetuate established interpretations of morality and decency in a period of great social change. Evangelical Protestantism became a vehicle for promoting general stability and order. Former Federalists and their allies who backed the benevolent societies had long believed that the country should be ruled by a few superior people; now that the political power of the privileged was threatened, they hoped to retain control through religion. The moral tenets of Christianity somehow would civilize and subdue the West, and pacify the urban poor, who were seething with unrest. As an agent of the Tract Society wrote, Christianity would "bridge over the dangerous chasm between the rich and the poor; so that instead of mobs and outbreaks destroying . . . life and property, there will be between these two great classes a reciproca-

Museum of the City of New York.

The American Tract Society and various state organizations disseminated religious literature throughout the nation. This illustration is from an 1858 certificate of lifetime membership in the New York City Tract Society; the membership cost $50.

From the original in the New Jersey Historical Society, Gift of the estate of Elizabeth Mary Frelinghuysen, 1967.

Theodore Frelinghuysen was active in the benevolent societies and was known as the "Christian statesman".

tion of confidence and good feeling, as there will be also a ready recognition of their mutual dependence, their harmonious interests, and their immortal brotherhood."

Lay officers of these societies were men of rising social and economic station such as industrialist Anson G. Phelps (1781–1853), whose firm was involved in manufacturing, railroads, and copper and iron mining, and Theodore Frelinghuysen (1787–1862), a New Jersey lawyer who, while serving as United States Senator from 1829 to 1835, delivered a six-hour speech condemning the Indian Removal Bill of 1830. His objections to the bill earned him the nickname, "Christian Statesman." From 1846 until his death in 1862, he was president of the American Bible Society, and at other times he served as an officer of the American Tract Society, the American Sunday School Union, and the American Temperance Union.

Unitarianism

During the 1820s and 1830s the bulwark of Calvinism was thoroughly dismantled by a little man who was an invalid all his life. William Ellery Channing (1780–1842) may have been sickly in body, but his mind reshaped American theology. Born in Rhode Island, raised by stern Calvinist parents, and educated at Harvard, Channing became the minister of Boston's Federal Street Congregation. From his pulpit he preached a new doctrine that human beings had free will and were rational ("God has given us a rational nature and will call us to account for it," he said). At the same time, he retained the idea of a personal God, the authority of Scripture, and the existence of miracles.

Channing, however, was more impressive for the spirit of his beliefs than for his theological innovations. Squarely on the side of the ordinary citizen, Channing created a religion of optimism and common sense for the average American. He was father of Unitarianism (so-called because he and his followers rejected the belief in the Trinity as a concept not justified by Scripture and impossible to understand). Although the Unitarian de-

Library of Congress.

William Ellery Channing, the father of Unitarianism.

nomination never became numerous, it exerted a great influence on such New England thinkers as Ralph Waldo Emerson and ultimately on a vast Christian public. The main thrust of Channing's religion was its emphasis on man's divine nature, his resemblance to his maker. Even God was refashioned from a stern Puritan patriarch into a true nineteenth-century Democrat: "It is not because his will is irresistible, but because his will is the perfection of virtue, that we pay him allegiance. We cannot bow before a being however great who governs tyrannically," Channing declared. And having spurned tyranny in 1776, Americans found it easy (and comforting) to accept such views. One might even interpret this phenomenon as the "Americanization" of God.

Transcendentalism and Perfectionism

Unitarianism was, however, too much the faith of established, well-to-do New Englanders to reach the masses. But its tenets reached a broader audience through a philosophical movement known as transcendentalism.

The leader of transcendentalism was Ralph Waldo Emerson (1803–1882), the descendant of a long line of ministers who himself served the Second Church of Boston until 1832, when he resigned because he felt he could no longer administer the bread and the wine in the Lord's Supper—articles of faith in which he no longer believed.

Emerson was thirty when he traveled to England and became a friend of the historian Thomas Carlyle, the poet Samuel Taylor Coleridge (who had introduced the English to German idealism), and the poet William Wordsworth. His contact with English Romanticism (and indirectly with German philosophy) gave him a new approach to nature. When he returned to Boston, Emerson made public addresses in which he advanced the Romantic idea that human beings are at the center of the world, godlike creatures who can fully realize their divinity by immersing themselves in lessons to be drawn from nature. Emerson attacked the formalities of established religion in a shocking speech to the graduating class of the Divinity College at Cambridge. In the place of organized religion, he exalted instinct, insight, and intuition. Transcendentalism stressed that the mind and soul can go beyond all intellectual limitations and grasp intuitively the realities of life. The transcendentalists assumed that human nature is perfectible—and this stand naturally linked them to the reform movement. In the

National Archives, Washington D.C.

Ralph Waldo Emerson, the leader of Transcendentalism.

1840s Emerson allied himself (though with reservations) with the abolitionists; he thought the slave must elevate himself and sincerely doubted whether this was possible. But, by the late 1850s his antislavery position was no longer equivocal in any way, and Emerson openly championed emancipation.

Emerson associated with many of the great minds of his day, including Margaret Fuller, Henry David Thoreau, James Russell Lowell, and Nathaniel Hawthorne. But his activities were not confined to a small circle of intellectuals. He made his living by giving public lectures across the country, and he went on many speaking tours of the West in particular. Even more people read his poems and printed essays.

What made the transcendentalists characteristic of their age was their emphasis on personal morality. For them true reform emanated from the individual and worked outward through the family, the community, and finally into the social and political life of the nation. As Emerson noted in one of his essays, "God enters by a private door into every individual."

Humanitarian Reform

While benevolent societies used reform and religion as a means of social control, as a way of preserving the status quo, a more dynamic and liberal reform movement sought to change American society radically for the better. These reformers had a high, undauntable sense of optimism. They were certain that America's mission was to set a moral example for the rest of the world, and they were eager to make that example as glowing as possible. Emerson asked, "What is man born for, but to be a Reformer, a Remaker of what man has made?" and many of his fellow Americans could only agree with this sentiment. Science, technology, democracy were all American pursuits that were prospering and that suggested progress was boundless; this was the orientation derived from the Enlightenment. The great rebirth of religious fervor contributed to the growing sense that human nature was perfectible; if only the conscience of the sinner could be awakened, he or she could be made to reform. Once saved, the sinner could demonstrate salvation in performing good works.

The Temperance Movement

One of the most energetic reform activities in the antebellum period was the temperance movement (not necessarily total abstinence from all alcoholic intake). The crusade against "ardent spirits" was launched in the pulpit by evangelists who warned that excessive drinking was sinful (the temperance movement was, according to one stalwart, "Christ's work. . . , a holy war, and every true soldier of the Cross will fight in it"). Others argued that drinking made voters unsuited for choosing their leaders wisely; as Lyman Beecher put it, drink could "dig the grave of our liberties and entomb our glory."

The most popular argument against drink was that it directly contributed to poverty. Not only was the urban worker kept by alcoholism in his wretched state, incapable of rising in the world and only with difficulty retaining his miserable job, but his family also suffered. Employers complained of frequent absenteeism and accidents owing to liquor. Much of the violence of the cities, temperance workers argued, could be attributed to drunkenness.

Modern commentators on the temperance movement sometimes discuss it with a smirk, as though it were merely an outgrowth of "Victorian" prudishness. But a closer look reveals that the problem of heavy drinking was immense in eighteenth-and early nineteenth-century America. Taverns virtually lined the turnpikes, a traveler in the West rarely could find an inn where he would not be kept awake all night by drunken brawls, and every public occasion (even the installation of a new minister in a church) called for a liberal round of drinks. Early U.S. census reports estimate that in 1792 the per capita production of spirits was 2.5 gallons a year; by 1823, the figure had risen to 7.5 gallons. Almost every grocery store sold beer or liquor, and the 1810 census revealed there were 14,000 distilleries in the country, producing some 25 million gallons of liquor every year, for which the public spent about $12 million—more than the total budget of the federal government. Even in staid Boston there was one grogshop for every twenty-one adult men. The old American tradition of heavy drinking was only exacerbated with the influx of German beer-drinking and Irish whiskey-drinking immigrants who believed in a festive and none-too-dry Sabbath, preceded often by an equally uproarious Saturday evening.

Why Americans drank so much is a question that has elicited many theories. Liquor was, first of all, cheap and plentiful; in the early days of the West, for instance, whiskey was used as currency and even taxes and the salaries of ministers were paid in liquor. In rural areas many farmers ran stills, which helped to fend off boredom, fatigue, and loneliness. In the cities the poverty and confusion of people newly arrived from American farms or from Europe could be forgotten, at least for a moment, in drink. Also, drinking was often a cultural tradition, one means of keeping alive "old ways." The problem was that imbibing was done on a massive scale, and each group—native Americans, the Irish, Germans, and so on—had their favorite drinks and ingrained social habits that rivals often found offensive and crude.

To reformers, this cause-and-effect pattern seemed strange; in their eyes liquor was not a symptom of poverty but rather the disease that created it. During the antebellum period, Americans were not equipped conceptually to see poverty as anything but the result of vice or laziness on the part of the underprivileged; to be poor was, in some sense, to be immoral. For the temperance worker liquor—rather than low wages, unemployment, or lack of opportunity—was the cause of urban poverty.

Temperance societies sprang up across the country, all of them working hard to convince Americans to sign the pledge against drinking. As early as 1826 a broader society, known as the American Society for the Promotion of Temperance, was formed in Boston. It was a dynamic group that sent lecturers throughout the country, published numerous pamphlets, placed stories in newspapers, and awarded prizes for the best temperance essays. By 1835, 3,000 ministers had signed a pledge promising to abstain altogether from liquor; with the aid of a large number of women supporters, schoolteachers, and hundreds of doctors, these ministers, in turn, campaigned for the cause. Local, state, and national temperance meetings were held in the early 1830s. A congressional society was formed to exert a moral influence upon the nation. Temperance hotels accommodated travelers who had taken the pledge. College students created their own temperance societies and graduation exercises, previously riotous brawls, turned into sober occasions.

In 1836 the first national convention of the American Temperance Union, a federation of temperance societies, met, and it was during this convocation that the movement split into two factions. The controversy was over how to define temperance. The majority of the delegates opposed only the consumption of hard liquor or "ardent spirits"; but they stopped short of demanding total abstinence. A radical minority (the "ultras") wished to broaden the abstinence pledge to include malt and fermented liquors, even wine taken during communion. This group supported legislative action to ban the production and retailing of all alcoholic beverages and introduced a resolution that "the traffice in ardent spirits, as a

The *Drunkard's Progress,* a lithograph published in 1846, when Neal Dow was crusading for prohibition.

Library of Congress.

drink, is *morally wrong;* and that the inhabitants of cities, towns, and other local communities, should be permitted by law to prohibit the said traffic within their respective jurisdictions."

The dissension aroused by this proposal contributed to the decline of the temperance movement, as did the Panic of 1837, which sapped the energy from all kinds of reform activity. In the South the temperance movement never really caught on, primarily because leading advocates of temperance in the North also were abolitionists.

The cause of temperance, however, received new inspiration as a result of a dramatic incident in 1840. In April of that year six men who met frequently to drink and gamble in Chase's Tavern in Baltimore sent a few of their number, as a joke, to attend a temperance lecture in a nearby church. Surprisingly, the pranksters were deeply moved by the arguments advanced by the lecturer and spent the entire night discussing their own drinking. They decided to abstain entirely from then on and proudly proclaimed themselves reformed drunkards. Naming themselves the Washingtonians (after the first President of the country), they set as their goal the salvation of unregenerate drunkards. By the end of the year, more than a thousand drunkards had joined the Washingtonians in Baltimore alone and soon missionaries were being dispatched to every state. The revivalist appeal of a reformed drunkard seeking the salvation of other drunkards was astonishingly effective.

One result of a resurgent temperance movement was a new effort to legislate an end to the traffic of "ardent spirits." Several states experimented with regulating intoxicants. Enthusiasm for prohibition ran especially high in Maine; under the leadership of Neal Dow, that state passed the first comprehensive statewide prohibition act in 1846, a measure that was strengthened five years later. In 1845 New York approved a bill giving local communities the option to forbid the sale of alcohol. Soon five-sixths of the state voted against licensing liquor stores, although the communities rescinded their hasty action in 1847. In 1852 the legislatures of Vermont and Rhode Island enacted statewide prohibition. Michigan became dry in 1853; Connecticut and New York in 1854; and New Hampshire, Tennessee, Delaware, Illinois, Indiana, Iowa and Wisconsin by 1855. By the end of the 1850s, thirteen states had approved prohibition legislation. The statutes on the books were flagrantly ignored, however, and the sale of hard liquor continued in scores of communities. Also, as numerous states learned, one group of legislators could quickly undo the work of their predecessors. By 1868, only Maine still retained its law establishing statewide prohibition.

Although the temperance crusade was not a great success, it did make Americans conscious of the evils of excessive drinking. Yet being aware of evils and shunning them are two quite different things. From 1850 to 1860, the decade when reformers scored their most impressive legislative victories, annual per capita consumption of whiskey, wine, and beer grew from 4.08 to 6.43 gallons. Beer consumption jumped almost threefold as German beer gardens and breweries flourished as never before. One thing the temperance movement had accomplished, however, was the training of a large number of men and women, black and white, in the techniques of organizing and propagandizing for reform. Many of these temperance advocates later distinguished themselves in other reform activities.

Wards of the State

One of the most significant areas of reform in the antebellum period was the movement to ameliorate the conditions of social offenders, paupers, deaf-mutes, the blind, the insane, and the retarded. The fervent belief of the humanitarian reformers that human beings were bascially good and rational except when corrupted by evil institutions and a bad environment produced dramatic innovations in the teatment of prisoners, delinquents, dependent children, and other wards of the state.

Penal reform was influenced by the idea that human beings were made antisocial by the society about them. Rather than being born criminal, offenders learned to be that way by imitating bad examples. This notion lay behind the theory of solitary confinement, considered humane in the nineteenth century, though today most people regard it as cruel. In the eighteenth century (and well into the nineteenth) prisoners were confined in large groups, men and women together, young and old, debtors with hardened criminals. This mixture of people allowed confirmed wrongdoers to corrupt first offenders. Isolated cells were introduced in 1829 in the construction of Pennsylvania's new Eastern State Penitentiary just outside Philadelphia; though theoretically the cells were designed to make the prisoner reflect on his wrongdoing and to isolate him from bad influences, in actuality the system caused many prisoners to suffer from extreme

Library of Congress.

Neal Dow
(1804–1897)

The "Napoleon of Temperance," father of the Maine Law, and a leading citizen of his native Portland for several decades, Neal Dow was a well-to-do businessman and landowner who waged an unending campaign against liquor and spirits in all forms, tobacco, slavery, and failure to observe the Sabbath in proper fashion. Temperance, however, was his special adversary, and it was an on-going battle because no legislation, no matter how contrived, could be properly enforced if local authorities winked at bootleggers and "blind tigers" (illicit saloons). During Dow's long life, most Maine residents undoubtedly endorsed his views, but lumberjacks piling into brawling cities such as Bangor after a season in the woods and sailors ashore for a few hours of fun made a mockery of most efforts to regulate the sale of whiskey, rum, and beer.

Dow, born into a family of English-Quaker descent, wanted to be a lawyer, but after basic academic schooling he entered his father's tanning business. A short, alert man (5 ft. 6 in.), Dow soon was married, raising a family, and in the thick of civic affairs; and, as his real estate investments grew, he devoted more and more time to thwarting Demon Rum. Soon a center of controversy, Dow took boxing lessons in order to protect himself, if necessary.

In 1846 Maine passed an anti-liquor law which authorities were unable or unwilling to enforce. Five years later, as mayor of Portland, Dow engineered more stringent measures at both local and state levels. These moves won him national, even international attention as the prime spokesman for temperance.

During the Civil War, Dow became a colonel in the Maine Volunteers, was twice wounded and captured while recuperating behind Union lines, but eventually was exchanged for Robert E. Lee's nephew, Fitzhugh Lee, later governor of Virginia. With peace, Dow resumed the liquor fight, running for President on the Prohibition party ticket in 1880.

A spirited campaigner almost until his death, Neal Dow wrote extensively and accumulated a fine library. His battles against evil were waged on many fronts; even celebrities who were guests in his home had to conform to his views. In 1885, for example, neighbors watched with amusement as the Reverend Phillips Brooks leaned far out of a bedroom window to puff contentedly, if precariously, on a huge cigar. ■

psychological tension and evidence signs of insanity. Even before this new facility opened, critics were alarmed by the harshness of such confinement.

In New York state, the prison that opened at Auburn in 1816 confined prisoners in tiny cells at night but gathered them by day in general workshops—or hired them out as contract labor. This contract labor arrangement turned the prison into a paying concern; in 1829 its operating expenses were about $34,000, but its receipts were nearly $40,000. Profits were given to prisoners when their sentences were up in order to encourage them to enter an honest occupation. Life at Auburn was harsh indeed. Convicts had to remain silent at all times, shuffle to and from work with one hand on the shoulder of the person in front of them, and risk flogging for even the most minor violation. These two systems—inmate silence and separate confinement—were widely imitated in other states, but by mid-century the Auburn method of silence had triumphed over that of Pennsylvania.

Prison reform naturally led to the notion that juvenile offenders might be better treated in correctional institutions. Reform schools were started in which an equal emphasis was placed on education and moral rehabilitation. New York took the lead and built the New York House of Refuge in 1825. In the next few years, other areas of the Northeast established institutions for juvenile delinquents (in 1847 Massachusetts started the first home for girls). By 1850 Americans generally accepted the principle that a youthful offender should be a ward of the state.

Imprisonment for debt also came under attack, especially after the depression in 1819 sent many new debtors to jail. In 1816, even before the panic, there were almost two thousand imprisoned debtors in New York alone, half of them confined for debts of less than $50. Imprisoning debtors was not only cruel but also futile and self-defeating, since in jail the debtor could not earn the money necessary for paying his creditors. In effect, debtors' prisons held people for ransom: some relative usually came forward and paid the debt so an individual could be released.

In 1817 New York passed a law making $25 the lowest amount for which a debtor could be sentenced. Other states imitated New York, some of them adding clauses stipulating that women could not be imprisoned for any amount of indebtedness. In 1821 Kentucky became the first state to abolish imprisonment for debt altogether. A western state where many small farmers had fallen into debt during the Panic of 1819, Kentucky legislators simply responded to the interest and needs of their constituents. In older states of the East, workingmen's parties fought vigorously for abolishment of imprisonment for debt, but the merchants and lawyers there campaigned to retain the practice. Richard Mentor Johnson (1781–1850), a native Kentuckian sponsored a bill in his state that ended imprisonment for debt. With the support of President Andrew Jackson, he championed bills in Congress to abolish imprisonment for debt in federal court actions. In 1832 his proposal became federal law. That same year, New York abolished imprisonment for debt and within a decade it was eliminated from the statute books of almost all of the states.

The mentally ill also received the attention of the reformers. In fact, an interest in the treatment of the insane grew out of prison reform, since the mentally ill were often incarcerated with prisoners. Before the Enlightenment, the general public had all too often thought that insanity robbed an individual of human status, reducing him or her to bestiality. But during the Enlightenment, a few doctors came to see that the insane were not monsters or beasts. As Phillipe Pinel, a French physician, wrote, the insane man "is but one of ourselves, only a little more so. Underneath his wildest paroxysms there is a germ, at least, of rationality and of personal accountability. To believe in this, to seek for it, stimulate it, build it up—here lies the only way of delivering him out of the fatal bondage in which he is held."

The Quakers opened the first asylum to experiment with more humane forms of treatment in Philadelphia in 1817. In 1836 New York built a state lunatic asylum at Utica to house insane patients formerly lodged in almshouses and jails. A few other institutions that offered more humane treatment to the mentally ill opened during the next few years.

But as late as 1841, most of the insane in America still were brutally neglected and mistreated. Large numbers were housed in cages, jail cells, poorhouses, and even in outhouses. After a chance visit to the women's division of the House of Correction in East Cambridge, Massachusetts, Dorothea Dix (1802–1887), a schoolteacher, was so moved by the spectacle of suffering she observed that she resolved to conduct an investigation of the plight of the insane. In 1843 she presented a report of conditions endured by the indigent insane in almshouses and

Library of Congress.

Dorothea Dix, a pioneer in the movement to provide specialized treatment for the insane.

local jails throughout Massachusetts. She declared in blunt tones, "I tell what I have seen," and called attention "to the *present* state of insane persons confined within the Commonwealth, in *cages, closets, cellars, stalls, pens! Chained, naked, beaten with rods, and lashed into obedience!*"

Dix's exposé prompted the Massachusetts legislature to appropriate funds to build a large addition to a hospital for the insane. Her success in that state was followed by similar triumphs in other parts of the country. She was aided in her campaign by Samuel Gridley Howe (1801-1876), one of the great humanitarians of the day. He not only aided Dix but also pioneered in the education of the blind, the deaf-mutes, and the mentally retarded. He instructed blind children in reading with the aid of raised letters—the Braille system of raised dots representing characters, which was invented in France, was not introduced until later in the century—and he taught deaf-mutes to speak rather than to rely exclusively on sign language.

In the 1850s Dix vainly attempted to obtain land from Congress for institutions for the care of the insane. Since land had been given for educational purposes and some citizens thought it should be granted to railroads to promote construction, she believed the federal government might provide for national hospitals as well. The bill passed after a hard fight but was vetoed by President Franklin Pierce. In his opinion, it was unwise for the federal government to support the nation's poor and unconstitutional to grant land for such purposes. Only long after the Civil War was her ambition to build such institutions realized. When she died in 1887, an American doctor wrote, "There has died and been laid to rest in the most quiet, unostentatious way the most useful and distinguished woman America has yet produced."

Prison reform and improvement in the treatment of the afflicted and handicapped reflected the antebellum conviction that every aspect of human existence—from the soul of the sinner to the ravings of the lunatic—could be cured. Christian charity, Enlightenment optimism, and scientific confidence had come together to usher in an age of unbounded confidence—what has been dubbed "the cult of curability."

The Peace Movement

Confidence in the perfectibility of human nature naturally led American reformers to condemn warfare and espouse pacifism. As early as 1783, Benjamin Franklin wrote that "there never was a good war or a bad peace," and ten years later another Philadelphian, the universal reformer, Benjamin Rush, urged the federal government to establish a Peace Department. As he described it: "In the lobby of this office let there be painted the representations of all the common military instruments of death; also human skulls, broken bones, unveined and putrefying dead bodies. . . . Above all this group of woful [*sic*] figures, let the following words be inserted in red characters, to represent human blood:—'NATIONAL GLORY'."

The War of 1812 spawned new pacifists. David Low Dodge, a New York merchant, condemned war in his little book published in 1815, *War Inconsistent with the Religion of Jesus Christ,* and at about the same time a New England clergyman, Noah Worcester, proposed that all international disputes should be settled peaceably and by an international congress and tribune.

A truly organized peace movement, however, emerged only in 1828 when William Ladd (1778-1841), a retired merchant living in Maine, founded the American Peace Society. Although Ladd's enthusiasm was inexhaustible (he once said, "They might as well throw snowballs into the crater of Vesuvius in the hopes of extinguishing it as to expect to cool me"), the peace movement was torn by internal strife after 1837. Two factions arose: one a forceful minority that condemned all war, recommended nonresistance to violence, and recognized no government as legitimate; and the other that simply condemned "offensive" wars. This second faction, for instance, maintained that the uprisings of Indians against white encroachments such as the Seminole War in Florida were justified—in fact, were "defensive" wars that should be applauded.

Although sympathetic to the conditions of American Indians and black slaves in revolt, William Lloyd Garrison (1805-1879) believed in moral suasion rather than force. Garrison, a nearsighted young man from a broken, poverty-stricken home, served a seven-year apprenticeship on the Newburyport (Mass.) *Herald.* In 1826 he set up his own ill-fated newspaper in that seaport community, remembered today only because the first verses of John Greenleaf Whittier (then a shoemaker's apprentice) appeared in its pages. Moving on to Boston, Garrison dabbled not only in peace reform, but temperance and abolition as well. The latter eventually became his road to fame and national recognition. By the late 1830s, Garrison advocated absolute nonresistance and total nonparticipation in government. With other radical pacifists, Garrison withdrew from the American Peace Society in 1838 and founded the New England Non-Resistance Society. He argued that all believers in a Christ who had preached the Sermon on the Mount must "suffer themselves to be defrauded, calumniated and barbarously treated, without resorting either to their own physical energies, or to the force of human law, for restitution or punishment."

Most pacifists, however, remained within the American Peace Society. The entire peace movement, whether preaching nonresistance or simply an end to wars of aggression, was thrown into confusion by the Mexican War, which broke out in 1846. One strong opponent of the war was Charles Sumner (1811-1874) of Massachusetts; he feared the annexation of potential slave territory in the Southwest. In Boston on the Fourth of July, 1845, Sumner had given a rousing oration in which he concluded that "War is utterly and irreconcilably inconsistent with true grandeur."

Courtesy Chicago Historical Society.

William Lloyd Garrison, pacifist and abolitionist.

Shortly thereafter, Elihu Burritt (1810-1879), a blacksmith, who had taught himself Latin, Greek, Hebrew, French, German, Spanish, and Italian, founded the League of Universal Brotherhood in 1846. This man, called "the Learned Blacksmith," became an advocate of international peace after a study of languages and science convinced him that all people are interdependent. He attempted to secure pledges from the members of his League that they would not serve in the military and would not support war in any way. Although Burritt enlisted some 30,000 converts in England, his campaign was a failure in America. By 1850, the peace movement was dying out in the United States. For scores of pacifists the cause of abolition was far more important than the cause of peace, and as the Civil War approached, many reformers (including Garrison) discarded their pacifist sentiments.

Abolitionism

Of all the reform movements of the antebellum period, abolitionism was the most explosive since it threatened the economic basis of the South. Yet, given the widespread belief that progress was unlimited and perfection inevitable, the antislavery movement was only natural.

The crusade encompassed many different schemes for freeing the slaves. The mildest plans called for planters to free their slaves voluntarily, without legal pressure, and in return the slaveowners would be compensated for their financial loss, but how and by whom was never quite clear. The emancipated slaves presumably would go back to Africa, where they would become colonists in a new country. Some abolitionists called for compulsory manumission of all slaves, suggesting that slaveowners be compensated by the various state governments. The most extreme schemes demanded immediate, uncompensated emancipation by federal law.

Talk of freeing the slaves gained momentum in America for a time as a result of the natural rights philosophy of the Revolutionary period. George Washington, like many other liberal southern planters, freed his slaves in his will upon his death. His neighbor in Virginia, George Mason (1725-1792), who owned 300 slaves, went so far as to declare that slavery exerted a damaging effect on the character of the slaveholder and was, therefore, a school of tyranny for future leaders of the South.

One obstacle always stymied even those most troubled by slavery—what was to be done with the slaves once they were freed? For no matter how sympathetic some whites were to the plight of the slaves, most feared that a large, free black population could not be integrated into American society.

The first Southerners to work actively for emancipation were the Quakers of the upper South. They tirelessly distributed antislavery literature, and in 1819 Elihu Embree (1782-1820), a Quaker from Tennessee, began to publish the *Manumission Intelligencer* (later the *Emancipator*), the first periodical in America dedicated exclusively to abolitionism. Other publications soon appeared, including the *Genuis of Universal Emancipation*, published by Benjamin Lundy (1789-1839) in Baltimore in the 1820s. To agitate for abolition, Quakers in the upper South organized societies that called for gradual abolition of slavery and an immediate improvement of the lives and fortunes of slaves by repealing laws that forbade whites to educate them. The number of abolition societies grew rapidly in the South. By 1827 three southern states—North Carolina, Tennessee, and Virginia—had more abolition societies than existed in the North. In addition to participating in such societies, Quakers in the South protested slavery by boycotting products made with slave labor and by helping runaway slaves.

The movement to send freed slaves to Africa resulted in the founding of the American Colonization Society in 1817. This organization, with its headquarters in Washington, D.C., purchased land in Africa and created the Republic of Liberia ("Land of Freedom") with its capital at Monrovia (named after President Monroe, who supported this colonization plan). The effort was a failure, however, because it did not receive federal support, transportation to Africa was too costly, and former slaves opposed the undertaking. As a result, though the United States had a slave population of nearly four million in 1860, only about 15,000 blacks had moved to Liberia—and many of these soon died from tropical diseases.

The rise of evangelical religion and the spirit of reform caused abolitionists in the North to abandon a gradual approach and demand an *immediate* end to slavery. This doctrine, called "immediatism," was championed by the most famous abolitionist of all, William Lloyd Garrison. About 1828 Garrison met Benjamin Lundy and the next year began to work with this Quaker on his *Genuis for Universal Emancipation.* In 1831 Garrison founded his own paper, the militant *Liberator,* published in Boston. In the very first issue he announced why he was directing his publication to readers in the North: "During my recent tour for the purpose of exciting the minds of the people by a series of discourses on the subject of slavery, every place that I visited gave fresh evidence of the fact that a greater revolution in public sentiment was to be effected in the free states—*and particularly in New England*—than at [*sic*] the South. I found contempt more bitter, opposition more active, detraction more relentless, prejudice more stubborn, and

Library of Congress.

The masthead from *The Liberator,* published in Boston by William Lloyd Garrison. Most of the subscribers to this abolitionist paper were free blacks in the North.

apathy more frozen, than among the slave owners themselves."

Garrison told his readers that moderation in the face of such a great sin as slavery was unthinkable. As he put it, "Tell the mother to gradually extricate her babe from the fire into which it has fallen, but urge me not to use moderation in a cause like the present." Garrison's approach, as embodied in the American Anti-Slavery Society, which he helped found in 1833, demanded immediate abolition without compensation on the grounds that, since slavery is immoral, slaveholders should not be rewarded for their sinful behavior. Garrison and his followers opposed colonization in Africa and fought to achieve full equality for blacks within the American social system. And, the Garrisonians pursued these goals with militant determination; Garrison himself announced, "I am earnest—I will not equivocate—I will not excuse—I will not retreat a single inch—AND I WILL BE HEARD."

Garrison's assault, coupled with the shock waves from the Nat Turner rebellion in Virginia in 1831, marks a turning point in this crusade; and, as a result, the 1830s became a watershed in the saga of American reform. Within a decade or so, backed by experienced workers and some 1,350 societies with a quarter of a million members, abolition was a force to be reckoned with; and, as antislavery agitation moved from the local to national level and grew more and more political, it also emerged as *the* reform. Nearly all other movements had to mark time until this great question was resolved. Three main centers of abolitionist strength emerged: New England dominated by Garrison, New York state where wealthy Manhattan philanthropists such as Lewis and Arthur Tappan provided considerable assistance, and Ohio with Lane Seminary and Oberlin College as training grounds for both leaders and workers. Since the movement grew so fast, great diversity as well as conflicts and contradictions were evident. Some societies were segregated and others barred blacks from membership. By no means did all abolitionists subscribe to Garrison's "immediatism," and many were unsure how to play their cards in the political arena.

Thousands of northern whites, who were alarmed by the turmoil of this antislavery protest, detested Garrison and frequently mobbed him when he gave public speeches. His chief supporters were free blacks. Unlike many reformers, Garrison felt at home among blacks and they with him; his demand for black equality in northern white society was repugnant to the vast majority of Yankees. Even many of his fellow abolitionists were dismayed by Garrison's support of other controversial causes such as women's rights.

The abolitionists used various means, not unlike the tactics of civil rights workers in the 1960s, to fight prejudice. In 1841 and 1842, fifty abolitionists, both white and black, protested segregated trains in Massachusetts by sitting indiscriminately in cars reserved for each race. A boycott of the trains, coupled with a threat of coercive legislation against segregation, led the railroads in that state to desegregate by 1843. Some abolitionists also attempted to integrate churches (most blacks were forced to occupy the "Negro pews" in the backs of churches or in balconies). They believed that the various Christian sects were responsible in large measure for the perpetuation of slavery; if the churches would band together and condemn slavery, they argued, blacks would soon be set free. By the end of the 1840s, abolitionists had integrated hundreds of churches in the North, though many blacks, frustrated by the ill will they continued to meet, began to organize their own sects and independent houses of worship. Segregation in northern schools also was very widespread, and invariably the blacks had inferior primary schools, if any at all. By the 1840s, however, most of the secondary schools and half of the institutions of higher learning in New England were accepting black students.

Abolitionists attempted to attack slavery at its economic roots by boycotting all produce made or raised by slave labor. Yet another abolitionist strategy was to call for the voluntary dissolution of the Union. As the abolitionist Wendell Phillips (1811–1884) explained, "To propose a dissolution of the Union is the best way of holding up such a mirror to the national mind, as makes it to see its own deformity. . . . Disunion startles a man to thought. It takes a lazy abolitionist by the throat, and thunders in his ear, '*Thou* are the slaveholder'."

Garrison was the most outspoken abolitionist, but not always the most effective, since his techniques often alarmed white Northerners, even those sympathetic to his general views. Charles G. Finney, the well-known evangelist, won many supporters to the cause of antislavery through his religious approach. And Theodore Dwight Weld (1803–1895) may have secured more converts to abolitionism than any other figure of his day. He was a Presbyterian evangelist who first preached with Finney; in 1830 Weld declared war on slavery. After that, not only did he preach abolitionism throughout the West but he also organized a band of seventy agents of the American Anti-Slavery Society. After training them for weeks, he sent them on speaking tours in the East and the Old Northwest. Weld and his band of preachers were remarkably successful in reaching ordinary citizens. They saturated towns with lecturers until a sufficient number of converts were found to form local abolition societies.

Abolitionist propaganda struck Southerners, especially after Nat Turner's revolt in 1831, as a dangerous and inflammatory encouragement of slave uprisings. In the summer of 1835, a mob of whites in Charleston, South Carolina destroyed sacks of mail containing abolitionist literature. In response to pressure from southern whites, President Andrew Jackson recommended to Congress in December 1835 that it prohibit circulation through the mail in the South of all "incendiary publications" designed to promote slave insurrections. The measure was not adopted, but from 1836 until the eve of the Civil War, the U.S. Post Office permitted the extralegal censorship of the mails. Local postmasters in the South reviewed and destroyed publications they thought offensive.

In an effort to silence the abolitionists, southern influence in the House of Representatives produced a gag rule, which was in force between 1836 and 1844. Under this rule, petitions against slavery were automatically tabled without debate so that the subject of abolition could not be discussed in Congress. The fight against tabling was led by former president John Quincy Adams, who was now a congressman from his native state of Massachusetts. Converted to the antislavery cause by Theodore Dwight Weld, Adams never was an abolitionist stalwart, but he was greatly concerned over the rights of citizens to petition Congress on any subject. And, during those eight years when the gag rule was in force, he presented hundreds of petitions against slavery, many of them from women in various states. In the flood of papers from his desk were suggestions for dissolving the Union, plans for a huge "Chinese Wall" between the North and the South, and calls for his own ouster from the House. All were duly laid aside according to the prevailing gag rule since his opponents assumed any petition he offered related to slavery.

Even in the North abolitionists found considerable opposition. In 1835, when an English abolitionist canceled a speech in Boston, Garrison spoke in his place. An angry mob of several thousand people, who had come to tar-and-feather the Englishman, vented their anger on Garrison, dragging him through the streets with a rope around his neck. In Alton, Illinois, the abolitionist newspaper editor, Elijah P. Lovejoy (1802–1837) defied the townspeople and published fiery articles calling for an

Library of Congress.

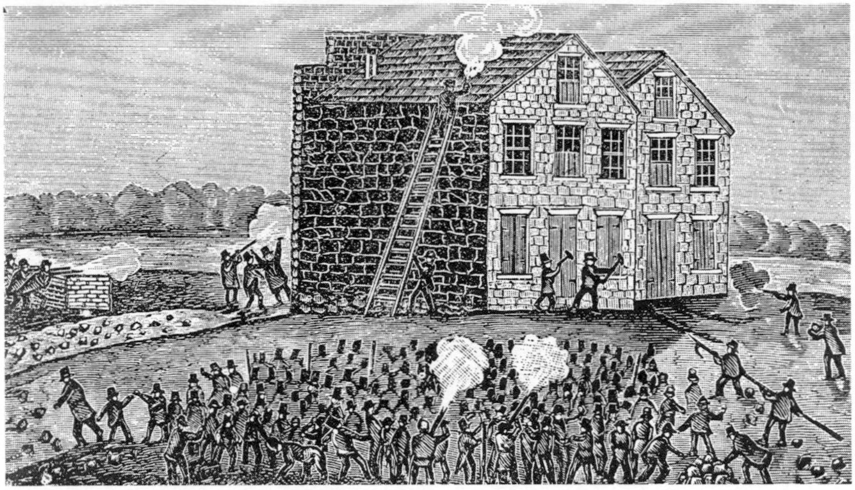

On November 7, 1837, an antiabolitionist mob in Alton, Illinois stormed and set fire to the warehouse where Elijah P. Lovejoy stored his newspaper press. Lovejoy was killed as he left the building.

immediate end to slavery. When he announced in 1837 the organization of a state branch of the American Anti-Slavery Society, some Alton citizens destroyed his press. Each time he received a new press, mobs wrecked it until on November 7 Lovejoy recruited sixty young abolitionists to protect a newly arrived press. That night an armed mob stormed the warehouse where the press was stored. When the citizens attempted to set the warehouse on fire, Lovejoy rushed out to drive them away and was shot dead.

Antiabolitionist riots broke out in such diverse places as New York, Cincinnati, and Boston. Northerners often considered abolition to entail complete equality of the races, and it was the prospect of full integration that aroused their hostility. That quite a few of the leading abolitionists were English only heightened the antagonism. Some hostile whites feared that abolition would lead to intermarriage, and others in the North often perceived the movement as a threat to the established social order and national unity.

Although public opinion in both the North and the South pictured abolitionists as advocates of black equality and miscegenation, in fact many abolitionists were not free of a condescending paternalism towards blacks, whom they could describe as a race that was "genial...docile...in whom the affections rule...and who overflow with the exuberance of childhood." Indeed, few white abolitionists treated their black counterparts as equals, and even Garrison once suggested to a former slave, Frederick Douglass, that he talk more like a slave and less like an educated man when addressing white audiences.

The North was no haven for either free blacks or abolitionists, but during the antebellum period, public sympathy for their cause grew, especially after irate Southerners began to suppress freedom of speech and use extralegal efforts to insulate themselves from antislavery sentiments. Many Northerners not sympathetic to abolition came to support the movement once the South violated constitutional rights.

Education and Reform

Romanticism, the great intellectual and artistic movement that swept Europe and America in the late eighteenth and early nineteenth centuries, held that people are born good and that only a corrupt world turns them evil. If a child is innately innocent, then education should strive to retain and enhance that purity; as Bronson Alcott, the New England transcendentalist and educator, put it, the true reformer "studied man as he is from the hand of the Creator, and not as he is made by the errors of the world." This sentiment was echoed by the Massachusetts educator, Horace Mann (1796–1859), who saw popular education as "a reform to end the need for reform."

In the early decades of the nineteenth century, American primary and secondary schools generally were expensive, private, and affiliated with some religious group. Although New England had a tradition of public education, the reality had declined sadly from the ideal.

Library of Congress.

Frederick Douglass (ca. 1817–1895)

Born into slavery, Douglass was the son of an unknown white man and a slave mother. He was born along the Eastern Shore of Maryland under the name of Frederick Bailey, which he later changed to Douglass after he escaped to the North. At an early age he learned to read, which was forbidden by slave laws, and throughout his life he remained an avid scholar. And when still an adolescent, he evidenced his fighting spirit by being so rebellious that his master sent him to a professional slavebreaker; however, six months of continual punishment only strengthened his will to escape and lead his own life.

In 1838, at the age of nineteen, he borrowed the identification papers of a free black sailor and took public transportation to freedom. He settled in Massachusetts and became active in the abolition movement. Douglass was such a well-educated and eloquent speaker that he was hired by the Anti-Slavery Society as a lecturer. In 1845 he published his *Narrative,* an autobiographical account of his slave days. The book, however, revealed his true identity; in order to avoid being recaptured, Douglass fled to England where he enjoyed a great success as a lecturer. When he returned to the United States, he edited a newspaper, *The North Star,* later called *Frederick Douglass' Newspaper,* published between 1847 and 1864. It was the leading black newspaper of the antebellum period. In its pages Douglass not only espoused abolition but also numerous other causes including women's rights. In fact, Douglass perceived the connection between the plight of women and slaves at an early date, and he was among those who encouraged feminists to fight for the vote. Similarly, Douglass urged Abraham Lincoln to turn the Civil War into a battle to end slavery.

After the Civil War Douglass became a leader of the Republican party and worked hard to obtain voting rights for newly freed blacks. He held several government posts, the most important of which was that of U.S. minister to Haiti between 1889 and 1891. ■

Schoolhouses were dilapidated, teachers incompetent, textbooks inadequate and scarce, and school terms extremely short (often no more than two months long). Elementary schoolteachers were very poorly paid; the emphasis was on religion, with the Bible central to the curriculum of elementary schools. Those attending primary grades were taught to be obedient and industrious, and most students—regardless of the educational level—were in church or private schools. Or they learned their lessons from tutors, especially if destined to go to college. No state had a public education system that was truly free in 1830, but in the decade that followed, considerable innovation occurred. These changes were engineered by reformers who feared what might happen if voters remained ignorant and illiterate and by factory workers and immigrants who were increasingly eager to have their children learn at least the "three Rs." There also was a general desire on the part of many citizens to teach nationalism (as they understood it) in order to strengthen the republic.

The *American Journal of Education,* established in 1826, publicized the need for reform. As a result of such efforts, the cause of state-supported primary education for all children, regardless of family background, gained popular support except in the South where education remained largely a personal matter for each family. A turning point in the fight for free, public education was the decision by Massachusetts in 1827 to make tax support of common schools compulsory; seven years later a permanent school fund was established. By 1850, every state in the Union had a similar fund, and all except Arkansas had experimented with permissive tax legislation in one form or another. Instruction and enrollment in public educational facilities differed greatly from state to state and between urban and rural areas within states. In the state of New York, 675,221 students were attending public classrooms while in Virginia, which had a white population about half as large as that of the Empire State, only a tenth as many students were in public classrooms. And in California, the ratio was far poorer: out of a population of 92,597 white inhabitants, a mere forty-nine students were enrolled in courses of public instruction.

However, at least in theory, the concept of the common school free to all children, one that was supported and controlled by the community where they lived, had won widespread acceptance. All states had made some progress toward this goal, although New England, New York, Pennsylvania, Ohio, and Michigan led the way. Of 3,644,928 individuals enrolled in all of the nation's educational institutions at mid-century, 90 percent were in a public facility of some sort. Nevertheless, only about one school-aged white child out of seven actually was in a classroom.

Educational reform extended not only to children but also to adults throughout the entire community be-

Museum of the City of New York.

A lyceum lecturer, a meteorologist, and his audience about 1838, in New York City.

cause of the growth of a system of lyceums that sponsored lectures, debates, scientific demonstrations, and other educational activities. The American Lyceum, founded in 1826 by Josiah Holbrook (1788–1854) was the name of this system, which had branches in every state in the Union within two years after it was established. The lyceum also served as a platform for proponents of the various reform programs.

The leading educational reformer of the day was Horace Mann. A frail youth who grew up in poverty, Mann had a dismal educational background and did not begin to prepare for college until he was twenty. Nevertheless, he posted a brilliant record at Brown University, after which he became a lawyer and then enjoyed a successful career in the Massachusetts legislature from 1827 to 1837. To everyone's surprise, he suddenly abandoned politics to accept a position as secretary of the state's new board of education. In this capacity he worked hard to win public support for improvements in the quality of instruction, teachers' salaries, school buildings,

Library of Congress.

Horace Mann, nineteenth-century educational reformer.

and educational materials. As secretary of the Massachusetts state board until 1848, Mann set the minimum school year at six months, persuaded the legislature to put up $2 million for better schoolhouses and equipment, doubled appropriations for public education, and increased the salaries of public school masters by 62 percent. During his administration, some fifty new high schools were built in Massachusetts.

With the help of Henry Barnard (1811–1900), who later became the first U.S. Commissioner of Education in 1867, Mann successfully campaigned for free public education throughout the North. Teacher training institutes were opened, textbooks were improved, and bills were passed providing for public tax support of the schools. Although Mann envisioned schools as agents promoting social control, he was not willing to see them become sectarian. As a Unitarian, Mann agreed that the Bible could be read in classrooms, but he insisted that it be read without comment. One church after another attacked him for raising a generation of godless children. Mann, however, courageously defended his ideals and triumphed. All the same, the schools of his day were far more moralistic in their instruction than are schools of today. Even ordinary textbooks such as the *McGuffey Reader* carried a message of moral uplift. The poetry and prose selections in McGuffey's fourth reader, for example, reveal considerable emphases upon Christian ethics and development of admirable qualities; among them are "Perseverance," "Try, Try Again," "The Good Son," "When there is a Will there is a Way," "True Manliness," "Waste not, Want not," "Consequences of Idleness," "Advantage of Industry," "The Right Way," "The Golden Rule," "Knowledge is Power," "Dare to do Right," and "The Sermon on the Mount." A typical McGuffrey lesson, "The Creator," included several paragraphs concerning the glory and perfection of God and four verses by the English clergyman John Keble, one of which reads as follows:

The glorious sky, embracing all,
Is like the Father's love;
Wherewith encompassed, great and small
In peace and order move.

At the end of each selection there were definitions of difficult words ("*En-cóm'passed,* surrounded") and questions to be answered: "Who is more beautiful than the rose, stronger than the lion, and more glorious than the sun?"

At the same time that public primary and secondary education was gaining ground, America's colleges and universities began to take the business of learning more seriously as better prepared students applied to enter their classrooms. They raised their standards and, for the first time, became much more than glorified preparatory schools. However, change and expansion in higher education depended directly upon the success of Mann, Barnard, and their associates. The true revolution at that level did not occur until after the Civil War.

A handful of colleges, in keeping with the spirit of the times, opened their doors to women as well as men—or devoted their efforts exclusively to the education of the "fair" sex. Yet, for the most part, neither coeducation nor women's higher education made much headway until after the Civil War. Seminaries founded by Emma Willard at Troy, New York (1821), by Catherine Beecher at Hartford, Connecticut (1823), and by Mary Lyon at South Hadley, Massachusetts (1836) were noteworthy, but Georgia Female College at Macon, which opened in 1836, was the first woman's college in America. One year later in 1837, Oberlin College in Ohio enrolled four females in its freshman class, but fewer than a half dozen other institutions of higher learning became coed before 1860, one of these being the University of Iowa (1855). Although several would-be female colleges appeared in the 1850s, of these only New York's Elmira Female College, which awarded its first diploma in 1859, was probably doing first-rate academic work. Simultaneously, cheap newspapers and periodicals were making an increasing readership better informed than ever before about the great moral and political questions of the day.

Utopianism

Paradoxically, although the spirit of the antebellum reform movement was highly individualistic, it found its purest expression in idealistic schemes for communal living. One obvious way to create the perfect world, at least in miniature or experimental form, was to live apart from the imperfect world with other fellow believers. If the new version proved superior, and no dedicated reformer ever had any doubts concerning the outcome, then the "old" imperfect world would soon emulate the perfect.

The Mormons

One such effort was the Mormon Church. This faith, also called the Church of Jesus Christ of Latter-day Saints, was founded in 1830 by Joseph Smith (1805–1844), a young man of Yankee stock who was cast into the turmoil of religious controversies swirling around him. Smith claimed visions and personal meetings with two persons of the Trinity—the Father and the Son. These and other revelations allegedly led Smith to the discovery of buried gold plates on which were inscribed the scriptures of the new sect, *The Book of Mormon* (Mormon was an angel who had created the plates originally). This work, which resembles the King James translation of the Bible, is believed by Mormons to be the record of ancient Hebrew settlers who came to America and the coming of Christ to the New World after the Resurrection. The central message of *The Book of Mormon* is the need for repentance. Rejecting Calvinist determinism altogether, the Mormon text states that all people are free to choose and attain salvation if they give up their life of sin and seek Christ.

Smith attracted large numbers of followers who believed his claim that he was a prophet chosen by God to receive direct and continuing heavenly revelations. The sect was attractive to some Protestant Americans, in part because of its strong emphasis on equality, its endorsement of democracy, and its assertion that America is the Promised Land. The Mormons formed a closely organized communal group; Joseph Smith expected all laymen to serve as priests in the church and advocated the communal sharing of goods.

Other Americans were much less receptive to Smith's ideas, and for a decade and a half (1831–1846) the sect faced violent opposition as the members tried to build their new Zion in various parts of Ohio, Illinois, and Missouri. Critics were incensed by their success, their missionary work with Indians, and their religious innovations, such as plural marriage, which were, in the eyes of some, heretical. When in 1844 a mob killed Joseph Smith and his brother in their fourth settlement at Nauvoo, Illinois, 148 of the faithful set out for the Far West, although a large number dissented and refused to go. Their six months' trek, begun in the dead of winter of 1846–1847 and marked by considerable hardship, was led by Brigham Young (1801–1877), who emerged as a very able organizer, a shrewd leader, and a man of great determination. At Salt Lake in Utah, where Young and his

Library of Congress.

Brigham Young, the Mormon leader who led the mass migration to the valley of the Great Salt Lake.

band finally settled, the religion flourished and became a worldwide movement. Young and his followers set up an elaborate irrigation system that turned the valley of the Great Salt Lake into an agricultural paradise. At the time of his death, the Mormon community had 357 towns and villages with some 140,000 residents, many of them lured by promises of free land and a new life. This strongly communal religion is one of the most lasting legacies of antebellum revivalism.

The Shakers

In the second quarter of the nineteenth century, another religious sect attracted a substantial number of followers—the Shakers, or more properly, the United Society of Believers in Christ's Second Appearing. Called the "Shakers" because of the bodily movements some members evinced during religious ecstasies, the group was founded in the late eighteenth century by Ann Lee (1736–1784), an uneducated Englishwoman. After her four children died in childbirth, Ann Lee had a revelation in which she learned that the source of all sin and evil was sex. Soon "Mother Ann," as she was addressed, had a number of adherents, all of whom joined her in practicing celibacy.

An additional revelation instructed the Shakers to move to America in 1774. By 1787, Mother Ann and her followers had established a successful community at New Lebanon, New York. By the Civil War era, there were some 6,000 believers living in nineteen different communities in the United States.

The Shakers suffered from public scorn and ridicule in antebellum America because of their celibacy and what opponents considered peculiar religious practices. Yet, they attracted considerable attention as well. In 1841, James Silk Buckingham visited the Shakers, and reported that about half a dozen women "whirled themselves around, in what opera dancers call a *pirouette*, performing at least fifty revolutions each—their arms extended horizontally, their clothes being blown out like an air balloon all around their persons—their heads sometimes falling on one side, and sometimes hanging forward on the bosom—till they would at length faint away in hysterical convulsions and be caught in the arms of the surrounding dancers." The Shakers clearly had succumbed to a wave of spiritualism. Little girls, seized by fits of shaking and turning, supposedly held conversations with spirits and sang songs taught them by angels. Mediums spoke in many languages as they were seemingly possessed by spirits of Chinese, American Indians, Greeks, and others.

Nevertheless, the Shakers slowly won grudging respect because of their organized and benevolent way of life. Members were strictly segregated according to sex in church, in dormitories, at meals, and on the job. Shaker farms were well run and prosperous; diversified agriculture was the rule, and members processed and sold dairy products and herbs. They were responsible for numerous practical inventions, including the buzz saw (invented by a woman), the apple parer, metal pen point, and flat broom. All work was shared, and all profits distributed equally among members.

The Shakers taught that the sexes were totally equal, and male and female elders ruled the communities. These authorities had absolute power, and the Shaker world was not in any sense democratic. Since the Shakers did not have children, they had only two ways of recruiting new members—through making converts and through adopting orphans. The Shakers, however, were not interested in forcing people to join their faith. Even the orphans they raised were free to leave the sect upon reaching twenty-one. Although scattered Shaker outposts appeared in various states east of the Mississippi River, the center of strength at their peak (perhaps 6,000 members in 1850) was in New England. Today only a handful of Shakers remain, yet the industrious, practical nature of their nineteenth-century counterparts, and especially the handsome, simple furniture they created, are now universally admired.

The Oneida Community

John Humphrey Noyes (1811-1886) carried the idea of Christian perfection farther than any other American of the antebellum period. He believed that true Christians could live without sin altogether and organized a community at Putney, Vermont, in 1836, where this ideal might be attained.

This group, soon forced to move elsewhere by horrified neighbors, was both Christian and socialistic. As Noyes put it, "The Revivalists had for their one great idea the regeneration of the soul. The great idea of the Socialists was the regeneration of society, which is the soul's environment. These ideas belong together and are the complements of each other."

In Oneida, New York, their new home, the Perfectionists, as they were called, became extremely prosperous from farming and manufacturing various items including silverware. All property was held communally, the sexes were regarded as equal, and women adopted the Bloomer costume of short skirts worn over pantalettes. Children remained with their mothers until they could walk and then entered nurseries, freeing most of the women to pursue trades and occupations. The community was regularly entertained by plays, concerts, and lectures.

The most controversial aspect of Oneida was the form of sex relationship. The conventional family system of parents and children remained, but Noyes felt a deep hostility towards the institution of marriage. In its place he introduced the practice of "complex marriage." Every woman was considered the wife of every man, and every man the husband of every woman. Sexual intercourse was permitted, but the act could only be performed with the agreement of both partners and community approval, and only certain members were supposed to produce offspring. The exclusive love of one person for another (called "special love") was frowned on and forbidden. Another unique feature of life at Oneida was a session or "cure" devoted to criticism of a member. The entire community participated in this ordeal, but such measures helped to maintain social control and provided an opportunity for the release of aggression and guilt feelings. Although this was a successful experiment, facing mounting hostility from nearby towns and villages, the Oneida group abandoned complex marriage in 1879 and in the following year incorporated as a joint-stock company. Noyes and a few followers then went to Canada, the others set up a joint-stock company which carried on various manufactures such as silverplate.

Robert Owen and New Harmony

Robert Owen, who was born in North Wales in 1771, grew up in a poor, religious family, and before he was fourteen he lost his faith. "But my religious feelings," he later wrote, "were immediately replaced by the spirit of universal charity—not for a sect or a party, or for a country or a colour—but for the human race, and with a real and ardent desire to do them good."

Although Owen rose to be one of the major industrialists of Great Britain, he never lost sight of this commitment to universal charity. In Scotland he built a model factory town for his employees and at all times took up the cause of the poor and the unemployed.

Finally, in 1825, he decided to put his ideas into practice. He bought a tract of land at New Harmony, Indiana, where he, his sons, and about a thousand settlers from Europe and the northeastern part of the United States established a utopian community. Owen sought to free people from the dogma of religion by attacking institutionalized churches. (On Sunday mornings lectures were delivered at New Harmony.) To combat the alleged destructive influences of capitalism, he socialized the means of production and declared that after the first nine months, a complete communism would be in effect. And Owen attacked sexism by making women full partners in this enterprise. Legislative power was delegated to an assembly made up of all adult residents, both male and

Joslyn Art Museum, Omaha, Northern Natural Gas Company Collection.

Robert Owen's socialist-cooperative community at New Harmony, Indiana.

female. Indeed, in his Declaration of Mental Independence, issued on the Fourth of July, 1826, Owen condemned private property, organized religion, and the institution of marriage—thereby alienating most Americans outside of his little community.

Internal dissension over ideological questions—combined with a liberal admissions policy—quickly ended this dream. By 1827 Owen, having lost four-fifths of his fortune, began to dissolve New Harmony. Critics attributed the failure to many causes. Some pointed to Owen's ambitious program to reform every aspect of ordinary life all at once. Others asserted that the community devoted too much time to music and dancing and too little to meeting the practical problems of survival. Still others observed that true democracy had been missing at New Harmony, since members from the upper classes refused to mix with those from the lower ranks of society. As one working-class member stated, "The people of the town continued [to be] strangers to each other, in spite of all their meetings, their balls, their frequent occasions of congregating in the hall, and all their pretense of cooperation."

Fourierist Phalanxes

Like some abolitionists, the Fourierists were utopian thinkers who rejected gradualism in favor of immediatism. As Albert Brisbane (1809–1890), a communitarian philosopher, put it, "Whoever will examine the question of social ameliorations must be convinced that the *gradual perfection of Civilization* is useless as a remedy for present social evils, and that the only effectual means of doing away with indigence, idleness and the dislike for labor is to do away with civilization itself, and organize Association."

Brisbane, sometimes referred to as America's first socialist, was a follower of Charles Fourier (1772–1837), a French philosopher and socialist who left a great impact on American social experimentation. Fourier believed that the passions of people could attain harmony only in a simple society close to nature. He rejected a society based on the machine, and proposed in its place a reorganization of society into so-called "phalanxes" or associations large enough for all social and industrial requirements and arranged in groups according to occupations, capabilities, attractions, and so on. According to Fourier, the phalanxes would guarantee every participant the means of self-support and the opportunity to develop personal interests. Each phalanx was to have 1,620 people cultivating 5,000 acres of land and working on handicrafts. Unlike Owen's New Harmony, which attempted to change human nature from competitiveness to cooperation by altering the social environment, Fourier's phalanxes took into account individual differences.

Albert Brisbane, a New Yorker who studied with Fourier for two years, began to lecture in Philadelphia and New York on Fourier's ideas in 1839, and the following year published his *Social Destiny of Man.* Horace Greeley, editor of the *New York Tribune,* was very impressed by Brisbane and gave him a column in the newspaper so he could expound on social utopianism. The Panic of 1837 had left many Americans destitute and doubtful of the validity of capitalism and industrialization, and some of these disillusioned people turned to Brisbane for guidance.

Many phalanxes were formed—almost fifty in all, including six in New York, six in Pennsylvania, eight in Ohio, and three in Massachusetts. The longest-lived was the North America Phalanx, established in 1843 and situated near Red Bank, New Jersey. The colony lasted until 1854, when the members voted to disband it. Almost a hundred people worked the farmlands and operated a few small industries in a congenial atmosphere. The phalanx did not fail because of economic difficulties, since the value of the property alone was increased 1,000 percent during the years of its existence. Surplus vegetables were shipped to Manhattan, only fifty miles away, and everyone—male and female—received wages. Members worked only as much as they chose to and were paid accordingly; higher wages were given to those who performed "necessary but repulsive" jobs. Although the system functioned smoothly, the quality of life at Red Bank was extremely severe and without many comforts of that era.

Brook Farm

The most famous experiment in utopian socialism was Brook Farm in West Roxbury, Massachusetts. Organized in 1841 by a group of New England intellectuals headed by a Unitarian minister and transcendentalist, George Ripley (1802–1880), it grew dramatically in size when Brisbane and Greeley persuaded the colonists to turn the community into a Fourierist phalanx in 1845.

Life at Brook Farm was highly stimulating, since some of the best minds in the country were members or frequent visitors. Margaret Fuller, Ralph Waldo Emerson, Bronson Alcott, Nathaniel Hawthorne, Robert Owen, and many others took a strong interest in the community. The educational system was outstanding and for the first time in American history students were instructed in the subtleties of the music of Mozart, Haydn, and Beethoven and became familiar with the literary works of the present as well as of the past. Classes in agriculture also were part of the curriculum, and students did many chores about the farm, since the objectives of the community, according to Ripley, were "to insure a more natural union between intellectual and manual labor than now exists; to combine the thinker and the worker, as far as possible in the same individual."

Yet the experiment was not an economic success, and it dissolved in 1846 after a major fire destroyed the largest building. Bankruptcy seemed inevitable, and a few cases of smallpox frightened off whatever members remained. Nevertheless, Brook Farm was a utopian community that came close to realizing the dream of a peaceful, fraternal organization in which the life of the mind and the life of labor were fused.

Étienne Cabet and Ícaria

Utopianism was as much a European as an American phenomenon, and one of the longest-lived experiments in communal living was founded and peopled almost entirely by French radicals. Étienne Cabet (1788–1856) was exiled from France for five years as a punishment for his political beliefs. While living in England, he became friendly with Robert Owen. Under Owen's influence, Cabet wrote an enormously popular novel titled *Voyage en Icarie,* published in 1840. By 1847 there were, according to one estimate, some four million European adherents to Cabet's utopian ideas. The following year some 300 men set out for the American state of Texas to found a community of their own. There the French and German Icarians hoped to live in a society in which elected officials would control all economic activity and supervise social affairs in an environment free of the constraints of organized religion.

The original settlement proved to be a disaster. The million acres Cabet bought in Texas were arid desert and scattered in many small plots, far from all forms of transportation. Early in February 1849, Cabet himself arrived in New Orleans with fresh manpower. This group, hearing that the Mormons had abandoned Nauvoo, Illinois, for Utah, purchased the community. All went well at Nauvoo for five years, and the Icarians prospered from the profits of their sawmill, flour mill, and distillery. But soon an anti-Cabet faction developed, and Cabet withdrew with 180 faithful followers and moved to St. Louis. A week after the migration Cabet died of apoplexy. The Panic of 1857 impoverished the two communities, although a group in Iowa survived until 1895 before disbanding and distributing the property to the individual members.

Contributions to American Life

These various utopian societies, whether religious or secular, sometimes have been dismissed as naive experiments in folly. Nevertheless, although almost all of the communities were short-lived and many were poorly planned, some made important contributions to American life. They served as a testing ground for ideas about equality of the sexes, the integration of physical and intellectual labor, and the viability of socialist ideas. Utopian leaders seriously challenged such hallowed institutions as private property, the family, and marriage. In the second half of the twentieth century, these questions again have been raised as Americans reevaluate industrialization, racial and sexual equality, and the prevailing forms of social organization.

During the decades just before the Civil War, these would-be reformers of American life faced tremendous, seemingly impossible, obstacles. Their experiments, in the eyes of their critics, were often much too radical and failed to come to grips with what many Americans viewed as the most serious defect in the "Grand Experiment," which was, of course, slavery. Living through the decades from 1820 to 1860 was, at times, somewhat like going to a circus. One could see action in all directions, on every hand; there were many sideshows but only one big tent. Those streaming into it may have been interested in—perhaps even sympathetic to—various social reforms and changing attitudes towards the family, women, sex, and property, but one reform took precedence. That was abolition. Until something was done about the black man's place in the emerging democracy, little could be gained by discussing secondary issues. In fact, if the slave-free controversy was not resolved, then the "Grand Experiment" itself was in jeopardy.

Essay

To the Health of the American People

Today the World Health Organization (WHO) defines public health as "the science and art of preventing disease, prolonging life, and promoting health and efficiency through organized community efforts." But, during a rather fumbling often uncertain career, public health in America has masqueraded under a variety of names such as public hygiene, preventive medicine, community sanitation, and even social welfare. To a great extent, modern medical knowledge was the work of the Old World, not the New, and at least until 1850 Americans who resided some distance from "doctors" may have been better off and may even have lived longer than those who had them as neighbors. Yet during the preceding century two vital innovations were evident in Europe. First, leading researchers in England, France, and Germany abandoned the age-old often fruitless hunt for miraculous "quickie" cures and began to study the nature of various diseases. The second step was careful examination by microscope, stethoscope, clinical statistics, experimentation, and autopsies to learn still more about the nature of human illness.

Colonial Americans certainly passed health ordinances; tried, at times, to isolate those thought ill with contagious diseases in pesthouses; drained marshes; sought out adequate supplies of fresh water; and endeavored to keep streets free of garbage, refuse, and sewage. But as cities grew and industrialization increased, these efforts were not enough. The life expectancy of school-aged children actually declined somewhat between 1789 and 1850.

The basic problem was a series of great epidemics that swept through the nation from time to time until the 1870s. The worst offenders—yellow fever, cholera, smallpox, and malaria—ravaged not only cities and towns but the countryside as well. To complicate matters, most doctors blamed uncontrollable natural phenomena or cosmic conditions and failed to realize how diseases were transmitted from one individual to another. Even if they suspected this possibility, they rarely understood the incubation period of germs and similar factors basic to disease control. Of course, vaccination for smallpox was known, but it was done from arm to arm until 1870 (not with calf lymph), and this method sometimes spread erysipelas, syphilis, and other dreaded maladies. Many consequently shunned vaccination and with good reason.

For the most part, these epidemics can be attributed to

Vaccinating the baby, from *Harper's Weekly,* 1870.

environmental factors such as polluted water, poor housing conditions, bad milk, decayed food, great swarms of flies, poor nutrition, overwork, ignorance, and carelessness. In their eagerness to stem these disasters our forefathers cleaned up their cities substantially (especially the more affluent neighborhoods), which was a step in the right direction. But, since they did not comprehend how epidemics spread, these onslaughts continued. Researchers of today can pinpoint the ship that brought cholera, for example, to New Orleans, list its first victims, and trace its progress into the countryside and upriver to St. Louis and beyond. Asiatic cholera is a devastating, swift killer. A healthy young man who feels dizzy in the morning, by noon becomes ill with vomiting and diarrhea, then grows steadily weaker and dies, not in a few days, but in hours. An estimated 50,000 Americans succumbed to cholera in 1866 alone, but the last great epidemic five years later had one solid

Courtesy New-York Historical Society, New York City.

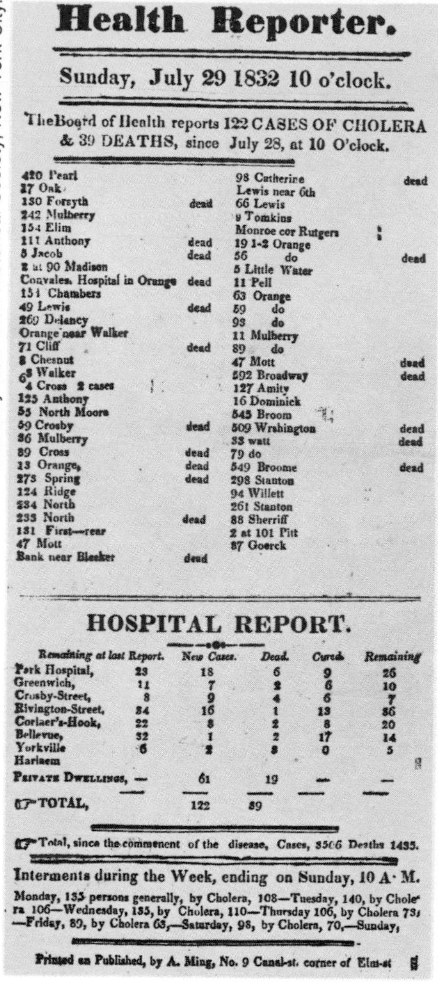

Health Reporter.

Sunday, July 29 1832 10 o'clock.

The Board of Health reports 122 CASES OF CHOLERA & 39 DEATHS, since July 28, at 10 O'clock.

420 Pearl		98 Catherine	dead
27 Oak		Lewis near 6th	
130 Forsyth	dead	66 Lewis	
242 Mulberry		9 Tomkins	
154 Elim		Monroe cor Rutgers	
111 Anthony	dead	19 1-2 Orange	
5 Jacob	dead	56 do	dead
2 at 90 Madison		5 Little Water	
Convales. Hospital in Orange	dead	11 Pell	
151 Chambers		63 Orange	
49 Lewis	dead	59 do	
269 Delancy		93 do	
Orange near Walker		11 Mulberry	
71 Cliff	dead	89 do	
8 Chesnut		47 Mott	dead
6 5 Walker		592 Broadway	dead
4 Cross 2 cases		127 Amity	
125 Anthony		16 Dominick	
55 North Moore		545 Broom	
59 Crosby	dead	509 Wrashington	dead
36 Mulberry		33 watt	dead
89 Cross	dead	79 do	
13 Orange,	dead	549 Broome	dead
273 Spring	dead	298 Stanton	
124 Ridge		94 Willett	
234 North		261 Stanton	
233 North	dead	88 Sherriff	
131 First—rear		2 at 101 Pitt	
47 Mott		87 Goerck	
Bank near Bleeker	dead		

HOSPITAL REPORT.

	Remaining at last Report.	New Cases.	Dead.	Cured.	Remaining
Park Hospital,	23	18	6	9	26
Greenwich,	11	7	2	6	10
Crosby-Street,	8	9	4	6	7
Rivington-Street,	34	16	1	13	36
Corlaer's-Hook,	22	8	2	8	20
Bellevue,	32	1	2	17	14
Yorkville	6	2	3	0	5
Harlaem					
PRIVATE DWELLINGS,	—	61	19	—	—
TOTAL,		122	39		

Total, since the commencent of the disease, Cases, 3506 Deaths 1435.

Interments during the Week, ending on Sunday, 10 A·M.

Monday, 135 persons generally, by Cholera, 108—Tuesday, 140, by Cholera 106—Wednesday, 135, by Cholera, 110—Thursday 106, by Cholera 73, —Friday, 89, by Cholera 63,—Saturday, 98, by Cholera, 70,—Sunday,

Printed an Published, by A. Ming, No. 9 Canal-st. corner of Elm-st

The statistics for one day during a cholera epidemic, in the New York City *Health Reporter* for July 29, 1832.

dividend: it gave birth to a nationwide program of ship quarantines. This quarantine program was an outgrowth of a congressional act of 1798—the first move by the federal government in behalf of public health—that sought to provide medical care for merchant seamen. In time, this quarantine program of 1871 grew into the United States Public Health Service. The Constitution, by the way, is silent on the subject of health, so most measures designed to promote community or public health in the nineteenth century originated in cities and state capitals, not in Washington.

Although cholera, yellow fever, smallpox, and malaria were dramatic, the real enemies of much of nineteenth century America were familiar illnesses that aroused little interest. These killers invaded every household and claimed their victims in a slow, occasionally casual manner. They were tuberculosis, infant diarrhea, dysentery, typhoid fever, pneumonia, and childhood diseases such as scarlet fever and diphtheria. Tuberculosis, a disease closely associated with industrialization and poor living conditions, evidently reached its peak at mid-century; after that date, a slow decline in the death rate is apparent. Just why is not entirely clear since the true nature of the disease was not yet understood. Some historians believe more intelligent citizens began to appreciate the value of fresh air, good food and water, and the dangers of indiscriminate coughing and spitting; thus a sanitary awakening turned the tide against "TB." Others point to better nutrition as a key factor, and still others maintain that those most susceptible died off, producing a naturally immune populace.

A Massachusetts native, Lemuel Shattuck (1793–1859), who taught in frontier Detroit for a few years and organized Michigan's first Sunday School, laid the foundations for modern public health in America with his *Report of the Sanitary Commission of Massachusetts* (1850), although initially few listened to his words of warning. Shattuck, an amateur genealogist, became interested in vital statistics while writing histories of his own family and of the town of Concord. In 1847, as a member of the Boston City Council and the state legislature, he engineered creation of a "Sanitary Commission" empowered to prepare a statewide survey. This undertaking clearly was Shattuck's own idea. He became commission chairman and, not surprisingly, also prepared the now famous report. At every step Shattuck faced stern opposition from medical men because he seemed to be invading their territory.

In his four-part study, Shattuck paid special attention to diseases caused by industrial-urban growth, demonstrating that the average age of all those who died in Boston between 1810 and 1820 was 27.85 years, but in the 1840s it was only 21.43

years, a decline in life expectancy of 6.42 years. Data collected for New York and Philadelphia revealed similar disturbing trends. Shattuck presented fifty recommendations aimed at creating local and state health programs, thirty-six of which now are accepted throughout America. These included state boards of health, local boards, careful compilation of vital statistics, special emphasis upon environmental factors such as smoke abatement; supervised construction of buildings; control of the sale and manufacture of food, drink, and medicine; compulsory vaccination against smallpox; schools for nurses; and institutions to train sanitary workers. Most important of all, Shattuck stressed the prevention of disease, not its cure.

"The great object of sanitary science is to teach people the causes of disease,—how to remove or avoid these causes,—how to prevent disease,—how to live without being sick,—how to increase the vital force,—how to avoid premature decay. And one of the most useful reforms which could be introduced into the present constitution of society would be, that the advice of a physician should be sought and *paid for* while in health, to keep the patient well; and not, as now, while in sickness, to cure disease, which might in most cases have been avoided or prevented."

Despite an appeal to practical New England common sense, a bill incorporating Shattuck's far-reaching proposals got nowhere in the Massachusetts legislature. He and his ideas were much too radical, far ahead of the times. Nevertheless, recurring epidemics and conditions created by the Civil War pushed sanitation to the forefront of the public mind and slowly some of his concepts began to be accepted. Because of yellow fever, Louisiana in 1855 set up a quarantine to be administered by a state board of health, the first in the nation. Massachusetts established a similar body in 1869, and during the early 1870s, six other states followed these examples: California, Minnesota, Virginia, Michigan, Maryland, and Alabama.

Emergence of the United States Sanitary Commission in June 1861, a voluntary group designed to promote the health and welfare of northern volunteers, was not viewed with much enthusiasm by Abraham Lincoln. Like Franklin Pierce who crushed Dorothea Dix's hopes for federally supported mental institutions with his veto in 1854, at first Lincoln was not impressed with the aims of a group composed of clergymen, do-gooder women, and a few doctors who, in his opinion, might become "a fifth wheel to the coach." Nevertheless, he gave reluctant approval, and a few weeks later the first battle of Bull Run demonstrated that the Army's medical service alone could

Historical Picture Service, Chicago.

The United States Sanitary Commission at work; engraving by Thomas Nast.

not possibly cope with thousands of sick and wounded.

The primary work of the commission was to inspect camps (this made workers very unpopular with military officers); to supply furniture, blankets, clothing, and some food to hospitals; and to provide nurses. Dorothea Dix, by the way, headed up the corps of nurses. Out of these wartime experiences, considerable information was gained concerning malaria and "crowd" diseases, the proper disposal of human waste, the value of fresh vegetables, the use of ether and chloroform during surgery, and the need for nursing training.

During the next century, the pace of public health awareness quickened considerably throughout America, but progress often has been uneven as four sectors struggled to stake out their jurisdictions and protect their special interests. These were local health departments in cities, counties, and towns; state services under the control of state boards; federal departments and agencies; and voluntary groups and associations. Cooperation and competition were clearly possible and, predictably, both have occurred. Perhaps the most dramatic developments in these decades since the Civil War have been the increased emphasis upon health care and personal hygiene in the public school systems of the nation, the sustained growth of vast medical schools and research centers backed by private donors, and the continued expansion of financial support of health services by federal and state agencies.

Like the Civil War, the crisis of the Great Depression of the 1930s stimulated considerable interest in public health, especially when local and state coffers were empty. Franklin D. Roosevelt's

Social Security Act of 1935 contained sweeping provisions authorizing annual grants to states for health purposes and greatly increased federal-state cooperation in this realm. However, not until 1953 did public health win cabinet status with creation of the Department of Health, Education and Welfare (HEW). At last, the nation had a national health organization, but whether it has a national health program is another matter. Despite this reorganization, public health work continues to be carried on by a variety of agencies and boards in the federal government, and efforts to pass national health care legislation have met stiff opposition from doctors and physicians who belong to the American Medical Association.

What has been accomplished in America during this century is indeed impressive. In 1900 the death rate from all causes was 17.2 per 1,000 population; in 1970 it was 9.4. Since the turn of the century, the life expectancy of Americans has increased by more than two decades, from forty-seven to seventy years. Epidemics have been eliminated, and tuberculosis—once the silent killer—has been virtually wiped out. Chronic diseases such as cancer, cardiovascular disorders, arthritis, neurological defects, and mental illness—often problems associated with aging—now are the special concern of public health research.

Yet, somewhat like the medical men of the nineteenth century who saw only epidemics and overlooked the true killers, current research and development in the health field while improving the quality of health care have contributed to higher costs. Treatment for any sickness, even basic hospital care, has become so expensive that a substantial number of Americans cannot bear the costs involved. A prolonged illness may mean heavy debt and mental anguish perhaps fully as disruptive as the illness itself. A cure that cripples cannot be viewed as a true corrective.

To assist the elderly, those hit hardest by expensive bouts with sickness, the Congress in 1965 created Medicare, two insurance programs administered by the Social Security Administration, now part of HEW, and financed by funds working Americans pay to that agency. Medicare provides hospital benefits and voluntary medical insurance to everyone over sixty-five years of age. Since 1973, Medicare also has provided help for some disabled individuals who are less than sixty-five. Closely related to Medicare is Medicaid, a state-administered program to give medical assistance to persons with low incomes. Supported by local, state, and federal funds, both eligibility and benefits vary somewhat from state to state.

For the past four decades, legislation designed to provide similar health care for all Americans, regardless of age, has failed to win congressional approval, and the merits of such proposals are hotly debated. Epidemics, wars, and economic disasters seem to have been the phenomena that nudged public health along the path of its hit-and-miss development and growth. And, as medical bills and hospital costs continue to soar, too many Americans can only pay lip service to Lemuel Shattuck's plea to seek the advice of a physician "while in health." Yet, although public health activity in America is a hodgepodge of boards and agencies, public and private, at various levels of society, the system works reasonably well; it certainly has come a long way since the days when a President dared to veto a bill designed to provide hospitals for the mentally ill and when another chief executive, a man known for his charity and wisdom, could approve, only with reluctance, voluntary efforts to ease the pain and suffering of wounded soldiers.

Selected Readings

General Accounts

Alice Felt Tyler, *Freedom's Ferment: Phases of American Social History from the Colonial Period to the Outbreak of the Civil War* (1944)

Harvey Wish, *Society and Thought in Early America* (1950)

Russell B. Nye, *Society and Culture in America, 1830–1860* (1974)

E. Douglas Branch, *The Sentimental Years, 1836–1860* (1934)

Religion and Religious Benevolence

William W. Sweet, *Religion in the Development of American Culture, 1765–1840* (1963)

Whitney R. Cross, *The Burned-Over District: The Social and Intellectual History of Enthusiastic Religion in Western New York, 1800–1850* (1950)

Bernard A. Weisberger, *They Gathered at the River: The Story of the Great Revivals and Their Impact upon Religion in America* (1958)

Timothy L. Smith, *Revivalism and Social Reform in Mid-Nineteenth Century America* (1957)

Clifford S. Griffin, *Their Brothers' Keepers: Moral Stewardship in the United States, 1800–1865* (1960)

John R. Bodo, *The Protestant Clergy and Public Issues, 1812–1848* (1954)

Some Varieties of Reform

Frank L. Byrne, *Prophet of Prohibition: Neal Dow and his Crusade* (1961)

David J. Rothman, *The Discovery of the Asylum: Social Order and Disorder in the New Republic* (1971)

Helen E. Marshall, *Dorothea Dix: Forgotten Samaritan* (1937)

Peter Brock, *Pacifism in the United States: From the Colonial Era to the First World War* (1968)
Merton L. Dillon, *The Abolitionists: The Growth of a Dissenting Minority* (1974)
Frederick M. Binder, *The Age of the Common School, 1830–1865* (1974)

Utopianism

Arthur E. Bestor, Jr., *Backwoods Utopias: The Sectarian Origins and the Owenite Phase of Communitarian Socialism in America, 1663–1829* (2nd. ed., 1971)
Mark Holloway, *Heavens on Earth: Utopian Communities in America, 1680–1880* (rev. ed., 1966)
Thomas F. O'Dea, *The Mormons* (1964)
Edward D. Andrews, *The People Called Shakers: A Search for the Perfect Society* (1953)
Robert D. Thomas, *The Man Who Would be Perfect: John Humphrey Noyes and the Utopian Impulse* (1977)

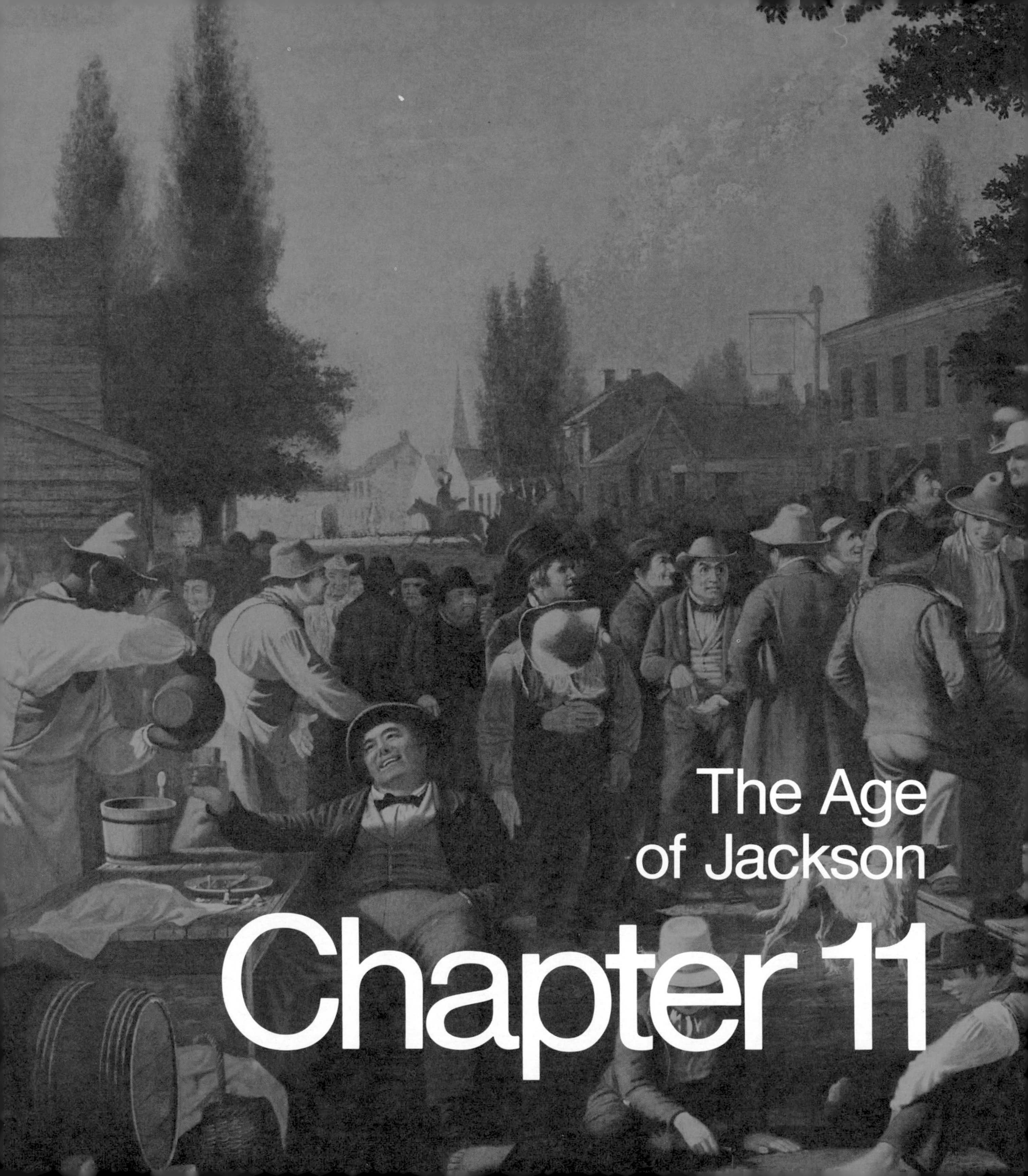

The Age of Jackson

Chapter 11

TIMELINE

1825
House of Representatives elects John Quincy Adams President

1828
Congress enacts "Tariff of Abominations"

1828
John C. Calhoun writes *South Carolina Exposition and Protest*

1828
Democrat Andrew Jackson elected President

1829
Peggy Eaton Affair

1830
Webster-Hayne Debate

1830
Land law permits purchase of up to 160 acres for $1.25 per acre

1831
Nat Turner slave revolt

1832
Jackson vetoes renewal of BUS charter

1832
South Carolina declares "Tariff of Abominations" null and void *in Ordinance of Nullification*

1832
Andrew Jackson reelected President

1833
Jackson issues *Nullification Proclamation*

1836
Democrat Martin Van Buren elected President

1837
United States recognizes Republic of Texas

1837
Onset of severe depression

1840
Congress approves Independent Treasury Plan

1840
Whig William Henry Harrison elected President

1841
John Tyler assumes Presidency after Harrison's death

1841
Pre-Emption Act encourages frontier land settlement

1842
Webster-Ashburton Treaty

1844
Democrat James K. Polk elected President

1845
Texas annexed to the United States

1846
Clash between Mexican and American troops leads to war

1848
Treaty of Guadalupe Hildago ends war with Mexico

CHAPTER OUTLINE

The ballyhoo that surrounds presidential elections today began with Andrew Jackson's campaign in 1828 as shrewd politicians realized that the public would respond more fully to slogans, rallies, cartoons, and other forms of propaganda than to sober discussions of the issues. Jackson's campaign not only marked the introduction of new tactics but also the "rise of the common man"—if not in fact, at least in political rhetoric. Once in office, Jackson strengthened the presidency and wrestled for a position of dominance over Congress.

Some themes of Jackson's age strike a familiar note even today; other matters were of more immediate concern. A two-party system of sorts developed around Jackson as opposition to his policies and programs increased. Territorial expansion was tied increasingly to the question of slavery in the new territories. The split between the North and South over this expansion widened after the Mexican War in the late 1840s and the acquisition of vast new lands.

New Political Competition

Between 1808 and 1824 the Jeffersonian Republicans faced little opposition and as a result suffered a decline in party discipline and national organization. Spared the rod of political competition, the Republican child became spoiled.

After the War of 1812, the Federalist party, which had long been ailing, finally died as a national organization. During James Monroe's term as President, from 1816 to 1824, Republicans became more national in outlook and actively modified their party so it might accommodate the view of ex-Federalists who wanted national government to do more than play a small, strictly custodial role.

But the country was growing, and the rise of sectionalism did not foster national political harmony. More and more the outspoken representatives of the West refused to accept party decisions, especially as the voting strength of that region increased.

Although the election of 1824 revolved to some extent around national questions such as internal improvements, the fate of slavery, the direction of banking policy, and the disposition of public lands, to a greater degree the competition was regional. Of the four candidates, Henry Clay was from Kentucky, Andrew Jackson from Tennessee, William Harris Crawford from Georgia, and John Quincy Adams from Massachusetts.

Since all four candidates were Republicans, they could not each expect to be the choice of their party's caucus in Congress; that group could select only one candidate and chose Crawford. His rivals then turned to other means of nomination—including endorsement by mass meetings and state and local legislatures. These methods were popular, since they were presumably more democratic than the caucus and more responsive to the majority will. Adams, of course, had the support of New England, while the others garnered backing from various parts of the rest of the nation.

Election of 1824

Competition for votes caused the aspirants to search for issues with broad, national appeal. These issues, however, were often vague, and the candidates descended to attacking each other on the basis of personal characteristics: Adams was ridiculed for the way he dressed; Calhoun for his overzealous ambition; Clay for his drinking and gambling; Crawford for once having advocated intermarriage of whites and Indians as an alternative to the latter's removal from Georgia; and Jackson for his alleged lack of experience in politics.

Nevertheless, each man did have a program. Henry Clay had promoted his economic plan, The American System, since 1815. To Clay the old states' rights philosophy of the Republicans was unsuitable for contemporary America, which would be better served, he thought, by a comprehensive national economic plan. Clay argued that higher tariffs would benefit the country by protecting American manufactured goods and agricultural products. At the same time, tariff revenues could finance a national network of canals and highways for increased internal commerce. In many ways Clay's ideas resembled those of the arch-Federalist whom the Republicans once had despised—Alexander Hamilton.

Many Southerners found Clay's American System unacceptable. They wanted no restrictions on foreign trade; since they exported cotton and imported many manufactured goods (and produced little of their own), they could see no advantage in excluding or reducing foreign trade. Moreover, a national transportation network, financed by duties on imports, held little attraction for them, since most states of the Deep South had good natural waterways and no need for improved roads or canals.

Clay's personality was not so appealing as that of Crawford or of Jackson. Nor was he as well-educated as some of his rivals. Many Northerners thought that Clay was too rowdy and uncouth; even his fellow Westerners found his economic theories too complicated and preferred the military glory of Jackson.

Crawford, choice of the congressional caucus, enjoyed the support of older Republicans, including the aged Jefferson. In public life since 1803, he had served as a state legislator, as a senator from Georgia, as a U.S. minister to France, as a Secretary of War, and as Monroe's Secretary of the Treasury. Crawford was dedicated to the interest of the South and believed in the old Republican doctrine of federal nonintervention, but to attract a national following, he supported a moderate tariff program and the maintenance of the National Bank of the United States. His opponents made much of the undemocratic way in which "King Caucus" had nominated him. Shortly after this triumph Crawford became seriously ill in 1823.

Andrew Jackson, the hero of New Orleans, was a strong contender despite the fact that he had served only two years in Congress and had a reputation of being a duelist and gambler. Though actually a man of strong convictions who found it difficult to take advice, he was viewed as a man of the people and as such seemed the natural choice of newly enfranchised segments of the

Courtesy National Gallery of Art, Washington D.C.

This painting of "Old Hickory" by Thomas Sully, a student of Gilbert Stuart and Benjamin West, depicts Andrew Jackson as the hero of New Orleans.

population. The depression of 1819, which extended well into the 1820s, encouraged debtors (many of whom had speculated in land in the West) to think of themselves as a class, and for these men, Jackson was the most appealing candidate, for like them he was a landholder and a self-made man. As John C. Calhoun observed to John Quincy Adams in 1820, the Panic had brought about "an immense revolution of fortunes in every part of the Union, enormous multitudes in deep distress, and a general mass of disaffection to the Government not concentrated in any particular direction, but ready to seize upon any event and looking out anywhere for a leader." That leader was Jackson.

In fact, Jackson was far from being a poor commoner. His estate, The Hermitage, was the finest in Tennessee—and he owned many other tracts of land. He was a former slave trader, a slaveholder, and a breeder of thoroughbred horses as well as a collector of cut glass, vintage wines, and costly furnishings. Although his friends, who were called the "Nashville Junto," presented him to the public as a child of the soil, he was a peculiar blend of pioneer and aristocrat. True, he was born in humble surroundings, and was self-made, but on economic issues in Tennessee, he tended to side with the "haves" against the "have-nots." His views on most public issues, were not generally known, and this vagueness gave him real advantages as a candidate seeking the votes of a restless, undecided public.

John Quincy Adams, son of a former President, John Adams, and Monroe's Secretary of State, seemed an obvious choice for the White House. He had held several important diplomatic posts abroad, including that of minister plenipotentiary to Russia and minister to England, and had served in the U.S. Senate. His economic views corresponded closely to Clay's. But Adams lacked the common touch and seemed disagreeably patrician and puritanical to many Americans. He was opposed to partisan politics, and this aversion distressed his fellow Republicans.

John Quincy Adams, scholar, diplomat, and president. This daguerreotype portrait was taken in 1843 when Adams was serving in the U.S. House of Representatives.

The Metropolitan Museum of Art, Gift of I.N. Phelps Stokes, Edward S. Hawes, Alice Mary Hawes, Marion Augusta Hawes, 1937.

Finally, South Carolinian John C. Calhoun, at age forty-two, was the youngest aspirant to the presidency. During the War of 1812 he had become an ardent nationalist, much in the fashion of Clay, and now advocated internal improvements, a strong army and navy, a protective tariff, and a second National Bank of the United States. In 1817 he became Secretary of War; convinced that Britain would draw the United States into yet another conflict, Calhoun asked Congress to give the country a large fighting force. Though he was unsuccessful, nonetheless Calhoun held office with distinction. As the contest seemed to narrow down to Jackson and Adams, Calhoun withdrew from the race and successfully sought the vice presidency instead.

In the election, Jackson won more popular votes than Adams, 151,271 to 113,122, and had a plurality but not a majority of the electoral votes. Clay and Crawford received enough votes in the Electoral College to send the election to the House of Representatives, where each state would cast only one vote. Henry Clay, Speaker of that body, now became a crucial factor. Clay was determined to stop Jackson whom he regarded as his rival. Since Clay knew Adams held economic views similar to his own, he threw his support to Adams, who was elected on the first ballot on February 9, 1825. Adams carried 13 states, Jackson 7, and Crawford 4. In addition to New England, Adams received the support of New York, Maryland, Ohio, Illinois, Missouri, Kentucky, and Louisiana; New Jersey, Pennsylvania, South Carolina, Alabama, Mississippi, Tennessee, and Indiana backed Jackson; and Delaware, Virginia, North Carolina, and Georgia voted for Crawford.

Once President, Adams appointed Clay as Secretary of State, and the Jacksonians cried that a "corrupt bargain" between the two men had cheated "the People." Although Adams and Clay probably reached an understanding about Clay's appointment, the agreement was neither unusual nor devious. Adams reciprocated Clay's support, and the appointment was a logical one. In no other way, however, did Adams use his power of patronage for political advantage; while in office he removed only twelve men from the federal bureaucracy, and these were for well-justified causes.

The Adams Presidency

The idealism (or lack of political self-interest) that Adams displayed in refusing to exert patronage powers also was revealed in his first annual message to Congress, delivered on December 6, 1825. In it he asked the legislators to remember that "The spirit of improvement is abroad upon the earth" and to implement his vision of a strong central government that would finance a unified system of roads and canals.

Adams proposed a reasonable protective tariff that would aid native industry, provide domestic markets for farmers, and enrich the federal government. He asked for the creation of a department of the interior that would sell lands at low rates but discourage wildcat speculation and an overly rapid settlement of the West. Such a government agency would facilitate a rational allocation of lands and provide for the conservation of natural resources. The sale of public lands would provide money to be used in removing Indians on a voluntary basis to areas west of the Mississippi River. Indian removal, Adams urged, should not violate treaty rights.

Finally, Adams called for reforms that would benefit the nation intellectually. He asked for funds to support scientific research (especially explorations), to build a national observatory, and to pay for public lectures on scientific subjects. Reviving an old idea of George Washington, Adams suggested Congress build a national university in Washington, D.C. He recommended a more effective patent law and a uniform standard of weights and measures based upon the metric system. Adams's proposed reforms extended even to the navy; he pointed out to Congress the "want of a naval school of instruction," corresponding with the Military Academy at West Point, for the formation of scientific and accomplished officers.

Adams obviously had great faith in the ability of reason and science to bring about a better world. To Adams the responsibility of government was to "promote the highest welfare of our country," and he warned Congress of the evils that would follow should it "slumber in indolence."

The nationalistic plan that Adams outlined won little support since it required extensive central planning and control. In citing the need for internal improvements, Adams tactlessly pointed to the superior record of several European countries, a comparison most Americans found irritating. Even if more adroit, Adams would have had a hard time securing congressional support for his ideas, since he had not won a majority of the popular vote and had been elected in the House through what was widely condemned as a corrupt bargain.

In general, Adams failed to understand the changing nature of American politics. He did not recognize that the ordinary voter had become more influential. Rather than taking his controversial proposals to the people, Adams addressed himself to Congress alone. He held fast to the eighteenth-century idea that the voters elected the best and wisest men who, in turn, were free to make policies and laws without referring back to their constituents. This concept of government was fast being replaced by one more responsive to public opinion. Characteristically, Adams instructed Congress to adopt his program and not be "palsied by the will of our constituents"—an unfortunate phrase that his opponents used later to convince the voters that the President was an enemy of the people.

Adams was, after all, the son of John Adams, the old foe of Thomas Jefferson, founder of the Republican party. Though the Republicans gradually had abandoned their original adherence to the ideal of a small caretaker federal government, nevertheless many of the old Jeffersonian Republicans still feared the strong central government advocated by Adams. His enemies declared that "all Adamses are monarchists." Southerners especially feared that a strong national government would interfere with slavery and erect high tariffs that would hurt the international cotton trade and benefit a program for internal improvements—which the South had no desire to finance. As Adams later put it, "When I came to the Presidency the principle of internal improvement was swelling the tide of public prosperity, till the Sable Genius of the South saw the signs of his own inevitable downfall in the unparalleled progress of the general welfare in the North, and fell to cursing the tariff and internal improvement, and raised the standard of free trade, nullification, and state rights."

Even in the area of foreign affairs, in which Adams was an expert, he had little success. His efforts to increase trade with the British West Indies were rebuffed, and an attempt at hemispheric cooperation ended in confusion. The Adams Administration received secret information that Spain was intent upon recovering its lost colonies in South America. Wanting to block Spain's ambitions, Adams proposed in December 1825 that the United States send a diplomatic mission to a congress of newly independent Latin American states. The meeting was to be held in Panama, and attendance by the United States would signal hemispheric solidarity.

A number of leading senators opposed the President's proposal. They had not been informed of Spain's plans, which Adams kept secret. Even had they known, they still might have fought the President in order to embarrass him. Some of the senators, including New York's Martin Van Buren (1782–1862) and Missouri's Thomas Hart Benton (1782–1858), argued that attending the conference might lead to a war between the United States and Spain, though this expressed fear of "entangling alliances" was probably only a coverup for a desire to hurt Adams and advance the Jacksonian cause. A group of southern senators, led by Robert Y. Hayne (1791–1839) of South Carolina, opposed the meeting because attending it would amount to official recognition of the new black nation of Haiti. Since the black Haitians had overthrown their white French rulers, the slave-owning South was obviously adverse to endorsing the new government. In March 1826, after many delays, Congress complied with the President's request—but so late that the diplomatic effort had been wrecked. One of the American delegates to Panama died en route, and the other arrived after the conference was over.

One of the deep differences between Adams and his enemies was over states' rights. In 1802 Georgia ceded its western land claims to the United States and assumed its present boundaries in return for the promise that the federal government would extinguish Indian title to lands within the state as soon as possible. Georgia was to be given full jurisdiction over those lands. Although the federal government had pledged to dissolve Creek and Cherokee land holdings in Georgia, this process was very slow. Finally, in 1825, the Treaty of Indian Springs was signed in which the "Creek Nation" agreed to surrender its lands in Georgia and a portion in Alabama in exchange for a tract in present-day Oklahoma.

Adams discovered that the chiefs who signed the treaty represented only eight of the forty-six Creek towns and that federal officers backing the treaty had acted more as Georgians than as representatives of Washington. Accordingly, Adams ordered Georgia to halt sale of Creek lands to white settlers until a new, fairer treaty could be drawn up. The governor of Georgia threatened civil war if Adams attempted to stop the proceedings. "From the first decisive act of hostility," he told the President, "you will be considered and treated as a public enemy . . . , and, what is more, the unblushing allies of the savages whose cause you have adopted."

Some Southerners warned that if the federal government could defend the existence of Indian "nations" within states it could also interfere in the internal affairs of the slave states and emancipate bondsmen. Like the tariff issue, the Indian question caused Southerners to suspect the intentions of the federal government. The dispute, as historian James W. Silver has noted, was "a crisis between nationalism and localism."

Before leaving office, Adams recommended removal of the Indians on a voluntary basis to territory west of the Mississippi. Yet no one emerged from the conflict unscarred. Georgia and the other southern states no longer held the federal government in high repute. The Creeks and other southern tribes soon lost their homeland. Adams later wrote, "We have done more harm to the Indians since our Revolution than had ever been done to them by the French and English nations before. . . . These are crying sins for which we are answerable before a higher jurisdiction."

The Tariff of Abominations

The rise of American industry during the antebellum period made the tariff an important political issue. New

England manufacturers and sheep raisers, hurt by the Panic of 1819, sought protective tariffs. Congress responded by enacting the mild Tariff of 1824. It failed to satisfy the protectionists, who pressed for higher duties. When the tariff question came up again at the end of Adams's term, some of Jackson's supporters backed a bill designed to appeal to the Middle Atlantic states of New York and Pennsylvania and the Western states. If Jackson could win the large bloc of electoral votes of these regions, he would enhance his chances of winning the upcoming election.

The Tariff of 1828 was a hodgepodge, poorly thought out and unfair, nothing more than a naked bid for votes. Oddly enough, the very Jacksonians who framed the bill never thought it would be passed. They had reasoned that the South, opposed to tariffs of any sort, would vote it down, and that the North, irritated by the high rates on raw materials, would also reject it. Defeat of the bill would win affection for Jackson from the antiprotectionist South. At the same time, Jackson would presumably secure the devotion of farmers in the West and manufacturing interests in the Middle Atlantic states for supporting the bill in the first place. Thus Jackson would be considered a friend of the western farmer, a protectionist in the North, and a freetrader in the South.

When the bill unexpectedly passed in mid-1828, it was immediately labeled "the tariff of abominations" by the South. John Calhoun, the Vice President, wrote the *South Carolina Exposition and Protest* (though he did not sign the essay) in which he called the tariff unconstitutional and recommended state nullification. Calhoun, once an ardent nationalist, was now a strong sectionalist. This switch reflected an economic trend. The average price for cotton had been dropping steadily for several years, bringing hardship to South Carolina (in 1816 cotton sold at 27 cents a pound, in 1820 at 17 cents, in 1824 at 13 cents, and in 1827 at 9 cents). The Tariff of 1828, by imposing high duties (and thus reaffirming the principle of protection), aroused great resentment in South Carolina. Calhoun's *Exposition* was an early sign that some Southerners, if frustrated, would be eager to reduce federal power and possibly even call for dissolution of the Union.

The Election of 1828

Between Jackson's defeat in 1825 and his triumph in 1828, his supporters in and out of Congress forged a new political entity, the Democratic party, with the sole purpose of putting "Old Hickory" (a nickname given to Jackson by his men in the War of 1812) into office.

A key figure in this campaign was Martin Van Buren (1782–1862), a politician possessed of considerable shrewdness, wit, charm, and a keen sense of public relations. Schooled in the rough cockpit of New York state politics, Van Buren became a U.S. Senator in 1821, yet kept his hand in affairs at Albany with the aid of a small band of associates, so much so that this group dominated by Van Buren became known as the "Albany Regency." In 1824 he supported Crawford, but three years later was in Jackson's camp; and, in 1828, Van Buren became one of "Old Hickory's" closest advisors. At the same time, he carried on a successful bid to become governor of New York; however, that political base securely in his pocket,

Chicago Historical Society.

Martin Van Buren was a brilliant political manipulator. This daguerreotype portrait of the "Little Magician" is from the late 1840s.

he resigned to become Jackson's Secretary of State and easily the dominant figure in the new Cabinet.

Historians have written of the "Revolution of 1828" and the sudden "rise of the common man." Actually ordinary citizens gained new prominence before Jackson's victory. In the election of 1824, the voters in all but six states chose presidential electors, and by that time universal white male suffrage was common in many areas. The great change that took place in 1828 had more to do with the creation of elaborate political machinery through which the ordinary citizen could make his influence felt.

The political race of 1828 also signalled renewed emphasis upon smear tactics. The Jacksonians spent about a million dollars to elect their man. No lie, insult, or calumny was excluded from their attacks on President Adams. They accused the puritanical man from Massachusetts of having procured an American girl for the sexual pleasure of the Czar of Russia; this favor was alleged to be the basis of Adams's success as a diplomat. Adams also was reputed to have had premarital sexual relations with his wife. Other charges held that Adams nursed dreams of becoming a king, a fantasy that the Jacksonians attempted to substantiate by listing White House expenditures (later proved false) with public funds for ivory chessmen, a billiard table, and other "royal extravagances." The Jacksonians told recent immigrants the President's father was the author of the Alien and Sedition Acts and that the son was equally prejudiced against foreigners, whom he reputedly insulted daily. The most publicized accusation was that Adams struck a corrupt bargain with Clay to win the election of 1824.

The supporters of the President were equally active in vilifying Jackson. Even Jackson's mother was smeared. As one writer put it, "General Jackson's mother was a COMMON PROSTITUTE brought to this country by the British soldiers! She afterwards married a MULATTO MAN, with whom she had several children, of which number GENERAL JACKSON IS ONE!!!" More damaging was the story that Jackson was an adulterer. His wife, Rachel, previously was married to Lewis Robards. Unbeknownst to her, she married Jackson before the divorce being sought by Robards actually was granted; as a consequence, Jackson and Rachel were forced to marry a second time. All of this was ancient history in 1828, since the second marriage took place in 1794, but the slurs continued and contributed to Rachel's death after the election. The General's personality was not exempt from criticism. Enemies portrayed him as a drunken bully, a rowdy, a duelist, and a gunfighter, as well as a villain who indulged in cockfighting, horse-racing, and sabbath breaking, to say nothing of fornication, murder, and treason.

The election campaign of 1828 was among the dirtiest in American history. Much of the mudslinging was done in the columns of the nation's 600-odd newspapers. The Jacksonians were particularly effective in organizing a partisan press. Interestingly enough, much of the cost of reaching the public was ultimately borne by the American taxpayer since partisan congressmen used their franking privilege to distribute campaign literature. In the opinion of many observers, it was not spontaneous anti-Adams sentiment among the populace that drove the President from the White House but rather it was a well-coordinated campaign against him.

The Jacksonians used stump speeches, parades, public rallies, barbecues, dinners, cartoons, and jokes. At the same time, they aroused the fears of minorities, implying, for example, that the Unitarian President was anti-Catholic and had made vague promises to special interest groups. The Jacksonian Democrats, anticipating modern tactics, even published results of public opinion polls favoring their candidate—in the hope of convincing fencesitters that Jackson was the inevitable choice, the winner whom they must support. In addition, they built up local political organizations in various states.

The Adams campaign never matched this effort, despite the efforts of Clay, members of the Cabinet, and other supporters. Adams himself was hard to sell. As he once said of himself with deadly accuracy, "I am a man of reserved, cold, austere, and forbidding manners. My political adversaries say, a gloomy misanthrope, and my personal enemies an unsocial savage. With the knowledge of the actual defects of my character, I have not the pliability to reform it."

Jackson won a sweeping electoral victory, taking 178 votes in the Electoral College compared to 83 for Adams, though in the popular election he secured only 56 percent of the vote. Despite scattered opposition, John C. Calhoun easily won the vice presidency. The election demonstrated that reduced suffrage requirements had given the vote to a greater populace, and more than a million of these new voters had been lured to the polls by a vigorous campaign. (The turnout, however, did not exceed the previous highs in most recent state elections.) Once again, the nation seemed to have a two-party system, and this rebirth of competition meant that from now

Jacksonian stump speakers extolled "Old Hickory's" virtues, made vague promises to special interest groups, and played upon the fears of recent immigrants in order to convince voters that "Andrew Jackson is the *candidate of the People.*"

on candidates would have to fight for mass support. Though the situation encouraged demogoguery, it also had the merit of drawing huge numbers of Americans into the democratic process.

Establishing Jacksonian Democracy

Soon after Jackson was in office, the bitter John Quincy Adams confided to his diary that "the only principles yet discernible in the conduct of the President were to feed the cormorant appetite for place, and to reward the prostitution of canvassing defamers."

It was true that handing out political appointments was one of the first acts performed by the new President. Even during his inauguration in March of 1829, some 20,000 people swarmed into Washington, D.C., many of them stampeding through the White House in search of jobs. During his first month in office, as Jackson told a friend, he received thousands of applications for government positions. "If I had a tit for every applicant to suck the Treasury pap, all would go away well satisfied, but, as there are not office[s] for more than one out of five hundred who applies," he lamented, "many must go away dissatisfied."

Jackson's cabinet selection paid off political debts. Martin Van Buren of New York, as previously noted, became Secretary of State. Although Van Buren became an important advisor, Jackson generally relied less on his official Cabinet for guidance than on a small group of political friends who came to be known as his "Kitchen Cabinet." Amos Kendall and Isaac Hill, both Treasury officials for a time, and Francis P. Blair, on his way to becoming editor of the Washington *Globe*, were prominent members of this inner circle.

Jackson and his followers were eager to place loyal men in control of the national patronage. John Quincy Adams had refused to dismiss anyone simply on the basis of political affiliation and had thereby retained in fact many enemies who busily plotted his downfall. Such high-mindedness was not Jackson's style. He went so far as to defend "rotation in office" as a democratic process and justified his sometimes careless appointments on the grounds that "the duties of all public officers are . . . so plain and simple that men of intelligence may readily qualify themselves for their performance," adding that "no one man has any more intrinsic right to office than another."

Jackson did not originate the spoils system, but he certainly contributed to its rise. Yet he did not initiate a clean sweep in 1829. Indeed, in 1830, after 18 months in office, only 919 of 10,093 officeholders had been replaced.

Library of Congress.

The inauguration of Andrew Jackson as depicted in Robert Cruikshank's drawing entitled "The President's Levee, or All Creation Going to the White House."

Museum of the City of New York.

This lithograph portrays Jackson as a devil dangling the spoils of office above the heads of political supporters.

Unfortunately, not all of the former employees were removed for good cause. Jackson and his followers sanctioned replacement of subordinate officers for personal or purely partisan reasons; all other Presidents (with the exception of Jefferson who was bent in 1801–1802 on ridding the government of Federalists) had replaced most office holders on well-justified grounds. Although Jackson's dismissals were not extensive (he probably divested himself of no more than 20 percent of all officeholders during his tenure), the spoils system was much more apparent on the state level, especially in New Hampshire and New York. Indeed, it was New York Senator William Learned Marcy, a Jacksonite, who had coined the phrase "to the victor belongs the spoils."

Nor did Jackson's appointments coincide with his stated concern for "the common man." Most of his choices for the higher public offices were rich, educated men from the same ethnic groups that Adams and his other predecessors had favored. Unfortunately, the spoils system led to a decline in the efficiency of public service, since incompetent men sometimes used their new offices to fill their pockets through graft and corruption. As the historian Edward Pessen has put it, Jackson's presidency marked "not so much the democratization of politics, as their commercialization."

The evils of the "rotation" policy can, however, be overdrawn. The backbone of Washington continued to be experienced civil servants long in office. And not all of the new appointees were unqualified. Some were capable men with a broad experience in public life who had a strong desire to compile a record of constructive achievement.

The Jackson-Calhoun Split

Jackson's victory in 1828 was, in part, the result of support in the North by Martin Van Buren and in the South by John C. Calhoun. Both men wanted to be President, and each hoped to succeed Old Hickory, who had intimated he would serve only one term (he was sixty-one in 1828). Soon after Jackson came into the White House, it became clear that his sympathies lay with Van Buren.

One cause of the break with Calhoun was the Peggy Eaton affair. On January 1, 1829, Jackson's Secretary of War and fellow Tennessean, John Eaton, married Margaret ("Peggy") O'Neale Timberlake. A vivacious, beautiful widow, daughter of a Washington tavernkeeper, it was rumored that she "kept company" with Eaton, who frequently stayed at her father's establishment, while married to another man. Gossips seized upon the fact she married Eaton only four months after the death of her first husband. Jackson refused to admit that Peggy Eaton might be a loose woman. His own wife, Rachel, died shortly before Jackson became President, and he was certain that the slanderous accusations of adultery against her had hastened her death. Jackson drew a parallel between the persecution his wife suffered and the coldness that official Washington was showing Mrs. Eaton.

Although at first Calhoun was not involved in the Eaton controversy, his wife, Floride, refused to acknowledge the woman's existence and other cabinet wives followed her example. Soon the President became convinced that Calhoun himself was leading the conspiracy against Mrs. Eaton. As John Quincy Adams, observing the fracas from a safe distance, drily observed, "Calhoun heads the moral party, Van Buren that of the frail sisterhood." Van Buren—a widower without daughters and thus having no women in his family who might be "stained" through contact with Mrs. Eaton—ardently defended the lady's virtue and became her patron, arranging dinner parties in her honor and being extremely solicitous of her welfare. In doing so, Van Buren gained the President's confidence at the same time that Calhoun lost it, although the New Yorker's very obvious political

Courtesy New-York Historical Society, New York City.

Peggy Eaton meets President Andrew Jackson and his cabinet. The so-called "Eaton Affair" contributed to the split between Jackson and Vice President John C. Calhoun.

skills had won his approbation long before Floride refused to receive Peggy. In 1829, when he was so seriously ill that he thought he was dying, Jackson wrote a letter to a friend praising Van Buren as "well qualified . . . to fill the highest office in the gift of the people. . . . I wish I could say as much for Mr. Calhoun. You know the confidence I once had in that gentleman. However of him I desire not now to speak."

Other factors of much greater importance than any social fracas underlay the break between Jackson and Calhoun. Calhoun opposed most of Jackson's cabinet appointees and attempted to fill some vacant government offices with his own allies. To add to the tension, Jackson learned that Calhoun, as Secretary of War, had wanted to punish him back in 1818 for his invasion of Florida, then Spanish territory. But the most substantial issue that divided the President and the Vice President was the nullification controversy.

States' Rights and Nullification

Jackson's view of states' rights versus federalism is subtle and difficult to pinpoint, though it can be argued that he acted in accord with his attitude, elusive as it might seem to be. At times he was an old Jeffersonian Republican upholding the doctrine of state sovereignty, but he also could be a fervent nationalist, a role especially suited to the occupant of the White House. He entertained a vision of Americans from every state and territory indissolubly bound together in a common destiny unfolding as their nation expanded across the continent—though without direction from the federal government.

The President's nationalism gave him ample room to make use of federal authority to set aside any impediments to the fulfillment of the great destiny he felt certain was awaiting America. The Indian removal policy, for instance, was a natural corollary to his views about the American Union and its glorious future. Regretable as the harm done to the Indians might be, they could not be allowed to stand in the way of the white man's westward expansion, Jackson thought. Yet, as differences with Calhoun developed, Jackson, a man of emotions without deep philosophical reflection (that, indeed, was Calhoun's specialty), did not think deeply concerning the issues involved. First and foremost, he was thoroughly angry that his will was being thwarted by his own Vice President.

In 1830 a debate arose in the Senate between Daniel Webster (1782–1852) of Massachusetts and the South Carolinian Robert Y. Hayne (1791–1839) concerning sectionalism. This issue developed when senators from Connecticut and Missouri became embroiled over a proposal to limit land sales in the West. New Englanders clearly hoped to curb the emigration of settlers from their region—a population drain that diminished their wealth, manpower, and political influence. Southern senators came to the aid of Westerners in opposing this scheme, which would have stunted the growth of the West. What seemed to be in the offing was a strong coalition of the South and the West against the Northeast, which favored high tariffs and high land prices. Hayne attempted to bolster this coalition by introducing the subject of states' rights.

He warned against the dangers of a strong central government and, basing his arguments on Calhoun's *South Carolina Exposition*, declared that each state possessed the ultimate authority to determine whether or not acts of Congress were constitutional.

Webster dropped in on the middle of Hayne's speech and decided that a reply to it would provide him with an excellent opportunity for speaking out against the dangerous doctrine of states' rights. The federal government and not the states, he reasoned, is sovereign over the people. Acts of Congress passed in accordance with the Constitution are the supreme law of the land. At the end of his second reply to Hayne, Webster concluded, "Liberty *and* Union, now and forever, one and inseparable!"

Webster had not always been a nationalist. During the War of 1812, he adopted a states' rights position when New England's merchants opposed a war with England that would interfere with trade and profit. But the rise of industrialization was shifting the economic interests of the Northeast from commerce to manufacturing, which prospered under high tariffs enforced by a strong central government. Webster's movement from states' rights to nationalism reflected the concerns of his part of the country, just as Calhoun's shift in the opposite direction revealed South Carolina's economic interests.

Webster's second reply to Hayne is the most famous congressional oration in American history. Its glowing patriotism and its forceful assertion that the authority of the federal government rests with the people, not with states, has resounded down through the years from the throats of both orators and school children. Webster himself recognized its importance and spent a month

Chicago Historical Society.

Daniel Webster
1782–1852

One of the greatest northern statesmen of the antebellum period was the son of a New Hampshire farmer. His father, who served in the state militia and was a judge in the county court of common pleas, was determined that Daniel would have a first-rate education. He sent the boy to Phillips Exeter Academy and to Dartmouth College. Following graduation, Webster studied law and taught school until he went to Boston and opened a law practice.

There Webster became associated with the conservative mercantile interests of the population and soon became their champion. At the outbreak of the War of 1812, Webster opposed the federal government so vigorously and espoused the cause of peace so eloquently that the Federalists sent him to Congress. Though he never suggested that New England secede from the Union, he did recommend nullification of the conscription bill that would have drafted soldiers into the federal army (the bill failed and so was not put to the test).

In Congress, Webster originally opposed high protective tariffs (duties designed to protect manufacturers and industrials), for at this point he was the friend of merchants and shippers whose interests would be hurt by protection. After the war, Webster withdrew from Congress and became a famous lawyer representing clients before the Supreme Court. His brilliant performance in court earned him the reputation for being the best legal mind in the country.

By the time Webster became a senator in 1827, his loyalties had shifted from the mercantile to the industrial sector of New England. In part this change reflected the basic metamorphosis of the New England economy, but it also represented a change in Webster's own interests, for he now owned stock in the Merrimack Manufacturing Company, a cotton mill. In Washington, he became an aggressive defender of the protective tariff and of the central government. During the nullification crisis, Webster championed nationalism in his most famous oration, his second reply to Hayne in January 1830. In that speech he argued that the Constitution set up a government that was sovereign over its own domain and was not a compact that could be dissolved; the only body that could judge constitutionality was the Supreme Court, not the states. For this position Webster came to be known as the "Defender of the Constitution."

At this time Webster also championed the Bank of the United States against Andrew Jackson and the Democrats. Once again, principle and personal interest came together, for Webster was deeply in debt to the Bank. His defense of the Bank brought him one of the regional

Whig nominations for the presidency in 1836, but in the election he received only the electoral vote of Massachusetts.

When Harrison became President in 1841, he appointed Webster Secretary of State, a position he retained after Tyler succeeded to the presidency. As Secretary of State, he brought a peaceful and successful conclusion to the border dispute between Canada and the United States in the Webster-Ashburton Treaty of 1842.

Throughout his life, marked by several changes of attitude, Webster was always consistent in his opposition to slavery; and toward the end of his life, he fought against the acquisition of Texas, which he felt certain would trigger new North-South friction. Although he believed that the question of continuing slavery within the southern states was a matter "within the exclusive control of the States themselves," Webster consistently supported the Wilmot Proviso, which would exclude slavery from territories acquired as a result of the Mexican War. In 1852, when he died of cirrhosis of the liver exacerbated by excessive drinking, Webster was worried about the fate of the Union he had done so much to preserve. ■

Courtesy Massachusetts Historical Society.

Daniel Webster replies to Robert Y. Hayne, who is sitting in the front center with his hands together. Vice President John C. Calhoun, at the extreme left, is listening intently and leaning on his desk.

"The man who has filled the measure of his Country's Glory."
JEFFERSON.
Jackson,
DEMOCRACY,
And our Country.
"The Union must be Preserved."
1. Samuel M'Kean,

The Tennessee State Library and Archives, Nashville.

A pro-Jackson and pro-Union broadside distributed by the President's allies during the nullification crisis.

polishing the speech before he allowed it to be published. Americans everywhere responded to it enthusiastically, not only in New England but also in the South and West. A Virginian, former president James Madison, wrote, "It crushes 'nullification' and must hasten an abandonment of secession." A possible coalition between the South and the West on the basis of free trade and cheap land had been stymied.

The nullification crisis completed the break between Jackson and Calhoun. At the annual Jefferson Day Dinner, held on April 13, 1830, Jackson pointedly made the following toast while looking at Vice President Calhoun: "Our *Federal* Union—It *must* be *preserved*." Van Buren, perhaps not the most impartial reporter, later asserted that the Vice President shook under Jackson's harsh gaze. In any event, Calhoun was ready with his reply: "The Union—Next to our liberty most dear."

Meanwhile the decline in the price of cotton led some South Carolinians to speak of nullifying the "Tariff of Abominations." Calhoun counseled delay, hoping that the new Congress scheduled to assemble in December 1831 would write a more moderate tariff, but former President John Quincy Adams, now a congressman from Massachusetts, secured a victory for protection in the Tariff of 1832, a bill that removed most of the aspects of the 1828 measure objectionable to manufacturers.

South Carolina, one of two states (the other was Virginia) whose senators solidly opposed the new tariff, responded by calling a state convention that on November 24, 1832, declared the tariffs of 1828 and 1832 "null, void, and no law, nor binding upon this State, its officers or citizens." Furthermore, South Carolina's Ordinance of Nullification threatened secession from the Union if the federal government used force in implementing the tariff. Calhoun, who resigned the vice presidency late in 1832, was elected to the Senate, where he proceeded to defend energetically his state's actions.

The virtual hysteria with which South Carolina responded to the Tariff of 1832 concealed another fear that was plaguing the rich Low Country plantation owners—the abolition of slavery. Although the abolition movement was only in its infancy in 1832, the ferocious congressional debate over admission of Missouri as a slave state, which had raged during 1819 and 1820, was still fresh in the minds of many white Southerners. They feared that the federal government might someday ban the further expansion of slavery, or even intrude on the legality of slavery where it already existed. Worse, South Carolina had witnessed a bloody slave uprising, led by Denmark Vesey in 1822, and many whites lived in terror of a general insurrection among blacks. This fear was only heightened when Nat Turner led his unsuccessful revolt in Virginia in 1831. White Southerners began to blame abolitionists for these outbreaks of violence. The fear of slave uprisings fostered "a garrison mentality," especially in Low Country counties where blacks greatly outnumbered whites or where blacks had access to ports that sailors who were "infected" with the abolitionist virus might visit. Actually, the years from 1822 to 1831 (Vesey to Turner) represent a high point of known slave conspiracies. How much influence rising abolitionist fervor and southern indecision played in that decade is unclear. But, once Southerners established a firm policy, few slaves dared plot any sort of mass action.

New York Public Library, Prints Division.

This contemporary comment on the nullification crisis depicts John C. Calhoun reaching for a crown while his victims, the Constitution and the Union, lie dead at the bottom of the steps leading to despotism. President Andrew Jackson at the far right restrains a nullifier and threatens to hang all disunionists.

President Jackson responded to the nullification crisis with a determination to enforce federal law and to preserve the Union. He transported troops to the forts in Charleston harbor, sent arms and ammunition to nearby areas in North Carolina, named General Winfield Scott (1786–1866) as his special emissary to South Carolina, and encouraged Unionists within the rebellious state to temper the situation and oppose nullification and secession.

On December 10, 1832, after being reelected by an overwhelming majority with Van Buren as his running mate, Jackson was in an excellent position to issue his *Nullification Proclamation,* in which he declared that the federal government was supreme, nullification absurd, and "disunion by armed forces" treasonous. "I consider . . . the power to annul a law of the United States, assumed by one State, incompatible with the existence of the Union, contradicted expressly by the letter of the Constitution, unauthorized by its spirit, inconsistent with every principle on which it was founded, and destructive of the great object for which it was formed."

Jackson was prepared, if necessary, to use federal troops to enforce the tariff. While Congress was at work drafting legislation that would give him the power to do so, Henry Clay introduced a compromise tariff. On the same day, March 1, 1833, that Congress gave Jackson power to enforce his *Proclamation,* it also passed Clay's tariff. This measure called for a gradual reduction of duties over a ten-year period; it was championed by Calhoun, still ambitious for the presidency and eager to head off an open war between his state and the Union. The new tariff and Jackson's Indian removal policy appeased all of the southern states except South Carolina, which had no option now but to rescind its *Ordinance of Nullification.* As a last face-saving gesture, however, South Carolina went so far as to nullify the congressional Force Act authorizing Jackson to crush their secession threat—but by that time no one cared. South Carolina could claim that its actions had won a new tariff, while Jackson could claim credit for preserving the Union. Though everyone seemed satisfied, the issues involved in this controversy would erupt later and lead to the Civil War.

The Bank War

If Jackson is remembered today as the friend of the "common man" and the defender of democracy, to a large degree it is because of his actions in the Bank War, and even more so to the rhetoric generated by his supporters in that conflict.

The Second Bank of the United States (called BUS) was incorporated in 1816 under a twenty-year charter. Its constitutionality was upheld in *McCulloch* v. *Maryland* (1819) by Chief Justice John Marshall. Although the BUS was mismanaged and suffered during the Panic of 1819, it subsequently recovered under the capable management of the Philadelphian Nicholas Biddle (1785–1844), who assumed control in 1823. Biddle led the bank to great prosperity, and during his rule it did a business of $70 million a year and had branches in twenty-nine cities. The bank provided sound currency and inexpensive commercial credit. Among the advantages it offered the country were a source of money for industrial expansion, a clearinghouse for the nation's finances, and a deterrent to poorly capitalized, wildcat banks that, if left unchecked, overheated the economy by making easy loans and encouraging speculation in western land.

But not everyone appreciated these advantages. Many Westerners, including Andrew Jackson, despised the BUS. Jackson saw the institution as a vast, powerful monopoly with all the influence of a branch of the government but not subject to federal supervision. As a Westerner, Jackson knew that during the panic of 1819 the Bank caused many state banks and investors to declare bankruptcy, and its actions, in time, had foreclosed the mortgages of countless farmers; Jackson himself suffered financial losses. More importantly, Jackson regarded the BUS as a dangerous foe to American liberties. He was convinced that the Bank, responsible only to its American and foreign stockholders and possessing almost limitless funds, could buy off congressmen, rig elections, and shape public opinion through newspapers owned by or indebted to it. This conviction was only strengthened in 1829 when several of his advisors assured him that Bank officials had campaigned against him in the recent election.

In spite of the Supreme Court's 1819 assertion of the constitutionality of the BUS, Jackson, in his first annual message to Congress in 1829, questioned its constitutionality, but he was reluctant to take on "the Monster," as Westerners had dubbed the bank, until he consolidated his own power. In 1832 Henry Clay, who had just received the National Republican presidential nomination, urged Nicholas Biddle to submit the Bank's charter to Congress for renewal. Although the charter of the BUS would not expire for four years, Clay hoped to gain a major campaign issue if Jackson vetoed the new charter. Biddle thought that Jackson would never make the Bank a political issue, so he decided to follow Clay's suggestion.

This proposal enraged the President. As he told Van Buren, "The bank is trying to kill me, but I will kill it!" And, indeed, he did when Congress failed to override his veto of the recharter bill. More importantly, it became a factor in the 1832 election since the veto message was political propaganda designed to arouse the public to vote for Old Hickory in his struggle against "privilege and aristocracy."

The Democrats won a sweeping victory; Clay did not carry a single state of the lower South or the New West where the BUS was held in such disrepute. In the Electoral College, Jackson had 219 votes, Clay, 49, but his popular lead was not quite so impressive (701,780 votes to Clay's 484,205). In fact, Jackson's overall total was slightly less than what he had received four years earlier.

Jackson now decided to remove federal deposits from the BUS. When his Secretary of the Treasury, Louis McLane, opposed this move, Jackson replaced him with William J. Duane, who also spoke out against the policy. A few months later, Jackson nominated yet another man, Roger B. Taney (1777–1864), to head the Treasury. Clay's supporters delighted in calling Jackson a tyrant because of this constant reshuffling of the Cabinet.

Jackson then took funds withdrawn from the BUS and deposited them in "pet banks" controlled by his allies, among which were the Union Bank of Baltimore, The Girard Bank of Philadelphia, three banks in New York, and two in Boston. Before the end of 1833, Clay introduced Senate resolutions censuring Jackson for his actions; these resolutions were aimed primarily against his war on the BUS but also against repeated vetoes of congressional bills (Jackson used the veto more often than any previous chief executive), and his constant tampering with the Cabinet. When Jackson's opponents gained a temporary majority in the Senate in 1834, they passed a formal act of censure against the President for his "executive tyranny." Jackson vigorously protested the move, but only after a three-year battle was he able to succeed in having it expunged from the Senate record. However, by the time these resolutions were being discussed, the Bank issue was no longer a sectional matter;

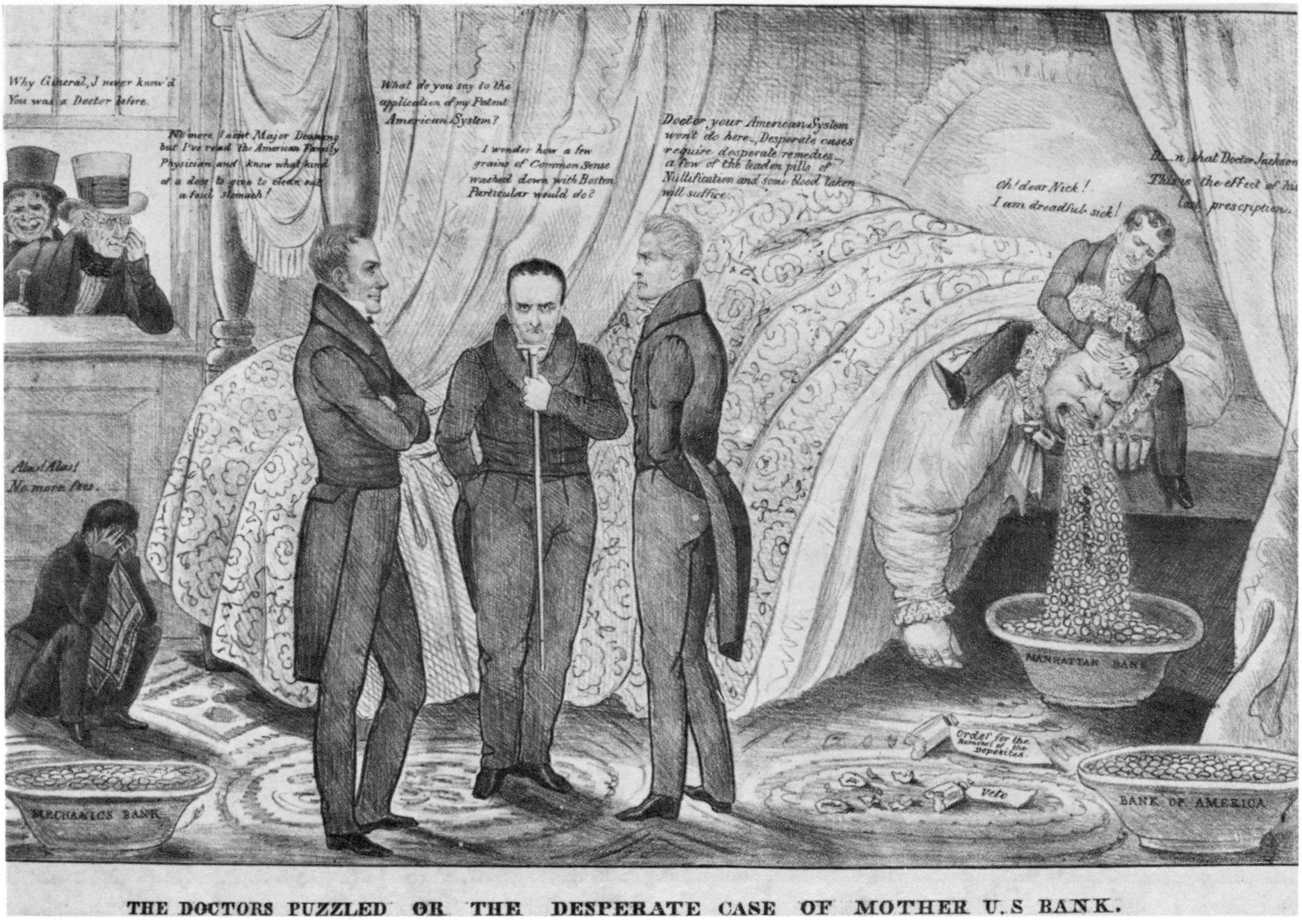

Courtesy New-York Historical Society, New York City.

"Doctor" Jackson's prescription for "Mother U.S. Bank." At the far left, Jackson insists that his medicine will "clean out" the bank's "foul stomach." In the center, leading anti-Jacksonites—Clay, Webster, and Calhoun—discuss remedies for the bank's predicament, while, at the far right, Nicholas Biddle tries to stop the removal of the bank's deposits.

instead it was a political question being hotly debated by Henry Clay's new Whig Party and Jacksonian Democrats.

Jackson's war against the Bank of the United States contributed to a series of severe economic reverses, including a nationwide financial crisis in 1833–1834. Biddle only hastened this disaster when he called in outstanding loans and contracted credit, partly to protect the Bank's investors but mainly to force congressional reconsideration of the BUS charter.

The "Biddle panic" lasted only a short time, and the country soon returned to what seemed like prosperity. But actually the economy had entered a dangerous inflationary spiral brought on, at least in part, by the tendency of state banks to lend newly acquired federal funds for the purpose of speculating in public lands and internal improvements. A land law of 1830, which authorized settlers to purchase up to 160 acres at the very low price of $1.25 an acre, greatly increased public land sales and encouraged reckless speculation. Between 1831 and 1836 federal land sales totalled 46 million acres as opposed to only 10 million for the years 1821 to 1830. To finance the construction of roads, canals, and railroads, states piled up enormous debts and local banks extended extensive credit. Between 1830 and 1838, states went into debt to the amount of $150 million, and two-thirds of the money was spent for internal improvements.

The state banks that fueled this speculative mania were generally short of specie—gold and silver. They issued paper money without sufficient specie to back it up. The currency expanded from $124 million in 1834 to $200 million in 1836. Jackson himself finally noticed this dangerous trend and attempted to curtail it on July 11, 1836, when he published his Specie Circular ordering the U.S. Treasury to stop accepting paper money for the sale of public lands; only gold and silver could be received in the future. This policy not only curtailed land sales but contributed to a loss of public confidence in state banks. Distrustful of paper money, people began to hoard gold and silver—and this damming of the flow of specie helped to bring on a severe depression shortly after Jackson left office. Although Jackson justified his war on the Bank of the United States in the name of the common people, it was ultimately the average small investor who suffered the most in the depression that followed.

Jackson and Foreign Policy

Jackson had far more success in foreign affairs than his predecessor who once had been a diplomat. Great Britain long had restricted U.S. trade with the West Indies, and the United States, in turn, had forbidden American goods to be carried in British ships to the islands. The British hinted to Adams that they might change this policy, which was detrimental to both countries, but Adams, mistakenly thinking that British officials were being pressured by their government to grant concessions, took the wrong tack. Rather than *requesting* the reopening of trade as a favor, Adams *demanded* it as a right. This irritated the British Foreign Minister, George Canning, who dropped the negotiations.

Jackson, admittedly a convinced anglophobe, approached the question anew. He specifically disowned the view of the Adams Administration, and on October 5, 1830, a proclamation was issued announcing that West Indian and American ports would be free and open to ships from either nation. The trade, so beneficial to southern planters and northern merchants, reopened two months later.

France never compensated Americans for ships and goods seized from 1803 to 1815 during the Napoleonic wars. At the end of 1834, Jackson recommended that French property in the United States should be seized if American claims were not promptly settled. Talk of war rumbled on both sides of the ocean, but finally in April

THE DESTRUCTION OF THE GOOD SHIP, PUBLIC CREDIT.

Courtesy New-York Historical Society, New York City.

This 1836 anti-Jackson cartoon blames the monetary crisis on the effects of Andrew Jackson's Specie Circular.

1835 the French Chamber of Deputies voted the necessary funds—but the American debt was to be paid only after Jackson had offered an explanation and an apology for his threats. *"From me, she will get neither,"* Jackson exclaimed, damning France. Despite these brave words, Jackson was careful to tell Congress that he had no intention "to menace or insult" the French government, and those words sufficed to appease the French. By the spring of 1836, Jackson was able to announce that four of the six installments on the debt had been paid.

Jackson also was watching events in Texas closely. In March 1836 Texas declared its independence from Mexico and established itself as a republic under President Sam Houston. When Texas asked for diplomatic recognition from the United States, Jackson moved cautiously, for he feared war with Mexico. More importantly, if Texas was admitted as a state, the annexation could engender a new dispute between Northerners and Southerners over whether the region would be slave or free, and that dispute might jeopardize the chances of Jackson's party in the 1836 election. As a result, Jackson moved with circumspection and did not recognize the republic until the day before he left the White House in 1837.

The Jacksonian Heritage

In 1837 Martin Van Buren, Jackson's handpicked heir, assumed the presidency. The former Vice President won a narrow victory and Jackson's popularity and his achievements between 1829 and 1836 probably tipped the balloting in his favor. Jackson had braved and bested the South Carolina advocates of nullification. He had waged an antimonopoly war against the Bank of the United States that was more attractive to some voters than it was sound economically. The country was enjoying what seemed to be a lasting prosperity and under Jackson the United States had settled important disputes in foreign affairs and made Europe take America more seriously.

But Jackson's most significant accomplishment was his redefinition of the presidency. Forceful in manner and confident of his popularity, Jackson reshaped the office into a position of enormous power and influence by using his veto power, by removing government workers from office and naming their replacements and by heading up a political party based on mass participation and organized for national action. Jackson became a symbol of the people's aspirations for democracy and participation in government. Yet the expanded presidency was a mixed blessing. The positive aspects of a strong chief executive are quick, well-directed responses to domestic needs and international crises. The negative aspects are the distortion of the traditional constitutional balance among the three branches of government and the possibility that the executive branch may mislead the people or limit their options through biased propaganda and management of the news.

A New Party System: Whigs and Democrats

Jackson's conduct as President won him both friends and enemies. Members of the coalition opposed to him formed a new political party—the Whigs, named after the party that fought royal supremacy in England and sought to restore a "proper" constitutional balance by giving more weight to Parliament. In American terms, "King Andrew" was the monarch and foe and Congress the friend of liberty. The Whigs brought together disparate elements, such as the National Republicans of John Quincy Adams and Henry Clay, the states' rights Democrats led by John C. Calhoun and John Tyler of Virginia, and the Anti-Masons led by William Wirt. The Anti-Masonic movement was a short-lived reaction against the secrecy of the Masonic Order fueled by the alleged murder of a member who allegedly divulged its secrets. This group, the first real "third party" in U.S. political history, was especially strong in Vermont, New York, and Pennsylvania during the 1830s. In 1832 it drew support from Clay and helped reelect Jackson, but by 1838 the party merged with the Whigs. More important interest groups that came together in the Whig party included industrialists and merchants from the Northeast, led by Daniel Webster; champions of internal improvements from the West, led by Clay; and states righters and wealthy planters from the South, led by John Tyler.

Although opposition to Jackson was the immediate goal of the Whigs, they offered voters an optimistic picture of the nation's future and, in contrast to Jacksonian laissez-faire, recommended a vigorous role for the federal government as a promoter of a healthy economy. Clay's American System lay at the heart of the Whig economic program; the Whigs called for a protective tariff that would promote American economic independence and lessen the country's reliance on foreign products and backed internal improvements that would bind together the industrial Northeast, the agricultural West, and the cotton South.

The Whigs, staunchly Protestant, tended to be churchgoing men who admired respectability and feared the alarming influx of foreigners, especially Irish Catholics. In spite of the elitist temper of the party, it included workers (especially those who resented immigrant competition for jobs). The Whigs also won support from free blacks in the North, since Jackson and most Democrats opposed equal suffrage rights for blacks and the Whigs, despite some doubletalk, seemed more sympathetic to black political aspirations.

The Bettmann Archive.

Andrew Jackson portrayed as "King Andrew," using his veto power to place his will above that of the Constitution, the federal courts, and the needs of the people.

A major factor that forged these disparate elements into a new political party was support for the Bank of the United States. After Jackson waged his war on the BUS between 1832 and 1834, various anti-Jackson groups buried their differences and came together in support of the Bank. Unity on the issue of the Bank and a general dislike for Jackson joined those Southerners, who abhorred the idea of a protective tariff and had threatened secession, with New Englanders who favored the tariff and abhorred states' rights. The Bank was very useful to southern planters, to northern manufacturers and merchants, and to western entrepreneurs. The battle over rechartering the BUS had very significant results in the political realm since it helped to create the Whig party and establish rigid alignments that lasted for nearly a quarter of a century.

The Election of 1836

The election of 1836 pitted the Whigs against Van Buren, Jackson's Vice President. The Whigs knew that their party was not yet well organized, that it was full of conflicting views. In choosing a candidate, the party bypassed Clay, who had not done well in the 1832 election and put up strong sectional candidates in various states. In New England, Webster was the candidate. In Tennessee, Hugh L. White ran with Whig support after he broke with Jackson when it became clear that Van Buren, never popular in Tennessee, had received the Democratic nomination. William Henry Harrison of Ohio campaigned under the Whig banner in the West and the Middle Atlantic states.

The Democrats were riddled with factionalism. Many Southerners refused to support New Yorker Van Buren, and others were still seething with discontent over Jackson's handling of the South Carolina nullifiers. The party attempted to stress its record, accusing the Whigs of being for that bastion of privilege, the BUS, for a "wasteful" system of internal improvements, for nullification, and for a high tarriff.

Jackson's own personality, however, was the chief issue, and the election returns were not much comfort to Old Hickory. Van Buren received only 51 percent of the popular vote. No vice presidential candidate received a majority of the electoral votes, so the Senate eventually chose Richard M. Johnson, the Democratic contender for that office. The two parties, with almost an equal number of supporters, appeared to dominate no particular region and a truly national two-party system seemed to be emerging.

Van Buren and Economic Problems

In his inaugural address, Van Buren stressed the need for national unity—an emphasis that reflected the factionalism he knew existed within his own party. To still the fears of southern whites, Van Buren promised that his administration would not interfere with the institution of slavery—a promise that infuriated abolitionists. But also he intimated that he would not push for annexation of Texas, which Southerners wanted to become a slave state.

Slavery, however, was not the first problem Van Buren had to tackle. Rather, it quickly became apparent that he had inherited a major depression. The Panic of 1837 was brought about by Jackson's destruction of the BUS, which had restricted the issuance of paper money by state banks. The Specie Circular of 1836 shifted supplies of gold and silver from the East to the West and cast doubt on the paper money in circulation. Finally, a depression in England lowered the price of southern cotton. By mid-1837 banks all over the nation were in deep trouble, plantations were selling at low prices, food prices were soaring, and factories were shutting down.

Van Buren's closest associates saw the crisis as a healthy interlude during which the economy would stabilize and rid itself of parasitical speculators and gamblers. Although many people, including loyal Democrats, clamored for the President to revoke Jackson's Specie Circular, Van Buren refused. A complete break between the government and all banks was what Van Buren wanted, and in 1840 Congress finally passed his Independent Treasury Act, which required the deposit of all federal funds in government-owned vaults in various parts of the country. In the process, Van Buren lost the support of those Democrats who had a personal interest in keeping federal funds in state banks. The only political gain of Van Buren's move was the return of Calhoun to the Democratic party. Calhoun never had been at ease with such Whig policies as the advocacy of a strong central government in charge of high tariffs and extensive internal improvements. He had long been in favor of an independent Treasury, and he welcomed Van Buren's bill as an opportunity for returning to the Democratic fold.

Although northern and southern Whigs disagreed about the efficacy of a Bank of the United States, a protective tariff, and internal improvements, nevertheless they closed ranks in blaming the depression on Democratic policies. Other issues also hurt Van Buren's chances for reelection. Some southerners held that the President's failure to arrange for the annexation of Texas meant that he was secretly sympathetic to abolition. Conversely, abolitionists led by Congressman Joshua R. Giddings of Ohio maintained that Van Buren had shown his pro-

The J. Clarence Davies Collection, Museum of the City of New York.

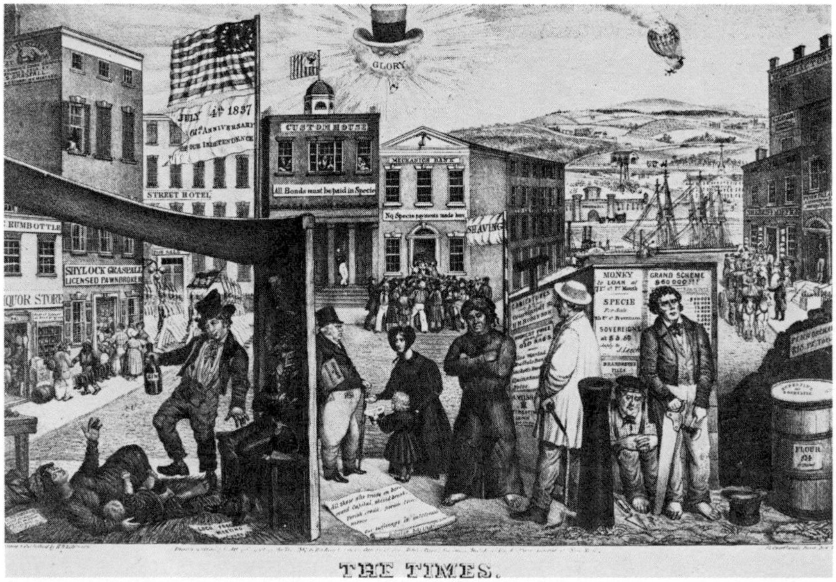

A Whig cartoonist's view of the Panic of 1837. A caricature of President Andrew Jackson watches over idle ships and workers while bank depositers clamor for their money, a mother and child beg, a husband drinks his troubles away, and a pawnbroker's shop prospers.

HUNTING INDIANS IN FLORIDA WITH BLOOD HOUNDS_

Library of Congress.

A pro-Indian view of the Seminole Indian War.

slavery sympathies by endorsing the costly and bloody Seminole War in Florida. Between 1835 and the end of 1842, the Seminoles, aided by many runaway slaves, fought U.S. forces; to many abolitionists the war appeared to be merely an effort to help slaveholders regain their escaped bondsmen. Van Buren therefore had the disadvantage of seeming antislavery in the South and proslavery in the North. Abolitionists were especially incensed by the refusal of both houses of the Congress to discuss petitions relating to slavery. After 1836, by tacit agreement, the Senate received antislavery petitions but rejected them. At the beginning of each session from 1836 to 1844 the House adopted a gag rule that automatically tabled any petition relating to slavery.

Whig Triumph of 1840

As the election of 1840 approached, the Whigs sensed victory. Remembering that William Henry Harrison had made the best showing in the previous election, winning 73 electoral votes as opposed to White's 26 votes and Webster's 14, they offered Harrison the nomination. An attractive candidate, he had defeated Tecumseh's forces at the Battle of Tippecanoe in 1811. Harrison, who was of southern ancestry (born in Virginia), had a popular following in the Old Northwest. Best of all, his political sentiments were vague.

Harrison was the choice of the New York Whig boss, Thurlow Weed, a man who did for the Whigs in 1840 what Van Buren did for the Democrats in 1828. Weed, grasping the nature of modern politics, argued that tactics not principles won campaigns. To assure Harrison's election, Weed secured the vice presidential nomination for Virginian John Tyler, a states' rights Democrat alienated from his party by Jackson's war on the Bank and by his handling of the South Carolina nullifiers. Weed hoped that Tyler would attract southern votes.

The Whigs followed the Democratic precedent of 1828 by using parades, rallies, songs, and slogans in order to paint Van Buren as an aristocrat and Harrison as a frontiersman and military hero. They decided not to have a platform at all, since their fragmented party might fall apart over stated principles. Instead the party relied exclusively on ballyhoo. When a Democratic newspaper said derisively that if Harrison had a small pension he would spend the rest of his days in a log cabin sipping hard cider, the Whigs cleverly turned this slur to their advantage. Harrison was portrayed as a rustic farmer, and hundreds of floats with log cabins were drawn through parades and Harrison was billed as the "log-cabin and hard-cider candidate." Horace Greeley went so far as to issue a special Whig newspaper called the *Log Cabin*. More than 5,000 Whigs scoured the country giving stump speeches. In catchy tunes the Whigs sang, "Tippecanoe and Tyler too, Tippecanoe and Tyler too! Farewell, dear Van. You're not our man; To guide the ship, We'll try old Tip."

Harrison garnered 53 percent of the popular vote and won 234 electoral votes compared to 60 votes for Van Buren. The popular margin was about 146,500 votes.

Library of Congress.

Joshua Reed Giddings (1795–1864)

A savage voice against slavery during the middle decades of the nineteenth century, Joshua Giddings represents a maverick point of view that maintained that the federal government should have nothing whatsoever to do with the troublesome institution of slavery. Only later in his life did he, in fact, become an avowed abolitionist.

Born in Pennsylvania to a restless frontier family of New England stock, Giddings grew up in Ohio. After rudimentary schooling and a brief career as an Indian fighter during the War of 1812, he taught school, farmed, married a girl from Connecticut, and began to study law in the town of Canton. Admitted to the bar in 1821, he set up a general practice in nearby Jefferson and, except for a term in the state legislature (1826), showed little interest in politics.

It was the financial crisis of 1837 and association with the abolitionist Theodore Dwight Weld that altered this man's life. The money panic ruined his dreams of a real estate fortune, and new anti-slavery zeal inspired him to seek a seat in Congress when the local incumbent decided to retire. During the next two decades Giddings moved from Whig to Free Soiler to Republican, always on the attack against slavery. The illicit slave trade, Texas, the Mexican War, the Wilmot Proviso—all felt his scorn. In 1842 his outspoken views won him the censure of the House of Representatives. Giddings immediately resigned but won the overwhelming endorsement of his district when he ran for reelection, a vote of 7469–393.

During the 1847–1848 session Giddings and young Abraham Lincoln shared the same lodgings, but not the same opinions. Giddings found the tall man from Illinois too timid on slavery and several of their table discussions led to heated words. Nevertheless a relationship emerged that lasted for many years. Because of ill health, Giddings quit Congress in 1858 and in that same year published *The Exiles of Florida: or, The Crimes Committed by our Government Against the Maroons, Who Fled from South Carolina and Other Slave States, Seeking Protection Under Spanish Laws.* This attack upon the machinations of southern Presidents (Madison, Monroe, Jackson) brought to light the cruelty experienced by both runaway slaves and Indians of the Southeast.

Despite misgivings, Giddings backed Lincoln in 1860 and also worked hard (and successfully) to get cabinet posts for Ohio politicians. In 1861 Lincoln named Giddings consul-general for Canada; here he died suddenly three years later at the home of a Montreal friend while analyzing a difficult, three-cushion billiard shot. ■

HARRISON
AND
TYLER.
TIPPECANOE LOG CABIN
corner of Main & Eagle Streets. _ Erected on the 18th. March, by the
WHIGS OF BUFFALO;
and dedicated to the cause of
HARRISON and TYLER
on the 20th March 1840.
Pub. & Lith. by Hall & Mooney
Size 20 feet by 30.

Courtesy New-York Historical Society, New York City.

An 1840 Whig campaign poster.

Now politicians were certain that ballyhoo techniques could capture the White House.

Politics, Expansion and Slavery

Victory in 1840 did not bring the factions in the Whig party together. Harrison never really commanded much respect among his fellow Whigs, and one month after he assumed office he died of pneumonia. His death brought party factionalism out into the open.

John Tyler, the first Vice President to inherit through death the position of chief executive, shared very few of the ideas of Whig leaders, and Henry Clay had no intention of letting him head the party. Tyler used the presidential veto to stop Whig efforts to revive the Bank of the United States, to pass internal improvement bills, to institute higher tariffs, and to distribute proceeds of public land sales to the states. All of the original members of Harrison's Cabinet except Secretary of State Daniel Webster resigned in disgust after six months.

Webster remained in the Cabinet because he was entering upon delicate negotiations with Great Britain. American feelings toward England, never too cordial, became still more hostile in the late 1830s. In 1837 Canadian insurgents, dissatisfied with London's rule, fled to an island in the Niagara River, where Americans supplied them with recruits and arms. One American steamer, the *Caroline,* aided the rebellious Canadians. The British sent a small force to seize the vessel; when they discovered that the *Caroline* had moved to the American side of the Niagara River, the British force continued its mission and burned and sank the ship. One American was killed and others wounded.

In 1840 a Canadian deputy sheriff named Alexander McLeod was arrested in Lockport, New York, and indicted for the murder of the American who died in the *Caroline* incident. The British protested that a man could not be tried for something done under orders as a member of an army; Daniel Webster rejected this reasoning and said that the state of New York had proper jurisdiction. Luckily, McLeod was acquitted.

The *Caroline* affair was only one of several border incidents. There was also an undeclared, bloodless war between Canadian and American lumbermen in the Aroostook River valley, claimed by both Maine and New Brunswick. In March 1839 General Winfield Scott, President Van Buren's emissary, negotiated a truce with

John Tyler, known as "His Accidency" by Henry Clay and his supporters, was a states' rights Democrat who had left his party because of opposition to Andrew Jackson.

New Brunswick officials. The border, however, continued to be vaguely defined.

To end this ambiguity, Webster met with England's envoy, Lord Ashburton, in a series of conferences and worked out a compromise by which the United States retained some 7,000 of the 12,000 square miles of wilderness under dispute. The *Caroline* affair was patched up through an exchange of diplomatic notes. Webster and Ashburton worked together with remarkable friendliness; Ashburton was sympathetic since he was a businessman married to a Philadelphia heiress and had made large investments in the United States. Both men recognized that Britain's colonial holdings were less important to its economy than continued trading with America.

Though Webster conducted an extensive propaganda campaign to sell the Webster-Ashburton Treaty of 1842, the citizens of Maine resented Webster and felt shortchanged. And nearly a century later it turned out they were right. The famous "red line" map found in Madrid in 1933, a copy of the map used during the peace negotiations of 1783, validated American claims in that region. Nevertheless, the treaty preserved peace between England and the United States, firmed up the border and awarded the United States 6,500 square miles in Minnesota that contained the priceless Mesabi iron deposits. Webster resigned from the cabinet in 1843 at the completion of the negotiations.

His Accidency and Whig Troubles

Despite the fact that he was a chief executive almost without a party, Tyler's administration produced other solid results such as reorganization of the navy, establishment of facilities that developed into the National Observatory, promotion of the use of the telegraph, and negotiation of a treaty opening up trade with China. Early in 1841 Tyler supported the successful effort by Whigs in Congress to repeal Van Buren's Independent Treasury law; for the next five years the federal government deposited its money in state banks.

The Jacksonian Democrats long had wanted a land policy that would benefit the poor settler, and in 1841 the Preemption Act finally realized this goal. It allowed settlers to squat on land—up to 160 acres. When the land was put up for sale by the government, the squatter had the right to buy it without fear of competitive bids and at the lowest government price. Preemption was a major triumph for the West. Called the "Log Cabin Act," it was linked to a proposal made by Henry Clay to distribute some of the proceeds of public land sales to the debt-burdened states, but this distribution bill was further connected with a provision for low tariff rates (distribution would be stopped if tariffs exceeded 20 percent). Since the tariff rate soon moved upward, distribution never went into effect.

In fact, in order to pay the growing national debt, Tyler was forced in 1842 to sign a high tariff bill, which restored duties back to the 1832 level. Statesmen of that period had a horror of federal debt; although the country had been quite free of debt in 1836, the government debt rose to $13,500,000 by 1842. The new tariff had to be revised three times before it could get past Tyler without a veto; many congressmen, including John Quincy Adams, were so angry at "His Accidency," as they called the President, that they unsuccessfully attempted to pass a constitutional amendment that would allow Congress to override a veto by a simple rather than a two-thirds majority.

The day after Tyler signed the Tariff of 1842 into law, Clay resigned from the Senate to prepare for the 1844 election. Tyler, anxious to win the presidency in his own right, now looked for new sources of support. To create a power base of his own, Tyler appointed a fellow Southerner, Calhoun, as Secretary of State in 1844. He also worked to add Texas to the Union, an area that would be likely to vote for him and would be a new slavery stronghold. Even after he failed to win the party's nomination and while serving as a lame-duck President, he sent American forces to the Gulf of Mexico and along the southwestern frontier of Texas without telling Congress or receiving the necessary authorization. Later, when Tyler submitted a treaty of annexation to the Senate, antislavery senators blocked its ratification, and Whig newspapers began to call for the President's impeachment. Tyler then proposed annexation by a joint resolution of Congress, one that would require only a simple rather than the usual two-thirds majority. Although some old Jeffersonian Republicans denounced this step as a violation of the Constitution, Texas finally was annexed by a joint resolution as Tyler was preparing to turn the White House over to James K. Polk in March 1845.

The Election of 1844

By 1844 the two-party system was fully established and party loyalty had begun to outweigh the merits of the individual candidates. Ignoring Tyler, the Whigs nominated Clay as their candidate; Clay then received a visit from Van Buren, who seemed the obvious Democratic candidate, and the two men probably agreed not to bring up the issue of Texas, which could plunge the country into sectionally divisive debates over the explosive issue of slavery. Shortly before the Democrats met in Baltimore, both Clay and Van Buren published letters against the annexation of Texas on the grounds that it would lead to war with Mexico, since that country did not recognize the independence of Texas. The Whigs indeed remained silent on the subject of slavery, wary of alienating voters in both the North and South.

But the Democrats undermined this strategy by passing over Van Buren and the ambitious Calhoun as well: because he was too closely identified with nullification, an unpopular stand even in the South, and Van Buren because of his stand on Texas. Instead the party nominated a dark horse, James K. Polk (1795–1849), Speaker of the House of Representatives and a former governor of Tennessee. Polk was a hard-money, Independent Treasury Jacksonian, an expansionist, and a Democratic stalwart who enjoyed the confidence of Andrew Jackson. When it became clear that Southerners would not accept Van Buren, Polk was drafted on the ninth ballot as the only candidate everyone could agree on. The news of Polk's nomination was carried from Baltimore to Washington on the first telegraph line in America. Whigs laughed at Polk's qualifications and asked, "Who is James K. Polk?", but they had not reckoned with his campaign strategy to remove the proslavery stigma of annexation of Texas by linking Texas with the "reoccupation" of Oregon.

The contest between Polk and Clay was complicated by the entrance of a third party, an antislavery faction active on the national scene since 1840 known as the Liberty party. In 1840 its candidate, James G. Birney (1792–1857), polled only 7,000 votes, despite the fact that there were some 1,500 antislavery societies in the country. At that point most abolitionists rejected a political solution to the slave issue and relied on moral suasion. By 1844, however, the party was gaining ground and won nearly 16,000 votes in New York alone—votes that otherwise might have gone to the Whig candidate Clay. Indeed, the Liberty party votes in New York allowed Polk to take that state—and thereby win the election, despite the fact that his views on slavery were even less acceptable to abolitionists than Clay's.

The Liberty party may have inadvertently given the election to Polk, but it received only 2.3 percent of the popular vote. Polk won with 49.6 percent compared to Clay's 48.1 percent; in the Electoral College Polk took 170 votes, Clay 105. Despite the Liberty party's poor showing, it soon won more converts as the events of the Polk administration convinced many Northerners that southern slaveholders were conspiring to control the federal government and promote their own interests over those of the rest of the country. As the debate over slavery heated up, the old coalition of Northerners and Southerners began to break down in both of the major parties.

Sophia Smith Collection, Smith College.

James Gillespie Birney (1792–1857)

Born in Danville, Kentucky, only son of an Irish immigrant who became one of the state's wealthiest men, Birney was educated at Transylvania University in Kentucky and at the College of New Jersey (now Princeton). The elder Birney, though a slaveholder, favored emancipation and obviously imparted some of his ideas to his son, who returned to Kentucky to practice law and became, by marriage, master of several slaves.

In 1818, Birney moved to Alabama where, although not a member of a state constitutional convention, he seems to have influenced certain provisions designed to encourage emancipation and prohibit the introduction of slaves into the state for sale. As a result of gambling and neglect of his lands he plunged into debt; early in 1823 he sold his plantation with its slaves and moved to Huntsville where he developed a successful law practice.

The decade from 1825 to 1835 marked Birney's transition from emancipationist to active abolitionist. Brought up an Episcopalian, at the urging of his wife in 1826 he became a Presbyterian, a move that coincided with his interest in African colonization for freed slaves and in the general restriction of slavery. A visit to New York and New England three years later convinced him of the superiority of free institutions, and in 1832 he began touring the South as an agent of the American Colonization Society.

In 1834 he freed six of his own slaves and soon after quit the colonization movement. No longer able to reconcile colonization and gradual emancipation with his religious and social ideals, he took up the cause of immediate emancipation. As his campaign against slavery intensified, Birney had to leave the Deep South, living briefly in Kentucky and Ohio before moving to New York in 1837. While living in Ohio he aided the "Underground Railroad." Even though by 1837 Birney's standing as an abolitionist was sufficient for him to be elected executive secretary of the American Anti-Slavery Society, he was not in total accord with the more radical abolitionists headed by Garrison. They were opposed to the Constitution (since it endorsed slavery) and felt that moral suasion, not political power, should bring about emancipation. Birney, by contrast, supported the Constitution and argued for political action. Accordingly, Birney was nominated in 1840 as the first presidential candidate of the new antislavery organization, the Liberty party. He was the presidential candidate of the Liberty Party again in 1844 and received 62,000 votes. A fall from a horse in the summer of 1845 partially paralyzed him and led to his retirement from public life.

Birney, a prize catch for northern abolitionists, nevertheless was a strange figure in their midst. He never supported slavery yet owned slaves, accepting the institution as he found it and seeking gradually to change it. He was a reasonable man who understood the law and thus faced the wrath of radicals such as Garrison. ■

Young Hickory in Office

As his nickname indicates, Polk was a convinced Jacksonian and, like his mentor, an enemy to the Bank of the United States, a foe of federally financed internal improvements, and a champion of cheap land. As he said in his first message to Congress, the duty of government is to help citizens "become the owners of small portions of our vast public domain at low and moderate prices." But Polk also pledged to work for a lower tariff, a policy that made him attractive to Calhoun and many Southerners. After his election but before his inauguration, Polk, the youngest man to be elevated to the presidency up to that time, worked hard to promote the annexation of Texas, which Congress approved by joint resolution in February 1845.

With the Texas issue settled, Polk announced four objectives in his inaugural address on March 4, 1845. These were: (1) reduction of the tariff; (2) reestablishment of the Independent Treasury; (3) settlement of the Oregon boundary; and (4) acquisition of California. Polk accomplished the first three goals with the cooperation of Congress before the end of the first session of the Twenty-Ninth Congress. The acquisition of California was achieved by the end of his term.

Polk's administration, in many ways the culmination of the Jacksonian philosophy, was an outstanding success—if one accepts these goals as criteria. He revived the Monroe Doctrine (the first to use that term) to prevent European colonization in Yucatan, even though residents there were eager to accept rule by either Spain or Great Britain. He struggled mightily with the spoils system and was an unusually conscientious administrator; yet, the intra-party feuds within the Democratic party led him to pledge that he would only serve one term.

Continental Expansion

The Democratic platform of 1844 called for the "reoccupation of Oregon," a sop to Northerners alarmed by that party's efforts in behalf of Texas. Presumably addition of both Texas and Oregon would retain the delicate slave-free balance within the nation. Under the Treaty of Joint Occupation of 1827, the Oregon country, stretching northward from the forty-second parallel to the line of 54° 40′, was open to both the United States and England. Before the election, the Democrats issued a campaign pledge—"Fifty-four forty or fight!" But after the annexation of Texas, Polk was no longer so eager to fight. Though he still maintained a public pose of insisting on the line as the northern boundary for the northwestern United States, privately he was willing to settle for the forty-ninth parallel. This duplicity misled many Westerners. When the English offered in 1846 to set the line at the forty-ninth parallel, Polk agreed, as did the Senate, but Americans on the West coast objected. Antislavery forces grumbled, since they felt that Polk, suspected of southern sympathies, had fought hard to annex all of Texas, where slavery was already established, but had not held out for all of the Oregon country, where slavery would not be introduced. If many senators readily accepted England's offer of the forty-ninth parallel, they did so primarily because the United States already was involved in a war with Mexico and could not risk another international conflict.

The Mexican War

While staving off war with mighty England, Polk provoked weak Mexico into open hostility. In determining the southern border of Texas, Polk was in no mood for compromise; he demanded the Rio Grande. To secure that border (and to acquire California in the process), Polk was willing to shed American blood. He sent General Zachary Taylor to occupy the disputed territory between the Rio Grande and the Nueces rivers. In April 1846 American and Mexican troops engaged in a skirmish. Polk, disregarding the constitutional stipulation that Congress alone had the power to declare war and aware that many Northerners were opposed to war, sim-

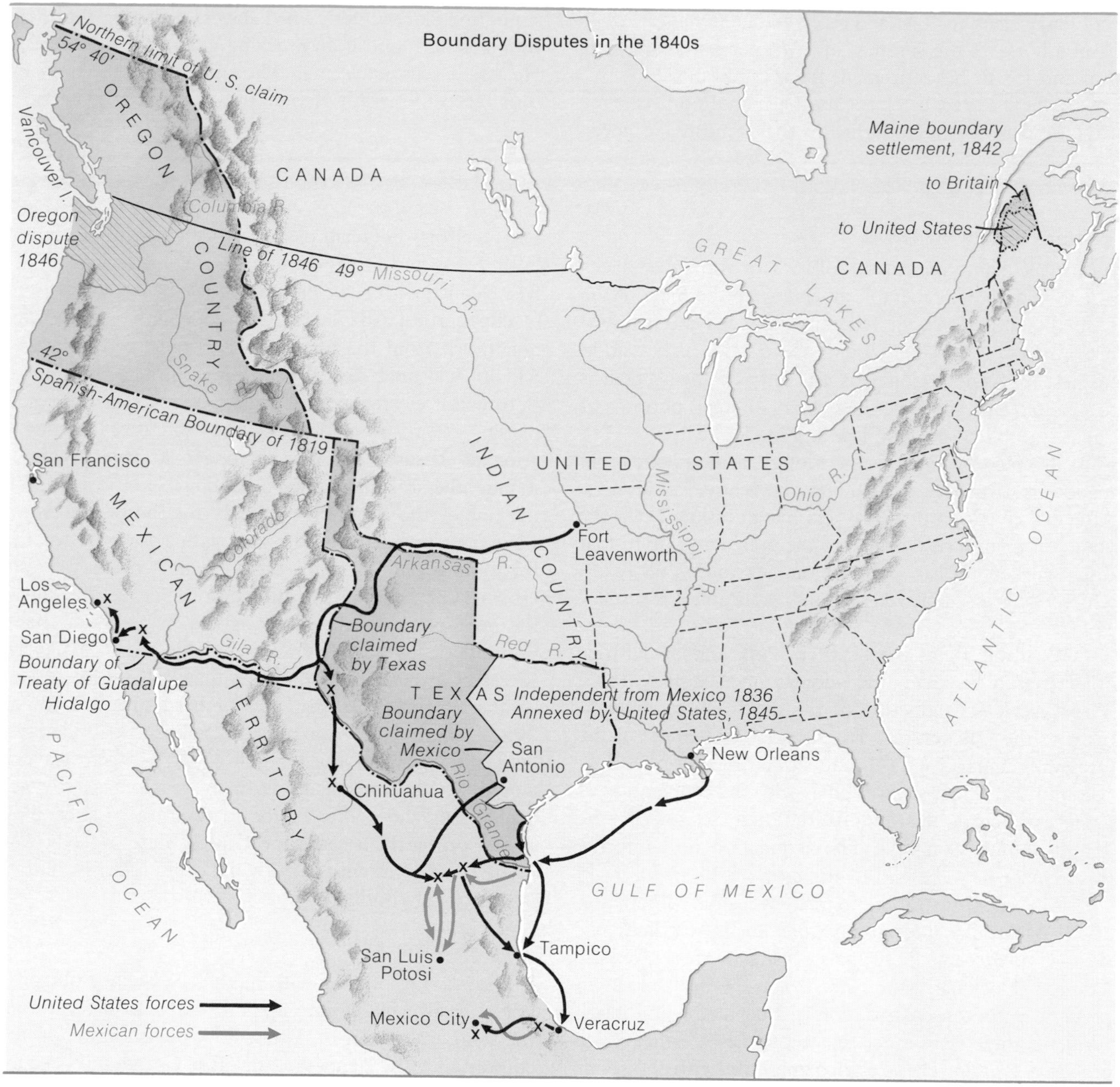
Boundary Disputes in the 1840s
Northern limit of U. S. claim
54° 40'
OREGON
COUNTRY
CANADA
Vancouver I.
Columbia R.
Oregon dispute 1846
Line of 1846
49°
Missouri R.
GREAT LAKES
CANADA
Maine boundary settlement, 1842
to Britain
to United States
42°
Snake R.
Spanish-American Boundary of 1819
San Francisco
MEXICAN TERRITORY
Colorado R.
INDIAN COUNTRY
UNITED STATES
Mississippi R.
Ohio R.
Fort Leavenworth
Arkansas R.
Los Angeles
San Diego
Boundary of Treaty of Guadalupe Hidalgo
Gila R.
Boundary claimed by Texas
Red R.
TEXAS
Independent from Mexico 1836
Annexed by United States, 1845
Boundary claimed by Mexico
San Antonio
Rio Grande
Chihuahua
New Orleans
PACIFIC OCEAN
ATLANTIC OCEAN
GULF OF MEXICO
San Luis Potosi
Tampico
Mexico City
Veracruz
United States forces
Mexican forces

ply announced the opening of hostilities. He then shrewedly attached the declaration of war to an appropriations bill designed to pay for fighting already in progress. If congressmen now failed to endorse the war, they would be accused of refusing to fund loyal American troops already in the field—a stand that would appear unpatriotic, even treacherous. This ploy was a striking demonstration of Polk's determination to compel a reluctant Congress to support his aggressive foreign policy in the Southwest. In reality, Polk was interested in much more than Texas; he hoped to seize the northern provinces of Mexico and all of California.

Many political leaders opposed the war, calling it unnecessary and unconstitutional. Abraham Lincoln, a first-term Whig congressman from Illinois in 1847-1848 was among those who denounced Polk. For the most part, this opposition was both sectional and partisan, that is, it came largely from northern Whigs. The President had defended his actions by saying that the war was not aggressive but defensive. Lincoln aroused intense controversy when he introduced his "Spot Resolutions" calling upon Polk to name the very "spot" where American blood had been spilled on American soil. According to Lincoln, the land where the first skirmish took place was not legitimately part of the United States but rather Mexican (and certainly the boundary was unclear). Lincoln called upon the President to "answer, fully, fairly, and candidly. Let him answer with *facts,* and not with arguments. . . . As a nation *should* not, and the Almighty *will* not, be evaded, so let him attempt no evasion—no equivocation."

Antislavery Whigs and abolitionists called the conflict "Mr. Polk's War." Early in 1846, Pennsylvania Congressman David Wilmot, a Democrat, introduced a proviso to an appropriations bill stipulating that none of the territory won from Mexico should be open to slavery. Although the Wilmot Proviso passed the House twice, it met defeat in the Senate. Nevertheless, the proviso became a rallying point for free soil Northerners and helped to dramatize the split between the North and the South.

The War, lasting about twenty-one months (1846–1848), consisted of a frustrating and inconclusive invasion southward from Texas by forces led by General Zachary Taylor (1784–1850) and another more successful march inland from Vera Cruz to Mexico City by units under the command of General Winfield Scott. Although Polk provoked this war, Mexican leaders must share blame. Political opportunists were more than willing to stir up feelings against the United States; but, if Polk had not been determined to have California, the other issues probably could have been settled. The war cost $73 million ($58 million in military operations, $15 million to Mexico for territory given up) and during the next four decades $64 million in pensions. Some 120,000 Americans were in uniform; of these, 1.5 percent died in battle, over 10 percent of disease, and nearly as many (9,207) deserted.

The war ended with the Treaty of Guadalupe Hidalgo in 1848, which gave the United States its present southwestern boundaries, save for a small area along the Mexican border acquired in 1853 in the Gadsden Purchase. The treaty also brought many problems in its wake—a fight over the extension of slavery into the newly won territory, which intensified sectional strife and encouraged the disruption of political parties—circumstances that contributed to outbreak of the Civil War. In fact, this war served as a training ground for young officers who would be facing each other in battle after April 1861. "The United States will conquer Mexico," Ralph Waldo Emerson had prophesied, "but it will be as the man who swallows the arsenic which brings him down in turn. Mexico will poison us."

Essay

The Polk Home, Columbia, Tennessee.

James K. Polk, The People's Choice in 1844.

Polk and the Problems of a Powerful Presidency

James Knox Polk, a rather frail man of iron will, is unique among the small band of men who have lived at 1600 Pennsylvania Avenue. He conceived and accomplished a very ambitious program in one term; he apparently never intended to seek another four years; he kept an extensive diary; and he literally worked himself to death as chief executive. Every Tuesday and Saturday he held Cabinet meetings at which he demanded reports, and he sometimes visited departments to see how his orders were being carried out. Polk's only diversion was daily walks, one just before sunrise and another after sunset. After more than a year in office, he noted with pride that he had dined out on one occasion and made only four social visits; only once had he been outside of the District of Columbia, a brief excursion to Mount Vernon.

A humorless, serious-minded individual who thought pleasure wasteful, Polk aged more dramatically during his White House tenure than most presidents have. Portraits of him at age forty-nine, the youngest man up to that time to win the presidency, and at fifty-four look almost like those of son and father. Within three months of his successor's inaugural, Polk was buried in the garden of his new home in Nashville, Tennessee, although his remains and those of his wife later were removed to the state capitol.

Polk was inaugurated in the rain, amid what John Quincy Adams called "a large assemblage of umbrellas," and his address left little doubt that he planned to assert American claims to Oregon, reduce the tariff, and set up an independent treasury system. Privately Polk told friends that he also hoped to acquire California, and he might have added that he planned to annex Texas, since, though such a step was approved by Congress several days before he took office, the final negotiations with that young republic were still going on.

James Knox Polk, protégé of Andrew Jackson, did all of these things but is best remembered today as a strong chief executive who had his way and rounded out the western half of the nation from Texas to Puget Sound. Polk hoped to use money, bluff, and diplomatic bargaining to get what he wanted. But the Mexicans refused to sell and Polk soon found himself involved in a bitter confrontation between the White House and Capitol Hill.

Before this skirmishing ended, Polk greatly enlarged

presidential power and the right of a President to withhold information from Congress. Polk's predecessor, Tyler, had given Webster $5,460 to defray his expenses while negotiating the border dispute between the United States and England. Later, when the House wanted to investigate how the money was spent, Polk refused to surrender the necessary documents. "The experience of every nation on earth," he told the House, "has demonstrated that emergencies may arise in which it becomes absolutely necessary for the public safety or the public good to make expenditures the very object of which would be defeated by publicity." If the President yielded to the House's request, then "he must answer similar calls for every expenditure of a confidential character, made under every Administration, in war and in peace, from the organization of the Government to the present period." The only time the House could *force* a President to hand over such documents was when it was conducting an investigation leading to possible impeachment. In an impeachment proceeding, Polk said, "the power of the House in pursuit of this object would penetrate into the most secret recesses of the Executive Departments."

The greatest outcry to that time against executive secrecy had concerned relations with Texas and Mexico. Without consulting Congress, Tyler had sent American forces to protect Texans against a possible Mexican invasion—before Texas had become part of the United States. When these secret arrangements and his treaty engineering the annexation of Texas were revealed, many Whig newspapers began to call for Tyler's impeachment. Once the annexation of Texas seemed assured, these objections died out, however.

When the Mexican government refused to receive Polk's envoy offering money for its lands between Texas and the Pacific, Polk concluded war was inevitable. Since many northern Congressmen opposed hostilities that they thought were designed solely to increase "The Slave Power," he looked for a way around this impediment. Mexico long had owed American citizens money for damage claims; the country was too poor, however, to honor these claims, and Polk considered declaring war on Mexico, using the unpaid debts as his pretext. He was on the verge of asking Congress to authorize war when he received information that gave him a better excuse.

Polk had sent General Zachary Taylor and a large force into the area between the Rio Grande and the Nueces River. Texas, partly at Polk's insistence, claimed the Rio Grande as its southern border; the Mexicans had a good case for designating the Nueces as the border, since when Texas was a department of Mexico that river had been its boundary. When Taylor moved into the disputed territory, Mexico regarded the action as a provocation. Polk instructed Taylor to consider any Mexican crossing of the Rio Grande as an act of war. Late in April a force of 1,600 Mexicans did just that and killed a small deputation of American soldiers. When this news reached Washington on May 9, Polk had his excuse for action.

In his war message to Congress, Polk announced that a state of war already existed since Mexico "has passed the boundary of the United States, has invaded our territory, and shed American blood upon the American soil." Polk declared war against Mexico without waiting for a congressional declaration as specified in the Constitution. He then stuck the declaration in the preamble to an appropriations bill for the prosecution of a war already in progress.

John Quincy Adams, formerly president and now a congressman, denounced Polk in 1847. He said the war "has never to this day been declared by the Congress of the United States. It has [only] been recognized as existing by the Act of Mexico, in direct and notorious violation of the truth. . . . The

Richard Caton Woodville, Courtesy National Academy of Design, New York. Photo by Teri Leigh.

"War News from Mexico"

most important conclusion from all this, in my mind, is the failure of that provision in the Constitution of the United States, that the power of declaring War is given exclusively to Congress.'' Adams dreaded the consequences of Polk's act. "It is now established as an irreversible precedent that the President of the United States had but to declare that War exists, with any Nation upon Earth, by the act of that Nation's government, and the War is essentially declared. It is not difficult to foresee what its ultimate issue will be to the people of Mexico, but what it will be to the People of the United States is beyond my foresight, and I turn my eyes away from it.''

Abraham Lincoln, a first-term member of the House of Representatives, also understood the dangerous implications of Polk's act. He felt that if the President was allowed to determine on his own when a foreign country was threatening invasion and must be repelled by a "defensive" war, then the chief executive had taken warmaking powers away from Congress. Warmaking had been the prerogative of kings, and the Constitution, Lincoln said, specifically denied this royal privilege to the President. The founding fathers, Lincoln wrote, "resolved to so frame the Constitution that *no one man* should hold the power of bringing this oppression upon us.''

Polk clearly got what he wanted, claiming as he pursued his goals that he represented the will of the American people and that Congress could speak only for various districts and states. This stance was rather dangerous since reading the minds of millions of Americans was and always will be an obscure, uncertain art; in addition, his narrow victory at the polls in 1844 certainly was no mandate to do much of anything. To get his way, he withheld patronage, twisted arms, and evoked patriotism.

Yet, although Polk enhanced the power of the office he held and remained steadfast in the "continental vision" that greatly enlarged the territory of the United States of America, he was, in a sense, a failure. It is the duty of every President, as leader of his party, to keep his party unified so as to win reelection or to be sure his successor will continue the policies of his administration. This Polk did not do. Also, while he may have been blessed with "continental vision," this man did not comprehend the changing nature of the slavery debate nor the awesome effect the acquisition of new territory would have upon that controversy.

Just as other chief executives striving to be known as "strong" Presidents would learn, an aggressive foreign policy may turn sour; what the electorate seems to want at the outset—an overseas empire or complete victory in Korea or Vietnam, for example—can become so elusive and so costly that the voters change their minds. Polk was luckier than some of

Library of Congress.

This 1845 cartoon illustrates that the Texas and Oregon questions aroused strong feelings among Americans.

those who followed in his wake. The Mexican War was soon over, successful and relatively cheap; the Civil War, which followed, was a quite different conflict. But, by the time the true cost of Polk's adventure in nationbuilding became apparent in the heightened rhetoric over slave and free territory, he was dead. Polk evidently thought that whatever domestic ruckus he stirred up by seizing some 5,000 square miles of territory could be resolved by compromise, but by the early 1860s effective compromise on this smoldering issue was no longer possible.

Selected Readings

General Accounts

John R. Howe, *From the Revolution Through the Age of Jackson: Innocence and Empire in the Young Republic* (1973)

Edward Pessen, *Jacksonian America: Society, Personality, and Politics* (rev. ed., 1978)

Leonard L. Richards, *The Advent of American Democracy: 1815–1848* (1977)

Arthur M. Schlesinger, Jr., *The Age of Jackson* (1945)

Glyndon G. Van Deusen, *The Jacksonian Era: 1828–1848* (1959)

Politicians and Political Parties

Samuel Flagg Bemis, *John Quincy Adams and the Union* (1956)

Marvin Meyers, *The Jacksonian Persuasion: Politics & Belief* (1960)

Richard P. McCormick, *The Second American Party System: Party Formation in the Jacksonian Era* (1966)

Lee Benson, *The Concept of Jacksonian Democracy: New York As a Test Case* (1964)

Ronald P. Formisano, *The Birth of Mass Political Parties: Michigan, 1827–1861* (1971)

Robert V. Remini, *Andrew Jackson* (1966)

Lorman Ratner, *Anti-Masonry: The Crusade and the Party* (1969)

James C. Curtis, *The Fox at Bay: Martin Van Buren and the Presidency, 1837–1841* (1970)

Robert G. Gunderson, *The Log Cabin Campaign* (1957)

Robert J. Morgan, *A Whig Embattled: The Presidency Under John Tyler* (1954)

Charles A. McCoy, *Polk and the Presidency* (1960)

Kinley J. Brauer, *Cotton Versus Conscience: Massachusetts Whig Politics and Southwestern Expansion, 1843–1848* (1967)

Special Studies

John William Ward, *Andrew Jackson: Symbol for an Age* (1955)

Leonard D. White, *The Jacksonians: A Study in Administrative History, 1829–1861* (1954)

William H. Freehling, *Prelude to Civil War: The Nullification Controversy in South Carolina* (1966)

Robert V. Remini, *Andrew Jackson and the Bank War* (1967)

Peter Temin, *The Jacksonian Economy* (1969)

Ronald N. Satz, *American Indian Policy in the Jacksonian Era* (1975)

Frederick Merk, *Manifest Destiny and Mission in American History: A Reinterpretation* (1963)

Charles G. Sellers, Jr., *James K. Polk: Continentalist, 1843–1846* (1966)

Chaplain W. Morrison, *Democratic Politics and Sectionalism: The Wilmot Proviso Controversy* (1967)

David M. Pletcher, *The Diplomacy of Annexation: Texas, Oregon, and the Mexican War* (1973)

America at Mid-Century

Chapter 12

TIMELINE

1842
William Gilmore Simms publishes *Beauchampe*
1844
Treaty of Wanghia opens Chinese ports to American trade
1846
Iowa becomes a state
1848
Wisconsin becomes a state
1848
Discovery of gold in California
1849
Francis Parkman publishes *The California and Oregon Trail*
1850
The nation's population reaches 23,191,876
1850
California admitted to the Union
1853
Gadsden Purchase adds land south of the Gila River
1854
Know-Nothing party becomes a strong political force
1854
Graduation Act reduces price of unsold federal lands
1854
Commodore Perry secures treaty with Japan
1857
Panic of 1857 increases unemployment
1858
Minnesota becomes a state
1859
Oregon admitted to the Union

CHAPTER OUTLINE

By focusing upon the decade before 1860 as merely a prelude to the Civil War, some historians have obscured many significant developments that were shaping the character of the United States in the first half of the nineteenth century. Now that the tragic division of North and South is finally being healed, historians are in a better position to analyze the decade before the Civil War. The focus is shifting to what previously were dismissed as secondary issues, such as the growth of industry and cities, the dramatic increase in immigration, and the territorial and economic expansion of the country. Of all these factors, only territorial expansion is of little concern today. The other matters now are more pressing than ever before as modern Americans wrestle with the problems of decaying cities, a troubling economy, and the inclusion of minority populations within the dominant society.

Expansion and Growth

In 1850, the nation had a population of 23,191,876 composed of 19,553,114 whites, 3,204,313 slaves, 434,449 free blacks, and, according to the compiler of the 1850 Census there were 400,764 "unrepresented and untaxed Indians." During the years since the first census in 1790, the white sector had grown from 80.7 percent to 84.3 percent, while the slave portion slipped steadily from 17.8 percent to 13.8 percent. The free black population, on the other hand, had fluctuated, going from 1.5 percent in 1790 to 2.5 percent in 1810 and then declining steadily to 1.8 percent in 1850. There were, in 1850, 100 white males to 95 females (a ratio that had remained virtually unchanged since 1790). At mid-century the male-female slave population was about equal, although free female blacks outnumbered males 108 to 100.

Virginia had the largest number of slaves (472,528), and five other states had a quarter of a million or more: North Carolina (288,548), South Carolina (384,984), Georgia (381,682), Mississippi (309,878), and Alabama (342,844). New Jersey (236) and the Utah Territory (26) were the only areas in the traditionally "free" sector which reported slaves within their borders that year. Maryland had the nation's largest free black population (74,723), followed closely by Virginia (54,333), Pennsylvania (53,626), and New York (49,069). About four-fifths of all free blacks lived in the state where they were born.

Only five states had more than a million inhabitants: New York (3,097,394), Pennsylvania (2,311,786), Ohio (1,980,329), Virginia (1,421,661), and Tennessee (1,002,717), although Massachusetts, Georgia, Kentucky, and Indiana each had almost that many residents. Massachusetts and Rhode Island were the only states with over 100 inhabitants per square mile. The national average was 7.90 persons, but ranged all the way from 861.45 in the District of Columbia to .04 in the Utah Territory.

New York, with slightly more than half a million people, was the nation's largest metropolis, followed by Philadelphia (340,045), Baltimore (169,054), Boston (136,881), New Orleans (116,375), and Cincinnati (115,435), with 6 percent of the total population living in these six cities. Some 2.2 million Americans were foreign born, Ireland (961,719), Germany (573,225), England (278,675), and "British America" or Canada (147,711) providing nearly all of this immigrant population. About two-thirds of these individuals lived in six states, each of which had over 100,000 foreigners within its borders: New York (651,801), Pennsylvania (294,871), Ohio (218,512), Massachusetts (160,909), Illinois (110,593), and Wisconsin (106,695).

The nation was, of course, overwhelmingly agricultural. About half of all free male workers over the age of fifteen worked on farms, and about a thirteenth of all land was improved and used for that purpose. This included 26 out of every 100 acres in New England, 16 in the South, 12 in the Northwest, and 5 in the so-called "Southwest," really the lower Mississippi Valley. The South had the largest farms, but those in southern New England and the Middle Atlantic region were the most valuable (on the average about $4,000), with two notable exceptions: 267 farms in the District of Columbia and Louisiana's famed sugar plantations had an average worth of $6,500.

By far the most important crop grown on America's farms was Indian corn, valued at nearly $300 million in 1850; three other crops each were worth about a third as much: wheat, hay, and cotton. Nevertheless, it was cotton that figured most prominently in overseas exports, 70 percent of the total production going to British factories. Butter valued at $50 million was produced in 1850, slightly surpassing the oat harvest ($43 million). Other crops of considerably less importance included Irish and sweet potatoes, tobacco, cane sugar, rye, orchard products, buckwheat, peas, beans, and market garden produce.

Wages varied greatly, so much so that no distinct pattern emerges. A laborer working without board could get as little as 54 cents a day in North Carolina, about twice as much in Florida, Louisiana, Maine, Massachusetts, Texas, and Wisconsin, and ten times as much on the Pacific coast.

Census takers of that year recognized over twenty major religious groupings from Baptist to Universalist with 38,183 churches and property valued at $87.4 million. The Methodists with 13,338 congregations and the Baptists with 9,360 clearly dominated the religious scene. In 1850, about four million young people were attending schools, colleges, and universities; only 26,461 of these students were black. College and university libraries were small, few having more than 25,000 volumes, although several societies and state governments had somewhat larger collections.

Although manufacturing did not loom large, employing less than one-fifth of all free workers, factories of one sort or another could be found everywhere throughout the nation. New York, with 199,349 establishments having an annual output worth $500 or more, led the list, followed closely by Massachusetts (165,938) and Pennsylvania (146,766); the territories of Minnesota (63) and Utah (51) brought up the rear. Cotton and woolen mills and factories turning out pig iron and iron castings could be found in virtually every state, although, as one would expect, New England dominated textiles; Massachusetts, New York, Pennsylvania, Kentucky, and Ohio, the iron industry. Some 1,217 distilleries and breweries scattered throughout the nation (Pennsylvania had 371; Alabama, California, the District of Columbia, Vermont, and Utah Territory, one each) employed 6,140 individuals and in 1850 produced 1,179,495 barrels of ale, 6,500,500 gallons of rum, and 41,364,224 gallons of "whiskey and high wines."

Expansion into New Lands

The settlement of the Oregon question with England in 1846, the acquisition of land from Mexico in 1848, and the Gadsden Purchase in 1853 together gave the United States its present continental limits (except for Alaska). By 1853 the nation stretched from the Atlantic to the Pacific and embraced three million square miles. Of this land, three-quarters was in the public domain of the federal government, which could sell the lands as it saw fit. Despite the rapid settlement of the West, in 1860 two-thirds of the American territory was still in federal hands.

The acquisition of new lands led to a shift in the population. Only a quarter of the total population of 12,866,020 Americans lived west of the Appalachian Mountains in 1830, but by 1850, half of the total population of 23,191,876 had moved west. As a result of this pattern of settlement, by 1860 about one-fourth of all the 31,443,321 people in the United States were living in a state other than the one they had been born in.

Cheap land and opportunity (fact or fiction) lured Americans beyond the mountains. The Preemption Act of 1841 guaranteed squatters the right to purchase up to 160 acres of land at the lowest government price; nor were squatters subjected to competitive bidding. Despite these generous concessions to venturesome, land-hungry settlers, Westerners pressed Congress for still more liberal terms. In 1854 the Graduation Act provided that all unsold public lands that had been on the market for ten or more years were to be offered up at a price varying between 12.5 cents and $1 an acre, depending on how long the land had gone without a buyer. During the next eight years, nearly 40 million acres were settled under these provisions. Agitation for free land continued in the 1850s as Americans and recent immigrants sought homesteads and real estate for farming, herding, or speculation.

Southerners violently opposed a free land policy for two reasons. First, they feared that such a policy would deprive the Treasury of necessary funds and the government would make up the difference by raising tariffs—which would hurt the South, dependent as it was on international trade. Second, free land in the West would attract antislavery settlers from the North, thereby making it likely that western territories would eventually enter the Union as free states. Southern opposition was so adamant that the nation did not embark on a free land policy until after the Civil War began. Nevertheless, the Preemption and Graduation Acts were sufficiently generous to promote rapid settlement. Iowa became a state in 1846, Wisconsin in 1848, California in 1850, Minnesota in 1858, and Oregon in 1859; they were all free states.

The Transportation Revolution

The development of new communities in the western part of the United States owed a great deal to the transportation revolution begun after the War of 1812. In the late 1840s there were only six thousand miles of railroad track in the United States, most of it along the East Coast. In 1860 there were 30,626 miles, and most of the increase was west of the Appalachians. Milwaukee, St. Louis, Memphis, and New Orleans all were served by railroads, and Chicago had become the very hub of transportation in the West, the terminus of fifteen separate lines. This explosion of railroadbuilding not only increased traffic, it also moved it faster. For instance, the trip from New York to Chicago required three weeks in 1840 via water and land; in 1860 the same trip by train took only forty-eight hours.

Most cities of the Old Northwest were joined to the East coast by lines emanating from Baltimore, New York, and Philadelphia. The economic interdependence of these two regions welded together a solid political unit, the North. This alliance dashed efforts of the South

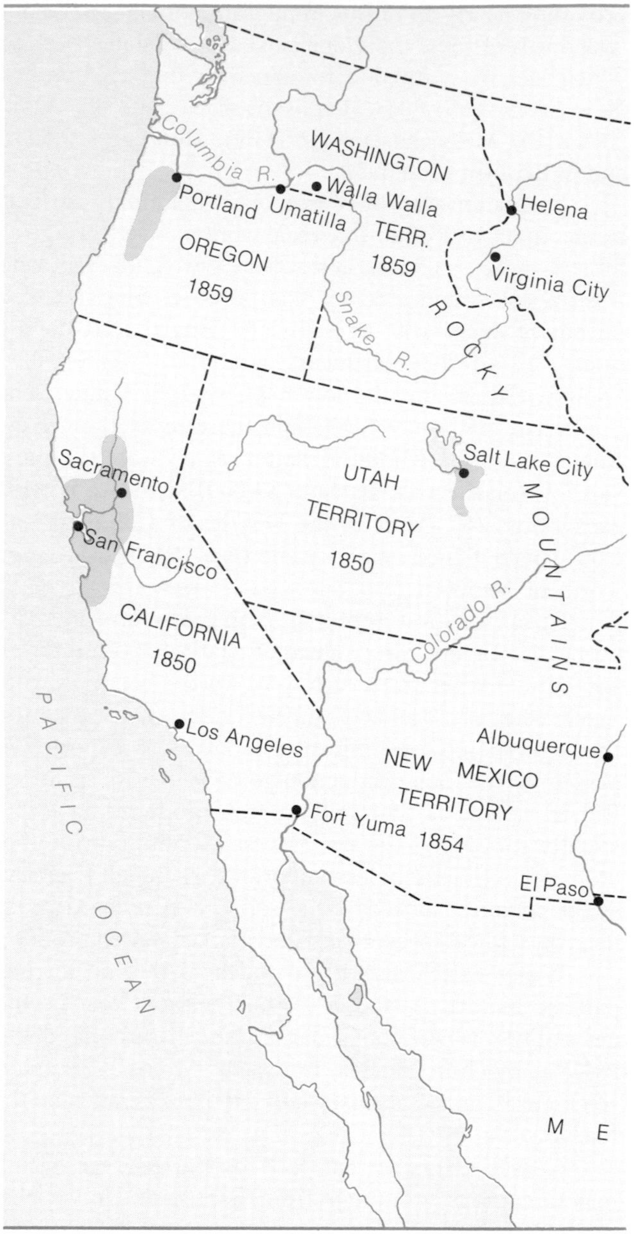

to form ties with the West. Western crops and other commodities that once went to southern markets (especially New Orleans) were now being diverted to the Northeast.

The emerging national system of transportation also stimulated regional specialization. The West was pro-

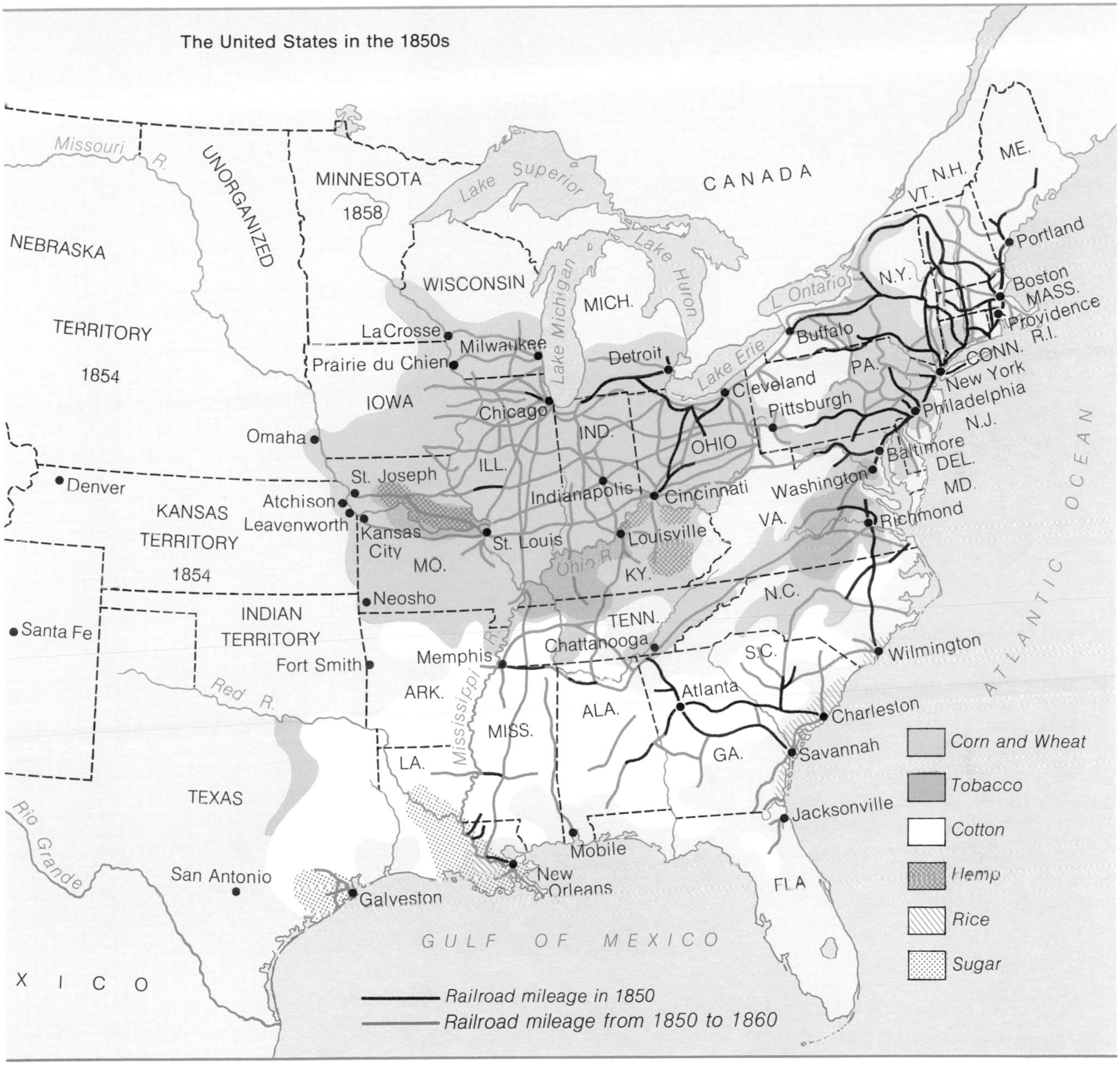

ducing foodstuffs that could be shipped to the industrial and financial centers of the Northeast, which in turn supplied the West with manufactured goods and capital. The South participated in this flow of goods and cash by sending cotton bales to the mills of the Northeast. All of these transactions were facilitated by trains, though railroads affected the South much less markedly than the West and the Northeast. The South had far fewer tracks, and what it had often failed to form a continuous network. The railroads of the South frequently did little more than carry goods from a plantation to a river or bay to be shipped to foreign or domestic ports.

Courtesy Clarke Historical Library, Central Michigan University.

A pioneer farm family in Michigan in the 1850s. The Graduation Act of 1854 did not end agitation for free land by Americans and recent immigrants.

Library of Congress.

The Illinois Central depot in Chicago. The main line of this railroad, the first great north-south railroad in America, was completed in 1854 and ran from Chicago to Cairo. The Illinois Central helped to open for development a wide expanse of fertile land. Southern Illinois, which otherwise might easily have gravitated into the orbit of St. Louis, was tied to Chicago.

The chart below shows the rapid increase in railroad mileage in the United States between 1830 and 1860.

Year	Miles of Track
1830	23
1835	1,098
1840	2,818
1845	4,633
1850	9,021
1855	18,374
1860	30,626

Industrial Expansion

In 1843 George Tucker, a professor at the University of Virginia, observed that industrial employment was increasing more rapidly than agricultural employment and that towns with a population of 10,000 or more were growing faster than the overall population. Industrialization and urbanization were indeed remarkable aspects of the United States in the 1840s and 1850s. In these two decades the number of agricultural workers increased from 3,570,000 to 5,880,000; but, as a percentage of the total work force, farm labor declined from 63.4 percent to 53.2 percent; in the same years, factory employees rose from 13.9 percent to 18.5 percent (or, in actual numbers, from 500,000 to 1,530,000).

By mid-century many of the conditions necessary for a true age of industrialization were emerging. Railroad track linked most urban centers to one another, permitting relatively easy exchange of goods, raw materials, and machine tools. Extensive coal mining allowed factories to be built anywhere since they were no longer dependent on waterpower for fuel. Mechanized factory production benefited from the introduction of interchangeable and standardized parts, the rise of the machine tool industry, mass immigration from Europe (which provided a cheap source of labor), and new markets along the western frontier.

But industrialization requires capital, and a great deal of this capital that developed the United States came from overseas. One estimate holds that foreign capital in the United States rose from $222 million in 1853 to $400 million in 1860. Another source for industrial investment came from the gold mines of California. Between 1848 and 1853, more than half a billion dollars' worth of gold was extracted from California. Indeed, the nation's supply of hard money climbed from $90 million in 1843 to $283 million in 1862.

As industry grew, corporations developed to control more and more of the new factories. New York passed a general corporation act in 1848 which permitted any group of investors to incorporate if they met certain standardized requirements (previously each group had to apply individually to the legislature). This new law and similar legislation elsewhere facilitated incorporation; nearly half of the business corporations established in America between 1800 and 1860 came into existence in the last decade before the Civil War. Traditionally businessmen took a concerned, paternalistic interest in the welfare of their employees, but as the real control of any corporation passed into the hands of management and the number of employees grew, even managers were separated from the rank and file by an intermediate hierarchy of foremen. The owners of a corporation, in short, were absent, and the managers were sequestered away in private offices.

Most Americans took no part in corporation life. The country's farmers, laborers, retail merchants, and professionals remained unorganized, while business was becoming organized on a grand scale. But it would be a mistake to see the early corporations simply as sinister cartels, that is, combinations within a single industry designed to restrict competition and maintain high profits. They were merely the first indications of the high degree of organization that would eventually characterize almost every aspect of American life.

"Yankee ingenuity" accounted to a large extent for both the increased efficiency of American industry and the appeal of its products. Separate industries had grown up by 1850 around such inventions as the sewing machine, telegraph, reaper, Colt revolver, vulcanized rubber, and circular saws. The most impressive American inventions were improvements of agricultural machinery, only natural in a country still primarily devoted to farming. American farmers were quite alert to every innovation; the farm press described inventions in detail and farmers examined them at county and state fairs. American plows, cornplanters, revolving rakes, and wheat drills surpassed those produced in other countries. Western farmers were especially attracted to these implements, which augmented production and reduced human toil and which often performed much better on the flat lands of the upper Mississippi Valley than in the hilly Northeast.

After agriculture, transportation was the next most important field to be improved by American ingenuity.

State Historical Society of Wisconsin.

Instructions for assembling a McCormick reaper-mower dated May 1857.

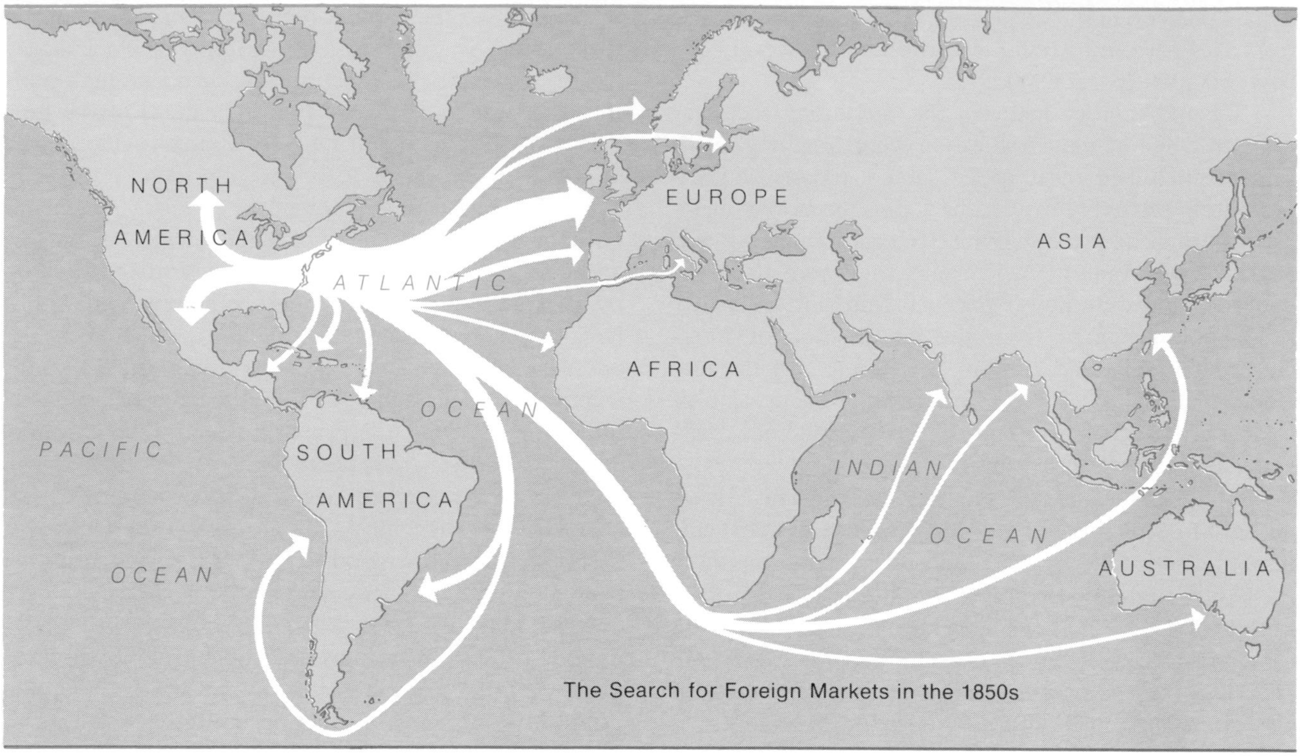

The Search for Foreign Markets in the 1850s

American locomotives were roomier, more comfortable, and more durable than their European counterparts, and the American T-rail was designed so that it could be laid rapidly and easily, thereby saving money and effort. Yet another American enterprise that benefited from inventions was the textile industry. Inventions involving most other industries, however, lagged behind; English machines were simply too good and too cheap to invite American competition. Nevertheless, the United States was caught in an inventive fever in the decades before the Civil War; the U.S. Patent Office registered one-third more inventions in 1856 than it had in 1855, and every subsequent year saw increases.

In the 1850s manufacturers became more interested in foreign markets. Total exports were double what they had been in the 1840s, though the main commodities sold abroad were not factory goods but agricultural produce. Cotton, in fact, made up more than half of all exports, and other kinds of southern produce (tobacco, sugar, and rice, for instance) accounted for another quarter. Whereas Europe in general and England in particular bought the bulk of American cotton, manufactured goods made in the United States were sold primarily to Mexico, the West Indies, and China.

The first American ship to sail to China left New York in 1785 and brought back exotic goods. But by the 1820s the China trade was becoming a two-way street. Instead of American merchants simply buying silks, porcelains, and other luxury products, the Chinese were buying American cotton cloth. Chinese exports to the United States continued to exceed imports, but farsighted American merchants considered the vast Chinese population as a great potential market, and the treaties that America and other western powers forced a weak Chinese government to sign all were designed to enhance the profits of foreigners trading there. The Treaty of Wanghia, signed in 1844, for instance, opened five major Chinese ports to Americans and stipulated that very low tariffs would be imposed on American goods.

In 1853 and 1854, the show of naval force by Commodore Matthew C. Perry led Japan in 1854 to conclude a treaty with the United States. The treaty permitted limited American trade on a most-favored-nation basis in two Japanese fishing villages. An abortive attempt to

U.S. Naval Academy Museum.

A Japanese view of the first encounter with Commodore Perry.

annex the Hawaiian Islands by the Pierce Administration and a treaty with Siam (Thailand) in 1856 represent other attempts to extend American overseas trade.

One of the strangest items exported was ice from New England, which, after some experimentation in the early 1800s, was shipped to India, China, Latin America, and even Australia. In 1856, for example, 363 cargoes totalling 146,000 tons left Boston and nearby ports, and merchants in Batavia, British officers in Bombay, as well as the rich of Charleston, Savannah, and New Orleans, cooled their drinks with New England ice.

Urban Expansion

The typical American citizen was a farmer or smalltown resident, but the population of many larger towns and cities began to soar after 1850 as industrial development drew people away from the countryside. Even before 1850 American industry became a serious rival of the frontier and soon factories, like the West, were seen as realms of opportunity.

By 1860 there were 6,216,518 Americans living in 101 urban centers with a population of 10,000 or more inhabitants. Port cities such as New York, Boston, and Philadelphia underwent tremendous growth between 1840 and 1860, and the inland cities on the Great Lakes experienced even more dramatic development. Chicago, for example, a settlement of about fifty people in 1830, quickly became the chief metropolitan center of the Midwest and the greatest railroad center in the nation. By 1840 there were 4,470 Chicagoans; by 1850, nearly 30,000 and by 1860, 109,260.

At first Chicago had served as a place where new arrivals could buy public farmlands; the city was little more than a real estate office. After the Panic of 1837 slowed down speculation in land, the city became a center for outfitting homesteaders with farm equipment. The railroad boom in the 1850s turned Chicago into a depot for farm produce streaming from the West to the East. Chicago's slaughterhouses and porkpacking plants enabled the city to process the livestock of the region. By 1853 Chicago had seven daily newspapers, factories such as those of Cyrus McCormick, which manufactured reapers and other agricultural machines, as well as numerous iron mills and lumberyards. The city owed its size and prosperity to its role as a center of industry, finance, and transportation.

Two other centers, older and somewhat larger, reflect similar trends, although both Cincinnati and St. Louis clung for too long to river commerce and saw Chicago and its railroads overtake them. Cincinnati grew rich supplying salt pork, flour, and foodstuffs to the one-crop cotton South. By the 1850s river gamblers, boxes of manufactured goods, and barrels of pork (Cincinnati for a time led the world in hog processing) came and went on innumerable steamers. In 1859 the city had two high schools and sixteen elementary schools with some 17,000 pupils, 180 Christian societies, 6 synagogues, 53 periodicals and 16 insurance companies. St. Louis, its commerce much like that of Cincinnati—supplying the lower South—had nineteen flour mills in 1850 and an assortment of foundries and food-processing plants. Both cities had other similarities: very large immigrant populations (more than 30,000 Germans settled in St. Louis before 1850) and close ties to the South. As a result, these commercial centers were torn apart by divided loyalties in 1861.

Cleveland and Buffalo, much more closely allied

Library of Congress.

Matthew Calbraith Perry (1794–1858)

Son of a distinguished naval officer four times taken prisoner during the Revolutionary War, brother to four other U.S. Navy officers and brother-in-law to still two more, the sea and service to the nation clearly shaped the life of this Rhode Island-born youth and that of his family as well. At one time no less than 17 Perry cousins were enrolled at Annapolis.

After basic schooling in his native Newport, Perry became a midshipman in 1809 and during the hectic years leading up to the War of 1812 saw action on a vessel commanded by his brother, Oliver Hazard Perry (1785–1819); however, he spent most of that conflict aboard a ship bottled up in New London by the British. Late in 1814 he married Jane Slidell, sister of John Slidell of Civil War fame. They had ten children, one of their daughters marrying wealthy August Belmont.

During the next 20 years Perry traveled widely suppressing piracy, conducting diplomatic missions, and helping to establish the ex-slave nation of Liberia. In 1833 he began a decade of shore duty in Brooklyn and New York City where he developed an interest in steam transport, naval education, and nautical engineering. Elevated to captain in 1837, this brusk, irascible, and somewhat pompous man soon was in the forefront of a nautical revolution that culminated a few years later in establishment of the U.S. Naval Academy and radical changes in sea warfare.

In 1843 Perry commanded a squadron dispatched to Africa to suppress the slave trade, subsequently directed a large naval force sent to Vera Cruz during the Mexican War, and then was selected to lead a fleet to Japan when the United States decided to establish diplomatic ties with that mysterious realm. President Millard Fillmore's personal letter to the emperor stressed that America desired trading rights because of increasing commerce between California and China. Vessels wrecked near Japan and those requiring coal might need assistance, the president added. The objects of Perry's visit, he stressed, were "friendship, commerce, a supply of coal, and provisions and protection for our ship-wrecked people."

In November 1853 Perry set out from Norfolk with a fleet of ten vessels. Sailing by way of the south Atlantic, the Indian Ocean, and China, he reached Japanese waters six months later. After nine days marked by boldness, threats, and cajoling, Perry departed for China, promising to return the following year.

Alarmed by the sudden appearance of French and Russian warships and fearing their commanders might also be seeking special privileges in Japan then enjoyed only by Holland, in February 1854 Perry hurried back and within six weeks secured trading rights in two ports. This agreement, perhaps aided by the emergence of a new regime, was cemented by the exchange of a strange assortment of gifts.

The emperor received a miniature train, a telegraph set, agricultural implements, the *Catalog of the New York State Library and of Post Offices,* three boxes of tea, a telescope, maps of various states, assorted swords and firearms, a sheet-iron stove, two mail bags filled with padlocks, and a substantial supply of Madeira, champagne, and whiskey. The empress got only a dress, a gilded box, and some perfume, but commissioners representing the emperor, depending upon rank, received varying amounts of cloth, pistols, cherry cordials, and whiskey. In return, the Americans got silks, brocades, porcelains, four small dogs, several tons of rice, and a dried fish wrapped in seaweed.

Perry's arrival back in New York was barely noted by the Pierce administration, but in 1856, assisted by Francis Lister Hawks, he published three remarkable volumes describing his exploits. Even more remarkable perhaps is the possibility that Nathaniel Hawthorne or Herman Melville could have coauthored these reports; but, for various reasons, the task fell to Hawks who also conducted Perry's funeral when he died suddenly two years later while preparing to assume command of a Mediterranean squadron. ■

with the industrial Northeast and the burgeoning frontier states of Illinois, Michigan, and Wisconsin, present a somewhat different picture. In 1850, Cleveland was about one-tenth as large as Cincinnati but recently had "planked" its main streets and built a huge pier out into Lake Erie, the first of its kind. Like Buffalo, which was much larger, Cleveland was producing a variety of goods to be shipped westward to new settlements of the upper Midwest or to the East via the Erie Canal. By 1845, for example, Buffalo was manufacturing tools, steam engines, stoves, nails, mirrors, and picture frames, soap, candles, millstones, and porcelain bathtubs. Neither city had much difficulty deciding where its sympathies lay as the Civil War approached.

The South was much more agricultural than urban, but nevertheless some major cities had arisen before 1860. Urbanization, to be sure, was less vital in the South than in the North, but it was still apparent, especially around its perimeter. Ringing the heartland of the South were the major cities of Baltimore, Charleston, Savannah, Mobile, St. Louis, Louisville, New Orleans, and Memphis—all located on a major body of water and sustained by extensive trade with the hinterland.

The census of 1860 numbered some thirty towns or cities in the South with a population of 8,000 or more. Most of these communities were state capitals or crossroads trading centers. Memphis, the largest city in antebellum Tennessee, was a typical southern boomtown. It was founded in 1819, the year after Andrew Jackson freed west Tennessee of Indian title. Until the late 1840s, Memphis remained a sleepy Mississippi River town. But a good railroad connection with Charleston on the Atlantic coast (completed in 1857) and prosperous cotton production in the hinterland turned Memphis into a true metropolis. In 1850 factors, agents who bought and sold agricultural produce, were handling 150,000 bales of cotton valued at $7,520,000; by 1860 the figures had tripled. Accordingly, prosperity brought a leap in the city's population, which increased from 8,841 in 1850 to 22,623 in 1860.

New Orleans, by far the South's largest city in 1850 (116,375), was fed by the produce of the Mississippi Valley and the commerce created by bumper crops of corn, tobacco, and cotton. Exotic and somewhat un-American because of its rich French-Spanish heritage, this city battled fires, hurricanes, and yellow fever throughout the decades from 1812 to 1860 but continued to prosper despite the competition of railroads in the upper Midwest. It was a colorful, highliving mix of bars, gambling, red-light districts, immigrants, opera, and theater that set it apart from all other southern towns and cities and from most urban centers of the rest of the nation as well.

Compared with the thriving, thronged northern cities of New York, Philadelphia, and Boston, southern cities often appeared sleepy and a bit forlorn, especially

Historic New Orleans Collection.

This illustration of urban life in the antebellum South shows a scene in LaFayette Square in New Orleans.

since their well-being was tied to agricultural cycles and little influenced by immigration and industry. Streets, except on Saturdays or during the busy fall harvest season, frequently were deserted. Many cities lacked adequate sidewalks, paved streets, sewers, or supplies of fresh water. Lurking just behind the imposing homes of white citizens were the miserable shanties of urban blacks, whether free or enslaved. Fear of a nocturnal black uprising haunted many southern cities; New Orleans employed more night watchmen than daytime police, and these nighttime officials patrolled the streets accompanied by trained dogs. Free blacks, moreover, were required by the city council to wear badges and to obey a strict curfew.

These disadvantages were to some degree offset by the attractions of urban life in the South. The public schools were better and more numerous than in the country. Typically, the town of Lexington, Kentucky, spent a fourth of its revenues to support schools, which almost all white children of school age attended. There they studied, among other subjects, Latin and Greek. Towns and cities also offered other educational advantages, including lyceums, public libraries, theaters, circuses, concerts, and musical performances of many varieties. In the 1850s, athenaeums and mechanics' institutes sprang up in the larger southern cities; they sponsored lectures on useful subjects and provided both libraries and exhibits to the public. By 1860 nearly a thousand readers belonged to the Kentucky Mechanic's Institute in Louisville. In the last decade before the Civil War, libraries showed marked growth in the South, especially in South Carolina, which rivalled Massachusetts in its number of books per capita.

Social and Cultural Diversity

The sheer size of the United States and its division into distinctive regions often dominated by quite different groups of people—urban and rural; slave and free; New Englanders, New Yorkers, cotton-growing Southerners, and trans-Appalachian Westerners; residents of stable, settled areas and wild, untamed frontiersmen; native and newcomer—created an unusual social and cultural diversity. Probably at no earlier time in American history could one have found such marked differences in outlook and in social habits as in the middle decades of the nineteenth century. The War of 1812 and the Mexican War had not woven these random viewpoints into distinctive themes, and changes wrought in communication, transportation, and industry, although certainly impressive when compared with earlier times, had not yet drastically altered American life.

Immigration and Nativism

By 1860, about one-eighth of the American population of some thirty-one million people were foreign born. Although many immigrants settled in the Old Northwest, an even larger number moved into enclaves already established in America's rapidly growing cities, especially in the Northeast. About 4.2 million foreigners arrived in the United States between 1840 and 1860 seeking new jobs and opportunities. Although many "native" Americans looked with hostility and fear upon this flood of new arrivals, others found it exciting; as the novelist Herman Melville wrote in 1849: "We are not a narrow tribe of men . . . whose blood has been debased in the attempt to ennoble it, by maintaining an exclusive succession among ourselves. No: our blood is as the flood of the Amazon, made up of a thousand noble currents all pouring into one. We are not a nation, so much as a world."

Most of the new immigrants came from Britain and Ireland or Germany; almost all the rest came from Scandinavia, Switzerland, and Holland. In fact, about 95 percent of the immigrants in the decades before the Civil War were from northern Europe. In general the immigrants were in the prime of life, able-bodied and productive workers; relatively few were under ten years old or over forty.

The Panic of 1857 reduced the rate of immigration drastically. Although an expanding economy previously had been able to absorb many foreign laborers, during the depression unemployment rose and immigration dropped from 251,306 in 1857 to 123,126 in 1858.

The largest group of immigrants were the Irish. Driven out of their own country by the potato crop failure and the famine that followed it in 1845 and 1846, more than 1.5 million of them had arrived in the United States by 1860, and they constituted about 40 percent of all foreign-born residents in America. Generally, the Irish were too poor to move inland from the coastal cities after they landed in the United States. They settled mainly in the port cities of the Northeast, though some traveled west and south seeking employment as day laborers building canals or railroads; only a very few ever turned to farming in America. The next most numerous nationality were 1,301,136 Germans.

Foreigners were unevenly distributed in the nation with more than 85 percent of the new arrivals in the North. Indeed, in such rapidly expanding cities as Chicago, Milwaukee, and St. Louis, almost half of the population was foreign born. The heaviest concentrations of immigrants were in eastern states such as Massachusetts, New York, and Pennsylvania and in such states in the Old Northwest as Illinois, Ohio, and Wisconsin. The Irish tended to concentrate in northeastern industrial cities, the Germans on farms or in the cities of the Ohio and Mississippi River valleys such as Cincinnati, Milwaukee, and St. Louis. The percentage of foreign-born citizens in various cities in 1860 is given in the table below:

Over 50%	45% to 50%	35% to 45%	25% to 35%
Chicago	Buffalo	Boston	Baltimore
Milwaukee	Cincinnati	Brooklyn	Philadelphia
St. Louis	Detroit	Louisville	
	New York	Newark	
		New Orleans	
		Pittsburgh	

Based on Ira M. Leonard and Robert D. Parmet, *American Nativism, 1830–1860* (New York: Van Nostrand Reinhold, 1971), p. 33.

From the collections of the Michigan History Division.

"Come to America." This advertisement encouraged Germans to settle in Michigan. During the antebellum period, entire German villages left en masse for America which was attractively pictured in numerous pamphlets and letters.

Library of Congress.

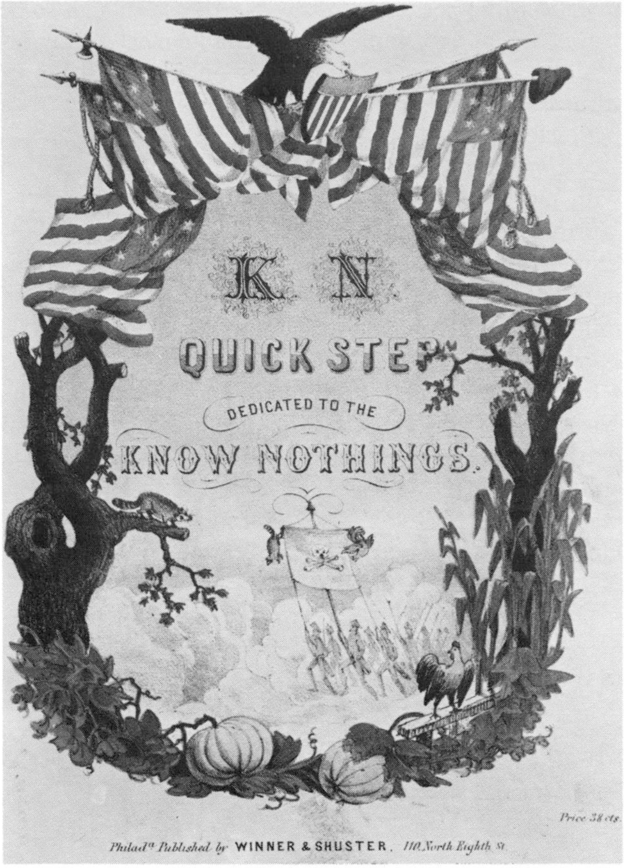

Title page of the "K N Quickstep" (1854), "dedicated to the Know Nothings"— a movement that attracted recruits from the middle class who were fascinated by secret handshakes, passwords, and distress signals, and who supported efforts at anti-immigrant legislation. Public opinion, however, was largely outraged by nativist mobbings and other excesses.

The influx of immigrants brought feelings of anger, anxiety, and despair to many Americans. The Catholicism of the Irish aroused in native Protestants deep suspicions that had subtle, long-range effects. The political radicalism and antireligious convictions of some German refugees also frightened conservative Americans. A wave of unsuccessful liberal uprisings in Germany in 1848 sent many revolutionaries fleeing to the United States, bringing with them ideas that alarmed many Americans. Irish Catholicism on the one hand and German liberalism on the other were distressing and unsettling; when these ideological differences were coupled with the frustration and despair resulting from rapid social and economic change and severe competition for jobs, the result was the rise in the 1850s of a virulent nativism. The nativist or Know-Nothing party (so named because of the vow of secrecy members swore) emerged as a strong national force in 1854 and enlisted many adherents to its platform calling for restrictions against immigrants. The Know-Nothings wanted to ban all foreign-born citizens from holding political office, deprive aliens of the vote, and delay naturalization of foreigners for at least twenty-one years after their arrival in this country.

Immigration to the South never matched the flood that inundated the North. The foreign-born were reluctant to settle in the South for a number of reasons. Southern cities were less industrialized than those in the North and consequently did not have as many factory jobs. Nevertheless, some southern cities had surprisingly high proportions of foreign-born citizens. As the table on page 409 shows, New Orleans and several border state cities such as St. Louis and Baltimore had substantial immigrant populations. Nevertheless, immigration to the South in general remained low during this period. The climate was unfamiliar, and growing conditions in the North more closely resembled those of northern Europe. Passage from Europe to southern ports was less frequent than to New York, Boston, or other northern cities. Finally, many immigrants had a strong aversion to slavery.

Among those foreigners who did go to the South were Germans, Irish Catholics, and Jews, often lured below the Mason-Dixon line by relatives or neighborhoods in seaport communities long dominated by their fellow countrymen. Most immigrants settled in cities where they became merchants, peddlers, skilled craftsmen, or laborers. Relatively few became farmers. Although there were notable exceptions, most immigrants who settled in the South soon accepted the southern proslavery view.

Despite this assimilation of beliefs, immigrants often encountered a strong hatred of the foreign-born in the South. In the 1850s the Know-Nothings often dominated southern city elections. In an effort to find an issue that would distract attention from more dangerous sectional rivalries, the Know-Nothings fanned the sparks of xenophobia (hatred of foreigners) and mobs killed more than a score of foreigners in Louisville on election day in 1855 and led riots against immigrants in several other cities. Nativists won control of most of the large cities of the South by contending that immigrants were opposed to slavery. Southern nativism, unlike that in the North, was more antiforeign than anti-Catholic, partly because there were fewer Catholic immigrants in the South and partly because Catholics who settled in the South became defenders of slavery.

Cultural Diversity

By its sheer numbers and through its control of the leading printing presses, growth of metropolitan centers, and development of a convergent network of railroad tracks, the Northeast and its institutions tended to dominate the cultural life of mid-century America. As one might expect, this influence often ceased or declined markedly at regional borders. The Appalachians, the Mason-Dixon line, the Mississippi and Ohio Rivers, even the Hudson, to some degree, delineated areas that sought guidance from some center in its midst with its colleges, theaters, emporiums, and great churches. The best example of this phenomenon was Boston, unquestionably New England's capital. Although the boundaries and "capital cities" of other regions are less easy to identify, New York, because of its size, wealth, and close ties to Europe, exerted some influence throughout the entire nation and was, in a sense, its cultural capital, perhaps sharing the educational and literary realms with Boston to some degree. If nothing else, much that was done in Savannah, St. Louis, Buffalo, Baltimore, and even Boston or Philadelphia, was measured against standards set in Manhattan.

Immigration turned much of the North into a rich cultural mix. Scores of newspapers published in foreign languages gave enclaves of newcomers a sense of community and informed them of events back home. Each nationality, moreover, practiced in America the arts of its native land. The Germans of Cincinnati, for instance, were dedicated to music and the city had numerous choral societies and instrumental groups. Similarly, the Irish of Boston formed Catholic and fraternal organizations in which they preserved their own customs.

Most Americans were too busy and too unsophisticated to appreciate the fine arts, but they nonetheless had cultural activities, some of them unfamiliar to their twentieth-century descendants. For instance, oratory was highly admired during the antebellum period. The orator was esteemed as the rival to the poet, and public speaking was considered an art both entertaining and edifying. Whether addressing a court room, a legislative body, or a church congregation, the orator won praise for a fine voice, effective gestures, perfect diction, and well-organized ideas. People would travel miles to hear an outstanding preacher or a stirring political speaker.

Literature and History

The prewar decades mark the declaration of American independence from European literary traditions. In the 1840s and 1850s American writers in the Northeast were no longer content to imitate the works of older cultures.

Library of Congress.

The Columbian Artillery in 1852. Militia companies like this Irish one were primarily social organizations. In addition to target practice and parades, the companies provided immigrants with such activities as balls, picnics, and lectures. The Columbian Artillery eventually became the Columbian Literary Association.

The National Archives.

Nathaniel Hawthorne, of Salem, Massachusetts, wrote *The Scarlet Letter* in 1850 and *The House of the Seven Gables* in 1851. These novels established him as the classic interpreter in fiction of the Puritan mind.

The essays of Emerson and Thoreau, the novels of Nathaniel Hawthorne (1804-1864) and Herman Melville (1819-1891), and the poetry of Edgar Allan Poe (1809-1849) and Walt Whitman (1819-1892) are all examples of a new American voice. Hawthorne's *The Scarlet Letter* and *The House of Seven Gables* treated native themes—in both cases the Puritan heritage. The stern morality of New England, the religious, even mystical, approach to experience, and the pessimism about the sinfulness of humanity imbue these brilliantly written novels, much acclaimed on both sides of the Atlantic. Melville's *Moby Dick,* a far more original exploration of the nature of evil, dealt with a maritime way of life—whaling. Melville and Whitman both were virtually self-educated and thoroughly steeped, as were so many Americans, in the Bible. The freedom from the constricting formalities of Victorian prose and verse enabled these writers to invent a rich, complex language characterized by ringing, Old Testament cadences. Whitman wrote boldly about sex and society in free verse lines unfettered by rhyme and even metrical regularities.

The favorite author of all Southern readers was a Scotsman, the author of *Ivanhoe,* Sir Walter Scott (1771-1832). It was he who pictured a medieval era of chivalry and courage, of deference to ladies and *noblesse oblige* towards servants—a view of society that Southerners were able to translate into the terms of their own world. The best-known counterpart to Scott in the South was the South Carolinian novelist William Gilmore Simms (1806-1870). In 1842 he published his *Beauchampe,* the tale of an aristocratic Southerner who kills a Kentucky colonel in order to avenge the seduction of his wife. Simms wrote more than twenty novels and sixty stories and became well known in the North and in European literary circles. Among his numerous romances based on South Carolina's history and frontier was *The Yemassee,* a story of Indian warfare in colonial times and one of the great American historical novels. In *The Sword and the Distaff* (later called *Woodcraft*), published in 1852, Simms pictured a slave, Tom, who accompanies his master onto the battlefield in the Revolutionary War, enjoys high adventures, and is invariably treated by his owner with the greatest affection.

The most popular writers of the day were poets; indeed poetry dominated American letters between 1830 and 1870. William Cullen Bryant (1794-1878) with his lyrical hymns to nature, and the American laureate, Henry Wadsworth Longfellow (1807-1882), with epics on native themes ("Evangeline" and "Hiawatha"), reached a vast public. Longfellow's poems were memorized by schoolchildren and his birthday was a national holiday for students. John Greenleaf Whittier (1807-1892) also won recognition for his fine regional poem about winter in New England, *Snowbound.* For all of these writers the one great subject was Nature (which they always capitalized); Romantics on both sides of the Atlantic believed that God's ways could be deduced by the painter and poet from a flower, a bird, or a landscape.

One of the South's greatest poets, Edgar Allan Poe, was actually born in Boston in 1809 but moved to Virginia as a child. Like many other Southerners, he was lost in fantasies about an earlier, chivalrous, semimythical era, although for Poe this dream world was not ordered and calm but streaked through with doom and despair. Though he edited the *Southern Literary Messenger* for a brief period, he lived much of his adult life in the North, primarily in New York. Creator of the first detective stories, he was a master of psychological thrillers, an astute critic at a time when virtually no other Americans could express any opinion about literature beyond simple approval or disapproval, and the inventor of a kind of poetry so melodious and so original that it inspired generations of writers, not only in the United States but also in Europe.

With the exception of Poe, the South produced no major literary figures before the Civil War, and this paucity of talent can be attributed in part to slavery. Slavery was an institution so under attack from northern abolitionists that southern white intellectuals devoted much of their energy to defending it. Another penalty slavery imposed on southern culture was repression. As the slaveowning society became more and more embattled, the local post offices refused to distribute inflammatory publications from the North, professors in southern universities were dismissed or harassed for their criticism of the system, preachers who condemned slavery were replaced, and in general, the free play of ideas and inquiry was stifled.

Then as now Americans were addicted to a non-artistic form of literature—self-improvement and how-to-do-it books. As *The Farmer's Companion* optimistically observed, the "agriculturalist . . . may devote his earnings, or most of them, to study." He could learn ways to rebuild his house from an issue of a popular magazine, *The Horticulturist.* Or he could study one of the many technical treatises, such as *The Useful Arts Considered in Connexion with the Applications of Science.* If he had a taste for more abstract subjects, he could read Professor Denison Olmsted's *Letters on Astronomy* or a book written by three New England scholars, *Essays on Ancient Literature and Art.* His religious appetite was fed by millions of religious tracts.

The sacredness of the family was an entrenched aspect of the American ethic. Indicative of this attitude was the popularity of *Godey's Lady's Book* in which the editor, Sarah J. Hale reputedly the author of "Mary Had a Little Lamb," dictated manners, dress, and taste to millions of women in all parts of the nation. Hale was a crusader for female education and teaching careers for women but otherwise shunned the women's rights movement. She retired as editor of the *Lady's Book* in 1877 after a half century of writing, editing, and, above all, producing for four decades the publication she considered to be "a beacon-light of refined taste, pure morals, and practical wisdom."

Fashions for June.
Furnished by Mr. G. Brodie, 51 Canal Street, New York, and drawn by Voigt from actual articles of Costume.

Fashions from *Godey's Lady's Book* in 1857, showing a bridal gown, young lady's outdoor costume, and girl's dress. *Godey's* stressed the role of the family in society and women's work in the home. During Sarah J. Hale's career as editor, the magazine gained a then impressive circulation of 150,000 subscribers.

The most famous American historian of the antebellum period (and for many years after the Civil War) was George Bancroft (1800–1891). In 1834 he published the first book of his ten-volume *History of the United*

Library of Congress.

Sarah Josepha Buell Hale (1788–1879)

Born on a farm in New Hampshire, Sarah Buell had an appetite but few opportunities for education, though her mother taught her to read and an older brother instructed her in Latin and philosophy. When, at the age of twenty-five she married David Hale, a lawyer in Newport, she found in him a new teacher. Her husband also encouraged her to submit occasional articles to local newspapers.

The death of her husband in 1822 left her with the responsibility of providing for five children. She then entered upon a serious career as an author and began to publish poems and fiction. In 1828 she was named the editor of a Boston magazine for women, the *Ladies' Magazine.* In 1837 Louis A. Godey bought out the magazine and established his highly successful *Godey's Lady's Book,* with Sarah Hale as the literary editor. It became the most famous and widely read American periodical for women. In its pages she argued for sensible dress, better homes, scientific housekeeping, and women doctors.

Although Hale never endorsed feminism and even opposed feminists of her day, she was a champion of education for women, and her articles on this subject profoundly influenced Matthew Vassar, the founder of Vassar College for women. Sarah Hale also made the public aware of the accomplishments of women through the 2,500 biographical sketches she wrote and collected under the title *Woman's Record, or Sketches of Distinguished Women,* first published in 1853. (She omitted Lucy Stone, Elizabeth Stanton, and Susan Anthony. Her mention of Lucretia Mott, another feminist, was acidic.) She herself was one of the most distinguished women of her era. In 1877 she retired after half a century of editing the *Lady's Book.* Though she always believed that women were best suited to act as moral guides to men, her role in promoting higher education for women left an enduring mark on America. ■

States, a gigantic effort that came to a conclusion only in 1876. In the intervening years Bancroft, a staunch Democrat and one-time political boss of Massachusetts, served as Secretary of the Navy under Polk and then as minister to Great Britain and later to Berlin. His *History,* which covered only the colonial and Revolutionary periods, was strongly patriotic and as such enjoyed wide popularity. As a defender of Jacksonian democracy,

Everyday Life

The agricultural fair became a standard feature of the American scene by 1850. This painting of a Pennsylvania fair in 1824 shows a plowing contest, new machinery and farmers discussing new breeds of stock.

Collection of Harry T. Peters, Jr.

Baroness Hyde de Neuvelle.
CORNER OF GREENWICH STREET JANVIER 1810.
I.N. Phelps Stokes Collection.
The New York Public Library.

This watercolor of Greenwich Street, New York City in 1810 shows people busy with everyday duties. Children pump water at the local well to take home, someone sweeps the sidewalk, cellars are open for deliveries and people stop to talk in the streets.

By the nineteenth century, childhood was recognized as a separate stage of development. Eunice Pinney captured these children at play in a watercolor done about 1815.

Abby Aldrich Rockefeller Folk Art Center, Williamsburg, Virginia.

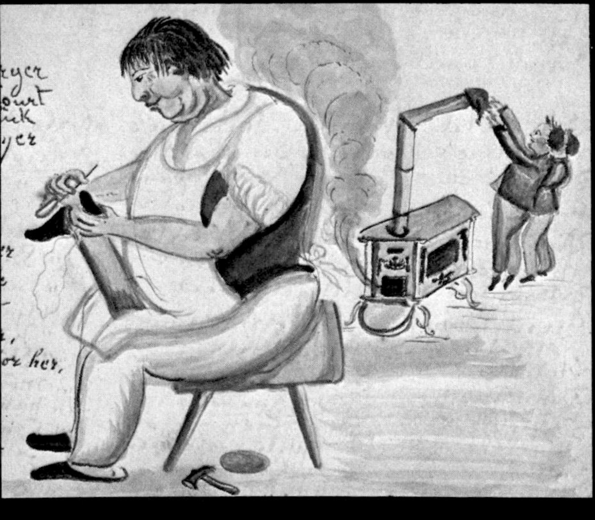

A Pennsylvania carpenter painted this view of a neighbor making boots. The boys in the background are playing with a sheet-iron stove. By the 1840s and 1850s the stove was replacing the fireplace for heating.

The Historical Society of York County.

FLAX SCUTCHING BEE
Linton Park
National Gallery of Art, Washington
Gift of Edgar William and Bernice Chrysler Garbisch.

This painting shows a rural work gathering. Flax is being processed by those present as they take time out to tease, court and gossip. Such rural gatherings not only made light of tedious chores but provided a rare opportunity for socializing in isolated rural areas.

Collection of Edgar William and Bernice Chrysler Garbisch.

The portrait of this Hartford family in 1836 illustrates the growing idealization of the family as an oasis of peace in a busy world. The children play with dolls, pets and a music box while one son does his lessons. The mother holds the ever-present sewing in her lap while the father watches all over the top of his newspaper.

Museum of the City of New York.

By the middle of the nineteenth century delivery trucks brought many goods directly to the homes of their prosperous customers in cities. This New York milkman of the 1840s made his rounds without the aid of individual milk bottles.

Collection of Hirschl & Adler Galleries, New York

Motherhood had become idealized by the mid-nineteenth century. James Goodwyn Clonney's painting "The Good Breakfast" reflects this idealization while catching a rare domestic scene. The good breakfast referred to is pancakes and coffee.

Collection of the Newark Museum

Most Americans did not live in towns and cities in the nineteenth century. Thus the peddler brought shop goods to the countryside and became a standard figure of folklore with a wagon filled with goods and a smooth sales pitch. These women are looking at a coffee mill.

Courtesy of the Western Reserve Historical Society

The home might be one oasis from the world but the tavern and club provided another for men. The men in this 1859 painting are smoking while they discuss politics, hunting, and local news. Women had no equivalent meeting places and certainly would not have been welcome here.

Foster Hall Collection, University of Pittsburgh.

Stephen Foster (1826–1864)

Born in Pittsburgh, Pennsylvania, Foster displayed at an early age a gift for music; however his parents opposed a musical career (a pursuit that scarcely existed as a full-time occupation in America at that time) and sent him to Jefferson College in July 1841 when he was barely fifteen years of age. Within a few weeks he quit, planning to continue his studies with tutors as home. Even at this tender age he had written several compositions, including "The Tioga Waltz," a melody for four flutes. Other songs followed, but five years later his parents sent young Foster to Cincinnati to keep books for his brother. There his ballads of the black American became so popular that in 1848 he published a collection, *Songs of the Sable Harmonists,* that proved music could be profitable. With this success behind him, Foster left Cincinnati and returned to his family's home in Allegheny City to pursue his chosen career in earnest.

His early songs were written for minstrels—that is, white singers wearing blackface—and his ballads were performed by such groups as the famous Christy's Minstrels and the New Orleans Serenaders. His connection with E. P. Christy proved to be a very profitable arrangement for both men, each contributing greatly to the popularity of the other. "The Old Folks at Home" appeared in 1851 and "Massa's in the Cold Ground" in 1852, two of Foster's best-loved songs. The following year he deserted black dialect for a time and produced "My Old Kentucky Home" and "Old Dog Tray," the latter selling 125,000 copies in only eighteen months. For the next few years, Foster remained in Pittsburgh where he wrote little of any consequence; then in 1860 he reasserted his former power with "Old Black Joe," one of his most enduring ballads. Despite the fact that most of these lyrics celebrated the South, Foster paid only one visit to that region, a brief excursion to New Orleans in 1852.

In that same year he moved to New York, having separated from Jane Denny McDowell whom he married in Pittsburgh in 1850. Poverty and obscurity marked Foster's final years as he drank heavily and wrote constantly (forty-eight songs in one twelve-month period), but his output was repetitive and uninspired. Frequently he sold these songs to music stores, not publishers, for only a few dollars. He died in 1864 in a charity ward at Bellevue Hospital after a brief illness. Foster's work was somewhat limited and obviously uneven, but his most enduring songs evoking a nostalgia for the security of bygone times and faraway places clearly express a unique, even exotic phase of American life and development. ■

Bancroft read the early events of American history as sure signs of the rise of the common man.

In an address to the working men of Northampton (1834), Bancroft clearly enunciated this view: "Where the people possess no liberty, their rights obtain no respect. . . . Show me one instance where popular institutions have violated the rights of property, and I will show you a hundred, nay a thousand instances, where the people have been pillaged by the greedy cupidity of the privileged class. There is more danger from monopolies than from combinations of workmen. There is more danger that capital will swallow up the profits of labor, than that labor will confiscate capital."

The other major historian of the period was Francis Parkman (1823–1893), less grandiloquent but more scholarly. Throughout his life Parkman was tortured by a mysterious nervous ailment that kept him in a nearly constant state of exhaustion and confusion, sometimes allowing him to write only six lines a day. Despite this terrible disorder, he was able to write *The California and Oregon Trail* in 1849 and the two-volume *History of the Conspiracy of Pontiac,* published in 1851. In subsequent years he published several impressive histories of the struggle between the British and French for the domination of North America, a theme developed with genuine literary distinction in his monumental series, *France and England in North America* (published between 1865 and 1892). Parkman set a new level of careful scholarship in American history. He was an indefatigable researcher, a careful compiler of original materials and despite his anti-Indian bias, an astute critic of the historical merit of various sources.

Contrasts and Contradictions

The very nature of the federal system of government, complicated by the addition of vast new lands, millions of immigrants, and industrial growth in what still was an agricultural economy, not only created cultural diversity within the United States but numerous contradictions as well. The greatest of these was, of course, slavery in an emerging democracy.

Because of these regional contrasts, any attempt to measure the achievements of a reform movement or even compare conditions in various regions ends up in a sea of qualifying statements. Different states reported different statistics in different ways. Perhaps this was inevitable in any age not yet accustomed to standardization even within a single state. A simple matter such as basic, primary education can become hopelessly confused. Many states by 1850 did not have free common schools and the length of school terms varied greatly (as did instruction).

The 1850 census indicates that the illiteracy rate among native-born whites in the South over the age of twenty was 20.3 percent, compared with 3.0 percent in the Middle Atlantic states, and .42 percent in New England. Yet these statistics ignore the immigrant population of the North and disguise the fact that southern cities such as Charleston, New Orleans, Memphis, and Louisville were developing creditable school systems, certainly better than those found in smaller communities in many other states. And, in the 1850s, while the common school flourished in the North and languished in the South, private academies abounded below the Mason-Dixon line. Virginia, for example, had more colleges and more college graduates and was expending more money on higher education than Massachusetts.

Yet much more than differing educational standards set one region—the Deep South—apart from all others. There slavery had few critics, industry and immigrants were sparse, and economic well-being rested, in the final analysis, on one crop. As the antislavery fury mounted, an arc of states from South Carolina to Texas became more and more unified in their opposition to abolition (and everything else northern as well) and came to see themselves and, in turn, be seen as a distinct section somewhat apart from the main pulse of national life. What confounded many southern spokesmen was the uncompromising attitude of their critics—citizens like themselves, of a nation that was born in compromise and had solved numerous crises in that same spirit; in time, naturally enough, they became equally adamant that *their* way was right.

Cotton and Slavery

In 1850, U.S. exports were valued at $135 million and cotton bales produced by slave labor constituted over 50 percent of that total, or $72 million. Ten years later exports had increased to $316 million, and cotton's share was even greater, $192 million, or about 61 percent. About two-thirds of all cotton and tobacco grown in

America was shipped overseas, virtually all other agricultural produce being consumed within the nation, although grain (corn) exports were mounting rapidly.

One of the unexpected results of the cotton economy was the way it tied the South to the North economically; in fact, the Deep South was almost a northern "colony." In the first half of the nineteenth century, northern men and particularly New Yorkers dominated southern commerce. They furnished credit on their own terms, and a protective tariff policy tended to increase dependence of the South on the North. Northern businessmen were the middlemen, shippers, bankers, and insurers who took a large share of the South's agricultural profits.

The end of the War of 1812 marked an important shift of cotton production to the West as settlers moved into the fertile soils in Georgia, Alabama, and Mississippi. The rich bottom land of the lower Mississippi River and its tributaries provided an excellent environment for growing cotton. Western Tennessee, eastern Arkansas, and western Texas also became centers of cotton production. The Indian removal policy made possible white expansion into most of these areas. By 1860 these cotton-producing states outstripped the older states of Georgia and the Carolinas.

There were fifteen slave states in the Union in 1850. The dramatic rise in cotton production—which was generating more national income, for instance, than the entire Northern iron industry—was based on slave labor. As slavery became more and more central to the southern economy, prospects of gradual and peaceful abolition became dimmer.

Yet it would be a mistake to think of the typical Southerner as the owner of a large plantation staffed with hundreds of slaves. In 1860 there were 1,516,000 free white families in the South, but only 385,000 owned slaves—that is, almost 75 percent of the free southern families owned no slaves at all. Of those families that did own slaves, in 1850 almost 50 percent owned fewer than five. The planter aristocracy (that is, the group that owned more than fifty slaves numbered only 10,000 families).

The well-to-do farmer who held ten to thirty slaves typically lived on his own land and personally supervised the management of his estate. He usually did not hire an overseer. Among the slaves there was some specialization of labor; a few of the slaves worked part-time as carpenters or cooks, but they generally had to do field work as well. Only on farms with more than thirty slaves was there much specialization. For instance, one wealthy Virginia planter in 1854 had eight plowmen, ten hoe hands, two wagoners, four oxcart drivers, a carriage driver, a hostler (a person who takes care of horses), a stableboy, a shepherd, a cowherd, a swineherd, two carpenters, five masons, two smiths, a miller, two shoemakers, five spinners, a weaver, a butler, two waitresses, four maids, a nurse, a laundress, a seamstress, a dairymaid, a gardener, and two cooks.

During these antebellum decades, because of an abundance of cheap land, an expanding economy, and a rapidly developing democracy, the plain people of the South, less affluent whites, did not think of themselves as a distinct class. In fact, the northeast with its native-foreign, urban-rural, industrial-agricultural divisions perhaps had more easily defined class groupings. In the South, as elsewhere, it was not impossible for a poor lad to become a lawyer, editor, doctor, or politician, and perhaps, at the same time, a slaveowning planter. Most importantly, whites, regardless of wealth or education, considered themselves superior to blacks and maintained a high degree of solidarity to ensure white supremacy. And the general association of rich and poor at church and at various social functions created a sense of unity between the plain folk and the cotton aristocracy, a unity often supplemented by kinship and a bond that would speak louder than politics in 1861.

While industrialization and urbanization were transforming the North (for better or worse), the South in many ways remained much as it had been in the eighteenth century—rural and agricultural. Immigrants brought to the North new ideas, customs, and trades, and in the big Northern cities these cultural innovations passed quickly from one individual to another. But in the South most of the citizens were farmers, living in isolation, slow to change their ways, and most prominent citizens usually were large commercial planters.

In recent years there has been a heated debate among historians over the question of whether slavery was truly profitable in the South. There is considerable evidence that it was. The steady movement of slavery into the cotton and sugar cane land of the Southwest can be explained only by the fact that the system must have worked. Similarly, only the success of the slave system could have justified the rising cost of prime black field hands. In 1840 such a slave cost about $700 in Georgia; in 1850 the cost had risen to about $1,000 and by 1860 it was nearly $2,000. Funds invested in slave labor brought high return to most owners. Indeed, the purchase of a black woman often yielded a high return on the original investment because her offspring could either be sold or used as additional labor.

By 1860 the Southern population consisted of about four million blacks and eight million whites. The concentration of blacks in the South varied. In the cotton lands of the Deep South, the concentration was particularly dense, as it was in the bottom lands of the Mississippi River and in the parts of southern Texas that drained into the Gulf of Mexico. By 1850 the Gulf area was the largest cotton-growing region in the world, far surpassing Egypt and the East Indies, the closest rivals. Of the 2.8 million black slaves engaged in agriculture in the United States in 1850, at least 1,815,000 were employed in the cotton fields.

As a result of the Deep South's marriage to cotton and its general indifference to industry, the region was producing less than 10 percent of the nation's manufactured goods by 1860. Some Southerners repeatedly attempted to industrialize the South, but to little effect. During the middle 1840s William Gregg (1800–1867) of South Carolina returned from a tour of textile mills in New England and the Middle states and published a series of newspaper articles later republished as *Essays on Domestic Manufacturing: or, An Enquiry into the Expediency of Establishing Cotton Manufacturers in South-Carolina.* Gregg argued persuasively against the South's continued adherence to cotton and its neglect of industry. In 1846 he established the Graniteville Manufacturing Company, a paternalistic cotton mill village, in Aiken, South Carolina that employed poor whites. This operation soon was bringing in annual dividends in excess of 12.5 percent.

The South's heavy reliance on agriculture entailed constant financial problems. Planters used factors (commission merchants) to sell their crops for them, as they had in colonial days. The factors, usually residing in a port city such as New Orleans, shipped crops, provided planters with credit, and sent supplies for their plantations in return for a commission. Between 6 to 9 percent of the sale price of cotton went to the factor in return for providing services, such as insurance, storing the cotton, handling it at the wharf, and so on. The planters borrowed money from the factors, usually at the going rate of 8 percent. In return, a planter promised most or all of a crop to his factor. This crop lien system, which became the principal means of borrowing money in the South, reinforced reliance on cotton as the mainstay of the economy, since factors regarded it as the safest crop and generally required planters to grow it in return for loans and advances.

Slavery and Southern Society

The presence of slaves created special pressures in southern life. A slave could not be educated, even taught to read or write; to do so was against the law. Nevertheless, on some occasions the laws were broken. The Grimké sisters, the daughters of a liberal South Carolina judge, recalled the excitement of teaching blacks in an atmosphere of secrecy: "The lights were put out, the keyhole secured, and flat on our stomachs before the fire, with spelling books in our hands, we defied the laws of South Carolina." White supremacists were convinced that education would arouse a spirit of rebellion in blacks. Thus schools for free blacks were closed and masters were forbidden to teach their slaves. Georgia prohibited blacks from holding jobs requiring education (such as typesetting); and Virginia refused to let its free blacks educated in the North return to their homes. Nevertheless, in the face of an almost total banning of black education, some slaves did manage to learn—in secret schools run in the city, from the white children on plantations, and through self-instruction.

Southern Protestanism in the decades before the war was characterized by anti-intellectualism; the philosophical skepticism and deism that captivated such southern leaders as Jefferson during the Revolutionary era all but disappeared, and the names of such Enlightenment thinkers as Voltaire, Hume, and Paine were despised. Although the Romantic movement (the dominant intellectual trend of the first half of the century) found expression in the North through reform groups, in the South it became a reaction against eighteenth-century rationalism and turned into a veneration of sentiment, feeling, and intuition.

Specifically, the fundamentalism of southern Christianity, linked with a Romantic adherence to intuition, led many Southerners in the 1850s to take up arms against the dangerous ideas of modern science. The new study of geology, of the cosmic system, of fossils and the remains of ancient civilization—all of these scientific pursuits brought into doubt many of the literal statements in the Bible concerning the age of the world, human origins, and the creation and development of the earth. As a result, by 1860 a Protestant dogma emphasizing the infallibility of the Scriptures and the vital need for conversion, along with a belief in the inherent good of slavery, had become firmly rooted in the southern way of life.

The rise of abolitionism in the North after the 1830s and the growing fear of slave rebellions caused Southerners to seek new ways of justifying slavery. The Baptist, Methodist, and Presbyterian churches, which had earlier condemned slavery, now defended the institution. By the mid-1840s, southern churches separated from their counterparts in the North as a result of the split over slavery. Leading southern ministers wrote books and delivered sermons demonstrating that slavery was upheld in the Old Testament and that, according to the New Testament, the Apostle Paul urged fugitive slaves to return to their masters.

A Clash of Cultures

Although it is incorrect to think of the United States as divided into two distinct regions, North and South, by mid-century the Northeast and the satellite regions tied to it by railroad tracks (such as the upper Midwest) were becoming more urban and more industrial, less agricultural, and increasingly unwilling to tolerate much longer the institution of slavery. A fringe of states stretching from Maryland and Virginia westward through Kentucky and Missouri exhibited some aspects of this emerging urban-industrial life, yet by sentiment and blood tended to be deeply rooted in an agricultural past. To the South, except for a mere handful of river and sea ports, agriculture's sway was unchallenged and so was the belief in a slave society. In some regions such as North Carolina, east Tennessee, and upland areas of several states, there was diversified, general farming, but cotton and those who grew it represented the real power throughout much of the Lower South.

While the North felt it was surging forward into a new era of greater prosperity for greater numbers of its citizens, much of the South was clinging to a romantic image of its slave society. Southerners often regarded Yankees as money-grubbing city slickers desperate for gain, indifferent to the suffering of their employees, and devoid of all personal charm; at the same time, they liked to see themselves as refined gentlefolk, more interested in a life of stately, cultivated ease than in making money, as kindly masters to their slaves, and as excellent hosts and fluent conversationalists. The North, however, saw the South as a land of moral and educational backwardness, perversely indifferent to progress, unjustifiably snobbish, more emotional than intellectual, and, above all else, as a land of slavery.

The North was a region marked by considerable cultural, linguistic, and religious diversity, the result of mass immigration; the South remained Protestant and Anglo-Saxon, except, of course, for millions of blacks who had a subtle but passive influence upon southern folkways. The mobility of people in the North (from farm to city, from city to frontier) was loosening the ties of family solidarity; in the South individuals grew up amongst relatives and maintained lasting loyalties even to distant cousins. The North was the scene of widespread and effective reform movements; the South was more content with traditional social arrangements. Education in the North was more and more directed towards practical benefit; in the South it continued to be oriented towards classical learning and the other ornaments of "civilized" life.

But the growing conflict over protective tariffs and slavery were the great divisive issues, and different styles of life, of thought, and of temperament merely exacerbated sectional hostilities. To the Southerner, the Northerner was an unfeeling machine; to a Northerner such as Henry Adams, historian and grandson of John Quincy Adams, the Southerner was a mindless creature of impulse. As Adams put it, "Strictly, the southerner had no mind; he had temperament. He was not a scholar; he had no intellectual training; he could not analyze an idea and he could not conceive of admitting two; but in life one could get along very well without ideas if one had only the social instinct." No matter how great the differences between Northerners and Southerners might have been, they were only exaggerated by ignorance. "We are, I fear," wrote one astute Southerner in 1857, "within a few years of disunion & perhaps of civil war; and all because neither side knows the other."

Essay

The Emergence of American Painting

At a time when the artists of Europe, inspired by Romanticism, were searching out exotic subjects in foreign lands or in fantasy or legend, a generation of American painters emerged who had only to record the wonders of their own land in order to satisfy the Romantic taste for the sublime and the marvelous. Most of these American painters were self-taught, many were sorely neglected, but all created an image of the United States both brilliant and enduring.

Painting was not a pursuit that commanded much respect in the American public during the colonial period and the early years of the Republic. Most of the itinerant artists were naive and untutored in even the bare rudiments of composition, perspective, drawing, and the use of color. Their work may seem charming to twentieth-century observers, but contemporary Europeans probably regarded it as laughable. Those American painters who were well trained, such as Benjamin West and Gilbert Stuart, spent long periods in England, where they achieved their greatest renown.

Americans frowned on painting for two major reasons—it was thought worldly and sinful and not a useful occupation. A carpenter or a silversmith turned out furniture or utensils that were practical; a painter produced nothing of use—save for a portrait of a political leader or a wealthy merchant or planter. But even these likenesses seemed tributes to mere vanity, not entirely acceptable to people bent on being other worldly and pious, such as the Puritans in Massachusetts or the Quakers in Pennsylvania.

In the Jacksonian era, however, this point of view went through a transformation, attributable primarily to the Romantic cult of nature. In the thinking of European and English Romantic artists and writers, which was echoed by Americans, nature was God's handiwork. The artist was peculiarly gifted to see and capture the spiritual qualities of nature in landscape painting. Thus, for an ordinary man or woman to contemplate a landscape painting was much the same as attending a sermon—it was a religious act. Armed with this reasoning, Americans suddenly felt justified in patronizing an art form that had previously struck them as frivolous and trivial.

An impressive new development in American art, called the Hudson River School, came into being about 1825 under the leadership of Thomas Cole. Born in England, Cole came to the

The Metropolitan Museum of Art, Gift of Mrs. Russell Sage, 1908.

"The Oxbow (The Connecticut River near Northampton)" by Thomas Cole (1846).

United States with his family when he was seventeen. Two years later, an entirely self-taught painter, he began to do portraits, wandering from house to house and eking out a living from tiny commissions. In his travels, however, he saw the moody landscapes of Thomas Doughty, an older American artist. Despite the fact that young Cole never had seen a first-rate landscape painting by a major artist, he nevertheless fused this brief glimpse of Doughty's work with his own stored-up impressions of the American wilderness to produce canvases of an astonishing originality and power. When he took a walking tour through the Catskills along the Hudson River valley, Cole sketched directly from nature. Later, after meditating on these subjects, he executed his vast canvases. Even his earliest works speak of the grandeur of the American scene and reveal in startling clarity every detail of the vast panoramas he executed. After he converted to the Anglican Church in 1842, his works were infused with a more religious tone.

When Cole died in 1848 at the age of forty-seven, the American poet William Cullen Bryant revealed in his funeral oration the religious way in which Americans looked at painting. Bryant said that Cole's paintings "are of that nature that it hardly transcends the proper use of language to call them acts of religion." In fact, the canvases were "the sincere communications of his own moral and intellectual being."

Soon a whole school of painters had formed around Cole's concept of nature. Among the most outstanding was Asher B. Durand, a man who worked as an engraver until he was forty

"Kindred Spirits" by Asher B. Durand (1849).

years old and only then turned full-time to painting. Like Cole, Durand painted the Catskills, the White Mountains, the Adirondacks, and the Berkshires. Ironically, at the very moment when the countryside in the Northeast was becoming almost daily more and more built up and industrialized, American artists decided to create their immense, empty wilderness scenes. Perhaps something of the compensatory function of art can be deduced from the fact that when American painters began to celebrate nature and religion, both already were entering an era of change. One of Durand's most famous canvases is *Kindred Spirits,* which shows William Cullen Bryant and Thomas Cole communing with nature, a fitting tribute to two of the American architects of the cult of nature.

The last of the great artists of the Hudson River School was

Frederic Edwin Church (1826–1900). Church was Cole's only student, and under his influence painted the ambitious, allegorical landscape, *Moses Viewing the Promised Land.* After Cole's death, Church took on a mighty subject that his teacher considered but rejected as too demanding—Niagara Falls. When Church exhibited his *Niagara* in New York and London in 1857, it drew hordes of excited spectators, and the dean of English art critics, John Ruskin, finally had to admit that perhaps there was such a thing as American landscape. Breathtaking vistas, scrupulously observed details, and religious symbolism imbued most of Church's landscapes; typically, in 1862 he pictured the reflection of the sun in a lake as the sign of the Cross.

American painters of the antebellum period achieved recognition not only for their landscapes and awesome technique. John James Audubon and George Catlin both left imaginative records of the wonders of a new land.

Audubon was born in Haiti in 1785 and raised in France but immigrated to the United States when he was eighteen. There he married and settled in Kentucky, earning his living as a merchant and land speculator. When he was thirty-five, in 1820, he exhibited his first bird drawings in Cincinnati, Ohio. They were greeted with such acclaim that Audubon, who was barely scratching out a living, decided to turn his attention to paintings of the birds of America. This new occupation soon became an obsession, and Audubon often worked seventeen hours a day. He collected specimens of birds from everywhere in the United States and, after eighteen years of hard work, completed more than 1,000 paintings and 435 engravings. This monumental effort was unappreciated in America; consequently, in 1826, Audubon sailed to England. There he arranged for some of his plates to be published, but it was not until 1838 that Audubon was able to issue in England his four-volume *The Birds of America, from Original Drawings, with 435 Plates Showing 1,065 Figures.* It proved a beautiful and nearly comprehensive record of the winged life of North America.

Courtesy New-York Historical Society, New York City.

"Carolina Paroquet" by John James Audubon (c.1825).

Audubon's zealous study of birds was matched by the vivid and fascinating pictures of American Indians by George Catlin. Like Cole and so many other American artists of this period, the Pennsylvania-born Catlin was entirely self-taught. To please his father he practiced law for a few years, but when he was twenty-seven, in 1823, he became a full-time artist. He did many unimportant portraits until one day, in the 1820s, he saw a delegation of splendidly dressed Indians in Washington, D.C. Catlin then and there resolved to devote all his talents to portraying Indians. In 1830 he went to St. Louis, where he remained for the next two years, painting the Indian chiefs who came to that city, which was then a territorial capital. He

New York Public Library, Astor, Lenox & Tilden Foundations.

"Four Bears, Chief of the Missouri River Mandans" by George Catlin (1832).

subsequently made a trip up the Missouri River as far as South Dakota, sketching members of various tribes he encountered.

A year later Catlin, after polishing his paintings, showed them to enormous crowds in Pittsburgh, Cincinnati, and Louisville. The exhibitions were so successful that he next journeyed through the Southwest, visited the Rockies, and then sailed up the Mississippi to its headwaters, all the while painting the Indians, their regalia, their dwellings, and their weapons and tools. Aside from its considerable charm and vivacity, his work remains a valuable anthropological record of Indian ways of life. In 1837 Catlin opened an exhibition of 600 pictures in New York City, charging each visitor 50 cents. With the profits he sailed for Europe, taking along with him "Catlin's Indian Gallery." In London, Paris, and in Holland immense crowds flocked to the exhibitions, all eager to see the various colorful guises of the fabled Red Man.

By 1851, unfortunately, the public, both in Europe and in America, was losing interest in traveling exhibits of this sort, perhaps because of the increasing vogue of photography. Catlin attempted to sell his paintings to the United States government. As the modern art critic John Canaday has written, "Daniel Webster and the northern senators sponsored the acquisition, but the southern block fought it. They saw the West as an area for the expansion of slavery at the expense of Indian rights and feared that Catlin's paintings would stir up sympathy for the tribes—as well they might have." As a result of southern opposition, the paintings were not bought by the government but rather by a rich American manufacturer.

At a time when Romantic artists in Europe were picturing medieval knights and ladies or conjuring up fantasies of devils and fair maidens or studying the exotic faces of Morocco, American painters were expertly capturing in paint the vast, haunting depths of the American landscape, the imposing splendors of the country's wildlife, and the haunting faces of its Indian population. The antebellum period saw the emergence not only of the first internationally important American writers (Hawthorne, Emerson, Poe, Melville, Thoreau, and Whitman) but also of its first major painters.

Selected Readings

Many of the books listed in Chapters 8 through 11 are relevant to the topics covered in this chapter. In addition, see the following sources.

General Accounts
Allan Nevins, *Ordeal of the Union,* (2 vols., 1947)
Rush Welter, *The Mind of America, 1820–1860* (1975)

Expansion and Growth
Ray Allen Billington, *Westward Expansion: A History of the American Frontier* (4th ed., 1974)
Everett Dick, *The Lure of the Land: A Social History of the Public Lands from the Articles of Confederation to the New Deal* (1970)
Paul W. Gates and Robert W. Swenson, *History of Public Land Law Development* (1968)
Robert W. Fogel, *Railroads and American Economic Growth* (1964)
Albert Fishlow, *American Railroads and the Transformation of the Ante-Bellum Economy* (1965)
Richard W. Van Alstyne, *The Rising American Empire* (1960)
Arthur Walworth, *Black Ships off Japan: The Story of Commodore Perry's Expedition* (1946)
Wyatt W. Belcher, *The Economic Rivalry Between Chicago and St. Louis, 1850–1880* (1947)
Peter R. Knight, *The Plain People of Boston, 1830–1860: A Study in City Growth* (1971)
Merl E. Reed, *New Orleans and the Railroads: The Struggle for Commercial Empire, 1830–1860* (1966)

Social and Cultural Diversity
Donald B. Cole, *Immigrant City: Lawrence, Massachusetts, 1845–1921* (1963)
Earl F. Niehaus, *The Irish in New Orleans, 1800–1860* (1965)
Irving H. Bartlett, *The American Mind in the Mid-Nineteenth Century* (1967)
David Grimsted, ed., *Notions of the Americans, 1820–1860* (1970)
Perry Miller, *The Life of the Mind: From the Revolution to the Civil War* (1965)
Francis O. Matthiessen, *American Renaissance: Art and Expression in the Age of Emerson and Whitman* (1941)
William R. Taylor, *Cavalier and Yankee: The Old South and the American National Character* (1961)

Contrasts and Contradictions
Clement Eaton, *The Growth of Southern Civilization, 1790–1860* (1961)
Clement Eaton, *The Mind of the Old South* (1964)
Clement Eaton, *A History of the Old South* (3rd ed., 1975)
Eugene Genovese, *The Political Economy of Slavery* (1965)
Eugene Genovese, *The World the Slaveholders Made* (1969)
Eugene Genovese, *Roll, Jordan, Roll: The World the Slaves Made* (1974)
Howard R. Floan, *The South in Northern Eyes, 1831–1861* (1958)

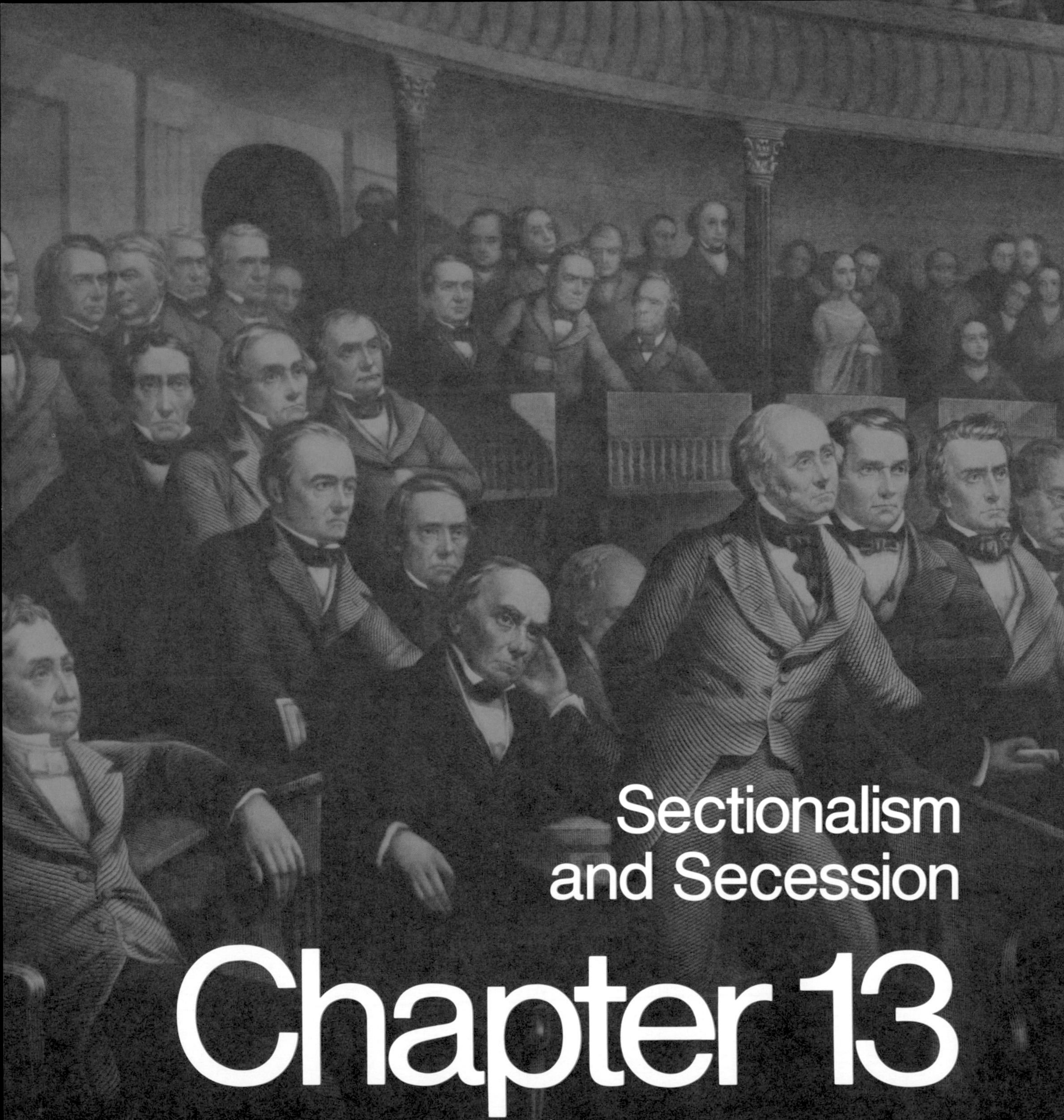

Chapter 13

Sectionalism and Secession

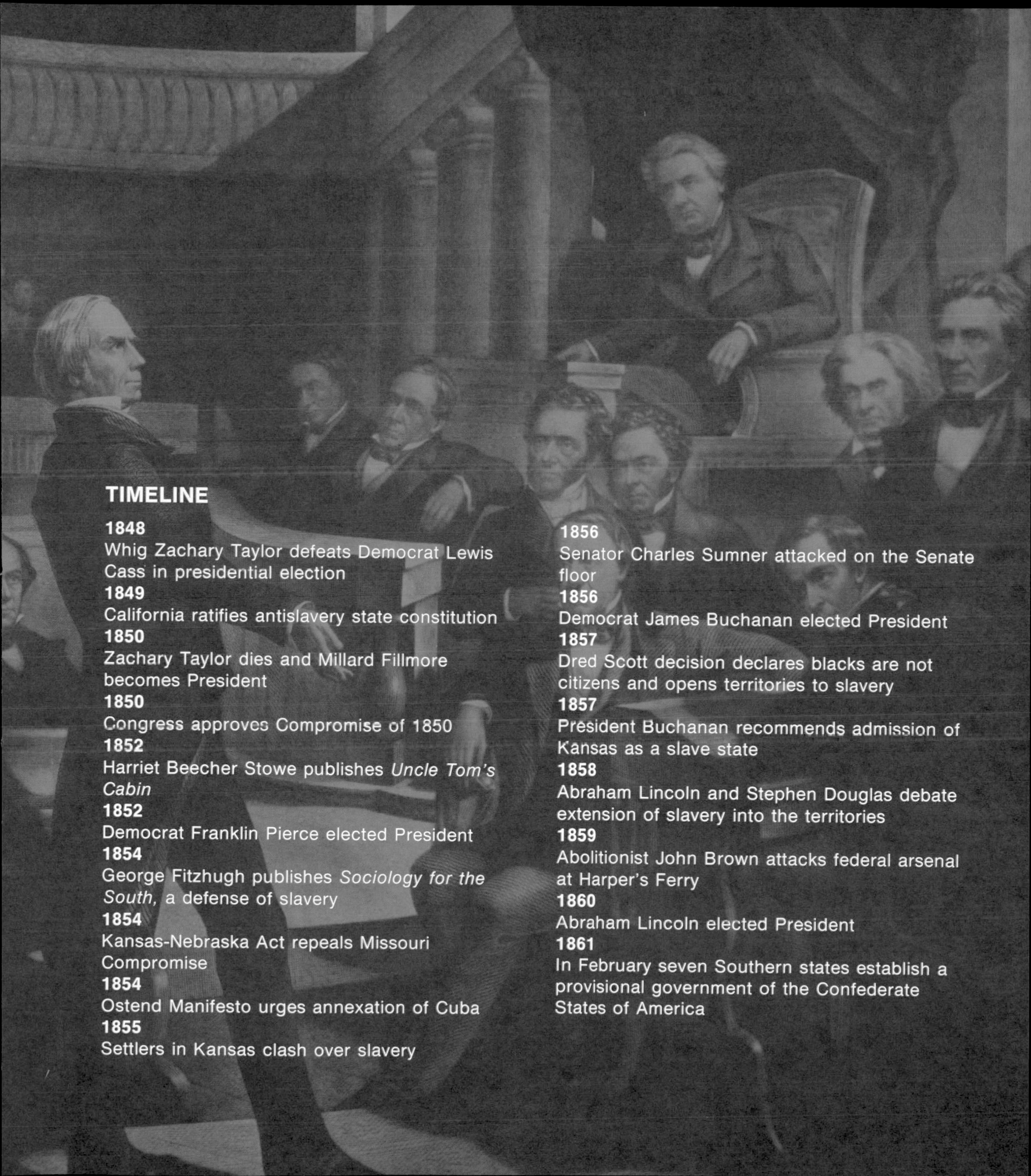

TIMELINE

1848
Whig Zachary Taylor defeats Democrat Lewis Cass in presidential election
1849
California ratifies antislavery state constitution
1850
Zachary Taylor dies and Millard Fillmore becomes President
1850
Congress approves Compromise of 1850
1852
Harriet Beecher Stowe publishes *Uncle Tom's Cabin*
1852
Democrat Franklin Pierce elected President
1854
George Fitzhugh publishes *Sociology for the South,* a defense of slavery
1854
Kansas-Nebraska Act repeals Missouri Compromise
1854
Ostend Manifesto urges annexation of Cuba
1855
Settlers in Kansas clash over slavery
1856
Senator Charles Sumner attacked on the Senate floor
1856
Democrat James Buchanan elected President
1857
Dred Scott decision declares blacks are not citizens and opens territories to slavery
1857
President Buchanan recommends admission of Kansas as a slave state
1858
Abraham Lincoln and Stephen Douglas debate extension of slavery into the territories
1859
Abolitionist John Brown attacks federal arsenal at Harper's Ferry
1860
Abraham Lincoln elected President
1861
In February seven Southern states establish a provisional government of the Confederate States of America

CHAPTER OUTLINE

Idealists may prefer governments that always pursue clear and consistent ends, but in a pluralistic society such as that of the United States, almost nothing occurs save from a variety of reasons, some worthy, others questionable, and still others inscrutable. The sectional conflicts that dominated American life in the 1850s arose from issues not always sharply defined in the minds of most Americans of the time.

In one sense this very obscurity was deliberately cultivated in the mid-nineteenth century by the nation's major political parties. Just as many elected officials today frequently back away from decisive statements on such controversial questions as welfare, busing, and economic planning by the central government, so the Whigs and Democrats in the decades before the Civil War attempted to retain their followings by straddling the great problems—abolition, the tariff, and the spread of slavery into new territories. After 1854, the new Republican party took a much different course and forcefully advocated the controversial policy of the containment of slavery.

To be sure, the question of slavery had long been festering. By the 1830s it was already a source of bitter contention between Northerners and Southerners. The land acquired from the Mexican War made the United States a continental nation, but the price paid for a gain in size was a loss in unity. The wrangling over the Wilmot Proviso in August 1846 was the opening round of a debate that would split the nation asunder.

Territorial Expansion and Politics

By the end of Polk's administration (1845–1849), congressmen were heatedly disputing the status of slavery in the territories. Southerners claimed the right to bring their property, including slaves, into any new area. They denied the contention that Congress had the authority to prohibit the movement of slavery into the territories. Democrat Lewis Cass (1782–1866) of Michigan tried to reduce tensions by advocating the principle of "squatter sovereignty," whereby the people of each territory might decide for themselves whether or not to permit slavery within their borders. Although this position might seem, at first glance, to favor southern ambitions, in fact southern extremists rejected it. They argued that territorial legislatures possessed no autonomy and ruled only by permission of Congress; they could not ban or endorse slavery. Congress alone had authority over territories, and that body, the Southerners reasoned, was constrained by the Constitution to guarantee an individual the freedom to use property (slaves) as he or she saw fit.

In the election of 1848, neither the Democrats nor the Whigs took a strong stand on the extension of slavery. The Democrats nominated Lewis Cass, thereby endorsing his principle of squatter sovereignty, but avoided any mention of the containment of slavery in their platform. The notion of squatter sovereignty was in any

Chicago Historical Society.

Lewis Cass, advocate of Squatter Sovereignty.

event a calculated appeal to moderates on either side of the Mason-Dixon line. The Whigs nominated Zachary Taylor (1784–1850) of Louisiana, a man who owned slaves and cotton fields but who stated that, if elected President, he would not abuse his veto power. With this statement Taylor implied that he would not fight decisions made by Congress concerning slavery in recently acquired lands. But his party refused to adopt a platform or announce its principles.

The Whigs attempted to capitalize on the war record of Taylor, who had won distinction during the Mexican War by defeating a superior Mexican force under General Santa Anna at Buena Vista. But Taylor, dubbed "Old Rough and Ready," was one of the strangest choices for the presidency in American history, since he had no previous political experience, had never cast a vote, lacked formal education, and could only remark when asked if he would accept the nomination, "I will not say I would not serve if the good people were imprudent enough to elect me." This was, of course, a repeat of the "Tippecanoe and Tyler, too" strategy of 1840; once more the Whigs hoped to ride the coat tails of a celebrated battlefield hero to victory. Taylor's running mate was Millard Fillmore (1800–1874), a dignified, high-minded political leader from New York state.

Cass, the Democratic nominee, was a loyal party man with considerable ability and political experience. A confirmed expansionist in the 1840s, he was, above all else, a nationalist. Even slavery with all of its ramifications was, in his view, a subordinate issue. The selection of Cass was an effort to win the western vote and to promote sectional harmony. While "squatter sovereignty" was not written into the Democratic platform, it offered—or at least suggested—a way to prevent the question of slavery from rigidifying sectional disunity.

Antislavery politicians in both parties found it difficult to live with either Taylor or Cass. In New York and New England, Democratic dissidents were called "barnburners" by their enemies. Because of their dislike for Cass, it was said these dissidents were treating their party as the exasperated farmer did his barn. They were burning it down to kill the rats infesting it. Antislavery or "conscience" Whigs, who bolted from their party as a result of Taylor's nomination, joined the barnburners and members of Birney's Liberty party to create the new Free Soil party founded on the principles of "Free Soil, Free Speech, Free Labor, and Free Men." The Free Soilers nominated ex-President Martin Van Buren, who had openly opposed the annexation of Texas and forthrightly repudiated slavery. The Free Soil party took away enough Democratic votes in New York to give that state—and the election—to Taylor and the Whigs. Nationwide, Van Buren won 10.1 percent of the popular vote; Cass, 42.5 percent; and Taylor, 47.3 percent.

Although Taylor was a Southern slaveholder, his military experience had given him a national outlook. He recommended that California, along with the rest of the land ceded by Mexico, be allowed to bypass territorial status and apply for statehood as quickly as possible. Immediate statehood, he believed, would settle the issue of slavery in the West without subjecting the nation to bitter sectional debates in Congress. With the discovery of gold in California in 1848, a flood of people, most of them Americans but some Mexicans and Europeans, entered the region; obviously statehood was advisable. Taylor stressed the need for the "law and order" that statehood would bring California, and although a slave owner himself, he insisted that the people there should determine for themselves whether slavery would be permitted in their state. But Taylor did not dare mention the inflammatory word, *slavery;* instead, he used the circumlocution "questions of domestic policy." This stand was tantamount to squatter sovereignty, a proposal previously advocated by Cass.

By October 1849, Californians had drawn up a state constitution outlawing slavery, which was overwhelmingly ratified two months later. The prospect of California's entrance into the Union as a free state alarmed Southerners, since it would upset the existing balance of slave and free states: fifteen slave states and fifteen free states. Should any new territory (New Mexico, Oregon, or Utah) also become a free state in the near future, the political power of the South in the Senate would be destroyed. Nevertheless, President Taylor, a Southerner, steadfastly urged the admission of California and warned that any attempt to block its entrance into the Union on purely sectional grounds would be unwise. In spite of Taylor's warning, southern extremists called for a convention to meet in Nashville, Tennessee, in the summer of 1850 to consider the possibility of secession from the Union. At the same time, many Northerners were agitating to prohibit slavery in the new territories and to outlaw slavery and the slave trade in the District of Columbia.

The Compromise of 1850

Henry Clay, always a great nationalist, attempted to stage a reconciliation between the North and the South. Though he was seventy-one and in poor health, he recognized that sectional hostilities were explosive; a majority of Northerners in the House of Representatives were ready to pass the Wilmot Proviso, banning slavery from all territory acquired from Mexico, and southern congressmen under the leadership of Calhoun were openly threatening secession.

Beginning on January 29, 1850, Clay presented a number of compromise proposals to the Senate, which later were organized into an omnibus bill. He recommended that Congress admit California without any stipulation concerning slavery (he knew it would be free), and organize the Utah and New Mexico territories so that the people there could decide the slavery question for themselves when they applied for admission to the Union (and he assumed these areas would be free, too). He suggested that the federal government pay part of the debt of the republic of Texas, in return for which Texas would give up its claims to land that would become part of the New Mexico territory. He urged the prohibition of the slave trade in the District of Columbia in order to end the spectacle of manacled slaves being led through the streets of the nation's capital. To pacify the South in return for ending that trade, he urged enactment of a stronger fugitive slave law; Northerners, he said, must return runaway slaves to their owners. The last of Clay's eight resolutions stated that Congress "has no power to prohibit or obstruct the trade in slaves between the slaveholding states; but that the admission or exclusion of slaves brought from one into another of them, depends exclusively upon their own particular laws." These proposals were a strong bid for nationalism, and Clay closed with a fervent plea that everyone consider carefully before advocating secession or war: "I implore them to pause—solemnly to pause—at the edge of the precipice before the fearful and disastrous leap is taken in the yawning abyss below which will inevitably lead to certain and irretrievable destruction."

Southerners were deeply unhappy with these suggestions, though they were offered in the spirit of compromise. Calhoun, too feeble to speak, had his objections voiced for him by Senator James M. Mason of Virginia. The South Carolinian threatened secession if the North took any action to thwart the spread of slavery or to curtail the domestic slave trade. What Calhoun did not anticipate was that his extreme remarks, by raising the distinct possibility of disunion and civil war, actually worked against his purposes and convinced moderate Southerners to cooperate with Clay.

But strong opposition to Clay's proposals also came from the North. William H. Seward of New York supported the Wilmot Proviso and, as an antislavery man, denounced the Clay proposals as a failure of principle; even if the protection of slavery should be considered constitutional, Seward said, "there is a higher law than the Constitution"—an assertion that outraged conservatives, especially in the South. Jefferson Davis (1808–1889) of Mississippi upheld the right of the South to extend slavery to the territories. He argued that the proposals offered nothing of value to the South and insisted

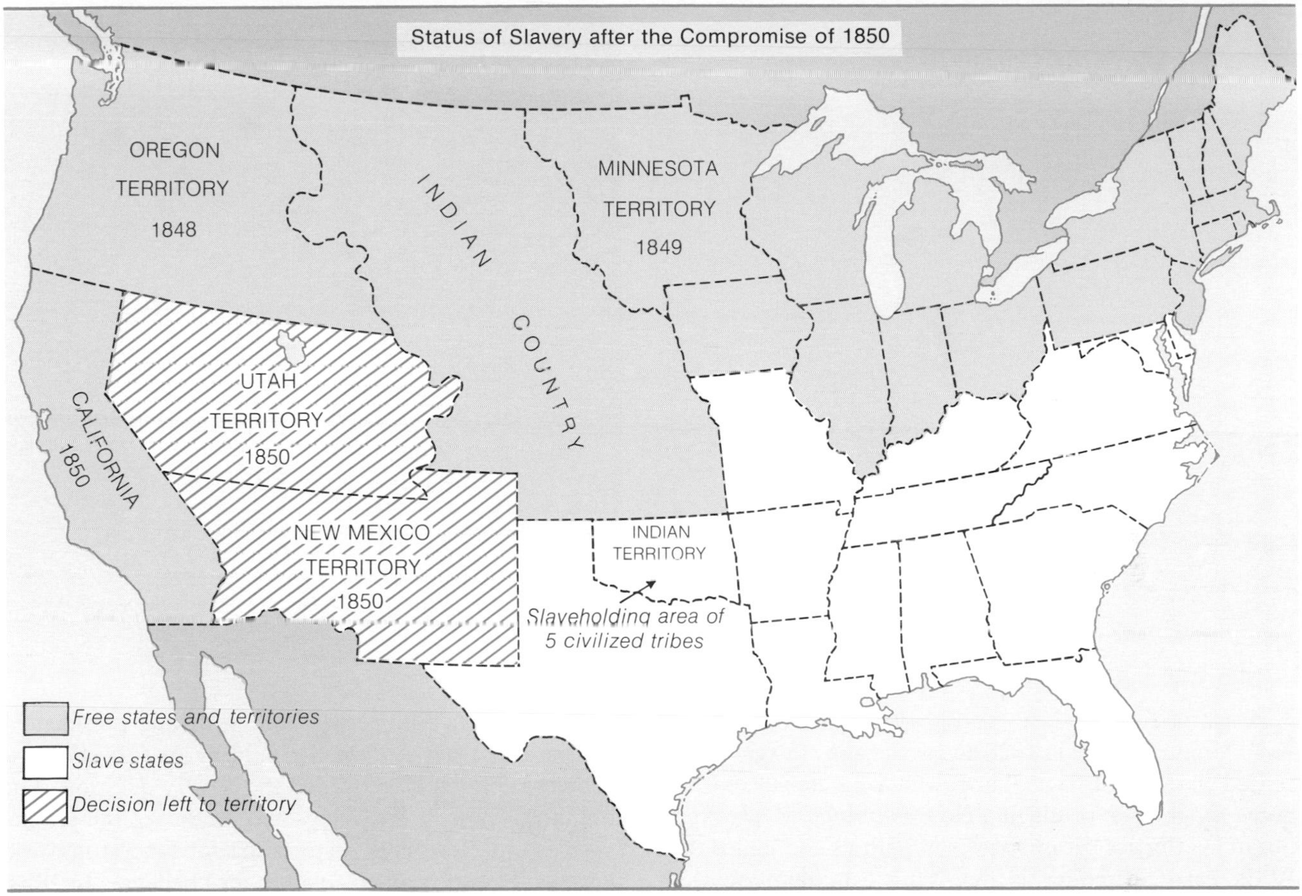

that the least the South would accept would be an extension of the Missouri Compromise line to the Pacific, permitting slavery to exist everywhere south of that line. Clay refused this counterproposal, pointing out that Mexican law had prohibited slavery, that it did not exist in new lands acquired from Mexico, and that he, Clay, would not have future citizens of California and New Mexico reproach his memory for introducing the institution into places where it had not flourished.

Daniel Webster made the most important speech on behalf of Clay's proposals. On March 7, 1850, in a beautifully written speech, Webster assured his northern colleagues that agricultural, climactic, and geographic conditions made the new western territories acquired from Mexico unsuited for slavery. Thus it was not necessary to include the Wilmot Proviso or any similar prohibition against slavery, which would only stir up destructive passions, in a bill for organizing new state governments there. As he put it, "I would not take pains uselessly to reaffirm an ordinance of nature, nor to re-enact the will of God."

Despite the efforts of Clay and Webster, dissension reigned between northern opponents to the extension of slavery and southern advocates of it. With the death of President Taylor in July 1850, Vice President Millard Fillmore, a strong advocate of Clay's compromise resolutions, moved into the White House and began to exert his influence. Even with the President's help, those favoring compromise faced serious opposition in the Senate until a thirty-seven-year-old Democrat, Stephen A. Douglas from Illinois (the man who framed the bills providing territorial governments for Utah and New Mexico), spoke eloquently in their behalf. Douglas decided to separate the various measures that were part of

National Archives.

William Henry Seward
(1801–1872)

Born in Florida, New York, Seward graduated from Union College in 1820 and at the age of twenty-one settled in Auburn, New York, which he considered his home for the rest of his life. He was trained as a lawyer, but in his thirties became active in politics and joined the Whig party. Running as the Whig candidate, he was elected governor of New York in 1838, a position he held for four years. As governor, Seward was able to establish nonsectarian schools in New York City, despite the violent opposition of nativists.

Although at first rather lukewarm to the slavery issue, Seward had moved squarely into the abolitionist camp before his second term as governor ended. Fearful he was too far in advance of public opinion and eager to replenish his financial resources, he chose not to seek another term and returned to his lucrative law practice. By 1848, however, antislavery sentiment was rising and Seward won a seat in the United States Senate. There he engaged actively in the debates concerning the Compromise of 1850. Seward was guided by a "higher law than the Constitution" and sought to abolish slavery and the slave trade in the District of Columbia and exclude slavery altogether from the western territories.

The early 1850s were difficult years for Seward, the Whig politician. He had backed both Taylor and Scott wholeheartedly; but, perhaps bitten by the presidential bug, he chose not to lead the fight against the Kansas-Nebraska Bill which reopened the slavery question. The declining power of the Whigs and the rise of the Know-Nothings in New York state called for fancy footwork; however, Seward proved equal to the challenge. In 1854, seeking reelection, he took a strong, antislavery stand to please local Whigs and managed to secure Know-Nothing backing, although their program was alien to his philosophy as an ardent expansionist and champion of the Irish. A year later the Know-Nothings were disappearing along with the Whigs as the Republican party became a recognizable entity, and Seward—forced on by a mixture of ambition, humanitarianism, and impulse—now was in the forefront of the antislavery campaign.

From 1855 to 1860, Seward, the Republican, served as one of the most vehement spokesmen of this growing movement. In 1858 he made a speech in which he characterized the North-South dispute over slavery as "an irrepressible conflict," a phrase that soon became famous. In 1860 Seward hoped to win the Republican presidential nomination, but he was judged too outspoken against slavery. After Lincoln won the election, however, he was quick to name Seward as his Secretary of State.

During the Civil War, Seward was in charge of the

difficult task of keeping England and France from coming to the aid of the Confederacy. In this assignment Seward performed admirably, by appealing to the antislavery sentiment in Europe.

Seward was by temperament an expansionist. During the slavery extension controversy, this impulse was held in check, but after the Civil War he felt free to indulge it—and did so by negotiating the purchase of Alaska in 1867. He also advocated the annexation of Hawaii, but this step was not taken while he was in office.

In the Reconstruction period, Seward continued to act as Secretary of State under Andrew Johnson, and he was influential in convincing the President to take a conciliatory posture towards the defeated South. Although Seward often made reckless statements, sometimes showed poor judgment, and occasionally shifted opinions in order to appeal to voters, he was one of the earliest and staunchest antislavery leaders. As such, he earned the respect of many of his northern contemporaries. ■

---

an omnibus bill and to push them through Congress one by one. Soon, all but the District of Columbia bill, which banned the slave trade in Washington, passed, and on September 17 even that bill became law. Douglas's successful strategy involved finding different coalitions in Congress to support each measure. For instance, he secured the admission of California as a free state by putting together an alliance of Clay supporters and those antislavery men who, though they were against some of the other measures (such as the Fugitive Slave Law), were naturally in favor of gaining another state where slavery would be outlawed. The Fugitive Slave Law was in turn passed by a different coalition of proslavery Southerners and moderate Northerners.

The so-called Compromise of 1850 was hailed as the final, lasting settlement of the slavery issue, a thorny matter that had so long troubled the nation. In reality, the Compromise only marked a lull in the storm of controversy; indeed, it was not really much of a "compromise." Although southern secessionists lost ground to southern moderates who supported it, the decision not to secede did not arise from genuine Union sentiments; even some southern moderates agreed secession might be the only course if the North did not enforce the Fugitive Slave Law.

The Fugitive Slave Law

The one provision of the compromise that everyone scrutinized carefully was the new, stricter Fugitive Slave Law. Southerners were waiting to see if it would be upheld in the North, and antislavery Northerners recommended that it be ignored. As early as September 1850, one Ohio newspaper was predicting that the law "will be a dead letter upon the statute book," and an editorial in Maine recommended strenuous resistance. As one Florida editor complained, "No sooner has this Fugitive Slave Law gone into effect, [than] the cry of repeal . . . resounds from one end of the Northern States to the other."

Antislavery Northerners objected to several provisions of the new law in particular. The law denied a fugitive slave the right of trial by jury. Federal marshals were authorized to call on bystanders to help them enforce the law. Citizens preventing the arrest of a fugitive, or aiding in his or her concealment or rescue, were subject to a heavy fine, civil damages, and imprisonment for up to six months.

Southerners viewed the election to the Senate in 1851 of Charles Sumner, an antislavery champion from Massachusetts, as a victory for Northern opponents of the Fugitive Slave Law. Despite considerable evidence of northern opposition to the law, state election results indicate that a slight majority of southern voters looked upon the compromise with hope, or at least with a wait-and-see attitude. In Mississippi, South Carolina, and Alabama, moderates won narrow victories over secessionists. Nevertheless, some of these moderates warned that the success of the compromise depended largely on northern willingness to obey the Fugitive Slave Law.

The "underground railroad," a secret system for conveying escaped slaves on boats, wagons, and trains from one hiding place to another, brought a substantial number of fugitives to northern cities before 1850. Under the new law, those fugitives who settled in the North found their freedom once again threatened. Even free blacks who were not escaped slaves feared for their

Worcester Art Museum.

'CONQUERING PREJUDICE,'
or
"Fulfilling a Constitutional duty with alacrity."
"My God!... My Child!... Will no one help!... Is there no mercy!"
"Any man can perform an agreeable duty... it is not every one that can perform a disagreeable duty."
"By Heaven! he exceeds my most sanguine expectation—he marks his way so clearly & treads so loyally on the track of the Constitution... It is more than great... it is sublime... I feel a great sense of relief."

This lithograph is an attack on the Fugitive Slave Law. The slave master at the far right is quite pleased with the assistance being rendered by a Northerner as they pursue a fugitive slave in front of a church.

safety since they might be falsely charged with having escaped from their "owners" and "returned" to whites posing as former masters. One result of the passage of the law of 1850 was the movement of about 3,000 fugitive slaves to Canada within three months. Harriet Tubman (ca. 1821–1913), a slave who escaped from Maryland's Eastern Shore, was one of the most able conductors on the underground railroad. Known by the slaves as "Moses," she made nineteen trips into slave territory to lead fellow blacks to freedom; and, after 1850, she guided runaways to Canada.

In order to prevent enforcement of the Fugitive Slave Law, many northern communities formed "vigilance committees" to protect fugitives. In Boston, for example, such a committee headed by Unitarian minister Theodore Parker (1810–1860) smuggled two slaves out of the country in 1850 to put them beyond the reach of slave catchers. Although from 8,000 to 15,000 blacks fled from slavery in the period from 1850 to 1860, only 191 slaves were claimed in the courts under the provisions of the Fugitive Slave Law. In New England, where hostility to the law ran highest, only three claims were made before 1854, and none after that year.

Two of the best-publicized cases of slave rescues occurred in 1851, and they were so notorious that many Southerners became convinced that the new law was unenforceable. Shadrack, a black who escaped from Virginia and was working as a waiter in Boston, was found by an agent of his master and taken to court. But a crowd of free blacks burst into the courtroom and rescued him; as one observer remarked, the crowd hurried Shadrack "through the square into Court Street, where he found the use of his feet, and they went off toward Cambridge, like a black squall, the crowd driving along with them and cheering as they went." Not only did Shadrack elude his pursuers, but the district attorney was unable to convict a single accomplice.

In Syracuse, New York, a fugitive slave named William Henry (called "Jerry") was arrested on October 1, 1851. He submitted to arrest because he was falsely informed that he was being detained for a New York state offense. Once in custody, Henry learned that he was

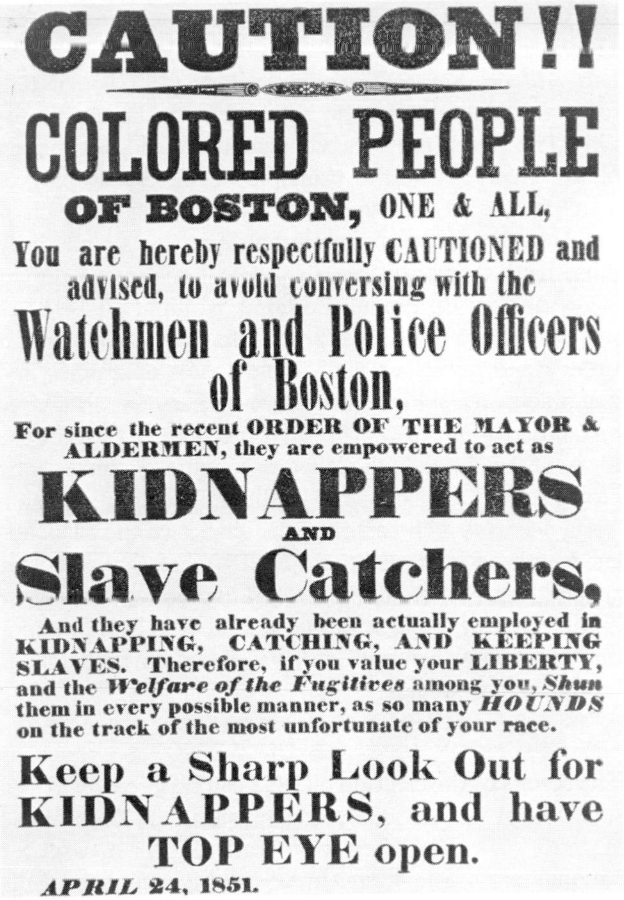
CAUTION!!
COLORED PEOPLE
OF BOSTON, ONE & ALL,
You are hereby respectfully CAUTIONED and advised, to avoid conversing with the
Watchmen and Police Officers of Boston,
For since the recent ORDER OF THE MAYOR & ALDERMEN, they are empowered to act as
KIDNAPPERS
AND
Slave Catchers,
And they have already been actually employed in KIDNAPPING, CATCHING, AND KEEPING SLAVES. Therefore, if you value your LIBERTY, and the *Welfare of the Fugitives* among you, *Shun* them in every possible manner, as so many *HOUNDS* on the track of the most unfortunate of your race.
Keep a Sharp Look Out for KIDNAPPERS, and have TOP EYE open.
APRIL 24, 1851.

Library of Congress.

A Boston Vigilance Committee's warning to the black people of that city.

being held under the Fugitive Slave Law. Incensed by what was happening, a group of abolitionists plotted his rescue. Led by Gerritt Smith and black minister J. W. Loguen, the abolitionists were confident that Henry would be released should he stand trial, but they felt, in Smith's words, that "the moral effect of such an acquittal will be as nothing to a bold and forcible rescue. A forcible rescue will demonstrate the strength of public opinion against the possible legality of slavery and this Fugitive Slave Law in particular. It will honor Syracuse and be a powerful example everywhere."

Smith's rescue plan was put into effect and a mob of black and white abolitionists broke into the police station and freed William Henry. He was quickly taken to Kingston, Ontario, where he lived until his death in 1853. Although a grand jury indicted twenty-six individuals for their role in the liberation, nine blacks and four whites fled to Canada, and only one of the remainder was convicted (no evidence of the exact nature of his sentence is extant). Each year until the Civil War, the city of Syracuse celebrated the "Jerry Rescue" with great pride.

The South bristled when it heard the news of this event. As the Savannah *Republican* wrote, "We warn the press and the people of the North that there is a point, not far distant, when forbearance on our part will cease to be virtuous or honorable, and that they, and they alone, will be responsible for all the ills that may betide this Government." Actually, though fugitive slaves were difficult to apprehend, once brought to trial, most of them were remanded to their rightful owners. In forty-seven cases calling for enforcement of the Fugitive Slave Law in 1851, some 82 percent of the fugitives were sent back to their masters. What Southerners thought was happening (wholesale disregard of the law) was not actually taking place. Although most Northerners opposed slavery, only a few citizens actively tried to thwart the Fugitive Slave Law. In spite of hostility and opposition, federal court officials generally did their duty.

While the Fugitive Slave Law may have been enforced in the North, nevertheless, it incurred considerable sectional animosity. Earlier the slavery question centered around whether slavery should be allowed to enter the western territories, but the 1850 Fugitive Slave Law raised a more sensitive question for some Northerners—the treatment and fate of individual blacks in their own hometowns.

Northern antislavery feeling was further aroused by the publication in 1852 of *Uncle Tom's Cabin,* written by Harriet Beecher Stowe. The book was inspired by Stowe's revulsion against the Fugitive Slave Law, which she regarded as immoral and un-Christian. This influential bestseller was an enormously popular fictional indictment of slavery. The most dramatic scene portrays a fugitive slave girl crossing an icebound river pursued by a slave trader. Many Northerners, never before sympathetic to the abolitionist propaganda, came to view the return of fugitive slaves as insupportable on humanitarian grounds. The Fugitive Slave Law unified the abolitionists since it was a common rallying point for all shades of opinion; those favoring pacifism, political action, and even disunion found it an issue upon which they could all agree.

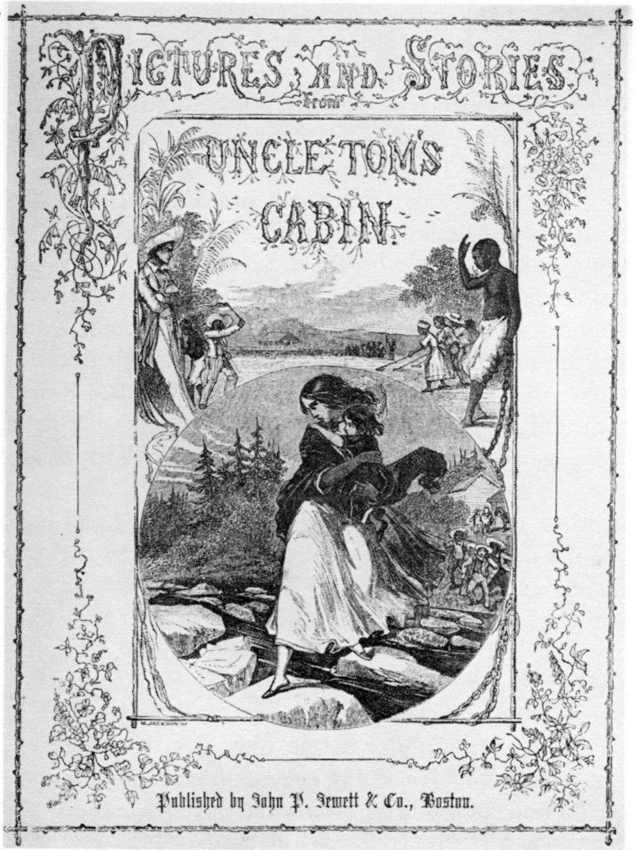

Courtesy New-York Historical Society, New York City.

"God wrote it," Harriet Beecher Stowe once said of her famous novel *Uncle Tom's Cabin.*

Defense of Slavery

As abolitionism and antislavery sentiment grew in the North, more and more Southerners came to the defense of their peculiar institution. South Carolina, with the largest proportion of slaves to whites in the South in 1850 (57.6 percent) and Virginia, with the greatest number of slaves (nearly half a million) led in forging the proslavery argument that became, in time, an ingenious defense of an institution condemned earlier by the South's finest minds.

Southerners cited the Scriptures, turned to the words and deeds of colonial statesmen, and drew upon the Roman and Greek classics—and they pointed to the prosperity of their region and to the living and working conditions of factory workers in the North—to prove the superiority of their slave society. Two books by Virginian George Fitzhugh (1806-1881)—*Sociology for the South; or, The Failure of Free Society* (1854) and *Cannibals All! or, Slaves Without Masters* (1857)—tried to forge this thought into an aggressive, positive philosophy. The South must, he concluded, defend not merely black slavery, "but the principle of slavery as part of man's nature," a view that sent chills throughout much of the North, especially immigrant quarters peopled by those fresh from Europe.

Another Virginian, Edmund Ruffin (1794-1865), was one of slavery's most ardent defenders. An agriculturalist and publisher who wrote scores of articles and pamphlets on a subject that became a personal obsession, his *Anticipations of the Future* (1860) went beyond the ideas of Fitzhugh, who always sought to convert the North to his point of view. Ruffin argued that secession was a necessity as he extolled the glories of an independent South. (Ruffin was permitted to fire the first shot against Fort Sumter in April 1861 and a few weeks later participated in the first Battle of Bull Run as a "temporary" private. When the Civil War ended four years later, he committed suicide.)

The Election of 1852

The results of the election of 1852 can be interpreted as a sign that most American voters favored the Compromise of 1850, or at least they were searching for a basis for national unity. The Whigs bypassed the incumbent, Fillmore. Southerners tended to back him because he supported the compromise, but many Northerners looked elsewhere for a variety of reasons; some because he had southern support, others because they thought another military man like Harrison or Taylor could lead them to victory, and still others because they were already thinking of an antisouthern, abolitionist, and purely sectional movement. To replace Fillmore, the Whigs nominated vain, pompous General Winfield Scott (1786-1866), nicknamed by his enemies "Old Fuss and Feathers" because of his notorious punctiliousness, quarrelsome nature, and pompous bearing. Scott was chosen—though on the fifty-third ballot—because he was a hero of the Mexican War. Although Scott himself was a champion of the 1850 compromise, many Whigs, especially in the North, deplored that settlement; in fact the compromise badly divided the party.

The Democrats, by contrast, endorsed the compromise, though they did not proclaim it to be a final settle-

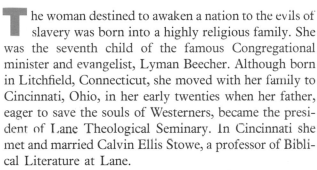

The Metropolitan Museum of Art, Gift of I. N. Philips Stokes, Edward S. Hawes, Alice Mary Hawes, Marion Augusta Hawes, 1937.

Harriet Beecher Stowe (1811–1896)

The woman destined to awaken a nation to the evils of slavery was born into a highly religious family. She was the seventh child of the famous Congregational minister and evangelist, Lyman Beecher. Although born in Litchfield, Connecticut, she moved with her family to Cincinnati, Ohio, in her early twenties when her father, eager to save the souls of Westerners, became the president of Lane Theological Seminary. In Cincinnati she met and married Calvin Ellis Stowe, a professor of Biblical Literature at Lane.

During the first seven years of marriage Mrs. Stowe bore five children, and for a time the cares of maternity kept her from pursuing a career as a writer. In 1843 a collection of her stories was published under the title *The Mayflower.* Her husband supported her in this career, saying, "God has written it in His book that you must be a literary woman, and who are we that we should contend against God?"

In 1850 her husband received an appointment as a professor at Bowdoin College and the family moved to Brunswick, Maine, where they existed in genteel poverty. Mrs. Stowe began to immerse herself in published accounts of slavery, such as Theodore Weld's *American Slavery As It Is,* and she contemplated writing a novel on that subject. While living in Cincinnati she had crossed the Ohio River into Kentucky on several occasions and even visited briefly a plantation; she and her husband had also helped one of their own black servants, who was claimed as a slave, to escape from federal officers. Aside from these incidents, Mrs. Stowe had few direct contacts with slavery, though she lived among fiery abolitionists, including two of her brothers, who were constantly denouncing slavery from their pulpits.

Mrs. Stowe's response to the Fugitive Slave Law of 1850 was to begin writing *Uncle Tom's Cabin: or, Life Among the Lowly,* one of the most widely read books of the nineteenth century, not only in America but also in Europe. Within a year after its publication in 1852, this antislavery work had sold 300,000 copies and was still going strong. The book not only won her the vast admiration of Northerners but also the undying hatred of southern whites, although her "concluding remarks" pointed out that the North must share the blame and burden of slavery: "Northern men, northern mothers, northern Christians, have something more to do than denounce their brethren at the South; they must look to the evil among themselves." Her book spawned some thirty anti-Uncle Tom novels in the South within three years. To defend herself against accusations of inaccuracy and ignorance, Mrs. Stowe decumented her case against slavery in *A Key to Uncle Tom's Cabin* (published in 1853). And in 1856, Mrs. Stowe published yet another antislavery novel, *Dred.*

Mrs. Stowe's family was supported chiefly by earnings from her writings, and between 1862 and 1884 she turned out about a book a year. Stowe's family responsibilities were large, since she supported a number of poor relatives, but her skill at handling money was faulty. Nevertheless, she was able to build a modest house in Hartford, Connecticut, and buy a home in Florida with the profits of her pen. The best of her later novels (*The Pearl of Orr's Island* and *Oldtown Folks,* for instance) were based on recollections of her girlhood in New England. ■

---

ment of the slavery problem. This adroitly calculated position appealed to both Northerners and Southerners. The Democratic candidate was Franklin Pierce (1804-1869) of New Hampshire, who was selected as a compromise candidate on the forty-ninth ballot. Though only forty-eight at the time of the election, Pierce had served in the legislature of New Hampshire and in the United States Senate. A loyal, Jacksonian Democrat, he followed party leaders on all issues except internal improvements, to which he was opposed. Although from the North, Pierce respected southern rights and harbored an antipathy for abolitionists, whom he considered dangerous activists bent upon destroying the Union. He was an ardent nationalist who hoped to promote the public well-being by harmonizing the conflict evident among various sections of the nation.

Pierce carried a majority of northern and southern states and received the largest plurality of votes ever counted up to that time. He garnered 1,607,510 popular votes, or 50.8 percent; Scott won 1,386,942 or 43.9 percent of the popular vote. The Free Soil candidate John P. Hale (1806-1873) of New Hampshire polled only about 5 percent of the votes with a platform that condemned the Compromise of 1850 and the institution of slavery. Despite Pierce's large plurality, his majority was slender—just 51,896, or 1.6 percent of the votes. Although his victory may have been a sign that the public endorsed the compromise, some historians believe the voters saw little real choice between Scott and Pierce. Few were willing to change their party allegiance unless presented with sharp, clear issues. Beginning with Jackson's election in 1824, the country had gone Democratic four out of six campaigns; this habit continued with Pierce.

Nevertheless, the election of 1852 had an important impact on the political party system. Both major parties recognized that the Catholic vote was becoming important, and their candidates attempted to demonstrate they were not hostile to that religion or that their opponent was. Scott even tried to revive his sagging fortunes by personal appeals to Irish and German immigrants, many of them suspicious of his military-nativist background. In addition, defeat at the polls indicated the further disintegration of the Whigs into "cotton" (proslavery) and "conscience" (antislavery) factions. The Whigs were never again a national party after 1852. The Free Soil party also showed weakness. The Democrats appeared to be the only political organization in which both Northerners and Southerners still were trying to accommodate sectional differences.

The Kansas-Nebraska Controversy

When Pierce entered the White House in March 1853, most Americans felt that the slavery question was settled—if not forever, then at least for a long time to come. Almost two-thirds of both the House and the Senate were Democrats. The country was prosperous and seemingly peaceful. Yet during the first years of the Pierce Administration the question of slavery in the territories arose again.

Until 1854, only the territories of Utah and New Mexico were open to slavery on the basis of local self-determination. In that year, however, Senator Stephen A. Douglas of Illinois (called "The Little Giant") proposed the territorial organization of the land west of Missouri and Iowa. Douglas was a prominent leader of the movement within the Democratic party called "Young America." The Young Americans believed that the United States must intervene directly in European politics and aid revolutionaries there who were eager to establish republican forms of government. Young Americans,

Courtesy, New York Historical Society, New York City.

George Fitzhugh
(1806–1881)

A native Virginian, Fitzhugh was educated as a lawyer and served in the office of the Attorney General under President Buchanan. About 1856 he made a trip to the North, where he lectured in Boston in defense of slavery.

Fitzhugh, greatly distressed by the poverty and misery of the industrial poor in the North, concluded that the socialists were right in believing that capitalism led to the exploitation of workers. But Fitzhugh did not think that a socialist revolution was the solution to America's problem. Rather, he proposed that the entire country should embrace the paternalistic relationship between master and slave that supposedly existed on southern plantations. This idea Fitzhugh expressed in his two best-known works, *Sociology for the South; or, the Failure of Free Society* (1854) and *Cannibals All! or, Slaves without Masters* (1857). Only if a person actually *owned* workers, Fitzhugh argued, would their health and morale be guarded. Until the eve of the Civil War, Fitzhugh still was hoping to introduce slavery into the North as a more beneficient system than free labor. Somewhat more realistically, Fitzhugh was also an early advocate of the industrialization of the South, though he hoped it would be accomplished, of course, with slave labor which could be made readily available by reopening the African slave trade. ■

buoyed up by the recent victory in the war with Mexico, also favored a bold expansionist program. As one leader put it, "Great, powerful and rich as are the United States, they must become greater, more powerful, more rich."

Douglas was a firm advocate of continental expansionism. The Little Giant viewed slavery as a "curse beyond computation" but he refused to acknowledge that a moral issue was at stake. He seemed to see slavery as a local issue and tried to relegate the question to the sidelines as he dealt with territorial government and problems presented by national growth. Whatever his reasoning, Douglas did not want the question of slavery to interfere with the rapid settlement and exploitation of the continent. He focused on two specific goals: first, removal of the Indian barrier to expansion and settlement west of Missouri and Iowa, that is, in Kansas and Nebraska; second, the building of a railroad to the Pacific. Like many advocates of the Young America movement,

Library of Congress.

Stephen A. Douglas, the Little Giant from Illinois who advocated the doctrine of popular sovereignty.

Douglas wanted to make the United States a two-ocean country, welded together by a transportation network into a single nation.

In order to accomplish these goals, Senator Douglas, who was Chairman of the Committee on Territories which had jurisdiction over such matters, was ready to make concessions to Southerners. The most important of these was repeal of the Missouri Compromise of 1820, which had prohibited slavery north of the 36°30′ parallel in all lands acquired by the Louisiana Purchase. Douglas, who supported rapid settlement of Kansas and Nebraska, which lay north of this line, proposed that the people of those regions be allowed to determine the slavery question for themselves according to the principle of "popular sovereignty," which already had been instituted in New Mexico and Utah by the Compromise of 1850. Unfortunately, Douglas's Kansas-Nebraska Bill only further endangered the already uneasy truce achieved by the Compromise of 1850.

From many northern members of Congress, Douglas faced very strong opposition to his proposals. Senator Charles Sumner of Massachusetts denounced the Kansas-Nebraska Bill and warned his constituents that "the Nebraska bill opens anew the whole slavery question." Sumner joined other antislavery Democrats in publishing "An Appeal" against Douglas's bill. This document declared that the new bill was "a gross violation of a sacred pledge" made in 1820. That pledge was the Missouri Compromise. The "Appeal" charged that Douglas had joined hands with southern slaveholders to violate the Compromise of 1820. Douglas himself, Sumner claimed, was "that human anomaly—a Northern man with Southern principles."

Despite such opposition, Douglas fought very hard for the passage of the bill. He was a combative man, and Sumner had aroused his fighting spirit. If the bill were enacted, it would win Douglas southern votes should he run in the 1856 presidential election. Popular sovereignty, Douglas believed, was necessary to break up the Indian barrier in the West and provide a pathway to the Pacific Coast for white settlers. Finally, he had a personal motive: he was associated with real estate and railroad interests and had speculated in land along the projected central and northern routes to the West. If Kansas and Nebraska were not immediately open to settlers upon the principle of "popular sovereignty," Douglas feared that Secretary of War Jefferson Davis (an apologist for slavery) might decide to run the transcontinental railway line through Texas and New Mexico. Davis actually supported the Gadsden Purchase in 1853 with this end in mind, that is, acquiring land from Mexico to permit a southern route.

The debates over the Kansas-Nebraska Bill were long and heated in both houses of Congress. Missouri Senator Thomas Hart Benton, who referred to himself as "the most extreme Southern Senator upon this floor," for example, urged his southern colleagues to repudiate the measure. *"Maintain the Missouri Compromise!* Stir not up agitation! Give us peace!" Finally, after a remarkable session lasting seventeen consecutive hours, the Senate, with the strong support of southern Democrats, passed the bill by a vote of 37 to 14 at 4:55 in the morning.

Douglas's allies fired cannons in Washington to rejoice, but one antislavery senator said to Sumner, "They celebrate a present victory, but the echoes they awake will never rest till slavery itself shall die." Later, with almost the unanimous support of southern Democrats, the House passed the Kansas-Nebraska Bill, voting 113 to 100. On May 30 President Pierce signed the bill into law.

The immediate result of the passage of the bill was the fragmentation of both political parties. Northern Democrats in the House had split over the issue, 44 in favor and 42 opposed to it. Opponents of the new law burned Douglas in effigy in every free state. The Whigs also were divided by the measure. Northern "conscience" Whigs fought the bill as had some southern Whigs. Most southern "cotton" Whigs joined the overwhelming majority of southern Democrats who supported it—a step that led to the absorption of most southern Whigs into the Democratic party. In short, the Whigs had split irrevocably over the bill and the Democratic party was badly divided as well; the Kansas-Nebraska Bill had clearly weakened both national parties.

Northern "conscience" Whigs drifted into other parties, some into the nativist Know-Nothing or American party, whose hostility to foreigners seemed to offer a national cause transcending sectional rivalries. An outgrowth of a secret patriotic society formed in New York in 1849, the Know-Nothings experienced phenomenal success for a few years as a result of the Kansas-Nebraska turmoil. Their name came from the universal answer to any question concerning the secrecy involved: "I know nothing." Many voters found temporary refuge with this group; however, the slavery issue quickly did to the Know-Nothings what it had done to the Whigs.

Some Whigs joined the anti-Kansas-Nebraska

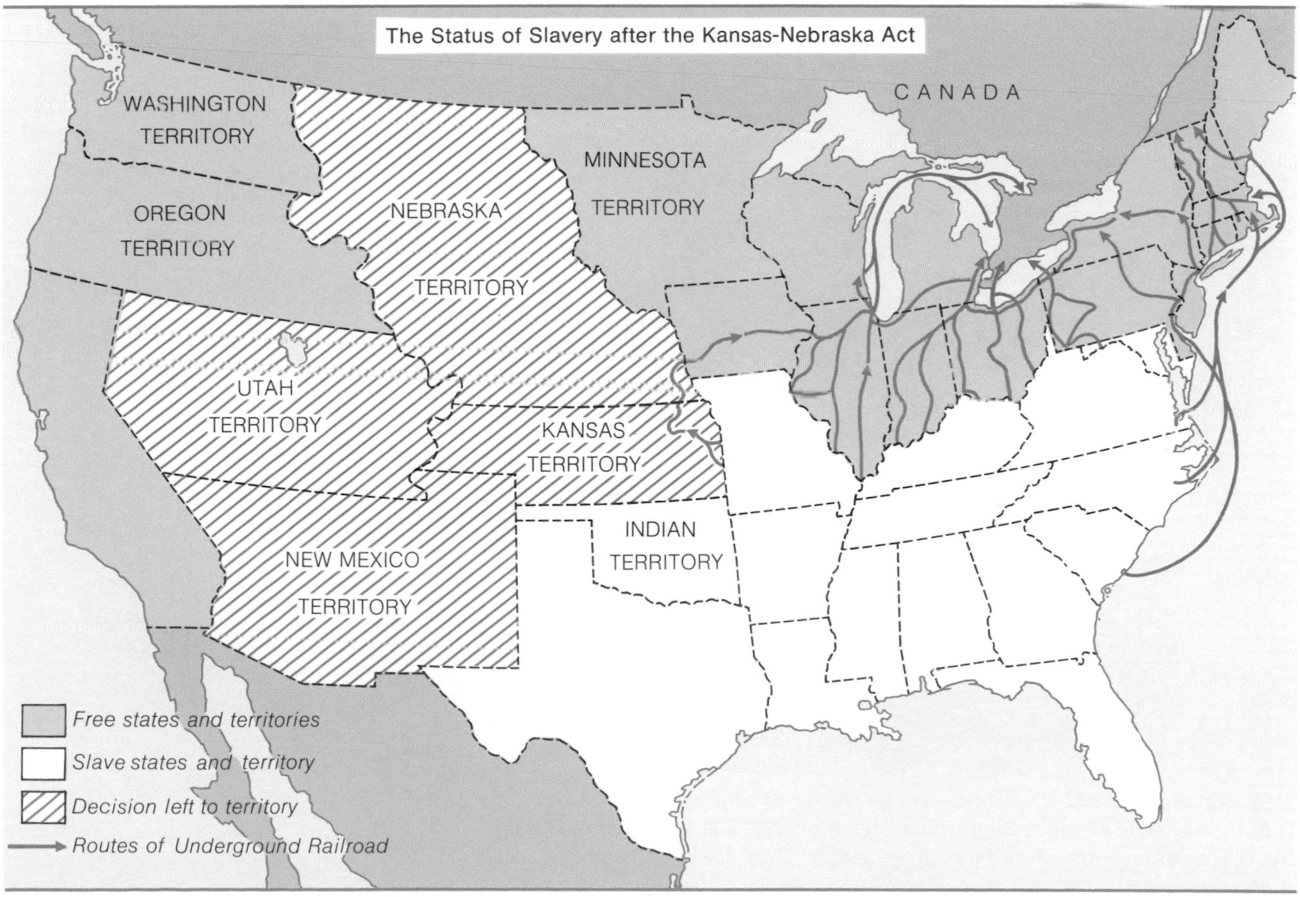

Democrats and former Free Soilers in creating a new political organization known as the Republican party. The Republicans included many diverse elements—abolitionists and other moral reformers, antislavery proponents, Negrophobes who disliked blacks as well as slavery, and zealous Protestant evangelicals, among others. All of these elements shared a common antipathy to the spread of slavery in the western territories. The Republican party grew with startling speed because millions of Americans in the North regarded the Kansas-Nebraska Act as the opening battle in a last-ditch struggle between the southern and northern ways of life. Some citizens viewed slavery as an immoral institution while others only concerned themselves with the prospect that it might become a national institution and force white workers to compete with slaves for jobs. As early as the Mexican War, a northern publicist had warned: "Chaps that make black slaves o' niggers—Want to make white slaves o' you." Regardless of their particular orientation, the diverse elements comprising the new Republican party all agreed that slavery was a menace that had to be contained.

The Ostend Manifesto

While this new political realignment was forming, sectional suspicions were growing as a result of the efforts of proslavery American ministers in Britain, France, and Spain to annex Cuba. Southerners were worried that Spain, which owned Cuba, was planning to free the slaves there and turn it into a black republic much like Haiti. The Ostend Manifesto—actually a secret dispatch issued by James Buchanan, American minister to Britain, John

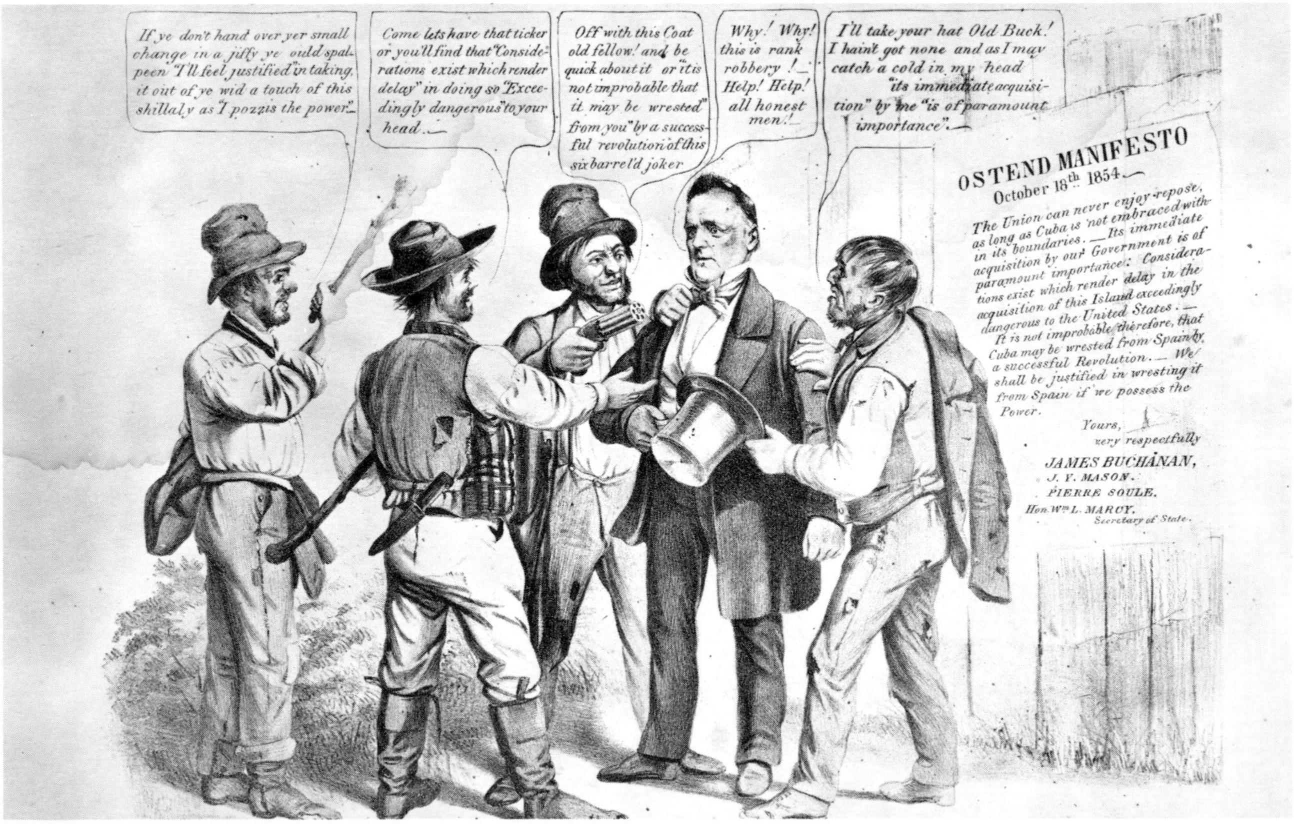

This cartoon ridicules the jingoism of the Ostend Manifesto. James Buchanan, one of the cosigners of the Manifesto, is being assaulted by "Practical Democrats" who are "carrying out the principle" he had enunciated.

Mason, minister to France, and Pierre Soulé, minister to Spain, and sent to Secretary of State William Marcy in October 1854—offered two recommendations. The United States should make an earnest attempt to buy Cuba from Spain, but, if unsuccessful, the American government should seize the island by force. If the continued presence of Spain in Cuba should endanger American liberties, the manifesto read, "then by every law human and divine, we shall be justified in wresting it from Spain, if we possess the power. . . ." When news of this communication leaked to the press, northern politicians found additional grounds for denouncing southern schemes. And the new Republican party found its membership growing.

Bleeding Kansas

In Kansas, a race was on between free soilers and proslavery Southerners to determine whether the territory would enter the Union as a free or slave state. Nebraska faced no such problem. It lay west of a free state and would be settled by an antislavery population, but proslavery Missourians saw Kansas as a natural area for slave expansion, some Missourians even insisting that the security of their state depended upon proslavery government in Kansas. While the New England Emigrant Aid Society and other organizations financed free soil settlers to the region, Missourians poured into Kansas and packed the Kansas territorial legislature with proslavery representatives. Of course, the proslavery men, since they lived close by, had an easier time of it than antislavery advocates migrating from afar. The free soil voters, however, refused to recognize the proslavery government. They drew up their own constitution that prohibited slavery as well as the entrance of blacks into Kansas, and in January 1856 elected a governor and a legislature. Virtual civil war erupted between supporters of the two rival governments as troublemakers on both sides staged frequent raids on each other. Brooklyn clergyman Henry Ward Beecher (1813–1887) gave his blessings to shipments of rifles to free soilers in Kansas; the weapons came to be known as "Beecher's Bibles." Missourians and free soilers came to the aid of their beleaguered brethren, and both sides added fuel to the guerilla war that was ravaging Kansas.

On May 19, 1856, Charles Sumner rose to speak about what he called "The Crime Against Kansas." In a three-hour diatribe he denounced the "murderous robbers" of Missouri seeking to turn Kansas into a slave state. During the course of his loftily worded speech (which included quotations from Cicero, Livy, Vergil, Dante, and Milton), Sumner lowered his tone to aim some choice insults at Senator Andrew P. Butler of South Carolina, whom he called the Don Quixote of Slavery, a man who had "chosen a mistress to whom he has made his vows and who, though ugly to others, is always lovely to him; though polluted in the sight of the world, is chaste in his sight . . . the harlot, Slavery." Several days later in retaliation for this affront to the absent Butler, South Carolina Congressman Preston Brooks, Butler's nephew, attacked Sumner at his desk and struck him repeatedly over the head with a cane. The assault on Sumner by "Bully Brooks," in conjunction with the news

Kansas State Historical Society, Topeka.

Kansas free soilers and proslavery advocates became engaged in a bloody civil war.

SOUTHERN CHIVALRY — ARGUMENT VERSUS CLUB'S.
KANSAS

This 1856 lithograph portrays the attack on Charles Sumner by Preston Brooks and ridicules "Southern Chivalry."

of more and more raids and skirmishes in Kansas, increased sectional tension and influenced the 1856 presidential campaign.

The Election of 1856

The political unrest surrounding the Kansas-Nebraska Act surfaced again during the presidential election of 1856. The Democrats passed over Douglas since his Kansas-Nebraska Act was so unpopular in the North. Instead they chose the shrewd and conservative Pennsylvanian James Buchanan, a sixty-five-year-old bachelor who had served as U.S. minister to Britain during the controversy over the Kansas-Nebraska Act and thus escaped association with that issue. Despite his coolness and impartiality, gained during some forty years in public life, Buchanan was known as a "Doughface"—a Northerner with southern principles. By taking the southern side during the recent Ostend Manifesto affair, Buchanan made gains among slaveowners but repelled many Northerners. Buchanan was a strict constructionist of the Constitution who believed that the slavery question could best be solved by the judiciary.

The Nativist American or Know-Nothing party chose ex-President Millard Fillmore who, like Buchanan, saw compromise as the only way the nation could survive sectional tensions. The Republicans, reflecting the Whig inclination for military heroes, selected the glamorous soldier-explorer, John C. Frémont, as their standard-bearer. In 1846 and 1847 Frémont had fought the Mexican army in California and served briefly as civil governor of the region. He knew little about politics, having spent only a year as a United States Senator, but came out vigorously in favor of a free soil Kansas and against the enforcement of the Fugitive Slave Law.

Buchanan won the election, but Frémont and the Republican party showed extraordinary strength in many former Democratic strongholds in the North. Buchanan, with 45.3 percent of the ballots and 174 electoral votes, swept the South but carried only five of the free states. Frémont, with 33.1 percent and 114 electoral votes, took the rest of the free states. Ominous for the future of the Democratic party was the fact that the Republican vote in the free states exceeded that of the Democrats by well over 100,000. Millard Fillmore and the Know-Nothings ran a poor third, garnering 21.5 percent and carrying only the state of Maryland.

The Dred Scott Decision and Its Effects

Two days after Buchanan's inauguration on March 4, 1857, the Supreme Court rendered a decision in the case of *Dred Scott* v. *Sanford.* Buchanan knew in advance of the Court's decision because two justices—Robert C. Grier and John Catron—had violated judicial ethics and advised him of the Court's intention. Buchanan commented during his inaugural address that the "happy conception" of popular sovereignty regarding the status of slavery in the territories had created some problems but these were of "little practical importance" since the

This cartoon presents Republican John C. Fremont as the candidate of "Popery, Fourierism, Free Love, Women's rights, the Maine Law, and Equality of our Colored bretheren."

whole matter was a "judicial question" that would soon be "speedily and finally settled." Unfortunately for Buchanan and the Court, many Americans drew the easy conclusion that the two were working in collusion.

Dred Scott had been a slave who belonged to Dr. John Emerson of Missouri. In 1834 Emerson took Scott with him to the free state of Illinois and in 1836 to the upper Louisiana Purchase territory, which, under the Missouri Compromise of 1820, was also free. Two years later, in 1838, Emerson returned Dred to Missouri. After Emerson died, Scott and his family were inherited by Emerson's widow. Asserting that his earlier residence in a free state and a free territory made him free, Scott then sued in the courts of Missouri. The lower court decided in his favor, the Missouri Supreme Court decided against him—and after several years the case finally reached the Supreme Court.

After the Supreme Court heard arguments on the case in February 1856, seven of the justices concluded that the Court had no jurisdiction, a ruling that would have sustained the Missouri Supreme Court. However, two antislavery justices, John McLean and Benjamin Curtis, declared that they intended to dissent and defend Dred Scott's freedom. Since this involved discussion of the status of slavery in the territories, each of the judges in the majority decided to write an opinion. Therefore, when the ruling against Dred Scott was issued on March 6, 1857, there were seven different majority opinions, no two of them stressing the same arguments and statutes.

Since the majority opinion was so divided, Chief Justice Roger B. Taney's opinion received the greatest attention. According to Taney, Dred Scott was not an American citizen since the Constitution recognized a "perpetual and impassible barrier" between blacks and whites and denied citizenship to blacks. Dred Scott was a black and also possibly still a slave; he had no right, on either score, to sue in the courts of the nation. But Taney did not stop with the fate of Dred Scott. He proceeded to deliver an opinion concerning the whole gnarled question of slavery in the territories. Citing the Fifth Amendment, which prohibits the government from depriving persons of life, liberty, or property without due process of law, Taney condemned the Missouri Compromise of 1820 as unconstitutional. The Compromise, he said, had attempted to deprive Southerners in the Louisiana Purchase territory north of 36°30′ of their slaves—that is, their property—and it therefore was invalid.

The Dred Scott decision not only damaged the prestige of the Supreme Court at a critical period when the judiciary might have pointed the way towards a solution of sectionalism; it also had other serious political consequences. The decision wrecked the machinery of political compromise. The Republican party's opposition to slavery in the territories thus suffered a serious blow. As a result, the new party denounced Taney's ruling. The fate of the Democrats, the only national party remaining, depended on its various factions accepting popular sovereignty and compromise. Yet, if the Constitution and the Supreme Court prohibited Congress and territorial legislatures from excluding slavery, how could the settlers themselves ever do so? Even if the northern Democrats accepted "popular sovereignty," would southern Democrats be willing to substitute the uncertainty of popular elections for the certainty of the Dred Scott decision? When they refused to do so in 1860, the Democratic party split and hope for compromise dwindled.

Showdown in Kansas

The question of the status of slavery in the territories came to a showdown in Kansas where there were two territorial governments, each vying for authority. One, located in Lecompton, was proslavery and passed strong laws protecting the peculiar institution in the territory—though the status of slavery in Kansas once it became a state could be settled only after a state constitution had been drawn up and approved by residents. The other legislature was in Lawrence, and it was just as vigorously free soil in its sentiments as Lecompton was proslavery. President Buchanan officially recognized the Lecompton legislature, but the Lawrence government maintained its own militia—and eventually commanded the allegiance of the majority of settlers.

In March 1857 President Buchanan appointed a new territorial governor of Kansas, Robert Walker, who called for the election of delegates to a new constitutional convention. But the free soilers, who deliberately abstained from voting, claimed with considerable accuracy that the election was rigged. The constitution drafted by the proslavery delegates contained a clause that protected slavery. The constitution as a whole was not submitted to a popular vote. Kansas voters were only given the option of ruling on the future introduction of slaves to Kansas. In an election marked by fraud and the abstention of free soilers, the proslavery forces easily triumphed.

Under pressure from southern leaders, President Buchanan recommended that Congress accept Kansas as a slave state governed by the Lecompton Constitution. Buchanan owed his election to the South, and his cabinet was full of powerful southern politicians.

By recognizing the proslavery constitution, the President betrayed the principle of "popular sovereignty," the brainchild of Senator Douglas. As a result of Buchanan's actions, the Democratic party split sharply into northern and southern factions, and Kansas was not admitted until 1861. By this time, Buchanan was preparing to leave office and a number of southern states had seceded. Kansas entered the Union as a free state in 1861, following the admission of Minnesota in 1857 and Oregon in 1859.

The Dred Scott decision and Buchanan's recommendation of the Lecompton Constitution destroyed the principle of "popular sovereignty." Consequently, more and more Northerners, disillusioned with the President, the Supreme Court, and the Democratic party, turned to the Republicans.

Growth of the Republican Party

The Compromise of 1850, the Kansas-Nebraska Act, and the Dred Scott decision, as well as numerous other political facts of life—the demise of the Whigs, the failure of the Know-Nothings, the conflict in Kansas, and the apparent impossibility of compromise on the expansion of slavery—aided greatly the youngest of political parties, the Republicans. Their ideology, very appealing to an emerging middle class and those who were or sought to become part of it, was centered on the concept of free as opposed to slave labor. They came to believe that the expanding, competitive society was nothing less than the direct result of free labor, and social, upward mobility was an integral part of that society. This doctrine, of course, ran counter to everything held sacred in much of the South.

The nation's problems were only exacerbated by the Panic of 1857, a depression that lasted until 1859. The industrial areas of the Northeast and the agricultural Midwest were hardest hit. Unemployment was greater than at any previous time in American history. Only in the South were the effects of the depression negligible. Southerners saw their own continued prosperity, which was based on the steady and lucrative cotton export trade, as confirmation the cotton and slave economy was preferable to the free northern industrial and agricultural economy.

The Panic of 1857 also had important political consequences. The Republicans took up the cry of impoverished Northerners for free homesteads of 160 acres in the West. To court the votes of eastern business interests, the Republicans called for a higher protective tariff, thus appealing to businessmen who were convinced that the low tariff had brought on the depression. By taking up these two causes, the Republicans hoped to attract farmers, industrial workers, and businessmen in the North who might be indifferent to the whole question of slavery. The Republican party was seeking to broaden its base in order to gain the allegiance of a vast number of voters.

The Lincoln-Douglas Debates

In the midst of the terrible depression that had begun in 1857, the Republicans in Illinois convened in Springfield in June 1858 to nominate Abraham Lincoln as their candidate for the seat in the United States Senate held by Stephen A. Douglas. An admirer of Henry Clay and a former Whig who had served in the Illinois legislature (1834–1842) and the United States House of Representatives (1847–1849), Lincoln was an outstanding lawyer and an energetic campaigner. Though not an abolitionist, Lincoln regarded slavery as an evil that should not spread. He joined the Republicans only after it became clear that their party was not merely a collection of abolitionists. Although he was an ambitious man, membership in the Republican party was not a cynical move. Lincoln considered the containment of slavery a paramount issue and the Republican party as the proper vehicle for addressing the problem. As he once remarked:

Chicago Historical Society.

Abraham Lincoln, advocate of the containment of slavery and political adversary of Stephen A. Douglas.

“The sentiment that contemplates the institution of slavery in this country as a wrong is the sentiment of the Republican party . . . They look upon it as being a moral, social, and political wrong; and while they contemplate it as such, they nevertheless have due regard for . . . the difficulties of getting rid of it in any satisfactory way and to all the constitutional obligations thrown about it. Yet . . .

they insist that it should, as far as may be, be *treated* as a wrong; and one of the methods of treating it as a wrong is to *make provisions that it shall grow no larger.*"

Between August 21 and October 15, 1858, Lincoln and the incumbent he was challenging, Senator Douglas, met in various locations in Illinois for seven joint debates. The major topic at issue was the status of slavery in the territories.

Douglas still defended the principle of popular sovereignty, but the Dred Scott decision and Buchanan's acceptance of the Lecompton Constitution seriously undermined that solution to the slavery problem. Lincoln, by contrast, was determined to contain slavery, although he pledged to support the Fugitive Slave Law and to oppose northern interference with slavery where it already existed in the South. He favored gradual, compensated emancipation as the best way to end slavery.

Douglas, eager to denigrate his rival, accused Lincoln of thinking "that the negro was made his equal, and hence is his brother, but for my own part, I do not regard the negro as my equal, and positively deny that he is my brother or any kin to me whatever." Lincoln hastened to contradict this assertion. He announced that he was opposed to citizenship and suffrage for blacks and did not approve of racial intermingling. As he put it, "I have no purpose to introduce political and social equality between the white and black races. There is a physical difference between the two, which . . . will probably forever forbid their living together on the footing of perfect equality." Lincoln shared and accepted prevailing northern racist attitudes. He desired freedom for blacks but not social and political equality. Nevertheless, Lincoln believed that blacks were entitled to "all the rights enumerated in the Declaration of Independence," and that position was in itself remarkably progressive in his time.

Before Lincoln encountered Douglas in the debates, he had made a speech accepting the Republican nomination that inflamed Southerners. Lincoln argued:

"A house divided against itself cannot stand. I believe this government cannot endure, permanently half *slave* and half *free.*

I do not expect the Union to be *dissolved*—I do not expect the house to *fall*—but I *do* expect it will cease to be divided.

It will become *all* one thing, or *all* the other.

Either the *opponents* of slavery will arrest the further spread of it, and place it where the public mind shall rest in the belief that it is in course of ultimate extinction; or its *advocates* will push it forward, till it shall become alike lawful in *all* states, *old* as well as *new*—North as well as South.

Have we no *tendency* to the latter condition?"

In this last ominous-sounding question, Lincoln was pointing out that the Kansas-Nebraska Act and the Dred Scott decision indicated a tendency toward the expansion of slavery. Popular sovereignty, Lincoln reasoned, was a step towards the "Africanization" of the United States—that is, Douglas's popular sovereignty was really a proslavery doctrine.

In the seven debates with Douglas, Lincoln maintained that slavery was the principal threat to the Union and that the Kansas-Nebraska Act had only intensified sectional conflict. There could be no middle ground on slavery, he said, the alleged neutralism of Douglas's popular sovereignty was designed to dull the northern conscience and clear the way for legalized slavery throughout the nation. The American people needed to recognize slavery as an evil and, within the limits of the Constitution, to treat it as an evil. Above all else, slavery had to be contained and marked for eventual extinction.

Lincoln urged the exclusion of slavery from all territories despite the Dred Scott decision and warned that popular sovereignty, if allowed to go unchecked, would eventually lead to the reopening of the African slave trade. As Lincoln put it, "For years he [Douglas] has labored to prove it a *sacred right* of white men to take negro slaves into the new territories. Can he possibly show that it is *less* a sacred right to *buy* them where they can be bought cheapest? And, unquestionably they can be bought *cheaper in Africa* than in *Virginia.*" Although Douglas had specifically condemned the clamor of southern extremists for a renewed African slave trade, Lincoln argued that, given the senator's popular sovereignty position, such a condemnation was logically inconsistent. And Lincoln's equation of popular sovereignty and the Africanization of America gained credence when reports reached Illinois that Douglas had the support of Pierre Soulé, a Louisiana advocate of the reopened slave trade. Reports of illegal cargoes of Africans arriving in southern ports also aroused northern fears.

Douglas not only denied his alleged approval of the African slave trade, he also reaffirmed his belief that popular sovereignty was the only democratic means for putting the slavery question to rest. "I don't care if slavery is voted up or down," Douglas said. "What could be more democratic than allowing the people of a region to decide the issue for themselves?"

At Freeport, in northern Illinois, Lincoln forced Douglas to admit that the Dred Scott decision had badly eroded the popular sovereignty argument. If a territory could exclude slavery only when it voted to become a state, might that not be too late to take effective action against the institution? Was there any lawful way for residents to exclude slavery from a territory *before* it became a state? Douglas responded with what has come to be known as his "Freeport Doctrine." As Douglas put it

> "It matters not what way the Supreme Court may hereafter decide as to the abstract question whether slavery may or may not go into a territory under the constitution, the people have the lawful means to introduce it or exclude it as they please, for the reason that slavery cannot exist a day or an hour anywhere unless it is supported by local police regulations. These police regulations can only be established by the local legislature, and if the people are opposed to slavery they will elect representatives to that body who will by unfriendly legislation effectually prevent the introduction of it into their midst."

Lincoln challenged the Freeport Doctrine as a "bare absurdity" that maintained "a thing may be lawfully driven from a place where it has a lawful right to stay," but in 1858 it served to win Douglas reelection in Illinois. Yet Douglas's Freeport Doctrine angered southern voters who already were disturbed by his stand against the admission of Kansas into the Union under the proslavery Lecompton Constitution. (Douglas took the view that the constitution had to be submitted to the voters to become legal.) Traditionally, historians have asserted that although the Freeport Doctrine won Douglas reelection to the Senate in 1858, it lost him the presidency in 1860. But the treatment accorded Douglas in the southern press during the early months of 1858 provides adequate proof that Douglas had already sacrificed much of his southern support long before he began to debate with Lincoln.

In the debates Lincoln held his own against Douglas, one of the most formidable figures in American politics. And he received remarkable publicity. The Chicago *Times* and the Chicago *Press and Tribune* printed all seven debates—an innovation in American political coverage. The campaign of 1858 marked Douglas's last triumph and Lincoln's emergence as a national figure in the Republican party.

Emotionalism at High Tide

Republican gains in the 1858 elections alarmed even moderate Southerners, and their uneasiness was only intensified when Republican Senator William H. Seward predicted that the nation was headed toward an "irrepressible conflict" between freedom and slavery. Although Lincoln was careful to word his "House-Divided" speech in such a way that it urged the containment—not the abolition—of slavery, some Southerners quoted it out of context to imply that Lincoln actually was an abolitionist.

As mutual animosity increased, Southerners sometimes seemed to equate their entire way of life with the cause of slavery. Jefferson Davis of Mississippi and others demanded a federal slave code protecting the institution in the territories. Davis also asserted that attacks on slavery violated the Constitution. Even more obnoxious to Southerners were the personal liberty laws that many northern states passed in order to make the recapture of fugitives more difficult; in 1859 the Supreme Court decided that such laws were unconstitutional.

Southerners became still more apprehensive when they learned that on July 5, 1859, the Kansas constitutional convention had replaced the proslavery Lecompton Constitution with a new document that prohibited slavery; this free soil constitution was ratified by the people of Kansas on October 4. Thoroughly alarmed by the drift of events, the South was already beginning to take desperate measures. In May 1858, the Southern Commercial Convention meeting in Montgomery considered the possibility of reopening the African slave trade. This movement was backed by Leonidas W. Spratt of Charleston, South Carolina, and New Orleans editor J. D. B. DeBow. Yet not all Southerners approved. The editor of the Richmond *South,* for example, warned that "neither history nor posterity" would applaud revival of that commerce. But prominent Southerners, especially in South Carolina, Louisiana, and Mississippi, were eager to reopen the trade, partly because the cultivation of new plantation lands near the mouth of the Mississippi River had caused a shortage of slaves and hence rising prices. But more importantly, the reopening of the slave trade had become a true test of southern resolve. In May 1859, delegates at the Southern Commercial Convention in Vicksburg adopted resolutions in favor of reopening the African slave trade and offering prizes for the best sermons supporting that traffic. Emotionalism was at high tide.

Harper's Ferry, Virginia

On October 16, 1859, abolitionist John Brown (1800–1859) and a group of eighteen devoted followers, both white and black, attacked the federal arsenal at Harper's Ferry with the hope of instigating a slave revolt. The entire nation was electrified by the news. President Buchanan immediately instructed Colonel Robert E. Lee (1807–1870) to lead a group of marines and defeat the insurgents. The battle lasted two days and no slaves came to Brown's aid. Two of Brown's sons died during the night, eight other members of his band were either killed or mortally wounded, and seven taken prisoner. Brown refused to surrender but was finally seized by force.

Brown has been variously described as a fanatic whose sanity was doubtful and as a saint devoted to a great cause. In actuality, he was a poor farmer who settled in Kansas and was convinced that he had been appointed by Providence to set up a stronghold somewhere in the mountains from which fugitive slaves and their white friends could incite a general rebellion among the blacks in the South. On a visit to New England, Brown got money, supplies, and arms from various abolitionists.

Physical invasion and the attempt to incite a slave insurrection played into the hands of southern disunionists who charged that the "Black Republicans" had supported the raid. Brown's actions, they warned, were only a logical step in developing the program of Republicans. To some Northerners, the raid seemed an unnecessary and misguided act of violence, but to others Brown was a martyr. Within a week after the raid, the Circuit Court of Virginia convicted Brown of treason against the state and of conspiracy to incite a slave rebellion. Throughout the proceedings Brown behaved with dignity and even cheerfulness. On the day he was hanged, he said that "the crimes of this guilty land will never be purged *away:* but with Blood." In the North, Emerson stated that Brown had made the "gallows glorious like the cross."

The Election of 1860

By 1860 the nation was teetering on the brink of disun-

New York Public Library.

John Brown's execution created a martyr for Northern Abolitionists.

ion. In 1857 Hinton Rowan Helper (1829–1909), a disgruntled, middle-class nonslaveholder of North Carolina, had published a book called *The Impending Crisis of the South; How To Meet It.* In 1859 the Republicans printed 100,000 copies of an abridged version of this work to distribute during the presidential campaign of 1860. Helper, while no friend of the black man, nevertheless attacked the slave system as the means by which rich Southerners had impoverished free white labor. The overthrow of the slave system, even by violence if necessary, was the only eventuality Helper could foresee.

On December 5, 1859, three days after John Brown was hanged, a two-month struggle began in the House of Representatives over the election of the Speaker. Republican John Sherman of Ohio, a leading contender for that office, had casually endorsed *The Impending Crisis* without carefully reading it. Southerners, who considered the book a tract advocating slave insurrections, thought that Sherman and other Republicans as well were guilty of condoning, and perhaps even planning, the raid on Harper's Ferry. Many members of Congress attended sessions fully armed, so heated had the political climate become. Southerners eventually blocked Sherman's bid to become Speaker of the House.

The South was now on the defensive. Some leaders urged measures such as the proposal to reopen the African slave trade, which were outrageous and lacked general support, even in the South. But other measures did find support. Alabama, for instance, forbade slaveowners to free their bondsmen under any conditions. Viewed from a wider angle, the South felt cornered by circumstances. Many Southerners feared that the North was growing at a much faster rate than the South and soon a majority of free states would easily outvote the slave states. In border states from Maryland to Missouri slavery was on the decline. Europeans were condemning slavery ever more vociferously.

Secession, a concept bandied about in some circles since the nullification fight of the early 1830s, gradually became more attractive to many Southerners. Whether it was a practical solution or not, talk about secession provided southern whites with an emotional release—a means of getting rid of tension aroused by outside criticisms of southern institutions. At the same time, the South was limiting freedom of expression; for an editor to print criticism of southern policies became extremely dangerous. Free blacks were banished from many areas, manumission was forbidden, and apologists for the South were promulgating the theory that slavery, far from being a necessary evil, was a positive good.

Many Americans in the North and the South believed that Stephen A. Douglas was the only person who, if elected President, could prevent a fatal rupture between the North and the South. But the struggle between Douglas and Buchanan over the admission of Kansas into the Union had badly disrupted the Democratic party. When the Democrats met in Charleston on April 23, 1860, to nominate a candidate for President (Buchanan refused to serve more than one term), Southerners proposed that the party endorse a statement stipulating that no territory could abolish or prohibit the introduction of slavery and that it was the obligation of Congress to protect slavery in the territories. When this proposal was voted down by a small majority of 165 to 138 and when a proposal was sponsored by supporters of Douglas and adopted by the convention to leave the question of the power of territories over slaves to the Supreme Court, the delegates from most of the southern states withdrew. These southern Democrats held their own meeting at Richmond, Virginia, and nominated Vice President John C. Breckenridge of Kentucky; the northern faction of the party, reconvening in Baltimore, nominated Douglas.

The national party that had dominated American politics for over thirty years had split over the issue of the spread of slavery to the territories. Douglas stood on a platform of "popular sovereignty," while Breckenridge maintained that the federal government must protect slavery and ensure its right to expand into the territories.

Bypassing such leading candidates as William H. Seward, who seemed too radical, and a contender from Missouri, Edward Bates (1793–1869), who offended immigrant voters because of his flirtation with nativism, the Republicans picked a moderate, Abraham Lincoln. As a candidate, Lincoln had much to offer. He had taken a strong moral stand against slavery over a number of years and had quietly but firmly built a historical and ethical case against the institution. Now that the country was polarized and the Republican party could hope to appeal only to the northern antislavery and free soil vote, Lincoln's reputation as a foe of slavery stood him in good stead. Since 1856 Lincoln had been building his own power base in the North, and he had the advice and aid of a shrewd political manager, David Davis (1815–1886), a wealthy and flamboyant 300-pound circuit court judge

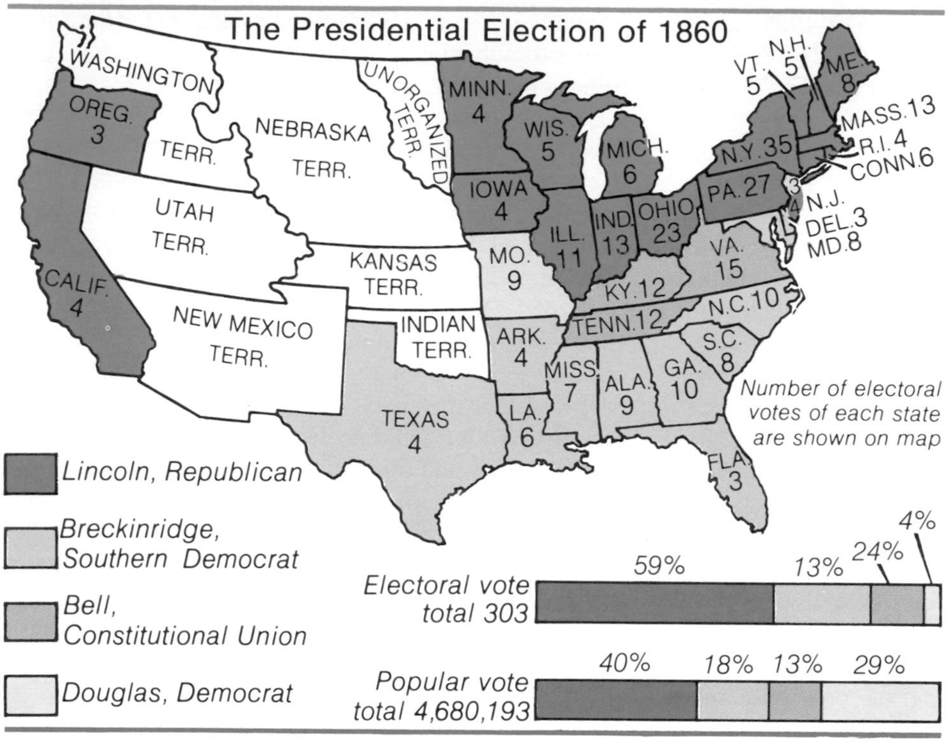

from central Illinois who made a series of deals to ensure his nomination. As Lincoln was named the party's candidate on the third ballot, Judge W. D. Kelley of Pennsylvania echoed the general feeling when he said, "Well, we might have done a more brilliant thing, but we certainly could not have done a better thing."

In the following months Lincoln did little campaigning beyond growing a beard because a young girl informed him that "all the ladies like whiskers." But if the candidate was dignified and inactive, his party was energetically soliciting votes. The Republicans appealed to many different groups by standing for a higher tariff, free homesteads, a transcontinental railroad, and the rights of immigrants. The strongest and most solid arguments, of course, were those against the extension of slavery and revival of the African slave trade.

The campaign of 1860 was complicated even further by the presence of a fourth presidential candidate. The Constitutional Union party, composed of conservative remnants of several defunct parties, especially American party members and old-line Whigs in the border states, chose John Bell of Tennessee as their candidate. Though Bell was a slave owner, he was one of only two Southern Whigs who voted in 1858 against admitting Kansas into the Union as a slave state. The Constitutional Union party condemned sectionalism and recognized "no political principle other than the Constitution." Bell was the choice of moderates who stood simply for the Constitution, the union, and the enforcement of all federal laws.

In the presidential race, then, Douglas stood for local self-determination or "popular sovereignty," Breckenridge upheld slavery and its extension into the territories, Lincoln preached containment of slavery, and Bell stood for "no political principle other than the *Constitution of the Country, the Union of the States, and the Enforcement of the Laws.*"

The question of the status of slavery in the territories was the crucial issue of the campaign, for by 1860 Southerners had come to recognize that the power to

PROGRESSIVE DEMOCRACY_PROSPECT OF A SMASH UP.

New York Public Library, Prints Division.

This Currier and Ives illustration depicts Abraham Lincoln and his running mate ready to take advantage of the divided Democratic party.

decide the status of slavery in the territories was the power to determine the future of slavery itself. Of the four nominees, Douglas was the only one to campaign actively, a practice considered unseemly in those days. Perhaps the best known politician in the country, Douglas understood that the Union was imperiled. He traveled everywhere reaffirming the principle of popular sovereignty and pleading with voters to stand by the Union, even if Lincoln were elected.

When the votes were counted, the worst fears of the South were realized. Despite the fact that Lincoln's three opponents piled up a plurality that surpassed his count by nearly a million votes, he had a clear majority in the electoral college. Lincoln's support, however, was the most sectional of all of the candidates. He won the electoral votes of every free state except three of New Jersey's seven electors, received no votes in the southern states, and won only fourth place in the border states. Breckenridge received more popular votes in the North than Lincoln in the South. His strength, however, was in the lower South; in the border states, he carried only Delaware and Maryland. Bell received the electoral votes of Tennessee, Kentucky, and Virginia. Douglas, whose popular vote fell short of Lincoln's by 485,706 ballots, won only the electoral votes of Missouri and four of the electors in New Jersey. Douglas obviously enjoyed widespread support, and only the four-man race denied him more votes. Indicative of the fact that a majority of voters were moderates, Douglas and Bell between them received 100,000 more votes than Lincoln, and their votes were more evenly distributed around the country than those received by Lincoln or Breckenridge.

Candidate	*Electoral*	*Popular*	*Percentage of Popular Vote*
Lincoln	180	1,865,908	39.8
Douglas	12	1,380,202	29.5
Breckenridge	72	848,019	18.1
Bell	39	590,901	12.6

Southerners were irate because a Republican would be inaugurated as a "minority president" in March 1861. Had they paid closer attention to the election results, however, they might have found some solace. The Republicans would be only the minority party in Congress. But the prospect of a "Black Republican" in the White House enraged Southerners, and many subsequently focused on their state capitals rather than the national capital as centers for political action.

Secession

A South Carolina woman traveling in Florida recorded in her diary for November 8, 1860:

"Yesterday on the train . . . before we reached Fernandina a woman cried out—

That settles the hash."

Tanny touched me on the shoulder.

—"Look out!—Lincoln's elected."

"How do you know?"—

"The man over there has a telegram. . . ."

"Now did you ever!" was the prevailing exclamation, and some one cried out: "Now that the black radical Republicans have the power I suppose they will Brown us all. No doubt of it."

Lincoln's election was seen as the beginning of more assaults like John Brown's. On December 20, 1860, a South Carolina convention announced the state's secession from the Union, saying that "a sectional party" had engineered the "election of a man to the high office of President of the United States whose opinions and purposes are hostile to slavery." For these reasons the "People of South Carolina" announced that their union with "the other states of North America" was "dissolved."

By February 1, 1861, all of the other states of the lower South had followed suit. A week later, at Montgomery, Alabama, a provisional government of the Confederate States of America was established composed of South Carolina, Georgia, Florida, Alabama, Mississippi, and Louisiana. Soon, Texas joined the Confederacy. Meanwhile, Delaware, North Carolina, Maryland, Virginia, Kentucky, Tennessee, Arkansas and Missouri were still clinging to the Union, but strong secession groups in most of these states were campaigning for withdrawal from the Union.

Although southern moderates had kept Breckenridge from sweeping their region in the election, a few months later Southerners had established their own confederacy. The movement was achieved through representatives sent by the electorate to state conventions; only in Texas was the decision to secede submitted directly to the voters. In each convention, except that held in South Carolina, members voiced both objections to and serious reservations about the momentous course upon which they were embarking.

Although there was still strong support for the Union in the South, especially in areas where there were few slaves, numerous influential Southerners were eventually emboldened to secede because they became convinced that the North would not fight. These leaders believed that northern merchants were too interested in making profits through trade to wage war against both their best market and their prime source of cotton—customer-suppliers who owed them $200 million. Nor

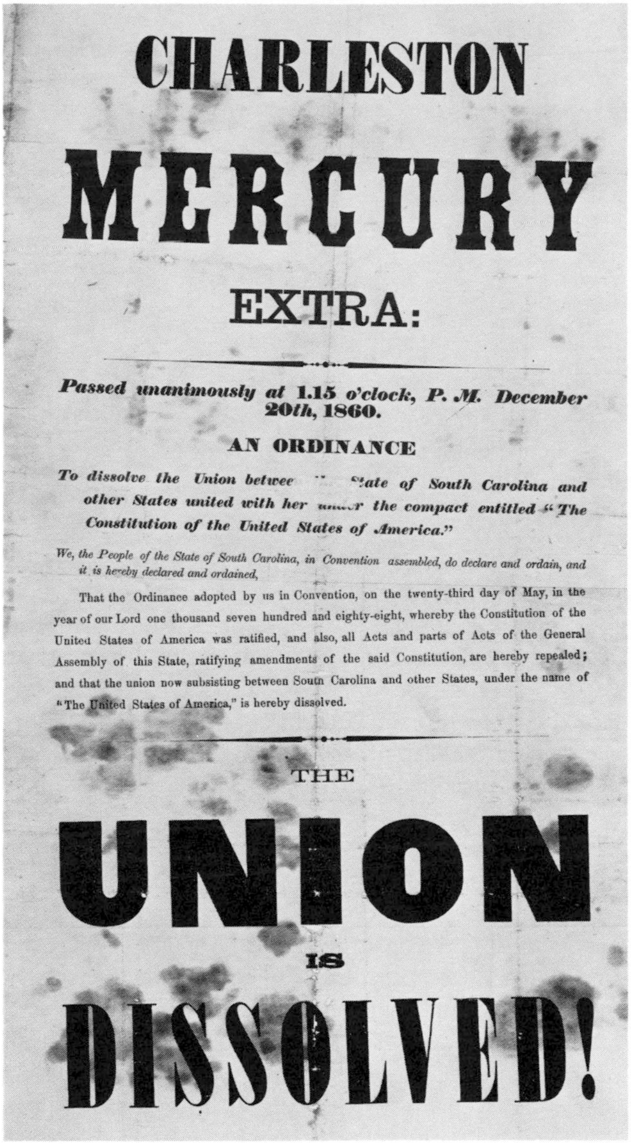

CHARLESTON MERCURY

EXTRA:

Passed unanimously at 1.15 o'clock, P. M. December 20th, 1860.

AN ORDINANCE

To dissolve the Union betwee[illegible] State of South Carolina and other States united with her [illegible] the compact entitled "The Constitution of the United States of America."

We, the People of the State of South Carolina, in Convention assembled, do declare and ordain, and it is hereby declared and ordained,

That the Ordinance adopted by us in Convention, on the twenty-third day of May, in the year of our Lord one thousand seven hundred and eighty-eight, whereby the Constitution of the United States of America was ratified, and also, all Acts and parts of Acts of the General Assembly of this State, ratifying amendments of the said Constitution, are hereby repealed; and that the union now subsisting between Soutn Carolina and other States, under the name of "The United States of America," is hereby dissolved.

THE UNION IS DISSOLVED!

Library of Congress.

The Charleston *Mercury* announces South Carolina's secession from the Union.

Courtesy New-York Historical Society, New York City.

This cartoon depicts the American eagle as it appeared when James Buchanan became president in 1857 and again when Buchanan left office in 1861.

could the North fight, some Southerners reasoned, since factory workers were "white slaves" who were obviously too weak and spiritless to enter combat; in addition, the North lacked tested military leaders whom the South had in abundance. But should war break out, secessionists pointed out, the South would win. Also, in Britain and France, the South had powerful allies who were dependent on southern cotton. And if the South did not act now, some extremists argued, soon it would be too late, for every year the North was becoming stronger, richer, and more populous.

President Buchanan proved totally inept in his handling of the secession crisis. The events in the wake of Lincoln's election would have taxed any lame-duck administration, but for a chief executive as weak as James Buchanan, they were overwhelming. To make matters worse, Lincoln, who promised not to interfere with slavery where it already existed, was regarded in the South as a symbol of the abolitionists, and his "House Divided" speech of 1858 was quoted to prove he was an enemy of slavery. The first Confederate Vice President, Alexander H. Stephens, emphasized the fact that his country had been established as a protector of slavery: "Our new government is founded upon . . . the great truth that the Negro is not equal to the white man; that slavery—subordination to the superior race—is his natural and normal condition." And Stephens was careful to add, "Our new government is the first in the history of the world, based upon this great . . . truth."

What Caused the Civil War?

As the major internal disruption in American history, the Civil War has invited many different interpretations, which often reflect as much about the period in which they were written as about the Civil War. During and immediately after the conflict, some historians explained it as a struggle between the principles of freedom (the North) and of bondage (the South) and others as a struggle between the principles of "localism" (the South) and of uniformity (the North). When the United States was emerging as a world power in the 1890s, historians wrote accounts of the war which stressed the deep-seated, irreconcilable differences such as slavery between sections of the nation. The war, according to their interpretation, made possible America's rise to greatness because it preserved the Union. In the 1920s economic and class determinism began to color historical thinking and Charles and Mary Beard in their *Rise of American Civilization* (1927) construed the war as a struggle for power between two economic sections of the country; in this context "the institution of slavery as a question of ethics was not the fundamental issue." Since the 1920s other interpretations have flourished. Some scholars have argued that the conflict was "irrepressible" while others have doubted that the war was inevitable and point to the "fanatical" abolitionists and the southern "extremists" as major contributing factors to the outbreak of hostilities. In recent years, the whole question of the causation of the Civil War has been lost in general discussions of racism and the subordination of blacks, not only during the Civil War but throughout American history. As historian Oscar Handlin has put it, "There is surely a difference between being a fanatic for freedom and a fanatic for slavery."

All these theories can be reduced to four basic interpretations. Especially fashionable among antislavery writers during and after the war was the *slavery interpretation.* According to this view, the war was a crusade against the South's evil and "peculiar" institution. The South was blind and irrational. The various compromises worked out in 1820, 1850, and 1854 had failed to stop the growth of "The Slave Power." The war was the result of the ideological differences between a free and a slave society. And in the opinion of the writers subscribing to this view, everything that preceded the war must be read in this light—North-South conflicts over states' rights or the tariff, for instance, were only disguised disputes about slavery. Those who adhere to this interpretation today frequently argue that moral judgments are necessary in an evaluation of the past and that slavery clearly was an abominable institution that had to be destroyed.

Critics of the *slavery interpretation* hold that good and evil are never so neatly divided that one side can be considered to be composed of "the good guys" and the other of "the bad guys." And they point out that while many northerners opposed the extension of slavery, only a very few were actually abolitionists or even sympathetic to abolitionism. Lincoln, for example, was not an abolitionist. Moreover, there was little concern for the welfare of blacks among segments of northern society. Nor can the slavery argument explain why a Southern man such as Robert E. Lee went to war; his loyalty to the South was not based on devotion to the institution of slavery.

Secondly, there is the *states' right interpretation,* which holds that the oldest debate in America was between champions of states' rights and nationalists. According to southern apologists, the North was threatening the South, and states' rights and secession were legitimate means of self-defense. This position was expressed by the President of the Confederacy, Jefferson Davis, whose two-volume *Rise and Fall of the Confederate Government,* published in 1881, summarized the major arguments. Davis claimed that secession was a conservative and legal action to preserve the Constitution and laws of the "Old Union" against northern assaults.

Opponents of this view maintain, however, that states' rights was only a derivative issue worked up by Southerners who were really concerned about more pressing matters. States' rights had not led to civil war in 1798, 1814, 1828, or 1850. Why should 1861 be any different? States' rights was not a conservative action to preserve the "Old Union" but a radical action to destroy it.

The third main point of view can be called the *economic interpretation.* This was especially popular in the late 1920s and 1930s. According to this position, the war was a "Second American Revolution" or a struggle of self-conscious economic groups for control of the government resulting in the triumph of capitalists, laborers, and farmers of the North and West over the southern plantation aristocracy. What the North wanted and achieved as a result of the war was a protective tariff, land grants, cheap southern raw materials, southern markets, internal improvements at federal expense and national banks. The South fought the North to protect its property and its profits, both embodied in slavery. This point of view was expressed in Charles and Mary Beard's previously mentioned *Rise of American Civilization.* This work traced the evils associated with the rise of big business to the triumph of northern capitalists in the Civil War.

Criticism of the *economic interpretation* points out that northern crops and manufactures sold in southern markets just as southern crops sold in northern markets. Indeed, big business in the North, far from promoting the conflict, actually worked for compromise in 1860. Nor was the South truly threatened by the North. Lincoln was not an abolitionist, and the Congress would not have been in Republican control if the southern states had stayed in the Union. The Supreme Court as led by Chief Justice Taney had, moreover, acted to protect the property interests of southern planters.

Finally, there is the interpretation that highlights the importance of *emotions.* This approach flourished markedly as the threat of war grew during the Great Depression. According to this interpretation, southern nationalism may have been growing before the war, but the war itself was brought on by extremists in both the South and the North who inflamed sectional prejudices. Abolitionists began to malign the South itself rather than just the institution of slavery. Southern fanatics demanded the reopening of the nefarious African slave trade. All the pride, fear, frustration, and hatred to be found in each section became focused on the North-South division, which led to a breakdown in democratic processes and a release of the same powerful passions that were earlier vented in waves of religious revivalism and in the hysteria of various nativist groups. This *emotional argument* was voiced by Avery O. Craven in *The Repressible Conflict, 1820–1861* (1939) and by James G. Randall in an article, "The Blundering Generation" (1940).

Some of those dissenting from this *emotional interpretation* hold that moral judgment in politics is necessary. According to them, the problem of slavery in a free society had to be solved and the abolitionists were right in calling slavery an evil that had to be eradicated.

If the question "What caused the Civil War?" is so difficult to answer, the difficulty may in part lie with the question. A direct answer assumes that the causes were equal to the events leading to secession. But this is not necessarily the case. Few people, in either the North or the South, expected war; it came about through a series of incidents and miscalculations. A more fruitful question might be, "Why did the southern states secede from the Union?" Secession was a deliberate decision prompted by specific causes and motives. Some of these causes can be quickly summarized. Southern nationalism had matured by 1861. The states' rights arguments, similarly had been worked out by 1860 and many southerners believed that their rights were being abused. Northern abolitionists were aiding slaves to flee the South and preventing their return under the Fugitive Slave Law. In Congress northerners were denouncing southerners as agents of Satan or as proud, unrepentant sinners. Southerners were being denied the right to take slaves into western territories. John Brown's raid only strengthened the southern belief that their property was being jeopardized. Thus, champions of states' rights were willing to join with southern nationalists to plot secession.

Yet another cause of secession was the personal interests of southern leaders. Some owed considerable sums of money to northern creditors; secession might cancel these debts. A southern republic also would provide new opportunities for ambitious politicians. And once the excitement of the moment swept aside all caution and deliberation, many southerners—those trained in the ideals of valor and martial glory and gallantry—could not turn back. Instead, they looked forward to the prospect of chivalrous exploits in battle.

Essay

The Supreme Court and Its Work

Alexis de Tocqueville, that often quoted nineteenth century observer of American life, customs, and mores, noted that "scarcely any political question arises in the United States that is not resolved, sooner or later, into a judicial question." And, he might have added, if that question becomes important enough it ends up before the United States Supreme Court. Various justices, of course, have heard arguments in thousands of cases since 1789. For the most part, the Court is an appellate court, that is, it listens to appeals regarding decisions rendered by lower courts. According to Article III of the Constitution, it has original jurisdiction "in all Cases affecting Ambassadors, other public Ministers and Consuls, and those in which a State shall be a Party."

The regular term of the Supreme Court opens on the first Monday of October and usually lasts about nine months. During the first six months or so, the justices hear arguments for perhaps three days of each week, spending the remainder of their time in conferences concerning matters before them. Once an appeal by someone dissatisfied with a lower court ruling reaches the Supreme Court, the justices can deal with it in several ways. They may decide rather quickly that the case is not worth hearing and merely reaffirm the lower court's action, in effect letting that decision stand. Sometimes they proceed a bit further and, without hearing arguments, issue short, unsigned

Culver Pictures.

A nineteenth century view of the chamber of the Supreme Court.

opinions on an issue they believe needs clarification. If an appeal involves a question that deserves consideration—perhaps circuit justices are ruling differently on an important matter—then lawyers representing those involved in a case will be invited to present oral arguments lasting thirty minutes to an hour. Even at this point the justices may conclude a case contains nothing of much relevance and decline to proceed further. However, if arguments are completed, then the justices weigh the issue involved.

Some weeks or months later, but within the same term, an opinion is announced, usually on a Monday. One of the justices customarily delivers a brief summation for the majority of the Court; and, if a dissenting member feels strongly about the matter, he may speak for the minority. At the same time, rough copies of these opinions, later polished and published, are distributed to some thirty or thirty-five reporters, and the basic elements of the decision are soon communicated through the nation's newspapers and its television and radio networks. Some cases elicit little attention, others deserve and get bold headlines. The *Dred Scott* decision of 1857, delivered two days after President Buchanan took office, was clearly a landmark case which fueled passions that led to war. There have been other cases, less emotionly charged, which have also influenced profoundly national growth and development.

In *Marbury* v. *Madison* (1803), Chief Justice John Marshall used the appeal of a would-be justice of the peace for his commission as an instrument to affirm that the Supreme Court alone had the power to interpret the Constitution and to decide if laws conflicted with that document. In 1824, the Court faced a very different matter in *Gibbons* v. *Ogden,* a case originating from a state-granted monopoly to a steamboat company owned by Colonel Aaron Ogden that served New York harbor and nearby areas. Thomas Gibbons had a small coastal boat in New Jersey that supplied customers to Ogden's line, which in turn took them on to New York. Gibbons decided to challenge the New York monopoly, claiming that he was involved in coastal trade that was actually interstate commerce; hence, the federal government had authority in this realm, not an individual state. A key question was, of course, whether navigation was commerce. The Marshall Court agreed it was, emphasizing that the federal government was already regulating interstate commerce. Within months, fares dropped drastically on steamboat lines along the East Coast as service increased. This decision meant that the federal government would have considerable influence on the development and growth of railroads and other modes of transportation that followed in the wake of the steamboat.

Dred Scott, the slave who sought his freedom through court

Missouri Historical Society.

Dred Scott, the slave who looked in vain to the Supreme Court for his freedom.

U.S. Supreme Court.

Chief Justice Roger B. Taney ruled that blacks were not included under the word "citizen" in the Constitution and were, therefore, ineligible to claim the rights and privileges guaranteed to American citizens.

action as a result of residence in free Illinois and on territorial soil controlled by the U.S. Congress, raised a perilous issue in troubled times. Chief Justice Taney's opinion, one of seven majority opinions issued, was much more than a simple ruling. He concluded that Scott, a slave, could not sue in the courts; and, in addition, being property, the Constitution could not deny his master the right to transport him to territorial land. And, even if Scott had become free while living in Illinois, upon his return to a slave state (Missouri), state law, not national, established his status. Ironically, a few months after Dred Scott's name became known throughout the nation, his new owner granted him his freedom. So Scott got what he wanted despite Taney's provocative ruling.

A half century later a quite different case with implications similar to those flowing from *Gibbons* v. *Ogden* changed the nature of American capitalism. A group of railroad potentates, J. P. Morgan, James J. Hill, and Edward H. Harriman, decided to organize a supermonopoly to control transportation in the northwestern United States. The Northern Securities Company, organized by Morgan, was supposed to end competition among his Northern Pacific, Hill's Great Northern, and Harriman's Burlington. In February 1902, President Theodore Roosevelt let the press know that he and his Attorney General planned to enforce the Sherman Antitrust Act of 1890 and break up the Northern Securities Company.

Since the Sherman Act was previously ignored, Morgan was dazed by this revelation and hurried to the White House where he reportedly told the President:, "If we have done anything wrong, send your man to my man and they can fix it up." As Morgan viewed matters, one corporation (his) was dealing with another of equal status (The United States of America). Roosevelt did not agree. The administration first sought relief in the federal courts of Minnesota, which had state legislation forbidding a railroad to buy control of parallel or competing lines; however, the railroads won, the courts concluding that a stockholding company such as Northern Securities was a legal venture.

But a short time later, Morgan, filled with self-confidence, told a group of New York reporters that his Northern Securities actually was "a community of interests," an admission that it was not merely a stockholding company as claimed. During ensuing months Roosevelt went on the offensive, charging that a too powerful monopoly such as Northern Securities actually destroyed the rights of others, and in 1904 the Supreme Court agreed with him. This decision by no means ended efforts by American businessmen to create monopolies, cartels, and similar groupings designed to restrict competition and to increase profits, but Roosevelt's aggressive policy put new teeth into antitrust legislation, serving notice that the U.S. government would not tolerate blatant restraints of trade that threatened the public interest.

Elsie Parrish, like Dred Scott, was one of the last people one would expect to become the principal in a Supreme Court case. In 1935 Parrish, a chambermaid in a Washington state hotel, received notice that she was being discharged. She had been getting 25 cents an hour when, by state law, her hourly income should have been 35 cents. The management refused to pay $216.92 in back salary, so she and her husband went to an attorney. In time, a local court said the state minimum wage law was unconstitutional, but a state court reversed that ruling.

Unhappy with the latter decision, Mrs. Parrish's former employers appealed to the Supreme Court. Unfortunately for the justices, *West Coast Hotel Co.* v. *Parrish* arrived before them in 1937 at a most inopportune time since they were involved in a bitter confrontation with President Franklin D. Roosevelt. They were striking down much of his hastily contrived New Deal legislation, and the President, in turn, fresh from a sweeping reelection victory, was threatening to enlarge the Court's membership so as to get his own way. This case created a special dilemma for the entire Court: should they uphold the state minimum wage law (similar to much of FDR's social legislation); or should they rule against it and thus take an indirect slap at their adversary's overall program? Elsie Parrish won, and with this decision and others in the same vein, much of the rancor embittering the relations between the White House and the Supreme Court was dissipated.

Undoubtedly the most celebrated decision of recent years was *Brown* v. *Board of Education of Topeka* (1954), overturning previous racial segregation rulings such as *Plessy* v. *Ferguson* (1896), which had sanctioned a dual, segregated society throughout much of the United States. The *Brown* case, really an amalgam of several similar cases, climaxed at least three decades of change as separation on the basis of race alone in schools, transportation, and housing came under fire. It proved very graphically that the court *can* change its mind, a fact that distressed thousands of conservatives as integration in nearly all aspects of everyday life became increasingly common.

The justices, led by Earl Warren who rendered the *Brown* decision, produced yet another ruling that the Chief Justice thought even more important: *Baker* v. *Carr* (1962). This case challenging the failure of state legislatures to reapportion voter representation as dictated by the movement of people from rural to urban areas originated in Tennessee. The moving force behind it was Walter Chandler, a Memphis attorney, who used

"GET RID OF YOUR FRIENDS"

Culver Pictures.

President Theodore Roosevelt's offensive against monopoly and illegitimate practices in railroad transportation was supported by the Supreme Court in 1904.

Charles W. Baker, a local justice of the peace, to sue Joe Carr, Tennessee's Secretary of State.

Chandler and his associates demonstrated that, because of inequalities similar to those existing in Tennessee, majorities in the legislatures of forty-three other states could be elected by less than half of the voters. Unable to get the Tennessee legislature or local courts to act on this matter, they sought satisfaction in the federal circuit courts; however, the justices said they were not certain they had the authority to order reapportionment. Eventually, in 1962 the Supreme Court said they did, thus unlocking the path to effective reapportionment— "one man, one vote."

In July 1974, the Supreme Court, headed by Chief Justice Warren Burger, heard and quickly disposed of one of the most sensational cases of recent decades: *United States* v. *Nixon, President of the United States.* Leon Jaworski, special prosecutor appointed by Nixon to probe the Watergate affair, was seeking White House tapes and documents he thought vital to his investigation. Nixon, claiming "executive privilege," refused to turn over those materials to Jaworski. By executive privilege, Nixon meant the acknowledged need to protect communications between high government officials and those who advise them, also asserting that this dispute was within the executive department and that to accede to Jaworski's request would violate the doctrine of separation of powers.

Ruling against Nixon, the Court observed that nowhere in the Constitution was there "any explicit reference to a privilege of confidentiality," yet the justices agreed that to exercise his office the President must be able to speak in confidence with his associates. But, since the materials that were sought related to criminal proceedings, to withhold such evidence "would cut deeply into the guarantee of due process of law and gravely impair the basic function of the courts." In short, no President is above the law.

This case, like *Marbury* v. *Madison,* which was quoted several times in the Supreme Court opinion, did not affect great numbers of people, nor did it, like *Brown* v. *Board of Education of Topeka* and *Baker* v. *Carr,* open the door to a flood of similar appeals. It reaffirmed the widely held belief that all citizens are equal before the law and, interestingly, substantiated Alexis de Tocqueville's observation made nearly 150 years ago that almost any American political question is resolved "sooner or later" into a judicial matter.

General Accounts

Joel H. Silbey, ed., *The Transformation of American Politics: 1840–1860* (1967)

David M. Potter and Don E. Fehrenbacher, *The Impending Crisis, 1848–1861* (1976)

Allan Nevins, *The Ordeal of the Union* (2 vols., 1947)

Territorial Expansion and Politics

Frederick J. Blue, *The Free Soilers: Third Party Politics, 1848–1854* (1973)

Holmon Hamilton, *Zachary Taylor: Soldier in the White House* (1951)

Robert J. Rayback, *Millard Fillmore: Biography of a President* (1959)

Holmon Hamilton, *Prologue to Conflict: The Crisis and Compromise of 1850* (1964)

Stanley W. Campbell, *The Slave Catchers: Enforcement of the Fugitive Slave Law, 1850–1860* (1972)

Larry Gara, *The Liberty Line: The Legend of the Underground Railroad* (1961)

Harvey Wish, *George Fitzhugh: Propagandist of the Old South* (1944)

William S. Jenkins, *Pro-Slavery Thought in the Old South* (1935)

Roy F. Nichols, *Franklin Pierce: Young Hickory of the Granite Hills* (2nd ed., 1958)

The Kansas-Nebraska Controversy

Basil Rauch, *American Interest in Cuba, 1848–1855* (1948)

Robert W. Johannsen, *Stephen A. Douglas* (1973)

James C. Malin, *The Nebraska Question, 1852–1854* (1953)

Roy F. Nichols, *The Disruption of American Democracy* (1948)

James A. Rawley, *Race and Politics: "Bleeding Kansas" and the Coming of the Civil War* (1969)

David Donald, *Charles Sumner and the Coming of the Civil War* (1960)

Stanley I. Kutler, ed., *The Dred Scott Decision: Law or Politics?* (1967)

Philip S. Klein, *President James Buchanan* (1962)

Growth of the Republican Party

Ronald P. Formisano, *The Birth of Mass Political Parties in Michigan, 1827–1861* (1971)

Michael F. Holt, *Forging a Majority: The Formation of the Republican Party in Pittsburgh, 1848–1860* (1969)

Don E. Fehrenbacher, *Prelude to Greatness: Lincoln in the 1850's* (1962)

Harry V. Jaffa, *Crisis of the House Divided: The Lincoln-Douglas Debates* (1959)

Allen Nevins, *The Emergence of Lincoln* (2 vols., 1950)

Eric Foner, *Free Soil, Free Labor, Free Men: The Ideology of the Republican Party before the Civil War* (1970)

Emotionalism at High Tide

David M. Potter, *The South and the Sectional Conflict* (1968)

Ronald T. Takaki, *Pro-Slavery Crusade: The Agitation to Reopen the African Slave Trade* (1971)

Stephen B. Oates, *To Purge this Land with Blood: John Brown* (1970)

William L. Barney, *The Road to Secession* (1972)

Ralph A. Wooster, *The Secession Conventions of the South* (1962)

Kenneth M. Stampp, *And the War Came: The North and the Secession Crisis, 1860–1861* (1950)

What Caused the Civil War?

Thomas J. Pressly, *Americans Interpret Their Civil War* (1962)

Edwin C. Rozwenc, ed., *The Causes of the American Civil War* (2nd ed., 1972)

Kenneth M. Stampp, ed., *The Causes of the Civil War* (1959)

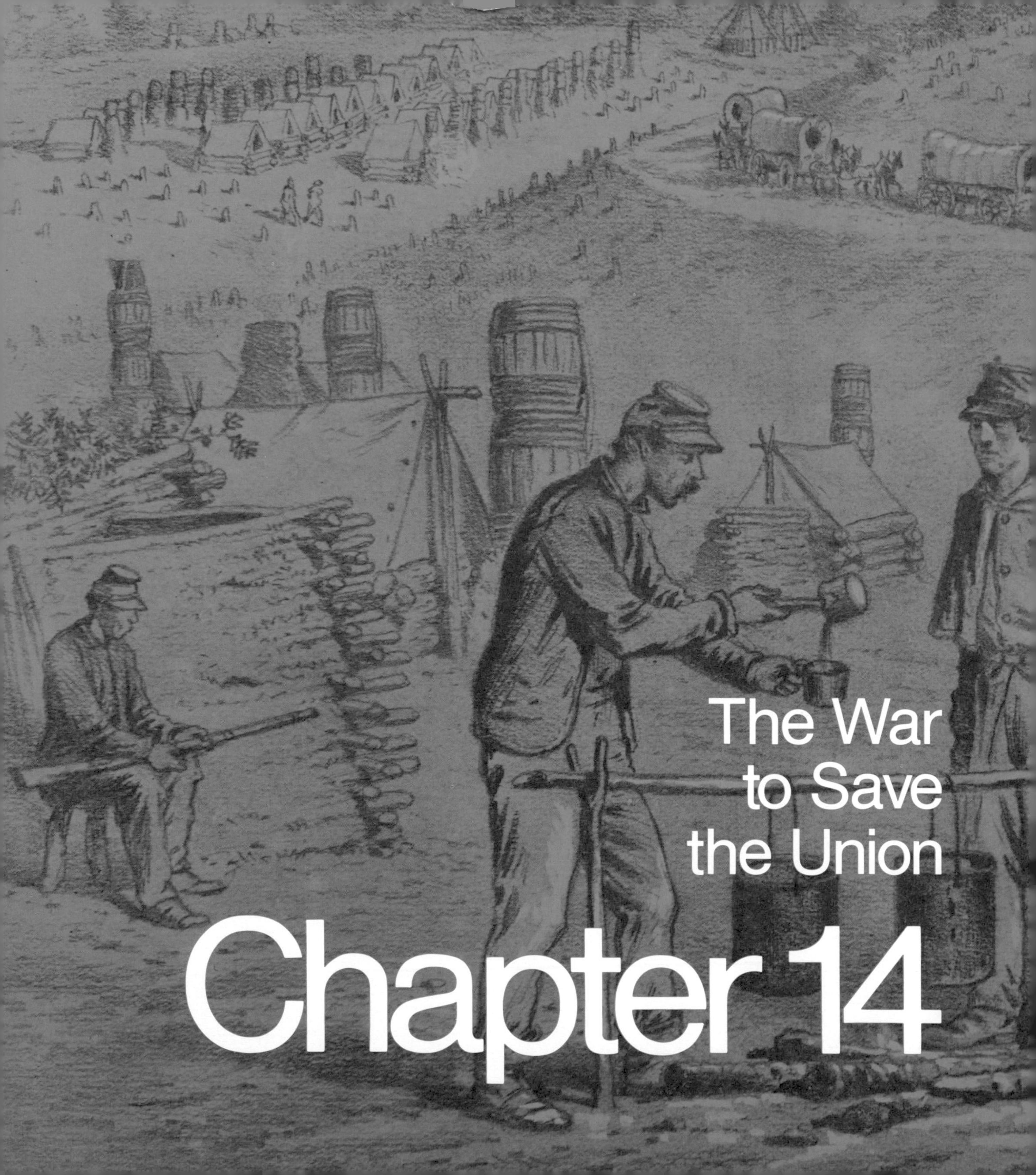

Chapter 14
The War to Save the Union

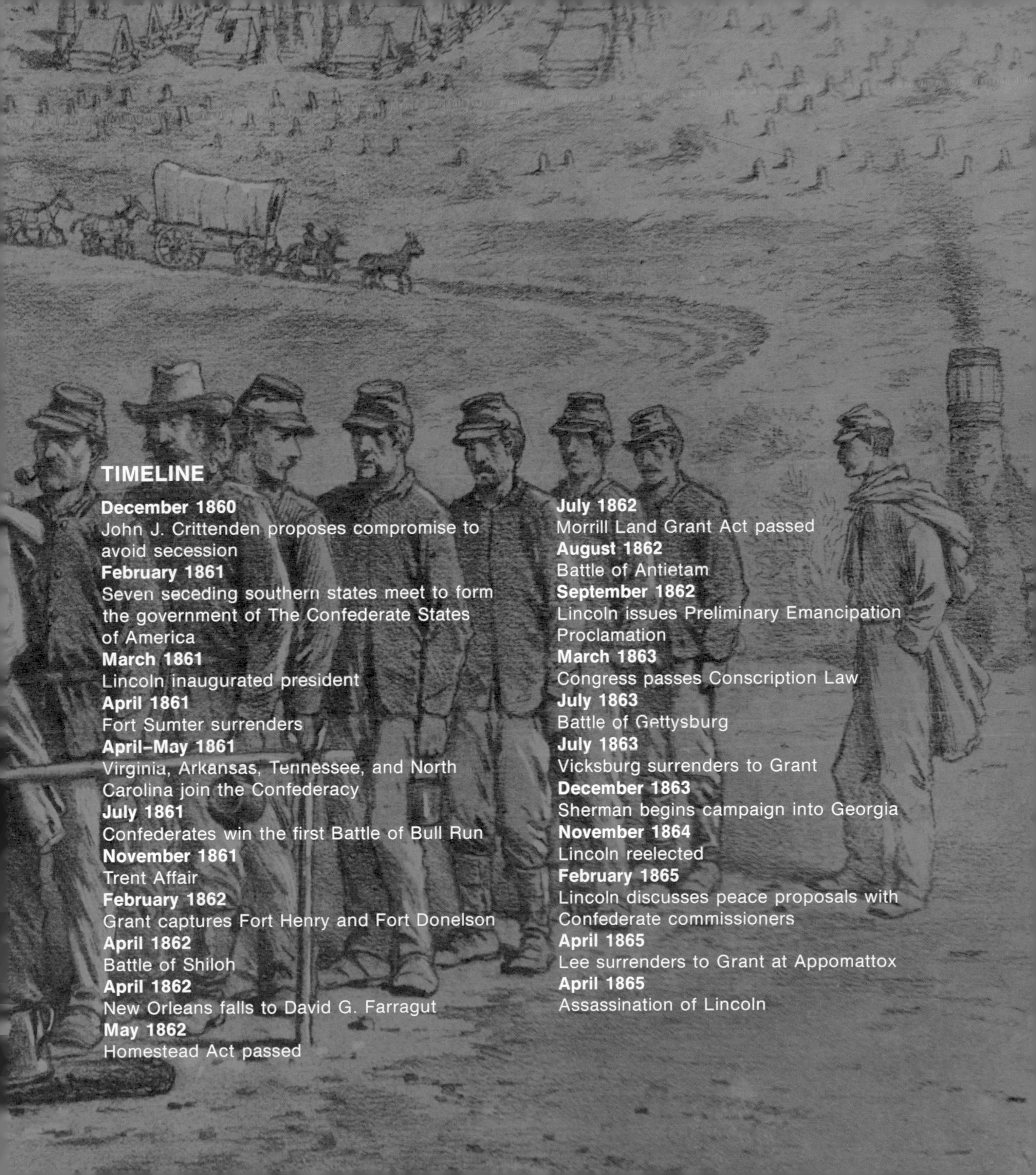

TIMELINE

December 1860
John J. Crittenden proposes compromise to avoid secession

February 1861
Seven seceding southern states meet to form the government of The Confederate States of America

March 1861
Lincoln inaugurated president

April 1861
Fort Sumter surrenders

April–May 1861
Virginia, Arkansas, Tennessee, and North Carolina join the Confederacy

July 1861
Confederates win the first Battle of Bull Run

November 1861
Trent Affair

February 1862
Grant captures Fort Henry and Fort Donelson

April 1862
Battle of Shiloh

April 1862
New Orleans falls to David G. Farragut

May 1862
Homestead Act passed

July 1862
Morrill Land Grant Act passed

August 1862
Battle of Antietam

September 1862
Lincoln issues Preliminary Emancipation Proclamation

March 1863
Congress passes Conscription Law

July 1863
Battle of Gettysburg

July 1863
Vicksburg surrenders to Grant

December 1863
Sherman begins campaign into Georgia

November 1864
Lincoln reelected

February 1865
Lincoln discusses peace proposals with Confederate commissioners

April 1865
Lee surrenders to Grant at Appomattox

April 1865
Assassination of Lincoln

CHAPTER OUTLINE

The Civil War marked the beginning of the modern American nation, a major economic power governed by a strong chief executive. This dramatic turning point in American history established the supremacy of the Union over the individual states and brought a dramatic shift in the country's political life. In a sense, the original republic of 1789 collapsed in 1860, and a four-year struggle brought an effective end to the dual sovereignty of a federal-state system. Lincoln's bold decisions as commander-in-chief marked an increase in presidential power that raised the specter of unrestrained executive authority.

Before the Civil War, state governments were strong and often self-reliant entities. For many Americans of 1860, the original joining of the states together to form the nation in 1787–1789 was an event in their personal, not mythical, past, since the Constitution was adopted during the lifetimes of their parents or grandparents. After the Civil War, the Union no longer seemed to be a federation of quasi-independent states but rather a solid political body in its own right. Similarly, the role of the President was transformed from that of a caretaker to a potent leader. Equally important, the victory of the North represented the triumph of one economy and way of life over another. The impersonal, urban, industrial Northeast, which was dependent on free labor (much of it supplied by immigration), had conquered the paternalistic, rural, agricultural South, based on slave labor and a static caste system.

Few people on either side foresaw how long and bloody a struggle lay ahead of them when war broke out in April 1861—or realized how profoundly their world would change before the fighting ceased. Few understood that the outcome of the war would be the transformation of the United States into a centralized, modern nation. Northerners imagined that the Confederacy would be quickly defeated and just as swiftly restored to the Union. Confederates believed that the North would have to accept the independence of the Confederacy once it secured the diplomatic recognition of European powers and proved that its armies were formidable on the battlefield.

The Path to War

When the first southern states seceded following Lincoln's election, James Buchanan was still President. Although eager to preserve the Union, he was hamstrung by his interpretation of his own powers as stated in the Constitution. He believed that secession was unconstitutional and declared that "the Constitution of the United

States is as much a part of the constitution of each State and is as binding upon its people as though it had been textually inserted therein." But at the same time, Buchanan was convinced he had no right to make aggressive war upon any state, though he was empowered to use military force defensively to overcome resistance to federal officers and to protect federal property.

Moreover, Buchanan sympathized with advocates of southern rights. Many of his advisors were from the South, including several members of his Cabinet (the Secretary of the Treasury was from Georgia, the Secretary of the Interior from Mississippi, and the Secretary of War from Virginia). The President, nearly seventy, was dismayed by the crisis and worried lest an overtly hostile act by the North would provoke the South into war. He and his colleagues worked for a reconciliation through various compromise proposals.

Efforts At Compromise

In Congress, Kentucky's Senator John J. Crittenden attempted conciliation through the so called Crittenden Plan. Crittenden, hoping to inherit the mantle of the great compromiser Henry Clay, wanted to break the tension between the lower South and the North by taking slavery out of politics altogether. His plan of December 18, 1860, called for reestablishment of the old Missouri Compromise Line of 36°30′ and for extending it to the Pacific. First, slavery would be prohibited in territories north of this line and maintained by federal protection in territories south of the line. When those territories north or south of the line entered the union as new states, they could determine for themselves through popular sovereignty whether they would be slave or free. Second, a provision called for the earnest prosecution of the Fugitive Slave Law, but when and if that law could not be enforced in the North, then the federal government should compensate slaveowners for their losses. Third, another provision stated that Congress could not abolish slavery in the states, nor in the District of Columbia, nor prohibit the interstate transportation of slavery where it already existed. Fourth, Crittenden urged that the African slave trade be suppressed and asked Congress to recommend that the personal liberty laws enacted in the North be repealed. When these various suggestions were ratified, they would become Amendments to the Constitution, and no future Amendments on the subject of slavery would be entertained or enacted.

Crittenden's compromise did not gather much support. Southern congressmen said they would consider the Amendments only if endorsed by the Republican party; Crittenden's effort to recognize slavery in new territories south of 36°30′ was unacceptable to President-elect Lincoln, who advised Republicans to reject the measure. Naturally enough, when this endorsement failed to materialize, southern leaders lost interest and attributed the failure to Republicans. Indeed, two days after Crittenden introduced his proposals, South Carolina passed an ordinance of secession.

On February 4, 1861, a Peace Convention, called by the state of Virginia, assembled in Washington, led largely by old men whose views on the question of the hour were well-known. Ex-President John Tyler was the presiding officer of the convention. Representatives from twenty-one states attended the secret meetings, though the seven seceded states of the lower South boycotted the convention and many northern delegates took little inter-

Chicago Historical Society.

John Jordan Crittenden made a last-minute attempt in December 1860 to take the slavery question out of politics forever.

est in its proceedings. On February 27 the Convention recommended to Congress that seven Amendments to the Constitution be adopted; they echoed the provisions of the Crittenden Plan for the most part and guaranteed that Congress would never have power over slavery in the states. The plan, however, received little support in Congress.

Throughout this interregnum period, President-elect Lincoln refused to make any concessions to the South regarding the question of the extension of slavery. As he wrote to a congressman from Illinois at this time, "Entertain no proposition for a compromise in regard to the *extension* of slavery. The instant you do, they have us under again; all our labor is lost, and sooner or later must be done over. . . . Have none of it. The tug has to come, & better now than later." Though Lincoln was willing to say that he would not interfere with slavery where it already existed and would back a rigorous enforcement of the Fugitive Slave Law, his conciliatory attitudes on these points either were not known or not believed in the South. He was invariably pictured by Southerners, who quoted his "House Divided Speech" as evidence, as an implacable foe to their way of life.

Rival Governments

Delegates from the seceding southern states meeting in Montgomery, Alabama, on February 4, 1861, adopted a constitution and established a provisional government. The Confederate Constitution largely copied the federal Constitution, lifting wholesale much of its language, but there were some significant changes. First, the "sovereign and independent character" of the individual states in the

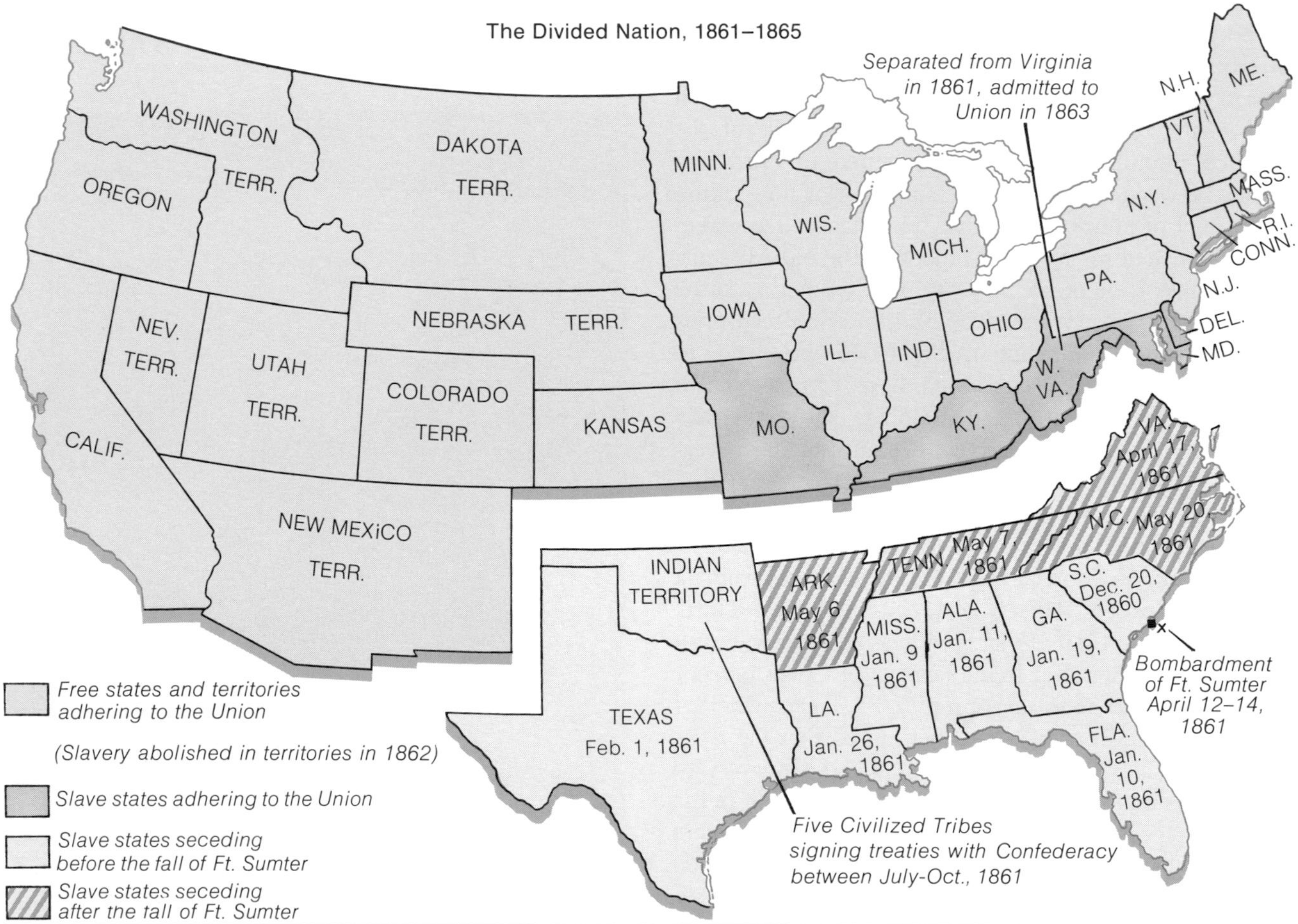

Confederacy was recognized and states' rights specifically guaranteed. Second, the southern politicians clearly sanctioned and safeguarded slavery; no law, "denying . . . the right of property in negro slaves" was to be passed. Extremists, however, were disappointed by the prohibition of the reopening of the Africa slave trade, a provision designed to win diplomatic recognition from the British and French governments. Many of the mechanics of government were also altered. For instance, the President, elected for a six-year term, was ineligible for reelection. Presumably this would give him more freedom in formulating policies since he would not be compelled to maneuver for reelection. There were to be no protective tariffs; this stipulation dispensing with a practice that the South had long resented and opposed.

Though Jefferson Davis (1808-1889) was not a rabid secessionist, Confederate leaders chose him to be their President and Georgia's Alexander H. Stephens (1812-1883), a Douglas Democrat who actively opposed secession in his state's convention, to be Vice President. Davis clearly was an outstanding, well-experienced statesman, but his course during these months caused some diehard Southerners to question his credentials. He had said little during the weeks following Lincoln's election and apparently was willing to concede all points so long as slavery would have the potential for expansion into the territories. Once Lincoln made his position known, Davis knew what his decision must be; however, he wanted to command the South's armies, not be President, a factor that caused much confusion during the war that followed.

The breakup of the Union proceeded by fits and starts, as most federal arsenals and forts in the Deep South, presided over by mere caretaker detachments, passed under the control of seceded states without any fuss. Commissioners from the Confederacy, like traveling

Chicago Historical Society.

President Jefferson Davis.

National Archives.

President Abraham Lincoln.

salesmen peddling their wares, scurried and lobbied throughout the rest of the slave states in an effort to increase the size of their nation. In general, their travels were unproductive; politicians in the upper South (Virginia, North Carolina, Tennessee and Arkansas) and in the Border states (Delaware, Maryland, Kentucky, and Missouri) were adopting a "wait-and-see" attitude. Yet the anxiety created by delay aided the secessionist cause. Congressmen from states that might secede hurried home to keep an eye on conventions debating the issue, to mend political fences, and to seek, perhaps, positions with the government of a new nation. This vacuum at the national level decreased the last hope of compromise and, since most of those who left Washington were Democrats of one sort or another, enhanced the power of the Republicans in Congress.

Army and navy officers of southern birth also debated their loyalties and, in time, had to choose between state and nation. This was a heartrending process without hard and fast rules, and the ultimate decisions depended upon local and federal ties, attitudes toward slavery and the Republican party of Abraham Lincoln, and numerous emotional and personal factors. Since its society valued military-naval careers highly, the South fared quite well and began the conflict with experience far in excess of what its population warranted. With that experience, however, came age, and before the war ended younger, more aggressive northern men frequently turned the tide of battle in their favor.

Meanwhile, on March 4, 1861, Lincoln was inaugurated as the President of the United States. In his inaugural speech, Lincoln urged a reconciliation, but he stated clearly, "The power confided to me will be used to hold, occupy, and possess the property and places belonging to the Government and to collect the duties and imposts; but beyond what may be necessary for these objects, there will be no invasion, no using of force against or among the people anywhere." In an eloquent conclusion, he spoke these moving words: "I am loath to close. We are not enemies, but friends. We must not be enemies. Though passion may have strained it must not break our bonds of affection. The mystic chords of memory, stretching from every battlefield and patriot grave to every living heart and hearthstone all over this broad land, will yet swell the chorus of the Union, when again touched, as surely they will be, by the better angels of our nature."

Lincoln faced grave problems. Through his speeches and actions, he attempted to keep the upper South and Border states from seceding. Even within his own administration, however, he was beset by anxieties. Like all new chief executives, he faced a swarm of officeseekers eager for appointment to government positions. To add to his trouble, his own Secretary of State, William Seward, tried to dictate policy. He suggested that Lincoln pick a fight with a foreign power, involve the nation in a war—and thereby unify the country. And Seward fancied himself the actual leader of the United States, Lincoln's prime minister. Quietly and firmly the President established his own rule and won Seward's respect.

Jefferson Davis had his problems as well. He was looking for ways to bring the remaining slave states into the Confederacy; without them the new "country" would find it difficult to stand up to the Union. Not only would the upper South and the Border states supply valuable manpower and industry, but their admission would provide a badly needed psychological boost for the young government and deal a severe blow to the old one. But even among the seceded states there were warring political factions and a conflict in ideology between those who envisioned the Confederacy as a loose federation of independent states and those who recognized that a certain degree of central authority was necessary in order to survive. Another conflict existed between those who demanded southern independence and those who wanted—or were suspected of wanting—to have the South rejoin the United States under more favorable terms. Jefferson Davis often was accused of belonging to this second group, dubbed the "reconstructionist" faction. Numerous other tensions also existed. Old Whigs disliked old Democrats, early advocates of secession were suspicious of recent converts, those eager to reopen the African slave trade villified their opponents, and those content with a slave-based Confederacy condemned anyone who advocated the admission of free states.

The First Shot

Lincoln's inaugural address failed to cool the nascent nationalism of the Confederacy. The new President faced the vexing problem of what to do about federal forts in the seceded states. Efforts of the Buchanan administration to resupply Fort Sumter in Charleston Harbor, for example, had failed. Lincoln inherited this unresolved problem. Any action that provoked the Confederacy might lead to the secession of the Border states, but any indecisiveness on Lincoln's part might be disastrous to the Union. Finally, Lincoln decided to provision the fort and notified South Carolina in early April that an expedition was on its way; the expedition would be peaceful if possible but would use force if necessary. President Davis wired the Confederate general in Charleston: "If you have no doubt of the authorized character of the agent who communicated to you the intention of the Washington government to supply Fort Sumter by force you will at once demand its evacuation, and if this is refused proceed, in such manner as you may determine, to reduce it." When Major Anderson refused to surrender the fort to General Pierre G. T. Beauregard (1818–1893), the Confederate forces opened fire at 4:30 A.M. on April 12, 1861. The next day Anderson surrendered.

There are conflicting opinions among historians concerning Lincoln's role in the Sumter affair and also about which side began the war. Some argue that Lincoln deliberately maneuvered the Confederacy into firing the first shot, while others place the blame on Davis and the Confederates, who, they believe, were spoiling for a fight and also were in an increasingly desperate position. The Confederacy needed Border state help to survive, and its leaders were confident that after the first shot rang out, Virginia and Maryland, even Delaware, would join the rebels. One Alabaman, fearful of Unionists in the Confederacy, wrote, "There is another way of avoiding the calamity of reconstruction and that is war. Now pardon me for suggesting that South Carolina has the power of putting us beyond the reach of reconstruction by taking Fort Sumter at any cost." In any event, the war had begun; the attack on Sumter instantly won public opinion in the North to the defense of the Union.

The Role of the Upper South and the Border States

On April 15, 1861, following the Confederate attack on Fort Sumter, President Lincoln called upon the states to provide him with militia to resist the "insurrection," to enforce the federal law, and to preserve the Union. But the great question, for both Lincoln and Davis, was what would the upper South and Border states do?

Although seven states in the lower South seceded from the Union before the attack on Fort Sumter, not a single state of the upper South had joined the Confederacy. Their reluctance to pull out of the Union derived from several sources. If they joined the Confederacy, they would be cut off from their markets and sources of credit and manufactured goods in the North. But if they remained in the Union, they would lose their sources of some agricultural staples and would forfeit the money lent individuals in the Confederacy. Furthermore, the cultural affinity between the upper South and the lower South was not absolute. Although the states of the upper South had slaves, most of them had far fewer than states

Public Building Services, National Archives.

The Confederate flag flies over Fort Sumter in mid-April, 1861.

in the Deep South, and these slaves were generally treated far more mildly.

The firing on Fort Sumter, however, forced the upper South states to take sides. Virginia (April 17), Arkansas (May 6), Tennessee (May 7), and North Carolina (May 20) went over to the Confederacy. Now that Virginia was part of the Confederacy, Richmond became the southern capital, despite the veto of President Jefferson Davis. The move to within 100 miles of Washington was one of defiance because the new capital was vulnerable indeed, but it also rewarded Virginians for casting their lot with the Confederacy and provided lawmakers with a more congenial urban setting of 40,000 in which to deliberate. With the addition of Virginia, the Confederacy also gained a great military leader—Robert E. Lee. When his native state withdrew from the Union, Lee resigned from the U.S. Army, despite the fact that Lincoln offered him command of it.

Yet none of these events led to the secession of the Border states. Delaware, Maryland, Kentucky, and Missouri remained loyal to the Union. This decision, however, was preceded and followed by fierce debates in each of the states except Delaware. In Missouri, for instance, prosouthern citizens frequently were arrested for burning bridges, tearing up railways and telegraph lines, and for opposing the Union in every possible way; indeed, only military coercion kept Missouri in the Union.

In addition to these four Border states, the mountainous western section of Virginia refused to secede. The western counties, physically isolated from slavery and long resentful of the economic and political dominance exerted by slaveholders along the coast, entered the Union as the new state of West Virginia on June 20, 1863. Lincoln, although he disapproved of splitting Virginia in this fashion, accepted the admission of West Virginia on the basis of expediency. He dodged questions about the constitutionality of the action. "Can this government stand," he asked, "if it indulges constitutional instructions by which men in open rebellion against it, are to be accounted man for man, the equal of those who maintain their loyalty to it?" There was practically, if not constitutionally, a difference between secession in favor of the Union and secession in favor of the Confederacy.

The Opposing Forces

The North's strength was strikingly superior to that of the South, though Confederates usually refused to admit their handicaps. Indeed, Confederate General Beauregard said, "No people ever warred for independence with more relative advantages than the Confederates. . . . The South, with its great material resources, its defensive means of mountains, rivers, railroads, and telegraph, with the immense advantage of the interior lines of war, would be open to discredit as a people if its failure could not be explained otherwise than by mere material contrast."

Yet the "material contrast," at least in hindsight, certainly favored the Union. There were twenty-two million people living in the twenty-three states remaining in the Union. Continued high immigration increased this numerical superiority; immigrants were encouraged to settle in the North in order to free factory workers to fight on the battlefield. In 1861 some 91,918 immigrants came to America and settled mostly in the North; in 1862, 91,985; in 1863, 176,282; in 1864, 193,418; and in 1865, 248,120. The foreign-born not only worked for the Union in factories, some 400,000 also served in the Union army.

The North enjoyed a balanced economy that was highly diversified. In 1860 the North had 110,000 manufacturing establishments employing 1,300,000 industrial workers. Numerous farms provided plenty of food for its citizens. It had sound banks and other financial institutions. The wealth of the North can be gauged by the value of its manufactured products ($1,700 million) and its iron production (480,000 tons). A railroad system, some 22,000 miles long, bound the Northeast to the Mississippi and Ohio River valleys. Moreover, the North could boast of naval supremacy.

The Confederacy, by contrast, had only nine million people living in the eleven states. Of this population, some four million were blacks, most of them slaves, and, though the blacks contributed to the southern economy, they were not used as soldiers. The agricultural South had little banking capital and few industrial resources. Manufactured products were valued at $156 million and annual iron production was only 31,000 tons. It had only 9,283 miles of track, much of it scattered sections not joined to one another. The South had only a few good ports, and these could be blockaded easily. An even greater disadvantage to military security were the Mississippi and Tennessee rivers and the Great Valley of Virginia, which offered tempting routes for invasion. Despite these disadvantages, the Confederacy did possess excellent military leaders.

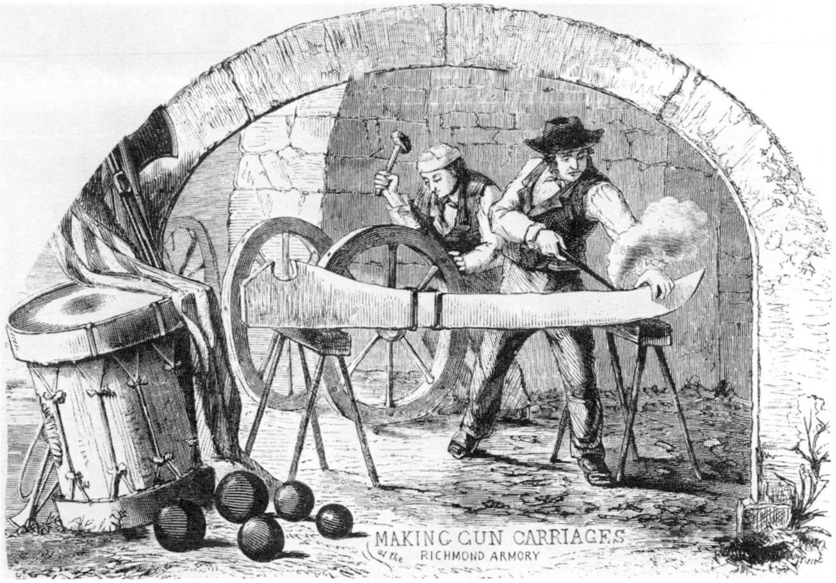
MAKING GUN CARRIAGES
at the RICHMOND ARMORY

Harper's Weekly.

Although, following secession, the Confederacy seized many federal forts and arsenals within its territory, the new government badly needed additional supplies of weapons and ammunition. This is a sketch of the famous Tredegar Iron Works in Richmond where gun carriages were made by hand.

Confederate Strategy

The Confederates were confident of their ability to maintain independence. They thought that the North would not wage war; since Northerners were primarily interested in profits, why would they bother fighting good customers and suppliers? Moreover, the South was confident that Great Britain and France, both dependent on southern crops, especially cotton, would grant the South diplomatic recognition and aid; backed up by these European powers, surely the South would be invincible.

The chief strategy of the Confederacy, once the war broke out, was defensive. As Jefferson Davis put it, the South sought peace "at any sacrifice, save that of honor and independence." As Southerners in the seceded states reasoned, if the Confederacy still remained in existence after the fighting ceased, then it would be the victor, regardless of which side won on the battlefield. This defensive posture had advantages and disadvantages. Although it was easier to hold a city than to take it and better to fight on familiar than on unfamiliar terrain, nevertheless this defensive strategy forced the Confederacy to spread its armies over the full length of its northern borders as well as along the Atlantic coast. This dilution of manpower made the Confederacy vulnerable to heavy concentrations of Union soldiers attacking at a particular point. A "perimeter defense" meant that Union forces generally had the initiative in battle.

Union Strategy

The problem of reuniting the nation quickly led Lincoln and his Cabinet to reject the strategy of the elderly General Winfield Scott (1786–1866). Scott's plan, referred to as the "Anaconda" by impatient Northerners, seemed to require too much waiting and too much time. It called for a policy of tightening the grip of the North around the body of the South by blockading Confederate ports until a Union invasion was organized. Scott recommended that some Union forces protect the nation's capital while others be sent down the Mississippi River to fragment the Confederacy and thereby force it into submission.

The blockade proposal was immediately adopted. Because Northerners were looking for a speedy conquest of the South and a swift reunification of the country, they decided to go on the offensive. Only after numerous failures and defeats did the Union finally revert to Scott's plan—the Anaconda pattern that eventually brought success. After the Confederate attack on Fort Sumter, Lincoln called for volunteers to suppress the "insurrection," and Northerners predicted the war would last only three months. Northern hopes for a short war received a dramatic setback when Union troops under Brigadier General Irvin McDowell (1818–1885) came rushing back to Washington in July 1861 after a brief encounter with a smaller force of Confederate troops under General

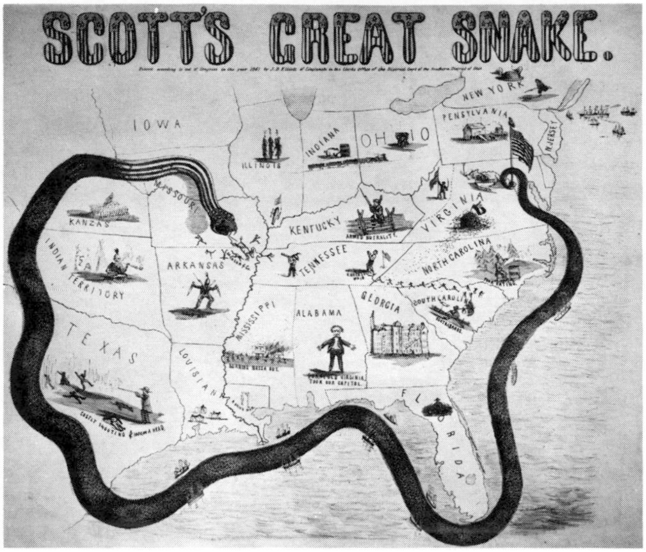

Courtesy New-York Historical Society, New York City.

A contemporary depiction of General Winfield Scott's "Anaconda" strategy that eventually brought success to the Union.

Courtesy Museum of Fine Arts, Boston. M. and M. Karolik Collection.

This hastily drawn pencil sketch by an unknown artist captures the panic that swept through the Union lines following the first Battle of Bull Run.

P. G. T. Beauregard, reinforced by General Joseph E. Johnston (1807–1891). This was the first Battle of Bull Run (also called Manassas), won by the Confederates; during this conflict, the gallant Thomas J. Jackson (1824–1863), a Confederate officer, won his nickname of "Stonewall" by repulsing a Union charge. The ill-prepared Union troops at first left the field in an orderly fashion, but the retreat soon deteriorated into a rout. One witness reported that the soldiers went off in all directions, throwing away their blankets, knapsacks, canteens—and finally muskets, cartridge boxes, and everything else in order to run faster.

This defeat led the North to a sobering reappraisal of the military situation. President Lincoln replaced the defeated McDowell with General George B. McClellan (1826–1885) and, in November 1861, upon Scott's retirement named McClellan general-in-chief. There was an effort to raise not just short-term militia units but a real army in which soldiers would serve for longer periods. The army in the West was regrouped, placed under the command of General Henry W. Halleck (1815–1872) and based at St. Louis. In Congress a group of Republicans pressured Lincoln to bring the war to a speedy and triumphant conclusion. This faction was led by Senators Benjamin F. Wade of Ohio and Zachariah Chandler (1813–1879) of Michigan and Representative Thaddeus Stevens (1792–1868) of Pennsylvania. Known by 1862 as the Radical Republicans, this faction established a congressional Joint Committee on the Conduct of the War that called for immediate military success and the emancipation of the slaves.

A Contest of Arms and Ideas

From July 1861 to March 1862, McClellan methodically trained and drilled his troops, believing that if he could put together a well-organized force of a quarter of a million soldiers he could simply march on Richmond and end the war quickly. Every detail attracted his attention, even to assembling balloonists for surveying enemy territory and telegraph operators for reporting the expected good news to Washington, D. C.

But Lincoln, impatient with continuing delay, ordered McClellan to take Richmond immediately. McClellan, however, preferred to advance on the city by way of the peninsula between the York and James River—an oblique approach quite different from the frontal assault Lincoln preferred. By the first of May, McClellan was leading an army of 112,000 men up the peninsula and was ready to clamp a giant pincers on the Confederate troops at Richmond. The general kept demanding more soldiers, but Lincoln deprived him of 40,000 men in order to protect the national capital.

While McClellan moved cautiously up the peninsula, a Confederate force of 85,000 men was preparing for battle. In the early stages of the peninsular campaign, Robert E. Lee, commander of the Army of Northern Virginia, replaced the Confederate general (Joseph E. Johnston), who was wounded. Together with "Stonewall" Jackson, Lee forced McClellan to retreat after the so-called Seven Days' Battle, fought between June 26 and July 2, 1862, near Richmond. The last battle of this engagement occured at Malvern Hill and was one of the bloodiest encounters of the war. McClellan failed to capture Richmond and was driven back. Some 36,000 men were killed, wounded, or missing in action—over twenty thousand of them Confederate and nearly sixteen thousand of them Union men. Despite such heavy losses, Lee's defense of Richmond encouraged the Confederacy.

Second Bull Run and Antietam

Lincoln was so dissatisfied with McClellan's failure to capture Richmond that he named Halleck general-in-chief of the Army and Halleck then brought John Pope (1822–1892) from the West and placed him in command of the forces in Virginia. Pope, a handsome, dashing, Kentucky-born West Point graduate, had scored some easy victories in the West; he also had denounced McClellan for his "incompetency and indisposition to active movements." What pleased Radical Republicans still more was Pope's prediction that "Slavery must perish," an attitude much more congenial than McClellan's refusal to liberate and arm slaves. Yet Pope actually was a weak leader given to incessant smoking, storytelling, and vanity; and despite his fierce words, Jackson and Lee easily outmaneuvered him in August 1862, and his effort to seize Richmond failed. Jackson led his force to the rear of the Union army and broke its communications; then, before Pope could isolate Jackson, the Confederate detachment had rejoined Lee. United, Lee and Jackson defeated Pope on August 29–30 at the second Battle of Bull Run and forced him to retreat.

Pope headed back toward Washington, some thirty miles away, with a badly demoralized army in disarray. Lincoln replaced Pope with McClellan, whose name now had been vindicated. McClellan's task was to stop Lee, who decided to press his advantage by seeking a decisive victory on northern soil and perhaps isolating the city of Washington. Such a victory might persuade England and France to recognize the Confederacy and aid its cause. In early September Lee crossed the Potomac into Maryland and part of his troops under "Stonewall" Jackson seized the federal garrison at Harper's Ferry, capturing 11,000 men and 13,000 small arms. But Lee soon walked into a trap. Lee's orders giving the disposition of troops fell into McClellan's hands. A Union private found the orders wrapped around three cigars that a Confederate

Cook Collection, Valentine Museum, Richmond, Virginia.

Robert E. Lee
(1807–1870)

This peerless Confederate leader was the son of a famous cavalry officer of the Revolution and governor of Virginia, Henry ("Light-Horse Harry") Lee, who was ill-fitted for civilian life and died when Robert was eleven, overwhelmed by a sea of debt. The youth grew up in Alexandria where his widowed mother was supported by her father's estate. In 1825 he entered West Point, where he distinguished himself as a student and as a military man, graduating in 1829 second in his class.

After winning a name for himself in the Mexican War, Lee served as superintendent of West Point. In 1859 he commanded the troops sent to quell the rebellion at Harper's Ferry. At the outbreak of the Civil War, he commanded the Department of Texas. Lee had mixed feelings about secession. He did not approve of the Confederacy, but he was torn between allegiance to his native state of Virginia and fidelity to the United States. On April 18, 1861, Lincoln offered him the command of the United States Army, but Lee declined the offer and cast his lot with Virginia and the Confederacy.

After Confederate General Joseph E. Johnston was wounded in May 1862, Lee took command of the "Army of Northern Virginia" (as Lee himself dubbed his troops). It was not until February 1865 that Lee became general-in-chief of all Confederate armies. Nevertheless, in the intervening years Lee was certainly the ablest southern general and the author of most of the Confederate strategy. His early military successes were brilliant. Aided by the daring and intelligent "Stonewall" Jackson, Lee won virtually every encounter in the early years of the war. He was turned back and defeated only in early July 1863 at the Battle of Gettysburg. After that defeat Lee was on the defensive—from the Battle of the Wilderness in early May 1864 until the final surrender at Appomattox Courthouse on April 9, 1865. Gifted with a great acumen for strategy and rare courage, Lee lacked only one quality, the ability to force his subordinates to conform to his own plans. Too courteous to browbeat his officers, Lee all too often went along with the ideas of lesser men.

After the war Lee applied for a pardon. Though indicted for treason, he was never brought to trial. He became president of Washington College in Lexington, Virginia (later renamed Washington and Lee). Avoiding all discussion of politics, until his death in 1870 he urged fellow Southerners to work hard, keep the peace and accept the decision reached at Appomattox. No other Confederate leader was so revered; he was a man in whom the South saw the embodiment of its best ideals and a man who, in time, became a national hero as well. In 1976 the United States Congress, in a final act of forgiveness and reconciliation, belatedly restored Lee's citizenship. ■

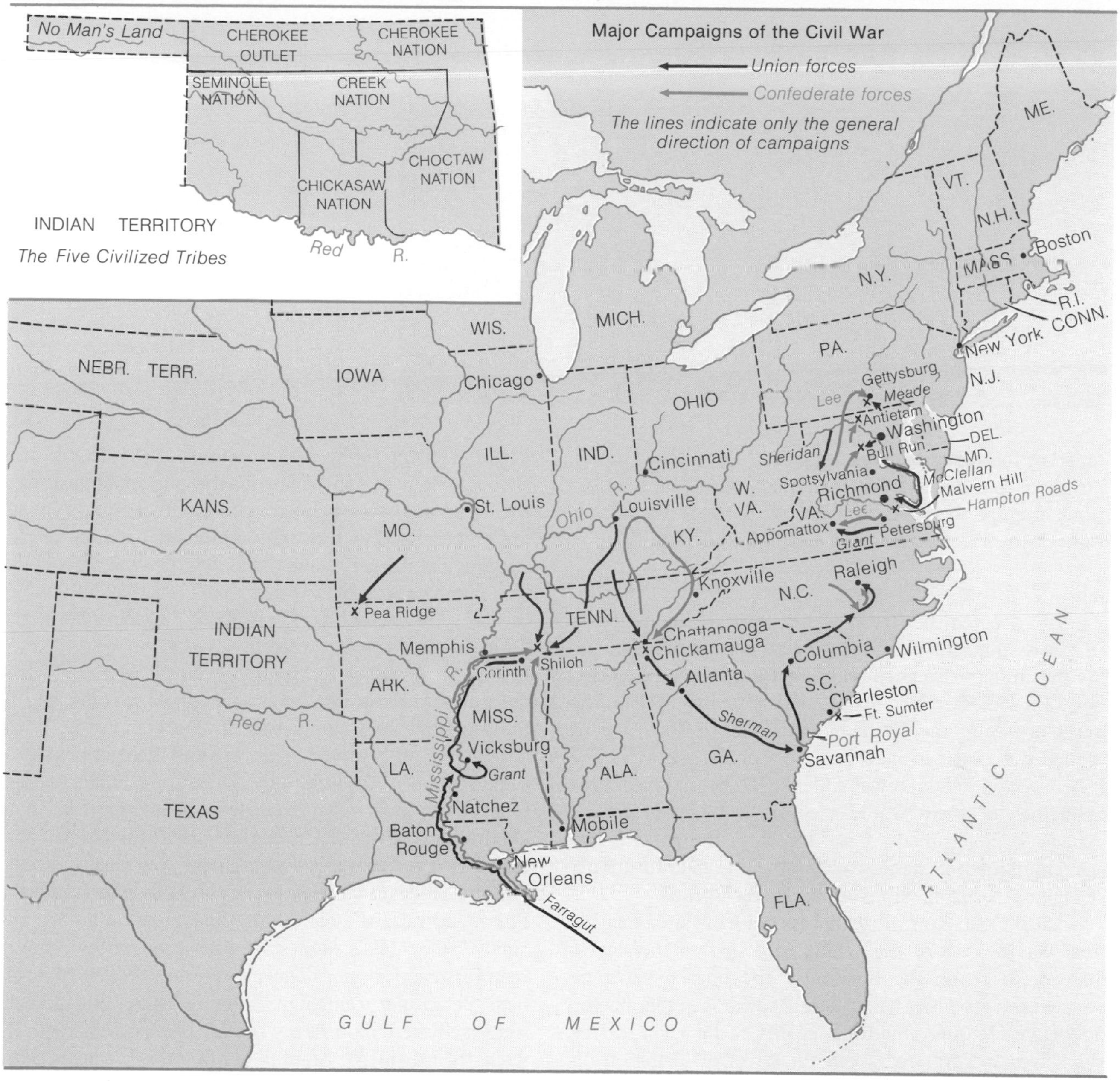

officer had accidentally dropped. Lee quickly recognized the hazards of his smaller army facing McClellan's forces with the Potomac River at his rear and made plans to withdraw back across the river into Virginia.

On September 17, McClellan attacked Lee at Sharpsburg on Antietam Creek, the goriest battle in American history up to that point, a massacre so grim that it has been called a "defeat for both armies." Lee had 40,000 men with him and all were actively engaged; McClellan, 70,000, but only about 46,000 took part in the engagement. Lee lost one-fourth of his army—killed, wounded, captured, or missing, McClellan, about 12,000. McClellan

Library of Congress.

Antietam, Maryland, in September 1862, was the scene of the goriest battle in American history up to that time.

failed to follow up his advantage, and Lee slipped out of his hands and back to Virginia. The South's most ambitious attempt so far to threaten Washington by cutting the rail lines to the city had ended in defeat.

The Abolition of Slavery

Lincoln deemed the Battle of Antietam a Union victory that was sufficiently encouraging to permit him to issue his Preliminary Emancipation Proclamation on September 22, 1862. Two months previously he had been on the verge of freeing the slaves, but Secretary of State Seward argued that, if an Emancipation Proclamation was published while the Union was suffering defeat on the battlefield, the document would seem a "last measure of an exhausted government, a cry for help, the government stretching forth its hands to Ethiopia, instead of Ethiopia stretching forth its hands to the government."

At the outset of the war, Lincoln had stated that his goal was to restore the Union, not to free the slaves. Indeed, to retain the loyalty of the border states he resisted the growing demands of Radical Republicans for abolition. He questioned the legality of his right to free the slaves and worried about the effect of liberation on the country. What changed his mind? On the field of battle, northern military officers were taking the matter into their own hands. In May 1861 at Fortress Monroe in Virginia, General Benjamin F. Butler (1818–1893) refused to return to their masters slaves who escaped to his lines. Simon Cameron, Lincoln's first Secretary of War, recommended to the President as early as the end of 1861 that slaves be emancipated and armed. In the West, Major General John C. Frémont (1813–1890) proclaimed a state of martial law in Missouri in August 1861 and freed all slaves belonging to Confederates. Lincoln was embarrassed by this order and made Frémont retract it, though at the very same time Congress was passing the first Confiscation Act, which provided that any slaves used for "insurrectionary purposes" in war against the United States would be freed.

Not only were there good military reasons to free the slaves; there were also humanitarian reasons, and to these arguments Lincoln was always responsive. Week after week he received petitions and delegations from religious and reform groups demanding emancipation. One of the most outspoken proponents for immediate abolition was Frederick Douglass, the former slave, who urged the President to enlist northern free blacks into the Union Army and let these black soldiers "march into the South and raise the banner of Emancipation among the slaves." Douglass's suggestion was seconded by military men for practical, not idealistic, reasons. When McClellan's peninsular campaign faltered, some Northerners suggested the Union Army recruit blacks to increase its strength. Edwin M. Stanton (1814–1869), who became the new Secretary of War in January 1862, was an early advocate of black enlistment. This proposal was closely tied to the question of abolition since slaves were flocking to Union lines and eager to fight for the Union cause, which they perceived as a war to end slavery. Meanwhile, Congress was taking steps towards general emancipation. In April 1862 Congress abolished slavery in the District of Columbia; in June, Congress abolished slavery in all

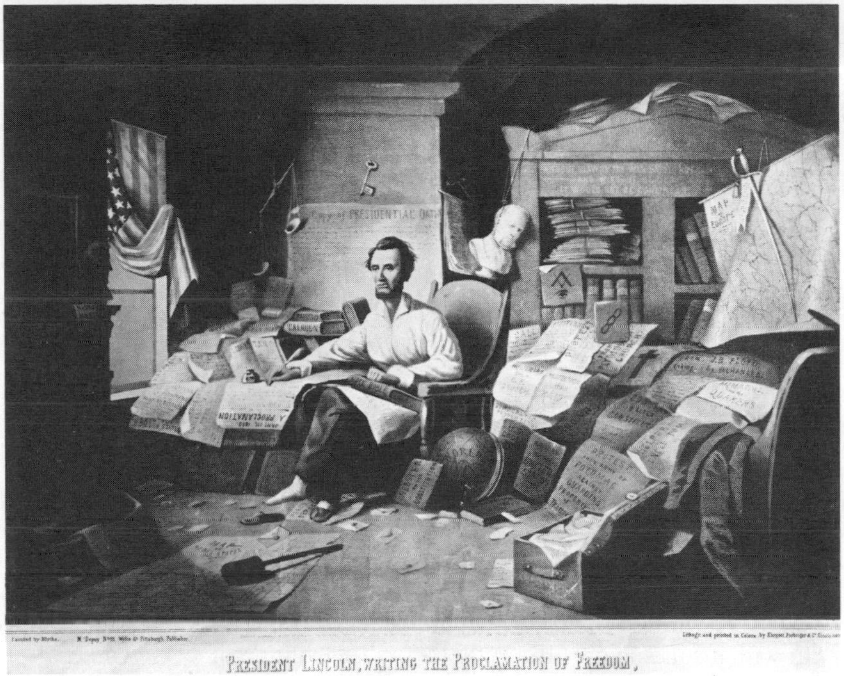
PRESIDENT LINCOLN, WRITING THE PROCLAMATION OF FREEDOM,

Library of Congress.

Lincoln ponders the question of abolishing slavery by presidential decree.

U.S. territories. And in July, the second Confiscation Act declared "forever free" all escaped or captured slaves in Union hands who belonged to any master in rebellion against the federal government.

Lincoln himself favored abolition by state law (not federal decree) with compensation for masters and eventual colonization of the blacks. Indeed, the April 1862 act abolishing slavery in the capital provided $1 million for compensation to masters (not to exceed $300 for any one slave) and $100,000 for the voluntary emigration of freed men to Haiti and Liberia. The colonization plan, however, did not succeed. Lincoln addressed a deputation of blacks from the District of Columbia on August 14, 1862, and outlined the advantages of settling in Central America. He pointed out that the proposed homeland was only seven days away by steamship from the United States, that its climate resembled Africa's, and that it was rich in coal. Colonization, Lincoln argued forcefully, would end much suffering by whites and blacks by separating the races. As he told the black delegates, "The aspiration of men is to enjoy equality with the best when free, but on this broad continent, not a single man of your race is made the equal of a single man of ours. . . . There is an unwillingness on the part of our people, harsh as it may be, for you free colored people to remain with us." The free blacks, however, did not respond favorably to the idea of colonization.

By the middle of 1862, Lincoln concluded that a presidential proclamation freeing the slaves in Confederate-held territory was becoming a military necessity. On July 22 Lincoln told his Cabinet of his intention to issue a proclamation of emancipation but hesitated until the right strategic moment. The proclamation was issued in the interests of the Union, not that of the slaves. Lincoln wrote New York editor Horace Greeley on August 22, 1862, before the proclamation had been made public: "My paramount object in this struggle *is* to save the Union, and is *not* either to save or to destroy slavery. If I could save the Union without freeing *any* slave I would do it, and if I could save it by freeing *all* the slaves I would do it; and if I could save it by freeing some and leaving others alone I would also do that. What I do about slavery, and the colored race, I do because I believe it helps to save the Union; and what I forebear, I forebear because I do *not* believe it would help to save the Union." He concluded his remarks by noting, "I have here stated my purpose according to my view of *official* duty; and I intend no modification of my oft-expressed *personal* wish

Harper's Weekly.

Thousands of slaves fled from their masters after news of Lincoln's Emancipation Proclamation reached them.

that all men everywhere could be free."

McClellan's success in turning back Lee's invasion of Maryland in the middle of September provided Lincoln with a suitable opportunity to act. The abolition of slavery, he now believed, was necessary for winning the war. The freed slaves would swell the ranks of the Union Army, and the act of freeing them would win the sympathy of European powers and persuade them not to recognize the Confederacy. During the Mexican War, Lincoln expressed fears about President Polk's unprecedented wartime powers, and now he felt that freeing the slaves went beyond the President's constitutional authority. He issued his proclamation "as a fit and necessary war measure" supposedly "warranted by the Constitution upon military necessity."

The Preliminary Emancipation Proclamation of September 22, 1862, warned the Confederacy that after January 1, 1863, all slaves in areas still in rebellion against the United States would be "thenceforward, and forever free." Lincoln's proclamation was designed to entice the slave states back into the Union; if they returned to the fold, he was saying, they could keep their slaves. Should a majority of qualified voters in any southern state elect representatives to Congress before January 1, 1863, that state would escape enforced emancipation. At the same time, Lincoln was willing to seek federal aid for any state that voluntarily put into effect a program of compensated emancipation.

In spite of the limited nature of Lincoln's Proclamation, it was the turning point of the Civil War. It shattered the Confederacy's hopes for foreign recognition, gave Union commanders presidential authority to recruit ex-slaves, and turned the war into the crusade that blacks and abolitionists had hoped for—a war to end slavery. Not until the Thirteenth Amendment was ratified in 1865, however, was slavery abolished *everywhere,* rather than in areas only in rebellion.

Wartime Diplomacy

The South waged an aggressive campaign during the first two years of the war to win both aid and recognition as an independent nation from England and France. Cotton, of course, was the trump card. The United States, on the other hand, fought just as hard to convince Europe that the Civil War was an internal matter, a family feud to be resolved without outside meddling. As an established power, moreover, the North had distinct advantages such as a functioning foreign service with considerable experience in diplomatic affairs. Although the South began the struggle basking in the overwhelming approval of European aristocracy, slavery was a heavy burden and Confederate diplomats never seemed to appreciate the depth of antislavery feeling throughout the Continent. And, while many aristocrats in England and France (the only nations that really counted) disliked the liberal, emerging democracy of the Union and rubbed their hands in glee at the prospect of a weaker, divided United States, once Lincoln transformed the Civil War into a struggle to end slavery, the Confederacy's hopes of European aid or intervention vanished.

Several factors played into northern hands and frustrated southern schemes. England began the war years with a huge surplus of American cotton and, despite some shortages, was soon importing bales from Egypt and India. Also, England was becoming increasingly dependent upon northern wheat, and the British faced a naval dilemma as well. As the world's leading sea power, Great Britain had long insisted upon the blockade as a recognized weapon of war. Breaking the northern blockade to aid the Confederacy could establish a dangerous precedent. In addition, England was booming as a result of the Civil War; she was selling supplies to both sides, and Confederate raiders were sweeping rival Yankee merchantmen from the seas, diverting more and more trade to British bottoms. Yet the key issue was the failure of the South to mount a sustained drive that promised ultimate victory. As a result, no European nation granted official recognition to the Confederate States of America, although several southern statesmen lobbied hard throughout various capitals.

Despite Union objections, the European powers proclaimed their official neutrality soon after war erupted. This diplomatic maneuver granted the Confederacy belligerent status. In the years that followed, there were transatlantic crises from time to time, but Charles Francis Adams (1807–1886), the son of one President and the grandson of another, was Lincoln's minister in London. He performed brilliantly and no break in diplomatic relations with Great Britain ever occurred. The most provocative episode, the *Trent* affair, took place in November 1861 when an impetuous Yankee captain, Charles Wilkes, stopped a British steamer, the *Trent*, and seized two southern diplomats, James M. Mason and John Slidell, who respectively were heading for London and Paris, and took them in triumph to Boston. The British were furious; the populace of the North elated. But cooler heads won out, and eventually the two men were permitted to proceed to Europe where they accomplished little.

Confederate purchase of sea raiders and ironclad warships from English shipyards precipitated more angry words, but nothing as volatile as the *Trent* affair. (After the war ended, the United States presented Britain with a huge bill for damages done by these raiders and, in time, collected.) Following McClellan's limited victory at Antietam and issuance of Lincoln's Emancipation Proclamation, the North was in a position to speak more forcefully, and the British government belatedly decided to terminate Confederate contracts with English shipbuilders. Displeased at the failure of cotton diplomacy, Southerners became increasingly critical of the British and late in 1863 gave up any hope of diplomatic recognition and expelled all British consuls from the Confederate states.

Napoleon III of France, eager to meddle in America to promote his colonial dreams, also helped the Confederacy outfit raiders and used a Mexican debt to French, English, and Spanish creditors as an excuse to occupy Mexico City in June 1863 and to set up a puppet empire in that country. This was, of course, a flagrant affront to the Monroe Doctrine, but the United States could do nothing about it until the war ended.

From Antietam to Appomattox

Lee may have been turned back at the Battle of Antietam and the engagement may have afforded Lincoln an opportunity to issue the Emancipation Proclamation, but northern public opinion was dismayed by Lee's escape and McClellan's failure to pursue and capture him. After so many bloody battles, Lee and the Confederate armies still were a force to be reckoned with. In October 1862 a gallant southern officer, James E. B. "Jeb" Stuart (1833–1864), led a cavalry raid behind McClellan's army, rushed up into Pennsylvania, and then returned to Lee's side, virtually unharmed. Stuart covered eighty miles in twenty-seven hours, and only one of his men was wounded. This daring feat made the cautious McClellan look ridiculous. When he told Lincoln that his horses were too tired to move, Lincoln caustically asked "what [have] the horses of your army done since the battle of Antietam that fatigues anything?" In early November Lincoln replaced McClellan with General Ambrose E. Burnside (1824–1881). Although the army nearly mutinied upon hearing of McClellan's removal, Lincoln expected great things of his new commander.

A month later at Fredericksburg, Burnside committed one of the worst blunders of the war. After neglecting to move against smaller Confederate forces that were exposed to attack, Burnside then foolishly struck, charging the musketry and artillery fire of well-entrenched Confederates, where the Southerners were strong and united and enjoyed a superior position on the field. When the smoke cleared, Burnside's losses totalled 12,600 men killed or wounded as compared with Lee's 5,300 casualties. "It's well that war is so terrible," Lee told a comrade, "we should grow too fond of it!" In January 1863, a few weeks after Fredericksburg, Lincoln replaced Burnside with Major General Joseph Hooker (1814–1879).

The year 1863 was filled with dramatic events. It opened with Lincoln's proclamation that slaves in areas still in rebellion were henceforth free. In the spring, Hooker led an army twice as large as Lee's, and crossing the Rappahannock River above Fredericksburg, he attempted to cut southern supply lines in Virginia and force the Confederates to retreat. But "Fighting Joe" Hooker failed to take the initiative, and Lee, with the aid of "Stonewall" Jackson, defeated the Union Army on May 3 near Chancellorsville. The Confederate victory at Chancellorsville, however, was marred by heavy casualties, including the death of Jackson, who was accidentally shot by his own troops—thereby robbing the Army of Northern Virginia of one of its great commanders. Nevertheless, Lincoln still had not found a general who could outmaneuver Lee.

The War in the West

Union armies were having greater successes in the West. In February 1862, General Ulysses S. Grant struck hard at several western Confederate positions. Aided by a gunboat flotilla, Grant took Fort Henry on the Tennessee River on February 6, but most of its garrison retreated to Fort Donelson on the Cumberland River, which Confederate General Albert S. Johnston (1803–1862) regarded as the major defense of Nashville. Following a four-day seige in mid-February, Grant accepted the "unconditional" surrender of the fort's garrison. Control of the Tennessee and Cumberland rivers gave Grant easy access to the heart of the South. Shortly after the capture of Fort Donelson, Nashville fell to Union forces.

Meanwhile, General Johnston was assembling a large force of Confederate soldiers at Corinth on the Tennessee-Mississippi border. Grant began advancing toward Corinth in early spring, but Johnston's forces attacked Grant's army of 33,000, near Shiloh Church just over the Tennessee border from Corinth. The two-day Battle of Shiloh (April 6 and 7, 1862) was one of the bloodiest battles of the war with both sides suffering heavy casualties. The death of General Johnston and the loss of about 11,000 Confederate troops so weakened southern forces that they were unable to push Grant out of western Tennessee and Corinth fell to Union troops without a struggle. Shiloh had one very important byproduct: it convinced Grant that only by waging a war of "complete conquest" against the Confederacy could the Union be preserved. As for the Confederacy, one contemporary wrote, "the South never smiled after Shiloh."

Further South, naval Commander David G. Farragut (1801–1870) of the West Gulf Blockading Squadron launched the Battle of New Orleans on April 18, 1862, and went on to destroy most of the Confederate fleet, which hastened the fall, ten days later, of the city. During the summer of 1862 federal gunboats defeated the remnants of the Confederate fleet at Memphis and opened up most of the Mississippi River to Union forces. A year later, when Grant captured Vicksburg on July 4, 1863, the entire river came under Union control, severing the southwestern portion of the Confederacy (Texas, Arkansas, and most of Louisiana) from the rest of the South.

From Gettysburg to the Wilderness

The fall of Vicksburg in the summer of 1863 coincided with Lee's second unsuccessful invasion of the Union in the East. Confederate President Jefferson Davis and General Lee hoped that a successful thrust into northern territory might force the North to sue for peace. This strategy was a gamble, since Lee's invasion required a large force and to amass such an army soldiers had to be diverted from the western front and the defense of Vicksburg. In short, Davis and Lee decided to risk everything on an assault into Pennsylvania and to expose Vicksburg, which had been under seige since May 19.

The gamble failed. In early June, Lee led his army up the Shenandoah Valley toward Pennsylvania, which he entered on June 28. At the same time Major General George G. Meade (1815–1872) replaced Hooker as the Commander of the Union Army of the Potomac. Lee and Meade locked horns at Gettysburg early in July in the greatest battle of the war when the two armies chanced upon one another on June 30. The next day the Confederates drove the northern troops back to Cemetery Ridge and Culp's Hill and entrenched themselves on Seminary Ridge. In the opening maneuvers, Lee was clearly victorious. But during the next two days, July 2 and 3, the tide turned. On the afternoon of July 2, Lee's men battered mercilessly at Union positions, but did not succeed in

National Archives.

Ulysses S. Grant
(1822–1885)

This Civil War hero was born in humble circumstances and grew up in Georgetown, Ohio, the son of a poor tanner. In his late teens he attended the United States Military Academy at West Point but was graduated without distinction at the middle of his class. Upon graduation in 1843 he served in the army in Missouri and Louisiana. He first saw action two years later during the Mexican War.

In the early 1850s, Grant was transferred to the Pacific coast where, lonely for his wife and young son, he became so bored and despondent that he sometimes drank too much and was urged to tender his resignation to the Secretary of War, Jefferson Davis. After eleven years of service, Grant was without money or employment and had the responsibility of supporting a family. He tried farming, selling real estate, and clerking in a customs house, but he was unsuccessful in all these enterprises.

His prospects improved considerably with the outbreak of the Civil War. He received an appointment as colonel of the Twenty-first Illinois Volunteers and, soon after, as a brigadier general. He fought for two years in the West where he scored some stunning successes, especially at the Battle of Vicksburg, which he captured on July 4, 1863. This victory cut the Confederacy in half and gave the Union control of the Mississippi River.

After another victory that fall near Chattanooga, Grant was appointed general-in-chief of the Union armies and subsequently devised the strategy that eventually helped to win the war. He recognized that the North must fight not to capture southern cities but to destroy southern armies. In addition, the Union had to engage all the Confederate armies at once, so that the various enemy forces could not come to each other's aid. Finally, he sought to cut the Confederacy into fragments. In all these goals, Grant was successful.

After the war Grant was acclaimed everywhere as a great hero and, in time, became a contender for the presidency. In 1868 he ran as the Republican candidate and won. Unfortunately, he made many inept decisions during his two terms and surrounded himself with advisors who were both corrupt and involved in major scandals. After his second term, Grant entered the world of business and again encountered failure. In the last year of his life, as he was dying of cancer, Grant recouped his fortunes, repaired his reputation, and bequeathed his family a fortune by writing his memoirs, two volumes that had an enormous sale and earned his survivors almost half a million dollars. ■

taking either Culp's Hill or Cemetery Ridge. Meade held on—though at a terrible cost, since he lost 20,000 men. At noon on July 3 the Confederate forces fired 140 cannons at the Union lines on Cemetery Ridge. The whole valley, two miles long and half a mile wide, was filled with thick black smoke. But when the smoke cleared, Lee could see that his gunners had failed to knock out the Union artillery. Grimly, Lee ordered 15,000 of his infantry to charge the Ridge. Union muskets and artillary mowed down the brave Confederate soldiers but on they came. When they reached the top of Cemetery Ridge, the mass of Union and Confederate soldiers was so thick that some men were firing accidentally at their own comrades.

Lee's army eventually was driven back and permitted to retreat into Virginia once more. Each side had casualties numbering about 25,000 men, but the North could far better afford such losses than the already weakened South. This invasion of the North took so terrible a toll of lives that Lee never again was able to mount an attack north of the Potomac. The day after the Union victory at Gettysburg, Vicksburg surrendered to Grant as some 30,000 Confederate soldiers laid down their arms. This capitulation meant that now the Confederacy was split in half, and the Mississippi, in Lincoln's phrase, now "rolled unvexed to the sea." Stunning Confederate defeats on the eastern and western fronts in the summer of 1863 put the Confederacy completely on the defensive and rendered its hopes for European recognition futile. On November 19, 1863, several months after the battle, a cemetery at Gettysburg was dedicated. The principal oration was delivered by a famous public speaker, Edward Everett (1795–1865), but President Lincoln made a few remarks that have resounded over the decades—the Gettysburg Address.

Four score and seven years ago our fathers brought forth, upon this continent, a new nation, conceived in liberty, and dedicated to the proposition that all men are created equal.

Now we are engaged in a great civil war, testing whether that nation, or any nation, so conceived and so dedicated, can long endure. We have met here on a great battle field of that war. We have come to dedicate a portion of that field as a final resting place for those who here gave their lives that that nation might live. It is altogether fitting and proper that we should do this.

But in a larger sense we can not dedicate—we can not consecrate—we can not hallow—this ground. The brave men, living and dead, who struggled here, have consecrated it, far above our poor power to add or detract. The world will little note, nor long remember, what we say here, but it can never forget what they did here. It is for us, the living, rather, to be dedicated here to the unfinished work which they who fought here have thus far so nobly advanced. It is rather for us to be here dedicated to the great task remaining before us – that from these honored dead we take increased devotion to that cause for which they gave the last full measure of devotion – that we here highly resolve that these dead shall not have died in vain – that this nation, under God, shall have a new birth of freedom, and that this government of the people, by the people, for the people, shall not perish from the earth.

Following the Battle of Gettysburg, there was a period of relative calm on the eastern front. In the West, General Grant cleared Tennessee of Confederate troops and opened the way for a Union drive eastward through the mountain barrier into Georgia and South Carolina. President Lincoln rewarded Grant for his successes by naming him General-in-Chief of the Union forces in March 1864.

Three major campaigns eventually resulted in the Union's victory in the war. Grant led one of these campaigns toward the Confederate capital of Richmond. On May 5 and 6 Grant and Meade, leading 100,000 men, met Lee in the Wilderness region of Virginia; the engagement was inconclusive. From May 8 to May 12, Grant suffered heavy losses at Spotsylvania Court House, but continued to march toward Richmond. On June 1 Grant attacked Lee at Cold Harbor and was driven off. Though Lee lost only 30,000 men in these engagements, compared with Grant's loss of 60,000 soldiers, Lee could ill afford any losses, however small. In June Grant settled down to a prolonged siege of Petersburg, just twenty miles below Richmond.

In August 1864 Grant sent his ablest cavalry commander, Philip Sheridan (1831–1888), to push the enemy south and destroy all supplies in the Shenandoah Valley. Sheridan defeated Confederate General Jubal A. Early (1816–1894) in several engagements in the fall and proceeded to devastate the valley in order to deny its crops to the Confederate Army. As Sheridan himself put it, "A crow would have to carry its rations if it had flown across the valley." Later Sheridan turned the flank of the Confederate Army on April 1, 1865, thus forcing it to evacuate Petersburg and retreat to Appomattox Courthouse.

While Grant and Sheridan were hammering away at Confederate forces in the East, General William Tecumseh Sherman (1820–1891) was completing his campaign against Atlanta in the fall of 1864. Sherman had left Chattanooga in May with about 100,000 men. Early in September, his "march through Georgia" led to the capture of Atlanta. Sherman, an early practitioner of total war, then led 60,000 men from Atlanta to Savannah, destroying everything in his path—war supplies, public and private buildings, railroads, homes, and household goods. His army wreaked more destruction than he had intended, and he often found it difficult to maintain discipline. Nevertheless, Sherman believed that only such extreme measures would convince southern civilians that their cause was hopeless. The pillaging of Georgia, moreover, devastated a vital source of food and supplies for the Confederate armies. The city of Savannah was occupied on December 21 and presented to Lincoln as a Christmas present. Then Sherman began a march northward through the Carolinas. In mid-February 1865 the Union Army reached Columbia, South Carolina's capital city, much of which was burned to the ground.

Wartime Politics in the North

In Grant, Lincoln finally found a general who could fight, but this discovery did not instantly win Lincoln much support from weary, restless Union voters. Grant's heavy losses in his drive toward Richmond did not inspire Northerners with much enthusiasm. As a result, the Democrats gained supporters from a growing peace movement that undoubtedly harbored southern sympathizers eager for a negotiated settlement of some sort. Some of these individuals, especially Southerners who had settled along the Ohio River in Illinois, Indiana, and Ohio, formed secret societies (clubs such as the "Knights of the Golden Circle," later known as the "Order of the American Knights" and finally known as the "Sons of Liberty") ostensibly designed to promote the interests of the Democratic party and to unseat Lincoln. Republicans accused the members of these organizations of plotting to aid the South with arms or attempting to establish a separate Confederacy in the North that would side with the South. The Republicans did have cause for alarm. In fact, some members of these secret organizations promoted resistance to the draft, encouraged and protected deserters, and engaged in outright acts of espionage and sabatoge. As a result of such activities, loyal Unionists came to view all Peace Democrats as "Copperheads"—poisonous snakes that strike without warning. Most Peace Democrats, however, did not deserve the label. The groups comprising the ranks of the Peace Democrats, excluding southern sympathizers, included eastern merchants eager for the restoration of profitable southern markets, workers and poor farmers suffering from inflation and fearful of the draft, and numerous citizens who were weary of a seemingly endless bloody war. Although most were loyal Unionists, they became stigmatized as "Copperheads."

From the beginning of the war, Lincoln was dissatisfied with the failure of the courts and government prosecutors to convict and punish people guilty of conspiracy and treason. Accordingly, he suspended the habeas corpus privilege, designed to protect citizens from arbitrary arrest, and imprisoned thousands of people without benefit of trial. And in 1862 he issued a general proclamation providing that all persons who discouraged enlistment, resisted the draft, or were disloyal in any way were subject to trial by courts-martial or military commissions. Over 13,000 individuals eventually were arrested and confined in federal penitentiaries or state prisons.

Lincoln's best-known northern opponent was Clement L. Vallandigham (1820–1871). A lawyer, editor, and Democratic politician, Vallandigham lived most of his life in Ohio, but his father's family was from Virginia and he idealized the southern way of life. Vallandigham led the Peace Democrats in the Old Northwest, and during the Civil War he called for compromise, freedom of expression, and peace on virtually any terms. In 1863 General Ambrose E. Burnside, Commander of the Military District of Ohio, warned the Peace party against continuing to declare its sympathy with the enemy. When Vallandigham ignored the warning, Burnside arrested him. Lincoln shrewdly arranged his release and banished him to the South under threat of imprisonment should he return north.

Throughout the war Lincoln faced political opposition that threatened his political future. Republican defeats in the 1862 congressional elections cut the Republican majority to a narrow margin of just eighteen votes in the House of Representatives. Even this slim majority was achieved only through intervention by the Lincoln Administration in the border states; in Kentucky, for instance, federal soldiers arrested anyone seeking office who was opposed to Lincoln. Despite the slight advantage the Republicans still maintained, their hold on the government was weakening. Pennsylvania, for instance, with a Republican majority of 59,000 in 1860, reported a Democratic majority of 3,500 in 1862 and the same pattern held true in New York, Ohio, Indiana, and Lincoln's own state of Illinois. Indeed, the Union Army's failure to force Lee's surrender led many Northerners to question Lincoln's wartime leadership and his choice of generals.

In March 1863 Lincoln's popularity suffered another blow when he issued a conscription law. Drafting soldiers into the army seemed an ominous extension of the central government's powers, and the law produced draft riots. The law was relatively mild and, like conscription in the South, riddled with exemptions—substitutes were allowed and one could buy his way out for $300. When authorities published the draft calls, the names of the poor and foreign-born dominated the list. Enraged workers in many communities protested against the distinction between "rich men's money and poor men's blood." The outburst in New York in mid-July 1863 was an especially ugly affair as gangs, often led by Irish-Americans, turned their wrath against blacks, killing, pillaging, and looting. Several hundred people were killed and the Colored Orphan Asylum was burned to the ground before troops could restore order.

Courtesy New-York Historical Society, New York City.

The Conscription Act of 1863 triggered an antidraft riot in New York City that cost hundreds of lives and $1.5 million in property damage. The troops used to quell the riot came from the army of General George G. Meade. The lack of these soldiers contributed to Meade's failure to stage an offensive against Lee after the Battle of Gettysburg.

In spite of strong dissatisfaction among Republicans with his handling of the war and efforts by some to find another candidate, Lincoln received the nomination of his party in June 1864. To improve his chances of winning the election, his supporters picked Andrew Johnson (1808–1875), a Tennessee "War Democrat," as his running mate and the two men campaigned under the banner of the National Union party.

In August, War Democrats chose General McClellan as the candidate of the Democratic party and permitted Peace Democrats to draft a platform calling for the immediate cessation of hostilities and the restoration of the "Federal Union of the States." After serious soul-searching, McClellan repudiated this peace plank—though he was not above playing on the widespread feeling of frustration with both Lincoln and the war which permeated the North.

By mid-summer the strength of pacifism and defeatism made Lincoln's reelection seem doubtful. Even within Republican ranks there was much dissension. Although the party agreed on three aims—victory in the war, reunion of the North and South, and emancipation of slaves everywhere in the country—it was split over the crucial question of reconstruction. Lincoln hoped that when the war was over, the southern states would swiftly reenter the Union with a minimum of rancor. Accordingly, he proposed that when 10 percent of the voters of 1860 in each rebel state had pledged allegiance to the United States, they could form a new state government and rejoin the Union. But two Republicans, Senator Benjamin Wade (1800–1878) and Representative Henry

Winter Davis (1817–1865), pushed a bill through Congress that required a majority of voters of 1860 in each southern state to pledge allegiance to the United States and to declare that they had never held office or voluntarily fought for the Confederacy before civil government could be restored. Lincoln was already setting up reconstruction governments in Louisiana and Arkansas and feared the Wade-Davis Bill might jeopardize their foundation. He found its terms so unacceptable that he pocket-vetoed it. Sponsors of the bill then published a manifesto condemning Lincoln, and there was a short-lived movement to nominate another Republican candidate for President. Lincoln himself conceded that he probably would not be reelected.

Sheridan's scorching of the Shenandoah Valley and Sherman's entry into Atlanta greatly aided Lincoln's search for votes and finally won the Radical Republicans to his side. Indeed, it was probably the votes of Union soldiers that put New York, Connecticut, Pennsylvania, Maryland, Indiana, and Illinois (a total of 101 electoral votes) in his column. McClellan carried only one state, Kentucky, decisively and won less handily in New Jersey and Delaware. Overall, Lincoln amassed 2,218,388 ballots, 55 percent of the popular vote, to 1,812,807 for McClellan. He had an electoral majority of 212 to 21.

Wartime Conditions in the South— and Collapse of the Confederacy

By the beginning of 1865 the South was collapsing. The federal blockade cut off badly needed imported supplies. The breakdown of transportation and Union occupation and destruction of production centers created chaos throughout large areas. Four years of conflict took a huge toll, reducing agricultural production, depreciating land values, stifling industry, demoralizing commerce, and disrupting whatever banking facilities existed. Omitting slave property, southern wealth shrank in value by some 43 percent.

Morale in the Confederate Army was shattered; desertions were high. Jefferson Davis even contemplated arming the slaves, but the Confederate Congress acted too late for this measure to take effect before the conflict ended. Davis also had trouble commandeering goods and services from some states, especially from South Carolina, which jealously guarded its rights as a sovereign state. The Confederate government found it increasingly necessary to tighten laws against conspiracy and to suspend the *habeas corpus* law. The southern plight became so desperate that Davis permitted Vice President Stephens and two other Confederate officers to meet with Lincoln and Secretary of State Seward aboard the Union vessel *River Queen* at Hampton Roads on February 3, 1865, to discuss peace proposals. But the Confederate commissioners stubbornly insisted that a prerequisite for peace was Union recognition of southern independence. Lincoln found this stipulation unacceptable, and this last ditch effort at peacemaking failed.

The end of the Confederacy came in the spring of 1865. By continually bludgeoning Confederate forces and cutting Lee's supply lines, Grant and Sheridan forced the Confederate military leader to abandon both Petersburg and Richmond early in April. Fearing that Lee might escape into central North Carolina and join up with another large Confederate force, Grant and Sheridan rushed after Lee and trapped him in south central Virginia. On the 9th of April Grant and Lee met in the village of Appomattox Courthouse southwest of Richmond. In accordance with President Lincoln's desire to treat the South with generosity, Grant seized all weapons but gave the soldiers their freedom after they had pledged not to take up arms against the United States again. Grant also permitted the men to retain their horses, which they needed for spring ploughing. The Union general did not even demand that Lee surrender his sword. The once magnificent Army of Northern Virginia disbanded, and the last major Confederate forces surrendered on May 26.

The People Who Fought the War

In both the North and the South the actual waging of the war involved hundreds of thousands of people. Estimates of the sizes of the two armies are only approximate, but one expert calculated that during the war 1,556,678 men served the Union and 1,082,119 fought on behalf of the Confederacy. The war cost about a million casualties, including 360,222 deaths on the Union side and 258,000 on the Confederate side. No one in 1861 expected the war to last long. Both armies were badly supplied, inadequately uniformed, improperly housed, poorly paid, and their health seriously neglected.

The Blue and the Gray

The northern army faced many problems. In the first years of the war uniforms differed from regiment to regiment, which led to terrible confusion on the battlefield. Greedy and unscrupulous private contractors supplied soldiers with expensive but inadequate food. At the beginning of the war, each soldier cooked his own food; only much later were cooks detailed to prepare food for large numbers.

Weapons also were inadequate in the Union Army. Only after Edwin Stanton (1814–1869) took over the War Department in January 1862 did the supplies of weapons begin to improve; by 1864 most northern troops were outfitted with the Spencer breech-loading, single shot rifle, which allowed a soldier to fire several rounds a minute. This efficient weapon raised Union morale considerably.

Health conditions remained inadequate through much of the war. The Union Army constantly camped in unsanitary locations. Food, clothing, and campsites were so dirty that the army was plagued by bouts of diarrhea, dysentery, and typhoid, which killed thousands of soldiers. The army ambulance corps was so small that after the second Battle of Bull Run in 1862 many Union soldiers lay wounded on the field for days. Only toward the end of the war did the Union have more stringent rules of hygiene, a larger medical corps, and an increased number of hospital beds. The United States Sanitary Commission, a quasi-volunteer women's auxiliary to the Army Medical Corps, coordinated care of Union soldiers, providing nurses, supplying and staffing hospitals, and doing whatever it could to aid the sick and wounded. The Commission spent $50 million, most of it raised at local sanitary fairs.

Harper's Weekly.

An improvised hospital, flanked on the right by reserves waiting to be called into action. On the outdoor operating table, in front of the house, is a bottle of whiskey—the only anesthetic available; about the table, scattered on the ground, lie amputated limbs.

The democratic quality of American life made it difficult for officers to maintain discipline. Soldiers ignored orders with which they disagreed. After repeated defeats on the battlefield, the morale of the northern troops deteriorated steadily. Only toward the end of 1863 did army discipline improve, though desertions remained frequent. There were about 200,000 men who permanently deserted their outfits, many of them in order to return to support their impoverished families; the federal government did nothing to compensate the wives and children of soldiers, and army wages were low—eleven dollars a month at the beginning of the war, though by 1864 this amount had risen to sixteen dollars. However, because of inflation a soldier's pay in 1864 actually purchased less than in 1861.

Reports filtering back about southern camps for prisoners of war did not help Union morale. Until 1862, captured Union soldiers were released or exchanged, but after that they were interned in prisons such as Andersonville, where some 13,000 prisoners died. Of the nearly 200,000 Union prisoners captured during the war, about 30,000 died in various prisons.

The Conscription Law of 1863 also produced discontent. Before the law was passed, most of the soldiers were volunteers, moved by patriotism or enticed by bounties paid by federal, local, or state governments. (These bounties also caused problems, since many men would desert as soon as they had collected the money and then reenlist in order to receive more money.) The 1863 Conscription Law made men between twenty and forty-five subject to the draft and made them liable, if drafted, for three years' service. But prosperous men could hire substitutes or pay the federal government $300 in order to get out of fighting; this provision angered the working class and led to draft riots.

Southerners faced these same problems and generally to a greater degree. Pay was low, inflation high, soldiers suffered from a poor diet, and medical care was inadequate. The Confederacy found it difficult to maintain discipline, a problem aggravated by the 1862 Conscription Act, passed a year earlier than in the North. This law discriminated against the poor. Men who owned more than twenty slaves were exempt from the draft, which led angry soldiers to call the conflict "a rich man's war and a poor man's fight." The morale of southern troops in the closing years of the war was far lower than that of the northern troops, since the Confederates were conscious of their dwindling fortunes. Defeat at Antietam, Gettysburg, Vicksburg, Sheridan's operations in the Shenandoah Valley, and Sherman's campaign in Georgia—all these defeats undermined southern confidence.

Blacks

For a time, at least, the Civil War focused attention on black Americans. Their presence was a root cause of the war, and both North and South needed their active support to achieve victory. When this support was invited, it was not due to a sense of solidarity with blacks. Military necessity prompted white Americans to seek black assistance. Blacks soon discovered that white supremacy was by no means one of the war's casualties.

The war was a mixed experience for blacks both in the South and in the North. Northern blacks argued that the war could not be won or the Union restored without ending slavery. Their expectations were buoyed up especially by the Emancipation Proclamation of 1863, which sanctioned the enlistment of black soldiers, and by the Thirteenth Amendment (ratified in 1865), which ended slavery.

The early years of the war revealed continued discrimination against blacks on the part of northern whites. Union armies did not allow blacks to enlist, northern generals sometimes returned escaped southern slaves to their masters, and Lincoln announced that the purpose of the war was not to end slavery but to preserve the Union. After the Emancipation Proclamation, however, blacks were allowed to serve in the army. In Massachusetts blacks formed the famous Fifty-fourth Regiment, and soon filled another, the Fifty-fifth. In the Mississippi Valley some 76,000 blacks formed twenty black regiments. Northern officers recruited nearly 100,000 black volunteers in the South.

Equal service in the army did not lead to equal benefits. Black soldiers were paid lower wages, received fewer and shoddier supplies, and suffered from very inadequate medical care; the last accounted for an astonishingly high death toll among black soldiers—some 37 percent of their number. Nor did emancipation and military service ensure northern blacks the vote. Only the New England states (with the exception of Connecticut) allowed blacks to vote on the same terms as whites; elsewhere, they generally were denied the ballot. Only the ratification of the Fifteenth Amendment in 1870 opened the polls to all northern blacks.

Library of Congress.

Blacks preparing to enter the Union Army.

In the South conditions for blacks were still worse. Black slaves were forced to serve in the armies, not as soldiers but in noncombat positions as cooks, teamsters, and laborers. Some free blacks volunteered to serve in the Confederate Army, but they were never used in combat; and others, like their slave brothers, were compelled to aid the Confederate cause in numerous ways. Many more blacks deserted their masters and formed armed bands that lived off the land. Still other fugitive slaves joined the Union Army.

The Five Civilized Tribes

While Southerners had been extremely reluctant to recruit blacks for battle, they eagerly sought military alliances with the Indians living west of the Arkansas-Missouri line. In particular, Confederate supply officers hoped to secure beef, hides, horses, grain, salt, and lead from the "Five Civilized Tribes"—the Cherokees, Chickasaws, Choctaws, Creeks, and Seminoles. The Confederacy was also eager to recruit Indian warriors to guard its western border from Union troops. The territory inhabited by the Five Civilized Tribes was located between Kansas and Texas. If the Confederates controlled this area, they would be able to defend the western approaches to Arkansas, Texas, and Louisiana against a Union invasion from Kansas. In order to accomplish this end, the Confederacy sent Albert Pike (1809–1891) of Arkansas to negotiate treaties of alliance with the Five Civilized Tribes.

The Confederacy found numerous allies among the Five Civilized Tribes. Many Indian leaders were mixed-blood slaveowners who identified with the South. Furthermore, as Union forces withdrew eastward from the vicinity of the Indian territory, the Five Civilized Tribes found themselves surrounded by the Confederacy on three sides. Between May and October 1861, while public attention in the North focused on battlefields in Virginia, Confederate Commissioner Pike negotiated treaties with leaders of the Five Civilized Tribes. In return for their pledges of military support for the Confederacy, the Indians received several concessions including the right to control white traders, the exclusive right to exercise police power in their domain, and a guarantee that the Confederacy would be financially liable for the actions of any intruders on Indian lands. Although Pike's efforts to secure treaties were successful, not all the members of the tribes supported the Confederacy.

Indians fought on both sides during the Civil War. Some like Cherokee Chief John Ross urged their fellow tribesmen to "do no act that shall furnish any pretext to either side of the contending parties to overrun our country and destroy our rights." Factionalism within each of the tribes led to the creation of rival governments, each claiming to be the legitimate spokesman for the tribe. Outstanding leaders among the Indians included Opothleyahola (1790–1862), a Creek who headed the Union faction, and Stand Watie (1806–1871), a Cherokee

Division of Manuscripts, University of Oklahoma Libraries.

Stand Watie, Cherokee Confederate General.

who accepted a commission in the Confederate Army.

In early March 1862, Stand Watie commanded a regiment of Cherokee Indians at the Battle of Pea Ridge in Arkansas. The Union forces were victorious, but Stand Watie's warriors continued to harass and raid Union settlements on the western border until the end of the war. Indeed, Stand Watie, who surrendered two months after Lee's surrender at Appomattox, was one of the last Confederate generals to lay down his arms.

The Civil War wreaked havoc in the Indian Territory inhabited by the Five Civilized Tribes. Union Indians fought their Confederate tribesmen, and Union volunteers from Kansas participated in numerous operations in the Indian Territory. Guerilla bands from Arkansas and Missouri such as the one lead by the infamous William C. Quantrill (1837–1865) roamed through Indian communities stealing livestock and spreading destruction and slaughter. These bushwhackers, though proslavery in sympathy, were indiscriminate in their raiding and attacked both Union and Confederate Indian settlements.

In addition to the Five Civilized Tribes, the Civil War also had a significant impact on other Indians in the trans-Mississippi West. As Union military forces withdrew eastward during the war, the situation of various tribes differed. Some Indians seized the opportunity to avenge previous wrongs and went on the warpath. Others were harassed by local Indian-haters or by other whites who coveted their lands and became emboldened as the American public focused its attention on eastern battlefields. These events provide the background to the earliest of the Indians wars on the plains, which increased in numbers and intensity after the Civil War.

Women

Except for the blacks in the South, no group in American society was more deeply affected by the Civil War than were the women of this nation. Union women and Confederate women supported the war effort by encouraging

Harper's Weekly.

This sketch by Winslow Homer depicts the federal arsenal at Watertown, Massachusetts, where women participated in munitions-making.

enlistment, aiding in the provisioning of the soldiers, caring for the wounded, raising funds, serving as spies, and assuming the tasks of their husbands or brothers back home. Yet male chauvinism did not die easily.

Male doctors, especially in the North, were hostile to the idea of using women nurses, and they never constituted more than 20 percent of the Union nursing staff. Although this hostility was veiled as concern for the welfare of the "weaker sex," it was in fact more often an antifemale attitude. Yet one female doctor, Mary Walker, won the coveted Medal of Honor, the only member of her sex ever to do so, for her work on behalf of Union troops. Nevertheless, women nurses tended the wounded and dying on the battlefield, some 3,200 of them on both sides making it their career during the Civil War.

In the North, they were under the direction of Dorothea Dix, who stipulated that only women over thirty who were "plain in appearance" could serve. Clara Barton (1821–1912), who helped organize the International and American Red Cross in the 1880s, was one of the best-known nurses of the war. Born in Massachusetts, she gave up a teaching career because of a throat ailment and moved to Washington in 1854 to work in the Patent Office. Distressed by the treatment given Union soldiers, she went out to the Virginia battlefields without any official affiliation to care for the wounded and sick and to cook nourishing food for them. In time, she became superintendent of nurses with the Army of the James.

In the South, only the tremendous need for medical aid tempered male chauvinism and resulted in some women nurses gaining official status. The Confederacy on occasion even used slaves and black women as nurses. One white woman, Sally Tompkins (1833–1916) organized a hospital in Richmond, and Jefferson Davis commissioned her a captain in order to keep "Sally's hospital" open. Another woman, Ella Newsom (1838–1919) dedicated herself and her deceased husband's substantial fortune to establish military hospitals in the South. Her dedication won her the title "Florence Nightingale of the South."

Women aided the war effort in many other ways. One of their chief activities was forming clubs and societies that raised money to finance the commissioning of troops or to provide care for the wounded. The United States Sanitary Commission, largely an enterprise organized, supported, and staffed by women, performed noble service.

Some women participated in the war more directly; about 400 of them presumably posed as male soldiers and actually saw combat. Other women, working either for the Confederacy or the Union, functioned as spies; Rose O'Neal Greenhow (ca. 1815–1864), a society hostess in the District of Columbia, for instance, fed valuable information to Confederate officers which helped them win the first Battle of Bull Run. Still other women became camp followers, some of them traveling with their husbands, others working the camps as prostitutes.

On the home front, women stepped into the jobs abandoned by soldiers. For the first time they became "government girls," clerks in federal offices. In the retail trades, women found jobs as salesladies. Northern women followed Union troops into the South and established schools to educate newly liberated slaves; eventually southern women took their places teaching school, and by the turn of the century most of the nation's teachers were women. In the South, women turned their houses and farms into supply centers and improvised factories, manufacturing clothes, shoes, and medicines needed by troops. In many ways, the Civil War was a watershed in the struggle of women for new roles outside their homes.

Aftermath

The northern victory in the Civil War firmly established the supremacy of the federal government over the seceded states. Lincoln assumed sweeping powers as commander-in-chief in the spring of 1861 and vigorously asserted the powers of the presidency. The federal government also gained control of new areas of American life. Americans always had resisted heavy government taxation, but during the war they accepted the burden, including income taxes. And the government also drafted thousands of soldiers. Conscription struck some Americans as an invasion of their personal liberty, but wartime necessity seemed to justify the practice.

The war functioned as a stimulus to northern agriculture. Manufacturing also flourished as the Congress, dominated by the Northeast after the exodus of Southerners, pushed through legislation long sought by industrialists. Republican congressmen secured the passage of the long-disputed protectionist tariff designed to foster

Massachusetts Commandery, Military Order of the Loyal Legion and the U.S. Army Military History Institute.

Sarah Chase (bottom left) and Lucy Chase (bottom center) with a group of Normal School teachers in Norfolk, Virginia, in 1865.

Lucy Chase
(1822–1909)
Sarah Chase
(1836–1913)

Lucy Chase and her sister Sarah grew up in a large, intellectually stimulating, and prosperous Quaker household in Worcester, Massachusetts. They both shared the reforming fervor of the pre-Civil War decades, and when war erupted, proposed to become army nurses. However, perhaps because of protests from their brothers and father, they decided to work instead among freedmen now under the control of the U.S. Army. In December 1862 they received appointments as teachers and orders to report to Craney Island near Norfolk, Virginia. Each received $20 with which to purchase "an outfit"; their salary was to be $25 per month.

A few weeks later they were in the midst of 2,000 homeless, hungry, destitute ex-slaves. They worked from dawn to dusk handing out clothing, patching and sewing, and visiting the aged and ill. They encouraged the industrious, scolded those who were lazy, listened to complaints, wrote letters for their charges, and, incidentally, taught the three Rs to all eager to learn. Although under nominal military discipline, these sisters operated with considerable independence, striving to prepare blacks to take their place in a postwar South.

For all their zeal, the Chase sisters also looked out for their own well-being much of the time. They spent each summer back in Worcester far from the heat of Virginia, managed to attend inaugural balls in Washington in March 1865, and a month later joined a party touring Richmond, capital of the defeated Confederacy. During the winter of 1865–1866, they visited Georgia with an eye to teaching there but decided not to do so. Lucy, the stronger of the two and fourteen years older than Sarah, taught in Richmond and Florida until 1869, but Sarah retired to the serenity of Worcester.

The Chase sisters spent the rest of their lives in genteel repose. Lucy died in 1909, Sarah a few years later. Their work of the 1860s is chronicled in penetrating, detailed letters, some of them surprisingly modern in outlook, edited for publication by Henry L. Swint in 1966: *Dear Ones At Home.* Their words provide a dramatic portrait of an aspect of life in the Civil War period—contraband camps for ex-slaves—about which we know little. ■

Library of Congress.

In his second inaugural address, President Abraham Lincoln announced his intention to "bind up the nation's wounds."

native industry—the Morrill Tariff of March 2, 1861, and its subsequent revisions during the war (in 1862 and 1864) and after Appomattox. Another controversial government function also won approval—federal participation in the banking business, embodied in the national banking system erected in 1863 and amended in 1864.

The Civil War resolved several issues that had long divided the nation. The South's "peculiar institution" was finally abolished by the Thirteenth Amendment. The federal government under President Lincoln had forcefully asserted its dominant role in the nation's political structure. By the end of the war, business values had clearly emerged as the national ethic. Other issues, however, were still left pending. The nation would now have to grapple with the vexing problems of reconstruction and race relations in the defeated southern states.

After Lee's surrender at Appomattox, Lincoln's major concern was to bring the South back into the Union quickly and without malice. In his second inaugural address on March 4, 1865, about a month before Lee's capitulation, Lincoln made his intentions explicit: "With malice toward none; with charity for all; with firmness in the right, as God gives us to see the right, let us strive on to finish the work we are in; to bind up the nation's wounds; to care for him who shall have borne the battle, and for his widow, and his orphan—to do all which may achieve and cherish a just and a lasting peace, among ourselves, and with all nations."

On April 14, five days after Lee's surrender, Lincoln attended a play at Ford's Theater in Washington. The President's party arrived after the curtain went up, and an ovation from the audience interrupted the actors. Less than a block from the theater, four men were conspiring to kill Lincoln. The ringleader was John Wilkes Booth (1838–1865); a handsome, twenty-six-year-old actor from a Maryland family. Booth, who was subject to fits of temper, had a sentimental attachment to the South but had ignored its plight throughout the war and continued to act on northern stages. Now that the Confederacy was collapsing, Booth saw an opportunity to make a dramatic gesture and avenge the South's defeat. He first plotted to kidnap Lincoln and hold him as a hostage for the release of Confederate soldiers, but he eventually decided on assassination.

At a little after ten P.M. Booth gained access to the presidential box and coolly shot the President through the head, leapt to the stage, and shouted "*Sic semper tyrannis!* The South is avenged!" The Latin words, the motto of the state of Virginia, meant loosely that a tyrant will always be destroyed. In the jumping from the box, Booth broke a leg; with great pain he limped to the stage door and rode away into the night. A few days later, federal troops tracked him down in a barn near Bowling Green, Virginia. One of his accomplices surrendered, but Booth refused to do so and federal authorities set the structure on fire. In the uproar Booth either committed suicide or was shot by his pursuers. Although rumors of his escape persisted for many years, little doubt exists that Lincoln's assassin met his death in the Virginia tobacco barn.

The wounded President did not die immediately. He was taken across the street and attended by a host of anxious doctors and officials. Finally, at 7:22 in the morning of April 15, 1865, Lincoln breathed his last. His death was a national calamity. Even some Southerners openly wept at the news. With Lincoln's death, it seemed to many people, the chances of a moderate reconstruction of the South had vanished.

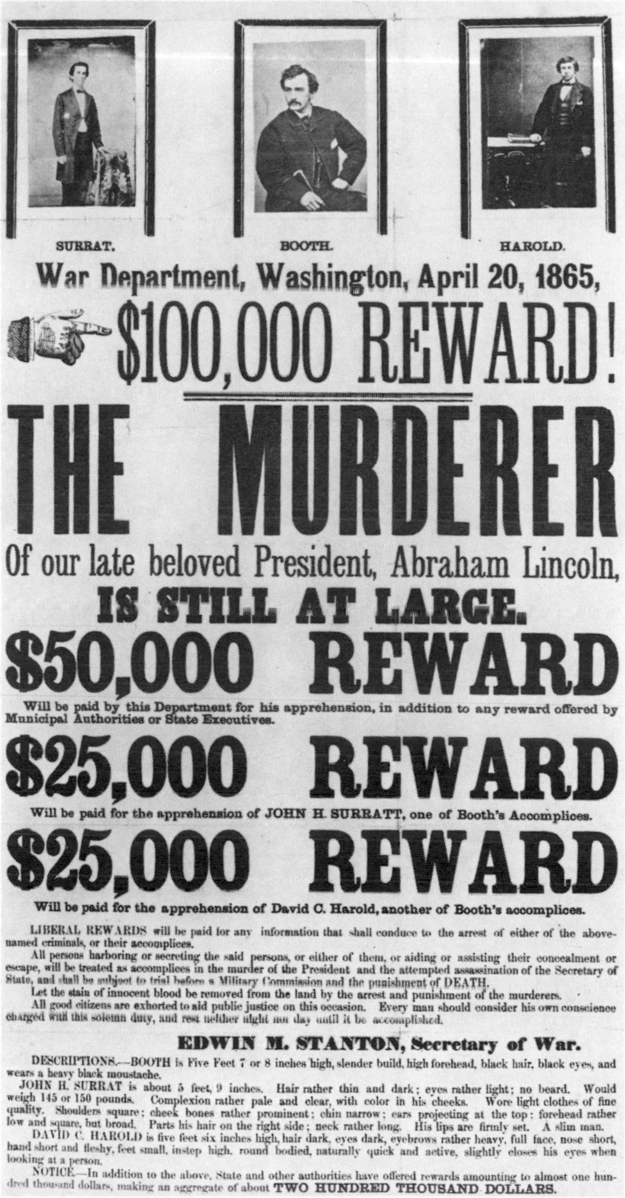

SURRAT. BOOTH. HAROLD.

War Department, Washington, April 20, 1865,

$100,000 REWARD!

THE MURDERER

Of our late beloved President, Abraham Lincoln,

IS STILL AT LARGE.

$50,000 REWARD

Will be paid by this Department for his apprehension, in addition to any reward offered by Municipal Authorities or State Executives.

$25,000 REWARD

Will be paid for the apprehension of JOHN H. SURRATT, one of Booth's Accomplices.

$25,000 REWARD

Will be paid for the apprehension of David C. Harold, another of Booth's accomplices.

LIBERAL REWARDS will be paid for any information that shall conduce to the arrest of either of the above-named criminals, or their accomplices.

All persons harboring or secreting the said persons, or either of them, or aiding or assisting their concealment or escape, will be treated as accomplices in the murder of the President and the attempted assassination of the Secretary of State, and shall be subject to trial before a Military Commission and the punishment of DEATH.

Let the stain of innocent blood be removed from the land by the arrest and punishment of the murderers.

All good citizens are exhorted to aid public justice on this occasion. Every man should consider his own conscience charged with this solemn duty, and rest neither night nor day until it be accomplished.

EDWIN M. STANTON, Secretary of War.

DESCRIPTIONS.—BOOTH is Five Feet 7 or 8 inches high, slender build, high forehead, black hair, black eyes, and wears a heavy black moustache.

JOHN H. SURRAT is about 5 feet, 9 inches. Hair rather thin and dark; eyes rather light; no beard. Would weigh 145 or 150 pounds. Complexion rather pale and clear, with color in his cheeks. Wore light clothes of fine quality. Shoulders square; cheek bones rather prominent; chin narrow; ears projecting at the top; forehead rather low and square, but broad. Parts his hair on the right side; neck rather long. His lips are firmly set. A slim man.

DAVID C. HAROLD is five feet six inches high, hair dark, eyes dark, eyebrows rather heavy, full face, nose short, hand short and fleshy, feet small, instep high, round bodied, naturally quick and active, slightly closes his eyes when looking at a person.

NOTICE.—In addition to the above, State and other authorities have offered rewards amounting to almost one hundred thousand dollars, making an aggregate of about TWO HUNDRED THOUSAND DOLLARS.

The nation was still in a state of shock five days after President Lincoln's death when the War Department offered a large reward for the President's assassin and his accomplices.

Courtesy New-York Historical Society, New York City.

Essay

War: Its Effects and Costs

The costs of waging war, both apparent and hidden, are enormous. Almost any historian or statistician can dredge up eye-boggling figures detailing how many millions or billions a modern conflict cost in money for bombs, materiel, manpower, and aircraft . . . how many buildings were destroyed in air raids . . . how many people were killed or maimed . . . how many thousands of dollars were spent on veterans' pensions after the fighting ceased . . . how many dams, schools, and hospitals could have been built with the funds expended in battle. The 600,000 men lost in the Civil War or the 291,000 Americans who died in World War II and the destruction accompanying their deaths obviously are only a small part of the total picture that has its positive side, too. Under pressure of war, in the race to outwit an enemy, nations often undertake research in medicine, technology, and industry that, because of great cost, might be unthinkable in peacetime. The growth of the American automobile industry in 1917–1918 and of atomic research during World War II are examples of this phenomenon.

Yet, in the final analysis, the true costs of war have little to do with dollar signs, daring projects rushed to completion in hush-hush secrecy, cities destroyed or cities not built. The real costs are to be found in the impact of a war experience upon those who survive and upon their way of life.

The Civil War greatly increased presidential power, made an industrial giant out of the northeastern quarter of the nation, paralyzed the South for half a century, and sowed anew seeds of racial turmoil and misunderstanding that still bear bitter fruit. It released pent-up forces favoring nation building such as transcontinental railroads, land-grant education, and a more centralized federal banking structure—measures frustrated by southern voices in the halls of Congress until April 1861.

The Civil War had a definite impact upon northern farms where an acute manpower shortage produced a dramatic shift from handheld to horsedrawn machinery. Even during the war itself, observers remarked upon this unexpected development. An official of the Ohio State Board of Agriculture wrote that "machinery and improved implements have been employed to a much greater extent during the years of the rebellion than ever before. . . . Without drills, cornplanters, reapers and mowers, horse-rakes, hay elevators, and threshing machines, it would have been impossible to have seeded and gathered the crops of 1863 with the implements in use forty or fifty years ago. . . ."

World War II produced a similar shift on the nation's farms from horses to tractor-drawn or gas-propelled machinery. Before 1940 many farmers tilled their fields with a combination of animal- and gas-power implements, but by 1945 the sturdy horse and mule had all but disappeared.

Many of these wartime results were by no means anticipated. In fact, Americans usually have fought for what seem to be very specific goals such as independence, preservation of the Union, making the world safe for democracy, or the containment of Communism. At the outset, they were secure in the belief that

Cornell Capa/Magnum.

Inger Abrahamsen/Rapho-Photo Researchers.

These scenes of business activity on the floor of the New York Stock Exchange and the rows of graves in Arlington National Cemetery provide two different perspectives on the impact of war on American society.

victory would guarantee an automatic return to things as they were before the current trouble erupted. But peace very often has arrived hand-in-hand with unforeseen dilemmas and numerous byproducts, some bad, some good. The Peace of Paris (1783) brought an independence of sorts and a chaotic five- or six-year interim that gave birth to a stronger, more workable federal structure. The War of 1812 perhaps nailed down the fact of independence and certainly stirred a flurry of national spirit; more importantly, as European imports declined, that brief encounter and the acrimony surrounding it generated an economic boom that gave birth to scores of mills and factories and set into motion forces that would come into conflict at Fort Sumter a half century later. And, of course, the Mexican War hastened the showdown on slavery.

The major conflicts of this century—two world wars and the so-called Cold War with its warmer moments in Korea and Vietnam—also have had profound economic impact. World War I fed a boom that ended in a depression which, in turn, had much to do with the onset of World War II. That conflict certainly provided jobs and ended unemployment, ushering in a generation of prosperity; but, by the 1970s, many Americans were beginning to question seriously the merits of unrestricted growth and development.

The specific effects of World War I include a quickening of the black migration from the South to the North with vast social and political implications, a disillusionment with the great crusade to make the world safe for democracy, and a lowering or a shift in social mores that produced flappers, bathtub gin, and the Roaring Twenties. World War II greatly accelerated the black demand for full equality, increased the flow of women into the work force where many remained, and initiated a baby boom with an untold effect in ensuing decades for realms such as education, housing, department-store sales and even for the protest marches of the 1960s. Korea gave us the conservative backlash of McCarthyism and a silent generation of young people fearful to speak out, eager to hide within a safe corporate structure by day and in suburbia at night. The slow involvement in Vietnam, apparently engineered or at least condoned by forces Americans had been taught to revere—officials at the highest level of the federal government, corporate executives, and military experts—eventually produced anything but silence. In fact, the ongoing ripples from faraway Vietnam are still felt today in recurring waves of inflation and hot debate over national goals.

Over a quarter century of "nonpeace" has bestowed upon America something it never had before: a gigantic peacetime military force centered in the Pentagon that seems to wield more

Brown Brothers.

The great migration of Blacks from the South to northern cities that began during World War I was a major watershed in the history of American blacks. Today, blacks mainly live in urban areas.

and more power in many realms of American life. No less a military man than Dwight D. Eisenhower (West Point graduate, career man, five-star general) in his farewell address as President (1961) leveled a warning finger at America's military-industrial complex.

> “Now this conjunction of an immense military establishment and a large arms industry is new to the American experience. The total influence—economic, political, even spiritual—is felt in every city, every state house, every office of the Federal Government. We recognize the imperative need for this development. Yet we must not fail to comprehend its grave implications. Our toil, resources and livelihood are all involved; so is the very structure of our society.”

The answer, according to the retiring President, was to guard against the unwarranted influence of the military-industrial complex. It was the duty of the nation's leaders, he concluded, to mold, balance, and integrate such forces so as to be certain that a free, democratic society would survive.

Sidney Harris.

An important question facing contemporary society is: how can America meet the demands of a permanent war economy—a large standing army and an ever-expanding industrial sector relying on military contracts—while still preserving traditional principles and values?

Many persons in and out of Congress are much concerned with this very problem of balancing military needs and expenses with those of the domestic sector. Everyone agrees that the United States needs a military guardian of some sort, but perhaps on a less expansive scale. Yet it is most difficult to "bell" the military cat. The menace of Communism—real or exaggerated—has been the rallying cry for the forces President Eisenhower sought to curb, and those who shout the loudest in behalf of the military-industrial complex tend to be conservative in economic, social, and political matters as well and eager to buttress the status quo both at home and abroad. This means that social reforms, even if badly needed, may be shelved or delayed. After all, this was what the uproar of the 1960s was about: money expended in a questionable effort to uphold the status quo in Vietnam supposedly at the expense of domestic reform in the United States.

Just as the Civil War elevated industrialists to a position from which they ruled America for over half a century. World War II and its aftermath did much the same for the Pentagon generals and their think-tank, computerized satellites. Only the future can tell whether their reign also will go unchallenged for five or six decades, but chinks in the armor are evident, Vietnam being the most obvious. Nevertheless, the military-industrial complex, a necessary fact of life in present-day America, clearly is the most obvious byproduct of World War II. This combination of military and industrial self-interest influences all of our lives and pocketbooks directly and if reckoned as a "cost of war" becomes too staggering to contemplate.

In essence, war is an unpredictable force for much evil and perhaps some good in the life of any nation. Even the victor discovers it does strange things to his civilization and to the daily life of his fellow countrymen. In fact, sometimes those who win face the greatest dilemmas. The vanquished wipe the slate clean and begin anew; their adversaries are encumbered by the spoils of war and the responsibility for reestablishing peacetime modes of life, if that is truly possible. Clearly the costs and the effects of war extend far beyond the months or years between the first and last salvo; they are, in fact, intricately woven into the fabric of every nation, sadly even those who choose to remain aloof and neutral.

Selected Readings

General Accounts

James G. Randall and David Donald, *The Civil War and Reconstruction* (rev., 2nd ed., 1973)

Civil War (1973)

David Donald, ed., *Why the North Won the Civil War* (1960)

Allen Nevins, *The War for the Union* (4 vols., 1959–71)

The Road to War

William B. Catton and Bruce Catton, *Two Roads to Sumter* (1963)

Kenneth M. Stampp, *And the War Came: The North and the Secession Crisis, 1860–61* (1950)

Robert G. Gunderson, *Old Gentleman's Convention: The Washington Peace Conference of 1861* (1961)

Richard N. Current, *Lincoln and the First Shot* (1963)

Military History

Bruce Catton, *The Centennial History of the Civil War* (3 vols., 1961–65)

Shelby Foote, *The Civil War: A Narrative* (3 vols., 1958–74)

John F. C. Fuller, *Grant and Lee* (1957)

James A. Rawley, *Turning Points of the Civil War* (1966)

William B. Hesseltine, *Civil War Prisons: A Study in War Psychology* (1930)

The Union: Special Studies

George M. Frederickson, *The Inner Civil War: Northern Intellectuals and the Crisis of the Union* (1965)

Louis S. Gerteis, *From Contraband to Freedom: Federal Policy Toward Southern Blacks, 1861–1865* (1973)

Norman B. Ferris, *The Trent Affair: A Diplomatic Crisis* (1977)

James McCague, *Second Rebellion: The Story of the New York*

William L. Barney, *Flawed Victory: A New Perspective on The Civil War* (1975)

Robert Cruden, *The War that Never Ended: The American City Draft Riots of 1863* (1968)

Frank L. Klement, *The Limits of Dissent: Clement L. Vallandigham and the Civil War* (1970)

The Confederacy: Special Studies

Emory M. Thomas, *The Confederacy as a Revolutionary Experience* (1971)

Thomas L. Connelly and Archer Jones, *The Politics of Command: Factions and Ideas in Confederate Strategy* (1973)

Charles W. Ramsdell, *Behind the Lines in the Southern Confederacy* (1944)

Frank L. Owsley and H. C. Owsley, *King Cotton Diplomacy: Foreign Relations of the Confederate States of America*, (rev. 2nd ed., 1959)

Robert F. Durden, *The Gray and the Black: The Confederate Debate on Emancipation* (1972)

The People Who Fought the War

Bell I. Wiley, *The Common Soldier of the Civil War* (1975)

James M. McPherson, *The Negro's Civil War: How American Negroes Felt and Acted During the War for the Union* (1965)

Annie H. Abel, *The American Indian as Participant in the Civil War* (1919)

Frank Cunningham, *General Stand Watie's Confederate Indians* (1959)

Mary E. Massey, *Bonnet Brigades: American Women and the Civil War* (1966)

Marjorie B. Greenbie, *Lincoln's Daughters of Mercy* (1944)

Bell I. Wiley, *Confederate Women* (1975)

Chapter 15

Restoring the Union

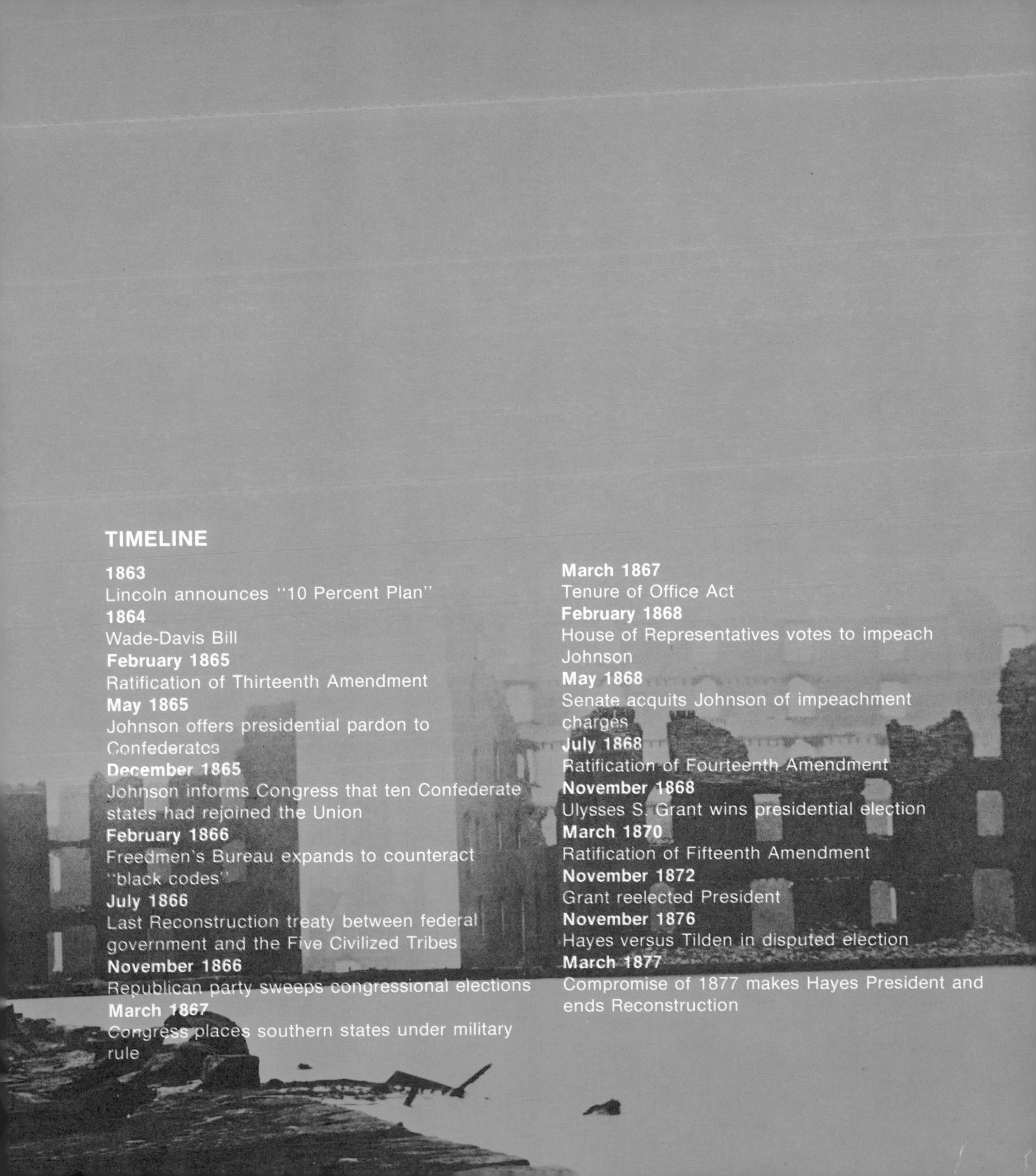

TIMELINE

1863
Lincoln announces "10 Percent Plan"

1864
Wade-Davis Bill

February 1865
Ratification of Thirteenth Amendment

May 1865
Johnson offers presidential pardon to Confederates

December 1865
Johnson informs Congress that ten Confederate states had rejoined the Union

February 1866
Freedmen's Bureau expands to counteract "black codes"

July 1866
Last Reconstruction treaty between federal government and the Five Civilized Tribes

November 1866
Republican party sweeps congressional elections

March 1867
Congress places southern states under military rule

March 1867
Tenure of Office Act

February 1868
House of Representatives votes to impeach Johnson

May 1868
Senate acquits Johnson of impeachment charges

July 1868
Ratification of Fourteenth Amendment

November 1868
Ulysses S. Grant wins presidential election

March 1870
Ratification of Fifteenth Amendment

November 1872
Grant reelected President

November 1876
Hayes versus Tilden in disputed election

March 1877
Compromise of 1877 makes Hayes President and ends Reconstruction

CHAPTER OUTLINE

The end of the Civil War on the battlefield ushered in many problems relating to the restoration of the Union. Lincoln's Emancipation Proclamation of 1863 abolished slavery in the areas in rebellion and the Thirteenth Amendment (declared in force on December 18, 1865) eliminated that institution throughout the rest of the nation, yet many dilemmas existed. Could the bitterness of four years of fratricidal strife be forgotten, or would it remain an emotional legacy for years to come? What would become of the black man in a South so ravaged and traumatized? Would he be able to keep his freedom? The South, stunned by defeat, lay prostrate and bloody. Four years of war had disrupted business and agriculture, labor was in chaos, and many institutions of normal daily life—especially in Virginia, the Carolinas, and Georgia where fighting only recently ceased—were virtually nonexistent.

One month after Lincoln's assassination on April 14, 1865, the British actress Ellen Kean reflected on the future of the American Union:

> "The South is *crushed,* there is no doubt of that, their army was killed out by the never-ending supply of fresh men in the Northern army. All the flower of the Southern youth is under the sod, all that remains of them are lads, old men, and broken-hearted women. Utter ruin stares them in the face. Not only are their houses burnt, and the system of labour destroyed but they even destroyed all the agricultural instruments. They have neither money nor tools. The iron heel is on them and they will be trodden out of existence. All the sweet Plantation life is gone for ever, and I fear the poor Negro will suffer with the Planter. The hopes of the South are ended. The difficulties of the North are *beginning.*"

Ellen Kean. *Death and Funeral of Abraham Lincoln with Some Remarks on the State of America at the Close of the Civil War* (London: Privately Printed, 1921), pp. 26–27.

An immediate question for the North was the readmission of the seceded states: when, how, and under what terms were they to rejoin the Union? Though the North was solidly committed to the ideal of unification, no such solidarity was evident in proposals concerning readmission, treatment of the defeated South, enfranchisement of blacks, and reestablishment of state governments.

W. L. Sheppard, Museum of the Confederacy, Richmond

A Confederate soldier's homecoming.

Lincoln and Preparations for Reconstruction

The question of reconstruction arose as early as 1861, when Lincoln raised the subject, though not the word, in his address to a special session of Congress on July 4th. Lincoln assured Congress that he would be guided by the Constitution in his policy toward the rebellious states after their insurrection was suppressed. Lincoln's foresight reveals both optimism and political pragmatism. The Constitution provided no guidelines for reconstruction, since nowhere in it was the issue of secession raised. This, in fact, was the great argument of the southern states: they had not violated the Constitution, since it had not explicitly forbidden secession. Lincoln argued consistently that the perpetuity of the Union was implied if not expressed in the Constitution. He insisted that, since the Union was older than the states, no state could reserve for itself the power to secede, nor could an individual state have entered the Union in the first place without having tacitly surrendered some of its sovereignty. "Our States have neither more, nor less power, than that reserved to them, in the union, by the Constitution—no one of them ever having been a State *out* of the Union," Lincoln contended. He concluded that the South had, in fact, not seceded at all; it was in the hands of revolutionaries or insurrectionists. Though Lincoln in his April 15, 1861, proclamation had called on the militia to suppress disloyalty, the implications of his policy were not carried out: Confederate prisoners were regarded as prisoners of war and were not tried for treason.

Attitude of Conciliation

From the beginning of the war, Lincoln maintained a conciliatory and generous attitude toward the South. In December 1863 he informed the nation of his intention to provide for the full restoration of the southern states to the Union. Such restoration could occur after one-tenth of the citizens in each state who voted in the presidential election of 1860 swore allegiance to the Constitution and formed a new state government that abolished slavery and repudiated secession. Lincoln's 10 percent plan, as it came to be called, provided a system whereby the states could reestablish their former relationship with the federal government.

Since Lincoln insisted that the states had never left the Union, he asserted that as President he had the power to grant pardons to individuals or even amnesty to groups. He believed that this executive prerogative would be the speediest possible way to restore the belligerent states to the Union. If the method of restoration were left up to Congress, Lincoln believed, this approach would invite delay as well as open the door to northern dissension.

Lincoln's plan aimed at a speedy restoration with a minimum of federal intervention in internal state affairs. He intended to give the majority of Southerners amnesty and full powers to restore loyal state governments. Even Confederate leaders might be pardoned, though the primary architects of rebellion, Lincoln hoped, would go into exile. Southern Whigs, who had been at the forefront of opponents to secession, would be established in powerful positions in state governments and affiliate themselves with the Republican party.

Long before Robert E. Lee surrendered at Appomattox in 1865, there were rehearsals for reconstruction in Tennessee, Louisiana, Arkansas, and the sea islands off South Carolina soon after these areas fell to the Union forces. As early as 1862, Lincoln established military governors in areas under Union control and encouraged loyal citizens to establish pro-Union governments. Indeed, he was willing to pardon Confederate soldiers who would take oaths of loyalty to the Constitution and to exonerate all citizens who had not borne arms. Because he wanted to be certain that southern defeat did not produce martyrs and because he realized that the Republican party would need the support of ex-Confederates if it were to make significant inroads into the South, Lincoln promised full pardons.

In 1864, before the end of the war, Lincoln had already made some progress toward the formation of loyal or pro-Union state governments; in particular, his emissaries worked closely with former Whig politicians in Tennessee, Louisiana, and Arkansas.

While Lincoln's benevolence influenced his policy toward the South, he was nevertheless a shrewd politician. He adhered to the conservative principles of the Whig party which had given him his start. Throughout his difficulties with Congress, particularly with Radical Republicans, he remained an astute statesman whose political acumen alone kept Congress and the administration functioning with reasonable harmony and efficiency. If Lincoln had a personal hero, it was the Whig statesman Henry Clay of Kentucky. Lincoln clung to the ideals of the Whig party well into the early 1850s and was not one of the original organizers of the new Republican party. This ideological legacy—combined with his acute awareness of the fact that Southerners generally held him personally responsible for beginning the war—was a major factor in his decision to treat the South as liberally as he could. At the same time, his innate conservatism and eagerness for harmonious reconciliation clashed with the goals of a group of Republicans on Capitol Hill.

The Wade-Davis Bill

As noted earlier in Chapter 14, Lincoln's plans ran into some difficulty when Congress asserted its own jurisdiction over reconstruction in July 1864. Radical Republican Senator Benjamin F. Wade of Ohio and Representative Henry W. Davis of Maryland introduced a severe reconstruction proposal, the so-called Wade-Davis Bill, which required a majority of the electorate in each southern state to take a loyalty oath and banned ex-Confederates from participation in state government. Lincoln easily blocked the measure by a pocket veto since Congress passed the Wade-Davis bill on the last day of its session.

Despite opposition from Radical Republicans, Lincoln adhered to his ten percent plan. By January of 1865, Tennessee followed Louisiana and Arkansas in offering Washington a loyal state government. Technically, these states were ready to be restored to their full privileges within the Union under Lincoln's plan, but Congress remained adamant in its refusal to seat senators and representatives from these states.

The Thirteenth Amendment

Actually, Republicans in Congress faced several political dilemmas. The Thirteenth Amendment abolishing slavery throughout the nation in February 1865, was now being considered by various states. Since acceptance would void the three-fifths clause of the Constitution, the southern states might return to the Union with larger congressional delegations than they had in 1861. Southern whites might even to able to coerce the freedmen into supporting conservative Democrats rather than Republican candidates. Also, black suffrage in the South might bring increased black suffrage in the North—but would northern whites accept black voters? Such matters perplexed congressional Republicans, and the stalemate between them and the President continued until Lincoln's death.

If formation of loyal state governments led to severe disagreement between the executive and the legislature, the question of dealing with the active Confederate supporters was also thorny. Both Lincoln and Congress agreed as early as 1862 that no mass executions for treason would take place. But in the summer of that same year, Congress passed a sweeping measure based on the idea of treason, the so-called Second Confiscation Act. The first act (August 6, 1861) had ordered the seizure of all property used for insurrectionary purposes. The second (July 17, 1862) provided for the punishment of treason by fines and imprisonment as well as by death and the punishment of actions of "rebellion or insurrection" by fine, imprisonment, and confiscation of property, including slaves. Although the Act of 1862 confirmed the

Library of Congress.

Benjamin Franklin Wade (1800–1878)

One of Lincoln's severest critics during the Civil War, Wade was a Republican Senator. He was reared in New England but moved to Andover, Ohio when he was a young man. There he tried a number of professions, working as a farmer, drover, laborer, medical student, and teacher before he finally decided to study law. As a lawyer he had one of the most successful practices in northeastern Ohio, but quickly turned to politics. From the very beginning he allied himself with the antislavery forces.

After serving as a state senator and as a judge and an antislavery leader in 1851, he was elected by the Ohio legislature to the United States Senate, where he served continuously until 1869. Wade attempted in 1852 to repeal the Fugitive Slave Law and later denounced the Kansas-Nebraska Bill. During the secession crisis of 1860 and 1861, he took a militant stand against all compromise plans including the Crittenden proposals.

Once war broke out, Wade was a passionate advocate of a stern, relentless offensive. When McClellan stalled after the first Battle of Bull Run, Wade tongue-lashed him repeatedly. As chairman of the Committee on the Conduct of the War, a congressional group that heaped criticism on the administration, he personally lashed out at the President and his generals. He disliked Lincoln intensely, especially after the President suggested a moderate reconstruction policy in 1863. In response to that proposal, Wade and Henry Winter Davis drew up a punitive congressional plan, dubbed the Wade-Davis Bill.

Lincoln vetoed this measure, prompting its authors to issue the Wade-Davis Manifesto, condemning Lincoln's action as a "studied outrage on the legislative authority" of Congress; according to Wade, Congress alone should establish a policy for the reconstruction of the South. The President's plan, Wade announced, was "absurd, monarchical and anti-American."

After Lincoln's assassination, Wade fully expected President Johnson to cooperate more fully with the policies of the Radical Republicans against the defeated South. But when Johnson surprised the Radicals by endorsing Lincoln's plan, Wade joined forces with his fellow Radicals Charles Sumner and Thaddeus Stevens in attacking the new President. In 1867 Wade became president pro tempore of the Senate, a position that in those days made him next in line for the presidency. Wade fully expected that the impeachment proceedings against Johnson would lead to the President's removal from office; accordingly, the Ohioan began to choose his own Cabinet members. When Johnson was acquitted, Wade had to abandon his presidential ambitions. In 1868 he made an unsuccessful attempt to win the nomination as Grant's vice-presidential candidate. Failing to win reelection to the Senate, Wade returned to his law practice in Ohio. ■

Library of Congress.

The Thirteenth Amendment freed all slaves.

government's position against wholesale executions, enforcement would have redistributed the huge landed estates and destroyed the planter aristocracy. Lincoln, however doubted the constitutionality of this measure and his attorney general made no serious effort to enforce it. In December 1863, Lincoln announced his 10 percent plan, which offered full pardons as well as protection from the Confiscation Act to those taking the oath of allegiance.

On March 4, 1865, the day after Congress established the Freedmen's Bureau to care for freed slaves, Lincoln made his second inaugural address, pleading for moderation: "With malice toward none . . . let us strive . . . to bind up the nation's wounds." In his final public appearance, in April, he again called for a generous reconstruction. Lincoln's assassination was a blow to the South as well as to many citizens of the North.

Just hours after Lincoln's death, Senator Wade and a small group of Radical Republicans who were members of the Congressional Committee on the Conduct of the War met in Washington to plan their reconstruction strategy. Some of them believed, as Representative George W. Julian (1817–1899) of Indiana put it, that the President's death was "a godsend to the country." Julian was not a fanatic; he sincerely felt that a "soft" peace, which enabled Confederate leaders to regain political and economic power, would make a mockery of much of the hardship the Union had endured. During his entire political career, Julian had been a fervent abolitionist. Like Wade and his colleagues, Julian hoped that Lincoln's successor would sympathize with their views on reconstructing the southern states.

Johnson and Reconstruction

Tennessean Andrew Johnson (1808–1875), the new Vice President, was a dedicated Unionist. Johnson, a Democrat, repudiated secession and refused to abandon his seat in the Senate when Tennessee seceded. In addition, he served at Lincoln's request on the Committee on the Conduct of the War and worked without rancor with such Radicals as Wade and Chandler. In 1862, after Union troops occupied much of Tennessee, Lincoln appointed him military governor, and in 1864 the President made him his vice presidential running mate.

Johnson was a self-educated man who had risen from poverty in North Carolina and Tennessee and who hated the aristocrats of the South. The Radicals hoped that he shared their views on reconstruction, and they had good reasons to believe he did. He had fought hard to preserve the integrity of the Union. Like them, he had supported ratification of the Thirteenth Amendment. Moreover, his vitriolic remarks about the southern aristocrats who had "dragooned" the ordinary Southerners, the humble men, into the war warmed their hearts as did his contention that the aristocratic class had to be destroyed. Johnson's efforts to undermine the southern planters helps to explain his reconstruction program, which barred those with sizable property from taking the oath of allegiance. This prohibition, Johnson hoped, would transfer political power and economic benefits from large property holders to the yeomanry.

The Radicals soon discovered, however, that Johnson was not *their* man. Congress was in recess when Lincoln was assassinated, and Johnson was President for nine months, from April to December 1865, before it reconvened. His actions during this period dismayed the Radicals. He recognized the loyal governments of Arkansas, Louisiana, Tennessee, and Virginia established under Lincoln's 10 percent plan. On May 29, 1865, Johnson offered presidential amnesty to Confederates taking the oath of allegiance, although he excluded several classes (holders of taxable property worth $20,000 or more, for example). But even the wealthy under Johnson's plan could petition the President for special pardons.

Indeed, to the surprise of Confederates and Unionists alike, Johnson granted these pardons rather liberally. Moreover, he began organizing provisional governments

Library of Congress.

Andrew Johnson in a photograph taken in 1865.

for the remaining ex-Confederate states and empowered provisional governors to assemble conventions composed of "loyal" citizens to amend state constitutions, ratify the Thirteenth Amendment, and repudiate the Confederate war debt. By December 1865 when Congress reconvened, every Confederate state except Texas had fulfilled Johnson's requirements (Texas did so by April 1866). Johnson then informed Congress that these states were ready to seat their Senators and Representatives in Congress. Although the Radicals were alarmed by these moves, they reacted slowly until by the summer of 1866 they had won sufficient support from other Republicans to challenge Johnson's role in reconstruction.

Johnson's Motives

Why did Johnson take a new approach to reconstruction after he had convinced the Radicals that he and they had so much in common? There is a distinct possibility that Johnson was influenced by his adroit Secretary of State, William H. Seward, who had been urging the establishment of a new national conservative political party that would attract Southerners. Perhaps Johnson wanted the presidential nomination in 1868 in his own right and realized he needed a firm political base in order to achieve that goal. Some historians have maintained that, sobered by the responsibility of power, Johnson began to see no alternative to leniency once he recognized duly elected southern officials. Others suggest that his change of policy resulted from weakness or fear: either he lacked the ruthlessness necessary to implement a harsh reconstruction plan or his growing fear of northern capitalists made him see the political value of retaining the planter class as a balancing force.

It is quite possible that Johnson's experiences as a Jacksonian Democrat gave him a political orientation at variance with that of Lincoln and the Radical Republicans. But part of the reason for Johnson's failure to implement either Lincoln's plan or the policy of the Radical Republicans lies in the fact that the planter aristocrats proved to be far more astute politicians than he. Johnson's vanity was fed when members of the planter aristocracy came to him seeking special pardons. Had Johnson not been a vain man, they would have found nothing to exploit. But once they discovered his weakness, they easily led him to compromise his positions to such an extent that finally he had to side with them against the Radicals or to admit he had failed—and thus invite Congress to take over the responsibility of reconstruction.

Johnson's reputation has undergone a number of historical reevaluations. In the 1920s he usually was portrayed as courageous, a man who defended constitutional rights and popular democracy in a spirit of reconciliation against vengeful Radicals and rapacious northern capitalists. In 1960, Eric L. McKitrick challenged this view, portraying Johnson as stubborn, provincial, and inept, a President who misunderstood public sentiment, particularly in the North and who misled the South about northern intentions. Johnson, according to McKitrick, alienated moderates in Congress, thus losing whatever bargaining power he may have had there. In McKitrick's view Johnson's failures can be attributed to his being an "outsider." Though he had undeniable abilities, he was a maverick. The same plebian origins that made him independent, also made him vulnerable.

Black Codes

Perhaps Johnson's greatest failure was his decision to abandon the southern freedmen to the mercy of their former masters. Johnson demanded that the southern states accept the Thirteenth Amendment, but he did not require Southerners to deal fairly with the freedmen. The new governments in the South barred freedmen from

Library of Congress.

The Black Codes replaced slavery in the South and virtually established a system of peonage for blacks. Here, a freedman is being sold to pay his fine.

voting, failed to make any provision for educating them, and took other steps to keep them illiterate, unskilled, and without property. These governments enacted *black codes* between 1865 and 1866 as a system of social control to replace slavery.

These codes condemned blacks to a subordinate and carefully regulated position in the social order in the hope of providing a manageable and inexpensive labor force for southern planters. The codes declared that blacks who were unemployed or without permanent residence should be treated as vagrants subject to fine, arrest, imprisonment, or forced labor. The words "master" and "slave" actually appeared in the labor contracts utilized in some of the southern states. Laws were passed that legalized marriages between blacks but banned interracial marriages. Blacks in South Carolina were required to obtain special licenses before they could enter any occupation other than agriculture. In Mississippi, blacks could not rent or lease land. Throughout the South, the codes led to racial segregation in public facilities and subjected blacks to discrimination in court procedures and in making contracts.

Within a few years *sharecropping* emerged as the replacement for the former slave-labor system in the South. As the freedmen were forced to buy their goods at plantation stores, a system of taking liens on their crops emerged. Crop liens led to debt peonage. Peonage and debt servitude blended so well into the southern way of life after the Civil War, bolstered by labor laws, customs, and governmental apathy, that its existence became widely known only in the early 1900s. Thus, the new postwar governments in the South promoted disenfranchisement, discrimination, segregation, sharecropping, and debt peonage.

Library of Congress.

Thaddeus Stevens, Radical Republican leader.

Congressional Reconstruction

When the first session of the Thirty-ninth Congress assembled in December 1865, Radical Republicans Thaddeus Stevens (1792–1868), Charles Sumner, and Benjamin Wade sought to have Congress take control of the course of reconstruction. Although only a minority in Congress, and, indeed, in the Republican party itself, the Radicals soon came to impose their policies on the majority. At that time, there were four different caucuses in Congress including the Radicals. Two groups, smaller even than the Radicals, were the demoralized remnants of the Democratic minority, led by Senators Samuel S. Cox of Ohio and Thomas A. Hendricks of Indiana. There was also a small group of conversative Republicans committed to the President, men like James R. Doolittle of Wisconsin, James Dixon of Connecticut, Edgar Cowan of Pennsylvania, and Henry Raymond of New York. But the most potentially powerful group was made up of moderate Republicans who wavered between supporting the President and siding with the Radicals. When Congress convened, Johnson still held the favor of the moderates, partly because he had nearly completed his reconstruction program and partly because it seemed to have won general approval throughout the North.

Soon, however, the Radicals began to exert new strength. First of all, President Johnson became increasingly inflexible and tactless in dealing with Congress. In addition, politicians in control of governments he had helped establish in the southern states took actions that angered northern public opinion. Not only had they passed the black codes, they were also completely indifferent to the effects of their actions in the North. Second, the Radicals knew what they wanted in terms of reconstruction in contrast to Johnson's seemingly inconsistent policies, and they were prepared to work strenuously to achieve their ends. As a result, some moderate Republicans were drawn into their camp. By the summer of 1866, the Radicals had made sufficient alliances within their party to control Congress and to take over the direction of reconstruction.

The Motivation of the Radicals

What motivated the Radicals in their policies toward the South? Long historical debate has not yet settled this controversy. Some men like Thaddeus Stevens of Pennsylvania apparently were motivated by a combination of factors: vindictiveness toward the South, idealism, and an equally powerful desire to maintain the ascendancy of the Republican party in the South. Some historians have suggested, with good evidence, that a commitment to the interests of northern capitalism was a fourth and perhaps even the principal motive of some Radicals.

Almost from the beginning of the historical examination of Reconstruction, American writers have been of one accord in condemning it as "tragic," a national disgrace, and "an age of hate." In the 1890s, James Ford Rhodes (1848–1927) branded the Radicals as "uncivilized." Early in the twentieth century a talented professor of history, William A. Dunning (1857–1922) of Columbia University, defined the attitude toward radical reconstruction that was to dominate American thought for the next fifty years. Supported by political popularizers such as Claude Bowers in *The Tragic Era* (1929), this view distorted the post-Civil War period in the public mind.

This interpretation held that the Radicals were motivated by a vindictiveness that nothing could abate. Driven by hatred of the South and selfish economic and political interests, only Lincoln's compassion for human suffering held them in check. Once Lincoln died, they used that tragedy to push through Congress their program for southern humiliation. In this view, Johnson is seen as sincerely trying to foster Lincoln's original plans, for which the Radicals viciously attempted to impeach him. Failing this, they elected Ulysses S. Grant President and engineered a corruption of government hitherto unprecedented. Finally, the triumph of states' rights in the South with the removal of federal troops signalled the redemption of decency in politics.

This view held, in short, that Radical Republicanism was sheer hypocrisy. More recently, scholars such as Kenneth M. Stampp have reminded us that the program of the Radicals had its roots in the antislavery crusade. Like the abolitionists, the Radicals spoke of regenerating the South and talked much of their sacred duties, of the will of God, and of the evils of compromise. Thaddeus Stevens declared in a speech to the House of Representatives on January 3, 1867: "I am for Negro suffrage in every rebel state. If it be just, it should not be denied; if it is to be necessary, it should be adopted; if it be a punishment to traitors, they deserve it."

Black suffrage was politically advantageous for the Republican party. Stevens himself frankly admitted that he favored black suffrage in the South because "it would insure the ascendancy" of the party. Before he became an advocate of black suffrage, however, he had hoped to

Library of Congress.

This cartoon shows President Andrew Johnson and Radical Republican leader Thaddeus Stevens on a collision course concerning Reconstruction.

provide the freedmen with an economic base of confiscated land to protect them from the exploitation of southern planters. He had argued that forty acres, a mule, and a hut would be more valuable to the freed blacks than suffrage.

Other Northerners had always pinned their hopes for the freedmen on their obtaining the right to vote. President Johnson, in contrast, demanded that the South continue to be a "white man's country" since "it must be acknowledged that in the progress of nations negroes have shown less capacity for government than any other race of people. . . . Of all the dangers which our nation has yet encountered, none are equal to those which must result from the success of the effort now making to Africanize the [southern] half of our country." These comments were part of Johnson's third annual address to Congress, and they incensed Radicals like Charles Sumner and Benjamin Wade. They warned that the franchise was needed to provide protection for freed blacks. Moderate Republicans, however, hoped to find some alternative between the black codes of the southern states and the position of these Radicals. Eventually, Sumner and Wade won other Radicals and the moderates over to their suffrage ideas. They were unwilling to reward the South by allowing the seceded states to return to Congress with more representatives than when they had left the Union as a result of the abolition of slavery and of the three-fifths clause. Many Republicans thus saw the enfranchisement of blacks and a vigorous campaign to align them with Republicanism as the only solution to this perplexing problem. Gideon Wells (1802–1878), Johnson's Secretary of the Navy, described the root of the movement for black suffrage as political advantage rather than philanthropy, though his strong support for Johnson's reconstruction program raises serious questions about his objectivity.

Even moderate Republicans feared the prospect of a southern-western agrarian alliance in the Democratic party dominating national politics. In addition, opposition to the black codes helped cement an alliance of Radicals and moderates. The adoption of the codes convinced many congressmen that a plot existed to maintain slavery in disguise. Thus they decided upon an independent course and proceeded to carry out a more radical reconstruction program than that proposed by President Johnson.

The Radicals, like the early nineteenth century reformers, viewed their work as a great crusade. Although these men were experienced politicians who had learned to accommodate themselves to the practical realities of public life, many had come from the ranks of the abolitionists or at least shared their moral idealism. The pleas of Radicals for justice to blacks and their warnings that the black codes were restoring a form of slavery reflect this idealism.

The Freedmen's Bureau

Congress sought to counteract the black codes by an act of February 19, 1866, that enlarged the Freedmen's Bureau. Established in March 1865 as a temporary bureau to care for the freedmen and the abandoned lands of the South, this paternalistic agency headed by General Oliver C. Howard (1830–1909) helped thousands of refugees, white Unionists, and freed blacks obtain food, shelter, and jobs.

Within four years the Bureau, which worked closely with the U.S. Army, issued twenty-one million rations, established forty hospitals, and spent more than $2 million in treating 450,000 sick people of both races. Although few blacks ever got their "forty acres and a mule," harrassed Bureau agents were especially active in the fields of labor relations and education. They fought hard to make certain that ex-slaves were treated fairly and that, in turn, ex-masters received a reasonable amount of work for wages paid.

The Bureau's greatest success was in education. Its agents established a variety of schools that included day schools, Sunday schools, industrial schools, and even colleges and universities. By 1870, more than 250,000 blacks were in 4,300 schools aided by the Bureau and various philanthropic and religious groups. Howard University (named for the Bureau's director), Hampton Institute, and Atlanta and Fisk universities are among the best known of the institutions that flourished with Bureau help.

Nevertheless, the Bureau had its troubles. Though Howard, known as "the Christian General," viewed the problems of the ex-slaves as an opportunity for evangelical and charitable service, some bureau agents were incompetent, some corrupt, and others were converted to the argument that white Southerners "knew their people best." Also, the Bureau always faced open scorn from conservative white Southerners and, in time, incurred the enmity of President Johnson as well. Despite

Library of Congress.

A contemporary artist's view of the role of the Freedmen's Bureau.

Library of Congress.

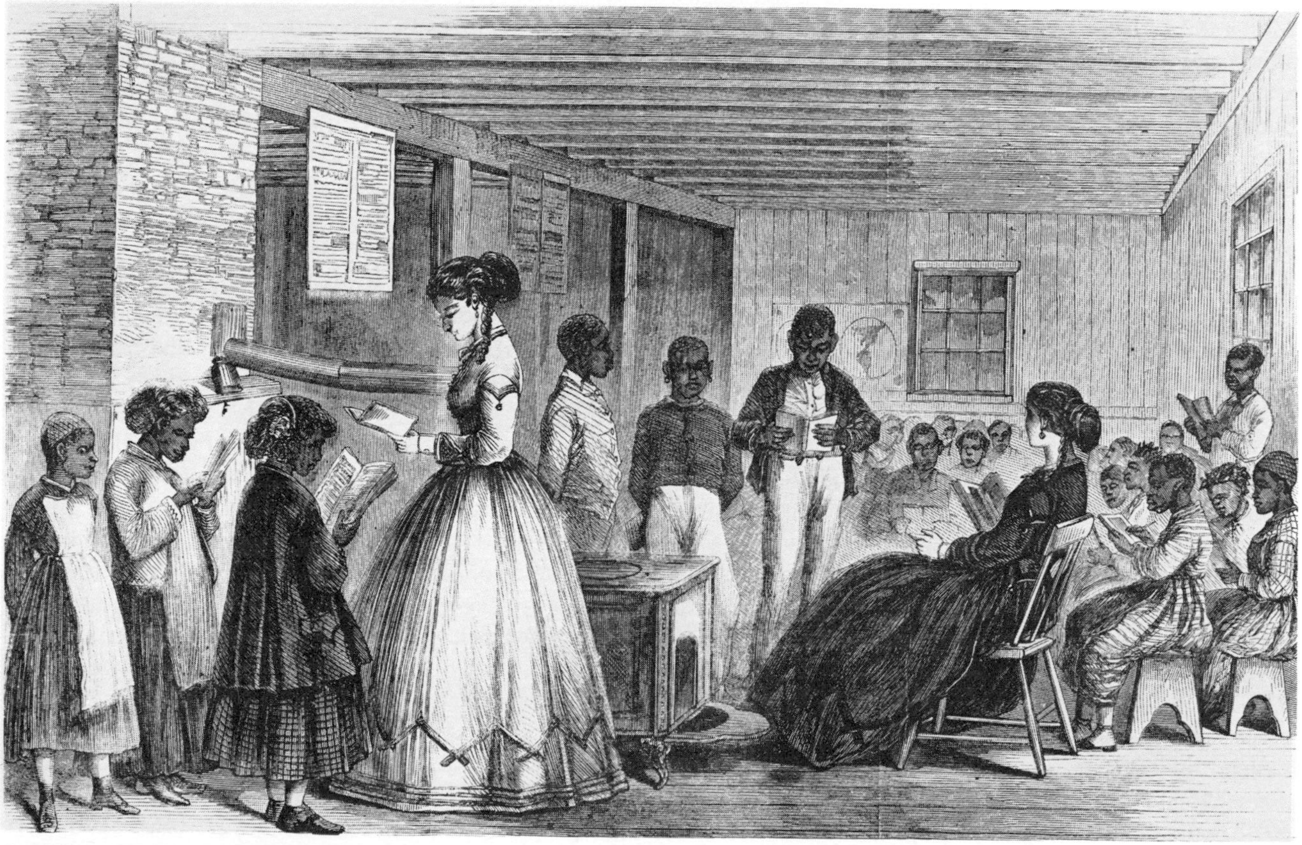

An 1866 sketch of a schoolroom in Richmond, Virginia operated by the Freedmen's Bureau.

these handicaps, the Bureau accomplished a great deal for the freedmen, and the Radicals still hoped to make the agency even more effective by extending its life and by empowering its agents to protect the civil rights of the freedmen.

Johnson's Responses

Early in 1866, President Johnson vetoed a bill seeking to extend the life of the Freedmen's Bureau. The President also vetoed a civil rights bill that guaranteed blacks the same rights and protection as whites, regardless of local laws; this bill authorized the use of federal troops to enforce the rights of black citizens. These vetoes alienated even the moderates and precipitated open warfare between Johnson and Congress. The reasons for both vetoes were simple enough. These bills, in Johnson's opinion, violated the rights of the States. The President even suggested after his vetoes that the Radical Republican "traitors" were trying to seize control of the government. Johnson's arrogance and intemperance, as much as his vetoes, united moderate and Radical Republicans as never before, and together on April 9, 1866, they overrode his veto of the Civil Rights Act. Then Congress passed a new Freedmen's Bureau Bill, and again the President vetoed it. Finally, on July 16, 1866, despite Johnson's obstinate insistence that the legislation encroached on states' rights, moderate and Radical Republicans worked together to override that veto as well.

The open political conflict between the majority of Congress and the President set the stage for the congressional elections of 1866. Many Northerners condemned President Johnson's abortive attempt to forge a new national political party composed of moderates and conservatives of both major parties. Radicals interpreted Johnson's move as an effort to form a coalition of northern Copperheads and ex-Confederates. Johnson's "swing around the circle"—a speaking tour between late August and mid-September that took him as far west as St. Louis—was a disaster. His speeches were vindictive, and they met with jeers from crowds in the Midwest. The heckling in turn provoked him to make statements that demeaned the dignity of his office.

Johnson's continued opposition to the Fourteenth Amendment (passed by Congress in mid-June and submitted to the states for ratification) also provided the Radicals with ammunition against him. This Amendment, one of the most detailed of the three so-called Civil War Amendments to the Constitution, had four principal provisions: (1) all persons, born or naturalized in the United States and subject to its jurisdiction, are entitled to all the privileges of citizenship and no state can deprive anyone of life, liberty, or property without "due process of law" or deny anyone "equal protection of the laws"; (2) if any state seeks to deprive any *male* citizen of the suffrage, then its representation in the Congress will be reduced proportionally; (3) anyone who renounces his oath to uphold the federal government and engages in rebellion cannot hold state or federal office (however, by a two-thirds vote in each house Congress can remove this disability); and (4) the public debt incurred by the federal government during the Civil War "shall not be questioned," but all debts and obligations of the Confederacy and its states, including "any claim for the loss or emancipation of any slave" are "illegal and void."

Radicals, eager to form a firm alliance with the moderates in the struggle against Johnson, supported the measure even though they preferred a less ambiguous definition of black rights. President Johnson opposed the Fourteenth Amendment and encouraged Southerners to reject the measure. In 1866–1867, ten ex-Confederate states followed his advice and rejected the Amendment because it barred southern leadership and permitted black suffrage. Johnson emerged from the 1866 congressional elections discredited. The Republicans waved "the bloody shirt of the rebellion" (a tactic by which they portrayed the Democratic party as the standard-bearer of rebellion) and obtained more than two-thirds of the seats in both houses of Congress, won every gubernatorial contest, and captured control of every northern state legislature.

There are many explanations for this sweeping victory. The Republicans, of course, capitalized on Johnson's political mistakes as well as northern opposition to the "black codes" and a bloody race riot in Memphis. They also persuaded businessmen that a Democratic victory would reverse policies favorable to commerce and industry. Moreover, the Republicans received the support of the Civil War veterans, who were beginning to organize the Grand Army of the Republic, a group that would be a considerable political force in the next two decades. The Republican victory, however, was based primarily on the fear among Northerners that Johnson was encouraging unreconstructed southern whites to ignore their defeat in war and to reestablish their old privileges—and even to reintroduce slavery. This fear caused northern voters to give the Republican Congress a mandate to carry out its own reconstruction policies.

Radical Reconstruction

Two years after the Civil War ended, the Republicans, firmly in control of Congress, voted to return the defeated states of the South to military rule, thus beginning the process of reconstruction anew. Congress deemed its actions necessary for a number of reasons: the President, who remained hostile and uncooperative, had to be chastened; ten of the former states of the Confederacy refused to adopt the Fourteenth Amendment; and the freedmen in the South were still subject to continual abuse. On March 2, 1867, Congress passed its First Reconstruction Act over Johnson's veto. This measure divided the South into five military districts subject to martial law. In order to return to their original status within the Union, the southern states were required to call new constitutional conventions elected by all adult males, black and white, except ex-Confederates. These conventions had to establish state governments guaranteeing black suffrage and had to ratify the Fourteenth Amendment.

When Southerners failed to follow the procedures outlined by the Reconstruction Act, Congress passed supplementary acts to put the earlier law into effect. Recalcitrance was to be expected from an experienced ruling class in the South that had no intention of reducing its own privileges, but President Johnson's reluctance to enforce laws Congress enacted was an even more frustrating obstacle. Though Congress could easily override his vetoes, only the President could execute the laws of the land. The Radicals saw the enfranchisement of two million southern black males as their best chance to offset the power of the southern ruling class and to maintain their supremacy.

Military authorities were required to register voters and to supervise the election of delegates to the constitutional conventions. Yet Southerners again defeated ratification of the proposed constitutions by staying away from the polls. The laws clearly had provided that the new documents were to be ratified by a majority of *registered* voters. In March 1868, Congress ruled that the new constitutions could be ratified by merely a majority of voters, no matter how small the turnout.

State conventions dominated by Radical Republicans met in ten Southern states in 1868. Blacks participated in every state convention, though they formed a majority only in South Carolina.

State Convention	Delegates: Black	White	Total	% Black
Alabama	18	90	108	17
Arkansas	8	58	66	12
Florida	18	27	45	40
Georgia	33	137	170	19
Louisiana	49	49	98	50
Mississippi	17	83	100	17
North Carolina	15	118	133	11
South Carolina	76	48	124	61
Virginia	25	80	105	24
Texas	9	81	90	10

Based on W.E.B. DuBois, *Black Reconstruction in America* (New York: Atheneum, 1969 reprint), p. 372.

The new constitutions, the most progressive the South had ever known, were similar to those in effect in the rest of the nation except for the articles guaranteeing civil rights for blacks, establishing universal manhood suffrage, and disqualifying ex-Confederates from voting or holding public office. Some documents introduced more equitable systems of legislative apportionment and made appointive offices elective. Most of these constitutions encouraged state support of education, the poor, and the physically and mentally handicapped. Other subjects addressed by the various constitutional conventions included the rights of women, reform of penal codes, and establishment of a more equitable tax structure. Indeed, the new constitution adopted in South Carolina was that state's first truly democratic frame of government.

By June 1868, seven states satisfied the requirements and their representatives were readmitted to Congress: Arkansas, Alabama, Florida, Georgia, Louisiana, North Carolina, and South Carolina. Early in 1869, Congress proposed the Fifteenth Amendment to the Constitution, which forbade any state from depriving a citizen of his right to vote because of race, color, or previous condition of servitude, though it failed to include sex as a basis for deprivation. By 1870, Mississippi, Texas, and Virginia were restored to the Union. Their admission was delayed

Library of Congress.

Blanche Kelso Bruce (1841–1898)

One of the first black men to win a seat in the United States Senate, Blanche K. Bruce was born into slavery in Farmville, Virginia, the son of a wealthy planter and a slave woman. In the late 1850s, Bruce was taken to Missouri, where he received a basic education. After teaching school for a time, Bruce attended Oberlin College for two years (1866–1868). In the late 1860s, he moved to Floreyville, Mississippi, where he became a planter.

A man of some means and possessing obvious executive ability, with the aid of the military government then ruling Mississippi, Bruce began a swift rise through a series of local and state posts to national prominence. In 1870 he became sergeant-at-arms of the state senate; the following year he was named tax assessor of Bolivar County; and in 1872 became sheriff. Two years later Bruce won the Republican nomination for the U.S. Senate and subsequently was elected to that high office by the state legislature. When he appeared at the Capitol in March 1875, the outgoing Mississippi Senator, J. L. Alcorn, refused to escort his successor to the swearing-in ceremony, but New York's Roscoe Conkling agreed to do so.

A man of tact and sound judgment, Blanche K. Bruce established a creditable record during his six-year term. He spent much of his time fighting in behalf of minority groups and in this capacity investigated vote fraud and civil disorders in the South, opposed Chinese exclusion, and spoke out in behalf of Indian rights. Bruce also was a firm advocate of navigational improvements on the Mississippi.

In 1878, Senator Bruce married Josephine B. Wilson. After Bruce retired from the Senate at the close of his term, he spent the rest of his life in Washington where Republican presidents duly appointed him to patronage jobs. Garfield named him Register of the U.S. Treasury Department, and Harrison appointed him Recorder of Deeds for the District of Columbia. Shortly before his death in 1898, Bruce was restored to the Treasury post by McKinley. ■

Library of Congress.

An interracial jury during Reconstruction.

Library of Congress.

Between 1869 and 1901, two blacks served in the United States Senate and twenty in the House of Representatives. This illustration shows those serving in the 41st and 42nd Congress, 1869–1873.

because of their refusal to approve constitutional clauses disenfranchising ex-Confederates, but these states finally were readmitted following ratification of the Fifteenth Amendment. Georgia, first admitted in 1868, was returned to military rule by Congress after whites there expelled duly elected blacks from the state legislature. The state was readmitted in 1870 only after the Reconstructions Acts and the Fourteenth Amendment were fully enforced there; Georgia also had to ratify the Fifteenth Amendment and to seat expelled black legislators.

In essence, the era of congressional Reconstruction was relatively brief. Within a short time, the former Confederate states were back in the Union and their governments once more were being directed by old-line conservatives. There are, however, several exceptions to this general picture: Tennessee was restored to the Union in July 1866 before congressional Reconstruction began; conservatives were in power in Virginia before its readmission; and three states (Florida, Louisiana, and South Carolina) experienced a measure of military rule until after the disputed election of 1876.

State	Readmitted to Union	Conservatives Win Control
Alabama	June 25, 1868	November 14, 1874
Arkansas	June 22, 1868	November 10, 1874
Florida	June 25, 1868	January 2, 1877
Georgia	July 15, 1870	November 1, 1871
Louisiana	June 25, 1868	January 2, 1877
Mississippi	February 23, 1870	November 3, 1875
North Carolina	June 25, 1868	November 3, 1870
South Carolina	June 25, 1868	November 12, 1876
Tennessee	July 24, 1866	October 4, 1869
Texas	March 30, 1870	January 14, 1873
Virginia	January 26, 1870	October 5, 1869

Based on John Hope Franklin, *Reconstruction: After the Civil War* (University of Chicago: Chicago Press, 1961), p. 231.

Congress versus President Johnson

The anti-Johnson Republican victories in the 1866 congressional elections enabled the Radicals to override President Johnson's vetoes of their Reconstruction Acts. Radical Republican leaders next sought to take advantage of their increased strength to weaken Johnson's ability to thwart their measures. Between 1866 and 1868, the Radicals passed several acts that increased congressional control over the military, over the process of amending the Constitution, and over presidential appointments. Congress even sought to prevent the Supreme Court from declaring its Reconstruction Acts unconstitutional by limiting the Court's jurisdiction over civil rights cases.

The passage of the Tenure of Office Act in March 1867 precipitated a confrontation between Congress and the President. This law prohibited Johnson from removing officials appointed by and with the advice and consent of the Senate without that body's approval. It was designed to prevent Johnson from undermining the Radicals by using his patronage power against them; it also was calculated to keep him from removing Secretary of War Stanton, the only member of the Cabinet still in sympathy with the Radicals. Johnson decided to test the constitutionality of these inroads into executive authority. While Congress was in recess in the summer of 1867, he dismissed Stanton. In close communication with the Radicals, Stanton barricaded himself in his office and refused to leave.

Johnson's attempt to oust Stanton outraged Congress. On February 24, 1868, the House of Representatives voted to impeach the President for "high crimes and misdemeanors." Strictly speaking, Johnson had done nothing to justify such a drastic procedure, but the Radicals were convinced that he meant to sabotage their programs, and some felt that he actually was planning to return ex-Confederates and Copperheads to power. In addition to his alleged violation of the Tenure of Office Act, the Radicals charged Johnson with attempting to bring disgrace and ridicule upon Congress. Yet only after Congress had decided to impeach Johnson did it actually appoint a committee to prepare the articles of impeachment. In the eyes of many congressmen, Johnson unquestionably was unsuited for office and assembling a list of his misdemeanors constituted, as it were, only an afterthought.

President Johnson's trial lasted from late March to mid-May, 1868. According to constitutional provisions, Chief Justice Salmon P. Chase (1808–1873) presided over the Senate proceedings. During the war, he had been Lincoln's Secretary of the Treasury and as a member of the Cabinet had assisted him in formulating policy. He and Lincoln had frequently disagreed, for Chase felt that the administration was lax and the President's cautious emancipation policy was too conservative. Always sympathetic to the cause of antislavery, Chase was a strong advocate of black suffrage and accordingly favored Radical positions. Despite his sympathies for Radicals, he soon was accused by members of Congress of being in Johnson's party. In fact, Chase questioned the constitutionality of the Tenure of Office Act and the procedures of the Senate; his avowed purpose was to sustain the integrity of the Supreme Court and prevent Congress from reducing the Chief Justice to a mere figurehead in the proceedings.

If two-thirds of the senators sitting as a court had found Johnson guilty, Benjamin Wade, the acting president of the Senate, would have become the next President, a prospect moderate Republicans found rather unpalatable because of his radical views on public finance, labor, and women's suffrage. Finally, on May 16, 1868, the Senate voted on whether or not Johnson had com-

Both: New York Public Library, Picture Collection.

In late February 1858, Thaddeus Stevens gave formal notice of the beginning of impeachment proceedings against President Andrew Johnson.

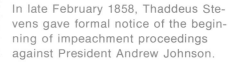

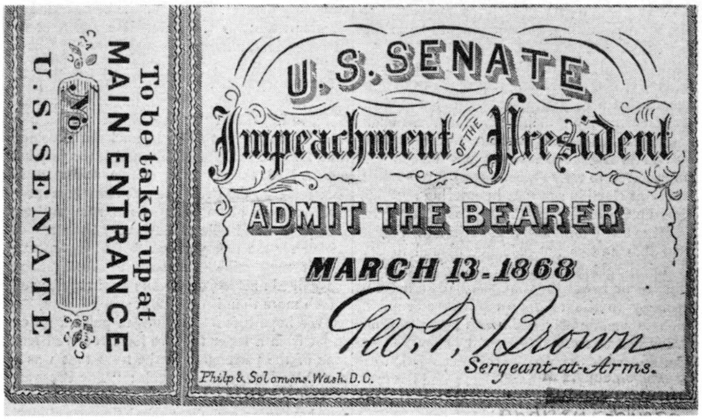

Facsimile of a ticket of admission to the impeachment trial of President Andrew Johnson.

mitted high misdemeanors as charged. The vote was 35 for conviction and 19 for acquittal, *one* vote short of the two-thirds necessary for conviction. Voting for acquittal were seven Republicans and twelve Democrats, who could not bring themselves to convict Johnson for dismissing a cabinet member whom he had not even appointed. Following the impeachment trial, Stanton resigned his office, and Congress went into adjournment.

The Election of 1868

A few days after Johnson's acquittal, the Republican national convention met in Chicago to prepare for the 1868 presidential campaign. On the first ballot the Republicans nominated General Ulysses S. Grant, the Union war hero.

Indiana Radical Schuyler Colfax (1823–1885), former Speaker of the House, was selected as Grant's running mate. The Republican platform condemned Johnson and the Democratic party, and praised the Reconstruction Acts of Congress. It equivocated, however, on the question of black suffrage by calling for black suffrage in the South but stating that the "question of suffrage in all of the loyal states properly belongs to the people of those states." The Radicals attracted a number of formidable enemies by insisting on black suffrage. This issue not only divided Republicans but became the rallying point for unity among Democrats who attacked the incumbents for advocating the "Africanization" of the South and black equality for the rest of the nation. In fact, Grant himself had little sympathy with the Radical view of racial relations. He lived much of his life in border states and was married to a Missouri lady whose father, an unreconstructed rebel, declared that the President really was "a good Democrat but did not know it."

The Democrats convened in New York on July 4. Although President Johnson received considerable sup-

Virginia State Library.

Black suffrage in the South helped to elect Ulysses S. Grant to the presidency in 1868. This engraving depicts blacks being herded to the polls and bribed to vote the "right" way.

port, both his questionable conduct and recent impeachment precluded his nomination. After considerable political maneuvering, the delegates nominated Horatio Seymour (1810–1886), a former governor of New York, as their candidate and Francis P. Blair, Jr. (1821–1875), as his running mate. Blair, a Kentucky-born lawyer, had risen to power in Missouri politics and in 1861 led a successful fight to keep that state in the Union. His career included service in the Missouri legislature, the Congress, and the Union Army. During the Civil War, he raised seven regiments for the North.

Throughout the campaign, the Republicans again made "the bloody shirt of the rebellion" their primary campaign issue. (Invoking the Republicans' role in the Civil War remained a standard party tactic for many years to come.) The result in 1868 was an easy electoral victory for Grant, 214 to 80, though the popular vote was much closer: 3,013,650 to 2,708,744 (52.7 percent to 47.3 percent). Interestingly enough, Grant's popular margin of slightly over 300,000 votes was provided by more than 500,000 black voters who were mostly southern blacks enfranchised by the Reconstruction Acts. Viewed in this light, it can be argued that a large number of white voters actually opposed the Radical programs and that Seymour was the choice of a majority of white voters both North and South. Indeed, the closeness of the vote in such states as Indiana (where Grant won by only about 10,000 votes) and New York (where he lost by a similar number) convinced many Republicans that their continued political hegemony necessitated enfranchising blacks in the North as well as in the South.

The Fifteenth Amendment

The ratification of the Fourteenth Amendment in July 1868, along with the enactment of reconstruction measures enfranchised southern blacks, but the idea of extending the suffrage to blacks in the North met considerable resistance. The Republican platform of 1868 had come out strongly for black suffrage in the South but, in deference to northern opinion, took no stand at all on giving the vote to blacks in the North. While Republicans avoided the black suffrage question in the North during the 1868 campaign, they later acted as if the election provided them with a mandate in favor of northern enfranchisement.

On February 27, 1869, Congress passed the Fifteenth Amendment to the Constitution, which forbade *any* state from depriving a citizen of his vote because of race, color, or previous condition of servitude (no mention was made of sex). Passage of the Amendment had divided Republicans in Congress and the Radicals, fearing an uphill battle for ratification, saw the ex-Confederate states as a ripe field to be exploited. There was good reason for concern. Voters in Connecticut, Ohio, Michigan, Minnesota, and Kansas had rejected proposals for black suffrage after the Civil War. Indeed, ratification of the Amendment in March 1870 was assured only by the support of southern states. Ironically, four of the southern states listed as ratifying the Amendment (Texas, Mississippi, Virginia, and Georgia) had not yet been fully restored to the Union by Congress when they participated in the task of amending the Constitution.

The passage of the Fifteenth Amendment was praised by blacks and former abolitionists, yet failure to put the supervision of elections under federal control eventually allowed Southerners to subvert the law. Blacks in the South found they were denied the vote on technicalities; thus there was no effective way of securing true national suffrage. Only in the twentieth century was the Amendment invoked by the Supreme Court to strike down discriminatory practices.

The South under Radical Rule

The eleven states of the former Confederacy were under the control of the Radical Republicans during all or part of the decade between 1867 and 1877. The legend of "Black Reconstruction" enunciated by conservative Southerners and propagated by such prosouthern historians as Dunning claims that a Radical coalition of carpetbaggers, scalawags, and blacks ruined the South and brought dark days until the region was "redeemed" by white conservatives and white supremacy. According to this interpretation, the new governments imposed by the Radicals expelled from power the South's experienced leadership and replaced it with untrained, incompetent, and corrupt men. The most notorious of these men were carpetbaggers, northern adventurers who supposedly invaded the postwar South for political and economic gain. Assisting them were two groups—the scalawags, poor southern whites who were allegedly depraved and greedy betrayers of their race and section, and blacks who supposedly were ignorant and illiterate people who merely cast their ballots according to the instructions of the Radicals. The members of this coalition, according to this interpretation, increased state and local taxes until they nearly ruined the white property-holding class. The governments controlled by the coalition were corrupt and wasteful. Indeed, they incurred shocking increases in state debts and brought some states to the edge of bankruptcy. Finally, according to the proponents of this view, the governments run by this coalition were destroying southern civilization by Africanizing it.

Many of these charges remained unchallenged as late as the early 1950s. In the last twenty years, however, historians have done much to correct this distorted picture of Reconstruction. Admittedly, the carpetbaggers were recent northern settlers who actively supported the Radicals. But many were simply experienced frontier promoters and developers who moved South rather than West. Reconstruction, in other words, entailed a diversion of the frontier movement into the relatively undeveloped South. A large number of so-called "carpetbaggers" (so named because they could supposedly carry all their assets in a satchel) were Union army veterans who believed the South was a land of opportunity. Hostile southern whites included among the carpetbaggers all the teachers, clergymen, and officers of the Freedmen's Bureau as well as many other agents of charitable organizations sent to relieve and give aid to the blacks. Clearly, some of these men and women were motivated by personal gain, some by humanitarian-

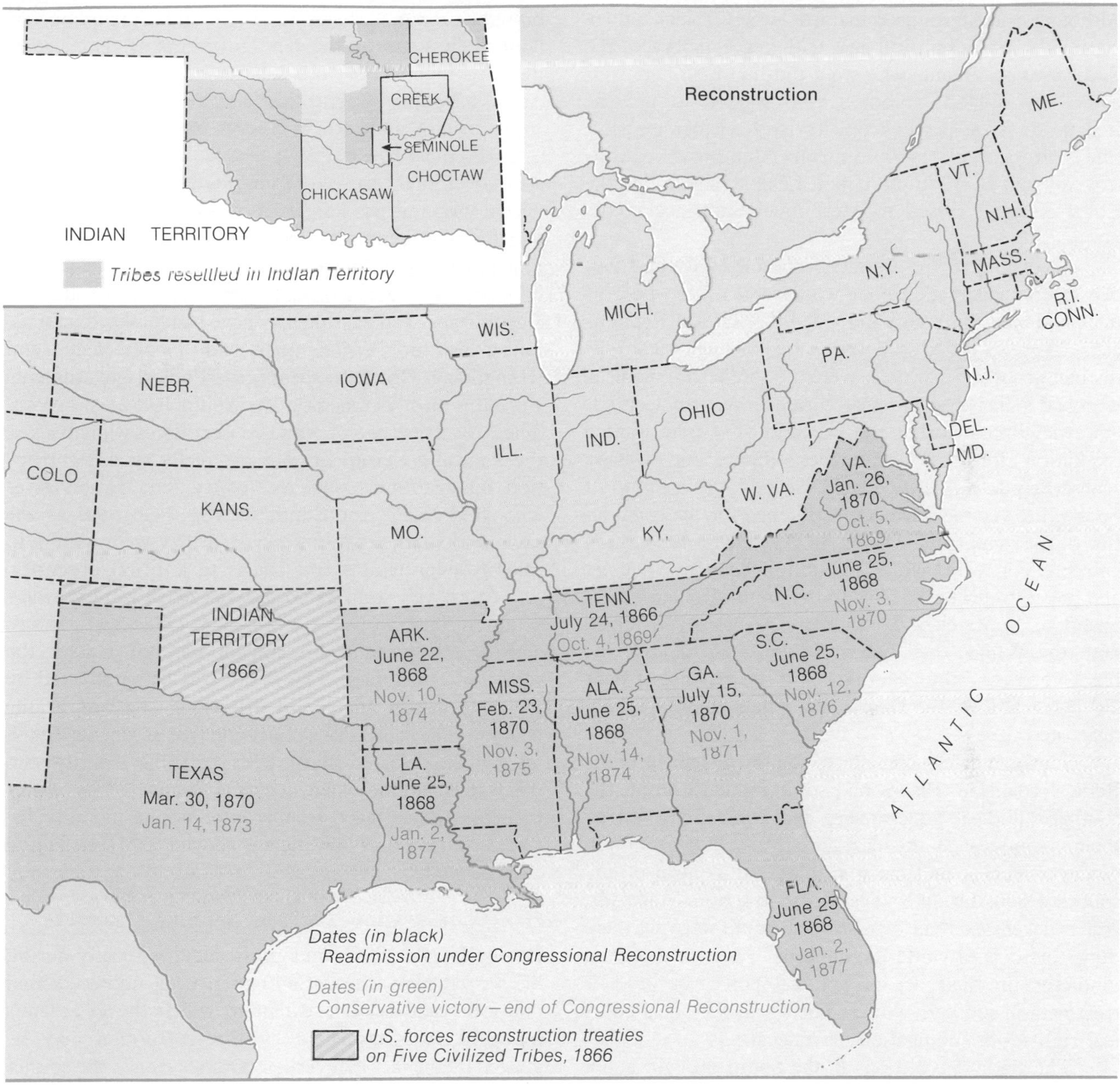

ism, and some by a combination of both. There were, undeniably, some plunderers and parasites who fitted the stereotype invented by Southerners, but no matter how carpetbaggers behaved, southern whites denounced them as corrupt. The real complaint, however, was that these Northerners were organizing blacks for political action.

Most white Southerners were especially contemptuous of groups such as the Union League. Organized in the North in 1862 to bolster sagging wartime morale, the League demanded unconditional loyalty to the Union.

Although some groups remained largely social, others became blatantly political and, with peace, embraced the Radical cause. Agents who went south at first were welcomed by upland Unionists who wanted to use the League to wrest power from lowland aristocrats; however, admission of blacks to membership provoked controversy and by 1870 the Union League (also called the Loyal League) ceased to exert much influence in the South.

According to the southern version of Radical Reconstruction, degraded poor whites and other opportunists betrayed the South and aided the Radical Republicans. These so-called scalawags actually consisted of four distinct groups. First, there were the southern Unionists, who had suffered severe persecution from their Confederate neighbors during the war and who now wanted retaliation for their grievances; this group usually scorned equal rights for blacks. Second was a group of poor white yeomen farmers who hoped for the confiscation of the rich planters' lands. Third were those southern entrepreneurs who favored Republican economic policies and hoped to bring industry to the South. Fourth were a group of upper-class Southerners previously affiliated with the Whigs; they believed they could control the black voters and thus gain power at the expense of their old political foes, the Democrats, whom they especially distrusted.

Southern blacks constituted the third element in the Radical coalition. Blacks had some influence in all the southern Radical governments but controlled none of them. Contrary to the charges advanced by southern conservatives, at *no* time were blacks in control of any southern state during Radical Reconstruction. Moreover, blacks developed their own leadership and were not mere dupes or tools of white Republicans. They were seldom vindictive in their use of political power or in their treatment of southern whites. Their goal was equal political rights, not subjugation or vengeance.

The Radical coalitions in the South brought about positive achievement in the various states. The adoption of more equitable tax systems, the promotion of physical reconstruction, the expansion of state railroad systems, the increase of public services, and the creation or expansion of public school systems—these are just some of their accomplishments.

Southern conservatives and their later apologists contended that the carpetbaggers, scalawags, and blacks brought economic chaos to the South. Corruption did flourish in some of the new governments. Legislators awarded themselves high salaries and padded their expense accounts. Corruption admittedly increased the high cost of state government. Yet blame for such activities must be carefully assessed. The highest cost of state government arose, for example, from corruption connected with railroad construction and railroad subsidies, and in these ventures Democrats participated fully as much as Republicans, and the post-Reconstruction governments as much as more than those of the Radical Republicans. Radical rule may have had its shortcomings, but it was not synonymous with incompetence and wrongdoing. On the contrary, the Radical governments were the most democratic the South had ever known. The basic grievance of white conservatives who attacked the Radical governments was not really against corruption, but against a liberal race policy. The conservatives who "redeemed" the South viewed themselves as the saviors of southern democracy, but they were willing to relegate poor whites and blacks to political obscurity.

Moreover, contrary to the charges of contemporary southern conservatives, the presence of blacks, scalawags, and carpetbaggers in government was not in itself the source of corruption. The South was being affected by the same forces that were disturbing the rest of the country. The social disorganization that accompanied the war hit the defeated South with particular severity, and postwar economic expansion was dominated by entrepreneurs whose loose standards of public morality infected contemporary politicians above the Mason-Dixon Line as well.

Grantism and the Nadir of National Disgrace

During Ulysses S. Grant's presidency, especially during his second term, the nation experienced unprecedented political scandals. The extent to which the President's reputation was tarnished by this corruption may be guaged by the fact that contemporaries coined the epithet "Grantism" to connote the moral degradation into which American politics had fallen. One astute biographer, quoting King Lear, notes that Grant was "a man more sinn'd against than sinning." But before he left office, the nation suffered what some scholars have referred to as "The Nadir of National Disgrace."

Grant came to the White House in March 1869 with little prior political experience. He had voted for James

Buchanan in 1856 and, while not voting in 1860, he favored the election of Douglas. It was only when he broke with President Johnson in 1867 during the controversy over the dismissal of Secretary of War Stanton that the Radicals began to view Grant with favor. Thus, political availability propelled the nation's foremost military hero, who was seen only a few years earlier by some friends as a failure, into the White House. Lacking administrative experience outside of the military, Grant ran his office with the aid of a military staff. He failed to consult with party leaders in Congress and ended up, through inept appointments to important offices and poor decisions, alienating liberal Republicans and naming several scoundrels to high positions.

Perhaps the most notorious of these scandals was the Crédit Mobilier, a construction company that helped build the Union Pacific Railroad. That company, owned by a few Union Pacific stockholders, received fraudulent contracts from the railroad, enabling it to pocket huge sums, some of which came from federal subsidies. To thwart a government inquiry, the company gave Crédit Mobilier stock to key politicians, among them, Schuyler Colfax, later Grant's Vice President.

Exposure of the Crédit Mobilier scandal by the *New York Sun* in September 1872 cast an ugly shadow upon Grant's bid for reelection in 1872. Joining the Democrats in their distrust of Grant were a number of Liberal Republicans (as those who favored civil service reform and opposed corruption in government came to be known). The election of 1872 saw an attempt at coalition between Democrats and Liberal Republicans. Its founders and supporters, men such as Edwin Godkin, editor of *The Nation,* felt that only if the country were run by the "best class of men" (meaning the intelligensia and the educated rich) could it be reformed. The Liberal movement, which was a conservative movement by modern definitions of the word, was composed of political neophytes. The nomination of Horace Greeley, well-known editor of the *New York Tribune,* as the Liberal party's candidate for President not only shocked the Democrats, but stunned many within the Liberal Republican ranks as well. Yet, Democratic leaders, anxious to overtake the Republicans, gambled and endorsed Greeley.

The result of the election was a second term for Grant, which proved even more reprehensible than the first. On March 3, 1873, just one day before Grant's second inauguration, Congress approved a bill that doubled the President's salary and raised other government salaries, including their own. Grant signed the bill. Public indignation against the so-called "Salary Grab Act" led to a repeal of portions of the law less than a year later. To make matters worse, serious political scandals involving a member of the President's office staff and his Cabinet plagued the administration. Grant's private secretary, General Orville E. Babcock, was indicted in 1875 for involvement in a whiskey ring that defrauded the government of the tax on whiskey. Secretary of War William Belknap (1829–1890) resigned from office in 1876 under threat of impeachment because of charges that he had accepted bribes from an Indian trader. Corruption in office appeared to be rampant.

In his last annual message to Congress, noting that his civil career commenced "at a most difficult and critical time," Grant made an astonishing apology for his shortcomings. He conceded he had no "previous political training," had witnessed only two presidential campaigns before 1868, and had been eligible to vote in only one election previous to that date. "Under such circumstances it is but reasonable to suppose," he added, "that errors of judgment must have occurred."

Similar conditions, most of which cannot be excused by "errors of judgment," were evident at the state and municipal levels. New York's William Marcy Tweed (1823–1878) was an infamous example of political corruption. His organization, Tammany Hall, dominated Manhattan politics from the late 1850s until 1871. It is estimated that he and his ring filched between $30 million and $200 million during their regime.

The public reaction to Grantism greatly encouraged Democrats. In the 1874 congressional elections, the Democrats regained control of the House of Representatives for the first time since before the Civil War, improved their standing in the Senate, and won control in many states. These accomplishments were clear signals that Radical Reconstruction was coming to an end.

The End of Reconstruction Politics

In the 1860s and the 1870s, as in the 1960s and 1970s, many southern whites perceived blacks as a threat to their economic security and dominant status. During the 1870s, white Southerners used a variety of methods to "redeem" the South from Republicanism and black rule.

Rutherford B. Hayes Library.

The Ku Klux Klan used physical violence to keep blacks from voting and to overthrow Radical Republican rule.

Southerners joined a number of secret terrorist societies such as the Ku Klux Klan (the KKK), the Knights of the White Camelia, the Pale Faces, and the Shotgun Club. The Klan, founded in Pulaski, Tennessee, in the winter of 1865-1866, was the most notorious of these organizations.

Redeeming the South—The KKK

The KKK, originally organized as a social club, was soon transformed into a powerful political organization. Ex-Confederate General Nathan Bedford Forrest (1821-1877) became "Grand Wizard of the Empire" in 1867. "Realms," or state organizations headed by "Grand Dragons," began to appear throughout the South in the late 1860s. By such tactics as night rides of white-robed and hooded men to frighten the allegedly superstitious blacks, by physical violence and by keeping blacks from the polls, the KKK sought to overthrow Radical rule. In addition to blacks, carpetbaggers, and scalawags, the chief targets of the KKK also included the Union League. The *Southern Enterprise* of Greenville, South Carolina, published the following warning to these groups in April 1868:

Niggers and leaguers, get out of the way,
We're born of the night and we vanish by day.
No rations have we, but the flesh of man—
And love niggers best—the Ku Klux Klan;
We catch 'em alive and roast 'em whole,
Then hand 'em around with a sharpened pole.
Whole Leagues have been eaten, not leaving a man,
And went away hungry—the Ku Klux Klan;
Born of the night, and vanish by day;
Leaguers and niggers, get out of the way!

Quoted in E. Merton Coulter, *The South During Reconstruction 1865-1877* (Baton Rouge: Louisiana State University Press, 1947), pp. 167-168.

The violence that ensued not only offended northern public opinion, but also led to the withdrawal of the more respectable members of the KKK. In 1869 Imperial Wizard Forrest ordered the dissolution of the organization. One problem the Klan faced from the outset was lawlessness and crime committed in its name by those who took advantage of their anonymity to pillage and steal. Shortly after Forrest told members to disband, Congress passed the first of several Enforcement Acts designed to protect blacks. These measures provided for federal supervision of elections and, in time, specifically declared the KKK an illegal organization. They also gave the President power to suspend the writ of habeas corpus and to proclaim martial law in areas where unlawful combinations were inciting "rebellion." In 1871 Grant used this authority to quell unrest, notably in North and South Carolina. Meanwhile, Congress held hearings in Washington and sent committees scurrying about the South to investigate the Klan. Despite passage of the Enforcement Acts, the congressional probes of the

A Prospective Scene in the "City of Oaks," 4th of March, 1869.
K.K.K.
OHIO
Alabama Department of Archives and History.

A Ku Klux Klan warning to carpetbaggers.

KKK, and several thousand indictments of suspected Klan members, few convictions were obtained. In 1894 Congress repealed many of the Enforcement Acts.

In retrospect, the rise of the Ku Klux Klan had both immediate and long-range effects. Federal investigations into its activities brought to light often chaotic conditions in the South, paving the way for changes (largely on southern terms), and the work of the Klan left a legacy of violence directed at keeping blacks and "outsiders" in subservient roles. Klan terrorism (or the threat of it) weakened the will of those white Republicans who had little sympathy for racial equality and had themselves intimidated a large number of blacks. The net result was that conservatives regained control of the state political machinery in Tennessee (1869), Virginia (1870), North Carolina (1870), and Georgia (1871). By 1874 Southerners elsewhere were openly using economic pressure and physical violence to keep blacks from exercising their right to vote. The "Mississippi Plan," or the so-called "shotgun policy," used in that state's election of 1875 was quite successful in overthrowing Radical rule by intimidating Republican voters. By the autumn of 1876, only Florida, South Carolina, and Louisiana were still under Republican rule.

The Contested Election of 1876

The Republicans, looking for a reform candidate to help overcome the criticism that they were the party of "Grantism," nominated Rutherford B. Hayes (1822-1893) of Ohio as their presidential candidate. Hayes was a former Union army general whose military service was varied and capable but not very distinguished. In addition, he had served a brief term in Congress (1864-1867) before his election to the governorship of Ohio. In that office he proved to be an astute politician and acquired a reputation as an honest and courageous administrator.

The Democrats nominated Samuel J. Tilden (1814-1886) of New York as their candidate. Tilden, who was a corporation lawyer, had opposed the election of Lincoln, disapproved of the war from the beginning, and was detached in his attitude toward that long struggle. In 1866 he became chairman of the Democratic state committee, a position he held for the next eight years. While occupying this position, Tilden helped break up the infamous Tweed Ring in New York and reform the state judicial system. In 1874 he was elected governor of the state on a platform of reform, which he continued to champion during his tenure, notably his fight against "bossism" in Manhattan and the "Canal Ring," which had milked the state treasury of appropriations intended for repairs and extension of the state's canal system. His determination to head a truly honest administration resulted in lower taxes, less expensive government, and the exposure of numerous fraudulent practices.

Democrat Tilden received a popular margin in the presidential election of over 250,000 votes. The Republicans, however, refused to concede Tilden's election and claimed that the returns in Florida, Louisiana, and South Carolina were in dispute. Both the Democrats and Republicans sent representatives to watch the official election count in these critical states. The situation in all three states was similar. The Republicans, in control of the state governments and the election machinery, relied upon the black masses for votes and practiced widespread frauds. By threats, intimidation, and even violence, the Democrats kept the blacks from the polls and, where possible, also resorted to fraud. While the efforts of white conservatives made a full and fair *vote* impossible, Republican control of the states made a fair vote *count* impossible.

On January 29, 1877, with inauguration day in early March quickly approaching, Congress created an Electoral Commission to settle the disputed election. The original plan called for the selection of seven Republicans and seven Democrats, while the fifteenth member was to be Supreme Court Justice David Davis, an independent. Davis became ineligible, however, when he resigned from the Court to become a senator from Illinois. A Republican justice was then appointed to fill his place on the commission which, by a vote of 8 to 7, proceeded to support the Republicans in each disputed state election. On March 2, 1877, a final count gave Hayes the victory by one electoral vote, a decision that was approved by the Senate, and Hayes, after one of the most disputed and uncertain elections in the nation's history, was inaugurated three days later.

The Compromise of 1877

In order to secure southern support for the decisions of the Electoral Commission, the Republicans made several promises to southern leaders. The unofficial negotiations that led to the so-called Compromise of 1877 were lengthy. The Republicans made three basic pledges: (1) they would withdraw federal troops from the South; (2) they would be fair to Southerners when it came time to distribute federal patronage and make sure a Southerner would be appointed to the Cabinet; and (3) they would provide federal funds for internal improvements in the South. In return, southern Democrats acquiesced in the election of Hayes and promised to deal fairly with blacks.

Both the South and the North were in a severe depression in the winter of 1876–1877. Unemployment provoked radical labor groups into a violent mood foreboding insurrectionary rioting. Among the Republicans, deep concern for the privileges promised by various new statutes regarding money, banks, tariffs, land, and railroads overshadowed whatever civil libertarian sentiments still remained among them. In addition, both parties feared that the election crisis would result in violence reminiscent of the crisis of 1860–1861.

The South's extreme poverty and desperate need for capital, coupled with its longstanding hatred for the remaining carpetbaggers, were primary causes for the cooperation between southern Democrats and Republicans. In return for the promise of state autonomy over civil rights, for a share of the federal patronage, and for access to federal funds, the Southerners agreed to the election of Hayes. Upon entering office, Hayes appointed David M. Key of Tennessee, who had served in the Confederate Army, as Postmaster General and ordered the withdrawal of federal troops from all former Confederate states. The Compromise of 1877 signaled the end of Radical Reconstruction and the "redemption" of the South.

Reconstruction in Retrospect

The Republicans retained the White House in 1877, and a basis for sectional reconciliation was laid, but both achievements were accomplished at the expense of the black people of the South. In the rural South, sharecropping and debt peonage replaced slavery. Despite the Fourteen and Fifteenth Amendments, whites in the "redeemed" South denied blacks civil and political rights.

Several factors help to explain why the North abandoned blacks. The old Radical leadership was no longer in the ascendancy; many Radicals had died or retired. Others showed little concern or understanding of the problems of the ex-slaves. Indeed, as immigrants from southern and eastern Europe poured into America in the 1870s, many old middle-class families—with whom most Radicals identified—came to view the problems of southern whites in a new light. Although some Republican congressmen continued to push for civil rights laws, the Congress, the Supreme Court, and the executive branch increasingly turned their attention to other issues. A new group of Republican leaders with ties to industrialists was emerging. Consequently, economic development in the South rather than the promotion of black suffrage there increasingly received greater attention. This new group of Republican leaders also discovered that northern public opinion was tiring of the Reconstruction issue. The business panic of 1873 and the severe economic depression that followed in its wake were uppermost in the minds of most Americans, not the plight of blacks.

By the 1870s, the Republicans no longer needed southern black votes to win elections. The states of the Old Northwest, which had consistently voted Democratic before 1860, were now Republican strongholds. The growth of urban industrial centers in this region had helped to align it with the industrial Northeast and the Republican party. In the eleven presidential elections between 1868 and 1908, the states of the Old Northwest went Republican eight times. All of these factors contributed to the demise of idealism and zeal for social reform engendered by the antislavery crusade. These factors also help to explain why the North abandoned the ex-slaves of the South. The Republican party was becoming a party of the status quo.

Ironically, neither the Republican party's abandonment of southern blacks to local white rule by the Compromise of 1877 or Congressional repeal of the Force Acts in 1894 necessarily alienated northern blacks from the party. Frederick Douglass, for example, continued to assure blacks that the Republican party was their party.

Segregation

Although the Thirteenth Amendment brought an end to slavery, a caste system arose that relegated blacks to second-class citizenship. Historians still disagree about the origins and development of segregation. Clearly, there was de facto segregation in parts of the South soon after emancipation, but it is disputed whether this pattern prevailed throughout the South. Jim Crow laws (the term is derived from white minstrel songs stereotyping blacks), which made segregation a rigid institution everywhere in the South, emerged only in the 1890s.

Racial prejudice provided fertile soil for Jim Crow laws. The hatred of blacks by lower-class whites, the hard times of the agricultural South in the decades after the war, the spread of urbanization and industrialization in that region, and the coming of age of a generation of freedmen with basic education who knew nothing of slavery, all these factors somehow contrived to establish a hodgepodge of laws and ordinances which embittered black-white relations.

Segregation had emerged in southern cities before the Civil War as a mosaic of customs, ordinances, state laws, public pressures, and convenience intended to serve as a means of social control over slaves who often performed various services without close supervision. The avowed goal of antebellum segregation was to prevent fraternization between whites and blacks, and between slaves and freemen. During the period of congressional Reconstruction, some Radicals such as Charles Sumner hoped that the due process and equal protection clauses of the Fourteenth Amendment would protect the civil and personal rights of the former slaves. In order to guarantee blacks "the full and equal enjoyment of the accommodations . . . of inns, public conveyances on land or water, theatres, and other places of public amusement" and to "mete out equal and exact justice to all," Congress passed the Civil Rights Act of 1875.

Southerners denied that Congress had the right to interfere with matters that were supposedly purely social, and the Supreme Court supported this contention. The Court held in *Hall* v. *DeCuir* (1878) that a state law forbidding discrimination on public carriers was an undue burden on interstate commerce. In the *Civil Rights Cases* of 1883, the Supreme Court declared the Civil Rights Act of 1875 unconstitutional and ruled that the federal government had no legal jurisdiction over discrimination practiced by individuals or private organizations. The federal government had jurisdiction only over the invasion of civil rights by states.

The situation of blacks in the South following Reconstruction was deplorable. The Thirteenth, Fourteenth, and Fifteenth Amendments had ended slavery, pledged equal protection of the laws and due process, and guaranteed black males their voting rights. Yet blacks were denied these rights by spurious arguments, devious subterfuge, and extralegal coercion. They were, in truth, only half-emancipated.

Indian Territory

Not only the eleven former states of the Confederacy, but the Five Civilized Tribes as well underwent a reconstruction process. Following the collapse of the Confederacy, the tribes living in Indian Territory (present-day Oklahoma) were subjected to new federal policies. Although large segments of the Creeks, Seminoles, and Cherokees had remained steadfastly loyal to the Union, other members of these tribes as well as the Chickasaws and the Choctaws ultimately joined the Confederacy.

The Five Civilized Tribes signed reconstruction treaties with the federal government in 1866. Washington officials wanted to adjust tribal affairs between "loyal" and "disloyal" Indians and to dictate the status of the freedmen. All five tribes soon recovered from the hard

"MOVE ON!"
HAS THE NATIVE AMERICAN NO RIGHTS THAT THE NATURALIZED AMERICAN IS BOUND TO RESPECT?

This Reconstruction cartoon depicts blacks and immigrants at the ballot box, while an Indian is being rudely pushed away.

times that "the white man's war" brought to Indian Territory. The mixed bloods, with the aid of hired laborers who replaced their slaves, rebuilt their homes, and raised livestock and were soon relatively prosperous once more. The full bloods also returned to their homes and resumed a subsistence agriculture, which kept them as comfortable as they ever had been in the West. With the signing of the treaties in 1866 and the subsequent restoration of their annuities, the tribes reopened their schools for the first time in five years.

But the Reconstruction treaties also provided a convenient opportunity for the federal government to attempt to achieve two long sought goals: (1) the reduction of tribal land holdings; and (2) the establishment of a territorial government over the Indians in order to regulate their activities. The latter effort failed, but the first goal was accomplished. The Reconstruction treaties of 1866 took away nearly one-half of the domain previously granted the Five Civilized Tribes "in perpetuity" under the removal policy of the Jacksonian era. In essence, the Reconstruction treaties were used as a means to circumvent the old removal treaties and concentrate other tribes in the territory guaranteed to the Five Civilized Tribes, thus releasing additional land for white settlement in other states as well as in Indian Territory. The treaties also forced the tribes to allow railroads to pass through their territory. The building of railroads had a tragic influence on the lives of these Indians. Their land lost its alleged protection from white society; railroad promoters, lawless and disorderly railroad crews, and many unscrupulous whites preyed on the Indians.

Reconstruction was both a unique and tragic experience for the Five Civilized Tribes. The federal government conveniently ignored important factors that led some Indians to side with the Confederacy, such as the abandonment of their territory by the Union at the outbreak of the war, their proximity to the Confederacy, and the federal government's cessation of Indian annuities. Even the loyalty of large numbers of Indians was overlooked. The treaties of 1866 served as a convenient means of reasserting social control over the Indians, regardless of whether they had been "loyal" or "disloyal" to the Union.

Women's Rights

During the Civil War, American feminists generally subordinated their own programs to an all-out effort to abolish slavery. In return, they expected the support of the abolitionists in the campaign to enfranchise women. But, inexperienced in politics, these women failed to estimate the extent and complexity of male chauvinism. They expected conservatives to maintain that society would crumble if women got the vote, but were totally unprepared for the opposition of their erstwhile Republican friends in Congress. Some abolitionist leaders, like Wendell Phillips, believed that merging women's rights and the rights of blacks could only confuse both issues in the public's mind. Other politicians, eager to acquire at least two million potential Republican male black voters in the South, were reluctant to endanger ratification of the Fourteenth and Fifteenth Amendments and passage of civil rights legislation by incorporating women's suffrage in their bills. Indeed, the Fourteenth and Fifteenth Amendments not only failed to prohibit discrimination by sex, but the former actually highlighted sexual discrimination in federal law by specifying that its guarantees were for *male* voters and citizens.

To some women like Susan B. Anthony (1820–1906) and Elizabeth Cady Stanton (1815–1902) the reiteration of the word "male" three times in the Fourteenth Amendment, always in connection with the term "citizen," opened the question of whether or not women were really citizens of the United States. Nevertheless, some women did try to vote during the Reconstruction years. Virginia Louisa Minor (1824-1894), filed suit in 1872 against an election official who refused to let her vote. The supreme court told her that the Fourteenth Amendment did not apply to women.

In 1869, some feminists responded to events they perceived as a betrayal of implicit pledges by setting up the National Woman Suffrage Association. This organization pushed for a constitutional amendment enfranchis-

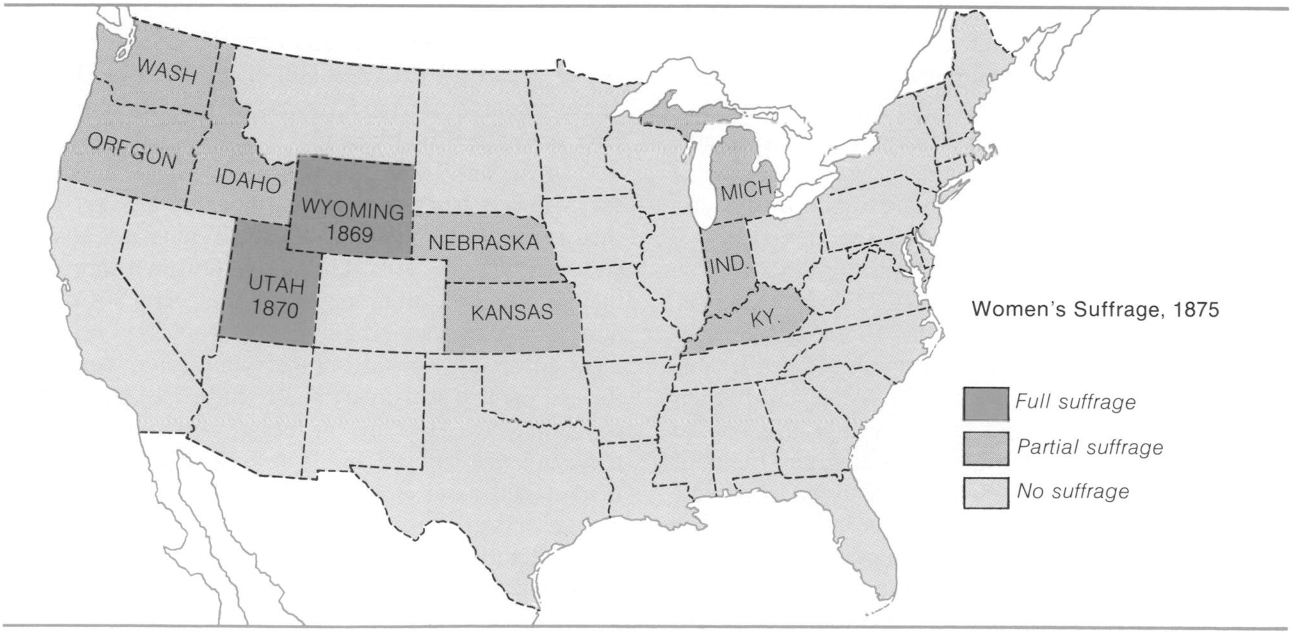

Courtesy New-York Historical Society, New York City.

Victoria Claflin Woodhull (1838–1927)

During the decade after the Civil War, the first woman to campaign for the presidency, Victoria Claflin Woodhull, flashed across the American scene like a meteor. A woman of great charm and considerable beauty, she scorned the moral code of her day, acted as if the fight for women's rights had already been won, and ended up dying at 89 much revered and very rich.

One of ten children, Victoria was born in near poverty in the country village of Homer, Ohio, not far from Columbus, Three of the children—Victoria, Tennessee Celeste, and Hebron—possessed a mix of remarkable guile, ambition, and showmanship. Along with their shiftless father, they put together a troupe that bottled and sold a variety of nostrums, including an "Elixir of Life" with Tennessee's lovely features on the label and a cancer cure concocted by brother Hebron. To amuse the rubes, the two sisters went into trances, communicated with the dead, and tried to heal the sick by means of mesmerism and the laying on of hands. By the time Victoria was sixteen, she had married in a loose fashion a young doctor named Woodhull. They had two children, one of whom, Zula Maud, was associated with some of her later enterprises in England.

In the late 1860s, the two sisters shook the dust of the Midwest from their skirts; more or less got rid of their father, Hebron, Woodhull, and Tennessee's husband; and showed up in New York City. Within a short time, they captured the attention (if not the heart) of Commodore Cornelius Vanderbilt, age 74, who for a brief moment apparently considered marrying Tennessee; nevertheless, the trio remained good friends. He enjoyed their company, their dabbling in mesmerism and the occult; they, in turn, enjoyed his favors, his tips on the stock market, and above all else, his willingness to set them up as a full-fledged brokerage house: Woodhull and Claflin. Soon Victoria went on the lecture circuit as a women's rights advocate. As the complete antithesis of what the public thought such creatures should look like, she was slim, utterly feminine, and a tremendous success, even though she sometimes expounded her free love philosophy along with other more acceptable views.

In 1870 *Woodhull and Claflin's Weekly* appeared, a bizarre publication designed to propel Victoria toward the White House; to promote feminism, a single standard of morality, and free love; and to attack injustice in all forms. The *Weekly* was the first U.S. journal to publish the *Communist Manifesto* of Karl Marx. In 1872 the Equal Rights party nominated Victoria for the presidency with ex-slave Frederick Douglass as her running mate. Douglass, who preferred Grant, ignored the nomination and Victoria received virtually no votes.

While Victoria was lecturing and trying to unseat Ulysses S. Grant, Tennessee was using the *Weekly* to blackmail some of her boyfriends. She let it be known that the records of a famous Manhattan brothel would soon be published in its columns—names, addresses, everything. Apparently, a lot of money appeared instead since the brothel records were never published.

In November 1872, the *Weekly* broke the story of Preacher Henry Ward Beecher's presumed intimacies with Mrs. Theodore Tilton, a parishioner. Tilton, who eventually sued Beecher, was a close friend of Victoria, and the trial, which ended in a hung jury, was one of the most sensational of the century. To get even, the Beechers and their friends drove Tennessee and Victoria to the brink of financial ruin. Then, in 1877, two years after the trial was over, Commodore Vanderbilt died, leaving the bulk of his estate to his son William. The rest of the family contested the will, claiming that Vanderbilt was incompetent because of his involvement with the Clafin sisters. Fearful of what Tennessee and Victoria might reveal if called as witnesses, William hustled them off to England to live, presumably with a large sum of spending money. Victoria married a very rich banker; Tennessee, a prominent businessman who subsequently became a baronet . . . and everyone lived happily ever after. ■

ing women, but insisted upon excluding men from its membership because the founders believed that male abolitionists had betrayed women's interests. Susan B. Anthony and Elizabeth Cady Stanton, with the aid of an eccentric financier and Democrat, George Francis Train (1829-1904), founded the weekly newspaper, *The Revolution,* whose motto was: "Men, their rights and nothing more; women, their rights and nothing less!"

A division in the ranks of the women's movement occurred when Henry Blackwell and his wife Lucy Stone joined with others in November 1869 to establish the American Woman Suffrage Association, which worked to enfranchise women through state organization and through the efforts of men *and* women. In early 1870, on the anniversary of the founding of *The Revolution,* Lucy Stone began a rival publication, *Woman's Journal.* The field was too small for more than one feminist paper, and *The Revolution* failed several months later. Part of the explanation for this schism was economic and political, rather than ideological. The American Woman Suffrage Association and *Woman's Journal* represented the interests of clubwomen, writers, and women in professions—in short, middle class women who were more or less conservative by feminist standards. The National Woman's Suffrage Association and *The Revolution* were concerned with the exploited workingwoman, the social outcasts, and women who were far more radical in their political orientation.

The split between "respectability" (The American Woman Suffrage Association) and "radicalism" (The National Woman's Suffrage Association) greatly weakened the women's rights movement for more than a century. Even a unified movement, however, would likely have faltered. The 1870s and 1880s were years of intense economic development, and most men and women were too absorbed with the momentous changes taking place in American society to take up the cause of women's suffrage.

Reconstruction, a decade of tension, high drama, some successes and many disappointments, left the nation a bit tired in body and spirit. As Americans celebrated their first hundred years, most citizens were quite eager to put behind them the war, the turmoil in its wake, the fate of the freedman, and, in great measure, social reform as well. Instead, they turned their energies inward to develop the West and the South, to build new industries and new factories, and to truly make one unified nation out of what almost had become two.

America at age one hundred

THE STRIDE OF A CENTURY.

533A

Granger Collection.

Opening day crowd at the Centennial.

Library of Congress.

Dignitaries start Corliss engine which powered exhibits.

Bettmann Archives.

Main Street, Rufus, Oregon, a wheat shipping community.

Bureau of Reclamation.

Farmer with four horse plow.

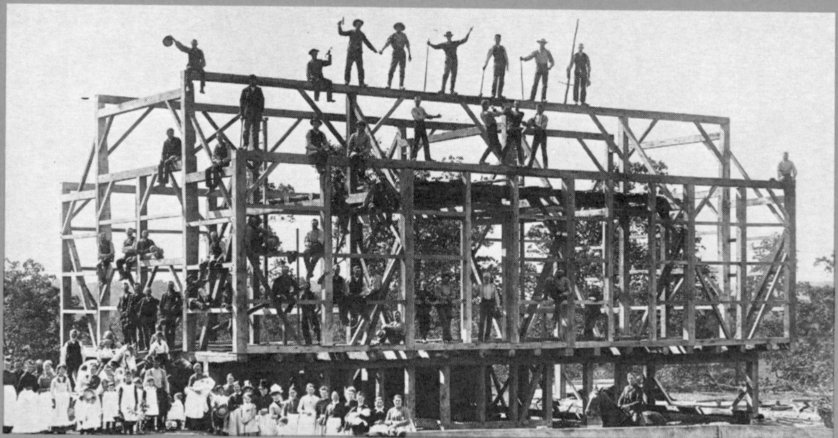

Courtesy Marlite Paneling, Selz, Seabolt & Associates, Inc.

Barn raising in Ohio.

Thomas Eakins. "Cowboy at the B.T. Ranch, North Dakota—summer of 1887", The Metropolitan Museum of Art, Gift of Charles Bregler, 1961.

North Dakota cowboy.

Denver Public Library Western Collection, Photo by Pont Soderberg.

Kokomo, Colorado, a typical mining town.

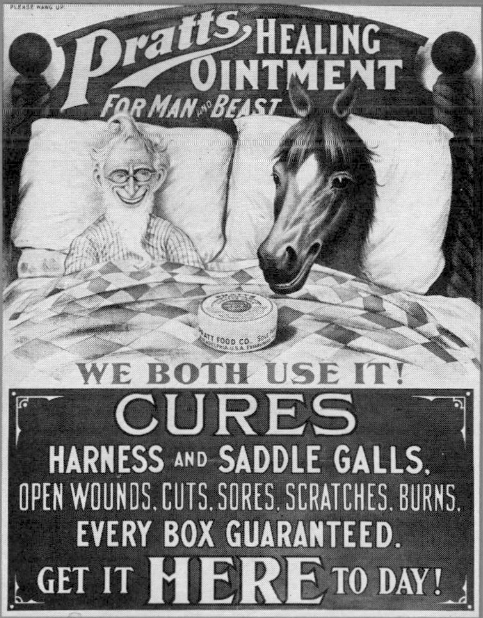

Granger Collection.

Typical patent medicine ad.

Granger Collection.

New York elevated railway.

Library of Congress.

Lawn tennis.

Library of Congress.

Kindergarten class.

Granger Collection.

Plantation hands en route to polls in South Carolina.

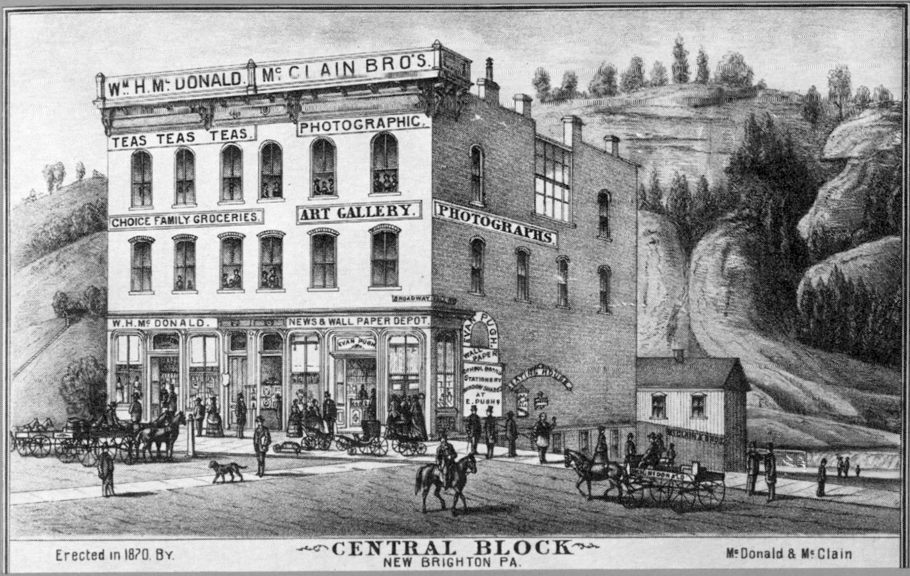

Library of Congress.

Downtown New Brighton, Pennsylvania.

Essay

Congress: Special Committees, Special Problems, and Public Opinion

Nowhere in the Constitution does the word "committee" appear; yet, it was obvious from legislative experience gained prior to 1789 that members of Congress soon would form themselves into small working groups in order to carry on their day-to-day business. What was less apparent was that occasionally, especially in times of crisis, these panels might become *special* committees designed to probe the activities of the executive branch of government. This could mean prodding a reluctant chief executive into action, monitoring his decisions and those of various cabinet officers, investigating past events, or perhaps—somewhat short of impeachment, though a step toward it—actually questioning the conduct of executive officeholders. For the most part, however, these "fact-finding" bodies have dealt with matters both mundane and exotic which, in the opinion of some legislators, did not fit into the standing committee framework.

Through the years the upper house of Congress has been especially fond of special or select committees. During the first half of the nineteenth century the Senate established temporary panels to discuss (among other things) roads and canals, excessive use of executive patronage, the strife-torn Bank of the United States, the circulation of abolitionist literature, the state of the coinage, fishing bounties, sickness and mortality on emigrant ships, the occupation of Oregon, and French spoilation claims prior to 1800.

During those same decades House members formed select committees to study coins, slavery in the District of Columbia, boiler explosions on steamboats, an assault upon a distinguished colleague, conditions in the gold assay offices in North Carolina and Georgia, and proposals for a Central American railway linking the Atlantic and Pacific oceans. Occasionally the two bodies formed joint committees to deal with such matters as the Library of Congress and arrangements for a presidential funeral.

The first joint panel to concentrate its full attention upon the executive branch of government with much force was the Joint Committee on the Conduct of the War, created in December 1861. Anxious, distressed by Southern successes, and wary of Abraham Lincoln's leadership, Congress authorized three

Culver Pictures.

Confederate victories at Bull Run and elsewhere early in the war led Radical Republicans in Congress to establish a Joint Committee on the Conduct of the War. Pictured here is the Union defeat at Ball's Bluff, near Washington in October 1861.

senators and four representatives to investigate the Union's war efforts.

This body, headed by Ohio's Benjamin F. Wade, also included at the outset Senator Andrew Johnson of Tennessee. Radical in tone and often impetuous in action, these men were authorized to probe military affairs, contracts, and expenditures; however, their investigations dealt principally with the competency of Lincoln's generals, and all who commanded the Army of the Potomac, except Grant, had to answer their incisive and often biased questions. In fact, some 2 million words of testimony seemed designed to dissect only one disaster: the Peninsula Campaign of 1862. This seven-man body played a major role on the Washington scene, but its work (summarized in eight volumes) often was overzealous, resulting in more harm than good.

One noted historian, James G. Randall, even credits the group with considerable mischief. None of the members had any military experience; yet, they tried to second guess those who did. In his view their investigations amounted to "elaborate inquisitions" that took generals and department heads away from their proper duties at crucial times, ruined the reputations of able commanders (especially if Democrats) while building up those of their "pets" (always Republicans), and created dissension and mistrust by bandying about unsubstantial charges of treason. These Congressmen pestered Lincoln unmercifully, stripped McClellan of all support, and even drove General Charles P. Stone out of the U.S. Army and into the employ of the Khedive of Egypt. At least four generals (McClellan, Stone, Fitz-John Porter, and Franklin) could thank these seven men, not the enemy, for most of their wartime difficulties. Speaking succinctly, Lincoln once said the committee's "greatest purpose seems to be to hamper my action and obstruct military operations." And General Lee apparently agreed. The Confederate leader reportedly once remarked that the Congressional panel was worth two divisions.

When Lincoln vetoed the Wade-Davis plan for Reconstruction in July 1864, Wade, the Ohio Radical was furious, since it expressed the fundamental beliefs of the Joint Committee on the Conduct of the War.

"A more studied outrage on the legislative authority of the people has never been perpetrated. . . . The President has greatly presumed on the forbearance which the supporters of his Administration have so long practiced, in view of the arduous conflict in which we are engaged, and the reckless ferocity of our opponents. But he must understand that our support is of a cause and not of a man; that the authority of the Congress is paramount and must be respected; that the whole body of the Union men in Congress will not submit to be impeached by him of rash and unconstitutional legislation; and if he wishes our support, he must confine himself to his executive duties—to obey and execute, not to make laws—to suppress by arms armed rebellion, and leave political reorganization to Congress."

A few weeks later the Wade-Davis Manifesto expressing similar views appeared, but it proved to be a disastrous political error in a presidential election year. The Manifesto won the endorsement of few leading Republicans and even Wade's hometown newspaper thought it "ill-tempered and improper."

More than anything else, this joint committee—persistent, energetic, resolute, determined—became the spearhead of the Radical assault upon administration policies that they viewed as soft and overly considerate of Southern sensibilities. By law, the body ceased to function ninety days after the end of hostilities.

Within a few weeks, however, its place was taken by the Joint Committee on Reconstruction, established in December

1865. A bigger group, it contained several prominent Radicals but, as work got underway, it was controlled essentially by Moderates. The chairman of the fifteen-man panel (six senators, nine representatives) was Maine's William P. Fessenden. Two of the best-known members were Thaddeus Stevens, the Pennsylvania Congressman who had proposed the creation of this body, and New York's Roscoe Conkling.

During its two-year life span, this joint committee held numerous sessions and collected a huge amount of testimony. Although this panel heard all points of view expressed by witnesses from the North and the South, its reports tended to give solace to Radicals, not their adversaries. In April 1866 the members concluded that, at the war's end, the defeated Confederacy consisted of "disorganized communities without civil governments." Hence, they stressed, elections held under such chaotic conditions obviously were invalid. Unfortunately, during these months by both deed and word President Johnson strengthened the hand of his Radical foes and, thus, gave credence to widely expressed opinions. This joint committee's chief triumphs were the Reconstruction Act of 1867 and the Fourteenth Amendment.

These two special panels of the 1860s are somewhat of an aberration in American history and perhaps can best be explained by the unusual pressures of those years. During the remainder of the nineteenth century no similar groups ever achieved such power. Senate committees were set up to analyze such matters as Indian affairs, woman suffrage, irritating delays in the day-to-day work of the executive branch of government, collection of internal revenue taxes in North Carolina, and creation of a University of the United States. Meanwhile, select House committees pondered illegal election returns, civil service reform, and depressed economic conditions. Joint bodies of those years arranged a proper funeral in 1886 for Senator John A. Logan (Republican stalwart, backer of generous pensions for Union veterans, and three times president of the Grand Army of the Republic) and seven years later discussed plans to reorganize the executive departments of the federal government.

As one would anticipate, the complexities of twentieth century life have fostered a virtual avalanche of special and select committees in both houses of Congress. In recent years even select *sub*committees have appeared, and some panels, such as the House Select Committee on Small Business, have achieved permanent status. Since 1900 special groups have scrutinized almost every facet of the national scene: crime, pornography, crop insurance, veterans' affairs, nutrition and health, aging, conservation, unemployment, bilingual education,

"IT'S A TELEVISION FIRST — TWO COMMITTEES ARE INVESTIGATING EACH OTHER."

assassinations, professional sports, and the inner workings of executive departments, as well as those of Congress itself.

Yet, despite such a varied shopping list, only a handful of inquiries has had much impact upon the majority of Americans. They perhaps remember the Teapot Dome and Pearl Harbor investigations, Gerald Nye's assault upon the munitions makers, Harry Truman's efforts to promote efficiency among World War II defense contractors, and the so-called Watergate hearings. On the other hand, most Americans have long since forgotten discussions relating to pneumatic tube mail service, dirigible disasters, the M-16 rifle, and alleged executions of American soldiers in France during World War I without proper trials and court-martial proceedings.

During the 1920s two special committees looked into the Teapot Dome scandals that grew out of the leasing of naval oil reserves in Wyoming to private producers. In 1922 Senator Thomas J. Walsh of Montana spearheaded an investigation examining the involvement of several cabinet members in this scandal, which led to a lengthy round of court battles but only one conviction, and that on procedural technicalities. These revelations, part of an emerging picture of general wrongdoing in high places, cast a dark shadow over the Harding administration, although Calvin Coolidge shrewdly maneuvered the Republicans out of troubled waters. In the late 1920s Gerald P. Nye, a

Republican senator from North Dakota, headed a special panel that reopened a probe of the controversial leases that led to the Teapot Dome fiasco.

A few years later, Nye turned his attention to World War I and alleged "cosy" relationships between Allied governments and American bankers and munitions makers even before the United States became involved in that struggle in April 1917. The Nye Committee (1934–1935) turned up mountains of material but no solid proof of any international conspiracy to lure America into war. Nevertheless, these hearings strengthened isolationist sentiment, and in 1936 Senator Nye was co-sponsor of the Neutrality Act forbidding the shipment of arms to nations at war. A prominent member of the America First Committee pledged to keep the United States out of Europe's struggles at all costs, Nye's extreme isolationism led to his defeat at the polls in 1944.

At the same time that Gerald Nye was fading from public view, a little-known Missouri senator was gathering headlines as chairman of a Special Committee to Investigate the National Defense Program. Under Harry Truman's guidance, its members tried to promote efficiency among defense contractors by dispatching investigators to plants and factories where alleged evils were said to exist. Truman's dedication and ability won him many friends and admirers and a place on the Democratic ticket as vice-presidential nominee when Franklin D. Roosevelt decided to run for an unprecedented fourth term in 1944.

Truman, fully aware of Lincoln's Civil War problems, was

J.P.I.

Senator Harry S. Truman's work as chairman of the Special Committee to Investigate the National Defense Program helped the war effort and won for him a place on the Democratic ticket in 1944.

determined his group would help, not hinder, the war effort, and shortly before his death in 1973 he described its accomplishments to Merle Miller, author of *Plain Speaking.*

"I believe it was established that we saved the taxpayers about fifteen billion dollars. And the lives of some kids. I don't know how many. It was said . . . some reporters estimated we may have saved the lives of a few thousand kids."

The most recent select committee to garner widespread attention was a panel of seven senators established in February 1973 (by a vote of 70–0) to investigate rumored irregularities in the 1972 presidential campaign. In fact, this group, headed by North Carolina's folksy Sam J. Ervin, Jr., probed only the Watergate affair and little else. This complex series of scandals initiated by a bungled burglary at the headquarters of the National Democratic Party in Washington soon ensnared numerous prominent Republicans, various White House aides and advisers, and even President Richard Nixon. In the summer of 1973 the four Democrats and three Republicans on this committee saw their names become household words as television took the hearings into millions of homes throughout the nation. Revelations at the hearings (assisted by ongoing grand jury probes) led ultimately to sensational trials and the impeachment and resignation of Nixon, the only man ever to quit the presidency.

Except for special Congressional committees designed to perform minor ceremonial duties—burying a deceased politician or welcoming a conquering hero—the avowed goals of these panels seem to fall into three general categories: investigation of past irregularities, solution of current dilemmas, and analysis of future problems. In a sense, the creation of these bodies often is tacit admission by Congress as a whole that some of its members have been asleep at the switch. Had they been alert and doing their jobs, rumored misdeeds might not have occurred; and, at the same time, it would seem to the casual observer that the standing committees of Congress, if functioning properly, should be able to handle both current and impending problems with as much success as any special panel. However, this view may well ignore the pressure of public opinion, for nothing arouses the interest of a Congressman so much as the aroused interest of a significant number of constituents (voters) in a specific problem or issue. Yet, once a special committee gets steam up, all too often its proceedings become little more than a noisy sideshow or a public platform for one political viewpoint. This certainly was true of the Nye committee that focused its attention on World War I almost

J. P. Laffont/Sygma.

Senator Sam J. Ervin, Jr., and the Senate Watergate committee and staff probe the rumored irregularities in the 1972 presidential campaign.

twenty years after the guns stopped firing, as well as the principal Congressional panels which emerged during the 1860s. And a minority of Americans remain convinced that Ervin and his associates, with the assistance of the press and television, "hounded" Nixon from office.

These special or select bodies undoubtedly are most effective when they address current affairs and remain essentially nonpartisan. Truman's World II group and Ervin's Watergate panel are prime examples of how such bodies can work for the public good. Yet the fact remains that the success, failure, momentum, and direction of any such inquiry depend ultimately upon the whims, leadership ability, and basic integrity of its chairman. Even more disturbing is the realization that he and his associates, elected to be spokesmen for the legislative branch of government, often are meddling—for better or worse—in the workings of the executive branch.

This can, of course, be viewed as a blunt challenge to the much revered "separation of powers" doctrine and lead to noisy and bitter confrontation that may paralyze the federal bureaucracy, even the life of the nation itself. Nixon's eighteen-month battle with the Watergate Committee—a donnybrook of courtroom proceedings, subpoenas, accusations, "leaked" information, and angry words—left both participants and spectators exhausted.

The truth is, these special and somewhat extralegal investigative bodies frequently are treading on dangerous ground, since the federal machinery, as complex and cumbersome as it may be, seems to provide the means to deal with alleged and sometimes imaginary evils. Only a true crisis, then, furnishes good cause for the creation of such panels, and without sound and able leadership the members may well exacerbate the very conditions they claim they have set out to correct.

Selected Readings

General Accounts

James G. Randall and David Donald, *The Civil War and Reconstruction* (rev., 2nd ed., 1973)

Kenneth M. Stampp, *The Era of Reconstruction, 1865–1877* (1965)

John Hope Franklin, *Reconstruction after the Civil War* (1961)

W. E. B. DuBois, *Black Reconstruction, 1860–1880* (1935)

Reconstruction During the Civil War

Herman Belz, Reconstructing the Union: *Theory and Policy during the Civil War* (1969)

Herman Belz, *A New Birth of Freedom: The Republican Party and Freedmen's Rights, 1861 to 1866* (1977)

William B. Hesseltine, *Lincoln's Plan of Reconstruction* (1960)

T. Harry Williams, *Lincoln and the Radicals* (1965)

Willie L. Rose, *Rehearsal for Reconstruction: The Port Royal Experiment* (1964)

Reconstruction After Appomattox

Michael Les Benedict, *A Compromise of Principle: Congressional Republicans and Reconstruction, 1863–1869* (1974)

David Donald, *Charles Sumner and the Rights of Man* (1970)

William S. McFeely, *Yankee Stepfather: General O. O. Howard and the Freedmen* (1968)

Eric L. McKitrick, *Andrew Johnson and Reconstruction* (1960)

Hans L. Trefousse, *Impeachment of a President: Andrew Johnson, the Blacks, and Reconstruction* (1975)

Martin E. Mantell, *Johnson, Grant and the Politics of Reconstruction* (1973)

Blacks, Indians, and Women

Roger L. Ransom and Richard Sutch, *One Kind of Freedom: The Economic Consequences of Emancipation* (1977)

Robert Cruden, *The Negro in Reconstruction* (1969)

Annie Heloise Abel, *The American Indian Under Reconstruction* (1925)

M. Thomas Bailey, *Reconstruction in Indian Territory: A Story of Avarice, Discrimination, and Opportunism* (1972)

Elinor R. Hays, *Lucy Stone: One of America's First and Greatest Feminists* (1961)

Alma Lutz, *Susan B. Anthony: Rebel, Crusader, Humanitarian* (1959)

The End of Reconstruction

Allen W. Trelease, *White Terror: The Ku Klux Klan Conspiracy and Southern Reconstruction* (1971)

C. Van Woodward, *Reunion and Reaction: The Compromise of 1877 and the End of Reconstruction* (rev. ed., 1966)

Keith I. Polakoff, *The Politics of Inertia: The Election of 1876 and the End of Reconstruction* (1973)

Samuel P. Hirshon, *Farewell to the Bloody Shirt: Northern Republicans and the Southern Negro, 1877–1893* (1962)

C. Van Woodward, *The Strange Career of Jim Crow* (3rd rev. ed., 1974)

Chapter 16

The New South and the New West

TIMELINE

1867
Oliver Kelley organizes the Grange

1869
First transcontinental railroad completed

1870
Congress appropriates funds for Indian education

1873
Discovery of the Comstock lode in Nevada

1874
Greenback party is organized

1875
Army subdues Comanche Indians

1876
Munn v. *Illinois*

1876
Custer defeated at battle of Little Big Horn

1879
Southern Baptist Convention rejects national reunification

1880
Milton George organizes Northern Alliance

1880
Greenback party nominates James B. Weaver for President

1885
Last cattle drive

1886
Geronimo surrenders to U.S. Army

1887
Dawes Severalty Act

1889
Oklahoma land rush

1890
James B. Duke forms American Tobacco Company

1890
"Battle" at Wounded Knee

1896
Plessy v. *Ferguson*

1898
Williams v. *Mississippi*

1898
Birmingham, Alabama, the nation's largest exporter of pig iron

CHAPTER OUTLINE

The most important fact in American life during the final decades of the nineteenth century was growth that changed all parts of the nation. Overall population rose from 39.8 million in 1870 to 76.2 million thirty years later, influenced in no small measure by the influx of nearly 12 million immigrants, most of them from Europe. By dividing the United States into four general regions, one can get some sense of what was happening.

It is obvious that all sections enjoyed substantial population growth during these three decades, and by the turn of the century the farms and industrial towns and cities of the midwestern heartland were home to slightly more Americans than lived in the South, a predominance that the North Central region clung to from 1880 to 1930 when the South regained first place once more. To some extent, this momentary eclipse of the South, traditionally the most populous of the four vast areas, was caused by the outward migration of whites during Reconstruction and after, the failure to attract immigrants in large numbers, and the movement of blacks to other regions in the twentieth century. Nevertheless, nine out of ten black Americans still were living south of the Mason-Dixon Line in 1900, and as census figures demonstrate, the population of the South nearly doubled (1870–1900).

This growth, coupled with the rise of cotton mills, the emergence of a tobacco industry, and the spread of new rail lines—though owned and controlled by Yankees—created the image of the "New South." This was a South of hard-working people eager to throw off some aspects of a troubled, slave past and to develop a judi-

POPULATION DISTRIBUTION (by millions)

	1870	1900
Northeast (New England, New York, New Jersey, Pennsylvania)	12.3	21.0
North Central (12-state area north of Ohio River between Pennsylvania and Colorado, including the Great Plains)	12.9	26.3
South (Confederacy, plus Oklahoma, Kentucky, West Virginia, Maryland, Delaware)	13.5	24.5
West (11 states and territories west of a line from Montana to Texas)	.9	4.3

cious marriage of raw materials and machines that would take advantage of natural resources as well. In part, the "New South" was an elusive dream, but it was a goal to which millions aspired, and rhetoric in praise of southern progress created a chorus of hope during the last years of the nineteenth century. Yet "southern progress" often was a statistical fairyland. Only after World War II did per capita income in much of the South begin to approach that of the national average.

In some ways, the "New West" is also an elusive concept because its chronological beginnings and geographical boundaries are indistinct. Certainly the Rocky Mountains and Pacific coast states are part of it, but so are sections of the Dakotas, Texas, and the Great Plains. Both the "New South" and the "New West" are a mixture of fact and fiction. During these years, both regions grew with the aid of capital from the Northeast and exhibited similar trends. They were heavily rural and agricultural, eager for the expansion of railroads at almost any price, and equally determined to develop (even ravage) their natural resources. This was an age of rampant exploitation and words such as "conservation" and "ecology" were seldom, if ever, heard.

Thanks to Hollywood and the cowboy, the "New West," more so than the "New South," has gained a secure niche in American history and folklore. But it is not the Great Plains farmer tilling wheat and corn but the range kingdom of six-guns, cattle drives, and outlaws that usually makes the pulse beat faster. Yet like all legends, both are based upon truth. There clearly was a new spirit throughout the South after 1877, a determination to rebuild and expand, and the same dreams of new towns and cities, new commerce, new transportation routes, and new industry are evident in the West as well. Ironically, while both regions often rejected the leadership of the rest of the nation as old-fashioned, too "citified," or too Yankee, at the same time their people eagerly sought investment dollars and measured their "progress" against that of centers such as Chicago, St. Louis, Pittsburgh, and New York.

The New South

The most pressing problem facing the South was how to get money needed to develop the region. The year 1877 was a depression year marked by violence throughout the nation. Those most severely hit by economic reversals were the poor, and few could have been worse off than the impoverished blacks and whites of the South. The southern economy had fallen behind that of the rest of the nation even though more cotton was being exported to foreign consumers, particularly the British. But this increase in volume did not make up for the reduction in price. Since cotton was the South's major agricultural asset, low prices hurt southern farmers—and benefited northern textile manufacturers.

Poor whites were often worse off than they had been before the war. Agriculture was becoming more mechanized, and few could afford the machines that were now turning out bumper crops in the Midwest; in addition, their place in the social order was threatened by the rise of the freedman. Prosperous Southerners, like their counterparts in the North, seemed inclined to blame the poor for poverty. Southern poverty was explained as the result of racial conflicts, Yankee interference, and "cracker" intransigence. (Strictly speaking, a "cracker" is a poverty-stricken resident of southern Georgia or northern Florida living in hilly or backwoods country; however, the term generally means any poor white of the southeastern region.) The real underlying causes—unfair economic and agricultural policies such as free trade and the crop lien system—were rarely mentioned.

A One-Crop Economy

Southern farmers had long been used to cultivating a single crop, either cotton or tobacco, supplemented with some corn, wheat, or other grains, and this specialization kept them economically dependent on the fluctuations of world market prices. The end of slavery and the shortage of money among planters led to tenancy or sharecropping, a system that had been practiced in a small way even before 1860. Under sharecropping, a planter, who was often landowner, merchant, and banker all in one, provided land, tools and equipment, seed, and credit at his store throughout the year. The tenant and his family supplied the labor to raise the crop.

The concomitant crop lien system enabled a tenant to receive supplies from a merchant by promising the merchant a share of whatever was harvested. Both parties faced certain risks. A tenant might not be a good worker and perhaps would abandon the crop before harvest time. The planter-merchant, who probably could read and write and had the law on his side, might not keep his

Brown Brothers.

This sharecropping scene of the 1890s suggests that little had changed for black laborers since slavery. The well-kept appearance of this cropping family, however, hints of affluence, pride, and perhaps independence.

word. In any case, one thing was certain: the tenant would be overcharged at the store and find himself in debt to the planter-merchant even after the crop was divided up. However, these high interest rates and inflated prices were not always unjustified. Sharecropping was, of course, a barrier to agricultural diversity since it meant that more and more land was planted in cotton, the major cash crop, and one that most tenants knew how to grow.

The roles of the landowner and merchant in this unique arrangement have been a subject of historical debate. Historians Monroe Billington and C. Vann Woodward deplore the practices of sharecropping and crop lien, since landowners used the system to intimidate "croppers" and transform them into virtual peons. In 1880 only 30 percent of all farmers in the lower South were tenants, but their numbers continued to rise until they reached a high of 60 percent forty years later. On the other hand, Joseph D. Reid has viewed the system more sympathetically. He argues that the decline in available supplies of agricultural capital and labor, rather than the practices of sharecropping and crop lien, explains the fall in relative income in the South. Reid goes on to cite advantages of the sharecropping system. It enabled people to find credit and employment at a time when the state banks had collapsed and money was in short supply. As late as 1900 only 500 state and national banks existed in the entire South. Reid even argues that sharecropping could join the interests of tenants and landlords—which may in part explain how the system became self-perpetuating. Landlords sometimes provided managerial expertise to their tenants; after all, increased productivity of the land, benefited landlords as well as tenants.

A definitive conclusion about sharecropping and the crop lien system is difficult to reach because social and economic historians tend to examine different sources. Reid's positive assessment of the system is no doubt a minority opinion; most historians argue that the combination of crop lien laws, tenancy, single-crop economies, and exhausted soils kept the South impoverished until the end of the century.

Although sharecropping may have been a necessary stopgap measure in the South of the late 1860s and early 1870s and may have provided the means by which many an ambitious young farmer got started, all too often it only opened the door to continuous debt, hard work from sunup to sundown, and unending poverty. The creditor held virtually all the cards. If dissatisfied or cheated, the only thing a tenant, who was often illiterate, could do was quit, and this meant finding a new home for his family and a new landlord while facing possible legal action by his old planter-merchant "boss."

The South appeared "solid" to the rest of the nation, but actually class distinctions divided Southerners along economic lines that seemed insuperable—tenant versus landlords, cracker versus freedman—and, in general, black versus white. The devastation caused by the war and the hardships during Reconstruction threw these class and racial differences into stark relief. By the end of the century, however, whites had generally agreed to forget class differences and to work jointly to control a rising generation of blacks who knew nothing of prewar plantation ways.

Religion

Southern religion was always a striking institution in the life of the people, but its potency in social, cultural, and intellectual affairs was remarkable in the postwar period. More than any other institution, religion reflected as well as permeated regional political and economic life. The political and economic rupture between North and South because of slavery had also entailed a split in Protestant churches, and this division was slow to heal. In 1879 the Southern Baptist Convention rejected a minority attempt to reunify the church with its northern counterpart—and this isolationism is still observable today. Only the Episcopal Church was successfully reunited in the nineteenth century, a short-lived Confederate branch rejoining the national church body in 1865.

The conservatism of the southern religion is apparent in the rejection of three vital new forces in American religious life: biblical criticism, Darwinism, and the Social Gospel movement. Biblical criticism was the application of methods of literary and historical scholarship to the Bible, a pursuit that often raised questions about which books of the Bible were authentic and about who had written them. To southern Protestants the Bible throughout was the literal word of God, accepted totally on faith. Darwinism as an intellectual movement, of course, conflicted with literal readings of the Scriptures, particularly Genesis and the story of creation. Charles Darwin (1809–1882) rejected the idea of the separate creation of the species and proposed instead a theory of evolution—which was completely at variance with the Biblical account. The Social Gospel movement, which stressed the social responsibility of Churches, grew in the North out of a desire to improve social conditions by educating the illiterate and by feeding the hungry. In the South, the churches ignored this movement and empha-

Library of Congress.

Baptismal ceremonies, like this one in the James River in Virginia, provided spiritual support to thousands of downtrodden blacks who needed refuge from daily problems.

sized individual redemption, not the resolution of social problems.

In the last quarter of the nineteenth century, when revivalism was at its height, Southern Baptist and Methodist churches accounted for 85 percent of church membership, in contrast to 47 percent membership in these two sects in the nation at large. In addition to these major faiths, there were scores of loosely affiliated sects that believed in premillennialism, the doctrine that the Second Coming of Jesus Christ would signal the beginning of a thousand years when faithful Christians would reign over the earth.

The growth of these revivalist sects and of the two major Protestant denominations was due largely to increased membership among southern blacks. With emancipation, southern white churches tried to maintain control over their black brethern, often by setting up "associate" congregations segregated by race and administered by whites. But blacks were quick to reject unequal status in one of the few areas of their lives where they could exercise choice. In 1860, the Southern Methodist Church could claim more than 200,000 black members; in 1865 it could barely count 50,000.

As early as the first days of Reconstruction, freedmen began to organize their own churches, free of the domination of their former masters. Denominations such as the Colored Primitive Baptists of America, organized in 1865, and the Colored Cumberland Presbyterian Church in 1870 attracted large numbers of blacks eager to experience religious independence. By the end of the century, an overwhelming majority of blacks belonged to their own churches, and membership was in the millions. Very quickly these churches became centers of secular activities, including recreation and politics. Many of the architects of black progress in the twentieth century, such as Martin Luther King, Jr., were ministers or prominent lay church leaders.

To some degree, Southerners, long adherents of stern individualism and self-reliance, were staggered by defeat and hard times, and the church provided a refuge, a secure, unchanging sanctuary. Their clergy proclaimed exactly what most of the faithful wanted to hear in an age of industrial growth, racial tension, migration, and expansion: a conservative social and intellectual philosophy supported by orthodox theology. An unchanging God, church, and Bible gave many the strength to sustain themselves morally if not economically in difficult days.

Race Relations

There is still considerable debate concerning the treatment and position of blacks during these years, though all historians agree that blacks were often exploited and treated unjustly. In most parts of the New South the color line hardened, but the process varied from region to region. In older, established communities some aspects of the master-slave relationship lingered on as whites sometimes provided as best they could for their former charges. In frontier or newer parts of the South, however, this spirit of noblesse oblige usually was absent.

The inequities of segregation are well-documented; the hypocrisy of the "separate-but-equal" policy was evident to both whites and blacks from the beginning. The segregation laws of the late nineteenth century were the South's way of institutionalizing the status of blacks so that change was illegal and the subordinate place of blacks guaranteed, or to put it another way, the superior position of all whites was maintained.

As the formal end of Reconstruction approached, the Supreme Court began to lose interest in the rights of blacks. In 1876 the justices held the Enforcement Act of 1870 to be unconstitutional and said the Fifteenth Amendment did not guarantee citizens the right to vote; merely the right not to be discriminated against by states on account of race, color, or previous condition of servitude. So far as the Court was concerned, the South was free to settle its problems as best it could—an outlook that became public policy with the so-called Compromise of 1877, which settled the Hayes-Tilden embroglio.

Democrats in the South at first pursued a rather contradictory course. Blacks usually were terrorized, harassed, or in some manner prevented from exercising the right to vote. On election day roads were blocked, ferry service suspended, ballots printed in foreign languages, and polling places changed without notice. South Carolina, the state with the highest percentage of blacks, invented an eight-box ballot scheme requiring voters unassisted to match up their vote with the offices being voted for. This meant, of course, one had to be able to read the labels (governor, lieutenant governor, and so on) in order to vote correctly. On the other hand, since the Democrats often were composed of rival cliques at the local and state level, they sometimes vied for black votes, feting would-be voters or simply herding them to the polls like cattle.

So long as competing groups could use the black

Library of Congress.

Lynching was one of the most hideous practices in the United States. Many of the blacks who suffered under vigilante injustice committed offenses no stronger than engaging in arguments with whites. A crowd of thousands watched this lynching in Texas in 1893.

vote to their advantage from time to time, no one was quite ready for complete and legal disfranchisement; however, in the 1890s alarmed by agricultural unrest and the rise of third parties, most Southern whites concluded that was the best course. Once the black man lost his vote the rest of the intricate structure of segregation was constructed with case.

Some historians argue that blacks had no choice but to accept segregation. They lacked entrepreneurial experience; they had little or no formal education (in 1870, 90 percent of all black adults were illiterate). The deliberate policies of southern banks against extending mortgage money to blacks, though part of a general hostility toward all farmers, made owning land especially difficult for blacks. In 1880, most blacks worked someone else's land; by 1900, only 8 percent of all farms in the five major cotton states were owned by blacks, and in acreage these farms represented only 6.5 percent of the arable land.

Despite this gloomy general picture, scholars recently have pointed to scattered examples of black autonomy, independence, and success in some parts of the South. Blacks actively entered politics when they joined the rebellion of farmers, which was initially known as the Farmer's Alliance. By 1889, at the St. Louis convention, the black Knights of Labor, the Colored Alliance, and the Farmers' Mutual Benefit Association joined forces with their white counterparts.

In this experience of cooperative effort and united political concern, blacks learned the value of solidarity and communal effort. If they were to escape from the treadmill of sharecropping and the crop lien system, they knew that they must either own their land or free themselves from the landlord-storekeeper. In spite of poverty and hostile labor laws, many blacks had, as Thomas E. Miller told Congress in 1891, "achieved a success founded upon material prosperity and accumulated wealth the equal of which has never been accomplished by pauperized serfs or peasants in any part of the universe." By that date some 15,000 blacks had risen from being hired hands to tenant farmers and gone on from there to purchase their own land.

Because of the unique character and history of New Orleans, blacks living there were probably more skilled and their occupations more varied than anywhere else in the South, or perhaps the nation, during the last decades of the nineteenth century. Negro males were engaged in 75 different occupations in 1860; 153 in 1870; and 156 in 1880. Although most skilled blacks were concentrated in the building trades, a few worked as cabinetmakers, jewelers, engineers, bookkeepers, pilots, florists, photographers, and druggists. By 1880, the first black capitalists in New Orleans succeeded in establishing brokerage houses, real estate firms and small businesses, notably groceries.

Clearly, a few blacks achieved in agriculture, on the labor market, and even in the world of finance and business some prominence. These successes, to be sure, represented the experience of only a small minority of blacks, though they are all the more remarkable for being won against overwhelming odds.

Although some blacks left the South for other regions, a handful even heading back to Africa, blacks of those years were moving for the most part from rural areas to towns and cities within the New South, usually in search of better jobs, better schools for their children, and a better way of life. William Pickens, later an outstanding early leader of the NAACP, remembered that his family moved no less than twenty times before his eighteenth birthday.

The decade of the 1880s represents a turning point in black-white relations within the New South and in the nation as well. Old abolitionists and their progeny, more

Library of Congress.

A carpenter's union composed of skilled black artisans from Jacksonville, Florida, c. 1890. Many southern blacks moved North, but few were permitted to practice their trades or join the American Federation Labor locals.

interested in a stable, growing economy than in the welfare of ex-slaves, began to look the other way as segregation by law, not custom, loomed on the horizon. At first, state laws regulating marriage, education, and transportation were defended on the basis of social mores, but by the turn of the century even many well-intended Northerners viewed the poll tax and similar stratagems designed to keep the black man away from the ballot box as a means of reforming and purifying politics by eliminating the potential for fraud.

The Supreme Court, having decreed that control of suffrage was a state matter (once local political battles subsided and a white clique gained a firm upper hand in a southern state, it soon held a convention and wrote a new constitution), put its stamp of approval on both disfranchisement and segregation. In a series of important decisions the Supreme Court gave its benign endorsement. *Plessy* v *Ferguson* (1896) upheld the constitutionality of a Louisiana "Jim Crow" law requiring "separate but equal" railway coaches. Only one man protested, Justice John M. Harlan, appointed by President Hayes, who insisted the Constitution was "colorblind" and the Louisiana statute unconstitutional. (Of course, in 1954 his views finally prevailed.) Two years later in *Williams* v. *Mississippi,* the Court held that a law permitting local authorities to ask voters to read and interpret any part of the Constitution as a requirement for registration was valid. And in 1899 in *Cumming* v. *Board of Education,* the justices by implication accepted "separate-but-equal" schools for black and white students. By that date legal segregation was fast becoming a way of life for millions of Americans.

Like those who were writing the rules for this caste system, blacks also pursued a rather erratic course of action. During the years from 1877 to 1900, the black voter vacillated between supporting the planter class and the poor whites and hoped to extract promises and political advantage from both, although he generally marked a Republican ballot in national elections. Usually he got only promises and after 1900 not even a ballot.

His most prominent spokesman during the last decades of the nineteenth century was Booker T. Washington (1856–1915), a remarkable educator who stressed immediate, practical goals. Amid a hostile Alabama environment Washington almost singlehandedly made Tuskegee Institute an outstanding example of black progress. At the same time he always counseled respect for the law and cooperation with white authority. By not antagonizing the dominant power structure and generally training farmers, mechanics, and domestic servants that southern society needed, Washington won respect, approval, and financial support. This program of vocational education comported well with the mood of the times, although after 1900 Booker T. Washington would face mounting criticism from black intellectuals who thought he had compromised too much in order to achieve short-range goals. He publicly accepted disfranchisement and segregation and worked within that framework; privately he helped to finance court cases against segregation.

Pressures for segregation varied from place to place

Library of Congress.

The loyalty of southern blacks to the nation can be seen in this photograph of children saluting the flag. Neither segregation nor ill-prepared black instructors nor paternalistic white teachers could dampen the enthusiasm for education of blacks of every age.

Library of Congress.

Booker T. Washington.

and decade to decade, but by the turn of the century the South was pretty much of one mind. Ironically, increasing standardization of American life meant—in a large segment of the nation at least—a "double" standard, a two-track, biracial society in which all public facilities such as hotels, schools, churches, hospitals, orphanages, poorhouses, jails, penitentiaries, and cemeteries were separate. Yet the truth is, this system of barriers was never wholly effective or complete. There always were exceptions to the general rule which merely served to highlight the ridiculous aspects of any such scheme in a democratic, changing society.

Industry

The importance of industrialization in the New South is still a matter of disagreement among historians. Some scholars, such as Broadus Mitchell, have argued that industry brought some real prosperity to the area. Others, such as Paul Gaston, have asserted that much of the postwar rhetoric about industrial benefits to the South was based more on hope than on reality.

In the late 1870s the depression that was besetting the entire nation showed signs of coming to an end. As the economy improved, spokesmen for the South presented their region's cheap and plentiful labor, its natural mineral resources, and its big cash crops of tobacco and cotton as inducements for northern investments. In addition, the new state governments welcomed speculators and investors with promises of low taxes.

Smithsonian Institution.

A primitive cotton manufacturing factory in Alabama. Poor whites from the hills and flatlands entered southern towns and cities to work. Though this scene is similar to the immigrant sweat shop of the North, the South remained backward industrially and succeeded only in diversifying its white labor force.

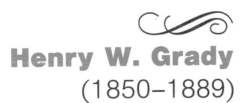

Library of Congress.

Henry W. Grady
(1850–1889)

Orator, journalist, architect of racial segregation, Henry Woodfin Grady was born in Athens, Georgia, where he attended local schools and the University of Georgia, graduating in 1868. Grady then studied law at the University of Virginia for a year, but journalism, not law, was to be his chosen career.

As a student he wrote for the *Atlanta Constitution* and in August 1869, as a representative of that newspaper, set out on a state press association tour of northeastern Georgia, Tennessee, and Alabama. Smart-alecky and brash, young Grady tried to prove the excursion was an attempt by railroad executives to corrupt Georgia newsmen and quit the group in Rome to become editor of the *Courier*. Unable to criticize local politics, he deserted the *Courier*, bought two other Rome newspapers, and formed the *Daily-Commercial*, which soon collapsed.

In 1871 he married Julia King of Athens, a childhood sweetheart, and a year later formed an Atlanta newspaper, which soon went the way of the *Daily-Commercial*. After working for a variety of papers, Grady spent some time in New York City, returning to Atlanta as a special reporter for the *New York Herald*. Then, in 1879, with the help of a $20,000 loan from Cyrus W. Field, he bought one-fourth interest in the *Constitution*. This new responsibility seemed to sober young Grady considerably.

During the next decade Henry W. Grady became a serious journalist dedicated to popular causes that would sell papers and increase advertising revenues. With the emergence of his New South theme—industrial development, diversified agriculture, and manufacturing—he became an almost instant celebrity.

A teetotaling, sentimental, pious man who sought an end to Civil War animosities, Grady mounted at the same time a bitter campaign to eradicate black influence in American life. In June 1887 his *Constitution* attacked white Atlanta University faculty members whose children were attending that private institution established primarily for blacks. Within a short time the college, which had been getting an annual state appropriation pending establishment of a school for blacks, lost this source of revenue.

And in November 1888 Grady noted in an address that "when the Negro was enfranchised, the South was condemned to solidity as surely as self-preservation was the first law of nature." A few months later, following another significant statement on the New South to a Boston audience, Grady, only thirty-nine, succumbed to pneumonia. With his death the New South lost a very forceful and eloquent voice. ■

In 1876, federal land, rich in coal and timber and long reserved for homesteading, was given over to speculators for unrestricted exploitation. Fearful that northwestern lumber was becoming scarce, Congress welcomed buyers to join in a carnival of spending. One national legislator bought 111,188 acres in Louisiana, and various northern companies purchased even larger lots in neighboring states. Between 1877 and 1888, 5.7 million acres of federal lands were disposed of in this fashion throughout the South. This development resulted in new settlements and further industrial growth as well as great improvements in transportation. Between 1880 and 1890, northern and foreign capital increased railroad mileage in the South by 135 percent. This expansion made available previously inaccessible mineral resources of iron and coal, particularly in the mines of Tennessee, Virginia, and Alabama. By 1898, Birmingham had become the nation's largest exporter of pig iron.

With the influx of northern money, southern towns vied for status by encouraging the establishment of cotton mills; between 1880 and 1900 the number of mills increased from 161 to 400. Mill building involved whole communities, especially in the Carolinas, Georgia, and Alabama. The South with its unorganized laborers accustomed to long hours and poor pay soon attracted millowners from New England, where the textile industry suffered a decline in direct proportion to the growth in the south.

The tobacco industry also prospered owing in sort to the business expertise of R. J. Reynolds and James Buchanan Duke. Such technological innovations as the cigarette-making machine, introduced in 1880, helped reduce labor costs. In 1890 Duke combined the five leading tobacco companies to form the American Tobacco Company. Virginia and Carolina expanded their production of "bright" tobacco, a variety much in demand among the smokers of the newly popular cigarettes. By 1890 Duke was making half the cigarettes manufactured in the country.

Lumbering was also thriving by 1880. In the next twenty years the five Gulf states increased their sales of lumber from $13 million to $73 million. Unfortunately, this prosperity was achieved at the enormous ecological cost of the reckless destruction of whole forests.

Cook Collection, Valentine Museum.

The tobacco industry brought thousands of dollars into the South. Blacks in this Virginia factory probably earned more money than blacks on farms. The factory foreman (visible between the two women with brooms) was white.

Despite all these advances, the South continued to lag far behind the rest of the country. Economic expansion in the North and West was far more rapid than in the South. As late as 1900 the South still had a smaller percentage of the nation's factories and capital than it had had in 1860. The South's industries produced unfinished textile goods and unfinished or unprocessed raw materials of every sort, the final processing usually being done in the North, and that step in manufacturing also brought the highest profits.

The South was trapped into remaining a raw material economy by a host of practices adopted during the Civil War to suit private northern interests, such as inequities in railroad freight charges that later had been sanctioned by the Interstate Commerce Commission. These unfair practices made it difficult for the South to compete in the Northeast, the nation's richest market, but they permitted northern manufacturers to sell at low prices in southern markets.

To some extent, historians who have pictured the South as a colony of the North have constructed a useful metaphor. The South produced the raw supplies for the workshops and factories of the North, where most industrial profits were made. By any yardstick—per capita income, general economic wealth, living standards—the South and the North were still as divided in 1900 as they had been in 1865, perhaps even more so. Roughly, the South was 40 percent poorer than the rest of the nation. The Old South had ended in military defeat; the New South endured an economic inferiority that was equally humiliating.

The New West

Unlike the New South, the origins of the New West cannot be limited to the years following 1876. Indeed, the history of the Far West dates back to the discovery of gold in California in 1848, the gold rush of 1849, and California statehood in 1850. The California rush in 1849, the Colorado rush of 1859, and the rush to the Black Hills in 1876 follow a similar pattern. Some historians have theorized that these events took place in a time of national instability or upheaval. The Mexican War provided the background for the 1849 rush, and the economic panics of 1857 and 1873 seem to have been the catalysts for the following two rushes.

By the middle 1850s, most of the rich sites in California had been thoroughly worked, and the remaining lodes of untapped ore could be unearthed only with heavy industrial machinery. As a result, the tide of settlement washed back from the Pacific coast. Dissatisfied miners from California drifted eastward in search of new buried treasure. In their wake, settlers and businessmen followed and gradually transformed some of the crude mining camps into frontier towns. By 1864, Nevada, with a population of only 20,000 people, had become a state, nine years before the discovery of the rich Comstock lode turned it into a boom area whose prosperity was to last until the 1890s.

Of all the gold strikes, the one in Colorado in 1858 was the most colorful. Two miners from California, John Beck and W. Green Russel, set out to pursue the myth of an El Dorado of gold in the Southwest. Accompanied by a party of about a hundred people, they began panning for gold in the region near Pikes Peak. Not until that summer did they strike "pay dirt," and even then, the yield was small. But wild rumors began to spread west

George Eastman House, International Museum of Photography.

An eight-mule team travels through the Ute Pass in Colorado, carrying ore from mines to nearby towns. More than 28 million dollars in gold and 21 million in silver was extracted from Colorado mines between 1860 and 1900.

and east. By the spring of 1859, the wildest and least rational of gold rushes was underway. "Pikes Peak or Bust" became a slogan heard from California to New York. According to one historian, by the end of June more than 100,000 "fifty-niners" overran the Pikes Peak country. They spread over the eastern Rockies, laying out mining camps as they went, panned every stream, chipped every rock outcropping, and found nothing. As disappointment spread, they started east again, the slogan of "Pikes Peak or Bust" on their wagons replaced by merely "Busted, by God." By midsummer half of the 50,000 miners who reached Colorado were back home once more, and one of the greatest fiascos in the history of the frontier was over.

Meanwhile, the real discovery of the century was taking place in the Nevada mountains surrounding the Carson River valley. There two prospectors, Peter O'Riley and Patrick McLaughlin, and a drifter named Henry Comstock, struck ore in 1873. The Comstock lode soon became the richest of all mines in the United States. Only a dozen or so of the hundreds of claims proved profitable, for the dense gold and silver ore required mills and heavy machinery, but for those who could afford such equipment profits were enormous. Two hundred million dollars was the total value of the yield, and this wealth transformed Virginia City into a high-living town of instant potentates.

By 1874 most of the western mines were passing into the hands of eastern investors. One of the few areas reputed to be rich in ore which the miners had not yet tapped was in the Black Hills of Dakota, the homeland of the Sioux Indians. Though military authorities initially tried to keep adventurers out of the territory, the army finally realized it was virtually impossible to hold back the miners. When the Sioux refused to concede any of their lands to white prospectors, federal agents simply closed their eyes and let the miners rush in. In October 1874, the Black Hills were opened to all comers.

The contents of a journal kept by an army engineer assigned to the expedition of General George Custer in the Black Hills has prompted some historians to reexamine this event, which was to prove so disastrous to the

Denver Public Library, Western Collection.

Small, hastily constructed towns like Telluride, Colorado, shown here in 1890, supplied miners with necessities and respite from the drudgery of mining life. Many merchants made far more money than individual prospectors, who toiled in the mountains and streams.

Sioux. Captain William Ludlow was a reflective man aware of the full situation, both the aggressive avarice of the miners and the legitimate land claims of the Sioux. He concluded in his diary that the government was, in fact, deliberately pushing the Indians into war. The gold mines were reputed to be fabulous, and the possibility of pushing the Indians out of their territory in one simple stroke was irresistible.

After the Black Hills were opened up, the mining frontier no longer existed. Of course, much gold and silver was still locked in the mountains of the West, but after 1875 trained engineers and heavy machinery were required to extract it. Though the day of the prospector and individual miner was at an end, they left behind them a scattering of busy new towns and farming communities.

The quarter century of mining fever that followed on the heels of the California gold rush represents a bizarre twist in American life. This frontier, in contrast

The Opening of the West

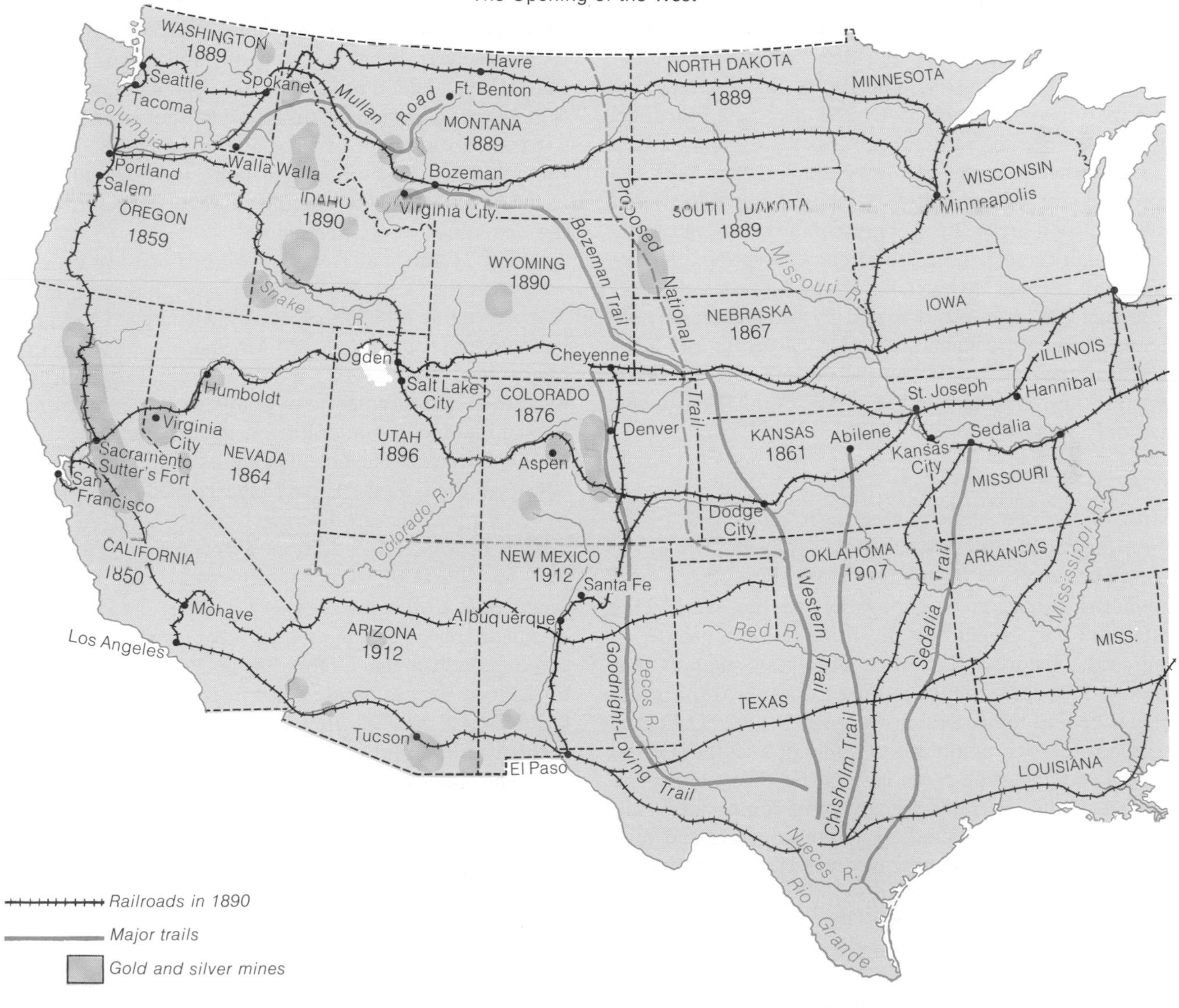

to most found in U.S. history, moved from west to east and often very fast indeed. Some communities were abandoned even before they got organized, lasting perhaps only a season as cardsharps, saloonkeepers, and prostitutes followed the action elsewhere. Yet if diggings were good, a city with an opera house, bookstores, newspapers, and fine restaurants, a community that maintained daily contact with the outside world by stage and telegraph and had an aura of luxury and stability, emerged much more rapidly than in an agricultural or pastoral setting. Although scores of these communities—Virginia City, Golden, Boulder, Helena, and others—had brief moments of glory, they also demonstrated an air of impermanence and insecurity since their life's blood depended on one industry. The future lay, in fact, with distribution points such as Denver and San Francisco, which also became railroad centers.

Nevertheless, each primitive camp viewed itself as a potential city. Upright citizens, including merchants and lawyers, soon arrived to supply commodities and settle legal conflicts; and these "solid citizens" proved instrumental in curbing lawlessness. Despite legends of shootouts and vigilantes promulgated by the writers of pulp fiction, law enforcement and orderly communities actually were the rule rather than the exception. Even Deadwood, South Dakota, the last of the Wild West towns, had only four shootings in 1876.

The Growth of Railroads

Most of the new settlers were eager to recreate in the West the orderly life of their home communities in the East. The success of the mining frontier depended largely upon the extension of civilization to the West. This extension was graphically illustrated by the growth of railroads. Historian Ray Allen Billington suggests that the rapid expansion of the mining frontier was the prime mover behind the federal government's subsidization of railroads. Easy communication would protect the isolated miners and bring the potentially lawless West under the control of the East, but perhaps most important of all, new railroad tracks bound the nation together and provided a means of exchanging raw materials and manufactured goods over vast distances.

Most historians agree that the construction of railroads and the impetus to commerce they provided were the most dynamic causes of economic growth in the country during the last half of the nineteenth century. By lowering the cost of transporting agricultural products and ore to eastern cities, the railroad furnished food for a burgeoning urban population, supplied raw materials for expanding factories, and generated much of the capital that financed America's industrialization. By opening the West for settlement, the railroad increased markets for eastern goods. More than any other single agency, railroad tracks converted a land of diverse sections into "one nation, indivisible."

In 1862, two companies began construction of the first transcontinental railroad. The Union Pacific was to build westward from Council Bluffs, Iowa; the Central Pacific, eastward from Sacramento. Each company eventually received twenty sections of public lands for each mile of track laid, a total of 181 million acres, as well as thirty-year government loans. The government lent $16,000 for each mile of track across the Plains, $48,000 for each mile in high mountain areas, and $32,000 a mile in the Great Basin, the varying amounts gauged to varying difficulties of construction.

The Homestead Act of 1862 had already brought settlers to the West eager to promote railroad building. The Mormons of Utah especially encouraged the great undertaking, and some 5,000 Mormons worked on railroad crews. But most of the men who built the railroads were Irish and German immigrants working the eastern line and Chinese immigrants on the western line.

The Central Pacific encountered more severe problems than the Union Pacific. Materials had to be shipped by sea, capital was hard to come by in the West, and labor extremely scarce. In addition, an even greater obstacle was the natural barrier of the Sierra Nevada mountain range near California's eastern border. Federal loans eventually raised capital, but the labor shortage remained severe. Because the Union Pacific was already laying track at the pace of a mile a day in 1866, outbuilding the Central by a ratio of eight to one, officials of the latter decided to hire and import Chinese laborers.

The Chinese had been coming into California since the gold rush days of 1849, though they were soon driven out of the gold camps by white miners. By 1866, about eleven thousand Chinese were hired for railroad crews, and from then on, four out of every five men hired by the Central Pacific were Chinese. Chinese laborers were a foreman's dream; not only were they paid substantially less than their white counterparts but they were also easy to manage. Moreover, there were no anxious relatives

University of Washington.

Railroads played an enormous role in opening the West. Here, a group of workers, among them a Chinese, rests on a mountain trestle on the line between Washington Territory and Minnesota.

around to bemoan the deaths of those Chinese laborers who collapsed under grueling construction work. Indeed, the Chinese had the grim virtue for their white overseers of being totally expendable.

Ironically, in the years immediately after a war fought to abolish slavery, Chinese labor was indentured. Chinese laborers knew neither the language nor the law; they were at the mercy of merchants and agents, who often cheated and exploited him. The position of Chinese workers was closer to that of slaves than of free laborers. And Chinese servitude was sponsored and condoned by the same Republican government that had just emancipated black slaves in the South.

On April 9, 1869 at Promontory Summit, the two sections of the railroad line met, thereby completing one of the most daring and difficult enterprises in the nation's history. In the wake of this achievement, four other transcontinental railroads appeared. By 1883, these lines had been completed: the Northern Pacific; the Atchison, Topeka, and Santa Fe; and the Southern Pacific. By 1893 the Great Northern Railway was also in operation. Within thirty years after the Civil War more than 70,000 miles of railroad track were built west of the Mississippi.

In addition to providing income to Westerners and promoting colonization and settlement, the railroads stimulated the growth of cattle raising and heavy mining. Finally, the railroads made it possible to locate factories near the source of raw materials. Now industry was free to begin developing in the West. Within twenty years after the completion of the first transcontinental railroad, the populations of the western states grew enormously; Nebraska rose from 100,000 people to more than a million and the Dakotas from 15,000 to 500,000. The center of agriculture moved from Indiana and Illinois to Iowa, Kansas, and Nebraska. In 1860 there were two million farms in the nation; in 1900 there were six million.

Cattle Country and the Great Plains

By the end of the Civil War, Texans realized that wild cattle could be domesticated. Since cattle that cost $3 or

Utah State Historical Society, Collection of Union Pacific Museum.

Ads like these, promising fast and inexpensive travel over long distances, played a prominent role in opening western states to settlement.

$4 a head in Texas sold for ten times that amount in the Mississippi Valley, the great cattle drives from Texas eastward began. Often as few as six to a dozen cowboys drove thousands of heads of beef north to railroad stations. At first the route for such drives followed the Sedalia Trail to Sedalia, Missouri. Later, the cowboys took the Chisolm Trail to Abilene, Kansas. Between 1868 and 1875 approximately 1,500,000 head of cattle were driven to Kansas.

By 1885, however, the era of the cattle drive was ending. In that year, 350,000 Texas beeves arrived in Kansas; in the next year, none. This phenomenon can be explained in part by the economic factors in the cattle industry. Farmers in the Midwest had been importing breeding cattle for several years, and by the early 1880s the supply of cattle, whether raised in the Midwest or in Texas, was exceeding demand. This glut on the market was forcing the price of beef down and making it less profitable for Texans to undertake arduous drives.

Furthermore, settlers in Kansas and northern Texas were blocking the open trails with barbed wire fences. And in 1885 many Texas cattle became infected with Texas fever, and Kansas and several other states passed quarantine laws. Finally, the newly built railroads made it more profitable to ship cattle for slaughter directly from the Southwest to Chicago by rail rather than to drive them overland to Kansas and then to ship them by rail from Kansas to Chicago. Moreover, cattle transported by rail lost less weight than those driven on foot.

The Cowboy

The myth of the cowboy is almost as popular in contemporary television programs as it was a century ago when Owen Wister wrote *The Virginian,* a bestseller that depicted the cowboy as the purest and noblest Anglo-Saxon, a western knight without armor. In reality, at least 25 percent of the 35,000 men who ran the cattle trails were black, and another 12 percent were Mexican.

Black cowhands were particularly numerous along the Texas Gulf coast and in the Indian country. In some sections of Texas, they formed the majority of the ranch hands, and a few ranches were worked almost exclusively by blacks. Though it would be naive to think that black cowhands were treated with total equality, nevertheless they enjoyed a camaraderie with their fellow workers that was rare in many parts of post-Civil War America.

It is not the black or Mexican cowhand, however, who has emerged in American folklore, but a stalwart, taciturn, hard-drinking sort of noble savage who tamed the West, saved the girl (but often neither kissed nor married her), and rode off into the sunset on his best friend, a faithful horse. Until the 1880s, at least in eastern eyes, the hired worker who tended cattle in the New West was not heroic at all. These "herders," as they were called, usually were portrayed as semibarbarous laborers living dull monotonous lives of hard fare and poor shelter. Those taking part in a Wyoming roundup in 1875

Western History Collections, University of Oklahoma Library.

Contrary to the general view that all cowboys were white Anglo-Saxons, in fact, Mexican-Americans and blacks, like the two seated in the front of the chuck wagon, belonged to typical trail crews punching cattle on the range.

were described as "rough men with shaggy hair and wild, staring eyes, in butternut trousers stuffed into great, rough boots." At that time these individuals were getting a dollar or so a day and their grub; their trail boss, perhaps $125 a month. Yet within a very few years these uncouth roustabouts became much more honest, virtuous, and colorful; in short, they became romantic figures who have cast a long shadow upon American life and culture.

It is, of course, impossible to generalize about such a full-blown legend. Some of these men, hardened by outdoor life and continuous physical exercise, were probably lean and tough and perhaps even honest and virtuous to boot; others, ignorant, mean, and dirty, may or may not have stood "tall in the saddle." Some, for example, joined the Knights of Labor in an effort to improve their lot. Most dreamed of getting their own ranch some day, and all endured a hard, arduous routine during certain months of the year. The "cowtowns" they crowded into, centers such as Ellsworth, Dodge City, and Abilene, certainly had barrooms and saloons, but dance halls and brothels were less common. Abilene, for example, did not have a dance palace until 1871 and then for only a single season. In its heydey Dodge City boasted of only two, one for whites and one for blacks. In such communities the rule of the day—and night—was order, and regulations against the carrying of guns were rigidly enforced. Few men died of gunshot wounds and rarely, if ever, from six-shooters. The "shootout" so dear to Hollywood never occurred. Yet at least one element of the western saga is true, the romantic cattle drive cowboy of the New West quickly realized that his most deadly foe was the settled farmer, whose barbed wire fences were putting an end to the age of the nomadic, footloose cowpoke.

The Farmer's Last Frontier

In the last years of the nineteenth century, millions of farmers surged into the Great Plains, filling Kansas,

Great Plains Black Museum, Omaha.

Jim Kelly
(ca. 1839–1912)

Jim Kelly, a tall, spare, black cowboy, was born to free parents, Uncle Amos and Aunt Phoebe Kelly, who worked for a Texas pioneer named James Olive. Amos and Phoebe, like a few lucky pre-Civil War slaves, had been set free upon the death of their master. Kelly, obviously named for the owner of his frontier birthplace near Georgetown, about 50 miles north of Austin, grew up with the Olive youngsters and later became a trusted associate of I. P. (Print) Olive for several decades.

As a young man, Kelly went to west Texas to work but about 1865 returned to the Olive lands where he did most of the bronco busting, becoming a peerless horse trainer. A sound, reliable individual to whom fear was a stranger, he soon was teaching a new generation of Olives to ride, rope, shoot, and how to do less exciting general ranch work as well.

Within a few years he joined his boss and other cowhands on the trails developing to the railheads, first in Kansas, then in Nebraska, where after the mid-1870s Kelly and the Olives made their home. He sometimes cooked during these long drives but more often worked as a rider. Whatever his role, he frequently was involved in gunplay, for the Olives were an aggressive, hotheaded lot.

In Ellsworth, Kansas, he once winged an adversary who was about to pump a fourth bullet into his employer as the result of a disagreement. Kelly then stayed behind until Print Olive was able to travel home once more. On another occasion, Olive, ill in a cowtown hotel, sent him to a local saloon to get him a bottle of whiskey. The barman refused to serve a black man, that is, until Jim flourished his six-shooter with obvious professional skill.

On yet another occasion, Print Olive, Jim Kelly, and several friends lynched several men they considered to be frontier criminals. Their trial, held in Hastings, Nebraska, in 1879, was so sensational that the governor eventually called out the militia to prevent further bloodshed. Jim was cleared of all charges, but Print spent some time behind bars. Kelly, like the Olives, lived out his last years in Nebraska, full of memories of the brawling frontier legend of which he was an integral part. ■

James Butler Hickok (1837–1876)

"Wild Bill" Hickok, born of Irish stock in La Salle County, Illinois, in 1837, went west to Kansas when only eighteen. An industrious worker, he became an active free-state man and soon was elected constable of a frontier township. This large, handsome, quiet youth then became a driver for a stageline on the Santa Fe Trail. After nearly being killed by a bear, he recovered from his wounds and transferred his operations to the famed Overland Stage Line on the Oregon Trail. In July 1861 Hickok tangled with the notorious McCanles gang. When the gunfire ended, McCanles and two of his associates were dead.

During the Civil War, Hickok was a Union spy-scout attached to a base in Springfield, Missouri. He was captured by the Confederates on several occasions but managed to escape, and in 1865 in a Springfield square he shot and killed a Union soldier who had turned traitor and joined the Rebels.

The following year Hickok moved to Fort Riley, Kansas, where as deputy U.S. marshal he ruled a wild 20,000 square-mile domain. From time to time he also served as a scout for Custer, Sheridan, and other generals grappling with frontier problems. In 1869 he became marshal of Hays City, Kansas, then two years later, of Abilene, the wide-open cowtown. In each region "Wild Bill's" justice was firm and fair and he only shot in self-defense or in the line of duty.

In 1872–1873 he toured the East with Buffalo Bill's traveling show. During these years he married a Cheyenne matron who survived him when he was murdered in August 1876. The setting for this tragedy was the notorious community of Deadwood in the Dakota territory, and the man who did the deed was the outlaw Jack McCall. ■

Denver Public Library, Western History Collection.

Many of those who risked their lives to homestead on the Great Plains were poor people unable or unwilling to compete in the industrial East. Self-sufficient, hearty, determined, and willing to endure cold winters and equally uncomfortable hot summers, these daring pioneers were unsung heroes whose endurance would amaze contemporary Americans.

Solomon D. Butcher Collection, Nebraska State Historical Society.

The Sprey family, proud residents of a sod house in Custer County, Nebraska in 1887. All homesteaders had the same experiences. The discrimination and segregation found elsewhere often had little relevence in the hostile western environment, where all races and creeds suffered equally.

Nebraska, the Dakotas, Wyoming, and Montana in a final rush for vanishing unsettled land. Ultimately, they pushed the Indians from their sanctuaries and also crowded the rancher and cowboy westward or onto more limited spreads.

Three interesting groups can be identified among the masses who moved westward: former slaves; white farmers who either sought a better living elsewhere or could no longer tolerate the growing density of population in the Mississippi Valley; and new immigrants, mostly from northern Europe.

The chaos of Reconstruction and the racist policies implemented in the New South impelled some blacks to seek the promise of land and freedom in the West. In 1879 between 20,000 and 40,000 Negroes followed a former Louisiana slave named Henry Adams to Kansas, some walking over the Chisholm Trail, some coming by boat on the Mississippi. Penniless, inexperienced, and friendless, a number of them were driven out by bigoted white Kansans or were unable to afford farming land.

Those who survived spent a miserable winter at the town of Nicodemus, the only Negro community in the state, but their example lured still more southern blacks who eventually owned 20,000 acres of Kansas farmland and proved themselves to be successful farmers.

A second and much larger group were from the Mississippi Valley which some people thought was becoming overcrowded in the 1870s. During this decade, every state bordering the Mississippi River (except Arkansas and Minnesota) either lost population or remained static.

Between 1870 and 1900 these restless folk, aided to some extent by blacks and much more by foreign migrants, occupied 430 million acres of land and put 225 million of those acres under cultivation. This compares with 407 million acres occupied and 189 million improved between 1607 and 1870. Most settled, at least for a decade or so, in the region just beyond the tier of states stretching from Minnesota to Louisiana, and while some Americans might not consider Kansas, Nebraska, Iowa, Missouri, and Arkansas as "west," in the late nineteenth century this area was clearly the eastern fringe of the "New West." By the turn of the century, however, hard times and the lure of the city altered this westward surge of humanity, one of the greatest movements of people in our history.

The third group, less numerous than native Americans but much more so than blacks, were immigrants from Ireland and northern Europe, particularly Germany and Scandinavia. In 1882 alone, 105,362 immigrants arrived from Norway, Sweden, and Denmark. The rugged climate of the Dakotas, and especially Minnesota, was reminiscent of their homeland and appealed to many of these people.

What drew ex-slaves, immigrants, and native-born whites westward was virtually free land (sometimes as low as $2 to $8 per acre and on easy credit terms), expanding rail lines providing ready access to markets, and radical changes in agriculture. Improved methods of milling wheat, better ways of handling and marketing grain, and wonderous machines for doing farm chores—all conjured up visions of sudden wealth and great opportunity which land speculators and railroad companies exploited to the fullest. And it is true that fortunes were made during some years. In the late 1870s, for example, one could cultivate an acre of wheat in the Dakotas for $9.50, anticipate a yield of perhaps 25 bushels per acre, and sell each bushel for 90 cents back East. Even after paying for the land and allowing for taxes, salaries and other costs, profits of 100 percent were not unusual. As a result, eastern and foreign investment capital quickly moved in.

Yet this "boom" picture has a sober side as well. The hardships of the environment were enormous. First, there was little wood for building, and adequate housing was an immediate problem. The solution was temporarily found in the sod house, often no more than a hole in the side of a hill with a front wall of cut sod and a roof of prairie grass and dirt. These dwellings were warm in winter and cool in summer and could not be burned

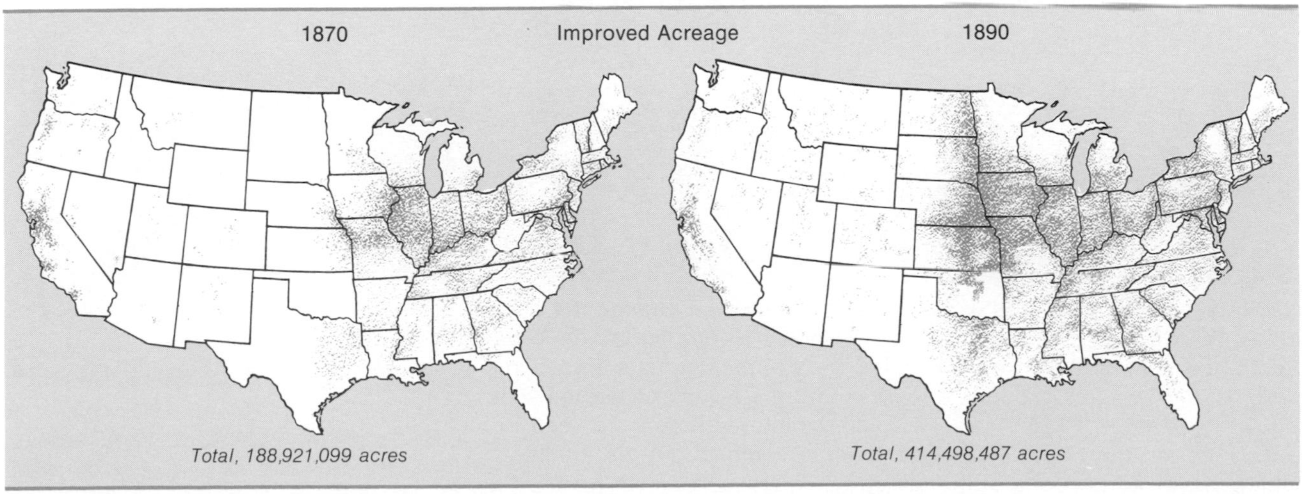

down, but they were also dank and dirty, crowded and unpleasant.

Water was as scarce as wood, and fuel was as hard to find as water. The climate of the plains was often intolerable to all but the hardiest. Spring floods were common and devastating; summers were normally scorching hot and dry. The autumns of the 1870s and the 1880s witnessed a worse plague: invasions of grasshoppers. In years when insect hordes did not consume crops, the farmer still faced the danger of prairie fire after months of arid summer heat.

There was yet another ominous cloud on the horizon of the Great Plains farmer. Using similar methods and at virtually the same time, his counterparts in Canada, Argentina, Russia, and Australia were doing much the same thing—a state of affairs that could only lead, in a few years, to depressed world prices for much that he was producing.

The reasons for the westward push, one of the most enduring themes in American history, have long fascinated scholars, both young and old. To Frederick Jackson Turner, the cutting edge of the frontier democratized and "Americanized" Europeans; and, as he saw it, the appeal of virtually free land and a more democratic way

Frederick Lewis.

Using bicycles, horses and wagons, eager ''sooners'' awaited the opening of the Cherokee strip by the United States Government at noon on September 16, 1893. Cowboys wearing broad-brimmed hats, dudes in derbies, and women in bonnets represented the myriad of fortune seekers who moved to Oklahoma. The soldiers pictured here were used to police the territory. The Cherokee Indians assembled outside the Land Office are to witness one of the last great seizures of Indian land.

of life pulled millions toward the setting sun. Their experiences, in turn, altered and transformed almost every aspect of American culture. Walter Prescott Webb believed that this flow was halted momentarily at the ninety-eighth meridian—the boundary of what was once called the "Great American Desert"—until the Industrial Revolution provided new tools such as barbed wire, the six-shooter, inexpensive windmills, new agricultural machinery, and new farming methods.

Such theories are attractive and obviously possess elements of truth, but the fact is the United States was largely an agricultural nation throughout much of the nineteenth century, and most blacks who left the South as well as immigrants who came to our shores (1870–1900) either could farm or were eager to learn how to do so. Ideas of democracy and invention aside, nearly 12 million new citizens arrived at eastern ports and the native-born population rose by 25 million during the closing decades of the 1800s. Thirty-seven million people had to find homes and make a living some place—and for many that someplace was the relatively cheap farmland lying beyond the Mississippi River.

The Oklahoma Land Rush

The occupation of Indian lands in Oklahoma was the last major invasion of Indian Territory. For years, the rich lands of Oklahoma had been eyed by farmers, ranchers, and investors. As early as 1874, railroad companies were petitioning Congress to open the region to white settlement. Elias C. Boudinot, a disgruntled Cherokee who had broken with his tribe, was encouraged (probably by railroad interests) to circulate everywhere exaggerated stories of 13 million acres of unoccupied land that supposedly belonged to no tribe. In fact, there were in the heart of the Indian Territory some 2 million acres of land not yet assigned. Over the next ten years, farmers and railroad propagandists slowly eroded federal protection of the sanctuary.

Finally, in the spring of 1889, the government opened up one part of Oklahoma. All along the northern border of the Oklahoma territory were massed feverish crowds of farmers, speculators, and adventurers on horses or in carriages and wagons. At Arkansas City fifteen crowded trains awaited the signal for the beginning of the invasion. Astoundingly, some 1,920,000 acres of land were claimed in a few hours.

Indian Pacification: National Dishonor

The expansion of the mining and agricultural frontiers and the invasion of the railroads into the Great Plains and the New West brought the federal government and its citizens into a final and tragic confrontation with the Indians. No doubt the Indians sometimes were a hazard, particularly to miners and farmers and ranchers who embarked upon difficult lives with high hopes and modest means of protection. But it is also clear that most confrontations were provoked by white intruders.

Warfare in the West

In the first half of the nineteenth century most of the tribes in the East had been transported west of the Mississippi where their presence soon precipitated clashes with other Indians, frontiersmen, and new settlers. The years from 1850 to 1890 were marked by numerous bloody clashes, broken treaties, and efforts by whites to acquire Indian lands by means usually corrupt and unfair.

The great warrior tribes of the Sioux and the Crow in the Northwest and the Kiowa and Comanche in the Southwest had guarded the Plains against all adversaries since the days of the Spanish conquerors. Essentially a nomadic people dependent upon the buffalo for all their needs—food, clothing, and shelter—the Plains Indians remained aloof from white intrusion as long as their hunting grounds were safe and their means of survival were not imperiled.

During the Civil War, the withdrawal of federal garrisons from the Western frontiers encouraged many Indians to seek revenge for their grievances against whites. At the same time, white Indian-haters in the West cheered as their militia committed atrocities against the Indians. By 1865, Indian-white skirmishes had spread throughout the Plains and the Southwest. In order to pacify the West, Congress established in 1867 a Peace Commission to convince the various tribes to relocate on reservations, one in present-day Oklahoma and the other in the Black Hills of the Dakotas. In spite of treaties to this effect and President Grant's adoption of a "Peace Policy" in 1869, warfare continued as the United States found it difficult to keep the Indians on the reservations and the whites off Indian lands.

At the end of the Civil War, the buffalo population was estimated to be between 12 and 15 million animals.

In 1871, a single herd, according to one estimate, contained 4 million buffalo. By 1883, however, the species was nearly extinct, after only a few years of unbridled hunting by whites. The animals were killed for their meat and for their valuable hides—or just for sport. The fencing in of grazing lands robbed the surviving buffalo of food. More than any other pressure, this destruction forced the Indians to submit. Starvation all too often completed the job the army had begun.

In 1865, most of the nation's 300,000 Indians lived in the West. Some of these Indians for 250 years had successfully fended off all intruders—the Spanish, the French, the English, and finally the Americans. The key to their mastery was the horse. Most observers of the Comanche described them as the finest riders in the world. Their horsemanship gave them their superiority as hunters and warriors and enabled them to migrate vast distances from depleted hunting grounds to land rich in game. One observer has left this description of Indian expertise: "In warfare, the most celebrated Comanche stunt was the useful one of riding horizontally on the *side* of the mount while moving at full speed and shooting arrows or bullets from behind the horse's neck or even from under its belly. Bow or gun, shield and a lance 12 to 14 feet in length were carried during this remarkable exercise, the weight of the body being upon the upper arm, which was inserted into a braided hair halter descending from the withers and passing under the neck. The rider left one heel only in view on the horse's back."

The final confrontation of the Comanche and the army, known as the Red River War, took place in Texas in the winter of 1874-1875. The army's success was achieved by Colonel Ranald S. Mackenzie, who understood that the only way to defeat his Indian opponents was to destroy their horses. Systematically, the cavalry pursued the horse herds, commandeered the best mounts, and slaughtered the rest. In the battle of Palo Duro Canyon, Mackenzie trapped a herd of 1,400 Indian horses; he saved 375 for army use and killed the remainder. After Palo Duro Canyon, the Comanches were effectively "pacified." Deprived of their horses and most of their winter supplies and harrassed unrelentingly by the army, the demoralized Comanches scattered in every direction. By the end of the year, they began to appear at the federal agencies on the reservations seeking government rations which, meagre as they were, represented the only alternative to starvation.

In 1877 when a band of the Nez Percé refused to open the Walla Walla Valley in Washington Territory to white gold miners, a tragic episode occurred. When troops moved in to force the Indians to accept new territorial boundaries, their leader, Chief Joseph, decided to move his band of 200 warriors and 450 women, children, and old people to Canada. Chief Joseph managed to elude the pursuing troops for more than four months, as the band traveled more than 1000 miles. The troops overtook the Nez Percé a few miles from the Canadian border and sent them to Indian Territory.

As the white man and other Indian tribes encroached on their lands, the fierce Apache became the scourge of New Mexico, Arizona, and parts of northern Mexico. Treaties were made with various tribal groups in the 1860s and 1870s, and in 1884 Geronimo, a fierce Indian leader, finally agreed to enter the San Carlos Reservation in Arizona.

A year later, Geronimo (ca. 1829-1909) fled to Mexico again and in March 1886, after three days of talks, agreed to return to the reservation once more. During these conversations, Geronimo blamed federal officials for disagreements that had arisen. Speaking bluntly, he told a U.S. general, "Whenever I meet you, I talk good to you, and you to me, and peace is soon established; but when you go to the reservation you put agents and interpreters over us who do bad things."

By "bad things," Geronimo meant corrupt practices (spoiled food, motheaten blankets, foul liquor), an often idle, humiliating existence, and constant threats of imprisonment. One tribute to this famed warrior is that when he and his thirty-six braves agreed to a surrender, 5,000 U.S. Army troops were searching for them.

As it turned out, Geronimo had a change of heart, fled once more, but finally gave up for the last time in September 1886. He and his small band were removed as prisoners of war to Florida and later resettled at Fort Sill, Oklahoma, in 1894. Now a celebrity, Geronimo attended the St. Louis World's Fair and other expositions and was a guest at Teddy Roosevelt's inaugural in 1905. He died at Fort Sill of alcoholism and pneumonia in 1909.

Indians living on reservations on the northern plains might have remained there peacefully had not miners invaded the Black Hills looking for gold. Sitting Bull and Crazy Horse, who earlier had refused to live on the reservation, declared war in 1876, and in June of that year achieved a stunning victory at Little Big Horn over General George Custer. But this was the high watermark of Indian success. By 1881, even Sitting Bull, who had

Western History Collections, University of Oklahoma Library.

Geronimo, seated in the left center, meets with General Crook (perhaps an appropriate name), second from right, in January, 1886. This meeting, like many others between soldiers and Indians, came to nothing.

Library of Congress.

A common grave, devoid of coffins, served as the last resting place for Indians killed at Wounded Knee.

escaped to Canada, was on the verge of starvation and was forced to surrender. He was then imprisoned and later allowed to return to the reservation where news of the Ghost Dance in 1889 once again gave him hope of defeating the white man.

The end of outright Indian-white confrontation came in 1890. The last incident of the Indian wars was the so-called "Battle of Wounded Knee" (actually a massacre) during which, according to one estimate, 300 Sioux were either killed or died of exposure. This tragic event occurred when a group of Sioux Ghost Dancers following the death of Sitting Bull left the Standing Rock Agency in the Dakotas, and when overtaken by Custer's old cavalry regiment, put up scattered resistance. Within minutes, shells and rifle fire raked the Indian ranks, showering death indiscriminately. Among the victims were some 100 women and children; about thirty-one troops also lost their lives in this senseless encounter. Some contemporaries saw this episode as the triumph of brave soldiers over treacherous warriors while others saw it as the slaughter of helpless Indians by an army seeking revenge for the Little Big Horn. The truth probably lies somewhere between these two views. Following Wounded Knee, Indian resistance on the Plains ended.

Relocation and Reform

During these decades the West, naturally enough, was openly hostile to the Indian; the East, much more interested in the fate of the black man, was generally indifferent. Once open warfare ceased and most Indians were on reservations, the Army's role in Indian affairs began to decline. As a result, friends of the military in Congress mounted a campaign to have the Bureau of Indian Affairs transferred from the Interior to the War Department. To support this change, they produced convincing proof of mismanagement, fraud, and even cruelty on the part of Indian agents. Although this effort failed, it stirred new public interest in Indian affairs. Until the 1880s most government officials believed that subduing the Indian, putting him on a reservation, and caring for him would solve the "Indian problem." But the pressure of settlement again and again forced dwindling tribal groups to move elsewhere. This happened so frequently

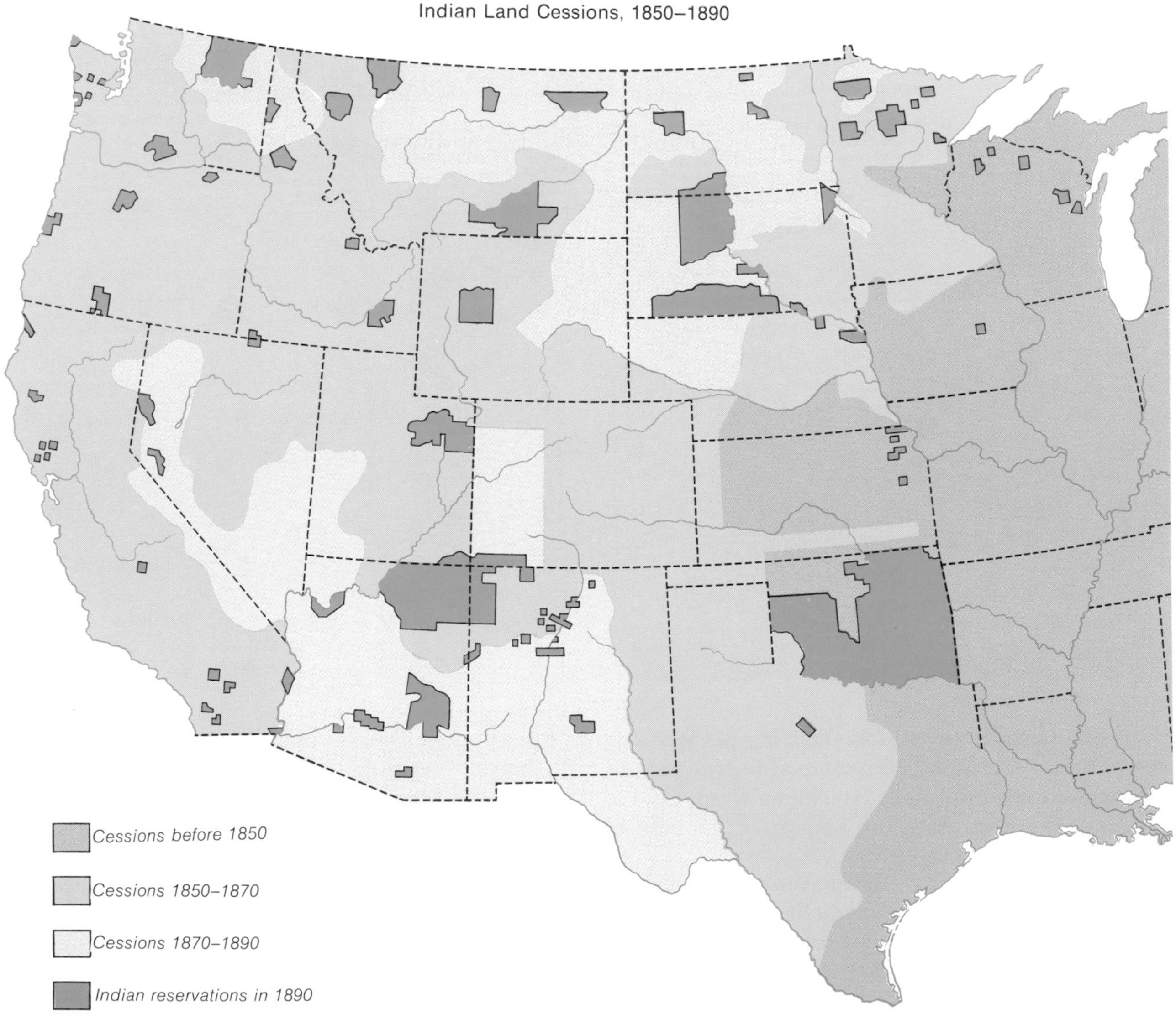

that one chief suggested all "red children" should be put on wheels so the "Great White Father" could move them at will.

Prodded by reports of Indian-white skirmishes and inept reservation management, several eastern associations, the most influential being the Philadelphia-based Indian Rights Association, began to speak out in behalf of the native American. So did Helen Hunt Jackson whose *Century of Dishonor* (1881) and *Ramona* (1884) dramatized the condition of the Indian.

During these same years numerous missionary groups joined the government in its effort to "educate" the Indian. In 1870 federal authorities appropriated the first funds specifically earmarked for the purpose and by the turn of the century were expending $2.5 million each year on 148 boarding schools and 225 day schools serving some 20,000 children. The best known of these institutions was Carlisle in Pennsylvania, purposely far from a reservation so as to encourage young Indians to shed their tribal past.

By the early 1880s many white Americans believed that the Indian reservation policy was no longer viable. Instead, assimilation of Indians into a white culture and way of life was preferable. Assimilation, of course, required the breakup of reservations, the dissolution of tribal government, and conversion of Indians to settled farmers. The Dawes Severalty Act of 1887, by far the most important development of federal policy toward Indians in the late nineteenth century, was intended to convert Indians to the white man's way of life. This law, which had been taking shape in a piecemeal fashion for a decade or so, authorized the President to allot tribal lands in 160-acre parcels to individuals and heads of families who agreed to adopt "the habits of civilized life." U.S. citizenship was to be granted to Indians who accepted allotments. The land could not be disposed of for twenty-five years to protect the Indians. Any surplus land, after the Indians had been taken care of, would be sold to the general public.

Clearly designed to obliterate tribal structure, this Act had the support of humanitarians, friends of the Indians and selfish landgrabbers. Henry L. Dawes, the humanitarian Massachusetts senator for whom the bill was named, sincerely believed in assimilation. Unfortunately, it soon became apparent that the legislation was a terrible mistake and virtually impossible to enforce. Allotments became complicated in legal tangles as heirs tried to assert their claims and questionable leasing procedures to white speculators further complicated the picture. Between 1887 and 1934 the Indians sold or lost an estimated 86 million acres of land, about 60 percent of the 138 million acres held when the Dawes Act was passed. Much of what was left was desert, scrawny forests, or poor scrub-covered land. But one handful of Indians had the last laugh: some of those who were forced onto inhospitable acres in Oklahoma later saw their poor land spout oil.

The Agricultural Malaise

Despite resolution of the "Indian problem," expansion of the New West, and a spirit of progress throughout the New South, farmers in all parts of the nation were disgruntled and unhappy during much of the last quarter of the nineteenth century. True, there were good years now and then and some individuals who produced specific crops geared to the needs of urban America—truck farmers of the Northeast, for example—did relatively well. But the great mass of farmers were irritable and uneasy, apprehensive of a changing nation, so much so that before the century ended they mounted an unprecedented political revolt.

The Causes of Discontent

To a great extent the farmer's problems were rooted in increasing industrialization and the growth of big business, but none of the shock waves and various side effects created by factories, corporate mergers, urbanization, and railroads would have caused much of a stir if agricultural income had been adequate to cover costs. Sadly, it wasn't. In the early 1880s wheat and corn prices began a steady decline that lasted for some fifteen years, and the producers of nearly every other commodity faced equally bleak times. Bills for fertilizer, seed, equipment, and transport to market often exceeded the costs of growing and harvesting a crop.

To add to the farmer's woes, he also suffered a concomitant loss of prestige and political power. No longer did his voice have the same force as it once did in Washington or the state capital, perhaps not even at the county seat. Instead, lawyers, business tycoons, and especially railroad executives and their hirelings were calling the shots. They had the money and with it went influence

Library of Congress.

Helen Hunt Jackson
(1830–1885)

Born Helen Maria Fiske, this poet, novelist, and philanthropist was one of the first individuals of her era to focus national attention upon the predicament of Indians. She grew up in Amherst, Massachusetts, where her father was a scholar of the classics and philosophy. Among her schoolmates and neighbors was Emily Dickinson who became a lifelong friend despite rumors of a romance between Miss Dickinson and Edward Bissell Hunt, whom Helen married in 1852. Bissell, a U.S. Army engineer, was killed in 1863 while experimenting with a submarine invention. Two years later their second son died, the first having succumbed to an infant malady a decade earlier.

Helen Hunt was now alone, and to this date had written nothing. In 1866 she settled in Newport, Rhode Island, where she and her husband had once lived, and began to publish poems. In the late 1860s she traveled abroad and then commenced to take her publishing career more seriously, producing numerous articles for *Scribner's* and other national magazines, most of them unsigned.

In May 1872 Helen Hunt went west and the following year took up residence in Colorado Springs. There she met and married William Sharpless Jackson, a financial promoter and railroad manager. In that setting she became interested in Indian life and culture, and the result was *A Century of Dishonor* (1881), a 457-page documentary account of Indian-white relations which she sent, at her own expense, to each congressman.

In 1882 Helen Hunt Jackson was named to a special federal commission to investigate conditions among California Indians. When the published report stirred little interest, she turned to fiction and produced *Ramona* (1884), her best-known work. This book had great appeal, but most readers were intrigued by the romance of the Old West, not the "Indian problem."

She died the following year at the age of fifty-four. Described by her contemporaries as brilliant, impetuous, charming, fascinating, and a keen business woman, Helen Hunt Jackson is also something of a mystery: her devotion to anonymity has made it impossible to identify much of the published work of this "Indian Harriet Beecher Stowe." ■

and legislation favorable to their special interests.

Equally galling was the ever-increasing gap between farm and city life. Most of the wonders of those years—gas and electricity, streetcars, indoor plumbing, better basic education, even the telephone and the railroad—were, to a degree, urban phenomena. Trains, of course, passed through the countryside, but sleek, well-dressed passengers and connections to a more comfortable, more exciting "outside world" often only served to remind farm families of their backwardness and their poverty.

Between 1870 and 1900 rural America reacted to this social-cultural-financial crisis by embracing numerous experiments designed to improve their lot. These included schemes to decrease rural isolation, increase income and cut operating costs, curb excessive rates charged by railroads, and eliminate middlemen (twin targets of special concern); in short, to raise the standard of living for all farm families through cooperation. As the decades progressed, these associations scored some successes, but not many. As a result, in the face of seemingly unending hard times, their programs and proposals became both more daring and more political in tone.

The National Grange

The first of these groups was the National Grange of the Patrons of Husbandry organized in 1867 by a Department of Agriculture employee named Oliver Kelley. Kelley's initial intent was to improve the social, cultural, and educational life of rural Americans. Assisted by William Saunders, an experienced organizer, by 1872 he had local lodges (or granges) in fourteen states with 800,000 members. Although these Grangers enjoyed the social gatherings and various programs provided for them, they quickly turned their meetings into economic forums.

At a national convention in 1874, they announced their twofold intention: to become both cooperative buyers and cooperative producers. As buyers who could eliminate dealers and their profits, the Grangers were enormously successful. Purchasing reapers, wagons, and sewing machines in quantity, they cut costs in half, often with the aid of well-known supply houses such as Montgomery Ward. As founders of packing plants, grain elevators, mills, and even banks and insurance companies, they were less successful since those undertakings required considerable capital and much expertise. In addition, large corporations countered by lowering prices on commodities the Grangers tried to manufacture themselves, a victory of sorts for farmers if these reductions proved to be permanent.

Another area of great concern to Grangers was railroad rates. During these years railroads were emerging as the first American enterprise to operate on a grand scale. Fierce competition resulted in rate wars that led to artificial restraints on competition through agreements to divide either traffic or earnings (pools) or by territorial understandings (one line would not extend service into the territory served by another). Some lines gave cheap, favorable rates to large customers such as Standard Oil; some increased charges for short hauls where competition was less fierce. For example, it cost less to ship wheat from Chicago to New York City than from some parts of the Dakotas to Minneapolis.

Farmers were not the only group to suffer from this kind of discrimination. Frequently, small business and commercial groups felt the impact of the railroad rates. Sometimes, as in Iowa, the rate structure benefited those towns and communities served by more than one line and penalized other towns and communities served by only one line. Given this shared economic grievance, Grangers, especially in the Midwest, turned to politics. In cooperation with businessmen from one or the other of the major parties, they gained control of several state legislatures and enacted laws regulating rates charged by grain elevators and railroads.

In 1871 the Illinois legislature authorized creation of a board of railroad and warehouse commissioners to regulate the rates charged by railroads for transport and the rates charged by operators of warehouses and grain elevators for storage. A Chicago warehouse company was found guilty of violating the law and appealed to the courts. The Supreme Court ruled in *Munn* v. *Illinois* (1876) that the business was in the public interest and public control was justified. The Court also declared that any state could regulate interstate commerce until Congress exerted such powers. This upheld the constitutionality of similar laws in Minnesota, Iowa, and Wisconsin.

The Grange's greatest success was the *Munn* v. *Illinois* decision, although it soon became apparent that effective regulation required federal legislation. By 1880, as various Granger cooperatives foundered on the rocks of inexperience and times improved somewhat, the Grange had only 100,000 members. Despite its failure as a political pressure group, the Grange focused attention upon an economic grievance of farmers, especially in the Midwest. Its rapid rise to power suggested that a potential base for broad political action existed and could be harnessed to address other grievances.

The Greenback Party

One such political group was the Greenback party, which was organized in Indianapolis in 1874. It urged currency inflation by demanding that the government continue placing greenbacks (paper currency not matched by gold reserves) in circulation. Except for the Civil War era when "greenback" notes were issued as a temporary measure, gold had been the basis of the national currency. Prices now were low, it was argued, because the supply of money (gold) was limited. The solution was to print more "greenbacks" not backed by gold. An increase in the supply of money would result in higher prices, a prospect that obviously appealed to farmers and debtors struggling to pay off their notes in an increasingly tight currency market.

Although Peter Cooper (1791–1883), an elderly New York philanthropist who ran for President on the 1876 Greenback ticket, did not win many votes the party subsequently widened its appeal to farmers and workers by advocating the taxation of national bonds, a federal income tax, the exclusion of Chinese immigrants, a restriction of working hours in industry, and the abolition of child labor. In 1880, their candidate, James B. Weaver (1833–1912), did somewhat better, but the party was still a minor national force because the boom years of 1880–1887 in the farming West allayed serious unrest. Money from eastern banks and loan companies was now readily available despite high interest rates, and farmers went into debt and mortgaged their homesteaded land in an attempt to improve their generally harsh living conditions.

But from 1886 to 1896, the West had ten dismal years of ruinously bad weather. For a decade, the annual rainfall was less than the twenty inches needed for farming. Cold winters and hot, dry summers ruined crops—and subsequently the farmers. Foreclosures of mortgaged farms in Kansas soared, and tenant farming, resembling the sharecropping of the South, began to appear. Farmers now became embittered by the nation's financial structure. "In God we trusted, in Kansas we busted" read many a wagon returning from the disastrous Midwest. Between 1888 and 1892 half of the people living in western Kansas moved out and 30,000 left South Dakota; in 1891 alone 18,000 prairie schooners entered Iowa from Nebraska.

Although the Greenback party, like the Grange, was a true political force and had a brief moment of glory, it created a powerful idea that did not die with it—the idea of stimulating the economy by increasing the supply of money. This idea, which became dormant in the good times of the early 1880s, would surface once more in the 1890s as a major political issue.

The Farmer's Alliance

Borrowing various ideas, concepts, and techniques from both the Grange and the Greenback party, in the 1880s a new group of farm organizations, loosely called "The Alliance," began to take shape. More so than either of its ill-fated predecessors, this body stressed cooperatives, and in some states flirted openly with political action, usually joining forces with the minority party in an effort to seize control and pass legislation favorable to farmers. At the same time, the Alliance was a social-educational force trying to improve the lot of farm families. The basic problem plaguing the Alliance was that various units tended to cling to regional, not national goals.

One group, the Southern Alliance, was a secret order founded on the Texas frontier in 1875 to combat horse thieves and loan sharks. For a decade it remained rather small and insignificant until C. W. Macune, an aggressive organizer, breathed new life into that body. During the late 1800s the Southern Alliance spread rapidly throughout the South, established a separate Colored Farmers' Alliance and Cooperative Union to look out for the welfare of blacks, and was well on its way to capturing the Democratic party machinery in several states.

Meanwhile, Milton George, editor of the *Western Rural,* a Chicago farm journal, created in 1880 the Northern (or Northwestern) Alliance to combat unfair railroad rates. Its growth encouraged efforts toward a union of the two main groups, and in 1889 representatives met and approved a platform espousing a graduated income tax, government ownership of railroads, laws against excessive land holding, strict government economy, the abolition of national banks, and greenbacks as currency.

However, sectional differences were too great and nothing came of this union. Southern whites refused to join with blacks and insisted that the Alliance remain secret and ostensibly non political since overt third-party action might, in much of the former Confederacy, split the dominant Democratic party and pave the way for black-Republican rule. Northern Alliance members, on the other hand, facing economic disaster, insisted on political action and in the early 1890s began organizing the Populist party. This meant the end of the Alliance as a force in rural life. Alliance men living in the New South generally abandoned the movement, and those living in the New West usually became Populists.

The Legacy of Agricultural Discontent

This mixture of hard times and organizational schemes to aid rural folk, in addition to fomenting a full-fledged political upheaval, produced an unusual crop of aggressive, outspoken leaders. Nearly all of them, regardless of temporary party labels, were at heart Democrats of one sort or another. Often, especially in the South, they did not call themselves Grangers, Alliance men, or Populists. Virginia had its Farmers' Assembly and South Carolina a Farmers' Association, which were often much more potent than Granges or Alliance groups in those states.

After a brief crusade in behalf of farmers in South Carolina, "Pitchfork Ben" Tillman (1847–1918) used the Farmers' Association to oust conservative Democrats from power, gain the governor's mansion in 1890, and then move on to Congress.

Leonidas L. Polk (1837–1892), a talented North Carolina agriculturalist, who founded the *Progressive Farmer* in 1886, three years later became president of the National Alliance. Then at its height and perhaps about to become a truly unified body, the Alliance counted its membership in the millions and this post catapulted Polk into national prominence. Polk tried unsuccessfully to operate within the old political framework, but in the early 1890s reluctantly became a Populist. His sudden death shortly before the first national convention was a severe blow to the young party.

Two spokesmen from the new West—James B. Weaver and Ignatius Donnelly (1831–1901)—were cast in a somewhat different mold, since they were associated with nearly every third party of the late nineteenth century, not just those related to agriculture. Weaver, Greenback nominee for the White House in 1880, had no difficulty identifying with the Alliance and Populism. Donnelly, a Philadelphia-born reformer who moved west to Minnesota, was allied with the entire spectrum of discontent from Liberal Republican to Populist.

The New West, embittered by hard times, mortgages, and poverty, and the New South, its goals frustrated and seemingly unattainable, would listen to and sometimes heed the siren cry of new political voices. Yet the disappointments of the early 1890s were largely temporary. Despite bad weather and trying seasons, both regions—in fact, all of the nation—had grown mightily during the years from 1870 to 1900. But much of that growth was uneven. The United States of America was still something of an adolescent requiring much guidance and direction. And some of the proposals of the Grangers, Alliance men, and Populists, thought wild-eyed and anarchistic when voiced, would provide the leavening so badly needed. Their ideas would find their way into party platforms, since that was the only way party leaders could retain control, and ultimately into statute books, since that, too, was the only way elected representatives could stay in office.

Essay

The Ghost Dance: A Ritual of Hope and Despair

The decision reached at Appomattox did much more than end our nation's bloodiest war and set free millions of blacks; it also decreed that the industrial-minded Northeast would run the country pretty much on its own terms for nearly half a century. Farmers, labor leaders, reformers of various persuasions, and minority groups would have little voice in national affairs as a United States made of coal, steel, oil, and railroads waxed strong, flexed its bulging muscles, and plundered its resources in the name of progress.

In times of rapid change which result in cultural stress, people often seek the security of old and more traditional ways of life. Although messianic movements stressing a return to the "good old days" have appeared in many cultures throughout the ages, the "Ghost Dance" of the Western Indians baffled and aroused the fears of white settlers, frontiersmen, and government agents. The Ghost Dance originated with the prophecies of Tavibo (ca. 1810–1870), a Paiute Indian in Nevada. "The Paiute Prophet," as he was known, claimed to be invulnerable to weapons, also had visions and therefore was visited by many Indians from Nevada, Oregon, and Idaho. His prophesies promised a time, not too distant, when the entire Indian races, living and dead, would be reunited upon an earth free of white men where the various tribes would live in a state of perfect happiness and the land would be rich with game. Tavibo died in 1870, his prophecies unfulfilled. However, within twenty years a prophet said to be his son would inspire what came to be known as the Ghost Dance.

During the 1880s, however, as the white population of the Plains and Rocky Mountain area increased, pressures upon the Indian grew apace. President Chester A. Arthur, in his first annual message to Congress (1881), called for a three-part Indian program: extending state and territorial law to reservations within their borders, granting homesteads to Indians who would sever tribal ties and become independent farmers, and establishing schools for Indians. These measures, all clearly designed to obliterate whatever native culture remained, foreshadowed the Dawes Act of February 8, 1887, which promised full citizenship to Indians who renounced tribal ways and "adopted the habits of civilized life."

Meanwhile the teachings of Tavibo lay dormant. In the late 1880s there appeared among the Paiute Indians a man named Wovoka ("Cutter"), also known as Jack Wilson (1858–1932). Wovoka, said to have been a son of the deceased holy man, Tavibo, was a dark, handsome youth, nearly six-feet tall, and a shrewd individual. A fast worker and a quick learner, he was virtually adopted by the David Wilson family, among the first settlers in Mason Valley, Nevada, who employed him as a hired hand for a number of years.

In his teens and early twenties, Wovoka/Jack Wilson lived in two worlds, working for the Wilson family from time to time, then going back to the Paiute way of life. Through this association with Wilson, his wife, and their children—all of whom Wovoka apparently admired greatly—he learned much about the Bible, Jesus Christ, Adam and Eve, the Garden of Eden, and how to eat and pray like a white man. During travels away from Mason Valley he also attended Shaker meetings and gained some familiarity with the Mormon faith.

Wovoka apparently assumed the mantle of a messiah sometime early in 1889, shortly after a severe illness during which he experienced delirium and saw visions. He preached a message of peace: "You must not fight. Do no harm to anyone. Do right always." Also, he preached that if the faithful performed a special dance, then miracles would occur. They would see their departed friends once more. The white man would disappear. Elk, buffalo, and antelope would return. The Indian would live in a land of plenty, undisturbed by the U.S. Army, reservation officials, and government agents. Within months his Ghost Dance doctrine had been embraced by some thirty or thirty-five tribes with an aggregate population of about 60,000. The most notable of these included the Paiute, Shoshoni, Arapaho, Cheyenne, Caddo, Pawnee, and Sioux, some of whom sent delegations to confer with Wovoka. The Navaho, the Pueblo Indians, and tribes of the Columbia River basin generally shunned the Ghost Dance.

Within two or three years, however, for a number of reasons, these people abandoned this fascinating ceremony with its promise of a better life and a message based in Biblical lore. The basic causes for the decline of the Ghost Dance were widespread disappointment engendered by predictions that failed to come true and perversion of the message by some adherents (especially the Sioux) who transformed the dance into a holy war against whites.

In October 1890, Sioux medicine men promised their warriors that the Indian millennium would occur as soon as the grass became green again. Their decimated ranks would be swelled by all the Indians who ever had lived and their spirits would drive before them immense herds of buffalo and ponies. The Great Spirit, who had deserted the red man for many years, now would turn against the whites and make their bullets powerless against the Indian. A huge landslide would overwhelm and cover all whites; those who might escape would become small fish in the rivers. But, to bring about this desired state of affairs, the Sioux must believe in and organize the Ghost Dance.

To the distress of those Indians who were convinced that whites would be eliminated by supernatural forces, the Sioux chose to take matters into their own hands; the Ghost Dance and special Ghost Shirts, they claimed, would protect them from U.S. Army bullets. The Sioux, once the largest and strongest tribe in the United States, had suffered one disaster after another for over two decades. Their lands, their numbers, and their herds of cattle had dwindled. Disease decimated whole families, and the drought of 1890 wiped out crops. Despite promises to the contrary, the government cut beef rations, and starvation was at hand.

At that moment a bizarre psychotic, Albert Hopkins, appeared with his "Pansy Banner of Peace" (a flower child of sorts) and claimed that he was the Indian Savior. Alarmed by Hopkins, the Ghost Dance, and the stubborn attitude of Indian holy men such as Sitting Bull, agents at Pine Ridge in the Dakotas called for troops. On December 15, 1890 Sitting Bull was killed during an attempt to arrest him. The flight of his followers led to a confrontation between Sioux braves dressed in Ghost Shirts and a contingent of the Seventh Cavalry at Wounded Knee, South Dakota. When the troops tried to confiscate their weapons, the Indians fired their rifles at the soldiers, confident that their Ghost Shirts would protect them

Smithsonian Institution, National Anthropological Archives.

Every Indian man, woman, and child became deeply involved in the ghost dance ritual. Although this was a religious ceremony, it created fear among white settlers.

from the white man's bullets. The soldiers returned their fire with Gatling guns, cutting down men, women, and children.

This bloody incident made a mockery of the basic tenets of the Ghost Dance as envisioned by Wovoka. In time, the ritual of the Ghost Dance, stripped of its original significance, became part of the tribal life among groups such as the Arapaho, Cheyenne, Caddo, Wichita, Pawnee, and Oto. As for Wovoka, for some years he was an attraction at various fairs on the West coast and, when he died at the age of seventy-four, was buried at Walker Lake Reservation at Schurz, Nevada, near the scene of his triumphs.

Although this yearning for miracles—a halcyon past restored by a ritualistic dance, holy garments, brotherly love, and righteous behavior—never was fulfilled, the tragic message of the Ghost Dance is there for all to see: a proud people who can only dream as their lands are being taken from them and their culture diluted. The most tragic irony of all is that even in the depth of their despair they based their hopes, not upon their own folkways, but largely upon fragments of various faiths practiced by their oppressors.

Smithsonian Institution, National Anthropological Archives.

Led by a spiritual leader, Indians asked their Great Spirit to help them reclaim land seized by land-hungry whites.

Selected Readings

General Studies

C. Vann Woodward, *Origins of the New South, 1877–1913* (1951)

Ray Allen Billington, *Westward Expansion* (1974)

The New South

C. Vann Woodward, *Reunion and Reaction. The Compromise of 1877 and the End of Reconstruction* (1951)

Broadus Mitchell, *The Rise of the Cotton Mills in the South* (1921)

Monroe Lee Billington, *The American South: A Brief History* (1971)

Southern Blacks, 1865–1900

George B. Tindall, *South Carolina Negroes, 1877–1900* (1952)

John Blassingame, *Black New Orleans, 1860–1880* (1973)

The New West

Lewis Atherton, *The Cattle Kings* (1961)

Joe B. Frantz and Julian E. Choate, Jr., *The American Cowboy. The Myth and the Reality* (1955)

Wayne Gard, *The Chisholm Trail* (1954)

Fred A. Shannon, *The Farmers' Last Frontier, 1860–1897* (1945)

Henry Nash Smith, *Virgin Land. The American West as Symbol and Myth* (1950)

Walter Prescott Webb, *The Great Plains* (1931)

John D. Hicks, *The Populist Revolt* (1970)

Norman Pollack, *The Populist Response to Industrial America* (1962)

Indians

Robert M. Utley, *The Last Days of the Sioux Nation* (1963)

Dee Brown, *Bury My Heart At Wounded Knee. An Indian History of the American West* (1970)

Angie Debo, *A History of the Indians of the United States* (1970)

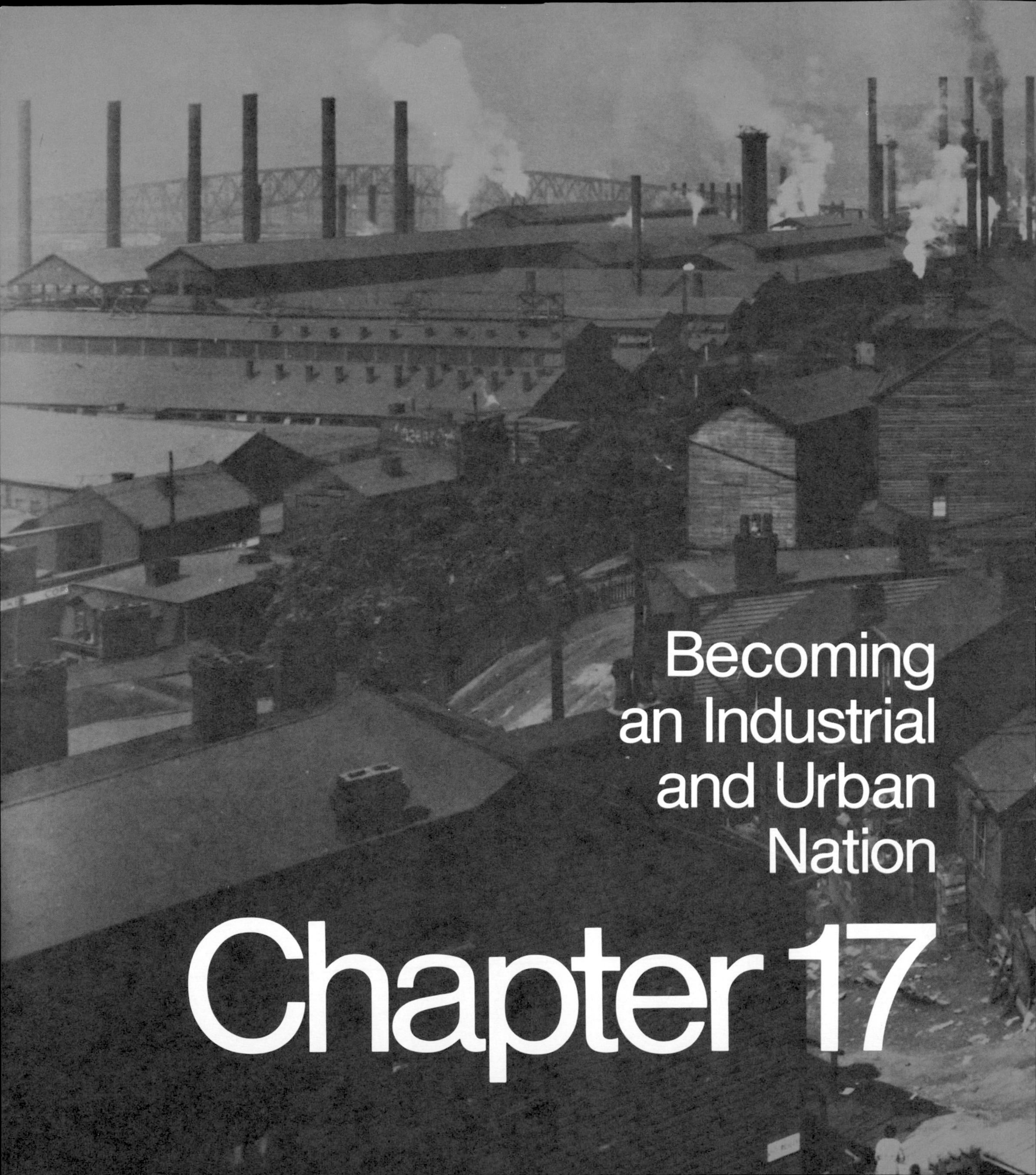

Chapter 17

Becoming an Industrial and Urban Nation

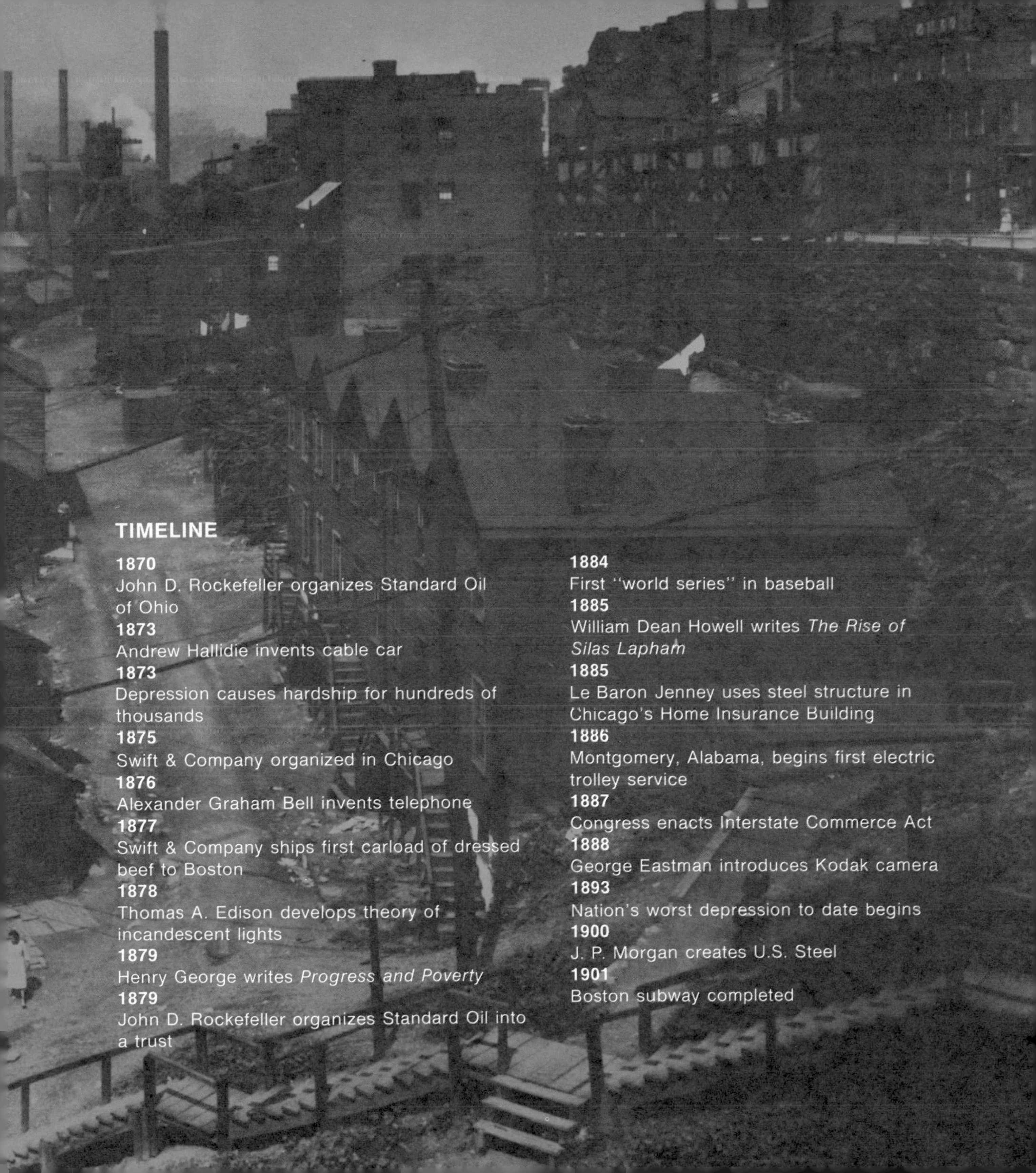

TIMELINE

1870
John D. Rockefeller organizes Standard Oil of Ohio
1873
Andrew Hallidie invents cable car
1873
Depression causes hardship for hundreds of thousands
1875
Swift & Company organized in Chicago
1876
Alexander Graham Bell invents telephone
1877
Swift & Company ships first carload of dressed beef to Boston
1878
Thomas A. Edison develops theory of incandescent lights
1879
Henry George writes *Progress and Poverty*
1879
John D. Rockefeller organizes Standard Oil into a trust
1884
First "world series" in baseball
1885
William Dean Howell writes *The Rise of Silas Lapham*
1885
Le Baron Jenney uses steel structure in Chicago's Home Insurance Building
1886
Montgomery, Alabama, begins first electric trolley service
1887
Congress enacts Interstate Commerce Act
1888
George Eastman introduces Kodak camera
1893
Nation's worst depression to date begins
1900
J. P. Morgan creates U.S. Steel
1901
Boston subway completed

CHAPTER OUTLINE

Phenomena related to growth touched all of America during the final years of the nineteenth century as the nation's industrial muscles waxed strong, as villages and towns grew into cities, and as established metropolitan areas developed sprawling suburbs. These expansive forces both influenced and drew strength from the New South and the New West; no region was totally immune from the impact of railroads, the growth of factories, the effects of new technological wonders, and the recurring waves of immigrants. It is true, however, that industrialization and urbanization tended to be more evident in older, more settled communities found in the northeastern quarter of the nation.

Large accumulations of capital, extensive pools of laborers with varied skills, small enterprises that could develop through expansion and merger into huge corporations, close networks of rail lines and waterways, and educational facilities that could provide levels of management expertise were all found in that region. Thus it was that cities such as New York, Boston, Philadelphia, Chicago, Pittsburgh, Cleveland, Cincinnati, Milwaukee, and Minneapolis emerged as centers of power and influence. Sometimes these communities were linked to a specific industry—Pittsburgh and steel, Minneapolis and milling, for example—but most were multipurpose, industrial-urban complexes that grew because of geographical and transportation advantages, coupled with shrewd investment by farsighted leaders.

The Rise of Big Business

Several factors encouraged the growth of big business during the last four decades of the nineteenth century. These included industrial expansion in the North to meet the demands of the Civil War—demands that continued to flourish in peacetime despite occasional business recessions, federal and state legislation favorable to business interests, and above all else, a tremendous growth in population (it more than doubled between 1860 and 1900), which provided native industry with millions of new customers. Moreover, during the 1890s new foreign markets in Canada, Asia, and Latin America opened up, steadily increasing the volume of manufactured exports. Although Yankee salesmen had to do battle with the products of European factories, in certain fields—sewing machines and agricultural machinery, for instance—they enjoyed clear superiority. And to aid American industry the federal government, largely at the insistence of the dominant Republican party, erected high tariff barriers that kept many foreign goods out of the U.S. market place.

A High Tariff Policy

A high tariff had been passed by Congress in 1861. Although public figures such as Carl Schurz and E. L. Godkin (editor of the *Nation*) advocated lower rates, in succeeding years tariff reform always failed. When a commission was formed in 1883 to review the government's tariff policy, powerful lobbyists representing the interests of iron, steel, oil, sugar, wool, and similar basic products were able to render the body ineffectual. The tariff was a dominant issue in the election of 1888, and the victorious Republicans honored their campaign pledges by passing the McKinley Tariff of 1890. In it was a reciprocity clause that gave the President the right to impose duties on foreign sugar, molasses, tea, coffee, hides, and other goods, if countries exporting these commodities to the United States imposed unjust duties on American products. This right served as a powerful weapon to force trade concessions from foreign countries, particularly those of Central and South America.

But the McKinley Tariff was unpopular at home because it greatly increased the retail price of imported goods and was one cause of the Republican defeat in 1892. A tariff reduction proposal, the Wilson-Gorman Act, was then passed, but once more congressmen allied with big business rendered it ineffective. Upon these

Courtesy New-York Historical Society, New York City.

The variety, complexity, and immensity of the burgeoning American metropolis were epitomized by Broadway in New York City in 1885. The array of advertisements and peddlers illustrate the close relationship between commerce, the city, and sheer size.

foundations, particularly the support of business by government, American industry entered the twentieth century well prepared for its all-out campaign for economic world supremacy.

The Dimensions of "Bigness"

In 1860, 140,000 manufacturing establishments were turning out products worth $1.9 billion. Four decades later 207,000 machine shops and factories produced goods valued at $11.4 billion. Two facts are readily apparent: production grew by leaps and bounds, while the number of individual producers failed to keep pace with this growth. Even allowing for the proclivity of the Census Bureau to alter the precise meaning of "a manufacturing establishment" during these forty years, it is apparent that numerous mergers and takeovers occurred. In the process some companies disappeared and a few became huge corporations. By the turn of the century only one percent of all manufacturing plants had annual production worth over one million dollars, but those establishments were turning out nearly two-thirds of the nation's manufactured goods.

To a large extent, fierce competition and hard times during the decades after Appomattox led to "gentlemen's agreements" within specific industries, pacts that were often not kept very well. Railroad magnates whose tracks frequently were overbuilt and ran through areas served by rival lines were quick to develop "pools," arrangements designed to maintain prices and split up business.

Since it was virtually impossible to enforce these pooling agreements (in 1887 the Interstate Commerce Act made this specific strategy illegal), by the early 1880s pools were giving way to holding companies and trusts. These were combinations of firms or companies, usually with a common product such as oil, steel, or perhaps rail service. The holding company, controlled by a single member concern, soon fell from favor since its operations, like those of a pooling agreement, could not stand the scrutiny of emerging regulatory commissions. The trust, however, proved more resilient and therefore became popular.

This was an independent entity, the creation of the stockholders of individual member companies. By a legally binding agreement, these stockholders exchanged their shares for others representing a proportionate interest in the principal and the income of the new combination thus created. They also surrendered management and operation of the combined firms to the trust. In this manner a board of directors (or trustees) could direct the affairs of the new concern and do so with a greater supply of capital and less fear of competition. In general, subsequent efforts at "trustbusting" rarely achieved much lasting success; instead, the various trustees merely "cleaned up their act" for a time.

A trust, of course, was innately neither good nor bad. Responsible management could bring order and efficiency to an industry and reduce costs to consumers; however, the prime goal of such a business arrangement was profit, and any advantages accruing to the general public were merely byproducts of this quest for a greater return on capital investments.

Nowhere was this tendency toward combination and consolidation greater than in the railroad industry. By 1900, with an overall value of slightly less than $10 billion, railroads represented one-tenth of the nation's wealth. A few years later, two-thirds of the tracks were controlled by seven groups which, because of mysterious board room agreements, really constituted only four combinations: Morgan, Hill, Vanderbilt, and the Pennsylvania interests.

During the final decade of the nineteenth century, the five most important manufactures (by the value of their products) remained at the top of U.S. industry, but their order of priority shifted, and those shifts indicate what was happening throughout much of America. Iron and steel jumped from fourth to first place, pushing slaughtering and meat products to second. Foundry and machine-shop products moved from fifth to third, lumber and timber products slipped from third to fourth, and flour and gristmill products (second in 1890) now were in fifth place. During that decade alone iron and steel production nearly doubled.

In short, factory and foundry output was increasing in importance, that of farm and forest decreasing. By 1900 more and more of the raw materials used in manufacturing were coming from mines, not from fields and woodlands as they had in the past. And at the turn of the century, not surprisingly, 35.5 percent of the nation's labor force (10.2 million workers) were industrial wage earners.

So many diverse factors fed this industrial expansion that it is virtually impossible to single out any one as being all-important. Thanks to immigration from overseas and from farm to city, labor was plentiful during

Library of Congress.

John Pierpont Morgan
(1837–1913)

Banker, financier, and organizer of industry, J. P. Morgan was the man during the Gilded Age whom the robber barons and the federal government turned to "when the going got rough." Morgan, who grew up in Hartford and Boston, represented the third generation of substantial wealth. Well-educated, including two years at Göttingen where mathematics interested him most, Morgan had formed by 1871 a powerful banking house linking Philadelphia and New York interests, Drexel, Morgan & Company. A quarter of a century later it became simply J. P. Morgan & Company.

During these years—in fact, from 1873 until his death—Morgan was a towering force for the integration of industrial life and stabilization of the U.S. economy. He and his father both were instrumental in encouraging European investment in America. Young Morgan at first turned his attention to railroads, then helped to organize steel and other industries. In 1895, when the U.S. government faced a deep crisis, he formed a syndicate that dumped $65 million into the U.S. Treasury, for a fee, of course.

In essence, his powerful banking house was a dealer in bonds, stocks, and notes; he and his associates were the directing power in the railroads, public utilities, and industries that issued those bonds, stocks, and notes; and, they also were the directing power in the life insurance companies and banks that invested in them. Shortly before Morgan's death, his firm controlled or exerted considerable power over companies worth more than $1 billion.

Although widely respected, Morgan was by no means infallible in business affairs. Icy, aloof, a man of violent dislikes, he was the essential aristocrat who had no interest in social reform and cared little for public opinion. He was an enthusiastic yachtsman, world traveler, avid art collector, and a devout, active Episcopalian. During his lifetime he gave lavishly of his wealth (especially to New York's Metropolitan Museum of Art, of which he was president for many years), although this philanthropy was less methodical than that of Carnegie and Rockefeller.

Twice married, he was the father of four children. At his death he left a net estate of $68 million and art worth an estimated $50 million. ■

these decades. In an era when farmers faced hard times and depressed prices, both new and native-born Americans, often with great reluctance, became urban dwellers and thus factory workers. Also, if one accepts the well-known thesis of Frederick Jackson Turner, by 1890 the frontier and cheap land were no more.

At the same time a gigantic rail network had developed which facilitated the flow of people, raw materials, and finished goods throughout all parts of the nation. In 1860, 30,000 miles of track, many of them narrow gauge and owned by small, inefficient companies, linked older Atlantic coast communities with the Mississippi Valley. Four decades later, 193,000 miles of railroad track (40 percent of the world's total) had spread to almost every corner of the United States; and, as noted, a small group of managers—efficient but often ruthless—now operated the trains that served millions of customers each year.

Much like the railroad, by 1900 telegraph and telephone lines also tied the nation together, and the latter provided a new and vital means of business communication within and between growing urban centers. Alexander Graham Bell's telephone, invented in 1876, was only one of the wonders of this age which businessmen quickly adopted for their own purposes.

New inventions saved time and labor and money. Thousands of patents were granted during these years, the number rising from 77,000 in the 1860s to 230,000 in the 1890s. The impetus of business and the needs of industry fostered an unprecedented era of technological innovation. In addition to the telephone, to name a few, there was electric power, Thomas A. Edison's electric light bulb, and refrigeration, to say nothing of the air brake, the trolley, the cash register, the steam turbine, and—that harbinger of profound social change—the automobile. One innovation frequently was the father of another, electricity, for example, giving birth to scores of inventions as this new source of power found countless applications.

Within the industrial community more stable conditions created by pools, holding companies, trusts, and mergers allowed for experimentation and innovation in internal business organization. Soon a new managerial class arose as distinct from those who actually owned mills and factories. The latter, because of the nature of the trust-corporate structure, had less and less to do with day-to-day operations. Frequently this managerial expertise had little or nothing to do with whatever was being produced, instead operating a business venture successfully and returning a profit on capital invested in it became the crucial goals.

In this atmosphere, national advertising acquired an increasingly important role. For the first time in American history, aided by a huge transportation-communication network, widespread basic education, and the growth

Museum of the City of New York.

Growing cities required a fast and efficient transportation network to move people from home to office or factory. Even the temporary inconvenience of track-laying crews at Broadway and Fulton Streets in New York City was accepted as a means to that end.

THE MUNSING
PLATED UNDERWEAR
for WOMEN
MISSES
CHILDREN
and MEN
THIS fabric—one cotton strand between two of wool—insures wear, appearance and shape. The **elastic flat seam** gives all the advantages of full-fashioned garments, at
POPULAR PRICES
Ask your dealer for our **free Booklet** showing styles **photographed on living models**, or address
The Northwestern Knitting Co., MINNEAPOLIS, MINN.
Courtesy Minnesota Historical Society.

Advertising techniques used today were fashioned years ago. This ad appeared in an 1897 edition of *Ladies Home Journal*. Note the subtle hint at sex appeal, promising underwear "photographed on living models."

of newspapers and magazines, millions began to become conscious of "brand name" labels in certain fields. In 1860, the nation spent only $27 million on advertising, by 1900, $95 million. This increase, a byproduct of urban living, was devoted to a new idea: advertisement of brand names coupled with catchy slogans. For example, Proctor and Gamble's Ivory Soap was said to be "99 and 44/100% pure." From its inception, however, modern advertising did much more than popularize brands and products; it also tried to create demand where previously none had existed.

The same concentration evident in the railroad industry, to some degree, could be found in food processing, the manufacture of soap, and the production of new appliances such as Singer sewing machines, all of which made excellent use of new advertising techniques. Each of these items also reflects great change within households, which often no longer had gardens or the facilities or time to make soap and clothing by slow, time-honored methods; it simply was much easier and cheaper to buy than to manufacture much that once was produced within the home.

And all of this industrial growth and expansion occurred during decades of general peace (if one overlooks frontier clashes with the Indians, an upsurge of lynching, and a minor fracas with Spain) and under the protective blanket of high tariffs that virtually eliminated foreign competition. Tariffs did not, however, keep out overseas investment, which was indeed welcome and played an important role in the emergence of modern America.

Railroads: The First Big Business

Between the 1850s and the 1880s, railroads were the prime generators of spectacular and sudden wealth. Only in the last two decades did industry (which railroads certainly helped to foster) become the major source of profits. During the eight years following the Civil War, 35,000 miles of new track were laid, virtually doubling the extent of U.S. rail lines. In the 1870s Pullman sleeping cars, steel rails instead of iron, a uniform gauge (four feet, eight and one-half inches), double tracks, greatly improved roadbeds, and expanded terminal facilities with switching yards and round houses became more and more common in all parts of the nation. Giant bridges also began to span rivers, increasing the speed and ease of transportation. Although the Panic of 1873 dealt railroads a momentary setback, in 1880 the United States had 93,000 miles of track and ten years later, 163,000 miles. By 1890 the full outline of a national rail system was apparent and only 30,000 miles of subsidiary or feeder lines appeared after that date.

This system was financed largely by stock sales and local, state, and federal loans and subsidies. By far the best known source was federal land given to proposed rail lines if constructed. (By 1943 various companies had received final title to 131.3 million acres, 90 percent of them located in states west of the Mississippi.) Whether this largesse was a wise policy has long been debated. It encouraged construction companies, always ready to inflate building costs, and entrepreneurs, equally eager to lay claim to land, to push tracks forward recklessly—and into unproductive areas. And, in time, competition, excessive expenditures, business recessions, emerging state and federal regulation, and inept (even fraudulent) management all took their toll. Some companies grew into big ones, and others were swallowed up by more aggressive and perhaps more efficient management. During the hard times of the 1870s, for example, 450 railroad companies (two-fifths of all those in the nation) went bankrupt.

In this process of building, merger, and experimentation, the beginnings of modern corporate finance evolved. Construction and operation required huge sums of money which often came, especially during hard times, from investment bankers. Men such as J. Pierpont Morgan could provide the funds needed but they increasingly began to play a role in management as well in order to protect the interests of their customers. These individuals, fully as much as competition and common sense, encouraged consolidation, careful cost accounting, and sound fiscal policies.

The original goal of a pre-Civil War railroad had been to siphon produce from the hinterland and stimulate trade with a specific port city such as New Orleans, Charleston, Norfolk, Baltimore, Philadelphia, or New York. But as America became an industrial-urban nation, ocean connections declined somewhat in importance, and the goal of emerging rail systems was to control vast areas, especially regions lying between growing centers of commerce. The first man to knit a number of short lines into a giant company was Cornelius Vanderbilt who, having made a fortune in steamboats, by the time of his death in 1877 had created the New York Central System, which dominated transportation in the Northeast between New York and Chicago. Rivals in the same general area included the Pennsylvania Railroad, which, in time, gained control of several major southern lines as well. In the West the Great Northern, Northern Pacific, Central Pacific, and Southern Pacific (moving from north to south) monopolized trans-Mississippi trade and commerce.

James J. Hill (1838–1916), creator of the Great Northern, was a man much like Vanderbilt, a careful, conscientious builder whose efforts paid off in 1893. His was the only transcontinental system to weather the financial panic of that year. The 1890s also shook up several fragile southern lines, among them the Southern and the Norfolk & Western, which soon came under the direction of New York and Philadelphia interests. By the early twentieth century, seven major combinations (with some occasional interlocking financial connections) dominated the American railroad industry:

1. Vanderbilt Roads—New York Central; Chicago & Northwestern
2. Pennsylvania Group—Pennsylvania; Baltimore & Ohio; Chesapeake & Ohio
3. Morgan Roads—Erie; Southern
4. Gould System—Missouri Pacific
5. Rock Island System—Rock Island
6. Hill Roads—Great Northern; Northern Pacific; Burlington
7. Harriman Roads—Union Pacific; Southern Pacific; Illinois Central

Library of Congress.

Cornelius Vanderbilt as he appeared one year before his death in 1877.

Recreation

An outing by the sea in the 1870s that must have been slightly uncomfortable for these overdressed pleasure-seekers.

Beach Scene, 1879, by Samuel S. Carr, Smith College Museum of Art.

Missouri Historical Society.

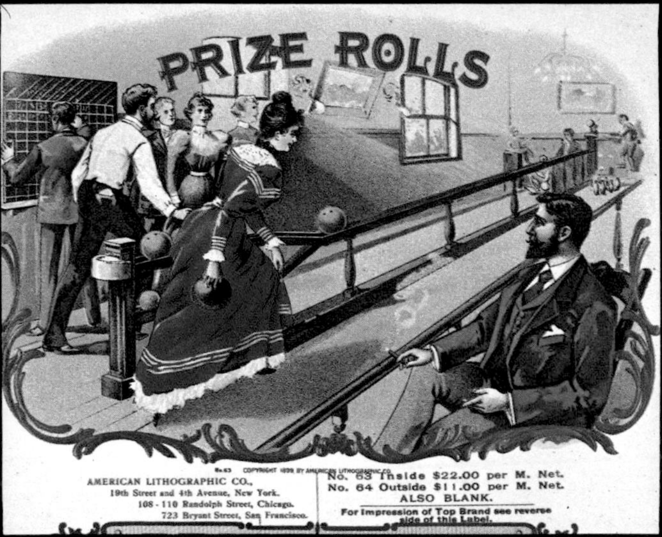

Bowling, like cycling and horseback riding, was enjoyed by members of both sexes during the 1890s.

Circus World Museum—Baraboo, Wisconsin.

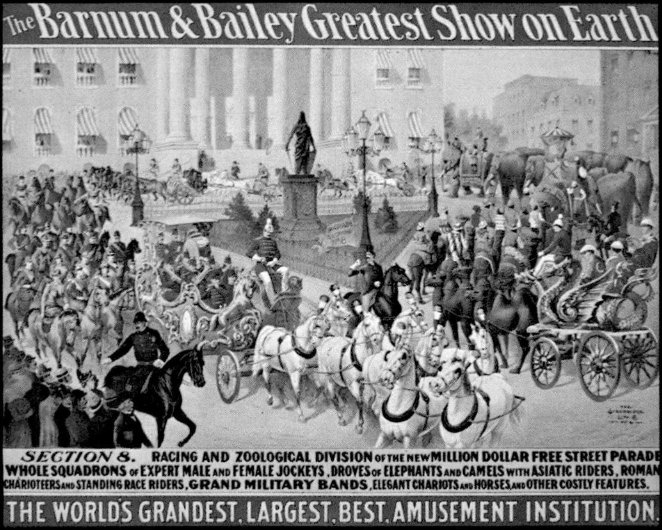

Though less popular as a pastime today, the circus was once the most exciting activity in rural America. Hundreds came to view the parades and applaud the daredevil performances of acrobats and animal trainers.

Bettmann Archive

As cities grew, organized spectator sports became popular. This 1887 baseball game at the Polo Grounds in New York City provided respite from the tensions of everyday urban life.

Culver Picture

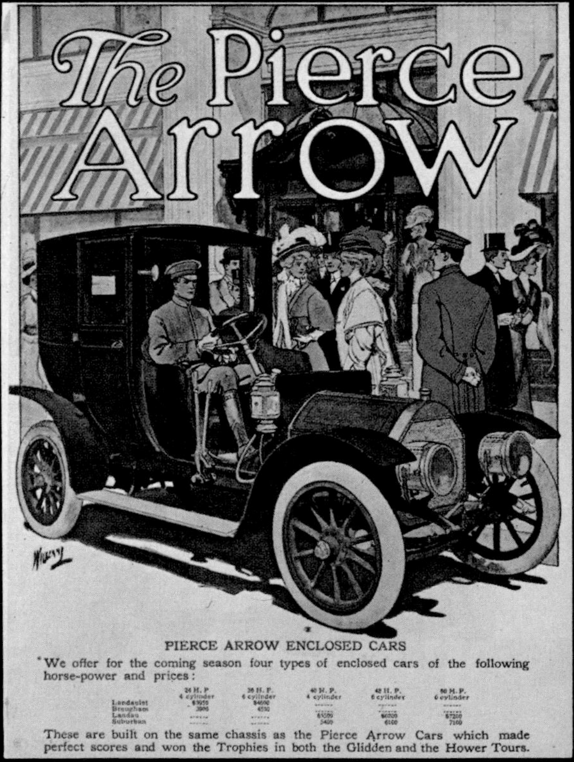

The automobile offered mobility to thousands of Americans seeking recreation during evenings and weekends. This 1908 ad suggested the additional pleasure to be derived by attending social functions in a fashionable car.

By the 1950s, the "sport of kings" was attracting hundreds of thousands of gambling spectators each year.

The postwar emphasis on family life led to a revival of traditional recreational activities like camping and picnicking.

Russ Kinne/Photo Researchers

Richard Steedman/Image Bank

Ordered living in the suburbs after World War II was paralleled by the rise of organized activites for children. Little League baseball, sometimes as competitive a sport for the parents as for the children, was the forerunner for youth leagues in virtually every sport.

Homecoming Queen, College of William and Mary.

In the 1950s, teenagers took center stage. Rock and roll led to many variants of the "jitterbug," some of which appalled an older generation of Americans.

Wayne Miller/Magn

Mitchell B. Reibel/F.O.S.

In the 1970s, health-conscious Americans took to jogging — in parks, in the countryside, and on city streets.

© Gabe Palmer/Image Bank

Along with the luxuries of our technological age comes an inclination toward passive entertainment. In an earlier period of our history these children would have been frolicking in this meadow.

Strobe lights and electronic sound systems characterize the disco-mania of the 1970s.

Ted Thai/Sygma

F.O.S.

Football has probably surpassed baseball as America's favorite spectator sport. Not only the complicated football formations, but also the precision marching bands and card tricks in the stands — often with patriotic themes — capture the imagination of millions of fans throughout the nation.

For city youths, opportunities for recreation have remained somewhat limited. One of the favorites is the "pick up" basketball game on a public school playground, or even on the street.

This weeding out process did not occur without considerable anguish and protest. Management waged all-out warfare in an effort to remain both solvent and independent. Favored shippers such as John D. Rockefeller demanded and got rebates not granted to other customers. Charges in regions served by a single line usually were everything the traffic would bear; where competition existed, rate wars, pooling, holding companies, deception, and fraud all too often were the rule of the day. Capricious and often unpublished freight rates were common, and a company might charge more for a short haul where no competition existed than for a long haul where it did.

This seeming chaos eventually inspired efforts to bring order and was thus a force for considerable good. Consolidation in transportation became the model for other industries, and its corporate methods—finance, management, labor relations—were quickly adapted to oil, coal, steel, and electricity. Almost any executive, stockholder, or employee could see benefits accruing from stable prices and was eager to emulate what was happening in the railroad industry.

Library of Congress.

No man was more representative of the robber baron in an age of high-risk financial intrigue, unscrupulous stock dealings, and extreme competitiveness than Jay Gould.

Freight rates, although they seemed excessive to western farmers, fell more rapidly than agricultural prices in the years following the Civil War. The cost of farm produce dropped 37 percent (1870–1900), freight rates nearly 70 percent. In the twenty years from 1880 to 1900 they declined 59 percent west of the Missouri River. However, such statistics cannot hide two truths: farmers went west anticipating better, not worse times, and distances beyond the Mississippi were so great that falling freight rates meant little.

Nevertheless, the rail system pioneered by Vanderbilt and Hill, nearly ruined by men like Daniel Drew and Jay Gould, and salvaged by the Harrimans and Morgans was much more than a corporate wonder: it literally bound the nation together. By 1900 one could travel in relative speed and comfort to all parts of the nation. Between 1870 and 1900, for example, the Chicago–New York travel time was cut from thirty to twenty hours, and the fare sliced almost in half, from $42 to $23. A vast region, free of tariff barriers like those splitting Europe into competing states, was now a unified market which was, after all, one key to America's industrial power.

Oil, Steel, and Electricity

Petroleum, long recognized as a source of illumination and said to possess magical restorative powers as well, was the fluid that literally lubricated the wheels of industrial progress throughout the final decades of the nineteenth century. During the Civil War era an "oil rush" of sorts engulfed western Pennsylvania and parts of Ohio and West Virginia as oil lamps became increasingly popular and industry found still other uses for this new product. Sudden emergence of a major commodity, soon the nation's fourth largest export, attracted the attention of a successful young produce executive, John D. Rockefeller, whose name is entwined not only with the rise of the oil industry but also with the development of trusts, ruthless monopolistic practices, shrewd, farsighted management, and philanthropy.

Rockefeller (1839–1937), who had only a common-school education, quickly demonstrated a keen head for business. During the Civil War he backed an oil refinery that had already proved itself, and shortly after

Courtesy Rockefeller Family Archives.

John D. Rockefeller at approximately 25 years of age.

hostilities ended and profiting from his experience, turned his entire attention to oil. To an industry marred by violence, lawlessness, and waste he brought order and stability—but on his terms. Rockefeller surrounded himself with very able talent, embraced new techniques, demonstrated the advantages of large-scale production, and by 1867 was the largest refiner of oil in the Cleveland area. In 1870 he organized Standard Oil of Ohio and then moved swiftly against rival firms in other parts of the populous Northeast. Those who accepted his offers shared in the profits, those who resisted became his enemies. He usually won out in the price wars that followed, and within a decade he controlled about 90 percent of the nation's refineries.

Rockefeller was a taciturn man, a devout Baptist who taught Sunday school and gave dimes to children. He detested waste and ostentation and lived a frugal personal life. He never seemed to doubt the correctness of his actions and once reportedly remarked, "God gave me my money." Standard Oil, the nation's first trust (founded in 1879 and reorganized three years later), consolidated twenty-seven different companies into a single giant corporation and, much as railroads were doing, demonstrated the advantages of "bigness" to others.

Although Rockefeller's organizational methods would not be tolerated today and his Standard Oil trust frequently came under scrutiny by the courts, it continued to flourish and prosper. In his rise to power Rockefeller left a trail of hatred. He forced railroads to grant rebates, used industrial spies to ruin competitors, and built his own factories and warehouses to eliminate middlemen and cut costs. Few industrial giants have risen so swiftly, been so ruthless, and perhaps, at the same time, been so shrewd and so perceptive.

Steel actually is a better barometer of the new industrial age than oil which, although very important, really came into its own with the automobile and the twentieth century. Before the Civil War only tools, knives, and similar small articles were made of steel. It was a costly process and few envisioned the day when

Drake Well Museum.

Pennsylvania was the original setting for what would become the multibillion-dollar oil industry. Derricks dotted the landscape in this early 1860s scene. At that time oil was shipped in barrels loaded on flatcars; by 1869 "boiler-shaped" tank cars had come into use and by the 1870s pipelines carried oil from the fields to the refinery.

Courtesy U.S. Steel Corporation.

The J. Edgar Thomson Steel Works in greater Pittsburgh was the first United States factory to mass-produce steel by the Bessemer process. Andrew Carnegie (shown below) took advantage of production and management techniques to create a virtual monopoly in steel.

Courtesy U.S. Steel Corporation.

steel would replace cast iron in railway tracks, bridges, and general construction work.

In the early 1850s two men—William Kelly, an American, and Henry Bessemer, an Englishman—began experimenting independently with methods to force molten metal to burn out carbon impurities by introducing a blast of cold air. In essence, steel is a more malleable form of cast iron with a very low carbon content, so-called "soft steel" possessing the least carbon of all (roughly less than 0.25 percent). Within a decade plants utilizing methods pioneered by Kelly and Bessemer began to appear in Pennsylvania and other regions close to supplies of iron ore and coal. Although Pittsburgh became a prime center, in the 1880s some fifty new steel plants were also opened near Birmingham, Alabama, and in parts of Tennessee and Virginia. As the price of steel dropped, its uses multiplied. In the decade after Appomattox, U.S. production soared from about 30,000 tons per year to over 600,000 tons. Meanwhile, yet another innovation, the "open-hearth" method, which could utilize cheaper ore, was introduced from England and in time became much more popular than the Kelly-Bessemer process.

Just as Rockefeller came to dominate oil, Andrew Carnegie, a poor Scottish immigrant, did the same in steel. Carnegie (1835–1919), a man whose career presents the classic rags to riches saga, used Rockefeller's methods but for various reasons never enjoyed the same degree of public scorn. Son of a humble but very intelligent weaver, Carnegie was a bobbin boy, messenger, and telegraph operator as a youth. His obvious talents earned him a position in 1853 as private secretary to Thomas A. Scott, an executive of the Pennsylvania Railroad and the financier who gave him his first lessons in stock speculation.

During the next fifteen years Andrew Carnegie entered various fields, among them phases of railroad construction, bridge building, oil refining, and even the sale of railway bonds in Europe. By 1868, at age 33, his annual income from investments totaled $50,000 a year, and he contemplated retirement, writing on one occasion, "The amassing of wealth is one of the worst species of idolitary [*sic*]. No idol is more debasing than the worship of money."

But a short time later, while on a business trip to England he saw the Bessemer process in action and returned to Pittsburgh determined to put all of his energy and money into a single industry: steel. Already a millionaire, Carnegie profited mightily from the financial disaster of 1873, buying out several hard-pressed competitors and thereby gaining a dominant role in a fast-growing field. Unique among the empire builders of those years, he always exercised direct control. His only stockholders were close associates, and he used a system of partnerships to create an integrated production line. With the aid of men such as Henry Clay Frick and Charles M. Schwab, he put together a huge combination of coal and iron mines, limestone quarries, coke ovens, ore-carrying ships, and railroads.

In 1900 Carnegie sold his empire to J. P. Morgan for half a billion dollars, giving birth to a giant corporation, United States Steel. He devoted the rest of his life to philanthropy, especially in the form of magnificent libraries given to towns and cities throughout America. In 1889 he wrote "The Gospel of Wealth" in which he endorsed the accumulation of capital as the necessary foundation for civilized progress; in it he emphasized the moral obligation of the rich to spend their money for the public welfare.

To many Carnegie was a new symbol of what could be the exemplary American experience: the poor immigrant boy who makes good and then benefits society. He himself was a realist and understood that by his very success he had proved more effectively than any socialist that free enterprise no longer worked—or even existed. In 1909 he wrote that the age of competition was over and advised the national government to regulate industry and to fix all wages and prices.

While the high-level manipulations of men such as Rockefeller, Carnegie, Frick, and Morgan had an indirect impact on the lives of most Americans, only a relative few were buying oil and steel in great quantities or were intimately concerned with the merger of railroads and the schemes of Wall Street financiers. The electric light and the telephone, on the other hand, were appearing in more and more households and businesses during the last decades of the nineteenth century and were exerting a profound effect on how millions lived and worked.

Library of Congress.

Many promoters lived off Thomas A. Edison's celebrity. Besides fostering the American need for gadgets, men like Professor Fritz also played a useful service by enlightening the public about technological innovations.

Thomas Alva Edison (1847–1931) was the most renowned inventor-businessman of these years, but without J. P. Morgan's money, Edison's discoveries would not have spread to every part of the country. The relationship between these two men is perhaps one of the best examples of the ability of private enterprise to foster technological inventions and to utilize them on a major scale. Born in Ohio, Edison received virtually no formal schooling and his knowledge of science and electricity in particular came from reading and experimentation. As a young telegrapher he worked in various eastern cities, often being fired because he allowed his experiments to take precedence over his routine duties. Before he was twenty-two, Edison had perfected a vote recorder, a stock ticker, and an alphabetical dial telegraphic device—none of which brought him any financial gain. (Between 1868 and 1900 he would register nearly 800 patents, all but a few of them in the electrical field.)

In an effort to improve his prospects, Edison went to New York City in 1869 where he got a job as a repairman for a telegraph company. Invention of an improved stock ticker netted him $40,000, and with this nest egg he became, for a brief time, a manufacturer of tickers and other telegraphic devices. By 1876, however, he was able to cease manufacturing and devote all of his time to research and experimentation.

In the fall of 1877, at age thirty, Edison began work on an incandescent light but soon interrupted his experiments to perfect the phonograph. Considered to be this remarkable man's only truly original invention, it also was his favorite. Numerous other individuals were interested in electric light research, among them George F. Brush, who had devised for Cleveland's streets (1879) an arc light system, which was soon being duplicated in several European cities. The arc, however, had distinct disadvantages since it was suitable only for simultaneous illumination of large outdoor spaces, not private homes. Edison rejected this method because he was interested in a complete lighting system that could compete successfully with gas.

By October 1878, Thomas Edison had developed the basic theory of his incandescent bulb and formed the Edison Electric Light Company with sufficient financial support to enable him to move forward with his experiments. Four years later his first commercial electrical station, which was centered at Pearl Street in New York City, opened with about eighty-five customers and some 400 lamps. Although successful, Edison's desire to see electricity adopted in other cities was frustrated by cautious backers and his strange insistence on the use of direct (as opposed to alternating) current, which severely limited the size and range of his central stations. Ironically, general use of alternating current, despite Edison's personal objections, eventually established his fame and made possible widespread use of electric light and power.

Among Edison's most influential backers as the potential of electricity was realized were J. P. Morgan and several of his associates. (Morgan's Manhattan home, interestingly, was one of the first in the city to have its own electric-lighting plant.) In the late 1880s these men helped Edison form a variety of companies designed to manufacture his products. In the years between 1889 and 1892, the Edison interests merged with several competitors, among them the Sprague Electric Railway and Motor Company, the Brush Arc Company, and the Thompson-Houston Electric Company, to form the General Electric Company. Throughout all this one can discern the hand of J. P. Morgan treating electric power much as he did railroads and steel.

Edison's most serious rival in this rush to fame and fortune was George Westinghouse (1846–1914), inventor of the air brake that made high-speed rail travel possible. In 1884, long before Edison could be persuaded that the use of alternating current was feasible, Westinghouse was attracted by its potential. Within a few years he and his engineers pioneered with large-scale municipal lighting, lit up the Chicago World's Fair, and began harnessing the waters of Niagara Falls. His Westinghouse Electric Corporation emerged as General Electric's most serious competitor, although after 1896 many patents were shared under a cross-licensing agreement.

Alexander Graham Bell (1847–1922), born in Scotland, came from a well-to-do family whose interest in phonetics and teaching of the deaf led to research on his famous invention. In 1870 the Bells moved to Ontario, and in the following year their twenty-three-year-old son began teaching in Boston and experimenting on a mechanism that could relay the human voice over great distances. His telephone, an obscure and late entry at the Philadelphia Centennial Exposition of 1876, won widespread acclaim. Within two years, the carbon transmitter improved voice quality considerably and the switchboard made the telephone both practical and commercially feasible.

Few inventions have won such immediate acceptance. In 1880 there were 50,000 phones in the United States; a decade later, 250,000; and by 1900, about 800,000. By 1892, intercity lines connected Boston and New York with Washington, Pittsburgh, Chicago, and Milwaukee. Four years later, during the election campaign, McKinley could talk by telephone to his campaign managers in 38 states.

For a time, Western Union Telegraph Company tried to set up its own telephone system in competition with Bell, but eventually gave up the fight and devoted its attention solely to wire service. Theodore Vail, Bell's general manager, was largely responsible for the telephone's very rapid expansion since he insisted that uniform equipment be used everywhere. He further enforced standardization by leasing rather than selling franchises. In 1885 Bell and his associates organized the American Telegraph and Telephone Company. Thanks to the poli-

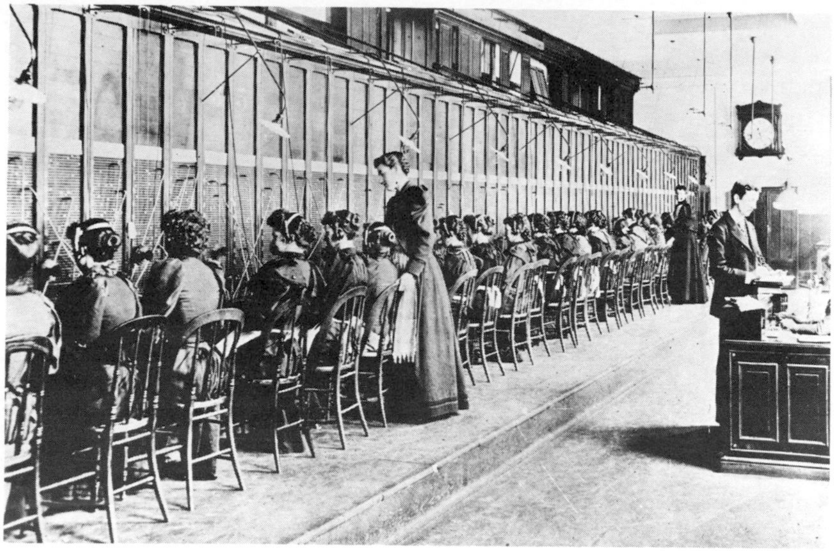

Reproduced with permission of American Telephone and Telegraph.

The central telephone office in New York City in 1888. From the beginning, women predominated as switchboard operators while men acted as managers and supervisors.

cies of Vail, AT&T's first president, that company defeated efforts to nationalize the system, enabling it to remain a unique private corporation in control of a national utility.

Unlike Edison who seemed mesmerized by electricity, Bell had much more varied interests, among them experimental air-conditioning, sheep breeding, speedboats, air flight, and geographical exploration. He was a founding member of the National Geographical Society in 1888, served as president from 1898 to 1903, and his heirs have long guided the destiny of that organization.

Other Growth Industries

In a less spectacular fashion than railroads, steel, electric lights, and telephones, several industries of considerable everyday importance experienced change and innovation during these years. These included meatpacking, flour milling, prepared foods, and tobacco. In each the same trends were evident: mechanization, consolidation, widespread use of new railroad lines, great expenditure of capital, and very often dominance by one or two aggressive individuals.

Meat, especially pork, had been cured, packed, and shipped great distances for generations, but the growth of railroads and the development of refrigeration brought transformations to this vital industry. In fact, meatpacking became organized into three basic functions: slaughtering and packing, storing and distributing, and utilizing byproducts. A key leader in this process was Massachusetts-born Gustavus Franklin Swift (1839–1903), who by 1875 had established Swift & Company in Chicago. Two years later he revolutionized the meatpacking industry when he shipped his first carload of dressed beef to Boston, thus changing radically established marketing procedures. Until that time cattle were shipped to the East and slaughtered close to metropolitan markets. Swift hired an engineer who designed an ice-cooled refrigerator car for use in warm weather. He faced considerable opposition from eastern butchers but eventually prevailed. In 1902 Swift merged with Armour and Morris, two of his competitors, to found the National Packing Company, a trust subsequently dissolved by the courts.

The flour-milling enterprise, once dominated by eastern cities such as Rochester, Baltimore, and Richmond, had shifted westward by the eve of the Civil War to St. Louis and Milwaukee. After 1870 wheat grown in the Dakotas and Minnesota made Minneapolis the "flour city" of the nation, largely because the invention of the middlings purifier made the hard red spring wheat of that region suitable for bread flour. By 1882 Minneapolis was the largest milling center in the world, although in the 1890s Kansas City began to challenge this supremacy with wheat from the Central Plains and the Southwest.

The Civil War, more than anything else, stimulated

the canning and preservation for commercial sale of fruits, fish, vegetables, and dairy products. The Union army ordered vast quantities of canned goods and, with peace, packers found public acceptance greatly enhanced. Gail Borden opened his first condensed milk factory in New York state in 1861. Soon other commercial canneries began to flourish in all parts of the nation—California fruits, Maine lobsters, and West coast salmon, to name a few. By the end of the century trade names such as Heinz with 25 factories, 85 pickle-salting stations, and far more than 57 varieties (a slogan chosen for its appeal) were well-known and widely recognized.

Tobacco, America's first exported crop, experienced growth and change as the sale of cigarettes—once thought effete—boomed as never before, although even greater returns would be realized in the twentieth century. Cigarette-making machines, aggressive and provocative advertising, and relentless exploitation of new markets at home and overseas brought prosperity to several sections of the New South. In 1890 James B. Duke (1856–1925), one of the most farsighted of these tobacco industrialists, formed the American Tobacco Company which within two decades held a virtual monopoly of all aspects of the industry except cigars, controlled 150 factories, and represented a half-billion dollar investment. In 1911, by court decree, this trust was broken up into sixteen parts, one of which retained the company name. Duke, a forceful, self-confident go-getter, is remembered today as the benefactor of the university that bears his name.

Panics and Depressions

This superficial picture of progress, prosperity, growth, and expansion was marred by recurring financial problems. Major depressions in each decade (1870–1900) lasted three or four years and caused more hardship than any other periods of "hard times," that is, until the Great Depression of the 1930s. During much of the thirty years following the Civil War, prices fell, leading to a deflation that was especially burdensome for agricultural debtors. Having contracted loans and mortgages at fixed sums, they had to repay those obligations with crops and money worth less than when the notes were signed.

The worst of these cyclic economic disasters occurred in 1873 and 1893, although on both occasions there were storm warnings and recovery came only after three or four chaotic years. In 1871, for example, 3,000 businesses failed and in 1872, another 4,000. Although statistics on unemployment are virtually nonexistent, it is safe to assume that hundreds of thousands were out of work and that this unrest fostered political instability. True, the situation in the United States was repeated elsewhere in the industrialized world, particularly Great Britain, but the English depressions were shorter and less ruinous.

The 1893 onslaught was somewhat more sudden, although agriculture had been in the doldrums for several years. Prices for raw materials and manufactured items were declining, and in 1891 goods were cheaper than they ever had been in the nation's history. Boots and shoes, woolen goods and cotton fabrics, the best white oak and ash used for furniture, and machinery were selling for 25 to 50 percent less than they had a decade before. As prices fell, production was often curtailed and unemployment grew, which further reduced consumer spending and slowed down the economy still more. The only advantage was that manufacturers, hurt by low prices, were forced to make production more efficient and less wasteful.

In 1893, 500 banks and 16,000 businesses collapsed and the following year railroad traffic and railroad construction both declined. By June 1894, one-fourth of the capitalization of all U.S. railroads was in receivership. Wages and prices had dipped 10 percent, and an estimated 20 percent of the labor force was unemployed. About 20,000 individuals were actually homeless in New York City and this grim picture was repeated in scores of cities and towns. It was not until 1898 that firm recovery began.

Why? What went wrong? There is, of course, no agreement on what caused any of these disasters. One political party tended to blame the other; farmers blamed middlemen and railroads, labor blamed capital, and so it went. But in the 1890s there were several factors that clearly led to trouble. Because of low prices for their crops, farmers were not playing their natural consumer role. Both agricultural and industrial goods were much too plentiful, and this overproduction drove prices still lower. Railroads and some other industries, much overexpanded, had outstripped the public's demand for their products and services. The fortunes of steel and banking, of course, were tied closely to those of railroads and industry in general.

At the time, none of these explanations enjoyed popular approval; instead voters, politicians, and reform-

Library of Congress.

The floor of the New York Stock Exchange was pandemonium on Friday morning, May 15, 1893, as brokers and stockholders tried to dispose of declining stocks. The panic contributed to a recession that afflicted many unsuspecting Americans. The 1890s were hardly gay for most citizens.

ers argued over the circulation of money. Many felt, rightly or wrongly, that if the supply of silver and greenbacks was increased, easy credit and "cheap" money would expand opportunities for investment and increase consumption. Some modern historians agree, but others emphasize that, in fact, considerable American capital was idle in the harsh 1890s and investment opportunities were scarce.

The dynamics of the economy were as baffling to nineteenth century Americans as they are to their twentieth century counterparts. Then, as now, leaders in finance and government worried about how to combat unemployment, increase productivity, find new markets for manufactured goods, and curb monetary fluctuations—a set of often contradictory goals virtually impossible to achieve all at once. What was clear to everyone as America entered the twentieth century was that, despite considerable progress and tremendous growth and expansion, the nation had not achieved a stable economy. Its capitalistic structure was plagued by ups and downs, fits of great energy interspersed with mass unemployment, business failures, and much hardship.

The Complexities of Urbanization

In 1850 almost four-fifths of the twenty-three million inhabitants of the United States resided in rural areas or in communities of 8,000 or less. By 1900 the Atlantic and Pacific coasts and America's northern and southern boundaries were linked by an intricate rail network, which made possible the shift from river and coastal settlement to new patterns of population distribution. Freed from the dominance of water transport and able at last to take advantage of rich soil and other natural resources abundant in the American terrain, the nation's commerce began to expand its horizons. Between 1870 and 1900 more than 495 million acres of land came under cultivation for the first time—a tract as large as all of Europe and Great Britain, excluding Spain. As late as 1910 the majority of Americans still lived in rural areas, but *how* they lived was dictated more and more by urban, not rural life. It is true that throughout much of the nineteenth century a rural, agricultural civilization shaped American culture, but in these post-Civil War years that dominance was shattered.

The Growth of Cities

In 1860, the United States had nine cities with populations of more than 100,000 people. Most were located in the East, which because it was the oldest was also the most densely populated area of the country, the gateway for immigrants from Europe and the center of industry. Boston, New York, Brooklyn (a separate city until 1898), Philadelphia, and Baltimore ruled the East, as New Orleans did the South, and Cincinnati, St. Louis, and Chicago led the Midwest.

Between 1860 and 1910, urban population increased

Photo by Byron, The Byron Collection, Museum of the City of New York.

Tenements housed thousands of people, who spilled out into the streets during fair weather. This photo is of the Jewish section of New York City, 1898.

seven times. The nation moved from a country of rural dwellers to one of town and city dwellers. Although the city offered workers the greatest number of opportunities, life there was also more constricted and individual rights fewer. In 1860, approximately five million people lived in cities; in 1900, the figure was closer to twenty-five million, and grew to thirty-five million ten years later. Such growth was unprecedented, a migration of staggering numbers, and created overwhelming problems. From the failing farms of many regions in America and from the shores of Europe, streams of newcomers turned scores of villages and towns into ever-larger communities.

Until the end of the century, with each successive generation the nation's population increased both on farms and in cities, but it was apparent that the cities represented the country's destiny. America was becoming urban. By 1900, Pittsburgh with its great steel plants was the symbol of the new industrialism. The commerce of the Great Lakes region had made Buffalo, Cleveland, Toledo, Detroit, and Milwaukee major inland ports and hubs of transportation. The expansion of the West had given rise to San Francisco and Denver as important urban centers. Railroads spurred the growth of Omaha, Salt Lake City, Kansas City, St. Paul, Ft. Worth, Spokane, Los Angeles, Portland, and Seattle. Industry and manufacturing turned Minneapolis and St. Paul into wheat-processing centers, Kansas City into the biggest meatpacker, and Milwaukee into the brewry capital of America. Though some industry remained in rural locations, particularly in the South, by the turn of the century 90 percent of all industrial production took place in urban factories.

Urbanization was not only reshaping the terrain of various regions but also introducing new institutions into the business life of the country. Accelerated commerce everywhere resulted in new activity in financial centers. In Chicago people speculated in agricultural futures, but New York's Stock Exchange was the clearinghouse for the nation's trading. Huge department stores replaced scores of small specialty shops and emporiums; cheaper newspapers, magazines, and widespread basic education fueled an advertising industry; and improvements in transportation revolutionized marketing practices.

The walking city, compact and limited in size to five to eight square miles, gave way to urban sprawl surrounding a distinctive interior structure. There was a downtown and central business district, the inner city, and close by it were the slums. The periphery was often the domain of the rich; the middle class lived between the slums and the neighborhoods of the wealthy.

These changes were part of the natural evolution of any country going through the process of industrialization, and certainly a similar pattern was unfolding in western Europe, particularly in England. But in the United States the rise of the city was more often characterized by enormous confusion, which was due partly to a lack of urban planning and partly to the influx of people who had been raised on farms. These rural people from either America or Europe felt alienated and hopeless in their new city environment.

There was little or no continuity between rural and urban living. Old ways ceased, along with the rural institutions that had supported them. Family life was altered radically. Families rented, rather than owned, their homes. Children were often a liability in the city, not an asset. Social relationships in general became more complex as socioeconomic differences were more sharply defined. In short, a class structure of sorts began to emerge, more stratified than anything America had ever experienced before.

By 1880, 28 percent of the population lived in cities; by 1910 the figure had risen to nearly 46 percent, or almost forty-five million people. During these years, as a result of population pressures and radical improvements in regional transportation, cities began to develop contiguous suburbs. Such satellite communities were not really new, for the railroad already had fostered commuter towns outside of New York, Boston, and other older, established eastern cities. What was new was the boost urban transit lines gave to suburban real estate development and how they altered the pattern of city life.

Urban Transit

In 1873, Andrew S. Hallidie, a Scottish immigrant, invented the cable car. This innovation was the first mechanically powered form of public transportation; an underground cable pulled cars through streets on rails. But the car was slow, not much better than horsedrawn cars that moved along iron or steel rails, and it was expensive to build. Cable cars eventually disappeared, except for the famous lines still in use in San Francisco.

Library of Congress.

The Brooklyn Bridge, one of the great technological achievements of the late nineteenth century. Street cars and els transported thousands of commuters daily between Manhattan and Brooklyn.

For a time, however, New York, Philadelphia, and Chicago had extensive cable roads.

The cable car lasted for twenty years, until the turn of the century when electric trolleys became the major means of urban transportation. Charles Van Depoole, a Belgian sculptor and engineer, was hired by James Gaboury to construct an electric railway for Montgomery, Alabama. In 1886, service began, and during the same year, Frank Sprague built a similar system for Richmond, Virginia. The trolley was a car powered by electricity transmitted through overhead wires. These wires were cheaper to install than underground cables. Though trolleys were often noisy and ugly and had a maximum speed of only 12 miles an hour, by 1890 fifty-one cities had adopted the system. A few also built electric elevated railways, the "els" that soon were part of the cityscape in New York, Philadelphia, Chicago, Boston, and Kansas City. (Manhattan's famous "el," a steam-powered version, first appeared in the 1870s.)

The cost of building transit systems was staggering. Boston, the first city to have both subways and elevateds powered by electricity, completed a major subway tunnel in 1901 at a cost of $4.25 million. That cities were willing to expend such sums on public transportation indicates the urgent need.

Two factors impelled city fathers to build: inward migration turned cheap, inner city housing into slums and pushed out the older, more prosperous residents, who could usually exert considerable influence on the mayor and city council. Second, new factories and businesses transformed residential areas into commercial districts. Well-to-do taxpayers demanded and got the transportation networks that they and their employees had to have to commute from the new suburbs to the factory or shop or business where they were employed.

No matter how fast transportation systems expanded, public lines were always crowded; demand was always ahead of supply. Since lines ran through major streets, they created traffic problems. They also disfigured urban vistas; the elevateds cast streets into shadow and blocked views. The high voltage wires were dangerous, and skilled maintenance help was in short supply. In one month in 1907, New York had 5,500 passenger injuries, forty-two of which were fatal.

These were also the decades that saw the paving of city streets: cobblestone, brick, macadam, and finally asphalt replaced dirt, which turned to mud in spring and winter and to dust in summer. It was also the age when urban bridges began to link closely related communities. The Brooklyn Bridge, completed by John Roebling and his son Washington in 1883, became a sightseeing wonder, the longest suspension bridge in the world. About 3,500 feet long, built at a cost of $15.5 million over a thirteen-year period, it served thousands of daily commuters traveling between Brooklyn and Manhattan.

Technological Breakthroughs

New techniques learned in the construction of railroad and streetcar lines were easily adapted to structures such as the Brooklyn Bridge and to the first so-called skyscrapers. Welding, electric motors, earth-moving equipment, and the use of hot rivets all played a role in the transformation of the urban scene. At the same time, the telephone, the arc lamp, and the incandescent light, as well as the extensive use of gas lights, radically changed how many city dwellers were living. They could now work and play round the clock. Factories instituted night shifts, and cafes stayed open till the early morning.

City life also became more hospitable as improvements in water supply, sewage disposal, and pollution prevention measures were implemented. Once the water supply was purified, typhoid fever was no longer epidemic in New York and Boston. Cincinnati installed the nation's first salaried steam fire department in 1853, although Manhattan still had a volunteer force a decade later. By the end of the century all major cities had full-time paid fire departments.

Great fires in Chicago (1871) and Boston (1872) stirred considerable interest in fire prevention, although the nation's most tragic blaze occurred simultaneously with the Chicago disaster when 1,152 people perished in Peshtigo, a small lumber town in Wisconsin. By 1877, fire sprinklers and fire alarms were in wide use in many cities, and eventually chemical engines were purchased and high pressure mains installed. Catastrophic fires such as the one in Chicago made the use of fire resistant materials an increasing necessity in building construction: concrete, terra-cotta, brick, steel, and asbestos were all employed with greater frequency. Also, enforcement of building codes, standardized fire hose threads, which enabled one fire department to assist another, and creation of electrical codes helped to reduce the hazard of fires somewhat. Needless to add, insurance companies were in the forefront of this effort to cut urban fire losses.

Electrically powered elevators permitted a new kind of architecture to develop that was uniquely suited to cope with urban crowding. The new urbanism was most clearly symbolized by the skyscraper. Chicago architects Le Baron Jenney, John Root, Daniel Burnham, and Lewis Sullivan erected at first spires of cast iron, and then of steel, to alter the skylines of cities forever. Jenney used a metal skeleton for Chicago's Home Insurance Building in 1885. Sullivan's ten-story Wainwright Building erected in St. Louis in 1891 proved to be an architectural masterpiece of the age.

The New Immigrants

Much of the growing population that crowded into America's cities during these years to build its street railways and new office buildings, to fill up its slums, and to fight its fires was of foreign birth. These European immigrants came to the United States in the last decades of the century for the same reason immigrants had always come: to better their lot economically and to escape political and religious oppression. Those who settled in the cities were responding to the same attractions that were luring American farmers into town. Many, perhaps like farmers and their families, thought their new surroundings only temporary. They planned to make money fast, save up a "nest egg," and return to their birthplace; for most, however, this separation—from a farm in Maine, a village in Ohio, or a town in Ireland—proved to be permanent.

From the 1840s to the 1880s, approximately two and a half million immigrants arrived in the United States every decade, but in the last twenty years of the century the figure was closer to nine million a decade, and many of these newcomers chose to remain in the eastern cities they first entered. Not only were the numbers unprecedented but also most of these immigrants were from southern and eastern Europe—from Italy, Austria-Hungary, Poland, and Russia. Earlier immigrants, by contrast, usually had been from Scandinavia, Britain, Germany, and Ireland. The new arrivals also frequently were Catholic or Jewish, not Protestant, and they brought with them cultures that seemed alien to native Americans.

By 1890 one out of every four Philadelphians and one out of every three Bostonians were foreign-born. New York and Brooklyn were the largest centers of immigrants in the world. Four out of every five residents in greater New York City (including Newark, New Jersey) were foreigners or born of foreign parents. The New York area had half as many Italians as Naples, as many Germans as Hamburg, twice the number of Irish as Dublin, and two and a half times the number of Jews found in Warsaw.

Photo by Edwin Levick, Library of Congress.

To thousands of forlorn, destitute, but hopeful immigrants the United States was the "land of opportunity."

Photo by Lewis W. Hine, George Eastman House Collection.

The poor and wealthy were not just in different classes, they inhabited different worlds. Tenements in Washington, D.C. and the Vanderbilt mansion on Fifth Avenue in New York City.

Photo by Byron, The Byron Collection, Museum of the City of New York.

The labor these immigrants supplied enabled the cities and industry to expand with breathtaking speed. Slavs worked the slaughterhouses of Chicago and the steel mills of Pennsylvania. Italian men in New York built the subways while their wives and daughters sewed garments in sweat shops. Other Italians worked in construction projects and constituted the majority of the city's bootblacks and sanitation workers. With their meager earnings many Italians bought small businesses, often pushcarts selling fruits and produce. Eventually, they would come to dominate the fruit business in all its phases, from produce market to retail outlet.

Urban Life

The problems of American cities in the late nineteenth century were common to large cities everywhere. What was special was the shocking juxtaposition of misery, poverty, and deprivation against great prosperity and

Photo by Hiram Myers, New York Public Library, Picture Collection.

Immigrants eager for work found employment in sweat shops. Entire families labored for long hours, at low pay, in unhealthful surroundings.

privilege. Luxurious mansions were only blocks away from some of the world's worst slums. Palaces on parks or waterfronts, elegant apartment buildings and town houses with gardens adjoined tenements and lodging houses. Because wealth was so conspicuous, it served as a temptation and a goal. America fulfilled its promise of opportunity by enabling some of the poor immigrants or their children to rise in the world. Luck and hard work could alter the lot of the poor within a lifetime; what could take a century to accomplish in Europe could be done in a generation in the United States.

But life in the present was often unbearably harsh. Compounding the problem was the indifference of most affluent and powerful people. The efforts of such reformers as Jane Addams, Jacob Riis, and John Spargo were those of a minority, and considering how few they were and how little political power they wielded, their endeavors were heroic—and amazingly successful.

Tenements often were so decrepit and unsafe that they collapsed—and such disasters were seldom reported in newspapers. One report that was printed in Philadelphia in 1881 remarked that the slum landlord had been ordered by the city to pull down his rickety tenement. He neither obeyed the injunction nor closed the building. His name was hard to discover. Slum tenements were in the hands of agents who worked for percentages but who denied all responsibility for upkeep. Slum landlords occasionally did not even know they were property owners; the rich sometimes left their investment in the hands of lawyers and banks.

Overcrowded, filthy, dangerous, and disease-ridden, the urban slum teemed with vice. Every block had its tavern; drunkenness was commonplace, as were prostitution and street violence. Low income meant families lived in depressed conditions where crime flourished. Between 1880 and 1890 the number of prison inmates rose by 50 percent. Homicides escalated dramatically in those same years, largely a product of the saloon and the tensions created by urban living.

Critics feared that slums would become breeding grounds for socialism and political radicalism. According to one such critic the city was "a serious menace to our civilization," because its citizens are susceptible to "socialistic propagandism" and many recent arrivals from overseas apparently could not easily be assimilated into American culture.

Polish sweatshop women, working six days a week from 7:00 A.M. to 6:00 P.M. for $4, could live on $3 and save $1 (men doing similar work could earn as much as $16 a week). Not only did many women manage to save, but they also found the energy to go to night school. The young, single immigrant woman, of course, did have some fun. As one wrote, "The machines are all run by foot power, and at the end of the day one feels so weak that there is a great temptation to lie right down and sleep. But you must go out and get air, and have some pleasure. So instead of lying down I go out, generally with Henry. Sometimes we go to Coney Island, where there are good dancing places, and sometimes we go to Ulmer Park to picnics. I am very fond of dancing, and, in fact, all sorts of pleasure. I go to the theater quite often, and like those plays that make you cry a great deal."

But such energy was not available to everyone. Children apprenticed in sweatshops before their teens looked like old men and women by the time they reached their mid-thirties. Child labor was one of the worst of the abuses of immigrant labor. John Spargo in *The Bitter Cry of Children* (1906) reported that in 1900 there were 1,752,187 children under sixteen working fulltime—a figure that probably is unrealistically low.

The poor—young and old, foreign-and native-born—elicited little sympathy from many intellectual leaders of these years. "God has intended the great to be great and the little to be little," said Henry Ward Beecher. ". . . no man suffers from poverty unless it be his own fault—unless it be his sin." Richard "Acres'of' Diamonds" Conwell expressed a similar view: "The richest people in the world are generally those of the best character. It is wrong to be poor." Poverty might be "wrong" and a "sin" in the eyes of the rich and well-born, but to a few it was an opportunity. They were the men who emerged as the political leaders and managers of the new cities.

Bossism

The urban crisis deepened with the creation of ethnic ghettos and crowded slums. The clash of cultures produced violence: strikes, brutal brawls at election times, and racial antipathies that often erupted into ugly street wars. Living conditions in immigrant neighborhoods were appalling. As the cities rapidly expanded, the demands for water, sewer systems, gas and electric power, fire and police protection, and school and health services became urgent.

The structure of city governments had always been weak, because under U.S. law the municipality is chartered by the state. As a result, state assemblies (until recently dominated by rural interests) have given city executives limited power, a policy usually endorsed by both urban and rural voters. Politicians rarely had succeeded in forging a reliable coalition out of a heterogeneous, urban population. Into this chaos of inefficient city administration came the bosses and their bureaucracies, which created efficiency and order. Their organizations provided jobs that won both loyalty and votes. They controlled urban politics for the next fifty years. Indeed,

Photo by Lewis W. Hine, Library of Congress.

The health, education, and general well-being of thousands of children was sacrificed so that impoverished families could afford food and shelter, and businessmen and industries could maintain high levels of production.

in cities such as Chicago, machine politics guaranteed the votes that often swayed the balance in the state for yet another half century.

The machine-dominated city sometimes created almost instant millionaires, and graft all too often was the order of the day. William Marcy Tweed and his New York pals apparently made off with over $200 million in the late 1860s, and similar "rings" operated in numerous other cities. One political boss, George Washington Plunkitt, went so far as to make the interesting distinction between "Honest Graft and Dishonest Graft," and ingenuously defended his machine against "unfair" accusations:

"Yes, many of our men have grown rich in politics. I have myself. I've made a big fortune out of the game, and I'm gettin' richer every day, but I've not gone in for dishonest graft—blackmailin' gamblers, saloon-keepers, disorderly people, etc. . . . There's an honest graft, and I'm an example of how it works. I might sum up the whole thing by sayin': I seen my opportunities and I took 'em. . . . My party's in power in the city, and it's goin' to undertake a lot of public improvements. Well, I'm tipped off, say, that they're going to lay out a new park at a certain place. I see my opportunity and I take it.

Threc Democratic bosses in Maryland—George N. Lewis, John S. Kelly, and John J. Mahon.

I go to that place and buy up all the land I can in the neighborhood. Then the board of this or that makes its plan public, and there is a rush to get my land, which nobody cared particular for before. Ain't it perfectly honest to charge a good price and make a profit on my investment and foresight? Of course, it is. Well, that's honest graft.”

That it was not illegal but merely immoral seemed an irrelevant issue to Plunkitt, who reflected the business values of his day with perfect accuracy, if with an unusual candor. Police graft was a commonplace of life. In 1895, a committee of the New State Senate reported payoffs in Manhattan amounting to about $7 million a year, some of which went to the police, ranging from patrolmen, who kept 20 percent of the take, to precinct commanders who took between 35 percent and 50 percent, and on up to inspectors who pocketed the rest. Most of this graft money was provided by businesses for franchises and contracts. The granting of monopolistic privileges for providing gas, water, electricity, transportation, construction, sewage systems, and street pavements made both businessmen and politicians rich.

This picture of the graft-ridden boss, seen largely through the eyes of contemporary reformers, is much too dark. Recent research indicates that not all bosses were venal crooks, nor every reformer a saint. The bosses stepped into a vacuum where the traditional levers of government—city, county, state, federal—either would not or could not function. That they used corrupt methods, stuffed ballot boxes, bought votes, paid bribes, and so on, cannot be denied, but such practices are by no means limited only to an urban setting nor to the decades from 1870 to 1900.

The men who ran these machines were generally recent immigrants and maintained close ties to their origins. They had much to offer slum dwellers in return for their votes. The boss provided jobs, either civic ones or positions in private firms franchised to the city. The boss also dispensed charity—coal and rent money, legal aid, picnics, and country outings away from the sweltering summer heat of the slums. He protected the immigrants' customs against the hostility of native-born Americans by paying for parades and festivals during religious holidays and by providing foreign language classes in public schools. The boss was, in a sense, a forerunner of the twentieth century city manager who, as shorn of political power (at least in theory), he did much to create. Both tried to make the city "run." The difference is, a city manager is hired to do the job, while the boss simply moved in and took over.

Library of Congress.

George Cox.

George Cox, the man who ran Cincinnati during the last decades of the nineteenth century and early years of the twentieth, is a prime example of the truly effective "bossism" tinged with pragmatism, shrewdness, and even reform. Born in 1853, the son of British immigrants, Cox worked from the time he was eight. He acquired a saloon and with it he entered the world of backroom politics. From 1878 to 1885 Cox served on the city council, then he joined forces with a Republican reform candidate for major and ran unsuccessfully for the post of county clerk. Cox tried again three years later for the same position and once more went down to defeat. That was his last bid for public office.

During the next few years Cox worked with, and then took over, more and more Republican strongholds of patronage and power. Within a short time he was working hand-in-glove with the president of the gas company, leading newspaper editors, and some of Cincinnati's most influential families such as the Tafts. The reasons were obvious: Cox and these individuals both possessed power, and he could give them something they wanted very much: stability and order.

Merchants and middle class interests desperate to protect their property also turned to him; and, in time, he was supported by an odd coalition of Germans, Jews, blacks, and members of the city's elite. In 1894 this working arrangement provided the Republicans with a plurality of 6,500 votes, the first decisive municipal election in a decade. In addition to providing more stable government, enfranchising Negroes to prevent polling place violence, and cutting down on petty graft, the Cox machine embraced reform. He and his allies accepted voter registration, the secret ballot, and state laws creating more centralized and municipal government. Administrations backed by Cox built up fine police and fire departments, supported growth of the University of Cincinnati, paved streets, constructed sewers and parks, suppressed (but did not close down) centers of sin, brought order in the public utilities field through progressive management, and yet kept the tax base low. In short, Cox and his Republican allies made the city of Cincinnati "work."

Of course, their Democratic opponents and assorted

reform elements were not satisfied and hammered constantly at "machine" methods and graft. In 1911, Cox was indicted for perjury and that same year a Democratic-reform coalition seized power. But by that time George Cox was no longer the "boss"; after he retired from his organization, the press and influential citizens turned against him. For at least two decades, however, he had put together a strange grouping of supporters and given his native city reasonably good government. More than anything else, Cox forged a voluntary political grouping that bridged cultural, racial, and class barriers and embraced moderate reform, a unique accomplishment in the annals of municipal history which indicates "bossism" is not always a force for evil.

American Culture in an Industrial-Urban Age

During these years of bossism, urban growth, immigration, industrialization and vast change, cultural life in towns and cities continued to flourish, often influenced both directly and indirectly by the general process of "nationalization." Railroads, advertising, publishing and other means of communication were tying the nation together as never before. Yet in retrospect the so-called "Gilded Age," with its rampant capitalism, urban poverty, and blatant ostentation, has been the subject of considerable controversy.

Critics and Defenders of Capitalism

The post-Civil War decades clearly marked a departure from tradition and from what had previously been regarded as normal. Everything seemed larger and more significant. Business and industry not only acted as catalysts for change, they also became institutions of unprecedented size and power. Never before had government ever been so entirely under the spell of businessmen.

Some of the great industrialists of this period seemed to prove that the average poor boy could rise to great wealth by dint of hard work and talent. Andrew Carnegie, one of the greatest of the millionaires, declared that poverty was the sternest but most efficient of all "schools." This may be true, but Carnegie was not typical. Men such as Rockefeller, for example, came from comfortable backgrounds, got at least a basic education, and—perhaps most important of all—took advantage of business opportunities presented by the Civil War.

These high-riding capitalists often called "robber barons" because of their ruthless business methods of empire building, were unquestionably men of considerable talent who were acting within generally accepted codes of contemporary behavior. Shrewd, energetic, aggressive, rapacious, domineering, and insatiable, in a time of change and expansion they tended to be objects of admiration and reverence, not scorn. Of course, the competitors they squeezed out and trampled upon viewed them somewhat differently. In their defense, the robber barons pointed to the industrial nation they were creating, a nation soon to dominate the world's markets. If tyrannical and greedy, they argued, at least they were turning America into a first-rate power. If wasteful, there seemed to be an inexhaustible supply of natural resources that made their plundering appear trifling.

Apologists for industrial capitalists invoked the ideas of Charles Darwin (1809–1882), whose *Origins of the Species* (1859) viewed the natural world as a jungle of fierce and incessant struggle where only the strong survived. In time, some individuals merely applied these ideas to the business realm as well.

Although the theories of Darwin were not widely known in America until a few decades later, their adaptation by Herbert Spencer (1820–1903) to social ethics was. Spencer, an Englishman, developed a philosophy of Social Darwinism that glorified progress and preached a message dear to the hearts of every American capitalist. He argued that commerce and trade must be allowed to evolve without interference, especially from reformers. Such a theory of economic life (to the extent that it was known in U.S. business circles) gave a "scientific" veneer to simple greed. In any event, the general sentiment of the period roughly equated wealth with virtue and poverty with vice or laziness. There was little or no appreciation of social factors responsible for a "culture of poverty" and no belief in the obligation of the rich to help the poor (charity was all too often regarded as a very rare act of individual Christian piety).

A few economic-minded reformers began to question these views. One of the most persistent was Henry George (1839–1897) who, as the result of shocking conditions he had seen in California and New York City, published *Progress and Poverty* in 1879. What disturbed this self-trained economist most was the evil of concentrated land ownership, and his solution was to tax land in such a way as to eliminate advantages of location and growth of a community (what George called "unearned increment"). Instead there would be a "single tax" which, he claimed, would make it unprofitable for real estate to lie idle, reduce the size of landholdings and increase the number of landowners, abolish poverty, provide employment, and "carry civilization to yet nobler heights." Revenue would be so great that no other taxes would be needed, and the federal government, rich with funds, could run railroads, telegraph companies, and numerous social services.

The single tax idea appealed especially to farmers who hoped to profit from rising land values, yet George was influential among city dwellers, too. He did surprisingly well in an unsuccessful bid to become mayor of New York City in 1886. His "single tax" concept actually enjoyed more success in England and Australia than in America; nevertheless, it did direct attention to the need for local tax reform measures.

A more direct critic of big business was Henry Demarest Lloyd (1847-1903), who opened his assault on Rockefeller's Standard Oil with a scathing article in the *Atlantic Monthly* (March 1881) entitled "The Story of a Great Monopoly." By 1894 he wrote in *Wealth Against Commonwealth* "that completion has killed competition, that corporations are grown greater than the State and have bred individuals greater than themselves, and that the naked issue of our time is with property becoming master instead of servant." He strongly denounced application of Darwin's "survival of the fittest" to the economic and social order and, in time, noted scornfully that "U.S.A." really meant little more than "United Syndicates of America."

Despite this outcry, to millions those who made millions were heroes. Carl Sandburg, poet and biographer of Lincoln, has told how deeply impressed he was as a youth by the story of Cornelius Vanderbilt, whose biography was serialized and circulated free as a cigarette premium in the 1880s. Writers such as William Dean Howells and Henry James saw the financier and speculator as representing not only "the ideal and ambition of most Americans" (as Howells put it) but also the most interesting American figure in the eyes of the world. In an early novel by James, *The American,* the hero is an attractive self-made man living in Europe.

This heroic image has held up quite well in the public eye except in times of economic disaster. In the 1890s and again in the 1930s the reputations of these swashbuckling industrialists declined markedly. Matthew Josephson's *The Robber Barons* (1934) popularized the idea that the prosperity of the Gilded Age was not the product of hard work and thrift but one of bold rapaciousness and corporate immorality. By the 1940s—and especially when U.S. industrial might helped win World War II—the pragmatism of the nineteenth-century industrialist was looked upon in a more favorable light. Today, most historians are not much interested in delineating Gilded Age heroes and villains; instead, they stress the accomplishments of industrialization; the stimulation of economic growth and the achievement of a higher standard of living than most other industrial nations of that era.

Smalltown America

The variations of the Gilded Age—urbanization, immigration, industrialization—had an uneven impact throughout smalltown America, depending largely upon geographical and economic factors. Rural centers of the South and West often changed little during those years, especially if bypassed by railroad lines; but towns of the industrial Northeast and the upper Mississippi Valley often exhibited, in miniature, many contemporary features of nearby city life.

Of course, a sense of community, the influence of the church, and the impact of the seasons and farming were strong in all small towns everywhere. The absence of paved roads, a product of the twentieth century, more than anything else, regulated the flow of everyday life in rural smalltown America of those years. But, in time, Sears, Roebuck catalogs, rural free delivery, parcel post, and better highways began to dispel some of this seasonal isolation.

A community on a railroad—or better yet at the juncture of two rail lines—often became a marketing-distribution center. If a county seat, it also could count on some courthouse business, and Saturdays and holidays when farmers, cowboys, or tenant farmers crowded into town always meant laughter, cash sales, some drunkenness, and perhaps an upsurge of petty crime. The railroad, of course, both brought and also took away. It brought circuses, traveling salesmen, vaudeville shows, revivalist preachers, new industrial wonders, newspapers,

Courtesy Montgomery Ward and Company, Inc.

Aaron Montgomery Ward (1843–1913)

An innovative dry goods merchant who joined up with the Grange to market his wares to rural Americans and who also saved the Chicago lakefront for all citizens to use and enjoy, Ward was born in New Jersey but soon moved westward with his family to Niles, Michigan. After a basic education, he began working in 1857 at a variety of trades, finally becoming a clerk in a general store. By the end of the Civil War, Ward was employed by a Chicago emporium; when it went broke, he joined a St. Louis company as a "drummer" (traveler). This association took him into rural communities where he developed the idea of buying in quantity and selling directly to farm families, thus eliminating many costs.

In 1872, following a momentary delay caused by the great fire, Ward set up his own dry goods business in Chicago. He invested $1,600 of his savings, his partner, George Thorne, $800. They began small and their first "catalog" was a single sheet of paper. From the outset Ward dealt only in cash transactions, promised complete satisfaction, and permitted customers to exchange or return goods they did not like. For a few years he was marketing agent for the Grange, a venture that earned him both money and goodwill in hundreds of farm homes. By 1888 Montgomery Ward had annual sales of $1 million; by the time of his death in 1913 the company was grossing $40 million, had 6000 employees, and was serving customers throughout the world.

A public-spirited man, Ward battled successfully to save Chicago's Lake Michigan shoreline for the use of all citizens, not just the rich. He retired in 1901; and, since he had no sons, management of the company passed to Thorne's five boys. Thorne and Ward had married sisters from Kalamazoo in the 1870s, and Ward's widow honored his memory with huge bequests to Northwestern University to establish medical and dental schools.

Ward's famous rival and contemporary, Richard Warren Sears (1863–1914), founder of Sears, Roebuck, and Company, because of rail connections also centered his operations in Chicago after 1893. Sears who began by selling watches in Minnesota, was a quite different man, a promoter, not a true merchandiser. After being in and out of the retail trade in the 1880s and 1890s, he sold his company to Julius Rosenwald in 1895, but continued as president until 1909. Almost single-handedly Sears created the Sears, Roebuck catalog, writing nearly all of the advertisements himself. (Roebuck, by the way, was associated with Sears only briefly as a watch repairman.) Ward and Sears—as salesmen, ad writers, and business executives—left an indelible mark on U.S. life, altering the way both rural and urban America shopped. ■

and magazines, but most of all it brought excitement and the "outside" world. It took away farm produce and scores of young people who, either unable to find employment in small towns and in rural areas or unwilling to do so, left for the "bright lights."

During most of the nineteenth century, small towns were an important part of the American landscape. A community of only a few thousand people could exert considerable influence, but the trends of the times were in favor of cities. Too many of the inventions of the day such as gas or electric lights, indoor plumbing, streetcars, and telephones (for the most part) could be enjoyed only in an urban setting. The growing metropolis not only seemed to present the possibility of better living and working conditions, it also had better schools and an overall atmosphere which, by contrast, often made small towns seem drab and uninteresting. However, as millions learned during this era, the potential of urban-industrial America frequently was exaggerated. Slum life and long factory hours were even more depressing than conditions back in Elm City or Centerville.

Education

Nevertheless, better education systems in both towns and cities gave the immigrant and the poor a chance for social mobility. "Book learning" was no longer for only the middle class and the well-to-do. As society became increasingly urban and industrial, educators responded by broadening the scope of basic classwork and by undertaking to make the nation literate. This was, of course, a vital first step in creating both an intelligent labor force and a consuming public.

The impetus for this policy came from the federal government, which had created a bureau of education as early as 1867. In 1870, compulsory attendance laws were enforced in the North and the West; a typical statute required children between eight and fourteen to attend school for twelve to sixteen weeks a year. Between 1878 and 1898, the number of children attending school grew from nine and a half million to fifteen million, and the number of public schools rose from 200 to 3,000. Teachers were paid higher salaries in cities than in rural areas, city school terms were longer, the buildings were better, and the organization of the city system was more responsive to the needs of the community. In the cities, the idea of kindergarten and of high school quickly caught on.

A literate populace reduced governmental inefficiency. Civil service examinations were set up to detect and reward ability. School curricula now included manual training at the elementary level, as well as such innovations as nature study, drawing, and home economics. Corporal punishment was eliminated in the cities in the 1880s. Illiteracy fell from a national average of 17 percent in 1880 to 11 percent by 1900.

The rapid expansion of school systems was of course chaotic, and political interference by bosses and party machines condoned corruption and incompetence. Reformer Joseph Mayer Rice (1857–1934) investigated and exposed such problems as the hiring of untrained political hacks as teachers. William Torrey Harris (1835–1909), U.S. Commissioner of Education, brought some order to the system. As a former administrator in the St. Louis schools, he had firsthand knowledge of crowded and understaffed classrooms. He abandoned the system of having students of all ages study together and set up instead the graded school. He made school personnel keep attendance records and careful school statistics. Standardization of education was increased by the adoption of textbooks.

The Arts

This educational revolution, as much as anything else, paved the way for new interest in the arts, especially literature. This output was marked by regionalism, vitality, and realism. Joel Chandler Harris (1848–1906) and George Washington Cable (1844–1925) wrote about the South; Hamlin Garland (1860–1940), about the Great Plains; Bret Harte (1836–1902), about California; and Sarah Orne Jewett depicted life in rural New England.

The best-known writer of this era was Samuel Langhorne Clemens (1835–1910), known as Mark Twain, who re-created life on the Mississippi River during his boyhood days in the adventures of Tom Sawyer and Huck Finn and became one of our nation's outstanding humorists. Twain was, however, a bundle of contradictions. He wrote glowingly of the West and Midwest but lived in the East, satirized the nouveau riche while scheming how to join them, and lived long enough to see some of his humor and democratic spirit deteriorate into bitterness and pessimism.

Born in New York, Henry James (1843–1916) was a quite different figure. A prolific novelist, he spent most of his life in England and wrote about the misunderstandings generated by the differences between the cultural values of Europeans and Americans. Keen inquiry into the minds of his characters initiated the psychological, stream-of-consciousness approach, which has had profound influence upon many other writers. Clearly critical of America, James eventually rejected his birthplace. His choice of Europe over America and the complexities of his style made him unpopular in his own day on this side of the Atlantic.

William Dean Howells (1837–1920), as editor and writer, had much immediate impact. He was able to spot ability and opened the world of naturalism, then flourishing in Europe, to many young writers. In *The Rise of Silas Lapham* (1885) and *A Hazard of New Fortunes* (1890) he himself confronted problems created by city life, new wealth, and the demand of women for a larger role in society. Frank Norris (1870–1902), Stephen Crane (1871–1900), and Jack London (1876–1916) converted realism into naturalism as they—along with Theodore Dreiser (1871–1945), who lived much longer—probed and portrayed the harsher aspects of American civilization. This quartet ranged over the entire spectrum of war, death, violence, sin, and class conflict, subjects that many Americans of those decades thought were wholly unworthy of "literature."

Music, poetry, painting, sculpture, and architecture generally failed to demonstrate similar vitality during the Gilded Age, as much of the work in these fields imitated European models. Also, native-born sons and daughters trained in those arts in Europe often chose to remain there. Only in the construction of clean, straight office buildings and huge bridges did Americans show the world anything new and different.

Leisure

During these decades nearly all classes had more free time than earlier in the century. Wage earners worked shorter hours, the new rich hired servants to perform chores they once did for themselves, and the householders of moderate means began to acquire a few laborsaving devices such as the sewing machine. Even the unemployed, one might add, enjoyed more leisure time than in previous decades, a fact that undoubtedly boosted urban crime statistics.

For the very wealthy this was an age of social climbing, which sometimes took bizarre forms. In 1897, with unemployment high and thousands roaming the streets, a millionaire named Bradley Martin gave a costume ball at New York's Waldorf-Astoria that cost more than $350,000. Two years later, social economist Thorstein Veblen coined the phrase "conspicuous consumption" in his *Theory of the Leisure Class,* meaning, of course, the craving to be seen spending money lavishly. Some of Martin's contemporaries also spent thousands building up a presentable family tree or grafted to it, through marriage, a duke or an earl. By the turn of the century ambitious U.S. parents had aided impoverished European nobility to the tune of an estimated $200 million.

At a somewhat lower level, fraternal lodges, a byproduct of urban conditions and often rooted in business, religious, or ethnic connections became extremely popular. Between 1865 and 1901, 568 different such groups appeared; by 1890, Boston, Chicago, and St. Louis had three times as many lodges as churches.

Like so much of America during these years of urban-industrial growth, the hallmark of leisure was *organization.* Fishing, hunting, walking, gossiping, visiting—recreation of older decades—still continued, but entertainment was more and more organized. The railroad facilitated the expansion of circuses, minstrel shows, and vaudeville troupes and made it possible for baseball and football teams to travel great distances. Princeton and Rutgers met in the first intercollegiate gridiron contest in 1869 (with 25 men on each side), and by 1884 well-developed baseball leagues could stage the first "World Series," a typical bit of Yankee bravado since this was hardly an international spectacle. With the invention of basketball seven years later, the nation got its first truly homegrown sport. Introduction of the bicycle in the 1880s created a craze that reached epidemic proportions in the 1890s when over a million were sold in some years.

For the less active there were more libraries, magazines, and newspapers than ever before—and more Americans who knew how to utilize them. Public lecture series were common in both town and city. During these years the daily newspaper, thanks to urbanization, increased literacy and imaginative innovations made enormous strides. In 1880 there were 971 dailies in the United States; by 1900, 2,225. Joseph Pulitzer, a clever businessman, in 1893 published the first colored comic strips in his New York *World.* Other metropolitan dailies soon followed his lead, and by the end of the century sports coverage and columns of special interest to women were also standard fare throughout the nation.

Sarah Orne Jewett
(1849–1909)

A gifted, meticulous writer, Sarah Orne Jewett was born in South Berwick, Maine, and lived there all of her life. Her father, whom she adored, was the community's leading physician. As a child she began to write poems; then at the age of nineteen, she submitted to the *Atlantic Monthly* a story that attracted the attention of the editor, William Dean Howells. As other short pieces followed, he suggested she develop them into a book. The result was *Deephaven* (1877), her first major work, telling of everyday life in a Maine coastal village.

During the next quarter century, Sarah Jewett traveled widely and got to know literary figures in both Boston and England. A very cautious worker who read much, she never married. In 1901 Bowdoin College, her father's alma mater, granted the author the first honorary degree that institution ever bestowed upon a woman.

Her best-known work, now considered a minor classic, is *Country of Pointed Firs* (1896). With great clarity and precision, it gives permanence to a disappearing rural way of life. ■

Culver Pictures.

Court of Honor, World's Columbian Exposition in Chicago in 1893.

The Chicago World's Fair

Officially known as the World's Columbian Exposition, this extravaganza opened in May 1893 to commemorate both the discovery of the New World and American progress during the Gilded Age. It ran for six months, cost $31 million, attracted 27 million visitors (and may or may not have produced a profit—the records are unclear on this point). The Fair consisted of 150 buildings located on a 666-acre plot converted from swampland into a dazzling panorama of white plaster, canals, and electric lights along Lake Michigan. An Australian visitor, in writing home, described it as "a city of palaces sprung up in a short time as if the wand of a Magician was waved over the shores of that inland sea and produced from its sandy depths the turrets and towers, domes and spires of an enchanted land." He admitted it was "very instructive" to see so many exhibits but also "tiresome."

Tiresome or not, "the Fair" became a national attraction. Millions saw displays from nearly all of the states and forty-six nations, marveled at an electric dynamo, Westinghouse's alternating-current generator, and rode in the world's first Ferris Wheel. They also listened to 5,978 speeches (many national and international bodies held conventions there) and watched the bawdy contortions of "Little Egypt" as well.

Perhaps better than its promoters realized, this ostentatious "White City" summarized much that was good and bad in America during the last decades of the nineteenth century. Nearly all of the buildings were temporary structures made of plaster and jute to look like marble. The elaborate displays within were the epitome of garish, overdecorated Victorian lavishness—"conspicuous consumption" at its worst. This opulence was cheek by jowl with sordid poverty, and the Fair opened (unfortunately) just at the onset of a very serious business depression and at a time when both lynching and political unrest reached new heights.

This exposition was an industrial marvel in an urban setting and thereby spoke plainly of what was happening in America. But even its amusement center, the famed Midway Plaisance, was highly *organized*, the first such display ever seen at an international fair of this sort. Its most lasting effect was upon architecture, which bestowed the classic style upon scores of government buildings and university campuses throughout America during the next half century. At the same time, garishness and poverty, racial and ethnic tensions and rural and labor unrest sounded a clear message to those who were listening.

Essay

George Eastman, Kodak, and the Origins of the Photographic Industry

It is very difficult to imagine a world without photographs and cameras. At least two major twentieth century industries—movies and television—depend upon the photographic process for their very existence, and several other enterprises such as journalism and book publishing would be drab indeed were it not for the photographer's magic art.

Photography has its roots in the work of a handful of French inventors of the 1830s, the best known of whom, L. J. M. Daguerre, gave his name to the daguerreotype. This process captured a single reverse image on a sensitized metallic surface that was later "developed" with liquid mercury. Although the daguerreotype had several drawbacks—no copies could be made from a plate and viewed from certain angles one saw little or nothing of the intended picture—it soon became very popular on this side of the Atlantic, and by 1853 about a thousand American photographers were turning out some three million prints.

Among the best known of these individuals, all of them professional photographers, was Mathew Brady. In the 1840s this youth from upstate New York set up his own gallery near P. T. Barnum's American Museum in Manhattan and quickly became the darling of that city's carriage trade. There one could get a reasonable likeness for $3 to $5. Brady actually did little of the work now credited to him since he often was more of a manager of sorts and dealt only with "important" customers. Yet, with the aid of a steady stream of overworked assistants he assured himself of a special niche in history by capturing the features of the men who lived at 1600 Pennsylvania Avenue (in all he "shot" seventeen presidents during his lifetime) and by sinking his life savings and considerable effort into recording for posterity the high drama of the Civil War. In fact, within a decade of Appomattox, because of bumbling recordkeeping and inept business practices Brady was bankrupt, although he continued in the photographic trade until his death in the 1890s.

During the middle decades of the nineteenth century, glass and then paper replaced Daguerre's metallic surface. Both had distinct advantages: one could get a true image (not transposed from right to left), copies could be made from the original negative, the result could be viewed from all angles, and, most important of all, the process was much cheaper. These innovations ushered in the tintype photo on black-japanned iron, the bulky family portrait album, and the stereoscopic slide, which gave a sense of perspective and depth when viewed in a special holder. Soon no self-respecting parlor was complete without these viewers and a fat album, both usually displayed very prominently in a place of honor close by the family Bible.

Despite these improvements, as long as pictures had to be developed with a hodgepodge of mysterious wet chemicals, each photographer concocted his own materials. Thus this art form interested few amateurs and remained the realm of professionals such as Brady with their galleries and assistants. However, in the 1870s several English inventors began to experiment with dry plates, paving the way for rapid change. Also, in that same decade another upstate New York youth, George Eastman (1854–1932) became intrigued with photography, and his hobby, soon a profitable business, would transform our world.

Eastman, an organizing genius with vision and one of the great tycoon-philanthropists of the early twentieth century, is reminiscent of Rockefeller, Carnegie, and other such figures. He was a poor boy who worked hard as a bank clerk, saved his money, and shrewdly put together a new industry so as to reap maximum personal gain. Yet, in at least three ways, Eastman differed from his multimillionaire contemporaries: from the outset he thought on an international, not a national scale, perhaps because he had to gobble up patents as fast as they appeared in various countries; he organized his chosen field so skillfully that by the time he was fifty or so it no longer had need of his guidance; and, bored with life and fearing prolonged ill health, in his seventy-eighth year he calmly put a pistol to his heart and pulled the trigger.

At fifteen, young Eastman, a resident of Rochester, New York, a city that would reap great rewards from his many benefactions, first became interested in photography. Within a decade he gave up his bank job, took on a partner, and began the business of empire building.

For the next quarter century Eastman pursued several complementary goals. He wanted to perfect a camera that the man in the street could use, gain firm control of the emerging photographic industry throughout the entire world, and develop a laboratory staffed with skilled engineers and researchers which would make his economic position impregnable. For the most part, despite frequent court battles and numerous patent disputes, he succeeded.

In 1884 Eastman began the search for transparent, flexible film. Four years later, his first Kodak appeared. He coined this name to attract attention, also secure in the belief that it could not easily be imitated. The first Kodaks cost $25 and were by no

Courtesy Eastman Kodak Company.

A probable production picture in which Eastman shows the advantages of vacationing with a camera.

Courtesy Eastman Kodak Company.

Courtesy Eastman Kodak Company.

The first Kodak camera mass produced for American consumption was marketed in 1888 for $25.00.

means an instant success. Many early models were faulty and had to be returned for service. But in the 1890s he began supplying Edison with film for pioneer movies, produced a daylight-loading camera, and began marketing a pocket Kodak which cost only $5. By 1896 more than 100,000 Kodaks had been sold.

By the turn of the century, Eastman was a true industrialist with some 3,000 employees at his plants in Rochester and Harrow, England. He also was a dictatorial "loner" who had little time for his board of directors or any employee who disagreed with him. For many years he adamantly refused to bargain collectively with his workers and fought to corner all of the patents related to the photographics industry, but shortly after 1910 he suddenly reversed field. General labor practices of other corporations and the threat of antitrust action by the federal government undoubtedly encouraged this change in attitude. In 1912, for example, Eastman controlled from 75 percent to 80 percent of the photographic business in the United States and was reaping an average profit of 171 percent upon goods he was marketing.

Although court battles with various rivals dominated the World War I decade (suits that Eastman usually won), it was during these years that he became a quiet, behind-the-scenes philanthropist. By the time of his death in 1932, Eastman had given upwards of $100 million to the Massachusetts Institute of Technology, Hampton Institute, Tuskegee, and especially to the University of Rochester, where he established medical and dental schools. Also well-known is the Eastman School of Music, which he founded in Rochester in 1919.

A very reticent, even shy bachelor, who, strangely, rarely was photographed, George Eastman spent his last years immersed in calendar reform, cultivation of exotic plants, and a growing detachment from the personal empire he had created. Each Sunday he staged public organ recitals at his great house on Rochester's East Avenue and continued to endow dental clinics throughout the world.

In 1925 he retired as president of his vast enterprise and was elevated to the position of chairman of the board. His various companies now had manufacturing plants in the United States, England, France, Germany, Austria, and Hungary, and subsidiary operations in numerous other countries as well. In all, the "Kodak King" employed some 19,000 workers who were producing goods each year worth $200 million.

But for all his vision and unique skill in developing a truly superior research laboratory that could spew out one wonder after another and overwhelm most would-be rivals, Eastman made one crucial mistake: he had created an ongoing organization that he could no longer understand and that also no longer needed him. Shortly after noon on March 15, 1932, he told a doctor and a nurse that he had a note to write, and they left him alone at his desk. A few moments later they heard a shot and rushed in to discover that Eastman had committed suicide. Methodical and scrupulously neat to the very end, he had carefully written the note he had in mind, put the cap back on the fountain pen, removed and folded his glasses, and then calmly pulled the trigger. His last words were these: "To my friends, my work is done. Why wait?"

Few men have dominated an industry as Eastman did photography. Not a true inventor like Edison, he nevertheless made himself both rich and famous by doing for that field what Rockefeller and Carnegie did for oil and steel. The tragedy of his story is not that George Eastman killed himself, but that he apparently lost touch with the world he had created. The truly outstanding research facilities that he developed and fostered evidently were exploring realms he could not understand or even begin to comprehend. In a sense, the brief note he wrote to his friends was all too true.

Courtesy Eastman Kodak Company.

George Eastman and Thomas Edison.

Selected Readings

General Studies

Thomas C. Cochran and William Miller, *The Age of Enterprise. A Social History of Industrial America* (1942)

E. C. Kirkland, *Industry Comes of Age. Business, Labor, and Public Policy, 1860–1897* (1961)

Arthur Meier Schlesinger, Sr., *The Rise of the City, 1878–1898* (1933)

Urban Development

Blake McKelvey, *The Urbanization of America, 1860–1915* (1963)

Zane L. Miller, *The Urbanization of Modern America. A Brief History* (1973)

James F. Richardson, *The New York Police* (1970)

Sam Bass Warner, Jr., *The Private City. Philadelphia in Three Periods of Its Growth* (1968)

Sam Bass Warner, Jr., *Streetcar Suburbs: The Process of Growth in Boston, 1870–1900* (1962)

Industrial Development

John Chamberlain, *The Enterprising Americans. A Business History of the United States* (1963)

Joseph Dorfman, *The Economic Mind in American Civilization, 1865–1918* (1946)

Richard Hofstadter, *Social Darwinism in American Thought* (1945)

Matthew Josephson, *The Robber Barons* (1934)

Robert Green McClosky, *American Conservatism in the Age of Enterprise: A Study of William Graham Sumner, Stephen J. Field, and Andrew Carnegie* (1951)

Industries

G. R. Taylor and I. D. Neu, *The American Railroad Network, 1861–1900* (1956)

Thomas C. Cochran, *Railroad Leaders, 1845–1900* (1953)

Allan Nevins, *Study in Power: John D. Rockefeller* (2 vols., 1953)

Ida Tarbell, *The History of the Standard Oil Company* (1904)

Joseph Frazier Wall, *Andrew Carnegie* (1970)

Immigrants

Will Herberg, *Protestant, Catholic, Jew* (1960)

John Higham, *Strangers in the Land* (1955)

Oscar Handlin, *The Uprooted* (1951)

Bosses

Alexander B. Callow, Jr., *The Tweed Ring* (1965)

Lyle W. Dorsett, *The Pendergast Machine* (1968)

Melvin G. Holli, *Reform in Detroit* (1969)

Zane Miller, *Boss Cox's Cincinnati. Urban Politics in the Progressive Era* (1968)

Popular Culture

Larzer Ziff, *The American 1890s. Life and Times of a Lost Generation* (1966)

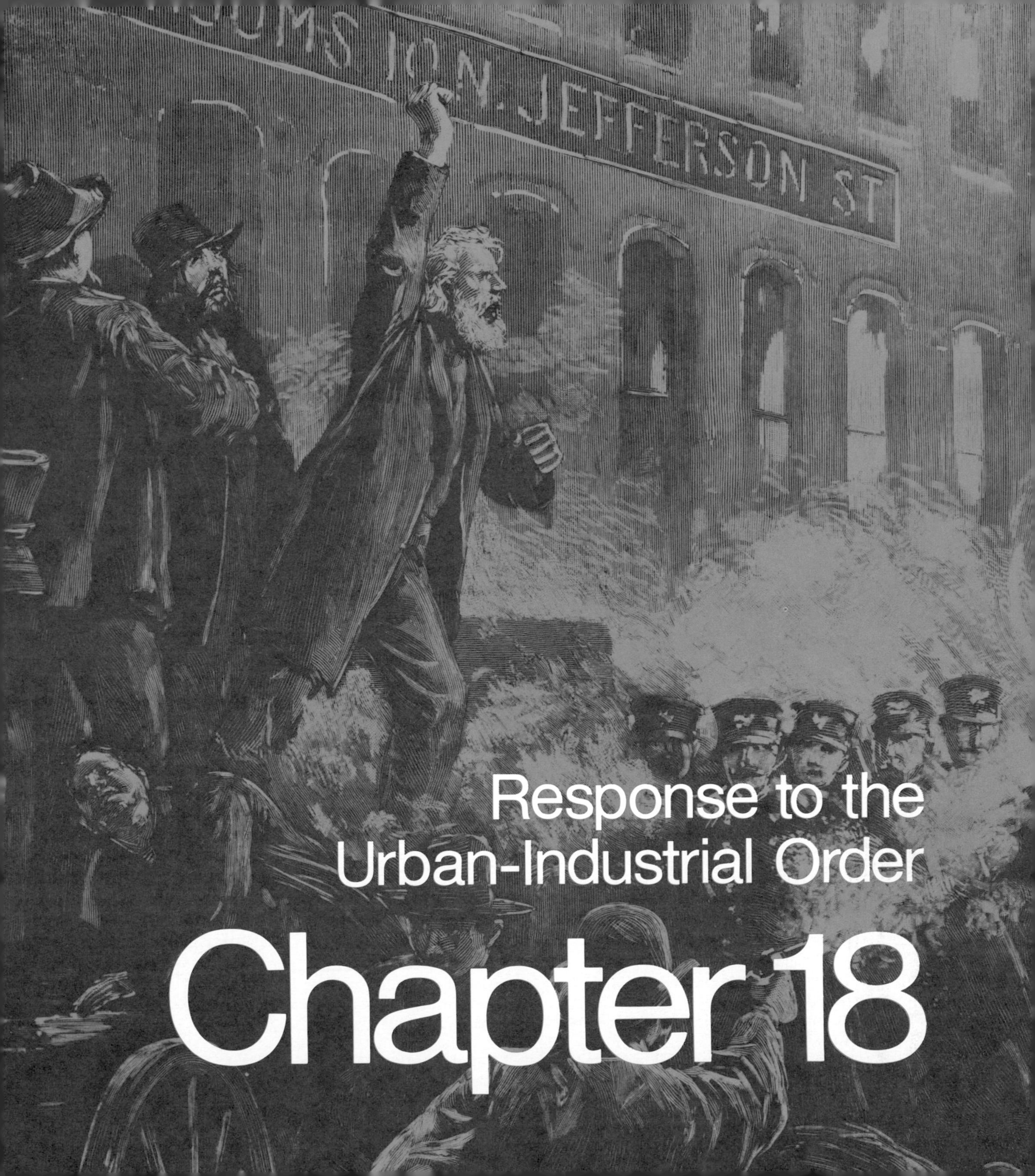

Response to the Urban-Industrial Order

Chapter 18

TIMELINE

1866
National Labor Union (NLU) is organized
1874
Women's Christian Temperance Union (WCTU) is organized
1876
The Johns Hopkins University begins modern university education in the United States
1881
Terrence V. Powderly becomes leader of the Knights of Labor
1883
Pendleton Act creates Civil Service Commission
1886
Samuel Gompers becomes the first president of the reorganized American Federation of Labor
1886
In *Wabash v. Illinois* the Supreme Court reverses *Munn v. Illinois*
1886
Haymarket Square riot
1887
Interstate Commerce Act attempts railroad regulation
1887
Denver establishes first Community Chest campaign
1888
Louisville, Kentucky adopts Australian ballot
1889
Jane Addams establishes Hull House in Chicago
1890
Sherman Antitrust Act outlaws trusts in restraint of trade
1890
National American Women's Suffrage Association (NAWSA) organized
1890
Wyoming enters the union with woman's suffrage
1892
Homestead strike
1894
Urban reformers organize the National Municipal League
1894
Chicago railway strike
1894
Immigration Restriction League is organized
1894
Coxey's Army marches to Washington, D.C.
1895
U.S. v. E. C. Knight Company
1905
W. E. B. DuBois forms the Niagara Movement

CHAPTER OUTLINE

The closing decades of the nineteenth century were times of overwhelming change and great contrast. Values, goals, and institutions designed to serve a settled, agricultural way of life were unable to meet the challenge of urban growth, uneven economic development, waves of immigrant workers, and unprecedented wealth side by side with equally astonishing poverty and deprivation. Two general and closely related themes were evident throughout these years: continual search for a satisfactory political, social, and economic order; and widespread demands for reform.

No businessman, farmer, or worker could possibly cope by himself in mastering the intricacies that were developing in the price-market maze. The result was a collective effort in nearly all phases of American life, an attempt to make some sense out of what was happening. The first to organize was the business community, which caused farmers and workers to emulate their example. Only urban consumers failed to follow suit.

Although the resulting outcry against railroads and corporations got most of the headlines and has long fascinated historians, something much more fundamental was at work in America during the late nineteenth and early twentieth centuries. This reaction was, in fact, a response to conditions created by industrialism, not simply to industries themselves. It took many forms. Those most concerned with the marketplace (businessmen, factory workers, and farmers) fought for a larger share of the new wealth. Those interested in the quality of urban life (migrants from rural areas and from overseas) tried to find meaning in a rapidly changing, impersonal setting. These pressures also pitted rural areas against cities, the South and West against the more highly developed Northeast, and frequently one emerging class against another. The answer of every group was reform, which often looked to the past for inspiration and which was designed to enhance the role of the segment of the population that was urging it upon the new, industrial America.

For the most part, in an age when making money was more important than religion, education, and politics, the original reform impulse came from the once-comfortable upper middle class, now disturbed by changes on every hand which they could not seem to control. In 1890 Henry Adams, a member of the prestigious New England clan that had given the nation two presidents, published his *History of the United States During the Administrations of Jefferson and Madison.* Dissenting from Jefferson's point of view, Adams believed that "no new life could grow" without "the introduction of manufactures and the gathering of masses in the cities." While Adams realized urban-industrial growth meant problems, he also believed that it provided

America with the opportunity to establish a new order of civilization. Only twelve years later, however, in an autobiography that displayed all the disturbed feelings of a displaced patrician, Adams despaired of America's ever achieving his concept of civilization.

Reforming Political Institutions

Not every Bostonian was as pessimistic and there, as in many other cities, reform spirit emerged. Not surprisingly, leaders first focused their attention upon the political process at the local, state, and national levels in the hope of bringing about change by using levers they understood. One problem these reformers faced was the Tweedledum-Tweedledee nature of political parties of that era. Without scorecards and identifying emblems, it was most difficult to tell a Republican from a Democrat, and vice versa.

The result was a rather unstable political life, especially at the national level. No incumbent president won reelection between 1876 and 1896; only one winner (McKinley, 1896) garnered more than 50 percent of the total popular vote; the ranks of "independents" in both the Senate and the House were strong; and rare was the chief executive who could count upon the solid backing of the legislative arm of government. Harrison had a slender Republican majority in both houses (1889–1891), and Cleveland and the Democrats enjoyed firm support of the Congress over the next two years. At all other times during those decades the two major parties shared control of Capitol Hill and the White House. It should be noted, however, that the Republicans usually held the latter, Cleveland being the only Democratic President of those years.

The Republicans were a loose alliance of northeastern business interests and midwestern farmers, aided at times by blacks and Union veterans. Whenever dissension threatened, Republican orators "waved the bloody shirt," equating party loyalty with patriotism and assailing all Democrats as secessionists or Confederate sympathizers. Their opponents were a more regional coalition of the so-called "solid South" (a situation really only true after 1900) and urban political machines of the Northeast. This is, admittedly, a very general picture. One could find bankers, businessmen, factory workers, and farmers in both major parties, and just as the "bloody shirt" usually kept restless Republicans in line, fear of "black rule" helped conservative Democrats thwart most protest movements in the South.

Mugwumps

Yet there were times when appeals to party loyalty did not work, and the presidential election of 1884 was just such an occasion. Both major parties had a reform-minded wing that occasionally went its headstrong way. In 1872, for example, political leaders distressed by the nomination of "Uncle Horace" Greeley and U.S. Grant fielded at least five rival candidates, but to no avail. A dozen years later unhappy Republicans who deserted their party's nominee, James G. Blaine, apparently had much to do with deciding a very close election in favor of Grover Cleveland. Stalwart Republicans called this group the Mugwumps ("chief" in Algonkian), a derisive term that the malcontents adopted. As a group, the Mugwumps were a short-lived phenomenon, but their cries for good, clean, honest government were heard often during these decades.

Good Government

Although the Mugwumps of 1884 concentrated their fire on what they considered to be corruption by Republicans at the national level, other reformers who preceded and followed them had divergent goals. Some sought lower taxes; others wanted to oust corrupt public officials; still others devoted their time to civic and moral improvements. Out of these sporadic efforts a spirit of reform eventually arose that could respond to the challenges of the American urban industrial order. But changes were slow in coming.

The movement for "good" municipal government in the late nineteenth century is a tale of frustration and few accomplishments. Cities, in effect, are corporations created by state legislatures. Rural spokesmen dominated the latter, and nearly all voters were reluctant to give urban authorities much power; hence reformers made little progress until urban problems made action imperative. Appeals for home rule, shorter ballots, better law enforcement, city planning, stronger municipal control, and, of course, an end to corruption generally fell upon deaf ears.

Philadelphia, for example, experienced a flurry of reform drives in the 1870s, but well-entrenched Republican machines at the local and state levels continued for decades to run things pretty much as they pleased. Writing at the turn of the century, Lincoln Steffens noted that Philadelphia was "corrupt and contented." And apparently it intended to remain so.

A problem that reformers faced throughout America was the failure of their middle class values and goals to stir much interest among urban voters. A machine boss frequently made local institutions work tolerably well for the poor and illiterate, usually better than the reformers did whenever they seized power. Also, efficient, effective government can be boring. Getting "the rascals out" is exciting, but the impersonal, honest bureaucracy that ensues may persuade voters to bring them back.

Nevertheless, the stirrings of municipal reform in city after city (1870–1890) convinced reform leaders of the need to coordinate their programs. In January 1894, representatives from Chicago, Milwaukee, New York, Brooklyn, Boston, Baltimore, Minneapolis, Albany, Buffalo, Columbus, and Philadelphia met in the last-named city to found the National Municipal League. The League experienced steady growth, particularly in New York and New Jersey, where corruption was worst and the problems the most complex.

But their foes, the political machines, often received support from wealthy and respected businessmen and church leaders, who obtained privileges from the machines. Reformers, therefore, had to fight people from their own, if not higher, classes in order to achieve their goals.

If political reform was to succeed, the people at large had to support it. They had to vote against extravagant government spending, graft, and unearned appointments to important public posts. They also had to draw attention to evils created by or overlooked by political machines.

But getting people to the polls often was difficult. Many new urban residents, people of both European and American birth, had little knowledge of or interest in community affairs, and even less in state issues. Besides, it was easy for an urban voter to conclude in an age of rampant fraud that his vote was unimportant. Also, city elections were all too often held in conjunction with state and national campaigns, thus obscuring municipal matters.

Election Reform

In order to oust entrenched machines that were adept at providing the poor with jobs and food, at keeping hundreds of citizens long since dead on the voting rolls, and at stuffing ballot boxes on election day, reformers had to change the rules by which the game of politics was being played. Their first goal was to transfer the preparation and distribution of ballots for each election from individual parties to responsible government agencies that guaranteed them to be genuine. This innovation, the so-called Australian ballot, was instituted in a municipal election in Louisville, Kentucky in 1888 and soon spread

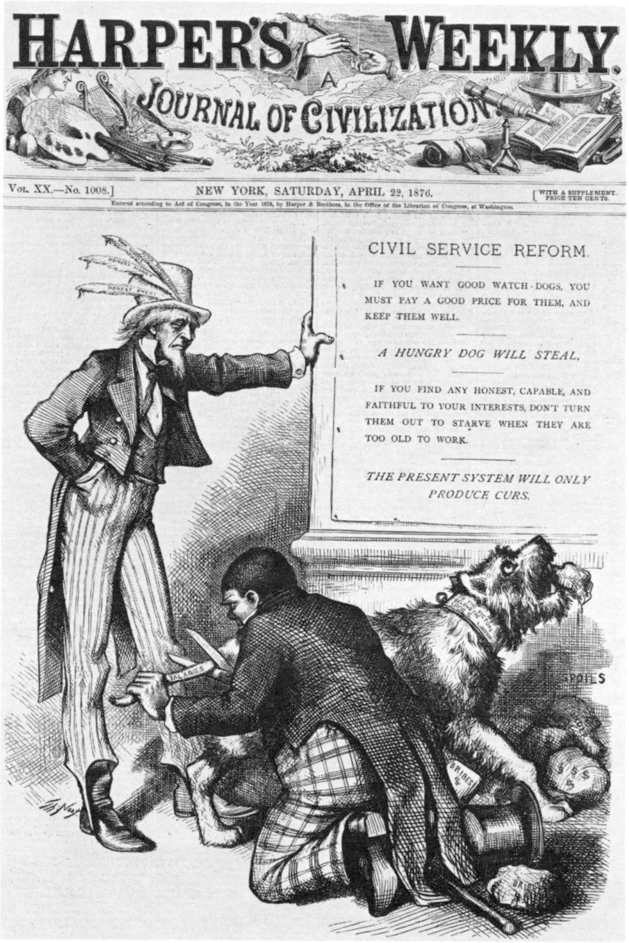

Library of Congress.

Harper's Weekly reflected the concern of reformers about corruption in government. Raising salaries to attractive levels was the primary reform method for obtaining honest and qualified government administrators until the Pendleton Civil Service Act of 1893.

to other cities and states. Although the Australian ballot hardly ended fraud, it made ballot-box stuffing and similar practices somewhat more difficult since numerous authorities (perhaps members of rival parties) knew how many ballots had been printed and circulated to various polling places.

Although they were of little importance until after the turn of the century, other election reforms included the initiative, recall, and referendum. The initiative, introduced in Georgia in 1777 and then largely forgotten, is a means by which voters can take direct action. If a hostile or indifferent city council or state legislature does not pass a certain measure, the electorate, by circulating petitions and collecting sufficient signatures, has the power to force the enactment of legislation. Recall, also instigated at the grassroots level by petition, gives voters the opportunity to oust a duly elected official from office before the end of his term. Los Angeles (1903) was the first community to institute the recall as a means of reforming city government.

Much more widely utilized than the initiative and recall is the referendum, perhaps because it gives lawmakers an opportunity to share responsibility for their actions with the public at large. This device, first used when Massachusetts adopted a new state constitution in 1780, is, in essence, a proposal to the voters. It gives them the chance to accept or reject legislative action that has already been taken. Occasionally a referendum is inaugurated by petitions circulated in opposition to a measure; more frequently it is simply a popular vote (engineered by legislators or city officials themselves) upon a law, ordinance, or proposed expenditure. Legislation dealing with public utilities, prohibition, finances, and the direct primary, as well as changes in local boundaries or governmental structure, have often been presented to the electorate in this manner.

Civil Service Reform

Liberal elements in both major parties were interested in doing something about the great number of inept and often unqualified workers at all levels of government. Throughout the 1870s several national figures embraced civil service reform, notably Rutherford B. Hayes, but without success. The assassination of his successor, James A. Garfield, by a disappointed officeseeker finally brought action. In January 1883, Chester A. Arthur—a man with a political past that exemplified what the reformers were against—signed the Pendleton Act creating a three-member Civil Service Commission on which both major parties were to be represented.

Inspired by the federal action taken in 1883, urban reformers soon tried to institute local civil service systems. New York state led the way, and in that same year the state legislature declared that cities with a population of 50,000 or more must establish specific requirements for civil service posts. By 1897 thirty-five cities in the United States had followed suit. Civil service laws were often written into new municipal charters. By 1900 Massachusetts, Maryland, Illinois, Indiana, Wisconsin, Louisiana, Washington, and Connecticut had joined New York in pressing for and encouraging cities to adopt civil service reforms.

Regulating Monopolies and Trusts

Private corporations were the creations of state legislatures, yet they frequently concentrated their activities in urban areas. Therein was the seed of many problems; for, to exercise its powers, a corporation often applied to and received a franchise from municipal authorities who conferred exclusive rights (a monopoly) to operate a ferry, a railroad, or some public utility. In a time of expansion, growth, and change, few Americans at first opposed these trends. Yet this also was an age of fraud and undefined business morality and, as one might expect, considerable sums could be involved in such transactions.

Corporations thought nothing of bribing city council members and judges to gain control of public utilities. In New York, for instance, the American Ice Company secured exclusive control of the docks in 1897. While pushing for municipal reform, state legislatures engaged in underhanded measures of their own. During these decades, a Massachusetts state commission levied gas and electric rates to the detriment of the municipalities serviced by those utilities. In Ohio and Illinois the state government granted special privileges to the railways in Cincinnati and Chicago without consulting the public. Throughout the United States, both the municipal and state bodies that administered laws governing corporations assessed corporate properties at far less than their actual value, thus providing unfair tax breaks for big business.

By the 1890s, largely because of blatant corporate excesses and difficult economic times, many Americans were becoming suspicious of and even hostile to the

Library of Congress.

Joseph Keppler produced one of the most famous antitrust statements of the late nineteenth century. In his 1889 cartoon monopoly, avarice, and intimidation of legislators prevailed because the capitalists had access to senators and the public was excluded.

activities of large regional companies. In a generalized way, the developing battle against the privileges enjoyed by railroads, Standard Oil, and various other monopolies that touched lean U.S. pocketbooks became known as the campaign against "the trusts." The mayors of a few large cities such as Chicago, Denver, Cleveland, Toledo, and Detroit were in the forefront of this assault upon what they and their supporters considered to be unfair practices. An outstanding example of a strong, effective mayor, who was scrupulous, honest, and devoted to reform, was Hazen Pingree of Detroit.

It was, of course, relatively easy for a man like Pingree to confront privilege on the local scene; "belling the cat" at the national level was quite another matter. Yet throughout these decades a variety of legal decisions, independent action by municipalities such as Detroit, legislation by numerous states, and a rising tide of general discontent caused business leaders to become wary. Further disregard for public opinion might provoke additional unrest and even increase the cry for much more far-reaching reforms. Thus, business leaders began to feel that regulation that they could control, or at least live with, was preferable.

In the 1870s the Supreme Court generally turned a deaf ear to the appeals of reformers to restrain the activities of corporations, especially railroads. They were, the court concluded, the creations of the states; furthermore, the Constitution implied that special privileges granted by one state were to be respected by all. The Fourteenth Amendment said states could not "deprive any person of life, liberty, or property, without due process of law." At first the justices said this did not apply to corporations, but in 1886 they reversed themselves in *Santa Clara County* v. *Southern Pacific Railroad* and expanded the "due process clause" to include corporations which, in the eyes of the law, were "persons." Thus a state could not tax or regulate a corporation it or another state chartered if the courts ruled such action was taken without "due process." This 1886 ruling, part of a general "nationalizing" process evident in America during those years, coupled with increasing outcry against "the trusts," set the stage for national legislation. Even as the Supreme Court struggled with these matters the states were acting on their own nevertheless. Antitrust advocates asked for an end to monopolies and the restoration of competition in business. The railroads were the first to be affected.

In the decade immediately after the Civil War the federal government took no steps against the favoritism shown by railroads to powerful shippers and to those cities where competitors had lines, and it ignored bribery, free passes, and outright gifts to secure land grants. It was then that states began to act. Some passed "Granger" laws (so-called because they were strongly backed by the

Courtesy The Burton Historical Collection, Detroit Public Library.

Hazen Pingree
(1840–1901)

Reform mayor of Detroit and then two-term governor of Michigan, Hazen Pingree was born in Denmark, Maine, in 1840, the son of a poor farmer, one of eight children. At fourteen he set out on his own and worked in cotton mills and shoe factories. Pingree enlisted in the Union army and participated in some of the worst of the Civil War battles until he was captured and sent to Andersonville. There he met prisoners from Detroit and went to that city as soon as the war ended.

After working a short time in a shoe factory, Pingree decided in 1866 to become a manufacturer. He and a partner invested hard work, careful supervision, and capital into a small factory; and, in time, Pingree became one of the nation's largest producers of boots and shoes. As a millionaire, he was generous toward the poor and a solid citizen interested in the welfare and growth of his adopted city.

In 1889 he ran for mayor on a reform ticket and won as a Republican in a normally Democratic city. Confronted with a system of patronage and existing franchises, Pingree gave preferential treatment to urban businesses and utilities, but he also paved streets, reduced public transportation fares to three cents, and cut rates for street lights, gas, and telephones. In the hard times of the early 1890s he won national attention by using vacant lots to raise potatoes for the poor ("Pingree's Potato Patches").

In 1896 he ran successfully for governor on the Republican ticket. Although often at odds with the party organization, Pingree was so popular with the voters that Republican leaders could not ignore him. He tried briefly to be both mayor and governor but was overruled by the courts. His chief adversaries as governor were the railroads, which he tried to tax more equitably. The public was with him on this issue but the legislature was not. Also, scandals connected with supplying Michigan troops in the Spanish-American War and that conflict itself diverted attention from Pingree's reform drive.

As a private citizen, he traveled abroad and began to write a history of the Boers, which he never finished. His chief contribution remained his service as mayor of Detroit. Lacking political experience, he was often inconsistent and seldom constructive, but he was a stern foe of corruption and thus one of a small band of reformers who stirred the public to action and paved the way for Theodore Roosevelt. ■

Grange) regulating charges for storing grain in warehouses and imposing restraints on railroad passenger rates.

In 1869 Massachusetts established a commission to supervise railroad activities and to investigate public grievances. Within ten years other states such as Minnesota, Wisconsin, Iowa, and Illinois followed suit. Illinois laid down explicit and detailed provisions against discrimination and gave the commission power to prosecute any railroad or grain elevator that refused to observe them. Although the Supreme Court upheld the right of an individual state to act (*Munn* v. *Illinois,* 1877), state authorities often lacked the power to enforce these laws. For, in truth, emerging railroad giants with expert legal talent and millions to spend were often much more powerful than state governments.

In addition, even in states where laws had been carelessly drawn to begin with and were consequently ineffective, the railroads waged a relentless war against such legislation. In 1886 the Supreme Court reversed its 1877 decision, declaring in *Wabash, St. Louis and Pacific Railway Co.* v. *Illinois* that an Illinois statute was invalid on the grounds that it was the exclusive power of Congress to regulate interstate commerce. Any further regulatory action against railroad abuses of that nature would have to be taken by the federal government, not that of the individual states concerned.

Even before the Wabash decision, some railroad managers had wearied of the ruthless competition raging among themselves and were more than willing to accept regulation. On February 4, 1887, President Cleveland approved the Interstate Commerce Act, which forbade railroads to engage in discriminatory practices, required them to publish rate schedules, and prohibited them from entering pooling agreements for the purpose of maintaining high rates. Further, the act declared that railroad rates should be "reasonable and just." Determination that rates on lines crossing state boundaries were "reasonable and just," as well as enforcement of certain provisions of the act, was placed in the hands of an Interstate Commerce Commission composed of five members. The Commission was to hear complaints, and to issue "cease and desist" orders when necessary. But if a railroad refused to comply, the Commission had to appeal to the courts, where the railroad companies enjoyed the advantage. (In eighteen years the Supreme Court heard sixteen such cases and decided all but one of them in favor of the railroads.) The ICC was, in fact, a passive factfinding body that lacked power to regulate rates; therefore, until the Clayton Antitrust Act of 1914, the Interstate Commerce Act did not really fulfill the hopes of reformers.

It was not only railroads, however, that felt the hot breath of public wrath. In the 1880s oil and steel companies also became the targets of protests. Both the Democratic and the Republican parties included recommendations for the regulation of trusts in their 1888 election platforms. In 1889 Republican Senator John Sherman of Ohio introduced the famous act that bears his name.

The Sherman Antitrust Act, passed in July 1890, made illegal "every contract combination in the form of trust or otherwise, or conspiracy, in restraint of trade or commerce among the states or with foreign nations." It also stipulated that "every person who shall monopolize, or combine or conspire with any other person or persons, to monopolize, any part of the trade be deemed guilty of a misdemeanor." The Sherman Act was passed in the House by a vote of 252 to 0 and in the Senate by a vote of 51 to 1. Violaters could be fined $5,000 and sentenced to a year in jail. This lopsided vote would seem to indicate overwhelming endorsement but, in fact, Congress was running scared. Virtually every state had passed antitrust legislation, yet inaction by New Jersey, Delaware, and West Virginia permitted corporations and combinations chartered in those "trust havens" to operate elsewhere. More important, shaken by public outcry, a Republican-dominated Congress put together a bill which, members hoped, would tide the party over until the next election.

This measure, poorly phrased and often ambiguous (perhaps intentionally), was difficult to enforce. Only eighteen suits were instituted under its provisions in the 1890s, some of them not against corporate trusts but labor unions. Effort to break up a sugar monopoly (*U.S.* v. *E. C. Knight Company,* 1895) floundered on the tenuous grounds that the federal government did not control the manufacture of a product (as opposed to commerce) exclusively within one state. Like the Interstate Commerce Act, the Sherman Act was not truly implemented until the early part of the twentieth century (with the Northern Securities decision of 1904).

Reforming Social Institutions

Innovations—such as the initiative, recall, and referendum; honest ballots; a civil service based upon merit; and regulatory legislation—merely shaped the framework within which governments operated. Reforming the social institutions which affected the day-to-day lives of millions, especially the growing mass of urban poor, was a much more complex affair. Yet for the good of American society as a whole, rudely shaken by the expansion of cities, slums, and industry, it was a step that had to be taken.

Charity Organizations

Private and secular charity organizations had existed in America since the 1650s. But only after the Civil War did such groups express much concern (for obvious reasons) for the plight of the urban poor. But American and European reformers of the mid-nineteenth century prided themselves upon their "scientific" approach; their programs stressed the rehabilitation and reconstruction of families and of individuals and an end to begging.

In 1877, the Charity Organization Society was established in Buffalo, New York; by 1893 more than fifty such bodies existed throughout the United States. These groups oversaw the dispersal of relief to the poor and needy in urban centers and worked to eliminate duplication of their efforts by similar associations so that maximum benefits could be enjoyed by all the interests served. They also attempted to keep charitable groups free of graft. Financial federations—popularly known as Community Chests—sprang up, the first one in Denver in 1887. Under the Community Chest scheme, private agencies within a community would submit budgets to a central committee, which then collected the total amount needed through an annual fundraising drive conducted by volunteers.

The Social Settlement Movement

The social settlement movement, begun in England in the 1870s, was based upon the idea that urban areas requiring improvement must have a community center that could become a club or meeting place of sorts for the needy. The staffs of settlement houses, as such centers were called, also used these facilities as laboratories for social research. They conducted investigations of slum areas to learn how best to alleviate existing conditions. Settlement workers trained slum inhabitants in ways to help themselves. They created clinics, dispensaries, and visiting nurse services. Programs were instituted that led to medical examinations, school lunches, and improved educational opportunities—particularly for foreigners who wanted to learn English. Settlement houses often had arts and crafts facilities to provide children and adults with a recreational respite from life in the slums. This activity proved to be an acutely important aspect of service; neighborhood playgroups, commonplace in rural America, virtually did not exist in the cities. In 1885 an organized play movement was inaugurated in Boston, and by 1887 ten playgrounds had been opened there. (In 1889 the first public gymnasium was added to the facilities offered to the poor.) Some settlement houses adopted the supervised playground technique as a means to establish friendly relationships among slumdwellers, to teach them citizenship and sportsmanship, and to guard them against unsavory social influences.

In 1886, Stanton Coit and Charles B. Stover established America's first settlement house in New York City. First called the Neighborhood Guild, it later was renamed the University Settlement. During the next three decades some 300 similar centers appeared in major U.S. cities, most of them supported by churches. The greatest single achievement of these settlements, although they did much to relieve the grim reality of poverty, was the Americanization of millions of immigrants by helping them to understand their new homeland and to take advantage of opportunities it presented.

Perhaps the most famous American settlement was Chicago's Hull House, founded in 1889 by Jane Addams and Ellen Gates Starr (1860–1940)—companions who had been inspired by visits to similar centers in London. Named for the man who had built a spacious residence at 800 South Halstead Street in 1856, Hull House added in time a dozen large buildings covering half of a city block and also operated a nearby playground and a summer camp in the country.

The success of Hull House attracted many volunteer workers, and their articles and books (as well as those of Jane Addams) brought the Chicago landmark widespread recognition. Visitors from all over the world came to study there and to learn from the experiences of this truly amazing institution. Other settlement houses included the South End House established in Boston by William J. Tucker and Robert A. Woods, the Henry Street Settlement of New York directed by Lillian B. Wald, the Kingsley House in Pittsburgh organized by William H. Matthews and Charles C. Cooper, and the Hiram House in Cleveland supported by George A. Bellamy.

Most of these settlements promoted and developed a sense of neighborhood in depressed areas, and some workers extended their interests and their activities to

University of Illinois Library at Chicago Circle Campus, Jane Addams Memorial Collection.

Jane Addams's Hull House in Chicago served as a model for settlement house workers in Boston, New York, Philadelphia, and other cities. Here, visiting nurses are hosted by a Hull House staff worker.

Photo by Jacob A. Riis, Jacob A. Riis Collection, Museum of the City of New York.

Jacob Riis documented the life and death of slum dwellers. Overcrowded tenements like New York City's Gotham Court made a premature trip to Potter's Field a certainty. Disease and violence claimed an inordinate number of the immigrants and members of racial minorities forced to reside in slums.

Photo by Jacob A. Riis, Jacob A. Riis Collection, Museum of the City of New York.

University of Illinois Library at Chicago Circle Campus, Jane Addams Memorial Collection.

Jane Addams
(1860–1935)

Like many leading reformers of her day, Jane Addams grew up in a well-to-do household and received a good education, but she felt impelled to help those less fortunate than herself. Born in Cedarville, Illinois and graduated from Rockford Seminary (later Rockford College) in 1881, she enrolled as a medical student in Philadelphia but had to quit after one year because of poor health. Seven years later, after a prolonged search for what she considered a useful occupation, she became interested in settlement work while visiting Toynbee Hall in London. Later on, Jane Addams and a college friend, Ellen Gates Starr, decided to found a similar institution in Chicago, and in 1889 they acquired Hull House. Although not the first settlement house experiment in America, Hull House soon became the most famous.

As a reformer, Jane Addams wore many hats. She was an effective public speaker, a prolific writer (10 books and over 500 articles), a shrewd businesswoman, a very capable fundraiser and manager, and an idealist in a sense but always striving for the possible—a trait that infuriated some of her associates. Not a humble woman, she was very proud and ambitious. Although Jane Addams had little interest in material possessions, she always stayed in the best hotels when traveling, ate in the most expensive restaurants, and was entertained lavishly by wealthy friends. Even Hull House, though not luxurious, provided genteel comfort for its residents.

Most Americans admired the work of this remarkable lady, yet some were disturbed by her defense of organized labor and willingness to welcome even anarchists to Hull House. Her outspoken opposition to World War I and suggestions that some doughboys might be less than heroes increased dramatically the ranks of her detractors. Throughout the 1920s, groups such as the American Legion denounced her as a Communist, "the most dangerous woman in America." She even was expelled from the Daughters of the American Revolution for her pacifist internationalism; nevertheless, in 1931 she shared the Nobel Peace Prize with Nicholas Murray Butler, president of Columbia University. ■

other fields such as the trade union movement, child-labor legislation, and child welfare in general. Out of such efforts came a new profession: social work. An unexpected development, however, was the publicity given both settlement houses and conditions they were endeavoring to correct. Among the most alarming testaments of need were two books by Jacob A. Riis: *How the Other Half Lives* (1890) and *Children of the Poor* (1892). His shocking photographs and impassioned prose exposed the horrors of slum life in grim detail and became landmarks of the social reform movement.

The Social Gospel Movement

The roots of experiments in charity settlements lay in urban religious forces. Troubled by the rise of tall business buildings (which symbolically looked down upon church spires), boisterous Sabbaths, and often dwindling congregations, leaders of the three dominant religious groups—Catholics, Protestants, and Jews—mounted campaigns both to help the poor and to breathe new life into decaying religious institutions. The result was the Social Gospel movement, a dramatic reshaping of religious outlook to encompass a general concern for all aspects of community life.

This "Social Christianity," a reaction against rampant American individualism and unrestrained capitalism, developed first among Protestant ministers who sought a pragmatic means of alleviating the sufferings of the poor. Since the congregations of Catholic and Jewish houses of worship consisted largely of immigrants, who were also often very poor and alienated from community life, these religious groups also entered the movement. Urban problems, in fact, were cross-denominational and did not discriminate on the basis of color, age, or belief. By the late 1890s Catholics, Jews, and Protestants were frequently cooperating to bring solace to the needy.

The Catholic Church had strongholds in Boston, New York, and Baltimore as early as 1860, but extended its influence within the next forty years to Cincinnati, St. Louis, and Chicago. To retain its hold on the growing host of poor and immigrant urban parishioners and to head off the loss of members to non-Catholic philanthropies, the Church established its own Society for the Protection of Destitute Catholic Children and annexed to its orphan asylums schools where manual labor skills were taught. The proliferation of societies within each church ultimately built strength in the immigrant neighborhoods of the rapidly growing cities.

Similarly, the first response of the Jews to urban social problems occurred through synagogues and their affiliated societies. The Reform (or Americanized) Jewish temples were separated by practice from the Orthodox synagogues. But the need to maintain orphan asylums, homes for the aged, industrial schools, settlement houses, and immigrant aid societies could not be met effectively by separate groups except in huge cities such as New York. By the 1890s divergent Jewish groups decided to end their differences in favor of joint action.

The rising tide of Jewish immigration to America in the 1890s helped hasten this development. Russian Jews fled from the Czar's pogroms, mostly to New York. When the efforts of Baron de Hirsch, an Austrian philanthropist, to develop farm and village settlements for these refugees proved unworkable, the cooperation of Hebrew welfare agencies in a dozen urban centers was enlisted. By 1910, 64,000 Jews had moved from slum ghettoes on New York's Lower East Side to some 1,400 cities and towns across the United States. The Interdenominational Educational Alliance, founded in 1887 in New York to promote the assimilation of eastern and southern European immigrants, was reorganized by trustees of the Hirsch Fund into the North American Civic League. The League brought Jews from various origins into a close working relationship with Gentiles as well as with their coreligionists in the Jewish faith, enlarged already existing classes for immigrants in nine cities and established new ones elsewhere. Sixty neighborhoods benefited from foreign language libraries opened by the League, while unskilled immigrants received instruction at the League's housekeeping-training centers.

Of the various religious groups, the Jews were the most oriented to the city. As a result, they often pioneered in significant urban movements. Samuel Gompers provided leadership in labor unions. Abraham Cahan, editor of the Jewish *Forward,* became a prominent spokesman for the burgeoning socialist movement. And in 1876 Dr. Felix Adler founded an educational organization, the Society for Ethical Culture in New York City—an establishment that survives to this day.

The Protestant response to the challenge of the cities took varied forms. A generalized grouping representing numerous denominations with conflicting goals and divergent interpretations of Biblical lore, they also were

Museum of the City of New York.

Jacob August Riis
(1849–1914)

Jacob Riis wrote several books and hundreds of articles, yet most Americans know this Danish born immigrant only as the author of a stunning exposé of tenement life published in 1890: *How the Other Half Lives*. Riis came to America in 1870 and wandered about in semipoverty until 1877 when he got a job with the *New York Tribune*. The next year he moved to the *Evening Sun* where for eleven years he was a police reporter. His office was located in the heart of Manhattan's immigrant district and Riis got to know the area and its inhabitants well.

This experience, coupled with his own background, made Riis generally sympathetic to and certainly perceptive toward the lot of the poor. In general, he accepted environment as the principal cause of poverty (a theory just beginning to win converts in 1890) and rejected earlier notions that the roots lay in sin, sloth, and depravity. Nevertheless, Riis was bound by some of the stereotyped views of his day. His rating scale of ethnic ability put Germans at the top and Chinese and blacks at the bottom. He considered an able black man superior to the lowest white, but essentially childlike, docile, eager to accept the most menial of jobs. "The Italian and poor Jew," he wrote, "rise only by compulsion." He was especially scornful of tramps, whatever their racial and ethnic characteristics, and thought them a form of humanity somewhat less desirable than thieves.

Jacob Riis obviously developed no systematic social theory nor did he offer any overall plan to solve problems he presented so graphically to millions of Americans. Yet he did join in reform efforts and helped to stimulate the muckraking era of American journalism. Above all else, by the power of his words and the dramatic quality of his photographs, some of them considered classics, Jacob Riis awakened a nation to the horrors of tenement life in growing urban centers. ■

buffeted by forces such as Darwinism, trade unionism, socialism, and other new ideas emanating from colleges and universities. Far less cohesive than Catholics and Jews, they had to deal with conditions created by migration from farm to city and the changing patterns of urban neighborhoods. Not surprisingly, Protestants espoused diverse solutions for the problems of the urban poor, solutions that one suspects may well have been little more than an outpouring of frustrated campaigns bottled up for several decades when one great crusade (abolition) dominated the reform scene.

The Christian Labor Union, founded in 1872 in Boston, brought several religious and labor leaders together in an attempt to deal with the hardships experienced by New England cotton-mill workers. The union attacked the inhumanity of the capitalist system and the churches' complacent attitude toward it; it also defended the right of labor to organize and helped it form Knights of Labor districts in Boston. The Union of Christian Work, established by Unitarians in Providence in 1868, maintained a school, a library, a clubroom and a lecture series to deal with the problems of intemperance, vice, and crime that were being aggravated by the growth of cities. Episcopalians followed suit, founding brotherhoods, sisterhoods, and workingmen's homes in various cities to shelter numerous poor craftsmen who were then migrating from England to America. Lutherans, Methodists, and other church groups also opened homes for needy immigrants and other destitute people.

A concept of Christian responsibility for the welfare of humanity was evolving. Washington Gladden (1836–1918), who came to be known as the "Father of Social Christianity," alerted church leaders to their responsibilities toward labor and other urban problems. Walter Rauschenbush (1861–1918) introduced Baptists to the social gospel; Graham Taylor (1851–1938), a professor at the Chicago Theological Seminary, led his students first into the slums and then into political and labor disputes on behalf of the poor. All three men envisioned the fate of urban religion as linked to the welfare of the laboring classes.

Gladden, for example, calculated in 1886 that the real annual wages of labor had gone up little, if any, since 1860. During those same years, he noted, America's wealth had increased from $16 billion to $43 billion, and the value of manufactured goods trebled. Since workers obviously were being denied a just share of their labors, he wrote, they naturally "complain and rebel" and see no alternative other than to organize "for mutual protection and defense."

Of course, the settlement movement and the rescue missions and institutional churches alone could not solve such problems nor meet all the needs of the slum poor. Their efforts did, however, awaken many church members to urban conditions.

Reforming Labor Institutions

While religious leaders and settlement workers could do much to invigorate social and spiritual life in urban areas and perhaps stir interest in campaigns to improve working conditions, workers themselves had to shoulder the responsibility for change and betterment in the industrial realm. The success of centralization and cooperation in the business community demonstrated to workingmen that they, too, must do the same thing. By forming trade unions they could wield considerable power in bargaining with management over wages, hours, and working conditions.

Labor Unions

During the first half of the nineteenth century most of the unions in America were city or regional groupings along craft lines. Leaders talked of political action and national organization, but not until 1850 did the first national union—the Typographical Union—appear. For the most part, union members stressed practical, immediate goals: higher wages, shorter working hours, improved working conditions, and protective labor legislation.

Immediately after the Civil War two aggressive labor organizations appeared—the National Labor Union (1866) and the Knights of Labor (1869). Within two years the NLU had 640,000 members. William H. Sylvis (1828–1869), its president, formerly headed the International Moulders' Union. He was an outspoken man and a talented orator, but his death at age 41 at the height of his career was a severe blow to the young union. The goals of the NLU included an eight-hour day; producers' cooperatives; arbitration of labor disputes; more rigid enforcement of the apprentice system; reservation of public lands for bona fide settlers; and development of lyceums, institutes, and reading rooms for workers. The NLU also favored direct political action, but the failure of its candidates to attract much interest in the 1872 election led to the demise of this pioneer union.

The Order of the Knights of Labor then assumed the leadership of American labor. Although this group experienced rough sledding during the hard times of the 1870s, by the close of the decade it had 700,000 members. This union emerged from local chapters in Philadelphia and originally was a secret order founded by Uriah S. Stephens (1821–1882), a tailor. Stephens preached that, unless checked, the aggressive accumulation of wealth in the cities would lead to the pauperism and degradation of the masses. A former schoolteacher, agitator for worker migration to the West, abolitionist, member of numerous secret fraternal orders, and active Greenbacker, Stephens was one of the most effective labor organizers of his day. However, various factors such as ruthless crushing of several strikes, economic unrest, and opposition of the Catholic Church to the secrecy of the Knights paved the way for a takeover of this union in 1881 by Terrence V. Powderly (1849–1924). Powderly, a machinist who had twice been elected mayor of Scranton, Pennsylvania, soon became the most prominent spokesman for the Knights. An idealist, he urged workers to form one integral body for protest through mutual cooperation. "Cooperation of the Order, by the Order, and for the Order"—a paraphrase of Lincoln's Gettysburg Address—was adopted by the Knights as their motto.

The violence of the 1870s led to the destruction of millions of dollars worth of property in many cities, some loss of life, and the construction of vast regimental armories bristling with men and ammunition earmarked to put a quick end to future unrest of this sort.

During the mid-1880s another upsurge of labor militancy occurred. The Knights of Labor were at the peak of their strength and, despite Powderly's opposition to strikes, they did support some railroad walkouts, work stoppages, nationwide boycotts, and political demonstrations. In 1886 610,000 men were out of work as a result of strikes, lockouts, or shutdowns due to strikes—more than three times the average for the five preceding years.

On May 4, 1886, anarchists gathered at Haymarket Square in Chicago to protest police brutalities. Amid fears of violence, the mayor attended the meeting, found the speeches harmless, and left. A short time later the police, disregarding his orders, tried to disperse a gathering which, in the public eye at least, was somehow related to the Knights of Labor who had, in fact, by sudden expansion welcomed socialists, radicals, and other diverse elements into the fold. A bomb was thrown, killing a policeman and fatally wounding six other people. A riot ensued. Eight anarchists were subsequently found guilty and four of them hanged. Although the identity of the bombthrower was never established, the incident smeared the whole labor movement and proved to be the death blow to the Knights of Labor. Within a year after the incident, the Knights lost their hold upon the large cities and became an organization consisting primarily of rural people.

In the same year that Powderly won control of the Knights of Labor from Stephens, two immigrants and an American-born carpenter founded the American Federation of Labor. Their names were Samuel Gompers (1850–1924), Adolph Strasser (1844–1939), and Peter J. McGuire (1852–1906). Under their leadership the AFL hammered out a philosophy somewhat more closely related to the realities of America's growing industrial economy than that of its predecessors. Rejecting the utopian radicalism of some of the Knights, the AFL devoted its efforts to gaining concrete benefits for skilled workers organized along craft lines. Unlike the Knights, the AFL was a loose alliance of national trade unions, each of which retained sufficient autonomy and jurisdiction over its own affairs to call its own strikes. The AFL did not hesitate to use strikes and boycotts as legitimate means to attain collective bargaining; the Knights of Labor had frowned officially on resorting to these measures. These principles were fully formulated by 1881 and reaffirmed in very strong terms in 1886 when the AFL was reorganized.

The AFL elected Samuel Gompers as its first president. (He retained the office for nearly forty years.) Born in London in 1850, Gompers had grown up in the trade-union movement. Originally a socialist, his experiences in America led him to adopt a more conservative approach to the problems of labor. Gompers felt that labor should accept the existing economic system and try to win a respectable place for itself as a "legitimate" group within that system. He believed that laborers in different crafts and callings would have to band together to struggle for higher wages and lower hours. Gompers strove to impose order by settling jurisdictional disputes between unions and by consolidating local unions into state and national federations. While the Knights of

Culver Pictures.

Mary Harris Jones
(1830–1930)

Through a strange twist of adversity, "Mother Jones," as she was called, became one of the most unusual figures in the American labor movement. A native of Ireland, she grew up in Toronto and worked as a teacher and a dressmaker until 1861, when she married a Memphis man who was a member of the Iron Molders Union. Six years later yellow fever swept through this Tennessee river town, killing her husband and their four children. Then, after she moved to Chicago, the famous Chicago fire of 1871 destroyed all of her possessions.

Alone and poor, Mother Jones began attending meetings of the newly organized Knights of Labor, and agitation for the rights of workers gradually became her life's work. Vigorous, witty, possessing a strong sense of drama, this little woman in a black bonnet developed into a symbol of defiance wherever strikers gathered. She was in Pittsburgh in 1877, in Chicago at the Haymarket Riot of 1886, and in Birmingham for the railway strike of 1894.

Working in southern cotton mills to gain firsthand knowledge of child labor conditions, Mother Jones attracted national attention at the turn of the century when she organized strikers' wives and paraded them forth with mops on their shoulders. On one occasion she marched a band of textile mill children from Kensington, Pennsylvania, to Teddy Roosevelt's Oyster Bay estate on Long Island. For more than half a century she was in the thick of labor protest and even at age 93 was in West Virginia cheering on striking coal miners.

On her 100th birthday Mother Jones was showered with greetings from both friends and former foes, including a telegram from John D. Rockefeller, Jr. She made a vigorous speech for movie cameras as she stood before her modest home in Silver Spring, Maryland, but six months later she succumbed to old age and was buried in a United Mine Workers' cemetery in Illinois.

A fiery agitator with a keen sense of humor, Mother Jones displayed considerable tolerance for those she opposed and usually won their respect. Not a socialist, she was sympathetic to socialist ideals; however, she was a determined foe of both prohibition and woman's suffrage. ■

Labor declined, the AFL grew. Within fifteen years its membership totaled more than a million.

One important group of unions associated with railroads—the four brotherhoods of engineers, conductors, firemen, and brakemen—chose not to join the AFL, though they generally made common cause with its members. The principal weakness of the AFL was not holdouts of this sort, but an emphasis upon skilled labor and a general exclusion of black workers and women from all craft unions. As such, it was the voice of a select few and banned perhaps 90 percent of all American workers from its ranks.

Nevertheless, despite such drawbacks, the militancy of the AFL combined with the reluctance of many employers to bargain with or even tolerate unions and harsh economic times led to considerable labor unrest during the last years of the nineteenth century. The most spectacular of these outbreaks included the above mentioned Haymarket riot of 1886 and strikes against Andrew Carnegie and George Pullman in the early 1890s.

Courtesy AFL-CIO.

Samuel Gompers as he appeared during the formative years of the American Federation of Labor.

The Homestead Strike

In 1892, 3,800 members of the Amalgamated Association of Iron and Steel workers at Andrew Carnegie's Homestead steel plant in Pennsylvania struck over wage cuts and working conditions. Henry C. Frick, the plant manager, called in 300 Pinkerton detectives, really strikebreakers, commonly called "goons," who paved the way for "scabs," substitute nonunion workers, to man equipment and keep production going. When the detectives arrived, they were met by the strikers. After a gun fight in which three detectives and ten strikers died and many more were wounded, the detectives surrendered. Public sympathy was aroused in favor of the strikers. Unfortunately Alexander Berkman, a misguided Russian anarchist, attempted to assassinate Frick and alienated public sympathy. The strike failed miserably, destroying unionism in the steel industry for years to come.

The Pullman Strike

The Pullman strike of 1894 proved even more disastrous for labor. The depression that began in 1893 brought on a new wave of wage cuts, layoffs, and strikes. In 1894 more men were unemployed owing to strikes than had ever been before, perhaps 20 percent of the entire labor force—that is, nearly 3 million may have been out of work. The most important strike of that year originated not among railway workers but among the factory workers in George M. Pullman's "model" company town (called Pullman, Illinois), which was located just south of Chicago. Wages were cut on five different occasions in the year prior to the strike, while rents for company houses remained the same. The Pullman workers became desperate. They had recently joined the New American Railway Union founded the previous year and headed by Eugene V. Debs (1855–1926). Debs urged caution, but his union voted to refuse to handle Pullman cars if management would not accept arbitration. Pullman refused. The General Managers Association then dismissed switchmen who boycotted Pullman cars. The union

Library of Congress.

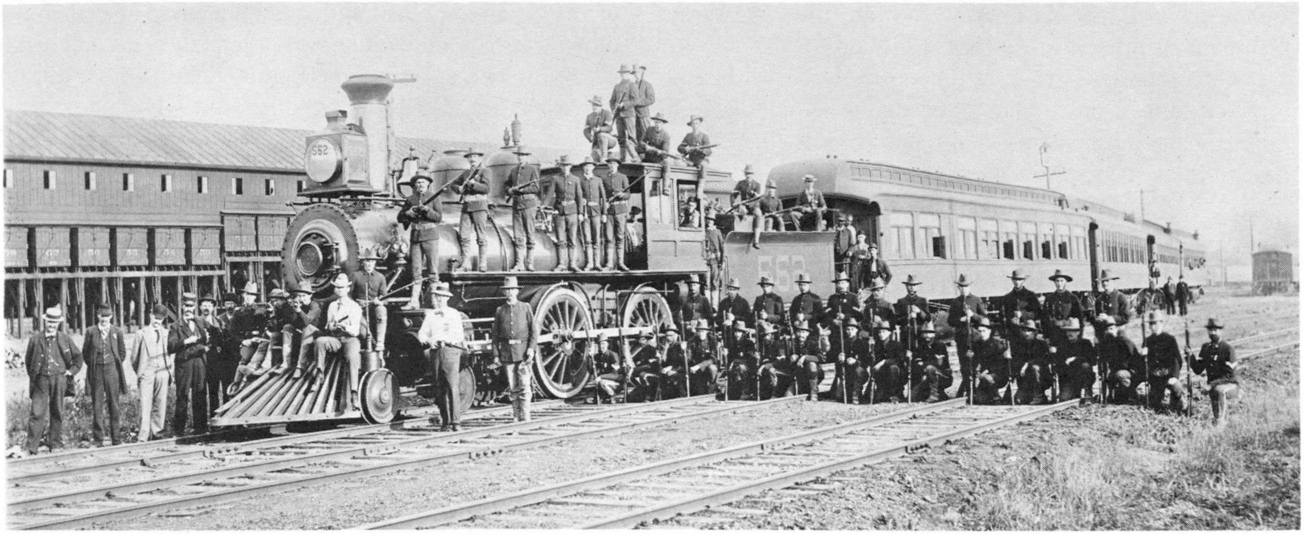

As a result of President Cleveland's antistrike policy, Federal troops "liberated" this train from unruly Pullman workers.

Tamiment Library, New York University.

Eugene V. Debs, born in Terre Haute, the son of Alsatian immigrants, was radicalized by being jailed for his support of the Pullman strikers.

struck. By the end of June almost all of the railroad men on roads west of Chicago were out of work.

The General Managers Association, acting on behalf of the railroads, appealed to the federal government to intervene with armed force and end the strike. So far violence had been avoided. Governor John P. Altgeld (an immigrant, former mayor of Chicago, and the man who had pardoned some of the Haymarket rioters) strongly opposed armed intervention. But lawyers for the railroads persuaded President Cleveland and Attorney General Richard Olney (a one-time railroad lawyer) that the strike was obstructing the delivery of United States mail and should be brought, therefore, to an end. In truth, mail deliveries had been cut off because the railroads themselves—against the union's wishes—refused to attach mail cars to trains boycotting Pullman cars. Choosing to overlook this fact, Olney secured an injunction against the union. On July 4, 1894, Cleveland sent some 2,000 federal troops into Chicago to enforce the injunction and to protect the mails.

With troops in Chicago the union lost control of the situation. Mobs of looters destroyed cars and burned and stole property. Twelve people were killed and countless arrests made at the scene. Although none of the arrested were strikers, the violence that occurred hurt the union in the eyes of public opinion. Olney had succeeded in breaking the strike, and in Pullman's favor.

Courtesy Pinkerton's, Inc.

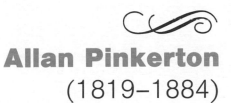

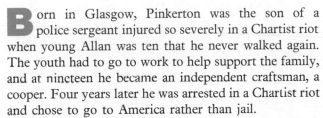

Allan Pinkerton
(1819–1884)

Born in Glasgow, Pinkerton was the son of a police sergeant injured so severely in a Chartist riot when young Allan was ten that he never walked again. The youth had to go to work to help support the family, and at nineteen he became an independent craftsman, a cooper. Four years later he was arrested in a Chartist riot and chose to go to America rather than jail.

Pinkerton settled in Illinois, resumed his trade, and one day, while cutting hoop poles in a deserted area, chanced upon a band of counterfeiters. He subsequently guided the party that captured them and this adventure led to police work. In 1850, Pinkerton, who was an ardent abolitionist and active in the underground railroad, was invited to become deputy sheriff of Cook County and, in effect, the young city of Chicago's only detective. That same year he organized a private detective agency, one of the nation's first, to probe railroad robberies. This business, a partnership at the outset, soon occupied all of his time.

During the 1850s the company prospered, and in January 1861 some of his employees were hired by eastern railroads to investigate threats to their property by southern sympathizers. In connection with this work they learned of plans to assassinate Abraham Lincoln en route to his inaugural. Pinkerton devised a famous scheme by which the President-elect got to Washington safely.

In April 1861, Lincoln invited Pinkerton to a conference on the organization of a secret service. Although this meeting produced no immediate results, Pinkerton and his men soon were working for General George B. McClellan, a former client, in the border states of Kentucky, Tennessee, and Virginia. Pinkerton (in disguise) even ventured into Georgia and Mississippi; and, using the name of Major E. J. Allen, began to direct counterespionage work in Washington as an aide to McClellan. Pinkerton quit when the general was removed in 1862 but continued to carry on investigations for the federal government throughout the war.

With peace, he set up branches in New York and Philadelphia. A stroke in 1869 ended Pinkerton's active career, although he actually ran the company almost until his death. His last years were devoted to writing his reminiscences. The eighteen volumes, filled with excitement and pleasant, novel-like prose, did much to enhance Pinkerton's prestige.

Another factor that brought him fame was his ardent opposition to labor unions. No analyst of social conditions, he sincerely believed that labor organizations were harmful to workers and especially in 1877 used all of his resources to crush strikes. After Pinkerton's death, his sons carried on the business, largely under policies initiated by their father. ■

Library of Congress.

Like many protest marchers, members of Jacob Coxey's Army (seen here marching en route to Washington, D.C.) perceived themselves as patriotic Americans working to enlist public support for their cause.

The failure of the Pullman strike had an important effect on the future of American labor. Debs and other union leaders were tried and sentenced to jail for contempt of court for having refused to obey the injunction against the union. When, on appeal, the Supreme Court upheld the sentence, it also bestowed upon the use of the injunction in labor disputes a prestige that it had never previously enjoyed. And, by suggesting that a strike might be construed as a conspiracy in restraint of trade under the Sherman Antitrust Act, the government placed a powerful weapon in the hands of management, one that could henceforth be used against the unions.

Another unforeseen consequence of the failure of the Pullman strike was the emergence of Eugene Debs, after six months in jail, as a confirmed Socialist. Within a few years Debs became the foremost leader of the American Socialist movement, and he remained in that position throughout the years when the movement enjoyed its greatest popularity and strength.

Coxey's Army

The most brutal year of the depression was 1894. One out of every five workers was unemployed. Some relief was offered by city governments, but it was wholly inadequate. When hungry men turned to the federal government for help, they were rebuffed or ignored. Jacob S. Coxey (1854–1951), an Ohio businessman, proposed a plan of federal work relief on public roads, to be financed by an issue of $500 million in legal-tender Treasury notes. (He even named his son "Legal Tender.") Coxey's "good roads" bill was designed to end the depression by injecting money into the economy by providing work and wages for the unemployed.

Congress rejected Coxey's proposal. "We will send a petition to Washington with boots on," vowed Coxey in response, and began gathering his forces. "Coxey's Army" marched peacefully from his hometown of Massillon, Ohio, to the White House lawn, accumulating sympathizers along the way. On May Day 500 marchers arrived in the Capitol and were greeted by cheering crowds. The police responded with something less than joy; policemen arrested the leaders, while trampling and beating at least fifty people in the process.

Coxey's Army disbanded, but at least seventeen other groups followed behind. During 1894 some 1,700 marchers in "industrial armies" arrived in Washington. They were usually sober and peaceful and met with public sympathy. The government became frightened. Even President Cleveland began to believe that a spirit of rebellion might result in mob rule.

Intolerance and Social Conflict

A population that almost doubled in the years from 1870 to 1900 created unprecedented problems and great social tension. Those whose positions in society and comfortable old ways were threatened by change sometimes mounted strange and even violent campaigns against forces they feared. These battles pitted liberal against conservative, rural against urban, black against white, Protestant against Catholic, those who drank liquor and beer against those who didn't, and "new" immigrants against "old," although all Americans (except perhaps Indians) can only be viewed as migrants of one sort of another. Set off by various sparks of intolerance, many of these campaigns were openly coercive, not simply quiet maneuvers to defend a set of values or to convert unbelievers. Instead, they aimed to impose forcibly on others certain "accepted" standards of behavior.

A Clash of Values

Reformers who are spurred to act by a sense of their own declining dominance usually approach those to be reformed with little sympathy, and certainly with less warmth. The reformables are not to be assimilated into the broader community and its culture; rather they must acknowledge the rightness of that community's existing patterns, keep to designated places, and act accordingly. Carried out in such a spirit, reform can only breed attacks and counterattacks and lead—as it did in late nineteenth century America—to virulent antagonisms throughout a country's social, political, and religious life.

The clash of values from 1870 to 1900 divided the American nation into warring groups, not quite ready to take up arms as in 1861, but willing and eager to use the classroom, pulpit, ballot box, and legislative chamber to effect reform. All of this activity must be viewed, of course, in the context of a burgeoning population that was becoming better educated and more mobile thanks to the spread of railway tracks. It was also becoming concentrated in large towns and cities, where agitation both for and against some proposal or social trend could elicit a dramatic and almost instantaneous response.

In a general way, middle class, smalltown, Protestant, native Americans were pitted against recent immigrants, largely Catholic (or at least not of the Protestant faith), who frequently settled in cities and lacked the virtues cherished by older settlers of Anglo-Saxon and northern European backgrounds. For many of the latter, the corner saloon, whether in a small village or in a city block, became the symbol of everything that was wrong with postwar America. It was, in their opinion (and they all too frequently were correct), a center of vice, prostitution, machine politics, ethnic or class unity, and most assuredly drunkenness. It also had the distinct advantage of being a visible enemy whose activities often were detestable, an adversary that could be attacked, and perhaps, overwhelmed. More than anything else, it was the saloon that led to the rise of a strong temperance movement.

The Temperance Movement

This phenomenon, largely a mixture of local and state campaigns before 1900, was an excellent example of "coercive" reform as thousands stormed forth, many of them women from rural or smalltown, middle class households, to vanquish Demon Rum. Yet within this crusade there were those who rejected both coercion and ties to reform in general.

The Woman's Christian Temperance Union (WCTU), organized in 1874, reflected these various attitudes. Annie Wittenmeyer (1827–1900), the first president, steadfastly resisted any association with other questions of the day and concentrated instead on moral arguments to promote total abstinence and perhaps to bring about a religious conversion as well. (It should be noted that the WCTU always meant abstinence when it said *temperance*.) In 1877, President Wittenmeyer, a Civil War nurse, teacher, and editor, told delegates to a national convention, "I trust the atmosphere of this meeting will be prayer. This society was born of prayer and must be nurtured and sustained by prayer. Prayer is the strongest weapon we can lay hold on." A year later she repeated this "singleness of purpose" and during the WCTU's first decade it held revival-type services in scores of cities, a precursor of the Salvation Army's efforts to rescue the underprivileged, downtrodden, and outcast.

In 1879, Frances Willard (1839–1898), representing a radically different viewpoint, became WCTU president, and until her death the organization embraced every reform of the age. Under Willard's direction the WCTU became involved in woman suffrage, dress reform, the Populist party of the 1890s, and even labor agitation. Frances Willard openly rejected the conservatism of her predecessors and charged forth to right every wrong which, in her opinion, was plaguing society. College-educated, she represented the new wave of intellectual feminism and, for the most part, had the support of the western, more liberal wing of the WCTU. Wittenmeyer, her experience rooted in good deeds during the Civil War and intimate ties to the Methodist Church, had the backing of an older, more conservative, eastern faction. Willard's victory in 1879 and her firm grasp on the helm for two decades made the WCTU a powerful force and a foundation stone of the Progressive movement of the early 1900s.

Another famous (and infamous) woman in her own day was Carry A. Nation (1846–1911), a somewhat irrational reformer who at times was an embarrassment to temperance forces. Her hatchet, zeal, and sheer physical strength struck fear into the hearts of scores of drinkers. This Kansas whirlwind garnered much publicity, but her accomplishments were few in number.

Much more effective than Carry's hatchet, and perhaps even the WCTU, in the actual reform of drinking practices was the Anti-Saloon League. Organized at Oberlin, Ohio, in 1893, it quickly gained national stature and led the fight to win state and national prohibition. Unlike the WCTU under Willard, the Anti-Saloon League (as its name suggests) had one goal in mind and soon found powerful allies in hundreds of Protestant evangelical churches. This alliance thus was strongest in

Frederick Lewis.

LUNCH
"I CANNOT TELL A LIE--I DID IT WITH MY LITTLE HATCHET!"

Carry Nation's fanaticism impelled her to enter saloons and wreak havoc upon "spirits," premises, and patrons alike.

Protestant, rural, nativist areas such as the South and Midwest, although Maine, New Hampshire, and Vermont also gave it strong support.

Before the Anti-Saloon League became a major force in American life two general waves of prohibition by state law occurred, one at mid-century and another in the 1890s. In 1889 both North and South Dakota entered the Union as "dry" states, but much of this fervor was short-lived or produced only technical prohibition and considerable "winking" at the letter of the law. By 1905 only Maine, Kansas, Nebraska, and North Dakota were "dry" states.

Although the real triumphs of the Anti-Saloon League occurred after 1900, a Prohibition party began fielding presidential candidates as early at 1872. During the group's early years it was strongest in New York and Ohio and sometimes (such as in the Cleveland-Blaine election of 1884) may have had considerable impact. The party reached its peak in 1892 when it garnered 264,133 votes; and, although the Prohibitionists have never broken into the Electoral College, they continue to try, the oldest and most indefatigable of all third parties. The problem they faced in the nineteenth century was that liquor reform often was a local or state issue not related to party and bipartisan support by contending forces frequently prevailed. Only in the early twentieth century (1916–1932) would prohibition become a matter of sufficient importance to gain major party and national attention at election time.

The Anti-Immigrant Movement

By 1900 recent immigrants constituted 40 percent of the population of America's twelve largest cities and another 20 percent were second generation. Between 1820 and 1930 three great migrations, each larger than the previous one, deposited thirty-seven and a half million people in the United States. The first two waves (1820–1860 and 1865–1890) came largely from northern and western Europe, the British Isles, Germany, and Scandinavia, but mixed in the second, and clearly dominating this flow of humanity after 1890, were many peoples from southern and eastern Europe—Italians, Poles, Bohemians, Slavs, and Russian Jews.

In the midst of strange and sometimes hostile surroundings, each new group sought to strengthen its more familiar institutions, especially religion, thus incurring even more hostility. And, in time, the antipathy toward new immigrants was shared both by native Americans and by old immigrants who had risen above the lowest rung of the industrial ladder and were no longer at the bottom of society. Respectable people, they said, lived in the better sections of town, had clean homes, did not frequent saloons and bawdy houses, led quiet and peaceful lives, did not consort with radicals and labor agitators, and never conversed in foreign tongues. Out of these differences arose a sense of innate Anglo-Saxon superiority and a fear that it might actually be endangered, a stream of proposals to exclude certain immigrants from America's shores, and an especially virulent strain of anti-Catholicism.

In an era when the sun never set on the British Empire, when the United States began to stretch from coast to coast and to covet overseas lands, and when a united Germany was beginning to flex its muscles, it was easy for some Americans to conclude that Anglo-Saxon peoples were destined to conquer the earth and to run it in an orderly fashion for the benefit of all mankind.

Josiah Strong (1847–1916), an Illinois-born minister, author, and social reformer, gave eloquent voice to these sentiments in 1885 in *Our Country: Its Future and Possible Crisis.* This volume, which had been a handbook for Congregational home missions, was revised by Strong into a sensational, even alarming, tract that sold over 500,000 copies. He called upon Protestant hosts to meet the "perils which threaten our Christian and American civilization" and demanded that public education become an arm of the Protestant church "because immorality is perilous to the state and morality cannot be secured without the sanctions of religion." In his view, a battle for civilization was already taking place in the American West with liquor, materialism, alien ideologies, and alien religious holding the initial advantages. A tall, vigorous, handsome man, Strong wrote enthusiastically of the "Anglo-Saxon mission," by which he clearly meant overt U.S. imperialism to cleanse the world of evil, un-American, un-Protestant tendencies. Catholics and immigrants, he argued, were dire threats to American life.

Even before Strong spoke out so firmly and eloquently, numerous individuals had begun to express concern that the nation and its culture were being overwhelmed by "inferior" immigrants. Contempt was mixed with fear as natives portrayed newcomers as breeders of crime, poverty, political corruption, and labor unrest. Strangely, one did not have to feel or even experience the

Courtesy New-York Historical Society, New York City.

Few minorities and ethnic groups were spared in this anti-immigrant cartoon. Note the anti-Catholicism in the depiction of the Pope and a pig-riding Irishman. Restrictionists who held that America sustained the world's rifraff and received nothing in return were incensed by liberal immigration policies.

alien presence in order to protest. Southerners who had seen few foreigners condemned conditions in northern cities, and scores of Americans who knew virtually nothing about the Mormons attacked their alien ways.

Francis Walker (1840–1897), superintendent of the census in 1870, an outstanding economist, and president of the Massachusetts Institute of Technology as it grew from one to four buildings, took a firm, anti-immigrant stand in 1892. The unfit of Europe, he said, were streaming across the Atlantic because of cheap transportation. This endangered the dominance of native Americans, Walker emphasized, because they were reducing their family size to compete with this tide of cheap labor rather than cutting their standards of living. In short, truly American society, a superior creation, was about to disappear under an alien flood superior only in numbers and nothing else.

To protect their way of life, in the late 1880s and early 1890s Americans began to experiment with restrictive measures. Although never so drastic or so intricate as those that white Southerners were designing at the time for black Americans, these proposals included strict enforcement of Prohibition, a quiet and sober Sabbath (not a time for feasting and relaxation in southern European style), literacy tests, and an end to the teaching of foreign languages in public schools. The great Prohibition battle, for example, pitted foreigner against native in state after state. Organized labor tried to restrict employment of foreigners as factory workers and, in time, used similar tactics to deny them white-collar jobs.

Yet these efforts all seemed to be after-the-fact measures; the only true solution was to deny entry to undesirable immigrants, despite the words shining forth from the great statue in New York harbor. In 1894 a group of New England leaders formed the Immigration Restriction League with Senator Henry Cabot Lodge of Massachusetts as its major spokesman. Joining with labor officials, the League lobbied for a literacy test for all new arrivals, a device that would keep out many southern and eastern Europeans. Between 1887 and 1917 such a bill was vetoed four times by Cleveland, Taft, and Wilson, but finally won approval during the hysteria of World War I. When the literacy test failed to have much effect, Congress finally adopted in the 1920s laws restricting the number of immigrants permitted to enter America each year.

There were, of course, those who opposed restriction. The business community, delighted with a steady supply of cheap labor, argued that the doors should be kept open to all. Immigrants through their various associations also fought the literacy test. Republican politicians, fully aware that after 1894 they received Italian, Slavic, and Jewish votes in urban areas, were reluctant to alienate this support. Although these forces could delay anti-immigrant legislation, as events demonstrated, with the onslaught of World War I they could no longer prevent it.

Anti-Catholicism

To a large degree, immigrant restriction was anti-Catholic in nature; or, to put the matter in proper perspective, the sudden flood of foreigners to America's shores, many of them devout Roman Catholics, reactivated an anti-Catholic bias long prevalent in an essentially Protestant culture. The battle line often was education. When priests proclaimed the need for parochial schools they reflected as well as stimulated sentiment within Catholic communities and also alarmed those interested in the general well-being of state-supported, public schools. Teaching of native languages in these private institutions and attempts to secure public funds for their support was nothing more, in Protestant eyes, than a blatant attack upon the bedrock of American patriotism, the classroom. During the late 1880s and early 1890s the struggle raged fiercely in various parts of New England and the Midwest. Massachusetts adopted public regulation of parochial schools, and in Ohio all students were required to attend public institutions. In Illinois and Wisconsin classroom instruction had to be in English, not German or some other foreign language prevalent in that region.

At about the same time (1887) a group of Iowans who felt threatened by Catholicism formed the American Protective Association (APA). This group, strangely enough, although clearly anti-immigrant in tone, enjoyed the wholehearted support of recent Protestant arrivals from northern Germany and Scandinavia. By 1893 the APA had only 70,000 members; but, fed by rumors that Catholics launched the depression of that year by making a run on banks in an effort to bankrupt the nation's economy, its ranks swelled enormously. During the first months of 1894 membership climbed to 500,000 as the group's influence spread rapidly from Iowa, Michigan, and Minnesota to western and eastern states.

To increase its strength, the APA allied itself with the Republican party in most regions, stirred up latent fears of popery in America, attacked Catholic influence in schools, and even circulated a bogus encyclical stating that 700,000 Catholics were organized into paramilitary units in various cities, ready to launch an all-out attack upon unsuspecting Protestants when the word was given. This weird brand of nativism gone amuck, a depression-fed movement, was generally forgotten in the free-silver agitation that followed. Nevertheless, both the Populist and the Democratic national campaigns of 1896 and 1900 carried ominous overtones of nativism, American Protestantism, and even of anti-Semitism, all essentially a rural reaction to the fast-changing urban scene. A half century later one could still hear tales of vast stores of arms secreted away in Catholic churches in preparation for the great "takeover" of American life. If this were not so, why did Catholics persist in building such big, fortresslike houses of worship? Catholics often countered this absurd charge with strong denials and yet another question. Their churches were always open to the public, while those of the Protestants were tightly locked much of the time. Why? What did the Protestants have to hide?

An Emerging New Order

Although temperance, religion, immigrants, and free silver captured headlines and occupied much of the attention of both voters and politicians in the closing years of the nineteenth century, these matters actually were relics and symbols of the past. In response to industrialization and urbanization a new order was taking shape, one that would guide and transform America. Elements of this complex structure included a new middle class with deep faith in specialization, professional training, higher education, and scientific management. Under the banner of progress and reform, a new bureaucracy appeared in city, state, and federal governments and in business offices as well; and women began to assume much more important roles in all phases of U.S. life. This same urge for reform relegated blacks to a special place outside of the new order although similar trends—specialization, professionalism, emphasis upon higher education, and strength through association—were evident in the black community. Far fewer individuals were involved, but considering the hurdles erected by American whites of those years, black progress was phenomenal. It was obvious to the most perceptive among both races that disfranchisement and segregation were stopgap, short-term measures. American society needed the black worker and to make him useful he had to be given some training and education. Once the faucet of knowledge was turned on one could neither turn it off nor direct the flow. This applied to millions of other Americans as well, regardless of skin color, sex, religion, and place of birth.

A New Middle Class

Just as important social trends of the 1880s and 1890s were obscured by noisy issues and went largely unnoticed, so did the development of a new middle class. It became a recognized class only in retrospect as historians were hard pressed to explain what happened in America during those decades. Now, it is apparent that two recognizable groups were emerging: professionals in their chosen areas such as medicine, law, economics, architecture, and social work; and a similar body of specialists in business, labor, and agriculture who were beginning to stress their distinctive roles and develop ties to others in the same general fields. Beginning in the 1870s a series of professional societies came into being such as the Public Health Association (1872), the American Library Association (1876), the American Bar Association (1878), the American Historical Association (1884), the American Economic Association (1885), and the American Political Science Association (1887).

More spectacular perhaps but part of the same general pattern were changes occurring in higher education. Technical and scientific courses, a necessity in an industrial age, had begun to reshape college curricula even before 1860. The Morrill Act of 1862 laid the groundwork for the new prominence of state universities (many of them labeled agricultural and mechanical colleges for several decades); and three years later the Massachusetts Institute of Technology opened its doors. Two basic principles that transformed American academic life during the next quarter century—elective courses of study and graduate work—had been pioneered by Thomas Jefferson's University of Virginia in 1825, but for some forty or fifty years most other institutions of higher learning continued to cling to rigid, mandatory programs and to ignore comprehensive plans for postgraduate work.

A magnificient, no-strings-attached bequest of Baltimore & Ohio railroad stock by the will of Johns Hopkins, probated in 1875, finally provided the impetus for modern graduate study. Although Yale granted the nation's first doctorate in 1861 and that institution, Harvard, Cornell, and Michigan were all struggling with problems posed by undergraduate and graduate study, it was Johns Hopkins University, which opened its door in Baltimore in 1876, that breathed new vigor into America's academic world.

Under the guidance of Daniel C. Gilman (1831–1908), president of Johns Hopkins from 1875 to 1901 and also the first president of the University of California (1870–1875), Johns Hopkins became a "faculty-centered" institution with money, facilities, able students, and milieu in which serious research was encouraged and promoted. Ironically, Gilman, who had fled from California because of fears that Grangers might "democratize" his fledgling school, was never quite happy with the word "research," even though his entire program was geared to that pursuit. By the turn of the century virtually all institutions of higher learning had copied much from the Johns Hopkins experiment and several other institutions—Harvard, Yale, Michigan, and Cornell, to name a few—were no longer merely undergraduate schools with a struggling medical or law school attached but true multipurpose universities.

Scientific Management

Modern industrial complexities gave birth to the specialty of scientific management, first systematized in the 1890s by Frederick W. Taylor (1856–1915), an engineer. Taylor sought the greatest output from workers with the least waste and cost. To him, scientific management was an interlocking pattern of rigid rules. Only a decade or so later did others revise his strict schemes to accommodate them to the attitudes and needs of various groups of workers and to particular products. As Taylor's scientific management techniques and as new sources of energy (especially electricity) were applied to more and more industries, production soared, increasing by 76 percent between 1899 and 1909. During that same decade the American labor force rose by only 40 percent.

Not everybody was wholly satisfied with conditions created by large-scale production and scientific management, but virtually everyone thought increased output would decrease poverty. They also agreed that the art of government had failed to keep pace with rapid changes occurring in industry. Their answer was to apply the same techniques of scientific management to public affairs by creating a blinding whirlwind of departments, commissions, boards, and agencies which, in the end, produced a bureaucracy that often seemed neither scientific nor manageable. And, even more regretably, it actually tended to increase at all levels the distance between the individual citizen and his so-called "public servants."

Bureaucracy

A bureaucracy consists of the machinery and the personnel that run an organization. The word apparently comes from a piece of woolen cloth ("burel") which the French used to cover writing desks, thus a group of desks became a bureau. Whether one is speaking in praise or criticism of a bureaucracy, it typically exhibits these features: a fixed jurisdiction, the authority to give orders limited to specific purposes, a more or less stable structure independent of the lives of its workers who possess (under ideal circumstances) expert knowledge and special skills, and much letter writing and recordkeeping.

Modern bureaucracy is tied to the rise of the new middle class and the concern for order and efficiency. Although bureaucratic ways have crept into business practices, a government bureaucracy is sustained, of course, by taxation and the rule of law. All twentieth century societies, regardless of their political views, have created a type of manager or bureaucrat who has the ability, or at least authority, to run the departments and agencies that modern life seems to require.

More than anything else, the bureaucratic approach to problems was concerned with what citizens were doing and how they were doing it. Moral teachings had no part to play in these new surroundings; only the social behavior of individuals deserved analysis and attention. In the 1890s urban reformers talked much about "good" citizens, "honest" men, and "good" laws; twenty years later the National Municipal League was urging the adoption of plans to harness urban energies to serve fluctuating needs. A "plan," it seemed, organized according to recognized rules and carried out by a functioning bureaucracy, presumably could work wonders. The administration of government at every level by complex formulas had become the key to progress and change, not the election of "good" men to replace those who were "evil."

Women's Rights

During the final decades of the nineteenth century, women made some modest gains in their struggle to participate in American public life; more important, however, were more fundamental changes occurring in education and in the attitude of the general public toward the activities of less radical feminists. By 1890, 80 percent of all colleges were coeducational, and two competing suffrage groups had merged into the National American Women's Suffrage Association (NAWSA). A few western territories had enfranchised women, usually in an effort to increase the "stable" vote of their electorate, and when Wyoming entered the Union in 1890, its women became the first to vote in national elections.

Between 1888 and 1897 three important bodies came into being which drew less adventurous and more conservative women into public affairs: the National Council of Women, the General Federation of Women's

Clubs, and the National Congress of Parents and Teachers. By 1900 the General Federation of Women's Clubs (GFWC) had 150,000 members who were using their influence to effect civic reforms, especially those involved with child welfare, education, and sanitation, and in 1914 the GFWC endorsed woman suffrage, admitting that it was, in fact, a feminist organization concerned with all reforms thought beneficial to women. Yet the most powerful women's group of those years was the WCTU. Even the Daughters of the American Revolution, formed in 1890, took a mild reform stance during the first twenty years of its existence.

The emergence of these organizations paralleled the rise of professional associations and service clubs among men, but they were, in essence, a response to quite different problems. More women were working outside of their homes and more of them were going to college. By 1890 they constituted one-sixth of the work force and very shortly 35 to 40 percent of all professional workers were women; by 1920 the majority of college undergraduates were women.

All working women, whether teachers, clerks, or secretaries, shared common problems such as unequal pay for work equal to that done by their male counterparts and other forms of job discrimination. Since unions took little interest in the welfare of women, they banded together in both general and specific groups in order to better their lot. Although these associations sometimes fought for the welfare of the most menial workers, leadership tended to come from the ranks of the middle class and even of the well-to-do or affluent. Increasing wealth and expanding higher education created a large class of women who had the spare time to do volunteer work; and, naturally enough, they pursued goals appropriate to their special interests.

By no means all of these women were suffragettes, but as they were exposed to public affairs they became much more sympathetic to NAWSA's ideals and goals. Many of those advocating social reforms became convinced that only with the help of the ballot could they succeed and others believed that denial of the vote on the basis of sex was an insult. Regardless of the merits of such arguments, by 1912 the women's suffrage movement was becoming much more militant and by that date—thanks to the developments of the past two decades—enjoyed the sympathy, if not the overt approval, of more Americans than ever before.

Black Progress

Although not part of the new order, which white Americans often perverted during the post-Civil War years to mean disfranchisement and segregation, black Americans were able to make substantial progress. By the turn of the century, two distinct schools of thought had gradually developed among their leaders. One group, led by Booker T. Washington, advocated pragmatic accommodation to the new order and realistic training of black youth for jobs they could get within it. For the most part, this meant no great leap forward but at least a step upward by means of a basic education stressing fundamental skills, manual trades, and scientific farming. These programs, developed at Washington's Tuskegee Institute in Alabama, and at his alma mater, Hampton Institute in Virginia, were typical of black education of those years. Although Washington never made his ultimate goals entirely clear, his critics feared that this accommodation might become an end in itself, thus relegating educated blacks to a place among the lower levels of the nation's work force.

The leader of the opposing school of thought was William E. B. DuBois (1868–1963), a native of Massachusetts who received his doctorate from Harvard University in 1895, writing his dissertation on suppression of the slave trade. DuBois, who taught at Atlanta University for a decade or so, believed that blacks had to prepare themselves to be much more than farmers, maids, and factory workers. If they did not, such would always be their fate. Shortly after 1900, DuBois and twenty-eight other black men formed the Niagara Movement to fight for civil rights, which developed in 1909 into the National Association for the Advancement of Colored People (NAACP). In 1910 DuBois became that group's director of publicity and research and, as editor of its official organ, *Crisis,* began to wield considerable influence. During the decades that followed he published essays, editorials, sketches, and novels, all designed to aid the cause of the black man in America.

However, the careers of both Washington and Dubois were far from typical. A mere handful of blacks were going to college and, as late as 1920 only three black institutions, Fisk University in Nashville, Lincoln University in Pennsylvania, and Howard University in the nation's capital, were offering college-level work. Laboring under legal and social restrictions imposed by Jim Crow laws and sanctioned by a white mentality for at

Historical Pictures Service.

William E. B. DuBois in the office of **Crisis.**

least three decades between 1900 and 1930, many blacks rarely publicly questioned such inequities.

No one could have predicted the responses of blacks, women, immigrants, and businessmen—or of *all* Americans—to changes wrought by a new urban-industrial order. True, various European nations were experiencing similar trends, but none in the setting of a vast landscape, a flood of foreign immigration, and a mosaic of tensions created by racial, religious, and regional differences. Misled by those who yelled the loudest, historians long have stressed the battle to curb corporations, when, in fact, most Americans were trying to cope with all of the ramifications of industrialization. Strangely, reform, was often led by the well-to-do, who needed it the least, and was occasionally resented by urban masses, who presumably would have benefited most. Perhaps a key to comprehending the nature of this general response to the new way of life created by factories, railroads, and cities is to visualize how various groups perceived what was happening to them at the time. That their analyses of events were often dead wrong seems obvious today, but no one can doubt the sincerity of their outcries or the depths of their discomfort as the world about them was transformed by forces beyond their control.

Essay

Florence Kelley, Ralph Nader, and the American Consumer

Florence Kelley (1859–1932), an indefatigable social worker who left a solid imprint upon American life, and Ralph Nader, born two years after her death, have much in common. Both grew up in politically active households, attended good schools, earned law degrees (although Nader subsequently referred to his alma mater, Harvard Law School, as "a high-priced tool factory"), became outraged by inequities created by mass industrialization, and essentially as lone crusaders set out to indict before the consuming public those guilty of "high crimes" committed in the name of profit. Florence Kelley was a dynamic, outspoken, dedicated individual who, for the most part, led a Spartan personal life, and Ralph Nader is apparently cast from a similar mold.

But there similarities end. Kelley's prime interest was how women, children, and blacks worked and lived in urban centers, especially those involved with the textile trade. The National Consumers' League, which she headed for nearly three decades, tried to arouse the concern of the buying public for such things as the wages, hours, and work, and the working and living conditions of those who made what they bought. By contrast, Nader is primarily interested in how giant corporations treat their customers. His goal, he concedes, is nothing less than "qualitative reform of the industrial revolution."

In short, Kelley wanted to use the consumer to improve the plight of labor; Nader, apparently convinced that labor is now strong enough to look out for itself, seeks to better the lot of a disorganized (and often disinterested) public. If nothing else, this indicates that the reform movements of the muckracking era registered some positive gains, however small they may have appeared at times.

Chicago Tribune.

Florence Kelley.

The daughter of a family of Philadelphia Quakers, Florence Kelley was educated at Cornell and in Europe. In 1884 she married Lazare Wischnewetsky, a Polish-German physician. After living on the Continent for two years, the couple and their first born came to America, but five years and two children later, Florence divorced Lazare, and she and their offspring took her maiden name.

That same year (1891) Florence Kelley joined the famous Hull House movement in Chicago and, while doing a survey of slums, became interested in child labor and immigrant problems.

Meanwhile, she studied law at Northwestern University and was admitted to the bar in 1895. Her work (and that of others) led in 1893 to a factory-workshop law in Illinois which limited women to an eight-hour day and created the position of factory inspector. Governor John P. Altgeld promptly named Florence Kelley to this post; and, in this capacity, she published four frank reports that shocked those who read them.

In 1899, Florence Kelley moved to New York City to head the National Consumers' League. For a quarter of a century she attended the national conferences, spoke, lectured, and scolded, all in an effort to get laws that would aid the working woman and create a sense of common responsibility for labor conditions prevalent throughout the United States. She was especially scornful of child labor, piecework done at home and not in factories, and fraudulent labels found in clothing, all of which added up to sweatshop conditions. A vigorous lady with a rich, commanding voice, one of her greatest successes—with the able assistance of her good friend and companion, Lillian Wald—was the establishment in 1912 of the U.S. Children's Bureau, a federal agency designed to draw attention of the government at the national level to the special needs of young people.

Ralph Nader, a tall, dark-haired bachelor, was born in the little town of Winsted, Connecticut, in 1934. His Lebanese parents had arrived in America nine years earlier and soon began operating a bakery and restaurant. With the aid of scholarships, young Nader attended Gilbert School in Winsted, Princeton, and Harvard. As a law student at Cambridge, he became especially interested in auto safety, research that led to his first major success in the field of reform.

Following a brief stint in the U.S. Army and a fling at law and teaching, Nader became a consultant to Daniel P. Moynihan in 1964, then an assistant secretary of labor. Together with Connecticut's Senator Abraham Ribicoff, they orchestrated a campaign that culminated in the National Traffic and Motor Vehicle Safety Act of 1966. This legislation was aided considerably by Nader's bestseller entitled *Unsafe at Any Speed,* published the previous year. Although this was a general attack on Detroit for its ability to forsake passenger safety for profits, the book zeroed in on a small compact produced by General Motors. That huge corporation, in turn, harassed young Nader with detectives, phone calls, and women, and eventually its president apologized publicly before a Senate committee for such unseemly and ridiculous conduct.

In addition to auto safety, Nader and his army of young lawyers, college students, and aroused citizens ("Nader's Raiders") have investigated working conditions in the nation's mines, the difficulties of Indians, the widespread use of x-ray

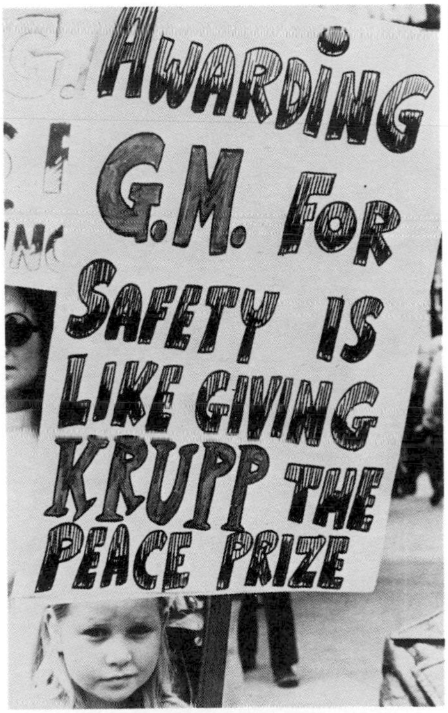

Wide World.

"Nader's Raiders" picketed the St. Francis Hotel in San Francisco on July 17, 1972 in protest when General Motors President Edward Cole received the first annual Excalibur Award for "outstanding contribution to automotive safety."

Wide World.

Ralph Nader joined teenage girls who testified before the Senate Special Committee on Aging. The girls inspected nursing homes and found conditions "horrifying, disillusioning, heart-breaking, and totally inexcusable."

machines by dentists, and meatpacking practices. Today, Nader heads a network of consumer-oriented research groups, all ploughing forward on shoestring budgets, but churning out scores of books, reports, articles, and statistical summaries designed to prod into action both the Congress and the voter.

These diverse operations are often criticized by Nader's critics. They say he has spread himself "too thin," that he is tilting at too many windmills. And Nader himself confesses to some frustration and disappointment. For example, his scheme in 1972 to publish extensive profiles of every member of Congress ended in near chaos; nevertheless, out of a great mound of research, inept planning, constantly revised schedules, and frayed nerves, there emerged at least one incisive book on the workings of our national legislature. This alone made the project worthwhile.

This man's reform efforts, unlike those of Florence Kelley and other socially conscious Americans of the early twentieth century, seem to have hit upon a formula for permanence which may make Ralph Nader a force to be reckoned with for years to come. His goals are less specific than theirs, more generalized and far more sweeping in nature; also, scores of battles are being waged by Nader and his associates at the same time. Because of his innate integrity and utter dedication to principle, Nader always can count upon recurring waves of college students and recent law graduates eager to go forth under his banner. Recruitment presents few problems.

The basic reasons for this widespread appeal are obvious. Nader offices may be pandemonium much of the time but successful alumni usually get excellent jobs, and in the meantime the work is fast paced and exciting.

The careers of Florence Kelley and Ralph Nader reflect the substantial changes that have occurred in our nation in recent decades, changes reminiscent of the abolition movement of the mid-1800s. The men and women who spearheaded that remarkable reform campaign soon learned that work at the grassroots level, although both helpful and necessary, was not the answer. In the pattern of nineteenth century reformers, Kelley labored in New York and Chicago at the local and state levels.

But almost from the beginning, Nader has centered the activities of his group in Washington because that is where the action is. Scores of workers who man the bastions of his low-rent think tank can easily charge up to Capitol Hill to accost congressmen or scurry about town to beard lobbyists and bureaucrats. Armed with facts, computer printouts, and the support of outraged consumers, they have become an established factor on the national scene. Perhaps, just perhaps, reform in America has become an ongoing entity and is no longer a hot-cold, on-and-off crusade given to spasms of frantic activity intermingled with decades of torpid lethargy.

Selected Readings

General Studies

Samuel P. Hays, *The Response to Industrialism, 1885–1914* (1957)

Richard Hofstadter, *The Age of Reform* (1955)

Social Responses to Change

Harry Elmer Barnes, *Society in Transition: Problems of a Changing Age* (1952)

Gilbert Seldes, *The Stammering Century* (1965)

Lawrence A. Cremin, *The Transformation of the School: Progressivism in American Education, 1876–1957* (1961)

Political Responses to Change

Robert W. Wiebe, *The Search for Order, 1877–1920* (1967)

Blacks and the "Color Line"

Seth Scheiner, *Negro Mecca: A History of the Negro in New York City, 1865–1920* (1965)

Rayford Logan, *The Betrayal of the Negro: From Rutherford B. Hayes to Woodrow Wilson* (1972)

C. Vann Woodward, *The Strange Career of Jim Crow* (1974)

Middle Class Responses to Change

Michael B. Katz, *Class, Bureaucracy, and the Schools: The Illusion of Educational Change in America* (1972)

Arthur Mann, *Yankee Reformers in the Urban Age* (1954)

Robert Green McCloskey, *American Conservatism in the Age of Enterprise: A Study of William Graham Sumner, Stephen J. Field, and Andrew Carnegie* (1951)

Stephan Thernstrom, *The Other Bostonians: Poverty and Progress in the American Metropolis, 1880–1970* (1973)

Morton and Lucia White, *The Intellectual versus the City, From Thomas Jefferson to Frank Lloyd Wright* (1962)

Labor and Agriculture

Robert V. Bruce, *1877: Year of Violence* (1970)

Foster Rhea Dulles, *Labor in America: A History* (1949)

Ray Ginger, *Altgeld's America. The Lincoln Ideal versus Changing Realities* (1958)

Grant McConnell, *The Decline of Agrarian Democracy* (1969)

Religion

C. Howard Hopkins, *The Rise of the Social Gospel in American Protestantism, 1865–1915* (1967)

Henry F. May, *Protestant Churches and Industrial America* (1967)

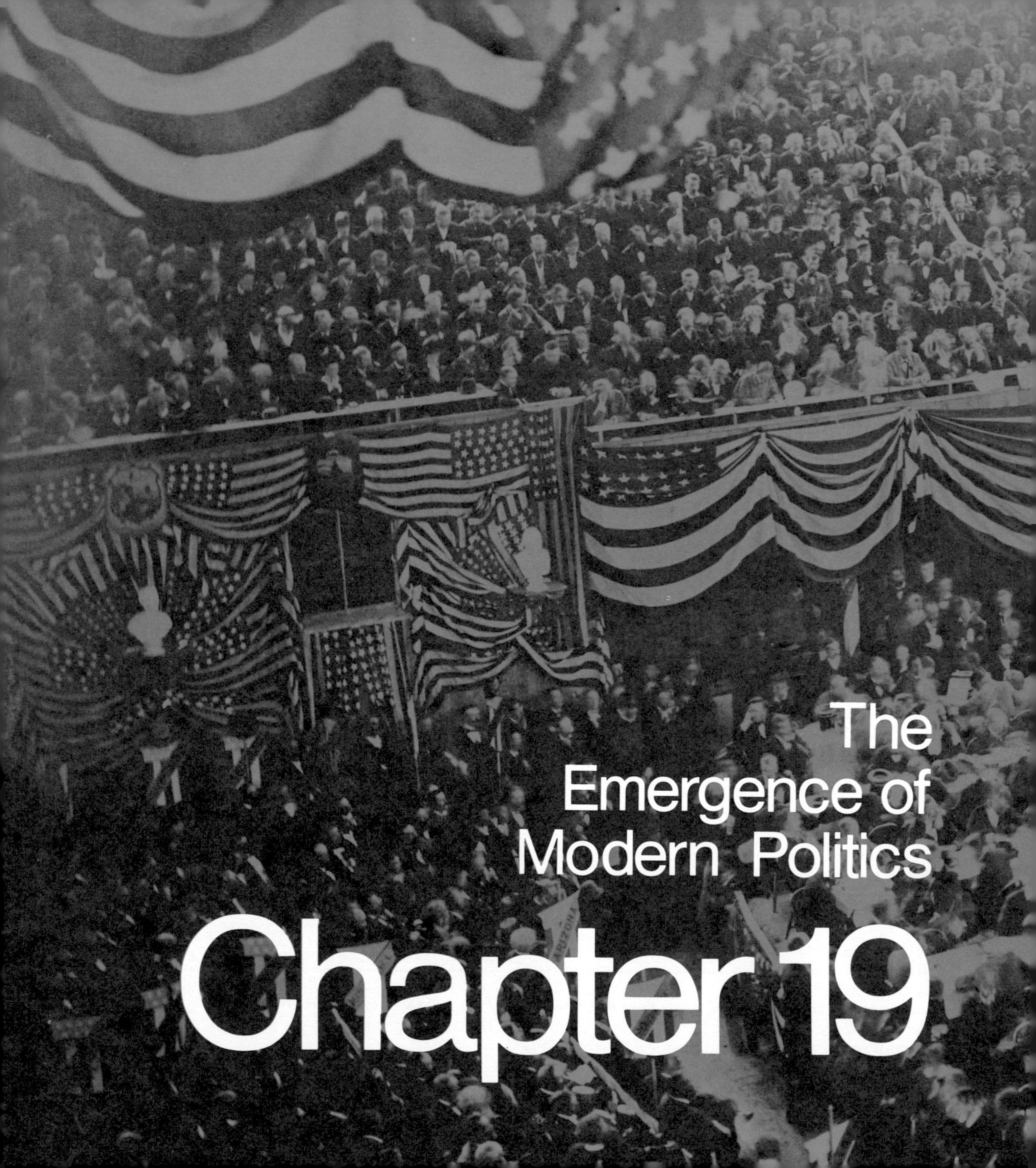

Chapter 19

The Emergence of Modern Politics

TIMELINE

1875
Resumption Act begins a period of deflation

1878
Bland-Allison Act authorizes limited coinage of silver

1880
James A. Garfield wins presidential election

1881
Garfield's assassination elevates Chester A. Arthur to presidency

1883
Pendleton Act establishes federal civil service

1884
Grover Cleveland wins presidential contest against James G. Blaine

1888
Benjamin Harrison defeats Cleveland for reelection

1889
Omnibus Bill authorizes statehood for the Dakotas, Montana, and Washington

1890
Henry Cabot Lodge proposes Force Bill

1890
Sherman Silver Purchase Act expands government purchase of silver

1890
Wyoming and Idaho become states

1890
Billion Dollar Congress convenes

1890
McKinley Tariff

1890
Mississippi rewrites election laws to exclude black voters

1892
Populist party adopts Omaha platform

1892
Cleveland defeats Harrison for reelection and Populist party wins 22 electoral votes

1893
Cleveland secures repeal of the Sherman Silver Purchase Act

1896
William McKinley defeats William Jennings Bryan for President

1896
Utah becomes a state

1897
Dingley Tariff increases tariff duties

1900
Gold Standard Act declares gold dollar as monetary standard

CHAPTER OUTLINE

The so-called "Compromise of 1877" is a true turning point in U.S. life. For reasons most Americans can appreciate and understand, their leaders rejected force and, after two decades of war and upheaval, returned to the political process as a means of settling disputes. The end of Reconstruction, however, deprived both Republicans and Democrats of basic platform planks, and for two decades neither party was able to create a stable majority. As a result, presidential elections were close affairs, with issues often murky and vague. The Republicans usually captured the White House, and this accomplishment has obscured the true weakness of their young party. Between 1874 and 1892, for example, the Democrats enjoyed sizable majorities in the House of Representatives; only on two occasions (in 1880 and again in 1888) could their opponents eke out slim margins, each time by fewer than ten seats.

This instability paved the way for numerous factors to exert unusual influence in the political realm from 1877 to 1900. These included big businesses such as railroads, local matters that otherwise would have been of little consequence, city machines often more potent than entire states, and third-party efforts tied to specific appeals that sometimes ignored geographical, political, and class boundaries. In a sense, this dilemma was the creation of the Republicans, for their success invited imitators to try to do the same. They had demonstrated how a group of insurgents could use a single reform (abolition) to form a new party and mount a successful challenge to the status quo. Their basic problem during these decades was what to do for an encore. How could they create an ascendant majority when their opponents had innumerable grassroots ties that they lacked? And, what issues could be developed to appeal to a sprawling, diverse, rapidly changing population?

By the mid-1890s the Republicans were on their way to effective answers that would cast a long shadow into the twentieth century. How had they done it? It was by making better use of the general cry for reform than their opponents and especially by espousing order and efficiency in government, a tactic that elicited the support of businessmen and a growing middle class. Perhaps one key to victory was an ability to think and act in *national* terms. But more than anything else, the Republicans projected the image of prosperity and economic expansion and pinned their hopes to a rising industrial America. This was, of course, the victory of Alexander Hamilton's ideas over those of Thomas Jefferson.

Many textbooks depict the Republican party of the late nineteenth century as the plaything of railroad magnates and oil tycoons, but by the 1890s the voters saw things differently. Although it was the party of wealth and respectability that had saved the Union in its darkest hour, it also represented progress, reform, prosperity, and national authority. During the previous two or three decades politicians struggled with limited success to make issues meaningful, and they developed numerous coalitions at all levels of government in a near-futile

Library of Congress.

Judge expressed obvious doubts about a Populist-Democratic coalition forged from a grass roots constituency. This cynical cartoon reveals the Illinois-based magazine's strong Republican inclinations.

effort to bestow meaning and identity upon their party. This battle, marked by an upsurge in congressional authority amid one-term Presidents and considerable economic unrest, eventually gave birth to our modern political system: two major parties jockeying for power, each quick to exploit all situations or proposals that elicited voter response and each deft at smothering in an embrace any third force that rose up to challenge their joint dominance of the political arena.

The Search for Identity

Once the Civil War and Reconstruction receded into the background, what Republicans and Democrats actually stood for was unclear to many voters and apparently to their elected representatives as well. For some years, in the South at least, this confusion was compounded by the reluctance of Old Whigs even to call themselves Democrats; instead they adopted the euphemism "Conservative." In the election of 1872, for example, voters throughout the nation could choose among electors pledged to candidates nominated by Democrats, Straight Democrats, and Independent Democrats. Also, one should keep in mind that the electorate of those decades had seen so many political groups come and go that to them a multiparty spectrum may well have seemed quite normal.

Major Issues of the Gilded Age

In this era of indecision and confusing party labels, local, state, and regional concerns often loomed large and specific issues, fanned by politicians themselves, enjoyed undeserved prominence. Such matters include civil service reform, tariffs, fiscal policies, and (at the local level) prohibition.

To some extent, those who were preaching reform were persons who were thwarted in their attempts to use the spoils system to their advantage. This was especially true of men and women formerly employed at every level of government. Simply put, the "outs" wanted "in." The morality and Puritan virtue of men such as Charles Eliot Norton who helped found the *Nation* in 1865 are unquestioned, but their zeal for change often arose from an inability to adjust to the business-industrial world of the late nineteenth century. Even Charles Francis Adams, Jr., bearer of a prestigious name and descendant of two Presidents, in 1869 could pull none of the traditional strings in Washington which previously had worked wonders for New England aristocrats with proper credentials. He and others like him decided to change a system upon which they could not work their will.

At the close of the Civil War the federal bureaucracy consisted of seven departments employing 53,000 individuals who received $30 million in annual salaries. The Post Office, with outlets in nearly every village throughout the land, employed more than half of these civil servants. The Treasury with its large central office and customhouses and agents at various ports and the Interior Department (which controlled lands, patents, pensions, and Indians) were somewhat smaller. War, Navy, State, and Justice had even less significant payrolls and less patronage to dispense.

The spoils system, to which most Washington workers and various employees in state and local offices owed their livelihood, was widely entrenched everywhere. Frequent elections often produced turnovers in personnel, but the system rested upon three basic principles well understood by all: appointments that enabled a mayor, governor, or party regular to build up a coterie of loyal workers (a "machine"); appointments made as a result of congressional pressure; and, because of decisions at the ballot box, rotation of officeholders. In a sense, the Civil War contributed in two ways to the downfall of this system. That conflict exposed its deficiencies and also created a band of "outs" bent upon reform so they could get "in."

Although the Grant administration was much maligned by Norton, Adams, and their friends and historians have perpetuated the picture they painted, the first competitive examinations for civil service positions were held in the Treasury Department in the early 1870s. And the administration of the New York Customhouse, scene of fraud, waste, and incompetence in the 1860s, improved markedly after Chester A. Arthur took over in 1871. It is quite possible, however, that Arthur, a spoilsman of the Roscoe Conkling machine, was kept honest by frequent investigations.

One solid achievement of reformers during these years was the abolition of the moiety system. When a shipment of goods was confiscated, one half (a "moiety") went to the federal government, one quarter to the informer and the rest was divided among various port authorities to encourage employees to uncover fraud. Abuse of this practice caused numerous protests, and in June 1874 it was outlawed by congressional action. Although the bill ending the moiety system also raised collectors' salaries, it is estimated that Arthur's annual income dropped from $56,000 to $12,000. Merchant reformers, eager to be sure that customhouses operated smoothly and efficiently, were largely responsible for this change, a giant step toward significant civil service reform.

Under President Hayes, reform of the notorious New York Customhouse went even further. Hayes decided to attack the Conkling machine (a Republican organization that failed to deliver its electoral votes in 1876) by attempting to remove Arthur. Eventually Hayes prevailed. In very blunt terms, the President told Arthur's successor to conduct the office on sound business principles and according to rules laid down during Grant's administration. "Neither my recommendation," Hayes declared, "nor Secretary Sherman's, nor that of any influential member of Congress, or other influential persons should be especially regarded. . . . Let no man be put out merely because he is Mr. Arthur's friend, and no man put in merely because he is our friend."

Similar improvements were made in the New York Post Office, apparently a nest of drunkenness, neglect, confusion, and incompetence until a Conkling appointee, Thomas L. James, in 1873 decided to set up his own civil service. By 1880, the volume of mail had increased by one-third, yet it was being delivered for $10,000 less, and both collections and deliveries had increased substantially. Nevertheless, these were only two efforts at civil service reform at two highly visible centers; elsewhere, despite the cries of reformers, all too often it was "business as usual." A general awareness existed that change was necessary at all levels of government, but only the assassination of a President and the emergence of Chester A. Arthur (of all people) as his successor made true civil service reform possible.

The campaign of Republican Hayes against the Republican machine that dominated New York state politics illustrates some of the confusion of this era. The party was a mixture of conservatives and liberals espousing various programs (as are most political parties), but in these decades of close election returns, the actions of a few could have dramatic impact. In three presidential canvasses of these years, the popular vote margin between the nominees of the two major parties was less than one percent. Throughout much of the period the Republicans' hold on the White House depended upon hard-won victories in such key states as Indiana and New York. Not once did they win a plurality of counties throughout the nation as a whole.

Library of Congress.

The stern, upright countenance of Rutherford B. Hayes belies his means to victory in 1876. His Republican supporters gained him the White House through fraud, intimidation, and compromise.

At times a Republican politician's conservative-liberal alignment was expressed in terms such as Stalwart, Half-Breed, and Mugwump. Stalwarts were down-the-line party men convinced that only the political organization that "saved the Union" was qualified to govern the nation. Half-Breeds, as the name suggests, straddled ideological boundaries and were somewhat more liberal, and the Mugwumps of 1884 deserted the party on the reform issue and went over to the enemy.

In 1880 the faction-ridden Republican party, really a grouping of congressional prima donnas with their troupes of lackeys, finally nominated James A. Garfield of Ohio, a man not closely associated with any wing but a Blaine partisan. To placate Blaine's arch rival, Conkling, who had fought hard to get U.S. Grant nominated for a third term, Chester A. Arthur of New York Customhouse fame became Garfield's running mate. Garfield won in a very close race (by fewer than 4,000 votes out of nearly nine million cast) with Winfield Scott Hancock, a nonpolitical Civil War general. This election is memorable mainly for the absence of issues and Arthur's brutal campaign as New York State Chairman to extort money from every Republican appointee down to the lowest postmaster. Even the night watchman at Albany's new capitol building, lighthouse keepers, and ship stewards all received a stern letter from Chester ordering them to remit 3 percent of their annual salary "for the good of the party." And these efforts paid off.

Within days of taking office, however, Garfield, a rather timid man, was in over his head. Overwhelmed by hordes of zealous officeseekers, he once expressed amazement that anyone wanted to be President. To add to his troubles, after reaching some sort of an agreement with Conkling, Arthur & Co. during the campaign, he antagonized the New York group by naming Blaine Secretary of State and appointing a non-Conkling man as collector for the Port of New York. In the midst of this furor, on July 2, 1881, a mentally unbalanced officeseeker named Charles J. Guiteau shot Garfield, shouting, "I am a Stalwart and Arthur is now President!" This boast was a bit premature since Garfield rallied and seemed to be on the road to recovery, but on September 19 he succumbed to his wounds and Chester A. Arthur, a Conkling ally, was President of the United States.

Reformers were horrified by this turn of events, but Arthur, an urbane man with considerable ability, rose to the challenge and gave the country a reasonably good administration. He did not bow to Conkling's dictates, supported civil service reform, prosecuted Post Office fraud, laid the foundations of a modern navy, and tried unsuccessfully to check congressional spending for unnecessary public works and to reduce the tariff. Also, with the aid of Tiffany's of New York he refurbished the White House in a rather grand manner.

The most important legislation of his three-year term was the Pendleton Civil Service Act (1883). Guiteau's shots more than anything else gave reformers the votes they needed in Congress to create a three-member commission to administer competitive examinations for federal jobs. This act also prohibited levying campaign assessments upon federal officeholders and protected those who refused to contribute if asked to do so. At first only the lowest employees were protected by civil service regulations, but the President was given the power to extend the classified list, which Arthur and his successors chose to do. By the end of the century 40 percent of all federal positions were governed by the Civil Service Commission.

Library of Congress.

James Gillespie Blaine (1830–1893)

One of the giants in an age of political stalemate, James G. Blaine was born in Pennsylvania, graduated in 1847 from what is now Washington and Jefferson College, and for six years taught school, first in Kentucky and then back in his home state where he also studied law. While in Kentucky he secretly married in 1850 a Massachusetts girl, Harriet Stanwood, also a teacher. To make certain everything was legal, they were married a second time in Pittsburgh a year later. Because her family had business connections in Maine which looked promising, they moved in 1854 to Augusta, the capital city, where Blaine made the *Kennebec Journal* into an organ for the new Republican party. His gracious home, located next to Maine's capitol building, later became the traditional residence of that state's governors.

A stalwart figure of a man, a persuasive orator, and an individual possessing great personal charm, he rose quickly through the Maine legislature to the U.S. House of Representatives where he served from 1862 to 1876 and then went on to a seat in the Senate. As such, he became a power in the Republican ascendancy, holding the position of Speaker of the House during some of these years. A loyal Republican but not an extreme Radical, he became leader of the so-called Half-Breeds and prime contender for his party's presidential nomination for the next two decades. Generally direct and forthright in his political dealings, he was nevertheless a true political boss of his age and never explained fully his dealings with land-grant railroads. Unfortunately for him, the only time that he actually won a place on the presidential ticket, these suspicions of graft cost him the support of the Mugwumps of his party in 1884 and contributed directly to Cleveland's victory.

For all of Blaine's activity as politician, his fame actually rests upon his role in foreign affairs. As Secretary of State in 1881 and again under President Harrison, he tried to develop concern for Latin American nations and to make the Monroe Doctrine less unilateral in its interpretation. He also took steps to gain U.S. sovereignty over the Ithmus of Panama and served in 1889 as the chairman of the first Pan-American Conference, which was held in Washington. In many ways Blaine's vision of "America for Americans" predates some of the policies enunicated by Theodore Roosevelt a decade or so later. From the days of William Seward to the time of John Hay, he stands alone as the only public figure with any consistent interest in and understanding of foreign relations. ■

A POPULAR MELODY APPLIED.
RC
We never speak as we pass by,
Altho' a tear bedims her eye; * * *
The spell is past, the dream is o'er,
And tho' we meet, we love no more!

Chester A. Arthur and Roscoe Conkling were the best of friends until Arthur became President. When Arthur decided he no longer needed Conkling and tried to limit the corruption and questionable patronage deals of earlier days, a break between the two men became inevitable.

In almost any political campaign there are disgruntled individuals who vow they will bolt the party and go their own way. Rarely do they actually carry out their threats on election day, and even more rarely has it made much difference if they did. But 1884 was an exception. James G. Blaine, dubbed on some occasions "the Continental Liar from the State of Maine" (though he was born in Pennsylvania) and on others "the Plumed Knight," was the Republican nominee. His opponent was Grover Cleveland, a politician from Buffalo, New York, with a reputation that held special appeal for reformers. Unique among presidential contenders of this era, Cleveland was not a Civil War veteran, and was a bachelor, and alleged father of an illegitimate ten-year-old son. Hence the Republican campaign cry: "Ma, ma, where's my pa?"

The Mugwump insurgency of that year was confined almost entirely to New York and New England and seems to have flourished only in urban areas where it enjoyed newspaper support. The Mugwumps were, for the most part, young, well-educated, articulate businessmen and professional folk. They were a new, restless generation bored with "bloody shirt" rhetoric and eager for change. The true impact of this movement is debatable since numerous other factors influenced the outcome in the state of New York, which Cleveland carried by a mere 1,047 votes (and with it won the election). Tammany Hall was against him and took some Irish voters into the Blaine camp. Two minor parties, Prohibitionists and an antimonopoly group, attracted more than enough support to claim they actually decided the outcome. Also, Roscoe Conkling, Blaine's archenemy, opposed the Republican ticket.

Yet, allowing for all of these intangibles, the vehemence with which Stalwarts attacked Mugwumps during a campaign devoid of real issues reveals how very seriously party regulars viewed this challenge. If nothing else, the Mugwumps created an atmosphere in which voting for the opposition was more acceptable and thus encouraged other reform-minded Americans to back Cleveland. In any case, his national margin of 25,685 votes provided victory, the first Democratic administration since before the Civil War, and a ready answer to the taunt of "Ma, ma, where's my pa?" "Gone to the White House, ha, ha, ha!"

Throughout these years, especially in the 1880s, duties paid on foreign imports began to emerge as a political issue of some importance. The tariff issue possessed several virtues. It set Democrats, who generally favored low tariffs and less federal regulation, apart from Republicans, who were fast becoming avid protectionists. Low tariffs usually could be translated into lower costs for consumers (and thus would attract voter support), and discussion of this rather vague national policy enabled politicians to ignore more substantive matters. At the same time, as a subject for discussion and as one upon which to take a stand, the tariff had drawbacks. Some prominent Democrats were stern high-tariff men, various

Library of Congress.

Another voice for Cleveland.

Cartoonist Frank Beard attempted to help the Republican cause during the 1884 election by depicting a hypocritical Cleveland frustrated by the cries of his alleged illegitimate child and former mistress.

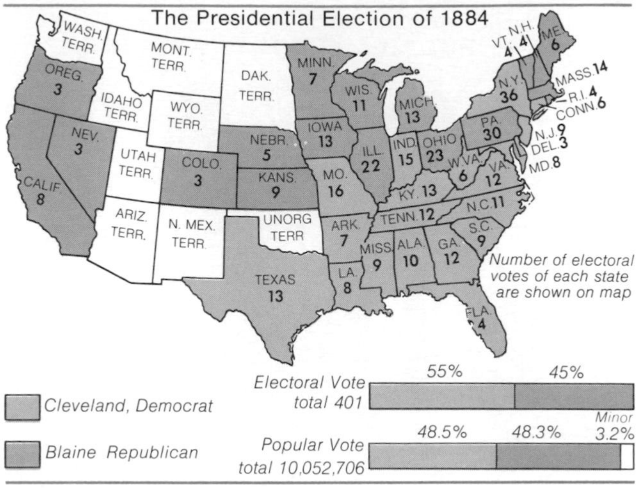

economic groups were determined to raise the tariff walls even higher, and no congressman, regardless of party, was eager to lower tariff regulations which were shielding specific goods produced by his constituents from foreign competition.

In December 1887, Grover Cleveland, who had conducted a very able administration, devoted his entire annual message to the tariff question, arguing strongly for drastic reduction. This move injected the tariff directly into the presidential campaign of the following year, but, like reform in 1884, it was only one issue in a close, bitter battle. His Republican opponent was Senator Benjamin Harrison of Indiana, grandson of the man elected in the "Tippecanoe and Tyler, too" campaign of 1840. Harrison was an able speaker, his party organized its forces well, and a high-tariff stance appealed to both industrialists and factory workers since it would presumably increase profits and wages. Cleveland, as chief executive, did not believe he should conduct an active canvass, the Democrats were less organized and had limited funds to spend, and, worst of all, their national chairman was a devoted high-tariff man who waged a halfhearted campaign at best. To add to their woes, the Republicans published two weeks before the election an indiscreet letter by the British minister in Washington. In it the minister hinted broadly that President Cleveland was a better friend of Great Britain than his opponent would be. Because of such blatant interference in internal affairs, Cleveland sent the diplomat packing, but the damage had been done—and the impact that such a statement had in Irish neighborhoods across the country is all too obvious.

Cleveland won the popular vote by a margin of 90,596 votes, but Harrison carried several crucial states such as Indiana, New York, and Ohio, gaining 233 electoral votes to 168 for Cleveland. Despite the furor over the tariff, the outcome seemingly did not hinge on that issue after all. Cleveland carried the manufacturing stronghold of New Jersey and Ohio and even increased his 1884 totals in several other pro-tariff states. In the end, astute organization by Republicans in crucial areas and shrewd use of money on election day probably were the key factors in Harrison's razor-thin victory.

Nevertheless, now in control of the White House and both houses of Congress for the first time since 1875, the Republicans proceeded to pass the McKinley Tariff of 1890. This measure raised rates, extended coverage to many items that had previously entered free, and was the first tariff to contain a complete schedule of protective duties on agricultural products. Regardless of its true impact, the Democrats used the McKinley Tariff to great advantage in the congressional elections of 1890 as they pointed to the higher prices they said it caused. The result was a disaster for the Republicans; even Congressman William McKinley of Ohio went down to defeat.

Four years later, with Cleveland once more in the White House, the Democrats tried to revise the McKinley Tariff but without much success. After months of bitter debate the Wilson-Gorman Act became law without the President's signature. Its rates, the result of much compromise and hard bargaining, were virtually the same as before. The problem was that the Democrats simply did not have enough Senate votes to effect true reform. As the original bill came from the House, it eliminated duties on raw sugar, had none on iron and steel, and had a mild income tax attached to it (later declared unconstitutional)—all features that many loyal Democrats in the upper chamber could not accept. The Republicans, who were outnumbered only 38 to 44, played upon these and other weaknesses and produced a stalemate. In addition, these debates were taking place in the midst of a severe economic recession, and the conviction was growing that monetary problems, not foreign imports and tariff regulation, lay at the root of the nation's ills.

The most enduring issue during the 1870s and 1880s—and one that would give both of the major political parties fits in the 1890s—was the question of the supply of money. Basic to this discussion was a downward drift in prices that farmers and many other Americans were receiving for what they produced. This three-decade decline kindled opposing views among those who benefited and those who suffered. Creditors lending money at a fixed rate of interest were able to buy more with that interest as years went by; borrowers had to work harder and longer to meet those payments. Lower prices generally were a boon to those on fixed incomes and often made little difference to anyone whose salary or profits were tied to general price fluctuations. But the crunch was that the mass of Americans were farmers, and they were hurting.

During the Civil War, as a matter of expediency, the federal government issued irredeemable Treasury notes called greenbacks. Since these were not backed by gold and continued to circulate long after the war ended, people tended to hoard gold dollars and spend cheaper, less valuable greenback dollars. Creditors, unhappy with payments made in "cheap" money, pushed through the Resumption Act of 1875 which obligated the treasury to redeem greenbacks in gold at face value on January 1, 1879. Greenback dollars, worth only 67 cents in relation to gold dollars in 1865, then rose to 100 cents before that deadline.

Inflationists (or debtors) fielded a Greenback party in the election of 1880 which had little impact, but even before that campaign, those favoring "cheap" money had turned their attention to silver as a solution to their ills. Before the Civil War gold and silver coins were minted at a ratio of 16 to 1, that is, there was sixteen times as much silver in a silver dollar as there was gold in a gold dollar. But as a result of the California Gold Rush of 1849, the price of gold fell, driving silver dollars out of circulation. In 1873 Congress quietly ended coinage of that medium of exchange. The opening of large western silver mines only a few years later created pressure for the return of silver coinage. Over the veto of President Hayes, Congress in 1878 passed the Bland-Allison Act, which authorized the Treasury to buy from $2 to $4 million of silver per month and to turn it into coins at the old ratio of 16:1. This did not really satisfy the demands of silver advocates since they wanted "free and unlimited" coinage and, moreover, the Treasury only purchased the legal minimum.

In 1890 the Sherman Silver Purchase Act increased the amount of silver the federal government would buy each month to 4.5 million ounces. Three years later as a financial panic turned into a severe depression, conservative business leaders (creditors) pointed to this legislation as a major cause and, with the help of President Cleveland, engineered its repeal. This action failed to end the depression and silverites (debtors) said the problem was that the Sherman Act had been too timid: only "free and unlimited" coinage of silver could solve the nation's woes. This debate set the stage for the great political crusade of 1896.

Party Structure

Since Presidents came and went every four years and political leaders often ignored true issues—whether tariff reform at the national level or the liquor question at the municipal and state level—the structure of political parties and how they tried to get and retain power were of utmost importance. As the self-proclaimed party of prosperity and national growth, the Republicans ultimately emerged in the mid-1890s as the party more in tune with the needs of an industrial, expanding America. The Democrats, more so than their rivals, were a collection of state organizations frequently at odds with programs proclaimed by their presidential nominees.

The foundation stones of both parties were local groups able to churn out votes by fair means or foul on election day. Any democracy must have a body of party loyalists willing to perform routine tasks, not only during campaigns but also in less exciting periods. In return, they expect something: money, jobs, favors, special consideration. The money to keep a party going comes from officeholders, candidates, and businessmen who are vulnerable because of frequent elections. Money collected and patronage are divided up by those who win, and the winners well realize that spreading both as thinly as possible obligates more of the electorate to them and translates into continuing support at the polls.

The word "machine" generally is used by disgruntled outsiders and reformers eager to build one of their own. It has a long history in American life. Aaron Burr, Thomas Jefferson, Andrew Jackson, and others were all backed up by organizations of some sort which helped them gain high office. However, development of the convention system for selecting presidential candidates and especially the growth of urban areas in the late nineteenth century made city machines more visible than ever before, and much more so than their rural counterparts. To some extent, old, established families in centers such as New York and Philadelphia created the urban political machine in its modern guise when they abandoned the field to newcomers. The flow of immigrants, growth of municipal services, development of utilities, and the pressing need for order in city life gave rise to machines headed up by men like Fernando Wood and William Marcy Tweed in Manhattan and similar organizations led by comparable men in Philadelphia, Boston, Chicago, Pittsburgh, Cincinnati, Kansas City, and New Orleans.

Occasionally, as in the case of the Roscoe Conkling machine in New York state opposing Rutherford Hayes and James G. Blaine, local groups were at odds with Presidents and would-be Presidents of the same political persuasion, but the purpose of such organizations was to deliver votes for their party's candidates, and they usually did so. It was especially important that they keep a wary eye upon elections to their state legislatures for throughout this period those bodies generally chose members of the U.S. Senate. Until 1866 each state was free to adopt whatever procedures it wished for the election of senators, but then Congress decreed that both houses must vote separately by roll call and meet jointly if it were necessary to iron out differences. One of the goals of reformers of this era was the direct election of senators by voters, an innovation that newer states often embraced in the late nineteenth century and one that finally became part of the Constitution by the Amendment of 1913.

Going from the urban (or rural) machine to the state legislature and then on to Congress, one finally arrived at the focal point of national political life during the Gilded Age. Although only one senator (Harrison) became President during those years, that body had a galaxy of "star" Republicans such as Blaine, Conkling, John Logan, and William E. Chandler, all of whom frittered away their talents and energies in bitter personal feuds. This arrogant group had overthrown Johnson, smothered Grant, virtually abandoned Hayes after risking war to give him the presidency, and kept every other Republican chief executive on a tight rein. Back in their home states, most were at the head of organizations of one sort or another which reached down through levels of city officials, bankers, influential businessmen (and equally influential saloonkeepers), and indispensable ward and precinct workers. For reasons somewhat difficult to comprehend today, no one from top to bottom seemed to realize that the crucial problem of the era was the adjustment of democratic America to industrial, urban life. And on this score reformers and those who attacked this political framework appear to have been equally guilty of faulty insight. They chased after will-o'-the-wisps such as greenback dollars, silver, prohibition, the tariff schedules, all of which related to but did not come to grips with changes everyone knew were occurring.

It took time and experience to nurture a group of leaders who, after 1900, would begin to grapple with economic and social problems. By prevailing views concerning the role of government, Republicans of the Gilded Age were conservative. They believed any government interference impeded progress and had to be kept at a minimum. Taxation should be limited, but they did not oppose spending tax dollars and erecting tariff walls to aid special interests. In this respect they differed from Democrats who thought the protective tariff and special subsidies wrong. All too often, historians have accepted the convenient reform argument of a corrupt alliance between Republican leaders and big business and portrayed this era as overwhelmingly corrupt, a period

Library of Congress.

Finley Peter Dunne
(1867–1936)

"But, Hinnissy, th' past always looks better thin it was. It's only pleasant because it isn't here."

"A rayformer thries to get into office on a flyin' machine. He succeeds now an' thin, but the odds are a hundherd to wan on th' la'ad that tunnels through."

"No matter whether th' constitution follows th' flag or not, th' supreme coort follows th' iliction returns."

"Those iv them that writes about their own times examines th' tongue an' feels th' pulse an' makes a wrong dygnosis. Th' other kind iv histhry is a post-mortem examination. It tells ye what a counthry died iv. But I'd like to know what it lived iv."

For over three decades the Irish dialect humor of Finley Peter Dunne, aided by his two most prominent characters, Mr. Dooley and his friend, Hennessey, delighted American readers. Dooley and Hennessey, like their creator, lived in Chicago and with philosophical wit analyzed the events of the day.

Born in Chicago of Irish parents, Dunne graduated from high school in 1884 and then worked as a reporter for a variety of local newspapers. In 1892 he began to write dialect pieces that soon became regular features. Six years later his first book of collected sayings and essays appeared and in 1900 he moved to New York City, his home for the rest of his life. There he soon married and raised a family.

Manhattan broadened Dunne's career as he consorted with artists (such as Charles Dana Gibson), crusading muckrakers of that era, and various political figures. A humorous review of Teddy Roosevelt's Spanish-American War memoirs, for example, sparked a lifelong friendship. In 1906 he became an editor of *American Magazine* and later was associated with *Collier's* and *Metropolitan.* After his last Dooley book appeared in 1919, Dunne tried to shed his Irish prose and launch other literary endeavors.

As a friend of Harry Daugherty he helped mount the Harding presidential boom of 1920 and subsequently appeared as a character witness for Harry Sinclair during the Teapot Dome probe. Always interested in politics, he backed Al Smith in 1928 and Franklin Roosevelt in 1932.

An essentially able man who set high standards for himself, Finley Peter Dunne rode the crest of an Irish cultural prominence in urban America (1890–1930). He yearned to become a more serious writer and perhaps even a politician. He was, however, essentially a great humorist, a verdict in which he would not have taken much pride. ■

Frederick Lewis.

Cleveland (seated, second from left) and his Cabinet. Notable members were William C. Whitney (standing, second from left), father of the modern United States Navy and founder of the Naval War College at Newport, R.I., and Lucius Quintus Cincinnatus Lamar (seated, far right), Secretary of the Interior, who had won fame for his efforts at reconciling the South and the North after the war.

when democracy was perverted. And while this thesis contains some truth, the question remains, why did voters acquiesce to such leadership and long give it their support? The best explanation is that these men represented the views of the mass of late nineteenth century Americans who, indoctrinated with Social Darwinism and laissez-faire ideas, regarded intervention by government as unnecessary and perhaps even immoral.

Congressional Dominance

The nature of party structure, a succession of one-term Presidents, and widespread conservatism among the electorate created three decades or more (1865-1900) in which Congress dominated the Washington scene and the political life of the nation. The roots of this legislative preeminence lay in the impeachment of Andrew Johnson and the disputed election of Rutherford Hayes. Hayes gained office under a cloud of suspicion and members of both parties referred to him as "the defacto President," "His Fraudulency," and "Old Eight-to-Seven." His program to end Reconstruction in the South, selection of a Cabinet that included both ex-Confederates and liberal Republicans, and bold attacks on a spoils-system machine headed by Roscoe Conkling have won Hayes the praise of historians but these moves infuriated his adversaries on Capitol Hill. At one time he had the support of only three members of the Senate, one of them a lifelong friend and another a relative.

Ohio's John Sherman (1823-1900), a Republican senator during the late nineteenth century and a perpetual aspirant for the office held by Hayes, once wrote, "The executive department of a republic like ours should be subordinate to the legislative department. The President should obey and enforce laws, leaving to the people the duty of correcting any errors committed by their representatives in Congress." George F. Hoar of Massachusetts said that if leading senators visited the White House, "it was to give, not to receive advice."

Cleveland, the only Democratic President of these years, tangled often with the Senate during his first term (1885-1889). Although he came to office billed as a reformer and a man of courage, he actually was rather stolid, lacking in imagination, and a bedrock conservative who agreed with his Republican foes on sound money and the rights of property. At first he tried to please both reformers and spoilsmen, eventually giving in to the latter.

Cleveland halted a widespread pension racket among Civil War veterans by vetoing hundreds of private bills individual congressmen had introduced for constituents previously turned down by the Pension Office. In January 1887 Congress passed a general pension bill covering all honorably discharged, disabled Union veterans who had served as little as ninety days and without regard to how they had been injured. Cleveland vetoed the measure, thus earning the enmity of the GAR. As President,

Library of Congress.

Library of Congress.

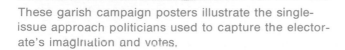

These garish campaign posters illustrate the single-issue approach politicians used to capture the electorate's imagination and votes.

he signed a substantial number of bills, more than Grant, Hayes, Garfield, and Arthur combined; at the same time, he was the first of this postwar group to wield the veto, clear evidence of the great power enjoyed by Capitol Hill. Three important measures passed during Cleveland's first term (although he could take little credit) were the Interstate Commerce Act, the Dawes Act outlining a new Indian policy, and a succession law detailing how Cabinet members would succeed to the White House upon the death of the President and Vice President. First in line was the Secretary of State, followed by others in order of the establishment of their departments.

Benjamin Harrison, the only President ever to receive that office from and hand it over to the same man, immediately signed the pension bill Cleveland opposed, and by 1899 annual expenditures for Union veterans would rise to the astronomical figure of $157 million. To get rid of an embarrassing Treasury surplus created by high tariff revenues, Harrison and what became known as "the Billion Dollar Congress" of 1890–1891 also distributed subsidies to steamship lines, passed lavish harbors and rivers bills, offered large premiums to government bondholders, and even returned taxes collected by federal agents during the Civil War. This plan worked brilliantly; by 1894 the surplus disappeared completely and the federal government has never been plagued by a surplus of funds since that time. Interestingly, this largess did not win many friends. Congressional elections wiped out the Republicans' seven-vote edge in the lower chamber with a dramatic reversal (235 Democrats, 88 Republicans) and in March of 1893 Grover Cleveland was once more living in the White House.

Party Coalitions

In decades of very close elections, unclear issues, and little personal leadership, both major parties found power an elusive entity. Advocacy of civil service reform, tariff revision, coinage of gold and silver, veterans' pensions, and even prohibition might cause a campaigner to lose as many ballots as he gained. Among the causes of voter uncertainty were dramatic changes created by the expansion of railroads, the growth of cities and industry in general, and a huge influx of migrants. Just as the electorate itself was being altered, so were the goals and hopes of individual voters. The result was rule by coalition, an occasional appeal to sectional loyalties, and flirtation from time to time with the demands of third parties.

In 1860 one-third of the United States was, in fact, neither united nor states. It consisted of vast territories under the direct control of the federal government, largely so-called Indian lands in the West. In 1870, the Dakota, Idaho, and Washington territories had 60,000 inhabitants; twenty years later, thanks to railroad expansion throughout the Northwest, 1,000,000. Similar trends were evident elsewhere, and by 1900 only Oklahoma, Arizona, and New Mexico still were territories.

For political reasons, four new states entered the Union during the Civil War and in the decade that followed: West Virginia (1863), Nevada (1864), Nebraska (1867), and Colorado (1876). However, aware of the crucial role these states played in the hotly disputed Hayes-Tilden affair—all except West Virginia supported Hayes—both parties backed away from endorsing further additions to the Electoral College. Although pressure for statehood continued unabated, it was difficult to measure its true strength. Frequently a campaign was merely the handiwork of a small faction eager to get federal jobs. Easterners also feared what they viewed as western radicalism, but finally in 1889 when the Republicans got a momentary grip on the White House and both houses of Congress, this logjam was broken. The result was the Omnibus Bill authorizing statehood for the Dakotas, Montana, and Washington, all of which entered the Union in 1889. Wyoming and Idaho were not covered by the terms of that legislation but held conventions anyway, and the following year shed territorial status. Six years later, the Mormons of Utah bowed to the inevitable, renounced polygamy, and also entered the Union.

When the tariff, pensions, and monetary matters failed to elicit much voter response, campaigners always could attack a distant enemy unable to retaliate. Northern Republicans again and again "waved the bloody shirt." The Democrats, they said, stood for disunion and secession; Lincoln's party had saved the Union in the 1860s and because it was the only "safe" political organization, it deserved the support of all truly patriotic Americans. Democrats, especially those living in the former Confederacy, answered by blaming the Republicans and their national legislation for that region's lack of progress and its relative poverty. In time, Westerners blamed eastern bankers for their agricultural woes, and farmers everywhere thought railroad magnates, the trusts, and city folk in general were the cause of low prices for their crops and hard times.

This politics by diversion was a means of adroitly ignoring pressing issues at home and demonstrated at least two fundamental truths of this era: the absence of substantive issues with which leaders and voters would concern themselves and the fact that America was not yet a unified "nation." Like its political parties, the country was a collection of divergent parts still warring against each other on occasion for short-term benefit.

This fragmentation, coupled with obscure issues and equally obscure leadership, was yet another factor promoting the politics of coalition. An extreme example occurred in the early 1880s when the Republicans and Democrats each held 37 seats in the U.S. Senate. Then Virginia sent to the Senate a gentleman who was not really aligned with either party—he had gained power as the result of a dispute over how to settle that state's pre-Civil War debt—and he held the deciding vote. Eventually he went with the Republicans, got control of patronage in his home state, and helped that party to organize the Senate.

Some voters and a few leaders of these years occasionally refused to coalesce with the two major parties and organized their programs around some other issue about which each felt very strongly. They could, of course, use the Republican party itself as a model since it had emerged from minor political status (1854–1856) and by embracing one major reform had gone "big time." Several groups such as those favoring labor reform, more greenback dollars, and prohibition fielded national tickets in the 1870s and 1880s. Those who sought an end to the liquor traffic proved to be the most durable of these movements and the only individuals who, without compromising their goals, eventually won out in the 1920s.

AMERICAN POLITICAL PARTIES SINCE 1789

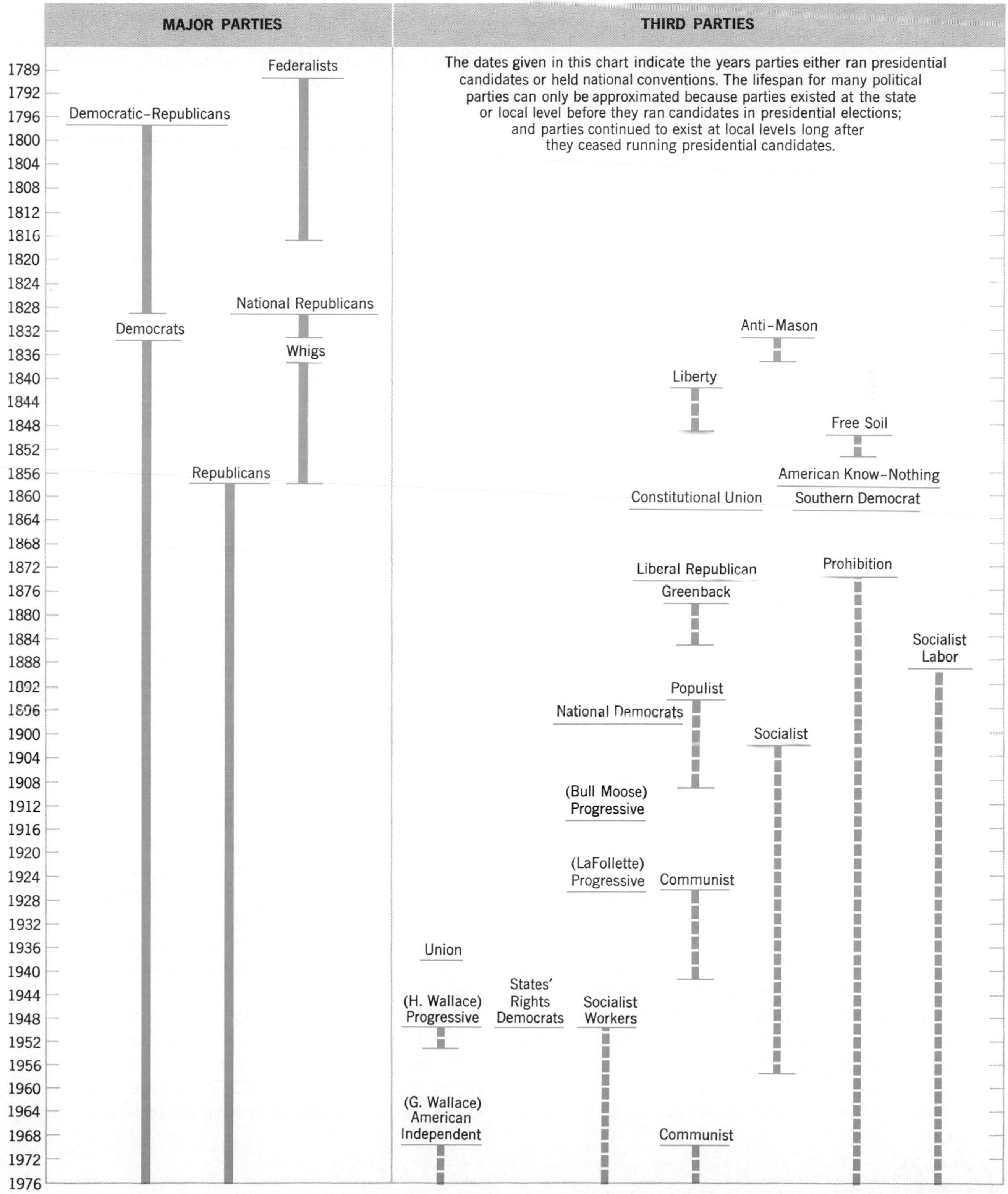
MAJOR PARTIES
THIRD PARTIES
The dates given in this chart indicate the years parties either ran presidential candidates or held national conventions. The lifespan for many political parties can only be approximated because parties existed at the state or local level before they ran candidates in presidential elections; and parties continued to exist at local levels long after they ceased running presidential candidates.
1789
1792
1796
1800
1804
1808
1812
1816
1820
1824
1828
1832
1836
1840
1844
1848
1852
1856
1860
1864
1868
1872
1876
1880
1884
1888
1892
1896
1900
1904
1908
1912
1916
1920
1924
1928
1932
1936
1940
1944
1948
1952
1956
1960
1964
1968
1972
1976
Federalists
Democratic-Republicans
National Republicans
Democrats
Whigs
Republicans
Anti-Mason
Liberty
Free Soil
American Know-Nothing
Constitutional Union
Southern Democrat
Liberal Republican
Prohibition
Greenback
Socialist Labor
Populist
National Democrats
Socialist
(Bull Moose) Progressive
(LaFollette) Progressive
Communist
Union
States' Rights Democrats
(H. Wallace) Progressive
Socialist Workers
(G. Wallace) American Independent
Communist

Although the direct impact of these groups was limited at the national level, their local presence was a source of constant concern in hundreds of precincts, towns, counties, and state capitals throughout the nation. Spokesmen of both major parties tried with varying success to support enough of their demands, generally rooted in economic change, in order to win votes. The Grangers of the 1870s, for example, who never formed a true third party, said they were a social order interested in improving the lot of rural folk everywhere, but they expended considerable energy upon railroad regulation and eventually developed sufficient power to bring about congressional action. The greenback furor was an effort to perpetuate "cheap" money favorable to debtors and borrowers. Had the Democrats and Republicans heeded these various appeals—or even merely paid lipservice to them (as they certainly did in some areas)—the great Populist upheaval of the early 1890s might never have occurred. But constant scorn from national political leaders and decades of frustration, combined with widespread hard times, fueled a political blaze of unusual proportions. By the time the smoke cleared, the equilibrium characteristic of American political life from Hayes to McKinley had vanished.

Race and Politics

A very troublesome factor in the political equation was the black voter. Republican Reconstruction gave black adult males the ballot, and one would think they would turn out on election day to thank their benefactors . . . and they usually did. Yet leaders of the great mass of ex-slaves realized many Americans were opposed to black suffrage and might well withdraw that right if it ever were politically expedient to do so. (Blacks were especially distressed by Cleveland's election in 1884, certain that this meant the end of their freedom.) They also knew that most black voters were ignorant of the true power of the franchise. And, more important, they quickly learned that without other civil rights—the protection of life and property—the ballot throughout much of the South was meaningless. Yet, properly organized, the black electorate could win elections in that region for the Republican party and, to put it another way, disorganization and frustration of that voting bloc could spell victory for the Democrats. Southern whites were especially disturbed by new public school systems, segregated and free, which obviously could increase literacy and meaningful political participation by blacks.

President Hayes, sticking to the commitments of 1877, adopted a laissez-faire attitude toward the black man in the South. His refusal to aid ex-carpetbaggers forced many Republicans of that region into a variety of "independent" movements, and the policies of Hayes and all of his Republican successors left the black man disgruntled and vulnerable. The party that gave him freedom and the ballot steadfastly refused to give him political offices or a share of the patronage. That same party also failed to protect his political and civil rights. At times, not surprisingly, blacks turned to conservative southern whites for guidance and protection; after all, the former owners and ex-slaves knew and understood each other. In truth, the Republican stratagem of courting blacks without giving them anything in return was doomed from the start. Blacks had to get along with their employers and those they associated with from day to day, not just politicians who sought them out only at election time.

In addition, the odds against Republican success in the South were staggering. The carpetbag regimes they had supported left a bad taste in the mouths of many citizens, regardless of color, place of residence, and political affiliation. Factional disputes among southern Republicans made any cooperation of "black-and-tan" and "lily-white" groups virtually impossible. In the closing years of the nineteenth century, Republican party platforms always promised the black man full protection, honest elections, and a new day. But in reality, Hayes, Arthur, and Harrison each did their best to jettison him and make the Republican party as white as possible, not only in the South but throughout the nation as well.

In an age of mounting racism, the problem was that support for blacks often alienated more votes than it attracted. Also, since both parties could easily buy votes (both white and black), the net advantage of such support was marginal. The answer, of course, was to eliminate this "troublesome factor" entirely and, so the argument went, end political corruption. But before that step was taken, the Republicans made one last effort to develop their southern strategy.

During the late 1860s and early 1870s, Republicans in Congress passed a number of acts designed to keep their carpetbag allies in power and to protect the civil rights of ex-slaves. Between 1876 and 1883 the Supreme Court quietly dismantled most of the legislation on various grounds, largely because these laws exceeded the letter and intent of the Constitution and its Amendments as interpreted by the justices.

In the late 1880s several northern Republicans—among them, Benjamin Harrison, John Sherman, and William C. Chandler in the Senate and a variety of House members, including a young Massachusetts congressman, Henry Cabot Lodge—introduced bills that would give federal authorities the power to supervise polling places during federal elections, thus preventing the exclusion of black voters. In the spring of 1890 Republican leaders asked Lodge to combine these bills into a single bill. On July 2, the same day that President Harrison signed the Sherman Antitrust Act, it passed the House, earning Lodge the enmity of most whites living south of the Potomac. Although this measure never won Senate approval, it stirred up a hornet's nest in many states and may have been a factor in the Republican defeat of 1892; on the other hand, it enhanced Lodge's standing in his home state and helped him move on to the U.S. Senate a year later.

Library of Congress.

This Thomas Nast cartoon, showing that black political rights in the South remained a vibrant issue throughout the late nineteenth century, appeared in *Harper's Weekly* in 1888.

In the same year that Lodge's Force Bill was a hot issue, the state of Mississippi held a constitutional convention, rewrote its election laws, and virtually disfranchised all black voters by creating literacy and property qualifications. Within a decade or so all other southern states had followed suit. The barriers were not high—the ability to read and write and the possession of taxable goods worth a few hundred dollars—but, more importantly, they were enforced by sympathetic officials who looked out for the interests of poor whites who otherwise might have lost their ballot. Some states adopted an "understanding clause" as a test for literacy. Any illiterate could register and vote if he "understood" any section of the state constitution read to him. Many white Southerners chafed under this absurdity and were happier with the "grandfather clause" concocted during Louisiana's convention. This device exempted from tests those who had been entitled to vote on January 1, 1867, as well as their sons and grandsons.

State conventions throughout the South borrowed freely from each other as they created tests and loopholes, and all wrote poll taxes into their new constitutions. One had to pay this levy well in advance of election day, perhaps as much as eighteenth months, retain the receipt, and take it to the polls. The result was a marked decline in voter turnout. In 1944, for example, Virginia cast 61,000 fewer votes than in the Cleveland-Harrison election of 1888, yet during the intervening decades women had gained the vote and that state's overall population had increased by 1,000,000.

The reasons and motives for disfranchisement were complex. Some political leaders were determined to eliminate certain classes of white voters along with blacks. The fact that thousands of less affluent white Southerners embraced Populism (1890–1896) stiffened the resolve of many Democratic party regulars to make certain no such movement ever again would threaten their state organizations. In North Carolina, Populists and Republicans joined hands and took over the state government for a few years. In general, those advocating disfranchisement (later sanctioned by federal courts) gave three basic reasons for their proposals: (1) removal of blacks from politics would end corrupt elections in which all factions bargained freely for black votes; (2) elimination of blacks as arbiters between various white groups would permit the latter to divide on basic issues and restore vigor to political life; and (3) disfranchisement would end false hopes among blacks since by showing them their "place" in society, race relations would both stabilize and improve.

Regardless of the consequences, the majority of white Southerners—in fact, probably most white Americans—viewed disfranchisement as reform. If nothing else, it snuffed out political independence among both races from Virginia to Texas, made black migration from that region to other parts of the nation inevitable, and created for nearly half a century (1900–1950) a "Solid South" that almost always could be counted upon to vote Democratic.

Politics Unsettled: The Crisis of the 1890s

Decades of equilibrium and tight elections began to unravel during the 1890s, largely because of a severe economic crisis. Agricultural problems that had been struggling to express themselves through a variety of semipolitical and third party movements suddenly exploded in the fury of Populism.

The Rise of the Populists

For the most part, Populism in its purest form was a western phenomenon, although it also enjoyed substantial following in some parts of the South and actually lingered on for decades in both regions, perhaps even to the present day. In states such as South Carolina, the Populists simply took over the regular party organization, usurped the name "Democrats," and ran things for the benefit of the "little" people. Southern Populism, more than anything else, was a class-oriented revolt against conservative urban business domination. It used much the same rhetoric as the Westerners, but its goals were limited by class, state, and racial boundaries. In general, Populists living in the South were a force for disfranchisement of black voters and for segregation, although they sometimes soft-pedaled such views and tried to enlist the support of blacks. It is no accident that legal disfranchisement by state conventions occurred largely *after* the Populist upheaval had run its course. White political factions saw the potential of the black vote for mischief and, alarmed lest their rivals might use it against them, agreed to deny it to all.

In the West, where Populism loomed largest, the thousands, even the millions of Americans who poured into the grain-growing states and territories beyond the Mississippi discovered soon after they arrived that relatively free land and hard work did not produce the expected good life. Their most serious problems as the years passed were transportation, money, credit, and tariffs. Railroads serving their region were soon consolidated into a few great lines owned by Gould, Harriman, Hill, Morgan, and others, all of them eastern business tycoons capable of controlling their destinies. When an Iowa or Nebraska farmer sold his crop for cash to pay off old debts, to finance a new crop, and to buy a few necessities, he got caught up in a financial system shaped by eastern bankers whose interests, he became convinced, contrasted sharply with his own. Consolidation of banking after the Civil War also seemed to work against him since local banks became fewer in number and less autonomous. The protectionist tariff of those years was another cause of the farmer's woes. He sold his produce in an unprotected market and bought his machinery, clothing, and household goods in one protected by a tariff written to please eastern financial and industrial interests.

Of course, how and where farmers lived and worked affected the nature of their protest. Transportation charges hit hardest the residents of Illinois, Iowa, Kansas, Minnesota, and the Dakotas, especially those who grew wheat since their annual income depended upon one crop. Although farmers had a few good years in the 1870s and 1880s, their plight generally worsened; and, regardless of the causes—dry seasons, poor farming methods, or unwise dependence upon a single staple—blame rested, at least in the opinion of farmers, squarely upon the unholy alliance of railroads, banks, and tariff-protected industry. In their view, these eastern interests constituted a great and evil conspiracy.

To give vent to his anger and frustration, the farmer joined, in turn, the Grange of the 1870s and the Farmers' Alliance of the succeeding decade. Both enjoyed limited success with antirailroad legislation and cooperative marketing schemes set up to bypass middlemen. For a time farmers also flirted with the Greenback party and a variety of antimonopoly reform movements, most of which had little or no impact on the national scene.

Then in the late 1880s various state alliances of farmers began to become aggressively political and the reasons were obvious. Over three-fourths of all Kansas farms, for example, were mortgaged at an average inter-

Library of Congress.

"MOWING 'EM DOWN! The politicians of both parties will have to lie particularly low to escape the new power in the political field." So ran the caption to this 1890 *Judge* cartoon. Serious threats from farm-supported candidates declined after the 1896 presidential election, however.

est of 9 percent, and droughts and poor crops made the future look bleak indeed. Since the Republicans traditionally dominated the Midwest, they felt the heat of this protest, just as it was the Democrats who suffered most in North Carolina, Alabama, and other parts of the South where, as the majority party, they were vulnerable. And herein lies one of the inherent weaknesses of the emerging Populist movement: to win votes it worked closely with the "outs" of any region. Such a policy made cooperation on a national scale difficult, if not impossible.

By 1890 two Alliance Senators, James H. Kyle of South Dakota and William A. Peffer of Kansas, appeared in Washington, and in July 1892 representatives of all of these dissident groups gathered in Omaha to form the Populist (or People's) party. Hundreds sang "Good-bye, Old Parties, Good-Bye" and endorsed enthusiastically numerous proposals: free coinage of silver, abolition of national banks, establishment of subtreasuries (government grain warehouses) or a better scheme, levy of an income tax, issue of sufficient paper money, government ownership of railroads, direct election of senators, nonownership of land by foreigners, limitation of the revenue of each state and the nation to expenses, adoption of an eight-hour day, establishment of postal banks, pay-

Kansas State Historical Society Topeka.

The studied demeanor of Mary E. Lease shown here misrepresents the fiery nature of this Kansas orator who instructed the Populist farmers to "raise less corn and more hell."

Library of Congress.

General James B. Weaver, presidential candidate for the Populist Party in 1892.

ment of pensions to Union veterans, and opposition to the prevailing contract law and immigrantion system. To head this long list, the platform committee composed a stinging preamble:

> "We meet in the midst of a nation brought to the verge of moral, political, and material ruin. Corruption dominates the ballot box, the legislatures, the Congress, and even touches the ermine of the bench. The people are demoralized. The newspapers are largely subsidized or muzzled, public opinion silenced, business prostrated, our homes covered with mortgages, labor impoverished, and the land concentrated in the hands of capitalists."

These former Grangers, Greenbackers, and Alliance folk then named James Baird Weaver of Iowa (a Union veteran and Greenback presidential hopeful in 1880) as their nominee for President. His running mate was James Gaven Field of Virginia, former Attorney General of that state, an ex-Confederate and a resident of Thomas Jefferson's Albemarle County. In November, although that ticket had little success east of the Mississippi, it carried the states of Colorado, Idaho, Kansas, Nevada, and North Dakota and won divided support in Oregon. For the first time since 1860, a third party had gained votes in the Electoral College, 22 of them. Out of 11 million ballots cast for president in 1892, the Populist party got 1,024,280, a quantity that definitely hurt the Republicans and gave the election to Cleveland. In addition, they elected 5 senators, 10 congressmen, about 50 state officials, and over 1,500 county officers and state legislators. Populism quite clearly was a force few politicians could afford to take lightly.

How had the Populists done it? How had these ineffective minor party malcontents put together an organization that finally exerted national impact? First and perhaps most important, they had developed experienced, competent leadership. Weaver of Iowa, Ignatius Donnelly of Minnesota, and "Sockless Jerry" Simpson of Kansas each had joined a variety of third party movements, learned how to manipulate crowds and issues with great effectiveness, and found at last an outlet for their energies. To enhance their appeal and add to the woes of both major parties, the year 1893, following hot on the heels of this unprecedented third party victory, turned out to be an economic wasteland.

Panic of 1893 and the Democratic Split

Within sixty days of his becoming President for the second time, Cleveland's triumph became a nightmare. Businesses began to fail and before the year was out 500 banks closed their doors and nearly 16,000 companies

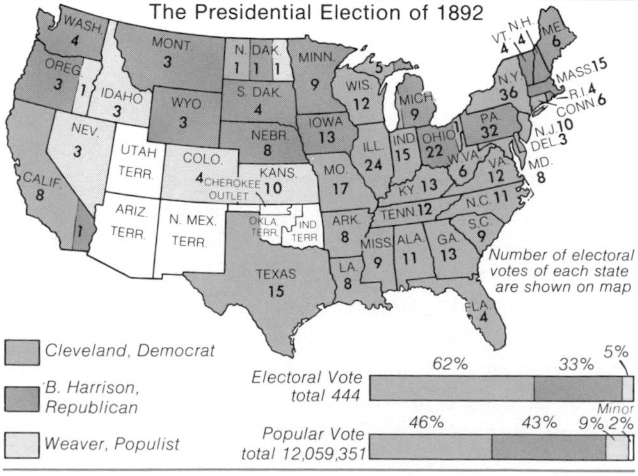

were bankrupt. The following year panic turned into depression, and by August 1896 stocks stood at 68 percent of their value four years earlier. At the worst moments perhaps as many as three million were unemployed, thousands hungry and destitute, and only by 1898 could one discern signs of recovery. Actually the nation did not function normally again until after the turn of the century. Not surprisingly, the party in power was ousted, but more surprising was the fact that it divided openly and fiercely on the question of how to meet this crisis. Even Republicans experienced some tug-and-pull within their ranks, yet they generally managed to maintain unity.

Political leaders differed violently on the question of causes and solutions. Cleveland himself blamed the Sherman Silver Purchase Act of 1890, eastern conservatives blamed western radicals (Populists), labor leaders singled out capitalists for special scorn, and agricultural spokesmen blasted federal monetary policies, especially failure to resume free coinage of silver. Also, Democrats and Republicans blamed each other for this economic chaos.

The true causes seemed to have been industrial expansion far in excess of consumer demand. Railroads had sent tracks into uninhabited regions just to claim territory, lines that might never become profitable. The fortunes of steel and banking were tied closely to those of the iron horse, and when it began to stumble, the entire economy faltered. Agriculture, especially in the West, was equally guilty of overexpansion (much of it as a result of zealous railroad promotion), but none of these factors held much fascination for the public. Instead, the American voter riveted his attention upon the fascinating and confusing gold-silver question. Although few knew what terms such as "free coinage," "gold standard," and "16:1" actually meant, they stormed forth, cheered, held rallies, and fought both for and against monetary reform, convinced that these proposals would either solve the dilemmas of their age or bring instant ruin to everyone.

In August 1893, President Cleveland asked a special session of Congress to repeal the Sherman Silver Purchase Act of 1890. Unwittingly perhaps, he put all of his eggs in one basket, proclaiming that the nation's ills were "principally chargeable" to that legislation. By so doing he held out promise that repeal would bring good times and also elevated the silver question to new heights. After heated debate that saw Congress split along sectional, not party lines, the House voted 239 to 108 for repeal. In the Senate, however, the battle was much closer. Recent admission of six western states—the Dakotas, Montana, Washington, Idaho, and Wyoming—gave the opposition at least ten additional votes. The silverites tried delaying tactics while Democrats at one point pressed the White House to compromise, but finally, late in October, Cleveland prevailed by a vote of 43–32.

It was a costly victory indeed since the promised economic recovery failed to materialize; in fact, conditions worsened. Also, having made silver a key issue, Cleveland was saddled with it for the remainder of his unhappy term. The drain of gold from the federal treasury became so great—largely because of an unfavorable trade balance, economic troubles in Europe, and demands of individual banks throughout the United States—that Cleveland had to go twice with cap-in-hand to Wall Street to float huge bond issues. The details of these transactions are not nearly so important as the impression created among voters. The President of the United States was borrowing from the great money trusts and naturally would be beholden to them in the future.

Meanwhile, the Populists scored even greater victories in local elections held in 1893, and in the following year, the Democratic majorities in both houses of Congress disappeared. After 1894 the Republicans enjoyed a four-vote margin in the Senate (which also had six Populists ready to wield their power), and in the House there were 244 Republicans, 105 Democrats, and 7 Independents. In short, Cleveland's policies were a disaster. They failed to solve the depression, won him a minor revision of the tariff (Wilson-Gorman Act), ended his party's control of Capitol Hill, and created the silver issue that would continue to split the Democrats.

The Election of 1896: Crisis and Realignment

Superficially at least, money was the overriding issue in the exciting presidential battle of 1896, but beneath silver and gold were moral questions. This was a struggle between two standard bearers who campaigned in a modern manner: one by traveling and speaking as no one had done before, the other by putting together a vast organization that tapped support at all levels of society. The result was a shift in loyalties, at least in the crucial Midwest, which gave the Republicans the base for a national dominance lasting (except for the narrow victories of Woodrow Wilson) into the early 1930s.

William Jennings Bryan, a powerful orator with

Library of Congress.

William Jennings Bryan
(1860–1925)

Descended from Virginia stock, Bryan was born in Illinois where he grew up, went to college, and dreamed of becoming a Baptist preacher. However, as he himself admitted, fear of baptism by immersion caused him to study law instead. In 1883 he began to practice in the town of Jacksonville, and the following year he married a local merchant's daughter, Mary Baird, an unusual woman who would exert considerable influence upon his life. In 1887, in search of a more lucrative setting, they moved west to Lincoln, Nebraska, where Mary studied law under her husband's tutelage and qualified for the Nebraska bar.

In the Democratic landslide of 1890, Bryan won a seat in the U.S. House of Representatives and two years later was reelected, his last successful bid for public office but far from his final attempt. In 1894 he failed in a try for the U.S. Senate and spent the next two years editing the *Omaha World-Telegram*, lecturing, and working for the free coinage of silver.

To the surprise of both political parties and much of the nation, in 1896 this thirty-six-year-old ex-Congressman became the Democratic nominee for President on a silver platform. He waged a whirlwind campaign but lost to William McKinley. Four years later they met again with similar results, and in 1908 Bryan lost out a third time to Teddy Roosevelt's handpicked successor, William Howard Taft. Still a very powerful figure at the Democratic convention of 1912, he engineered the nomination of Woodrow Wilson and secured for himself the position of Secretary of State. Although he had no experience for that post, he served creditably well, resigning in 1915 when his pacifist views clashed with Wilson's more aggressive stance toward Germany.

Bryan spent the last decade of his life as a newspaper editor and lecturer; he was for three decades one of the most popular figures on the Chautauqua circuit. In 1925 he went to Dayton, Tennessee, to oppose famed lawyer Clarence Darrow in the well-known Scopes "Monkey" trial. Scopes was accused of teaching Darwin's theory of evolution in public schools in defiance of state law. Bryan won but, under cross-examination by Darrow, his naive antievolutionist views were laid bare for all to see. He died in Dayton a few days after the trial ended.

A powerful orator and a sincere, honest man, William Jennings Bryan clearly was out of step with his times, whether campaigning for the White House or defending anti-evolution statutes. As both politician and lawyer, he was really at heart the Baptist preacher he dared not become because of his fear of water. ■

Library of Congress.

Bryan's brilliant "Cross of Gold" speech brought three divergent parties under his control and won him the Democratic nomination.

magnetic appeal and only thirty-six years old, stunned the nation when he captured the Democratic party in 1896. By both platform and candidate the Democrats repudiated Cleveland and everything he stood for. Many traditional "gold" Democrats and party machines of the Northeast, alarmed by this turn of events, either quietly supported Republicans or sat out the election, waiting for the storm to pass. Bryan, conscious of this defection, proclaimed himself the spokesman and savior of the common man, leader of a new moral force that would cleanse the Democratic party and rebuild it from within.

As candidate of the Democrats, Populists, and Silver Republicans he organized "silver clubs" in state after state, delivered 570 speeches to perhaps 3,000,000 people, and preached a great crusade for the mass redemption of America's soul. He used the language of revivalist clergymen and his rallies took on the trappings and the aura of old-time tent meetings: "You shall not crucify mankind upon a cross of gold!" He came to convert the people to the truth so they could rule and by honesty, virtue, and bimetallism redeem their corrupt and fallen nation. This political pietism had marked success in rural areas and among Methodists, Prohibitionists, and hordes of third party veterans who had never heard such eloquence before, but smalltown bankers, businessmen, and especially the urban-industrial Northeast were not impressed. If anything, they were frightened by what they viewed as rank, un-American radicalism.

The Republican nominee, William McKinley of Ohio, solid, safe, and equally as sincere as Bryan, led a counterattack that sought to demonstrate that free silver and other hairbrained schemes espoused by the wild man from the Platte would wreck the nation's already endangered economy, throw still more people out of work, cheat honest, God-fearing businessmen, and place in power a radical regime. Church leaders who learned the damage that free silver might do to their salaries and endowments tended to back McKinley, although their flocks sometimes disagreed. The Republicans, much more effectively organized than their opponents, tried to educate the public to what they perceived to be the dangers of Bryanism and the advantages of Republican protectionism by never letting them forget for a moment that their current economic miseries were occurring under a Democratic administration.

Mark Hanna directed McKinley's overall campaign with enormous helpings of literature, press releases, and money. He and his staff, centered in Chicago, produced nearly 200 pamphlets geared to the special demands of almost everybody—farmers, coal miners, woolgrowers, steelworkers, mechanics, and lumberjacks. More than a million copies of each pamphlet were printed, and the Chicago mail room had 100 employees busy distributing these booklets to all parts of the nation.

Two weeks before the election Hanna suddenly switched tactics and returned to old-style politics. Convinced that the money battle was won, he dispatched orators everywhere, called upon the GAR to stand by the party that "saved" the Union, and on October 31 staged a national "flag day" in every northern city resplendent with enormous pro-McKinley parades. At last, the Republican strategy became clear. The party was offering pluralism to the American people. Any ethnic minority that supported Major "Bill" McKinley was assured of its security (except perhaps blacks in the South). Every occupation, religion, industry, and section would receive

Smithsonian Institution.

Candidate William McKinley addressing a Republican gathering at his front porch in Canton, Ohio in 1896.

fair treatment under the protective tariff. Farmers' grievances would be investigated and, if necessary, corrective action taken. By contrast, Bryan seemed to be impaled upon a single issue: silver.

McKinley won by about 600,000 votes, carrying all of the Northeast, the upper Mississippi Valley, and California and Oregon, thus becoming the first President to win a true popular and electoral majority since 1872. Bryan, not surprisingly, won the endorsement of the former Confederacy and all of the new states except North Dakota. Many myths have grown up around this hotly contested campaign, and at least two of them should be dispelled. First, contrary to legend, the silver forces entered this battle well organized. Indeed, it was a confrontation for which they had been preparing for over two decades. Second, Bryan did not win the nomination by the mere accident of a powerful speech. Yet twist and turn as he might, in the minds of many voters Bryan was tied to a Democratic administration that was saddled with a severe economic depression. The Republicans fought the campaign hardest where the votes were—in the cities and in industrial areas—and won. Perhaps most important of all, while both parties were split by the monetary issue, the Democratic split was far deeper, and for Bryan and the hopes of millions who viewed him as a savior, that division was fatal.

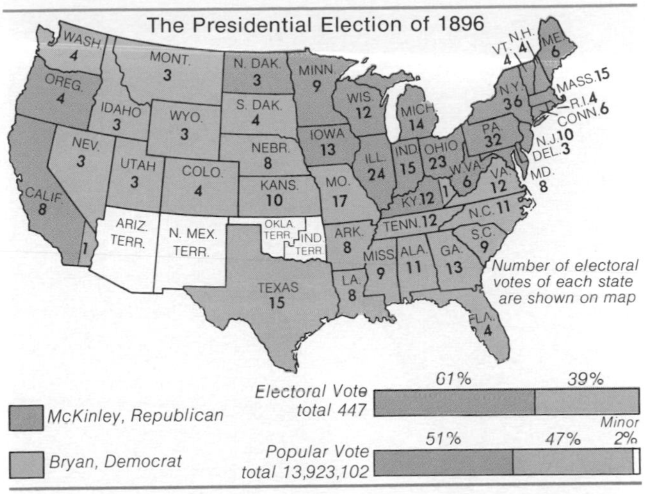

Republicans in Power

William McKinley began his term with very comfortable majorities in both houses of Congress. Although the Democrats gained 50 seats in the House in 1898, this left the Republicans with a 22-vote margin in the lower chamber, and they even increased their strength in the Senate. In fact, they retained firm control of the upper body until 1913, and except for the years 1913–1921, Republicans controlled the presidency until 1933.

A New Majority

Several factors help to explain the emergence of a Republican dominance after nearly a quarter of a century of indecisive national politics. The Democrats, with the support of the South, which was still basically an agricultural region, saw union with the disgruntled farmers of the Midwest as the key to victory. Unfortunately for them, their plans were upset by the disastrous depression of 1893, which occurred during a Democratic administration and by "free silver," a phantom issue capable of scaring as many voters as it attracted. Most important of all, Republican party managers decided to soften their ethnocentrism and to accentuate a positive response to the nation's economic plight.

The result was, in fact, a reversal of values by the two major parties, or at least a shift sufficient enough to create what some historians have called "the politics of realignment." This phenomenon was most apparent in the Midwest where Catholic and German Lutheran voters who had traditionally supported Democrats rejected the evangelical pietism of Bryan and began to cast Republican ballots. In their zeal to unite West and South, the Democrats of the 1890s had become, officially at least, the party of prohibition, sabbatarianism, nativism, and evangelical Protestantism. Those party planks, once owned outright by the Republicans, held little appeal for many ethnic groups, not only in the Midwest but also in the Northeast as well.

Of course, the McKinley-Hanna forces did not openly spurn morality, piety, and God in 1896 or after, but simply deemphasized those goals that pietists hoped to achieve by electing Republican officeholders. This approach was successful in that it quieted the fears of nonpietistic voters alarmed by Bryan, free silver, and Populism and swung them into Republican columns. Both parties spoke with different tongues in different regions in order to attract support, but in the national campaigns of the crucial 1890s the Democrats were burdened with the economic disaster of 1893, cheap money in the form of free silver, rural, pietistic morality in an age of increasing ethnic strength and urban growth, and, above all else, platforms and programs that held no special appeal for either the factory worker or his boss. By contrast, the Republicans seemed to stand for prosperity, industrial expansion, and national growth. Above all, they stood for the kind of pluralism that matched the needs of an increasingly diverse America. The Democrats all too often appeared as a disgruntled minority that could do little but criticize. Even reform, known as Progressivism after 1900, was largely carried forward by the Republicans, the majority party.

Library of Congress.

Marcus A. Hanna, influential Ohioan who became the power behind the throne as advisor to McKinley.

McKinley as President

William McKinley was no reformer, and his experiences in Ohio and in Congress had taught him the value of a middle-of-the-road approach. Long before 1896, as a campaigner for public office, McKinley's social and political background implanted in his mind the concepts that he and Hanna molded into pluralism, votes, and victory.

The last of the chief executives who fought in the Civil War, McKinley selected a Cabinet composed of orthodox, undistinguished, stable citizens much like himself; however, as vacancies occurred he named several men of considerable talent to key positions, among them, John Hay as Secretary of State and Elihu Root to head the War Department. McKinley, a former congressman and an ex-governor of Ohio, was a kindly, considerate man whose smile masked a life of great personal tragedy. His two children died when very young and his lovely, frail wife suffered from convulsions.

Possessing an innate ability to drift with the winds of public opinion, McKinley's greatest problem was that he seemed to lack resolve. To aid recovery he advocated and got greater protection for U.S. markets (the Dingley Tariff of 1897) and the Gold Standard Act of 1900, which declared that the gold dollar was to be the sole standard for the national currency. With the gradual return of good times, Populism faded from view and farmers abandoned independent politics for profits and lobbying.

The most exciting event of McKinley's first term was the brief Spanish-American War of 1898, which really was not much of a war as wars go. His business backers did not want the United States to get involved but, fearing that their hero would be defeated in 1900 if he did not give in to the public clamor (also, congressional elections were soon coming up), they reluctantly supported what turned out to be a very costly adventure in imperialism. It was at first a conflict that only concerned the mistreatment of Cubans by the Spanish government, but McKinley suddenly faced a decision in the Philippines, another Spanish possession halfway around the world. After Commodore George Dewey's startling naval victory in Manila Bay, should the United States keep those islands or not? Eventually, with God's help, McKinley, a Methodist, decided the answer was yes; he thus bestowed upon the nation a bloody guerrilla war, an empire of sorts, new markets, and new responsibilities in the Far East which would have much greater impact upon twentieth century America than anyone could have foreseen in 1898.

Campaign of 1900

The presidential canvass of 1900 was merely a pale rerun of four years before with the same candidates, the same results, and much the same issues. Rising prices and an improving economic outlook took much of the steam out of the silver issue, although Bryan continued to stress it wherever he talked. He also tried to make imperialism a key platform plank, but the majority of Americans were not concerned with that either. Fast-moving events had made both matters passé; with better times currency reform was unnecessary and arguing about an empire that already existed seemed futile.

Countering with the "full dinner pail" theme, the Republicans won somewhat more easily than in 1896 and increased slightly their comfortable margins in both houses of Congress. The most important event of 1900 really was not the campaign hoopla, or even McKinley's victory. It was the death of Garret A. Hobart and the selection of young Theodore Roosevelt, hero of San Juan Hill and the reform governor of New York, as the President's running mate. McKinley and Hanna certainly would have preferred someone else (almost anyone, in fact) but political pressures forced them to accept this aggressive, dynamic forty-one-year-old aristocrat turned politician.

In September 1901, six months into his second term, McKinley went to Buffalo to attend the Pan-American Exposition, was shot by a young anarchist, and died eight days later. With his passing, just as the nation was moving from the nineteenth into the twentieth century, the old order gave way to the new. A few months later in his first annual message to Congress, President Theodore Roosevelt sounded the dominant theme of a new age: changes must be made to meet the challenge of the social and economic problems created by an urban-industrial world. The old rules, he implied, were no longer adequate. Not only was modern politics emerging in America but also the search for an integrated economy capable of adjusting to local, regional, national, and even international pressures. That search, much more than Greenbackers, disgruntled farmers, Populists, and silverites then realized, would achieve in one form or another many of the goals they had long espoused. Under the name of "Progressivism," reform would shortly become both respectable and powerful, an entity both major parties would have to grapple with.

Essay

Slogans and Presidential Politics

The word "slogan" can be traced to a Gaelic expression meaning war cry; so, every four years as presidential hopefuls begin their quest for national power (amid considerable talk about sacrifice, service, and answering the call of duty), it is indeed appropriate that slogans take form and are heard throughout the land. Although any devoted fan of early leaders of the Republic undoubtedly can unearth high-sounding phrases related to their hero—Jefferson, "A Vote for Every Man, Whether He Owns Property or Not;" Jackson, "Let the People Rule"—only with the development of national convention in the 1840s did campaign slogans assume much importance.

One of the earliest and also one of the very best was "Tippecanoe and Tyler, Too" in 1840. Since the elderly Harrison died shortly after his inaugural, the fact his name was not even mentioned made little difference. "Van, Van is a Used-Up Man," referring to the defeated incumbent, Martin Van Buren, had a certain ring to it, but was soon forgotten along with "With Tip and Tyler We'll Bust Van's Biler" and "Van's Policy, Fifty Cents a Day and French Soup—Our Policy, Two Dollars a Day and Roast Beef."

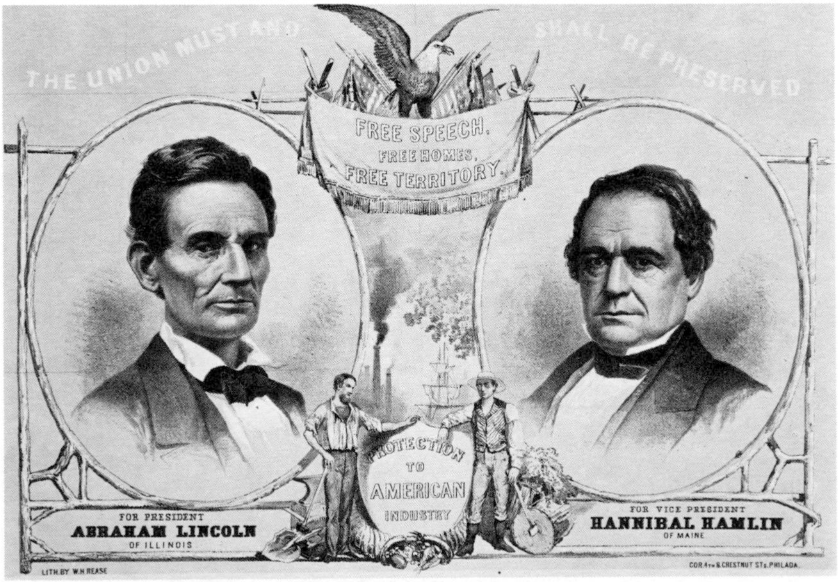

Library of Congress.

During the election of 1860, perhaps the most important in the nation's history, the Republican Party decided on a simple straightforward approach and slogans.

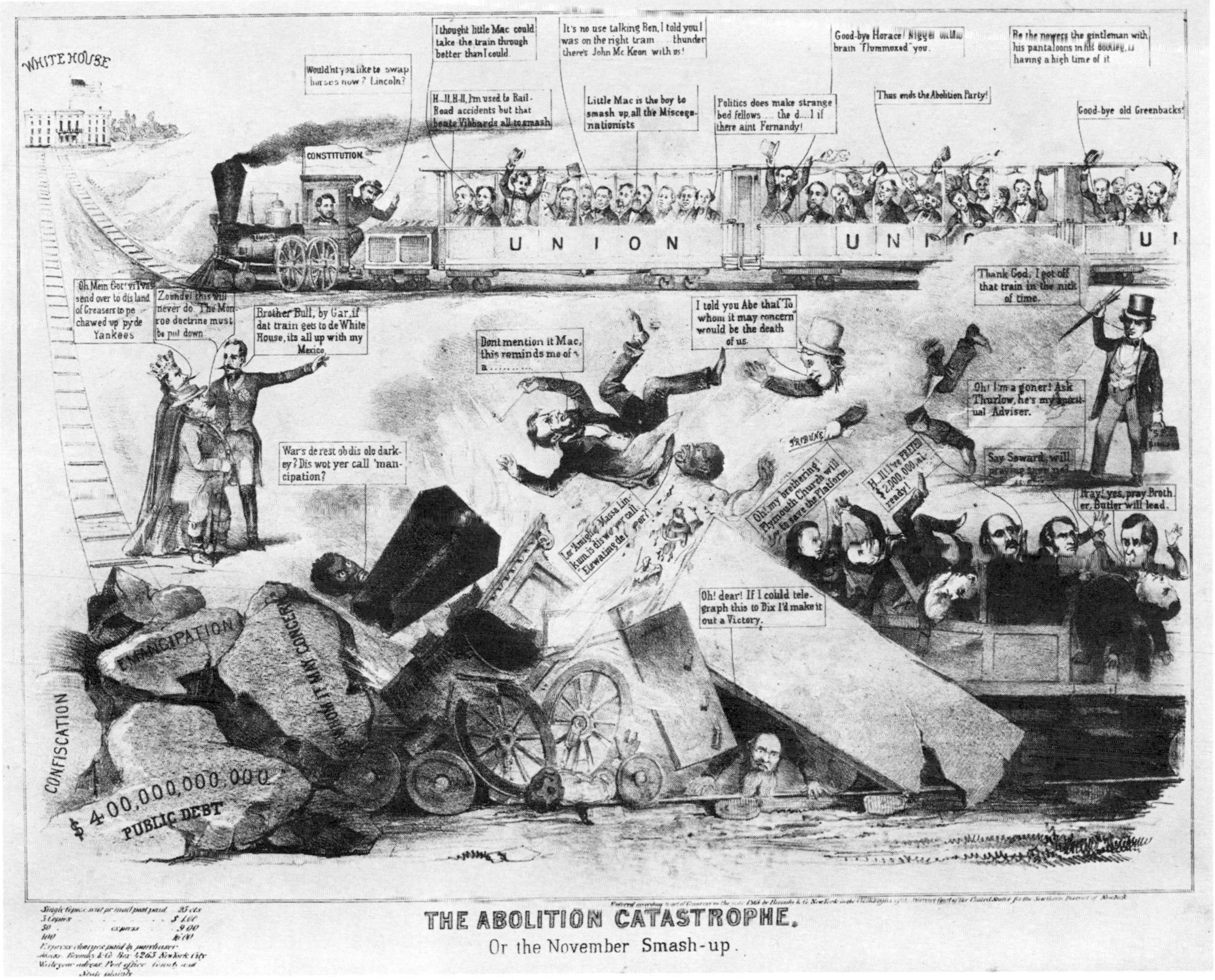

Apparently no details seem too small or points too insignificant for cartoonists involved in presidential elections. Popular themes of the late nineteenth century, notably fiscal policies and the race question, persist to this very day.

Library of Congress.

The campaign war cries of the next quarter of a century were generally of the french-soup-and-roast-beef variety, too wordy or too closely linked to current events to enjoy long life. Polk and the Democrats won in 1844 with "The Northwest and the Southwest," an oblique and rather vague reference to Oregon and Mexico which, nevertheless, had substantial voter appeal. Van Buren tried a comeback in 1848 and failed miserably with "Free Soil, Free Speech, Free Labor, and Free Men," and eight years later John Charles Fremont met a similar fate with "Give 'em Jessie" (a rather strange allusion to his secret marriage in 1841 to Senator Thomas Hart Benton's daughter, Jessie), although those three snappy words certainly were

Library of Congress.

Although the Democratic party ticket of Hancock and English campaigned in vain, appeals to freedom and nationalism had become a firm electioneering practice by 1880. Less than twenty years earlier the Democrats would have been loath to use the slogan "Union is Strength."

preferable to "We Are Buck-Hunting," "Fremont and Jessie," or "Jessie Bent On Being Free."

The hotly contested 1860 election produced a dozen or so slogans, "Free Territory for a Free People" being the words usually displayed on Republican posters; however, a much more apt war cry appeared four years later when Lincoln ran a second time. It consisted of a phrase he presumably coined when a loyal Republican congratulated him upon his renomination: "Don't Swap Horses in the Middle of the Stream." "Vote as You Shot" also was used that year, a rather blatant appeal to party regularity.

The slogans of the immediate postwar era, like the times themselves, lacked class. It is difficult to understand how words such as "Let Us Have Peace" (originated by U. S. Grant) rallied the faithful to the polls but apparently they did, not once but twice, in 1868 and again in 1872. Liberal Republicans who opposed Grant's renomination shouted "Universal Amnesty and Universal Enfranchisement," a mass of syllables that are virtually unshoutable and require considerable interpretation and reflection to be fully understood. Of course, since the Liberals did not have anyone's attention to begin with, that made little difference. In 1876 the Republican cry of "Hurrah! For Hayes and Honest Ways" countered the Democrats' "Democracy, the Last Refuge of Personal and Political Rights, Will Give Us Back the Ancient Purity of Government" and "We Demand a Rigorous Frugality in Every Department of Government." On this score alone, Tilden deserved to lose. "Anyone to Beat Grant," the slogan of anti-third-term Republicans at their convention in 1880, led to 36 rounds of balloting. Eventually, "anyone" turned out to be James Abram Garfield of Ohio.

One of the most unusual slogans appeared in 1884; not only was it in Latin but directed against a vice-presidential nominee, Republican John Alexander Logan. "Aut Caesar aut Nihil" (Either Caesar or Nothing), the motto of Cesare Borgia, meant to his critics that if Logan succeeded, four years later his zeal to become President would know no bounds. But 1884 was the year for Grover Cleveland and "Ma, Ma, where's my pa? Gone to the White House, ha-ha-ha," words and sentiments any red-blooded voter could understand even if he had flunked Latin. "A Surplus is Easier to Handle Than a Deficit," attributed to British statesman Benjamin Disraeli, was the 1888 Republican slogan. It referred to Cleveland's avowed intentions to cut tariffs in order to reduce the surplus in the U.S. Treasury.

In 1896 McKinley ran as the "Advance Agent of Prosperity" and in 1900 as the leader who could provide a "Full Dinner Pail." Eight years later the Republicans resorted to the simplest of slogans, "Stand Pat." This was the cry of conservative members harking back to a speech Senator Mark Hanna had made in Ohio in 1902 urging the Republican party to "stand pat" against all tariff reform. They "stood pat" and elected William Howard Taft.

The origins of one of the most famous and unfortunate of campaign slogans, Wilson's "He Kept Us out of War" (1916), are shrouded in mystery. Speeches made at the Democratic convention in St. Louis that year certainly stressed this general theme, much to the President's discomfort, but actually the party faithful seem to have left with these phrases ringing in their minds: "War in the East, Peace in the West, Thank God for Wilson," "You Are at Work, Not at War," "Alive and Happy, Not Cannon Fodder," and "Wilson and Peace with Honor, or Hughes with Roosevelt and War." Sometime in succeeding weeks, perhaps to counteract a Republican newspaper ad arguing that the President in fact had taken the nation into war with Mexico, Democrats emphasized the much more famous slogan.

Warren G. Harding coined his own battle cry in an acceptance speech at his home in Marion, Ohio. In brief remarks he talked in glowing terms of returning to a peaceful, orderly, prewar world, a state of "normalcy," a vague term that gave

Smithsonian Institution.

Somehow a hootennany hoot for L.B.J. seems incongruous given the serious visage of the President. Nevertheless, Johnson defeated Goldwater in 1964.

Smithsonian Institution.

Campaign slogans and platitudes alone hardly guarantee success. Presumably most Americans are advocates of peace and love, but not even these affirmative words could stave off a Democratic defeat in the 1972 election.

birth to "Back to Normalcy with Harding." Four years later the Republicans ran on "Keep Cool with Coolidge," a more refined version of "Coolidge or Chaos," and an obvious attempt to blot out memories of the man who had made the word "normalcy" so famous.

"A Chicken in Every Pot and a Car in Every Backyard to Boot" was Hoover's expanded and updated version of McKinley's "Full Dinner Pail." Like Wilson's inferred pledge of continued peace in 1916, Hoover's promise in 1928 of chicken stew and backyard flivvers very shortly had a hollow ring as the Great Depression deepened. Equally ironic was one of the Democratic slogans heard prominently throughout the land four years later: "Throw the Spenders Out!" The Republicans countered with "Prosperity is Just Around the Corner" and "The Worst is Past," but such words were no match for "Happy Days Are Here Again" (complete with music) and the enticing prospect of a "New Deal."

Four years later and again in 1940, the Democrats stole Abe Lincoln's "Don't Swap Horses" theme and used it to great advantage. "Defeat the New Deal and Its Reckless Spending" did little for Landon, although Willkie had somewhat more success with "We Want Willkie" (a precursor of "I Like Ike" in the 1950s). Other Republican slogans in 1940 included "We Don't Want Eleanor Either," "Roosevelt for ex-President," and "Roosevelt? No! No! A Thousand Times No!"

Any review such as this of presidential campaign slogans reveals how very ephemeral they really are. Most are so quickly forgotten that historians are forced to use several sentences to explain the true meaning of three or four words. The first and perhaps the most forceful, "Tippecanoe and Tyler, Too," only has pertinence because Tyler became President; had he not, it would have quickly been discarded. Lincoln's "Don't Swap Horses" has a special poignancy since it is so typically Lincolnesque in expression and humor. "Anyone But Grant" probably deserves a prize of some sort for not beating around the bush and getting right to the nub of the matter, but it is hardly fodder for the hustings. And "Aut Caesar aut Nihil" seems equally inappropriate for a real, fired-up rally.

What strikes one about twentieth century slogans is how often the words have returned to haunt those who once endorsed them with enthusiasm: Wilson's "He Kept Us out of War" (1916), Hoover's promise of chicken and automobiles for everyone (1928), and "America Needs Nixon" (1960). Two political slogans that no party ever dared use openly during a campaign nevertheless should be mentioned in passing since they permeate the very nature of political life and reflect the essence of all ballot box battles. They are "To the Victor Belong the Spoils," an attitude long prevalent and finally acknowledged in the days of Andrew Jackson, and five words attributed to John Van Buren, a New York lawyer-politician and son of Jackson's successor in the White House: "Vote Early and Vote Often."

Selected Readings

General Studies

H. Wayne Morgan, *From Hayes to McKinley: National Party Politics, 1877-1896* (1969)

Richard Hofstadter, *The Age of Reform: From Bryan to F. D. R.* (1955)

Richard Hofstadter, *The American Political Tradition* (1948)

Candidates and Presidents

Allan Nevins, *Grover Cleveland: A Study in Courage* (1932)

Louis W. Koenig, *Bryan: A Political Biography of William Jennings Bryan* (1971)

H. J. Sievers, *Benjamin Harrison, Hoosier Statesman* (1959)

R. G. Caldwell, *James A. Garfield, Party Chieftain* (1931)

D. S. Mussey, *James G. Blaine, a Political Idol of Other Days* (1934)

G. F. Howe, *Chester A. Arthur* (1934)

P. W. Glad, *McKinley, Bryan, and the People* (1964)

H. Wayne Morgan, *William McKinley and His America* (1963)

Margaret Leech, *In the Days of McKinley* (1959)

Political Strategy

Ari Hoogenboom, *Outlawing the Spoils: A History of the Civil Service Reform Movement, 1865-1883.* (1961)

C. Vann Woodward, *Reunion and Reaction: The Compromise of 1877 and the End of Reconstruction* (1951)

Richard Jensen, *The Winning of the Midwest: Social and Political Conflict, 1888-1896* (1971)

Stanley P. Hirshson, *Farewell to the Bloody Shirt: Northern Republicans and the Southern Negro, 1877-1893* (1962)

Matthew Josephson, *The Politicos, 1865-1896* (1938)

Samuel T. McSeveney, *The Politics of Depression: Political Behavior in the Northeast, 1893-1896* (1972)

Rayford Logan, *The Betrayal of the Negro: From Rutherford B. Hayes to Woodrow Wilson* (1972)

Stanley L. Jones, *The Presidential Election of 1896* (1964)

Political Reform

Gerald W. McFarland, *Mugwumps, Morals, and Politics, 1884-1920* (1975)

Agrarian Protest

Solon J. Buck, *The Granger Movement* (1913)

Russell B. Nye, *Midwestern Progressive Politics: A Historical Study of Its Origins and Development, 1870-1958* (1965)

John D. Hicks, *The Populist Revolt* (1970)

Norman Pollack, *The Populist Response to Industrial America* (1962)

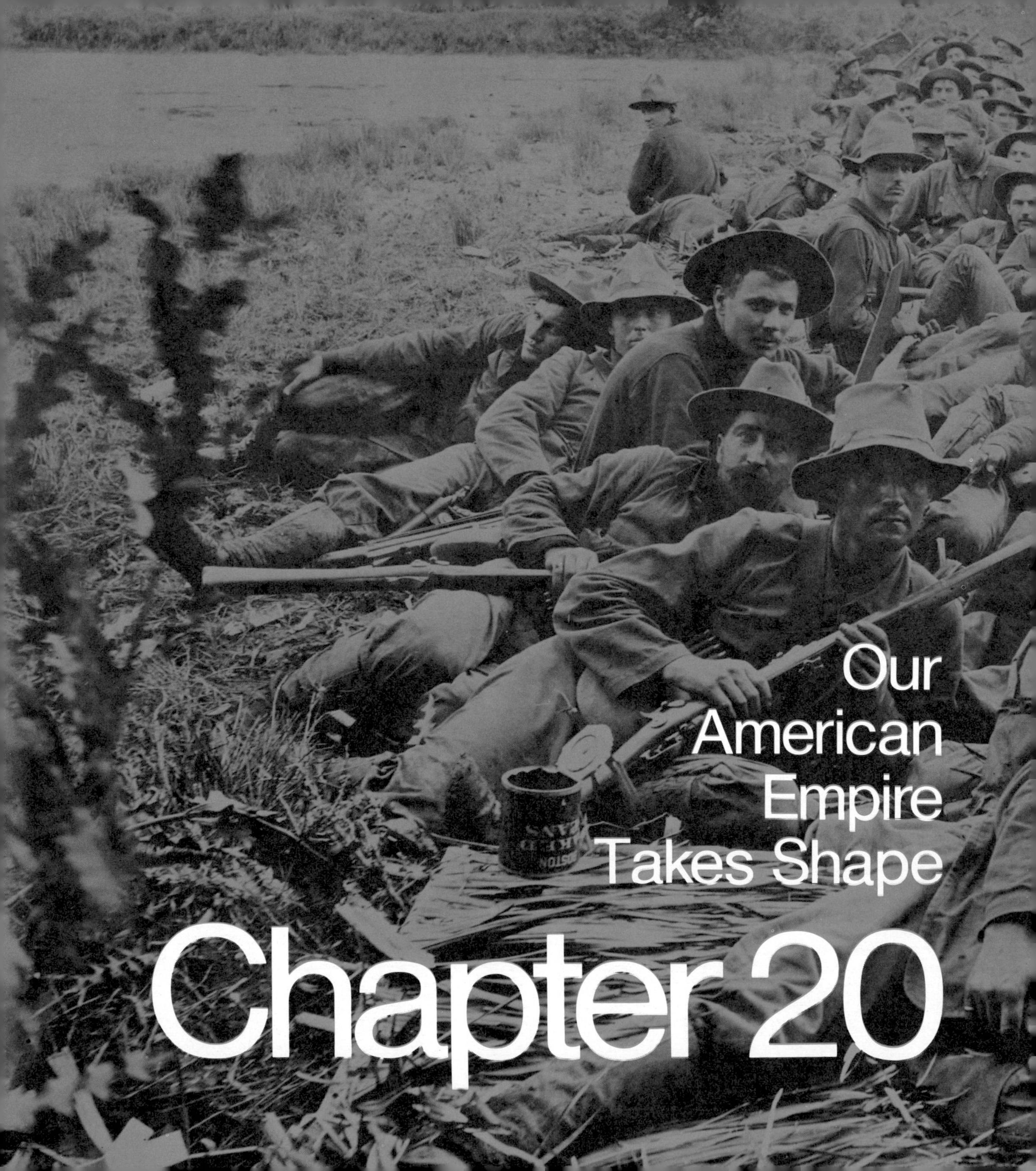

Our American Empire Takes Shape

Chapter 20

TIMELINE

1867
Withdrawal of French troops from Mexico

1867
Nicaragua grants United States transit rights for canal

1868
United States buys Alaska from Russia

1869
Grant Administration attempts to annex Dominican Republic

1871
Treaty of Washington settles Anglo-American differences

1875
Hawaii agrees to a reciprocal trade treaty with the U.S. and not to transfer territory to any other power

1878
United States acquires naval station in Samoa

1881
James G. Blaine promotes Pan-Americanism

1883
Congress appropriates funds for first modern steel ships

1887
United States abrogates Clayton-Bulwer Treaty

1889
Pan American Union established

1890
Alfred Thayer Mahan writes *The Influence of Sea Power Upon History, 1660–1783*

1891
U.S.S. Baltimore incident in Chile

1893
American settlers in Hawaii revolt against Queen Liliuokalani

1895
Secretary of State Richard Olney declares U.S. sovereign in Western hemisphere

1898
Battleship *Maine* explodes in Havana harbor

1898
Spanish-American War

1898
United States annexes Hawaii

1899
Secretary of State John Hay announces the Open Door policy in China

1899
Emilio Aguinaldo leads revolt against American rule in Philippines

1901
Platt Amendment to Army Appropriations Bill

CHAPTER OUTLINE

During the late nineteenth century, shifts occurred in American foreign policy which paralleled changes occurring in our nation's industrial and agricultural life. In fact, one could say with some truth that the United States did not have a foreign policy until that time. Its leaders and its people were so caught up in internal development and growth that whatever foreign relations existed were governed by nonentanglement in overseas affairs (Washington's Farewell Address) and recognition of our claims to a special role in the Americas (the Monroe Doctrine). Both of these essentially negative principles tended to stifle, not foster contacts with foreign powers. In the two decades after the Civil War this general indifference to what was happening overseas continued. But with the clamor for more markets to buy the goods of more factories and more farms, interest in a true foreign policy designed to promote American commerce mounted apace. Then in the 1890s America became a nation whose interests and boundaries extended beyond its seaboards. When a war with Spain brought the United States into possession of a far-flung empire of colonies and protectorates that included millions of subject peoples, a new phase of history began, during which foreign policy and domestic affairs were to become inextricably intertwined.

The Civil War and American Foreign Policy

European nations—particularly Spain—saw in the American Civil War an opportunity to press their own advantages in the Western hemisphere. In 1861, Spain reannexed the Dominican Republic. Although Secretary of State Seward immediately invoked the Monroe Doctrine and demanded that Spain withdraw, all American military resources were devoted to the struggle at home. Moreover, Washington feared that if it exerted pressure through diplomatic channels, Spain would recognize the Confederacy as a legitimate government. Consequently, when guerrilla resistance to the Spanish arose on the Caribbean island, Washington was helpless to send aid. However, exorbitant fighting costs and the deaths of troops from yellow fever caused the Spanish to withdraw their forces in July 1865.

European Intervention and Mexico

A still greater threat to autonomy in the Americas was European intervention in Mexican affairs, which lasted from 1858 to 1867. When a reform liberal group, headed by Benito Juárez, opposed a powerful conservative minority of landed aristocrats, Mexico launched its own Civil War. England, Spain, and France possessed large holdings in Mexico, much of which were damaged during the war. When Juárez won, these foreign governments demanded indemnity from him. Since the Mexican treasury was exhausted, Juárez declared a two-year moratorium on payments to foreign creditors. To the Europeans this move provided the perfect excuse for intervention. The Spanish landed in the new republic in December 1861, followed by the French and English in 1862. Americans, who had also suffered property damage during the Mexican Civil War, were invited to join in the attack, but, already involved in a war of their own, they remained neutral. Although the English and Spanish eventually withdrew their forces, European intervention brought Mexico much hardship and chaos.

The French, however, remained. Napoleon III, hoping to expand France's empire in the New World, established a Catholic monarchy in Mexico, a monarchy closely allied to French interests and dependent on France for survival. Napoleon believed that a Mexico loyal to Europe would serve as a buffer against American continental expansion. He installed the thirty-one year-old brother of the Austrian emperor, the Hapsburg Archduke Maximilian, as emperor of Mexico. For five years French troops kept Maximilian in power; the United States, uncomfortable but unable to act so long as its own Civil War still raged, did nothing. Once the American Civil War ended, however, the United States government threatened to invade Mexico and expel the French. This threat, coupled with persuasive diplomacy on the part of William Seward, persuaded Napoleon to withdraw his troops on March 12, 1867. Three months later a Mexican firing squad executed Maximilian (who refused to evacuate with the French), and Mexico was again a republic. The conclusion of this Mexican affair led American as well as European statesmen to a greater awareness of the principles of the Monroe Doctrine.

Library of Congress.

Archduke Maximilian before the Mexican fiasco.

After France withdrew from Mexico, the United States proceeded to exercise its own influence south of the border. During the 1870s Texas experienced a cattle boom, and Texans began greedily to eye Mexican territory. As the army neared the end of the Indian campaigns that had occupied it since the final days of the Civil War, professional soldiers were faced with the prospect of maintaining a peacetime force that would be relatively unimportant in national affairs. In 1876, using rustling and Indian raids along the border as an excuse, a coalition of Texas Democrats in Congress and cattle and military lobbies conspired to provoke a war with Mexico in the hope of annexing its northern lands. The coalition failed because business interests believed that foreign trade and investment would provide a more lucrative source of national revenue. At first, because of deals made in order to gain the White House, President Hayes refused to recognize the new Mexican government of Porfirio Díaz. But commercial interests again prevailed and he finally did so.

In 1881, Secretary of State James G. Blaine declared publicly that the United States had no interest in expanding its territory south of the border. Thereafter Mexico was seen as a profitable market for American trade and investments. Encouraged by the policies of Díaz, American capitalists invested heavily in railroad building, mining, and other ventures, finally surpassing even Great Britain as the most prominent foreign investor in Mexico's economic development. By 1910 the American investment probably totaled $1 billion, with perhaps one-third of that sum in mines and petroleum, a figure about equal to the entire European investment in Mexico at that time. Mexicans themselves profited little from this interest in their resources. The new American-built railroads went from American-owned mines to American markets, and most of the profits from American investments were drained out of Mexico back to the United States.

Canadian-American Relations

With the end of the Civil War, a parallel interest in expanding United States territory to the north also occurred. A group of Canadian dissenters who objected to British rule, known as the Fenian Brotherhood, were not only granted refuge by Americans for a time but also permitted to conduct raids on Canadian soil. Political unrest of this sort was fed by several factors during the first half of the nineteenth century. The eastern provinces of Canada profited from the War of 1812 but then suffered a general economic slump that kindled a cry for representative government. Other issues included Protestant-Catholic animosities, the power of absentee landlords, disagreements between commercial and agricultural interests, and anger at special fishing rights granted to the United States in 1818. By the 1850s the Atlantic provinces all had achieved substantial self-rule, but between 1815 and 1840 what is now Quebec and Ontario experienced even greater turmoil marked by sporadic outbursts of violence. The matters at issue, similar to those bedeviling eastern Canada, were complicated by intense Anglo-French bickering and pressures for expansion to the north and west. The American Civil War, British imperial policy, and the urge to expand (perhaps the crucial factor) led to the confederation of the colonies into a single dominion on July 1, 1867. Continental union and new political freedoms took the bite out of most of the protest movements north of the border, such as the Fenians, and laid to rest fears of American annexation; at the same time it invited U.S. investment. As they had with Mexico, American businessmen envisioned huge profits from Canada as a prospective market, one that also could provide access to Britain's colonial empire. In brief, by the closing years of the century, Americans had finally given up their schemes to annex Canada outright; instead they would use it as a back door to British customers throughout the world.

U.S.-British Relations: Boundaries and Arbitration

The post-Civil War years marked the beginning of a new era of relations between Great Britain and the United States as several key problems were resolved. The issues involved centered on the construction of raiders for the Confederacy in British shipyards (1861–1865) and American claims arising from the havoc caused to Union forces by cruisers such as the *Alabama.* After years of fruitless negotiation dating back to 1863, Secretary of State Hamilton Fish saw an opportunity to reopen the negotiations in July 1869 through Sir John Rose, the Canadian Minister of Finance. The British were embroiled at the time in a conflict with the Russians, who had abrogated the Treaty of Paris of 1856 prohibiting expansion of the Russian fleet in the Black Sea. Fearing war with Russia and the possibility that the United States would outfit Russian privateers to prey upon British ships, Britain was anxious to restore diplomatic harmony with America. Now mutually concerned but differently motivated, the British and the Americans agreed to submit their differences for arbitration to a joint commission comprised of five Americans, four British delegates, and one Canadian which met in Washington from February to May of 1871.

The United States surprised the British by presenting claims for the full cost of the Civil War from July 1863 until its conclusion, plus 7 percent interest—so-called indirect damages to the Union caused by Britain's actions. This strong stand appeased both critics of the Grant administration in the Senate and public opinion. Despite this bravado, the sessions were surprisingly cordial, aided by balls, receptions, and even a spring fox hunt in the Virginia countryside. The forty-three articles of the Treaty of Washington provided for further arbitration of four issues: the northwest water boundary near Vancouver Island, the *Alabama* claims, general claims by both the United States and Britain concerning damage to shipping as the result of Civil War action, and fishing rights in Atlantic coastal waters, the United States having abrogated a previous agreement in 1854. Although the most troublesome issue at the Washington talks proved to be that of fishing rights, the Americans eventually se-

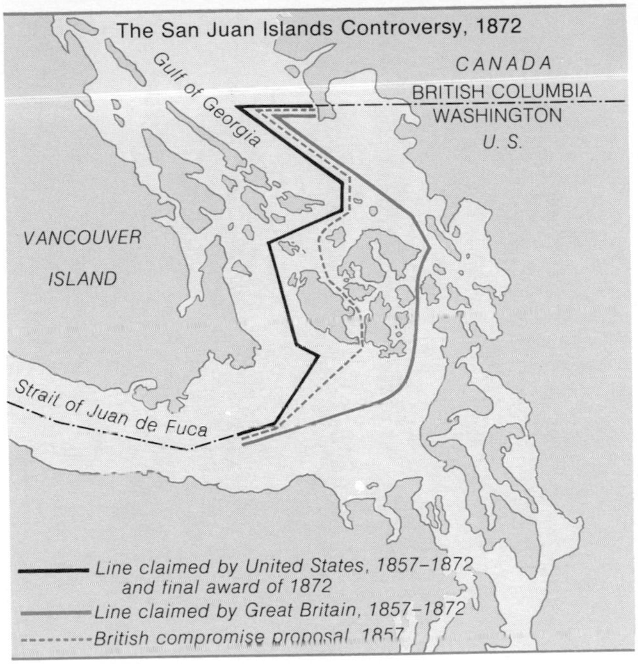

cured greatly increased privileges. This angered the Canadians who realized their own interests were being sacrificed because the Mother Country was eager to settle the vexing *Alabama* matter and to erase a precedent that could endanger her naval supremacy in time of war.

To consider the *Alabama* question, the treaty set up a panel to which members were to be named by Britain, the United States, Italy, Switzerland, and Brazil. It also included a frank admission by the British government that it deeply regretted what had happened and that in the future any neutral country must show "due diligence" to prevent the building, arming, or equipping of ships designed to prey upon a nation with which it has peaceful relations.

The *Alabama* commission, which met in Geneva in December 1871, experienced rough moments, especially when the U.S. representative, Charles Francis Adams, suddenly revived his nation's huge bill for the cost of the entire Civil War after Gettysburg, plus a 7 percent interest charge. On several occasions the talks broke down, but the commissioners eventually persuaded Adams to rule out his exorbitant indirect claim (a matter not before them for adjudication anyway) and to proceed to the heart of the issue. In September 1872 the members, with the notable exception of the British spokesman, awarded the United States $15.5 million for damage done by the *Alabama* and two other raiders, the *Florida* and the *Shenandoah.* British officials subsequently mounted the canceled draft on a wall of the Foreign Office as a warning to future ministries.

The other three questions were settled with less acrimony. The boundary issue was handed over to the German emperor who in 1872 upheld Washington's claims. In September 1873 a special commission granted Britain $1.9 million for damages her ships suffered as the result of the Union blockade. All American claims were disallowed. Another group, meeting in Halifax in 1877, awarded Britain $5.5 million for additional fishing rights conceded by the Treaty of Washington. Although U.S. spokesmen were less than happy with a net gain of about $8 million, the overall results were quite significant. Four arbitration commissions, three of them dealing with very troublesome issues in U.S.-British relations, had cleared the air and perhaps averted minor hostile clashes. This was, in fact, the greatest diplomatic triumph of these years, a note of sanity in the midst of domestic scandal and sordid national politics.

Expansionist Tendencies

William H. Seward, Secretary of State under Presidents Lincoln and Johnson, was the first cosmopolitan planner of American foreign policy. Most often associated with the purchase of Alaska, he was far more important as an advocate of aggressive expansion in foreign affairs. Seward wished to expand American boundaries as far north as the "icy barriers" would allow, eastward to the West Indies, and westward toward the Far East. His foreign policy was founded on two premises. First, the nation that controlled most of the world's raw materials would also be the strongest, able to use those resources to feed its own industries and to manufacture products for sale to other nations. Second, the geopolitical arena for any struggle for markets would be the Far East. Thus the economic domination of the Orient, especially of China, became a necessary step toward achieving world power.

Seward advocated establishing markets in Korea, Japan, and China for American goods as the first step toward fulfilling his vision. His second step toward the Orient required building a canal across Central America, with a strong navy and naval bases to protect it once completed. The bases, located strategically in Cuba, Puerto Rico, Santo Domingo, and the Virgin Islands, would assure the United States control of the canal. This control would be further secured by acquisition of colonies or protectorates in these areas. In the Pacific, American dominance was to be accomplished through acquisition of the Hawaiian Islands and the Aleutian Islands.

The need for a naval base in the Caribbean became apparent during the Civil War when the Union could not suppress Confederate operations there. In January 1866 Seward cruised the West Indies, ostensibly for his health, visiting those islands that might prove suitable sites for bases. St. Thomas in the Danish West Indies particularly impressed him, and he sought to buy the small colony for $7.5 million. Despite political maneuvering by Seward and President Johnson, Danish ratification of the proposed treaty and two plebiscites held in the islands to demonstrate that the native population approved of the sale, Congress considered the acquisition unnecessary and vetoed it. Soon after this defeat, Seward tried to obtain a base in the Dominican Republic. This attempt also failed. Finally, when Haiti offered (in January and February of 1869) to cede a port at Mole St. Nicholas to the United States, the House voted down resolutions for establishing American protectorates there as well.

Newly reunited and recovering from war, America was not interested in overseas expansion. In fact, the widespread sentiment of the time—called continentalism—held that the country should abstain from expenditures or commitments that would require large naval expenditures and confine itself to its existing continental boundaries. Moreover, the American tradition was by definition anticolonial, against governing without the consent of the governed. And a strong racist undercurrent in popular thought disapproved of acquiring possessions and peoples of alien races and cultures. Perhaps the strongest forces thwarting Seward's dreams were an inability to arouse popular support for most of his ideas and political bickering in the Senate itself. During the Johnson years, the Republicans were deeply split between Radicals and Conservatives, and virtually anything the administration proposed exacerbated their differences. Indeed, from Grant onward, the two major parties were so evenly balanced that getting two-thirds of the Senate to agree on any treaty was utterly impossible.

Seward's aspirations for Alaska fared better. The Russian settlement there had proved to be a militarily indefensible economic liability and the Czar wished to sell it. Such a sale would enable the United States to become stronger and to create a buffer zone between Russian and Canadian territory. Baron de Stoeckl, the Russian minister to the United States, offered the land at the bargain price of $7 million—a sum that was inexpensive even for the 1860s when it was known that Alaska had deposits of gold. The Russians also knew that ultimately the Americans would probably enter the territory and, once there, it would be difficult to expel them.

Despite these considerations Seward realized that the purchase of Alaska would not be received well in Washington, so negotiations were begun in secret. On March 30, 1867, the treaty ceding Alaska was signed; and, as feared, when President Johnson asked the Senate for approval, he was greeted with cries of "Seward's Folly" and "Johnson's Polar Bear Garden." Anti-expan-

New York Public Library, Picture Collection.

William Seward was an expansionist out of phase with the mood of the times. Postwar Americans focused their interests close to home.

Signing the treaty for the purchase of Alaska; Seward is seated second from left, Sumner second from right. The purchase was one of the least troublesome land acquisitions the United States ever made. There were few boundary disputes and conflicts with the indigenous population.

sionists dubbed Alaska "Frigidia" and "Walrussia". Yet within ten days the treaty was approved (37–2), largely because Radical leader Charles Sumner saw it as a step toward the annexation of Canada. In an effort to stimulate settlement, Seward launched a tremendous propaganda campaign extolling Alaska's rich fish, fur, and timber resources. Although the impeachment proceedings against Johnson caused delays, in 1868 Alaska became part of the United States, and proved to be the high-water mark of Seward's secretaryship. Deeply involved in the domestic crisis of impeachment proceedings, Congress allowed leadership in foreign affairs to fall entirely to the chief executive and his Secretary of State, thus setting a precedent for the future.

"Big Navy" Advocates

The primary instrument of implementing American foreign policy was the navy. Almost obsolete until the 1880s, the navy thereafter was in the process of modernization. One admiral commented in the 1870s that the rotting fleet reminded him of the dragons the Chinese painted on the walls of their forts to scare the enemy. Finally in 1883, despite outspoken opposition and considerable apathy, Congress appropriated funds for the construction of four modern steel ships, the beginnings of an armada that would give a good account of itself in 1898. By the close of the 1880s a "big navy" lobby, composed largely of junior officers fearful that limited naval expenditures would make them ensigns for decades, was becoming active in Washington.

To encourage the government to place more funds into the Navy Department, these officers began to cultivate the interests of businessmen and congressmen, whose firms and constituents would benefit from a large naval construction program. The most noted proponent of naval expansion and growth was Captain Alfred Thayer Mahan, author of *The Influence of Sea Power Upon History, 1660–1783.* Published in 1890, Mahan's book helped popularize the need to modernize naval forces. Others before Mahan had stressed the need to prepare for war in peacetime. Rear Admiral Stephen B. Luce, who had founded the Naval War College (1886) to train the men and officers who would man the warships, guided Mahan in his early career as a naval historian by stressing the need for a battleship fleet as well as for the study of strategy to win naval battles. Some historians regard Luce as the father of the modern navy, while granting that Mahan was its most successful propagandist.

Mahan's history was greeted with enormous enthusiasm by American expansionists and especially European leaders. British officers used the work to advance their program of naval imperialism; and the German

Library of Congress.

The Navy's White Squadron as it appeared in 1889. It is evident that the naval high command lacked confidence in steam power; indeed, the debate over the use of sails continued to the time of the Spanish-American War.

Kaiser William II had the book translated and copies placed aboard all his warships. Japanese admirals and captains also read the work with considerable interest.

Mahan believed that "The first law of States, as of men, is self-preservation—a term which cannot be narrowed to the bare tenure of a stationary round of existence. Growth is a property of healthy life." Out of these premises he fashioned a program to build a great navy, acquire colonies around the world, and establish naval bases in strategic areas. A great merchant marine would then serve as the instrument of economic domination. Mahan argued that armed might was the real arbiter of disagreements, rather than inept diplomacy that only hampered a nation's imperialism. He maintained that politicians and public alike had to be educated to accept this next step in a nation's destiny, if need be by repressing any laws that restricted the growth of arms. Mahan understood that his naked espousal of aggression would meet with opposition from liberals in America, but he was confident that his views were widely, if secretly, supported in political and commercial communities that were too "pious" to say so openly. Mahan provided American imperialists with a view of history that "proved" imperialism to be both inevitable and desirable.

Two of Mahan's disciples were to have a great effect on America's future. Theodore Roosevelt was, in the 1890s, already scorning the softness he felt was caused by capitalist wealth and proposing the strenuous athletic life as a cure. He admired militancy and approved of "righteous" warfare, maintaining that the country "needed" a good war to keep it from moral and physical decay. Like Mahan, Roosevelt envisioned America as a dominant world power whose strength would come from a formidable navy and from overseas bases and possessions. Roosevelt advocated the building of a Nicaraguan canal as well as the annexation of the Hawaiian Islands—by military force, if necessary. In an address to the Naval War College in 1897 he declared the national need for a navy powerful enough to dominate the Western hemisphere and to drive out the European powers, particularly Great Britain. "Peace is a goddess only when she comes girt with sword on thigh," he remarked, in a piece of rhetoric that foreshadowed his later foreign policy.

The young politician had to proceed cautiously at this stage of his career. It was not until an accident of politics put Roosevelt in the White House that he could "safely" unleash his naked imperialism, although as Assistant Secretary of the Navy (1897-1898), he exercised much indirect pressure to promote his and Mahan's ideas. For the time being he could only support Mahan in his secondary political role, but he was clearly waiting for his moment. In a letter to Mahan written in 1897, Roosevelt

The Huntington Library, San Marino, California.

Alfred Thayer Mahan

(1840–1914)

A slender, six-foot, sandy-haired man who was certain his views concerning the importance of naval warfare were correct, Mahan was the son of a West Point professor. After two years at Columbia College in New York, he entered the U.S. Naval Academy, graduating in 1859. Following blockade duty during the Civil War, he rose steadily in rank and responsibility and in 1885 became a captain. The following year he began lecturing on naval history and strategy at the Naval War College in Newport, Rhode Island; he soon became the president of that institution and served in that capacity until 1889.

In 1890 some of his lectures appeared under the title of *The Influence of Sea Power upon History, 1660–1783,* a book that opened new vistas in international affairs and elicited widespread attention abroad. A second volume published two years later, *The Influence of Sea Power upon the French Revolution and Empire, 1793–1812,* further enhanced his reputation, and the two books together did much to influence the worldwide buildup of naval forces before World War I.

Mahan retired from the navy in 1896 but was recalled to duty during the Spanish-American War. Much decorated by foreign nations and revered at home as well, Mahan turned out several more important works, writing almost until his death in 1914. He was a member of the U.S. delegation to the peace parley held at The Hague in 1899 and three years later was elected president of the American Historical Association. Without doubt his ideas had much to do with shaping the nature of the holocaust that just was getting underway when he succumbed to heart failure. ■

Culver Pictures.

Mrs. Bonney's Chinese Boarding School, a western outpost in Canton.

stated that Spain must be pushed out of the Caribbean: "I need not say that this letter must be strictly private. I speak to you with the greatest freedom, for I sympathize with your views, and I have precisely the same idea of patriotism, and of belief and love for our country. But to no one excepting Lodge do I talk like this."

Henry Cabot Lodge (1850–1924), a friend of Roosevelt from Harvard days, was another ardent convert to Mahan's views. After a brief stint in the House of Representatives, in the 1890s this Massachusetts "scholar in politics" who was married to a rear admiral's daughter became a senator. An ardent nationalist like Roosevelt and also a firm believer in a "big" navy, he sought a canal through Nicaragua and annexation of the Hawaiian Islands; he also advocated American dominance of Samoa and the purchase of the Danish West Indies and Greenland. Austere, cold, a towering political figure for nearly three decades, this senator favored closer cooperation with Great Britain in world affairs, but as events after World War I demonstrated, he never fully embraced internationalism. Lodge was a third and very powerful member of a growing faction of imperialists in American public life.

Missionary Zeal and Racism

American missionary work is rooted in a campaign begun in the early 1800s to "Christianize" the entire world by the year 1900; by that term, most of those who went forth to serve clearly meant conversion to a Protestant faith, preferably their own. The most active areas of operation were two troubled, declining empires, Turkey and China. Turkey held special fascination because it contained the Holy Land; China, because it had so many souls to be redeemed. For the most part, this drive was led by Presbyterians, Congregationalists, Baptists, and Methodists, although pre-Civil War splits caused some factionalism within their ranks, and after 1865 the trend was toward greater interdenominational cooperation.

The missionary story during the nineteenth century is complex and defies generalization. Converts, who sometimes joined up for political not religious reasons, were few in number and the missionary's task always remained incomplete and short of funds; otherwise he had no goals to pursue and no sound reason for soliciting support back home. Yet in many areas missionary schools and hospitals had such profound impact that they made Christianity and westernization inseparable allies. As a result, missionary schools aided American penetration of China and helped expand U.S. influence throughout the Far and Middle East, including such far-flung outposts as Hawaii, Samoa, Korea, and Constantinople. The brave men and women who served in these regions were, first and foremost, zealous workers for the glory of God, but they also were patriots interested in the glory of Uncle Sam who came to believe that secular work among "the heathen" might be more important than their immediate conversion. In addition, by the 1880s they constituted a propaganda lobby eager to persuade other Americans that overseas expansion was both highly desirable and in the national interest.

In 1885, Josiah Strong revived the tenets of Manifest Destiny, giving religious support to the notion of racial superiority. In his book *Our Country,* he argued that Anglo-Saxons had a "divine sanction" to be their brothers' keepers, particularly in Latin America. Others, such as the historians John Burgess of Columbia University and John Fiske of Harvard University, argued that the white man's burden was to "civilize" the world. When these spokesmen began to couch their arguments in economic terms, they also began to attract commercial interests at home.

Library of Congress.

The "White Man's Burden" was Rudyard Kipling's phrase summarizing the conviction that the West had a duty to seize foreign lands and "civilize" the natives. The view was not universal. William H. Walker's satire on imperialism appeared on the March 16, 1899 cover of *Life* magazine.

Economics and Imperialism

Especially prominent among these interests were merchant capitalists (shipbuilders, importers and exporters, owners of steamship lines) with a stake in international growth. Using the well-known argument of overproduction, they said that the nation's welfare required overseas expansion and helped to pressure Congress into passing the Mail Steamship Subsidy Bill of 1891. Victims of growing monopolies who had been pushed out of the domestic scene also turned their eyes to distant lands. Minor C. Keith, founder of the United Fruit Company, was one of many capitalists who saw in the sugar and mineral riches of the Caribbean a new source of millions. When they experienced difficulties with their foreign rivals or hosts, these men called upon the United States government for protection, claiming that the national interest was at stake.

Some of these claims of overproduction had a sound basis; for, as alleged, American farmers and manufacturers were producing far beyond domestic needs. Prices were erratic and the economy unstable as the law of supply and demand ruined many individuals and inhibited national growth. When an outbreak of trichinosis prompted most of Europe (Britain, France, Austria-Hungary, Italy, Greece, Germany) to ban American pork in 1881, a precedent was set for banning American agricultural products, and the Farmers' Alliance of that decade insisted that the federal government provide new markets to offset such losses.

All of these diverse factors—the desire of certain politicians to expand U.S. territory, the fears of career navy officers that they might never be promoted, A. T. Mahan's plea for a naval renaissance, the businessman's craving for new markets, and the missionary's confidence in the innate superiority of Yankee culture—created a public mood that would soon shatter America's traditional anticolonialism. The nation that had rejected colonial bonds in the eighteenth century and cheered lustily whenever other peoples followed their example was, by the close of the nineteenth century, giving serious consideration to building an empire of its own.

The United States and Latin America

The Grant administration's interests in Latin America centered on Cuba, the Dominican Republic (Santa Domingo), and an interocean canal; and, although the results were meager, only Secretary of State Hamilton Fish (1808–1893) prevented them from also being disastrous. Fish, a wealthy New Yorker with some political experience, joined the Cabinet reluctantly but ended up staying the full eight years (1869–1877). Grant, who adopted a hell-for-leather approach toward Carribean affairs, was especially eager to aid Cuban rebels and annex the Dominican Republic, or at least to secure a naval base there. In 1869 the President sent to the Dominican Republic a special agent who negotiated treaties providing for annexation and (as an alternative) a ninety-nine-year lease on Samana Bay with an option to buy. The Dominicans quickly conducted a plebiscite and agreed to join the United States, but the Senate turned thumbs down on the whole idea. Grant was so shocked that he never submitted the question of leasing Samana Bay to a vote.

Library of Congress.

By far the most astute member of Grant's Cabinet, Secretary of State Hamilton Fish acted as a force for both moderation and expansion in foreign affairs.

These developments precipitated a bitter feud between Grant and Charles Sumner, head of the Senate's Foreign Relations Committee (whom the President had mistakenly addressed as Judiciary Committee chairman). Grant even implied at one point that, were he not living in the White House, he would challenge Sumner to a duel. In the end he soothed his ego by maneuvering to have his adversary ousted from the Foreign Relations post. This fiasco actually had beneficial effects since it removed several obstacles to a more reasonable accommodation with Great Britain in 1871. Sumner, who opposed such a move, then had less power, and Grant, who at one time agreed with the senator's views, had changed his mind.

Grant also miscalculated the Cuban crises that arose during his administration. In the fall of 1868 fighting broke out between Spanish colonialists and rebel forces, starting what came to be known as the Ten Years' War. Since the rebel government was extremely weak, Fish opposed both recognition and intervention, offering instead to have Washington act as mediator for the opposing factions. Congress, on the other hand, proposed recognizing that a state of belligerency existed. This move, although giving moral encouragement to the Cuban rebels, would have complicated Fish's ongoing negotiations with Great Britain, since he was maintaining that London erred in 1861 when it recognized the Confederacy as a "belligerent." The Secretary of State eventually convinced the President not to get involved in Cuba, at least not in 1870. Five years later, however, he suggested that England, the United States, and perhaps other European powers should join in imposing peace on that island, a proposal that was sharply criticized in the American press since it seemed to disregard the fundmental precepts of the sacred Monroe Doctrine. Then in 1878, with the accession of a new monarch to the Spanish throne, a more liberal colonial policy evolved, and the Cuban question receded from view for seventeen years, smouldering but not demanding American attention.

Grant and Fish also attempted to follow through on

Library of Congress.

Dredges at work on the unsuccessful Nicaragua Canal venture in 1887.

Seward's plans for an interoceanic canal. Seward had concluded a treaty with Nicaragua in 1867, giving the United States transit rights across the country. When the Suez Canal was opened in 1869, public interest in a Central American canal intensified. Fish focused on the Isthmus of Panama, attempting to secure a right of way with the consent of the Colombian government (which governed Panama). But the Colombian Senate added so many unacceptable amendments to the treaty that negotiations collapsed. Grant then appointed an interoceanic commission to determine the best route for a waterway. Though Nicaragua was their unanimous choice, nothing was done at the time to implement the idea.

During President Hayes's administration interest in the canal was revived. Ferdinand de Lesseps, the French builder of the Suez Canal, obtained from the Colombian government the right to build a waterway across Panama. The action of de Lesseps' shocked the American public, which saw his project as a violation of the Monroe Doctrine. Despite attempts to allay public hostility, de Lesseps was informed by Secretary of State William Evarts that any canal joining the Atlantic and Pacific must be under American control.

To prove its seriousness, Congress initiated steps to void the Clayton-Bulwer Treaty of 1859 by which Britain and the United States had agreed that neither should have exclusive rights over future canal routes across Central America. By 1887, the treaty had been abrogated, and an American promoted and Nicaraguan-sponsored Maritime Canal Company began construction on a canal across Nicaragua. When the company went bankrupt, the U.S. government chose not to intervene and thus avoided an open diplomatic rift with the British. Meanwhile, in 1889 the French company collapsed because of bankruptcy, poor planning, and disease; nevertheless, despite these setbacks, it was apparent that the United States fully intended to build and to control a canal linking the Atlantic and Pacific oceans—and in the not-too-distant future.

James G. Blaine and Pan-Americanism

Latin America and a canal were special concerns of James G. Blaine, Secretary of State under Presidents Garfield, Arthur, and Harrison (1881, 1889–1892). Seward's failure had in part been due to his focus on the Far East, which most Americans felt was too far away to be of national interest. Like Seward, Blaine was a Republican who spoke for eastern industrial corporate interests. Blaine, a key Republican spokesman during the 1880s whether he was in office or out, also shared Seward's belief that foreign acquisitions were the best insurance of markets for America's industries. But he realized that Latin America was a more viable step toward a bigger share of world markets than acquisitions in the Far East. Consequently, his Latin American policy was not based merely on the desire to increase trade; it attempted as well to promote peace in a troubled area as the necessary condition for a flourishing trade. Latin America was a large exporter to the States, especially of sugar, coffee, fruit, and minerals. But it imported little in return, preferring to purchase manufactured goods from Europe, particularly from Great Britain. By promoting peace in Latin America, Blaine hoped to eradicate opportunities for European intervention in Latin affairs and at the same time to develop a more favorable balance of trade. But creating a stable peace throughout the Latin countries was no small task. Continual strife existed below America's southern border—particularly in the boundary areas between Mexico and Guatemala, between Argentina and Chile, and between the latter and Peru and Bolivia.

The Mexican-Guatemalan border dispute of 1881 opened the door to Blaine's first excursion into Pan-Americanism. When a similar problem arose in Chile, Blaine opposed the terms of a treaty requiring the ceding of rich nitrate deposits in Peru to Chile and earned thereby the enmity of Chile for America. This U.S. position was largely due to suspicions that Britain had instigated the hostilities. While most historians now agree that little evidence exists of British plans to intervene in South America, contemporary Anglophobes such as Blaine firmly believed that they would. Even after leaving office, Blaine retained this view. "It is a perfect mistake," he said, "to speak of this as a Chilian war on Peru. It is an English war on Peru, with Chili [*sic*] as the instrument and I take the responsibility of that assertion. Chili would never have gone into this war one inch but for her backing by English capital."

Blaine clearly undertook the role of mediator in Latin America to help establish a precedent of American arbitration in the volatile affairs of the southern continent. He hoped to increase U.S. prestige and at the same time to reduce South America's traditional ties to Europe. But Blaine was hampered by incompetent diplomats, by Washington's inexperience in such a role, and by lack of discipline in his own office. More important, with the death of Garfield, he no longer was in favor at the White House and after a few weeks resigned, ending a ten-month experiment in Pan-Americanism.

In 1889, however, with his wing of the Republican party back in power, Blaine got his job back and was able to move forward once more, often dealing with old, familiar problems. His return was, for obvious reasons, not well received in Chile. In 1891 civil war erupted there and a steamer loaded with arms for the rebels was seized by U.S. officials in San Diego; however, the crew overpowered their guards and made a successful dash to Chile. In time, the rebels, who won their war, reluctantly surrendered the vessel to American authorities, although U.S. courts ultimately ruled it should have been permitted to sail unmolested. These maneuverings set the stage for yet another confrontation between these two nations.

In 1891 a group of American sailors from the cruiser *Baltimore* were given shore leave in Valparaiso and became involved in a barroom brawl. Two of them were killed. In an address to Congress, President Harrison asked that American honor be avenged by a declaration of war on Chile. At the last minute, however, Chile offered apologies and promised compensation, and the war scare subsided. Only tense relations between the countries and a growing mood of imperialistic expansionism had made such a threat possible. Many cooler heads now realized that organization and policy were necessary if peace was to be maintained. And they looked to Blaine's ideas of Pan-Americanism as the answer.

As early as 1881, Blaine had tried to achieve his goals of economic and diplomatic supremacy in Latin America by means of an inter-American conference and even issued invitations to such a gathering a few weeks before he left office in 1881. Eight years later such a conference was belatedly convened in Washington by Thomas Bayard, Cleveland's Secretary of State. Blaine served as secretary of that gathering and, when he succeeded to Bayard's post, became its president.

The conference established the International Bureau of American Republics, later known as the Pan American Union. Although the conference became an agency for the exchange of economic, scientific, and cultural information, it failed to set up trade agreements or any effective instrument for diplomatic intervention. Despite obvious distrust on the part of Chile and Argentina and the misgivings of several other Latin American nations, the United States emerged as the dominant power in the Americas, able to set policy and to chart a more effective course for the future.

Cleveland and Venezuela

A few years after this unusual inter-American conference ended, Grover Cleveland, back in the White House for another term, found himself involved in a hot border dispute between Venezuela and Great Britain. The trouble between the two nations had started in the 1840s when disagreement arose between Venezuela and the British territory of Guiana. But the claims were so extreme on each side that nothing could be settled. And in the 1880s, when gold was discovered in the disputed border area, the conflict flared up anew. By then, the Venezuelans were deeply in debt to the British and apparently unable to pay them back. The British now demanded the controversial territory as payment and rejected a U.S. offer to act as mediator.

Americans felt that to sustain their role as arbiter of peace in South America they had to step in and resolve the dispute. They also were alarmed by Britain's increasingly imperialistic stance in Central America. In April 1895 four hundred Britain marines occupied the port of Corinto, Nicaragua, in retaliation against rumored abuses of British subjects. Simultaneously the British made important inroads in Brazil, threatening to control the shipping lanes and the major rivers, threats that made American mercantile interests nervous.

Meanwhile, William L. Scruggs, a former minister to Venezuela under Harrison, who was dismissed for corruption in office, became a powerful propagandist for that South American country. His role in shaping American intervention has since been revealed by journals and letters he kept. A skillful lobbyist, Scruggs published a pamphlet in 1894 that went through four editions and fired the public imagination. Called *British Aggressions in Venezuela, or the Monroe Doctrine on Trial,* this tract called for the deliverance of oppressed Venezuelans from British exploitation. That U.S. foreign policy could be influenced by lobbyists and business interests is no great surprise, but that such groups nearly involved America in war with one of Europe's most powerful nations is evidence of how dangerously ill-equipped both Congress and the presidency were to handle complex diplomatic issues.

Negotiations to settle the border dispute were initiated under Secretary of State Walter Gresham, who died in 1895 before they were completed. He was succeeded by Richard Olney, a far more abrasive diplomat. Olney had been a corporation lawyer who rose to the office of Attorney General with Cleveland's election in 1893. Olney informed Great Britain that the United States "is practically sovereign on this continent, and its fiat is law." The United States would tolerate no European interference in its domain. Furthermore, it had the indisputable right to interpose itself in any European-American conflict.

The British were asked to reply to Olney's declaration before the President addressed Congress in December 1895. Lord Salisbury, Britain's foreign minister, took four months to reply to what amounted to an ultimatum, and then refuted the broadly interpreted version of the Monroe Doctrine that Olney had presented. Cleveland delivered a militant address to Congress, demanding the formation of a commission to investigate the border dispute and intimating the strong possibility of war if the commission's findings were ignored.

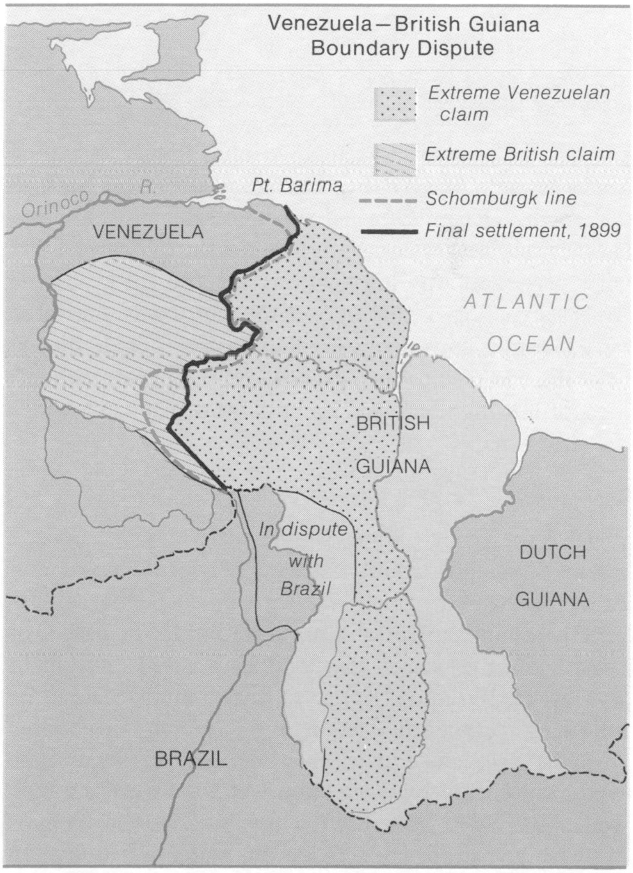

America was unprepared for such a struggle, but the British had to assume that the President's words might lead to hostile action. As it turned out, trouble in South Africa suddenly demanded all of Britain's resources, and they backed away from yet another confrontation in South America. Given the hostility of their European neighbors, they decided it would be wise to have an American ally and therefore agreed to American arbitration. A treaty was drawn up favoring the British claims over those of Venezuela. This document marked a new stage in Anglo-American relations and amounted almost to an alliance. But while the treaty pleased Britain and gave America the prestige it had demanded, it was negotiated without Venezuela's knowledge and agreed upon without her approval. The arbitration commission of two Americans, two Englishmen, and one Russian protected American interests by forcing Britain to relinquish control of the Orinoco River and its mouth, but ceded to Britain 90 percent of the remaining disputed territory.

The United States in the Pacific

During the years between 1878 and 1896 the United States became involved in several disputes over lands in the Pacific Ocean. One led to international arbitration, another to outright annexation, and a third to a brief war with very ominous implications for the future. Some American action in that part of the world was motivated by economic considerations and simple greed. In any case, the end result was a great increase in colonial holdings, promising markets, and both immediate and potential problems.

Samoa

In 1878 the United States signed a treaty with Samoa, a group of islands about halfway between Hawaii and Australia. Samoa, which was then independent, authorized the establishment of a naval station in the harbor of Pago Pago, the best in the archipelago. This agreement also granted trading rights to the United States; the following year both Britain and Germany negotiated with the Samoans and received similar privileges. The use of one harbor by three nations did not work out very well, and early in 1889 matters looked serious as warships of the three nations collected at the island of Tutuila. On March 15, 1889, two weeks before President Cleveland's term expired, a hurricane wiped out most of these foreign vessels, postponing any immediate confrontation. The three powers then met in Berlin later that same year and agreed to maintain the neutrality of Samoa and, in effect, to establish a tripartite protectorate over the islands.

That agreement also failed to end this triangular bickering, and in 1899 Germany and the United States divided responsibility for the islands, Britain being compensated by recognition of its rights to Tonga and the Solomon Islands. Between 1900 and 1904 the chiefs living in the American zone, Eastern Samoa, ceded their islands to the U.S. government, although this cession was not formally accepted by Congress until 1929. Western Samoa remained in German hands until 1914 when it was occupied by troops from New Zealand. These maneuverings were, of course, a triumph for the naval lobby that was keenly interested in Samoa, although not one American in a thousand (then or now) probably could

STUDYING TO PLEASE.
Samoa: I CAN'T SING ALL THESE NATIONAL AIRS AT ONCE!

New York Public Library, Picture Collection.

The Samoans had no control over their destiny and were absent from the Berlin Conference of 1899.

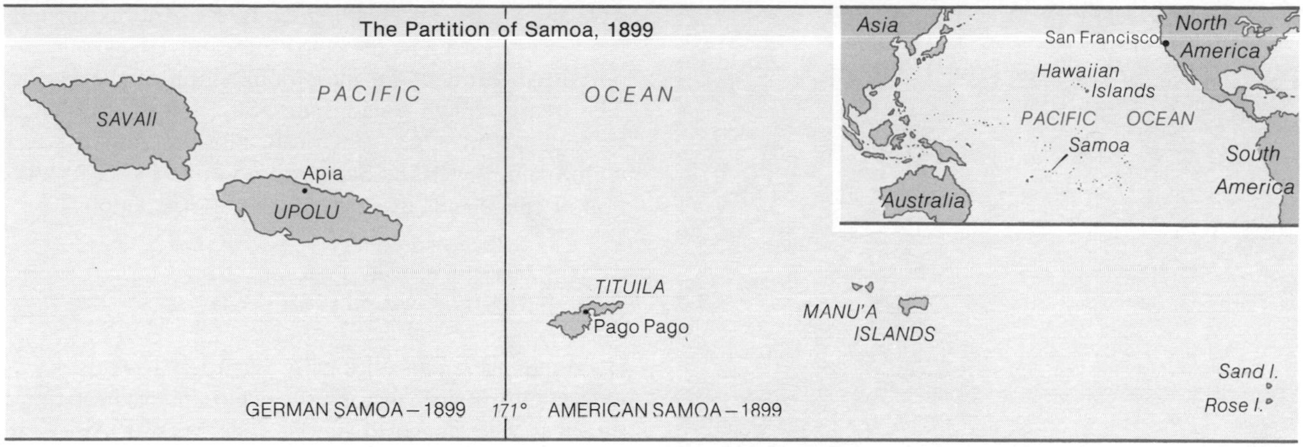

pinpoint the location of those islands wthout consulting an atlas.

Hawaii

When Cleveland began his second presidential term in 1893, he discovered that Harrison had left him an entirely new legacy. One of Harrison's final acts in office had been to smooth the way for the annexation of Hawaii. The nation's interest in these islands started during the eighteenth century when trade with China began to flourish. In the early nineteenth century the missionaries who had followed the traders had established converts among the natives. Soon sugar planters followed, establishing a growing American community which in time included numerous clergymen turned businessmen of whom it is often said "they went to do good and did well." Annexation was proposed as early as President Franklin Pierce's administration and again under President Grant. In 1875, a treaty was signed giving the United States dominant access to the sugar crops, which were increasing rapidly. By 1895, sugar production had increased ten times over what it had been during the previous two decades. The domestic industry that grew up in response to this rich supply provided a powerful lobby for annexation.

In 1887 the colonialists on the islands forced the reigning king, Kalakaua, to make large concessions, such as accepting a constitution that limited his powers and made his court responsible to a senate controlled by large landowners. But when the old king died in 1891, he was succeeded by his sister, Queen Liliuokalani (1838-1917), a strong-willed monarch who disliked the growing influence of whites in Hawaii and wished to reassert the independence of the islands.

In 1893 Queen Liliuokalani attempted to replace the constitution with one that restored power to the native population and returned to the throne the royal authority relinquished by her brother. In response to this move the sugar planters formed a revolutionary clique that set up a provisional government and sought annexation to the United States. If Hawaii became part of the United States, its sugar would be exempt from tariff restrictions and thus cheaper than that imported by the United States from the West Indies.

Using the Queen's new policies as an excuse, especially her rejection of constitutional government, the United States minister to Hawaii, John L. Stevens, ordered (without authorization) 150 marines from the cruiser Boston into Honolulu. This forced the monarch to capitulate. On February 15, 1893, Harrison submitted a bill to the Senate requesting the annexation of the islands. But Harrison was in his last days in office, and Cleveland's second inauguration was at hand.

After President Cleveland took office he sent an investigating committee to Hawaii. The committee reported that the vast majority of the native population supported Queen Liliuokalani. Hearing this, Cleveland decided to fight the Republican plans for annexation and even supported the idea that it was the nation's duty to assist the Queen to return to power. Cleveland did not reckon with the new rebel government of planters, both American and European, now firmly entrenched on Ha-

Hawaii State Archives.

Sanford B. Dole (seated), businessman and first governor of the Territory of Hawaii, with the last monarch, Queen Liliuokalani. Although the Queen was an ardent nationalist who wished to limit white influence, she succumbed to white culture, as her stylish Victorian garb suggests.

waiian soil. These men remained hostile to Cleveland. They refused to relinquish their hold on the local government and ignored Washington, preferring to wait for a presidential election that might bring a reversal in U.S. policy. With the support of John L. Stevens, the United States minister to the islands and an annexationist, the 150 men from the cruiser *Boston*, originally sent ashore to "protect" American lives and property, remained to insure the continuance of the new regime. This new regime now declared the islands to be the Republic of Hawaii.

In the election of 1896 the Republican party platform endorsed U.S. control of Hawaii. When McKinley won he soon sided with the annexationists, though he had previously shown little interest in American imperialism. On August 12, 1898, the Hawaiian Islands became United States territory. Nevertheless, McKinley did not have an easy time persuading Congress. Anti-expansionists were still strong and could not be moved, even by the purported threat of Japanese domination of the Pacific. The treaty, drawn up in June 1897, lay in the Senate without action. Only American entrance into the war with Spain moved the Senate to approve the incorporation of the islands as part of an emerging empire.

The Spanish-American War

Historians have conventionally regarded 1898 as a watershed in American history, the beginning of the nation's career as a great world power. The Spanish-American War, more than anything else, contributed to the creation of an American empire complete with colonies, protectorates, and territories in both hemispheres. At the time the war was enthusiastically hailed as "splendid." And although the electorate was still far more concerned with domestic affairs, it offered little resistance to the foreign policy that was made behind closed doors by the President's Cabinet. Nevertheless, anti-imperialistic and anti-expansionistic sentiment on the part of many of the nation's powerful politicians remained strong.

The Cuban problem was part of a long ongoing conflict between Spain and Cuban freedom fighters. When revolution again broke out in 1895, it was partly prompted by anger at Spanish corruption and incompetence. But the situation was also aggravated by the American tariff law of 1894, which raised duties on raw sugar and brought new hardship to the island. Like most of the mercantile world Cuba was still in the throes of the severe depression that had started in 1893.

The revolt that ensued was savage. Destruction of property and lives was widespread on both sides. When General Valeriano Weyler, the Spanish colonial commander-in-chief, began to relocate villagers in concentration camps in order to end their support of guerrilla forces, the American press started to fan the flames of war. William Randolph Hearst's *New York Journal* and Joseph Pulitzer's *New York World* vied for circulation with headlines about atrocities committed by the Spanish against the islanders. To arouse interest, Hearst dispatched famed artist Frederic Remington to Cuba to draw pictures of destruction caused by the rebellion. Remington allegedly telegraphed back that all was peaceful. "There is no trouble. There will be no war."

Hearst, it is said, replied, "You furnish the pictures and I'll furnish the war."

Americans had traditionally been sympathetic to the Cubans, who were struggling against a grossly unjust colonial monarchy. Cuba was seen by some as economically and politically strategic, a gateway to the proposed isthmian canal and a source of revenue from over $100 million invested by Americans in Cuban sugar. To profit from these sentiments, the Cuban junta set up an office in New York City to raise funds and to gain sympathy through a steady flow of propaganda against Spain.

Though it is clear that both public sentiment and vested economic interests pressed newly elected President McKinley and Congress to intervene, Washington's policy toward an independent Cuba was not yet defined. Most of those who urged intervention—both the Republican and the Democratic presses—insisted that they did so for strictly humanitarian reasons. Liberals, Populists, and representatives of American labor were all forces behind this sentiment. But others feared that an independent Cuba might become radical or unstable, unable to protect American lives and property or to honor its debts. These sentiments were expressed by imperialists such as Mahan, Roosevelt, and Lodge, who urged intervention for the purpose of annexation.

By the time McKinley took office, Hearst and Pulitzer had made "Weyler the Butcher" a household term throughout much of America. As his purported telegram to Remington indicated, Hearst not only reported but manufactured "news." When one of his reporters entered the cell of a female revolutionary and spirited her away to safety, the nation was delirious with joy. The Bishop of London wired his congratulations, and Missouri's governor suggested Hearst send 500 reporters to Cuba and free the entire island.

Yet fears remained that a rebel victory might not be in America's best interests after all. What was a very cruel racial and class war could lead to the establishment of a "black republic" with radical ideas. Both Cleveland and McKinley played for time, hoping this troublesome issue would resolve itself. But both agreed that if Spain proved unable to deal with the insurrection, then humanitarian motives would have to supersede diplomatic considerations, making American intervention unavoidable. McKinley held to his view until the summer of 1897 when Spain launched full-scale military operations in an effort to end the revolt.

American Intervention

By August of 1897 the McKinley administration recognized that it had two alternatives. It must either acknowledge Cuba's independence or enter the war and oust Spain from the island. In February 1898 a private letter written by Enrique Dupuy de Lome, the Spanish minister to the United States, was stolen and published. The letter described President McKinley as "weak," an ambitious politician who sought only to please crowds. The minister immediately resigned. But on February 15, six days after the publication of his letter, the American battleship *Maine* blew up in Havana harbor. Two hundred and sixteen died in the explosion. The American press immediately provoked public hysteria, while popular opinion convicted Spain of engineering the blast. The yellow press called for war, shouting "Remember the Maine! To Hell with Spain." The Spanish government disavowed any responsibility for the accident, offered condolences, and agreed to an immediate and joint investigation. The commission concluded that the explosion had been caused externally. But the mystery was never solved. Most historians think it improbable that the Spanish government sabotaged the ship, since it was clear that Spain wished to avoid war with the United States.

Before the commission made its final report Congress had already voted $50 million for defense. In late March President McKinley presented Spain with a proposal that an armistice be declared that would last until October 1 and that its policy of concentration camps cease. These steps apparently were what Washington considered minimum essentials for restoring peace to the wartorn island. In a less imperative tone, McKinley noted that the United States might eventually be willing to mediate the conflict.

In early April a peaceful solution still seemed possible. Spain agreed to end concentration camps and grant an armistice but only for so long as the army commander in Cuba thought necessary to prepare for eventual peace. In short, war could be resumed whenever Spain was ready to do so. This probably was about as far as the Spanish government could go without risking trouble at home. On April 11, the President implied in a message to Congress that Madrid was unable to fulfill its promises and that intervention in the name of "humanity and civilization" had become necessary.

Actually, Spain's reaction to McKinley's proposals made little difference, for pressures were mounting on

Library of Congress.

The *Maine* the day after the fatal explosion.

the President that made war almost inevitable. The clamor for action was loud within his own party, and even the business community, long wary of war, was changing its mind. Recovery from the debacle of 1893 seemed less secure than first thought, and many business leaders concluded that actual war might disturb the economy far less than constant rumors and indecision. Also, congressional elections were coming up in the fall and McKinley himself was looking ahead to 1900 and renomination.

For a week Congress seethed with excitement as legislators fought, called each other "liar" and "scoundrel," and threw books at those who opposed their views. In the halls groups eager for war sang "Dixie," "The Battle Hymn of the Republic," and "Hang General Weyler from a Sour Apple Tree." Then on April 19 the members passed a fateful, four-part resolution that (1) declared Cuba free, (2) demanded the withdrawal of Spain, (3) directed the President to use armed force to achieve these objectives, and (4) stated that the United States had no intentions of annexing Cuba. The last point, known as the Teller Amendment, won approval without dissent. It had the strong support of sugar interests who did not wish to see Cuba within the tariff walls and of all those who thought the United States was embarking upon a great and glorious crusade. It was however, a bit vague and left open the possibility that Cuba might become a U.S. protectorate; significantly, it replaced the largely ignored Turpie Amendment (first passed and then discarded), which would have pledged the independence of Cuba even before military intervention occurred. Madrid immediately severed diplomatic relations with Washington. On April 22, the U.S. Navy blockaded Cuban ports, two days laters Spain declared war on the United States, and the following day McKinley signed an act of Congress declaring that a state of war had existed since April 21.

The Spanish-American War lasted only ten weeks and was doubtless the most popular war ever fought by Americans. With the Teller Amendment agreed upon, Americans saw the war as an act of mercy, a fulfillment of the principles of the Monroe Doctrine, and the successful assertion of American dominance in the Western Hemisphere. The Spanish fought for their honor, although it was clear that they could not win.

The first blow of the war was not struck in Cuba or even in the West Indies. Less than a week after war had been declared Commodore George Dewey won a stunning naval victory in Manila harbor in the Philippine Islands. Dewey was an appointee of Assistant Secretary of the Navy Theodore Roosevelt and like his patron a firm imperialist. With the President's approval Roosevelt had warned Dewey to prepare for battle weeks in advance of the declaration of war. On April 30, after leaving Hong Kong, the American ships surprised and sank the ill-equipped Spanish fleet, thus destroying Spanish naval power in the Pacific. In the Caribbean the American fleet effectively blockaded the Cuban coast and thus bottled up the Spanish ships that had recently arrived from the Cape Verde Islands under the leadership of Admiral Pascal Cervera Topete. Although the U.S. Navy was brilliantly prepared and effective, the same could not be said for the Army.

At the outbreak of the war the United States Army was an ill-prepared force of some 28,000 men and officers. The War Department was outdated and supplies and weapons were inadequate for the battles ahead. No military strategy had been thought out; even the maps were antiquated. In charge of the forces assembling at Tampa, Florida, for the invasion of Cuba was General William Shafter, a hero of the Civil War. The embarkation was chaotic and inefficient. Men were supplied with winter woolen uniforms to fight in the tropics and given food from "patriotic" meat companies but quickly dubbed "embalmed" by the soldiers it was supposed to nourish. Medical supplies were inadequate. Casualty figures, initially low, soon rose catastrophically due to cases of dysentery and yellow fever.

The public, meanwhile, saw the war as a glorious adventure. The homefront celebrated with bands and parades, unaware of the total inadequacy of the armed forces to meet an enemy whose strength was unknown. Even more incompetent and ill-equipped, with its officer ranks riddled with corruption and its troops often indifferent, the Spanish forces gave America its quick victory. The most publicized and picturesque American unit was the First Volunteer Cavalry Regiment, or "Rough Riders." This group, composed of cowboys, ranchmen, Indians, hunters, and even graduates of Harvard and Yale, was commanded by Col. Leonard Wood (1860–1927) and the newly volunteered Lt. Col. Theodore Roosevelt.

With the Cuban fleet bottled up in Santiago Bay by the vastly superior American naval force under Admiral William Sampson (1840–1902), an expeditionary force landed 18,000 men without incident. Though there were over 200,000 Spanish troops on the island only 13,000 of them were in the vicinity of Santiago. So inefficient were

New York Public Library, Picture Collection.

United States troops departing for Manila. Most of their casualties in battle were to be inflicted by rebel Filipinos rather than the Spanish military.

the Spanish communication and transportation networks that these troops were left alone to deal with the Americans.

It was at the major battle of San Juan Hill that Theodore Roosevelt established his reputation for valor. In later years Roosevelt often described the battle as "great fun, a bully fight." The reality, however, was a bloody affair. The American army, low on supplies and morale, was near ruin; only the folly of the Spanish Navy saved the day. Admiral Cevera Topete decided to defend Spanish honor in an open confrontation with the superior American fleet. He sailed out of Santiago Harbor on July 3. Within hours his ships were sunk. There were 400 Spanish casualties, but only one American died. Stripped of naval support, the Spanish Army surrendered on July 16. Two weeks later Puerto Rico was occupied by American forces without incident. On August 12 a peace

Library of Congress.

George Dewey (1837–1917)

Born in Vermont, the hero of Manila Bay was educated at Norwich University and Annapolis, graduating from the latter in 1858. His career there revealed little indication of future greatness. He entered with a class of sixty, of which only thirty-five remained at the end of the first year; Dewey was thirty-fifth. By the time of graduation, however, he ranked fifth. He saw action during the Civil War under Admiral David G. Farragut and impressed superiors with his cool and efficient manner under fire.

By 1872, the year his first wife died, Dewey was a commander. A dozen years later he was a captain and in 1896 a commodore. From 1889 to 1896 he was associated with various bureaus that gave him great familiarity with modern battleships, and in 1897, at his own request, he was granted naval command in the Pacific. This move set the stage for his dramatic victory, for when war erupted with Spain, he and his men were in Hong Kong, poised, trained, ready for immediate action. In just a few hours on May 1, 1898, Commodore Dewey demonstrated the superiority of America's fleet and won for his nation new respect throughout the world. Ten days later he was promoted to rear admiral and formally commended by Congress. In 1899 Dewey returned home to a tremendous welcome and was given the rank of admiral of the navy, a position created especially for him and the highest rank ever held by an American naval officer.

That same year Dewey married a widow and took the tactless step of deeding over to his bride a Washington home that a grateful nation had bestowed upon him. From that moment America's love affair with Dewey cooled perceptibly. Mentioned as a presidential candidate in 1900, he compounded his errors by saying he would gladly serve (one should always appear a bit reluctant), adding he had studied the job and was "convinced that the office of President is not very difficult to fill." Not surprisingly, no great wave of support for his candidacy ever developed.

By special permission Dewey continued on active duty despite advancing age, serving as president of the navy's general board. Dewey published his autobiography in 1913 and died four years later, shortly before America became involved in World War I. ■

agreement was signed and U.S. troops then entered Manila as well. Though American deaths from combat were comparatively few in number—fewer than 400—fever and dysentery pushed the final toll to nearly 6,000.

Imperial Peace

The peace terms raised the question of defining the word "pacification." For McKinley pacification meant installing a stable, pro-American regime that would pay Cuba's debts and protect foreign-owned property and keeping American forces on the island for three years. To insure a pro-American government, a program of reconstruction was begun, which included restoration of most of the normal services, such as adequate sanitation. The rebel army was induced to disarm by giving the rank and file mustering-out payments, while its leaders were offered well-paid sinecures in the provisional government. In actuality, Cuban independence was withheld. America promised not to interfere in internal affairs if Cuba agreed to become, in effect, a political satellite. The new island republic had to pledge nonalignment, which prohibited it from entering into international agreements

National Archives.

Black troops resting at San Juan Hill. Shortly after this picture was taken, they helped save Theodore Roosevelt and his Rough Riders from a romantic but poorly conceived attack on the hill, but they received little credit for their exploits.

with powers other than the United States. A curb was placed on borrowing from European nations, and military bases were conceded to the United States in perpetuity at Guantanamo on Cuba's south coast. Moreover, the United States had the right to interfere in Cuban affairs if and when American interests seemed endangered. Cuba was now, in fact, an American protectorate much like Hawaii.

These goals were achieved through the Platt Amendment, named after Senator Orville B. Platt of Connecticut. This amendment to the Army Appropriations Bill of 1901 authorized the President to end the military occupation of Cuba only if these limitations were incorporated in Cuba's constitution. After vigorous protest by Cuban nationalists, the amendment was finally acceded to, a rare instance when one sovereign nation has "amended" the constitution of another. On March 2, 1901, Cuba was left to govern itself as independently as it could under the circumstances.

As a prerequisite for peace in August 1898, Spain had agreed to relinquish control of Cuba, give the United States Puerto Rico and an island in the Marianas in the Pacific (Guam), and permit American troops to occupy "the city, bay, and harbor of Manila" pending final treaty settlement. The last proviso was left intentionally vague because no one yet knew what to do with the Philippine Islands.

Bitter Legacy: The Philippines

Conditions in the Philippine Islands defied easy solution. The Spanish had recently suppressed a rebellion of Filipino patriots seeking independence and bribed the leader, General Emilio Aguinaldo (1869–1964) to go into exile. After Dewey's smashing victory at Manila Bay (1898), he immediately brought Aguinaldo back to Manila on an American warship so the guerrilla leader could reorganize his forces and resume the revolt against Spanish rule.

To this point the war had seemingly been a great humanitarian effort to help oppressed peoples, and it appeared unlikely that imperialistic groups in America would have their way. But occupation of Cuba and annexation of both Puerto Rico and Hawaii turned out to be stepping stones to still greater acquisitions and greater responsibilities as well.

President McKinley had declared that forcible annexation of the Philippines was nothing less than "criminal aggression." Now he began to see the matter in another light. In a communication to a Methodist delegation he declared:

> "The truth is I didn't want the Philippines, and when they came to us, as a gift from the gods, I did not know what to do with them....When I realized that the Philippines had dropped into our laps...I sought counsel from all sides—Democrats as well as Republicans—but got little help. I thought first we would take only Manila; then Luzon; then other islands, perhaps, also. I walked the floor of the White House...I went down on my knees and prayed Almighty God for light and guidance...And one night late it came to me this way. I don't know how it was, but it came. (1) That we could not give them back to Spain—that would be cowardly and dishonorable; (2) that we could not turn them over to France or Germany—our commercial rivals in the Orient—that would be bad business and discreditable; (3) that we could not leave them to themselves—they were unfit for self-government—and they would soon have anarchy and misrule over there worse than Spain's was; and (4) that there was nothing left for us to do but to take them all, and to educate the Filipinos, and uplift and civilize and Christianize them...."

The hand of God had laid the white man's burden on the shoulders of President McKinley. Accordingly, he instructed the War Department to add the Philippine Islands to the growing empire of the United States.

Although William McKinley probably did seek God's help as he claimed, earthly voices undoubtedly spoke to him in more resolute terms concerning the fate of the Philippines. Naval interests saw the islands as key bases. Businessmen eager to increase the China trade saw them as vital to extending American influence in the Orient. Missionaries were zealous to convert "the heathen," most of whom were loyal Roman Catholics and had been for centuries, together with a few hundred thousand Muslims. In the end, Spain sold the islands to the United States for $20 million and a distant, alien people were suddenly part of America's imperial responsibility.

The decision to keep the Philippines ignited an explosion in U.S. political and intellectual circles. Strange bedfellows such as Andrew Carnegie, Samuel

Gompers, William Jennings Bryan, Grover Cleveland, Mrs. Jefferson Davis, Mark Twain, and William Vaughn Moody lambasted government policy that, in a moral sense, was difficult to defend. True, most of the opposition came from Democratic ranks, but those who spoke out had a powerful argument: a people dedicated to the end of colonialism could not rule colonies themselves. But apparently they could. The alliance of the navy, commercial folk, and politicians eager to see America a world power was too strong, and the Senate agreed to acquire this controversial new possession while the international press quoted Rudyard Kipling, who urged America to "take up the white man's burden." One must assume from the trend of events that acquisition of the islands had the approval of the majority of Americans as well. The glamor of far-flung possessions in an age when rival nations were building empires simply was irresistible. At long last, a few spots around the globe would fly the American flag, and downtrodden millions could enjoy the benefits and advantages of an enlightened rule.

This was not, however, how the Filipinos viewed matters. A proud people with a long history, they felt betrayed, stabbed in the back by those who had come to deliver them from Spanish rule, only to remain as rulers themselves. Two days before the Senate agreed on February 6, 1899, to retain control of the islands, Aguinaldo resumed his fight for independence, this time waging war against his former allies, the Americans. This revolt, a bloody, hit-and-run, guerrilla-type affair, lasted four years and cost the United States at least $600 million dollars and some 4,000 lives. Filipino losses in life and property were much higher and, in all, this tragic rebellion proved to be much more costly than the Spanish-American War itself.

Institutions, Ideals, and Foreign Policy

In a period of eighteen months (1898–1899) the United States suddenly became a colonial power as it annexed, bought, and conquered lands in the Caribbean and Pacific. Congressmen who disavowed "any disposition or intention to exercise sovereignty, jurisdiction, or control over Cuba" as they went to war ended up adding the Platt Amendment to that nation's constitution, seizing Puerto Rico, Guam, and the Philippines by treaty, and waging a tragic war against Filipinos who wanted to be free and independent. How did all this come about? Was it normal American continental expansion and Manifest Destiny gone wild, an aberration in U.S. life, or simply a natural byproduct of the international empire-building climate of the closing decades of the nineteenth century? And, granted that most opinionmakers initially seemed to oppose imperialism, what caused them to change their minds?

Business and Foreign Policy

A key ingredient in this equation was the economic depression of the 1890s. Declining sales and lower salaries were endangering many middle class households and those who headed them may well have greeted both war and colonial markets with unabashed enthusiasm. And, while most Americans had rejected colonialism in the 1870s, conditions two decades later were much different. In addition to unusually hard times, the earlier debate came hot on the heels of a great war; now a new generation could have its own fight. Also, those who opposed colonialism after Dewey sailed into Manila Bay had to devise alternatives to colonialism. Giving lands taken in war back to Spain or to some other power did not make much sense, nor did immediate independence that might, in the end, deliver Filipinos, Cubans, and Puerto Ricans into the hands of yet another oppressor.

In general, the business community produced few, straight-out imperialist crusaders, perhaps because most influential businessmen were middle-aged and beating the imperialist drum was a job for younger men such as Theodore Roosevelt and his "big navy" associates. Most solid men of affairs, whether in business or government, tended to oppose colonies but not expansion that meant trade and influence. Their line of reasoning went something like this: the colonies might turn out to be bad bargains and the United States probably should not embark upon a full-blown imperialist career, but, all things considered, the advantages still might outweigh the disadvantages. Naturally enough, this ambivalence made the tasks of the Roosevelts and Mahans, who knew precisely what they wanted, very much easier.

Anti-imperialists tried to tie their campaign to other issues of the day such as prohibition, tariffs on sugar, trusts, and the "money power," but without much success. They claimed that those who imported liquor, tobacco, textiles, and sugar—and the financial houses that bankrolled these operations—were behind this lust for

Library of Congress.

Carl Schurz
(1829–1906)

Few men have lived such storybook lives as Carl Schurz. Student revolutionary, general diplomat, editor, confidant of Presidents, senator, Cabinet officer, a man of great charm and wit, he carved out a dazzling career in his new American homeland. Born near Cologne, he got into trouble as a student at Bonn during the revolt of 1848–1849 and had to flee from Germany. Schurz spent several years in various European countries but by 1856 had settled down in Wisconsin.

He soon became active in Republican party circles, campaigning unsuccessfully for state office even before he actually became a citizen. This German immigrant worked hard on behalf of Lincoln in 1858 and 1860 and, as a result, was named minister to Spain; however, two years later he resigned to become a brigadier general. His military career, which was not especially distinctive, required much tact since he carried on a personal correspondence with his commander-in-chief over the heads of his superiors.

In the immediate postwar years, Schurz vacillated between politics and journalism, ending up as a one-term senator from Missouri and a violent critic of the corrupt Grant regime. He had much to do with the defeat of plans to annex Santo Domingo, the first overt expression of his anti-imperialist stand. In 1876, to the distress of Liberal Republicans, he backed Hayes and later as a result became Secretary of the Interior. In this capacity he began development of national parks and instituted a much criticized but enlightened Indian policy.

In 1881 Schurz went to New York City where during the next two decades he held various official and unofficial editorial jobs with publications such as the *Evening Post, Nation,* and *Harper's Weekly.* He was a distinguished and strident voice against war in 1898 and fought hard against acquisition of the Philippines and Cuba. His arguments, summarized in an address at the University of Chicago, stressed these points: all previous U.S. territories were contiguous (except Alaska) and thinly populated, located in temperate regions "where democratic traditions thrive," and required no material increase of the armed forces. Although Schurz was being true to his heritage of revolution, liberalism, and active democracy, few listened. Intoxicated by visions of the Stars and Stripes flying in faraway lands, most Americans endorsed the policies of Lodge, Mahan, and Roosevelt. ■

empire. Some politicians accused McKinley of being a pawn of England and helping that nation "carry out her schemes of foreign colonization and foreign domination." They also fanned the flames of racism, noting that a dark-skinned empire could cause great problems in the future and that Anglo-Saxon peoples did not flourish in the tropics. To some extent, anti-imperialists were Democrats and intellectuals, although this issue respected neither the boundaries of class nor those of political party.

Their ranks included numerous famous names who joined up for a variety of reasons ranging all the way from sheer political partisanship and white supremacy to the most admirable of moral and humanitarian arguments. Among them were well-known politicians such as Benjamin Harrison, Grover Cleveland, William Jennings Bryan, Ben Tillman, and Richard Olney; reformers and independents such as Carl Schurz, E. L. Godkin, and Jane Addams; labor leader Samuel Gompers and steel magnate Andrew Carnegie; the presidents of Stanford, Cornell, Michigan, Northwestern, and Harvard; former abolitionists like Thomas Wentworth Higginson and the sons of others (Emerson, Garrison, and Birney); and a host of writers, including Mark Twain, William Dean Howells, William Vaughn Moody, Edgar Lee Masters, George Washington Cable, Thomas Bailey Aldrich, Ambrose Bierce, and Peter Finley Dunne.

A key issue was, of course, whether or not to retain control of the Philippine Islands. With the business community eager for markets and willing to gamble on the question of colonies and the general public stirred up by much flag waving, parades, and a brief, highly successful war, those who opposed annexation had a tough fight on their hands. The McKinley administration, through a variety of pressures and statements which claimed that ratification of the peace treaty with Spain really did not mean that the Philippines would become a U.S. colony, won by a two-ballot margin in the Senate; however, only a vote cast by the Vice President broke a 29–29 deadlock and defeated a resolution pledging independence for the islands. Whether American businessmen wanted markets or colonies they apparently now had both and whatever responsibilities that went with them as well.

Foreign Policymaking and the Open Door

Actually, what was going on during the years from 1898 to 1901 was a great debate over the proper strategy and tactics of American economic expansion, especially in the Far East. In essence this was a three-cornered battle between imperialists, anti-imperialists, and members of a coalition of forces that rejected traditional colonialism and advocated instead some means by which U.S. economic strength could enter and perhaps dominate various underdeveloped regions of the world. Most members of these groups had their eyes on one special prize (China), and each believed their programs and policies would enable U.S. businessmen to reap substantial profits in a market that seemed to hold great promise.

From the outset of the Spanish-American War, the McKinley administration clearly intended to retain at least a foothold in the Philippines, an "American Hong Kong" of sorts that could serve as a stepping stone to China and a center of U.S. power in the western Pacific. Manila Bay was simply part of a chain of bases—Hawaii, Guam, Wake (occupied at the time of the acquisition of Hawaii)—across the world's largest ocean. Once America got to the end of that chain, its foreign policymakers faced three alternatives: join other powers in a partitioning of China (a policy that might limit the U.S. share of the pie); link up with Great Britain and Japan to force Russia and others to accept nondiscriminatory trade in all of China (a policy that would have been unpopular at home and could lead to international squabbles); or devise some scheme to neutralize China and exempt it from the imperializing process (a policy that would be difficult to formulate and hard to pursue).

The third approach was eventually chosen and implemented through Secretary John Hay's famous Open Door notes of 1899 to interested powers. Although discounted in recent decades as futile and naive, the Open Door policy actually was a brilliant stroke that served American businessmen reasonably well for nearly half a century and became a cornerstone of U.S. foreign relations. In theory the notes rejected spheres of influence in China but in practice accepted them, suggesting that all powers levy the same tariffs and duties on other foreign merchants in such areas as they did on their own. To win approval Hay first approached the power most likely to agree (Great Britain) and then moved down the line to the most reluctant (Russia). That the replies were often vague and evasive misses the point; all Hay was trying to do was create a framework within which more meaningful diplomacy might operate.

Interestingly, the Open Door took the fury out of

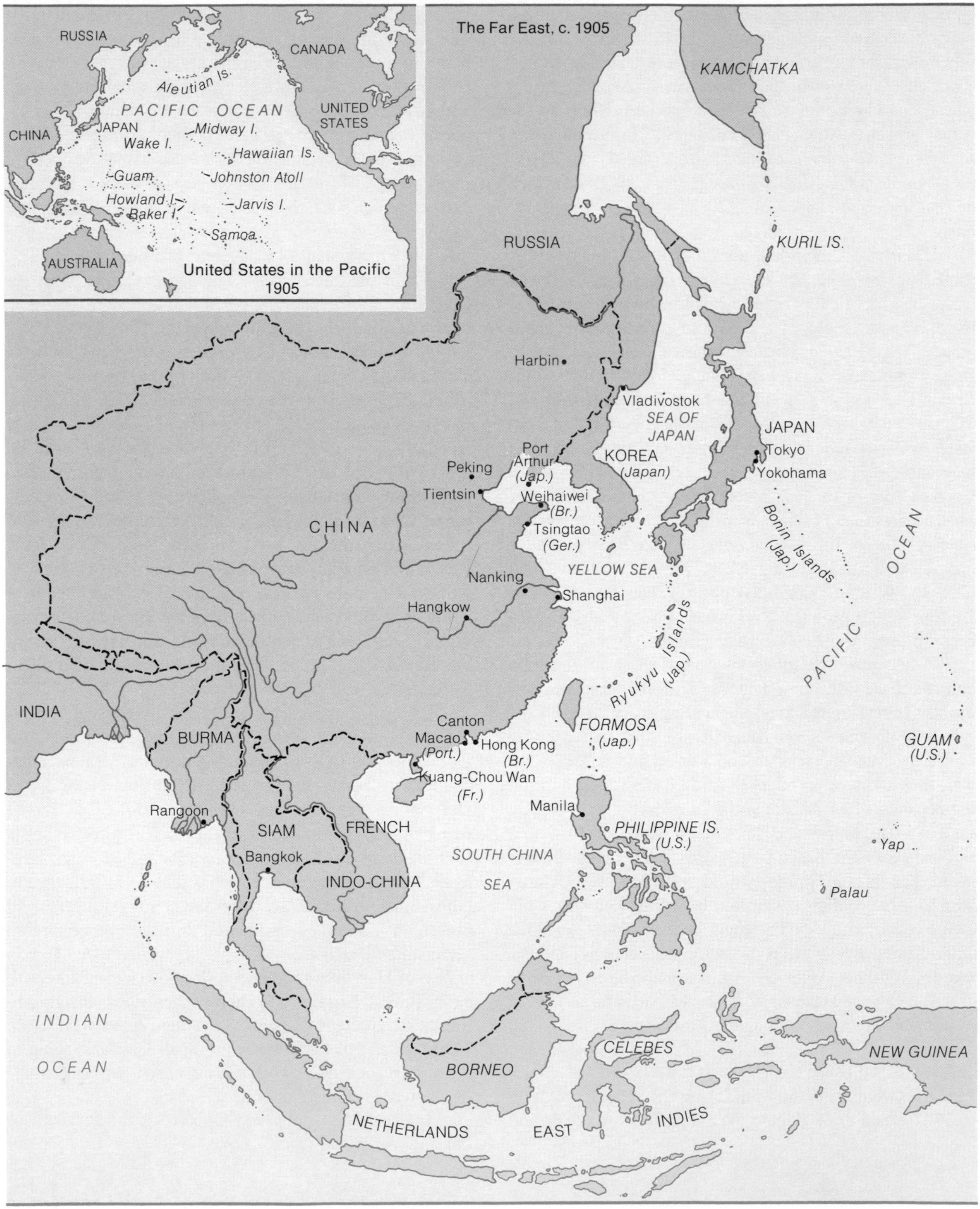
United States in the Pacific
1905
RUSSIA
CANADA
Aleutian Is.
PACIFIC OCEAN
UNITED
STATES
CHINA
JAPAN
Midway I.
Wake I.
Hawaiian Is.
Guam
Johnston Atoll
Howland I.
Baker I.
Jarvis I.
Samoa
AUSTRALIA
The Far East, c. 1905
KAMCHATKA
KURIL IS.
RUSSIA
Harbin
Vladivostok
SEA OF
JAPAN
JAPAN
Tokyo
Yokohama
Port
Arthur
(Jap.)
KOREA
(Japan)
Peking
Tientsin
Weihaiwei
(Br.)
Tsingtao
(Ger.)
CHINA
YELLOW SEA
Nanking
Shanghai
Hangkow
Bonin Islands
(Jap.)
PACIFIC
OCEAN
Ryukyu Islands
(Jap.)
INDIA
Canton
Macao
(Port.)
Hong Kong
(Br.)
Kuang-Chou Wan
(Fr.)
FORMOSA
(Jap.)
GUAM
(U.S.)
BURMA
Rangoon
SIAM
Bangkok
FRENCH
INDO-CHINA
SOUTH CHINA
SEA
Manila
PHILIPPINE IS.
(U.S.)
Yap
Palau
INDIAN
OCEAN
BORNEO
CELEBES
NEW GUINEA
NETHERLANDS
EAST
INDIES

Library of Congress.

John Hay.

the anti-imperialist storm and within a few years that issue had virtually disappeared. William Jennings Bryan as Woodrow Wilson's Secretary of State gave this policy firm support. Some of the most loyal backers, who should not have been surprised, learned that the pietistic midwesterner would not shirk from shouldering his share of the white man's burden and was as eager as any farmer or industrialist to secure and develop overseas markets.

The only variable Hay forgot in 1899 was the host nation, the country most interested in what was going on: China. And his policy helped to foster a massive uprising, the Boxer Rebellion, which forced the United States to take precisely the sort of military action it wanted to avoid. Five thousand U.S. troops were dispatched to China to help restore order, and fears that suppression of this outburst might trigger absolute partition caused American diplomats to attack any further development of spheres of influence, although they had no means by which to enforce such a policy.

In the end order was restored, at least momentarily, but within a few years Russia and Japan were at war on Chinese soil and a short time later the Chinese experienced the first throes of an ongoing revolution that would drag on until the middle of the twentieth century. Yet if the aim of Philippine annexation and the Open Door was to provide American businessmen ready access to the

Oriental markets, for whatever they were worth, then that goal was achieved. More important, perhaps, was the sobering impact of the Philippine insurrection and the Boxer Rebellion upon imperialists and anti-imperialists at home. Both groups had to temper their arguments considerably and deal with the realities of foreign policy in action, a new experience for many Americans.

The Election of 1900

All of these vital questions should have made the Democratic challenge in the presidential election of 1900 formidable, but that was not the case. As noted, the Open Door policy took much of the sting out of the anti-imperialist argument; and, as soon as he won renomination, McKinley announced that Cuba would soon be independent. Even McKinley's new running mate, Theodore Roosevelt, now that he had almost everything he wanted, disavowed any plans to grab more land. Democrat Bryan and Republican McKinley each garnered just about as many votes as they had four years earlier under much more exciting circumstances.

Perhaps it was the rebellions in the Philippines and in China, the return of good times at home, a sense of new responsibilities with troops stationed in far-flung

Library of Congress.

聯合軍北京皇城の内門突進之圖
清國戰乱画報其廿

A print from a Japanese album published in Tokyo in August 1900 showing American, British, and Japanese troops attacking the Boxers who held Peking.

outposts, or merely the turn of the calendar from one century to another, but America's mood was changing. The old Civil War leaders and the divisive forces of their generation were passing from the scene, and new men who thought in national and international terms were coming to the fore. Few doubted that the United States was maturing as a nation rich with potential and industrial growth. The drive for continental expansion and unity had been achieved and now a thirty-year campaign for foreign possessions and lucrative overseas markets was drawing to a close.

For better or for worse, the United States of America, born out of one imperial system, had now created its own.

Essay

Guerrilla Warfare in American History

Guerrilla warfare is essentially the art of war as practiced by the weak as a means of wearing down a better-equipped opponent. If successful, those who pursue this age-old discipline become, in time, stronger, gain the upper hand, and ultimately achieve victory. Some present-day guerrilla tactics had their origins in America as the Indians contended with the cutting edge of European settlement, and as the settlers, in turn, fought for their independence from Great Britain (1775–1783), often utilizing subtle tricks of combat learned from their aboriginal adversaries.

The word "guerrilla," the Spanish diminutive for *guerra* (war), thus indicating a "little war," arose during the Peninsular Campaign (1809–1813) when, with English assistance, the Spanish and Portuguese partisans harassed the forces of Napoleon. This was, in fact, a classic example of guerrilla warfare: relatively weak, poorly outfitted groups waging a protracted campaign in concert with a larger, friendly force so as to diminish ever so gradually the effectiveness of a common foe.

To be successful, guerrillas must have leadership, weapons, recruits, training, discipline, sanctuary, and supplies. They also should be tightly organized and willing to resort to terror tactics; however, indiscriminate murder and wanton pillaging may backfire, for every guerrilla has several objectives. He is trying to win popular support, or at least not incur the hostility of the populace, to present constructive reform proposals that are readily understood and appreciated, and to gain victory and political power with the aid of a sympathetic citizenry and an outside force.

The skillful maneuverings of Francis Marion ("the Swamp Fox") against Cornwallis in the Carolinas during the Revolution and the dashing cavalry exploits of men such as Nathan Bedford Forrest, John Morgan, and John S. Mosby in the Civil War are good examples of how guerrilla warfare should be waged. On the other hand, the hit-and-run tactics of the American Indians of the eighteenth and nineteenth centuries were doomed from the start. Theirs certainly was "the war of the weak," but they had little unity, no constructive program, and no larger force with which to coordinate their operations; and they made no attempt to carry on psychological warfare calculated to win the populace to their side.

America's experience with guerrilla opposition in the Philippines (1899–1902) is a sordid episode in our past that should have alerted this nation to pitfalls to be encountered in

Library of Congress.

The fire that severely damaged Manila in April 1800 could have been started by either American soldiers or rebel patriots.

Vietnam. The two tales are by no means identical, yet some of the lessons the United States Army learned at the turn of the century were forgotten all too quickly.

The Philippine disaster had its roots in American indecision and failure to realize that the Filipinos really wanted to be independent and free. Also, perhaps it should be noted that the United States went to war with Spain because of conditions in nearby Cuba. President McKinley's war message to Congress dealt exclusively with that island, which some Americans had coveted for nearly a century. It said nothing about the Philippines, a faraway region most of them knew nothing about.

Yet, once Admiral Dewey won a smashing victory at Manila Bay, no one knew what to do next. Should the United States of America keep a naval base there? Merely acquire special commercial privileges? Seize all of the islands as colonies? Set up a commonwealth under its protection? Or should Dewey and his men simply sail away and let the Filipinos look out for themselves? Editors, clergymen, politicians, military and navy brass, jingoists, and anti-imperialists argued and blustered for some six months; but, in the end, William McKinley (guided, he said, by God's help) decided it was our Christian duty to remain and civilize the Filipinos, most of whom had been Catholics or Muslims for several centuries. Apparently the Almighty helped the President in the Senate, too, where the treaty ending the war with Spain and ceding those islands to the United States faced a rough fight and was ratified by a vote of 57–27, only one more than the required two-thirds majority.

By the time this "civilizing" effort became truly effective some three years later, 4,000 U.S. soldiers, 20,000 Philippine guerrillas, and perhaps as many as 200,000 civilians were dead. As in Vietnam, during the early stages of this affair, the United States Army suppressed news of what was becoming a first-class revolution. Distressed by the slow pace of pacification and realizing that 1900 was an election year, McKinley dismissed the general in charge and replaced him with Gen. Arthur MacArthur, father of Douglas MacArthur of World War II fame.

Library of Congress.

Filipino prisoners guarded by U.S. troops in Manila.

By May 1900, MacArthur had 70,000 men at his disposal, but it was McKinley's victory at the polls that helped him turn the tide. The Filipinos, realizing they could expect no support from the Democrats (out of power but largely anti-imperialist), soon formed a native Federal party whose members were willing to accept U.S. sovereignty. The capture of General Emilio Aguinaldo, noted guerrilla leader, and the appearance of William Howard Taft as governor in July 1901 greatly increased the possibility of ending this insurrection.

Aguinaldo, a wily opportunist but also a fervent nationalist, led a revolt against Spanish rule in the 1890s and, when captured in 1897, agreed to go into exile if Spain would institute certain reforms and pay him a substantial sum of money. The following year, soon after Dewey's victory, he was back in

Manila. When he and his followers discovered that their newfound friends were not liberators but imperialist colonizers, they took to the jungles and became guerrillas again. However, once Aguinaldo was captured, he swore allegiance to the United States of America and helped bring three years of bloody warfare to a close.

Taft's role was that of a humane administrator. He realized that, in order to win, the Americans had to build up native support. By instituting land reform and stressing civil instead of military government, he had the situation well in hand by the end of 1902, although sporadic outbreaks of violence continued until 1916.

Guerrilla fighting returned to the Philippine Islands during World War II, although this time bands of Americans and Filipinos were fighting side by side against the Japanese who then occupied the region. Of course, by no means all of the Filipinos were openly anti-Japanese, and General Aguinaldo was among those who, for various reasons, became collaborators. Some of these men certainly acted out of patriotism and love of country since limited cooperation was one way to hold their nation together, others undoubtedly believed that the Japanese were "the wave of the future," and still others may have harbored (with good cause) deep-seated anti-American feelings. Although those who cooperated with the Japanese were treated in a very arbitrary manner by the Americans at the war's end—some ended up in jail for a time and some did not—on July 4, 1946, as promised a decade earlier, the Philippines became a free and independent nation.

America's most recent and most tragic experience with guerrilla warfare was, of course, in Vietnam. There in Southeast Asia, tactics reminiscent of those used by Americans themselves in the Revolution, the Civil War, and World War II were practiced with devastating success by the enemy. How this was accomplished is an ongoing controversy, and one can find substantial evidence to support opposing views. But one fact is clear: U.S. forces and their South Vietnamese allies eventually lost because they could not command the support of the people.

This war is, in fact, a fine example of a classic guerrilla conflict—weak, but well-organized partisan groups waging a protracted campaign of harassment in cooperation with stronger allies against a common foe. All of the combatants used terror; the massacre at My Lai in 1968 is a tragic example of how American GIs acted at times. All combatants also utilized psychological warfare, but throughout the 1960s and early 1970s, the slow, methodical approach of the North Vietnamese and their Communist associates began to pay substantial dividends.

Library of Congress.

Don Emilio Aguinaldo y Famy led the Filipino rebels against both Spain and the United States. Fighting against superior forces, Aguinaldo inflicted heavy casualties on the United States army.

Philip Jone-Griffiths/Magnum.

Vietnam, sixty years after the struggle in the Philippines. A different time, a different place, a different adversary, but the anguish, pain, and brutality were the same.

Clearly, 1972 was not 1902, and Vietnam was not the Philippines. Colonial empires had disappeared and the climate of world opinion had changed. All the great power that the United States could bring to bear—money, men, bombs—was not enough, and eventually the struggle was abandoned. In the meantime, that fight disrupted the normal course of America's domestic and foreign relations to a marked degree.

Guerrilla warfare is admittedly a nasty business. Those indulging in hit-and-run tactics and terror usually are not treated as bona fide soldiers when they fall into enemy hands. Passions run unchecked and one cruelty seems to justify another. Helpless civilians who perhaps have not taken sides in the struggle and do not want to usually suffer the most. Yet sometimes, as during our American Revolution and much more recently in Vietnam, it is the only way a weak force can hope to achieve victory. How one views guerrilla warfare and all of its sordid aspects merely depends upon which side one is cheering for.

Selected Readings

General Studies

Charles S. Campbell, *The Transformation of American Foreign Relations, 1865–1900* (1976)

Alexander DeConde, *A History of American Foreign Policy* (1963)

Foster Rhea Dulles, *Prelude to World Power: American Diplomatic History, 1860–1900* (1968)

Lloyd C. Gardner, Walter F. LaFeber, and Thomas J. McCormick, *The Creation of the American Empire: U.S. Diplomatic History* (1973)

John A. S. Grenville and George Berkeley Young, *Politics, Strategy, and American Diplomacy: Studies in Foreign Policy, 1873–1917* (1966)

David Healy, *U.S. Expansionism: The Imperialist Way in the 1890s* (1970)

Walter LaFeber, *The New Empire: An Interpretation of American Expansion, 1860–1898* (1963)

Ernest R. May, *Imperial Democracy: The Emergence of America as a Great Power* (1961)

William A. Williams, *The Tragedy of American Diplomacy* (1962)

Incipient Imperialism

Ernest R. May, *American Imperialism: A Speculative Essay* (1968)

Milton Plesur, *America's Outward Thrust: Approaches to Foreign Affairs, 1865–1890* (1971)

David M. Pletcher, *The Awkward Years: American Foreign Relations Under Garfield and Arthur* (1961)

Alice Felt Tyler, *The Foreign Policy of James G. Blaine* (1927)

Margaret Leech, *In the Days of McKinley* (1959)

Spanish-American War

Julius W. Pratt, *Expansionists of 1898* (1936)

Frank Freidel, *The Splendid Little War* (1958)

Anti-Imperialism

Robert L. Beisner, *Twelve Against Empire: The Anti-Imperialists, 1898–1900* (1968)

Open Door

C. S. Campbell, Jr., *Special Business Interests and the Open Door Policy* (1951)

Thomas J. McCormick, *China Market: America's Quest for Internal Empire, 1893–1901* (1967)

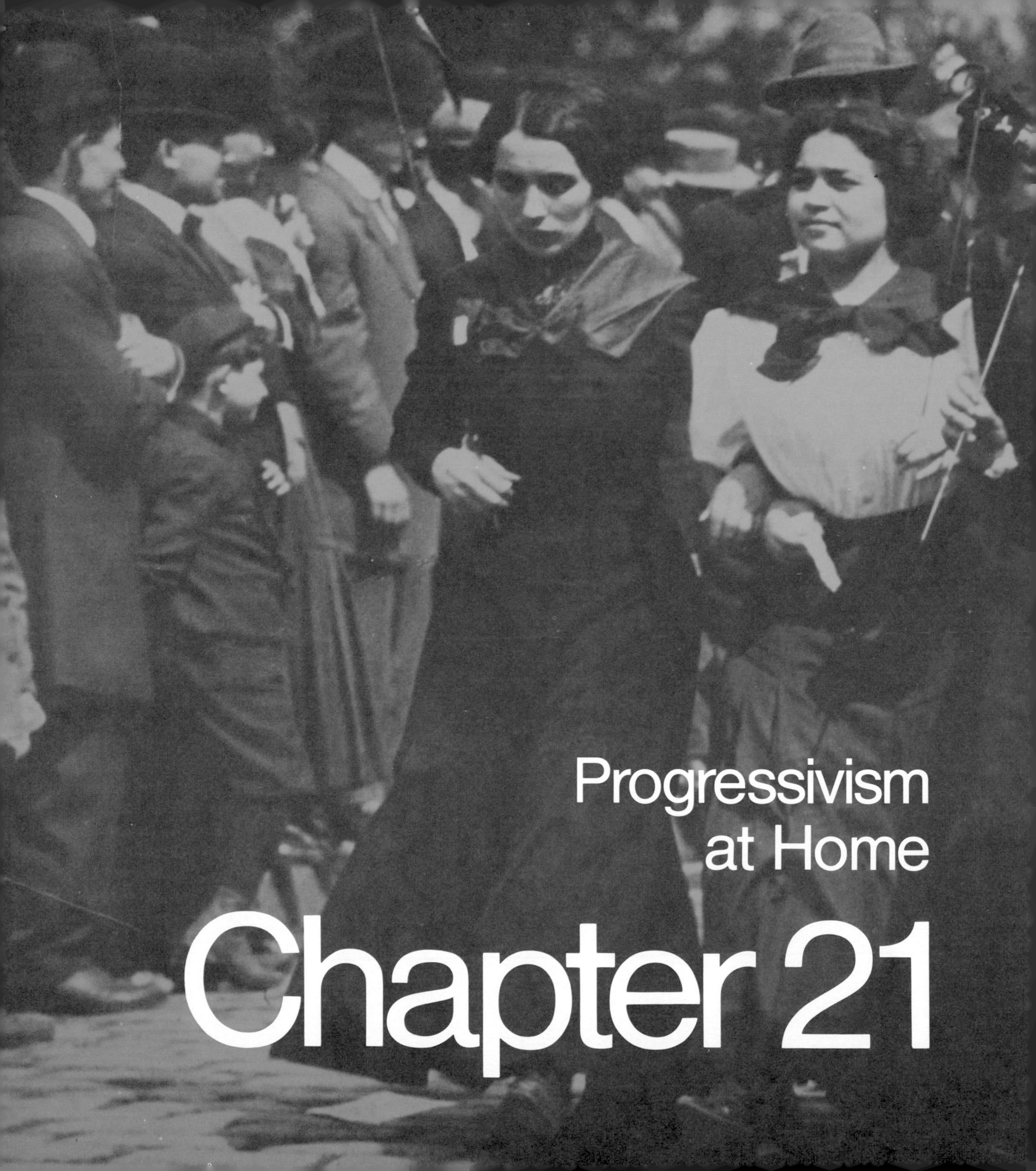

Chapter 21

Progressivism at Home

TIMELINE

1890
Jacob Riis vividly portrays poverty in *How the Other Half Lives*

1899
Thorstein Veblen writes *The Theory of the Leisure Class*

1900
Robert M. LaFollette elected governor of Wisconsin

1901
Theodore Roosevelt becomes President after McKinley's assassination

1902
Lincoln Steffens' first muckraking article appears

1902
Roosevelt calls for federal intervention in coal strike

1903
Bureau of Corporations established to investigate trusts

1904
Supreme Court orders dissolution of Northern Securities Corporation

1904
Roosevelt elected President

1905
Industrial Workers of the World organized

1906
Pure Food and Drug Act

1907
Panic of 1907

1908
Roosevelt popularizes conservation with a national convention

1908
Taft elected President

1909
National Association for the Advancement of Colored People (NAACP) is organized

1910
National Urban League is organized

1910
Ballinger-Pinchot controversy

1910
Mann-Elkins Act strengthens Interstate Commerce Act

1912
Roosevelt, Taft, and Wilson battle for the presidency

1913
Underwood-Simmons Tariff reverses high tariff policy

1913
Federal Reserve Act initiates banking and financial reforms

1914
Clayton Act strengthens antitrust legislation

1914
Federal Trade Commission is established

CHAPTER OUTLINE

The reform impulse that dominated much of U.S. life at local, state, and national levels from the turn of the century to involvement in World War I was a very complex phenomenon rooted to some extent in the past but promising hope of a better future. Unlike abolition (1845–1860), it had no single goal, was a force wherever politicians gathered, and drew its strength from many sources. In addition to Populism, these included a reaction to corporate power, a desire on the part of many—businessmen, executives, laborers, government officials, and farmers (taxpayers all)—for greater efficiency in public life, and a zeal—coupled with an innate sense of moral superiority—to improve the lot of all Americans. This zeal in the eyes of Progressive reformers, as in the case of prohibition, meant change and betterment for everyone, whether they wanted it or not.

Progressivism certainly was a crusade against big business, one that resulted in more regulation by both state and federal governments. It was, in essence, middle class reform as thousands tried to undo what they viewed as the excesses of industrialization and urbanization and to redirect the flow of American life according to the more "comfortable" rules of a rural, smalltown atmosphere they had either once known or perhaps still adhered to. Yet, since it had many goals, this reform movement was a weapon that cut both ways. Even though Progressivism generally was anticorporation and stressed the reshaping of urban life, one should keep in mind that business titans and city bosses often backed reform goals and used Progressive, liberal rhetoric for somewhat different reasons. Federal or state regulation could and did end much of the chaos created by unrestricted business competition and thus tended to improve the lot of well-established companies. A metropolitan politician speaking to immigrant voters who knew nothing about white, Anglo-Saxon, Protestant (WASP), smalltown America could use Progressive language but endorsement of some reform proposals (prohibition, for example) would have ended his career.

In addition to the many issues involved, several other factors help to explain the "why" and "when" of Progressivism. These include an enormous growth in wealth and population which brought tremendous change in its wake, a general recovery from the devastating effects of the economic turmoil of the 1890s, and an emergent citizenry which was acquiring a fundamental education and the ability to read and understand arguments broadcast throughout the land by scores of newspapers and magazines. In short, the spreading problems created by industrialization, urbanization, and immigration seemed to demand solutions. At the same time, because it was increasingly relieved of pressing economic concerns, a more literate society could now turn its attention to social ills.

Also, Progressivism emerged in a receptive climate of "newness." The United States of America suddenly was an imperial power with imperial majesty; this was the first decade of a new century; the New South and much of the nation had put the most divisive elements of the Civil War, Reconstruction, and race relations behind them (even Jim Crow was generally interpreted as reform since it seemed to give both stability and efficiency to political, economic, and social life); and new technology continued to promise a great new age.

In 1850 there were 23 million Americans, by 1900, 76 million, and in 1920, 106 million. This growth was due to both a decreasing death rate as health conditions improved, and a rising influx of immigrants. Between 1900 and 1915, for example, 14.5 million, many of them from southern and eastern Europe, settled in scores of U.S. cities.

During the first two decades of the twentieth century, the annual average per capita income rose from $450 to $560. In 1910 there were 38 million nonagricultural laborers, 8 million of them women. Although free public education was established through the land, in 1900 six million Americans were illiterate, and during the years from 1900 to 1920, only one-third of the children of industrial laborers completed primary school. For them, as for most Americans, high school was a luxury they could not afford.

Metropolitan growth, which was fed by migrations within the country, waves of foreigners, and successive phases of industrialization, was impressive indeed. In 1880 there were nineteen cities with more than 100,000 inhabitants; by 1900 that number had nearly doubled. During those decades more than six times as many people took up residence in cities as moved to farms, not a very surprising statistic in view of the Alliance-Populist outcry.

By the turn of the century America was a nation of big business with problems inherent in the expansion of corporate industries. These included cyclical unemployment, proliferating slums, and gnawing poverty. Although the new wealth had done much for some Americans, it seemed to have accomplished too little for all too many. Prosperity had brought with it waste; there were those who, caught up in change, had been swept aside by it. Woodrow Wilson, although speaking near the end of the Progressive Era and in partisan tones, expressed the fears and hopes of many Americans when he uttered these words during his first inaugural address in 1913:

"The evil has come with the good, and much fine gold has been corroded. . . . We have been proud of our industrial achievements, but we have not hitherto stopped thoughtfully enough to count the cost, the cost of lives snuffed out, of energies overtaxed and broken, the fearful physical and spiritual cost to the men and women and children upon whom the dead weight and burden of it all has fallen pitilessly the years through. . . . With the great Government went many deep secret things which we too long delayed to look into and scrutinize with candid, fearless eyes. The great Government we loved has too often been made use of for private and selfish purposes, and those who used it had forgotten the people."

The Varieties of Reform

The common bond linking many Progressives as their varied and often contradictory campaigns began to take shape in the early 1900s was a simple fear that, unless there was immediate reform, late nineteenth century radicalism might assume much more violent forms. Such arguments quickly won approval even in the most conservative circles whose members often interpreted specific reform proposals as a means of maintaining the status quo, not as a prelude to change. Yet, in the main, the central theme of Progressivism was a liberal, well-meaning, humanitarian-inspired effort to correct inequities existing in American life.

Progressive goals differed with time and varied with regional and urban or rural needs. And the movement as a whole sought political, economic, and social reform which emerged in that order chronologically. Of these areas, proposals for political change became the most important, those that affected the greatest number of people. Proposals for social change, which were the most radical features of the movement, touched the lives of the least number of Americans. On the whole, the middle and upper classes benefited far more quickly from these reforms than did the poor. At the same time, much Progressive legislation and many Progressive ideas became the foundation stones of New Deal legislation passed in the 1930s—accomplishments that did have, and continue to have, lasting benefit to the majority of Americans.

The Literature of Reform: Fact and Fiction

That the "people" were fundamentally decent was an assumption underlying much Progressive thought. Many believed that once the public was truly informed, it would inevitably demand change and erase corruption, poverty, and evil from American life.

But it was easier to believe in "the people" in the abstract than it was to define them. It was equally hard to find common goals. Those who advocated political Progressivism did not necessarily support Progressivism in the economic or social realms. Nevertheless, the dissemination of enlightened words by intellectuals, novelists, social workers, and journalists made it increasingly difficult for most Americans to remain complacent and uninvolved, or at least unaware of what was happening.

A pragmatic approach, encouraged by the writings of psychologist William James and educator John Dewey, made American intellectuals believe that the nation's problems could be attacked and solved in a straightforward, practical manner. Society (not nature) had created the problems, and society could rectify them. Thorstein Veblen's *Theory of the Leisure Class* (1899) and *Theory of Business Enterprise* (1904) were scholarly indictments of modern business. Veblen was careful to distinguish business from industry, finding only industry beneficial since, unlike business, it was concerned with more than profits. Industry produced goods, Veblen argued, whereas business merely merchandised goods. But Veblen was suspicious of all large enterprises. His *Instinct of Workmanship* (1914) showed how the innate desire to create was thwarted within the dehumanizing context of monopolistic enterprises. Though read by only a few, the works of these three men and others provided argument, theory, and technique for the initiation of progressive reform.

Information about poverty had been provided as early as 1882 by Helen Stuart Campbell (1839–1918), author, editor, and home economist, who wrote *Problems of the Poor: A Record of Quiet Work in Unquiet Places* (1882) about New York's slums. She also published articles in the *Tribune,* later collected as *Prisoners of Poverty* (1887). But it was the prose and photographs of Jacob Riis, *How the Other Half Lives* (1890) that stirred America's conscience, not the "quiet" reports of Mrs. Campbell. A Danish immigrant disillusioned by the unfulfilled promise of American society, Riis realistically portrayed daily life in the city slums. Robert Hunter's *Poverty* (1904), John Spargo's *The Bitter Cry of the Children* (1906), a study of child labor, Walter Rauschenbusch's *Christianity and the Social Crisis* (1907), and Frances Kellor's *Out of Work* (1915)—these books added to this literature of fact and made it difficult for many to believe that squalor and hunger were divine punishments inflicted on the lazy and morally degenerate.

Library of Congress.

Theodore Dreiser.

Library of Congress.

Frank Norris in 1898.

More widely read, at least by the middle class, were the novelists of the period. The son of an immigrant and one of nine children who had been raised in poverty, Theodore Dreiser said of *Sister Carrie* (1901) that it was "not intended as a piece of literary craftsmanship but was a picture of conditions." In this novel, as in *Jennie Gerhardt* (1911), *The Financier* (1912), and *The Titan* (1914), Dreiser depicted characters whose feverish pursuit of the American ideal of success had led them to pervert their values and often to commit acts of violence. The Southern Pacific Railroad was the subject of Frank Norris' 1901 novel, *The Octopus.* The first of an uncompleted trilogy on the production, distribution, and consumption of wheat, the book showed how the railroad was strangling wheat farmers; the second novel of the trilogy, *The Pit* (1903), dealt with a monopolistic railroad company's attempt to corner the market. Conditions in the Chicago meatpacking industry were exposed by socialist Upton Sinclair in *The Jungle* (1906), and the inhumanities of the stockyard and steel mill were denounced in the poems of Carl Sandburg. Another socialist writer, Jack London, told of poverty in London's East End in *People of the Abyss* (1903), and American novelist Winston Churchill described political corruption in *Coniston* (1906).

But those who reached the greatest number of readers and therefore had the greatest impact on reform were the muckrakers, the journalists who wrote about political and corporate corruption and made accusations supported with documented evidence. Theodore Roosevelt, impatient with journalistic exposures, coined the term in anger: "In Bunyan's *Pilgrim's Progress,* you may recall the description of the Man with the Muck-rake, the man who could look no way but downward with the muck-rake in his hands: who was offered the celestial crown for his muck-rake, but would neither look up nor regard the crown he was offered, but continued to rake the filth of the floor." Roosevelt used the term "muckraker" to insult journalists, but the writers in question

Library of Congress.

SENATOR SHARK

The great public-spirited philanthropist

The mythical Senator Shark in *McClure's Magazine* characterized the reformer's view of politicians: villains who squeezed millions from the public, passed on a token to their constituents, and became rich by pocketing the difference.

Culver Pictures.

McCLURE'S MAGAZINE

Christmas 1903

NINE SHORT STORIES
Pictures in Color

The Story of Rockefeller

OPENING OF THE SECOND PART OF THE HISTORY OF STANDARD OIL

By

Ida M. Tarbell

John La Farge on the Hundred Greatest Pictures, and Other Features

S. S. McCLURE CO., NEW YORK AND LONDON

The cover of *McClure's Magazine* for Christmas, 1903. Tarbell's series on Rockefeller and the Standard Oil Company roused wide public interest.

cheerfully embraced it. The muckrakers were heirs to a tradition that had evolved during the 1880s and 1890s in such popular magazines as *McClure's, Munsey's,* and *Cosmopolitan.* With technological improvements in production, the price of these periodicals dropped from thirty-five cents to a dime, increasing both their circulation and their importance as instruments for social change. The energetic S. S. McClure (1857–1949) was the first to publish contributions by such writers as Ida Tarbell (1857–1944), Ray Stannard Baker (1870–1946), and the most famous of the muckrakers, Lincoln Steffens (1866–1936).

Library of Congress.

Lincoln Steffens in 1912.

"Tweed Days in St. Louis," Steffens' first important article, appeared in the October 1902 issue of *McClure's,* followed by "The Shame of Minneapolis" in January 1903. These two articles, along with five others, were collected and published in 1904 as *The Shame of the Cities.* Steffens next exposed political corruption at the state level, in Missouri and Rhode Island, and then turned to the federal government. His target was the corruption of the Old Yankees—WASP leaders of old New England stock. Novelist David Graham Phillips (1867–1911) followed with another attack on the Yankees in *The Treason of the Senate,* which named those senators who were less loyal to constituents than to business interests.

Political Progressivism

The evils of machine rule were recognized in the late nineteenth century by the Mugwumps, who believed that only corruptible men obtained political jobs. The Mugwump solution was to support and elect to office "honest" men, by which they meant candidates were to be sought only among wealthy Anglo-Saxon businessmen. But Progressives, like the Populists, believed that all levels of government were controlled not so much by dishonest individuals as by special economic interests. It was, they concluded, in the public interest to oppose such groups—one of which was political machines.

At the municipal level, Progressives sought to make the political machines more responsible to the people than to political bosses; this shift would presumably restore self-rule and increase government efficiency. At the state level, Progressives advocated enlarging suffrage, especially to include women voters. Progressives worked to have candidates selected through direct primaries rather than by party officials, and by 1915 direct primaries had been adopted in 37 states. Progressives also expanded the ballot so that the public could vote directly for policymaking offices, leaving only the less important positions to be filled by the victorious party. While these measures helped limit the power of large interest groups, some Progressives sought still greater changes in the political realm. Toward this end, Progressives worked for the adoption of the initiative and the referendum. By 1916 more than twenty states had enacted these measures, and by 1914 eleven states had adopted the recall as well. Nationally, Progressives opposed the Electoral College, stressed the need for presidential preference primaries, and supported the direct election of senators, added by an Amendment to the Constitution in 1913.

It was at the municipal and state levels that Progressives made their most rapid and permanent gains, particularly in the West and Midwest. Of the eleven states that had instituted recall by 1914, ten were west of the Mississippi. In the East and in those midwestern states that had the strongest links with eastern industry, political Progressivism proceeded much more slowly. In the South such Progressive measures as the direct primary, regulation of insurance companies and railroads, and legislation governing campaign practices were all offset by increased disfranchisement of blacks and many poor whites.

Beginning in 1900, reform began to have impact in state after state as new faces and new forces took control. New governors in Iowa, Minnesota, Nebraska, the Dakotas, and Oregon all introduced successful Progressive administrations. But the most radical and best known of all Progressive leaders was Robert M. La Follette (1855–1925), a Wisconsin Republican who came from a working class background and who had roots in the agrarian-Populist tradition. Elected governor of Wisconsin in 1900 over the opposition of the Old Guard, La Follette had by 1914 achieved many of the Progressive goals of what was called the "Wisconsin Idea." Hailed by Theodore Roosevelt as the laboratory of democracy, Wisconsin had enacted by the outbreak of World War I a remarkable series of laws governing civil service and lobbying and campaign expenditures. It had also introduced the direct primary, initiative, and referendum, to say nothing of child and female labor laws, public health and pure food laws, conservation legislation, state control of banks and railroads, a workman's compensation act, a superior educational system, higher corporate taxes, and the nation's first state income tax.

Library of Congress.

The genteel appearance of Ida Minerva Tarbell disarmed the officers of Standard Oil. Suspecting her to be a gullible female reporter, executives fed her outrageously favorable stories about the company, which she used to Standard Oil's disadvantage in her published accounts.

Economic Progressivism

Like its political counterpart, economic Progressivism developed from currents in the late nineteenth century, when growing hostility toward trusts had resulted in the passage of the Sherman Antitrust Act. During the 1890s judicial interpretation of the act rendered it ineffective as a weapon against the continuing consolidation of large corporations. However, big business now came under attack by newspapers (especially those publications owned by Joseph Pulitzer and William Randolph Hearst) and by muckraking magazines. Among the most effective of these assaults was Ida Tarbell's *History of the Standard Oil Company* (1904), first published as a series of articles beginning in 1902. In *Other People's Money* (1914), Louis Brandeis (1856–1941) drew on the investigations of the Pujo Congressional Committee into the "money trust" and charged that those bankers led by J. P. Morgan were controlling financial credit—in short, Brandeis announced that the people's money was being used against the people.

Correcting economic abuses proved more difficult than solving political problems. Although Progressives wanted greater governmental control over the economy, they did not favor socialism. Nor could they agree on what business practices should be in the future. Followers of Brandeis opposed trusts on practical as well as moral grounds. They argued that large corporations were bad for the economy because monopolies eliminate competition and discouraged businessmen from seeking improvements and increasing production. These reformers looked to Congress to implement changes and to an informed public to support their goals.

Smaller businessmen feared large corporations and organized labor wherever it was strong. Many of them were the sons or grandsons of men who had brought about the rapid industrialization of the previous fifty years. Now these small businessmen felt that both their financial status and social prestige were threatened by the giants of the new wealth. They were interested in reform—but only to the extent that reform would maintain or improve their own interests.

Regardless of the nature of their operations, many businessmen were generally sympathetic to reform. At the same time, the Panic of 1907 reminded them strongly that general economic chaos not only endangered profits but also threatened their very existence. Although a sense of general self-interest brought them loosely together, once they began to organize (a step contrary to the principles of free enterprise that they were theoretically attempting to uphold), differences among them became more apparent. And factions crystallized as the business community attempted to develop a "practical Progressivism" that would solve economic problems throughout the nation.

Efforts to revise and regulate railroad rates were hampered by the conflicting regional interests of western shippers and those of the eastern businessmen who controlled the railroads. Large businessmen were not able to agree with smaller businessmen on the most appropriate methods by which to regulate the growth of trusts. Nor could an accord be reached on banking reform so long as urban and rural bankers found their differences irreconcilable. Parochialism was also a divisive factor. As one Virginia banker wrote: "I want to see the Southern funds of Southern banks controlled by Southern men familiar with Southern conditions." Perhaps all four of these interrelated areas—trains, trusts, banks, and parochialism—could be heard in the outcry of Oshkosh banker T. R. Frentz: "The effete East wishes to enrich itself at the expense of the rough and rugged West. Beware, Mr. Morgan, Mr. Keene and Standard Oil Crowd! You may form steel trusts and other kinds of trusts, but you cannot lick the cream out of Mr. Frentz' own saucers in his own home."

Social Progressivism

Advocates of social Progressivism went further than their political and economic counterparts in encouraging governmental paternalism to improve living conditions for the indigent. Reformers advocated the participation of government experts at all levels to help bring about these improvements. Their demands included better working conditions, on-the-job protection for women and children, employer liability for injuries incurred by workers, and social insurance. They were also interested in conservation and city planning and encouraged open discussion of sex and prevention and treatment of venereal diseases.

Perhaps their greatest area of influence was in the settlement house movement, which began in the 1880s in Great Britain and soon expanded to America. Chicago's Hull House (1889) and Boston's South End House (1891) were among the most influential and best known. Most settlement workers came from Anglo Saxon, middle class families; in many cases their fathers, working in the professions, had experienced a loss of status amid upheavals of post-Civil War America. Some young men and women who entered the settlement movement may have embraced social reform from a feeling of anxiety over such a loss of family status or from a sense of uselessness or isolation from the bulk of the American people. The plight of the poor may have served as an emblem of their own feelings of social disorientation. A few may have joined settlements to test social theories acquired in the classroom or to live cheaply until they decided upon a profession, especially when they discovered that their college or university training (often classical in outlook) did not prepare them well for a role in a changing, urban-industrial America. In addition, many college-educated women found that settlement houses provided a meaningful occupation and the opportunity for companionship with other similar women. But the majority of settlement workers, mostly unmarried, came because of a sincere and unquestioning desire to improve society. Nor was self-interest a significant factor among them. Many who engaged in settlement-house work did so from a strong religious impulse. A 1905 poll revealed that 88 percent of 339 settlement workers contacted were active church members.

More radical than other Progressives, these social reformers lived and worked among immigrants and laborers. Unfortunately, however, the majority of Progressives, those interested in political and economic change, often knew little about how the poor lived and their response to poverty was ambiguous and contradictory at best.

Tensions in the Reform Age

Not surprisingly, a variety of goals created a variety of tensions within this general movement. Some reformers thought that limiting the numerical strength of certain minorities such as blacks and immigrants would cure their community's immediate ills. Others believed that increasing the influence of organized labor in politics and society would exert beneficial effects. This lack of consensus, as much as anything, meant that Progressivism would lead a tumultuous, troubled life.

Anti-Immigrant Sentiment

Many Progressives believed the influx of immigrants an obstacle to political reform and were inclined to blame the new arrivals for poor city government. Part of the problem was that, except for the continuous presence of settlement workers and visits by candidates at election time, there was little direct communication between Progressive leaders and immigrants. Moreover, the immigrants tended to support the political boss, himself often a second-or third-generation immigrant; and, as a rule, Progressive doctrines failed to appeal either to the boss or his followers. Lower taxes were irrelevant to those who owned no property. Balanced budgets; the initiative, referendum, and recall; and government efficiency were of less importance to poor immigrants than were increased employment opportunities and better living conditions.

Among Progressives outside the area of social reform, a few of the more fastidious feared that the "foreignness" of new arrivals would prevent the creation of a "perfect" society. Such a utopia usually was seen in terms of an Anglo-Saxon heritage. Until 1850, most immigrants had been primarily from Anglo-Saxon origins and had therefore been more easily assimilated than those who came later from southern and eastern Europe. Western and southern states were least affected by these newest arrivals. The established presence of Japanese and Chinese in the West and blacks in the South made those regions reluctant to welcome newcomers unless they were well-to-do Anglo-Saxons who presumably would aid the economy and buttress the local establishment; nevertheless, the "foreign" neighborhoods of nearly all port cities throughout the nation grew markedly during the late nineteenth and early twentieth centuries. By 1909 newspaper headlines were denouncing Italian lawlessness and the existence of a shadowy Black Hand Society; the quick upward mobility of new Jewish arrivals had also increased discrimination based on economic as well as religious fears.

This resurgence of nativism was an undercurrent of the times, not its mainstream. And as immigrants became recognized as a political force, Progressive politicians sought their votes. In the three-sided presidential campaign of 1912, Woodrow Wilson lavished praise on them—in part to overcome negative remarks he had made about various immigrant groups a decade earlier in *History of the American People.* Frances Kellor brought the problems of the urban poor to the attention of Progressive party candidate Theodore Roosevelt who, influenced by social workers, called his party the "Party of Social Justice." Even the conservative incumbent William Howard Taft promised to veto literacy-test legislation for immigrants if elected.

Blacks

For black educator and writer W. E. B. DuBois, the central problem of the twentieth century was "the color line." At a time when immigrants were making some social and economic advances, conditions for blacks worsened in the North as well as the South, where 90 percent still lived and where reform legislation was designed to benefit only whites. The years from 1885 to 1900 witnessed a hardening of racial barriers and the onslaught of segregation by law, not by custom. Lynching, for example, peaked in 1893 and was by no means limited to the former Confederacy. In 1910 nearly one-third of all blacks were illiterate, and wherever they lived, they were subjected to discrimination in housing, employment, and travel. During this period two race riots—in Atlanta (1906) and Springfield, Illinois (1908)—marked a low point in race relations since Reconstruction, and blacks were being lynched as far north as Coatesville, Pennsylvania. Even among the Progressive vanguard there were many people who favored segregated facilities.

Woodrow Wilson (1856–1924), born in Virginia and raised in Georgia and the Carolinas, was especially vulnerable on this point. Writing in the *Atlantic Monthly* (1901), he endorsed suffrage restrictions then underway in the South, noting "the temper of the times has changed." A decade or so later his antiblack *History of the American People* (five volumes, 1902) provided material for the first half of a stellar movie production, "The Birth of a Nation." Wilson was so delighted with the result that at the end of a private White House showing he jumped up shouting, "It's like writing history with lightning!" The producers used his reaction in promoting the movie, but riots in the North soon eliminated several controversial scenes. During those same years official segregation increased markedly in the federal government, apparently with Wilson's acquiescence or approval.

Again, the most radical Americans were the social reformers, who included Susan P. Wharton of the wealthy Philadelphia family, William English Walling (1877–1936) of the University Settlement in New York and Henry Moskowitz (1880–1936), head resident of Madison House on New York City's Lower East Side. Investigations into black urban life were made by Mary White Ovington (1865–1951) in *Half a Man* (1911), by W. E. B. DuBois in *The Philadelphia Negro* (1899), and by Ray Stannard Baker (1870–1946) who, in *Following the Color Line* (1908), found discrimination to be advancing in the North as well as the South.

National black organizations were established, such as the National Negro Business League (1900), the National Medical Association (1904), the National Negro Bankers' Association (1906), and the National Negro Retail Merchants' Association (1913), all modeled along the lines of their white counterparts. In 1905 thirty black intellectuals led by DuBois met at Niagara Falls, Canada, to form a group opposed to the gradualism in race relations preached by Booker T. Washington. This group, known as the Niagara Movement, demanded that blacks be granted immediate economic and political equality. In 1909, the movement joined with both black and white liberals to establish the National Association for the Advancement of Colored People (NAACP). Its first president, Moorfield Storey (1845–1922), a Massachusetts-born lawyer with impeccable Yankee credentials and ties to abolition, served as private secretary to Charles Sumner and later wrote a biography of that statesman. A crusader for the rights of both Indians and blacks, in 1915 Storey argued successfully before the U.S. Supreme Court (*Quinn* v. *U.S.*) that grandfather clauses rendered Maryland and Oklahoma elections null and void. A year after the NAACP appeared, another interracial body, the National Urban League, was established in New York City with the goal of securing equal opportunities for blacks throughout the nation. Both associations faced lean, hard years, their work often being carried on more by whites and white money than by contributions from blacks themselves. Not until attitudes began to change, after 1930, did these groups begin to acquire more prestige, support, and influence.

Reformers, Radicals, and Labor

Labor was fighting for survival, but Progressives at first took even less interest in the movement than they did in the plight of immigrants and blacks. To the majority of Americans, labor unions seemed "un-American" in a number of ways.

Even Theodore Roosevelt had mixed feelings on this matter. Writing in the *Review of Reviews* (1897) he had praise only for "certain labor unions, certain bodies of organized labor," such as railway conductors, locomotive engineers, and firemen who, he thought, embodied "almost the best hope that there is for healthy national growth in the future." Eight years later, as President, he told Chicago strikers that he believed in unions and boasted that he himself was an honorary member of one but cautioned that a union, like a corporation or an individual, must obey the law. In 1910, out of the White

Library of Congress.

William E. B. DuBois (1868–1963)

A tireless, outspoken fighter for the black man, not afraid to embrace controversial, unpopular stands, William E. B. DuBois was born in Great Barrington, Massachusetts, and educated at Fisk and Harvard. His long and successful career included teaching, editing, sociological research, organizational work, and politics, all in behalf of his race. In contrast to the generalized effort of Booker T. Washington to help blacks by teaching them trades and skills that would enable them to find their place in a white-dominated world, DuBois preached a different message: education of the "talented tenth" who would create a self-sufficient black society. Washington favored practical accommodation, at least for the time being; DuBois, however, was eager to challenge the status quo.

DuBois taught at Atlanta University from 1896 to 1910 and again from 1934 to 1944, making that institution a center for racial and sociological research. In 1905 he helped found the Niagara Movement, which became four years later, with white cooperation, the National Association for the Advancement of Colored People (NAACP). From 1910 to 1923 DuBois was editor of *Crisis,* that group's prestigious journal.

In 1944 he returned to NAACP work once more but quit in another policy dispute four years later. Meanwhile, he had become a consultant to the United Nations and involved in Communist party activities. The latter led to a federal indictment (but acquittal) during the repressive postwar years. In 1950 DuBois ran unsuccessfully for the U.S. Senate on the American Labor ticket. That same year he won a World Peace Council Prize and in 1961, the Lenin Peace Prize. In his application for membership in the Communist party, DuBois conceded the path had been "long and slow." He told how he joined the Socialists in 1911 but then quit to support Woodrow Wilson. In 1962 he became a citizen of Ghana and at the time of his death was director of a government-sponsored *Encyclopedia Africana.*

A reserved, somewhat formal man and an immaculate dresser, DuBois always carried a cane. When he died in Africa, he still owned a home in Brooklyn, apparently reluctant to break the final tie to his native land. ■

House and itching to return, he gave all-out support to unions: "In our modern industrial system the union is just as necessary as the corporation." By 1917, T. R. was even willing to blame corporations for the shortcomings of the trade union movement, urging capitalists and workers to become partners and recognize their duty to the public as a whole.

Although Progressives supported improved working conditions and generally thought collective bargaining (determination of terms of employment by worker and employee representatives) a just goal, demands for a closed shop seemed to violate the individual rights of workers who did not want to join unions. Many also found labor methods disagreeable: boycotts seemed im-

Culver Pictures.

Alexander Berkman—with the receding hairline—addressing IWW supporters at New York City's Union Square in 1908. The Wobblies made a broad appeal to women, blacks, Jews, and other ethnic groups ignored by the AFL.

moral, and the violence and disruption of the social and economic order that accompanied some strikes, particularly those of the IWW under the leadership of "Big Bill" Haywood, were abhorrent to all but the most radical Progressives, something they saw as alien to the American way of peacefully settling labor disputes. In addition, labor leaders were often immigrants or sons of immigrants; for instance, Samuel Gompers, president of the American Federation of Labor, was an English-born Jew. The foreign origins of labor organizers alienated American nativists.

Curiously, organized labor itself was opposed to immigration. AFL union members were skilled workers and therefore felt superior to unskilled immigrants and blacks who might be trained by employers to replace them. Labor worked actively against immigration, demonstrating in 1902 for legislation that would continue excluding Chinese immigrants and in 1907 for laws against Japanese immigrants. When the Industrial Workers of the World (IWW) was established in 1905, AFL fears increased, both regarding competition between unions and further identification of all workers with radicalism. The "Wobblies," as the IWW members were called, were both radical and socialist and by 1918 had instigated almost 150 strikes. What was still more alarming, the IWW organized those workers whom the AFL had rejected—textile workers, miners in the West, and itinerant farm workers.

Like big business, organized labor was a special-interest group. Its numbers tripled from 1900 to 1904 and by 1914 reached two million. Although this figure represented only 10 percent of the total industrial work force, Progressives feared the formation of a party led by

Culver Pictures.

I.W.W. SONGS

TO FAN THE FLAMES OF DISCONTENT

THE PREACHER AND THE SLAVE

By Joe Hill

(Tune: "Sweet Bye and Bye")

Long-haired preachers come out every night,
Try to tell you what's wrong and what's right;
But when asked how 'bout something to eat
They will answer with voices so sweet:

CHORUS

You will eat, bye and bye,
In that glorious land above the sky;
Work and pray, live on hay,
You'll get pie in the sky when you die.

This IWW song expressed the contempt felt by labor activists for the impractical promises of religion to the downtrodden.

labor activists, one that would not take into consideration the needs of the general population.

It is perhaps significant that industrial workers and farmers, the nation's largest labor group, were unable to find any common ground for cooperation; in fact, they rarely even tried to do so. Their experiences and goals were much too different, as the election of 1896 had

Culver Pictures.

William Dudley Haywood
(1869–1928)

Unlike most labor leaders, who begin their careers as radicals and end them as conservatives, "Big Bill" Haywood began as a moderate and throughout his life became increasingly radical. After being a miner, then (at least according to legend) a cowboy in the 1880s, Haywood became interested in the labor movement during the next decade and by 1899 was a member of the national executive board of the Western Federation of Miners. A Socialist, he opposed the elitism of the AFL and in 1905 headed a labor convention in Chicago that established the Industrial Workers of the World ("Wobblies"). To achieve their goals (unification of all labor and control of production by workers), the "Wobblies" advocated passive resistance, strikes, and, when necessary, violence. Able to reach both intellectuals and the masses, Haywood preached the irreconcilable dichotomy between employer and employee and, at the same time, the brotherhood of man and elimination of race distinctions.

When Idaho governor Frank H. Steuenberg was assassinated in 1906, Haywood was arrested for complicity but was successfully defended by Clarence Darrow. He was active in the Socialist party until he was dismissed from the group's national executive board in 1913 for favoring the use of violence. In 1917, having opposed America's involvement in the war, Haywood, with other IWW members, was arrested under the Espionage Act for interfering with conscription and for conspiracy. In 1918 he was convicted, fined $10,000, and received a twenty-year sentence. Awaiting a motion for appeal, Haywood jumped bail and left the country for the Soviet Union. There he made several speaking tours but found the USSR as unresponsive to his revolutionary ideas as his homeland had been. His last years were spent in illness and confinement to a hotel room in Moscow. His autobiography, *Bill Haywood's Book,* was published posthumously in 1929. ■

clearly demonstrated. The farmer who owned his land was a capitalist in miniature to whom organization meant regimentation, and his hired hands usually looked forward to the day when they, too, had acres of their own to till. In addition, rural-urban rivalries stirred by political, economic, and social trends denied to the labor movement a vast reservoir of potential support. Nevertheless, as the voting bloc of industrial workers increased, Progressive politicians began to take more notice of them.

Even those Progressives who admitted that unions were needed could not agree on what their rights and limitations should be. Labor leaders were often personally ambitious, attempting to gain power at the expense of the established order. Organizers also made it difficult for leaders in other areas to identify with them because of a class consciousness that seemed to set them apart from American society. One reform mayor said: "I don't like Labor Day, except as a holiday. These parades of working men seem to proclaim a difference between them and the rest of us which ought not to exist." Union leaders also made themselves unpopular by their willingness to embarrass other reform movements in order to attain labor objectives. Because they did not play by the rules, labor leaders were regarded with suspicion by Progressives. In turn, labor leaders viewed Progressives as fair-weather friends, often with good reason. Some settlement workers opposed increased wages for workingmen, fearing that the extra money would be used to indulge "vulgar passions." Even Jane Addams, who supported labor vigorously and hired only union men for work at Hull House, admitted: "It is only occasionally that I get a glimpse of the chivalry of labor . . . so much of the time it seems so sordid."

As early as 1902, during a strike by miners in the Pennsylvania anthracite fields, labor had gained favor with the public by its willingness to arbitrate, which the owners refused to do even after President Roosevelt had intervened. By 1916, when railroad brotherhoods were agitating for an eight-hour day, labor had become strong enough to refuse arbitration, and management fearful enough to encourage it. Much of the settlement house support of labor was channeled through the Women's Trade Union League, which frequently met at Hull House, South End House, and the Henry Street Settlement. These groups gave both financial and moral backing, for example, to the strike of New York's garment workers in 1910. These efforts sometimes cost settlement houses contributions from industrialists, but by the outbreak of World War I most business executives had become less emotional about labor and the problems of unionization, foreigners, and a class-oriented society.

The Age of Theodore Roosevelt

The nation's twenty-sixth President came to the White House essentially a conservative. Nevertheless, his ambiguous response to Progressive thought had troubled both Old Guard Republicans and leaders of reform. Roosevelt was a man on whom the nation would project various images, all of them aggressive: cowboy, policeman, prizefighter, big-game hunter, champion of human rights. Yet he was, above all else, a politician eager to use power to bring about changes that he thought the nation needed. In 1905, for example, he even summoned three college football coaches to the White House and told them to clean up a sport marred by fatalities and serious injuries or he would have it banned. Whether the changes Roosevelt sought as President were liberal, conservative, radical, or reactionary in tone depended, of course, upon how one viewed the area of action concerned. Those coaches probably thought the President's 1905 ultimatum radical in the extreme; the families of dead players and others nursing broken bones undoubtedly viewed his words as both visionary and "progressive."

Roosevelt entered politics for reasons of principle as well as love of power; he felt that he could guard and advance the public interest. Although his background had led him to distrust the nouveau rich, experience had caused him to fear the mob; like most people of the time he was as critical of labor-Populist movements as he was of monopolies. Of a labor dispute that occurred while he was governor of New York, he said: "If there should be a disaster at the Croton Dam strike, I'd order out the militia in a minute. But I'd sign an employer's liability law, too." His use of public office reflected a moral belief in the "golden mean," and his political career had already led him to realize that corruption of public office resulted in the use of government to enhance interests of groups rather than those of the people as a whole. It was in part his dealings with a corrupt New York legislature that led him as governor to instigate a political housecleaning; this purge, in turn, caused state boss Tom Platt to secure for him the Republican nomination for the vice presidency (over the objection of Ohio political boss Mark Hanna) to make certain that Roosevelt left New York.

When William McKinley died in September 1901, he became the third President to have been assassinated in forty years. On hearing news of the shooting, Hanna said: "I told McKinley that it was a mistake to nominate that wild man at Philadelphia." But shortly thereafter, emerging from a conference with the new President, Hanna remarked: "Mr. Roosevelt is an entirely different

Library of Congress.

Theodore Roosevelt, in 1885, as a backwoods hunter in buckskin. Though this picture was staged, he had a profound interest in the frontier, which was later captured in his book, *The Winning of the West.*

Library of Congress.

Lt. Colonel Theodore Roosevelt in his "Rough Rider" uniform in 1898.

Library of Congress.

Roosevelt probably had more energy than any other President, but he was a reflective man as well.

Library of Congress.

Roosevelt as he appeared shortly before his death in 1919. Despite his advocacy of the "strenuous life," Roosevelt died at the relatively young age of 61. His eldest son's death during the Great War and Wilson's decision to prevent Roosevelt from joining the "bully" war in France hastened his early demise.

man today from what he was a few weeks since. He has now acquired all that is needed to round out his character—equipoise and conservatism." Mr. Roosevelt was proceeding cautiously. The mandate had not been his, but rather McKinley's, and McKinley had promised not to interfere with business interests. Roosevelt reassured businessmen and bosses both verbally and by keeping McKinley's Cabinet intact. He may also have been remembering that not one of the four Vice Presidents who had succeeded to the presidency—Tyler, Fillmore, Johnson, and Arthur—were nominated by their party at the next election. If Roosevelt wanted the nomination, he would have to conform to his party's expectations.

Roosevelt's first message to Congress in December 1901 revealed a President who saw economic problems in national rather than regional terms. He called for everything from trust and railroad regulation to an improved pension system for veterans, from extended powers for the Interstate Commerce Commisssion to conservation and reclamation programs, from a new immigration policy to better treatment of Indians. But the Old Guard was not alarmed by such liberal and reformist rhetoric, since Roosevelt had already shown a willingness to cooperate with conservatives on the tariff issue and monetary policy.

The Trust-Buster

In 1900 a government investigation showed that 185 corporations were capitalized at a total of $3 billion. According to a later investigation, by 1904 some 318 corporations controlled capital investments totaling $7 billion, representing two-fifths of the nation's manufacturing capital; 184 of these corporations had been established since 1898. Clearly, the Sherman Antitrust Act of 1890 was ineffective. From the beginning, Roosevelt was unsympathetic toward those who opposed trusts simply because of their size and was careful to distinguish between those trusts guilty only of success and those guilty of actual misconduct, "those combinations which do good and those combinations which do evil." Mergers, he believed, often reflected or furthered advances in technology, and in 1902 he remarked that "big aggregations" were "an inevitable development of modern civilization."

For Roosevelt, the central question was whether or not the government had power to regulate trusts. The legislation he advanced was intended to confirm that right. He promised to "proceed by evolution . . . not by revolution," a policy too moderate to please those who wanted to destroy all trusts and too progressive for the comfort of big business interests. "We are not attacking the corporations," Roosevelt explained, "but endeavoring to do away with any evil in them. We are not hostile to them; we are merely determined that they shall be so handled as to subserve the public good."

On the President's recommendation, a Department of Commerce and Labor was established in 1903 including a Bureau of Corporations with authority to investigate practices of interstate conglomerates. The legislation also provided for an act establishing the priority of antitrust suits. Although the bill was less controversial than other versions being considered, when its passage seemed endangered Roosevelt went to the people, announcing that the legislation was opposed by John D. Rockefeller's Standard Oil trust. The public support that followed helped secure passage.

At the same time, Roosevelt was working for a reinterpretation of the Sherman Antitrust Act. The Supreme Court decision in 1894 for the E. C. Knight Co., which had been involved in cornering 98 percent of the sugar industry's output, upheld laissez-faire in the extreme and suggested that trusts were beyond government control. In this case, the first involving the Sherman Act, the justices held narrowly that acquisition of manufacturing facilities within a state bore no direct relation to interstate commerce, a decision that had stimulated the growth of trusts.

By 1901 a complicated struggle for ownership of the Chicago, Burlington & Quincy Railroad and a battle for Northern Pacific Railroad stock created both a financial panic and the seeds of an important antitrust case. At the time J. P. Morgan, John D. Rockefeller, James J. Hill, and E. H. Harriman created the Northern Securities Company (a holding company for the Northern Pacific, the Great Northern, and the Chicago, Burlington & Quincy railroads). The immediate ostensible purpose of the company was to end the panic, but its executives intended that eventually the company would monopolize transportation in the growing Northwest. Early in 1902 Attorney General Philander C. Knox and Roosevelt discussed bringing suit against the Northern Securities Company for having violated provisions of the Sherman Act. On February 19, Knox issued a brief press release that caught the rest of the Cabinet and the financial world by surprise. Since Wall Street had always been advised in advance of any government action that would affect business, the unexpectedness of the attorney general's decision to file such a suit enraged the financiers as much as the suit itself.

On February 23, 1902, Morgan visited Roosevelt in Washington in an attempt to settle the matter. "If we have done anything wrong, send your man to my man and they can fix it up," said Morgan. "That can't be done," replied the President. "We don't want to fix it up," added Knox, also present at the meeting, "we want to stop it." After Morgan left, Roosevelt turned to Knox, "That is a most illuminating illustration of the Wall Street point of view. Mr. Morgan could not help regarding me as a big rival operator, who either intended to ruin all his interests or else could be induced to come to an agreement to ruin none." Two years later, by a five-to-four vote, the Supreme Court did "stop it" and ordered Northern Securities dissolved. The defendants held that the decision in the Knight case permitted them to acquire the properties involved and established a precedent that the Sherman Act covered only strictly commercial matters. The justices agreed with the government's contention that the holding company created was an illegal device for restraining trade since it eliminated competition in transportation in a large region.

During the Roosevelt years, suits against forty-four trusts and combinations were filed by the federal government and ninety more under his successor, Taft; yet it was Roosevelt's pioneering advocacy of government control that earned him the name of trust-buster as his legal aides investigated for the first time the complex dealings of tobacco, oil, steel, beef, railroad, and other interests.

Labor Gains

Theodore Roosevelt, as noted earlier, had mixed feelings toward organized labor, yet he went further than any of his predecessors in improving the status and general acceptance of unions. In 1902, 140,000 men led by United Mine Workers chief John Mitchell, struck the anthracite coalfields of Pennsylvania. As the strike dragged on, labor gained public support by its continued willingness to arbitrate; the mineowners (most of whom also owned the railroads that carried the coal) refused to do so, even after both sides had been invited to the White House in an attempt to settle the dispute. Nor was sympathy for the owners increased by Philadelphia and Reading Railroad president George F. Baer, who remarked: "The rights and interests of laboring men will be protected and cared for—not by agitators, but by the Christian men to whom God in his infinite wisdom has given control of the property interests of the country."

Although Roosevelt was sympathetic toward the miners' demands, his major concern was for the "rights and interests" of the public, who in the days before gas, oil, and electric heating, were confronted with a dire shortage of coal in the winter months ahead. The owners had called not only for an injunction against the strike but also for the protection of the militia. Roosevelt informed them he was disposed to call in the militia but only to take over the mines and keep them running. With the intervention of Mark Hanna, Secretary of War Elihu Root, and even J. P. Morgan, the owners finally submitted to arbitration. Although the union was not granted its

Culver Pictures.

THE LION-TAMER

This cartoon in *Harper's Weekly* in 1904 expressed popular support for Roosevelt's role as trust-buster.

Frederick Lewis.

Hundreds lined the streets in New York and other cities and towns for rations of fuel during the coal strike of 1902.

central demand, union recognition, the miners did receive a reduction in working hours to nine hours a day (in a few instances to eight) and a 10 percent pay raise, which the owners were allowed to pass along to consumers in a proportionate increase in prices. Roosevelt was the first President to call for federal intervention in a labor dispute, and in doing so he brought prestige both to his office and to the government in representing the public interests.

Nevertheless, Roosevelt advocated an open shop for all government employees and came into conflict with the American Federation of Labor when he reinstated a nonunion worker in the Government Printing Office. He did, however, advocate "the right of laboring men to join a union . . . without illegal interference." The attitude of the President represented the most significant gain won by labor since the Pullman Strike of 1894.

The Election of 1904

Campaigning for reelection in 1904, Roosevelt offered no systematic program, but rather a broad policy based on the "square deal" he intended to give all sides. His politics were thus rooted in the economic and cultural pluralism that voters had approved in the McKinley-Bryan race of 1896, a pluralism now being espoused by a dynamic personality admired by many Americans regardless of their political views.

To attract conservative business interests, the Democrats nominated New York Judge Alton B. Parker; however, most of the Wall Street community, including its biggest leaders—Morgan, Rockefeller, Harriman, and Gould—supported Roosevelt and vice presidential nominee Senator Charles W. Fairbanks of Indiana. (One financier, Henry Clay Frick, was later to remember ruefully that Roosevelt "got down on his knees before us.

We bought the son of a bitch and then he did not stay bought.") The reversal of form by the Democrats was a conscious effort to abandon Bryan's farm-labor coalition of 1896 and 1900 and forget his monetary schemes.

Roosevelt probably could have won without business support in 1904. His stand against the "malefactors" of the trusts and his increasingly benign attitude toward labor had swelled the ranks of his supporters, and he had appointed to office Catholics, Jews, labor leaders, and citizens of German, Irish, and Hungarian extraction. Black educator Booker T. Washington had been invited to the White House (although this was later downplayed), and he had, unofficially, advised Roosevelt on patronage.

The campaign was enlivened only by the President's personality and Parker's unsubstantiated charges that Secretary of Commerce George B. Cortelyou, as chairman of the Republican National Committee, had attemped to blackmail businessmen by demanding financial support in exchange for assurance that findings of the Bureau of Corporations would not be published.

Roosevelt's ability to placate opponents while achieving his own political ends already had been established. La Follette saw him as "the ablest living interpreter of what I would call the superficial public sentiment of a given time, and he is spontaneous in his reactions to it." Another, even less flatteringly, thought his gift was an understanding of the "psychology of the mutt." Whatever it was, the public wanted more and gave him a landslide victory: 56.4 percent of the popular vote (7,626,593) to Parker's 37.6 percent (5,082,898) and 336 electoral votes to the Democrat's 140.

The Presidential Election of 1904

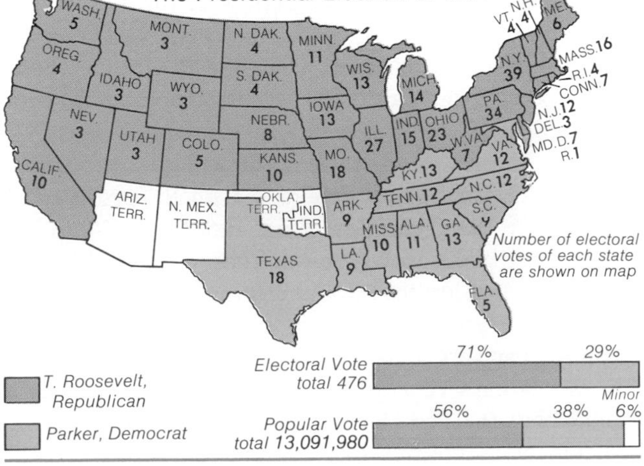

Railroads

Now that the presidency was clearly his by a verdict at the ballot box, not by inheritance, Roosevelt began to reinforce his idea of executive action. As he later wrote: "My view was that every executive officer . . . was a steward of the people bound actively and affirmatively to do all he could for the people, and not to content himself with the negative merit of keeping his talents undamaged in a napkin."

His first target was the railroads. Like the Sherman Act, the Interstate Commerce Act of 1887 had been weakened by subsequent Supreme Court decisions. By 1904 six major railroads, encompassing 800 independent lines, controlled 75 percent of the track mileage. Rates were up, but with no corresponding improvement of the lines and no increase in workers' pay. The Elkins Act of 1903, supported by the railroads, had made shippers as culpable for accepting rebates as railroads for offering them, but strong regulatory legislation was still needed. In 1904, testimony given during an Interstate Commerce Committee (ICC) investigation revealed continued corruption within the railroads and resulted in the Hepburn Act (1906), which authorized the commission to fix maximum railroad rates, subject to court review.

The Hepburn Bill got through the House easily enough, but in the Senate the President had to play hard and skillful politics. In effect, the House wanted radical reform, the Senate, only tacit regulation. Some features of the measure were phrased in general terms to attract maximum support, and this annoyed freshman Senator La Follette. He wanted ironclad rules for evaluating railroad properties and, breaking with tradition, took to the floor in an unsuccessful attempt to add amendments. Then, by cooperating for a time with key Democrats Roosevelt outflanked the Old Guard Republican conservatives and finally got the legislation he wanted.

For the first time the federal government was given the power to impose prices and, although appeals could be made, the burden of proof was now on the railroad owners, not on the ICC. Although more bark than bite, the Hepburn Act set precedents for federal regulation of American industry. Owners were still able to evade a "commodity clause" requiring them to dispose of steamship lines and coal mines they had purchased in order to eliminate competition, and the commission still lacked the power to evaluate railroad properties and service costs, the only equitable way to establish fair rates.

Food and Drug Legislation

Legislation was also enacted in the areas of food and drugs. Federal inspection of meat for export had existed since 1890, but there was no similar control over meat sold domestically. Dr. Harvey W. Wiley, chief chemist of the Department of Agriculture, had found extensive use of preservatives and adulterants in prepared and canned foods, and North Dakota Food Commissioner Dr. E. E. Ladd revealed in 1904 that "more than 90 percent of the local meat-markets in the State were using chemical preservatives," particularly "boric acids or borates." Advised by Wiley, Roosevelt in 1905 made recommendations to Congress, but not until 1906, with the appearance of Upton Sinclair's *The Jungle*, was Congress pressured to act. Sinclair had intended his novel to expose the exploitation of workers by industry, but what the public responded to was his description of unsanitary conditions in the Chicago stockyards. A special investigation followed the book's publication, and as a result a federal meat inspection act was passed; although Congress appropriated little money for enforcement, it represented a first step.

In 1904, "The Great American Fraud," a series of articles by Samuel Hopkins Adams, appeared in *Collier's Weekly*, warning against patent medicines. Outraged public response ensured the passage of a Pure Food and Drug Act in 1906, amended in 1911 to prevent misleading labeling of medicines.

Among other notable pieces of legislation of the period were the Employer's Liability Act of 1906, effective within the District of Columbia; a 1907 law that forbade corporate contributions to campaign funds by national banks and by any corporation "organized by authority of any law of Congress" in any election involving federal officials; and a 1908 act that limited the hours of trainmen.

Breach with the Old Guard

By 1907 Roosevelt's relationship with the Old Guard had deteriorated. By increasing the pace of reform, he had advocated policies that many businessmen blamed for the Panic of 1907 and the brief depression surrounding it. The panic, however, resulted not from reforms but from excessive financial speculation, a weak banking and monetary system, and the natural, temporary expansion of industrial output beyond the market's ability to consume.

Library of Congress.

The reality of spoiled, tainted meat—dubbed "embalmed beef" by outraged Spanish-American War soldiers—failed to rouse the public. But a novel by Upton Sinclair did stir them to demand passage of the Pure Food and Drug Act. One of its provisions was the establishment of inspection stations.

A run on New York banks began in October when the public discovered that a few trust companies there had tried to corner the copper market with funds from their own unstable accounts and had failed. Some banks, though uninvolved in the copper dealings, were forced to close. They recalled notes throughout the country. The panic ended when, under the supervision of J. P. Morgan, funds were pooled from larger Manhattan banks and, with Treasury deposits, transferred to threatened banks. A week or so later Morgan used this crisis to propose a merger of United States Steel and a small, hard-pressed competitor, the Tennessee Iron and Coal Company. When asked about such a union, Roosevelt gave his tacit consent, a decision that would return to haunt him. But neither the government nor bankers wanted a few wealthy financiers to have the responsibility of maintaining the nation's economy in times of emergency. As a result, both the President and his critics applauded the creation of a congressional committee, headed by Re-

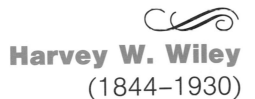

Library of Congress.

Harvey W. Wiley (1844–1930)

Born in an Indiana log cabin, Harvey Washington Wiley was a leader in improving the quality of the food Americans eat. Reformer, teacher, chemist, author, lecturer, he served as a corporal in the Civil War and then got a medical education in his native state and a B.S. degree at Harvard in 1873. He returned to Indiana to become professor of chemistry at Purdue University (1874–1883), during which time a year's study at Berlin stimulated his interest in food adulteration.

From 1883 to 1912 Wiley was chief chemist of the U.S. Department of Agriculture. His chief goals were research on sugar and syrup crops (greatly benefiting the sugar beet industry), chemical analysis of other agricultural produce, and a vigorous campaign against food adulteration. Despite considerable opposition, in 1906 he secured passage of a Pure Food and Drug Act. Wiley then released his famous "Poison Squad" to ensure enforcement. The findings created a sensation but, aided mightily by the White House, public outrage, and works such as Upton Sinclair's exposé of the meatpacking industry, *The Jungle,* Wiley prevailed. By the time he resigned in 1912, he had built up a solid core of 800 employees dedicated to protecting the health of all Americans.

Witty, author of numerous books, a good public speaker, and a sure-fire hit on the Chautauqua circuit, Wiley had a commanding presence and frequently declined offers to enter politics. He did, however, campaign for Wilson in 1912. A true son of the Progressive era, he saw his role as that of a crusader for better food, not as a politician. ■

publican Senator Nelson Aldrich of Rhode Island, to study financial reform.

Throughout these years, Roosevelt's benign attitude toward labor troubled conservative Republicans, and in the elections of 1906 the President found himself caught between the Old Guard and organized labor. The pressures on Roosevelt became more intense as the two sides increased their demands. The National Association of Manufacturers obtained several injunctions against strikes and boycotts, thereby threatening the growth of unions, and encouraged congressmen to oppose all labor legislation. On the other side, the AFL submitted to Washington a bill of grievances that demanded shorter working hours, improved conditions, union recognition and, above all, relief from injunctions against strikes provided for by the Sherman Act. The unions also actively campaigned against those who seemed unfriendly toward labor, and although Roosevelt supported all Republican candidates, he urged all party nominees to liberalize their views on labor.

The outcome was not very reassuring to the regulars and conservatives of either party. The returns showed a trend towards Progressivism among Republicans in the North and among Democrats in the South. Also, the Republican majority in the House was cut sharply, and it seemed that organized labor was beginning to adopt an anti-Republican stance.

An issue that was muddying the political waters was the conservation of natural resources. Fewer than 200 million of the country's original 800 million acres of virgin forest remained under government control by the time Roosevelt took office; four-fifths of those 600 million acres were in private hands and 10 percent was owned by two railroads and a timber company. In his first message to Congress, the President stated that "the forest and water problems are perhaps the most vital internal problems of the United States." Mineral resources had also been plundered as if the supply were limitless. In 1907 Roosevelt told Congress: "The mineral wealth of the country, the coal, iron, oil, gas and the like, does not reproduce itself, and therefore is certain to be exhausted ultimately; and wastefulness in dealing with it today means that our descendants will feel the exhaustion a generation or two before they otherwise would."

Under provisions of the existing Forest Reserve Act of 1891, Roosevelt set aside nearly 150 million acres of government land and, prompted by La Follette, withdrew an additional 85 million acres in the Northwest and Alaska from public entry. The Newlands Act (1902) apportioned some of the money received from the sale of public land to the construction of dams and reclamation projects. When it was discovered that cattlemen, ranchers, timbermen, and railroads were plundering these lands, Roosevelt transferred supervision of national forests to the Forest Bureau of the Department of Agriculture, supervised by the chief ranger, Gifford Pinchot. A close friend of Roosevelt, Pinchot had studied forestry in Europe and was an ardent conservationist, perhaps too zealous for his own good.

In 1908 the President called a national conservation council, which was attended by governors of forty-four states, Supreme Court justices, members of the Cabinet, and experts in science, education, and politics. The conference not only brought the issue of conservation to public attention but also led to annual meetings of governors, the establishment of conservation committees in a number of states, and a National Conservation Association (1909) which disseminated information.

Westerners who had grown rich exploiting the land were able to persuade Congress to prevent the creation of new forest reserves in six western states—unless such plans received congressional approval, which seemed unlikely. Congress also refused to make appropriations for flood control suggested by the Inland Waterways Commission and for publications of the Country Life Commission; the members of both groups had been appointed by the President. Despite these setbacks, Roosevelt succeeded in establishing the foundations of conservation legislation and with Gifford Pinchot put the word "conservation" into the minds and vocabulary of the American public.

Reform Politics and Party Competition

On election eve in 1904 Roosevelt promised not to seek reelection; when 1908 came around, he decided to keep that promise. His political strength allowed him to name a successor, and the man he chose was in many ways his opposite, William Howard Taft. Taft, whose lifelong ambition was to serve not as President but as a justice on the Supreme Court (a goal he would finally achieve in 1921), had held judicial and administrative positions—circuit court judge, governor-general of the Philippines, administrator of the Canal Zone, and Secretary of War. He had never been a candidate for elective office, nor had he wished to be. He was not used to politics and was unskilled at political maneuvering: "Politics, when I am in it, makes me sick," he once remarked. But the size alone of this portly, affable man inspired public confidence, and, though Taft was not Roosevelt's first choice, the relationship between the two men was a warm one. Moreover, Roosevelt had received Taft's promise to continue the program of reform.

Taft: Progressive as Conservative

Taft easily defeated Bryan, once again the Democratic candidate, but Republicans lost seats in the House and several governorships. Unlike the aggressive Roosevelt, Taft was a strict constructionist, convinced that the President should have only that authority specifically desig-

Library of Congress.

Utter disregard for conservation was the norm in logging. Besides the devastation of the land, mud slides could endanger ox teams and men hauling logs to saw mills.

nated by the Constitution. His reluctance to provide strong executive leadership or to intercede in legislation aggravated differences between Republican Progressives and the Old Guard. As party factions became more divisive, Taft recognized the necessity of keeping the party together. For him, the center of the party was, ultimately, the Old Guard, not the insurgent minority. Although some Progressive legislation was passed during Taft's administration, it did not keep pace with the public demand for reform.

Perhaps the suspicions of Progressives should have been aroused when Taft appointed a conservative Cabinet, which included five corporation lawyers, without seeking the advice of Roosevelt. Led by George Norris of Nebraska, House insurgents began to question Taft's commitment to reform when they failed to gain his support in limiting the powers of tobacco-chewing, ultraconservative Speaker of the House "Uncle Joe" Cannon of Illinois. And by the time the Payne-Aldrich Tariff had been created, Progressives were convinced they had been abandoned.

The 1908 Republican platform had included a promise of tariff revision, commonly understood to mean reduction; Taft himself had confirmed this during the campaign. To many critics, tariffs were "the mother of trusts" and allowed monopolies to grow unchecked. To allay the anxiety of business interests, Taft called a special session of Congress to resolve the issue. Representative Sereno Payne of New York introduced a bill that the House passed, placing iron ore, hides, and flax on the free list, reducing duty on lumber and steel, and including a graduated inheritance tax. But manufacturing interests were able to influence action in the Senate; of more than 800 changes made there, 600 revised charges upward, and the free list was subjected to the wit of contemporary humorist "Mr. Dooley": "Th' Republican party has been thru to its promises. Look at th' free list if ye don't believe it. Practically ivrything nicessary to existence comes in free. Here it is. Curling stones, teeth, sea moss, newspapers, nux vomica, Pulu, canary bird seed, divvy-divvy, spunk, hog bristles, marshmallows, silk worm eggs, stilts, skeletons, an' leeches. Th' new tariff bill puts these familyar commodyties within th' reach iv all." Senator Henry Cabot Lodge put it less humorously: "I have never come so close to tariff making before, and the amount of ruthless selfishness that is exhibited on both sides surpasses anything I have ever seen."

One by one the revised schedules were attacked by Progressive senators, little affecting the final version of the tariff but supplying information to consumers about

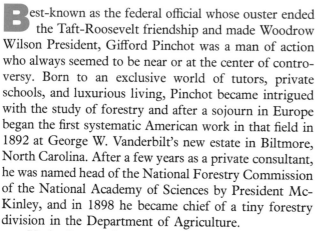

U.S. Department of Interior.

Gifford Pinchot
(1865–1946)

Best-known as the federal official whose ouster ended the Taft-Roosevelt friendship and made Woodrow Wilson President, Gifford Pinchot was a man of action who always seemed to be near or at the center of controversy. Born to an exclusive world of tutors, private schools, and luxurious living, Pinchot became intrigued with the study of forestry and after a sojourn in Europe began the first systematic American work in that field in 1892 at George W. Vanderbilt's new estate in Biltmore, North Carolina. After a few years as a private consultant, he was named head of the National Forestry Commission of the National Academy of Sciences by President McKinley, and in 1898 he became chief of a tiny forestry division in the Department of Agriculture.

Under Roosevelt, who quickly grew to admire this lean, tall, hardy aristocrat with handlebar moustache and intense eyes, Pinchot became an "empire builder." In 1905 his division was transformed into the U.S. Forest Service and gained control of the vast reserves of the General Land Office, formerly under the Interior Department. A catalyst for a general conservation movement, Pinchot clearly had the ear of the White House until March 1909 when Taft took over; then everything changed.

Richard A. Ballinger, once commissioner of the General Land Office and now Secretary of the Interior, quickly moved to dismantle Pinchot's Forest Service. In a feud over conservation practices in Alaska, Pinchot lost out and hurried to Italy to tell the touring Roosevelt of his troubles, thus precipitating the three-way election campaign of 1912. Pinchot even wrote Roosevelt's "New Nationalism" speech of August 1910, which started this political uproar.

A maverick Republican, Pinchot campaigned hard for Roosevelt in 1912 and then retreated to Yale where he taught from time to time (1913–1936) at a forestry school founded with his father's money. In 1914 he married a great-granddaughter of Peter Cooper, the first of two wives, a suffragette who once announced for the U.S. Senate and then withdrew with the frank admission that she saw no hope of winning the race.

In 1923 and again in 1931, Gifford Pinchot, a vigorous Prohibitionist, took advantage of the disarray in Republican machine ranks in Pennsylvania to become governor of that state. During his first term he modernized administrative techniques to make them more efficient and got tighter regulation of state utilities. His second administration, in the depths of hard times, was less noteworthy. Active almost until his death, in 1942 he showed the U.S. Navy how to extract drinking water from fresh fish, something he had learned during a South Seas cruise. ■

Library of Congress.

William Howard Taft, the largest man ever to occupy the White House, never possessed the energy or robust qualities of his predecessor.

the relationship between tariffs and trust interests. Nor did the compromise worked out by Taft and Aldrich achieve more than the downward revision of rates on iron ore, coal, oil, cotton and a few other items; it did, however, result in a constitutional Amendment that would provide for a personal income tax and establish a 2 percent corporate tax and a tariff commission. Politically, the opposition was polarized, and Taft made matters worse when he selected the heartland of midwestern Progressivism in which to call the bill "the best tariff bill that the Republican party ever passed." As the Republican Progressives interpreted the trend of events, the President had rejected their views and had gone over—lock, stock, and barrel—to the conservative, Old Guard wing of their party. La Follette of Wisconsin was especially distressed, and he soon became the leader of a thinly disguised revolt against the conservative wing of the Republicans, which was dominated, in his opinion, by business and industrial interests.

Railroads

When Congress met in 1910, the disgruntled Republican insurgents struck back. Norris and other indignant Republicans allied themselves with Democrats to strip Speaker Cannon of his membership on the powerful House Rules Committee. Initially the President and Progressives had agreed for the most part about railroad legislation, but by the time the Mann-Elkins Act was passed in 1910, Taft, who had made support of the bill a test of party loyalty, was openly and actively working against the reelection of Progressives in the coming fall elections and was withholding his patronage from them.

In its original form, the bill empowered the Interstate Commerce Commission to fix rates on its own initiative and to oversee any railroad securities that were to be issued. Taft was especially eager to establish a Commerce Court that would hear appeals on rate decisions. The Progressives, fearing judges would be too lenient towards the railroads, were opposed to the broad powers given to the Court and to a provision that allowed for certain mergers; also, they wanted to include a provision that would enable the government to assay the values of railroad properties—and to base rates on those values. House Progressives deleted the merger provision and added amendments. One amendment gave the government the right to evaluate property; the other included telephone and telegraph companies under the bill's jurisdiction. The proposed legislation was then virtually rewritten in the upper house where Senator Aldrich bargained with the Democratic minority; in exchange for Democratic support of the bill, ensuring its passage, Aldrich pledged Republican backing for the admission of Arizona and New Mexico to the Union—two states that were almost certain to fall into the Democratic camp in the election of 1912. Taft's Commerce Court was saved, but physical evaluation of the railroads postponed until 1913—a move that brought about further party disunity.

Less controversial accomplishments of Taft's administration included division of the Department of Commerce and Labor (established in 1903) into separate entities, and creation of a parcel post and postal savings bank. The civil service list was broadened; a Commission of Economy and Efficiency was established to examine federal administration; and an act was passed to make information about campaign expenditures public. A Federal Children's Bureau was set up under the direction of Hull House's Julia Lathrop, and Congress sent to the

States for ratification the Sixteenth Amendment which authorized a personal income tax. Ratification came in 1913 and a personal income tax was adopted as part of a Tariff Reform Program. Alaska was granted territorial status, and New Mexico and Arizona were added to the Union. Taft needlessly antagonized Progressives when he refused to certify Arizona's admission until it removed from its constitution a provision for the recall of judges. The legislation was quickly restored once Arizona became a state.

Ballinger-Pinchot Controversy

In the area of conservation, Taft closed a vast number of acres of public land to settlement and established the Bureau of Mines to safeguard mineral resources. But because he became caught up in the middle of a controversy between Secretary of the Interior Richard A. Ballinger and Gifford Pinchot, still head of the Forestry Service (and a symbol of the Roosevelt administration), Taft appeared to renounce the conservation program begun by his predecessor.

With information provided by Louis R. Glavis, an investigator employed by the General Land Office, Pinchot charged that Ballinger had allowed private interests to develop reserved coal properties in Alaska. Pinchot brought his charges to Taft, who dismissed them, along with Glavis. Pinchot next supplied *Collier's Weekly* with confidential information in two articles that attacked Ballinger and the administration; further, Pinchot admitted in a letter read before the Senate that he had leaked this information to the press and he went on to denounce Ballinger as an enemy of conservation. Pinchot's own dismissal was thus ensured. In 1910 a congressional committee cleared Ballinger. But Louis D. Brandeis, attorney for the opposition, proved that the document on which Taft had decided in favor of Ballinger had actually been written after he had made his decision. Although Taft continued Roosevelt's conservation policies, the Ballinger-Pinchot spat ignited passions in the Congress. Soon Republican Progressives teamed up with Democrats to strip the Republican Old Guard (Taft's most loyal followers) of much of their power.

In reality, ever since Roosevelt assumed the presidency in 1901, his party had been split on the issue of reform. Neither soft words nor quick slogans could conceal this fact and the Ballinger-Pinchot affair revealed how very deep these political differences really were.

The issue was headline news and solidified opposition to the increasingly conservative Taft. In March 1909 Roosevelt had discreetly gone to Africa to hunt big game, leaving only his shadow over the new administration. Before his return he was joined in Italy by Pinchot, who presented his version of the Ballinger incident, along with letters of complaint against Taft from Progressive Republican leaders. Roosevelt was never to feel the same about his successor. Returning to the United States in June 1910, he was besieged at his Oyster Bay home by insurgents who argued that Taft was endangering his policies. It was after the Ballinger-Pinchot controversy that Taft, too, cooled toward Roosevelt. He began to see a "socialistic tendency" in both Pinchot and Roosevelt and thought of his enemies as those "carried off their feet by Roosevelt's sermons and preachments."

The Taft-Roosevelt Split

Initially Roosevelt intended only to unite Republican factions, but his decision to participate in the New York state convention and embark on a speaking tour through the West made conflict with the Taft administration inevitable; Taft was actively seeking the defeat of all those Republicans Roosevelt could support most wholeheartedly. As Taft had moved to the right politically, Roosevelt had gone even further left. In August at Osawatomie, Kansas, Roosevelt not only repeated the demands of his last congressional message (even then too radical for Taft) but called for a New Nationalism that, among its more controversial features, would curtail the powers of conservative courts, which were seen by Roosevelt as impediments to social justice. "I stand for the square deal," he explained. "I mean not merely that I stand for fair play under the present rules of the game, but that I stand for having those rules changed so as to work for a more substantial equality of opportunity and of reward for equally good service."

The result of this split within the Republican party was a Democratic landslide in 1910. For the first time since 1892 Republicans no longer had control of the House, and their Senate majority was narrowed. Democratic governors won in many eastern states, including Woodrow Wilson in New Jersey, and Progressive Republicans triumphed in the West. If Democrats could form a coalition with Republican insurgents, they would control the Senate. It was clear that Taft probably would not be reelected in 1912.

Taft's obvious weakness as party leader, Roosevelt's growing disenchantment with his policies, and the revolt of La Follette created considerable political unrest and stirred hopes of victory in 1912 among Democrats, out of power since 1896. In January 1911, led by La Follette, insurgents established a Progressive Republican League, whose purpose was to liberalize the party; soon after, having received Roosevelt's assurance that he did not intend to run, the Wisconsin senator announced his candidacy for the presidency. On a speaking tour, La Follette collapsed, and though he soon recovered most of his supporters used this brief illness as an excuse to go over to Roosevelt, who in the meantime had supervised the drafting of a letter from six governors requesting that he run.

The contest became increasingly bitter and personal as Taft and his supporters sought to maintain the status quo that many thought Roosevelt and his followers were out to demolish. Taft had little chance of winning the election, but the Old Guard was determined to deny the nomination to Roosevelt. Although they conceded Roosevelt might be a strong candidate, he could not get their backing. The Old Guard manipulated Southern states through patronage, owned the majority of the delegates from New York and other boss-run states, and controlled the convention machinery. Presidential primaries held in thirteen states gave Roosevelt 278 delegates, Taft 48, and La Follette 36; of the remaining 254 contested seats, the national committee gave 235 to Taft. Irate Roosevelt supporters walked out of the convention, and Taft received the nomination on the first ballot.

In August, Roosevelt's followers convened in Chicago as the Progressive party. Hastily formed, the party attracted such social reformers as Jane Addams, economic Progressives, and many people who had bolted from the Republican party. One of them, William Allen White, (1868–1944), distinguished editor of the *Emporia Gazette* of Kansas, later wrote: "Roosevelt bit me and I went mad." The platform was a synthesis of current Progressive thought in all areas and was by far the most socially advanced program proposed up to that time. It advocated suffrage and a minimum wage for women, workmen's compensation, and social insurance; it called for limiting the use of government injunctions in ending labor disputes and for abolishing child labor. The platform also included demands for: initiative, referendum, and recall (including referendums on judicial decisions); a

The Evansville Courier.

The shifting relationship between Roosevelt and Taft became apparent to the entire nation by 1912.

national presidential primary; public exposure of campaign contributions and expenditures; a tariff commission to set rates scientifically; and a federal trade commission that would have broad powers of control over business and industry.

"I am feeling like a bull moose," Roosevelt cried; ever after the Progressive was the "Bull Moose" party. Having sung "Onward Christian Soldiers," the party nominated him, along with Governor Hiram W. Johnson of California as his running mate, by acclamation. "We stand at Armageddon, and we battle for the Lord," Roosevelt told his followers.

Woodrow Wilson

Although his family only settled in the South shortly before his birth in 1856, for Woodrow Wilson the South was the "only place in the country, the only place in the world where nothing has to be explained to me." Son of a Presbyterian minister, young Wilson quickly acquired a zeal for moral reform colored by a Calvinistic philosophy. Unhappy practicing law, Wilson left for the academic world, where both his teaching and the publication of six books impressed Princeton trustees, who in 1902 appointed him president of the university. During his administration he initiated many reforms, but during a controversy over plans for a graduate school, he left the university in 1910 to run for governor. Although recruited by state bosses, Wilson disassociated himself from the machine and adopted the cause of Progressives. After his election, he and the legislature of New Jersey (a stronghold of the corporations) began to regulate big business. Wilson also backed laws that established a primary, workmen's compensation, education reforms, and the regulation of utilities—accomplishments that made Wilson one of the foremost contenders for the Democratic presidential nomination.

Although Bryan was no longer a viable presidential candidate, he controlled the votes of a number of delegates to the 1912 Democratic national convention and his followers were suspicious of the former Princeton president in spite of his recent Progressive record. Westerners favored House Speaker "Ol" Hound Dawg" Champ Clark of Missouri; business interests disliked Wilson's stand against trusts in New Jersey. State political machines, wary of Wilson's renunciation of his own in New Jersey, worked actively against him. His enemies reprinted disparaging phrases written by Wilson about labor and immigrants in his *History of the American People* and persuaded many delegates in the South to support Alabama's Oscar W. Underwood.

Although Clark came to the Baltimore convention assured of a majority, he needed two-thirds of the votes to win, and Wilson's forces controlled at least one-third of the delegates. When, on the tenth ballot, New York switched into the Clark column, Bryan, an ancient foe of New York's Tammany Hall, announced that he would not support any candidate backed by his old enemy and switched his votes to Wilson. Aides of the New Jersey governor then made a number of deals on the convention floor, including an agreement to nominate Indiana's Thomas R. Marshall for the vice presidency. On the forty-third ballot Wilson won a majority and was nominated on the forty-sixth.

The Election of 1912

The battle for the presidency pitted Roosevelt's New Nationalism against Wilson's New Freedom, and although both were Progressive programs, they differed philosophically. Roosevelt had been deeply influenced by Herbert Croly's writings, particularly by his revolutionary concept of using traditionally elitist Hamiltonian methods to achieve popular Jeffersonian ends. Croly (1869–1930), an editor, political theorist, and founder of the *New Republic* (1914), stressed the necessity for strong leadership and pragmatic proposals. His concepts demanded a strong federal government that would accept the growth of industry not only as inevitable but as beneficial and would regulate it for the good of the people. Aided by Louis Brandeis in systematizing his own thought, Wilson was opposed to a stronger central government and to increased federal control of business. Wilson advocated free trade regulated only by the personal morality of business leaders. He compared the trust to an automobile and the corporate executive to its driver: if the driver becomes reckless, said Wilson, it is pointless to punish the car. Wilson saw the existing government as a "foster-child of special interests" and, at least initially, preferred to leave a great deal of authority to the states—a policy that would be made possible by eliminating the dangers of big business and thus the need for a strong central government. Unlike Roosevelt, Wilson supported a laissez-faire approach and was careful to point out that it was only "illicit" competition, not competition itself, that had enabled the strong to crush the weak. Roosevelt called the New Freedom "rural Toryism." Wilson saw the Roosevelt plan as "an avowed partnership between the government and the trusts," whereby the government was to guarantee that the trusts would be "kind." "I do not want the sympathy of the trusts for the human race," Wilson explained. "Free men need no guardians." Submission to them would lead to a "corruption of the will."

There were other areas in which the two platforms differed. In accord with Wilson's laissez-faire economics, the Democrats favored a downward revision of tariffs, while the Progressives advocated increased protective measures. In addition, the Democratic program for social reform was neither so systematic nor so inclusive as that of the Progressives. But to Wilson the heart of the matter was two radically different concepts concerning the role of government, and in October 1912 he prophesied:

"This is a second struggle for emancipation. . . . If America is not to have free enterprise, then she can have freedom of no sort whatever."

Library of Congress

The first and only Ph.D. to campaign for and win the presidency, Wilson undoubtedly found himself at ease addressing this college audience in Iowa.

The Democrats swept the House and Wilson won the presidency. Although he captured only 41.8 percent of the popular vote to Roosevelt's 27.4 percent and Taft's 23.2, in the Electoral College the tallies were 435, 88, and 8 votes, respectively. In addition, Socialist party candidate Eugene Debs received over 900,000 popular votes. However much the split in the Republican Party had contributed to Wilson's victory, the combined votes of the three parties running on reform-oriented platforms amounted to a clear mandate for change.

Democratic Progressivism: The Wilson Administration

Few men have entered the White House with less experience in the art of practical politics than Woodrow Wilson. He was long on theory and ideas but had never served as a legislator at the state or federal level and, except for two years as New Jersey's chief executive, knew little about governing. In his *Congressional Government* (1885) he had unfavorably compared the weakness of the presidency and the inefficiency of Congress with the British parliamentary system. Although Wilson restored the executive leadership Taft had lost, he believed at the same time that the government which governs least governs best. His political inexperience was partially offset by his ability to attract capable men as advisors. And he used this ability to further the cause of the New Freedom's first goal: tariff revision.

The Underwood-Simmons Tariff

Wilson told the nation: "The object of the tariff duties henceforth laid must be effective competition, the whetting of American wits by contest with the wits of the rest of the world." To achieve that end, Congress was called to a special session where Wilson personally addressed both Houses, the first President to have done so since Jefferson. While unremarkable in itself, his presence dramatized the issue and captured the attention of a generally approving public.

The Underwood tariff bill passed in the House with little debate and with voting along party lines. But special interest groups then descended on Washington, and

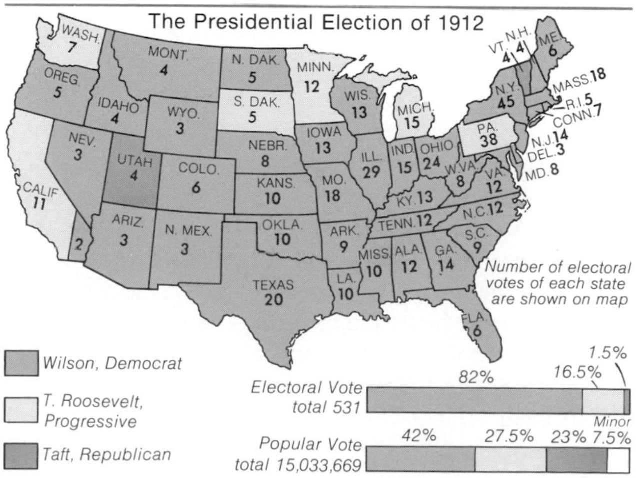

members of the Senate were besieged by lobbyists of every sort.

In May, Wilson brought the "sinister pressure" of the lobbyists to the attention of the public: "It is of serious interest to the country that the people at large should have no lobby, and be voiceless in these matters, while great bodies of astute men seek to create an artificial opinion and to overcome the interests of the public for their private profit. . . . The Government ought to be relieved from this intolerable burden."

With public opinion aroused, an investigation was conducted into the private investments and interests of all members of the Senate. It was shown that certain senators would profit from the demands to remove sugar and wool from the free list (on which they had been placed, with other items by the House) and, as a result, only two Democrats voted against the bill. When it was passed in September 1913, the Underwood Bill reversed the trend in tariff policy of the last fifty years; though still protectionist, it reduced tariffs on more than 900 items, raised fewer than 100, and maintained the old rates on 300. Wool and sugar remained on the free list. The bill also provided for a graduated income tax (constitutional now, with the ratification two months earlier of the Sixteenth Amendment) of from 1 percent to 6 percent on incomes of more than $3,000. Passage of the bill not only demonstrated the strength of Wilson's leadership but also promised that some of the goals set by the New Freedom would be fulfilled.

Banking and Currency Reform

Even before the tariff bill reached its final form, Wilson presented his plans for revising the banking and currency system. Although it was generally agreed that such steps were necessary, individuals differed as to what direction reform should take. The inelasticity of credit and shortage of currency (demonstrated during the Panic of 1907) had led Aldrich's Monetary Commission to publish a report that included a list of 17 major defects in the banking system, among them an overly great concentration of loanable funds and of surplus money in New York City banks. In 1911, a report was made public of the Pujo Committee's investigation into "money trusts." This report made clear the extent to which such concentration had grown: members or directors of those New York banks controlled by Morgan and Rockefeller interests held a total of 341 directorships in 112 U.S. corporations with an aggregate capitalization of more than $22 billion. The bankers themselves wanted reform and advocated the establishment of a central bank along the lines of the Bank of England and the Second United States Bank—an institution that businessmen, not the government, would control. Farmers of the West and South, long suspicious of concentrated wealth in the East, demanded that the issuing of notes be exclusively a government function. Taking a still different position, Wilson supported a central bank with regional branches that would be overseen by a federal board—but this proposal pleased neither bankers nor Progressives. As a result of the insistence of Secretary of State Williams Jennings Bryan, in its final form the bill stipulated that bankers would not be represented on the banking board and all notes would be issued by the government. Wilson promised farmers that he would, in the near future, attend to the matter of dissolving interlocking corporation directorates. The Federal Reserve Act thus passed the House in September 1913. To overcome opposition in the Senate, Wilson again presented his case to the people, charging that bankers were creating unfounded fears that panic would result from passage of the bill. Opponents nevertheless managed to limit the powers of the Federal Reserve Board and to raise the amount of gold reserves necessary to issue bank notes.

The bill was passed in December and, as a result, the United States had an efficient banking system for the first time in 100 years. Each of the twelve regional districts was given a Federal Reserve Bank owned by member banks, each of which put up 6 percent of its capital. A Federal Reserve Board supervised the regional banks, which issued short-term commercial notes backed by a gold reserve of 40 percent. That is, the government could theoretically redeem 40 percent of its commercial notes in gold. Private banking interests still prevailed, but the system was now controlled by the public sector to a greater extent than it had ever been before. New and established small businesses could obtain credit more easily; the flexibility of the system would eventually accommodate and survive the financial upheavals of World War I. Another purpose of the act, to provide farmers with more easily obtainable credit, was not achieved until passage of the Federal Farm Loan Act of 1916, which created twelve regional Farm Loan Banks similar to the Federal Reserve banks.

Trusts

With passage of the Federal Reserve Act, the second major goal of the Democratic platform was achieved. The New Freedom had also called for legislation against monopolies. Investigations showed that in 1913, in spite of advances made by the Roosevelt and Taft administrations, monopolies were more numerous and more powerful than they had been at the beginning of the century. Wilson again addressed in person both houses of Congress, making specific recommendations for the control of trusts—which included the abolition of interlocking directorates (as he had promised farming interests the previous year), the clear definition of antitrust laws, the empowerment of the ICC to regulate the finances of railways, the creation of an interstate trade commission to oversee businesses, and the punishment of individuals rather than corporations for violations of antitrust laws.

The overall intention of the Federal Trade Commission Act (1914) was to eliminate unfair business practices and thereby restore lawful competition, but an amendment giving the courts broad review over commission decisions weakened its effectiveness. Nevertheless, during Wilson's administration, the commission issued 379 "cease-and-desist" orders as the result of 2,000 malpractice complaints and, in its investigation of light and power companies, laid the foundation for Franklin Roosevelt's later regulation of public utilities.

Accompanying the Federal Trade Commission Act was the Clayton Antitrust Bill, which was also weakened by amendments attached by conservative senators. Because the Clayton Bill was more radical, it met with greater opposition. As Wilson had asked, the bill prohibited price discriminations that would be harmful to competition and beneficial to monopolies, forbade interlocking directorates (except—as amended by the Senate—those that did not decrease competition), and made corporation officers personally liable for illegal corporate acts. It also limited the use of government injunctions against strikers and exempted labor unions from the provisions aimed against corporations so long as the unions were pursuing legitimate aims (a phrase which, as interpreted by conservative courts, nullified such exemption).

The legislation did not at first appear to be so weak as it later became through court interpretation, and it seemed both a triumph for the administration and another example of Wilson's ability to achieve announced goals. Wilson's successes enabled his party to retain control of the Congress in the 1914 elections, although dissolution of the short-lived Progressive party enabled the Republicans to register some gains.

Wilson Moves Left

With this mandate, Wilson moved further left toward many of the tenets held by the now defunct Progressive party. In reality, this was the only course open to him since the Republicans were the majority party, and to win reelection he had to get the votes of as many liberal Republicans as possible. His task was to woo workers and farmers without appearing as radical as Bryan and thus alienating traditional Democrats. In 1916, in addition to the Federal Farm Loan Act, a Child Labor Act was passed (though later declared unconstitutional by the Supreme Court) as well as a Workmen's Compensation Act for civil service workers and the Adamson Act, which established an eight-hour day for railway workers. In that same year Wilson supported the establishment of a tariff commission comprised of nonpartisan experts and designed to prevent the American market from being inundated with foreign goods. Wilson's nomination of Louis Brandeis to the Supreme Court, against great opposition, demonstrated to the public and to Progressives his continued commitment to reform. While much of the legislation passed during Wilson's first administration was immediately effective, other achievements were dissipated by the conservative interpretations of the courts, and still others would be submerged by the tide of war, only to reemerge and to be revived by the legislators of the New Deal era. For, in truth, foreign matters and not domestic concerns weighed heavily upon the minds of many voters when they went to the polls in November 1916, although few probably realized the disastrous effect "foreign entanglements" would have upon the reform impulse dear to so many of them.

Essay

Margaret Sanger, Birth Control, and Population Trends

Brown Brothers.

Margaret Sanger in the 1940s.

Both the Populist and Progressive movements stirred up a whirlwind of reform movements. Some of them, badly needed, quickly won popular approval; others, controversial and far ahead of their time, were scorned and quickly forgotten. And a few, thanks to persistent, well-organized campaigns and changing social conditions, finally gathered sufficient strength to beat back opponents and gain general, if not complete, acceptance. Such a reform was birth control, and the lady who engineered this distinct change in American attitudes toward contraception and the size of families was Margaret Higgins Sanger.

A very attractive, complex individual, if she had begun her career in the last half of the twentieth century, Margaret Sanger would have been called an emancipated woman, although she might not have given much more than lipservice to the "woman's liberation" movement. Sanger had very little to do with any organization she could not control personally, and after flirting with the radical fringe of the IWW and Socialism for a few years, she retreated to the security of an upper-class world that had money to devote to her chosen cause: birth control.

Born in Corning, New York, in 1883, the sixth of eleven children, Margaret Sanger grew up in a middle class atmosphere. Her mother died at age forty-eight of tuberculosis, her father, a wayward Catholic, at age eighty. Margaret Higgins was hostile toward her father, firmly convinced that his passion had killed her frail mother, yet from him she inherited an iconoclastic nature and the ability to do battle against great odds.

Caring for her mother in her final illness led to a career in nursing in New York City. There, for the first time, as she worked on the Lower East Side, young Margaret Higgins saw how abject poverty and uncontrolled fertility could reap a grim harvest of maternal and infant mortality. At nineteen she married William Sanger, a young architect and budding Socialist who shared some of her reforming zeal.

The Sangers built a house in the suburbs, had three children, and for a decade lived a typical commuter existence. The only disturbing factors were a bout with tuberculosis which sent her to Saranac Lake for a time and an increasing sense of boredom shared by both young parents. So they gave up the suburbs and moved back to Manhattan where she could nurse and where they could attend meetings with fellow Socialists and assorted radicals who discussed exciting things such as anarchism, the writings of Freud, and the need for immediate change in the American way of life.

By 1913 the Sanger marriage was in deep trouble. Margaret was convinced that she had to go to France to study contraceptive methods, although such information had been available in the United States for many years. According to her most perceptive biographer, David M. Kennedy, the truth is, William probably took his family to Paris in one last, vain attempt to save the marriage; but, on December 31, 1913, Margaret Sanger sailed for home alone, leaving her husband and children in Europe.

The next six years were the most tempestuous in Margaret Sanger's life. In 1914, she became editor of *Woman Rebel, a* publication designed to encourage the use of contraceptive techniques. On its masthead were these words: "No Gods, No Masters." Although her father might not have approved of this newspaper's contents, he certainly would have endorsed that defiant phrase. Within a few months New York's postmaster said the *Woman Rebel* was indecent and could not be sent through the mails. In August 1914, Margaret Sanger was arrested, but subsequently fled to Canada and then to England. While there she met Havelock Ellis, famed sexual psychologist, who spent considerable time with her in the British Museum. In effect, Ellis gave Mrs. Sanger a cram course in sex and contraception, told her what to read, and gradually helped her refine her scattered thoughts.

Within a year, Margaret Sanger was back in New York City; but, meanwhile the birth control movement was beginning to take shape. Her husband was arrested after he gave one of her pamphlets to a police agent who had expressed an interest in birth control. His trial revealed that both Sanger and the movement had considerable support. He got thirty days in jail, during which time one of their children died of pneumonia. Soon, Margaret Sanger also was in court, but the government, not eager to bestow martyrdom upon this woman, eventually dropped the mail charges of the previous year.

There was, of course, a basic contradiction in the early stages of this reform movement. Although radicals paid lipservice to birth control, it hardly served their true goals since they were eager to increase the masses so as to increase their strength. In general, the poor greeted birth control with disdain; the middle class, already practicing birth control and producing smaller families, gave it their support, perhaps as a means of easing

Courtesy Planned Parenthood Federation of America, Inc.

Sanger (left) and her sister, Ethel Byrne, awaiting trial in 1916.

pressures from below which could, they feared, cause social dislocations.

In 1916, Mrs. Sanger opened a birth control clinic in Brooklyn, the first in the United States, and was soon back in court charged this time with "maintaining a public nuisance." She was convicted and served thirty days in the workhouse.

Four years later the Sangers were divorced. By that time Mrs. Sanger had also broken off her Socialist, radical ties and was looking for money—big money—that could give her influence and power. In 1921 she founded the American Birth Control League (ABCL), which she headed, and in 1922 found a very wealthy man, twenty years her senior, whom she married. J. Noah Slee, president of Three-in-One Oil, who admittedly pursued her, agreed to a unique marital arrangement that allowed both parties to keep their own names and live virtually separate lives. For two years the union was kept secret; nevertheless, Slee lavished thousands upon his wife's project, the ABCL.

In the late twenties, as a result of too much time spent traveling abroad, Mrs. Sanger lost control of the ABCL, and in 1929, she and her husband set up a rival group in Washington, the National Committee on Federal Legislation for Birth Control. From this body there emerged in 1942 the Planned Parenthood Federation of America and, in 1953, the International Planned Parenthood Federation with Margaret Sanger as its first president. The work of these groups was aided not only by Slee's money but that of George Eastman, the Rockefellers, and numerous other philanthropic fortunes.

The years between 1929 and 1942 were the most productive in Mrs. Sanger's long life, although progress sometimes was hampered by her contradictory, poorly conceived views. In time, she saw birth control as a means of reducing the suffering of the poor, limiting the number of unfit children, increasing both the quantity and quality of sexual relations, and ridding American life of Victorian taboos. She was very naive politically and, instead of cooperating with medical men eager to promote birth control, tended to fight them, never fully comprehending their insistence that the methods used comply strictly with state and federal laws. In 1936 an appeals court decision modified a federal act restricting the right of physicians to prescribe contraceptives in order to save life and promote the well-being of patients. The following year the American Medical Association finally endorsed birth control.

In 1942, Margaret Sanger moved to Tucson, Arizona, to care for her ailing husband, who died a year later. By 1945 she was merely a figurehead in the birth control movement, but her work of the previous quarter century had been indispensable.

Courtesy Planned Parenthood Federation of America, Inc.

After years of harrassment and toil, Margaret Sanger founded the American Birth Control League. It attracted mainly middle class women. The waiting room is pictured in 1921.

Ruthless, pragmatic, much too emotional at times, frequently adapting or distorting facts to fit arguments, and not above seeking out rather questionable scientific views to comport with her pet theories, nevertheless, Margaret Sanger prevailed. When she died in September 1966 at the age of eighty-two, no one doubted the true magnitude of her victory.

Although some New Deal programs of the 1930s quietly endorsed certain aspects of birth control, President Eisenhower came out flatly against it during his second term in the White House (1957–1961). His successor, John F. Kennedy, gave hesitant approval, and by 1965 two former Presidents, Eisenhower and Truman, were cochairmen of a planned parenthood association, and Lyndon Johnson was calling for family planning services both at home and abroad. In 1960 there were some 150 public and private family planning agencies in the United States serving about 150,000 women. By 1973, more than 3,000 agencies were providing birth control services for 3.2 million women.

Historically, as the United States and other industrialized nations became more urban and less rural, the birth rate has declined; thus in time population trends and social thought simply caught up with Margaret Sanger's reform movement. She battled federal and state governments, churchmen (both Catholic and Protestant), and apathy, but she eventually prevailed.

In recent decades, especially from 1945 to 1965, there was an unusual increase in the national birth rate born of affluence and a desire of many families to have three or more children; however, since that time the U.S. birth rate has declined perceptibly, aided by an increasing number of divorces and some rough spots in the economy. Although the general public attributes this decline to the availability of new means of fertility control, such as the pill and intrauterine devices, demographers point out that the national birth rate dropped sharply during the 1920s and bottomed out at 18.4 per 1,000 population in the 1930s, long before these methods were known.

What the future holds is not entirely clear, but most experts expect only a modest increase in the U.S. population in the decades ahead. Without immigration or unforeseen developments, it probably will level off at about 275 million sometime within the next fifty years.

General Studies

Herbert Croly, *The Promise of American Life* (1909)

Richard Hofstadter, *The Age of Reform: From Bryan to F.D.R.* (1955)

Samuel P. Hays, *The Response to Industrialism, 1885-1914* (1957)

James Weinstein, *The Corporate Ideal in the Liberal State, 1900-1918* (1969)

Gabriel Kolko, *The Triumph of Conservatism* (1963)

Henry May, *The End of American Innocence* (1959)

Roosevelt

W. H. Harbaugh, *Power and Responsibility: The Life and Times of Theodore Roosevelt* (1961)

George E. Mowry, *The Era of Theodore Roosevelt* (1958)

Taft

H. F. Pringle, *The Life and Times of William Howard Taft* (2 vols., 1939)

Wilson

John M. Blum, *Woodrow Wilson and the Politics of Morality* (1956)

Arthur S. Link, *Woodrow Wilson and the Progressive Era, 1910-1917* (1954)

Social Life and Social Progressivism

Walter Lord, *The Good Years: From 1900 to the First World War* (1960)

John Higham, *Strangers in the Land: Patterns of American Nativism, 1860-1925* (1965)

Allan Davis, *Spearheads of Reform: The Social Settlements and the Progressive Movement, 1890-1914* (1968)

Allan Davis, *Jane Addams* (1973)

Lincoln Steffens, *Autobiography* (1931)

Political Progressivism

Russell B. Nye, *Midwestern Progressive Politics* (1951)

Robert H. Wiebe, *The Search for Order 1877-1920* (1967)

David P. Thelen, *The New Citizenship* (1972)

Economic Progressivism

Louis D. Brandeis, *Other People's Money and How the Banks Use It* (1914)

Robert H. Wiebe, *Businessmen and Reform* (1962)

Blacks

Ray Stannard Baker, *Following the Color Line* (1908)

I. A. Newby, *Jim Crow's Defense: Anti-Negro Thought in America, 1900-1930* (1965)

Elliot M. Rudwick, *W. E. B. DuBois, Propagandist of the Negro Protest* (1969)

August Meier, *Negro Thought in America, 1880-1915* (1963)

Charles F. Kellogg, *NAACP, 1909-1920* (1967)

Chapter 22

Progressivism Abroad

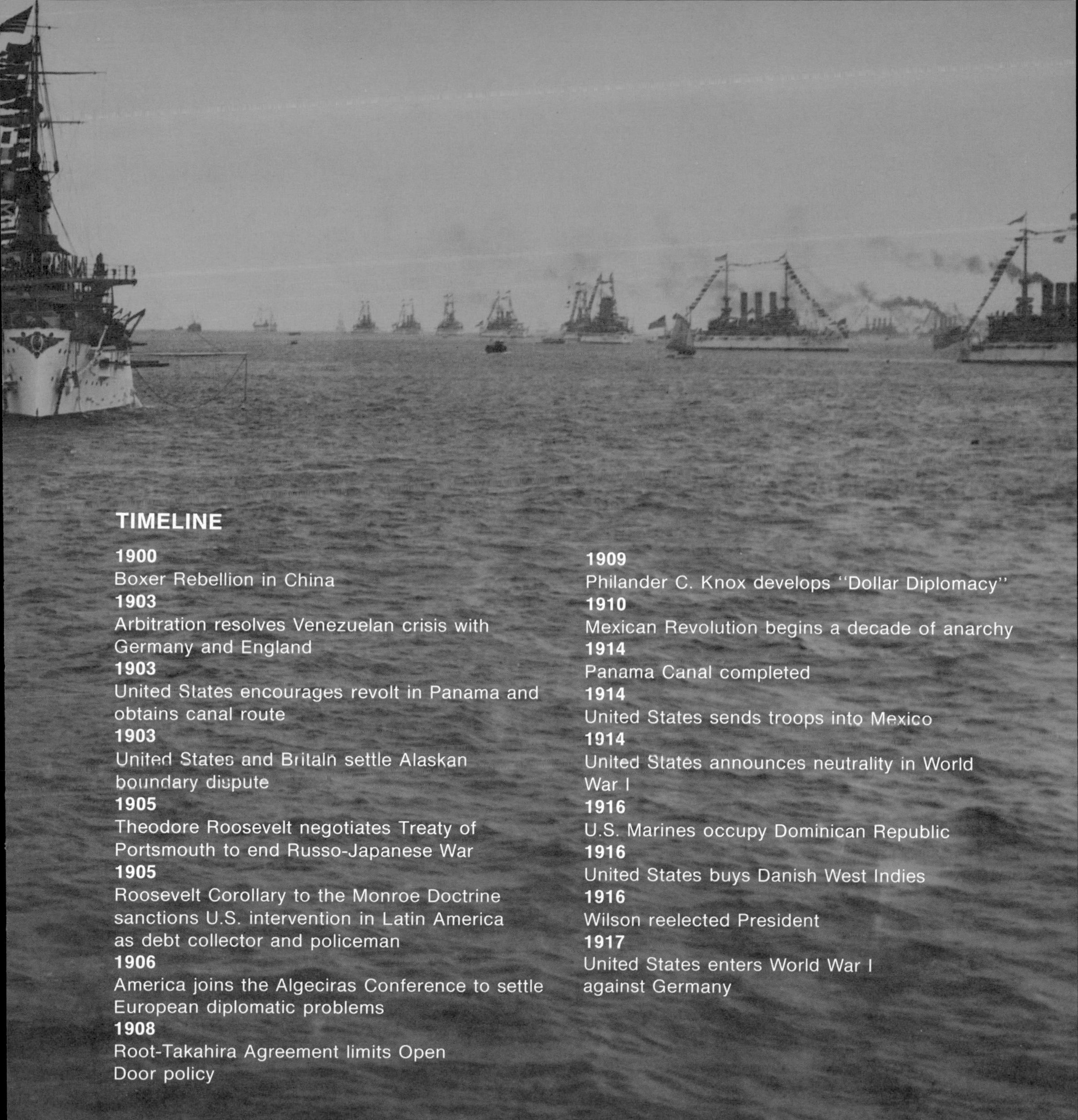

TIMELINE

1900
Boxer Rebellion in China

1903
Arbitration resolves Venezuelan crisis with Germany and England

1903
United States encourages revolt in Panama and obtains canal route

1903
United States and Britain settle Alaskan boundary dispute

1905
Theodore Roosevelt negotiates Treaty of Portsmouth to end Russo-Japanese War

1905
Roosevelt Corollary to the Monroe Doctrine sanctions U.S. intervention in Latin America as debt collector and policeman

1906
America joins the Algeciras Conference to settle European diplomatic problems

1908
Root-Takahira Agreement limits Open Door policy

1909
Philander C. Knox develops "Dollar Diplomacy"

1910
Mexican Revolution begins a decade of anarchy

1914
Panama Canal completed

1914
United States sends troops into Mexico

1914
United States announces neutrality in World War I

1916
U.S. Marines occupy Dominican Republic

1916
United States buys Danish West Indies

1916
Wilson reelected President

1917
United States enters World War I against Germany

CHAPTER OUTLINE

Simply put, Progressivism overseas was inspired by the same reform sentiments and the same forces that stirred American life at home after the mid-1890s. If the industrial might, organizational skills, moral superiority, and basic good sense of U.S. citizens could improve the quality of life on the domestic scene, why could those same elements not perform similar miracles for even more millions overseas? In a sense, the Spanish-American War, the Open Door, spirited jousting with various powers in all parts of the world (Asia, Latin America, and Africa), Dollar Diplomacy, outright intervention in the affairs of several neighbors to the south, and even involvement in World War I can be viewed as an effort to spread the benefits of Progressivism to foreign as well as native soil.

Yet there were marked differences between these domestic and foreign campaigns for change. The former fitted neatly into the years dominated by Theodore Roosevelt and Woodrow Wilson and exhibited a distinct liberal tinge at every level—local, state, and national. Progressivism abroad often enjoyed much more support from conservatives and big business than it did at home, and its time span was somewhat greater, perhaps because those opposing domestic change could see merit in reform overseas. There it might increase both sales and profits. The election of Wilson in 1912 and his policies as President made reform a true, interparty issue. Until that time, Progressivism had been largely the plaything of liberal-leaning Republicans and Democrats who sometimes cooperated to pass legislation they favored; Wilson, in effect, stole the ball and ran with it quite successfully during his first four years. In no small way, the Democratic interlude (1913–1921) forced the Republicans to close ranks and set their house in order; one of the casualties of that housecleaning splurge was Progressivism and its reforming zeal.

Entanglements in Asia and Europe

Regardless of who was leading this battle for reform and whether it was Progressivism at home or abroad, the rank and file exhibited a great sense of optimism, secure in the belief that America had a special mission to make the world a better place in which to live. Such an attitude on the part of a people growing in industrial power and in numbers can easily be understood, for it was a natural result of a culture saturated with missionary fervor and proud of its record of expansion and worldly success. It was not really a giant step from straightening out affairs in Cuba and the Philippines to taking on Standard Oil and Northern Securities and then trying to regulate life in Mexico and thwart the forces of reaction in Europe. All were part of the same general, never-ending struggle to right wrongs and undo evil wherever it existed.

Seen in this light, Wilson's self-righteous drive "to make the world safe for democracy" in World War I and the support America gave it become more intelligible. Also, the effort to export first capitalism (the basis of the American way of life) and then democracy (its essence), in the context of Progressive reform, made good sense. Without these fundamental ingredients, Progressives thought, true and lasting reform was impossible. Nevertheless, this lofty, benevolent campaign often was riddled with inconsistencies. The door opened in China to all comers was slammed shut in Latin America as the United States tried to monopolize trade in the Western hemisphere. Anticolonialism in one region was transformed into American colonialism elsewhere. Concern for subject peoples somehow did not spread to blacks within the United States as a Jim Crow society became ever more pervasive—nor to Asiatics within our continental borders—even though their welfare halfway around the world stirred considerable interest.

Consciously or unconsciously, this outpouring of muddled sentiments—domestic reform, corporate expansion, missionary zeal, international involvement appropriate to our new "imperial" status, and both military and economic conquest—had one very dramatic result: Never again would the United States of America be able to return to the comfortable, isolated way of life enjoyed during the first century of its existence. Perhaps sheer growth and technological change would have produced similar effects, but a cultural mind-set bent upon reforming the world made world involvement and world responsibilities inevitable.

The Russo-Japanese War

The stunning victory of Japan over China in 1895 revealed Japan to be a growing power. Nine years later Japanese confidence was so strong that after a series of confrontations with Russia over Manchuria and Korea, the Japanese made a surprise attack on Russia's fleet at Port Arthur. Two days later, on February 10, 1904, Japan declared war.

Both public and official opinion in the United States supported Japan. "I was thoroughly pleased with the Japanese victory," Roosevelt wrote his son, "for Japan is playing our game." By "our game," Roosevelt meant that the Japanese seemed to be reacting to internal reform impulses not unlike those being felt in American life. But as their victories continued, Roosevelt worried that a Russian defeat would upset the balance of power in Asia. Also, continued fighting on Chinese soil threatened the stability of the Open Door arrangements.

Working through personal friends in the diplomatic corps of Great Britain, Germany, and Japan—and without the knowledge of Congress or his Cabinet—President Roosevelt sought to mediate a peace that would preserve the status quo in the East. By the summer of 1905, Russia faced certain defeat in an unpopular war abroad while it combated revolution at home. At the same time, Japan's economy was near bankruptcy. When the Japanese indicated their willingness to accept arbitration, Roosevelt imposed one condition on both warring parties, to which they agreed: that they honor the Open Door policy in China.

Meetings were held in Portsmouth, New Hampshire, in August 1905. Russia agreed to withdraw from Korea and to surrender its special interests in southern Manchuria to Japan but threatened to break off negotiations when Japan demanded a large indemnity and the island of Sakhalin, which is at the mouth of the Amur River, the largest river in Siberia. Roosevelt then persuaded the Japanese to give up the indemnity and settle for half of Sakhalin, Port Arthur, and the South Manchuria Railroad. The treaty was signed on September 5, 1905, and for his efforts President Roosevelt was awarded the Nobel Peace Prize the following year.

The Portsmouth conference marked the second major involvement of the United States in Asian affairs, with results as ambiguous as those flowing from the Open Door policy. The Russo-Japanese War confirmed Japan's strength, aroused feelings of nationalism in Asia, and marked the decline of European influence there. And for the United States, a long and unfortunate involvement in Asia had begun. That war also had profound impact throughout the colonial world: for the first time in several centuries a non-European people had beaten an essentially European empire at its "own game."

Tensions with Japan

During the Russo-Japanese War, Washington made efforts to forestall any conflict with Japan over the Philippines. As Japanese victories mounted, Secretary of War William Howard Taft visited Tokyo for talks with Count

Taro Katsura, the Japanese prime minister. In the unofficial Taft-Katsura Memorandum of July 27, 1905, the prime minister assured the United States that Japan had no designs on the Philippines, while Taft reassured Japan that peace in the Far East would be furthered by Japanese "suzerainty" over Korea. With the closing of the American legation in Seoul in November 1905, the United States became the first nation to recognize Japan's complete control over Korea. The "Open Door," it seemed, did not apply to that large peninsula.

Nevertheless, the relationship between Japan and the United States deteriorated following the Treaty of Portsmouth. While Japanese leaders were satisfied with terms that recognized Japan as a world power and confirmed its hegemony over Korea, the Japanese people strongly criticized their ambassadors for their failure to win an indemnity. The ambassadors, in turn, blamed Roosevelt, and anti-American riots occurred in many parts of Japan.

Aggravating these feelings was the discriminatory treatment of an increasing number of Japanese immigrants on the West Coast of the United States. Like the Chinese before them, the Japanese in California were subjected to restrictive legislation, boycotts, and riots. But unlike China, Japan was an emerging power, and Roosevelt realized the contradiction in seeking equal and open treatment for the United States in Asia while placing restrictions on Asians in America. Nor did he underestimate the pride of Japan in being the first Oriental nation to defeat a Western power in modern times.

The Japanese were deeply offended when in October 1906 the San Francisco school board segregated 93 Japanese children from white students and placed them in a separate school. The Japanese government protested that segregation was "an act of discrimination carrying with it a stigma and odium impossible to overlook." Since the school board's action was a local affair beyond the immediate jurisdiction of the federal government, Roosevelt was frustrated in his attempt to have the decision reversed. He told his son: "The infernal fools in California, and especially in San Francisco, insult the Japanese recklessly, and in the event of war it will be the Nation as a whole which will pay the consequences." After his annual message to Congress in December, during which he called the school board's action a "wicked absurdity," Roosevelt invited the mayor of San Francisco, along with the board, to Washington. There he convinced them to desegregate the school; in return he promised to halt the immigration of Japanese laborers. Through an exchange of notes in 1907 and 1908, an informal gentleman's agreement was reached between the governments of the United States and Japan, stopping Japanese labor immigration to the United States mainland in exchange for Roosevelt's assurance that those Japanese already in the country would not be treated as inferiors.

Many people, both in America and abroad, felt that

Culver Pictures.

Kei-Kichi Aoki, the Japanese-American schoolboy to the left, applied for admission to a San Francisco primary school in 1907 and was refused by the woman principal and the board president (far right). The application was the first move in a test suit brought by the federal government against the school board. Though the government initially backed the Japanese, relations between the United States and Japan worsened after this incident.

Library of Congress.

Elihu Root
(1845–1937)

More than most men, Elihu Root had very close ties to his alma mater, Hamilton College in Clinton, New York. He was born there, graduated in 1864 as valedictorian of his class, eventually acquired an estate nearby, was chairman of the board of trustees from 1909 until his death, and in his last years served as superintendent of the college grounds, a task he took quite seriously. In addition, his father and brother (both named Oren) were professors of mathematics at Hamilton from 1849 to 1907, successively known to hundreds of students as "Square" and "Cube" Root.

After teaching school for a year, Elihu Root went to New York City to study law. He was admitted to the bar in 1867 and two years later had an annual income of $5,000, five times what "Cube" Root was making back in Clinton. His legal career prospered even more in the 1870s as courtroom work became his specialty. In time, his phenomenal memory, hard work, mastery of detail, precision, clarity, and, above all else, his wit made Root a leading figure among American lawyers.

In 1878 he married Clara Wales, daughter of a wealthy New Yorker, who would have considerable influence upon his career. By nature Root was drawn to Republican conservatives but he was also a friend of Chester A. Arthur and supported Theodore Roosevelt in his unsuccessful bid to become New York's mayor in 1886.

Until 1899 Root only dabbled in local politics, but in that year he agreed to become McKinley's Secretary of War. In this capacity he dealt with affairs in Puerto Rico, Cuba, and the Philippines; more important, and despite considerable opposition, he instituted much-needed reforms in the U.S. Army. Among other things, Root set up the Army War College and ended permanent staff jobs in Washington.

At the insistence of his wife, who disliked official life, he resigned in 1903 and also spurned overtures to run for governor and President. Had Root become New York's chief executive he, not Taft, undoubtedly would have succeeded Roosevelt. Instead, he became Secretary of State upon the death of John Hay in 1905, doing much to improve battered relations with Latin America and Japan.

As senator from New York (1909–1915) he was caught in the eye of the Roosevelt-Taft storm and stuck by his party; this ended his friendship with TR. Always an internationalist and recipient of the Nobel Peace Prize in 1912, Root favored the League of Nations with proposed reservations and was long active with the Carnegie Endowment for World Peace. ■

Library of Congress.

The fleet being readied for its world tour. When this picture was first published the title was "A flock of Uncle Sam's peace doves at the Brooklyn Navy Yard."

a war between Japan and the United States was nevertheless likely. Roosevelt recognized Japan as a "formidable new power—a power jealous, sensitive, and warlike, and which if irritated could at once take both the Philippines and Hawaii from us if she obtained the upper hand on the seas." To forestall that possibility Roosevelt decided that it was "essential that we should have it clearly understood by our own people especially, but also by other peoples, that the Pacific [is] as much our home waters as the Atlantic."

Toward that end, the President sent the United States Great White Fleet on a "practice cruise" to the West coast which, despite the protestations of Congress and East coast residents, soon grew into a world tour. Many feared an attack when the fleet got to Japan or the seizure of Hawaii and the Philippines while it toured the Mediterranean. But, surprisingly, a tumultuous reception in Japan was a high point of the tour since the people of that nation were flattered by such unexpected attention and interpreted it as a good-will gesture.

Publicly, the President played down any intention of impressing Japan with the naval might of America. And while the fleet steamed toward Japan, he took further steps to relieve tensions between the two countries. This overture culminated in the Root-Takahira Agreement of November 30, 1908, by which the two nations agreed to respect each other's possessions in the Pacific, to support the status quo in Asia, and to uphold the independence and integrity of China so all nations might enjoy equal commercial opportunity on the Asian mainland. Superficially, the agreement seemed a victory for the Open Door. Actually, by supporting the status quo it assured Japan's absolute control over southern Manchuria and Korea, areas of secondary importance to American foreign policy.

Algeciras

Even as tensions with Japan were waxing and waning in the Far East, Roosevelt became involved in North Africa. The curtain raiser on this new stage was a comic opera situation that developed when Ion Perdicaris, a Greek subject who presumably held U.S. naturalization papers, was seized in 1904 by a native chieftan named Raisuli. To rouse apathetic GOP convention delegates meeting in Chicago, Roosevelt brandished a telegram dispatched to the American consul at Tangier insisting the United States must have "Perdicaris alive or Raisuli dead." What he failed to disclose were several relevant facts. Orders not to use force without specific instructions had already been given; arrangements for the release of Perdicaris had already been made; and apprehensions had arisen that he was really Greek, not American after all.

The following year, and in the same area, smoldering friction between France and Germany burst forth as Britain lent support to French expansion in Morocco and as Germany, thanks to the Kaiser's new interest in colonization, came to the defense of the Moroccan sultan. Ostensibly the Kaiser's purpose was to protect the trade policy established by the Madrid Convention of 1880, which gave the United States and thirteen other countries equal commercial opportunities in Morocco.

Early in 1905 the Kaiser secretly asked Roosevelt to convince Britain to withhold support from France. At first Roosevelt refused: "We have other fish to fry and we have no real interest in Morocco." But by the middle of May newspapers on both sides of the Atlantic were predicting war. To remain consistent in his attempts to preserve world peace through mediation while defending the Open Door policy, Roosevelt agreed to act. Also, as mediator at Portsmouth and a firm believer in the balance of power principle in the Far East, Roosevelt recognized the dangers inherent in Germany's challenge to the workings of that same delicate concept in Europe and Africa. Once the Kaiser promised to support any fair decision the President proposed, Roosevelt was able to convince France that he was acting, not to promote German interests, but to avert a war that would destroy world peace.

In January 1906, representatives of France, Germany, Great Britain, and the United States met in Algeciras, Spain. Roosevelt justified U.S. presence on several grounds: eagerness to prevent a partition of Morocco, which might endanger the Open Door principle around the world; determination to keep Germany from gaining a stepping stone leading to the Western hemisphere; and, most important, concern to defuse a crisis that might erupt into a world war and involve the United States. Confirming the French presence in Morocco, Roosevelt proposed that France and Spain enjoy a preferred status in policing the country, thus fulfilling his intention to "stand by France" while keeping on reasonably good terms with Germany. The proposal was ratified by Congress but amended to state that such ratification involved no departure "from the traditional American foreign policy which forbids participation by the United States in the settlement of political questions which are entirely European in their scope." Yet precedent was broken with the assumption that a threat to world peace justified such intervention in continental affairs.

American participation in the Algericas conference had far-reaching effects. Roosevelt's action typified the interest of Progressives in preserving world peace by maintaining the balance of power, attempts that were to be taken up again by Woodrow Wilson. And America's participation in the conference revealed a new awareness that, through the network of European alliances, all major powers could become entangled in a conflict that might occur between any two of the nations.

As for the Moroccan Open Door, Secretary of State Elihu Root noted that "while it is to the advantage of the powers to secure the 'open door,' it is equally vital to their interests and no less so to the advantage of Morocco that the door, being open, shall lead to something." Within four years, the United States was involved both in a railway project in the Ottoman Empire and in the economy of Persia. And in World War I the State Department cited Algeciras as the basis for American claims to equal opportunity across the entire North African coastline. Participation in the conference marked a definite shift in American foreign policy toward closer ties with England and France; and, since those two powers would soon be at war with Germany, this was, after all, the single most important result of Theodore Roosevelt's little cruise into the troubled waters of European diplomacy.

Policing the Western Hemisphere

Unlike Asia, Europe, and Africa, the Western hemisphere was a vast area where Theodore Roosevelt could do more or less whatever he wished. The forces of no king, kaiser, czar, or emperor could thwart his will and, according to the Monroe Doctrine, the United States would make certain they never did. As a result, he intervened in the affairs of several Latin American nations (for their own good, of course), expanded the meaning of the Monroe Doctrine to fit his own ends, and began to dig a canal linking the Atlantic and Pacific oceans.

Venezuela

Roosevelt's first message to Congress (1901) set forth U.S. policy toward European intervention in Latin American affairs: "We do not guarantee any state against punishment if it misconducts itself, provided that punishment does not take the form of the acquisition of territory by any non-American powers." But events in Venezuela began to change that policy somewhat.

Dictator Cipriano Castro had borrowed heavily from European powers and now refused to repay his country's debts. In December 1902, having assured the United States that they were not interested in territorial acquisition, Great Britain, Germany, and Italy blockaded five

Culver Pictures.

Monroe Doctrine
UNCLE SAM—THAT'S A LIVE WIRE, GENTLEMEN!

During the early twentieth century the Monroe Doctrine became as sacred as the Declaration of Independence and the Constitution. And for the first time the United States had the muscle to force its will not only on feeble Latin American States but also on world powers, as in the Venezuelan crisis of 1902.

Venezuelan ports and bombarded forts at Puerto Cabello in an attempt to force payment. Castro, expecting little support either from Roosevelt or from Hay (Roosevelt thought Castro an "unspeakable villainous little monkey"), appealed directly to the American public, citing the Monroe Doctrine in an attempt to tie the interests of the United States to those of Venezuela.

The dictator then sent to Washington a formal request for arbitration, which Hay forwarded to the British and German governments "without comment." But as public opinion turned against Germany, Hay urged arbitration. Both Britain and Germany agreed, and when the two governments requested that Roosevelt act as arbiter, a conference was scheduled in Washington for January 1903.

Even before arbitration had formally begun, German demands seemed excessive, and a German ship bombarded a Venezuelan port and the village around it. The *New York Times* announced: "Worse international manners than Germany has exhibited have rarely come under the observation of civilized man." "Are people in Berlin crazy?" Roosevelt asked. "Don't they know that they are inflaming public opinion more and more here?" When Germany resisted a suggestion to refer the dispute to The Hague Court (an arbitration body set up in 1899), Roosevelt let it be known that the United States would accept no other solution. Not wishing to provoke further anti-German feelings in America, the Kaiser reduced his demands and submitted to arbitration by The Hague in February 1903. Roosevelt was to remember later that he had delivered an ultimatum to the German ambassador: If Germany refused to arbitrate, the American fleet would go to Venezuela. Whether he actually made this threat or not, it was clear that American policy regarding European intervention in Latin America needed a sharper definition.

Luis M. Drago, Argentina's minister for foreign affairs, suggested one such revision. To Latin American leaders, European intervention in Venezuela reinforced a dangerous nineteenth century precedent. Proposing a corollary to the Monroe Doctrine, Drago sent a message to Washington stating that it was wrong for European nations to collect debts forcibly from any American nation. The Drago Doctrine was not accepted by the United States until the Second Hague Conference in 1907 (and then only with modifications). The administration's official policy was instead reflected by Roosevelt's own corollary to the Monroe Doctrine proposed in December 1905.

The Roosevelt Corollary

Even by 1904 Roosevelt no longer felt that Latin Ameri-

Brown Brothers.

To some observers it seemed as if Roosevelt was playing with toy battleships in a private pond.

can misbehavior justified European intervention. In May he announced that "chronic wrong-doing or an impotence which results in a general loosening of the ties of civilized society, may . . . require intervention by some civilized nation, and . . . the adherence of the United States to the Monroe Doctrine may force the United States . . . in flagrant cases of such wrong-doing, or impotence, to the exercise of an international police power." Roosevelt had only to wait one year for the opportunity to become "policeman."

Like Venezuela, the Dominican Republic had borrowed heavily from European powers and by 1905, torn by internal strife, was unable to make payments from its customs income. Thus it was up to the United States to forestall a repetition of naval demonstration by European battleships in the Caribbean. While many favored outright American annexation of the republic as a solution, Roosevelt disagreed. In December he announced to Congress his "corollary" to the Monroe Doctrine: Since America could not allow European governments to collect debts by force in the Western hemisphere, the United States had to make sure that the financial obligations of "backward" states were met. As the Monroe Doctrine had forbidden European intervention in the Americas, Roosevelt's corollary sanctioned intervention by the United States when necessary to prevent "outside" intervention.

On December 30 the president of the Dominican Republic "requested" that the United States take over the operation of that nation's customs collections, and Roosevelt quickly established a trust fund to repay the European debts. When this measure was rejected by the United States Senate, Roosevelt signed an executive agreement that continued the custom collections until the Senate accepted a modified version in 1907. The United States, said Roosevelt, had "put the affairs of the island on a better basis than they had been for a century." But for their economic and political stability the people of the Dominican Republic paid a high price—a wound to their pride and a loss of autonomy. And a precedent had been established that would increasingly entangle the United States in both the domestic and foreign affairs of Caribbean and Central American nations.

Cuba

By the end of the Spanish-American War, the United States, in control of Cuba, was the dominant power in the Caribbean. The Platt Amendment to the Cuban constitution gave Washington a virtual veto power over Cuba's diplomatic and financial dealings with foreign governments. (In 1905, for example, the American minister vetoed a trade agreement between Cuba and Britain because it offered the latter significant advantages re-

"Progressivism" abroad: United States soldiers marching in cadence to the beat of drums in Santo Domingo City in 1905. The military authorities cunningly used black troops to "police" the local black population.

garded as "most unsatisfactory to the United States.") The amendment also gave Washington the right to intervene at will, required the sale or lease of lands to the United States for a naval base, and forced Cuba to ratify all actions made by the United States military government there. Further, all of these terms were also to be embodied in a permanent treaty with the United States—the Reciprocity Treaty of 1903, which virtually closed the Cuban economy to other outside interests.

The military governor of Cuba, General Leonard Wood (1860–1927), remarked frankly: "There is, of course, little or no independence left Cuba under the Platt Amendment." And although both Americans and foreigners still expected annexation to follow (in spite of the Teller Amendment, which forbade it), Roosevelt withdrew American troops in May 1902. But by September 1906 they were back at the request of Cuban President Tomás Estrada Palma. At that time a provisional government was established to prevent revolution by intervention—a policy that denied to the Cuban people the right to create their own institutions and become truly independent.

The Panama Canal

Of even greater strategic importance than Cuba was the possibility of an interoceanic canal under American control. The dream of creating an isthmian canal dated back to the 1850s. At the beginning of the twentieth century, as America's naval power was growing and the United States was acquiring islands in both the Pacific and the Caribbean, such a waterway seemed especially desirable, in fact, a necessity. The failure of America and French companies to build a canal through either Nicaragua or Panama convinced Washington that construction was beyond the means of private capital. But an obstacle to building was the Clayton-Bulwer Treaty (1850) by which Britain and the United States had agreed that neither would seek to control any canal built on the isthmus. Realizing that Congress was ready to ignore the terms of the treaty, Hay persuaded the British to amend it. With the approval of Congress on December 16, 1901, the second Hay-Pauncefote Treaty granted the United States the right to build an interoceanic isthmian waterway and to fortify it as well.

The question remained: Where to build, Nicaragua or Panama? In 1876 French interests had purchased rights from Colombia to build a canal in Panama. By 1889 Ferdinand de Lesseps, who engineered the Suez Canal, had spent more than $260 million in attempts to construct such a waterway. The New Panama Canal Company, which had taken over the bankrupt de Lesseps organization, was eager to sell its rights and assets to the United States. But Washington would need permission from the Colombian government to build there. Nicaragua had meanwhile cancelled its concession with a private construction company, and a new syndicate was formed to negotiate with the United States for construction rights in that region. While both groups had congressional support, Nicaragua was favored, based on reports of two official commissions. Even before the report of the second commission was delivered in 1899, the Senate passed a bill for a Nicaraguan canal. It needed only House approval to become law.

William Nelson Cromwell, general counsel for the New Panama Canal Company, had been working since 1896 to block a Nicaraguan waterway. Befriending powerful politicians, among them Ohio Senator Mark Hanna, he contributed heavily to the Republican campaign of 1900, during which that party endorsed a Panamanian canal. The Nicaraguan canal bill was subsequently defeated in the House, which called for new investigations of both routes.

The investigating commissions found that the route through Panama was shorter by one-third and valued the assets of the New Panama Canal Company at $40 million, almost $70 million less than the company's own evaluation. The company refused to accept the commission's figure. Consequently, on January 9, 1902, the House of Representatives appropriated funds for the Nicaraguan route. The French company then agreed to accept the lower figure proposed by the commission. When the House bill reached the Senate, it was amended to authorize the President to buy the concession of the New Panama Canal Company for $40 million and to arrange terms with Colombia to build a canal through Panama.

Still, Roosevelt had only a "reasonable time" to conclude negotiations, and Colombia's eighty-year-old president, José Manuel Marroquín, found himself in a difficult position. He realized that if he gave in to U.S. demands, political opponents would charge him with surrendering to American imperialism. If he refused, Nicaragua would reap the economic benefits of a canal, and the Panamanian Isthmus, over which thousands had traveled to and from California during the nineteenth century, would become worthless. Marroquín also realized that the United States might seize Panama by force.

At last he instructed Dr. Tomas Herrán, his chargé d'affaires in Washington, to accede to the wishes of the United States while securing for Colombia every possible advantage. But after Secretary of State John Hay presented him with an ultimatum, Herrán was forced to sign a treaty highly favorable to the United States. In exchange for $10 million and an annual rent of $250,000 to begin in nine years, the Hay-Herrán Treaty of January 22, 1903 gave America a 100-year lease on a strip of land six miles wide. The treaty was approved by the United States Senate but was rejected unanimously by its Colombian counterpart. The Colombian government demanded $25 million ($10 million from the New Panama Canal Company and $15 million from the United States) and expected to receive an additional $40 million by obtaining the New Panama Canal Company's franchise, which, it was claimed, would soon expire.

President Roosevelt was prepared to seize the isthmus and start digging "without any further parley" with the Colombian government. He told Hay: "I do not think that the Bogotá lot of jack rabbits should be allowed

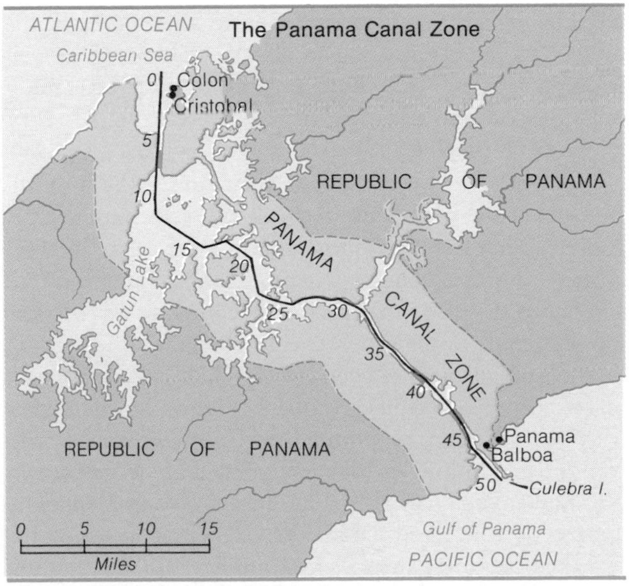

Library of Congress.

Philippe Bunau-Varilla (1859–1940)

A talented engineer and a highly successful lobbyist but an extremely inept diplomat, at least in the eyes of most Panamanians and many Americans, Philippe Bunau-Varilla claimed late in life that he became interested in Panama at the age of eleven when he heard his mother and an engineering student discussing the French triumph at Suez. As a young man he entered the employ of de Lesseps and at age twenty-six was chief engineer of his Panama project.

After five years of construction (1885–1890), Bunau-Varilla spent the next decade working to get American interests to resume building the canal. In 1902 he arrived in this country where he lobbied and lectured, convinced that the situation for his company was becoming desperate. Some of his friends thought he was going insane, and his brother even crossed the Atlantic to check on his health. When an earthquake ravaged Martinique in May of that year, he pointed out to congressmen who would listen to him the dangers of such an occurrence in Nicaragua, Panama's rival. And in succeeding months he apparently conceived the idea of a revolt against Colombia, then became Panama's first minister to Washington, quickly signed away a large piece of that infant republic's real estate, and sailed for home, the stockholders of his beleaguered company $40 million richer.

Bunau-Varilla subsequently became manager of the Congo Railway and president of a Spanish railroad. At some point in his erratic career he presumably designed the Paris subway, although only an adaptation of his plans was actually used. He also harbored a pet scheme for tunneling under the English Channel. A major in the engineers in World War I, Bunau-Varilla lost a leg at Verdun but returned to service and was mustered out as a lieutenant colonel.

In 1938 he issued a statement calling for a vast overhaul of the Panama Canal to make it a sea-level waterway: "Its locks must be eliminated, otherwise enemy agents can blast the locks and paralyze the exchange of American ships between the Atlantic and the Pacific." He thought the work would cost a billion dollars and take twenty years. Bunau-Varilla died in May 1940, just weeks before his eighty-first birthday and shortly before Nazi legions overwhelmed his homeland. ■

permanently to bar one of the future highways of civilization." Panamanians, who had often revolted against rule from Bogotá, feared the canal was lost. Some, especially those connected with the New Panama Canal Company, were prepared to do whatever was necessary to secure the canal. With the support of Cromwell, the tacit approval of Washington, and the promise of $100,000 from Philippe Bunau-Varilla (an engineer who had worked with de Lesseps and a large stockholder in the French company), the conspirators began planning a revolution that opened one of the most controversial chapters in U.S. history.

A treaty with Colombia going back to 1846 guaranteed the United States the right of transit across the Panamanian isthmus and allowed it to intervene, with the consent of the Colombian government, should a foreign power attempt to seize that strip of land. Now, to "keep the transit clear," Hay was prepared to twist those treaty terms and use them against Colombia to support a secessionist movement in Panama. On October 19, 1903, three American war vessels were dispatched to Central America. On November 2 their commanders were told that, should a revolution break out, they were to occupy the Panamanian railway (a subsidiary of the New Panama Canal Company), secure open transit and prevent Colombian troops from landing within fifty miles of the isthmus. On November 3, 1903, the State Department cabled the consul at Panama: "Uprising on Isthmus reported. Keep Department promptly and fully informed." That afternoon, the consul replied: "No uprising yet. Reported will be in the night." And, hours later: "Uprising occurred tonight 6; no bloodshed. Government will be organized tonight."

Led by a former commander-in-chief of Colombian troops, an army of less than 1,000—section hands from the railroad, bribed Colombian deserters and the city of Panama's fire brigade—arrested the governor of Panama, bribed a Colombian admiral to sail away, and prevented the landing of Colombian troops. On November 4 Panama proclaimed its independence. Two days later Washington recognized the Republic of Panama, and in a week Roosevelt officially received the first Panamanian minister to the United States, none other than engineer and conspirator Philippe Bunau-Varilla. Fifteen days after the revolution Bunau-Varilla and Hay signed a treaty granting the United States in perpetuity a canal zone ten miles wide, four miles wider than provided by the Hay-Herrán Treaty. In exchange, America was to assure Panama's independence. With ratification of the treaty by the U.S. Senate on February 23, 1904, Panama became yet another protectorate.

Construction of the canal began in May and was completed ten years later. After the seizure of Panama, a defensive Roosevelt argued that his action had been the result of a mandate from the civilized world. In 1909 he explained to Congress that he seized Panama "in accordance with the highest, finest and nicest standards of public and governmental ethics." But in 1911, out of office, the need to speak softly no longer great, Roosevelt enthusiastically told a university audience in Berkeley, California: "I took the Canal Zone." As President, Taft subsequently failed to placate Colombia. And Wilson, in an attempt at improving Latin American relations, began negotiations for an indemnity of $25 million, which was finally awarded Colombia in 1921. Not coincidentally, the indemnity also opened up Colombian oil fields to American companies.

Dollar Diplomacy

Military and naval intervention paved the way, of course, for economic exploitation; or, to put it another way, the purpose of threats, arm twisting, and international bluster was to make sure U.S. investment, not European, enjoyed preeminence in the Western hemisphere. So-called Dollar Diplomacy was, however, only a limited success at best; once exported outside of the Americas and not supported by U.S. force, it floundered hopelessly.

Knox and Dollar Diplomacy

With the death of John Hay in July 1905, Elihu Root became Secretary of State, tempering Roosevelt's aggressive policy in Latin America. "The South Americans now hate us," he wrote privately, "largely because they think we despise them and try to bully them. I really like them and intend to show it." This he did by embarking on a goodwill tour in July 1906. At the third Inter-American Conference in Rio de Janeiro, Root sought to reassure Latin American leaders: "We wish for no victories but those of peace; for no territory except our own; for no sovereignty except over ourselves." Set against the Roosevelt corollary, intervention in Panama and the Platt Amendment, his words were not convincing.

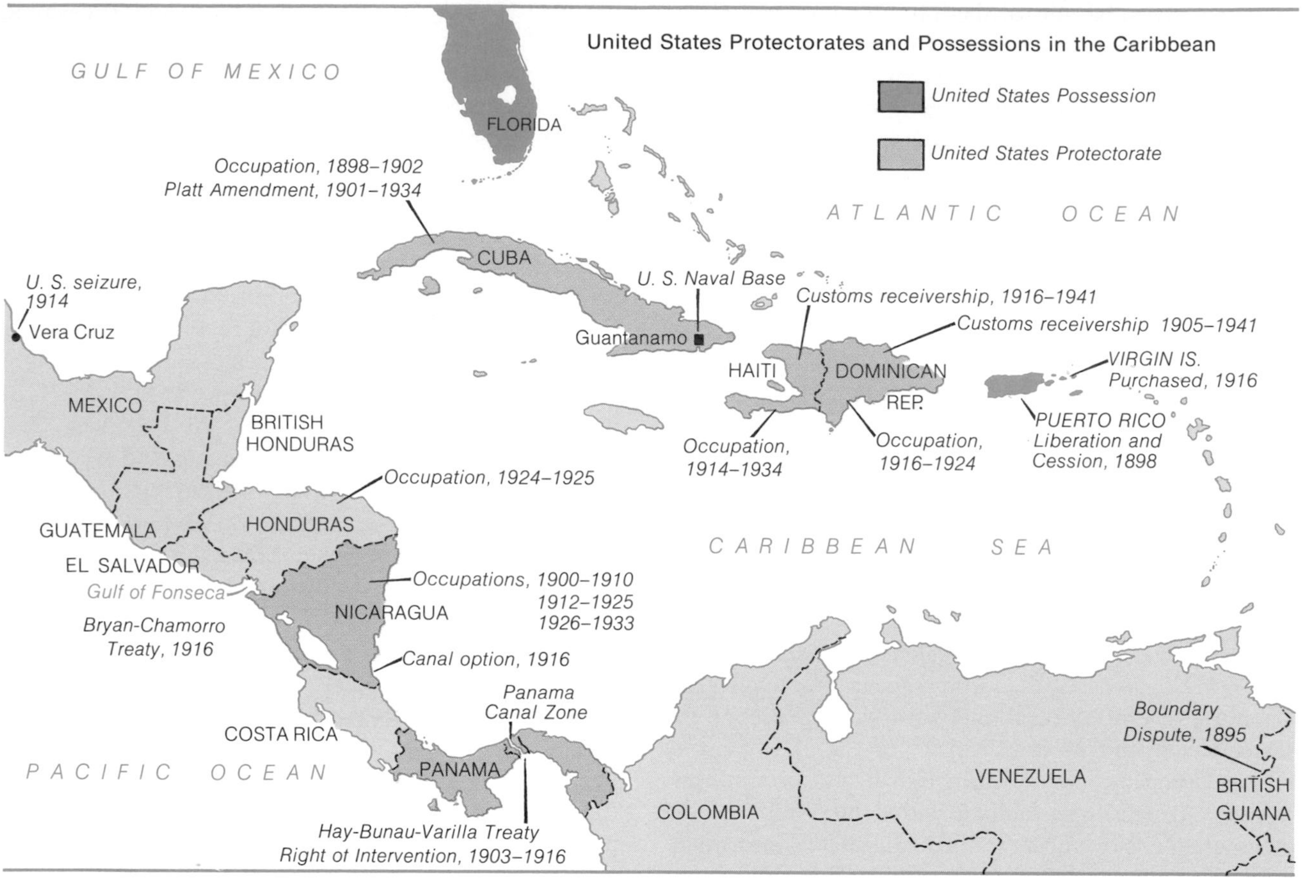

On his return, Root told Americans that Latin countries had now moved into "the stage of industrialism" and warned American businessmen that if they did not respond to this change, their European counterparts would take advantage of opportunities for investment there. Root's policy was to provide opportunities for business in the foreign arena without offering favors. With the election of Taft and his choice of Philander C. Knox (1853–1921) as Secretary of State in 1909, this policy changed. Under Knox, not only did the government help American businesses abroad, it also sought to give advantages to the strongest among them.

As the Panama Canal neared completion and American business interests expanded in Latin America, Taft and Knox became wary of European intervention. To protect both the canal and American investments, they, like Roosevelt, refused to tolerate any disorder in Latin America, and Taft subsequently intervened in Latin American affairs even more than his predecessor. Initially the intervention was economic. As American capital replaced European in Latin America, the United States achieved greater leverage in controlling the economies of those nations, and Taft gained the power to dictate policy there. If Dollar Diplomacy failed and diplomatic suggestions were ignored, punitive measures followed—as in Nicaragua.

Nicaragua

Since coming to power in 1893, Nicaragua's dictator José Santos Zelaya had tried to dominate the five Central American republics. He engaged in a number of petty wars with his neighbors, invaded Honduras in 1907 and deposed its president, and threatened El Salvador and Guatemala as well as American business interests in his own country. But perhaps his greatest mistake was a decision to finance Nicaragua's debt through an international syndicate of European investors based in London. Nicaragua's proximity to the Panama Canal, Zelaya's continued hostility toward the United States, and his decision to turn over his country's economy to European forces combined to pose a serious threat to American hegemony. If Nicaragua's debt was not paid, Europeans could seize the country's major sources of revenue. Washington warned Zelaya to change his policies, and when he did not, United States war vessels were ordered to the area to demand settlement of all outstanding issues involving American companies in Nicaragua. As Guatemalan strong man Manuel Estrada Cabrera put it, by offending Washington, Zelaya had "thus violated the first rule of behavior for a dictator of the Caribbean area."

In October 1909, Juan J. Estrada, a general of Zelaya's party, led a revolution backed financially by various sources, among them the United Fruit Company and Guatemala. (Under Estrada Cabrera, United Fruit received major concessions of plantations and generally dominated the economy of Guatemala for over half a century.) Nicaraguan forces soon captured and executed two Americans fighting with the rebels. On December 1, Knox sent a note to the Nicaraguan chargé d'affaires in Washington in which he denounced Zelaya as a tyrant and called his regime a "blot upon the history of Nicaragua." The Taft administration then broke off diplomatic relations with the country. Unable to withstand U.S. pressure, Zelaya fled to Mexico.

By August 1910 the rebels had established control and elected as President Adolfo Díaz, formerly a bookkeeper for an American mining company in Nicaragua. In July 1911 Diaz instructed his minister in Washington to sign a convention with Knox that would have made the Central American country a protectorate of the United States and guaranteed payment of its loans through American control of Nicaraguan customhouses. When the United States Senate refused to ratify the convention, two American banking companies negotiated a private contract that gave Nicaragua a loan of $1.5 million, with repayment guaranteed by a receivership of Nicaraguan customs duties. Thus the country became an "unofficial" protectorate of the United States. And when Díaz was faced with a revolution in July 1912, Taft responded by sending eight warships and 2,500 marines. To discourage further rebellion, a warship and a guard of 100 marines stayed in the country.

Library of Congress.

Philander Chase Knox, the man who tried to make Dollar Diplomacy work.

The Western Hemisphere

Only in Argentina was Dollar Diplomacy successful. There the government agreed to take out loans from J. P. Morgan and Company in order to purchase battleships and in January 1910 United States companies won the contracts to build them, thus undercutting British economic influence in Argentina.

Since all the Central American countries except San Salvador defaulted on payments to European creditors, Knox sought financial arrangements to forestall any possible control of revenues by European powers. In Honduras he tried to establish an American collectorship for payment of debts, but the treaty was rejected by both the United States Senate and the Honduran Congress. Similar attempts in other Central American countries were unsuccessful, with the State Department consistently negotiating treaties, the Senate regularly rejected them.

The spirit of the Spanish-American War had passed, and most Americans were either opposed to or indifferent toward the creation of more entangling alliances. The problems Taft faced at home in his dealings with Latin America were threefold: his political clout with Congress and the public was declining, "Dollar Diplomacy" was not producing the benefits throughout the world that had been anticipated, and that policy certainly was not sowing seeds of stability and democracy among neighbors to the south.

Asia

To Willard Straight, American consul in Manchuria, Dollar Diplomacy was "the financial expression of John Hay's 'Open Door' policy." Between 1905 and 1910 Straight tried to give the Open Door financial clout as he worked with railroad financier Edward H. Harriman to open China to Western investment. Through private banking interests, Straight sought to negotiate a loan that would provide China with economic reform. At the same time, he tried to devise a formula enabling Harriman and other interests to purchase the South Manchurian Railway, thus checking Japanese influence there, and the Chinese Eastern Railway, controlled by Russia, in northern Manchuria.

The plan complemented the Taft administration's policy, since Knox feared that Japanese control of trade, railroads, and minerals in southern Manchuria would close the area to American investors. In an attempt to neutralize Manchuria, Knox tried to organize an international syndicate that would lend China money for the purchase of all Manchurian railroads. With British acquiescence, Knox approached Japan and Russia. Japan, he believed, could not refuse without appearing to oppose the Open Door policy. But in January 1910, Japan, Russia, and Britain all rejected Knox's plan.

Knox had made two unfortunate errors. The business recession of 1907 blocked his original proposal as U.S. investors became much more interested in conditions at home than in Asia; and, unschooled in diplomacy, he failed to realize that London's tacit reply to his railroad scheme idea—given subject to Japanese approval—was, in fact, a rejection. Britain fully intended to stand by its ally in opposing any outside interference in Manchurian affairs.

Instead of opening Manchuria, Taft's Dollar Diplomacy in effect closed it. Knox's blunder resulted in closer cooperation between Russia and Japan in controlling their interests in the area. Both nations reaffirmed their desire to maintain the status quo and to take common action in defending their spheres of influence. Angered, American bankers threatened to withdraw from China completely. And China's distrust of the United States deepened, for the plan had involved both Russia and Japan, two of her enemies. The Chinese people saw the end result as an attempt by the United States to keep their country divided.

Compounding the ineffectiveness of Dollar Diplomacy in China, Taft persuaded England, France, and Germany to allow the United States to participate in a four-power consortium that in May 1911 agreed on a loan to the Hukuang Railway. The loan was unpopular with the Chinese, who continued to resent foreign exploitation, and helped set off the revolution that overthrew the Manchu dynasty that same year.

Woodrow Wilson and Missionary Diplomacy

Neither during his campaign nor in his inaugural address did Wilson give much attention to international relations. Yet what was happening outside of the United States played a significant role in his first administration and almost completely dominated his second. When Wilson took office, Japanese aggression in Manchuria jeopardized the Open Door policy in China. Colombia was still angry over America's participation in the secession of Panama. A small occupation force continued to control affairs of Nicaragua, as the United States directed that country's finances, intervening at will. And a revolution in Mexico threatened border communities from California to Texas.

Ideology

Wilson and his Secretary of State William Jennings Bryan were committed to a policy of pursuing peace and maintaining neutrality. Neither brought to office any practical experience in foreign affairs. What guided their policies was a missionary zeal to "help" less stable governments. Morality, not expediency, guided their actions. The United States, they felt, should be held up as an example that less fortunate governments must emulate. And while both supported the expansion of U.S. business interests abroad, they denounced Taft's Dollar Diplomacy, seeing in it an extension of the power and privilege of American capital.

Yet Wilson and Bryan sought to save Latin American and Caribbean countries from both internal disorder and European domination by extending Platt Amendment treaties to unstable governments there. By doing so, they continued and extended a policy of intervention, which was deeply rooted in the missionary impulse of the late nineteenth century. Wilson was, of course, the product of a stern Calvinistic household, his father being a Presbyterian minister; Bryan, almost a Baptist minister, always viewed the world through "moral-colored" glasses. Wilson called for a "spiritual union" between the Americas and promised that "the United States will never again seek one additional foot of territory by conquest." But to the inhabitants of the "other" Americas, it was difficult to distinguish between a United States foreign policy based on a big stick and hard cash and one founded on lofty evangelism.

Intervention in the Dominican Republic and Haiti

American control of Dominican customs in 1907 brought stability to the republic for six years. But in September 1913 a revolution broke out, and the United States–supported government of José Bordas Valdés seemed doomed. In the summer of 1914, as fighting continued, Wilson arranged for an armistice and sent an investigatory committee to the republic with suggestions for reform. In November, elections were held and Juan Y. Jimenéz, a revolutionary leader, became president. Old and enfeebled, Jimenéz could not rule effectively and another revolution occurred in May 1916.

After issuing warnings that the United States would not tolerate a continual state of anarchy, Wilson sent in American marines to occupy that nation. The Dominicans refused to sign a proposed treaty giving Washington complete control of the republic's armed forces and finances. So, by November 1916, the marines established military rule. Though Wilson had acted "with the deepest reluctance," he was convinced that it was "the least of the evils in sight in this very perplexing situation." And while the imposed rule returned stability to the country, the Dominicans had even more reason to distrust the moral pronouncements of Woodrow Wilson.

Meanwhile, neighboring Haiti, the only black nation in the Americas, was racked by internal unrest. Early in 1914 when the fourth regime in less that three years was overthrown, Washington expressed concern. In July, fearing further European intervention and wishing to safeguard American investments, the Wilson administration asked Haiti to sign a treaty that would surrender customs control to the United States.

Both the new dictators, the Zamor brothers and their successor Davilmar Théodore, refused to do so. In December 1914, after new disturbances, U.S. marines removed $500,000 from a Haitian bank and placed it aboard a warship. After another revolution in January, Wilson and Bryan sent a commission to negotiate a treaty with Théodore granting the United States a naval base and control of customs in return for American support. But before the commission reached Haiti, Théodore had fled, and the new president, General Vilbrun Guillaume Sam, refused to negotiate.

When another revolution erupted in June 1915, Sam executed 167 political prisoners. On July 28, 1915, an enraged mob took him from the French legation in Port-au-Prince, dragged him through the streets and tore his body apart. That same afternoon, marines landed in the city and within a week United States forces overran the country. The *cacos,* Haitian professional soldiers, retreated to the mountains, resisting fanatically, and the war almost became one of extermination as more than 2,000 of them were shot before fighting ceased.

By August, Admiral W. B. Caperton was overseeing the country, forcing upon the people a twenty-year treaty that gave the United States greater control than it had over any other nation in the Western hemisphere. The terms provided for American command of the country's armed forces, finances, public works, and foreign affairs. It passed the Senate in February 1916 without a dissenting vote. And although Haitians eventually approved a new constitution drawn up by Washington, it brought them neither democracy nor stability, a not unsurprising conclusion to an unhappy series of events.

Danish West Indies

With the outbreak of World War I in 1914, America became increasingly fearful that Denmark might sell the Danish West Indies (now the Virgin Islands) to Germany. Two years later in order to protect the Panama Canal, Secretary of State Robert Lansing (1864–1928) informed Denmark that the United States would seize the

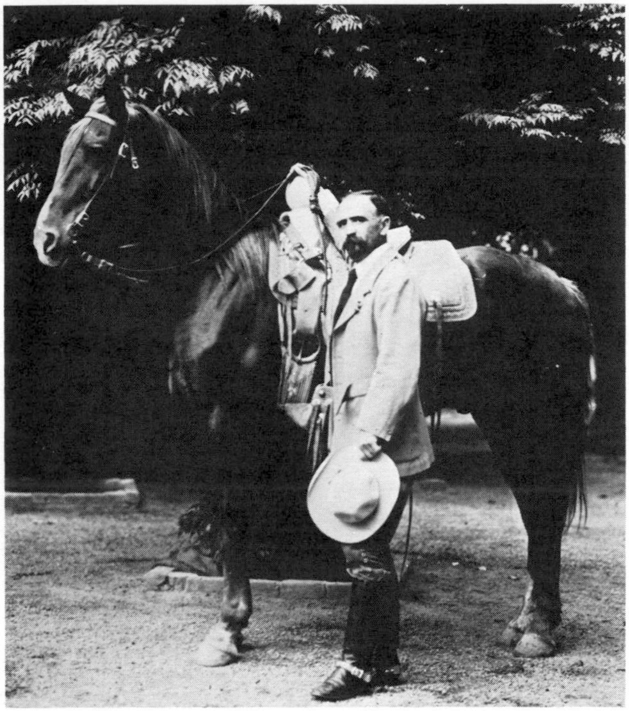
Library of Congress.

New York Public Library, Picture Collection.

Francisco Madero, at the left, the aristocratic reformer, and Victoriano Huerta, the military dictator, at the right.

islands if a German takeover seemed imminent. (Lansing, a New York lawyer married to the daughter of Benjamin Harrison's Secretary of State, assumed that office in June 1915 when Bryan, distressed by Wilson's increasing unneutral stance, decided to quit.) Therefore, Denmark agreed to sell the islands, and on August 4, 1914 the United States purchased them for $25 million, five times more than the American offer made fourteen years earlier. With this acquisition, American domination of the Caribbean was complete and would not be challenged until the rise of Fidel Castro nearly fifty years later.

Revolution in Mexico

Until the beginning of World War I, Mexico presented Wilson's greatest problem in foreign affairs. As early as 1910, while Taft was President and Porfirio Díaz (1830–1915) the dictator of Mexico, the United States had investments in Mexico totalling nearly $2 billion. In estimated value alone, Americans controlled 43 percent of all property there; Mexicans themselves, only 33 percent.

The programs of Francisco I. Madero (1873–1913), an idealistic young reformer, attracted many of his countrymen, while his election slogans—"Mexico for the Mexicans" and "Land for the Landless"—chilled American investors. In 1910, after Díaz tried to subvert elections, Madero seized power, vowing to destroy the privileged order and reestablish Mexico's society on a democratic basis. American ambassador Henry Lane Wilson worked to undermine the Madero government, throwing his support to a counterrevolution led by Felix Díaz, the deposed dictator's nephew. Through him, the ambassador saw an opportunity to reestablish the old order. Díaz was joined by Victoriano Huerta (1854–1916), Madero's chief general, and Ambassador Wilson offered the two the American embassy in which to meet.

Between February 9 and 18, 1913, Huerta executed a coup and had Madero murdered. Although the assassination shocked the world, Germany, France, Japan, and other powers extended recognition to the Huerta government. In spite of the urgings of Ambassador Wilson, Washington did not. While the Taft administration was embarrassed by the ambassador's implication in both the counterrevolution and Madero's murder, its policy of withholding recognition was based on politics, not morality. Not only did the State Department recognize the usefulness of withheld recognition in arbitrating outstanding disputes with Mexico, but in a few weeks a Democratic administration would inherit the problem as Woodrow Wilson became President.

The new President resisted pressure from both the ambassador and business interests to recognize the Huerta regime. He distrusted the Mexican ruler, and said privately, "I will not recognize a government of butchers." To resolve the dilemma, he sent former Minnesota governor John Lind to Mexico as a special agent. Lind was to offer Huerta a bribe in the form of a large loan if the dictator would agree to hold new elections in which he would not be a candidate. Huerta expressed the sentiments of many Mexicans when he refused: "I will resist with arms any attempt by the United States to interfere in the affairs of Mexico."

But on October 1, 1913, after Huerta imposed a military dictatorship on the country, President Wilson called for the dictator's resignation. At the same time he sent a note to governments of those nations with representatives in Mexico, asking that they withhold recognition. Wilson also informed them that he would use whatever means were necessary to force Huerta from power. The President explained his refusal to grant de facto recognition in his Mobile speech of October 27, during which he also restated America's disinterest in seeking Mexican territory and his administration's concern over European investments in Latin America.

In addition to isolating Huerta politically, Wilson also encouraged the Constitutionalists, who, under General Venustiano Carranza (1859–1920), a Maderista, had been fighting Huerta's forces in the north. Wilson sent a confidential agent to Mexico with an offer of American support in exchange for Carranza's promise to establish a democratic system of government. Carranza refused, vowing to oppose by force, if necessary, any American troops that might enter Mexico.

An opportunity to intervene came on April 9 when seven American sailors and an officer from the U.S.S. *Dolphin* were arrested while ashore in Tampico. The men were quickly released and the Mexican commander sent a personal note of apology to Admiral Henry T. Mayo. Mayo, however, with the support of Wilson, demanded a twenty-one gun salute, as the administration decided to use this petty incident to oust Huerta—who, they claimed, had offended the honor of the United States. Huerta agreed to the salute—if an American ship would return it volley for volley. The situation became more tense; Wilson ordered the North Atlantic fleet to Tampico and asked Congress for the right to use armed force against Huerta.

When the President learned on April 21 that a German steamer was on its way to Veracruz with a large shipment of munitions intended for Huerta's forces, he ordered the fleet to Veracruz, where it was to seize the customhouse in order to block the entry. On April 22, after fighting determined Mexican naval cadets, soldiers, and citizens, American forces occupied the city. Four hundred people, most of them Mexicans, were dead or wounded.

Though in fact the United States had intervened to bring about Huerta's downfall, President Wilson claimed

New York Public Library, Picture Collection.

Venustiano Carranza (seated) with Alvaro Obregón

Culver Pictures.

Pancho Villa
(1878–1923)

Facts concerning Villa's life are obscured by legend, hero worship, and hatred. During his tempestuous career he is alleged to have raped several women, married at least eight, forced a priest to marry a girl in a public ceremony, played Robin Hood to the poor of northern Mexico, and dazzled his adversaries with his military genius.

Pancho Villa, born Doroteo Arango, first got into trouble when he either killed or wounded the son of a wealthy landowner who either seduced or tried to seduce his fourteen-year-old sister. Soon after Arango's first brush with the authorities, he fled to northern Mexico and took the name of Villa, and began his career as an outlaw. By 1911 when Victoriano Huerta (with U.S. blessing) ended the long Diaz dictatorship, Villa and Venustiano Carranza had gained prominence in the north and Zapata in the South.

During the ensuing struggle to oust Huerta, Villa quickly became the darling of American journalists. The *New York Times* (December 14, 1913) published a picture of him labeled "Villa, the Robin Hood of Mexico," the man who stole from the rich and gave to the poor. In the meantime, Woodrow Wilson (who adamantly refused to recognize the Huerta government because of the manner in which it came to power) began to deal directly with General Villa, even making aid available to him. By the end of 1914, considerable friction had developed between Carranza and Villa. In October 1915 Wilson finally granted Carranza formal recognition, cut off all arms to Villa, and even allowed Carranza's men to cross American soil in order to attack Villa.

Meanwhile, Villa and his followers committed raids that led Wilson to order American troops to pursue him. In the eyes of many Mexicans, Pancho Villa became something of a national hero and Carranza's prestige—since he did little to counter the gringo thrust deep into Mexican territory—declined somewhat. However, on April 6, 1917, the entry of the U.S. into war against Germany and Austria reduced this south-of-the-border squabble to a minor sideshow.

Nevertheless, Villa continued to be a thorn in Carranza's side until 1919 when he agreed to retire to a huge ranch where he lived a life of ease, although a corps of bodyguards was always close at hand. On July 23, 1923, while he was returning from town, a hail of bullets struck Villa's automobile, killing the former general and several of his companions. Three years later someone pried open his tomb and made off with his head. Although there is no shortage of rumors, no one knows who killed Villa or who decapitated his corpse.

Nearly all of the leaders involved in this story of nation building south of the Rio Grande died violent deaths, yet only Pancho Villa, who failed to achieve the presidency, seems destined for immortality. In November 1966, the Mexican congress officially recognized Villa as a hero of the revolution. ■

publicly that the fleet had been sent in response to the national insult the United States had received at Tampico. Few could understand his policy. One English journal wrote: "If war is to be made on points of punctilio raised by admirals and generals, and if the Government of the United States is to set the example for this return to mediaeval conditions it will be a bad day for civilization."

On April 25, to avert war, the ABC powers—Argentina, Brazil, and Chile—offered to mediate the dispute. Wilson accepted the meetings, which were held from May 18 to July 2, 1914, but they accomplished little. Wilson had intended to use the conference to establish a provisional government that would turn Mexico over to the Constitutionalists. But Carranza refused to send representatives to the meetings and again denounced Wilson's attempts to interfere in Mexican affairs.

On July 15, yielding to internal and external pressures, Huerta resigned. The Constitutionalists entered Mexico City a month later but failed to establish a permanent coalition, and Mexico was plunged into civil war for another three years. Carranza turned down a series of recommendations made by Secretary of State Bryan, who noted that advice from the United States could not be

Brown Brothers.

General John Pershing's troops searching for the elusive Pancho Villa in 1916. Dusty throats and saddle sores rather than heroism and victory became their lot.

ignored "without deep and perhaps fatal consequences to the cause of the present revolution." Robert Lansing, Bryan's successor, interpreted Carranza's refusal as arrogant defiance and in August shifted American support to the illiterate former bandit Francisco (Pancho) Villa who had driven Carranza out of the capital. But when Carranza regained Mexico City in February 1915, the United States shifted to a policy of neutrality.

Meanwhile, as tension increased with Germany over the use of submarines against merchant shipping in the Atlantic, the State Department sought a policy that would avoid a war with Mexico, a war the German government was encouraging. Therefore, in October the United States extended de facto recognition to the Carranza government.

At first the relationship between the two countries was friendly, but on January 10, 1916, some of Villa's men removed 17 Americans aboard a train in northern Mexico and shot 16 of them on the spot. On March 9, Villa with 400 men raided Columbus, New Mexico, and destroyed the town, killing 19 Americans, perhaps in an attempt to gain badly needed supplies.

Demands for reprisals against the Mexican raiders could not be ignored in an American election year. In March, after negotiating a protocol with the Carranza government that allowed both countries to pursue bandits across their common border, Wilson sent General John J. Pershing (1860–1948) into Mexico to capture Villa. With specific instructions not to commit any act of aggression against Carranza's forces, Pershing and more than 6,000 men penetrated 300 miles into Mexican territory. Alarmed at the scope of the punitive expedition, Carranza began diplomatic action to force Washington to withdraw the troops.

As Villa continued to elude Pershing, the United States became convinced that Carranza was either incapable of or disinterested in controlling the gangs of bandits in northern Mexico. In April a clash between American and Mexican soldiers left 40 Mexicans and two Americans dead. After Wilson sent a new detachment to join Pershing, Carranza demanded the withdrawal of all American troops and ordered his generals to prevent any additional Americans from entering the country and to resist any movement on the part of the punitive expedition in any direction other than northward, toward the border. On June 18, Wilson mobilized the National Guard, incorporating it into the United States Army, and sent additional warships to both coasts of Mexico. Two days later, Lansing informed the Mexican government that American troops would not be withdrawn and that any attack on them would "lead to the gravest consequences." On June 21, Mexican and American forces fought at Carrizal, with casualties on both sides. War seemed imminent, and the State Department even prepared a war message.

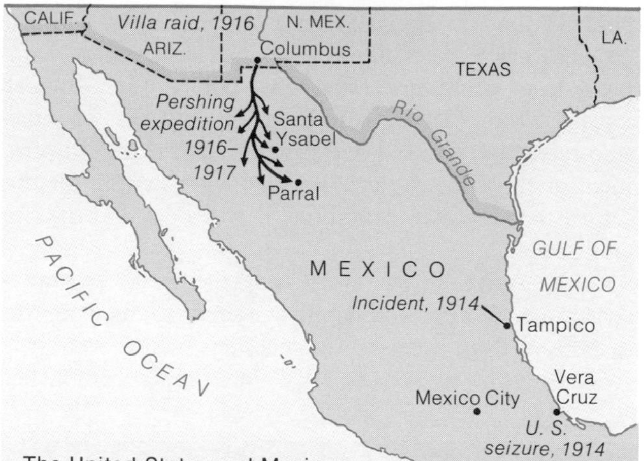

The United States and Mexico 1914–1917

But neither government wanted open conflict. Carranza soon released 23 American soldiers captured at Carrizal and on July 4 suggested that the two governments negotiate directly to relieve tensions. In September a joint high commission met in New London, Connecticut, but broke up in January 1917 when the two parties could not agree on terms. With the probability of U.S. involvement in Europe growing more certain daily, Wilson recalled Pershing's forces to Texas.

Meanwhile, the Mexican government had drawn up a new constitution. Although the United States found it objectionable because of restrictions against private foreign investment, Washington extended de jure recognition by sending an ambassador to Mexico City. The decision to go to war against Germany in April 1917 postponed the resolution of problems between Mexico and the United States, and relations remained less than cordial throughout Wilson's administration.

British-American Rapprochement

Throughout the period of ups and downs in foreign affairs between 1900 and 1917, an important theme was the evolution of an Anglo-American rapprochement. During the Boer War (1899), Britain stood virtually alone when she sought to suppress a German-supported rebellion of white South Africans. Although public sentiment in America favored the Boers, Secretary of State Hay and the Republican party were friendly toward England. In part, this was in exchange for Britain's support of the United States during the Spanish-American War. Moreover, it would have been difficult to condemn Britain's action in Africa while the United States was crushing rebels in the Philippines. The rapprochement progressed during Roosevelt's administration, disappointing those who thought that because of his Dutch ancestry the new president might throw his support to the Afrikaaners.

The Alaskan Boundary Dispute

In the light of this emerging friendship, the longstanding Alaskan boundary dispute between the United States and Canada seemed ripe for arbitration. For more than seventy years it had been commonly assumed by the United States, Russia, and Britain that the border of the Alaskan panhandle coincided with the Alaskan coastline. But after gold was discovered around Canada's Klondike River, near Alaska, the Canadian government claimed that the border actually followed a relatively straight line, measured from the heads of inlets along the coast, not the coast itself. The new border would allow Canadians to

Library of Congress.

Americans have always taken the discovery of gold seriously. Thousands of men sailed to Juneau and, undeterred by the snow, trekked over the treacherous Chilkoot Pass to the gold fields in search of fortune.

enter the mining region without going through Alaska and would thus also give Canadian gold an outlet to the sea.

Miners from the United States flocked to the area, and both countries feared a conflict. As early as August 1898 the dispute went (unsuccessfully) into arbitration. And in March 1902 Roosevelt, who found Canada's claims "an outrage pure and simple," sent troops to Alaska to keep the peace in mining communities. In January 1903, Secretary of State Hay signed with British Ambassador Sir Michael Herbert a treaty that called for another attempt at mediation. To the panel of "impartial jurists of repute" Roosevelt appointed then Secretary of War Elihu Root, ex-Senator George Turner of Washington and Senator Henry Cabot Lodge—hardly an unbiased trio. Dismayed, Herbert noted that "everything in this country is subservient to politics, and really an ambassador in Washington needs more than an ordinary stock of patience."

Roosevelt let it be known that he would use force if the dispute were not settled to the satisfaction of the United States. In October 1903, Britain's Lord Chief Justice Richard E. W. Alverstone, appointed along with two Canadian jurists, continually sided with the United States, thus not endangering the still fragile American-British rapprochement but inflaming Canadian public opinion. Roosevelt later noted that the settlement was "the last serious trouble between the British Empire and ourselves, as everything else could be arbitrated."

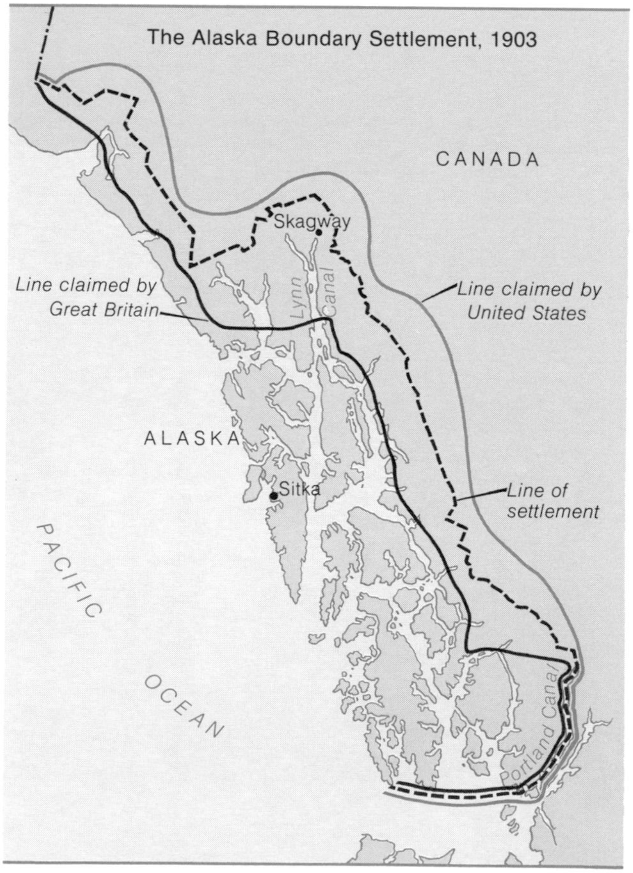

The North Atlantic Fisheries

A second area of contention between the United States and Britain also involved Canada and did threaten, in spite of Roosevelt's statement, the rapprochement. Canada and Newfoundland (separate entities until 1949) had long resented an agreement that since 1888 had allowed American fishing boats to buy supplies in Canadian harbors but offered no similar privileges to Canadian fishermen in American ports.

In November 1902, Hay signed a treaty with Newfoundland's prime minister permitting fish and other products to be sold in the United States in exchange for free American fishing privileges in the waters of that province. But American fishing interests refused to open their markets to foreign competitors, and three years later the Senate killed the treaty. As a result, Newfoundland enacted legislation that discriminated against American vessels. By January 1909 both countries had agreed to submit the dispute to The Hague's Permanent Court of Arbitration. Its findings in September 1910 allowed Britain to enact and enforce *reasonable* local fishing regulations. The court also modified Britain's exclusion of American ships from all bays. Closed to vessels of the United States were those bays less than ten miles wide at the mouth. Beyond the three-mile limit, American ships were allowed to fish along those bays with wider mouths. In July 1912 an Anglo-American commission confirmed the court's rulings, with some modifications, and so clarified the major points of one of the longest controversies in American foreign affairs.

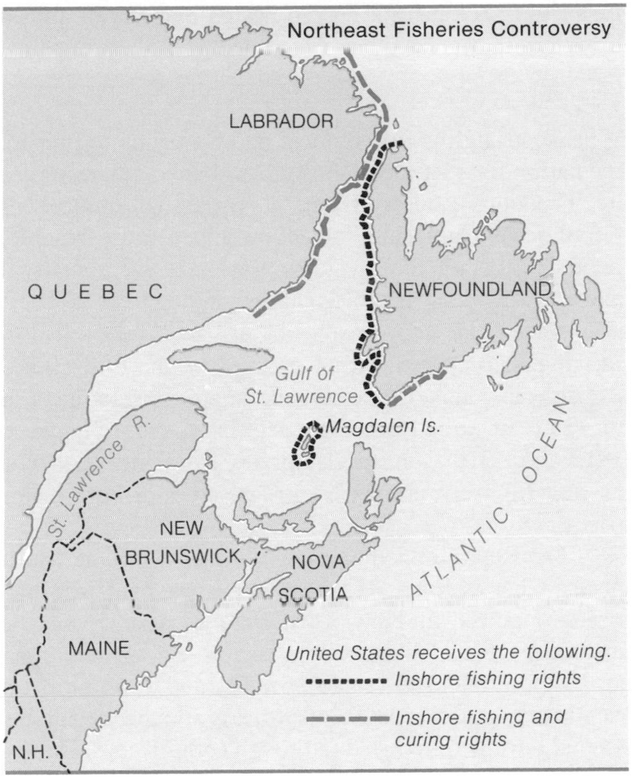

The Panama Tolls

The last important difference with Britain was the interpretation of the second Hay-Pauncefote Treaty concerning payment of Panama Canal tolls. In August 1912 Congress exempted from tolls those American ships involved in trading between the coasts of the United States. The original treaty, however, provided for use of the canal to all ships "on terms of entire equality." Britain charged that the exemption was discriminatory and would raise the tolls for foreign ships. Although the issue involved no interest vital to either country, it did involve the honor of the United States. Taft refused to adjudicate the dispute, arguing that "when the treaties are properly construed, owning the canal and paying for it as we do, we have the right and power, if we choose, to discriminate in favor of our own ships."

Though Wilson supported this policy during the campaign of 1912, once he assumed office he became convinced that national honor would be saved only if the disputed provision were repealed. Wilson told the Senate Foreign Relations Committee in January 1914 that British support of the administration's policies in Mexico might be won if the dispute over tolls were settled in a friendly manner. In March he presented his position on the tolls to an unreceptive Congress and in doing so alluded to the situation in Mexico: "I ask this of you in support of the foreign policy of the administration. I shall not know how to deal with other matters of even greater delicacy and nearer consequence if you do not grant it to me in ungrudging measure." By June 11 both houses of Congress had repealed the exemption, but only after much debate, thus resolving the last important difference with Great Britain before the advent of the Great War.

Thus as the end of Woodrow Wilson's first term drew near, the nation had put its hemispheric house generally in good order, at least from Washington's point of view. Numerous states vital to the defense of the Panama Canal were under direct or indirect U.S. control, affairs in Mexico were calmer—though still difficult—and minor differences with Canadians to the north had been ironed out more or less upon our terms, not theirs. If all of this sounded like the death knell of Progressivism abroad, it was, except for one great and glorious effort to reform not just the New World or Asia but the Old World as well.

America as a Pro-Ally Neutral

In the summer of 1914 the flaming pistol of a Serbian patriot ignited a general war that ended an era in Europe as firmly and completely as it did in America. Within a brief time, the Central Powers, consisting of Germany, Austria-Hungary, and ultimately Turkey and Bulgaria, were fighting the Allies led by Great Britain, France, Russia, Japan, and later Italy. Although President Wilson favored strict neutrality, neither he nor his fellow citizens were able to adopt such a stance. Many Americans maintained close ties to the nations involved and, in the main, were from the outset pro-Ally. Also, official relations with Britain had improved in recent decades as those with Germany had worsened. In addition, Germany's brutal military campaign through Belgium had hardened these views.

Admittedly, a common language helped British propagandists overcome latent Anglophobia, which was still potent in many parts of America, but Germany's U-boat war did even more to aid the Allied cause and eventually took the United States into the conflict on the side of the Allies. The mass of Irish, Germans, Poles, and Jews who favored the Central Powers, although large in numbers, did not exert much influence in government circles where key diplomatic decisions were being made.

Biased Neutrality

As hostilities opened, Germany's might depended upon land domination, Britain's upon control of the seas. To declare an embargo on the shipment of war supplies, as pro-Germans and pacifists urged, would have helped Germany and hurt England. Wilson's decision to accept the status quo appears to have been based upon a desire to adhere to traditional rules of neutrality and a fear of British defeat and German victory. Yet the President's ideas concerning traditional neutrality were indeed strange. He protested British action on occasions but never did much more than that, while by 1915 he was describing the Germans as "wild beasts" when talking with his Cabinet.

Early in that same year he permitted the Morgan banking house to extend a huge loan to France, rejecting German-American proposals to prohibit the export of war materials. Then, a few months later he lifted Secretary of State Bryan's ban on all loans. Very soon U.S. financial involvement increased dramatically, so much so that national prosperity became tied to the war itself, although it would be wrong to conclude that America entered the struggle in April 1917 solely because of this factor.

Germany's response, not surprisingly, was increasing pressure to limit American aid to its enemies. The result was a series of ship sinkings that troubled but did not break relations between Berlin and Washington. The ships destroyed included the *Lusitania* and *Arabic* in 1915 and the *Sussex* in 1916; despite the loss of American lives and angry diplomatic notes across the Atlantic, momentary outrage subsided when Germany agreed to be more careful. However, Wilson's insistence on America's rights as a neutral was so heated that Bryan quit as Secretary of State and was succeeded by Robert Lansing.

The Election of 1916

Wilson, struggling to avoid war and yet trying to prepare the nation for that inevitability, was baited at every turn by Theodore Roosevelt and a substantial number of Republicans clamoring for action and a more resolute policy. Although the President urged the Democrats to make "Americanism" their campaign slogan in 1916, it was instead "He kept us out of war" and Wilson had to accept it. Compared with the stand of the Old Guard Republicans, his attitude was moderation personified; at the same time, the Democrats' legislative record between 1912 and 1916 won special praise from independents, ex-Bull Moosers, and weary Progressives of both major parties.

The Republicans nominated former Supreme Court justice Charles Evans Hughes, an austere man who had risen to power in New York state as a critic of the insurance trusts. Wilson won a narrow victory, less than an absolute majority (since Socialist and Prohibitionist candidates got over 800,000 votes), and he began his second term with reduced (although comfortable) Democratic margins in both houses of Congress. Despite the opposition of ethnic groups opposed to his pro-Ally policy (Irish, German, Jewish, and Polish voters), most of the Progressive, liberal, and solidly Democratic vote supported Wilson.

Mediation, Frustration, and War

With the political campaign behind him, President Wilson began a concerted effort to end the war in Europe, now a bloody stalemate, by a negotiated peace. Addressing the Senate on January 22, 1917, he asserted the right of the U.S. to participate in any such deliberations and called for "a peace without victory." "Only a peace between equals," he asserted, "can last." Such idealism, perhaps noble in tone, was utterly unrealistic in the light of recent events. The United States had played no direct role in the struggle thus far and had bent over backwards to accommodate one side while maintaining it was "neutral."

Nine days later the German government submitted terms for discussion that assured continuation of the dominant military position it then enjoyed on the Continent and announced resumption of unrestricted submarine warfare. Wilson immediately severed diplomatic relations with Berlin. During the next sixty days a series of fast-moving events took the United States of America into European entanglements as a partner of the Allies against the Central Powers. These included interception of the Zimmerman Note, by which the German foreign secretary suggested to Mexico that it join Germany in war against the United States if hostilities erupted; and the sinking of still more vessels in the Atlantic, which caused the loss of American lives. Fearful that Britain and France were in such desperate condition that only immediate U.S. help could save them and overwhelmed by calls for war, Woodrow Wilson reluctantly gave in to those appeals early in April 1917. At the same time, he must have known from the beginning that his policies could have virtually no other outcome. Only a quick Allied victory could have made his "neutrality" feasible; and, had British-French power been able to dominate the struggle, then U.S. involvement, even in the form of loans and supplies, would have been largely unnecessary.

On April 2, 1917, the President asked Congress for a declaration of war against Germany and launched a crusade "to make the world safe for democracy." Four days later the Senate (82–6) and the House (373–50) concurred. It is difficult to say whether these totals reflected support for Wilson or an upsurge of fervent patriotism and national outrage. What is clear is that outright participation in World War I and the repressive mood it created meant that the Progressivism of Roosevelt and Wilson had run its course, not to be revived until the nation was convulsed by a far more serious crisis and yet another Roosevelt sat in the White House. It also meant that, for better or worse, America henceforth would be deeply involved in world affairs, not only as an imperial power but as banker, policeman, arbitrator, and counselor.

Essay

United States, Panama, and the Canal

At the heart of the long controversy concerning the creation and maintenance of the Panama Canal lie three basic truths. For three-quarters of a century (1825–1900) U.S. statesmen were interested in a waterway linking the Atlantic and Pacific; treaties were signed with various nations from time to time regarding such a project; and in 1855 American interests completed a railroad across the Isthmus. By the beginning of the twentieth century the United States of America was an abrasive, cocky new power feeling its imperial "oats" and eager to throw its weight around. And throughout all of the decades of debate leading up to the present day—150 years or so—this relationship between a small nation with something a large one wants and feels it must control has given Washington nothing but headaches.

Colombia (called New Granada in the mid-1800s) was always a weak nation compared with the United States, and Panama, part of Colombia until the "revolt" of November 3, 1903, was even weaker. That uprising, by the way, resulted in only one casualty: Wong Kong Yee, a native of Hong Sang, China, was killed by a shell from a Colombian gunboat as he sat eating dinner with his family in Panama City. Within seventy-two hours Washington recognized the insurgents as the de facto government and on November 13 granted full recognition to the new regime. That same day, Philippe Bunau-Varilla, a former engineer with the French company which had tried to build a canal in Panama, arrived in the United States and within a week had signed with Secretary of State John Hay on behalf of Panama a treaty that transferred construction rights (and much, much more, it turned out) to the United States government. On that august occasion Hay used an inkwell that once belonged to Abraham Lincoln. Bunau-Varilla then returned to France, his company $40 million richer, and subsequently penned this eulogy to Theodore Roosevelt: "You have rendered to your noble country and to the world the greatest of services by cutting, at last, the Gordian knot which for centuries has paralyzed humanity." Whether Roosevelt had cut one knot—or had tied several more equally hard to untangle—is problematical.

Library of Congress.

Theodore Roosevelt shows his commitment to building the Panama Canal—and to publicity—by operating a piece of heavy machinery himself.

On December 2, Panama ratified the Hay–Bunau-Varilla Treaty, and five days later Roosevelt summarized its contents to Congress. Ten weeks later on February 23, 1904, the Senate gave its approval and the legal niceties preparatory to digging the "big ditch" had been taken care of. All of this occurred during the first weeks of Panama's independence and that independence clearly depended upon prompt acceptance of a document that no Panamanian either negotiated or signed. It was almost as if an enterprising Dutchman, relying upon some defunct business deal, had engineered the transfer in 1782 of the Hudson River valley and a corridor northward to Canada to some foreign power, say Russia or China, without consulting the newly independent United States, yet tying U.S. freedom to prompt approval of that transaction.

There was in these proceedings one very tragic twist. Originally Bunau-Varilla wrote that Panama would "lease" a strip of land across the Isthmus to the United States but then changed that word to "granted," the source of much debate and misunderstanding since 1903. What is even more astonishing is that this Frenchman acted without specific instructions from the new government in Panama and rushed the agreement to completion before a Panamanian commission could get to Washington. To add to the confusion, the ruling junta in Panama, without seeing the text, promised ratification as soon as the document reached that young republic.

Several other facts concerning the development of the Panama Canal should be noted. Events during the Spanish-American War made the need for a canal apparent to all Americans, and there were only two possible routes: Panama and Nicaragua. The latter, however, was ruled by an uncooperative dictator, Zeyala, and the U.S. had also been unable to work out an agreement with Costa Rica, which would have been involved with any waterway in that region. In addition, southern Democrats in Congress, many of them the President's staunchest enemies, favored the Nicaraguan route since it was closer to their ports. But—and this was crucial—U.S. engineers reported that a canal at Panama was preferable to one in Nicaragua. It would be shorter, easier to build and maintain, and cheaper to construct and operate. Although lobbying efforts in Congress certainly aided Panama's cause, the Roosevelt administration undoubtedly decided to build there in the light of what engineering experts, not lobbyists, said. Just to be on the safe side, the President also dispatched two or three handpicked army officers in civilian dress to Panama early in 1903 to assess the area from a military point of view. Having settled on the Isthmus, the U.S. government faced a Colombia torn by revolution and unable even to consider an American offer (the Hay-Herrán Treaty) until June of 1903. After two months the Colombian Congress, torn by factionalism, rejected the agreement.

What happened during September and October of 1903 is

Historical Pictures Service, Inc., Chicago.

Cutting the canal through the backbone of the isthmus.

still wrapped in secrecy and controversy. That Panama, distant from and long disenchanted with rule from Bogotá, should consider revolution is not surprising since its economy depended upon travel across the Isthmus. That a revolt could solve many of Roosevelt's immediate problems is obvious. And that U.S. vessels prevented Colombian forces from snuffing out a brief uprising in Panama is equally apparent.

The official U.S. explanation was that Article 35 of its Treaty of 1846 with Colombia required America to guarantee free and uninterrupted transit across the Isthmus at all times. That same article also stated that the U.S. guaranteed the sovereignty of Colombia over that narrow strip of land. All of these phrases referred, of course, to railroad travel and in no way gave the Colossus of the North any rights concerning canal construction, much less to promote or to thwart revolution.

During the next decade one of the greatest engineering marvels in history unfolded. Despite landslides, yellow fever, and incredible odds, the canal slowly took shape. By March 1909, sixty-eight huge steam shovels were hacking away at the rugged earth, but shoveling, drilling, blasting, and hauling all had to be coordinated so one operation would not interfere with another. And even as the work went on the unfinished canal had become a tourist attraction, drawing 15,000 spectators in 1911 and another 20,000 in 1912. During the final years of construction a work force of about 50,000 (including 6,000 Americans and many more blacks) patronized some 350 saloons in Colón and Panama City and a large number of brothels, most of them run by enterprising American women. Yet there were also churches, YMCAs, and social clubs—some thirty-nine of them in all.

Meanwhile, back in Pittsburgh, some fifty mills, foundries, and machine shops were turning out rivets, bolts, nuts, girders, steel in innumerable forms and shapes, and no fewer than 19,000 roller bearings. The whole system, as it emerged, was run by electricity, something that would have been impossible a decade earlier. The total cost was $352 million (including $10 million paid to Panama and the $40 million Bunau-Varilla secured for his employers). By comparison, all territorial purchases from Louisiana to the Philippines cost only one-fifth as much. Taken together, the French and Americans spent about $639 million on the Isthmus. About 5,600 men died after the Americans took over in 1904 (only 350 of them white) and perhaps another 20,000 prior to that time.

Yet the Panama Canal actually cost $23 million less than the estimated price quoted in 1907 and opened six months ahead of time in August 1914. Since that time, three basic issues have embittered relations between Washington and Panama. First and foremost, has been the right of the U.S. to treat the Canal Zone as if it were sovereign territory. Panama, on the other hand, has insisted that America could only construct, maintain, operate, and protect the canal—nothing else. It denied that the United States could treat the zone through the heart of the nation as an outright possession.

The second major problem involved commerce. Hay vowed

National Archives.

The Gatun Locks—near the Atlantic Ocean entrance—as they appeared in June 25, 1913, approximately one year before completion of the canal.

that America could do whatever it wished in the Canal Zone, but Secretary of War William Howard Taft visited the region in June 1904 and devised an interim agreement concerning customs, postal rates, and commissary stores. However, Panama's businessmen, convinced that Bunau-Varilla conceded much too much, have never been happy with these arrangements, altered from time to time by subsequent negotiations.

And the last major point of contention, one of increasing importance since 1945 and the demise of colonialism, is the question of national pride. Having one's nation split by the colony of another where pay and living conditions usually have been better and visibly so, is galling in the extreme. If one can imagine a foreign power patrolling and virtually owning a strip for ten miles wide from Manhattan northward to the Canadian border, flying its flag, speaking its language, and practicing its customs within sight of millions of U.S. citizens year after year, then it is perhaps possible to appreciate sentiments felt and experienced by Panamanians.

Americans, long mesmerized by the scope of their engineering achievement at the Isthmus (which is not to be denied), proud and secure in the innate goodness of their national policy, often find it difficult to see the canal as anything less than a well-administered "possession." Yet in 1958 when Milton Eisenhower, brother of the President, made a special visit there (two years, it should be noted, after Egypt seized the Suez Canal), citizens of Panama gave voice to much the same demands they had been making for a half a century: The U.S. should cease economic activity not related to defense or operation of the waterway, give equal pay to Panamanians for doing the same work as Americans in the Canal Zone, grant an equal share of the gross profits to the Panamanian government, recognize Spanish as the official language of the zone, and display there the U.S. and Panamanian flags on an equal basis.

On September 22, 1960, upon orders of President Eisenhower, the flags of Panama and the U.S. were flown together for the first time in a public plaza *just outside of* the Canal Zone as a symbol of the Isthmian republic's "titular sovereignty" over that area. Although scattered disruptions marred the ceremony, 5,000 spectators watched in respectful silence. Even this minor concession brought howls from superpatriots in Congress. Daniel J. Flood, a Pennsylvania Democrat, was so angry that he talked of impeaching the President. Columnist Drew Pearson thought Eisenhower's action was designed to help his Vice President, Richard Nixon, who then was gearing up his first drive for the White House.

Despite such protests and wild assertions by various patriotic groups concerning what Bunau-Varilla did or did not grant to the U.S. in 1903, succeeding administrations held quiet, behind-the-scenes discussions culminating in a revision of U.S. rights in the Canal Zone.

In March 1978 the Senate, by a margin of 68–32 (one more than necessary for a two-thirds majority), approved a treaty assuring permanent neutrality of the waterway; the following month, by a similar vote, members of the Senate agreed to turn the canal over to Panama on December 31, 1999. Until that time a joint Panamanian–U.S. Commission will supervise operations. These moves by no means ended this controversy, and in May 1978 the U.S. Supreme Court turned aside an attempt by 60 congressmen bent upon undoing these agreements.

This would seem to end at least the U.S. "imperial" phase of the Panamanian imbroglio. Rarely in history have diplomats (and more especially, engineers) signed treaties with sovereign powers on behalf of nations with which they had very tenuous ties. That was, of course, precisely what Philippe Bunau-Varilla did, and Theodore Roosevelt, in his eagerness to get a canal across the Isthmus of Panama, grasped at this opportunity. It got him out of an embarrassing quandary but left two nations with a very troubled relationship, a magnificent engineering feat, and decades of bitterness which now, it is hoped, are drawing to a close.

Selected Readings

General Studies

Alexander DeConde, *A History of American Foreign Policy* (1971)

Ernest R. May, *The World War and American Isolationism 1914–1917* (1959)

Richard W. Leopold, *Elihu Root and the Conservative Tradition* (1954)

Rubin Francis Weston, *Racism in U.S. Imperialism: The Influence of Racial Assumption on American Foreign Policy, 1893–1946* (1972)

Foreign Policy Under Roosevelt

Raymond A. Esthus, *Theodore Roosevelt and the International Rivalries* (1970)

Howard K. Beale, *Theodore Roosevelt and the Rise of America to World Power* (1956)

Charles E. Neu, *An Uncertain Friendship: Theodore Roosevelt and Japan, 1906–1909* (1967) .

Dollar Diplomacy

Dana G. Munro, *Intervention and Dollar Diplomacy in the Carribean, 1900–1921* (1964)

Walter V. and Marie V. Scholes, *The Foreign Policies of the Taft Adminstration* (1970)

Wilsonian Diplomacy

Arthur S. Link, *Woodrow Wilson and the Progressive Era, 1910–1919* (1954)

The Military

Richard D. Challener, *Admirals, Generals, and American Foreign Policy: 1898–1914* (1973)

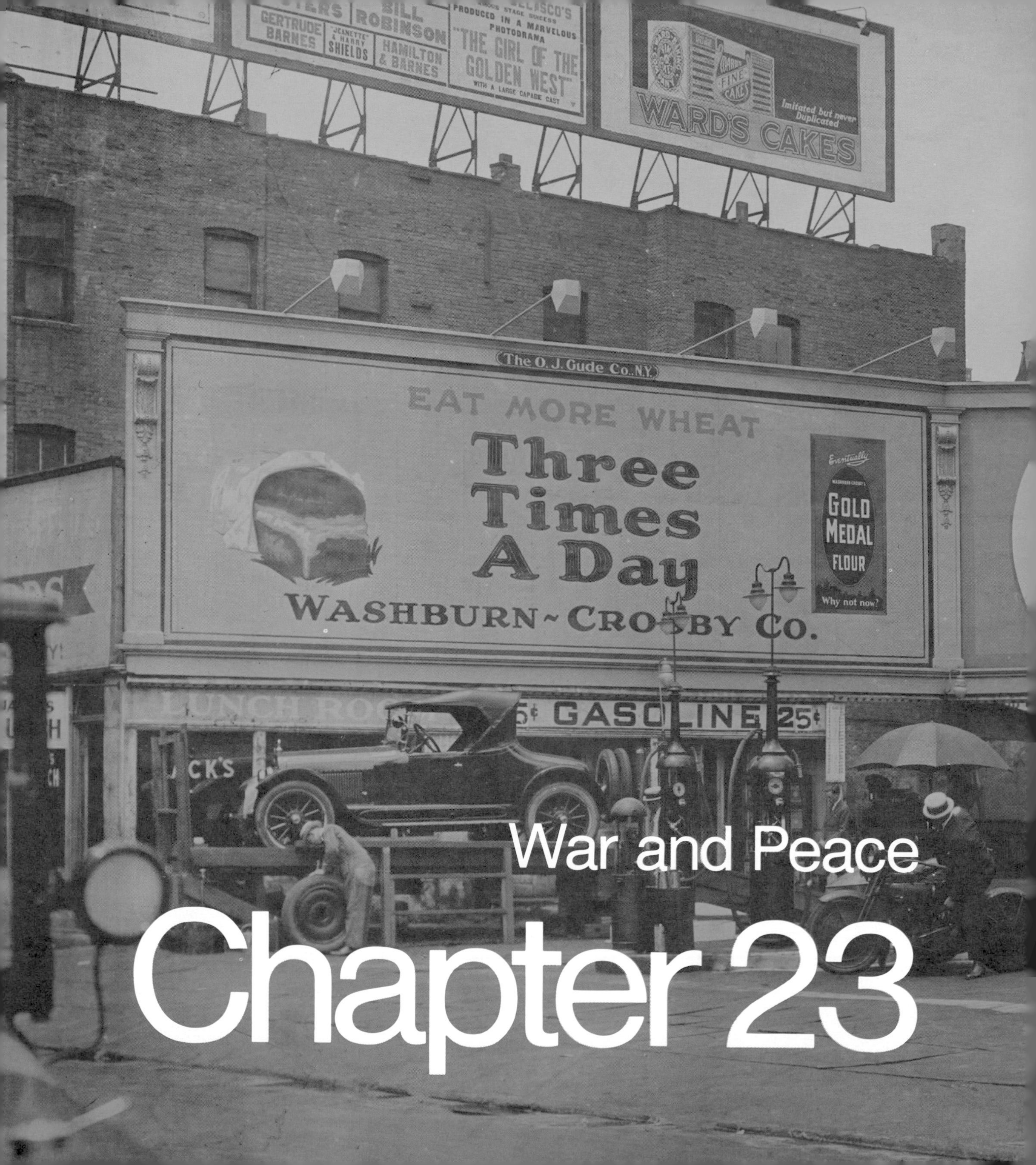

Chapter 23

War and Peace

TIMELINE

1917
President Wilson asks for declaration of war

1917
National War Labor Board recognizes collective bargaining, minimum wage, eight-hour day, and child labor regulation

1918
Wilson announces Fourteen Points

1918
National War Labor Board creates a national network of trade associations and unions

1918
1.2 million AEF soldiers fight in Europe

1918
Republicans gain a majority in Congress

1919
National Prohibition approved with ratification of Eighteenth Amendment

1919
Strikes end wartime harmony of labor and management

1920
The "Red Scare" intensifies with arrest of 6,000 people

1920
The Senate rejects the Versailles Treaty

1920
Women's suffrage approved with ratification of Nineteenth Amendment

1920
Republican Warren G. Harding elected President

1921
Sacco and Vanzetti are convicted of robbery and murder

1923
Teapot Dome scandal exposed

1923
Harding's death makes Calvin Coolidge President

1924
Henry Ford lowers cost of Model T to $290

1924
National Origins Act curtails immigration

1924
Indian Citizenship Act marks beginning of Indian policy reform

1925
Ku Klux Klan claims five million members

1925
Tennessee court convicts John T. Scopes of violating law prohibiting the teaching of evolution

1927
Charles A. Lindbergh makes first solo transatlantic flight

1928
Herbert Hoover defeats Al Smith in presidential election

CHAPTER OUTLINE

Often broken up into two separate phases, these twelve years are better understood as a single sequence. The war marked the culmination of an emphasis on "administrative reform" begun in the Progressive era. The government-business relationship achieved during the war became the accepted political order during the 1920s, a relationship symbolized by the career of Herbert Hoover, who first served as Federal Food Administrator, then as Secretary of Commerce and, finally, as President.

A number of new forces and problems pervaded this decade. The government instituted prohibition of alcoholic beverages, women won the right to vote, and agricultural surpluses caused discontent among rural Americans. Nativist and antiradical sentiment became more pronounced, especially in the countryside. And in the cities, immigrants and minorities began to band together to achieve shared goals. These and other forces or problems either were created by the war experience or resulted from it.

Woodrow Wilson remained in the White House until March 1921. The "normal" Republican legislative majority was, however, restored in 1918 when they won control of Congress. This majority prevailed for as long as prosperity lasted—that is, until the Great Crash of 1929 in the stock market. Until then the surface of national life appeared untroubled, although there were growing disturbances beneath it. But the crash of 1929 made the inadequacies of the administrative state in the "New Era" glaringly apparent. Subterranean forces erupted and eventually caused a transformation of the economic, political, and social order in the 1930s.

But the period from 1917 to 1929 laid the groundwork for the modern American life that was to follow. And perhaps the two most significant developments of this period were the energized role of the presidency in wartime and the construction of an ongoing relationship between government and the economy.

The United States and the Great War

On April 2, 1917, President Wilson delivered his war message to a special congressional session, while huge crowds of peace demonstrators and police gathered outside. As early as March the Cabinet had unanimously recommended that the United States abandon technical neutrality. However, Wilson had delayed. Unrestricted German submarine warfare, along with the Zimmerman telegram, helped make Wilson's decision to enter the war acceptable to the American public.

The President revealed the Zimmerman message to the American public on March 1, precipitating a wave of anti-German feeling across the nation. But Congress continued to withhold the kind of support Wilson wanted, such as arming American merchant vessels.

Angered by the sinking of U.S. vessels (three in March alone) and fearful that the Allies could not fight on without American aid, Wilson decided on war. He realized that this decision would change everything at home. Like other Progressives, he feared that if he committed American men and arms to the European struggle, political liberalism would be threatened and repression would follow.

Despite these fears Wilson became convinced that

German aggression would not be limited to Europe and that real peace would never be assured so long as this threat existed. His war message called for "a crusade," but not everyone was swayed by his words. Opponents of war, led by Senator Robert La Follette of Wisconsin, debated the resolution for four hours. But by April 6 Congress had acted and the U.S. was at war.

America's Military Contribution

America's military contribution to the war ultimately proved decisive, but it was slow in reaching Europe. The nation was unprepared and this created problems. The Selective Service Act, passed on May 18, 1917, initiated the eventual registration of over 24 million men between the ages of 21 and 45, over 2.8 million of whom were inducted. When the war ended in November 1918, there were over 4.8 million American men under arms (including volunteers). This new and untrained army was difficult to outfit immediately, especially with artillery and heavy equipment. When the first American Expeditionary Force (AEF) arrived in France, General "Black Jack" Pershing insisted on keeping the men under separate command (against the wishes of the Allies) and refused to send them into battle until they had completed basic training.

The Supreme War Council was set up at Versailles in November 1917, but President Wilson would not send a government representative to it, although a U.S. gen-

Library of Congress.

President Wilson asked Congress for a declaration of war against Germany on April 2, 1917. The actual votes in both houses occurred a few days later.

National Archives.

Although American troops came into World War I late, they engaged in many bloody and important battles.

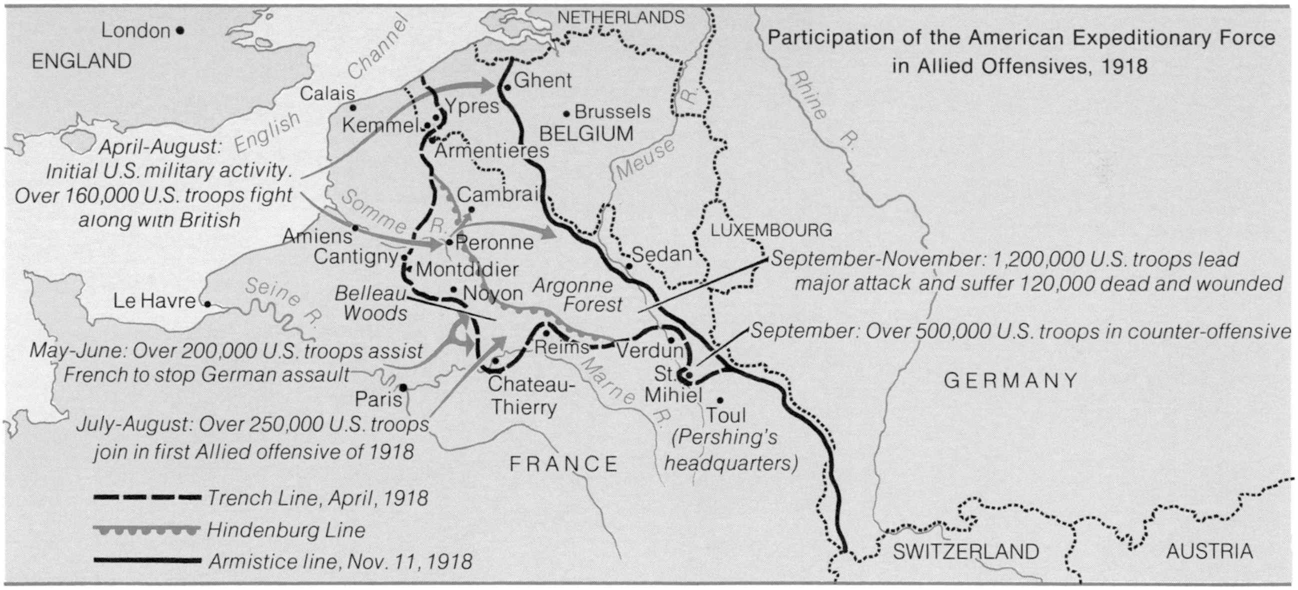

eral did sit regularly with the Allied military advisers as an adjunct to the Council. In addition, Wilson insisted on "associate," as opposed to "allied," status for the United States on the Council. These actions, in the opinion of the Allies, conveyed an annoying sense of American aloofness.

By March of 1918, however, Wilson and Pershing had to change their stance somewhat. The Germans had routed the Italians and crushed the Russian army during the fall of 1917. The consequent withdrawal of the Russians from the war left the Central Powers with a quiet eastern front, which enabled them to concentrate their efforts exclusively in the west, where the French and English troops were near exhaustion. Then in the spring of 1918 the Germans launched an all-out offensive and pushed the Allies back to the Marne River. With the Germans only fifty miles from Paris, Allied prospects were dim.

General Ferdinand Foch became Supreme Commander of the Allied forces, and Pershing finally allowed his troops to participate with the Allied forces. The first important action occurred in June at Château-Thierry. In July the Americans helped push back a German offensive in the Marne pocket. From July to November of 1918, during the last offensives, American troops began to flow into France at an increasing rate. By September over 1.2 million American troops were committed to the effort. The decisive battles that ended the war were won by the British on the central front and the French on the northern front and, with the AEF contributions, in the Meuse-Argonne sector. The Americans had come at the right time to supply the needed men and arms.

Fatalities were extremely high. The French lost 1.3 million men, the British 900,000, and the Russians 1.7 million. Compared with these figures the American loss of 116,516 men was low. All troops—American, Allied, and those of the Central Powers—suffered high incidences of shell shock (what in World War II would be called battle fatigue) and tuberculosis.

At sea the British had already bottled up the Ger-

Brown Brothers.

After the armistice, American soldiers returned to heroes' welcomes from an idealistic public. Here the returning Seventy-seventh Division marches triumphantly down Fifth Avenue in New York City.

man fleet (except for U-boats). But the Americans also made an important contribution in the naval arena. Admiral William S. Sims was in charge of the European division of the American Navy. To reduce submarine losses he devised the convoy system, with destroyers being used to escort troop and cargo ships across the Atlantic. In addition the American navy ran a highway of ships across the English Channel, transporting nearly a million troops to France. By the end of the war more than 2,000 American ships and 500,000 American naval men were aiding the Allies. If the American role was relatively small, it was nonetheless vital to Allied victory.

The Impact of War at Home

Historians disagree about the impact of the war on American Progressivism. For instance, Richard Hofstadter has argued that liberal traditions always fare badly in times of national crisis, so it was inevitable that the war would end reform in America. The idealism and patriotic self-sacrifice Americans experienced in 1917–1918 absorbed the nation's attention, and this experience led to a conservative reaction when peace came. Thus Democrat James M. Cox's resounding defeat in the 1920 presidential election can be seen as a repudiation of the self-control and altruism that Progressives had demanded of the nation during the war.

Throughout the war the American public thought United States intervention was an act of altruism, undertaken without hope of political or economic gain. Wilson saw America as Europe's redeemer and declared during the treaty debates that "America is the only idealistic Nation in the world." Since the war was linked to Progressive rhetoric and ideals of civic participation such as responsibility and sacrifice, any reaction against the actual ordeal of fighting might well produce rejection of both the ordeal and the values that had led to it.

More recently, other historians have stressed the ways in which the war, rather than betraying, actually fulfilled the goals of Progressivism, especially in the area of social justice. According to this view, the mood of the nation was growing weary and the vitality of the Progressive movement diminishing even before war began.

America's involvement, they say, enabled the Progressive movement to accomplish reforms that might never have been possible in peacetime. One example is the social justice movement. Led by social workers, ministers and intellectuals, this movement tried to humanize the cities and better the working conditions in industry.

During the war, both efficient management and manpower were in short supply. Thus, in the summer of 1917 those reformers who were called to Washington were surprised to discover that legislators actually wanted their advice and guidance. Congress passed bills providing workmen's compensation for longshoremen. Wartime agencies such as the National War Labor Board were ready to recognize issues such as collective bargaining, the minimum wage, and the eight-hour workday, as well as to consider programs to reduce the exploitation of workingwomen and children. Improvement of urban housing, another goal of the reformers, suddenly became a federal issue. The government built or controlled dozens of housing projects, often experimental in nature, patterned after the English Garden City with its graceful row houses, curved streets, and community recreation and shopping areas.

The social and health insurance movements also made gains because of America's participation in the war. The Military and Naval Insurance Act of 1917 provided for compensation to soldiers' families in the event of death or disability, thus insuring at least a minimum standard of subsistence. Despite resistance from private insurance companies and the medical profession, the movement to improve national health through compulsory health insurance gained support, and new standards of sanitation, mental hygiene, and physical fitness appeared.

The women's rights movement also profited from the war. After years of opposing suffrage, President Wilson finally endorsed it. The Nineteenth Amendment, giving women the right to vote, was passed in 1919 and ratified in 1920. Progressive values also supplied impetus to and strong support for Prohibition, resulting finally in ratification of the Eighteenth Amendment in 1919.

The mobilization of industry and agriculture and the nationalization of railroads under William G. McAdoo (1863–1941) in the winter of 1917–1918 were further steps towards "social control." But while reformers such as Helena Dudley and Jane Addams applauded these changes, they also realized that they were the product of national emergency and not of national conscience. Within a few years, as they predicted, social apathy and a mood of hedonism would again become commonplace.

Despite such reforms, there were many to whom the war brought no relief. Blacks who were drafted served in segregated units while racial bigotry at home remained undiminished. In 1918 William E. B. DuBois called for blacks to put aside their grievances and hope that, with the advent of peace, participation in the war movement would improve their living conditions. DuBois urged blacks to unite and close ranks: "Since the war began we have won: Recognition of our citizenship in the draft; One thousand Negro officers; Special representation in the War and Labor Departments; Abolition of the color line in railway wages; Recognition as Red Cross Nurses; Overthrow of segregation ordinances; A strong word from the President against lynching. . . . Come fellow black men, fight for your rights, but for God's sake have sense enough to know when you are getting what you fight for." But the war did not, as hoped, end racial strife, although it did stimulate a massive black migration to the North, as thousands sought jobs in industry.

One of the main goals of Progressivism had been the establishment of an "organizational" or centralized administrative government. Wartime needs led to the creation of a large federal apparatus designed to handle social and economic conflicts in an increasingly complex society. The war created the bureaucratic state, which in turn dominated the life of the nation in the 1920s.

Wilson perceived that the immediate and most important problem that the nation faced was mobilization, not merely of men but of industry as well. He realized that the war would not be won by sheer force of numbers of fighting men. Rather, victory depended upon industrial superiority. But there had never been a wholesale conversion of industry from peacetime to wartime needs in America. The government had no precedents for economic mobilization, no sense of how to supervise the production or distribution of goods that participation in the war made necessary. No stockpiles of arms or equipment existed, no inventory of supplies. And there was no one to offer leadership in these matters.

To solve such problems, in July 1917 the federal government created the War Industries Board (WIB). Run by Bernard M. Baruch (1870–1965), a wealthy New York Democrat with wide influence in the business world, the WIB had authority over all government purchasing and allocation of raw materials, as well as over production and labor relations. Acting as a liaison between industry and the army, the WIB was fairly successful in eliminating bottlenecks and speeding up production. But Baruch's activities were circumscribed by limits of time—the WIB appeared well after the necessity for it arose—and by the absence of sufficient power to enforce controls of pricing and manufacturing priorities.

In May of that same year Wilson established a food control program under Herbert Hoover (1874–1964), who had directed the Belgian Relief Commission and was experienced in such matters. Three months later he set up the Food Administration (authorized by the Lever Act) and gave Hoover power to control prices and thus to stimulate production, especially of wheat and meat. More than anything else, Hoover's efforts brought the fact of war into American homes. Millions soon were grappling with "Wheatless Mondays" and "Meatless Tuesdays," sugarless candy, and strange slabs of whale and shark flesh; but it all seemed to work, and by 1918 the United States was exporting three times as much wheat, meat, and sugar as it normally did.

Yet chaos continued in other areas, and in April 1918 Wilson prepared the Overman Act. Sponsored by Senator Lee Overman of North Carolina, it gave the President almost complete authority to reorganize and administer all government agencies.

The war years also witnessed the formation of a national network of trade associations, both public and private. In April 1918 Wilson created the National War Labor Board (WLB). Businessmen tolerated the increasing unionization of industry as a necessary step toward efficient negotiation and cooperation between management and labor.

Government, business, labor, and even universities and private law firms were becoming increasingly bureaucratic, and bureaucracy seemed to define the national idea of efficiency. Government usually adopted an attitude of "benevolent neutrality" toward business mergers, particularly in industries beset by shortages.

Sometimes, however, government acted directly. McAdoo's control of railroads and shipbuilding programs of the Emergency Fleet Corporation, for example, created such close partnerships between business and government that they paved the way for the lenient (and sometimes corrupt) attitudes of government towards business influence in the 1920s. They also created a common language and common assumptions that any bureaucrat, whether paid by private or government funds, could understand and appreciate. This apparatus could, however, be used in different ways, depending on the ideology of the moment. Thus, when the New Deal came to power in the 1930s, Franklin D. Roosevelt utilized the same structure to reverse relations between government and business that had existed in the 1920s. Whether business ruled government or government ruled business, this interaction was made possible by government agencies devised during the war years.

Wilson and the Wartime Presidency

In order to conduct the war President Wilson had to increase his own powers, which caused him to behave with increasing arrogance and rigidity both at home and in his relations abroad. He established what has been referred to as a "constitutional dictatorship." Nevertheless, Wilson saw to it that Congress "sanctioned" every unusual step he felt he had to take.

But many deemed Wilson's acquisition of presidential authority dangerous. To mobilize public opinion in his favor Wilson created the Committee on Public Information. Administrated by George Creel, the CPI convinced newspapers to accept censorship and then used them to launch an enormous propaganda campaign. Depicting the United States as a hero fighting to save democracy from Huns who committed atrocities against innocent civilians, the campaign further argued that work stoppages were unpatriotic and that pacifists were enemy sympathizers.

Although Congress passed sedition acts that helped exacerbate the situation, it also tried to oppose Wilson's accumulation of authority. Both Republicans and Democrats attempted to set up a Joint Committee on the Conduct of the War. Though their efforts failed, the Senate Military Affairs Committee did succeed in forcing Wilson to appoint Charles Evans Hughes (1862–1948) to investigate activities in the War Department.

Political activity was not altogether "adjourned," even if Wilson remained in firm control. The President urged that factional and party politics be put aside for the duration of the war, but he was nevertheless attacked, if indirectly, through the 1918 election. In October he asked Americans to endorse his policies by voting for a Democratic Congress, noting that a Republican victory would be a repudiation of his leadership.

The Republicans were determined to increase their strength in Congress and prevent the Democrats from taking all the credit for an American victory in Europe. And their opponents were hurting their own political cause. Although government restraints on profiteering were mild enough to allow reasonably generous profit margins in most industries, Southern Democrats lobbied to exempt cotton from all price controls, and Wilson acquiesced to their pleas in order to win support for his war measures. At the same time prices for wheat, set and enforced by the federal government, caused unrest. To remedy this situation Congress agreed to increase the price of wheat from $2.20 a bushel to $2.50. But half the harvest had been promised to the Allies and passage of the bill would cost the British another $100 million for food imports. On the advice of his Cabinet, Wilson vetoed the bill.

Other issues such as the peace negotiations also affected the 1918 election. As Allied victories on the western front increased, the Republicans clamored for unconditional surrender as the only way to end the war, claiming anything less would be a compromise, or at best an inconclusive peace. Supporters of prohibition and the women's suffrage movement wanted quick realization of their demands. (Prohibitionists argued that the production of alcohol was wasting precious food supplies, while suffragists insisted that women's role in war work entitled them to the vote.) Wilson's reluctance to support the Eighteenth Amendment alienated powerful members of the Anti-Saloon League. But the Democrats' prejudices against suffrage and their refusal even to consider the issue or to give in to the demands of expediency proved still more damaging. In contrast, the Republican caucus in the Senate moved to adopt the Nineteenth Amendment and grant women the right to vote. But the Democrats, led by southern Senators, defeated the bill. This persistent intransigence deprived the Democratic campaign of whatever merit it might otherwise have had in the eyes of many voters, particularly those in more Progressive regions of the East and West.

The overwhelming Republican victory in 1918 can, therefore, be ascribed to two forces: Democratic ineptitude and the reassertion of the "normal" Republican majority in the Congress. Wilson refused to believe polls that warned of impending defeat, stubbornly insisting that most Americans shared his concern for world affairs. His mistaken view may, of course, have altered the course of recent history to a marked degree, although one should not read too much into the Republican victory of 1918. They were, after all, the majority party. Wilson had won by a hair in 1912 and again in 1916, and the war in Europe had forced him and his party to implement coercive and often unpopular programs.

Yet the war itself was quite popular—at least the parades, patriotic fervor, and the hubbub of activity created—and it also offered an outlet for the messianic zeal of the Progressive era. On one hand it gave Americans a sense of national unity—part propaganda, part real. And World War I ushered in a new kind of ideology that obscured class, party, and race conflicts with what contemporary writers and orators called "100 percent Americanism."

These "100 percenters" equated loyalty with conformity with *their* views of what Americanism was. Never before had public opinion been so thoroughly marshalled behind such an idea. Conformity meant giving service to America and performing duties for the cause. Questioning the rightness of this notion was unpatriotic. The press held contests to find the best statement of what an American citizen's duties were, and the winner, "The American Creed," soon became part of every school child's morning ritual—an incessant reminder that patriotism meant service to country.

Americans flocked to serve the war effort. Bond drives and pledge signings were widespread activities. Voluntary organizations appeared almost overnight. But for some mere service was not enough. What was required was a new attitude toward government, one demanding obedience as the expression of "right thinking." The 100 percenters perceived no conflict between this hysterical demand for conformity and the traditional freedom of the individual. When thwarted or questioned, the 100 percenters turned to government enforcement of their ideas.

The Espionage Act of 1917 provided for a "fine of not more than $10,000 or imprisonment for not more than twenty years" for anyone engaging in espionage, sabotage, or obstruction of the war effort or attempting to "cause insubordination, mutiny, or refusal of duty." The Sedition Act of 1918 made it a crime to "utter, print, write, or publish any disloyal, profane, scurrilous, or abusive language" about the government, the Constitution, the flag, or the uniform of the army and navy. The Supreme Court upheld the Espionage Act in *Schenck* v. *United States* (1919), a case involving the conviction of a man who had mailed circulars to draftees urging them to refuse to report for induction. A unanimous Court concurred with Justice Oliver Wendell Holmes (1841–1935) that the Espionage Act did not violate the First Amendment since such action during wartime constituted "a clear and present danger that . . . will bring about the substantive evils that Congress has a right to protect." Also in that same year the Supreme Court upheld the conviction of Socialist leader Eugene V. Debs for encouraging an audience "to resist militarism where ever found."

These laws and court decisions did not satisfy superpatriots who mounted campaigns against anyone or anything that seemed unpatriotic. The immediate target of these campaigns was German-Americans. Any person or business with a German name was suspect. Rumors began circulating: German-Americans in the Red Cross

TELL THAT TO THE MARINES!
HUNS KILL WOMEN AND CHILDREN!
JAMES MONTGOMERY FLAGG

New York Public Library, Picture Collection.

Propaganda efforts by the Committee on Public Information and such posters as the one above helped to whip up patriotic fervor against the Germans, stimulate enlistments, and bring success for bond drives and conservation of materials and foods.

Randolph S. Bourne Papers, Rare Book and Manuscript Library, Columbia University Libraries.

Randolph Bourne

(1886–1918)

Randolph Bourne was born into a fairly well-to-do middle class family in Bloomfield, New Jersey, in 1886. Facially disfigured from birth and a victim of spinal tuberculosis, which left him a dwarf and hunchback for life, Bourne spent a lonely adolescence. But a precocious intelligence compensated for his physical disabilities. When his family suffered a financial setback, Bourne had to delay entering college for a time, but by 1909 he had saved enough money to enroll at Columbia. The four years at Columbia exposed him to the ideas of John Dewey, Charles Beard, and other prominent intellectuals; he soon embraced socialism and radicalism. Bourne gained notoriety as a critic of Columbia's intellectual atmosphere, publishing a series of essays in the *Atlantic Monthly* on the role of youth in shaping the renascence of American civilization (published in 1913 as *Youth and Life*). He took an M.A. in Sociology at Columbia in 1913, then went to Europe on a fellowship.

When he returned from Europe in 1914, Bourne joined the staff of *The New Republic,* founded by leading Progressives Croly, Weyl, and Lippmann. He chafed under his assignment (education editor and book reviewer), but had a forum to air his political views. He broke from the editorial policy of *The New Republic* over the question of American participation in World War I and became the single most important intellectual to oppose American entry into the war. (His old mentor, Dewey, wanted to use the war as a socially useful instrument; the *New Republic,* after some hesitation, also gave its approval.) Bourne abhorred war and scoffed at the intellectuals who supported it; he asked Dewey, "If the war is too strong for you to prevent, how is it going to be weak enough for you to control and mold to your liberal purposes?"

Bourne began publishing antiwar essays in June 1917, most of them appearing in the pacifist journal, *Seven Arts.* After *Seven Arts* folded, Bourne had no literary forum. He died of influenza in December 1918, and became a kind of cultural hero for later disaffected intellectuals. ■

were putting ground glass in bandages, or spreading influenza germs, or poisoning wells and water reservoirs. And many people believed these unsubstantiated rumors. A ridiculous and tragic drive to stamp out German culture in America began. German music was banned. The teaching of German in public schools was prohibited. Sauerkraut was renamed "liberty cabbage" and German measles became "patriotic measles." These seemingly harmless measures led to mob action neither harmless nor uncommon. German book stores were looted. Public beatings began to occur with alarming frequency, as well as tar-and-feather parties that ended in lynchings. (In southern Illinois a mob of miners lynched a German alien in the same bloody fashion of vigilantes who had killed Italians and blacks before the war).

Wilson invoked the Alien Enemies Act of 1798, which gave him arbitrary control over all unnaturalized subjects of a hostile power in wartime. Only a fraction of the half-million German aliens living in the United States were interned, most of them ending in camps in Georgia, North Carolina, and Utah. By the end of 1918, 6,300 were in U.S. internment centers (there were 45,000 Germans in British prison camps), and the government was rigorously enforcing its Espionage and Sedition acts. Meanwhile, with the unofficial blessing of the Justice Department, secret societies of volunteer spy hunters sprang up across the country.

Despite these witch hunts and punishments for criticizing the government or dissenting against the war, pacifists such as Jane Addams, Robert La Follette, and various Socialist party members remained firm in their antiwar stance. Other Progressives, however, finally joined the patriotic crusade. And *The New Republic,* the leading Progressive magazine, gradually came to favor American participation in the war.

Women and Blacks

By attaching themselves to the war effort, women, blacks, and prohibitionists hoped to make substantial gains. Prohibitionists had first argued against the immorality of drinking; now they emphasized the need to conserve grains and the fact that many liquor interests, especially the beer industry, were owned or operated by German-Americans. They won their cause and prohibition became a legal fact of life. But their victory over drink never really was complete.

Women consolidated earlier gains and finally achieved suffrage. Carrie Chapman Catt, president of the huge National American Women Suffrage Association (NAWSA) and a leading feminist, said that "The greatest thing that came out of the war was the emancipation of women, for which no man fought. War subjected women and war liberated them." It was Catt who had masterminded the suffrage victory, though she opposed the war on grounds of pacifism and because she felt that it would deflect the women's movement from its true course.

A group of radical suffragettes, known first as the Congressional Union and later as the Women's Party and led by Alice Paul, continued to demand that Congress approve a suffrage amendment to the Constitution. In 1917 they organized a march in Washington, D.C. which was attacked by angry onlookers. In another public protest the Paul group burned a copy of Wilson's Fourteen Points speech. There were other incidents that resulted in the arrest of many of the women protesters. Following the example of English radical suffragettes, many of the protesters when arrested went on hunger strikes that resulted in brutal forced feeding. Because of the unfavorable publicity and allegations of disloyalty, NAWSA and Catt, rather than aiding Alice Paul and her group, actually tried to avoid any connection with the radicals.

On June 4, 1919, Congress finally approved the Nineteenth Amendment calling for women's suffrage. The fight for ratification proceeded slowly as anti-suffragists claimed that the suffrage movement was radical, inspired on the one hand by Russian Bolshevism and on the other by German influences. Everett Wheeler (1840–1925), a lifelong New Yorker and chairman of the Association Opposed to Woman Suffrage, issued a platform that began, "Compelling another State to adopt your own ideals is the essence of German Kulture which is bringing woe to the world. It would be particularly unjust to impose it upon the Southern states involving, as it would, the votes of negro women." Despite these tactics and allegations, women's suffrage finally was won in the summer of 1920 when West Virginia and Tennessee—the last two states needed for ratification—approved the Amendment after long and bitter battles in the state legislatures.

Many women involved in war work came into increasingly frequent contact with feminists and feminist ideas, and these encounters sometimes produced unexpected results. In the spring of 1917 it appeared that a serious shortage of farm labor was imminent owing to the

Courtesy League of Women Voters.

By assisting in the war effort, putting pressure on politicians, and demonstrating for their cause, woman suffragists finally achieved success in 1920. In this parade in New York City, Carrie Chapman Catt (center) and Dr. Anna Howard Shaw (in academic robes) led the way.

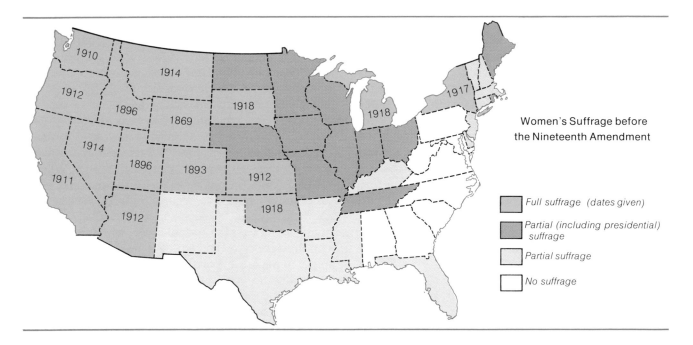

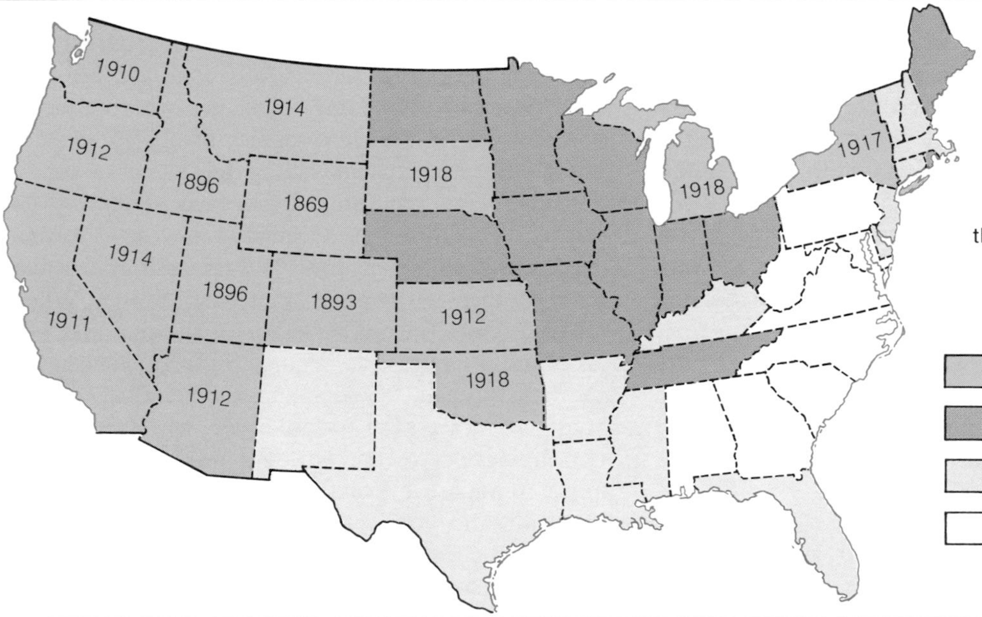

Women's Suffrage before the Nineteenth Amendment

transfer of working men to the war. To meet this crisis, the Woman's Land Army of America, a group of volunteers in agricultural service, appeared in New York. The mayor of New York City created a Committee on Women in Agriculture and appointed a supervisor. College women and those in seasonal trades were recruited, housed collectively and employed on nearby farms. Soon forty states had created similar "Liberty Farms."

In business and in the professions women also gained status, taking every opportunity to prove their equality to men. Nearly one-fifth of the nation's 66,000 nurses volunteered for army duty. At the urgent behest of the federal government, women entered civil service, thus relieving men for warwork. The Women's Lawyers' As-

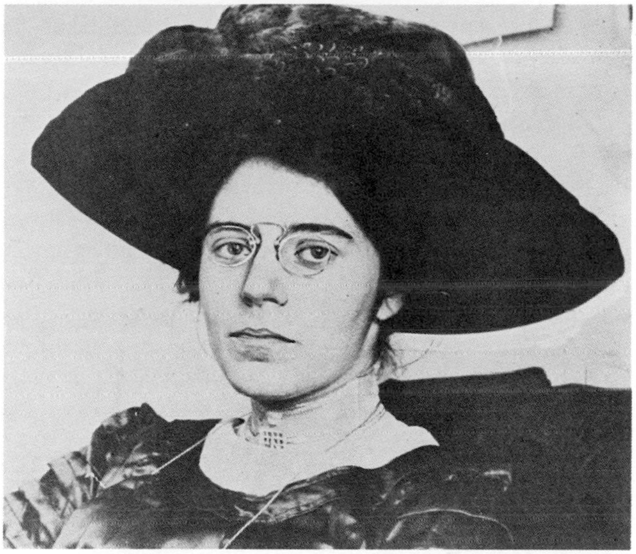

Brown Brothers.

Alice Paul
(1885–1977)

Born into a Quaker household in Morristown, New Jersey, in 1885, Alice Paul graduated from Swarthmore in 1905 and earned a doctorate at the University of Pennsylvania in 1912. From 1907 to 1910 she studied in England, where she took part in the militant suffrage movement and went to jail three times while she was there. A member of the National American Woman Suffrage Association, she broke in 1913 with Carrie Chapman Catt, head of that group, and formed the more militant Congressional Union for Woman Suffrage (later the National Woman's Party). In March of that same year, she led a suffrage march in Washington which coincided with Wilson's inauguration. In contrast to Catt's NAWSA, Paul's organization engaged in direct political action in an attempt to gain support for suffrage proposals and relied more heavily upon publicity to get attention.

In the 1920s Paul's NWP was the main proponent of specifically feminist goals such as the Equal Rights Amendment (ERA). Consequently that group came into frequent conflict with the "social feminists," typified by the League of Women Voters (virtual successors to the NAWSA). During that decade she earned three law degrees at American University and ran the NWP with an iron hand, evoking strong support and admiration from some while alienating others. During the 1930s she lobbied in Geneva for international recognition of ERA.

In 1941 Alice Paul noted sarcastically that the mounting world crisis had excluded women. They had, she emphasized, no voice at Versailles or at any deliberations since that time. By 1944, ERA had developed political clout and in July 1946 by a simple majority (38–35) won the approval of the U.S. Senate; however, Alice Paul would have to wait two more decades before this measure gained sufficient support in Congress (a two-thirds vote) to be put to the states as a proposed Amendment to the Constitution. ■

---

sociation urged its members to take the unique opportunity created by the war to serve their country on various boards and committees that needed legal advice. Women physicians tried to enlist in the Army Medical Corps but were rejected. Nevertheless, the Council of National Defense created a Volunteer Medical Corps in January 1918, after the American Medical Association adopted a resolution supporting equality for women in the Army Medical Corps. Although women eagerly filled the new corps, they were never given the equality of rank that they demanded and deserved. When Congress voted to give military rank to nurses but not to women physicians, Dr. Anna Howard Shaw (1847–1919), head of the Women's Committee of the Council of National Defense, remarked that "Women doctors should stand together and offer their services exactly as men offer theirs, and refuse to accept any other position. But the difficulty is that women are so willing to be door mats that they fail to stand together."

Dr. Shaw spoke from experience since she knew that the Women's Committee had only been a sop to emancipated women demanding a responsible share of the war effort. She won the post because she was well-known and used it to nag, cajole, and pressure government officials to improve the status of women. The committee did manage to coordinate a variety of volunteer activities and to promote food conservation. The organization's most lasting contribution was a nationwide drive in conjunction with the Federal Children's Bureau to provide physical examinations for five million babies.

Women in industry made great strides. Before the war the three million women in manufacturing and trades had been almost exclusively unskilled workers. Now they became typesetters, linotype operators, blacksmiths, mechanics, bricklayers, telegraphers, streetcar operators, lathe operators, and more. During the crisis, the War Labor Board protected them from exploitation. With peace, however, came displacement and disillusionment. The American Federation of Labor made little effort to organize and help women. Instead, unions often barred women from membership. As men returned home, the women who had replaced them and done their work were dismissed as "scab" labor—despite their willingness to join the unions that barred them.

Blacks, too, benefited temporarily. Urged by their leaders to close ranks and enlist wholeheartedly in the cause, blacks did so, hoping that Wilson's crusade for democracy would work at home. Although blacks were discouraged from volunteering for military service there were, proportionately, more blacks drafted than whites (32 percent of all blacks who were registered, 27 percent of all whites). Ultimately one black ROTC camp was established and over 1,200 black officers won commissions. But black soldiers usually were used in "support" regiments to do jobs that required labor and service; only two divisions actually were in combat, and they received the Croix de Guerre. Despite this partial acceptance, conflicts occurred, especially in training camps. The worst incident was at Houston, Texas, where twelve civilians were killed in September 1917. As a result, thirteen black soldiers were sentenced to death and executed, and another fourteen soldiers were imprisoned for life.

The response to war obviously was a mixed bag of sacrifice and selfishness, and even those who sacrificed often did so for selfish reasons. Both groups and individuals used this crisis to push toward or to achieve specific goals, a not-too-surprising development. More significant than this general reaction, perhaps, was the sense of frustration and unfulfillment that became widespread as the excitement of battle and the euphoria of victory receded into the distance. Yet despite these disturbing developments which fostered an era of isolation and apathy, World War I left a positive legacy as well. It gave a definite boost to numerous industries, among them autos, aircraft, and chemicals, created a greatly enhanced and more capable bureaucracy at all levels of government,

National Archives.

American women played many important roles in the war effort, including taking the place of men in heavy industrial jobs.

and above all else, taught Americans how to mobilize and organize in times of emergency. These lessons in organization would be put to good use during the Depression of the 1930s and when war returned once more in 1941.

The Aftermath of War

Americans received a number of jarring postwar shocks, partly because promises made to them could not be kept and partly because of demobilization and the readjustment to peacetime life. Labor experienced discontent when wartime contracts were cancelled and jobs eliminated. Just as the government had been unprepared to mobilize for war, it had no plans for demobilization now that the conflict was over. Soldiers were hastily discharged to take them off government payrolls. War industries closed and the economic controls established during the war disappeared.

Discontents and Disturbances

Industry could not make the switch to peacetime production smoothly. And consumers with savings from wartime jobs began pouring money back into the economy. Within one year the cost of living increased 33 percent. By 1919 inflation had struck and unemployment was high. A year later the nation faced a recession. Ultimately there were 30,000 bankruptcies, nearly 500,000 farm foreclosures, and over five million people out of work.

The harmony that labor and management experienced during the war years vanished. Unions now demanded recognition and wanted increased wages to combat inflation. Management fought to reestablish the open shop, using propaganda techniques to make people believe that unionization was a radical movement inspired by foreign influences. Textile and clothing workers, as well as telegraph and telephone operators, staged successful strikes. But their success inspired a rash of unrest that tried the patience of both the federal government and the American public.

One strike against the steel industry lasted four months in 1919 and proved a severe setback to the labor movement. Management rejected union demands to reduce the twelve-hour workday. The steel industry responded with violence, importing thousands of strikebreakers, and gained the help of state and federal troops. The strike failed. At the same time coal miners under the new leadership of John L. Lewis (1880–1969) struck with somewhat more success.

An especially notorious strike of the period occurred in Boston in August 1919. Denied a raise in wages from prewar levels, Boston police organized under a charter from the AFL and threatened to strike. The mayor and a

U.P.I.

Even policemen became "radicalized" by union sentiment in 1919. In Boston, when the Police Commissioner forbade his men to join an AFL affiliate, they voted overwhelmingly to strike. A militiaman directs traffic in this photo.

citizen's committee heard their grievances, recommending that most requests be granted. But the police commissioner was an avowed enemy of organized labor. He rejected these suggestions and fired nineteen of the leaders. On September 9 the policemen struck, leaving Boston at the mercy of looters and roaming gangs. Middle class groups across the nation registered shock and fear. When the city finally neared the point of anarchy, Massachusetts governor Calvin Coolidge (1872–1933) called in the National Guard. The strike was broken and many policemen fired. To labor leader Samuel Gompers's pleas that these men be reinstated, Coolidge replied, "There is no right to strike against the public safety by anybody, anywhere, any time."

Seattle's Central Labor Council called perhaps the most violent strike of the period, a general walkout in support of striking shipyard workers. This was an extreme step and Mayor Ole Hanson was determined to suppress it. Claiming Bolshevist agitation caused the unrest, Hanson put down the strike with army troops.

Brown Brothers.

In 1919 and 1920, the American public was gripped by fear of "bolshevists." Such terrorist acts as this bombing at Wall and Broad Streets in New York only heightened public hysteria and produced repression of all "suspicious" groups and persons.

Library of Congress.

A. Mitchell Palmer
(1872–1936)

A. Mitchell Palmer was born in 1872 in Moosehead, Pennsylvania, the son of devout Quaker parents. He graduated summa cum laude from Swarthmore in 1891 and was admitted to the Pennsylvania bar in 1893. Elected to Congress as a "reform" Democrat in 1908 and reelected in 1910 and 1912, he received considerable attention as a leading Progressive legislator. He co-sponsored the child labor restriction bill. Offered the post of Secretary of War in 1913 because of his role in keeping the Pennsylvania delegation behind Wilson at the 1912 convention, Palmer declined because of his Quaker beliefs. After running unsuccessfully for the Senate in 1914 (against Republican Boies Penrose), he retired to private life.

In October 1917, Palmer became Alien Properties Custodian in the Wilson administration, a position that embroiled him in controversies and gave him great power. In March 1919, Wilson appointed Palmer Attorney General. In this capacity, Palmer fought labor unrest by issuing an injunction against John L. Lewis and striking coal miners (1919), but also employed the antitrust laws against the price-fixing of the Beef Trust. He gained most publicity, however, for his initiation of raids (Palmer Raids) on private homes and offices of allegedly radical (mostly alien and immigrant) groups and individuals, bringing about massive deportations of aliens. Possibly political ambition fueled this crusade, as Palmer was a leading contender for the 1920 Democratic nomination (at least until the Red Scare fizzled in May 1920). Failing to get the nomination, he retired to private law practice. He died in 1936. ■

Whether or not Hanson's accusations were true, his charge of Bolshevism was typical of America's growing hysterical response to labor unrest.

The Red Scare

As public fears of foreign influences grew, all forms of radicalism came under suspicion. Political opportunists launched a "Red Scare." There was some, if little, real cause for concern. Communism and socialism were spreading in Europe as a result of the success of the Russian Revolution in 1917, and the new Soviet leaders had announced to the world at the Third International in March 1919 that Communism was to be an agent for world revolution. But in the United States there was little organized communist activity. The American Communist Labor Party had only 20,000 members and the

Communist Party of America (led by John Reed, a former Harvard student and journalist who had witnessed the Russian Revolution and written about it) claimed only 30,000–60,000 members. And the Socialist party, torn by debilitating inner conflicts, had only 40,000 adherents. So the total membership of all three organizations constituted less than one-half of one percent of the American population at the time. But scare headlines persisted, as well as propaganda generated by conservative business interests and opportunist politicians. Public fear of Red plots increased. When sporadic anarchist-initiated bombings occurred in April and June of 1919, the public nearly panicked.

In such a mood the nation welcomed the witch hunts of Attorney General A. Mitchell Palmer. Palmer used Justice Department employees to violate the civil liberties of thousands of immigrants by conducting raids on radical organizations and terrorizing the immigrant press. In a nationwide raid conducted on New Year's Day 1920, 6,000 people, many of whom were not Communists, were seized without warrants in their homes, herded into prisons, beaten, and held without counsel. Hoping to secure the Democratic presidential nomination, Palmer continued to uncover Red plots, although his raids revealed no corroborating evidence. His "reign of terror" lasted until May 1920, when his predictions of doom finally proved ludicrous and the hysteria they had engendered fizzled out.

But few Americans spoke out while Palmer was committing his outrages, although Assistant Secretary of Labor Louis Post did and helped to end both the raids and the scare. In reality the scare was a fabrication from beginning to end. There was no concrete Communist threat to America. Coming to its senses, the American press returned its attention to real concerns and the Red Scare became a thing of the past.

The Red Scare left scars, perhaps the ugliest of which was a strong nativist attitude and a lingering suspicion of all immigrants. Organizations such as the Ku Klux Klan espoused hatred not only of foreigners but of Catholics and Jews as well, and primarily of blacks. Congress passed restrictive quotas, effectively keeping out immigrants from central and south Europe and immigrants from Asian countries. In 1921 Italian-Americans Nicola Sacco and Bartolomeo Vanzetti, admitted anarchists, were tried for robbery and murder in Boston. Although there was no conclusive evidence against them, they were convicted. For six years artists and writers and liberal politicians protested that Sacco and Vanzetti were being punished for their political beliefs and begged (in vain) that a new trial be held. Despite these efforts the pair was executed in 1927.

Aliens and immigrants were not the only ones who experienced postwar violence. Again and again blacks encountered antagonism in their competition for jobs. Having migrated to northern cities during the war years in search of work and a freer life, unemployed blacks were now suddenly caught in an outbreak of race riots. The worst of these occurred in Chicago in the summer of 1919. Mobs of angry whites rampaged through ghetto areas for thirteen days, ultimately killing thirty-eight blacks.

Library of Congress.

Vanzetti's letter to his son — a personal testimony, portrayed by Ben Shahn.

© Chicago Tribune, 1976.

During the "red summer" of 1919, so labeled because of the bloody racial conflicts that occurred in those months, whites are seen driving out blacks by stoning their homes. The young boys running toward the corner spotted an unlucky black and stoned him.

More and more blacks returned from the army only to find the same inequities they had known before the war. Under the leadership of W. E. B. DuBois, the National Association for the Advancement of Colored People (NAACP) became increasingly militant in demanding long-denied rights for blacks. The response of white supremacists was terrorism. In 1919 alone Southern lynch mobs claimed seventy black lives (ten of them war veterans). Before the end of the year some twenty-five race riots resulted in death, injury, and widespread property damage. Whites blamed foreign influences for this unrest, and most blacks discovered the gains of the war years were illusory.

The Political Backlash

Repudiated in the 1918 election and beset by domestic social problems, Wilson faced the peace negotiations with uncertain political support. As early as 1916 the President advocated a League of Nations as a bulwark against future wars. To see this goal fulfilled, Wilson realized that the Allied leaders at Versailles must somehow avoid the extremist demands that the French were advocating. On the other hand, it was not unusual that leaders whose peoples had suffered should demand that Germany pay for its aggressions. The dilemma that Wilson faced was how to reconcile these divergent aims.

Wilson himself claimed that only a "peace without victory," would endure, one that included a reconciliation based on disarmament, the self-determination of minorities, and open diplomacy. What was needed to ensure such a peace was an international organization, one that would also control Germany. In addition, there was a rising tide of radicalism among the working classes, and this radicalism had to be dealt with.

Wilson favored a plan that would try to raise the general standards of the working classes on a worldwide basis. So he took AFL leader Samuel Gompers with him to the conference table. A strong antisocialist, Gompers was prepared to represent labor and to help Wilson avoid the demands of European socialists and radicals.

In January 1918 Wilson had announced his program for peace, which he called the Fourteen Points. Five of these "points" were broadly international: the end of secret pacts in favor of open diplomacy, freedom of the seas, disarmament, free trade among nations, and a fair method of responding to the claims of colonial peoples. Eight other points dealt with Europe and the issue of self-determination. These included German evacuation of Russian territory, return of Alsace-Lorraine to France, reestablishment of Belgian autonomy, creation of an independent Poland, and national autonomy for the peoples of the Austro-Hungarian Empire and of European Turkey. The fourteenth point called for the creation of a League of Nations.

Despite support from liberals in the United States and Great Britain, Wilson's objectives encountered strong opposition. Some points conflicted with the ambitions of the Allies. Among the Americans, there were some who resisted the idea of internationalism of any sort; to them protective tariffs remained the firmest means of assuring American economic superiority.

National Archives.

In 1919, President Wilson threw all his energies into securing a "just peace," spending months in Europe negotiating with leaders from the other victorious powers and making triumphant public appearances, such as the one in France pictured above.

By the time Wilson arrived in Europe, his political foes at home were cementing a solid opposition to his peace plans. (He also failed to take any important Republican with him to the conference table.) At Versailles Wilson bargained away several idealistic treaty provisions in order to insure that a League of Nations would be included in the final settlement. Although he had not expected a perfect peace, Wilson's views received much less support than he had hoped for. (Objections to Wilson's plan came primarily from Count Nobuaki Makino of Japan, Vittorio Orlando of Italy, Georges Clemenceau of France, and David Lloyd George of Britain.) The final treaty's fifteen parts and 440 articles were very punitive towards Germany, stripping that nation of its colonial possessions, slashing its army and navy, exacting huge reparations, and providing for long-term occupation by the victors and trials for "war crimes" committed by some of the defeated leaders. This was hardly what Wilson wanted, but he understood and accepted the Allied position. Moreover, his Fourteen Points had been followed as closely as political expediency permitted. Wilson had his League. Perhaps issues that Versailles could not handle could be resolved by the League at some future date. All Wilson had to do now was to convince at least two-thirds of the U.S. Senate to accept his League.

The struggle for ratification marked the final blow to Wilson's career. Twice he tried to win political opponents over to the League—first on a trip home from Versailles in March 1919 and then again in July. Both attempts failed. Although the idea of the League was popular among millions of Americans, only the Senate could ratify it. And forty-nine out of the ninety-six members of the Senate were Republicans. Of this majority only fourteen Senators, so-called "Irreconcilables," were unalterably opposed to the treaty and to the League. A coalition of liberal Republicans and Democrats, most of whom supported Wilson, could give the President the approval he so desperately sought. But the coalition felt that it should wait for instructions from Wilson about what to do. In return for cooperation, the Republicans in the coalition wanted the treaty to be subject to their party's amendments, under the leadership of Senator Lodge. Wilson denounced these demands as immoral and refused to heed his advisers—all of whom urged him to accept some form of compromise. Stubborn, sure he was right, he decided to go to the people.

In September 1919 Wilson embarked on an 8,000-mile trip across America. Although audiences at nearly forty stops greeted him warmly, Senate opposition remained firm. Wilson began suffering from severe headaches and had to cancel the rest of the trip. Back in Washington he was too weary to work. On October 2 a cerebral hemorrhage disabled him, and for the next six weeks his wife was the virtual President.

Lodge and his followers presented an amended treaty to the Senate in November. Wilson ordered his supporters to reject it and the bill failed. But the treaty was not yet a dead issue. Moderates in both parties, as well as millions of Americans, hoped that it would ultimately be ratified. Wilson, however, never changed his stance. The treaty was either to be adopted without amendment or to be rejected altogether. On March 19, 1920, a coalition of the fourteen "Irreconcilables" and Wilson's own supporters (mostly Southern Democrats) defeated the treaty for the last time. (In 1921 by a simple two-nation agreement the United States ended its formal state of hostility with Germany.)

Wilson vowed that the next presidential election would hinge on the treaty issue and called on Americans for a "great and solemn referendum" on the League as part of the election. Despite his ruined health he considered running again. Wilson's equivocation on the issue of nomination ruled out the candidacy of his son-in-law, William Gibbs McAdoo, who was among the most qualified of the candidates in any party. The Democratic nomination went to Ohio's governor James M. Cox, who supported the League and opposed prohibition. His running mate was a young Hudson River squire named Franklin Delano Roosevelt.

But other national problems overshadowed the issue of the League, and Wilson's own rigid and often offensive conduct did little to help his cause. As a result popular interest waned. Wilson had, in effect, played into the hands of his enemies, just as Senator Lodge had hoped he would. The question of the League never again came up for a vote in the Senate.

It is difficult to say just how important this decision was. The United States cooperated actively with many League agencies in the years that followed. Yet one can mount an argument that the absence of a U.S. voice in official deliberations contributed in some measure to the problems that led to World War II. However, such a thesis benefits greatly from hindsight. Even if the U.S. had joined the League, that is no guarantee that its spokesmen would have tried to alter policies and programs of the interwar period or, if they tried, would have been any more successful than their counterparts who met each year at Geneva to wrestle with international dilemmas.

Culver Pictures.

In the unsuccessful battle for ratification of the Treaty of Versailles and League of Nations Charter, Wilson's most formidable foe was Republican Senator Henry Cabot Lodge, Chairman of the Foreign Relations Committee.

The "New Era"

The Republican congressional victory in 1918, the general reaction to wartime controls instituted by a Democratic administration and to its inept handling of the conversion to peace, the drying up of the waters of Progressivism—all these factors ushered in a dozen years of Republican dominance. This usually meant conservative, probusiness policies; but, since the Republicans won handily in 1924 and 1928, apparently that was precisely what the voters wanted.

Republican Rule

To run against the Cox-Roosevelt ticket, the Republicans chose a handsome, gregarious, one-term senator from Ohio, Warren G. Harding (1865–1923). By no means inexperienced, Harding had worked his way to prominence in the rough world of Ohio politics, gaining special

Library of Congress.

Warren Harding and his wife Florence.

repute for his oratorical skills. At the 1912 Republican convention, Taft had personally selected Harding to place his name in nomination, and four years later Harding had served as that body's keynote speaker. His running mate was dour, but witty Calvin Coolidge, the Massachusetts governor who had crushed the Boston police strike.

As a campaigner, using the "front-porch" approach of McKinley, Harding exhibited several very attractive attributes. He was modest and spoke well, even if he did not always address the issues head on or say much that was worth remembering. Also his Marion, Ohio, background, his publishing-political career, his patriotism ("Stabilize America first, prosper America first, think of America first, exalt America first!") was a refreshingly pleasant change from the lectures of the professorial Wilson and the scare tactics of his Attorney General. His famous call for "normalcy" could be interpreted many ways—an emphasis upon traditional Republican values, a return to pre-Wilsonian programs, or perhaps even a revival of some of the Progressive ideas of Teddy Roosevelt. Most important of all, however, Warren G. Harding comported well with the mood of America in November 1920—so well that he got a smashing 61 percent of the popular vote. The Republican landslide also produced huge majorities in Congress (22 seats in the Senate and 167 in the House).

Harding created a favorable impression by assuming office without ostentation; but once there, his troubles began, and it soon became increasingly obvious that the President was a weak man incapable of true leadership. He chose a Cabinet that included some men with brilliant minds and others with questionable character, appointed very inept men to high positions, and, as Washington tongues wagged, spent much too much time playing golf and poker with his pals, and drinking liquor in an age when it was banned.

In this instance, as would be true a half-century later, the American people were not served well; by an overwhelming margin they had endorsed a national leadership that was seriously flawed. In the nineteenth century perhaps the nation could muddle along, but the complexities of the twentieth century, even in Harding's day, made the situation difficult.

The burden of governing fell heavily upon the shoulders of some of President Harding's more astute associates such as Coolidge, Secretary of Commerce Hoover, and the new multimillionaire Secretary of the Treasury, Andrew Mellon. Although outwardly this administration and the two that followed exhibited the firm imprint of Mark Hanna-William McKinley Republicanism, Progressive thought was never entirely absent. Hoover, for example, was from the Theodore Roosevelt camp and virtually all Republicans paid at least lipservice to the Progressive-inspired administrative "revolution" in the federal bureaucracy that had reached its culmination during the war years.

Following closely the Republican campaign platform, the new administration adhered to a high protective tariff and a policy of tax reductions (of benefit mostly to the wealthy). Mellon, one of Harding's most influential advisors and a man whose attitudes suited party interests perfectly, believed that government was "just a business," to be run on profit-motive principles. He continually advocated slashing the federal budget to achieve a reduction in taxes, particularly taxes on business profits. His view was that such taxes discouraged corporate investment and new production which, in turn, created unemployment. Harding (and later Coolidge) was also committed to economy in government. Paradoxically, despite this commitment, federal spending increased sharply during Harding's presidency and the bureaucracy expanded.

Harding was aware of his own shortcomings (a commendable attribute perhaps) and relied heavily on key Cabinet members. Besides Mellon, Harding leaned on Secretary of State Charles Evans Hughes. Hoover, Hughes, and Mellon put their stamp on the Republican "normalcy" program by establishing a national budget system, creating new farm credit legislation, and aiding the building of highways; yet in the main "normalcy" turned out to be a policy that—it should again be stressed—enjoyed the approval of most voters.

The Harding Scandals

If Harding had Mellon, Hughes, and Hoover to instruct him, he also had less suitable mentors—the hacks and dishonest men in his Cabinet. And the results were some of the most notorious government scandals in American history. Charles Forbes, head of the Veterans Bureau, pocketed a large share of the $250 million departmental budget allocated for hospitals and supplies. Upon discovering Forbes's misdeed early in 1923, Harding allowed him to resign. (Ultimately Forbes was exposed, tried, found guilty, and sent to prison.) This affair demonstrates yet another flaw in the President's character. He was much too kind and found it impossible to be stern or harsh when necessary.

Jesse Smith, an intimate friend of Attorney General Harry Daugherty, committed suicide in Daugherty's apartment after being exposed for peddling bribes to the Justice Department. Daugherty refused to testify at his own trial on the grounds of self-incrimination and was twice saved from prison by hung juries.

The most infamous misdeed of Harding's administration came to be known as the Teapot Dome scandal. Secretary of the Interior Albert Fall first persuaded Harding to let his department control the naval oil reserves at Elk Hills, California, and at Teapot Dome, Wyoming. Then he illegally leased these properties to private oil companies. Fall's secret was exposed in 1923. After a year-long Senate investigation into the matter, it was revealed that Fall had received $100,000 in cash, nearly a quarter of a million dollars in bonds, and a herd of cattle—all "loans" from the oil companies. In 1927 the government successfully sued to cancel these contracts. The oil executives and Fall were all acquitted of conspiracy to defraud the government, although Fall was later convicted of bribery in 1929 and sentenced to a year in

Wide World.

The first former Cabinet member to be imprisoned, Albert B. Fall (left), arrives at the District of Columbia Supreme Court for arraignment.

prison—thus becoming the first member of a President's Cabinet ever to go to jail.

Harding was aware of at least some aspects of what his less honest aides were doing and even spoke despairingly about it to Hoover. But he was saved from the humiliation of having to account for himself. On August 2, 1923, a heart attack ended Harding's career and his problems forever. The scandals involving Cabinet members came to light only after his death.

Luckily for the Republican party, Vice President Coolidge, who succeeded Harding as President, was able to counter the Teapot Dome issue through his own rectitude and the fact that he had not been involved in the affair. He not only permitted but even encouraged the continuation of the congressional investigations into the matter.

The Republicans were able to ride out the Teapot Dome storm because the nation was enjoying great prosperity. The new President was credited with having engineered the good times; the phrase "Coolidge Prosperity" quickly came into use in 1923 when he took office. Overproduction on farms was, however, causing some rural discontent. High protective tariffs made it almost impossible for European countries to sell their own goods in American markets and thus extremely difficult to purchase and import American surpluses. Nevertheless, general prosperity ensured Coolidge of an easy victory over his Democratic opponent, West Virginia's John W. Davis (1873–1955) in 1924.

Courtesy University of Iowa Libraries.

As Secretary of Commerce under both Harding and Coolidge, self-made millionaire Herbert Hoover dominated the Cabinet, gaining a say in the making of virtually all domestic policies. This cartoon captures the public image of the energetic Secretary.

The Associative State

General prosperity continued throughout Coolidge's term in office. Government policies of acquiescence to business were not only accepted by the public but acclaimed. Kept on as part of the Coolidge administration, Hoover continued to work at stimulating the economy through the voluntary associations he had established under Harding.

Secretary Hoover was transforming the Department of Commerce into the most massive of the federal agencies, expanding both the office and its functions. The paradox of Hoover's work during Coolidge's presidency is that while he distrusted big business, he instituted at the same time the largest peacetime bureaucracy—a sort of publicly owned business—that had ever been seen in Washington. Hoover believed in a New Era, one that would reconcile the old industrial nation to the benefits of science and social engineering and yet keep intact the values of individualism, private enterprise, and "grass roots" involvement in government. His method of using cooperative institutions such as trade associations and professional societies as political forces was dubbed "associationalism."

The goal of Hoover's "associative" state was to achieve a nation in which a government founded on cooperation with business would adhere to the principles of free enterprise. He wanted to operate federal agencies as if they were entities safe from selfish or greedy motives and from the whims of individuals. To implement his associative state, Hoover expanded the Department of Commerce and divided it into three divisions: one for industry, one for trade, and one for transportation and communications. The roots of Hoover's new bureaucracy would rest in cooperative private societies, which would in turn encourage local communities to help solve the nation's problems. Some 700 private national associations were functioning in 1919; a decade later, encouraged by Hoover, there were over 2,000.

Hoover was, in fact, attempting to establish a far more radical form of government than historians usually give him credit for. His imaginative idea of running government like a giant and efficient corporation represented Hoover's idiosyncratic effort to reconcile the increasingly inhuman aspects of a technological society with its liberal democratic heritage.

Hoover was not altogether typical of his party or his contemporaries, whose lack of foresight would soon become apparent. Hoover often worked to bring about positive changes, but like his fellow Republicans he also ignored "soft spots" that were developing in the economy and showed continued indifference to the woes of the mining and textile industries. An unchecked economic spiral was developing that would eventually destroy the entire business community. But most of Hoover's compatriots noticed none of these signs, not even that the industries which had accounted for much of the real prosperity of the mid-1920s—automobiles and construction—had peaked and by 1927 were in decline.

The Reign of Business

American business can rightfully claim much of the credit for the remarkable prosperity enjoyed by the public during the 1920s. Through its feats of efficient and low-cost production, business won the uncritical admiration of the majority of Americans. But since prosperity was closely associated with business leadership, the collapse of that prosperity dragged down the good reputation of that leadership.

What were the attitudes of management during this period of unprecedented quietude and "normalcy"? The cry for a return to the values of prewar America was recognized by many observers to be little more than political rhetoric. The public was in general complacent and unconcerned about problems that were developing—although the Red Scare, the rise of the Soviet state, the disenchantment of many American intellectuals, the growth of the federal bureaucracy and its expenditures, and the hard times felt in agriculture and the coal industry can hardly have gone completely unnoticed. Moreover, mass production and the ever-expanding corporate structure of business made it more necessary than ever before for business to project a favorable public image. In its efforts to cultivate a friendly climate of opinion, business formulated a code of ethics based on the ideal of service that had been widespread during the war. "Service as a basis for profit-making," said Henry Ford, "is coming to be recognized as the true motive for creative industry." Changing social and economic conditions demanded new responses from business. The recognition that it was profitable to exist in harmony with labor, consumers, and stockholders did much to bring about reforms within the business community.

Many members of the new generation of managers were themselves products of the age of Progressivism. More and more they were professionals trained by colleges and groomed by corporations rather than self-made entrepreneurs. These professional executives wished above all else to maintain self-regulation. The idea became prevalent that the manager was a trustee responsible to a vague community-at-large, and this "philosophy" was aired with increasing frequency at Chamber of Commerce luncheons. The same message about service to the community, ethics in business, and managerial trusteeship and its responsibilities was put forth in numerous articles and speeches of the period. Charles Cason, a vice president of the Chemical National Bank of New York, typified this new attitude when he remarked:

> "Today, there is a new point of view. We know that real success in business is not attained at the expense of others. Business can succeed only in the long run by acquiring and holding the good will of the people. To do this, it is necessary to render honest, intelligent service at a fair price. The best upper-class men in business are really genuine in their belief in service and are consistent in its practice. Most of them would not consider a policy which enriched them or their company and was at the same time against the public interest."

It is debatable how much of this idealistic talk was public relations rhetoric and how much of it was an actual attempt to implement a new policy. Certainly many businessmen did not like the materialistic image that the public had of them. And many businesses did

Library of Congress.

Bruce Barton
(1886–1967)

Bruce Barton, born in Robbins, Tennessee, in 1886, a son of a circuit-riding preacher and writer who later secured a pulpit in fashionable Oak Park, Illinois, attended Berea College for a year before enrolling at Amherst College. When he graduated in 1907, his classmates voted him "the man most likely to succeed." During the next dozen years Barton worked briefly at odd jobs in Montana and then in publishing in Chicago and New York. In 1919 he formed an advertising agency—Barton, Durstine, and Osborne—with two young men he had met while working on a World War I publicity campaign. Nine years later the firm became Batten, Barton, Durstine & Osborne (BBDO), one of the most successful in the annals of advertising. Among Barton's accounts, for example, was "Betty Crocker," for which he invented the well-known trademark.

In the 1920s Barton was launched on his career as a writer. *The Man Nobody Knows* (1925)—portraying Jesus as a businessman and was on the best seller list for two years. In seven chapters he described Jesus as a many-sided social executive, "the founder of modern business," who used simple, straight-forward advertising language to spread his message. Barton also wrote numerous magazine articles and a book about the Bible, *The Book Nobody Knows* (1926).

Barton's career also demonstrates the connections between business and the Republican party, since he served as GOP publicist from 1919 to 1940 and was himself a congressman from New York City, 1937–1941. An isolationist, his name was immortalized by FDR in his condemnation of "Martin, Barton, and Fish," whom he viewed as the worst the GOP had to offer. Barton was defeated in his campaign for the U.S. Senate in 1940 and returned to advertising work. He died in 1967.

Father of three children and a devotee of books and golf, Bruce Barton was much honored during his career but also subject to some criticism. While he talked much of personal freedom, his employees noted that Lucky Strike (a BBDO account) was the only brand of cigarettes sold on company premises. In defense of advertising's well-known excesses, Barton once remarked, "If advertising is sometimes long-winded, so is the United States Senate. If advertising has flaws, so has marriage." ■

attempt to turn the idea of service and trusteeship into a working reality—to create through corporate philanthropy and in their relations with labor a true "welfare capitalism," an ongoing "industrial democracy." Company-sponsored unions, employee stockownership plans, pensions, and welfare programs became increasingly common. Andrew Carnegie's fervent philanthropy was emulated in many new foundations, in the establishment of community chests and in the slow but steady acceptance by the rich of their obligation to alleviate some of the burdens of the poor.

It would be unfair to assume that big business actually set out to destroy its smalltime competitors in the twenties, although some key industries did move toward oligopoly (not monopoly). But small-to-medium-sized firms continued to dominate the national scene. Two-thirds of all American businessmen in 1929 were proprietors of small unincorporated shops with one to twenty employees. These small businessmen earned an average of $1,600 a year. They were the men represented in the National Association of Manufacturers and in the Chambers of Commerce across the country. The Gospel of Business was no myth to them; instead, it was a way of life. Bruce Barton, who was a pioneer in the field of advertising and later became a congressman (1937), typified their attitudes. Barton's favorite quote from the Bible was "Wist ye not that I must be about my Father's business?" He believed that the divine plan for redemption of mankind must certainly include free enterprise. In a bestseller called *The Man Nobody Knows,* Barton claimed that building a business was a Christian obligation. "Jesus built the greatest organization of them all. . . . He picked up twelve men from the bottom ranks of business and forged them into an organization that conquered the world."

Despite such smugness, the 1920s witnessed some genuine progress in industry. Hoover's associationalism aided growth and prosperity. Easy credit combined with the dissemination (through the associations) of information about new scientific techniques for eliminating waste in mass production increased productivity. Plants and facilities expanded, with "research and development" (R & D) becoming a new and important item in many corporate budgets. Productivity rose 40 percent in industry and 25 percent in agriculture, and profits in some enterprises were larger than ever. But these profits were not "distributed" to workers in the form of increased wages—and this oversight proved to be one of the weakest aspects of the New Era economy.

Despite the inequity between profits and wages, many businessmen made efforts to keep labor happy. They wanted not only to stimulate consumer power but also to retard the growth of unions. The unsuccessful postwar strikes had destroyed much of labor's organizational power, and management in the Twenties was engaging in "welfare capitalism" to keep unions weak. This meant higher wages (even if these increases were not proportionate to profits) and shorter working hours. Companies also hired "personnel managers" and labor experts to advise them. In 1928 one-third of all plants with over 250 employees had personnel managers. The overall effect of these efforts on the part of business was a decline in union membership.

Public relations and advertising became important adjuncts to business in the Twenties, helping to create a desire among consumers for the goods being produced. Advertising became widespread, especially for "name brands" sold nationally. Although much of this advertising was strictly factual and conservative as late as 1929, advertising agencies began to use psychological appeals (often that of snobbism) to enhance consumer demand.

A new "mass-consumption" society was developing, and this new society was symbolized by the rise of the chain store. Between 1920 and 1929 the A&P chain grew from 4,621 outlets to 15,418. J.C. Penney went from 312 to 1,395. Standard Oil of New Jersey increased its 12 stations to 1,000. Safeway outlets rose from 766 to 2,660; Piggly Wiggly, the pioneer supermarket chain, from 515 to 2,500; Western Auto Supply from 3 to 54; Lerner Shops from 6 to 133; and S.S. Kresge from 184 to 597. By purchasing goods in volume these new chains could pass savings on to consumers in the form of lower prices. Chains could also offer a greater variety of goods and at greater convenience to their customers. By the end of the decade, chain stores controlled about one-fifth of all the retail business in America. To counter the growth of chain stores some wholesalers worked out with groups of retailers—especially those who sold food and drugs—contractual agreements that granted them exclusive rights in an area. In return, the wholesalers provided national advertising and advice on how to display products and maintain inventory control.

A similar phenomenon in the Twenties was the

Library of Congress.

Among many other signs of modernity to appear during the 1920s was the supermarket. The first such store, pictured here, was the Piggly Wiggly in Tennessee.

flourishing of mail-order houses, which, although they dated back to the 1880s, were aided greatly by RFD routes and parcel post, instituted in 1912. Mail-order houses offered suburban and rural consumers easy credit, although some houses (such as Sears) also established their own retail outlet stores in cities in order to compete for the urban market. Sears, Roebuck was especially successful at capturing the new spirit of suburban America and geared its sales pitch accordingly.

Service establishments mushroomed during the 1920s. Restaurants, department stores, gas stations, beauty shops, insurance offices—the rising proportion of workers employed in these institutions (one-fourth of the working population in 1900; one -third in 1929) reflected the emergence of an economy that was becoming more and more service oriented. Since service organizations, unlike manufacturers, produce no goods and can improve their efficiency at only a very slow rate, this shift from goods to services impeded the general growth of the economy.

Though there was some criticism of the nation's increased preoccupation with materialism—coming mostly from intellectuals—the businessman and his values epitomized the age. Rhetoric borrowed from the struggle for social justice was now employed to identify progress with technological development; and progress, development, growth, and efficiency were virtues. Until 1929, the rhetoric worked quite well.

Stresses in the Social Fabric

Yet rhetoric, no matter how beguiling, is no substitute for facts and it is now apparent that the complacent, happy, "roaring" Twenties were, in truth, a troubled, divided era. It was "Custer's Last Stand" for some aspects of rural, smalltown America and much that it held dear. The nationalizing and suburbanizing of everyday life was like a tidal wave that could not be stopped.

An Urban Society

The census of 1920 revealed that for the first time a majority of Americans lived in cities. During the following decade this trend would be countered in part by development of "motorized suburbs." But cities continued to grow. The increasing use of the automobile, aside from contributing to the growth of the suburbs, facilitated contact between cities, with their diverse populations, and the traditionalist countryside. Naturally enough, conflict between urban and rural Americans intensified.

To rural-minded traditionalists the city represented all that was wrong with modern life. Even the conflict between the older and younger generations was subsumed by this complaint, as was much of the discontent that youth was experiencing at the time. Certainly the cities with their faster pace of life and their "speakeasies" where liquor could be had as though it were legal, offered a set of social and economic opportunities far different from those available on farms or in the rural towns. Traditionalists expressed increasing fears, often bordering on the irrational, about urban life and the values of the Twenties. Bigotry and prejudice were present everywhere, but rural resentments manifested themselves in the demand for restricted immigration, the spread of Ku

Klux Klan activities, the crusade against the teaching of evolution in public schools, and the continued support of prohibition.

A political fundamentalism developed across rural America that became the foundation of conservatism and reaction in the 1920s. This political fundamentalism attempted to impose a patriotic conformity on all Americans—based on a coercive worship of the Constitution, an effort to codify national standards of morality into law, and a return to the spirit of Protestantism that had dominated an earlier, mostly rural American landscape.

By 1924 Protestant fundamentalists were basing their campaign against modern life on an odd combination of the Bible and the Constitution, while the Ku Klux Klan's motto had become "Back to the Constitution."

The results of this growing antagonism were restrictions on immigration that were passed into law, restrictions founded on racism and rationalized away by pseudoscientific nonsense. Earlier books such as *The Passing of the Great Race* by Madison Grant (a virulent pro-Aryan, anti-Semitic tract) and *The Rising Tide of Color* by Lothrop Stoddard, a professor at Harvard (which warned the white races that they would soon be engulfed by "more fertile colored races"), were popular and respected. Kenneth Roberts stated (in the *Saturday Evening Post*) that America was being overrun by mongrel races from southern Europe and central Asia. Until the war an average of one million immigrants a year had arrived at Ellis Island and at other U.S. ports of entry. In the early 1920s the figures ranged from 300,000 to 800,000, annually in 1921 about 40 percent came from southern and eastern Europe. For a long time industrialists in need of cheap labor has opposed restrictions on immigration. By 1923, with the combined factors of

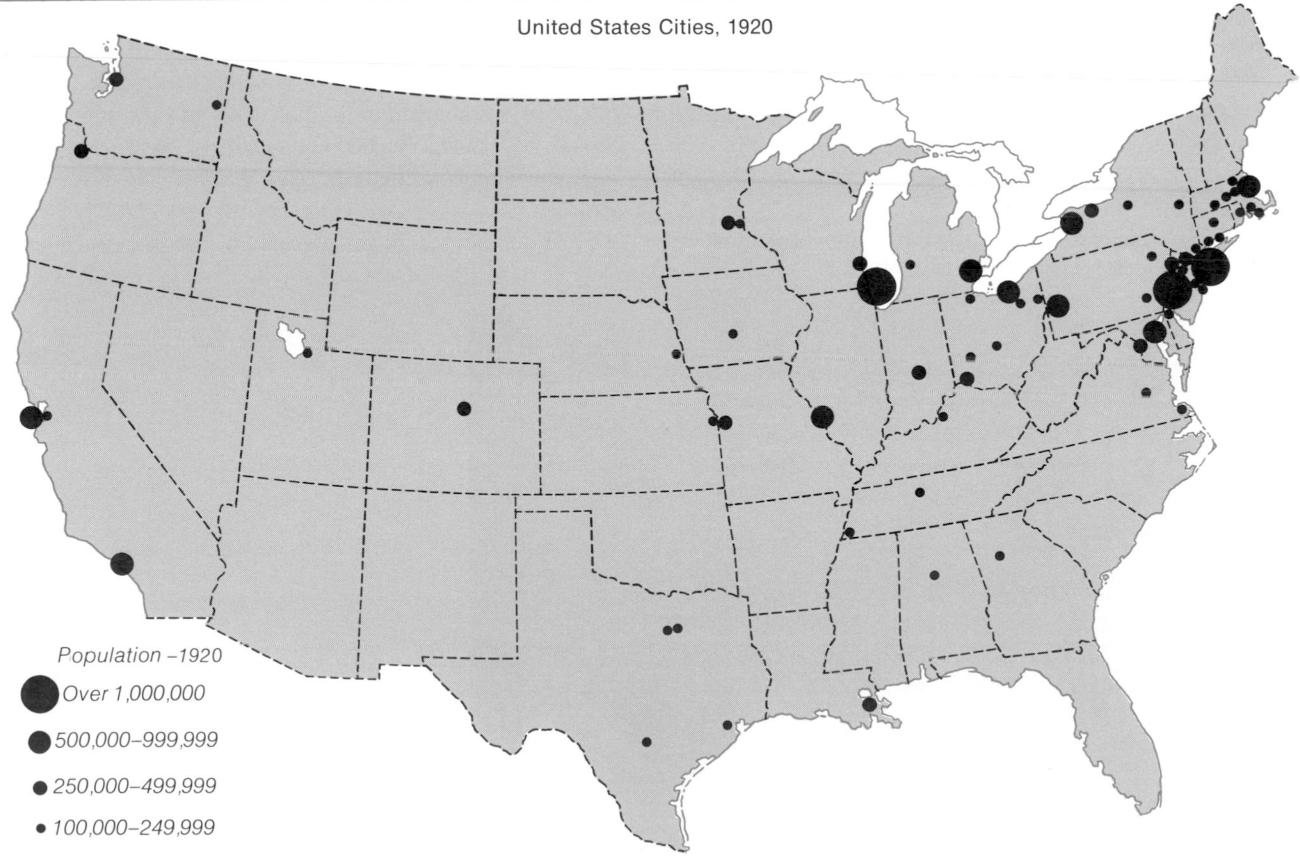

the Red Scare and new efficient means of production that reduced the need for unskilled labor, the last barrier against restricted immigration fell.

On April 13, 1924, the Coolidge administration gave its unofficial blessing to the nativist cause when, in his first annual message to Congress, the new President called on his countrymen to do "something" to keep America American. Coolidge had previously endorsed racist sentiment in an article entitled "Whose Country is This?" published under his byline in *Good Housekeeping* magazine in 1921. The article espoused the notion that Nordics deteriorate when they intermarry with "other" races—that is, with members of other ethnic groups.

Six weeks later the National Origins Act was passed, limiting the total number of immigrants entering the U.S. each year to 150,000, and classifying them by place of birth. This legislation provided a much more drastic limitation than an act passed in 1921; it cut immigrant quotas from 3 percent of the foreign-born in 1910 to 2 percent of those recorded in the 1890 census. These quotas shut out all but a handful of immigrants from southern and eastern Europe. And, as a concession to West coast prejudices, the act forbade all immigration from the Orient. The *Los Angeles Times* proudly announced in its headlines that a "Nordic Victory is Seen in Drastic Restrictions."

Yet another indicator of the pervasive intolerance of the 1920s was the reemergence of the Ku Klux Klan, a racist organization that had been active during Reconstruction. The new Klan, founded in 1915 in Georgia by William Simmons (1880–1945) as a fraternity of "native born, white, gentile Americans" and directly inspired by the remarkable film, *Birth of a Nation,* soon spread its activities to the Southwest, Midwest and Far West. By 1925 the Klan's membership had grown to five million—mostly lower middle class and working class white men—and had become both a political power and an agent of terrorism. About half of these Klansmen lived in metropolitan areas, especially in growing cities of the traditional South (Atlanta, Memphis, Knoxville, and Dallas) and in centers of the North and other parts of the nation undergoing population change (Chicago, Detroit, Indianapolis, Denver, Los Angeles, and Portland). In 1922 Walter Pierce, a Democrat running for governor in staunchly Republican Oregon, received the Klan's support after he came out in favor of an initiative proposal that would abolish parochial schools by requiring all parents with children between the ages of eight and sixteen to send them to public schools. Pierce was elected governor by a margin of 34,000 votes and the school bill passed by about 11,000 votes. Three years later the Supreme Court voided the law in *Pierce* v. *Society of Sisters.*

The Klan's power reached its zenith in Indiana

Library of Congress.

One of the dark sides of the twenties was the resurgence of the Ku Klux Klan, whose members appeared openly in the most public of places—as before the Capitol in Washington. At least until the middle of the decade, the Klan was very influential in the politics of several states.

when David Stephenson (who held the rank of Grand Dragon in the state organization) assumed control of the Republican machine. Stephenson had his henchman, Ed Jackson, elected governor; soon some 350,000 Klansmen took over Indiana state politics. In Kokomo police officers actually directed traffic while wearing Klan robes. But Stephenson overreached himself. He kidnapped and assaulted his secretary, Madge Oberholtzer, and prevented her from receiving medical attention after she attempted suicide, as a result of which she died. When Stephenson was convicted of manslaughter and sentenced to life imprisonment in 1925, he demanded that Jackson grant him a pardon. The Governor refused. In return for this "betrayal" of a fellow Klansman, Stephenson opened his own "little black book" to public scrutiny causing one congressman, the mayor of Indianapolis, and a number of minor officials to join the irate Dragon in jail.

Despite its claims to be a protector of American purity, the Klan was an overtly corrupt and sadistic organization, using floggings, kidnappings, cross burnings, arson, and even murder to keep entire communities under its collective thumb. When the scandals that had occurred in Indiana came to light the financial corruption, political bribery, and moral hypocrisy of the Klan were apparent to millions. The group never fully recovered from the debacle of 1924, although it continued to stir up anti-Catholic and anti-black sentiment for years.

When Charles Darwin's *The Origin of Species* was first published in 1859, it set off a long controversy between proponents of science and Christianity that had, it seemed, been resolved in England and America well before the turn of the century. But in America the Twenties witnessed a rebirth of hostility toward science and technology, particularly in rural areas. Science was the embodiment of change that was both frightening and mysterious; as a result, conservative fundamentalists carried on a crusade against the teaching of evolution in schools. And this crusade found a leader and hero in the rotund form of William Jennings Bryan.

For thirty years Bryan had been a folk hero in the heartland of the Mississippi Valley. Sincere and courageous, he was a political descendant of Jacksonian democracy and a spiritual heir to nineteenth century evangelical Christianity. With his blessing the Tennessee legislature passed a bill in 1925 that made it illegal to teach any theory that contradicted the description of the creation of the universe appearing in the Bible in the Book of Genesis. (Florida, Oklahoma, Mississippi, and Arkansas passed similar laws.)

The American Civil Liberties Union offered to defend any teacher who would test this new law. And John T. Scopes (1900–1970), in a spirit more of amusement than of social protest, decided to take advantage of this offer. Clarence Darrow (1857–1938), the most famous lawyer in America and a well-known agnostic, and Arthur Garfield Hays, a civil liberties attorney, were to defend Scopes. To assist the prosecution the World's Christian Fundamental Association chose the great Bryan himself. Bryan proclaimed that the trial was to be "a duel to the death" between Christianity and evolution. Staged in the little town of Dayton, the proceedings quickly came to be known as the "monkey trial" and attracted the attention not only of the American public but of much of the rest of the world as well.

At the climax of the trial Bryan took the stand on behalf of the prosecution—as an authority on both science and the Bible. Darrow's cross-examination was ruthless and merciless, exposing Bryan's intractable ignorance of both fields. The eminent authority did not know the literal length of a Biblical "day"; it could, Bryan admitted, actually be millions of years. He could only speculate—or in fundamentalist terms "interpret"—what the Scripture meant when it spoke of the world being created in seven "days." Bryan's admission of uncertainty undermined the literal fundamentalist position on the Bible and made further argument on his part impossible.

In spite of this defense, Scopes was convicted of breaking the law although the state supreme court nullified the verdict in an effort to prevent an appeal and further testing of the law that might then result. But no one had really expected Scopes to win his case. The point had been to draw public attention to the danger of giving legal sanction to religious thought and restricting academic freedom. The defense may have lost the trial, but it had won the day.

In another sense, however, the trial at Dayton symbolized the hostility existing between city and country at the time. The arrogance of a Darrow had been pitted against the shallowness of a Bryan—but the battle had been between modernist and traditionalist thought. And if the traditionalists represented religious fanaticism, the modernists had an equally self-righteous faith in the absolute nature of science.

Life in the cities in the 1920s was not, however, all intellectual freedom and enlightenment. Immigrants and workers participated in the battle between city and country in which they were potential victims. Some movement for reform had arisen to help cope with urban problems but, by and large, urban living conditions grew worse as the nation in general prospered.

Cities were growing poorer as the middle class had begun moving to the suburbs, taking with it a substantial revenue source. The political balance of power in both state and federal governments remained with rural America, which was indifferent to the plight of city dwellers. The traditional ally of the working classes had been the Progressives, but they were in disarray and unable to help effect social change of any kind.

After the failure of Wilsonian policies and the shattering experience of war, large and aggressive reform elements still existed, but they lacked national leadership and were, moreover, beset by internal conflicts and tensions. And the movement's stable middle-class component, made up of businessmen deeply committed to reforming government and to curbing oligopolies, was now eroding. Prosperity was making the middle class more and more conservative and less and less interested in reforms that would improve the life of working class Americans and farmers.

In addition, prohibition—the great experiment of the Progressive movement—created considerable chaos, inspired millions to break the laws who had never done so before, and made a shambles of law enforcement itself in towns and cities across the land. It was a final irony that this grand effort to improve the lives of Americans through drink reform ended up spawning gangsterism and further discredited whatever other Progressive proposals might be offered to a wary public.

In effect from 1920 to 1933, the Volstead Act culminated several decades of anti-drink activity that forced many states to go legally "dry"; yet, in the words of one social historian, the nation accepted prohibition "almost absent-mindedly." In a single stroke, wine and beer were denied to many immigrants who considered them normal, everyday fare, saloons closed down or became "speakeasies," and millions of irate customers created an immense demand for alcohol. This giant thirst was slaked

Library of Congress.

Although gangsters and rumrunners abounded during the prohibition era, at least as common were the "respectable" owners of stills, who flaunted the ban on alcohol—and made tidy profits for their efforts.

by means of deceit, official connivance, and considerable ingenuity on the part of all concerned.

Izzy Epstein and Moe Smith, dedicated prohibition agents, used numerous disguises to trap their adversaries. This hard-working pair made over 4000 arrests and confiscated more than $15 million worth of liquor, but they were the exceptions. In addition, their careers were brief; both men were dismissed in 1925, presumably because they were garnering more publicity than their superiors. For the most part, those breaking the law carried the day. Enforcement of this controversial federal legislation was often half-hearted and spasmodic at best, and nowhere was this more evident than in large cities, such as Chicago, New York, and Philadelphia.

In fact, Chicago was the pacesetter in crime during the 1920s, thanks largely to the organizational genius and firepower of Alphonse Capone (1899–1947). New York-born "Al," also known as "Scar Face," used the illicit liquor trade as a means to bring order to a chaotic mass of competing ethnic gangs eager to sell "protection" to scores of merchants. He was to crime what J. P. Morgan was to Wall Street, shaping a cohesive force by giving each participant a share in the profits and working hand-in-glove with both big business and politics. Capone, a dynamic and witty personality, once said of the U.S. Supreme Court justices, "They are nothing but precinct captains in long black robes."

By 1927 Capone ruled Chicago and he and his gang were enjoying an annual income of $60 million, much of it from beer sales. Two years later he staged an Atlantic City convention at which various mobs carved up the nation like so many fiefdoms. But Capone's days were numbered. His ostentatious behavior and craving for publicity—mistakes very few of his successors have made—led to a conviction on federal income tax evasion charges and an eleven year sentence. His attorneys offered federal officials a $4 million bribe, but to no avail. Capone was released in 1939, a pathetic shadow of his former self, suffering from the advanced stages of syphilis which caused his death eight years later.

Limitations of the "New Era"

However much the war reshaped American life, some aspects remained painfully unchanged. Experiences of both the newly liberated woman and the "New Negro" of the 1920s only underscored historic sexism and racism long prevalent throughout the nation. During this period women and blacks were able to lay only the groundwork for later gains. Neither group benefited much from New Era promises. American Indians benefited even less.

The women's movement began the decade on a moment of exhilarating success. Women had won the right to vote and seemed to be making other gains, especially (during the war) in the area of job possibilities. But the 1920s witnessed a split between social feminists and egalitarian feminists. Social feminists were more interested in broad social reforms than they were in the advancement of women as such; the primary concern of staunch feminists was equal rights for women. This split enervated both groups and ultimately produced nothing more than a holding action for women in American society.

The 1920s saw a rapid increase in the number of women officeholders (statistically proportionate to present-day levels). More and more women gained other government jobs, although they remained underpaid. Women in industry grew from 8.5 million to 10.7 million in the Twenties, but the labor movement continued its discriminatory policies. The findings of six separate investigations conducted by the Women's Division of the Labor Department proved conclusively that nearly all married workingwomen contributed their entire earnings to the support of their families, as did two-thirds of single workingwomen living at home. Nevertheless, the notion persisted that women worked to earn "pin money" and were supported by either husbands or their families. This view left workingwomen vulnerable to the exigencies of the labor market as the advent of the Great Depression of the Thirties demonstrated.

The clearest indication of division in the women's movement was the controversy that developed over the proposed Equal Rights Amendment (ERA). Led by the National Women's Party under Alice Paul, egalitarian feminists believed that passage of the ERA was an absolute necessity for their cause, Social feminists, especially in the League of Women Voters, thought the ERA would threaten other protective legislation that benefited women. Social feminists had in the past experienced some success in achieving consumer protection, election law reforms, and labor protection laws. (They had also, briefly, achieved child and maternity protection laws; that is, until the Sheppard-Towner Act of 1921 providing funds for instruction in baby care was repealed in 1929.) By 1925 social feminists were largely on the defensive and found themselves exerting their energies to protect their achievements from reactionary forces that were becoming both numerous and powerful. Many social feminists continued, nevertheless, to draw up plans and programs that later proved useful during the New Deal years. But for the most part the 1920s witnessed only a barely perceptible improvement in bettering the political and economic lives of women—and at the cost of the fragmentation of the feminist movement.

Blacks, too, failed to achieve the reforms they had hoped for in 1918. Their oppression by legal sanctions, though less formalized than before, continued. Violent persecution at the hands of the Ku Klux Klan was an

Photo Files.

Harlem, the center of New York's black population, was a thriving community in the 1920s. Its entertainments drew throngs of whites, as well as black patrons.

everyday occurrence throughout the country; the number of lynchings remained shockingly high. Although blacks continued to support the Republican party, they received no attention or aid from the federal government.

Blacks had begun their transformation from a rural people into an urban minority during the war. This trend continued after the war. There had been only 2.7 million blacks in American cities in 1910, as compared to the 6.9 million that lived in rural areas. By 1920 there were 3.5 million blacks in cities, while the number of rural blacks remained the same as it had been ten years earlier. And by 1930 the number of blacks in rural areas had dropped to 6.6 million, and there were 5.2 million blacks living in cities.

The mecca for urban American blacks was the section of New York City known as Harlem. Harlem became the center for Garveyism and the Harlem Renaissance—two important black movements in which the New Negro would emerge.

Harlem had been attracting black intellectuals since at least 1914. By the Twenties it boasted a well-established group of individuals who acted as unofficial leaders for blacks throughout America. The NAACP headquarters, established in 1909, was now located in Harlem. Its most prominent leaders were James Weldon Johnson (1871–1938) and W. E. B. DuBois. Johnson, a poet and writer who was born in Jacksonville, Florida, had been a professor of literature at Fisk University, while Du-

Bois, a doctoral graduate of Harvard, was a native Northerner. By the Twenties the presence in Harlem of Johnson, Dubois, and others attracted black intellectuals and artists—as well as ordinary black men and women—to the capital of the black world.

Three magazines of considerable influence among the black community were born and flourished in Harlem. *Crisis,* founded by DuBois in 1910 and edited by him thereafter, was published by the NAACP. It focused on lynchings, printing in every issue a statistical breakdown of violence against blacks throughout the land. In 1917 A. Philip Randolph and Chandler Owen began publishing the *Messenger,* the self-described "Only Radical Negro Magazine in America." During the war *Messenger* counseled blacks to resist military service on behalf of a white man's cause. When the Espionage and Sedition Acts came into force, the magazine was confiscated and its publishers arrested. In time *Messenger* became the organ for Randolph's larger enterprise, the Brotherhood of Sleeping Car Porters. In 1923 the Urban League began publication of *Opportunity,* a magazine that dealt with the problems of race in a more academic manner than either *Messenger* or *Crisis.* Edited by Eugene Kinkle Jones, a member of the League, and Charles S. Johnson (1893–1956), the pages of *Opportunity* were filled with scholarly studies by young social scientists.

A unique center of racial consciousness, Harlem began to attract not only the nation's most prominent black thinkers but black artists and poets as well. The Twenties witnessed a Black Renaissance with the emergence of poets Langston Hughes (1902–), Countee Cullen (1902–1967), and a host of less well-known writers and artists. Harlem sculptors and painters often employed African themes in their work. Scores of white patrons encouraged this cosmopolitan movement in black arts and letters in Harlem which aroused a new spirit of racial consciousness and interest in African roots. Though it was increasingly in evidence throughout the Thirties and in the years following World War II, this spirit would not flower until the late Sixties.

The most vivid expression of Afro-Americanism in the 1920s was a phenomenon called Garveyism. Named for its founder, Marcus Garvey (1887–1940), this movement advocated black participation in capitalist pursuits and a return to Africa. Rejecting the passive accommodation to the practices of whites advocated by Booker T. Washington and his followers, Garvey preached militant black nationalism as the path to independence. Born in Jamaica, Garvey wanted to establish a nation of American blacks in Africa where they could be free at last of racist American oppression.

In 1917 Garvey inaugurated his Universal Negro Improvement Association (UNIA) in Harlem. From the outset he was bitterly opposed by DuBois and Johnson, who feared that his flair and rhetoric masked a political demagogue. Garvey's UNIA proclaimed blacks to be a nation in exile. His followers were given exotic titles such as the Duke of Nigeria and the Lord of Uganda and then appropriately outfitted and decorated with medals. At a convention held at Madison Square Garden in 1920, Garvey appeared—in a purple, green, and black uniform with a hat of white feathered plumes—before a full house of delegates from Africa, Brazil, Central America, and the West Indies. He exhorted them: "We have changed from the old cringing weaklings, and transformed into full-grown men, demanding our portion as *men.* . . . Up, you mighty race!" In the UNIA newspaper, *Negro World,* Garvey urged blacks to take pride in their nobility and to cast off the self-hatred and servility of mind that colonialism and slavery had bestowed upon them.

Garvey's scheme for transocean shipping to Africa proved his undoing. The Black Star Line was to be wholly owned and operated by blacks. DuBois and others warned Harlem citizens that the Black Star Line was only a dream. Garvey's plans did not take into account the complexities of navigation, naval architecture, and international finance that his project required. Nor did he have any idea of the true nature of tribal life in Africa. In the end he was convicted of fraud, imprisoned, and finally exiled.

Black leaders such as DuBois dreamed of a pan-Africanism that would unite the cultures of two continents; Garvey preached a separatism that frightened Europeans and whites as well as many blacks. The failure of Garveyism was perhaps inevitable. But Garvey gave his followers a sense of their collective potential and commanded their loyalty as no subsequent black leader would again until the emergence in the 1950s and 1960s of the civil rights movement.

American Indians, a true minority of about 350,000

U.P.I.

Marcus Garvey founded the Universal Negro Improvement Association in 1917, which for a time gave millions of his black followers a new race pride and hope for establishing a black-controlled Africa.

in the 1920s, for the most part suffered in silence and privation. Tucked away out of sight, divided into many groups, and working at menial jobs (if any existed), they had few leaders or patrons to speak in their behalf. There were, however, small stirrings of activity that, just as among blacks, would be fanned to greater heights by World War II and an increasing sense of identity and racial pride.

In 1922 the Pueblo Indians of the Southwest held a council, their first since 1680, to discuss the threat of non-Pueblo settlers on their lands and the Bursum Bill (then before Congress), which would have required all Indians to prove ownership of property. John Collier (1884–1968), a young crusading Georgian who became interested in the Indians' plight while traveling in the West, became executive secretary of the American Indian Defense Fund and engineered the defeat of the Bursum Bill. He discovered that federal laws protecting Indian lands from white incursions did not apply to the Pueblo tribe since its members had been citizens of Mexico and were granted the same status in 1848 by the U.S. government; hence legally they were not Indians.

The council, debate over the Bursum Bill, and Collier's work led to the Indian Citizenship Act of 1924. By granting citizenship, this measure cleared away much of the confusion concerning the legal rights of Indians. Until passage, some were U.S. citizens as a result of special treaties and others had acquired a "conditional" sort of citizenship. Nevertheless, only as a result of court tests in Arizona and New Mexico in the late 1940s did Indians in those states gain effective use of the franchise.

In the mid-1920s the Secretary of the Interior asked the Institute for Governmental Research, a private foundation, to make a thorough survey of reservation life.

The result was the Lewis Merriam Report (1928) advocating considerable change in federal policies: more medical and educational aid for Indians, higher standards for those employed in the Bureau of Indian Affairs, and numerous long-range programs to assist Indians. The policies of Hoover's Commissioner of Indian Affairs, Charles J. Rhoads (1872–1956), an astute Philadelphia banker and a Quaker, reflected this changing attitude toward Indians.

Automobiles and Flying Machines

Perhaps more than anything else, the automobile—cheap, mass-produced—symbolized changing cultural patterns in the 1920s. It made suburbs possible, comported well with the needs of both bootleggers and cops, and tended to end or at least diminish rural isolation. Between 1895 and 1958, 2612 independent auto factories appeared in 664 communities in 46 states, and soon after the turn of the century nearly every town and city could boast of a few pioneer contraptions.

During the first decade of this century those intrigued by auto travel spent much of their time at race meets staged to demonstrate the speed potential of gas-powered vehicles or in long-distance tours designed to prove their practical durability. Since European manufacturers won most of the racing trophies, American auto enthusiasts soon lost interest in that form of competition; and, as the novelty of the auto wore off and these machines were no longer playthings for the rich alone, the appeal of cross country tours diminished greatly. Yet the emerging industry, which gradually became centered in the Detroit area (in 1916, for example, Michigan for the first time produced one million units), had to overcome two huge hurdles: high costs and poor highways. Both, to a large degree, were solved in the 1920s.

Profiting greatly from experience gained by filling government contracts during World War I, Henry Ford perfected his mass-production techniques and steadily lowered the price of his black Model T from $950 in 1909 to $290 in 1924. Ford even marketed a basic chassis and engine without a body for those who wanted bargain basement specials. By 1927 the American automobile industry had manufactured 20 million cars, half of them Model T Fords.

A nation on wheels meant great social change. Not only was this new industrial giant an important factor in the entire economy, it also spawned demands for road construction that were felt by every state legislator and congressman; it created subsidiary businesses—such as used car lots, garages, filling stations, auto financing, and auto insurance; and it gave a tremendous boost to tourism. By the close of the twenties, tourist cabins (simple, no frills, progenitors of the splashy, luxury-studded motels of today) lined most hard-surfaced highways. The standard family vacation was an exhausting drive to visit relatives, a camp-out in national and state parks, or perhaps merely a grand circle of states just to see how far one could go in two weeks.

The automobile also gave rise to bus transportation and the trucking industry. Neither innovation was of much importance until the late 1920s, yet both posed major threats to the nation's network of streetcar lines and railroads.

Although the airplane, like autos and trucks, received added attention as a result of knowledge garnered during World War I, only daredevils, the rich, and a few hardy military-naval pilots had much to do with them in the twenties. Numerous problems related to air travel had to be ironed out before public acceptance would be forthcoming. When transcontinental passenger service began in the summer of 1929, it actually was a combination of land and air travel. Sturdy pioneers went by train from New York to Columbus, Ohio—the Alleghenies were considered too dangerous to fly over in an era that lacked radio navigational aids, lighted airfields, and pressurized cabins. From Columbus, passengers flew to Waynoka, Oklahoma, where they boarded a train bound for Clovis, New Mexico, and then flew on to Los Angeles. This plane-train trip took 48 hours.

More than anyone else in the 1920s, Charles A. Lindbergh (1902–1974) gave a dramatic boost to aviation. He was not a builder like Ford but a "popularizer" whose exploits won him a unique place in the nation's heart and also demonstrated the potential of air travel. A quiet young man who dropped out of the University of Wisconsin because it was not teaching him what he wanted to know, Lindbergh puttered with various types of engines, became a flyer and a pilot for the U.S. Mail Service, and in May 1927 (with the backing of some Missouri businessmen) startled the world by crossing the

San Francisco Examiner

AN AMERICAN PAPER FOR THE AMERICAN PEOPLE — AMERICA FIRST

VOL. CXXVI. NO. 142. CC SUNDAY, MAY 22, 1927—ONE HUNDRED AND THIRTY-EIGHT PAGES DAILY 5 CENTS, SUNDAY 10 CENTS

LINDBERGH REACHES PARIS IN 33½ HOURS; RIOTOUS WELCOME GIVEN WEARY AIRMAN

"Lucky"— Smilin' Through!

ADMIRERS WRECK FENCE, ROUT POLICE TO GREET SEA HERO

By WILLIAM HILLMAN,
Staff Correspondent Universal Service

LE BOURGET FIELD, PARIS, May 21.—(By Special Cable Dispatch.)—Swooping down from the skies in a magnificent landing, cheered to the echo by thousands upon thousands of welcoming Americans and French residents, Capt. Charles Lindbergh, the intrepid "Flyin' Fool" from St. Louis, Missouri, landed here tonight at 10:22 Paris time, completing his marvelous non-stop flight across the Atlantic Ocean from New York to Paris, a distance of approximately 3,600 miles.

Lindbergh's time was 33 hours and 30 minutes, two and one-half hours ahead of his schedule. He maintained an average speed of 107½ miles an hour.

Pulled From Plane

The gallant Missouri boy was pulled bodily from his plane, the "Spirit of St. Louis," almost before the plane had glided to a standstill. Lindbergh was raised on the shoulders of his admirers and carried away in triumph, to the accompaniment of shouts and cheers from thousands and thousands of spectators.

The first peep that Paris had of Lindberg was characteristic—the crowds saw merely a grinning youngster.

Throwing open the tiny door of his plane—the cabin of which had been a death chamber for a day and a half—the young airman pulled off his helmet, as though glad to be rid of it, and then broke into his characteristic grinning smile.

Throng Crashes Fence

Twenty-five thousand people crashed through the wire mesh fence at Le Bourget Field and raced half a mile across the field to where the crowds were milling about the victorious aviator. The people went wild. Flags were waved, songs were sung, cheers were shouted, and the carefully planned official reception went by the board.

"It's he," was the great cry, and even the French enthusiasts cried, "America forever. Vive l'Amerique!"

Hats were smashed, costumes torn, suits ruined. But the temper of the crowd remained unchanged. It was a wild, warm welcome, with everything in the nature of welcome that the French knew.

Women, crushed by the crowds, fainted here and there. They were carried to the "side-lines" and the outburst continued.

Mob Out of Control

Police tried, but were unable to control the mobs. It was Lindbergh's day and all day at that.

One of the first to reach Lindbergh's plane was the International News Service correspondent.

The grinning boy looked around him and heard a clamor of French voices. For a moment he seemed startled, as though he was frightened at being in a strange land. Then he opened his mouth. The great flyer spoke his first words. They were not words of boastful claims of victory, but words of fear—

CAPTAIN CHARLES LINDBERGH'S smiling countenance—photographed shortly before he hopped off from New York on the epic flight that landed him in Paris safely. A dispatch from Paris says: "The first peep that Paris had of Lindbergh was characteristic. Throwing open the tiny door of his plane—the cabin which had been a death chamber for a day and a half—the young airman pulled off his helmet, as though glad to be rid of it, and then broke into his characteristic grinning smile." Women and men battled to greet him as he was carried high on the shoulders of the first to reach him. "Doesn't anyone speak English?" the flyer pleaded. "Get me a drink."

Young Charles Lindbergh became an instant national idol by becoming the first man ever to fly non-stop from New York to Paris, in May 1927.

New York Public Library, Picture Collection.

Atlantic alone in a tiny craft appropriately named "The Spirit of St. Louis." Known as "Lucky Lindy" and "The Lone Eagle," he received the adulation of millions; however, his battles with reporters, his withdrawal from society after the kidnap-murder of a son, and his association with unpopular political causes later tarnished this image somewhat.

Politics as Cultural Conflict

As in any age, the political life of the 1920s reflected the broader social realities of the era. The dominant factors that shaped the 1920s were the preeminence of business, the impact of administrative and bureaucratic reform instituted during the war years, and the rising tension between rural and urban dwellers and between nativists and immigrants. Though the Republicans continued to dominate Congress, there were nonetheless signs of unrest in the electorate that would erupt with full force once the Depression hit.

A McKinley-Hanna "pluralist" Republican majority of workers and businessmen had reassumed the political helm in 1920. Hard times among farmers produced a short-lived Progressive party in 1924 whose platform called for the nationalization of railroads and utilities and emphasized an appeal to agrarian sensibilities based on antitrust sentiment. The Progressive party's opposition to strike injunctions also made it attractive to labor. In 1924, the Democratic party, which was divided between rural advocates of prohibition (who wanted William G. McAdoo) and urban anti-prohibitionists (who supported Alfred Smith), chose a bland, colorless corporation lawyer as its standard bearer. But John W. Davis posed a threat to no one, least of all the Republicans.

The key issue in 1924 was "Coolidge prosperity." Both Coolidge and Davis ran antiradical campaigns against Progressive candidate La Follette. Only 55 percent of the voters cast ballots, and Coolidge won a lopsided victory. The Republicans lost considerable backing among German-Americans, Irish-Americans, Jews, and to some extent Italian-Americans—all of whom had supported them in 1920. The primary beneficiary of these defections seems to have been La Follette, whose party got almost 5,000,000 votes and made some inroads in the cities, yet his record of pacifism, his stand against prohibition, and his opposition to the Ku Klux Klan hurt him in rural areas. In addition to the poor showing of Davis (8.3 million votes to 15.7 for Coolidge), the Democrats lost strength in Congress (4 seats in the Senate; 22 in the House). They made modest gains in the 1926 mid-term elections but still remained a distinct minority in both houses.

With Coolidge out of the race in 1928, Hoover was nominated on the first ballot at the national convention.

Library of Congress.

Alfred E. Smith (1873–1944)

Born on Manhattan's Lower East Side to second-generation Irish and German parents who were both Catholic, Al Smith spent his childhood around the docks; in fact, he said later that he and the Brooklyn Bridge grew up together. Two years after his father's death he quit the eighth grade to begin a series of odd jobs. His only degree, he bragged, was "FFM" (Fulton Fish Market). A popular, affable youth, Smith joined a local theater group, a step that led into politics. When twenty-one, he became active in precinct work for the Democratic party and within a decade was in the State Assembly. At first ignored by the Tammany Hall machine, he rose quickly and soon had Tammany backing. When the Democrats won control of the legislature in 1913, Smith became Speaker.

During these years Smith split his efforts between protecting Tammany interests and working for various social reforms (sanitation, health and fire prevention laws, wage and hour legislation for women and children, and workmen's compensation). In 1915 he was elected sheriff of New York City, a post fat with rich fees; then in 1918 he became governor, beating out William Randolph Hearst. He lost the governor's race in the Republican landslide of 1920 but was reelected in 1922, 1924, and 1926.

In these years Smith was able to steer an independent course away from Tammany. He made significant strides in administrative reorganization, welfare programs, and tax reduction, although he remained a fiscal conservative. Yet, as the state's chief executive he was usually on the side of Progressive legislation, and a vital influence upon him was Belle Moskowitz, a social reformer and close advisor. Many observers believe her death in 1933 marked the demise of Smith's liberalism.

Defeated for the Democratic presidential nomination in 1924 (largely because of rural opposition and dry supporters of William G. McAdoo), he won on the first ballot in 1928. He fought a losing battle against Hoover and prosperity, hurt also by his Catholicism, wet views, and urban twang.

After 1928, cut off from politics by New York's new governor, Franklin D. Roosevelt (whom Smith had persuaded to run at the last minute), he became president of the Empire State Building Corporation. As his economic conservatism became more apparent, Smith feuded often with Roosevelt, although he belatedly supported him in

1932. Two years later he helped form the American Liberty League, a well-financed, anti-New Deal coalition of conservative Democrats and Republicans. Eventually, the approach of World War II brought Smith and Roosevelt together again. He died in 1944.

Of medium height, stocky, smooth-faced, usually puffing a cigar, the "Happy Warrior" was a witty, resilient campaigner whose New York manners, Catholicism, and anti-prohibitionist stance hurt him seriously at the national level. Shortly before his death, Smith declined to attend the national party conclave, noting he would be "as welcome as an electric razor at a barbers' convention." ■

Library of Congress.

Far from representing old-fashioned America, Republican presidential candidate Hoover campaigned in 1928 as the spokesman for a "New Era." Using the radio to take his message to the voters, Hoover outpolled Democrat Al Smith in the election by a wide margin.

A natural expression of an era dedicated to efficiency, management, growth, and big business, and a very able administrator, Hoover seemed to be an ideal candidate—although it is true that members of the Republican Old Guard distrusted his associational activities and regarded him as nonpartisan in spirit. Al Smith, his opponent, worked hard to help the Democratic party avoid the divisiveness of 1924. As a national campaigner, the "Happy Warrior" did his best to avoid open conflict with state and local leaders who resented his candidacy.

The Hoover-Smith contest was not a race of conservative Republicans against liberal Democrats. Rather it was a contest of cultures. Smith was more conservative on fiscal matters than Hoover, though as New York's governor he had supported urban-oriented social welfare programs. But he was the son of immigrants. He thus represented to rural Americans everything they feared; he in turn treated farmers with disdain. Coolidge's indifference toward farmers was less damaging to Hoover than it might have been. Smith picked up some votes in the Republican strongholds in the Midwest, but his religion and his opposition to prohibition lost him thousands of rural votes, even in the traditionally Democratic South.

Smith's candidacy did activate the immigrant vote, especially among women, and produced the first Democratic majority in the nation's twelve largest metropolitan areas. But only cities with high immigrant populations broke from the Republicans in 1928. It would take the Depression to shatter the Republican majority. In politics as in so much of American life, the Great Crash of 1929 would prove to be a major watershed.

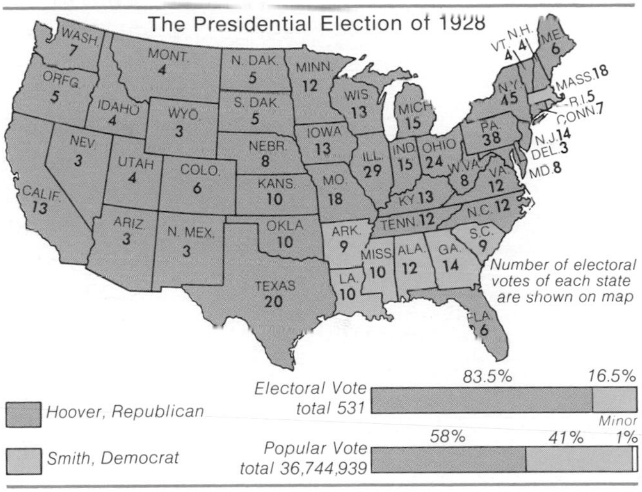

Essay

Life and Leisure

Four phenomena, so much an integral part of the American scene today that they often merit no special comment, exerted a profound impact upon the 1920s; they were the automobile, movies, radio, and advertising. And although all were adapted at times to practical pursuits, each nevertheless contributed directly to a new and sometimes puzzling factor in the daily life of millions: leisure time activities organized on a widespread scale.

The auto industry, which sold one million units in 1916 and more than five million thirteen years later, wiped out electric railway and street car companies, created new suburban living habits, and released farm families from centuries of isolation. Roads that were once dust-choked in summer, mud-filled in spring and fall, and rut-lined in winter became all-weather highways. Vacation plans changed dramatically as families went farther away from home, often to national and state parks where they met people from other sections of the country. School buses doomed the rural, one-room structure to oblivion, women drivers found long skirts a dangerous anachronism, and both lovers and criminals discovered the automobile to be possessed of attractive features its inventors had never dreamed of.

Average weekly movie attendance grew from 40 million in 1922 to 95 million in 1929 and 115 million in 1930. By 1931 there were 22,731 motion-picture houses in the nation, many of them truly living up to their name, "palaces." The introduction of "talkies" in 1927 staggered the film world momentarily, but soon business was better than ever. Although it is difficult to measure the effect of Hollywood, no one doubts that it was considerable. What stars did up there on the big screen—walking, dancing, talking, joking, crying, lovemaking, and feats of daring—was soon imitated from one coast to another, as were their cosmetics, their manner of dress, and their code of conduct both on and off camera.

Movie magazines, bulging with ads, furnished still more details to a breathless public, as did newspaper columns. Hollywood was "hot" copy, not only in the United States but throughout much of the world, and (unfortunately at times) the only America and the only Americans known to millions of foreigners was what that city churned out. One of the great culture shocks of World War II was the contrast between the real GI and his silver screen counterpart of the 1920s and 1930s.

Perhaps nothing illustrates the power of Hollywood better

than the death of screen lover Rudolph Valentino in 1926. Charles W. Eliot, ninety-two-year-old president emeritus of Harvard University and the nation's leading educator, died on August 26 of that year, about twenty-four hours before Valentino breathed his last. Eliot got a one-shot, single column send-off, but Valentino lingered on, or close to, the front pages for weeks. Of course, there were basic differences. Valentino lay in state in the Gold Room of Frank E. Campbell's Manhattan funeral parlor for ten days and was then carried across the country by train to California and yet another funeral service five days later. In addition, millions who had never heard of Eliot and, worse yet, even Harvard itself, saw this handsome Italian as ROMANCE in capital letters.

So many distraught American women either killed themselves in sorrow or gained momentary fame by bungling the job that Benito Mussolini exhorted Italian women to become mothers, not suicides. Screen star Pola Negri, who between swoons disclosed (to the great surprise of many of Valentino's friends, male and female) that they were lovers, nevertheless recovered sufficiently during a sensational interview to remember the duties of a hostess and to break open a case of whiskey for reporters.

Radio, at first regional but later national in its scope and influence, was largely a proper toy for little boys interested in science or something military officers played with until November 2, 1920, when KDKA in East Pittsburgh, Pennsylvania, began to broadcast regular programs, the first of which featured the Harding-Cox election returns. From that moment on, the growth of radio was spectacular. The total value of sets and parts produced in 1921 totaled a little more than $10 million, by 1929

Brown Brothers.

Rudolph Valentino, matinee idol of the 1920s, in a typically exotic costume for one of his films.

Brown Brothers.

The radio, which became commercially useable in the early 1920s, entered millions of American homes in that decade. Here an interested customer examines some of the home sets available.

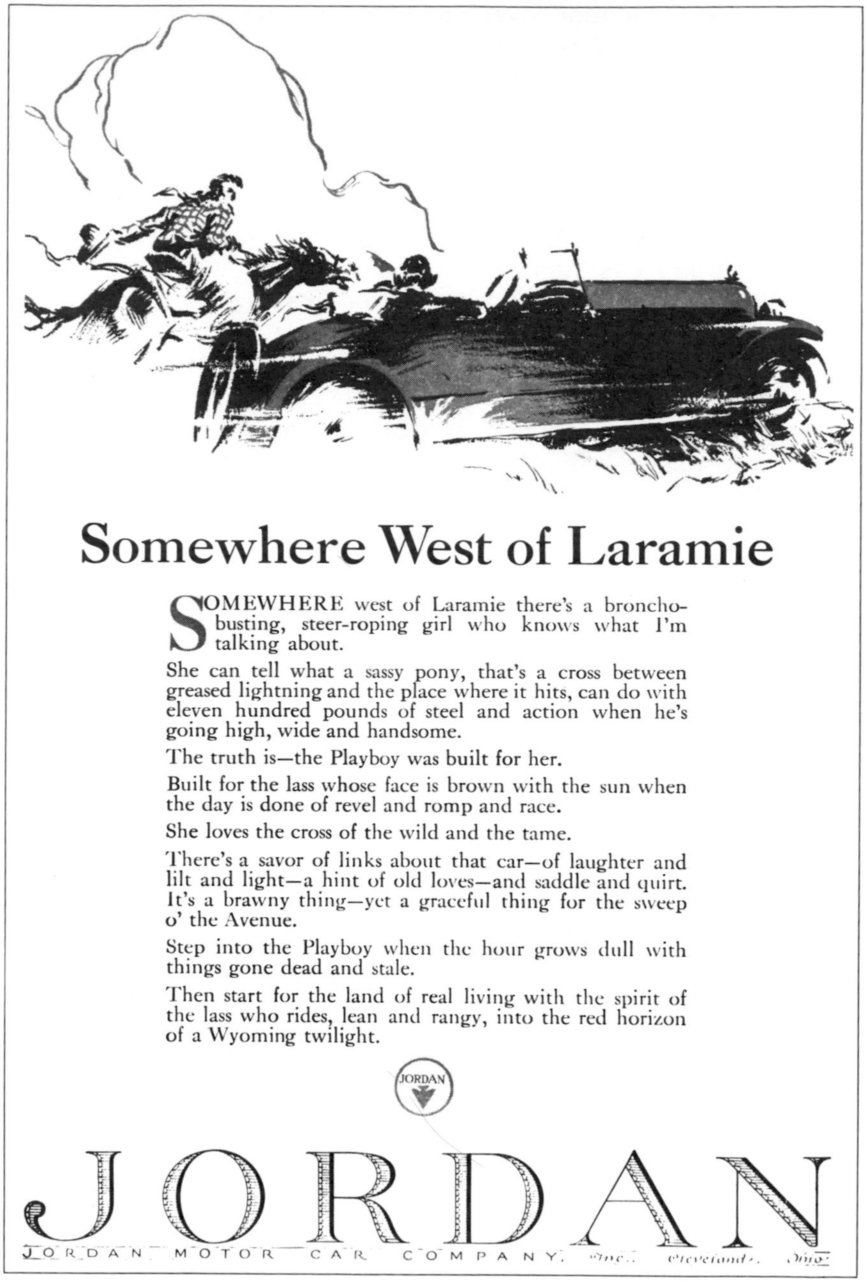

Somewhere West of Laramie
SOMEWHERE west of Laramie there's a broncho-busting, steer-roping girl who knows what I'm talking about.
She can tell what a sassy pony, that's a cross between greased lightning and the place where it hits, can do with eleven hundred pounds of steel and action when he's going high, wide and handsome.
The truth is—the Playboy was built for her.
Built for the lass whose face is brown with the sun when the day is done of revel and romp and race.
She loves the cross of the wild and the tame.
There's a savor of links about that car—of laughter and lilt and light—a hint of old loves—and saddle and quirt. It's a brawny thing—yet a graceful thing for the sweep o' the Avenue.
Step into the Playboy when the hour grows dull with things gone dead and stale.
Then start for the land of real living with the spirit of the lass who rides, lean and rangy, into the red horizon of a Wyoming twilight.
JORDAN
JORDAN
JORDAN MOTOR CAR COMPANY,

Bettmann Archives.

Advertising became big business in the 1920s, as producers of all sorts of consumer goods used adventure and sex appeal to enhance their products. This advertisement for Jordan automobiles was typical of the type found in popular magazines.

$400 million. And to that estimate must be added retail sales profits. According to the 1930 census, 12 million families (about 40% of all American homes) had radios. Of course, more radios were found in cities than in rural areas and the depressed South had proportionally fewer than other parts of the nation.

Major networks soon appeared—National Broadcasting Company in 1926 and Columbia Broadcasting System a year later—and in 1927 the federal government established a commission to license stations and assign each appropriate wavelengths. For the most part, early radio was viewed as an entertainment medium. There were occasional bits on the weather, news, and stock market, but these were overshadowed by children's hours, dramatic readings, church services, and—through it all—music. As late as 1927 about three-fourths of all programs featured tunes and melodies in some form, everything from classical recordings to jazz hits to hillbilly hoedowns.

Of course, in order to listen to this music one had to tolerate the advertising pitches that paid for the programs, just as one has to accept radio and television commercials of today. Billy Jones and Ernie Hare, two vaudevillians, for example, advertised Interwoven Socks with this jungle:

"Socks! Socks! We call each other Heel and Toe!
We're happy-go-lucky wherever we go!
Now it's time to entertain you."

Cereals, automobiles, and cigarettes got similar treatment, creating a mass market with national brand recognition from Maine to California. Perhaps the best-known of these radio performers was the "Amos 'n' Andy" team of Freeman F. Godsen and Charles J. Correll, two performers crowded off the live stage by Hollywood. Their black-life comedies enthralled nearly two generations of avid listeners.

"Dream world" advertising, found largely in slick magazines such as *Saturday Evening Post, Cosmopolitan, Vogue,* and *Time,* exuded an impact equal to that of radio commercials, perhaps even greater. The pursuit of happiness became synonymous with the pursuit of the opposite sex as ad executives pursued the account dollar with lavish pictures trumpeting the glories of soap, cold cream, shampoo, shaving cream, hair tonic, and so on. Sex, sex appeal, cleanliness, and keeping well ahead of the Joneses became hopelessly entangled as anxieties, some of them only recently diagnosed, were nurtured to increase corporate sales.

These diverse factors—the auto, movies, radio, and advertising—all in one way or another contributed to a great interest in sport. Professional baseball, already well established in several major cities, enjoyed new prominence in smaller, "minor league" communities. Memory of the Chicago "Black Sox scandal" in the World Series of 1919 faded away as baseball hero George H. ("Babe") Ruth of the New York Yankees hit a record making sixty home runs in 1927. College football, much less popular and not so well-known until after World War I, entered the golden age of Ernie Nevers, George Gipp, and Red Grange with huge stadiums, huge crowds, and huge traffic jams.

Courtesy Mrs. John Held, Jr.

This cover from the widely read *Life* magazine captures in exaggerated fashion the popularity of psychoanalysis and the greater public attention to sex in the 1920s. The reader is in full "flapper" costume.

Grange (1903–   ) scored five touchdowns for Illinois against Michigan in 1924—four of them in 12 minutes—and passed for a sixth.

This era also witnessed the birth pangs of professional football. The National Football League (founded in 1922) came out of swaddling clothes three years later when Grange signed with the Chicago Bears. Unprecedented crowds—36,000 in Chicago and nearly twice as many people in New York—turned out to watch the famed "Galloping Ghost." Eventually plentiful football talent after World War II injected new life into the sport and rival leagues, higher and higher salaries, and, above all else, television made "pro" ball a razzle-dazzle spectacle enjoyed by millions. Of course, the ubiquitous tube has rendered similar service to other sports—baseball, basketball, tennis, golf, horse racing, bowling, to name a few—and even introduced Americans to less familiar skills such as soccer, gymnastics, competitive swimming, practically anything encompassed by the Olympics.

Today it is not unusual—in fact it is commonplace—for groups of friends to organize their social life around sports events, movies, even TV programs. This is usually largely passive *in*activity on their part, exercising only their eyes, ears, mouths, and elbows, not their minds or bodies. What is essentially new is not organized leisure per se—various athletic events, dances, and games have long been an integral part of many cultures. But the extent to which this organization affects millions as mere spectators is unprecedented. And without the automobile, radio, television, and advertising (for better or for worse), it never would have come about.

Selected Readings

American Entry and Participation in the War

Ross Gregory, *The Origins of American Interventionism in the First World War* (1971)

Ernest R. May, *World War and American Isolation, 1914–1917* (1959)

Arthur Walworth, *America's Moment: 1918. American Diplomacy at the End of World War I* (1977)

Society and Politics: The War and Its Aftermath

John Higham, *Strangers in the Land: Patterns of American Nativism, 1860–1925* (1963)

Robert K. Murray, *Red Scare: A Study in National Hysteria, 1919–1920* (1955)

William M. Tuttle, Jr., *Race Riot: Chicago in the Red Summer of 1919* (1970)

The 1920s: General Accounts

Frederick Lewis Allen, *Only Yesterday: An Informal History of the 1920s* (1931)

Paul A. Carter, *The Twenties in America* (1968)

Paul A. Carter, *Another Part of the Twenties* (1977)

William E. Leuchtenburg, *The Perils of Prosperity, 1914–1932* (1958)

The New Era: Business and Politics in the Twenties

Robert K. Murray, *The Politics of Normalcy: Governmental Theory and Practice in the Harding-Coolidge Era* (1973)

Robert F. Himmelberg, *The Origins of the National Recovery Administration: Business, Government, and the Trade Association Issue, 1921–1933* (1976)

David Burner, *The Politics of Provincialism: The Democratic Party in Transition, 1918–1932* (1968)

Joan Hoff Wilson, *Herbert Hoover: Forgotten Progressive* (1975)

Race and Cultural Conflict

Kenneth T. Jackson, *The Ku Klux Klan in the City, 1915–1930* (1967)

E. David Cronon, *Black Moses: The Story of Marcus Garvey and the Universal Negro Improvement Association* (1968)

Norman H. Clark, *Deliver Us From Evil: An Interpretive History of American Prohibition* (1976)

Felix Frankfurter, *The Case of Sacco and Vanzetti* (1927)

Hazel Hertzberg, *The Search for an American Indian Identity: Modern Pan-Indian Movements* (1971)

Women and Youth in the 1920s

J. Stanley Lemons, *The Woman Citizen: Social Feminism in the 1920s* (1973)

Paula S. Fass, *The Damned and the Beautiful: American Youth in the 1920s* (1977)

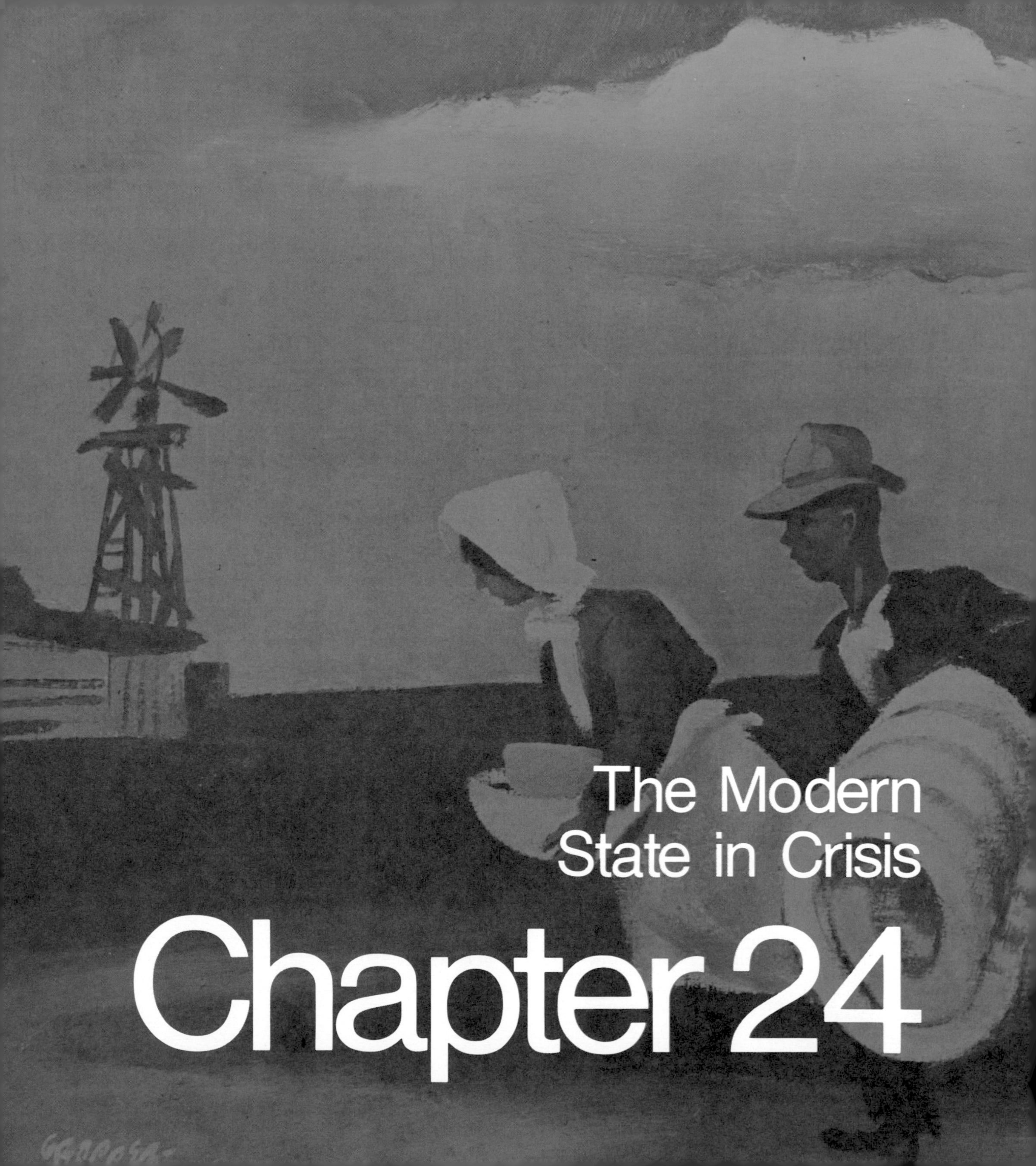

Chapter 24

The Modern State in Crisis

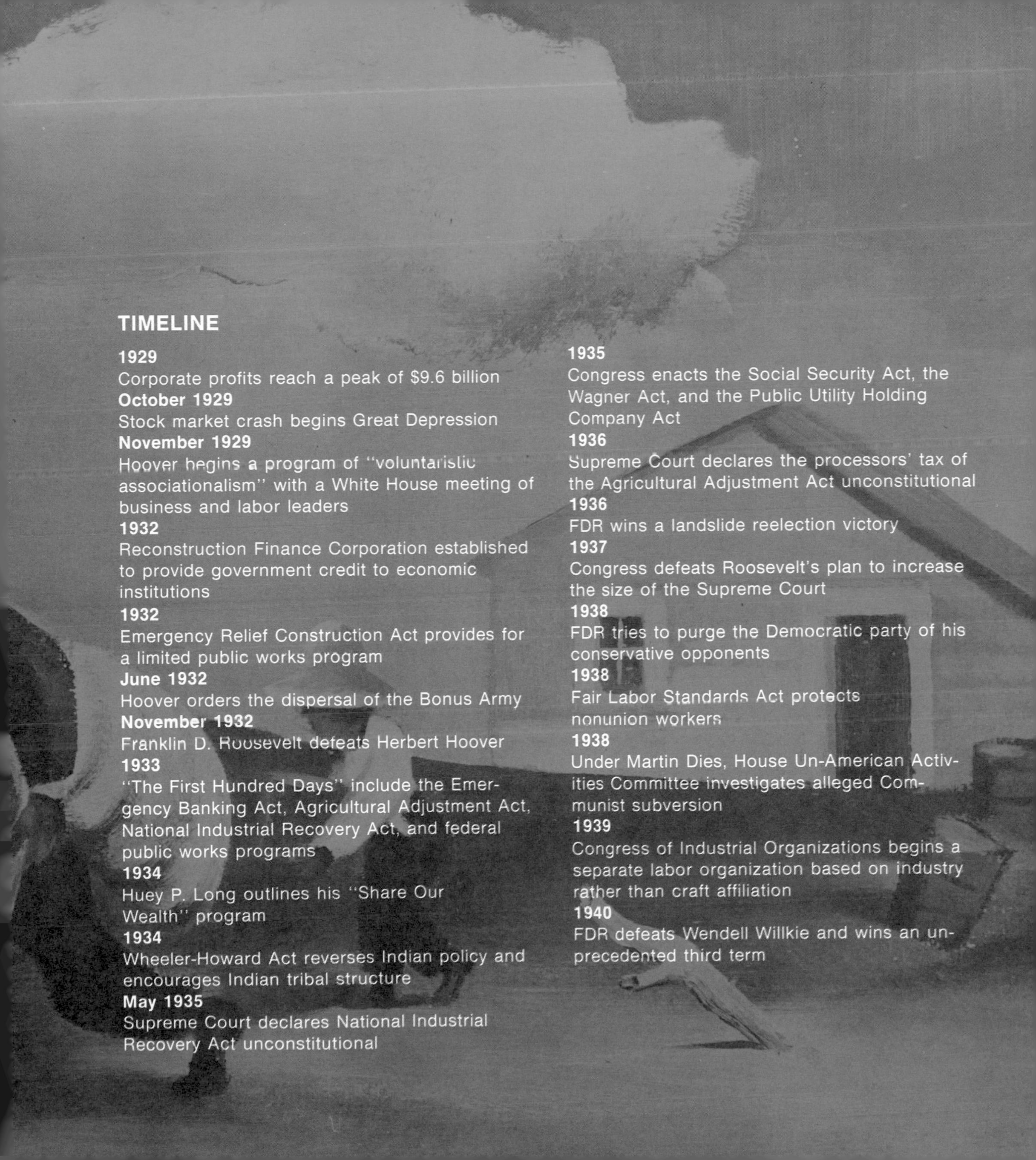

TIMELINE

1929
Corporate profits reach a peak of $9.6 billion
October 1929
Stock market crash begins Great Depression
November 1929
Hoover begins a program of "voluntaristic associationalism" with a White House meeting of business and labor leaders
1932
Reconstruction Finance Corporation established to provide government credit to economic institutions
1932
Emergency Relief Construction Act provides for a limited public works program
June 1932
Hoover orders the dispersal of the Bonus Army
November 1932
Franklin D. Roosevelt defeats Herbert Hoover
1933
"The First Hundred Days" include the Emergency Banking Act, Agricultural Adjustment Act, National Industrial Recovery Act, and federal public works programs
1934
Huey P. Long outlines his "Share Our Wealth" program
1934
Wheeler-Howard Act reverses Indian policy and encourages Indian tribal structure
May 1935
Supreme Court declares National Industrial Recovery Act unconstitutional
1935
Congress enacts the Social Security Act, the Wagner Act, and the Public Utility Holding Company Act
1936
Supreme Court declares the processors' tax of the Agricultural Adjustment Act unconstitutional
1936
FDR wins a landslide reelection victory
1937
Congress defeats Roosevelt's plan to increase the size of the Supreme Court
1938
FDR tries to purge the Democratic party of his conservative opponents
1938
Fair Labor Standards Act protects nonunion workers
1938
Under Martin Dies, House Un-American Activities Committee investigates alleged Communist subversion
1939
Congress of Industrial Organizations begins a separate labor organization based on industry rather than craft affiliation
1940
FDR defeats Wendell Willkie and wins an unprecedented third term

CHAPTER OUTLINE

In October 1929, as most Americans faced the future with optimism, the foundations of the present disappeared, giving way to an economic depression, the Great Depression, that dominated American life until the eve of war in 1940. President Hoover, prime mover of the New Era, caught between the achievements of his past performance and the confusion created by hard times, experimented with solutions that stretched the rather narrow limits of his ideological endurance. As his administration floundered, Americans, hungry for action as well as food, turned to a man about whom they knew little but who promised them a "new deal." And although the policies of Franklin Delano Roosevelt's administration were notably inconsistent, often contradictory, and only partially successful, the people elected him to office for an unprecedented four terms.

Legislation passed under the banner of the New Deal was not innovative in an ideological sense; it drew heavily from the lessons of the postwar period and elaborated on precedents established by prewar Progressives. Its goals, limited to economic recovery and politically acceptable social and economic equality, did not allow much opportunity for sweeping change. It was World War II rather than New Deal legislation that solved the problems of the Depression; yet Roosevelt's programs made the 1930s somewhat more tolerable than they might have been. During that decade women and minorities, "marginal" members of the work force, suffered setbacks, although unions expanded. Pockets of abject poverty remained throughout the country in 1940, despite legislation geared toward relief. And although civil rights and civil liberties began to receive attention, government action in those areas was more symbolic than concrete. Nevertheless, despite these and other disappointments, the New Deal was able to blunt most of the radical discontent during the Thirties.

While in office, Roosevelt instigated changes that were to have a great impact on American life, bequeathing to the nation an active presidency at the center of a government deeply involved in the economic and social welfare of its citizens. And of greater importance than the success or failure of individual pieces of New Deal legislation was the survival of the American system in the face of its greatest economic challenge.

From "New Era" to New Deal

In 1929 Americans could see substantial evidence that the New Era had indeed arrived. Even ordinary men and women were confident they could become rich. "Our situation is fortunate, our momentum is remarkable." So reported the President's Unemployment Conference in the spring of 1929 after a yearlong study. "Acceleration rather than structural change is the key to an understanding of our recent economic developments." This report stressed the stability of the country's price structure, praised the prudence of management, and noted that "with rising wages and relatively stable prices we have become consumers of what we produce to an extent never before realized." Prominent among those congratulated were New Era leaders, who had established "the organic balance of economic forces" without "serious cyclical economic fluctuations."

Statistics were encouraging: Corporate profits had reached a peak of $9.6 billion in 1929, with unemployment at a reasonable rate of 3.1 percent. During the previous decade the government had seen an annual yearly surplus accompanied by a total debt reduction of more than 20 percent. New capital issues totalled more than $10 billion, and there existed a favorable balance of trade of $840 million.

But all was not well. Hoover and his advisors stressed the high proportion of national wealth held by families earning less than $10,000 a year, but that high figure disguised real inequities in income distribution; other statistics showed that 5 percent of Americans were receiving one-third of the nation's personal income. This survey also ignored an agricultural depression, a decreased rate of investment in residential and community buildings, and a downturn of production in automobiles and other key industries. But blinded by bright promise, few Americans could see the precipice they were approaching.

Hoover and the Depression

Seven months after Hoover took over, the roof caved in. Although he had issued cautionary warnings in his capacity as Secretary of Commerce, few listened. Loans on stocks to New York brokers and bankers jumped from $3.5 billion in June 1927 to $8.5 billion by September 1929, and the price of common stocks nearly doubled. In those same months, business activity in general (commodity prices, factory employment, and freight-car loadings) rose by only a few percentage points.

Circumstances such as these—uneven growth, unrestricted loans, questionable banking practices, and an orgy of speculation by thousands who had never seen a stock certificate before—brought on the Great Crash of October 1929 and the long depression that followed. The New Era produced stable prices, substantial personal savings, and easy credit. With confidence in existing institutions, those with money were willing to invest heavily in stocks and securities, which were often unregulated and susceptible to erratic influences.

The roots of the dilemma, in the broadest sense, lay in the destruction of World War I when tangible wealth worth one-third of a trillion dollars vanished, leaving behind huge debts and a vast supply of unsupported paper money. The United States, the only power to emerge without heavy debts and the creditor of many less fortunate nations, refused either to cancel these obligations or to lower its tariff walls so debtors could gain the economic leverage to make payments on their loans.

Once the foreign financial scene became troubled, Wall Street turned its attention to the domestic realm, especially utilities. For example, Samuel Insull, head of electric, gas, and transportation companies in the Chicago area and veteran of Liberty Bond sales in World War I, turned his skills to the solicitation of funds from customers through stock sales. The result was a series of holding company pyramids in which Insull controlled large blocks of property with little actual investment. Between

STAGE BROADWAY SCREEN

VARIETY

PRICE 25¢

VOL. XCVII. No. 3 NEW YORK, WEDNESDAY, OCTOBER 30, 1929 88 PAGES

WALL ST. LAYS AN EGG

Going Dumb Is Deadly to Hostess In Her Serious Dance Hall Profesh

DROP IN STOCKS ROPES SHOWMEN

Kidding Kissers in Talkers Burns Up Fans of Screen's Best Lovers

Hunk on Winchell

Talker Crashes Olympus

MERGERS HALTED

Demand for Vaude

HOMELY WOMEN SCARCE; CAN'T EARN OVER $25

FILTHY SHOW OF SHUBERTS GOOD FOR SCREEN

Pickpocketing Dying Out

Ads for Execs

Soft Drink Smuggling

Flirting Contest

Studio in Church

BROOKS COSTUMES

New York Public Library, Picture Collection.

Although it was a long time building, the Great Crash occurred with seeming suddenness on "Black Tuesday," October 29, 1929. The Crash at first affected only those who owned stocks, but shortly spread into a Depression which ruined millions of Americans.

mid-1928 and early September 1929 the price of his stock rose from $12 to $159 a share. At the same time, other companies involved in new "miracle" industries enjoyed similar success. General Electric shares shot up from $130 to $396; Westinghouse, from $191 to $313; RCA, from $94 to $501. In October 1929, the period of overheated speculation came to an abrupt end; on the 21st, stocks began to decline; on the 24th, more than 12 million shares were exchanged; and on the 29th, came the crash.

Once the downward trend began, economic weaknesses caused the market to plummet further. America's corporate structure was not secure. New holding companies and investment trusts were forced to retrench, using any income they might receive to service existing debts rather than to invest in expansion. Nor was the banking structure sound enough to withstand the flurry of buying and selling since many banks were deeply involved in the stock market themselves, often like their customers buying "on the margin"—that is, paying only a small percentage of the price with an eye to making a quick sale as prices rose. The failure of one bank caused the assets of others to be frozen and people to fear for the safety of their investments deposited in still other banks. Consequently, a run on banks set off a chain reaction, and in the first six months of 1929, even before the crash, 346 banks failed, representing a loss to depositors of almost $115 million. By March 1933 two-thirds of the nation's banks had closed.

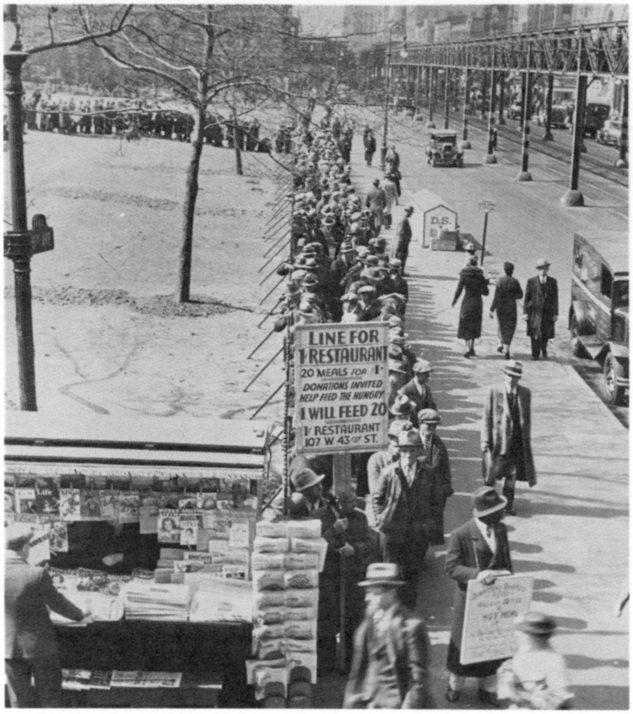

H. W. Fechner, Franklin D. Roosevelt Library Collection

A common sight during the Depression was the "hunger line," or "breadline." Here scores of unfortunates waiting their turn in a breadline in February 1932 solicit donations from passersby, calling attention to a participating restaurant.

Trouble overseas as nations defaulted on World War I debts and the Hoover administration's still higher tariffs caused a decline in exports, saturating the domestic market with durable goods. In part as a result of this, production levels decreased sharply and within a year of the crash had declined by 25 percent.

Between 1929 and 1933 the wholesale price index (with a base of 100 in 1926) plummeted from 95.3 to 65.9 and new capital issues sank from $10.2 billion to $709.5 million. Over the same period, unemployment rose from 3.1 percent to 25 percent, and between 1930 and 1940 the average number of unemployed dropped below eight million only once. In 1938 one out of every five Americans ready and willing to join the work force still could not find jobs.

It was appropriate that the leading symbol of the New Era was to oversee its time of greatest trial. But for Hoover, evidence of such prodigious failure was incompatible with the concrete advancements that the economy had made toward the American dream of success. Generally he called for "responsible individualism" and "voluntaristic associationalism"—neither of which would prove effective in coping with the magnitude of the Depression. Specifically, on November 21, 1929, he summoned a council at which business leaders promised to maintain production levels and wage rates while labor agreed to withdraw demands for wage increases. Hoover and his advisors felt that such cooperation would reduce price levels and production costs would be lowered enough to make profits possible. Neither industry nor labor was legally bound to terms contradicting the natural inclinations of both parties. Workers were not disposed to settle for less than they could get. Nor did industry want to maintain levels of production for a market that was not absorbing its goods. As a result, by the summer of 1931 industry leaders had reduced wage scales and decreased levels of production.

Rejecting the advice of those who prompted more drastic measures, such as General Electric's Gerard Swope who urged greater activism and public works projects, Hoover offered only renewed optimism: "We have come out of each previous depression into a period of prosperity greater than ever before. We shall do so this time." In spite of the realities of the nation's economy, he announced: "The fundamental business of the country, that is, the production and distribution of commodities, is on a sound and prosperous basis." On March 8, 1930, Hoover promised an end to the crisis in sixty days.

Although Republicans lost control of the House in the elections of 1930, Hoover continued to talk recovery; yet he admitted while addressing Congress in December of that year that the "origins of this depression lie to some extent within our own borders through a speculative period." Nevertheless, he insisted, the "major forces of depression now lie outside of the United States." To some degree, since Hoover obviously was disturbed by market trends before he entered the White House, the President was simply endeavoring to put the best face on a dismal situation and through soothing words to generate economic activity.

Except for the Emergency Relief Construction Act, a public works measure of 1932, Hoover tried to build confidence and stimulate the economy through personal exhortation and credit, not through direct governmental aid. In January 1932 the President signed into law the Reconstruction Finance Corporation, giving government credit to endangered savings banks and mortgage and life insurance companies in which millions had invested.

Hoover's reliance on political theory when confronted by human need, his continued belief in "American individualism" as individuals went hungry, was reflected in his attitude toward relief. He believed that relief was a local responsibility; as it turned out, local funds were insufficient in this crisis. Though the President assured the nation that federal money would be available should the need arise, people felt that need long before such funds were allocated. After the drought of 1930, Congress appropriated $145 million to save the livestock of Arkansas farmers. But Hoover opposed the distribution of an additional $25 million to feed the farmers themselves, preferring that help to be given, voluntarily, through the Red Cross. Eventually, with the President's approval, the farmers received $20 million in loans.

The response of both Hoover and General Douglas MacArthur (1880–1964) to the Bonus Army eroded even further public confidence and support. Hungry and out of work, World War I veterans demanded immediate payment of compensation Congress had deferred until 1945. In June 1932 they marched to Washington, D.C., camping within sight of the Capitol, to present their "petition in boots" to Congress. As their numbers grew to 20,000, guards appeared around the White House, increasing in the minds of many a sense of the President's isolation from the people. When two veterans were killed as authorities tried to dislodge them from temporary housing in abandoned buildings owned by the government, the National Guard was called in to disperse the "army." With sabers drawn, four troops of cavalry marched through the city, accompanied by six tanks and a column of infantry with fixed bayonets. Tear gas was thrown into the makeshift colony and shacks set on fire as veterans fled with their families. Even those unsympathetic toward the marchers' demands were outraged. The administration's mistake was compounded when newsreels contradicted official denials that the U.S. Army had used violence and that the marchers' camps had been set on fire.

By this time, Hoover's reputation was in a shambles. The self-made businessman and humanitarian who had distributed tons of food to an impoverished Europe and also aided strife-torn Russia, was unable to feed his own country. His image no longer inspired confidence, and few listened to his words of hope. Makeshift shantytowns in which many poor people lived were named "Hoovervilles." Old newspapers that they used for warmth were called "Hoover blankets." Empty pockets turned inside out were said to be "Hoover flags." Though condemned for his inability to seek solutions outside the framework of his own political ideology, Hoover went further than any previous President in mobilizing the federal government in an economic emergency. But he did not go far enough. And even if there still existed inherent processes in a free-enterprise system to maintain economic security and provide for economic recovery, much of the American public no longer had faith in them.

Roosevelt and Hoover

In its November 9, 1932, editorial, *The Nation* interchanged the first and last names of the presidential candidates to emphasize the ambiguous and indistinguishable

Franklin D. Roosevelt Library Collection.

A "Hooverville" on a vacant lot in New York City.

nature of their campaigns. But if the Democratic candidate's promises seemed no different from those of his Republican counterpart, Franklin Delano Roosevelt (1882–1945), in background and temperament, was quite unlike Hoover.

The only child of a wealthy New York family, Roosevelt spent his early years on a large estate overlooking the Hudson River at Hyde Park. There the services of governesses and tutors, a pony, and a 21-foot sailboat were provided for his education and pleasure. Before he was sixteen, Roosevelt had visited Europe eight times. After attending Groton and Harvard, he entered Columbia Law School and, though unhappy as a lawyer, eventually passed bar examinations. At twenty-eight he became interested in local politics and in 1910 was elected to the New York state Senate, where he led insurgents in opposition to Tammany leaders. For his active support of Wilson in the election of 1912, he was appointed Assistant Secretary of the Navy, a position once held by his fifth cousin, Theodore Roosevelt. His effectiveness as a campaigner and speechmaker established, Roosevelt was nominated by the Democrats in 1920 for the vice presidency; during the campaign he toured the country, making approximately 1,000 speeches.

With Harding's victory, Roosevelt once again became a private citizen—which it seemed he would remain after August 1921 when he was stricken with poliomyelitis. But by 1922, after a series of special exercises and water therapy, he was able to walk with eight-pound leg braces, supported either by crutches or a cane and the arm of a companion. The affliction was to help rather than to hurt his political career. Many Americans, themselves stricken with hunger and poverty, came to see in his courage an example to follow, and in his personal triumph, a promise for their own. Initial doubts about the limits of his stamina were dispelled when, at the urging of Democratic presidential nominee Al Smith, Roosevelt campaigned successfully for the governorship of New York in 1928. Reelected in 1930 by a majority of 700,000 votes, he became a leading candidate for the Democratic presidential nomination in 1932.

The Democrats were optimistic about their chances for victory in 1932, whomever they might nominate; Roosevelt's strong activist record as a governor from the outset of the Depression and the support of southern conservative delegations gained him the nomination on the fourth ballot. Traditionally, a nominated candidate did not make an acceptance speech until formally notified of his nomination several weeks after the convention. Shattering precedent, Roosevelt flew to the convention to accept the nomination in person. He announced: "You have nominated me and I know it, and I am here to thank you for the honor. Let it . . . be symbolic that in so doing I broke traditions. Let it be from now on the task of our Party to break foolish traditions. . . . I pledge you, I pledge myself, to a new deal for the American people." Although the phrase was of no special importance to

Scion of a wealthy New York family, Franklin D. Roosevelt fought his way back from poliomyelitis during the 1920s to become leader of the Democratic party. With FDR, in this 1919 photograph taken in Hyde Park, are his domineering mother, Sara Delano Roosevelt (seated next to him), his wife Eleanor, and his five children.

Roosevelt at the time, "new deal" was picked up by journalists the next day and later became the rallying cry of the new administration.

During the campaign most of Roosevelt's ambiguous proposals defied characterization, but his call to action and the fact that he was not Hoover were sufficient to attract the support of most voters, who believed a change was necessary. Hoover brought down the GOP with him as he used the campaign to "educate" voters with a vindication of his policies. A victim of a "credibility gap" as well as of his own stubbornness, he polled only 15,758,397 popular votes to Roosevelt's 22,825,016 and carried only six of the forty-eight states.

In his inaugural address the new President confidently announced: "This great nation will endure as it has endured, will revive and will prosper. So first of all, let me assert my firm belief that the only thing we have to fear is fear itself—nameless, unreasoning, unjustified terror, which paralyzes needed efforts to convert retreat into advance." Ironically, Roosevelt's cheerleading optimism differed little from that of his predecessor, which the

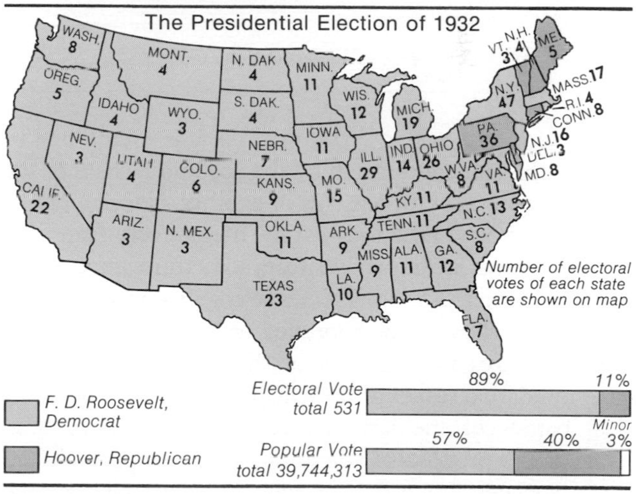

public had ignored; on the other hand, he followed up his words with action, which Hoover could not possibly have taken for at least three reasons: his political mind-set, the opposition of a Democratic Congress, and the unwilling-

Frederic Lewis.

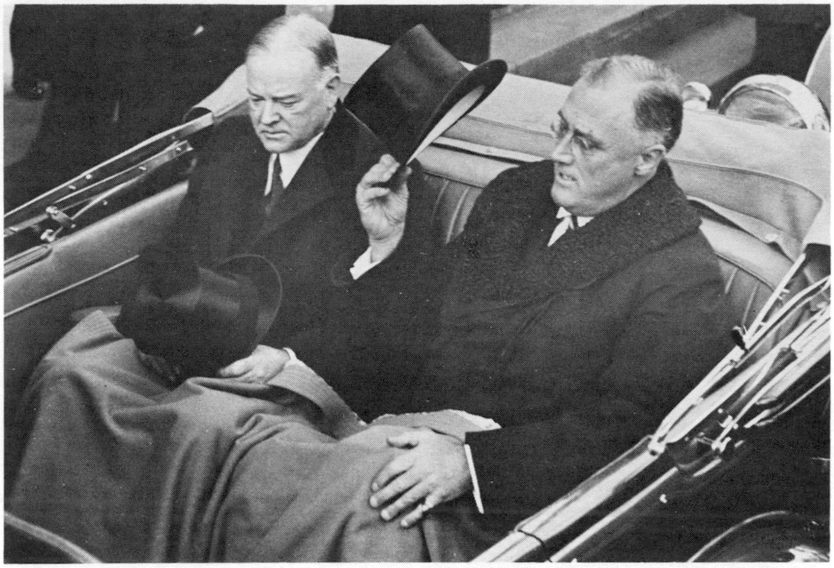

On Inauguration Day 1933, outgoing President Hoover hardly spoke to his successor. Relations between the two had been badly strained between the election and the inauguration, as Roosevelt had refused to work with Hoover on any of the latter's recovery programs.

ness of millions of Americans to accept dramatic changes until the crisis had deepened. Within the "First Hundred Days" of the Roosevelt administration, Congress would approve almost all the proposals made by the new President, and while these, and those to follow, would not form a coherent whole, they would affect almost every aspect of life in America.

The New Deal

The New Deal was a series of programs established to deal with problems created by the economic chaos of the Great Depression. In one way or another, before it ran its course, the New Deal touched the life of every American citizen. It was a complex venture, sometimes experimental and visionary, at other times strangely conservative in tone. Yet, whether one approved or disapproved of specific measures and innovations, the New Deal fashioned the foundation stones of present-day America. The political battles of the last half-century rarely have been waged over proposals to undo the work of Roosevelt and his associates. Instead, they have been waged over the system bequeathed to us.

The Roosevelt Circle

One man was at the center of the New Deal, but he brought with him a very talented wife (perhaps his intellectual superior), five attractive, athletic children well into their twenties by the time their father became President, and a cadre of dedicated workers from his days in Albany. Action, not intellectual achievement or philosophical reflection, was at the heart of their collective desires; and, in a sense, they revived the aura of an earlier Roosevelt White House. FDR himself was, above all else, a politician, a persuader, an aloof manipulator often distant from family, friends, and associates. He was confident, self-assured, apparently undismayed by the enormity of the task before him, but at the same time he had little understanding of economic realities, no sound, well-thought-out program, and no special residue of experience that would enable him to work miracles. Yet the Squire of Hyde Park not only had flair but also had the willingness—and the eagerness—to try new ideas. These qualities alone inspired confidence in an America drained of that precious commodity.

Eleanor Roosevelt (1884–1962), a distant cousin, married Franklin in 1905 at a wedding dominated by her dynamic uncle, President Theodore Roosevelt. A shy, awkward girl, she spent the next decade or so starting a family and living much in the shadow of her ambitious husband. When New York state granted suffrage to women in 1918, for example, she did not even bother to vote. Then, two shattering events changed her life: discovery of Franklin's intimate relationship with her social secretary and his bout with polio, which left him partially paralyzed. In the mid-1920s, as Eleanor Roosevelt was battling his domineering mother who wanted her son to give up public life, she embraced an aggressive political career on her husband's behalf and never again was far from the ferment of liberal reform. By 1939 she had traveled 280,000 miles, shaken thousands of hands, and made hundreds of speeches. Beginning in 1935 she also wrote a column ("My Day") and four years later was receiving 150,000 letters. A Gallup Poll conducted in 1939 showed that 68 percent of Americans approved of her activist role as First Lady (she often worked to help the poor, blacks, and other minorities), a much higher rating than that of her husband. An adroit, backstage manipulator, she often arranged for black leaders to call upon her at the White House and then made certain that her husband also met them, if only in passing. In this way she gave blacks access to the President which could have been politically embarrassing had minority spokesmen sought a formal meeting through direct channels.

Another member of the Roosevelt circle, cast in the same liberal mold, was Frances Perkins (1882–1965), Secretary of Labor and the first woman ever to hold Cabinet rank. A Massachusetts-born social worker famous for her tricornered hats and outfits some said were designed by the Bureau of Standards, she rose through experience gained in World War I to a position on New York's State Industrial Commission, becoming director of that body under Governor Roosevelt. Although organized labor scoffed at the idea of a woman heading up the Department of Labor, she did a competent job during difficult times. Her biggest failure was as a mediating influence in strikes that plagued the 1930s. After resigning from the Cabinet in 1945, she served as a member of the Civil Service Commission (1946–1952).

Other women who rose to positions of prominence included Nellie Tayloe Ross and Ruth Bryan Owen (1885–1954). Ross, governor of Wyoming from 1925 to 1927 and director of the U.S. Mint for two decades (1933–1953) was the first woman ever to become the chief executive of a state or to hold the prestigious Mint position. Owen, daughter of William Jennings Bryan and a member of Congress from Florida (1927–1933), served for three years as minister to Denmark, the first woman ever to head a U.S. diplomatic mission.

The two most powerful influences upon Roosevelt were Louis M. Howe (1871–1936) and Harry Hopkins (1890–1946). Both suffered from chronic ill health but were devoted completely and wholeheartedly to "the Boss." Howe, an ungainly, untidy little man who began life as a journalist, looked out for Roosevelt's interests from the time he was a newcomer in Albany until he was firmly established in the White House; then Hopkins more or less took over those responsibilities as Howe's health failed. Howe, a "behind-the-scenes" man and a brilliant political analyst, served as Roosevelt's key aide for nearly a quarter of a century, keeping his political spirit alive when polio struck. Hopkins, an Iowa-born social worker, joined the Roosevelt team in 1928, heading up temporary relief efforts at the state and then national levels. Unlike Howe, he was highly visible and held a variety of key positions, and even out of office he was recognized as a force of considerable consequence.

Franklin D. Roosevelt Library Collection.

During the New Deal years, women for the first time became visible in the federal power structure. Most visible of all was Eleanor Roosevelt (left), pictured here with Ruth Bryan Owen, the first woman ambassador.

The Early New Deal, 1933–1935

While Roosevelt awaited his inaguration on March 4, 1933, he conferred with Raymond Moley, Rexford Guy Tugwell, Adolf Berle, Jr., and others of his professorial advisors known collectively as the "Brain Trust." Bitterness between incoming and outgoing Presidents increased when Roosevelt rejected Hoover's pleas to join the discussions being held to retain banker confidence.

And it was banking interests that were the target of the first in a series of legislation by which the government intended to control investments and end, as Roosevelt put it, "speculation with other people's money." On March 6 FDR closed all banks throughout the country pending congressional action on his Emergency Banking bill. This legislation, passed on March 9, provided government insurance for those banks that proved sound; 600 banks received loans amounting to $1 billion, while 2,000 institutions were closed down. On March 12 some sixty million Americans gathered around radios to listen to the first of Roosevelt's "fireside chats," during which they were assured that it was again safe to entrust their funds to the nation's banks. Because all banks had been closed, it was feared that when they reopened many depositors might withdraw their money. But on March 13, with confidence restored, deposits in every city exceeded withdrawals.

Like other legislation that was passed swiftly by Congress during the First Hundred Days, the Emergency Banking Act was aimed at recovery and reflected the administration's intention to revise and shore up rather than to supplant established systems—to offer a new deal, but from the same deck. The act also typified the ad hoc nature of early emergency New Deal legislation. As Roosevelt said in 1933: "One thing is sure. We have to do something. We have to do the best we know how at the moment. If it doesn't turn out right, we can modify it as we go along." Also typical was the response of critics from both the right and left, the former insisting the measures went too far, the latter that they did not go far enough. As Congressman William Lemke charged: "The President drove the moneychangers out of the Capitol on March 4th—and they were all back on the 9th."

On March 12, Congress passed an economy measure that slashed $400 million from payments to veterans and $100 million from the wages of federal employees. The next day, Roosevelt asked Congress to repeal the Eighteenth Amendment and end prohibition; the states ratified the Twenty-First Amendment and by April 7 beer was being sold legally in the United States for the first time since 1920. The country was moving, and its people began to respond. If they did not know exactly where they were going, they at least experienced, for the first time in months, a sense of movement rather than stagnation.

Two of the most ambitious programs of the First Hundred Days were the Agricultural Adjustment Act (AAA) that the President signed on May 12 and the National Industrial Recovery Act—usually called NRA for the National Recovery Administration it created—which was passed a month later. The former reflected the new administration's concern over the plight of farmers who had been experiencing low prices and hard times for a decade; the latter, the realization that industry needed assistance immediately. The AAA assumed that agricultural problems plaguing farmers since the 1870s were based on overproduction, not underconsumption, and that compensatory payments to farmers to reduce crop production would solve these problems. Moneys for these payments were to be raised by licensing and taxing millers, packers, canners, and other processors, not from general revenue. The act was to be administered democratically—county by county, commodity by commodity—but this very decentralization soon led to control by larger owners, who often cut back production on lands leased to sharecroppers and tenant farmers. By 1935 the AAA had increased agricultural prices, but its popularity was limited by the fact that it cut back food production at a time when people were starving. In January 1936 the Supreme Court in a 6-3 decision (*U.S.* v. *Butler*) declared the processing tax unconstitutional. With the act thus invalidated, farm prices declined sharply, the Court was denounced, and those members responsible for the death of the act were hanged in effigy by distraught farmers.

The National Industrial Recovery Act had much in common with the Agricultural Adjustment Act in both its democratic construction and its fate. A major goal of early New Deal legislation was "reflation"—that is, a return to the price and wage levels of the "golden" years between 1919 and 1929 and thus to high consumer demand and high levels of production—but without the economic inequalities of that period. With the trade associations of the 1920s and the earlier War Industries Board as precedents, the NRA was to supervise industrial codes of fair competition. Under this administration,

Culver Pictures.

Hugh Johnson
(1882–1942)

"Everybody in the world is a rink-stink but Hughie Johnson and he's all right!" Neighbors living in Fort Scott, Kansas, in the 1880s long remembered this youthful cry, which symbolized Johnson's sixty-year battle with the rest of the human race. Able, opinionated, a mixture of gruffness, charm, wisecracks, and shyness, Hugh Johnson was born there in 1882. At the age of fifteen he tried to run away and join Teddy Roosevelt's Rough Riders, but his father stopped him at the railway depot with the promise of an appointment to West Point. He finally got there three years later, graduating in 1903.

During the next sixteen years he served in Texas, San Francisco, the Philippines, Mexico, and Washington, D.C. Before the Mexican imbroglio and World War I occupied his time, Johnson turned out numerous rousing adventure books for boys.

In 1917–1918 he served as judge advocate under General Pershing, a representative on the War Industries Board, and director of Selective Service. Retiring as a brigadier general in 1919, Johnson became president of the Moline Plow Company. One of Roosevelt's so-called "Brain Trust" in 1932, he soon was appointed to head up the National Recovery Administration. During that agency's brief, chaotic life Johnson held the most exciting news conferences to be found in the nation's capital. He dramatized the force of the New Deal with blunt phrases such as "cut out the guff," "hooey," and "bunk"; however, he turned out to be a rather inept administrator.

Johnson served for a short time as head of WPA, but then began to drift away from the New Deal and Roosevelt, especially after the President's court reform plan of 1937. He was violently opposed to FDR's third-term bid, fearing it meant the entry of the United States into World War II.

Much of this criticism appeared in his widely circulated newspaper column, "Hugh Johnson Says." Never really so hard-boiled as he appeared, Johnson, who died in 1942, was for a brief time one of the most interesting individuals on the national scene. ■

production, employment and wages were to be increased, work hours lowered, and labor, under Section 7(a), guaranteed the right to bargain collectively. Also, the provisions of this act encouraged cooperation throughout all levels of industry and suspended antitrust legislation in a desperate attempt to revive the economy.

The pugnacious administrator of the NRA was General Hugh Johnson who had helped organize the draft during World War I and was a veteran of the War Industries Board. Johnson viewed his job realistically:

"This is just like mounting the guillotine on the infinitesimal gamble that the ax won't work." The codes were to "eliminate eye-gouging and knee-groining and ear-chewing in business," said Johnson. "Above the belt any man can be just as rugged and just as individual as he pleases."

The government issued blanket guidelines for all industries until each could set up its own code, according to its needs. Although the largest industries were recalcitrant, by 1935 more than 500 had established such codes and more than 200 others were being formulated. Obviously, all industries did not require regulation, and wasted effort accompanied the inclusion of industries concerned with the manufacture of curled hair, horse hair dressing, shoulder pads, and other such products.

Johnson gave the NRA both its symbol (the Blue Eagle) and its slogan ("We Do Our Part"). And as the program gained public support, the eagle began to be seen everywhere. In New York 250,000 people, in the city's largest parade until that time, marched down Fifth Avenue under its banner. But by 1934 critics were attacking the NRA from all sides. Large businesses charged government interference with labor practices under 7(a); small businessmen and liberals objected to the suspension of antitrust laws; labor charged that 7(a) caused confusion and ultimately allied the government with big business; housewives complained of increased prices.

The NRA placed even more faith in the self-regulation and voluntarism of business than had the Hoover administration. According to Johnson, the fate of the man who violated the code was too terrible to contemplate: "As happened to [Kipling's] Danny Deever, NRA will have to remove from him his badge of public faith and business honor and 'takin of his buttons off an' cut his stripes away' break the bright sword of his commercial honor in the eyes of his neighbors—and throw the fragments—in scorn—in the dust at his feet. . . . It will never happen. The threat of it transcends any puny penal provision in this law." Yet the codes, which were to have been formulated democratically by business, labor, and consumer representatives, frequently became dominated by larger firms, whose executives and lawyers, with knowledge of specifics, had an advantage over NRA officials, who were familiar only with the broad outlines of the blanket code.

While even impartial studies found much wrong with the NRA, the program kept the economic situation from becoming worse. The deflationary spiral was halted as unemployment dropped from 25 percent in 1933 to 20 percent in 1935 and the national income increased from $40 billion to $57 billion. Business ethics generally improved, child labor and sweatshops were virtually abolished, and a national system of minimum wages and maximum hours was established. But the NRA did little to speed recovery and, as the sense of economic crisis faded, it created a series of private economies ruled by individual industries. Competition was stifled by the larger corporations in control of the codes, production was reduced and profits came not from an expanded industry but from price raising. Since the government

U.P.I.

A 1933 rally in San Francisco shows the NRA emblem, a Blue Eagle clutching a thunderbolt, formed by some of the 8,000 children present.

was unwilling to use punitive measures, private business interests expanded at the expense of public interest.

Like the AAA, the NRA was struck down by the Supreme Court. In May 1935, in a unanimous decision (*Schechter* v. *U.S.*), the Court declared that Congress could not delegate legislative power to the President "to exercise an unfettered discretion to make whatever laws he thinks may be needed or advisable for the rehabilitation and expansion of trade or industry." The Court also found the act covered more than interstate commerce. Although Roosevelt protested "the horse-and-buggy definition of interstate commerce," the passing of the NRA had few mourners. But it left in its wake no living body of legislation upon which other ideas of the New Deal could be centered. The NRA was neither pure voluntarism nor, as conservatives charged, a step toward national economic planning. It combined associationalism, licensing authority for government, recognition of consumer rights, and collective bargaining protection—all of which often worked at cross-purposes. In the tension among its components can be seen a microcosm of the New Deal.

Programs to reduce the number of unemployed workers were also initiated within the First Hundred Days. The Civilian Conservation Corps (CCC), the first of these, eventually employed 2.5 million youths between the ages of eighteen and twenty-five to rehabilitate forests and soil, dig ditches and canals, and stock streams and lakes with fish. This organization and its work held special fascination for Roosevelt, and he often visited CCC groups as they worked to control floods and extend state park lands. By 1939 over two million young men had served in the CCC, and in that same year the President and Mrs. Roosevelt proudly displayed one of their camps to the King and Queen of England. In May 1933, the Federal Emergency Relief Administration (FERA) was established to provide more than $500 million in direct relief to state and local agencies for routine construction work and education programs for adults and children. The following month, the National Industrial Recovery Act created the Public Works Administration (PWA) to coordinate all public works programs. It initially employed four million men on projects of clearance and construction and in clerical jobs, with wages adjusted to local rates. Under the direction of Secretary of Interior Harold Ickes, it was limited both by his caution with money at a time when rapid spending was required to stimulate the economy and by the President's raids into its funds for other programs.

In April 1935 public works programs increased sharply with the formation of the Works Progress Administration (WPA), which eventually spent more than $11 billion on some 250,000 projects and provided a basic wage for hundreds of thousands of unemployed, stimulated the growth of private business, and completed reforms that states could not afford to undertake. Under its provisions, within four years the Federal Theatre Project produced plays, circuses, and vaudeville shows in English, Yiddish, Spanish, and French to an audience of thirty million, many of whom had never seen a play. The Federal Writers Project initiated some 1,000 publications, including state and city guides, and employed such writers as Conrad Aiken, John Cheever, and Richard Wright. Under the Federal Arts Project the art of mural decoration was revived, employing the talents of such artists as Stuart Davis, Willem De Kooning, and Jackson Pollock. Because of murals painted in Manhattan, Davis (the eldest) was undoubtedly the best-known of this group in the 1930s. The trio, leaders in abstract modern art, soon confounded critics and patrons with their unorthodox techniques and untraditional productions. Pollock even abandoned his easel in time, putting canvases on the floor instead and using a trowel or stick in place of a brush. The National Youth Administration eventually gave part-time employment to 600,000 college students and 1.5 million high school students, largely in jobs related to their fields of interest.

Relief measures aimed specifically at rural areas began in March 1933 with creation of the Tennessee Valley Authority (TVA). Somewhat akin to the "socialism" with which conservative critics charged the administration's entire program, the TVA was to "use the facilities of the controlled [Tennessee] river to release the energies of the people." The area to be administered covered 40,000 square miles in seven states and was intended as a laboratory for social planning. Provisions for the construction and control of dams to develop waterpower resources and facilitate nitrate production were accompanied by other provisions for malaria control and recreational lakes. Although the government's development of waterpower was attacked as a threat to private utilities worth $12 billion, the Supreme Court in 1939 sustained the constitutionality of the TVA with only one dissenting vote in *Tennessee Electric Co.* v. *TVA*.

Frederic Lewis.

Harold Ickes
(1874–1952)

Harold Ickes, one of the most loyal members of Franklin D. Roosevelt's New Deal team, was Secretary of Interior from 1933 to 1946. Although that office is normally not a key Cabinet post, this thickset, bespectacled, vigorous champion of the underdog quickly became one of the most colorful and forceful personalities of that exciting era.

Born in Pennsylvania in 1874, Ickes went at age sixteen (upon the death of his mother) to Chicago to live with relatives, and the Windy City soon became his political laboratory. In 1897 he graduated from the University of Chicago, worked as a reporter for three years, and then returned to his alma mater to get a law degree. Within a short time Ickes was deep into politics, usually supporting Progressive Republican hopefuls. He was a Bull Moose stalwart in 1912, and backed Charles Evans Hughes in 1916, but four years later switched to the Democrats when he and his friends failed to prevent the nomination of Harding. In 1932 he worked hard for Roosevelt and a year later joined his Cabinet.

In Washington, Ickes also became administrator of the Public Works Administration (PWA), part of the National Industrial Recovery Act, which he administered so frugally that PWA gradually came under the aegis of one of his most astute rivals, Harry Hopkins. In 1940 he played a very prominent role in the controversial third-term campaign, speaking out vigorously on behalf of FDR and ridiculing his opponent as "a rich man's Roosevelt . . . a simple, barefoot Wall Street lawyer."

With the onset of war, Ickes took on the task of coordinating petroleum for defense needs and became a virtual czar of the oil industry. Always a strict conservationist and an outspoken foe of big business, to some he was simply "Harold the Meddler" or a "common scold"; but to others he was perhaps the wittiest tongue in Washington. Twice married and a collector of stamps and dahlias, he produced a three-volume *Secret Diary* that is a source of much information concerning the New Deal era. Ickes died in 1952. ■

Despite its achievements, the TVA never became the model for social planning that the administration intended it to be. More widespread in its impact was the Rural Electrification Administration, which in 1935 revolutionized the life of America's rural citizens. At that time, only one out of every ten Americans had electricity

Culver Pictures.

The WPA (Works Progress Administration) not only gave Americans jobs, but allowed states and cities to construct and upgrade needed public facilities. Here a band of WPA workers are shown working on the Richmond, Virginia, waterfront in late 1937.

in their homes. Farmers worked without electrical machinery, their wives without washing machines, refrigerators, or other electrical appliances. Under the REA, a series of nonprofit cooperatives allowed rural citizens to borrow money from the government to bring power lines into the countryside. By 1941 two-fifths of all Americans were equipped with electricity.

The Later New Deal: 1935–1938

Both contemporary observers and historians have long disagreed on what happened to Roosevelt's programs as the close of his first term drew near, especially whether his proposals became more conservative or more radical. Some see a "second" New Deal in 1935 quite different from that of 1933. As one scholar has observed, the "first" New Deal told business what it must do; the "second," what it must not do. To some extent, legislation passed in 1935 had been in the works for some time; in addition, more so than two years earlier, the President was thinking in terms of reelection. In any case, 1935 brought a distinct shift. The NRA and AAA, legislation central to the early New Deal, were dismantled in 1935 and 1936 respectively. Many new measures (such as the Wagner and Social Security acts) represented a different approach to solving economic problems and others (such as the Public Utility Holding Company Act) reflected a new commitment to antitrust activity. Both business interests and leftist groups, more critical than they had been during the time of immediate crisis, increasingly sought to influence administrative policies.

Nevertheless, characteristics shared by the two periods are greater than apparent differences. Legislation continued to be eclectic and consistent in that it was nonideological; in fact, most measures passed between 1935 and 1938 had been discussed in some form by Roosevelt and his advisors as early as May 1933. Essentially, commitment to "reflation" and the reduction of vast social and economic inequalities remained strong. But with the economic emergency over (and thus the necessity for purely ad hoc measures), the administration could more thoughtfully draft legislation designed to bring enduring reform.

The Second Hundred Days began in June 1935, when, after months of inactivity, the President called on Congress to pass a social security bill, the Wagner labor proposal, a banking bill, a public utility holding company measure, a "soak-the-rich" tax scheme (a misnomer for the Revenue Act of 1935), and additional minor measures, some of which were themselves highly controversial.

The Social Security Act (1935) was one of the most far-reaching measures enacted by the New Deal. Intended in part to steal the thunder of two pension advocates who might oppose FDR in 1936—Louisiana's powerful Senator Huey Long (1893–1935) and Francis E. Townsend (1867–1960)—it provided for a general agency to administer unemployment compensation, old-age security, and various social services. Payroll taxes, which have increased dramatically since the 1930s, were to provide the funds to run these programs.

The Wagner Act improved on Section 7(a) of the defunct NRA by clarifying the federal government's support of collective bargaining. It established a federally appointed, independent National Labor Relations Board to oversee elections determining bargaining units, to certify the victorious units, and to restrain interstate businesses from such "unfair labor practices" as dismissal of workers because of union membership and domination of unions by employers. Unions were not obliged by the act to make any concessions in return. Granted investigatory powers, in two years the board heard more than 5,000 cases involving "unfair practices."

In 1934, the Securities Exchange Act set up the

Securities Exchange Commission (SEC) to ensure federal regulation of trading practices. The act compelled both registration and disclosure of information on all securities placed on the stock exchange, thus preventing insiders in the stock market from manipulating securities. With passage of the Banking Act of 1935, government control extended to currency and credit. During the previous year, Roosevelt had appointed Utah banker and former Mormon missionary Marriner Eccles (1890–1977) to head the Federal Reserve Board. A Keynesian by instinct, Eccles favored government spending and an unbalanced budget long before he had heard of similar theories advanced by British economist John Maynard Keynes (1883–1946). Almost immediately, Eccles began drafting a bill that would significantly revise the Federal Reserve System. Although the bill was heavily amended (its chief opponent, Senator Carter Glass of Virginia boasted: "We did not leave enough of the Eccles bill with which to light a cigarette"), the Banking Act was, according to Walter Lippmann, a victory for Eccles "dressed up as a defeat." It established a seven-member board of governors appointed by the President for fourteen-year terms. Chief officers of regional banks could be appointed only with the board's approval. All large state banks were now required to join the Federal Reserve System if they were to benefit from the federal deposit insurance system.

Like the Securities Exchange Act, the Public Utility Holding Company Act of 1935 sought to control a specific problem area of business interests. Initially, Roosevelt had insisted on a "death-sentence" clause permitting the SEC to abolish any electric-power monopoly involved in illegal practices, along with those unable to justify their existence by January 1, 1940. Utility lobbyists descended on the capital and organized letter-writing campaigns—activities that, as congressional probes later discovered, included forgeries and evidence of bribes. Under such pressure, the "death sentence" was commuted; but the act that resulted only shifted the burden of proof from the holding companies to the SEC, with which all power combines were required to register. Within three years most of the electric-power monopolies were dissolved.

Less successful were the later antitrust efforts of Thurman Arnold (1891–1969), named Assistant Attorney General in charge of the Antitrust Division of the Justice Department. With 190 attorneys in his employ ("Trust buster" Teddy Roosevelt had had only five), in five years Arnold instituted 44 percent of all antitrust suits undertaken up to that time under the Sherman Act of 1890. Although he succeeded in breaking up a number of loose conglomerates, his attacks reflected no attempt to reform conditions encouraging their growth. And with the coming of war, charges that such attacks were in fact impeding efforts at mobilization limited his campaign.

The Resettlement Administration (RA) of 1935, like

Library of Congress.

This pea picker's shanty in Imperial Valley, California, was typical of the crude, makeshift dwellings in which the destitute were forced to live during the Depression.

the Rural Electrification Administration (REA) established a month later, tried to relieve rural poverty. Headed by Rexford G. Tugwell (1891-), the RA took over the rural rehabilitation and land programs begun by the FERA. But, with funds limited, of 500,000 poor farmers and their families only 4,000 were relocated from submarginal land to fertile soil with modern equipment. As the RA collapsed, a program for the relief of southern tenant farmers appeared. This plan resulted in the Bankhead-Jones Farm Tenancy Act of 1937, establishing a Farm Security Administration to replace the RA. This body erected sanitary camps for migratory workers and provided loans to small and tenant farmers which enabled them to establish cooperatives for medical care, crop marketing, and the purchase of equipment. By the end of 1941 more than $1 billion had been appropriated for these purposes, much of it in the form of loans to be repaid. But since those who benefited from the act were often voteless and voiceless croppers and migratory workers, and those who suffered were powerful business interests, especially huge farm corporations interested in maintaining cheap labor, pressure on members of Congress to limit allocations somewhat, appeared in the form of the Soil Conservation Act of 1936 with crop-reduction payments disguised as "soil-conservation" payments and the unconstitutional processors' tax replaced by general revenue funds. But large farmers continued to dominate these administrative bodies. The act did little to reduce crop surpluses. Late in 1938 Secretary of Agriculture Henry Wallace (1888-1965) noted that another good crop yield would "sink" the economy. Between August 1938 and December 1939, 128 million bushels of wheat were exported under subsidies established by the Department of Agriculture—at a loss of 50 cents per bushel in the summer of 1939. Only the war solved problems of overproduction and brought back good times for America's farmers.

A People in Economic Depression

Hard times tended to blur certain factors in American daily life and at the same time to highlight others. Nearly everyone shared the economic privation to some degree, thus creating common bonds; yet who got assistance from local, state, and federal agencies awakened ethnic, minority, and class awareness. And since each group was eager to use its clout to get its share, political passions mounted. The experimental nature of the New Deal invited both radicals and conservatives to offer up their nostrums for public consideration. The result was a political realignment of great importance, precipitating a conservative backlash, union unrest, and unusual stress upon the importance of civil rights and civil liberties. In no small degree, all of these trends were the natural result of decades of Progressive ferment followed by World War I, the chaotic 1920s, and the chilling experiences of the Depression years.

The Roosevelt Coalition

Hoover's defeat in 1932 was as decisive as his victory in 1928. Less apparent than the sweeping Democratic triumph was the political realignment that was taking place and would emerge as a new Democratic majority in 1936. This was a coalition formed primarily of urban Progressives, laborers, blacks, and immigrants.

In the cities, Roosevelt retained the support of ethnocultural groups (prominent among them were politicized immigrant women) who had voted for Democrat Al Smith four years earlier and whose percentage of voter turnout remained high. To this Roosevelt added substantial support from blacks and made significant gains in depressed farm areas, where, unlike Smith, Roosevelt did not have to contend with the issue of Catholicism and his urban associations. The results of the election showed a general repudiation of Hoover's policies among all social and economic divisions of the population. Roosevelt received a popular majority in every geographical region except New England (where he got just under 50 percent of the vote) and carried 90 percent of the nation's 3,000 counties.

In an off-year election the party in power traditionally loses congressional seats, but in 1934 the Democrats gained 13 in the House. Harry S Truman of Missouri was one of nine newcomers to the Senate who gave Democrats better than a two-thirds majority in that body. Election returns that year showed a repetition of the new urban attachment to the Democratic party and the effectiveness of "liaisons" between the administration and various constituent bodies of the coalition: Mary (Molly) Dawson strengthened the ties with newly activated Democratic women, Sidney Hillman and John L. Lewis those with organized labor, and Harold Ickes and Eleanor Roosevelt those with American blacks. While this body

Library of Congress.

Typical of criticisms of the New Deal by 1936 was this cartoon by J. N. Darling, portraying FDR, Harry Hopkins, and James Farley making off with the individual rights of citizens.

of liaisons augmented the traditional network of machine bosses prevalent in the years preceding the Depression, it did not end patronage, which was now dispensed to maintain the coalition. Women and blacks fared better than they had by previous standards.

While many speculated that Republicans would soon disappear as had the Whigs and Federalists, others—like the writer and social critic H. L. Mencken (1880–1956)—felt that the opposition to the New Deal was so strong that Republicans could win in 1936. The Democrats renominated Roosevelt by acclamation and promised to extend programs that he had begun. The Republicans selected a man who had cut his political teeth in the Bull Moose campaign of 1912 and the only Republican governor to be reelected in 1934, folksy Kansan, Alfred M. Landon (1887–), and promised to do everything the New Deal had done—but without the destruction of the "American system of free enterprise, private competition, and equality of opportunity" with which they charged Roosevelt's administration. Landon, it turned out, was a rock-ribbed conservative in everything except farm policy where his old-time Progressive thought was apparent. In a heated campaign, the Republicans argued that unemployment, at 12.8 million in 1933, had been reduced in three years to only 9 million. Democrats responded by saying that conditions would have been worse under continued leadership of the New Era. As the rhetoric grew hotter, the intensity of anti-New Deal venom mounted apace; nevertheless, in the greatest landslide in American presidential politics until that time, Roosevelt received a plurality of 10 million votes, won 523 of the 531 electoral votes and lost only Maine and Vermont—which prompted the rephrasing of an old political saying to read: "As Maine goes, so goes Vermont." Landon, whose victory the press predicted, polled only 36.5 percent of the popular vote; Roosevelt received 60.7 percent compared to 57 percent in 1932. Another dimension of Roosevelt's victory is seen in the fewer than 200,000 votes for Socialist party candidate Norman Thomas, less than one-fourth of the votes he received in 1932. A radical anti-New Deal party, the Union Party, secured only 900,000 votes.

For the first time the "Roosevelt coalition" gained support among cities with few immigrants. In seeking reelection the President had opposed the "economic royalists" who took "other people's money." The result was a sharp differentiation in the vote according to income level. The Gallup Poll showed that Roosevelt received 42 percent of the upper-income vote, 60 percent of the middle-income vote, and 76 percent of the lower-income vote. Democrats also rejoiced in the fact that two-thirds of first-time voters cast their ballots for Roosevelt.

The Supreme Court and the Opposition

Winning big can cause big problems in politics. As political victors often do, Roosevelt interpreted his new mandate as prior approval for any policy he might pursue and, as a result, committed serious blunders that undermined his leadership. His first serious miscalculation involved a traditional enemy of the New Deal—the Supreme Court. In February 1937 Roosevelt submitted to Congress a bill drafted by Attorney General Homer Cummings that would allow him to "pack" the Supreme

Library of Congress.

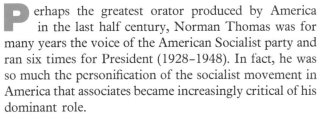

Norman Thomas
(1884–1968)

Perhaps the greatest orator produced by America in the last half century, Norman Thomas was for many years the voice of the American Socialist party and ran six times for President (1928–1948). In fact, he was so much the personification of the socialist movement in America that associates became increasingly critical of his dominant role.

Born into a middle-class family in Marion, Ohio, in 1884, he delivered Warren G. Harding's *Marion Star* as a boy, went on to Princeton (graduating in 1905), and then moved to New York City where he became a social worker. After further study at Union Seminary, Thomas was ordained as a Presbyterian minister in 1911. Charitable work in Harlem and marriage to a fellow social worker, Frances Violet Stewart, increased his interest in socialist doctrines.

Thomas opposed American entry into World War I and helped found the American Civil Liberties Union in 1917 to aid conscientious objectors. The following year he joined the Socialist party and during the 1920s ran unsuccessfully for city and state offices.

In 1926 Thomas gained control of the party machinery, making his first bid for the White House two years later. During the Depression years his platform—much of which FDR ultimately adopted—attracted considerable attention. Standing to the left of the New Deal, however, he admired the Russian economic system, that is, until he visited that country in 1937.

By 1934, Thomas was becoming increasingly critical of Roosevelt's policies. He had praised the early introduction of collective controls, but now thought the New Deal insensitive to the real needs of the nation's poor and to civil liberties as well. Disturbed by the growing militarism of the late 1930s, he opposed American entry into World War II and in 1940 headed the Keep America Out of War Committee.

Thomas lost control of the American Socialist party in 1950. He died in 1968 at the age of 84. A prolific writer and brilliant lecturer, Thomas was a tall, dignified man, a true gentleman exuding considerable charm and humor. One of his favorite platform techniques was to open a speech by quoting his campaign promises of 1928. Except for the nationalization of America's railroads, virtually everything he proposed had been enacted into law by 1950 in one form or another. No other defeated presidential candidate has been that successful. ■

Brown Brothers.

This 1937 drawing, titled "Nine Old Men" depicts the Supreme Court as President Roosevelt saw it: aged, infirm and negative. Chief Justice Hughes is standing, center.

Court under the guise of instituting broad judicial reform. "This brings forward," the President told Congress, "the question of aged or infirm judges—a subject of delicacy and yet one which requires frank discussion." Yet he preferred to stress judicial inefficiency, not age, noting that in the past year the justices had declined to hear 87 percent of the cases presented by private litigants without giving any explanation for their refusal. Roosevelt's bill proposed that no federal judge on the bench for ten years should wait longer than six months after his seventieth birthday to resign or retire; if a judge were to remain after that time, the President could appoint an additional judge—not to exceed six in the Supreme Court and forty-four in lower federal courts.

Loud protests were heard from Democrats as well as Republicans, from the general population as well as politicians. Democratic party leaders were angered because they had not been told in advance of these recommendations; in fact, Cummings was the only Cabinet member aware of FDR's scheme before it was announced to the press. Septuagenarian senators and congressmen, not surprisingly, were unwilling to admit the inefficiency of septuagenarian judges. Many Americans feared the destruction of a cherished symbol established by the Founding Fathers, the Supreme Court, unaware that the membership of that body had been changed several times during the nineteenth century. Even some liberals felt Roosevelt's goal was humiliation of the Court for past decisions he did not like rather than its reformation.

As the battle unfolded, events in the Court itself seemed to obviate the need for such "reform." In March 1937, in a 5–4 decision, the Court upheld the constitutionality of a minimum-wage law similar to an earlier measure declared invalid. Two weeks later, by the same margin, the Court declared the Wagner Act constitutional in *NLRB* v. *Jones & Laughlin Steel Co.* In May, conservative Justice Willis Van Devanter retired. Within weeks the Court upheld umemployment insurance provisions of the Social Security Act and declared old-age pensions constitutional.

Roosevelt compounded his initial mistake by continuing to press for passage of his "court reform" bill. One senator asked, "Why run for a train after you've caught it?" Vice President John Nance Garner (1868–1967), who loathed the court plan, demonstrated his displeasure by leaving the capital for an extended visit to his home in Texas. New York's Governor Herbert Lehman (1878–1963), a close political ally of Roosevelt, publicly denounced the proposal. Under such pressure, the President had to settle for a compromise bill which enacted procedural reforms but did not allow him to appoint new judges.

Perhaps Roosevelt lost the battle and won the war, as he later claimed; within two and a half years, five members of the nine-man bench were Roosevelt appointees. But as a result of this fiasco, both Republican and Democratic congressmen who had refrained from opposing other policies of the administration now felt bold enough to speak out against the President's programs. Roosevelt's attempt in the 1938 primaries to "purge" the party of conservative elements backfired and added to his woes. The President's third mistake was to

Library of Congress.

Wendell Willkie
(1892–1944)

Descended from German immigrant stock, Wendell Willkie was born in Elmwood, Indiana, in 1892. His family life was most unusual. When his father, a prosperous lawyer and landowner, fell upon hard times, his mother studied for the bar and became that state's first female attorney. Each morning the father woke up the six young Willkies by shouting classical quotations at them. The household was, in the words of one observer, "sort of a perpetual debating society."

After receiving his law degree from Indiana University in 1916, Willkie served as a lieutenant in the artillery in World War I but did not see combat. In 1920 he joined an Akron, Ohio, law firm and became a popular speaker for the League of Nations and against the Ku Klux Klan (he had supported Wilson's New Freedom during his college days). In 1929 Willkie was named chief counsel for the Commonwealth and Southern Corporation (an electric utility) and in 1933 became its president. An opponent of public ownership and federal control of utilities, Willkie became one of the most outspoken critics of the Tennessee Valley Authority and the Public Utility Holding Company Act.

Willkie began life as a liberal Democrat, even serving as a delegate to the 1924 national convention. His unhappiness with the New Deal led him to shift to the Republican party in 1939. As a foe of federal power policy, he gained a reputation among both businessmen and Republicans in general as a forceful spokesman. Coupled with his support of aid to the Allies, this reputation (and some very effective preconvention maneuvering) led to his nomination in 1940 by the party he had just joined.

Some of this "maneuvering" involved packing the balconies of the convention hall in Philadelphia with hundreds who, much to the distress of party regulars, kept chanting "WE WANT WILLKIE!" Never again would either major party permit "outsiders" to apply such pressures.

During the ensuing campaign, Willkie attacked FDR for trying to lead the nation into war, while at the same time he advocated aid to Britain. In the process his assault provoked the President into making several promises that later proved somewhat embarrassing. After losing the election, Willkie gave unqualified support to the Lend-Lease program and fought the isolationists at every turn; he spoke out for the cause of a postwar international organization (as well as for the protection of black civil rights). FDR sent him as his ambassador of goodwill on a global tour.

Though Willkie hoped for the 1944 nomination, he had alienated the right wing of his party by too close association with "the enemy" and had to withdraw from the race after his defeat in the Wisconsin primary. He died of a heart attack in October 1944.

An unusually forceful campaigner, Willkie, a shock of unruly dark hair hanging over his forehead, roared his way across the nation in 1940 and into the hearts of many Americans. Yet, as later events revealed, he agreed fully with his opponent's foreign policy, and any scheme he might have had for dismantling the New Deal probably would have been frustrated on Capitol Hill. Despite similar criticism, in the last four decades no Republican effort to undo FDR's program has met with much success. ■

push hard for reorganization of the executive branch hot on the heels of these two political rebuffs. Finally, by the late 1930s the economic situation was beginning to work in favor of New Deal opponents. In 1937 Americans glimpsed the Depression's end, but in 1938 that vision seemed to be vanishing. Roosevelt, worried about the possibility of inflation, cut back federal spending sharply. The result was a sharp recession, indicating that private business was not strong enough to take over the "pump-priming" mechanism of the economy.

The 1938 election resulted in a Republican comeback of sorts, which after the 1936 rout was probably inevitable. They gained seven seats in the Senate and seventy-six in the House, leaving the Democrats with still very healthy margins of 69–23 and 261–164, respectively. Nevertheless, the possibility of a workable anti-administration coalition of Republicans and disenchanted Democratic conservatives (including those who had survived Roosevelt's primary purges with little difficulty) loomed larger than before. The election also brought to state and national prominence a number of future Republican leaders, among them, Robert A. Taft (1889–1953) and John Bricker (1893–   ) of Ohio, and Harold Stassen (1907–   ) of Minnesota. Although the New Deal was fading, Roosevelt's popularity continued to dominate national politics, and in 1940, with the threat of war and the promise of an economic boom, he was able to defeat Republican candidate Wendell Willkie by a vote of 449 to 82 in the Electoral College; the popular vote, however, reflected a narrower margin of victory—27,263,448 to 22,336,260. Again, Roosevelt won in the cities, and the "Roosevelt coalition" remained healthy despite FDR's unprecedented and controversial bid for a third term, a decision that ended many long-time political friendships and breathed new life into his Republican-conservative opposition.

The Work Force

Although the number of those employed increased throughout the 1930s, unemployment and low wages continued to plague many workers. And while the government for the first time assumed direct responsibility for the welfare of laborers, not all benefited from this concern.

The growth of unions in the 1930s was the most dramatic in history. Membership rose from 3.6 million in 1934 to 4.7 million in 1936 and 8.2 million in 1939. Once the Wagner Act and the National Labor Relations Board replaced the old NIRA provisions, labor became a bulwark of the Roosevelt coalition, contributing to the new Democratic majority with campaign contributions as well as votes.

Nonunion workers were offered protection by the Fair Labor Standards Act of 1938, generally recognized as the last New Deal measure. This legislation tried to put "a ceiling over hours and a floor under wages." Roosevelt called it "the most far-reaching, far-sighted program for the benefit of workers ever adopted in this or any other country." Although employers often took advantage of provisions for numerous exemptions, over a two-year period the act reduced weekly hours to forty (benefiting some 13 million Americans) and increased the minimum wage to 40 cents (affecting more than 700,000 workers). One noteworthy provision abolished child labor in the manufacture of goods destined for interstate commerce.

Still unprotected and largely ignored by reformers were "marginal" laborers—agricultural workers, women, blacks, and others new to the industrial work force. Until the war boom revitalized the American economy, many farm laborers and migrant workers existed in conditions like those described in John Steinbeck's *Grapes of Wrath* (1939). When the depression struck, women and blacks

Library of Congress.

Tenant farmers, like these black families in Missouri, were among the most severely afflicted during the Depression. Evictions of tenants, black and white, frequently occurred when lands were taken out of production by their landlords seeking AAA subsidies.

tended to lose their jobs in industry. Both were also victims of wage discrimination. As collective bargaining and federal legislation set equal wages, both suffered, since they no longer received occasional employment as cheap labor. Then, as the economy improved and jobs became available again, women especially had trouble returning to the work force, and unions showed little interest in organizing them. While their position in government circles increased in both rank and jobs, entry into the professions remained difficult. Union membership among blacks increased—partly because the Congress of Industrial Organizations (CIO), though not free from bias, was less discriminatory than other unions.

A new breed of unionists accompanied the rise in membership. Prominent among them was John L. Lewis (1880-1969) of the CIO, which by 1938 was in direct competition with its parent union, the AFL. Founded in Pittsburgh in November 1938, the CIO grew out of a heated debate within the AFL. The latter favored organization along traditional craft lines; the former, by mass production industries as encouraged openly by the short-lived NRA. At the AFL convention held in 1935, craft advocates prevailed, prompting seven unions to form a "Committee of Industrial Unions." Suspended

Wide World.

Although the New Deal years witnessed important gains for unions, organizing efforts in mass industries frequently ended in violence. This conflict in 1937 between policemen and CIO strikers at Republic Steel in South Chicago was dubbed the "Memorial Day Massacre."

from the AFL a year later, this dissident group began to assume more definite form and openly challenged its parent organization, causing widespread violence and considerable unrest.

Through such innovative tactics as the sitdown strike, especially in Michigan's auto factories, the CIO was able to organize very effectively while the Roosevelt administration either looked on with benign neglect or helped behind the scenes. The success of the CIO changed the shape of organized labor as well as its size. While the largest unions before 1935 tended to be in noncentralized construction fields, a labor movement shaped by industry, not occupations as such, naturally enough became concentrated in various cities of the industrial East and Midwest, enhancing their political influence considerably.

Radicalism

Given the destitution and desperation dominating the period, it is surprising that radicalism attracted so few supporters. Certainly, radical groups existed, on the right as well as the left. William Dudley Pelley (1890–1965), a New England author and editor, hoped to become Hitler's American counterpart once Europe had been conquered and he had led his Silver Shirts ("the cream, the head and flower of our Protestant Christian manhood") in terrorizing Communists, liberals, and Jews.

More successful were other radical groups. By 1934 the "radio priest," the Reverend Charles E. Coughlin (1891–), had an audience of ten million. In the same year he decided that Roosevelt, whom he had initiallly supported, had sold out to bankers and began an attack on both the "Jew Deal" and, later, "Franklin Double-Crossing Roosevelt" himself. In the 1936 elections, calling the President "anti-God," Coughlin supported the Union party candidate, Representative William Lemke of North Dakota. After Roosevelt's decisive victory, Coughlin retired from politics, comparing himself to the persecuted Christ. He continued, however, to publish *Social Justice*, a periodical which grew increasingly anti-Semitic and was ultimately banned from the mails.

Another "leftist" group, the Townsendites, led by Dr. Francis E. Townsend, was influential in the formulation of the Social Security Act (of 1935). A California country doctor, Townsend was disturbed by the plight of the elderly who faced unemployment with no personal financial resources. The Townsend Plan would have given to every citizen over sixty a lifetime pension of $200 a month, provided he or she retired and promised to spend the sum within the month. Congress found the plan economically unfeasible, since it would have channeled one-half the national income to one-eleventh of the population. By the end of 1934 the doctor claimed 1,200 Townsend Clubs, most of them in the West.

With the passage of the Social Security Act in 1935, Congress created a compulsory national system of insurance that gave workers at the age of sixty-five retirement money financed by a one percent tax on their wages and matched by their employers. Beginning in 1942 (later changed to 1940) retired workers who were over sixty-five would receive from $10 to $85 per month, depending upon the amount they had contributed. In addition, the measure made funds available on a matching basis to states for distribution to qualified recipients who had already retired. The act also established a system of unemployment insurance and care for the destitute and handicapped elderly in which both federal and state governments participated. The act still left millions unprotected, among them farm workers, domestics, and others who most needed such insurance. It omitted coverage for illness and failed to establish adequate national standards for health care. It also created the only welfare system in the world based upon the wages of laborers themselves. But, despite its limitations, the Social Security Act helped to establish firmly the government's responsibility for the social welfare of its citizens.

The most formidable of the radical movements was "Every Man a King," led by Louisiana Senator Huey P. "Kingfish" Long. In 1932 the senator had supported Roosevelt, but in 1934, denied patronage, Long established his own "Share-our-Wealth" program. Through a redistribution of income, it would have given every American family a $5,000 homestead, $2,000 in income each year, a car, and a radio. Long soon enjoyed national support and in 1935 his organization claimed to have a mailing list of 7.5 million people.

The senator's appeal was based not only on promises but on personality. He would often wear a watermelon-colored tie with an orchid shirt, his cherubic face and red hair topped by a striped strawhat. He amused crowds with feigned stupidity, which masked a shrewd legal mind, and converted many through his brilliance as an orator. He began in 1918 as a state railroad commissioner, then became chairman of the Public Service Commission of Louisiana where he used his power to attack large oil companies such as Standard Oil. Defeated for governor in 1924 because he was caught between those espousing extreme views concerning the Ku Klux Klan, he gained a plurality four years later and the governor's chair but not firm control of state politics. By means fair and foul, working against and with powerful New Orleans groups and providing a program that helped the "little people" of Louisiana, Long eventually consolidated his power. To Gertrude Stein, among others, Long was "not boring in the way Harding, President Roosevelt and Al Smith have been boring."

In 1935, at the age of forty-two, Long announced

U.P.I.

U.P.I.

Two of the most popular (and demagogic) critics of the New Deal were Louisiana Senator Huey Long (left) and Father Charles Coughlin (right). Long's "Share Our Wealth" program made him a great political threat to the administration. Coughlin, whose weekly radio broadcasts and periodical *Social Justice* won him millions of followers, lost credibility in the late 1930s because of his overt anti-Semitism.

that he would run for the presidency. In September of that year, having returned to Louisiana, he was assassinated in the state capitol by a man whose family he allegedly insulted. With his death the most serious threat to the administration from the left came to an end.

Roosevelt's problems with Communism and socialism, traditional movements of the far left, eased somewhat, at least temporarily, between 1935 and 1937. To establish a Popular Front against fascism, Communists supported liberal parties, and in 1936 the American Communist party candidate Earl Browder (1891–1973) in effect supported Roosevelt for reelection. As the Roosevelt coalition of workers, farmers, and the economically less fortunate grew, support for the Socialist party declined.

The close cooperation of leftist groups in the nation's fight against fascism won the support of liberals, particularly college students, who often participated in "front" organizations, an involvement that would have serious repercussions for many. But by co-opting potential radicals, Roosevelt's policies prevented such groups from seriously threatening the existing economic and political system. This was not an unimportant achievement of his administration.

Civil Rights and Civil Liberties

Increased response to demands for civil liberties was more rhetorical than real during the Depression decade. The New Deal was partially committed to the protection of such liberties for *some,* but did not significantly improve on the achievements of the 1920s. The groundwork was laid for future advancement of some deprived groups, notably workers and blacks, but the administration's response to those outside the political mainstream was ambiguous. Nevertheless New Dealers did support creation of the Senate Civil Liberties Subcommittee headed by Robert La Follette, Jr. (1895–1953) to oversee the protection of workers.

The administration also was ambivalent toward any hunt for "subversives," although in 1936 Roosevelt began FBI surveillance of certain groups on both the right and left. The President identified himself with moderates in this area after the performance in 1938 of the newly created House Committee on Un-American Activities. Headed by Texas Democrat Martin Dies (1900–1972), the committee ignored the existence of Nazi groups in America and focused on Communist infiltrations. In the first days of hearings, witnesses, offering no evidence, branded as communistic 640 organizations, 483 newspapers, and 280 labor unions. Even the Boy Scouts, Campfire Girls, and Shirley Temple were not safe from charges that they had at the least been careless in lending their names to "Red" causes. The committee attacked the New Deal itself for using money "to advance the cause of communism in the United States." When testimony before the "nonpartisan" committee labelled several liberal candidates as Communist pawns, Roosevelt was forced to speak out against the group's "flagrantly unfair and un-American attempt to influence an election."

In that area of civil liberties known as civil rights, the record of the New Deal was relatively poor, despite the efforts of Eleanor Roosevelt and the appointment of a "black Cabinet" of advisers. Mrs. Roosevelt worked very closely with Mrs. Mary McLeod Bethune (1875–1955), president of the National Council of Negro Women, in focusing attention upon the plight of blacks. The NAACP, which employed a gradualist approach, was equally unsuccessful. Congress rejected an antilynching bill that the NAACP helped to draft and that Roosevelt supported. In 1935 the Supreme Court ruled in *Grovey* v. *Townsend* that the Democratic party was a voluntary political association, and blacks could be excluded from membership in a private political club and thereby barred from voting in primaries. One bright spot, though more symbolic than anything else, was the administration's response in 1939 to the refusal of the Daughters of the American Revolution to permit Marian Anderson to sing in Constitution Hall in Washington, D.C. With the approval of the President, Secretary of Interior Harold L. Ickes invited Miss Anderson to perform on Easter Sunday at the Lincoln Memorial. An estimated crowd of 75,000 heard her recital, which began with "America" and ended with "Nobody Knows the Trouble I've Seen." At the same time, Mrs. Roosevelt publicly resigned her membership in the DAR.

Despite these modest gains at the national level, black self-help organizations flourished in a number of northern cities. One goal of such groups was to persuade white employers in black communities to hire some black employees. Unsuccessful efforts at persuasion led such black leaders as the Reverend John H. Johnson of New York City to organize pickets of the stores and urge blacks "Don't Buy Where You Can't Work."

American Indians, thanks largely to the dedication of John Collier, the Atlanta-born social worker who became executive secretary of the American Indian Defense Fund in the 1920s and Commissioner of Indian Affairs under Roosevelt from 1933 to 1945, took definite steps toward self-sufficiency after years of confusion and neglect. As commissioner, Collier set about the task of diminishing his own power and authority as that of Indians increased. The first tangible victory of this campaign was the Wheeler-Howard Act (1934), which reversed federal Indian policy. Instead of trying to break up tribes and stamp out native cultures, the government now worked to encourage tribal unity and to foster cultural and artistic expression. Also known as the Indian Reorganization Act, this legislation was accepted initially by 74 percent of all tribal groups and later extended to Indians and Eskimos in Alaska.

In practice, the Indian Reorganization Act provided

U.P.I.

Eleanor Roosevelt served a vital function for the administration in the 1930s, maintaining contacts with black spokespersons and generally acting as the "conscience" of the government on civil rights matters. She is pictured here with Mary McLeod Bethune.

increased funds for education and for business loans, ended the land allotment scheme of the Dawes Act (1887)—which had cut Indian lands from 138 to 52 million acres (much of it arid desert and wasteland)—began to enlarge tribal holdings, and encouraged Indians to seek jobs with Collier's department. By 1940 more than half of his employees were Indians.

Although most Indians still existed in poverty and faced unique problems shared by few other Americans—an "invisible" minority lacking dynamic leadership and rarely possessing sufficient numbers to have political clout, for example—the tenor of Indian life was changing. As a white man familiar with this long-ignored corner of the American scene observed, "Since Collier came in, you can at least go on a reservation without feeling ashamed to be a white man."

The Permanent Revolution

Thanks to the temper of the 1930s, more complete press coverage than ever before and greatly increased use of radio, what Roosevelt and those about him did each day became instant news. This enhanced the role of the White House and the federal bureaucracy because millions looked to Washington for the guidance, direction, and assistance that states and localities could not provide. Nevertheless, this was an ambivalent relationship at best. Those who sought help often were quick to criticize growing federal power. The passage of time has not eased some of the rancor fostered by specific changes wrought by the New Deal and by similar programs that have followed in its wake.

The Roosevelt Presidency

Not only did Roosevelt expand the office of the President beyond its old bounds and his policies affect the lives of millions, but with advances in technology his voice came directly into people's homes. Never before had the President been able to appeal to the bulk of the population simultaneously. In return, the volume of mail sent to the White House—which during Hoover's administration had amounted to a few hundred pieces daily, opened by one man—soon averaged between 5,000 and 8,000 a day and required the services of a staff. Clearly, Americans felt engaged in a dialogue with their President. And with the rise of weekly news magazines and the growing number of news broadcasts, the public's interest in the political situation expanded far beyond election time.

Equally as permanent was Roosevelt's influence on presidential management. After the 1936 election, he appointed a three-man commission to propose legislation for reorganization of the executive branch. Because Congress was unhappy over the President's attempts at "court packing" and tended to view such reorganization in terms of Hitler's dictatorial ambitions, the Executive Reorganization plan was defeated. But a compromise version, omitting the more controversial features, resulted in 1939 in the creation of the Executive Office of the President. It provided for six administrative assistants not accountable to Congress and placed the Bureau of the Budget under the protection of the new office. Later, under other Presidents, such important agencies as the Council of Economic Advisers, the National Security Council, and the Central Intelligence Agency would be added.

In a 1938 fireside chat, Roosevelt remarked: "There is placed on all of us the duty of self-restraint. That is the duty of democracy. . . ." Certainly he could not have foreseen what this enlarged office, lacking such restraint, might become. And while the government was more visible by its intrusion into areas of life previously within the private domain, the new enlarged office could function beyond public view. The dangers of this were perceived by few, and during the war years such fears receded, to be forgotten until a later day.

New Deal Balance Sheet

The New Deal and its innovations will always have their critics. And criticism will come, as it did in the 1930s, from all points of the political spectrum. The New Deal did too much, not enough, moved in the wrong areas, failed to initiate true reform, and so on. Such criticisms are in a sense irrelevant because they miss the main point of the entire exercise: in a time of great crisis the New Deal worked well enough to keep a nation together, reasonably well cared for, and able to face great challenges in the 1940s. It had no central ideological thrust, even as it had sharp internal divisions ideologically. It was essentially conservative if that meant conserving the basic liberal-capitalist order. It was liberal and radical in tone, if that meant the injection of the government into realms of U.S. life previously left to private jurisdictions.

Although statistics showed gradual and almost steady improvement during the 1930s, the depression was not over when the New Deal came to a halt. World War II and the spending it demanded, not the programs of the 1930s, brought final economic recovery. Yet the repercussions of its legislation on economic life cannot be minimized. Formulas for agriculture, public housing, and labor-management relations, established by the early 1940s, were to serve as foundations for governmental programs into the 1970s. The New Deal pattern of spiralling public debt, accelerated by World War II, also seemed as permanent as other Roosevelt innovations by the end of the 1930s, as did the increased number of Washington bureaucrats.

But no ideological transformation accompanied these changes, and the basic liberal-capitalistic framework of the country remained unchanged. If all economic and social problems of the Depression were not solved, neither was there agreement on how they might be solved, as evidenced by conflicting ideas presented in the Temporary National Economic Committee's 1941 report covering an investigation into the concentration of economic power. This exhaustive, three-year study of the nation's economic health (552 witnesses, 31 volumes of testimony, and 43 monographs prepared by 188 government economists under the direction of the committee) shed some light upon existing business practices but tended to concentrate on monopoly, ignoring more general problems such as employment levels. Perhaps the "agreement to disagree" within this postmortem on the New Deal represented a tacit admission that there was no single "right" way. Given the rate of success of competing economic theories today, this may be another enduring aspect of the New Deal.

Essay

The President's Friends

As many men who have sat behind the desk in the Oval Office of the White House told us, being President of these United States can be a lonely, demanding job. In January 1941, shortly before beginning his unprecedented third term, Franklin Delano Roosevelt was host to his Republican opponent of a few months before, Wendell Willkie. As the two men talked, Willkie asked why the President kept Harry Hopkins, a controversial, sickly figure, at his side. Roosevelt replied quietly that if Willkie ever got his job he would understand. Nearly everyone who comes to the White House, Roosevelt said, wants something, but Harry Hopkins asked for nothing except an opportunity to serve.

Not every chief executive has been fortunate enough to have such a devoted aide, but several, especially during the twentieth century and with increasing frequency since Roosevelt's day, have made use of individuals who may or may not hold government posts. If these persons are of the same political persuasion as those discussing this phenomenon, they are known as assistants, aides, or advisors; if not, they are simply cronies.

In addition to providing companionship and a sounding board for ideas, these individuals can divert criticism from a President to themselves. As discussants, they fulfill a function once performed by the Cabinet, which, because of the growth of the federal bureaucracy, has tended to become merely a group of managers. Only on rare occasions do the Cabinet members gather as a group at the White House and truly debate and discuss issues confronting an administration.

In fact, within each President's official family a tight coterie of one or two prominent Cabinet officers and a group of aides and assistants usually emerges as being of key importance. Reporters watch very closely to see who has "the ear of the king," because, in truth, these men are powerful courtiers not unlike those who once walked the halls of Versailles and Windsor Castle. These are the men who shape policy and influence federal programs.

Historically, the first chief executive to use such a group in a more or less day-to-day fashion was Andrew Jackson. His so-called Kitchen Cabinet consisted of four or five men, including Martin Van Buren, his Secretary of State, one or two very able Treasury Department employees, and several local editors. The composition of this group was not fixed and membership changed from time to time.

Library of Congress.

A contemporary cartoon portrays Jackson and his "Kitchen Cabinet," the first of the informal presidential advisory groups.

Several reasons existed for such a body of advisors. Like every chief executive, Jackson had to pay off political debts and to select his official Cabinet from the leading lights of his Democratic party, men with whom he may or may not have felt at ease. Controversy with his vice president, John C. Calhoun, the Peggy Eaton affair, his advanced age, and his prolonged residence beyond the Appalachians were other factors that may have fostered creation of a Kitchen Cabinet.

Ulysses S. Grant tried a somewhat different approach with disastrous results. He moved his wartime staff, virtually intact, to 1600 Pennsylvania Avenue and let its members manage the daily business of the presidency.

Edward Mandell House (1858–1938), a Texas-born "colonel" and unofficial advisor to Woodrow Wilson during World War I, represents yet another type of aide. House, a small, soft-spoken man from a wealthy cotton family, was a political "fixer" with much experience in his home state when Wilson first met him in 1911. He and Wilson, then governor of New Jersey, took an instant liking to each other; and, although House played only a small role in the 1912 campaign, this diminutive Texan had a big hand in the selection of Wilson's Cabinet. Colonel House refused a post for himself, preferring to operate independently behind the scenes, and soon became an accomplished intermediary between the White House and the world of finance and business.

It was international affairs, however, which interested House most, and as soon as war erupted in Europe he was a very busy individual. for a time he tried his hand at mediation, but after April 1917 he was Wilson's direct personal link to the Allied governments. The colonel helped draft the famed Fourteen Points and, naturally enough, was a prominent member of the Peace Commission at Versailles.

Library of Congress.

President Wilson (seated), with confidant and advisor, Colonel E. M. House.

Unfortunately for House, who was fundamentally a compromiser, he caved in to heavy British-French pressure and, while Wilson was ill, yielded on several key points in the proposed treaty. The President felt he had been betrayed and never forgave House, who, when he returned to America, discovered he was no longer welcome at the White House. Colonel House lived out his days in New York City and worked in behalf of Roosevelt in 1932, but the two men were not close friends.

Since FDR's day, various chief executives have had intimate advisors who may or may not have been on the federal payroll. One of the most durable of these men is Clark Clifford, a handsome young associate of Harry Truman with a well-to-do St. Louis background. Charming, skillful, and a liberal influence upon Truman, he went on to become one of Washington's wealthiest lawyers. Clifford also was an advisor to John F. Kennedy and served as Secretary of Defense under Lyndon B. Johnson. His role in the Vietnam turnabout still is not entirely clear, but he apparently had much to do with decreasing U.S. involvement in Southeast Asia.

Yet it is Harry Lloyd Hopkins (1890–1946), a gaunt, ailing figure, who towers over all other presidential confidants and advisors. One observer once said that Hopkins, dying by inches from cancer and the side effects of treatment and surgery from 1937 to 1946, had "the weary, melancholy look of an ill-fed horse at the end of a hard day." And this was indeed true.

Hopkins, a first-class organizer and administrator, was born in Sioux City, Iowa, son of a harnessmaker and leather salesman. His family moved from place to place but finally settled in Grinnell, Iowa, where young Harry went to college and emerged as the "big man" of the Class of 1912.

Soon after graduation, almost by accident, he got into social work in New York City, an experience that led to top jobs with the American Red Cross and the New York Tuberculosis Association. During the Al Smith campaign of 1928, he met FDR. They liked each other immediately, and Hopkins was soon heading up Governor Roosevelt's temporary relief program in New York state.

In 1933, Hopkins moved on to Washington to continue the same work on a national level. During the next few years he held positions as head of the Federal Emergency Relief Administration (FERA), the Works Progress Administration (WPA), and the Department of Commerce. Between 1933 and 1938 he spent almost $8.5 billion and emerged as the second most powerful man in the United States.

His personal life was far from happy. Twice married, he separated from his first wife in 1930. His second wife died of cancer in 1937 and an eighteen-year-old son was killed early in World War II. Hopkins was something of a playboy, and to the

Franklin D. Roosevelt Library.

The two Roosevelts and FDR's jack-of-all-trades, Harry Hopkins, en route to Washington from Warm Springs, Georgia, 1938.

U.P.I.

U.P.I.

H. R. Haldeman (top) and John Ehrlichman (bottom), top assistants to Richard Nixon.

consternation of Eleanor Roosevelt, he liked the horses and often could be found at trackside cheering on the ponies. A nightclub habitué, Hopkins spent election night of 1936 at an elegant New York wateringhole, drinking champagne amid glum and glowering Landon Republicans.

Hopkins nearly died three years later, and his tenure as Secretary of Commerce was never taken seriously. He was so ill that he rarely went to his office. Outspoken, blunt, Hopkins created many enemies and, during FDR's bitter campaign for a third term, quit his Commerce post. Ostensibly he stepped aside "for reasons of health." The truth was, Roosevelt's closest friend had become a political liability. He had alienated too many people during the President's first eight years, and even more at the Democratic convention where he directed activities that led to "the Chief's" renomination.

With war in Europe, Harry Hopkins became a sort of "Colonel House," although with a somewhat different mission. It was his job in 1941 to find out how the United States (then still at peace) could help both Great Britain and Russia. The result was the formidable and very important Lend-Lease program, which he helped organize and administer for a time.

After 1941, however, this gaunt ex-social worker had no official position and no office except a card table in his bedroom. The difference was, of course, from the fall of France in June 1940 until Roosevelt's death in April 1945, that bedroom was in the White House.

Except in a time of crisis, it is doubtful whether another House or Hopkins will be seen around 1600 Pennsylvania Avenue. Congressmen, political party leaders, Cabinet members, and others holding down official government positions obviously resent such intrusions. Their work, planning, and hopes may be frustrated by these individuals, men very close to the President who know his every whim.

Neither elected by voters nor responsible to anyone but "the Chief," they nevertheless have wielded great power. Before Watergate, for example, H. R. Haldeman and John Ehrlichman, key aides to President Nixon, possessed considerable clout. These men, however, were not cast in the House-Hopkins-Clifford mold of earlier decades; and, in view of accusations and counterclaims made since 1974, one might question whether they were ever "the President's friends." Reared in the organization, button-down, computerized business world, they thought it their duty to merchandise and sell not issues and programs, but a product: the President of the United States. The Watergate tragedy has, of course, dealt a body blow to the "imperial presidency" they elevated to such heights and perhaps to all-powerful aides as well.

Yet any chief executive, isolated and wrestling with immense problems and great issues, needs all the help he can get. That of a friend holding no official post and ostensibly having no ax to grind or of a trusted aide and confidant eager to do his bidding should not be denied to him.

Selected Readings

The Great Crash and Hoover's Response

John Kenneth Galbraith, *The Great Crash* (1961)

Peter Temin, *Did Monetary Forces Cause the Great Depression?* (1976)

Albert U. Romasco, *The Poverty of Abundance: Hoover, the Nation, the Depression* (1965)

The Depression: General Accounts

Edward R. Ellis, *A Nation in Torment* (1970)

Studs Terkel, *Hard Times: Oral History of the Great Depression in America* (1970)

Charles H. Trout, *Boston: The Great Depression and the New Deal* (1977)

Franklin D. Roosevelt and the New Deal

James M. Burns, *Roosevelt: The Lion and the Fox* (1956)

Paul Conkin, *The New Deal* (2d ed., 1975)

William E. Leuchtenburg, *Franklin D. Roosevelt and the New Deal, 1932-1940* (1963)

Arthur M. Schlesinger, Jr., *The Age of Roosevelt* (3 vols., 1957-1960)

John Braeman, Robert H. Bremner, and David Brody, eds., *The New Deal* (2 vols, 1975)

Ellis W. Hawley, *The New Deal and the Problem of Monopoly: A Study in Economic Ambivalence* (1966)

Labor and the New Deal

Irving Bernstein, *The Turbulent Years: The American Worker, 1933-1941* (1970)

Sidney Fine, *Sit-down: The General Motors Strike of 1936-1937* (1969)

Opposition to the New Deal

Donald R. McCoy, *Angry Voices: Left-of-Center Politics in the New Deal Era* (1958)

George Wolfskill and John A. Hudson, *All But the People: Franklin D. Roosevelt and His Critics, 1933-1939* (1969)

Women and Minorities

William H. Chafe, *The American Woman: Her Changing Social, Economic, and Political Role, 1920-1970* (1972)

Raymond Wolters, *Negroes and the Great Depression: The Problem of Economic Recovery* (1970)

Dan T. Carter, *Scottsboro: A Tragedy of the American South* (1969)

Kenneth R. Philip, *John Collier's Crusade for Indian Reform, 1920-1954* (1976)

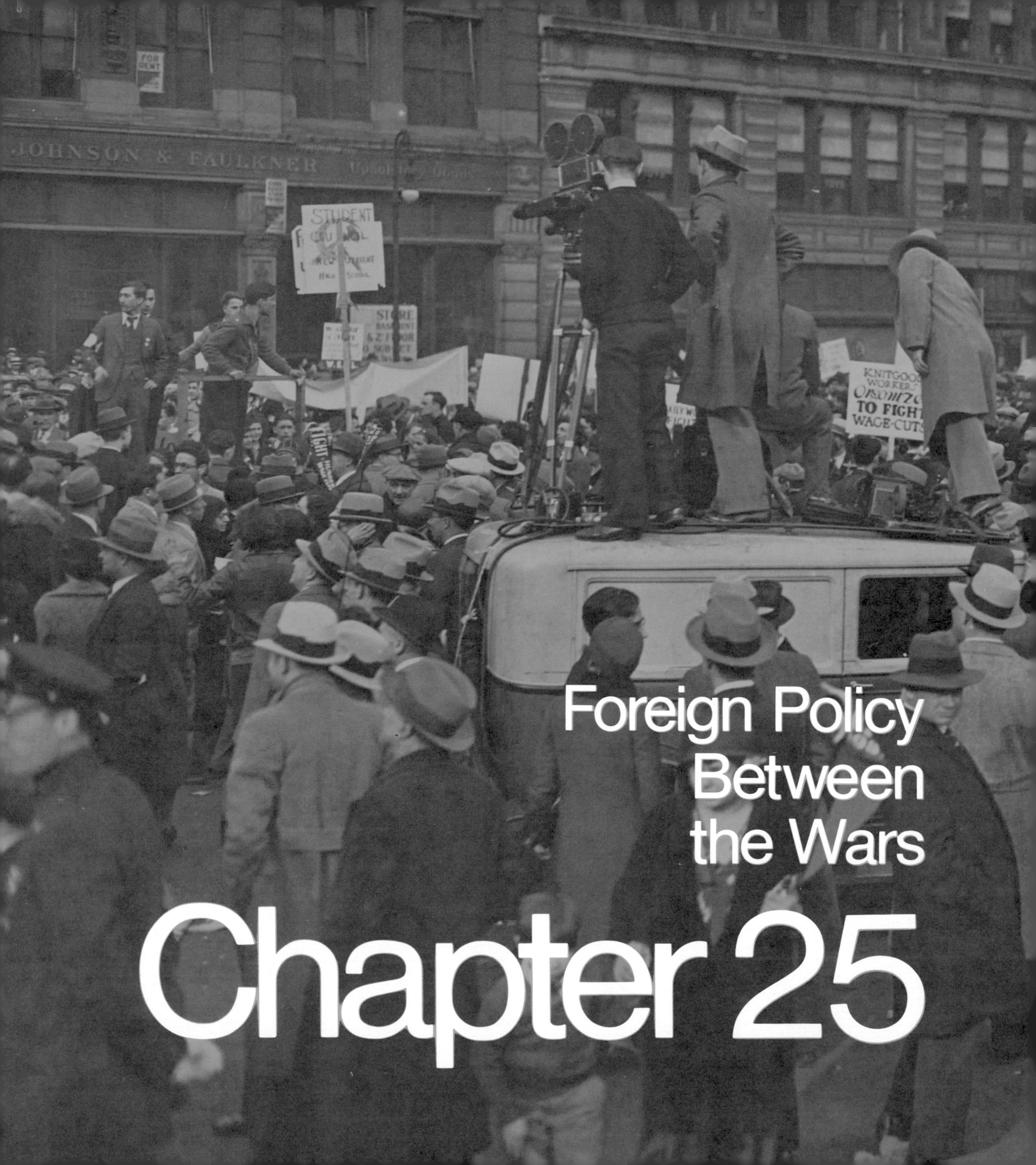

Chapter 25

Foreign Policy Between the Wars

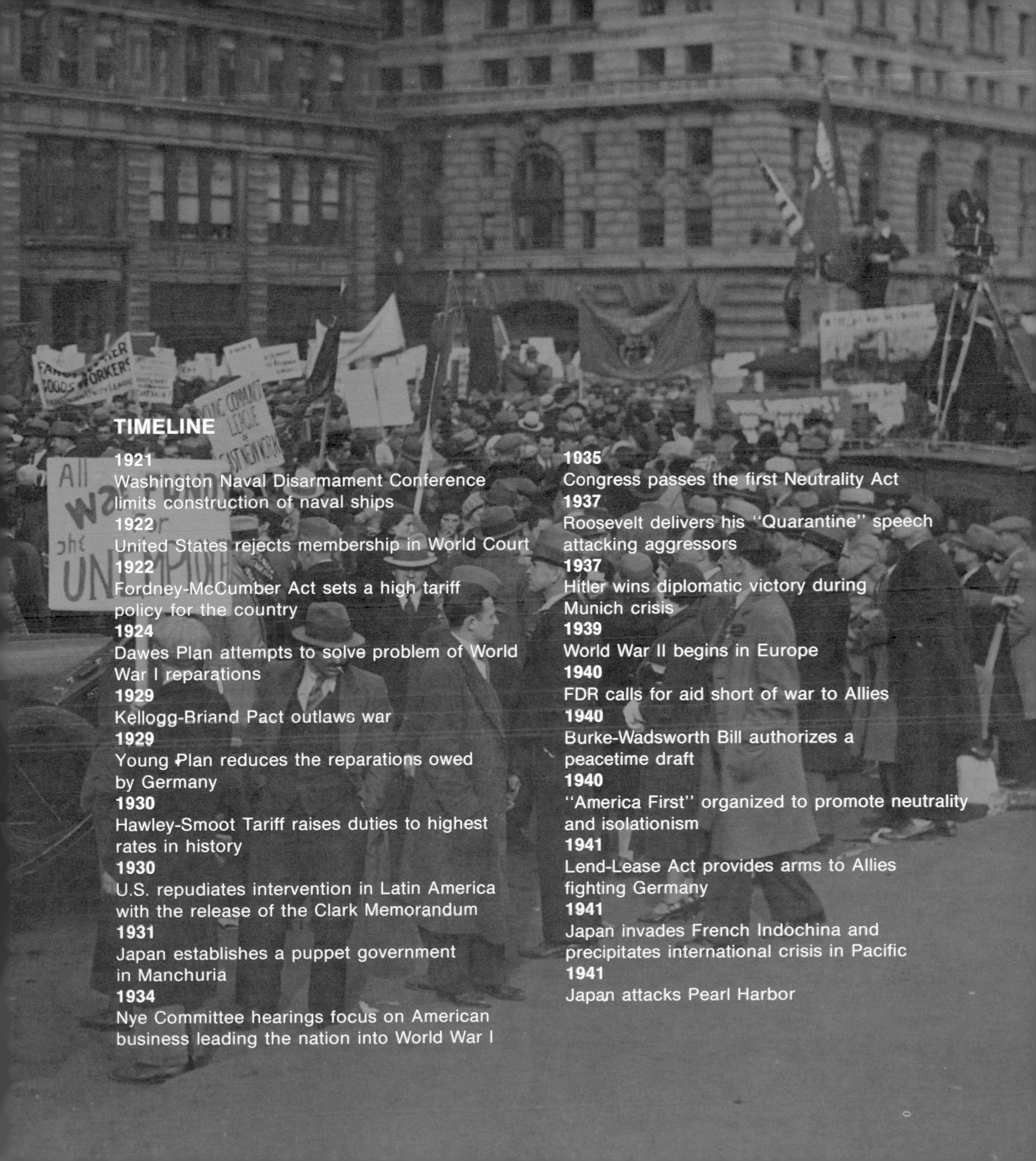

TIMELINE

1921
Washington Naval Disarmament Conference limits construction of naval ships
1922
United States rejects membership in World Court
1922
Fordney-McCumber Act sets a high tariff policy for the country
1924
Dawes Plan attempts to solve problem of World War I reparations
1929
Kellogg-Briand Pact outlaws war
1929
Young Plan reduces the reparations owed by Germany
1930
Hawley-Smoot Tariff raises duties to highest rates in history
1930
U.S. repudiates intervention in Latin America with the release of the Clark Memorandum
1931
Japan establishes a puppet government in Manchuria
1934
Nye Committee hearings focus on American business leading the nation into World War I
1935
Congress passes the first Neutrality Act
1937
Roosevelt delivers his "Quarantine" speech attacking aggressors
1937
Hitler wins diplomatic victory during Munich crisis
1939
World War II begins in Europe
1940
FDR calls for aid short of war to Allies
1940
Burke-Wadsworth Bill authorizes a peacetime draft
1940
"America First" organized to promote neutrality and isolationism
1941
Lend-Lease Act provides arms to Allies fighting Germany
1941
Japan invades French Indochina and precipitates international crisis in Pacific
1941
Japan attacks Pearl Harbor

CHAPTER OUTLINE

The years between the two world wars form a single fabric in American foreign policy. The period before 1914 and the decades after World War II were marked by very different attitudes toward world involvement, although many historians have overstated the sharpness of the breaks that 1918 and 1945 inaugurated. The traditional view, which held that isolationism prevailed during the 1920s and 1930s, saw this attitude as a reaction against President Wilson's activism in world affairs. In the 1920s the most conservative elements of both national parties attempted to disengage America from any involvement in world politics. In the following decade, the American public, insecure as a result of the Great Depression, encouraged disengagement. President Roosevelt and Secretary of State Cordell Hull, both old Wilsonian internationalists, were unable to reverse this tendency in foreign policy until the late 1930s, when they pointed to the danger posed by Axis aggressors in Europe. The Republicans of the 1920s, have, therefore, been regarded as isolationists; the Democrats of the 1930s, as torchbearers of Wilsonian internationalism. (Wilson's ideal finally triumphed when the United States sponsored the formation of the United Nations.)

Such generalizations are, however, too simple to describe accurately the formation of American foreign policy in the interwar years. The public and the media did recoil from Wilson's goals and methods; both refused to accept his chosen instruments of internationalism, the League of Nations and the World Court. But the Republican administrations of the 1920s were not averse to world cooperation. They endorsed antiwar and disarmament agreements and provided government assistance to American business abroad. One recent student of American foreign policy calls this blend of economic self-interest and political cooperation for the creation of a stable world order "independent internationalism." A few historians believe that all Republican efforts toward international cooperation served a policy of singleminded probusiness imperialism; this view, however, is extreme. Many Democrats of the 1920s were not one bit more Wilsonian than their Republican counterparts. A majority of the members of both parties repudiated "Wilsonianism."

Some of the dispute over American foreign policy in the 1920s and 1930s was actually a disagreement over the policymaking process. Much of the criticism of Wilson's programs was a reaction against his highhanded style and use of executive prerogative. The isolationist stance on Capitol Hill was, therefore, based in large part on distrust of presidential power—a distrust that Roosevelt's domestic activism, New Deal, and threats to pack the Supreme Court only intensified. In 1935 Congressman Louis Ludlow (1873–1950) of Indiana proposed that the Constitution be amended to stipulate that war could be declared only by plebiscite (except in the case of invasion). Ludlow's proposal stirred serious national interest and only strenuous administration efforts during the next three years prevented House action on this matter.

Roosevelt, of course, wanted a strong presidency, and as the nation's attention turned from the troubles at home to those abroad, he sought changes in the Neutrality Acts which would allow him to use executive discretion in applying embargoes. When war finally came in September 1939, it obliterated any distinction between internationalism and economic self-interest and made a strong executive mandatory, setting a precedent perpetuated after 1945 by the Cold War and contemporary world politics.

The advent of the media as a shaper of public opinion and the rising importance of polls (such as the Gallup Poll in the 1930s) helped to influence the attitudes of public figures toward foreign policy and intensified the rivalry between Congress and the President. Although "independent internationalism," rivalry between branches of the government, and the growing importance of the media were not innovations of the 1920s and 1930s, these discordant elements now began to exert special influence.

Normalcy and Foreign Affairs

The traditional view that Republican foreign policy in the 1920s was isolationist is not unanimously supported by historians. Certainly the spirit of the 1920s was nationalistic, but it was unlike the stonewall isolationism of the nineteenth century. During the 1920s the nation's leaders accepted some participation in world affairs, if only in the form of a policy of involvement without commitment. Having been deeply implicated in European affairs in 1917–1918, America was now suspicious of any further entanglements. The brief depression, recovery, and boom that followed World War I left little opportunity to formulate a far-reaching policy toward world involvement. The isolationism of the 1920s is most clearly seen in a refusal to join the League of Nations. But terms such as "isolation" and "involvement" are at best unclear generalizations. For instance, America participated in the international disarmament movement and maintained its interest in Latin America and the Far East. Still American leaders were understandably afraid to risk tests of strength that might involve armed intervention.

Economic involvement was quite another matter. After the war the United States was an international creditor. The government had to seek out and encourage the expansion of trade and improvements abroad. Thus cooperation with foreign governments and concern for world stability, however minimal, became political necessities. By 1919 the United States was producing nearly half of the world's manufactured goods. The balance of trade was favorable: America controlled one-sixth of the total world exports and one-eighth of the total imports. Before the war the national debt to foreign nations was nearly $4 billion; after the war the United States was owed $12.5 billion by Britain and France, its wartime allies. Such extensive economic commitment abroad made America "isolationist" more in theory than in practice.

Rejection of Wilsonianism

When the Senate refused to ratify the Treaty of Versailles it effectively defeated Wilson's attempt to bring about a new political order based on "liberal capitalism" (as opposed to traditional imperialism and revolutionary socialism). Those on the political left and right formed a coalition to oppose Wilson; their combined efforts were to play a prominent role in shaping diplomacy during the coming decade. Opponents of the League of Nations appealed to nationalist sentiments to prevent American participation in the international body. The press, led by William Randolph Hearst, Robert Rutherford McCormick (1880–1955) of the *Chicago Tribune*, and Frank A. Munsey (1854–1925) of the *New York Sun* were powerful and vocal enemies of internationalism. In the Senate, Republican William Borah of Idaho worked especially hard to activate interested ethnic groups—Irish, Italians, German-Americans—against the League. Also, wealthy industrialists such as Andrew W. Mellon and Henry Clay Frick used their resources to oppose the League. It is doubtful, however, that "clever" politicians could have thwarted genuine popular support of the League. The truth is that the few Americans who cared about the issue at all (and those who did not care were a decided majority) came to believe that participation was not in the best interests of the nation. Wilson declared that the election of 1920 was to be a "solemn referendum" on the League of Nations; indeed the overwhelming Republican victory represented a resurgence of nationalism among the voters.

A number of superpatriotic organizations grew up in the period immediately following World War I. One popular magazine, *America First*, took patriotism into homes and schools. The League of Loyal Americans worked to get "One Tongue, One Ideal, and One Flag." The American Flag Movement pushed for a flag in every home. All of these groups, from the American Legion to the Ku Klux Klan, opposed the League of Nations. The Red Scare of 1919–1920 and the rising anti-immigrant sentiments that endured throughout the 1920s were symptomatic of the same public suspicion of anything deemed "not American."

Library of Congress.

William E. Borah
(1865–1940)

Born of German stock in Illinois in 1865, William Borah had his undergraduate days at the University of Kansas (as well as early plans to be an actor) cut short by ill health; however, he began to study law and was admitted to the Kansas bar in 1890. The following year young Borah moved to Boise, Idaho, where he began a stellar career as a criminal lawyer. As special counsel for the state he helped convict "Diamondfield Jack" Davis, a cattlemen's employee who murdered several sheepherders. Borah also prosecuted a number of sensational mining murder cases as well as the three labor leaders charged with conspiracy to murder a former governor. In the latter case, Borah faced Clarence Darrow who, by means of hung juries, managed to keep his clients out of prison.

Meanwhile, Borah's political life was beginning to take shape. Normally Republican, in 1896 he tried unsuccessfully to win a congressional seat as a Silver Republican pledged to support Bryan. In 1903 he was defeated for the U.S. Senate but three years later, with the aid of carefully cultivated popular backing, won the right to go to Washington. There he was named chairman of the Senate Committee on Education and Labor. In this role he disappointed conservatives by sponsoring a bill creating the Department of Labor and pushing through a law providing an eight-hour day on government contract work. He also led a Progressive crusade for the income tax and direct election of senators, but did fight for Idaho special interests against conservationists. A staunch supporter of Theodore Roosevelt from 1908 to 1912, he refused to bolt the party and join the Bull Moose movement.

An ardent nationalist and imperialist before World War I, Borah, fearful of entangling alliances, became a foe of the League of Nations; nevertheless, he encouraged U.S. participation in the Washington Naval Conference (1921). Widely hailed as a "statesman," Borah never visited a foreign nation but was instrumental in securing passage of the Kellogg-Briand Pact.

An accomplished orator and a confirmed political maverick, Borah recognized the people of Idaho as his only boss. Known in the Senate as the Great Opposer, he supported most New Deal measures, but was a leading isolationist-nationalist throughout the 1930s. Borah officially entered the presidential race in 1936 but did poorly in the primaries and soon dropped out. A very popular, approachable legislator, William E. Borah often was critical of Republican proposals and programs, but he usually returned to the fold at election time. He died in Washington in January 1940. Appropriately, Idaho's highest peak (12,655 feet) is named in his honor. ■

Death of the League and World Court Issues

President Harding entered the White House backed by both friends and enemies of the League. Harding, a "strong reservationist," told Congress in April 1921 that the United States would take no part with "super powers" in a "world governing" League. The President, together with his pragmatic Secretary of State Charles Evans Hughes, represented a middle ground within the Republican party. Harding advocated informal cooperation with the League that would permit observation of League affairs but only limited participation with various groups such as the League's humanitarian agencies.

On the other hand, Harding, Secretary of State Hughes and Vice President Coolidge favored United States membership in the World Court. The League of Nations established the Permanent Court of International Justice (the formal name for the World Court) in 1921 to arbitrate international disputes and to help develop a body of international law. In October 1922 Secretary Hughes proposed American membership—with a proviso that the United States would not become a member of the League of Nations. But isolationists in the Senate were suspicious, particularly since some advocates of the Court clearly hoped that such membership would provide a wedge to reopen the issue of League membership. Unwise propagandizing by these advocates reactivated the old anti-League coalition, ranging from insurgents La Follette and Borah to conservatives such as Democratic Senator James Reed of Missouri. The Senate Foreign Relations Committee insisted on adding yet another reservation to those Hughes proposed, one that would give the United States the right to withhold consent whenever a court decision involved the nation's interests. This meant that America could ignore any ruling it did not like. In 1926 the Senate voted to accept membership in the World Court on the condition that "any dispute or question in which the United States has or claims an interest" could be considered only with Washington's prior consent.

The Court requested clarification, whereupon President Coolidge announced bluntly that the United States could not adhere to the Court's decisions. The issue of membership was introduced again in 1930 (under Hoover) but lay bottled up in the Senate Foreign Relations Committee until 1934. When it emerged with President Roosevelt's approval (as it had with Hoover's), the isolationists again attacked it and the proposal failed in the Senate.

The record of the League of Nations during the 1920s did little to improve the possibility of American participation. Lacking military power, the League could only use diplomacy to protect and maintain peace. In 1923 the French occupied the Ruhr Valley; later that year Italy's Benito Mussolini bombed and invaded the Greek Island of Corfu. The League was powerless to stop these incursions; plans to draft mutual aid pacts proved eventually to be futile, though this failure was not immediately evident. The Locarno Pact (1925) sought to guarantee the status quo of Europe's borders. When Germany entered the League in 1926 it agreed to the pact; in the same year the League settled a boundary dispute between Greece and Bulgaria. The Peace of Locarno was, however, a short-lived settlement and general American indifference to League activities remained virtually undiminished.

In general, Democrats began to abandon the idea of United States involvement in that body as early as 1920. Their overwhelming defeat in 1924 forced them to drop the issue in an attempt to dissociate themselves from Wilsonianism and win back the Midwest and immigrant blocs in Northern cities. By 1928 even Roosevelt, although a member of his party's internationalist wing, gave up on U.S. membership in an article he published in *Foreign Affairs* magazine.

The reluctance of the Harding and Coolidge administrations to act on the issue of war reparations that Germany owed the Allies was further evidence of a disinclination to enter into European affairs. Congressional opposition limited American participation in the deliberations of the International Reparations Commission to an unofficial observer, Charles G. Dawes (1865-1951), who attended sessions in 1923. A year later, after the German mark became worthless, an American commission headed by Dawes set up a five-year interim reparations schedule, with flexible yearly sums based on Germany's ability to pay; the plan simultaneously provided for a $200 million Allied loan to Germany. By 1929 the Dawes Plan was superseded by the Young Plan (named for Owen Young, who carried on these negotiations), which scaled down the total German obligation in reparations to the European allies to $8 billion, with minimum annual payments of $153 million. In reality, American banking circles supplied most of this money. But tariff walls in both Europe and America frustrated this attampt to stimulate the German economy, generally depressing and hindering any true revival of postwar commerce.

Limiting Arms, Banning Wars

When the United States did become involved in international affairs it did so, paradoxically, in an effort to secure American insularity by limiting armaments and banning war. But the nation's lack of commitment even to these goals became obvious when no means of enforcement appeared. The major effort to limit arms was the Washington Naval Disarmament Conference of 1921–1922. Initiated by Secretary of State Hughes (partly to forestall the British plan for a general conference on Asian affairs), the Washington meeting attempted to reduce an Anglo-Japanese-American arms race.

Hughes, taking an unusually strong stand in his opening remarks, proposed huge cutbacks. He also startled the participants by revealing precise knowledge of the size of foreign navies, information obtained through American intelligence work. He quickly diverted the conference away from Asian concerns to the issue of arms and achieved a significant agreement on ratios for the navies of three major powers: the United States, Great Britain, and Japan. A four-power treaty respecting the status quo in East Asia, and a nine-power treaty pledged to maintain the Open Door policy and Chinese territorial integrity were also negotiated as a result of Hughes's efforts.

Nevertheless, this middle-of-the-road diplomacy invited criticism. Some called the results too entangling; others said they were too isolationist. The Senate ratified these agreements after attaching a contradictory reservation on armed commitment. Hughes's successor in the State Department, Frank B. Kellogg (1856–1937), tried unsuccessfully to expand the 1921 agreement beyond naval ships. In 1930, the Washington agreement was renegotiated at London with slight changes, which turned out to be advantageous to Japan.

The United States also joined efforts to outlaw war. The antiwar movement had supporters among friends and foes of the League, among pacifists and advocates of national defense alike. The Coolidge administration's symbolic gesture in behalf of peace in its closing months encouraged antiwar supporters. Herbert Hoover announced the resulting Kellogg-Briand Pact three months before the stock market crash of 1929. This pact had its origin in the theories of a Chicago corporation lawyer, Salmon O. Levinson, who discovered in 1919 that international law did not forbid war. He coined the phrase "outlawry of war," words that caught the fancy of many Americans, including William Borah, chairman of the Senate Committee on Foreign Relations.

Library of Congress.

Throughout the 1920s, public opinion ran strongly in favor of outlawing war by international law. This 1923 demonstration was typical of efforts which eventually helped to bring about the Kellogg-Briand Pact.

Supported by powerful isolationist politicians, rich lawyers, and prestigious academics, antiwar groups throughout America overlooked their diverse political points of view and worked together to pressure the President into acting on this matter. Philosopher John Dewey (1859–1952) brought liberals into the movement, pronouncing, "If the moral conviction of the world will not restrain a nation from resort to war, the world will not get rid of war under any system." In April 1927 French Prime Minister Aristide Briand issued a statement to the American press proposing a pact to outlaw war. Coolidge made little effort to disguise his irritation with Briand for bypassing diplomatic channels and going directly to the press. But he could no longer ignore public clamor at home.

Secretary of State Kellogg, deciding that the Briand appeal smacked of a Franco-American alliance, reluctantly offered his own ideas. Kellogg's plan, however, was to include all of the major powers, creating a multilateral rather than a simple bilateral pact. A year of diplomatic procrastination ensued. Finally, on August 27, 1929, representatives of fifteen nations signed the Pact of Paris, agreeing to renounce war. Most of these nations, including Japan and Germany, ultimately ratified the pact. Citizens all over the world rejoiced in this promise of a permanent peace; few bothered to notice the extensive provisos made by France and Great Britain about obligations to their colonial empires. The American Senate ratified the agreement, but with stipulations (recommended by the Foreign Relations Committee) that all of its provisions be subordinated to the Monroe Doctrine and the right of the United States to defend itself against aggression. Moreover, the Senate amended the pact so that America was not obliged to act against violators of the Kellogg-Briand plan.

Its probable effectiveness was summed up by Senator Carter Glass (1858–1946) of Virginia: "I am not willing that anybody in Virginia shall think that I am simple enough to suppose that it is worth a postage stamp in the direction of accomplishing world peace. . . . But I am going to be simple enough, along with the balance of you, to vote for the ratification of this worthless, but perfectly harmless peace treaty." On this cynical note the pact passed the Senate by a vote of 85 to 1. Immediately following this vote, the Senate took up a bill appropriating funds for the construction of fifteen new cruisers. This action caused one New York newspaper to ask, if signing a peace pact with the twenty-six nations meant the U.S. needed fifteen new warships, how many would have been required if the treaty had been rejected? This query went unanswered, but Kellogg, long very cool toward the pact that eventually bore his name, won the Nobel Peace Prize for 1929, which carried with it an award of $46,000.

The Public and Foreign Policy

Disillusioned after World War I, Americans in the 1920s were much more concerned with prosperity at home than with politics abroad. Moreover, many citizens felt that it would be simpler to leave foreign policy to politicians and diplomats. Apathy, rather than hostility, was the usual response to questions such as whether the U.S. should participate in the League of Nations and the World Court.

Although internationalism had not become a dead letter, the movement did die down in the 1920s until—in the words of one historian—it represented a "recessive characteristic," especially among groups who felt it unnecessary to *prove* their Americanness. Study and research organizations such as the Institute of International Education (founded in 1919), the Foreign Policy Association (1921), the Council on Foreign Relations, and the Institute of Politics (1921) flourished in academic surroundings. The goals of these study groups varied widely. The Carnegie Endowment for International Peace (led by Nicholas Murray Butler and James T. Shotwell), the American Peace Society, the Women's Peace Union, and the Convention of Student Volunteers all were interested in disarmament and world peace and played an important role in building support for the Kellogg-Briand Pact. Just as often, however, their efforts precipitated a backlash, especially in Congress, as when the attempt to insure American participation in the World Court failed. Two groups sought to promote peace by offering monetary awards. One was the Woodrow Wilson Foundation the other was the Bok Peace Award group.

Isolationists tended to be less well organized than internationalists and fragmented by divergent points of view. Some were politicians (Herbert Hoover, Senator William Borah) and some were members of the conservative press (Colonel McCormick of the *Chicago Tribune*). But their ranks also included historians, liberal journalists and representatives of the political left.

American historian Charles A. Beard exemplified the academic and intellectual isolationist. For Beard, America's priorities were defined in terms of a patriotic dedication to "the making in the United States of a civilization, as distinguished from a combination of aggregated wealth, economic distresses, almshouses, work relief and public doles. . . . Surely such a policy is as defensible as, let us say, one that leads to the killing of American boys in a struggle over the bean crop in Manchuria."

Beard's nationalism brought him closer to narrow isolationists such as Senator Borah than it did to socialists such as Norman Thomas. But Thomas was also a firm

Library of Congress.

Charles A. Beard
(1874–1948)

A tall, angular, white-haired Hoosier who was a newspaper editor, history teacher, political scientist, dairy farmer, and above all else extremely readable writer and man of principle not afraid to endorse unpopular stands, Charles A. Beard was a unique individual. Turning out twenty-nine historical studies, fifteen theoretical studies, and fifteen textbooks, he was a towering presence in the U.S. academic world for four decades yet was rarely a part of it.

Born into a Mark Hanna Republican household, Beard operated, with the aid of his brother, a rural weekly for four years before enrolling at DePauw University in the mid-1890s. During the succeeding decade, he studied twice at Oxford, picked up graduate degrees at Columbia University, and married Mary Ritter of Indianapolis, herself a very able writer who often assisted her husband. A dynamic lecturer, Beard soon joined the Columbia faculty where he virtually created the political science curriculum. In 1913 his eighth and perhaps most controversial book appeared, *An Economic Interpretation of the Constitution,* which demonstrated that some Founding Fathers had considerable personal stake in the deliberations leading to that famous document.

In October 1917, Beard resigned from his post at Columbia to protest the dismissal of two other faculty members opposed to American involvement in World War I and spent the next two decades writing, tending his Connecticut dairy herd, and advising foreign governments. The two most important byproducts of those years were *The Rise of American Civilization* (1927), a multivolume classic that he coauthored with his wife. In it, the Beards stressed the "Americanness" of U.S. institutions to the exclusion of Old World influences and the growing conviction that Europe really was little more than a "big Balkans."

Beard originally endorsed FDR's New Deal planning but as the drift toward World War II became apparent, he turned violently against the administration. During his last years, Beard again taught spasmodically at Columbia and Johns Hopkins. In the words of one contemporary, his books were a mix of history, economics, political science, and salt. Critics sometimes found his work weak, unreliable, and impressionistic—but never dull. ■

noninterventionist and a lifelong pacifist who, throughout his career, fought for liberty and economic justice and felt that inequities existing within the United States were serious enough to demand the nation's total attention. In Thomas's view, internationalism could embroil the United States in futile wars that would solve nothing so long as capitalism remained unchanged. Beard represented the intellectual position for isolation; Thomas, a more passionate leftist position.

The media, which changed dramatically in the 1920s, played an important role in communicating and shaping public opinion, usually coming down on the side of isolationism. Advances in radio, the growth of "news" periodicals such as *Time* magazine (founded in 1923) and the regular appearance of syndicated columnists and foreign correspondents in chain newspapers all helped to make the public more conscious of the international scene—and perhaps more suspicious of it as well. Some editors were mildly internationalist (for instance, those of the Gannet, Scripps-Howard, and Curtis publishing empires). But most were not; major independents such as the *Chicago Tribune* and the *Kansas City Star*, and the huge Hearst chain (with three million circulation) were staunchly isolationist.

Business—particularly small and medium-sized manufacturers—also lobbied for economic protection and isolationism. Local Chambers of Commerce and the National Association of Manufacturers (NAM) rallied to exert influence on Congress whenever the tariff issue arose. The American business community agreed upon the desirability of expanding foreign trade; but competing groups differed bitterly on how to accomplish this expansion. Manufacturers, of course, favored high tariffs. Bankers, with their international interests, and those involved in imports and exports naturally opposed restrictive nationalist policies.

Instead of pursuing a liberal free-trade policy after 1920, the newly elected Republican administrations bowed to the powerful NAM lobby, which feared foreign competition. New industries spawned by the war also demanded that high duties be maintained and economic troubles that followed the advent of peace swelled protectionist ranks. The result was an Emergency Tariff Act in 1921 to cope with these troubles and the Fordney-McCumber Act, passed a year later. This measure, designed primarily to protect "infant" war industries and the nation's farmers, generally restored high Republican rates of a decade or so earlier, and gave the President some flexibility to change levies so as to equalize foreign and domestic production costs.

Hoover came to power pledged to aid America's trouble-plagued agricultural economy and, in the end, his efforts (coupled with the crash and considerable logrolling) produced the Hawley-Smoot Tariff of 1930 and even higher rates. Despite much criticism from Europe and pleas that such measures hindered efforts to settle war debts, Hoover was convinced that American foreign economic policy had nothing to do with problems at home. In his view, defects of the Treaty of Versailles and unsound monetary practices of European nations had ruined world prosperity.

Presidents Harding, Coolidge, and Hoover lacked expertise in foreign affairs and generally delegated much of the responsibility for policymaking to the State Department, where a middle-of-the-road approach prevailed with the endorsement and approval of key congressional leaders. Secretaries Hughes and Kellogg were answerable to the Senate Foreign Relations Committee, chaired until 1925 by Henry Cabot Lodge and thereafter by William E. Borah. By the end of the decade the presidency recaptured the initiative from Congress but still retained the moderate Republican approach.

An area of special concern during the 1920s was Latin America. When revolution broke out in Nicaragua in 1925, Coolidge sent 5,000 American marines to help reestablish "order" and dispatched Henry L. Stimson (1867-1950) to help arrange for a truce and an honest election. Stimson, who headed the War Department under three presidents (Taft, Roosevelt, and Truman) and also served as Secretary of State under Hoover, managed to restore peace, but U.S. Marines stayed on in Nicaragua until 1933.

In 1925 President Plutarco Elías Calles of Mexico, who was newly elected, demanded that American oil companies renegotiate their Mexican leases and concessions within two years, something the four largest American companies refused to do. When the Senate passed a unanimous resolution insisting on a peaceful settlement of the dispute, Coolidge sent a new ambassador, Dwight W. Morrow (1873-1931), to Mexico City. Morrow, a classmate of Coolidge at Amherst College and a distinguished banker and lawyer, succeeded admirably but could not erase unpleasant memories of American diplomatic incompetence and interference.

Library of Congress.

The arrival of the first Marines at Matagalpa, Nicaragua, in 1925, beginning a military presence in that nation which was to last eight years.

Depression Diplomacy

The economic stagnation that engulfed much of the world in the late 1920s tended to push domestic affairs to the forefront in most nations. Many leaders thought finding jobs for millions of unemployed at home more important than matters beyond their borders, yet some governments—notably those of Japan, Italy, and Germany—tried to relieve internal pressures by means of external adventures. These moves stirred contradictory responses within the United States: calls for international cooperation to maintain peace and an upsurge of isolationist sentiment strengthened by bitter memories of World War I.

Hoover and Foreign Crises

Although Hoover supported United States economic expansion as both Secretary of Commerce and President, he was not an internationalist. Instead, he generally remained aloof from postwar reparations problems and yielded to nationalists on restrictive tariff policies. Hoover believed that Europe could now take care of itself and that once the arms race ended, world peace would be assured. The President visited Latin America on a goodwill tour, making promises as he went that the United States would cease its interference in that region; he then arranged to have marines withdrawn from Nicaragua and Haiti (although they did not actually leave until 1933). Even when Latin American revolutions nationalized property belonging to American citizens and cancelled debts owed to American businesses, Hoover refrained from interfering. In addition, to soothe Latin tempers, both Hoover and Secretary of State Stimson endorsed the Clark Memorandum, a 236-page document repudiating the interventionist twist given to the Monroe Doctrine by Theodore Roosevelt. This decision, revealed in 1930, helped lay the foundations for better relations throughout the Americas and a true Good Neighbor policy.

A decade of Republican policies left Hoover with still other problems abroad, such as postwar reparations, world trade made chaotic by economic disasters, and Japanese aggression in Asia. As in his domestic policy, the President showed too little flexibility in these matters. For the first two years of the Depression, he refused to reassess the question of World War I debts. Then he suggested a one-year moratorium on all debts rather than renunciation. By the time Hoover made a formal proposal to Congress, Germany, in the midst of widespread bank failures, had announced a virtual repudiation of all reparations.

American banks, which had loaned nearly $1.7 billion to Germany, were themselves suddenly brought to the brink of bankruptcy. Washington inaugurated an emergency freeze on payments by Germany. But it was too late to stop the spread of worldwide panic and the draining of gold reserves everywhere. Debtor nations other than Germany grew hostile, blaming American international economic policies for their own fiscal disasters. Like Germany, they repudiated their war debts and loan obligations to America; only Finland continued with its payments. (Cuba, Liberia, and Nicaragua had already paid off their debts.)

With the virtual default of debtor nations, hostility grew on both sides of the Atlantic. Despite the growing threat of Fascism (which thrived in this atmosphere)

Congress passed the Johnson Act in 1934, which banned further loans to nations that had defaulted and prohibited the purchase of securities or bonds from them.

In the 1920s the United States came much closer to collective action in Asia than in Europe. In an effort to stabilize the Asian situation, conferences were held to avoid naval races and to limit the building of warships. But it was the Japanese who benefited most from these proceedings, which allowed them to dominate the western Pacific with their powerful navy. As long as Americans clung to an aversion to armed interference, Japanese good will remained the only hope of peace in the Far East.

In 1928 Chiang Kai-shek, a Chinese political leader, broke with the Communists (his former allies against the old regime) and took over the central government. The United States soon recognized Chiang's claims to legitimacy. In the fall of 1931 Japan, alarmed by Chiang's drive for national unity, decided to seize Manchuria, a rich province in northeastern China. Soon Japanese troops overran the entire region and converted it into the puppet state of Manchukuo.

Such overt aggression violated the Nine Power Treaty, the Kellogg-Briand Pact, and numerous other diplomatic accords Japan had signed with the Western powers, and China turned to the League of Nations for help. The League set up the Lytton Commission, a five-member panel (including an American general) which was powerless to do anything. Even this small gesture infuriated U.S. isolationists, and business interests in both America and Europe were extremely reluctant to interfere and endanger their investments in Asia. This feeble effort at international cooperation aroused such an outcry that Hoover felt compelled to state in his annual message to Congress (December 1931) that he retained complete freedom of action in Asia.

Secretary of State Stimson suggested that Washington and the League agree to impose economic reprisals against Japan in lieu of active intervention; the President rejected Stimson's proposal as provocative, opting instead for moral condemnation of Japan. The Secretary of State then issued a statement—later called the Stimson Doctrine—which declared that the United States would not recognize any changes brought about by aggression or that violated China's territorial integrity. However, this measure proved to be completely ineffective.

In January 1932, the Japanese bombed Shanghai, killing thousands of civilians before taking the city. Again Hoover, a Quaker and unalterably opposed to violence, resorted to stern words, but refused to consider stronger measures such as a boycott. In 1932 the League finally voted to condemn Japan and request the return of Manchuria to China. Japan merely withdrew from the League, justifiably certain that no attempt would be made to enforce the condemnation.

Roosevelt as Nationalist-Isolationist

In the 1920s Roosevelt had moved towards isolationism; then in 1932 in return for the promise of political support from Hearst newspapers, he withdrew his support of the League of Nations. Although no longer an internationalist, Roosevelt could scarcely be called naive in matters of foreign policy. An Assistant Secretary of the Navy under Woodrow Wilson, he had learned much about international affairs. At the outbreak of the war in Europe in 1914, he urged the development of a formidable navy. By the time Roosevelt won the presidency, he had visited Europe thirteen times. Not personally familiar with Asia, nevertheless he was stirred by the political traditions in his family to take an active interest in that part of the world.

Roosevelt took office on March 4, 1933. In his inaugural address he declared that "The only thing we have to fear is fear itself." But he was referring to domestic crises, not foreign affairs (America was then in the fourth and worst year of the Depression). Issues overseas were even less clear than those at home, and the policies of Hoover's Republican administration left few guidelines for the new administration. Despite his repudiation of Wilsonian internationalism and the League, Roosevelt chose Cordell Hull—an ardent Wilsonian—as Secretary of State. An idealist and a moralist, Hull was also an astute politician whose acumen helped him survive for eleven years in Roosevelt's Cabinet.

Hull chose Norman Davis (1878–1944) as a chief advisor. Davis was an avowed internationalist whom Roosevelt might have selected to head the State Department had his deep involvement with the House of Morgan and banking circles not disqualified him. To the chagrin of Davis and Hull, Roosevelt named Raymond Moley (1886–1975)—the Columbia professor who organized the "brain trust" for Roosevelt's 1932 campaign—as Assistant Secretary of State. Although Moley remained in Washington in an official capacity for only six months, he continued to consult with FDR from time

Library of Congress.

Cordell Hull
(1871–1955)

Cordell Hull's father once said of his famous son, "Cord wasn't set enough to be a school teacher, wasn't rough enough to be a lumberman, wasn't sociable enough to be a doctor and couldn't holler loud enough to be a preacher. But Cord was a right thorough thinker." This "right thorough thinker" was born in a log cabin in Overton County, Tennessee, in 1871, a backwoods community which in 1937 still had only one telephone. His mother was part Cherokee; his father prospered on timber and moonshine. After a rudimentary education and a brief stint at Cumberland University Law School, Cordell Hull, not yet twenty, was admitted to the Tennessee bar.

He was in the lower house of the Tennessee legislature from 1892 to 1897, also serving briefly in the Spanish-American War. From 1903 to 1906 Hull was a state circuit court judge and thereafter always was known as "Judge" Hull.

An avowed disciple of Jefferson and a strong advocate of tariff reduction and an income tax, Hull served in the U.S. House of Representatives from 1907 to 1921 and again from 1923 to 1930. There he was strongly identified with Wilson's New Freedom and helped author the income tax law, as well as the inheritance and estate tax legislation of 1916. Convinced by the experience of World War I that trade barriers caused "economic wars," Hull increasingly dedicated himself to the reduction of trade barriers. Defeated for reelection in 1920, he served as Democratic National Chairman from 1921 to 1924. In 1930, after seven more years in the House, he won election to the Senate.

Named Secretary of State by FDR in 1933, Hull pushed successfully for passage of the Reciprocal Trade Act of 1934, which gave the President power to reduce tariff rates with individual nations in return for concessions. Although many observers at first thought this man was a weak, political appointee, he soon grew in stature. His easygoing, friendly, sometimes undiplomatic manner soon paid off as he almost singlehandedly made the Good Neighbor policy with Latin America a reality.

Although no interventionist, Cordell Hull took a firm stand against aggression and played an important role in the rejection of Japanese demands leading up to Pearl Harbor. During World War II he was overshadowed by various presidential advisors (especially Hopkins) and did not attend any Big Three conferences. After resigning in 1944, he accepted appointment as a delegate to the United Nations in 1945 and that year received the Nobel Peace Prize for his U.N. contributions. A man of sly charm, a bit Lincolnesque in appearance—6 feet 1 inch tall, lean as a rail fence—Hull died in Bethesda, Maryland, in 1955. ■

to time. By 1936, however, this blunt, practical man, who enjoyed considerable success as an editor, columnist, and radio commentator, was becoming more critical of New Deal policies, labeling them too internationalist in tone and antibusiness. Thus, it is not clear what Roosevelt's attitudes toward world involvement really were; probably he himself was unsure of how far he could depart from a decade of caution as the nation confronted the worst economic crisis of its history.

Nevertheless, there were some notable internationalist achievements in the early 1930s. The government in 1933 finally extended official recognition to Russia, which had previously been shunned because of widespread fears of Bolshevism. In 1934 the newly created Export-Import Bank began to encourage foreign trade through American loans and financing; that same year tariff rates were reduced. These moves reflected a growing business support for an enlightened internationalism that would foster world trade.

Roosevelt's major international achievement in his first years as President was his Good Neighbor policy, really a continuation of Hoover's friendly overtures. The president's first step in Latin American affairs was inauspicious. He recalled Sumner Welles (1892–1961), a former diplomat, to public life to serve as ambassador to Cuba, then suffering from the brutality of the Machado regime. When that government was ousted by a revolutionary coup, Welles handpicked a new president and cabinet, which the Cubans rejected; Washington, in turn, refused to recognize its successor. As a result, suspicion and hostility greeted Secretary of State Hull and Ambassador Welles in 1933 when they attended the Seventh International Conference of American States in Montevideo, Uruguay. But after promising that the United States would refrain from further interference in internal affairs, they were able to reverse the mood of the sessions. To prove the sincerity of the new administration, in 1934 Roosevelt abrogated the Platt Amendment giving the U.S. the right to interfere in Cuban affairs and recognized a new revolutionary government in El Salvador. By 1936 when American delegates attended the Inter-American Conference at Buenos Aires, their reception was as warm as could be hoped for.

Isolationism in Congress and the Public

Roosevelt's Good Neighbor policy helped to smooth relations in the Western Hemisphere, and the President and his Secretary of State generally avoided open involvement despite growing threats to world peace by aggressor nations—Italy, Japan, and Germany. These moves, unpaid war debts, disillusionment with world affairs, and domestic economic chaos reinforced American apathy and isolationism in the 1920s, blending with a growing antiwar sentiment in the 1930s.

By 1935 it was evident that war in Europe and Asia was imminent. Italy wanted an African empire; Japan seemed bent on the complete conquest of China. Astute observers realized that Germany was eager to resume its great power role. Nevertheless, most Americans felt they had no legitimate interest in either Europe or Asia. The American Institute of Public Opinion said this majority was overwhelming (95 percent).

Anti-entanglement leaders in Congress, suspicious of what America could gain from any foreign adventure, drew their conclusions from a careful if misguided study of foreign affairs and from the belief in the primacy of domestic problems. Republican Senator William Borah of Idaho was the most prominent foe of intervention, closely followed by Republican Senator Gerald Nye (1892–1971) of North Dakota. Their isolationist views were, however, not the same as the outdated nineteenth century indifference to the Old World. These men fought to avoid long-term commitments to other nations, thus leaving the United States free to act in its own best interests at all times.

Others feared that the shock of another war might alter the character of the United States. Total mobilization would ultimately concentrate power in the central government and invite totalitarianism in a country already weakened by the onslaughts of the Depression. Small ethnic pockets also had vested interests in American neutrality—German-Americans with family ties to the old country and Irish-Americans loath to aid Great Britain, their traditional oppressor.

Historians also contributed. As early as 1920, scholars began to reconsider the nature of World War I, challenging the prevailing opinion that Germany was solely responsible for the conflict. Sidney Fay's *The Origins of the World War* (1928) took this view while Hartley Grattan's *Why We Fought* (1929) accused France and Great Britain of deceiving the United States about their own imperialist ambitions. In the Thirties, revisionist attacks on American gullibility and the duplicity of the Allies became more overt.

Wide World.

Senator Gerald P. Nye, a fervent isolationist, was chairman of the special Senate committee established in 1934 to investigate the role of the munitions industry in American entry into World War I.

In addition, the severity of the Depression and the failure of banking and big business to provide economic safeguards inspired widespread distrust of both commerce and industry. The banks, with their foreign investments, and industry with its overseas markets would suffer most, it was said, from nonintervention. Suspicion of munitions manufacturers and bankers led to the creation of a Senate committee chaired by Gerald P. Nye to investigate the role of the munitions industry in bringing about the nation's entry into World War I.

The Nye Committee began public hearings in the fall of 1934 and soon accused magnates such as Pierre duPont and J. P. Morgan of being "merchants of death" who had pushed the United States into war. Headlines exposed allegedly unsavory details of munitions industry relations with the War Department and with events in Latin America and China between 1914 and 1934. Even though the Nye Committee did not offer documentary proof to support allegations of profiteering, many Americans accepted the view that the war had been fought primarily for private gain. Early in 1935 Walter Millis, a reporter for the *New York Herald Tribune,* published *Road to War 1914–1917,* a popular history that reinforced this opinion.

Suddenly pacifism became a national movement. College students staged huge antiwar strikes supported by religious groups who demanded withdrawal of ROTC units from universities. Senator Nye charged that Wilson had covered up the machinations of the House of Morgan, which sought to recoup its loans to the British and French through an Allied victory guaranteed by American troops. With these revelations the isolationists routed their critics. At one and the same time, the year 1935 witnessed the high tide of American isolationism and the beginnings of militant aggression in Asia and Europe.

In 1935 Roosevelt encouraged U.S. membership in the World Court as a gesture toward helping maintain peace. The Senate, however, turned thumbs down on this idea. Instead, Congress passed the first Neutrality Act (amended and extended in 1936 and 1937). These acts grew increasingly stringent; all denied the President the discretion to apply embargoes on war-related material, allowing him only to determine if war existed. The Neutrality Acts sought to insure that internationalists would have less power through the executive branch and also endeavored to limit the new power Roosevelt possessed in domestic affairs as he exercised presidential prerogatives in unprecedented ways.

The Path to Involvement

Despite the well-intended efforts of avowed isolationists and pacifists to assure peace and a grim determination on the part of many more Americans simply to ignore the rest of the world, a crisis atmosphere enveloped Asia, Africa, and Europe by the late 1930s. Headlines told of high-level conferences and last-minute agreements, aggression and threatened aggression, undeclared conflicts and civil war. Chinese, Ethiopians, and Spanish died by the thousands in the prelude to a general war that first erupted in Europe in September 1939. From that moment on, the United States wrestled with the complex problem of aiding its friends without actually becoming involved in what was fast developing into a worldwide struggle. Events at Pearl Harbor early on the morning of December 7, 1941, resolved this dilemma and, once more, America was at war.

FDR and International Crises

It is incorrect to view President Roosevelt as a frustrated internationalist pecking away at an isolationist Congress throughout the 1930s. Nor was Secretary of State Cordell Hull an all-out internationalist, aside from believing that free trade would foster world stability. Not until 1937 did Roosevelt make any effort to alert the people or Congress to the dangers of the international situation. Even then, much of his emphasis was on hemispheric preparedness and nationalism rather than on collective world security.

Roosevelt took essentially the same stance towards Japanese aggression in China as Hoover and Stimson: he refused to consider the use of force against the Japanese and invoked nothing beyond diplomatic protests against violations of the Open Door policy. Roosevelt tried somewhat harder to aid Chiang Kai-shek. But the combination of Chiang's ineptness, Japanese diplomatic hostility, and the demands of the Depression at home forced Roosevelt to abandon these efforts until 1938, when it was essentially too late.

The importance of Japanese trade to the American economy could not be ignored. Throughout the 1930s Japan was a leading importer of American goods, rising from the position of fifth to third most important foreign market throughout most of the 1930s. American cotton was a leading Japanese import, and Roosevelt needed southern cotton votes to get reelected. Refined oil, scrap iron, and steel were also major exports; all three industries had strong lobbies in Washington. The business community wanted to avoid a confrontation with Japan that might lead to violence. On the other hand, Japanese conquest of China was equally unthinkable, since it would make Japan more self-sufficient and close a lucrative market to Americans. The conflict in China was apparently unresolvable.

Japan left the League of Nations in 1933, and two years later renounced the naval arms limitations agreed to at the Washington Conference in 1921. The United States did nothing and assumed no important role at the Brussels Conference (1937) designed to contain the undeclared war between China and Japan.

The problem facing the U.S. and other democracies in those years was the rise and appeal of Fascism, a political system that puts the welfare of a nation-state or race at the center of life and history. Like totalitarian Bolshevism in Russia, it insists upon a single-party state and strict regimentation of all aspects of society and government by that party. The name "Fascism" comes from the Latin *fasces,* bundles of rods or sticks carried by ancient Romans to indicate authority, and it was first used as a similar symbol in modern times by Benito Mussolini's Black Shirt movement in Italy in March 1919. Social unrest and disillusionment engendered by World War I brought Mussolini to power in 1922, and a decade later similar conditions in Germany gave Adolf Hitler and his National Socialist (Nazi) party an opportunity to seize control of that nation. By the mid-1930s Fascism in various forms, again in response to war, depression, and economic turmoil, had also been accepted in Austria, Hungary, Poland, Rumania, Bulgaria, Greece, and Japan.

Although Roosevelt avoided taking action in the Pacific against Japanese aggression, the Italian invasion of Ethiopia in October 1935 precipitated his first major foreign crisis, testing the validity of the new and hastily contrived Neutrality Act. Under its provisions, whenever the President proclaimed the existence of war, he had to forbid the sale or transport of munitions to belligerents for six months. He also could warn Americans who traveled on belligerent ships that they did so at their own risk. (The ghost of the *Lusitania* was still very much alive.) Roosevelt wanted a more flexible measure enabling him to assist nations attacked by aggressors but eventually signed the bill and promptly invoked the arms embargo. He also proclaimed a moral embargo, a voluntary restriction of other exports. Both the Italian government and the American oil industry—which had increased shipments to Italy by 600 percent in the months prior to the invasion—protested. Of course, any "moral" restraint required the cooperation of all nations, which was lacking. Congress, alarmed by the outbreak of civil war in Spain in February 1936, then decided to strengthen the Neutrality Act by banning credit and other aid to belligerents and extending the six-months proviso to two years.

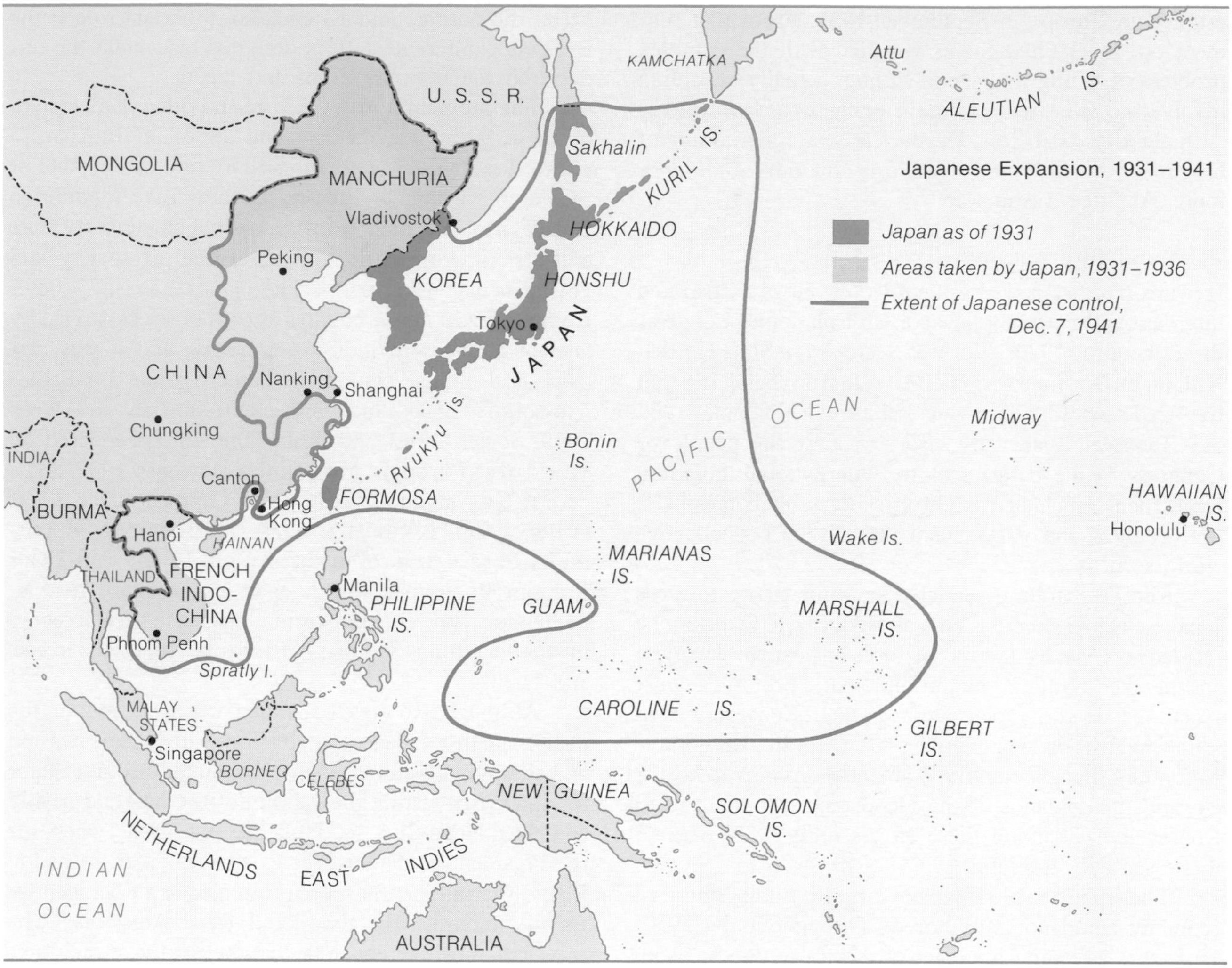

It is not surprising that, despite outright conflicts in several parts of the world, Roosevelt reflected the isolationist temper of the times, since World War I and its aftermath had left deep scars throughout America. In his annual message to Congress (January 1936), after largely ignoring foreign matters for three years, the President discussed the world crisis at some length, endorsing a policy of strict neutrality. As his reelection campaign of that year developed, he reaffirmed that view. Speaking at Chautauqua, New York, in August he said, "I hate war. I have passed unnumbered hours, I shall pass unnumbered hours, thinking and planning how war may be kept from this nation."

Some of Roosevelt's critics dismiss this as mere platform rhetoric, but the President clearly meant what he said. Roosevelt hoped that use of the Neutrality Act would provide the League of Nations with the support needed to widen economic sanctions against Italy and other aggressors. But in July 1937 the Japanese launched a full-scale invasion of the Chinese interior. American public sympathy was with the Chinese; but, since neither country had officially declared war, Roosevelt did not invoke the Neutrality Act—which would have hurt China far more than Japan.

On October 5, 1937, the President, speaking in Chicago, declared that the "present reign of terror and international lawlessness begun a few years ago . . . has now reached a stage where the very foundations of civili-

Library of Congress.

While American public opinion remained isolationist, Adolph Hitler of Germany and Benito Mussolini of Italy embraced increasingly militaristic and aggressive policies that threatened to bring war to Europe. The only American response through 1939 was a series of Neutrality Acts.

zation are seriously threatened. If those things come to pass in other parts of the world, let no one imagine America will escape, that America may expect mercy, that this Western Hemisphere will not be attacked, and that it will continue tranquilly and peacefully to carry on the ethics and arts of civilization." The famous "Quarantine Speech" calling for cooperative action against a spreading "epidemic of world lawlessness" was a bold step indeed. With it, Roosevelt repudiated any hope that the nation could remain aloof and, as clearly as he dared, warned the nation that overseas hostilities posed a distinct threat.

Public reaction to the speech was overwhelmingly negative. Critics such as historian Charles Beard saw in the speech evidence of the secret, longstanding internationalist sympathies of both Roosevelt and Hull. But the speech was vague, mostly calling for the same economic sanctions as in the past, only now on a far more extensive basis. Probably the President was deliberately ambiguous, reflecting his own uncertainty as to what course the nation should follow in undeniably worsening times, nor did Roosevelt attempt to build support for his views expressed in Chicago.

Courtesy Imperial War Museum.

Throughout the 1930s, Japan made increasing inroads in China, beginning with Manchuria in 1931. Here Japanese forces are shown attacking Tientsin in 1937.

Frederic Lewis.

Los Angeles Times

VOL. LVII — MONDAY MORNING, DECEMBER 13, 1937. — DAILY, FIVE CENTS

JAPANESE ADMIT SINKING U. S. SHIP

Heavy Seas Rip Out Three Piers

Convicts Slay Guard Captain in Prison Riot

SUNK IN PERILOUS CHINESE WATERS

Gunboat Goes Down in River

Floods Peril Many Homes

Sloan Donates $10,000,000

BRITAIN AROUSED BY THREE JAPAN ATTACKS ON GUNBOATS

Scientist Arrested in Hit-Run Killing

Stricken Babies Pronounced Cured

Liner Begins Rescue of 600 Marooned Hoover Passengers

IN THE 'TIMES' TODAY

OBSERVATIONS

Roosevelt Daughter Enters Hospital

The strafing and sinking of the *Panay* by the Japanese in the Yangtze River aroused an immediate outcry in the United States.

Two months later Japanese planes sank the American gunboat *Panay* in the Yangtze River, seeming to bear out Roosevelt's predictions. But the Japanese government offered profuse apologies and indemnities, which the United States accepted with a sigh of relief. America was moving into another economic recession. The domestic situation dominated public interest as fear of war grew somewhat less acute.

By the end of 1937, the Neutrality Act in more restrictive form had become a permanent fixture of U.S. foreign policy. Throughout 1938 diplomatic nerves became more and more frayed as events proceeded at a dangerous pace. In March, Hitler invaded and annexed Austria. Roosevelt invoked the Neutrality Act clauses governing nonrecognition and broke the commercial treaty between Austria and the United States. This action was scarcely more severe than America's reaction two years earlier when Germany had retaken the Rhineland.

After the *Anschluss* (union) with Austria, Hitler announced that he would annex a large part of western Czechoslovakia, using a German majority in the Sudetenland to justify aggression. The Czech crisis tested not only Great Britain and France but the United States as well, although the latter was not represented at a series of meetings held at Munich in the fall of 1938. Hitler, Mussolini, Prime Minister Chamberlain of Great Britain, and Prime Minister Daladier of France attended. No one spoke for Czechoslovakia, whose fate was being decided. Roosevelt's role remains unclear. When he heard that Chamberlain was accepting an invitation to Munich, the President wired him "Good Man." But the Germans, instead of reducing their territorial demands, increased them. William Bullitt, the American Ambassador to France, wired the President to call an international conference to avert war, suggesting that Roosevelt himself act as arbitrator. Secretary Hull and others advised him against so direct a step. Instead, Roosevelt publicly asked the European leaders to continue negotiating with Eduard Beneš, the Czech leader. Hitler refused. The President then appealed to Mussolini to intervene. An agreement reached at the end of September averted war, but only after a complete and humiliating capitulation of the democracies to Hitler.

The Munich crisis, more than anything else, ushered in a new era in broadcast journalism, paving the way for the television commentators of later decades. The Columbia Broadcasting System (CBS) dispatched youthful Edward R. Murrow to Europe in 1937 to establish programming from that region. He left with specific instructions to avoid international politics and to seek out instead bizarre and interesting happenings. Murrow, however, quickly proved that millions of Americans, sitting close by their radios throughout the tense weeks of September 1938, were indeed concerned about international affairs. (Public reaction a month later to a production by Orson Welles detailing an invasion from Mars and utilizing spot interviews and news bulletins similar to those heard from Munich proved that news broadcasting had come of age.)

Most historians believe that Roosevelt shared the hope of Daladier and Chamberlain that the Munich concessions would end German aggression. On March 15, 1939, however, Hitler invaded the rest of Czechoslo-

Wide World.

At Munich in September 1938, Hitler shakes hands with British Prime Minister Neville Chamberlain.

vakia. In April the President naively appealed to Hitler and Mussolini for ten-year assurances of nonaggression against thirty-one Near East and European states. At the same time he urged Congress to step up the arms embargo. Roosevelt's appeals were rejected with contempt by the Fascist leaders and ignored by Congress; the isolationist senators were confident that there would be no war. Perhaps Roosevelt made his appeals chiefly to awaken American public opinion, for by this time he was undoubtedly thoroughly alerted to the probability of serious trouble in Europe.

In March 1939, Fascist forces in Spain, armed by Germany and Italy, won that bloody Civil War. In May 1939, the same month that the Italian army overwhelmed little Albania, Germany and Italy signed a "Pact of Steel." During the summer, as Russia and Germany held secret negotiations, Hitler turned his gaze toward Poland.

On August 23, German and Russian diplomats concluded a nonaggression agreement in Moscow.

On August 24, Great Britain entered into a mutual assistance pact with Poland.

On September 1, Hitler invaded Poland.

Two days later France and Great Britain declared war on Germany.

World War II had begun.

War in Europe

We can only speculate as to what difference a stiffer stance by the United States would have made to world events. Some historians believe that Roosevelt's indecisiveness invited disaster; others feel that nothing could have contained German and Italian aggression, even in the period before Munich. Nevertheless, it seems that had Roosevelt been a more committed internationalist, he could have brought about revisions of the Neutrality Act earlier than 1939. Instead he concentrated on domestic legislation and on his 1937–1939 institutional reform packages (executive reform, court packing). Too often his half-hearted revision efforts were understood, probably accurately, as moves to increase the freedom of White House action.

Even after 1939, as the nation drifted toward intervention, Roosevelt continued to be reluctant to get involved, limiting himself to insuring Allied success (in order to keep the United States out of war) and to securing hemispheric neutrality. On the day war broke out in Europe, Roosevelt gave one of his famous fireside chats over the radio. He could not, he said, expect Americans to remain "neutral in spirit," and called for a special congressional session to revise the Neutrality Act. The "cash-and-carry" provision of the revised act would aid

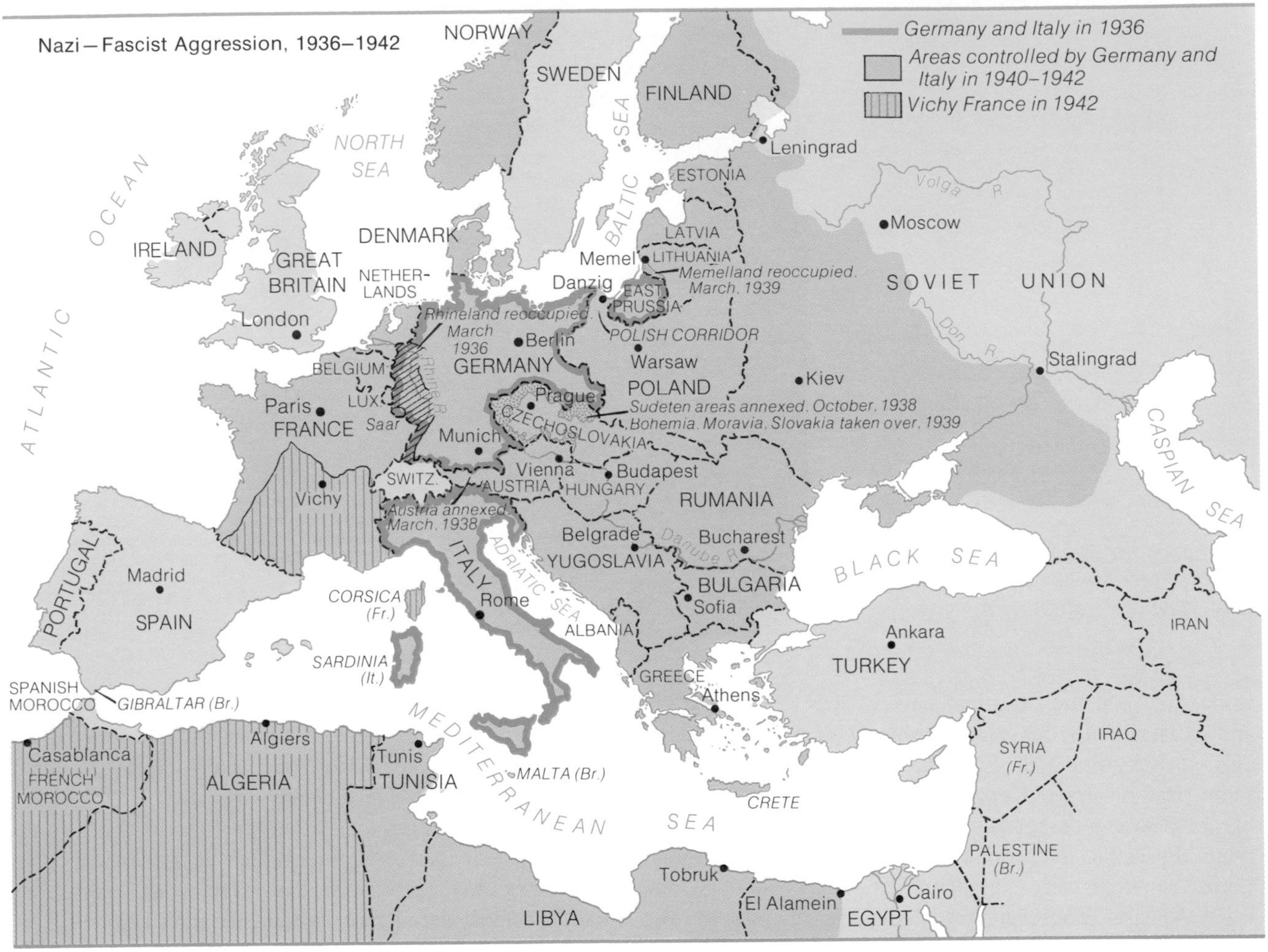

Britain, the possessor of a mighty navy and merchant-marine, since it required that foreign nations must use their own ships to transport goods bought in America. Hence it would also keep American ships out of the war zone and avoid direct American involvement.

The turning point for FDR was Germany's invasion of Norway and Denmark, the *Blitzkrieg* against the Netherlands, and the fall of the Low Countries and France in April–June 1940. Roosevelt gave a speech to his son's law school graduating class at Charlottesville, Virginia, in which he committed all U.S. aid to the Allies "short of war." He attacked the Italian government for its military alliance with Germany and its participation in the French invasion: "On this tenth day of June 1940, the hand that held the dagger has struck it into the back of its neighbor."

On June 20, Roosevelt appointed Republican Henry L. Stimson as Secretary of War and Frank Knox (1874–1944) as Secretary of the Navy, in a bid to form a bipartisan coalition in support of his new stance. He then secured a fivefold increase in naval and armed forces appropriations, calling specifically for an annual production of 50,000 war planes.

In July—after the evacuation at Dunkirk and while Britain suffered savage German air attacks—Winston Churchill (1874–1965), now Britain's leader, cabled Roosevelt requesting help and supplies. The British statesman specifically asked for destroyers to bolster the battered English fleet so as to repel an expected German invasion; Roosevelt's response was both humane and political—an "inspiration," according to Secretary of the Treasury Henry Morgenthau, Jr. (1891–1967). Fifty destroyers were given to Britain in September 1940 in exchange for ninety-nine year leases of bases in Newfoundland and in the Caribbean. Since the bases could be used for hemispheric protection, Roosevelt won the support of American isolationists and interventionists alike. In that same month, the Burke-Wadsworth Bill provided for the registration of all men twenty-one to thirty-five and induction of 800,000 draftees, the first time the United States ever had taken such a drastic step in peacetime.

During these crucial months Roosevelt had to proceed with caution and perhaps even some deviousness in foreign affairs. He was running for a third term against Wendell Willkie, who had gathered the support of liberal and conservative Republicans as well as the allegiance of many Democrats outraged at the dangerous precedent a third term seemed to suggest. The President had clearly become an interventionist ready to go to any lengths to insure a British victory, and his campaign for reelection sometimes was misleading: "Your boys are not going to be sent into any foreign wars."

Roosevelt's victory, although decisive, did not approach his landslide of 1936; he received only 54.8 percent of the vote. A month later Churchill informed Roosevelt that the "cash-and-carry" basis of American aid was in peril; Britain had nearly exhausted its supply of American dollars, and German submarines made transport increasingly hazardous. Roosevelt proposed the Lend-Lease Act. The United States would provide the arms Britain needed without regard to cost, and when the war was over, the British would repay the loan. Thus England would stand and America would act as an "arsenal of democracy." Isolationist Senator Robert A. Taft sarcastically remarked that lending war materials was "a good deal like lending chewing gum. You don't want it back."

The Lend-Lease Act, introduced in Congress in January of 1941, was so sweeping that it aroused isolationist antagonism. A parade of witnesses, including Charles A. Beard, Charles A. Lindbergh, and Joseph P. Kennedy (1888–1969), former ambassador to England and father of future President John Fitzgerald Kennedy, testified against the act. But the devastating German air raids of August-October had exerted profound effect upon U.S. public opinion and upon Congress, and the bill became law on March 11, 1941.

The most extreme opposition came from Senator Burton K. Wheeler (1882–1975): "Approval of this legislation means war, open and complete warfare. I, therefore, ask the American people before they supinely accept it, was the last World War worth while? . . . The lend-lease-give program is the New Deal's triple A foreign policy; it will plow under every fourth American boy." (Roosevelt called this last remark "the rottenest thing

Fox Photos.

The dramatic British evacuation from Dunkirk in June 1940 signaled the end for France, which fell to the Nazis.

that has been said in public life in my generation.")

The lend-lease program committed more than American economic resources to Britain. The Germans, already sinking some 500,000 tons of merchant marine ships a month and depleting Britain's transport fleet faster than it could be replaced, extended the war zone to the coast of Greenland. The Battle of the Atlantic for the lifeline to Britain was underway and American naval power soon was involved. No one—neither critic nor admirer of Roosevelt—denies that American participation in the war was all but complete at this point. Some critics, such as Stimson, pointed out that Roosevelt's major error was not to begin all-out armed intervention. When American convoys began to sail in the summer of 1941 the nation's active role in the European war became inevitable.

The End of Isolationism

Although Roosevelt faced considerable hostility, he perhaps genuinely hoped that aid to Britain could keep the United States out of war. He was most aggressive with Congress concerning this matter, but he knew from experience that some members would attack his stand.

The most notable recent campaign to safeguard the U.S. from drifting into war had been the Ludlow Amendment of 1937, providing that, except in the event of an invasion, Congress could not declare war unless a majority of Americans agreed in a nationwide referendum. An American Institute of Public Opinion poll indicated approximately 75 percent of Americans approved of the amendment. Ludlow and his allies launched a propaganda campaign, attacking their critics in radio speeches, but in January 1938 the House rejected the measure, by a vote of 209 to 188.

Even after war broke out in Europe staunch isolationists continued to keep an indecisive President at bay on the issue of the revision of the Neutrality Act. In fact, as late as 1941 the President had considerable difficulty whenever he tried to continue or increase his defense effort. In August of that year, by a single vote (203-202) the House of Representatives agreed to extend the period of selective service beyond the twelve-month limit set by the Burke-Wadsworth Act. And, less than one month before the Japanese attack upon Pearl Harbor, that same body (after considerable White House pressure) voted 212-194 to amend the Neutrality Act so as to permit the arming of U.S. merchant ships.

The internationalists were active but divided. Some advocated all-out aid to Britain short of war, while others pressed for a declaration of war against Germany. A small group of internationalists, such as those in the Council on Foreign Relations and the Foreign Policy Association, had always pressed for a greater involvement in European affairs. Americans of Anglo-Saxon descent and Anglophiles joined Clarence Streit's Union Now movement. Many American Jews also urged increased assistance in fighting Hitler since the virulence of German anti-Semitism was becoming a threat to their very existence. Theologian Reinhold Niebuhr (1892-1971), a leading pacifist until the Munich Pact, together with a number of former pacifists, organized the Union for Democratic Action in April 1941, asserting that a war against totalitarianism was the least immoral of a number of unhappy choices. With the fall of Norway and Denmark the Committee to Defend America by Aiding the Allies became the major spokesman for moderate intervention. This nationwide group, chaired by newspaper editor William Allen White, was committed to the all-out defense of France and England and extremely active in behalf of the destroyer deal.

But those who rallied around the banner of isolationism were even more varied in motive and origin. Traditional isolationists in Congress argued that intervention was unnecessary since, given its special geographical defenses, America was essentially invulnerable to attack. An invasion by sea was unthinkable. Republican Senator Henry Cabot Lodge, Jr. (1902-   ) of Massachusetts declared that Germany could not conquer the United States, even if England fell. It was fanciful, he scoffed, to suggest such a turn of events.

A strong element among the isolationists were pacifists, some of whom had fought in World War I, and others of whom—especially among the Protestant clergy—objected to the war on traditional grounds. Probably the most outspoken pacifists in the 1930s were eastern college students not eager to man the trenches. Thousands signed the Oxford pledge of nonresistance, which had started at Oxford University in 1933 when a large majority of students vowed that under no circumstances would they fight for king and country. The pledge began a movement that dominated student politics throughout the 1930s in Britain and even more in America, where it was reworded to read that the signer would not "support the United States Government in any war it

Library of Congress.

William Allen White

(1868–1944)

A short, chubby man who for several decades was the nation's small town conscience, William Allen White was born in Emporia, Kansas, in 1868. He attended the University of Kansas in the mid-1880s but left before graduation to become editor of the *El Dorado Daily Republican* of Kansas. After working on other regional newspapers, in 1895—with only $1.25 in his pocket and a $3,000 loan—he purchased the *Emporia Gazette* with which he would be identified for the remainder of his life. A year later he turned out an anti-Populist editorial, "What's the Matter with Kansas," which was circulated widely by McKinley's campaign manager, Mark Hanna.

White was active in the Progressive movement, joining Lincoln Steffens, Ray Stannard Baker, and Ida Tarbell as an editorial associate for *American* magazine in 1906. His 1909 novel, *A Certain Rich Man* (which sold 250,000 copies), reflected growing support for government regulation of business. In 1912 he bolted the Republican party to serve as national committeeman from Kansas for Roosevelt's Bull Moose party. He rejoined the Republicans after 1912 and became a force for reform. Chafing under the conservatism of the 1920s, White supported and admired Hoover. In 1928 this admiration, combined with his dislike of the city and his prohibitionist belief, made him a strong critic of Al Smith. In that decade he ran unsuccessfully on an anti-Klan platform for governor of Kansas.

During the New Deal, White backed most of FDR's measures—except at election time. He consistently supported the President's foreign policy and in 1940 helped found the Committee to Defend America by Aiding the Allies (CDAAA). He favored "all aid short of war," *not* outright intervention. After serving as liaison between FDR and Willkie in the 1940 campaign and thus keeping foreign policy from becoming a major issue, White resigned from the CDAAA in January 1941 after a dispute over convoying lend-lease aid to Great Britain.

A man of perception and humor, the "Sage of Emporia" began as a conservative and ended up a Progressive liberal. Personally he thought Bryan "shallow" and Debs "a charlatan." During the Spanish-American War he wrote that "Some great sentimental power—destiny, evolution or the Lord of Hosts—is guiding the course of this war." When this editorial was reprinted forty years later, White added a footnote: "Probably the devil." ■

Minnesota Historical Society.

Even in the face of aggression in Europe and Asia, American peace advocates continued to demonstrate in great numbers, as in this rally of over 2000 in Minneapolis during 1936.

may conduct." While many student organizations were politically radical or socialist, others were church-oriented or ethical in their bias against war.

Several ethnic groups also endorsed isolationism. Some 700,000 German-Americans, who feared the backlash of World War I might be repeated, made Chicago a center of midwestern isolationism. Irish-Americans resented aiding Britain more than they disliked Hitler. Some, such as Father Charles Coughlin of the Christian Front (which had a membership of 300,000) saw Fascism as a bulwark against the godlessness of Communism and Soviet Russia, arguing that interventionism was a Jewish conspiracy. Italian-Americans, for reasons similar to those of the German community, feared a separation from families and a severance of ties to Italy. Other extremist groups included a large assortment of "anti-Communist" organizations such as the Ku Klux Klan and the Bund (the American counterpart of the Nazi party). Ironically, after the Hitler-Stalin Nonaggression Pact was signed, the American Communist party turned staunchly isolationist.

But the most notable isolationist propaganda came from the group named "America First." Founded in September 1940 and led by the nation's most recent hero, Charles Lindbergh, America First argued that a German victory in Europe would not endanger any vital American interests or American security in the Western hemisphere. America First became a widely based coalition group whose charismatic leader attracted powerful friends, large public funding, and a considerable number of anti-Semites. The moral vacuity of America First reached its nadir in September 1941 when Lindbergh delivered a speech charging that the British, the Jews, and the Roosevelt administration were responsible for America's drift toward war. Lindbergh declared that, since Jews owned or influenced much of the motion picture industry, the press, and radio, they were "a danger to this country," and warned them that if war broke out, they should expect a widespread outbreak of intolerance. Lindbergh denied that his remarks were meant to be taken as threats of reprisals, but his longstanding admiration of Germany and its air force, three visits to Germany (1936–1938), and meetings with Hitler made the American Jewish community apprehensive. To many observers Lindbergh's remarks seemed symptomatic of a growing pro-Nazi stance among isolationists.

But the majority of Americans remained uncommitted. Public opinion, certainly against intervention, also was clearly sympathetic to Great Britain. The national survey organizations of Gallup and Roper, begun in 1935, published their polls regularly, and their findings were read carefully by the nation's politicians. The majority of Americans favored all-out support of Britain so that intervention would be unnecessary.

Library of Congress.

Jeannette Rankin (1880-1973)

Born in Montana in 1880, Jeannette Rankin grew up in Missoula and graduated from Montana State University in 1902. After teaching for two years, she visited her brother in Boston, where she was so moved by the poverty of that city's slums that she resolved to enter social work. A year later she returned to Montana to speak on behalf of the woman suffrage movement then being proposed in the state legislature. She took over the state suffrage movement and won national attention for her efforts when suffrage was adopted there in 1914.

Two years later Rankin announced her candidacy for Congress in Montana, a state known for its corrupt politics. She was the only Republican elected statewide in 1916 (though she later claimed "I never was a Republican"). As the first woman elected to Congress, she was under close scrutiny from press and public. Although her brother warned her that a "no" vote on the declaration of war in April 1917 would cost her her seat, she voted against U.S. entry. (The House vote was 373-50.) In 1918 she ran unsuccessfully for the Senate, her district having been gerrymandered against her by Montana Democrats.

In the 1920s Rankin worked for extension of the suffrage, for an amendment prohibiting child labor, and as a lobbyist for the National Council for the Prevention of War. In 1932 she helped organize marches on both political conventions to urge inclusion of a peace plank. Throughout the 1930s she lobbied for mandatory neutrality legislation.

Reelected to Congress in 1940 on a "keep-us-out-of-war" platform (over a pro-New Deal incumbent), Rankin cast the lone vote against war in Congress on December 8, 1941, an act met by hostility. After retirement from Congress in 1943, she made seven trips to India, homeland of Gandhi, to get the feel of the country. During the 1960s, Rankin reemerged in the public eye as an opponent of the Vietnam War, in 1968 leading the Jeannette Rankin Brigade in a March on Washington. She died in May 1973 at the age of 92.

The only member of Congress to vote against U.S. entry in both world wars, Jeannette Rankin was a lifelong pacifist. Her only concessions to advancing age were a cane and some weariness at seeing ideas she had advocated for decades treated as something radically new. Concerning elections she once said that voters all too often were given "a choice of evils, not ideas." Women, she observed, have been "worms." "They let their sons go off to war because they're afraid their husbands will lose their jobs in industry if they protest." ■

U.P.I.

Aviator hero Charles Lindbergh became the most prominent spokesman for isolationism during the "Great Debate" over American foreign policy in 1940–1941.

Courtesy Imperial War Museum.

The meeting of Roosevelt and British Prime Minister Churchill at Argentia, Newfoundland (August 1941).

With the Nazi invasion of Russia on June 22, 1941, the war picture changed dramatically. The lend-lease program was extended to the U.S.S.R. as a means of containing the European war on that continent. In August 1941 Roosevelt and Churchill met on a battleship off Newfoundland and agreed to the Atlantic Charter, committing the two nations to economic collaboration and an end to commercial and territorial aggrandizement after the defeat of Nazi Germany.

To Pearl Harbor

Ironically, with the nation's attention centered on Europe and the nation fearful of involvement there, war erupted instead in Asia. The surprise attack by the Japanese on Pearl Harbor on December 7, 1941, outraged and puzzled many Americans. Nor have commentators since that time understood why the nation was so poorly prepared for the events of that fateful day. Some years afterwards Robert Sherwood wrote, "Millions of words have been recorded by at least eight official investigating bodies and one may read through them all without arriving at an adequate explanation of why, with war so obviously ready to break out *somewhere* in the Pacific, our principal Pacific base was in a condition of peacetime Sunday morning somnolence instead of in Condition Red."

After the war and the death of President Roosevelt, a number of "revisionist" historians, including Charles Beard, offered a conspiracy theory, that the surprise element of the attack on Hawaii was in fact hatched in Washington to provoke the nation into war. The theory presumes that the Germans refused to attack the United States despite lend-lease, so a "back door" to the war in Europe had to be found. By provoking Germany's ally, Japan, into an aggressive "sneak" attack, by tempting Japan with the unprepared Pacific fleet, President Roosevelt and his advisers—principally Cordell Hull—would then be able to enter the war without domestic opposition. While there is no conclusive evidence supporting such a theory, an air of uncertainty still surrounds the vulnerability of Pearl Harbor to enemy attack.

Key issues were America's designs regarding China and the extent of real unpreparedness among the inner circles of the United States government. Japan had occupied most of the China coast since 1937, but the beleaguered Chinese held out. Between 1937 and 1941 American sympathy was almost entirely with the Chinese, who were given whatever aid a nation in the throes of a depression could afford in light of an explosive diplomatic situation. At the same time, the United States was the major supplier of raw materials fueling the Japanese war machine. During those years, Japan bought nearly all her scrap metal and copper from the United States as well as two-thirds of her oil. This lucrative trade lasted well into 1940. Although Washington could have declared an embargo on these goods, to do so would have meant recognizing that Japan and China were at war—a situation neither country would have admitted. If the United States applied an embargo to Japan, under the conditions of the Neutrality Act it would also have had to apply one to China. The Japanese would suffer from an embargo, but it might prove fatal to the Chinese. Indeed, until 1940 Roosevelt used the threat of embargo as a major diplomatic weapon in his negotiations with Japan, always hoping that the Japanese might retrench before he was forced to carry out his threat and risk a complete severance of relations. These commercial realities as well as Roosevelt's deep hope of avoiding a complete involvement in war are a far more logical assessment of the situation than the conspiracy theory.

In fact, American pacificism and the President's reluctance to actually use the embargo combined to assure the Japanese that the United States would not interfere militarily in the Sino-Japanese war. In return Japan avoided an alliance with Germany to prevent interruption of her vital U.S. trade.

But in 1940 Nazi successes in Europe left the vast French, Dutch, and British colonies of Asia vulnerable. The Japanese avidly eyed the oil, rubber, and iron ore resources of the East Indies and Southeast Asia. They remained, however, cautious. In June 1940, Japan agreed to respect the autonomy of the East Indies—provided that neither the Germans nor the British tried to occupy them. This pledge to the Dutch government in exile included a stipulation of no interference with Japan's trade with the islands.

But Japanese militants became impatient; in July 1940, fearful that the rich prize of Europe's colonies would slip away, they forced the government to change prime ministers. Prince Fumimaro Konoye (1891–1945), the new head of state, initiated plans to implement Japan's New Order (announced in 1938). The New Order was an economic plan for the complete domination of China and the western Pacific, excluding the United States from its former Asian markets and ultimately destined to make Japan free of her dependence on American resources.

The new military government of Japan was more belligerent than its predecessor and on July 25, 1940, Roosevelt barred the export of petroleum, petroleum products, and scrap metal to Japan without a license, and six days later restricted sale of aviation fuel to the Western Hemisphere. In a desperate effort to ward off a Rome-Berlin-Tokyo alliance, Roosevelt proclaimed in September an embargo on the export of all scrap iron and steel outside of the Americas, but in the same month the Tripartite Pact became a reality. The Axis powers recognized Japanese supremacy in Asia, and Japan acknowledged Italian-German supremacy in Europe. All pledged mutual support in the event of an attack on any one of them. At the same time, Tokyo began to occupy strategic bases in northern French Indochina.

The American embargo placed an enormous strain on Japanese domestic resources and manpower. Moreover, Roosevelt began to reinforce the American navy in the Pacific, particularly in the Philippines. In fact he was already in consultation with the British and the Dutch, making plans for the defense of Southeast Asia against a Japanese attack.

In March 1941 the new Japanese ambassador to America began regular meetings with Secretary of State Hull. The talks, intricate and evasive, impressed Hull as delaying tactics. In light of the Tripartite Pact, the State

Department grew skeptical of ambassador Admiral Nomura's assurances that Japan was seriously interested in peace. But when—shortly before the German invasion of Russia in June 1941—the Japanese signed a neutrality pact with Soviet Russia and then honored it by refusing to join Hitler's forces, an uneasy peace seemed possible.

Then in July 1941 Japanese troops invaded the rest of French Indochina and occupied Saigon, also setting up a puppet state in Siam. Meanwhile, pressure on Malaya and the Dutch East Indies increased. Roosevelt faced the dilemma of disengaging Japan from the Axis and stopping further moves in Southeast Asia without provoking war. Ambassador Nomura was informed that if Japan withdrew from Indochina, the United States would guarantee neutrality and reopen Japan's access to raw materials.

When Tokyo remained silent, Roosevelt decided on July 26, 1941, to freeze Japanese assets in the United States and proposed the cessation of all commerce with Japan. The Japanese then reappraised the situation. Premier Konoye, more moderate than his military cabinet, favored further negotiations, but insisted on meeting directly with Roosevelt. Secretary Hull and others dissuaded the President, who was interested in such a meeting. They reminded him of Munich and argued that Konoye was not prepared to make real concessions. Even if he were sincere, there was no guarantee a military cabinet would follow his lead. Despite urgent notes from Ambassador Grew in Tokyo, who thought such a meeting might provide at least temporary peace, Konoye's offer was rejected.

In September Japanese leaders reached a secret decision that, if the United States refused to resume normal trade relations (including export of iron and oil) within a month, they would begin preparing for war. The issue of China, they concluded, was closed; the war there was, in their opinion, no longer a matter of contention between Japan and the United States. Roosevelt considered American acceptance of this view tantamount to a betrayal of the Chinese, and Washington hardened in its commitment to the liberation of China.

Some historians have ventured that when war came it was really over China. They blame Washington for backing Japan into a corner from which war became the most feasible exit. Without doubt, China was the main obstacle to any peace settlement, although that does not mean it was the cause of the war. Konoye's failure to achieve his proposed meeting may, however, have prompted his resignation and that of his cabinet in mid-October. The new premier, General Hideki Tojo (1885–1948), the minister of war in the Konoye cabinet and former head of the secret police, was much more decisive than Konoye had been. Tojo set the end of November as the deadline for reaching a peaceable solution with Washington. He indicated that, although much else might be negotiable, the withdrawal of Japanese troops from China was not.

For some time Washington had been able to anticipate some of Japan's moves because it had mastered the Japanese secret cipher system known as Purple. The elaborate machines constructed to decipher intercepted messages were called Magic. By decoding messages sent to various embassies around the world, Washington knew by the end of November that war was imminent—but

Library of Congress.

Throughout 1941 Japanese ambassador Admiral Nomura (second from right) engaged in lengthy discussions with Secretary of State Cordell Hull in an attempt to compromise differences between the two nations.

was unable to anticipate where it would break out. Most experts thought Japan would attack the Dutch East Indies or the Philippines. Little thought was given to the possibility of an assault in the central Pacific or on Hawaii. Roosevelt sent a number of alerts to the Pacific fleet, including forces at Pearl Harbor. In Washington, Secretary Hull continued meeting with the Japanese ambassador. But by now Japanese demands were increasing, principally the resumption of trade in vital raw materials. Without a guarantee that aggression in Southeast Asia would cease, the talks came to a virtual standstill.

In view of the code breaking and the futility of diplomacy, there has been much debate over why the attack on Pearl Harbor was such a surprise. But even after decoding, it often was difficult to understand the import of information received. One such message, intercepted immediately before Pearl Harbor, was translated to read "Relations between Japan and England are not in accordance with expectation." So mild an understatement attracted little attention. But a few days after Pearl Harbor the same message was reexamined, and two serious errors in translation were discovered. "Not in accordance with expectation" should have read "are on the brink of catastrophe," and the vital code word meaning the United States had been omitted. What the message really said was "Relations between Japan and England and the United States are on the brink of catastrophe." Given the traditional restraint of the Japanese the message was tantamount to announcing war.

On December 6, 1941, President Roosevelt sent a message to the Emperor appealing for peace. Meanwhile on November 26 a convoy of Japanese aircraft carriers left home waters heading for Hawaii. On December 7 they launched their devastating attack, destroying two battleships and immobilizing six others as well as a number of lesser ships. In all, 188 army and navy planes were destroyed and 2,043 Americans died. The next day President Roosevelt asked Congress to declare war against Japan, saying that December 7, 1941 was a date "which will live in infamy." Only one dissenting vote, that of Congresswoman Jeannette Rankin, was cast against the declaration. Under the terms of the Tripartite Pact Germany and Italy declared war against the United States on December 11. For America, World War II had begun.

National Archives.

The American fleet was crippled by the Japanese attack on December 7, 1941. Three days later, the badly damaged remains of five once-proud battleships were still awash in the harbor.

Essay

The College Campus and Student Protest

There was nothing very unique about the protests of college and university students which rocked American society in the 1960s except their size and volume. The academic atmosphere long has harbored the potential for tumult and outcry, and from colonial times teachers and professors often have felt the ire of undergraduates.

To begin with, conflict in such a setting is normal. The job of instructors is to teach the young to think, and when they think and act differently from their elders, disagreement may arise. In short, to use a much overworked phrase, there is a "generation gap." A student's career at any institution usually is relatively brief, the professor's much longer. So, what seems an outrage to the young with limited experience and short perspective, in the general scheme of things may not ruffle their teachers at all. Like any bureaucrat, they may simply hunker down and ride out the storm. Also, while students, especially during their last year or so within ivy walls, may be thinking only of a job outside of those confines, their courses all too often teach only great truths and generalities that provide few solutions to the dilemma confronting them. Not surprisingly, two radical goals of recent decades have been (1) to make the university a force for reform, not stability or reaction, and (2) to get students involved in American life and politics instead of existing in some sort of "holding pattern" for four or more years.

Until the last half-century, the collegiate population of America has been small and most campus protests have been local affairs. Students have gone on short-lived rampages because their football team won a big game, it was a warm spring evening, visiting hours in the women's dorms were restricted, or food at the university-run cafeterias was swill. Rarely have these outbreaks had any coordination from one area to another nor have they been in any true sense political.

This last factor (political orientation) separates U.S. student protest from that in much of the world, even to the present day. Student voices have shaped government policy in Europe from time to time and occasionally even brought down regimes. A young activist by the name of Gavrilo Princip had much to do with igniting World War I when he shot Archduke Franz Ferdinand in June 1914.

In addition to an absence of political interest—that is, students committed to a definite program or party—those endeavoring to harness undergraduate power have faced other hurdles. The major concentrations of American higher education are diverse and lack a geographical center. It's a long way from Berkeley to Madison and from there to Washington, D.C. As a result, students have felt little sense of community, and they have failed to develop any concept of being "an incipient elite."

It is virtually impossible to keep up with classwork and organize rallies a thousand miles away, and it is equally difficult for students to view themselves as a distinct class within American society. They come from diverse backgrounds and, again, their role as students is temporary and fleeting.

But, perhaps most important of all, traditionally their ranks have been slim; and, even today, the great majority of American students are much more interested in sports, social life, sex, and jobs than they are in undoing great injustices or manning the barricades in behalf of the proletariat.

Between 1869 and 1900 the number of college students grew from 52,000 to 237,000 and by 1929 nearly quadrupled again, increasing to 1,100,000. Student population grew somewhat in the 1930s, but was nothing compared with the post-World War II campus explosion. In 1946, 22 percent of all Americans between eighteen and twenty-one were enrolled in colleges and universities and two decades later 45 percent of that age group were students. In 1967 some 6,000,000 young people were attending classes at 2,300 colleges and universities. These numbers—increasing from 237,000 to 6,000,000 six decades later—and cataclysmic events at home and abroad help to explain the rising tide of student protest on American campuses in this century. Two world wars, the rise of socialism and Communism, the Great Depression, frustrated peace efforts, the Cold War, atom bombs, Korea, Vietnam, segregation—all of these were ammunition for speeches, banners, slogans, and marches.

The 1930s saw the first crest of this clamor for change, although it was relatively minor compared with the uproar of the 1960s. The campus of that decade was a place filled with contradictions. Most colleges and universities were far from the mainstream of daily life and faculties tended to like it that way, but it was difficult to shut one's eyes to hunger, starvation, and loss of jobs, which affected students and teachers alike.

During those years political attitudes in America began to move to the left, although academic administrators resisted this change or ignored it. Many of them expelled students whom they thought radical or any who tried to establish Communist or socialist campus groups. The president of the City College of New York, one of the most "radical" schools in the nation, once flailed a group of activists with his umbrella and called them "guttersnipes." Radical faculty also felt the wrath of such men.

Minnesota Historical Society.

Women students at the University of Minnesota on strike for peace, April 1936.

Loyalty oaths for teachers were instituted in several states, in an effort to purge universities of such evil influences.

Compulsory ROTC at a time when pacifism was strong was an inflammatory campus issue. Many students of the mid-1930s vowed they were conscientious objectors. A survey of 65 colleges in 27 states, which was undertaken by researchers at Brown University, revealed that 39 percent of those contacted took an absolute pacifist stand and 33 percent said they would take up arms only if the United States of America were invaded.

This antiwar sentiment, fed by disillusion with the League of Nations, was the most vital element in student activism of the 1930s. Although such views did not originate in that decade (both the World Court and the League were important issues in the 1920s), numerous antiwar conferences, rallies, and strikes captured headlines, much to the distress of university presidents and red-blooded, patriotic groups such as the American Legion, the Veterans of Foreign Wars, and the Daughters of the American Revolution.

This movement reached its peak in 1936 when about 18 percent of all undergraduates in every part of the nation attended antiwar meetings deploring U.S. entry into World War I. Some Princeton students even formed a Veterans of Future Wars and demanded their bonuses in advance, and 400 young people from the Manhattan area picketed J. P. Morgan's home in an unusual display of antiwar sentiment.

After 1936, however, this campaign began to disintegrate amid acrimony and discord as more and more Americans became convinced that rearmament was a wise, necessary policy. The rise of Fascism and the outbreak of war in Europe effected a miraculous change; and, in 1942, many of the young men of 1936 who said they would not bear arms overseas did just that.

Campus groups with ties to Communists and socialists, liberal and conservative organizations, and various churches also exerted some influence during the 1930s, but their ultimate effect was minimal. The Communists represented the most dedicated faction, but even their ranks were torn by discord, few of them being certain of their ideology or which Communist doctrine they were dedicated to. A wise Columbia University dean once told a group of alumni distressed by opinions expressed in the student newspaper that they were colorblind. "What you mistake for red, is simply green."

Although the student activist movement of the 1930s must be considered a failure, it did arouse a sense of social awareness never before evident upon American campuses. The Roosevelt administration, for a time, embraced some of its leaders, thus increasing greatly the prestige of these individuals and their movement. Joseph P. Lash, head of the American Student Union (ASU) in the 1930s and later author of *Eleanor and Franklin* (1971), began a long relationship with the Roosevelts as a result of his activism. Lash, a graduate of New York's City College in 1931, spent the Depression years deep in the politics of the left. For a time, his ASU was

Frederic Lewis.

Campus peace demonstrators turned out 5000 strong to hear Socialist Norman Thomas speak against war at this 1936 rally at the University of California, Berkeley.

Black Star.

The anti-Vietnam protests of the late 1960s and early 1970s brought National Guard troops onto campuses in large numbers, as at Ohio State University in May 1970.

associated with the American Youth Congress, a "united front" of sorts against Fascism. Lash was, in fact, discussing a job with the Communist *Daily Worker* in August 1939 when news of the Hitler-Stalin pact shattered the ranks of young American liberals.

Three months later when he was summoned to Capitol Hill to testify before the House Un-American Activities Committee headed by Martin Dies, Eleanor Roosevelt was in the audience. Afterwards, to reaffirm her faith in the young people of the nation, she invited Lash and five of his friends to the White House for dinner. Although the President was wary of the Youth Congress and a year later spoke rather sternly to its representatives because of their pro-Moscow stance, his wife continued her support until the summer of 1941. Ultimately, however, the group's flip-flops on international policy, triggered by Hitler's invasion of Russia, were more than she could stand. Nevertheless, this break did not end individual friendships nurtured by these associations, notably that of Eleanor Roosevelt and Lash.

Despite the shortcomings of the student protest of the 1930s, that upsurge taught many organizational lessons and provided a residue of experience (rarely consulted, however) for those who would try once more in the 1960s to stir the undergraduate soul. Interestingly, it was antiwar sentiment—World War I in the 1930s and Vietnam three decades later—that was at the heart of student activism. Young radical voices apparently could stir thousands to act *against* something that was in the past or half a world away. Achieving a unified voice on civil rights, domestic reforms, or even suggestions for change on their own campuses was much more difficult. And developing lasting political muscle, if ever that was intended, remains an elusive goal.

Selected Readings

United States and the League of Nations

N. Gordon Levin, *Woodrow Wilson and World Politics* (1968)

Ralph Stone, *The Irreconcilables: The Fight Against the League of Nations* (1970)

Elmer Bendiner, *A Time for Angels: The Tragicomic History of the League of Nations* (1975)

Foreign Policy in the 1920s

Selig Adler, *The Uncertain Giant; 1921–1941: American Foreign Policy Between the Wars* (1965)

L. Ethan Ellis, *Republican Foreign Policy, 1921–1933* (1968)

Joan Hoff Wilson, *American Business and Foreign Policy, 1920–1933* (1970)

Isolationism and Pacifism

Selig Adler, *The Isolationist Impulse: Its Twentieth Century Reaction* (1957)

Manfred Jonas, *Isolationism in America, 1935–1941* (1966)

Franklin D. Roosevelt and Foreign Policy

Robert A. Divine, *The Reluctant Belligerent: American Entry into World War II* (1965)

Lloyd C. Gardner, *Economic Aspects of New Deal Diplomacy* (1964)

John E. Wiltz, *From Isolationism to War, 1931–1941* (1963)

Leonard P. Liggio and James J. Martin, eds., *Watershed of Empire: Essays on New Deal Foreign Policy* (1976)

Coming of War to America

Dorothy Borg, Shumpei Okamoto, and Dale K. Finlayson, eds., *Pearl Harbor as History: Japanese-American Relations, 1931–1941* (1973)

Charles A. Beard, *President Roosevelt and the Coming of War, 1941* (1948).

Mark Chadwin, *The Hawks of World War II* (1968)

Wayne S. Cole, *Charles A. Lindbergh and the Battle Against American Intervention in World War II* (1974)

Roberta Wohlstetter, *Pearl Harbor: Warning and Decision* (1962)

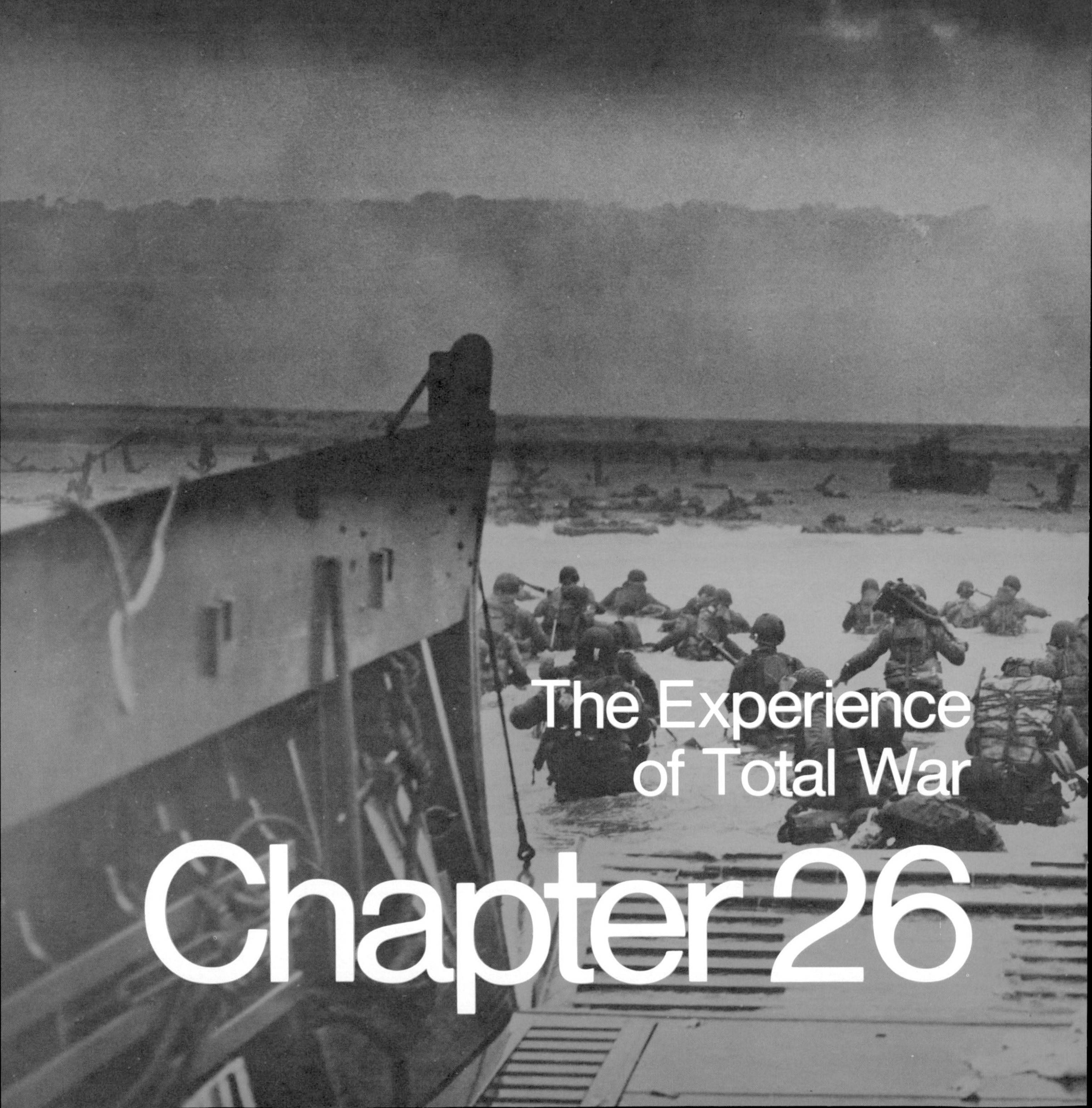

Chapter 26

The Experience of Total War

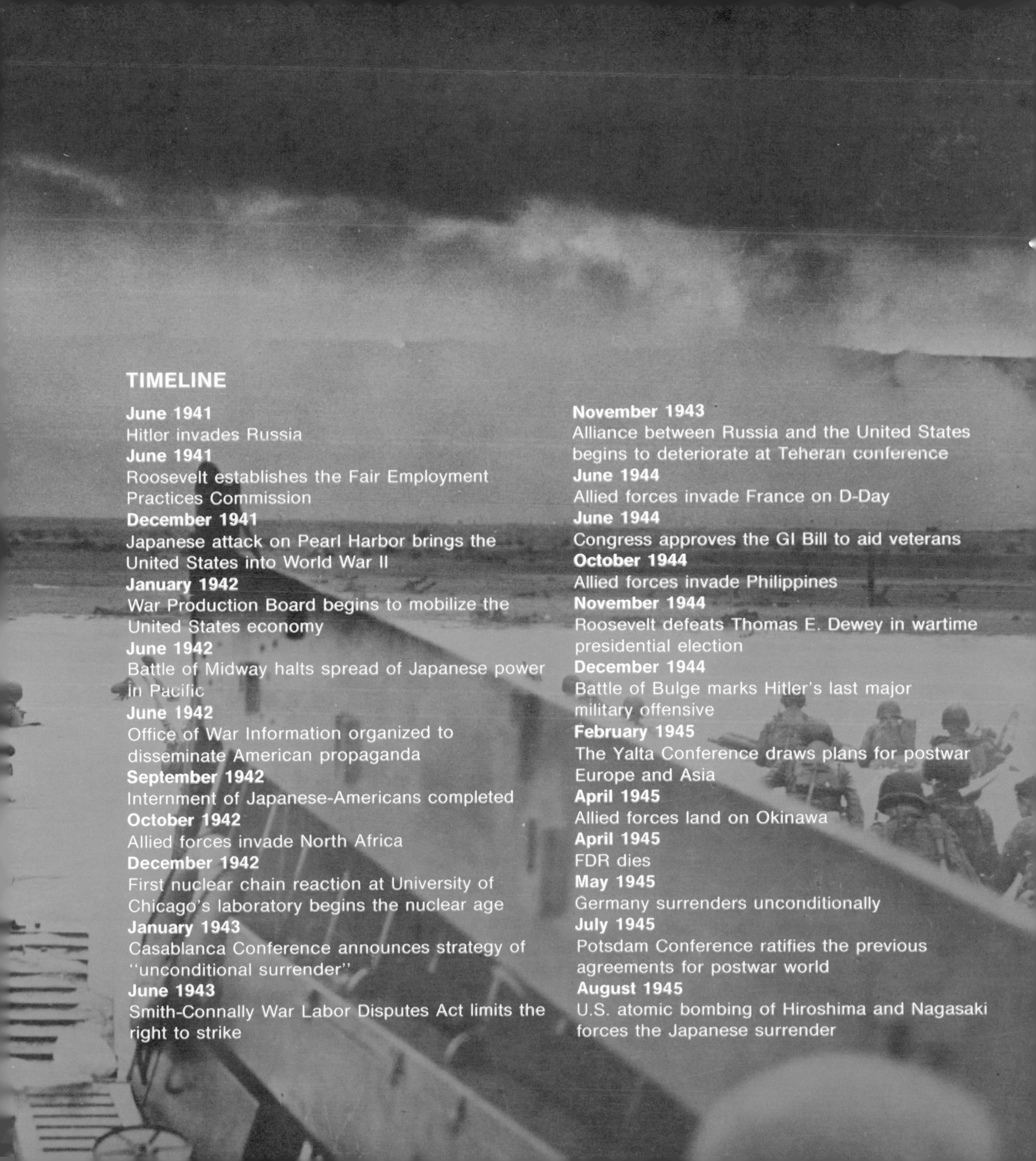

TIMELINE

June 1941
Hitler invades Russia

June 1941
Roosevelt establishes the Fair Employment Practices Commission

December 1941
Japanese attack on Pearl Harbor brings the United States into World War II

January 1942
War Production Board begins to mobilize the United States economy

June 1942
Battle of Midway halts spread of Japanese power in Pacific

June 1942
Office of War Information organized to disseminate American propaganda

September 1942
Internment of Japanese-Americans completed

October 1942
Allied forces invade North Africa

December 1942
First nuclear chain reaction at University of Chicago's laboratory begins the nuclear age

January 1943
Casablanca Conference announces strategy of "unconditional surrender"

June 1943
Smith-Connally War Labor Disputes Act limits the right to strike

November 1943
Alliance between Russia and the United States begins to deteriorate at Teheran conference

June 1944
Allied forces invade France on D-Day

June 1944
Congress approves the GI Bill to aid veterans

October 1944
Allied forces invade Philippines

November 1944
Roosevelt defeats Thomas E. Dewey in wartime presidential election

December 1944
Battle of Bulge marks Hitler's last major military offensive

February 1945
The Yalta Conference draws plans for postwar Europe and Asia

April 1945
Allied forces land on Okinawa

April 1945
FDR dies

May 1945
Germany surrenders unconditionally

July 1945
Potsdam Conference ratifies the previous agreements for postwar world

August 1945
U.S. atomic bombing of Hiroshima and Nagasaki forces the Japanese surrender

CHAPTER OUTLINE

American historians often have been criticized, and justifiably so, for finding too many "turning points" and "watersheds" in our past; yet World War II must be viewed as a climactic episode that divided and changed the life of this nation and the lives of its citizens as well. It had much more significance, for example, than either World War I or the Depression decade. On the diplomatic front, the United States, which took part in none of the high-level conferences held in Europe in the late 1930s, emerged as the leader of the "free" nations in the new Cold War and, thanks to an atomic monopoly, the most important military power in the world. At home, war produced a complex interweaving of the public and private sectors, which has continued to the present day. Permanent debt and involvement of the federal government in the economy "solved" the Depression, and a network of agencies and boards emanating from the White House greatly increased the power of the executive branch.

As awe-inspiring and pervasive as World War II was, the United States of America suffered the least from the direct effects of battle of all the major powers involved. No U.S. cities were bombed, the homefront was able to produce unafraid of enemy incursions, rationing and shortages were irksome but not crippling, and Americans witnessed none of the devastation visited upon Great Britain, much of Europe, Russia, the Middle East, North Africa, China, Japan, and various parts of Southeast Asia. This great struggle and America's commitment to it may have been "total," but the nation's experience, when compared with that of others, actually was not.

And when victory came in both Europe and the Pacific in 1945, it turned out to be a seriously flawed triumph. The problem in Europe was the incipient Cold War, which soon became a worldwide confrontation between former allies; and, in the Far East, America's unilateral decision to use the atomic bomb against Japan raised serious doubts concerning control of such weapons.

The social impact of the war upon the American domestic scene was mixed. The demand for labor created jobs for thousands of blacks and women, but that conflict did little to alter basic racial and sexual discrimination long evident in U.S. business and industry. Except for the cruel detention of Japanese-Americans—and that admittedly is a very large "exception" indeed—the record of civil liberties during World War II was somewhat better than might have been expected in the heat of conflict. Certainly most of the sillier aspects of anti-German sentiment evident in 1917–1918 were missing. The influence of the war upon well-established institutions undoubtedly was more profound than any purely social change, notably the growth of the military-industrial-scientific complex, which has dominated much of American life since 1945, and the tremendous expansion of presidential power in both foreign and domestic affairs.

The years from 1939 to 1945, very understandably, have given rise to considerable controversy. Widespread foreign commitment brought in its wake responsibilities and tensions that millions of Americans find unnerving. Comfortable old ways are gone, replaced by red tape, computerized business operations, and jarring events in lands that once appeared only in crossword puzzles. The paramount question perhaps concerns wartime decisions by Allied leaders, specifically "Doctor Win-the-War," Franklin Delano Roosevelt. If he had acted differently between 1941 and 1945, could the Cold War have been averted? Or, to put it another way, did an ailing man make decisions that redounded to the disadvantage of the anti-Communist bloc?

In attempting to answer these and other questions concerning those tempestuous years, one should keep several facts in mind. The United States perhaps was in *potential* danger during the first six months of 1942, but its existence never actually was threatened, and much of the effort expended both before and after December 7, 1941, was calculated to make sure it would not be. Roosevelt's policy was to support the enemies of the Axis powers (Germany, Italy, and Japan) with all-out aid and to keep warfare as far from the Western Hemisphere as possible. And, once shooting began, he was determined to achieve victory as quickly as possible with a minimum loss of American lives. Viewed in this context—substantial help for those fighting your enemies and unconditional surrender of common foes at the earliest possible moment—some of President Roosevelt's policies and decisions, later questioned and criticized roundly with the aid of hindsight, appear both reasonable and proper.

Total War, Limited Victory

As commander-in-chief and the man who shaped U.S. military policy, Roosevelt was influenced by six guiding principles. Three of these were obvious even before Pearl Harbor: the solidarity of the Anglo-American alliance, recognition of Nazi Germany as enemy number one, and all-out aid to Russia, which was invaded by Germany in June 1941. The other three emerged after disaster struck in the Pacific six months later. They were unconditional surrender of the Axis, sufficient assistance to China (which had been at war with Japan since the early 1930s) to keep that nation fighting so it could enter the postwar world as a great power, and development of the United Nations as a forum for international peace to be directed by the victorious allies: the United States, Great Britain and its Commonwealth, the U.S.S.R., and China. That same peace forum was to be, of course, the "policeman" of the world.

Pearl Harbor

On Sunday, December 7, 1941, a Japanese task force consisting of 31 ships (including 6 carriers), 432 planes, 1 large and 6 midget submarines carried out a brilliantly executed raid against the giant U.S. naval base at Pearl Harbor in the Hawaiian Islands. In a series of onslaughts (really a three-hour battle), the attackers lost all of their undersea craft and 29 of 353 airplanes actually involved in the raid. Fifty-nine Japanese airmen and about twenty submariners perished.

U.S. losses, by comparison, were huge. At the outset there were upwards of 100 American naval vessels—battleships, cruisers, destroyers, and smaller craft but no vital aircraft carriers (which were at sea)—spread out under the early morning sun. Nearby were about 400 army and navy planes, some obsolete and many without armament of any kind. By 10:00 A.M. 18 major warships, including 3 battlewagons, were sunk or seriously damaged, about 180 U.S. aircraft destroyed, and 2,403 Americans dead, nearly half of these fatalities occurring when the *Arizona* blew up. In addition, many more U.S. servicemen were injured, considerable property was destroyed, and the vital base lay in ruins.

The initial reaction at Pearl Harbor was one of utter confusion. During the first few moments army personnel thought the navy was carrying out a mock attack and the navy, of course, blamed the army; but, as bullets and bombs rained death and destruction, men of both branches of the service realized they were witnessing the impossible.

This sense of bewilderment quickly gave way to shock, fear, and anger, moods that spread throughout the U.S. mainland as news of this "sneak attack" disrupted Sunday afternoon dinners, concerts, and football games. The reaction was sudden and predictable: enlistments soared, Congress spoke with virtually one voice, and President Roosevelt led a unified nation determined to avenge this unprecedented "day of infamy."

There were, of course, extensive inquiries into Pearl Harbor in an attempt to find a scapegoat. But the truth is that all Americans must share the blame. Despite substantial warning—even sightings of submarines near the entrance to Pearl Harbor a few hours before the attack—everyone underestimated Japan's strength and capabilities and, in 1941, clearly misunderstood that nation's intentions.

Actually, the disaster of December 7 should not have come as any great shock. Several books had appeared detailing just how the Japanese might carry out an attack on Pearl Harbor, and American naval commanders had spent a quarter of a century in mock war games with Japan as the avowed enemy. In 1965, Chester W. Nimitz, much decorated admiral and hero of World War II, noted he had participated in such exercises at the U.S. Naval War College in 1923, adding that after hostilities got underway "nothing that happened in the Pacific was strange or unexpected."

Nevertheless, the Japanese who attacked Pearl Harbor and their leaders made several serious mistakes. They failed to destroy oil storage tanks there and left undamaged repair facilities soon put to good use. Had the initial strike been elsewhere in the Pacific, it is quite possible that the American public would not have supported a declaration of war. An assault against the Dutch East Indies (which was anticipated), the British colonies, or even the Philippines—then in the process of becoming independent—might have been rationalized in one way or another. But the deaths of so many American boys could not be ignored, even though the full extent of this disaster and the havoc wreaked at Pearl Harbor was kept secret for many months.

Library of Congress.

Three of the first Joint Chiefs of Staff at a luncheon in December 1942. (Left to right): Admiral Ernest J. King (Navy), General Henry H. Arnold (Army Air Force), and Admiral William D. Leahy (Chief). Absent is General George C. Marshall (Army).

Organizing for the Fight

America probably entered World War II better prepared to go into battle than its people had any right to expect. An organizational framework, in part operational already, had to expand immediately. Those in command could draw upon certain major sources for guidance: experience gained during World War I and in the New Deal fight to get the national economy rolling again and what Great Britain, long accustomed to international responsibilities and Germany's foe since September 1939, was doing. The most important innovations were formulation of the joint chiefs of staff, a tremendous growth in U.S. air power, and development of an extensive intelligence-gathering network. Each would have considerable influence upon American life long after World War II ended since they proved to be permanent fixtures, not temporary wartime measures.

Early in January 1942, President Roosevelt set up a joint staff group consisting of Admiral William D. Leahy (1875–1959) as chief, and General George C. Marshall (1880–1959), Admiral Ernest J. King (1878–1956), and General Henry H. Arnold (1886–1950); Marshall represented the army, King the navy, and Arnold the air force. This foursome, quartered in Washington, paralleled a similar British body in London with which it cooperated extensively during the next three years. To some extent this innovation foreshadowed the creation of the Department of Defense in 1947 with a civilian chief holding Cabinet rank.

The U.S. Army Air Force, only a "corps" within the army until June 1941, grew by leaps and bounds and was one key to Allied victory. As General Arnold later recalled, in forty-five minutes he was given $1.5 billion and told to go out and get an air force. Strongly backed by Roosevelt and public opinion, too, as a result of German air successes in Europe, the U.S. Army Air Force enjoyed every possible advantage. It got the best of everything — manpower, supplies, and money.

In March 1942 this new command was made equal to the U.S. Army's ground forces, creating two major combat groups within the army. Naturally enough, some tensions and animosities existed between GIs and "fly boys," but by the last eighteen months of World War II these differences had been largely resolved. As each group became more skilled in warfare, it began to appreciate the work of the other; however, cooperation among U.S. military forces—the Army, Navy, Army Air Force, Navy Air Force, Marines, Coast Guard, and so on—often left something to be desired, even during invasions when all were supposed to be working together to defeat a common foe. A well-known cartoon of the day showed a glum U.S. sailor staring at his GI counterparts as a friend reminded him, "You must remember, they're our allies just like the Chinese!" These rivalries proved to be ammunition once again at the war's end for those advocating a unified Defense Department.

The Office of Strategie Services (OSS), a conglomeration of intelligence-gathering groups massed together under the Joint Chiefs of Staff in June 1942, was directed by Colonel William J. Donovan (1883–1959), an energetic, zealous leader. The OSS, the most exciting new agency to emerge from World War II, was also the most controversial. Its 12,000 workers and agents made maps, conducted cloak-and-dagger espionage, killed people and saved lives, and analyzed everything from Hitler's sex life and psychological outlook to the economies of Nazi-held lands.

The OSS was the father of the Central Intelligence Agency (CIA) created in 1947, and any final analysis of the true effectiveness of either is virtually impossible since secrecy has surrounded so much of their work. On the plus side, the OSS proved that by bringing together operatives, scholars, military men, and bankers one could uncover facts required for vital wartime decisions. On the minus side, the OSS never actually developed a single, integrated clearinghouse for information collected but depended heavily upon British intelligence throughout the entire war. And, as with the CIA, a web of mystery and covert activity covered up blunders and sometimes success as well.

A Shaky Start

Soon after Pearl Harbor, Churchill hurried to Washington for the ARCADIA talks, the second of several vital wartime meetings with Roosevelt. The two leaders reaffirmed the provisions of the Atlantic Charter, set goals for American industry, and made public their already agreed upon "Hitler-first" policy. Yet words were no substitute for grim headlines and did little to hide the reality of worldwide successes by the Axis powers. Throughout much of 1942 they were able to campaign pretty much as they pleased wherever they wanted to, with little or no opposition.

Hitler held all of Europe in his grasp, his battle-tested forces cut ever deeper into Russia, and still other German armies under Field Marshal Erwin Rommel (1891–1944), a brilliant tactician much admired by his enemies, raced back and forth across the sands of North Africa more or less at will. On the other side of the world, Japan's new "Co-Prosperity Sphere" quickly encompassed Hong Kong, Malaya, Guam and Wake Islands, Singapore, the Dutch East Indies, and the Philippines. In short, the western half of the vast Pacific basin, virtually all of the islands north of Australia and the eastern perimeter of the Asian mainland from Siberian Russia to India, were in enemy hands.

During the spring of 1942 German U-boats sank scores of vessels within sight of U.S. coastal communities and even bottled up Chesapeake Bay for six weeks. In June these undersea raiders were sinking Allied ships at the rate of five per day in the Atlantic; however, this turned out to be their peak month. Blackouts, coordinated air and sea patrols, and especially new technical gear such as radar gradually turned the tide, and within a year the submarine menace was largely a thing of the past. Meanwhile, two hard-fought sea battles—Coral Sea (May 3–8) and Midway (June 4–7)—halted the spread of Japanese power, although, as noted, by that time the Rising Sun flew triumphantly over much of the Far East.

On October 24, 1942, American, British, and Free French forces landed in North Africa to challenge Rommel and his Italian allies. This invasion, dubbed TORCH and led by General Dwight D. Eisenhower (1890–1969), did not answer beleaguered Russia's constant demand for a second front on the European continent, but it fulfilled

Roosevelt's earnest desire to have American GIs in action against Germany before 1942 ended.

These developments hardly constituted victory, but they did dispel some of the gloom so evident in Washington. Of much greater importance was the Russian front where a titanic struggle was going on which would end early in 1943 with a momentous defeat for Hitler's men at Stalingrad. To find a turning point in World War II, one should look to the last months of 1942. There were no great triumphs. Due to a decline in U-boat sinkings, steady growth of U.S. factory production, Allied landings in North Africa, Japan's advance finally halted, and Nazi legions bogged down in the snows of Russia. Allied strength relative to that of their foes clearly was beginning to have an effect.

By January 1943 even Adolf Hitler was having second thoughts. During a quiet conversation at his headquarters in East Prussia, with Stalingrad very much on his mind, he asked no one in particular, "What should a leader do when he thinks he may be losing a great struggle?" After World War II was over, few of his associates had any difficulty pinpointing its most crucial days. For them the last three months of 1942 were decisive, but the fruits of Allied successes admittedly were not apparent until sometime in 1943. No longer were the Allies reacting to decisions made in Berlin, Rome, and Tokyo; instead they themselves were shaping the course of world events for the first time in several years: the initiative was now theirs.

Rounding the Corner

During 1943 the momentum of the war clearly shifted to the Allies, and plans for an invasion of western Europe became more definite. Yet, until the close of that year, the United States had, despite a Hitler-first policy, about an equal number of men committed to the Atlantic and Pacific sectors, some 1.8 million in each area. Before peace came, a far greater number of Americans (over 15 million) would be in uniform. Their ranks included both men and women and people of all colors, creeds, and backgrounds. The strength of the three major services in 1945 was (in millions): Army, 8.2; Navy, 3.3; Air Force, 2.3.

The North African campaign ended in a resounding victory in May 1943. Sixty days later Allied forces landed in Sicily and, sixty days after that, in Italy. These events led to the downfall of Benito Mussolini (1883–1945) as a new Italian government negotiated an armistice with the invaders; however, Mussolini soon headed up a puppet regime located at Lake Como, manipulated, of course, by the Germans. In a very short time the royal government, with Marshal Pietro Badoglio (1871–1956) as premier, joined the Allies. This was the first major defection from the Axis camp, but the results were not impressive. Nazi troops continued to control much of Italy, and relations between Italians and Americans, British, and French, recently foes, now ostensibly friends, were plagued by considerable suspicion and widespread misunderstanding. As a result, the Italian campaign

Frederic Lewis.

American troops engaged in successful amphibious landings at the Atlantic, Pacific, and Mediterranean. The troops here, departing from an LST craft during maneuvers, were training for the invasion of North Africa.

turned out to be a long, bloody, frustrating affair, tying down thousands of men that both the Axis and the Allies could have used to great advantage elsewhere.

Meanwhile, the war against Japan was carried on by air strikes and landings in the Solomons, which followed hard fighting under very demanding conditions in New Guinea and Guadalcanal. For the most part this business of nibbling away at the fringes of Japan's vast empire was the work of American, Australian, and New Zealander ground troops led by General Douglas MacArthur (1880–1964) and various units of the U.S. Navy and the U.S. Army Air Force.

In mid-March 1942, MacArthur left the beleaguered Philippines for Australia, where he organized training bases and used that continent as a bastion from which to counterattack. But in that part of the world 1943 was largely a time for preparation, for "softening up" the enemy by means of air strikes and increasing the tempo of the "island-hopping" technique, which would begin to push the Japanese back toward their homeland.

Allied leaders were so confident of victory that, by the end of 1943, they were beginning to make plans for the postwar era. Three high-level conferences—Casablanca (January), Quebec (September), and Teheran (November)—could be called both coordinating and planning sessions. At Casablanca, Roosevelt and Churchill sketched out the invasions of Sicily and Italy and agreed upon a policy of "unconditional surrender," and at Quebec they turned their attention to the Far East, giving Admiral Nimitz permission to move forward in the central Pacific and General MacArthur the go-ahead toward the Philippines.

Teheran, the first meeting held with Joseph Stalin (1879–1953), the Russian leader, brought into focus several complex issues. Stalin, angered by failure of his allies to invade western Europe and suspecting they might be quite willing to see the U.S.S.R. mortally wounded by its struggle with Nazi Germany, made his aims clear. Despite the words of the Atlantic Charter, he intended to expand Soviet influence and perhaps Soviet control over the Balkans and much of eastern Europe.

Even before Roosevelt went to Teheran, his old friend William C. Bullitt (1891–1967), a veteran diplomat, pointed out the dilemma facing the President. Victory over the Axis depended upon cooperation with Russia, yet that victory would mean an increase of that nation's power in both Europe and the Far East. Bullitt,

Library of Congress.

The brilliant American hero in the Pacific Theater, General Douglas MacArthur.

like Churchill, argued for an Anglo-American "second front" in southeastern Europe so as to deny much of that continent to the Soviets. Roosevelt agreed with Bullitt's logic but replied he had "a hunch" that if the U.S.S.R. were supplied with everything it needed in wartime that nation might feel less threatened by Germany in the future and would cooperate to achieve world order in peacetime. Also, he added, it was entirely possible that, if pushed too hard, the Soviets might still conclude a separate peace with Germany.

What Roosevelt failed to comprehend was that his overall policy of defeating the Axis with maximum use of American industry and minimum expenditure of American lives had created an atmosphere of suspicion in Moscow even before he met with Stalin at Teheran. The Russians could make no such choice between matériel and men, and the longer Roosevelt and Churchill put off launching a true second front—once scheduled to take place in 1942 and then delayed for two years—the more of their countrymen perished. When the Normandy landings finally came on June 6, 1944, the Soviet Union still faced 250 enemy divisions; the Allies, in France and Italy, fewer than 90. Casualty figures reflected this disparity even more dramatically. The Soviets lost an estimated sixteen million citizens (civilian and military) in World War II; British-American losses in all theaters totaled fewer than a million. U.S. authorities reported at war's end that 291,557 Americans had died and 670,846 had been wounded in battle.

In addition, whatever Moscow thought of Washington and London (and vice versa) must be viewed in the context of their relations (or nonrelations) during the two decades leading up to World War II. The "Grand Alliance" was simply a marriage of convenience and, like all such arrangements, might or might not prove to be lasting.

In any case, Roosevelt did his best at Teheran to allay Stalin's fears and secured a promise that the Soviet Union would join the war against Japan as soon as fighting ended in Europe. En route to that conference, Roosevelt and Churchill met with China's Chiang Kai-Shek (1887–1975) in Cairo on November 22–26, where they agreed that Manchuria, Formosa, and the Pescadore Islands, seized by Japan, would be returned to China after the war ended. They also pledged to continue their fight in the Pacific until Japan agreed to "an unconditional surrender," the same terms offered to Germany and Italy following the Casablanca Conference held ten months earlier.

Library of Congress.

Two of the best-known American commanders in the European theater were General George S. Patton (left) and General Dwight D. Eisenhower (right), shown here conferring in 1943.

Victory in Europe

Simply put, after the very successful Allied landings in Normandy under the leadership of General Eisenhower, Germany was caught up in a two-front war. Within two weeks of the opening of the long-awaited second front, more than a million British and American troops were spreading deep into France. More GIs invaded southern France on August 15, and ten days later the citizens of Paris joyously greeted their liberators. Meanwhile, Russia was clearing its soil of German invaders and by late 1944 the Allies were poised to strike at the heart of Hitler's once great empire from both east and west.

Despite very heavy Allied air attacks, which postwar analysis revealed were less effective than thought, Germany fought on doggedly, even making two desperate efforts to ward off inevitable defeat. Late in the summer of 1944, V-2 rocket bombs, flying faster than sound and impossible to intercept, began to rain death and destruction on English cities. More of a nuisance than an offensive weapon, nevertheless, these attacks killed 8,000 people and did considerable damage before Allied bombers were able to search out and destroy the launching sites.

Much more serious was a huge counteroffensive begun in the Ardennes forest of Belgium in mid-December 1944, the so-called "Battle of the Bulge." For about ten days the supposedly beaten enemy rolled back American troops, spreading gloom throughout Allied capitals

Library of Congress.

The Big Three: Churchill, Roosevelt, and Stalin held their last face-to-face meeting at Yalta in February 1945.

during the holiday season and raising high the hopes of their adversaries. German prisoners of war held in Great Britain reacted by rioting, and some 600 POW camps in the United States, containing upwards of half a million men, seethed with excitement. This proved, however, to be merely a "last hurrah," not the beginning of a true campaign, although the Battle of the Bulge did set back the Allied timetable by some six weeks.

Early in February 1945, Roosevelt, Churchill, and Stalin held their last and most controversial meeting at Yalta, a resort community in Crimea. Eager for Soviet aid against Japan and desirous of having the U.S.S.R. in the United Nations, Roosevelt tended to react favorably to most of Stalin's proposals. These included recognition of Russia's "special interests" in eastern Europe, tentative approval of a Russian-backed Polish government with the understanding that free elections would be held in that country, and consideration of substantial reparation payments by Germany. Later FDR's enemies would say that because he was gravely ill and not able to think clearly, he "sold out" to the Russians. This view ignores the full realities of the time. Soviet armies were in control of much of eastern Europe already. And, just as the United States and Britain concluded peace with Italy and reconstituted governments as their forces cleared western Europe of Germans without consulting Stalin step by step, his military leaders did the same thing in the East.

A few weeks after Yalta, in March 1945, German authorities contacted OSS agents in Berne concerning surrender of their armies in northern Italy. Within forty-eight hours American officials informed Moscow, and the Soviets asked to take part in these discussions. When Roosevelt replied these were merely tentative talks and their representatives could be present at any formal surrender, Moscow accused the western Allies of negotiating in secret while the Russians carried the main burden of the fight against Hitler.

Early in April, Stalin wrote Roosevelt that he understood the negotiations were now complete and included an understanding that the Germans would permit Anglo-American forces to advance unchallenged across Europe in return for easy peace terms. On April 4, FDR responded angrily that no such agreement had been arrived at or even considered. In fact, for the time being, nothing came of the Berne talks other than this controversy; however, the episode clearly showed the extent of suspicion in Moscow concerning American and British motives as victory approached. On the day President Roosevelt died, April 12, 1945, he drafted a telegram to Stalin noting that the Berne incident now was history and expressed the hope that such misunderstandings would not occur in the future. This incident revealed that Roosevelt's efforts to placate Stalin's fears had been for naught. He had given him vast stores of matériel, twice traveled to Russia for conferences, and agreed to Soviet hegemony over much of eastern Europe, but that was not enough. He had not made the one great sacrifice that might have changed Stalin's mind: massive American casualties in an early second front so as to relieve German pressure on the Russian homeland.

The final weeks of fighting in Europe created yet more controversy. Some Western observers later believed

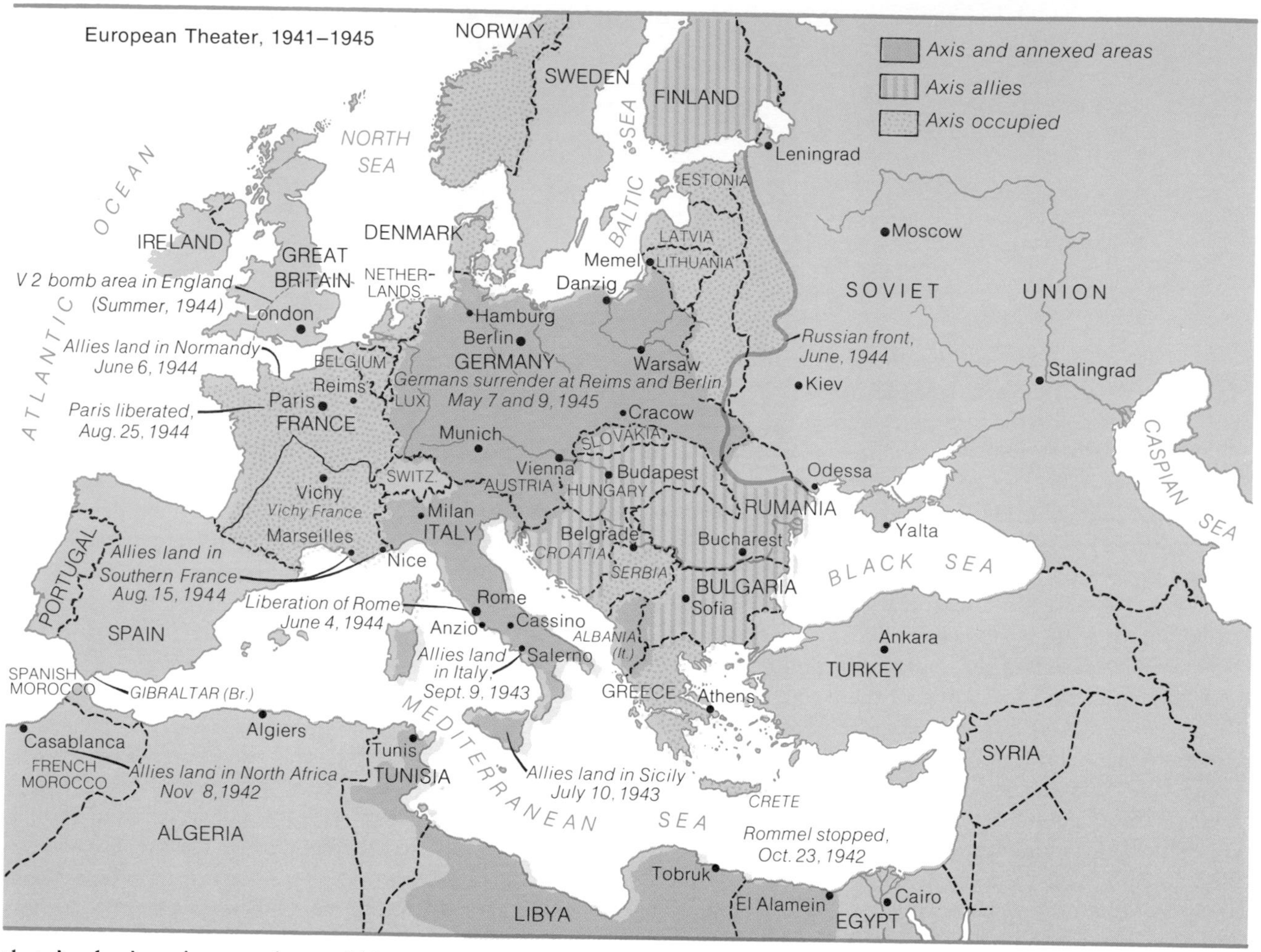

that Anglo-American armies could have gotten to Berlin before the Russians did; however, for various reasons General Eisenhower chose not to engage in such a race. These included fears of a possible enemy stronghold in southern Germany and unfortunate confrontations if the linkup with the Russians was not carried out in an orderly manner. Also, the Allies already had decided upon the division of Germany and of Berlin as well, so advancing into territory that would have been relinquished to the U.S.S.R. made little sense.

Hitler committed suicide in his underground bunker in beleaguered Berlin on April 30. Three days later, Admiral Karl Doenitz (1891–   ), his successor, tried unsuccessfully to surrender to the British while continuing to fight the Russians. Then, on the morning of May 7 Germany surrendered unconditionally to all of the Allied powers. Later that same day, President Harry S Truman, Roosevelt's successor, informed a joyful America that the fighting in Europe had come to an end, adding his wish that FDR could have lived to savor victory.

This was a bitter-sweet triumph, for peace seemed to create nearly as many problems as it solved. The totalitarian governments of Hitler and Mussolini were gone, but in their place were a divided Germany and a starving, destitute continent, much of it under the sway of Russian Communist might. Also, as all Americans knew, Europe was only half the battle: there still was a war in the Far East to finish.

Victory in the Pacific

During 1943 and 1944, at an ever-increasing tempo, air

strikes at island outposts followed by amphibious assaults began to decrease the scope of Japanese power in the Far East as MacArthur's troops and the U.S. Navy and Marines wrestled with fanatical resistance in one stronghold after another. The most crucial events of 1944 included Allied landings in the Philippines in October of that year, followed shortly by several naval engagements that virtually wiped out the Japanese fleet. These included the battles of Leyte Gulf (October 23–25) and Surigao Strait, Samar, and Cape Engaño (all on October 25). By late 1944 superfortresses of the U.S. Air Force were attacking Japan itself from bases in the Marianas. During the last ten months of fighting, American planes dropped 160,000 tons of conventional bombs on the homeland. Particularly devastating were fire bombs released over Tokyo. A single raid on March 9 left 185,000 dead.

Even before the Philippines were completely cleared of the enemy, on April 1, 1945, Allied forces landed in Okinawa, the last major Pacific battlefront of World War II. Here Japanese fanaticism took bizarre turns as kamikaze (suicide) pilots in planes loaded with bombs tried desperately to crash into U.S. ships. Once more, fighting virtually to the last man, 110,000 Japanese died on Okinawa by mid-1945. American troops suffered 49,000 casualties and took fewer than 8,000 prisoners; also, for the first time in the Pacific war, U.S. Navy losses were proportionally higher than those of ground troops. This suicidal, last-ditch stand cast a dark shadow on Allied plans to invade Japan, an assault scheduled to take place on November 1.

A few weeks after fighting ended on Okinawa—on July 17, 1945—Allied leaders met at Potsdam near Berlin. Truman and Stalin represented their nations, but Churchill, whose Conservative party was voted out of office during the talks, was replaced by Clement Attlee (1883–1967), leader of the Labour opposition. Truman was intent upon securing Russian assistance against Japan as soon as possible, but East-West difficulties clearly dominated these discussions. Much that Roosevelt and Churchill had viewed as tentative—the Polish-German frontier and reparation payments, for example—Stalin insisted was final. The three powers were able to agree that, in principle, Germany should remain united, although each (later France would get a zone, too) would exert temporary military control over specific areas. They also issued a joint demand for Japan's unconditional surrender.

While at Potsdam, Truman learned that an atomic bomb had been tested successfully in the New Mexico desert. This event, one of the war's best-kept secrets, meant that he faced awesome decisions. Should this power be used and, if so, where and when?

Although a new Japanese government was already sending out peace feelers through its ambassador in Moscow, that nation still had some five million men under arms, and no one could be certain that these preliminary discussions were serious. The Japanese premier's rejection of the Potsdam ultimatum (even though it contained a veiled threat concerning new weapons), set into motion a chain of events that led to the explosion of two atomic bombs, one at Hiroshima on August 6 and another at Nagasaki three days later.

Truman Library Collection/U.S. Signal Corps.

In July 1945 the new leaders of the United States (Truman) and Great Britain (Attlee) met with Stalin at Potsdam to discuss postwar plans.

National Archives.

The end of the war in the Pacific, marked by the signing of the surrender aboard the U.S.S. Missouri on September 2, 1945, closed six years of World War.

Meanwhile, as promised, the U.S.S.R. entered the Pacific war against Japan, yet the Japanese government hesitated to act as diehard elements tried to ward off the inevitable. Early on the morning of August 10, Emperor Hirohito (1901-) broke the deadlock by declaring that his nation must surrender, subject only to the condition that he retain his sovereign powers. Despite two awesome blasts, Russia's entry into the war, and a decision by the Emperor himself, staunch militarists still tried unsuccessfully to thwart these plans.

This decision quickly was relayed to President Truman via neutral Switzerland and he, in turn, informed other Allied leaders. Following a slight delay, all agreed that Hirohito could remain; and, after once more overruling the militarist faction in the government, the Emperor and the Japanese nation surrendered. On August 14 these behind-the-scenes maneuverings were made public, and World War II at last was over.

Yet, as in Europe, victory in the Pacific was tinged with haunting fears and misgivings. Use of the atomic bomb opened up a Pandora's Box of dilemmas, paramount among them, how to control such power? And China, torn by an unending civil war between Chiang's Nationalists and the Communists, hardly could exert much force in the postwar world. Even in the last weeks of August 1945, the days between Japan's agreement to surrender and the actual capitulation ceremony held in Tokyo Bay on September 2, vast stores of matériel flowed into the hands of Chiang's enemies. Japanese in Manchuria and Korea were supposed to surrender to the Russians, those in northern and eastern China, to the Nationalists. However, the Communists were at hand and with each day they became more powerful with the aid of Japanese military supplies. Peace in the Pacific was at best only a brief illusion as the Chinese chose up sides to fight each other instead of the Japanese, and Russia made a vain attempt to exert some control over Japan, now in the firm grip of General Douglas MacArthur, its postwar mentor.

Economic and Social Mobilization

Although the United States never was totally mobilized, World War II produced far greater government intervention in economic and social affairs than World War I or the Depression. Yet FDR came to economic regulation slowly and with much reluctance, shunning a truly comprehensive plan lest his political enemies see a "plot" on his part to usurp power.

Harnessing the Economy

By 1940 Roosevelt set up a flexible emergency planning organization within the executive office and added a number of allocation and supply boards as America became "the arsenal of democracy." This economic mobilization effort experienced many transformations, with FDR always retaining considerable power; however, it did not really become coordinated or move into "high gear" until after the attack on Pearl Harbor.

In January 1942 the President established a War Production Board under the direction of Donald M. Nelson (1888–1959), a Sears, Roebuck executive. Although an excellent organizer, Nelson was unable to force his will upon the civilian sector, and late in 1942 Roosevelt persuaded James F. Byrnes (1879–1972) to leave the Supreme Court bench and become an "assistant president" of sorts in charge of wartime production. In May 1943, this position was clarified when Byrnes became head of the Office of War Mobilization. Skill and obvious success made Byrnes a potential vice-presidential candidate in 1944.

Basic problems facing Roosevelt and Byrnes were four in number: how to convert civilian production to

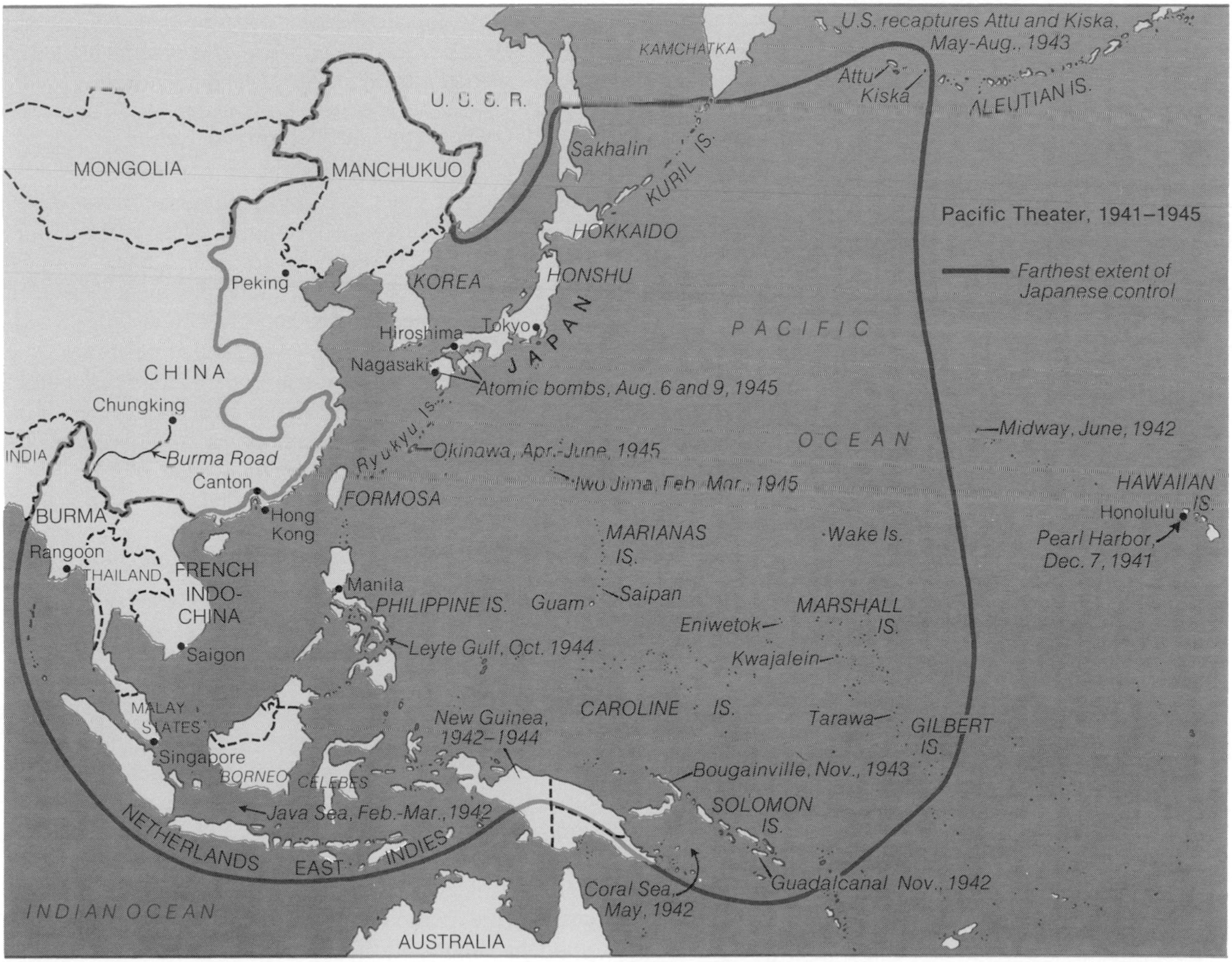

wartime needs and expand output as quickly as possible; how to allocate materials in short supply and perhaps find substitutes; how to recruit an adequate labor force and see that it was housed, fed, and paid, and its rights respected; and, at the same time, how to maintain adequate living standards for all citizens—for servicemen, factory workers, miners, and farmers; for the elderly, young, poor, and minority groups—in short, how to see that runaway inflation did not make a mockery of wartime prosperity.

The onset of World War II obviously solved some of the dilemmas of the Depression years. Labor shortages replaced unemployment. The income of war workers rose to dizzy heights, and the nation's farmers and coal miners, after some fifteen to twenty years of very rough times, were able to pay off loans and get out of debt.

To encourage business to convert to wartime purposes and also to expand production, the federal government offered numerous incentives. Expansion costs could be spread over several years, thus reducing taxes and increasing income. To relieve uncertainty, new products could be manufactured on a cost-plus-fixed-fee basis, allowing industrialists to meet all costs and be sure of some profit, no matter what happened. The federal government also eased antitrust laws to encourage pooling and similar cooperative arrangements so as to increase efficiency and production. In some instances, notably the vital rubber industry, the government even built huge plants and leased them to manufacturers with options to buy at the war's end. To avoid ocean travel and German U-boats, hastily constructed pipelines were soon carrying oil from Texas to the Northeast.

Wherever possible, as with industry itself, the government used incentives to attract workers. Between 1940 and 1943 more than fifteen million Americans entered the labor force or donned uniforms, most of them drawn from the ranks of the unemployed or from a large segment of the population which had never worked outside of home or farm before, notably women, blacks, and teen-agers. Yet this was a haphazard process at best. Forcing men into uniform and workers into jobs was a tricky business subject to scores of local political pressures.

Both skilled and unskilled laborers were often reluctant to go far from their homes or to experience true hardship. Absenteeism and rapid turnover were formidable problems, and leaders of a democratic state hesitated to adopt a system akin to forced labor. Congress fretted and struggled with these matters throughout 1942 and 1943, unwilling to draft fathers into service and receptive to demands that agricultural workers be kept out of uniform.

Not until the summer of 1943 was a partial solution achieved. On the West coast, where labor turnover presented a huge headache for shipyards and aircraft factories, a system developed that soon spread to other parts of the nation. A census determined how many workers were available in an area, and plants located there received new contracts only if the labor supply justified it. Also, a centralized system of referrals controlled hiring, which could proceed only with government permission. To some extent, this policy directed the flow of manpower to wherever it was needed. Though not outright compulsion, nevertheless, this scheme tended to limit a worker's freedom of movement somewhat.

The Government and Organized Labor

On the surface, the American labor movement waxed fat during the war years as membership grew from 10.5 to 14.7 million. By 1944, as a result of salary increases and overtime pay, real weekly wages before taxes were 50 percent higher than in 1939, and employment of women and young people tended to boost family income considerably. Nevertheless, labor-management relations were strained by the federal government's widespread concessions to business, by the relatively weak voice of labor on boards and in agencies directing war programs, and by the ceaseless upward spiral of living costs.

In December 1941, Roosevelt got a "no-strike" pledge from organized labor and shortly set up a National War Labor Board to resolve wage disputes. But strikes still occurred, especially in the coal industry in 1943 as miners struggled to combat rising prices for nearly everything they bought. Unwilling to create martyrs, the government did little about such outbreaks. In June 1943, the Congress, over FDR's veto, passed the Smith-Connally War Labor Disputes Act, which limited severely labor's right to strike at any plant or facility essential to the war effort (a definition which could cover almost any enterprise in the nation). This act, a reaction to walkouts in the coal mines, required notice before a strike occurred, a thirty-day cooling-off period, and then a strike vote. It also gave the President power to fine or to imprison union officials for defying his orders, and it

Library of Congress.

The militance of United Mine Workers leader John L. Lewis, depicted here as an unfortunate Samson, was instrumental in producing sharp congressional reactions, notably the Smith-Connally War Labor Disputes Act of 1943.

outlawed political contributions by unions.

Just as labor bristled at times under wartime controls, so did management. Sewell L. Avery (1874–1961), autocratic, antiunion head of Montgomery Ward and long a foe of FDR, precipitated a crisis in 1944 when he refused to allow a union election. (His employees often spelled their boss's name without periods after his initials to form the word "slavery.") When Avery's Chicago workers walked out, this affair came to a head. Eventually the federal government moved in and soldiers carried Avery from his office, seated majestically in his chair. Actually, Sewell Avery should have been among the very last men in America to challenge FDR, whose programs had channelled millions into Montgomery Ward cash registers. Deep in the red under Hoover, the company always showed a profit after 1933 and in 1944 made $21 million after taxes.

Financing the War

World War II cost the citizens of the United States and their government at least $300 billion. Some estimates even run as high as $350 billion. In any case, the sum was at least ten times greater than the cost of World War I to American taxpayers. By mid-1943 federal authorities were spending $8 billion a month, a sum equal to annual budgets in New Deal days. War bonds, borrowing, and new income levies helped to meet some of these costs. In July 1943 the now-familiar practice of withholding income taxes by payroll deductions was instituted. These revenues and other forms of taxation paid about two-fifths of the war's total cost. Nevertheless, the national debt soared from about $48 billion in 1941 to $247 billion four years later. So, in a sense, this unprecedented spending remained an outstanding, unpaid debt long after fighting ceased.

The year 1942 was the most frantic time as more than $12 billion, most of it federal money, poured into military installations and factories. This meant, of course, sudden wealth and a flurry of unprecedented activity in some areas, and continued (even accentuated) economic depression elsewhere. In that year alone 300,000 retailers went out of business, most of them small enterprises not located near boomtowns or run by entrepreneurs unable to get labor or specific materials.

Most of this windfall went to large companies able and ready to produce. Two-thirds of the $300 billion that the federal government eventually ploughed into the economy went to 100 of the 18,000 companies that fulfilled war contracts. Communities such as New York City, a center of small manufacturing concerns, did not share in this bonanza. By November 1942 only seven Manhattan firms had contracts valued at $2.3 million; instead, Detroit's autobuilders, shipyards on both coasts, new aircraft plants, and arms manufacturers benefited most from government spending.

The result was tremendous growth for General Motors, which received nearly 8 percent of all federal contracts. Other top moneymakers included Curtiss-Wright, Douglas, Lockheed, Chrysler, Ford, Bethlehem Steel, American Telephone & Telegraph, and du Pont. This meant increased economic concentration for America and great wealth for a few corporations. By mid-1945, the 63

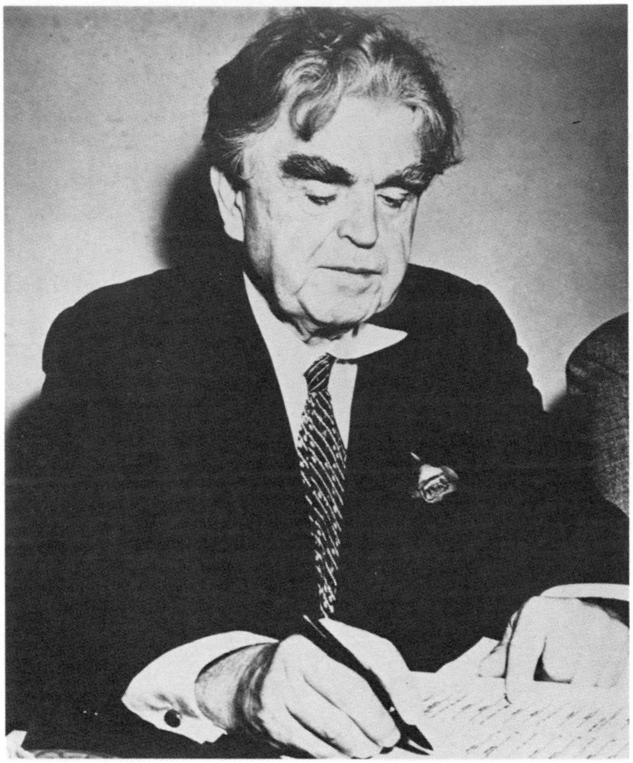

State Historical Society of Wisconsin.

John L. Lewis (1880–1969)

A formidable figure who awakened prophecies of greatness among those who met him, John L. Lewis was a potent force in American labor and politics for four decades. He was a remarkable orator whose glare, bushy eyebrows, and pointed finger accentuated his rolling, sonorous tones.

Born in Lucas, Iowa, in 1880 of Welsh parents, he ended his formal education in the seventh grade, although his wife later tutored him to aid in development of his career. His life represents an elitist problem that has long plagued American organized labor: an individual's drive to get power for his union followed by a keen desire to exert power over it. Lewis began working in coal mines when he was sixteen and a decade later, in 1906, started his climb to national prominence. He served as a legislative agent for the United Mine Workers (UMW) in Illinois from 1901 to 1911 where he won substantial victories and attracted the attention of executives of the American Federation of Labor (AFL). In 1920 Lewis became president of the UMW, a post he held for forty years, and, as a protégé of Samuel Gompers, vice president of the AFL. Impressed with this young man's skill, and on the advice of Secretary of Commerce Herbert Hoover, Calvin Coolidge asked him to become Secretary of Labor, but Lewis declined.

In 1935 Lewis and several other prominent labor leaders who were increasingly unhappy with AFL policies formed the Committee for Industrial Organizations. The issue was whether unions should organize all workers in an industry or organize along traditional craft lines favored by the AFL. In 1938 the break with the AFL became final when the Congress of Industrial Organizations (CIO) appeared. Lewis, who became CIO president and led successful mass unionization campaigns, was a strong supporter of FDR in 1936. After Roosevelt gave only lukewarm backing to additional union drives, Lewis refused to support him in 1940. Disgusted with the President's victory, this labor leader (as he had promised to do) quit as CIO head but remained as the UMW's chief. In 1942 he split with a pro-FDR faction in the CIO and took his union out of that group.

The next year Lewis aroused public condemnation when he and his miners went out on strike (despite a wartime no-strike pledge) in an effort to gain higher wages. This so-called "work stoppage," the most serious during World War II, cost over 9 million man-days. The federal government seized the coal mines, but eventually the strikers won their demands: portal-to-portal pay—that is, wages from the time they entered the mines until they departed.

Although John L. Lewis, who had a knockdown, drag-out struggle with Harry Truman in 1946, remained at the UMW helm until 1960, he is best remembered as Roosevelt's Depression-era friend and wartime foe. Few labor leaders have wielded so much power in America and attracted so much public attention, for Lewis, who was dedicated, eloquent, and impressive, was a very difficult man to ignore. ■

largest manufacturing companies with assets of more than $100 million had increased their net working capital to more than that held by all manufacturers in 1939. And, quite naturally, war workers and their families, often deserting farms, small towns, and small companies unable to secure wartime contracts, went where the action was.

Inflation and Rationing

Too much money and too few consumer goods equaled inflation as dollars bid against each other for scarce items. A simple ceiling on wages was not the answer since living costs continued to rise, and any measure of that sort might curb incentives to produce. The solution lay, in part, in taxation that would limit spending and in savings programs, a means of deferring spending until more goods were available.

The Revenue Act of 1942 broadened the tax rolls fourfold to cover nearly fifty million Americans. The following year the now familiar system of payroll deductions was instituted, and for the first time in their lives thousands began filing federal income tax returns. War bonds, peddled with much hoopla by Hollywood starlets and battlefront heroes, encouraged saving, but the results were not truly impressive. Sales reached nearly $100 billion before the war ended, but banks, insurance companies, and corporations accounted for three-fourths of that total. To make matters worse, the redemption rate of $25 bonds doubled (1942–1944), only increasing spendable income if they were cashed.

To some extent, any scheme to combat inflation had to include rationing. During World War II, the Office of Price Administration (OPA) introduced numerous rationing programs that limited the sale of such items as gas, coffee, canned goods, sugar, shoes, and meat. Often these goods themselves actually were not in short supply. For example, limiting gas usage saved tires and curtailing the use of cans saved precious tin. Gasoline rationing, for obvious reasons, did not begin until after the 1942 congressional elections.

No aspect of wartime America was enveloped in so much controversy as rationing. There was virtually no way to assure that political pressures could be eliminated from such a program, and any ruling that pleased one sector of the economy infuriated another. The result was the spread of "black markets" where one could buy goods, especially meat, without ration stamps or at higher than ceiling prices. Liquor, rayon goods, and shoes were also hot items, and sometimes wholesale operations flourished not unlike those of Prohibition days in the 1920s. Cattle rustling reappeared in the West. A Pittsburgh newspaper reporter, given $2,000 to work with, was able to purchase a ton of meat in three weeks without handing over any ration stamps; and, if he wished, he could have bought stamps at $6 per thousand. In addition to the "black market" there was also the lesser known "red market" in meat. This consisted of staying (somewhat) within OPA rules and regulations but upgrading cheaper cuts and selling them as prime.

All these problems could not overshadow substantial achievements. By mid-1943 many wrinkles in industry, manpower, wages, and inflation had been ironed out. In the beginning of 1944 factory output was so great that some cutbacks were in order. It was now double that of all the Axis powers combined. In the process of stimulating and organizing this tremendous expansion, the U.S. government, by necessity, became a potent, active force in all sectors of the nation's economy, expending between 1941 and 1945 a sum roughly twice as large as all federal outlays from 1789 to 1941.

Two unique aspects of this wartime experience should be noted. Washington imposed regimentation of sorts on nearly every citizen, while in an effort to stimulate production, it removed some business restrictions of New Deal days. And, whatever was done—in Presi-

Library of Congress.

HELP THEM JOIN THE AIR FORCE
F. H. LA GUARDIA
MAYOR
K·JULY 21ST to 28TH

During the war, government and private agencies alike sponsored conservation and collection drives.

Library of Congress.

Rationing was designed to limit consumption of scarce commodities, including foods. Storekeepers were to collect ration coupons from consumers and had to present the accumulated coupons in order to replenish their stocks.

dent Roosevelt's fashion of proceeding experimentally and with divergent forces in mind—came piecemeal. He was most reluctant to fight a war against dictatorship overseas by imposing ironclad rules at home. The best way, in his opinion, was to get people to do on their own what controls would have forced them to do anyway. In this manner, even in crisis, the form of democracy was retained even if its spirit was strained a bit at times.

Education

World War II affected education and technical research in diverse ways, both stimulating and inhibiting normal development. In the first two years of that conflict high school enrollment dropped by 17 percent. Some young men and women donned uniforms, others left to take high-paying defense jobs, and still others were too disturbed or distracted by events going on about them to continue their studies. Personal tension and family disorganization took a heavy toll. Divorces nearly doubled during the war, as did juvenile delinquency. (Crimes such as robbery and murder, on the other hand, tended to decrease, perhaps because war itself provided a release for violence or because those inclined to commit such acts were in uniform and busy training or fighting.) Adolescents, many of them old beyond their years, experimented with sex, liquor, and prostitution. Those who remained in high school classrooms usually concentrated upon technical and scientific subjects to the detriment of academic and liberal arts courses, a trend repeated at the college level as well.

Unlike World War I, when colleges for men almost ceased to exist, the armed services used campuses for language training and similar special programs. Occupational deferment for those involved in studies deemed vital to the war effort was also much more common than in 1917–1918. Nevertheless, many institutions experienced extremely rough times as classes dwindled to half their normal size, personnel left for other pursuits, and income fell drastically.

In 1944, with victory seemingly in sight, both the army and navy began to curtail their training courses. As a result, in June of that year Congress established a committee to study the plight of the nation's colleges and universities. The result was the famed "GI Bill" (Public Law 346). This measure was designed basically to ease the general transition from uniform to civilian status by providing $20 a week until an ex-serviceman or woman found a job. These allotments, paid for up to 52 weeks, gave rise to the so-called "52-20" clubs. But the educational benefits, not the unemployment provisions, were what attracted most GIs and also provided a tremendous boost to the nation's academic life. College enrollment in 1946 was 45 percent higher than two years earlier and in 1947 more than a million veterans were attending classes somewhere in the nation. In lecture halls recently nearly empty it was now "standing room only."

Meanwhile, during the war years much more dramatic events were occurring in the research laboratories of some of America's most prestigious universities, often amid great secrecy. Professors, physicists, physicians, and experts in many fields produced new detection devices such as sonar and radar, lifesaving blood plasma, and, above all else, the atomic bomb, which helped to hasten the end of the war in the Pacific. The first nuclear chain reaction at the University of Chicago's laboratory on December 2, 1942, set in motion programs that gave rise to huge new research centers such as Oak Ridge in Tennessee and Los Alamos in New Mexico.

Interestingly, much of this invaluable research in various fields (all related in one way or another to winning the war) was carried on at scores of colleges and universities and by people from many nations. It was a unique example of higher education serving directly the national interest. At the same time, this association had both immediate and long-range effects: it provided government money for badly depleted academic bank accounts and created ties between Washington and various campus departments that continued in postwar decades.

A Nation on the Move

The demand for wartime labor produced a vast migration that during 1941–1945 relocated about 15.3 million people in new counties, 7.7 million of these folk settling in new states as well. Interstate and interregional movement, although much greater than in the five years before Pearl Harbor, conformed to general patterns of that period. Between April 1940 and November 1943, thirty-five states showed a net loss in civilian population. The big gainers were in the Far West—California, Oregon, and Washington, and to a lesser degree, Arizona, Utah, and Nevada—and three South Atlantic states, Maryland, Virginia, and Florida. The District of Columbia, in a class by itself and responsible for some of the growth in nearby sections of Maryland and Virginia, gained 162,469 residents, registering a wartime population increase of about 25 percent.

Shipyards and aircraft factories lured thousands of Americans westward, and more shipyards and manufacturing plants drew still others to centers on the East coast. Many of those on the move were farm folk, the nation's agricultural population dropping by 17 percent during the war years; 5.5 million went to towns and cities to live and 1.5 million donned uniforms. The ten most congested areas included Mobile, Hampton Roads (Norfolk, Newport News, Hampton, Portsmouth), San Diego, Charleston (South Carolina), Portland (Oregon), the

Puget Sound region of Washington state, Los Angeles, San Francisco, and Muskegon County and Detroit-Willow Run in Michigan. The percentage of population increase over 1940 in these centers ranged from 8.2 percent in the Detroit area to 25 percent in San Francisco, to about 44 percent in Hampton Roads and San Diego, and to a whopping 64.7 percent in Mobile.

In absolute terms, the biggest gainers were Los Angeles and San Francisco, each of which picked up over 500,000 new residents. Farm boys from the northern Great Plains went to build aircraft on the West coast; southern whites and blacks, sharecroppers, tenant farmers, and their families, moved to shipyards on the Gulf and Virginia coasts or to factories in the Michigan-Indiana-Ohio area; and new plants and new opportunities drew thousands from the Northeast to the Midwest and Far West. Housing often was deplorable, as almost anything could be used temporarily and was. Frequently several workers rented the same bed and slept in shifts.

Women and the War

In 1940 the percentage of females in the labor force was almost exactly what it had been in 1910, and there seemed little reason to expect any change. Yet by 1945 a dramatic transformation had taken place. Almost overnight, out of sheer necessity, women were welcomed with open arms by employers who had long scorned them. They became railroad workers, shipbuilders, aircraft riveters, and white-collar personnel. Barriers fell everywhere as Rensselaer Polytechnic Institute enrolled its first woman, Curtiss-Wright sent 800 female engineering trainees to college, and duPont and Standard Oil hired women chemists. Women also became lawyers, stockbrokers, and journalists in unprecedented numbers. And many donned uniforms as nurses and joined auxiliary units associated with various branches of the armed forces. In all, over six million women took wartime jobs of one sort or another.

In addition, women who remained at home or were employed in factories and offices also did volunteer work such as rolling bandages, knitting socks, driving trucks, directing convoys, aiding civil defense programs—assisting the war effort in whatever way they could. Many women employees, plagued by their dual role as worker and mother/wife, created a high turnover rate and considerable absenteeism. Conditions also gave rise to "latchkey children" and demonstrated the need for child-care facilities. In 1943 federal funds were made available for such purposes, but red tape, shortages, and the failure of many families to be interested in such centers doomed the success of this venture.

This phenomenon produced some unexpected results. For the first time in history, American women experienced the luxury of occupational mobility. If they had the qualifications, they could move from menial tasks and home or farm labor to better-paying, more interesting jobs in industry and business. Black women benefited more than any other group as rigid employment barriers collapsed in the face of an acute labor shortage. War also enabled the workingwoman to become an accepted fact in middle class America. Although many quit voluntarily in 1945, some two million remained in the work force, especially those over forty-five who had diminishing responsibilities in family households.

By almost any standards, World War II represents a

Library of Congress.

American women were instrumental in keeping the industrial plant going during World War II. Women workers faced special difficulties, working long hours and running households unassisted during the war years. The women pictured here are arriving for work at a Niagara Falls aircraft plant in the spring of 1943.

Library of Congress.

Oveta Culp Hobby
(1905–   )

Director of the Women's Army Auxiliary Corps in World War II, better known simply as the WACs, Oveta Culp Hobby rose to prominence in politics and publishing in the 1920s and 1930s. Originally a Democrat, she was in the forefront of the Eisenhower movement in 1952 and later served in the Cabinet for two years (1953–1955), the second woman in history to attain such high rank.

Daughter of a Texas politician, Oveta Culp took an early interest in public affairs. She studied law at the University of Texas and at age twenty was both parliamentarian of the state legislature and Houston's assistant city attorney. Marriage in 1931 to Governor William Pettus Hobby, publisher of the *Houston Post,* catapulted her into journalism. Work at the *Post* streamlining women's news won her a $1-a-year public relations job with the War Department in July 1941. Three months later General George C. Marshall asked Oveta Culp Hobby to map out plans for the WACs.

Sworn in as commandant in May 1942, Colonel Hobby faced immediate criticism. Blacks were especially disturbed by her southern background, but Hobby's insistence that black women be represented among officer candidates in proportion to their numbers in the population quelled this outburst. The goal of the WAC program was to supply clerks, typists, dental hygienists, chauffeurs, cooks, and bakers, thus relieving soldiers for frontline duty. At the outset the Pentagon announced that it would enroll 10,000 women in 1942 and increase WAC strength to 150,000 by 1944. However, similar programs in other services and disenchantment with what often was drab, uninteresting duty cut peak size to only 100,000.

Hobby retired in July 1945 and returned to her duties at the *Houston Post,* becoming editor and publisher in 1952. Meanwhile, she supported Dewey in 1948 and Eisenhower four years later. In 1953 she became the latter's Social Security Administrator and subsequently Secretary of Health, Education and Welfare, the first person to head that new agency. Two years later she once more resumed her journalistic duties, continuing a very active role in civic and political affairs. Hobby is the mother of two children, one of whom succeeded her as head of the *Post* empire. ■

turning point for workingwomen. It laid the groundwork for greater personal freedom, more participation in the world outside of the home, and the feminist movement, which blossomed a quarter of a century later. Yet a paradox remains. Although the American public at war's end was willing to accept a woman employee (not on a level equal to that of her male counterpart, however) if she kept a good household and took care of her children—or especially if she was thirty-five or forty and perhaps single—most individuals still felt her true role was that of homemaker and housewife. Americans continued to believe that women only worked out of "necessity." Thus a married woman might venture forth after her offspring were safely in school, but she was not perceived as an equal in the labor force, and few considered any female job more important than dusting, cooking, cleaning, and mothering. Yet at the turn of the century, the young, single, and poor dominated the female labor force; fifty years later most workers who were women were married, middle-aged, and often middle class to boot. Here, then, were the roots of substantial social change.

Selling the War

Censorship, although not so extreme as that in 1917–1918, appeared immediately after Pearl Harbor. Byron Price (1891–   ) left the Associated Press to head up the Office of Censorship, which enjoyed good cooperation from publishers, radio broadcasters, and the public at large. To FDR, "explaining" the war was at least as important as censorship, and in June 1942 he set up the Office of War Information (OWI), which under the direction of Elmer Davis (1890–1958), produced advertisements, cartoons, and weekly digests. In Davis' view, his job was to tell America why the nation was at war, how things were going, and where they were going. In a sense, OWI was a huge city desk, a clearinghouse that handled most but not all of the news generated by the war itself and by various government agencies and departments.

Although the OWI was very active overseas as it bombarded both civilian and military, friend and foe alike, with millions of words (notably through "Voice of America" broadcasts), two of its most interesting arms were the Domestic Radio Bureau and the Bureau of Motion Pictures. The former turned out "educational" dramas and "spot" ads; the latter pushed for (and usually got) films proclaiming unity, progress, and eventual victory. These included "White Cliffs of Dover," "Wake Island," "Bataan," and "So Proudly We Hail"; however, pictures with comedians such as Bud Abbott and Lou Costello in "Buck Privates" and "In the Navy" with their slapstick humor made much more money at the box office.

World War II presented Hollywood with special problems. Every star had to be seen at work winning the war either at servicemen's canteens or in uniform. Agents looked high and low for potential leading men with football injuries, double hernias, or five children—anyone who would not be drafted halfway through a production; and they looked equally hard for Orientals to play sinister Japanese villains. Most of the latter were actually Chinese from the Los Angeles area—beer salesmen, bartenders, and poets—who suddenly were making $800 a week. But to most Americans, despite the fact that *Time* published a handy guide entitled "How to Tell Your Friends from the Japs" (December 22, 1941), all Far Easterners looked alike.

Coverage of World War II by American press and radio was perhaps the best and most complete ever seen or heard. As many as 500 reporters were overseas at any one time and more than three times that number were accredited to the U.S. armed forces. In their ranks were several well-known women writers and photographers, including Inez Robb, Peggy Hull (who also served in World War I), and Margaret Bourke-White. Their male counterparts included William L. Shirer, Edward R. Murrow, H. V. Kaltenborn, and Quentin Reynolds. Ernie Pyle, however, was the man who emerged as the best-loved reporter of the war. It was Pyle who lived the struggle day by day with the GI, won a Pulitzer Prize in 1944, and died the following year on Ie Shima during the Okinawa campaign, the victim of a sniper bullet.

There was GI journalism, too, as the *Stars and Stripes* produced both European and Pacific editions featuring Bill Mauldin's cartoons and Milton Caniff's sexy "Male Call." Most of the established military and naval installations both at home and overseas also published their own newspapers and magazines. By the war's end even German prisoners of war quartered in the United States were printing camp weeklies under the careful scrutiny of U.S. Army censors.

All of these efforts—radio broadcasts, movies, newspaper columns, advertisements of various kinds—

U.P.I.

Walt Disney
(1901–1966)

Creator of cartoons, movies, and fantasylands enjoyed by millions, Walt Disney was one of the nation's busiest citizens during World War II. He and his staff turned out hundreds of training films, drew scores of appealing emblems for aircraft and gunnery crews, and almost singlehandedly made the Good Neighbor policy a reality.

Walt Disney was born in Chicago but grew up in Missouri. Always a bundle of energy, at sixteen he was taking night courses in cartooning in Chicago but actually had little art training. Too young to fight in World War I, Disney drove a Red Cross ambulance overseas and then returned to Kansas City, where he got an advertising job. After several unsuccessful attempts to produce animated cartoons, in 1923 he went to Hollywood where his brother Roy already was employed in movies. With a $500 loan from an uncle, these young men set up a small studio.

Sometime in the mid-1920s, Mickey Mouse, Disney's best-known character, appeared. Just how is not entirely clear, although according to Disney's *New York Times* obituary, Ubbo Iwerks, an associate, actually created Mickey. Mickey's first two productions (silent cartoons) were not successful; but, with sound provided by Walt Disney's voice in 1928, the lovable little mouse quickly won a worldwide following.

During the 1930s the Disney studios grew by leaps and bounds with Walt handling production, and Roy, finances. Walt Disney was, in a sense, one of the last great movie moguls, daring to do almost anything. Hollywood scoffed at the idea of a feature-length cartoon, but *Snow White and the Seven Dwarfs,* costing $1.6 million, grossed six times that figure within a few weeks.

Much of the work done by Disney and his staff for the armed forces (1941–1945) was classified or consisted of training films. But one production, *Victory Through Air Power,* was released to the public. Millions also saw *Saludos Amigos* (1942) and *The Three Caballeros* (1945), feature-length cartoons designed for south-of-the-border audiences; for, on the eve of World War II, U.S. officials, much concerned about Axis activity in the Western Hemisphere, discovered that Latin Americans admired Mickey Mouse more than any other U.S. figure. As a result, the State Department hurriedly dispatched Disney and his artists south to research productions designed to foster goodwill.

After the war Disney turned to nonanimated productions such as Mary Poppins and to development of Disneylands in California and Florida. Unlike most studio heads, he refused to release many of his old films to television, noting with much truth that they found a new audience every seven years. Instead, Disney produced new films for this medium which, in turn, advertised his other ventures in the entertainment realm. He died in 1966.

In his amazing career Walt Disney received twenty-nine Oscars and was one of the few individuals ever to enjoy simultaneous praise from the U.S.S.R. and the American Legion. The secret of his success was a troupe of lovable, unsophisticated characters with universal appeal. Yet perhaps nothing amused or flattered Disney more than the password used at Supreme Allied Headquarters in Europe on D-Day: "Mickey Mouse." ■

---

had definite goals in mind. Until 1945 their aim was to explain the war, undermine the enemy's spirit and counter his propaganda, boost morale, and achieve victory. With success at hand, emphasis shifted to stressing the need for continued Allied cooperation in the United Nations and to unstinting praise for the glories of democracy, which a defeated Germany and Japan must be led to choose in the postwar world. Under the pressures of wartime propaganda and wartime necessities even Joseph Stalin became a hero of sorts, and his stern dictatorship was transformed into a semidemocracy in the eyes of many Americans. Ironically, just as the Czarist government was a dilemma for the Allies in World War I, Communist Russia caused similar problems in World War II.

"Fresh, spirited American troops, flushed with victory, are bringing in thousands of hungry, ragged, battle-weary prisoners . . ." (*News item*)

Army cartoonist Bill Mauldin's war-weary G.I.'s became familiar figures to readers during the war. Mauldin's ironic commentaries—such as this depiction of American troops entering Germany in 1944—were realistic reminders of the grimness of war.

Civil Rights in Time of War

Harnessing a nation to fight means that demands of the moment such as national unity and national survival may override temporarily the established rights of certain individuals. Although not legally correct, it is a truism that civil rights are often wartime casualties. At the same time that enemy action may create special pressures, vast movements of peoples, blatant propaganda, and the unsettling experience of war itself can foster animosities difficult to contain or suppress.

Racial Tensions

The fight against Fascism presented America with a very embarrassing situation. It badly needed black labor and was quick to denounce the racial theories of its foe. Yet it clung, sometimes tenaciously, to a Jim Crow past. The principal points of contention were the role of blacks in wartime jobs and the armed forces and the treatment of black GIs by local lawmen, especially in the Deep South. As they donned their uniforms, black Americans flowed North and West to work; or, without uniforms, they sought jobs previously denied to them. In both cases, they stirred up considerable consternation that, in turn, inspired a new militancy among all blacks throughout the nation. Unlike World War I, when blacks generally agreed to close ranks and ignore basic grievances until

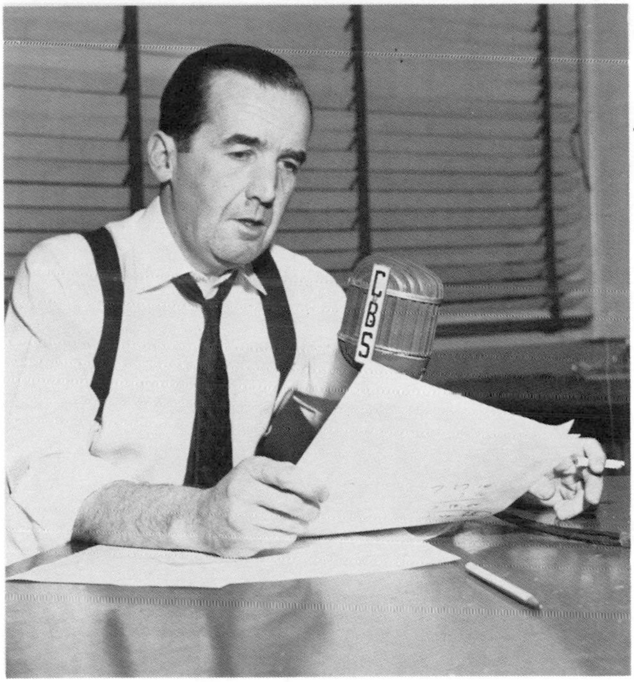

New York Daily News Photo.

Edward R. Murrow
(1908–1965)

A tall, handsome, almost fatigue-proof man who could easily have slipped into the role of foreign correspondent in an adventure movie (even though he never worked in a newspaper office), Edward R. Murrow was the voice of war and beleaguered Britain to millions of Americans. Long before Pearl Harbor, his somber "This is London" told listeners much about bombs, air raid sirens, disaster, and death.

Born in Greensboro, North Carolina, young Murrow moved west with his family in 1920 and worked his way through Washington State University where he was a campus leader, graduating in 1930. From 1930 to 1932 he was president of the National Student Federation of America, a job that earned him a position as director of the Institute of International Education. This work, backed by Carnegie-Rockefeller money, enabled Murrow to travel widely throughout Europe and make numerous valuable contacts. In 1935 he joined the Columbia Broadcasting System as a special events man and two years later was sent to Europe.

The only CBS employee on the Continent, Murrow was told by an executive as he left New York to search out such things as "the song of a nightingale from Kent," a program voted top honors by U.S. listeners in 1932. Instead, he soon was up to his neck in fast-moving events in Austria, Munich, and Poland and began to elicit expert help and opinion in various key capitals, including that of William L. Shirer in Berlin. Eric Sevareid and Howard K. Smith also became part of his team.

But Murrow himself *was* London to many Americans throughout World War II. During the blitz (even as his studio was hit), he broadcast eyewitness accounts that helped to undermine the isolationist cause back home. His praise of Churchill's leadership and English bravery against great odds shrewdly helped prointerventionists develop the argument that America must act while Britain was still a valuable ally, not a defeated nation.

An insatiable, enthusiastic talker, a wizard at darts, and an awful driver, Murrow held various jobs with CBS after the war and headed up the United States Information Agency (1961–1963), but nothing he did in television or as an executive equalled his wartime exploits. A loner with a rich, dramatic voice, he seemed to prefer radio because he thought it more flexible than its stepchild, television. Also, he had the unique satisfaction of bringing a new dimension to radio (and some would say to television as well), for he used that medium to both educate and improve American society. ■

John Phillips/Life Magazine © 1944 Time Inc.

Bill Mauldin
(1921–)

Although many writers and artists got invaluable experience as GIs on the staffs of the *Stars and Stripes, Yank,* and other wartime publications, none put it to better use than Bill Mauldin, now one of our nation's most respected political cartoonists. Born in New Mexico in 1921, Mauldin spent much of his early childhood bedridden with rickets in nearby Arizona. In high school he took an interest in drawing and later studied at the Chicago Academy of Fine Arts.

Despite poor eyesight and a record of ill health, Mauldin joined the Arizona National Guard in 1940, and when it was nationalized, found himself in the United States Army. His cartoons for both camp and local newspapers soon attracted attention; and, in 1943 Sergeant Mauldin joined the overseas staff of *Stars and Stripes.* He was wounded at Salerno and later saw action in other parts of Italy and in France.

Mauldin's work, extremely popular with enlisted men, featured two dirty, dull-eyed, unshaven GIs named Joe and Willie who reflected battlefront conditions much as they actually were. He refused to portray sex, death, or fear and was equally adamant that Germans should not be seen as ludicrous, bumbling idiots. Nevertheless, Mauldin did draw Army brass as they often appeared to men in the ranks—cartoons that drew the ire of General George S. Patton. At one point, Eisenhower even called General Patton and Sergeant Mauldin together to discuss their differences. By the time the war ended, despite Patton's criticism and a feeling among some stateside civilians that Joe and Willie were somewhat too realistic, Mauldin's cartoons were syndicated in seventy-nine U.S. newspapers. In 1945 he won a Pulitzer Prize.

Bill Mauldin, who now works and lives in Chicago, visited both Korea and Vietnam when war enveloped those lands. In 1973 he reflected upon these experiences in an article that appeared in the *New Republic:* "Ain't Gonna' Cover Wars No More: Evolution of a Dove." Like many Americans who made a similar journey in their minds, if not in a geographical sense, Mauldin eloquently described how visits to battle zones turned him into a hawk, crying for revenge. Then, slowly, influenced by his long-haired offspring, he had moved by the late 1960s to a dove viewpoint. Cartoons reproduced in the *New Republic* reflect this trend, which Mauldin wryly notes was marked by a rise in angry letters and a declining number of "Americanism" awards. ■

peace came, in World War II they tended to demand immediate action. Some even advocated prolonged warfare as the best hope for eliminating racial barriers.

Despite such views and serious riots in Detroit and Harlem in 1943, blacks made only limited gains during the war years. Still, a fundamental shift in the attitudes of both blacks and whites was evident. One result was issuance of Executive Order 8802 (June 25, 1941), setting up the Fair Employment Practices Commission (FEPC) assuring blacks of some consideration for wartime jobs; however, the President did so only to ward off a march on Washington threatened by blacks unless he met their demands. The President's principal black antagonist was A. Philip Randolph, head of the Brotherhood of Sleeping Car Porters, who planned to lead the march on the nation's capital on July 1, 1941. Roosevelt, who was always conscious of how much he needed the support on Capitol Hill of conservatives and southern politicos was unwilling to do more. Nearly 700,000 black youths who put on uniforms served in separate units, although the Navy experimented with limited integration after 1944. Not restricted to labor battalions alone (the general practice in World War I), black servicemen (7,000 of whom became officers) usually existed apart from whites; nevertheless, combat conditions sometimes made a farce of segregation.

Mexican-Americans often suffered abuses similar to those experienced by blacks, although they were not segregated by the armed forces during World War II. Yet, as a group, until they moved from rural areas to cities in postwar decades, Mexican-Americans were largely a "forgotten minority." Their numbers were much smaller than those of blacks, and segregation practices against them were more limited and sometimes less clearly defined. Only in communities along the Mexican border from Texas to California was the "problem" evident. Nevertheless, some outbreaks of violence occurred during the war years, notably the so-called "zoot-suit" riots of June 1943, when servicemen in Los Angeles clashed with Mexican-American and black youths dressed in exaggerated jitterbug-type costumes. To some extent, this racial antipathy was fed by unfounded fears that Mexican-Americans, like the Japanese, might pose a potential fifth-column threat on the West coast.

Far more important than the race riots, zoot suits, or even Roosevelt's reluctance to do much to aid the

U.P.I.

Overcrowded conditions and the migration of thousands of blacks into northern cities produced numerous racial clashes, as in Detroit in 1943.

plight of blacks was their migration by the thousands from the Deep South to other parts of the nation. By 1945 their presence alone made the "race problem" national in scope and also created a bloc of potential voters that astute politicians would soon discover. At the same time, subtle interaction between white liberals and once militant blacks produced a new milieu. By the end of 1943 more than a hundred local, state, and national commissions had been formed "to promote better race relations." And, although membership often drifted away into a mass of committees and surveys, some leaders took on the task of winning for blacks their constitutional rights.

These whites frequently were acting out of self-interest, eager to avoid Washington marches and riots. Blacks who joined them sometimes had similar motives, were jealous of new organizations such as the Congress of Racial Equality (CORE), or were convinced that any minority needed all the assistance it could get. Many of them, having risen up the social and economic ladder during World War II, wanted to retain their new affluence, which could be threatened by violence and unrest.

Culver Pictures.

A. Philip Randolph
(1889–)

Asa Philip Randolph, a valiant fighter for the civil rights of blacks during the last half century, was born in Crescent City, Florida, in 1889. Although his family was poor, he got a high school education and studied at the City College of New York after he moved to Manhattan to live. As a young man, he held various jobs and in 1917 helped found *The Messenger,* a magazine of black protest. Unlike DuBois and other black spokesmen, he opposed American involvement in World War I and was arrested for his criticism of U.S. policies. In the 1920s *The Messenger* and Randolph opposed Marcus Garvey, whom Randolph thought undemocratic. During that same decade young Randolph campaigned unsuccessfully for state office on the Socialist party ticket.

Randolph was also a leader in the labor movement for blacks. In 1925 he organized and became president of the Brotherhood of Sleeping Car Porters. This union, which gave porters new dignity, affiliated with the AFL in 1936 and the following year, after a long struggle, won wage increases from the Pullman Company.

Taking full advantage of New Deal legislation, Randolph pushed steadily for federal protection of blacks' rights to employment, threatening a march on Washington in 1941 in order to assure that they got wartime jobs. When Roosevelt responded with an executive order setting up the Federal Employment Practices Commission (FEPC), Randolph called off the march. During World War II he formed the League for Nonviolent Civil Disobedience Against Military Segregation, which was instrumental in pushing Harry Truman to order desegregation of the armed forces in 1948.

Randolph has continued to be a major force for black rights and in the American labor movement as well. He became a vice president of the AFL-CIO in 1957 and later served on that group's executive committee. Randolph also helped Martin Luther King, Jr., organize his famous March on Washington in 1963. ■

Japanese-Americans

During 1942 over 110,000 Americans of Japanese descent were evacuated from the West coast and herded into so-called relocation centers. Early enemy successes provided the impetus for this deplorable decision, but it is obvious that the federal government was responding to pressures from newspapers, politicians, and the public at large in the Far West, a region that long had resented Japanese residents. When the Justice Department declined to do the job, Roosevelt turned the matter over to the U.S. Army's Western Defense Command, which justified its action on the basis of "military necessity." The enormity of this injustice was compounded by failure of the Supreme Court in *Korematsu* v. *U.S.* (1944) to protect the rights of these individuals (two-thirds of them American citizens) and by the fact that later on most of them failed to regain prewar possessions and property. As a result, Japanese-Americans were the only socioeconomic group in the nation that did not prosper during World War II.

By September 1942, most all "evacuees" were in ten camps located in seven western states, each of which held up to 12,000 persons. The government, at the outset, had not expected to maintain these facilities throughout the war, and during 1943 began to devise various ways for those interned to depart. To get out, one had to prove loyalty to the United States of America, get a job away from the Pacific coast, and show that the community was willing to accept him as a resident. At the same time, somewhat strangely, the War Department registered all young males with a view toward enlistment. Eventually, some 8,000 internees decided to go to Japan and were permitted to do so, some having renounced U.S. citizenship in the face of such treatment.

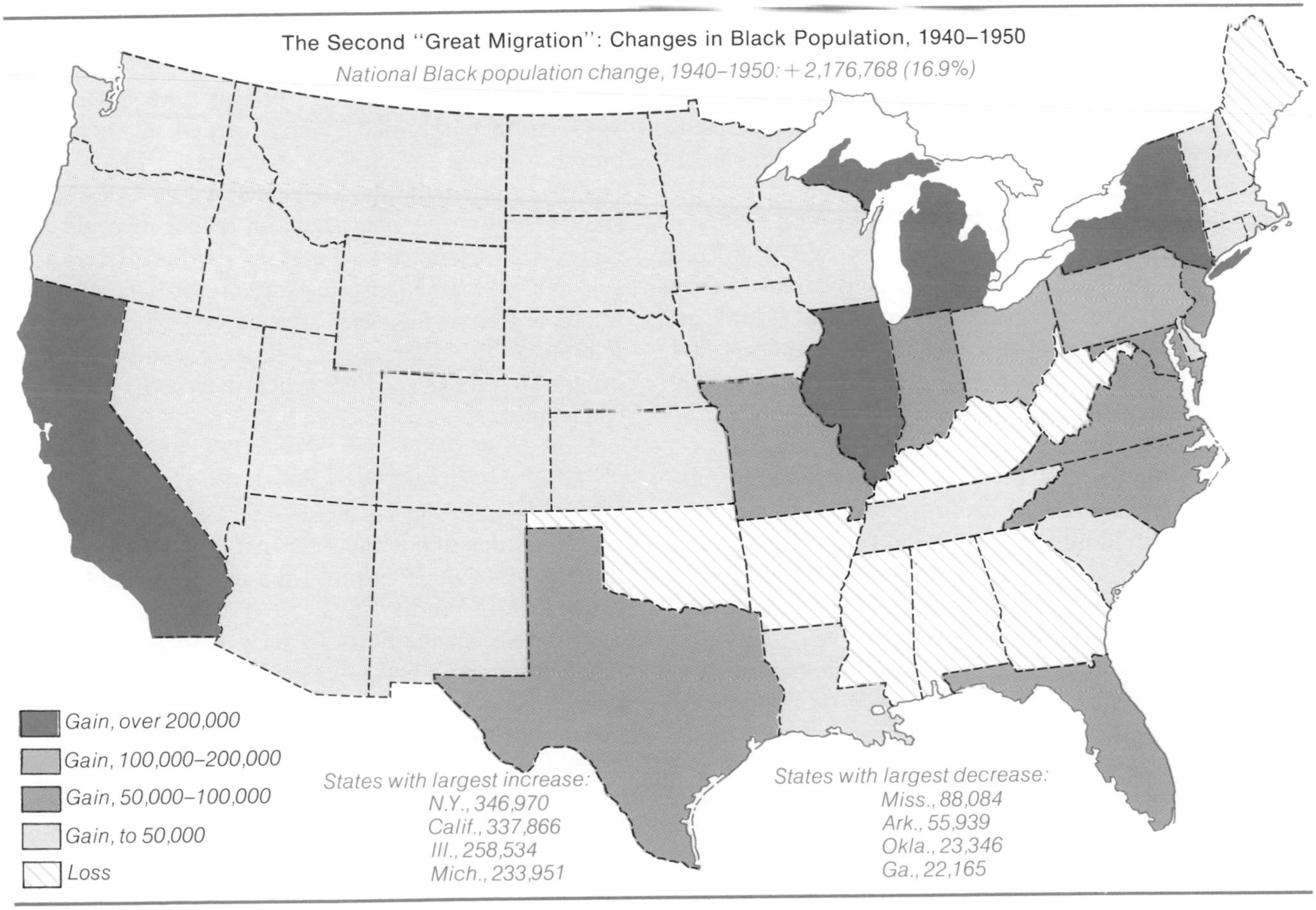

Library of Congress.

Japanese-Americans of all ages were evacuated from the West Coast in 1942; most of them were detained in relocation centers until 1944.

Library of Congress.

By the spring of 1944 the federal government realized there was no sound reason for continuing the detention camps; but, fearful of political repercussions in an election year, Roosevelt did nothing—until he carried the West and won his fourth term. On January 20, 1945, the Japanese-American relocation centers were ordered closed, and all but 5,000 evacuees considered security risks were free to go wherever they wished. However, things were not quite that simple. Many could not find homes and jobs and came back to camp, and by June 1945 the authorities were faced with the bizarre task of "forcing" the internees to leave.

The program cost the U.S. government $250 million; the Japanese-Americans lost income and property worth $350 million. Only about half of them initially returned to the Pacific coast states, but by 1960 70 percent of all Japanese-Americans (down from 88.5 percent in 1942) lived in that region.

These relocation centers, inspired by immediate fear and past prejudice, were not conceived or run by evil men, nor were they Nazi concentration camps. Yet widespread hysteria swept up many who should have known better. Respected political analyst Walter Lippmann (1889–1974) in February 1942 attacked "the Fifth Column" on the West coast and a year later California's new governor, Earl Warren (1891–1974), urged that the Japanese be permanently barred from his state. Yet early in 1945, as they returned, Warren urged all citizens to pursue a course "worthy of Americans." Much of the blame rests upon the shoulders of Franklin D. Roosevelt and his advisors. A bold stand on their part could have nipped this horrifying scheme in the bud. Even more culpable are the august justices of the United States Supreme Court who, long after any possible excuse for relocation had disappeared, chose to condone such a program by a vote of 6–3 when they had a chance to condemn it.

War and Civil Liberties

If one can push the Japanese-American tragedy to a far corner of the mind, then the nation's record of civil liberties was quite admirable in wartime, certainly much better than in World War I. Several factors account for these developments. Few Germans and Italians were recent immigrants, they often had sons and daughters in uniform, and, even before war erupted, Americans were making a distinction between the German and Italian peoples and their Fascist leaders. The scope of the war and the talk of a United Nations encouraged sympathy and understanding for foreigners whose assistance might well be needed. U.S. Communists, a noisy group on the far left that normally would have scorned any capitalistic struggle, were among the war's strongest backers after Hitler invaded Russia in June 1941.

With liberal elements eager and willing to support the war and cultural pluralism in vogue, this meant that those on the far right and anyone who opposed the fight (for whatever reasons) might feel the wrath of public opinion and federal authorities. Fear of sabotage and subversion was widespread, kept alive by wartime slogans and posters ("A slip of the lip may sink a ship"), although Roosevelt's interest in such matters seems now to have dated back to earlier days. Extremely sensitive to Communist activities and press criticism, as early as 1936 he instigated intelligence gathering by the FBI which later was expanded into a near witch hunt by the Dies Committee of the House.

Opposition to war was less common than in World War I, but the average American was no more tolerant of pacifism than he had been in 1917–1918. Ninety percent of those questioned during the war years were extremely critical of such views. The Selective Service held to a very narrow interpretation of a clause granting conscientious objector (CO) status to those who "by reason of religious training and belief" were opposed to war. As a result, some 5,500 young men, most of them Jehovah's Witnesses, were denied such a classification and ended up in jail where they often were badly treated.

Even those recognized as conscientious objectors fared poorly. Some 12,000 young Americans were sent to Civilian Public Service camps where, unlike draftees, they received no government pay, only whatever cooperating churches could give them. As a result of this treatment many eventually abandoned the camps and went to prison where they perfected the nonviolent resistance tactics so crucial to the civil rights movement of the 1950s and the antiwar protest of the 1960s.

In general, the Supreme Court, as was clear in the case of Japanese-Americans, chose not to interfere in civil rights matters. Most of the justices, led by Felix Frankfurter (1882–1965), felt that curtailment of rights did not mean their attrition; they could be restored once war was over. In June 1943 the Court, after much wrangling, spoke with one voice as it approved a curfew of Japanese-Americans on very narrow grounds, but eighteen months later, in December 1944, three justices questioned the entire detention program, terming the majority's ruling "a legalization of racism." Perhaps Frankfurter's views were valid; civil rights could be restored in full when peace came. Yet the question of how much damage is done in the process remains along with the haunting fear that some day peace might not bring a restoration of personal liberties vital to the concepts of democracy and individual freedom. Who knows, a Court that knuckles under to "military expediency" in war might bow to some other pressure in peacetime.

War and American Institutions

The presidency, the federal government, and the military and industrial communities changed considerably during World War II. Perhaps these elements of American society never will return to comfortable, old prewar days; and the same might be said of the nation that they either serve or dominate. Their final role at the moment is still not entirely clear.

Growth of Presidential Power

Franklin Roosevelt's authority, thanks to domestic and foreign crises, four successful election campaigns granting long-term incumbency, and his obvious gifts of leadership and persuasion, increased dramatically during World War II. Though, like Woodrow Wilson before him, FDR sought to have wartime powers sanctioned by Congress, he wanted them largely vague and unspecified. And, as usual, in the First and Second War Powers Acts of December 1941 and March 1942, the President had his way. No doubt exists, however, that he was prepared to use the war as an excuse to exert his will; and, on one occasion when asking for repeal of a farm parity provision in a price control measure, he told Congress that, if necessary, he would use his special powers to get what he wanted.

Both at home and abroad, and even within his own administration, Roosevelt always was a broker of sorts, playing one force off against another. Critics fumed about such disarray amid conflicting boards and agencies and feuding bureaucrats. What they failed to perceive was that FDR was primarily interested in dramatizing public goals, raising hopes and expectations, enunciating principles, harmonizing seemingly irreconcilable views, and, in the end, producing solid achievements of one kind or another. Careful, orderly management that might look good but not give desired results was not his way of operating. Roosevelt once told a friend that Treasury and

State were virtually impossible to deal with. Both seemed encrusted with age-old customs and resistant to change. Yet, nothing, he added, equalled the Navy. "The admirals are really something to cope with—and I should know. To change anything in the N-A-V-Y is like punching a feather bed. You punch it with your right and you punch it with your left until you are finally exhausted, and then you find the damn bed just as it was before you started punching."

Nevertheless, before his sudden death in April 1945, Roosevelt did a lot of "punching" and achieved many changes on the Washington scene. The result was an ever larger presidency with ever greater powers; some changes, such as the beginning of secret dossiers and security files, were somewhat ominous. FDR clearly laid the foundation stones of the "imperial" presidency of the 1960s and early 1970s, and his treatment of the office and its powers raises serious questions that cannot be answered. How does one reconcile democracy with the conduct of war—or, for that matter, with the demands of any crisis which an administration says entails "national security"?

Bipartisanship

Although the Republicans, many of them staunchly isolationist, fought Roosevelt and his party on lend-lease proposals and other measures leading up to all-out war, the first bomb that fell on Pearl Harbor took away most of their support, at least temporarily. Domestic issues suddenly seemed of little consequence, and everyone had to get behind "Dr. Win-the-War." However, this spirit did not last long; rationing, inflation, labor disputes, and wartime tensions gave the Republicans surprising strength in the 1942 elections. They ended up controlling half of the nation's governorships, won 42 new seats in the House and added nine in the Senate.

Bipartisanship in foreign affairs continued in 1942–1945 only because the Democrats accommodated to the new situation, as did the Republicans to some degree since the majority of voters seemed willing to accept the dualism of cooperation in foreign matters and competition and disagreement at home. In 1944 the Republicans ran on a strongly conservative platform, and FDR bowed to similar pressures in his own party, dumping Vice President Henry Wallace (1888–1965), a liberal.

This campaign, a strange affair in the midst of war and a true test of how democracy actually works under stress, saw Roosevelt's unprecedented bid for a fourth term. The Republicans, buoyed up by impressive gains in the 1942 congressional elections, spent much of their time making certain that Wendell Willkie, an avowed internationalist and now closely identified with the Democratic administration, did not get the nomination. When he ran poorly in the Wisconsin primary, Willkie dropped out of the race, leaving a clear field for Thomas E. Dewey (1902–1971), governor of New York.

Dewey, associated with the same international wing of the party as Willkie was in 1940 but not linked to FDR, was nominated on the first ballot with only one dissenting vote. His running mate was Ohio's John W. Bricker, a staunch conservative. Throughout the convention and the campaign, the Republicans loudly proclaimed their cooperation with the war effort, while at the same time leveling very partisan attacks at their political adversaries whom they accused of associating with radicals and "Reds." Ex-President Hoover even said the Communist party was trying to reelect Roosevelt and blamed the Russians for the rising tide of nationalism evident throughout the world.

Just a week before the Democrats met, Roosevelt indicated he would run. The real battle was over second place on the ticket. The President preferred to retain Henry A. Wallace as Vice President, but Wallace was much too liberal for many elements within the party. Somewhat reluctantly, FDR submitted two names to party leaders: Senator Harry S Truman of Missouri, who had gained prominence as head of a committee investigating government war contracts, and James F. Byrnes of South Carolina, once a member of the Supreme Court and now the very capable Director of the Office of War Mobilization. Fearing that Byrnes was both antiblack and antilabor, liberals quickly gave the nod to Truman, and even before the party balloted, the Roosevelt-Truman ticket was forged.

The campaign that ensued was not especially distinguished, for the minds of both FDR and the electorate were somewhere else much of the time. Dewey's charges of "tired old men" and federal government confusion were refuted by Roosevelt's occasional displays of oratorical vigor and military successes in both Europe and the Pacific. Although FDR's victory margin was the smallest in his four tries for the White House, he still won by 3,598,564 votes and an electoral count of 432–99. In the process, the Republicans lost eighteen House seats and some of the influence they had enjoyed during the previous two years.

The New Deal coalition held and Roosevelt won, but it was clear that Republican strength was on the upsurge in all sections except the South, which clung to its own brand of downhome Democratic conservatism. Of course, if the Republicans could somehow harness all of these antiliberal yearnings to their wagon they might be able to regain the White House once more. And it was no secret that a large segment of Republican party loyalists, never happy with bipartisanship in any form, would be quite willing to junk such wartime baggage as soon as peace came.

Toward the "Garrison State"

One of the most significant developments of World War II was formation of a network that later became known loosely as the "military-industrial complex." Although cooperation in defense planning and contracts between the armed services and U.S. manufacturers was evident in the 1920s and 1930s, only during the war years and after did this phenomenon become widespread and apparent to all Americans. During World War II, the federal government relied heavily upon "dollar-a-year" executives who ran agencies and boards as a patriotic gesture for the ridiculous annual salary indicated. In that capacity, they often tilted precious contracts in the "right" direction. The result was that the biggest companies, which admittedly had the know-how and capabilities to produce goods immediately, received the bulk of wartime business.

Also, because of the nature of the challenge, the scientific establishment joined hands with the military and industrial worlds to forge a new and seemingly all-powerful triumvirate. The most spectacular offspring of this union was the atomic bomb, but scientists, industrialists, and generals also produced radar-guided rockets, radio proximity fuses, amphibious tanks, and flame throwers fueled with napalm jelly and gasoline. The complexity of such weapons assured the rise of a permanent defense-oriented industry run by scientists and manufacturers. At the same time, worldwide responsibilities and superpower status meant that for the first time in its history the United States of America would have a large, peacetime military-naval-air arm ready to use those weapons. This intermingling of science, industry, and military services—along with academic laboratories as well—created innumerable ties and associations strengthened by both contacts and contracts that would become a permanent feature of the postwar world.

For anyone born since 1945, names such as Hitler, Roosevelt, Churchill, and the battles of Europe and the Pacific during World War II are almost as remote as Napoleon, Lee, and Grant or Jena, Bull Run, and Gettysburg. Yet that conflict shaped their lives much more dramatically than almost any event that preceded it. Washington, D.C.—resplendent with presidential power, scores of boards and agencies, tax forms, FBI and CIA secrecy and intrigue, and miles of seemingly endless red tape—has become an integral part of every American's daily life. Before 1940 only a minority of U.S. citizens had to file federal income taxes each year, rarely did one see a soldier in uniform unless he lived close by a military post, and one's world might well be centered upon the county seat or at best the state capital. Five years later millions of Americans were paying federal taxes, they had become accustomed to seeing thousands of their fellow citizens in uniforms (some of them with black skins, some of them wearing skirts), and they were becoming increasingly familiar with the names of exotic, faraway places. World War II was a "watershed" of staggering proportions with socioeconomic implications that would be revealed in their entirety only in the postwar decades.

Essay

The Beginning of the Atomic Age

Few months in recent history have encompassed so much drama as the 180 days between March and September 1945. A war in which millions died came to a sudden, cataclysmic conclusion, a handful of victorious leaders met to argue about peacetime policies and split up the spoils, and in an instant an awesome, fearful future became reality in the skies over southern Japan. Rarely has peace come with such ominous warning. Probably no other event in the twentieth century will divide its decades more neatly into two different eras—B.B., before the bomb, A.B., after the bomb—than that explosion at Hiroshima, a city of some 350,000 inhabitants, early on the morning of August 6, 1945.

The bomb, a uranium creation known as "Little Boy," destroyed almost everything within a radius of some 8,000 feet of the blast and killed 71,000 people. Many more later died of injuries and the effects of radiation. Almost 98 percent of the city's buildings were destroyed or seriously damaged. Three days later a plutonium bomb, nicknamed "Fat Man," was dropped on Nagasaki with similar results.

This devastation, wrought by Americans who consider themselves to be a humane, God-fearing people, not only ushered in the Atomic Age and a peace of sorts, it also precipitated loud debate over the necessity of these unprecedented explosions and the wisdom of policies that led to such widespread death and destruction. How had it all come about? Who had developed two bombs that could snuff out 150,000 lives with the snap of a finger? Why?

Two Hungarian refugee scientists, fearful of German research, provided the immediate impetus for the development of atomic energy in the United States when, in 1939, they persuaded Albert Einstein to sign a letter to President Roosevelt. In this message they argued for immediate action, but nothing much happened for over two years. Then, in August 1942 the War Department began its famed Manhattan Project, which, in time, spent $2 billion and employed some 150,000 people in huge plants in Oak Ridge, Tennessee, and Hanford, Washington, and at much smaller research laboratories at the University of Chicago and Los Alamos, New Mexico.

Even before the first bomb was tested secretly (and successfully) on July 16, 1945, many who knew what was going on were having second thoughts. Once the genie was out of the bottle, how would it be controlled? What effect would use of this awesome power by one nation have upon its postwar relations

Official U.S. Air Force Photo.

The atomic bomb, a grim novelty in 1945, soon became a grim permanent presence.

with both its allies and former adversaries?

To understand why President Truman and his advisors finally decided to deploy these two bombs against Japan, it is very important to get some idea of the sequence of events during these weeks and months. Here is a brief chronology that shows how U.S. policy evolved in 1945.

February 4–11	Yalta Conference. Russia agrees to enter war against Japan within three months after Germany surrenders.
April 12	Roosevelt dies and Harry S Truman, until then unaware of the atomic project, becomes President.
May 8	War ends in Europe. (V-E Day).
May 9	Interim Committee charged with advising Truman on development and use of atomic weapons meets for first time.
June 1	Interim Committee recommends dropping bombs on "dual targets" in Japan as soon as possible and without warning.
July 12	Japanese ambassador in Moscow, upon instructions from his home government, seeks Russian mediation to end war.
July 16	First atomic bomb tested successfully near Alamogordo, New Mexico.

July 17	Potsdam Conference opens.
July 24	Truman informs Stalin that the United States has developed "a new weapon of unusual destructive force." On that same day the President approves dropping the first bomb on Japan on August 3 or as soon as weather will permit after that date.
July 26	Powers at Potsdam call for Japan to surrender unconditionally or face "prompt and utter destruction." The so-called Potsdam Declaration does not mention the atomic bomb specifically nor assure the Japanese that they can retain their emperor (a key point), although they are told that ultimately they will be able to choose their own form of government.
July 28	Japanese premier dismisses the Declaration as "unworthy of public notice."
August 6	"Little Boy" dropped on Hiroshima.
August 8	Russia declares war on Japan.
August 9	"Fat Man" dropped on Nagasaki.
August 10	Japanese cabinet agrees to Potsdam peace terms if emperor can be retained as titular head of state.
August 11	U.S. reply implicitly recognizes status of emperor.
August 14	Japan accepts U.S. terms.
August 15	Despite last minute attempts by military diehards to thwart the emperor's plans, he goes on radio for the first time in his reign and tells Japanese people of surrender.
September 2	Formal surrender terms signed aboard *USS Missouri* in Tokyo Bay.

Official U.S. Air Force Photo.

Hiroshima—shortly after the atomic bomb was dropped.

To this rather stark list of events, several facts must be added. By July 1945, U.S. forces had completed a very costly conquest of Okinawa, the last island stepping stone leading to the Japanese homeland. Allied troops planned to invade the southernmost island of Kyushu on November 1.

In mid-July the Japanese army still had an estimated five million men under arms, about two million of them based in Japan itself. Although the navy, for all practical purposes, had ceased to exist, the air force had an estimated 5,000 Kamikaze (suicide) planes, a desperate form of warfare used with outstanding success during the Okinawa campaign. Thus the invasion planned for November 1 faced a considerable land force and, had it taken place, the death toll of both defenders and invaders might well have been awesome.

The atomic explosions that leveled Hiroshima and Nagasaki, cities crammed with military installations vital to the defense of Japan, certainly are to be deplored and since 1945 many individuals have attacked the U.S. decision to use atomic power against a wartime enemy. Some of these spokesmen, such as Hanson Baldwin, military analyst for the *New York Times,* have impeccable credentials. The arguments of others, however, often are rooted deep in hindsight, concern over the Cold War that developed in the wake of World War II, and anti-U.S. sentiment.

Library of Congress.

Hiroshima—a year after the bomb.

Pushing aside for the moment moral arguments, whether the bombs increased or decreased casualties, and what happened after August 1945, one might look instead at the wartime situation confronting Allied leaders as that month began. True, the Japanese now were fighting alone, but they possessed substantial resources and, from all indications, intended to fight to the bitter end as they had done throughout much of the western Pacific. Although the Japanese cabinet *seemed* to be leaning toward a negotiated peace of some sort, the premier said publicly that the Potsdam Declaration was ''unworthy of public notice.'' It was now known he was treading a knife edge between one group struggling desperately to end the war and another determined to fight on. Early in August 1945, no Allied statesman or general could be certain just what was going on as enemy leaders debated war and peace.

These atomic blasts, which actually snuffed out fewer lives than conventional fire bomb attacks that were being carried out over Tokyo at about the same time, must be viewed in context as weapons one wartime opponent used against another in order to gain an advantage. That they ended a great war rather promptly cannot be disputed. Neither can one doubt the tremendous psychological advantage they bestowed upon the Allies; yet, even as the smoke cleared from Japan's skies, controversy concerning what had happened was well underway and has continued unabated to the present day.

Selected Readings

American Military and Diplomatic Involvement in World War II

A. Russell Buchanan, *The United States and World War II* (2 vols, 1964)

James M. Burns, *Roosevelt: Soldier of Freedom* (1970)

Robert A. Divine, *Roosevelt and World War II* (1969)

Ralph B. Levering, *American Opinion and the Russian Alliance, 1939-1943* (1976)

Stephen A. Ambrose, *Eisenhower and Berlin, 1945: The Decision to Halt at the Elbe* (1967)

Gaddis Smith, *American Diplomacy During the Second World War, 1941-1945* (1969)

John L. Gaddis, *The United States and the Origins of the Cold War, 1941-1947* (1972)

Gar Alperovitz, *Atomic Diplomacy—Hiroshima and Potsdam: The Use of the Atomic Bomb and the American Confrontation with Soviet Power* (1967)

Martin J. Sherwin, *A World Destroyed: The Atomic Bomb and the Grand Alliance* (1975)

American Society During the War: General Accounts

John M. Blum, *V Was for Victory: Politics and American Culture During World War II* (1976)

Richard Lingeman, *Don't You Know There's a War On? The American Home Front, 1941-1945* (1970)

Richard Polenberg, *War and Society: The United States, 1941-1945* (1972)

Minorities and Rights During Wartime

Roger Daniels, *Concentration Camps, U.S.A.: Japanese Americans and World War II* (1972)

Paul L. Murphy, *The Constitution in Crisis Times, 1918-1969* (1972)

Lawrence S. Wittner. *Rebels Against War: The American Peace Movement, 1941-1960* (1969)

Jacobus Ten Broek, Edward Barnhart, and Floyd W. Matson, *Prejudice, War, and the Constitution* (1958)

Herbert Garfinkel, *When Negroes March* (1959)

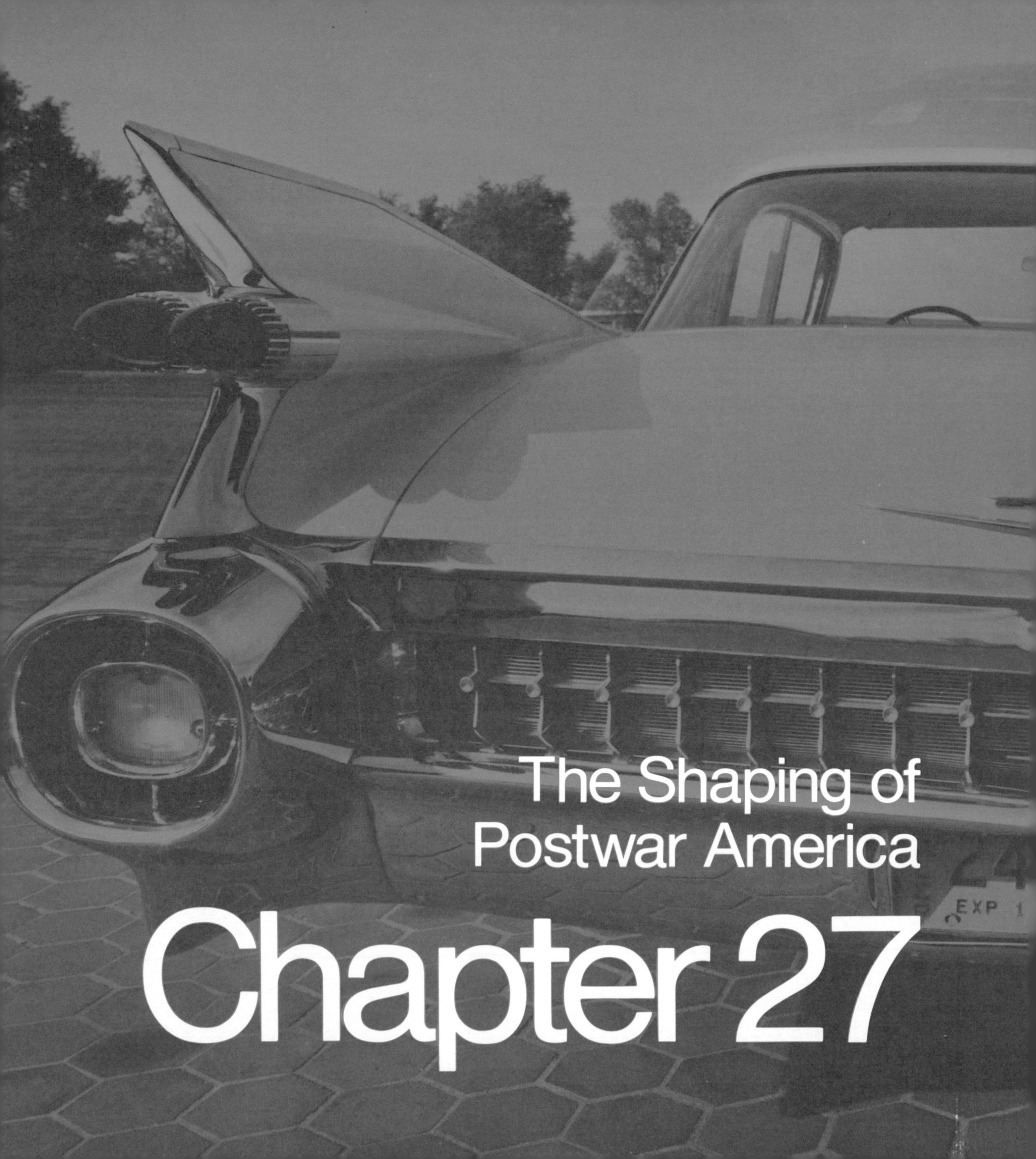

Chapter 27

The Shaping of Postwar America

TIMELINE

1944
Congress enacts the GI Bill of Rights to provide veteran benefits
1945
Truman becomes President on the death of Roosevelt
1945
Truman proposes a twenty-one-point domestic program later called the "Fair Deal"
May 1946
Truman proposes a law to draft strikers who endanger the national security
July 1946
Price controls from World War II abruptly end
November 1946
Republicans win a landslide victory in congressional elections
August 1946
Atomic Energy Act places atomic power in civilian hands
1947
Congress approves Taft-Hartley Act to limit the power of organized labor
February 1948
Truman proposes civil rights legislation
June 1948
Truman orders desegregation of federal employment
November 1948
Truman wins an unexpected victory over Thomas E. Dewey in presidential election
1951
Univac I becomes the first commercially available computer
1952
Dwight D. Eisenhower and Richard M. Nixon elected President and Vice President
1953
The Department of Health, Education and Welfare is created
1954
In *Brown v. Topeka Board of Education* the Supreme Court declares "separate but equal" schools unconstitutional
1955
Elvis Presley records "Blue Suede Shoes," "Heartbreak Hotel," and "Hound Dog"
1955
Dr. Martin Luther King, Jr. directs Montgomery boycott
1956
Federal Highway Act authorizes the construction of 41,000 miles of interstate highways
1956
Eisenhower wins second term as President
1957
Federal troops force integration of Little Rock Central High School
1960
John F. Kennedy narrowly defeats Richard M. Nixon in presidential election

CHAPTER OUTLINE

The experience of World War II brought great prosperity, interrupted New Deal social reform programs, precipitated a vast migration, and raised serious questions concerning the future role of women and blacks in American life. Above all else, it created a much expanded economy that was allowed to run free and unfettered because it was producing the goods that brought victory over the Axis. Just how these forces should be harnessed for maximum benefit in peacetime was the major challenge of postwar years. Not surprisingly, the mood of the public was a mixture of optimism born of victory and impatience arising from a liberal-conservative standoff over what economic and political courses were to be followed.

By 1960, after considerable groping and some confrontation, postwar America was assuming a distinctive, recognizable shape. Truman accomplished little in his attempts to revive New Deal programs (which he called his "Fair Deal"), but he held the advocates of a return to "normalcy" at bay. And those who felt as he did continued this "holding pattern" during the Eisenhower years with considerable success. Thus the United States entered the 1960s with the Roosevelt reforms intact, a firm foundation upon which to build.

Major social trends such as a population explosion and a continuing flight of millions to suburbs gave this decade and a half much of its unique flavor. The demands of upwardly mobile suburbia created a mass-consumption society with more and more of the consuming being done by the young, a segment of the overall population growing by leaps and bounds. Those producing the baby boom often commuted to work in offices run by massive corporations and by various levels of government—local, state, and federal—all of which were becoming increasingly interdependent.

This new corporate-government world solved some economic and social problems of the 1930s and the war years such as unemployment and shortages, yet it spawned new dilemmas as well. Whites who fled from established cities to growing suburbs took their leadership, experience, and money with them, leaving behind a decaying urban core increasingly filled with minorities unable to pay the taxes that were needed to maintain essential services. A strongly youth-centered society aroused both pressures and expectations for all family members. And high rates of production and consumption disguised fundamental defects in the emerging postwar economy as producers used both capital and know-how in frivolous "quick-buck" enterprises often extremely detrimental to the environment.

Tension, conflict, and even another war dominated the Truman years, but the Eisenhower era ushered in a kind of quiescence that America badly needed. At the same time, voters demonstrated a strange ambivalence. As a whole, they rewarded and praised Eisenhower's conservatism by voting for him; at the same time, some economic and social groups pressed ever harder for change. The byproduct of this interplay was the election of Democratic congresses, which were more attuned than the President to demands for new approaches and programs. It was almost as if the general public was intentionally checking both Congress and the chief executive by balancing control of the federal government. By 1960 the electorate clearly was on the side of Capitol Hill: it was time to energize the New Deal and move forward. John F. Kennedy became the spokesman for these forces and the period of inaction was at an end.

Reconversion—Political and Economic

Although Americans should have been prepared for the death of Franklin D. Roosevelt, sudden as it was, they clearly were not ready to accept a virtually unknown entity in his place. FDR, the august, jovial Hudson River squire, a father figure who occupied the White House for over a dozen years, cheered them up during the Depression, gave them jobs and food, and led them to the very brink of victory in the greatest war the world had ever seen. Now he was gone and in his place stood a twangy mid-westerner, Harry S Truman, who wore thick glasses and seemed the antithesis of his patrician, wise, confident, and seemingly all-powerful predecessor.

The Changing of the Guard

It is difficult to say which of three events in 1945—the death of Roosevelt, the Allied victory in Europe, or the exploding of atomic bombs over Hiroshima and Nagasaki—separated most clearly one era from another; but since all three occurred within a few months, it now makes little real difference. While those in uniform or overseas undoubtedly were more impressed by the onrush of peace, civilian America probably viewed the passing of the presidential mantle from Roosevelt to Truman as the beginning of a new age. A question everyone had to deal with was what sort of man was this ex-haberdasher who dared to follow in the wake of greatness.

Truman, born in a border state in 1884, grew to political maturity amid the Progressivism of William Jennings Bryan and Woodrow Wilson. In his rise to a seat in the U.S. Senate in 1934, he had rubbed shoulders with all of the diverse elements that made up the Democratic party: small town politicos, urban machine bosses, city minority groups, labor leaders, and civic reformers. He won a solid reputation for honesty and efficiency as a county administrator, worked closely with New Deal programs at the state level, and finally translated all of these contacts into votes. In addition, his border state heritage made him satisfactory to the South, a key element in the Democratic party.

During his first term in the Senate he was a liberal crusader. As was customary, he said little and stuck to committee work. His two major speeches did little to shed light upon his intellect and personality. In one he spoke out very forcefully against the great power of corporate interests; in the other he vehemently attacked the reappointment to a federal post of an enemy of Kansas City's corrupt Pendergast machine, which had done much to advance his own career. Despite Harry Truman's pro-New Deal stance, the White House backed his opponent, Governor Lloyd Stark, in the 1940 senatorial election. The man from Independence fought back and with the aid of black and labor votes won a second term. His work as chairman of an important wartime committee designated to probe government contracts with the business world gained the approval of liberals, as did his interest in planning for peacetime reconversion. Nevertheless, approval did not mean wholehearted support, and in the campaign of 1944 the darling of liberal groups was still Henry Wallace, not the man who replaced him on the ticket.

So, when Truman put his hand on a Bible and swore to uphold the Constitution, both liberals and conservatives were wary. He was a New Dealer who had been influenced by a midwestern Progressive heritage, but he was no intellectual—only a shrewd political animal who had aligned himself with the right groups at the right time: in Missouri, the Pendergast machine, rural courthouse cliques, labor, and blacks; in Washington, the Senate establishment and the New Deal. As Vice President he was not privy to the inner workings of the Roosevelt White House and knew virtually nothing more than the general public knew about foreign and domestic affairs. A typical reaction to news of FDR's death was, "My God, now Truman's President!" Truman himself was overwhelmed by his new responsibilities, and because of his background, fears of inadequacy, and unfamiliarity with the reins of power, hid his feelings in a mix of bluster and belligerence. But within a few months he had replaced Roosevelt's appointees with his own men and was beginning to put his stamp upon a crucial period in American history. For better or worse, a new political era had begun.

Truman Library Collection.

At the 1936 Democratic Convention Truman chats with party leaders. Thomas J. Pendergast, head of the infamous Kansas City machine, is next to Truman; James A. Farley is second from right.

The Postwar Economy

Conversion to peacetime pursuits is a difficult task, much more so than transition from peace to war. When girding for a fight, national leaders can evoke patriotism, national honor, and sacrifice and be certain of a ready response. Also, those donning uniforms are being corralled by a single employer, Uncle Sam. But no such unity of purpose is evident when dismantling a war machine. Millions rush about trying to find a comfortable slot in the emerging milieu, at the same time determined to retain recent social, economic, and political gains. They also often push for even greater benefits, which, in their opinion, wartime curbs on prices and wages have denied them. The first months of peace often tend to bring out the most selfish traits, and 1945–1946 was no exception.

Americans should have learned something from 1919–1920 and perhaps they did—the cruel race riots of that era were not repeated; yet, despite planning dating back to 1943 and President Truman's sincere attempt to convert gradually to peacetime, public pressure for immediate change was too great. Demobilization of the armed forces, for example, became a rout. Veterans' groups, wives with their "Bring Back Daddy" clubs, and even mass demonstrations by GIs themselves made a shambles of any efforts at an orderly transition. In 1945 the nation had twelve million men in uniform, a year later, three million, and in mid-1948, one-half that number. In the early months of 1946, Truman observed that the process was "no longer demobilization . . . it was disintegration."

This rush to discard khaki had tremendous domestic repercussions. Through the Servicemen's Readjustment Act (GI Bill of Rights) passed in 1944, the government had developed a broad program of veterans' benefits to cushion the shock, including money for education, hospitalization, home and farm loan guarantees, employment information services, and unemployment compensation. It worked quite well and, coupled with general prosperity, kept veterans relatively content. By 1955, for example, approximately half of all World War II veterans had used their education benefits. This eased pressures on the job market somewhat, gave higher education a badly needed shot in the arm, and provided advanced training for millions. At the same time, this program fostered upward social mobility and created increased expectations for the purchase of consumer goods, factors that in turn, aided the economy. During the same decade about 25 percent of all World War II veterans used loan guarantees to secure homes, most of them located in sprawling suburbs. The so-called "GI Bill," designed to prevent a repetition of the chaos of 1919–1920, more than achieved its varied goals. A major piece of social legislation, it touched and changed the lives of millions even as the headlong race to resume civilian ways accelerated.

Wide World.

Returning servicemen were greeted with enthusiasm in 1945 and 1946.

On September 1, 1945, the President called Congress into special session and submitted a 16,000-word message (one of the longest in history) detailing a twenty-one-point program for domestic legislation. It called for the extension of many wartime powers to ease the transition to peace, the construction of more new homes (fifteen million in ten years), an increase in the hourly minimum wage from 40 cents to 65 cents, reduction in tax levels, and a boost in congressional pay from $12,500 to $20,000 per year. Republicans and most business leaders howled in protest, claiming that Truman was trying "to outdeal the New Deal." However, this anguish was both premature and unnecessary. The President soon got caught up in other matters and failed to push any of these wide-ranging proposals with much vigor, although a few years later this same package would emerge as the Fair Deal.

Major problems facing the administration were the pace of events, which it could not really control, and the collapse of plans for gradual demobilization, which was a pattern repeated throughout the economy. Truman strove to be a hard-liner on retaining price controls during his first months in office, but he soon gave in to the wishes of steel manufacturers, farmers, and meatpackers. Consumers grumbled loudly and talked of organizing buyers' strikes, but failed to do so. Actually, he and his advisors had no other choice. Millions of consumers, greenbacks clinched in their fists, were willing to pay $5 for a pair of nylons worth $1.98, $20 for a recapped auto tire, and $100 "under the table" to get a $75 per month apartment. Republican congressmen sensed a wave of protest that might take them to victory, and even the President's closest associates in government advocated and carried out conflicting policies.

For all practical purposes, and over Truman's objections, price controls and the Office of Price Administration (OPA) virtually ended on July 1, 1946. Veal cutlets quickly went from 59 cents to 95 cents a pound in New York, and milk rose from 16 cents to 20 cents a quart. Then it was the consumers' turn to protest, and Congress hurriedly patched together a flimsy substitute bill, which, as one observer commented, did not provide the authority to control prices, only to decontrol them officially. Efforts to restore controls on the prices of meat, soybeans, and cottonseed oil in August 1946 met stiff resistance. Many restaurants ignored the new rules, and—more important—John L. Lewis said his miners would dig no more coal unless the meat regulations were lifted. Prodded by the political reality that "meatless voters are opposition voters," the administration gave up. Early in October, Truman held his largest press conference since the war ended and then addressed the largest American radio audience (forty-four million) since Roosevelt spoke to the nation when hostilities began. On both occasions his subject was the end of price controls on meat.

Wide World.

When the Office of Price Administration was unable to stop soaring prices in 1946, an irate public protested. Consumer demonstrations like this one in Trenton, New Jersey, were common.

Truman clearly lost the battle to restrain prices, yet in a sense he won the war. Two years later, as he stumped the country in his campaign to remain at 1600 Pennsylvania Avenue, the plain people of America knew what Truman was talking about when he spoke forcefully of his unsuccessful struggle to continue price controls and stop inflation.

For reasons not entirely clear, Truman was much less flexible on wages. Perhaps, having begun to knuckle under to demands to decontrol prices or possessing a residual probusiness outlook, he decided to make a stand on wages. In any case, the result was a rash of major strikes, dramatic confrontations between the White House and labor leaders (somewhat ironic considering how much the President needed their support), and widespread unrest that limited production. Inflationary trends increased even more than during the first twelve months of peace.

It was Truman's fate to be at the vortex of a determined effort by business titans to check the rise of organized labor once and for all. Late in 1945 a select group representing steel, motors, food processing, and the electrical industry met secretly in New York with Ira Mosher, the head of the National Association of Manufacturers. They pledged to fight labor's rising demand for a bigger share of the economic pie and to thwart further unionization, which had grown dramatically under the provisions of the Wagner Act of 1935. The nub of the question was whether management could raise prices to cover higher wages. Management said yes; the government, with OPA then still operative, said no, noting that wartime profits were adequate to meet any "reasonable" salary adjustments.

As tempers reached the boiling point, labor had one great advantage. Since wartime restrictions on strikes had expired, walkouts were legal; management, however, still was bound by price ceilings. During the first weeks of 1946 some two million workers were out on strike in Detroit, Chicago, and St. Louis as steel, auto, meatpacking, and electrical workers battled police, overturned cars, and smashed windows.

Then, in April and May, Truman faced a showdown with railroad workers and coal miners who also wanted to strike for higher wages. When negotiations bogged down, the President bluntly told two veteran railroad union executives, Alvanley Johnston (1875-1951) of the Brotherhood of Locomotive Engineers and A. F. Whitney (1873-1949), president of the Brotherhood of Railroad Trainmen since 1928, that if they thought he would sit still and let them tie up the whole country they were "crazy as hell." Truman's first reaction was to go over their heads to the public with a stinging rebuke in which he would name names and accuse his adversaries of being "Commie-leaning" traitors who had tried to sabotage the war effort and were now using the same tactics in time of peace. Fortunately, cooler heads prevailed and the President's radio address on May 17, 1946, was a sober appeal to reason tinged with obvious indignation. The next week, with talks still going on, Truman went before Congress to seek the right to draft strikers who endangered national security, but in the midst of his speech he received a note that the railroad impasse was broken. The lawmakers cheered, Truman finished speaking, and hasty plans to put strikers into uniform were soon forgotten. For the moment, however, the President was labor's number one enemy. Whitney vowed to spend $47 million (all the money his union had in its treasury) to defeat Truman in 1948; but, when it came time to campaign, he was back in Truman's corner once more. This brinkmanship brought the President substantial dividends. His actions in 1946 may have been intemperate and his proposed solution unconstitutional, but he did avert a major catastrophe and showed the "give 'em hell" spirit that would bring him success two years later.

Even as Truman was standing toe to toe with the railroad workers a crisis was building with John L. Lewis and coal miners. Unlike Whitney and Johnston, Lewis enjoyed the complete backing of the industrial sector he represented, the independent United Mine Workers; and, after months of feuding over wage demands and welfare benefits, 400,000 miners quit at the end of March 1946. This action was not felt immediately because of a thirty-day supply of coal above ground. In early May, as those stockpiles disappeared, pressure on Truman mounted. On May 9, the *New York Sun* said it was time for the nation "to talk turkey" to both the administration and the Congress. "The President has dodged and hedged and shilly-shallied with the problem of industrial unrest. What he has actually done about it can be summed up in one word—nothing." Finally, on May 21 Truman ordered the government to seize and operate the mines. A week later his Secretary of the Interior signed a contract with Lewis granting his union much of what it was seeking.

Five months went by and then, in a power play designed to gain supremacy over his rivals in the American Federation of Labor (AFL) and the Congress of Industrial Organizations (CIO), Lewis announced he was displeased with vacation pay provisions in the contract and wanted to reopen bargaining procedures once more. The government refused and on November 18—two

U.P.I.

John L. Lewis leaving court after being fined for refusing to end the UMW strike in the fall of 1946.

days before the miners were to walk out again—Truman obtained a temporary injunction restraining Lewis and his union. The miners quit anyway.

Lewis and the union were soon cited for contempt of court and convicted. The membership was fined $3.5 million and Lewis, $10,000, the stiffest penalties ever imposed in a labor contempt case to that time. Lewis and his lawyers thundered defiance and began plans to take the matter to the Supreme Court. Then, some four or five hours before President Truman planned to make a personal appeal to the miners to return to work, Lewis called a press conference and capitulated. In somber tones he lambasted the administration's "yellow-dog" injunctions before the courts but then said that judges deliberating such weighty matters should be free from "the hysteria of an economic crisis." Therefore, he continued, "all mines in all districts will resume production of coal immediately." The President, although his party had been badly bruised in the congressional elections a few weeks before, had prevailed.

Earlier in the wake of widespread industrial unrest, both Congress and the President had agreed that new legislation was necessary to control work stoppages. In December 1945 Truman had submitted his ideas on reform in labor-management relations to Capitol Hill. What the President apparently wanted, in his pragmatic, uncomplicated way, was some basic machinery that would weigh the arguments of both sides. He did not think labor should lose any of its hard-won rights; instead, strong rules to settle disputes should be laid down and, if necessary, the White House should enforce these rules. Congress thought differently and tried to enact tougher legislation in the Case Bill (June 1946), which Truman vetoed. But a year later, the Congress overrode his veto of another bill, the Taft-Hartley Act, which empowered the President to force a union to accept a sixty-day "cooling off" period before walking out. Then, if the dispute was not resolved, management's last offer would be put to a secret vote by all members. This act also banned closed shops, prohibited union contributions to political campaigns, required unions to make public their financial records, compelled union leaders to take oaths that they were not Communists, permitted management to sue unions for strike damage and broken contracts, and curtailed collection of union dues by employers. To the public at large, this measure seemed designed to do something about work stoppages in time of crisis—an issue Truman himself had stressed; to organized labor, however, it hit at various basic rights that had been enjoyed as a result of New Deal legislation.

Paramount among these rights was the closed shop, one in which an employer agreed to hire only union members as opposed to a "union" shop where nonunion members could be employed temporarily pending application for membership. The Taft-Hartley Act, to the distress of organized labor, opened the door to so-called "right-to-work" laws and within a decade nineteen states had enacted such legislation. In essence, these statutes stipulated that no one shall be denied the right to work because of membership or nonmembership in a labor union; that is, union membership may not be a condition for either getting or holding a job.

The problems that Harry Truman, Congress, employers, organized labor, farmers, workers—in fact all America were trying to deal with—were enormous. Between 1940 and 1945 the nation spent more than $300 billion on war; the gross national product (total of all goods and services) jumped from an annual rate of $99.7 billion (1940) to $211.9 billion (1945). In 1944, U.S. factories produced nearly 100,000 planes and only 70,000 passenger cars; in 1949 the trend was reversed: 3,700,000 cars and 6,000 planes. Average weekly earnings had almost doubled in the war years, from $24.80 to $44.39, and the forty-eight-hour week was standard. At war's end, thanks to rationing and price controls, Americans had $136.4 billion in savings and bonds, some of which they were determined to spend as quickly as possible.

As Truman's vacillating efforts to hold the line on wages and prices failed, the cost of living index, which normally fluctuated a couple of points a year, leaped from 76.9 at the end of 1945 to 83.4 a year later, soaring to 102.8 by 1948. Each price increase spawned new wage demands. Strikes, slowdowns, spiralling living costs, and shortages all tended to make the man in the White House the scapegoat. He had won a few victories, though, including passage in 1946 of an Employment Act that revitalized the machinery for economic planning (theoretically committing the government to full employment).

Truman also had taken substantial steps toward the unification of the armed forces and reorganization of the executive branch of government. The Atomic Energy Commission, created on the final day of 1946 by the Atomic Energy Act, put atomic power in the hands of a civilian body that would direct its use. David Lilienthal

(1899-   ), an experienced reformer-administrator who long had been associated with the Tennessee Valley Authority, was the first man to head up this organization. At the outset, all fissionable materials and most facilities producing and using them were government owned; however, in ensuing decades these restrictions were diluted somewhat to permit private ownership of nuclear fuels. The National Security Act (1947), in theory at least, united the U.S. Army, Navy, and Air Force into a new Department of Defense. This move was prompted by an obvious lack of interservice cooperation on the eve of the Pearl Harbor disaster and a duplication of activities fostered by war itself. The first man who tried to ride herd on this merger (which admirals and generals tried to prevent) was James V. Forrestal (1892-1949). Ironically, as Secretary of the Navy from 1944 to 1947, Forrestal initially was in the opposition camp, but once Truman decided to act, he gave the unification plan his full support. This was, however, a battle that exacted a high price. In March 1949, Forrestal resigned because of nervous exhaustion and a few weeks later committed suicide by jumping to his death from a hospital window.

Postwar Politics

To the average voter, the key problem was soaring prices, not atomic power, economic planning, and reorganization of government. In mid-1946 the Republicans hit upon a dramatic campaign slogan: "Had Enough?" And, on November 5, when the smoke cleared, they had picked up 11 seats in the Senate and 54 in the House. For the first time in sixteen years the party of Lincoln, Grant, and Hoover controlled Congress. Democratic machines in Chicago, Jersey City, and Detroit crumbled under the weight of consumer protests, unable to control their rank and file. Governor Thomas E. Dewey, the Republican presidential candidate in 1944, and his party carried New York City for the first time since 1926. The future looked so bleak for "Harry the Bungler," now viewed merely as a caretaker president, that Senator J. William Fulbright (1905-   ), a first term Democrat from Arkansas, suggested that Truman step aside and let a Republican successor take over.

Nevertheless, despite a tendency at the time to see the verdict of November 1946 as a repudiation of liberal New Deal policies and programs, it was merely a specific reaction to Truman's vacillation. He had shown spunk and spirit, which was admired, but also evinced a stop-go, yes-no approach to consumer-oriented issues, which was not. What the voter wanted was not an unraveling of the New Deal but an end to rampant inflation and constant friction on the domestic front (and perhaps an end to the emerging Cold War as well). The Republicans themselves may have misread the results of that November election; certainly some of them, in their eagerness to dismantle the New Deal, made that mistake.

Harry Truman, his prestige and leadership at a low ebb, had two more years in the White House and no place to go but up. He became both more accommodating and more tenacious, sincere in the belief that, as he once observed, "Any good politician with nerve and a program that is right can win in the face of the stiffest opposition." Having said that, Truman, a sturdy politician, set out to find the right program. In January 1947 he reiterated his Twenty-one Points that he had unveiled in September 1945, which he had not yet pushed very hard. Now the tone was milder, and much conciliation was evident. The administration obviously had been staggered by defeat.

Then, sometime in mid-1947 the White House mood changed as Truman concluded that his point-by-point extension and continuation of the New Deal was both good policy and good politics. His vetoes—there would be eighty of them in 1947-1948—began to strike a familiar theme: defense of the national interest and the poor against a heartless, rich, Republican Congress. By January 1948 there were many signs that Truman was gaining support out in the hinterlands, if not on Capitol Hill, and it was a more confident President who spoke to the Eightieth Congress as it commenced its second session, enunciating clearly all of the liberal issues buried in rhetoric twelve months earlier.

What Truman was doing was preparing the ground for the fall campaign. By asking for more than he knew the Republicans would give him, the President was building up his image as a vigilant liberal leader protecting the rights of the average citizen. At the same time, unwittingly perhaps, he was stirring expectations that within a decade or so would have to be dealt with. Throughout the winter and spring of 1948, Truman, assisted by a group of able advisors (Clark Clifford, Oscar Ewing, Leon Keyserling, and others), sent a message a week to Capitol Hill keeping Congress off balance. The only new item and the one that most stirred members of both parties and much of the country as well concerned civil rights.

Truman Library Collection.

Truman proved to be a surprisingly strong advocate of civil rights legislation. Here, he and Eleanor Roosevelt accompany NAACP Executive Secretary Walter White to the Lincoln Memorial, where they were to be guest speakers at the 1947 NAACP annual conference.

In mid-September 1946 the President met with a small delegation alarmed by lynchings occurring in the Deep South. Among those present were the NAACP's executive secretary, Walter White; Channing Tobias, a black executive with the Phelps-Stokes Fund; James Carey, secretary-treasurer of the CIO; and Boris Shiskin, an AFL economist. The following month the President set up a large committee of prominent citizens to study the issue of civil rights. Within the administration this body was known as "Noah's Ark" because it seemed to contain two of everything: blacks, women, Catholics, Jews, businessmen, Southerners, labor leaders, college presidents, and so on. Charles E. Wilson, president of General Electric, served as Chairman and Franklin D. Roosevelt, Jr., as vice chairman. Several weeks after the disastrous 1946 election, the President revealed the existence of this group, observing that democratic institutions cannot survive "where law and order have broken down and individuals . . . are killed, maimed or intimidated." He called upon the members to recommend whatever legislation or administrative action deemed necessary to protect the civil rights of all citizens.

Ten months later Truman received a sweeping report advocating use of existing federal machinery and new legislation to end both discrimination and segregation in American life. Their proposals included revision of laws and stiffer penalties to encourage compliance, elimination of segregation in interstate transportation, abolition of the poll tax, protection of voters in federal elections and primaries, recognition of lynching as a federal crime, termination of discrimination and segregation in the armed forces, and eradication of similar practices throughout the District of Columbia, including its public schools.

By the time Truman got this report the mood of the nation seemed to be turning in his favor and Henry Wallace (whom he had dismissed from his post as Secretary of Commerce) was about to become the Progressive party's candidate for the White House. Only by moving to the left could Truman hope to retain large blocs of urban Negroes and restless white liberal Democrats and perhaps his office as well.

On February 2, 1948, Truman surprised many people by asking Congress to enact into law most of the recommendations of his Civil Rights Committee. Yet, in essence, this was Truman the politician speaking and acting, not Truman the liberal crusader. His strategy was to make reasonably bold requests on Capitol Hill where they would not be granted (thus becoming excellent campaign fodder) and more cautious proposals in executive departments where he had greater powers. It should be noted that these recommendations presented only a moderate challenge to Jim Crow; except in interstate transportation, emphasis was upon "nondiscrimination," not the elimination of segregation per se.

During the months leading up to the 1948 Democratic party convention, Truman wavered a bit and even tried to placate Southerners with a mild platform plank on civil rights. Liberals, led by young Hubert Humphrey (1911-1978), then mayor of Minneapolis, took the fight to the convention floor and won. Again, this was not an outright attack on Jim Crow but an endorsement of equal opportunity for all Americans. Yet this split the convention. Mississippi and Alabama delegates walked out in protest and subsequently nominated Strom Thurmond (1902-   ) of South Carolina (then a Democrat, later a Republican) as the states' rights candidate for the presidency. Selection of Alben W. Barkley (1877-1956) of Kentucky as Truman's running mate helped paper over some of the party discord. Barkley, a popular, loyal New Dealer, a racial moderate, and a skillful compromiser, proved to be an excellent choice.

Truman, realizing that he needed urban northern support in order to win (especially in view of the Republicans' rather liberal platform), barred on June 26 by executive order all discrimination in federal employment and instituted steps leading to equality of opportunity in the armed services. And, at the same time that his civil rights policy was unfolding, Truman moved from lambasting to lampooning the Eightieth Congress. In a bold stroke he called the members back to a summer session where he demanded action to stop inflation and start housing construction. He then proceeded to list every other major proposal his administration had sent to Capitol Hill since 1945. "If this Congress finds time to act on any of them now," he added, "the country will greatly benefit. Certainly, the next Congress should take them up immediately." Congress did nothing much except talk about the Red menace as Truman whistlestopped across the country telling anyone who would listen how hopeless the "no good, do nothing" Eightieth Congress was.

Supremely confident of victory, the Republicans for the first time in their history renominated a defeated presidential candidate, Governor Thomas E. Dewey of New York, and picked as his running mate California's liberal chief executive, Earl Warren. This combination of popular, experienced leaders from key states, looked like a winning ticket to everyone except diehard conservatives, who soon would launch an all-out attack upon whatever remained of the wartime bipartisan foreign policy.

In the campaign Truman faced three challengers—Dewey, Wallace, and Thurmond—and seemingly impossible odds. His carefully orchestrated strategy was to preserve the New Deal and regain control of Congress by focusing attention—with the aid of folksy phrases, wit, and sarcasm—on domestic issues. As Truman told the story, this was a battle between the little man (whom he was defending) and rich Republicans eager to wipe out everything Roosevelt and the Democrats had done since 1932.

Although Truman's narrow "upset" victory (49.5 percent of the total vote cast) often has been seen as the political coup of the century, this view overlooks some basic truths. He was the candidate of the majority party and enjoyed the backing of almost all of labor and many influential Democrats throughout the nation. Dewey, confident and ahead in the polls in September, did not exert himself and ran a rather dull campaign. (*Life* magazine even hailed Dewey as "our next president" a few days before the balloting.) The Thurmond forces were able to control only four states (Alabama, Louisiana, Mississippi, and South Carolina). Wallace actually got nearly as many votes as the Dixiecrat leader (1.15 million), but, scattered in various large cities, they had no impact in the Electoral College. Postelection surveys revealed that Wallace lost strength as balloting approached; in fact, Truman was the only one who gained in September and October.

The result was an "upset" only in the sense that the pollsters failed to detect what was happening, especially the swing of the farm vote to Truman. More important, perhaps, was an extremely low voter turnout: 51.5 percent. No candidate had excited the electorate. When Truman saw a mandate for his Fair Deal, he was just as mistaken as the Republicans had been in 1946. This 1948 decision was merely a "maintaining" action. Truman continued in the White House by exploiting Republican weaknesses and Democratic strength. He and his aides

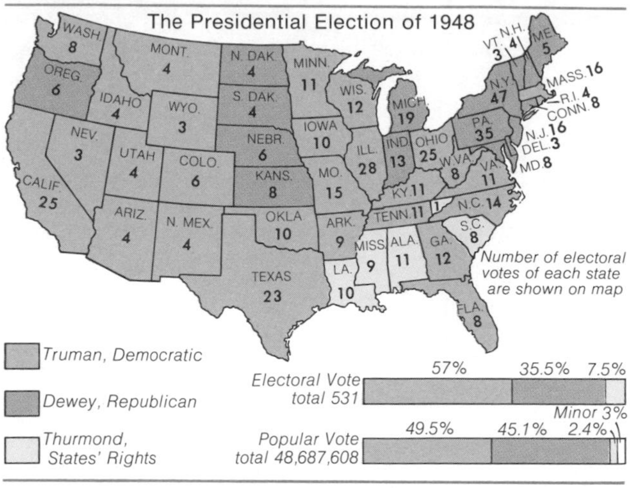

The Presidential Election of 1948

had achieved the immediate goal of staying in power, but they had not converted a substantial bloc of voters to a political faith embracing long-range liberal objectives. In short, despite victory, the man from Independence remained very vulnerable.

This inherent weakness became apparent when Truman's legislative program ran into trouble on Capitol Hill and foreign problems multiplied. Soon his overall approval rating with the American public skidded downward. In January 1949, he hit a low of 32 percent in public opinion polls in September 1946, 69 percent of Americans approved the President's actions. A year later his rating stood at 45 percent, in January 1951, at 36 percent, and in January 1952, at 25 percent. Not surprisingly, the conservative southern Democrat-Republican coalition in Congress blocked most of the Fair Deal; and, after the outbreak of war in Korea in June 1950, Truman had to spend more and more time with foreign, rather than domestic, affairs. He was, in fact, a reluctant liberal who was perhaps not fully committed to the immediate reforms he proposed. Yet, pushed by the NAACP and the political logic of the times, Harry Truman probably carried the civil rights struggle as far as he could; certainly, he did much more in this field than any of his predecessors, including FDR.

Truman's White House record remains controversial. His accomplishments were moderate at best and left the nation with many unresolved problems. He was ahead of public opinion in his proposals to Congress, but not in his actions, and he helped to unleash scores of expectations that his successors would have to satisfy.

Perhaps the most important fact revealed by national elections of the Truman years is that most Americans were groping for an existence free of conflict. War, Red-baiting, reform, and confrontation of any sort did not fit into their idea of peace. Untroubled by domestic and foreign distractions, they wanted to enjoy the restful ease earned in war. This did not mean a return to the normalcy of the 1920s or a dismantling of any New Deal legislation. What was needed was simply a time to relax and catch one's breath.

The New America

The outlines of postwar society had existed for several decades, but only after 1945 did mass consumption, autos, suburbs, youth, and technological organization become dominant factors in the nation's daily life. Ironically, the period was also marked by basic problems such as discrimination, segregation, racism, and poverty.

Mass-Consumption Society

As defined by experts, mass consumption exhibits three major features: a majority of affluent families possessing sufficient discretionary purchasing power to replace and enlarge their stock of consumer goods, a cycle of fluctuations in economic growth (inflation and deflation) controlled by the whims and needs of consumers, and a consumer psychology based not upon availability of money or actual need but on a willingness to buy. After 1945, for the first time in history, most Americans (not just the well-to-do and very rich) had a residue of spending money to buy new cars, excess clothing, boats, electrical gadgets, and so on above and beyond their basic requirements. Although one-fifth of U.S. families remained poor, discretionary spending power rose from \$40 billion (1940) to \$100 billion (1950) to \$200 billion (1959).

Availability of credit—"buy now, pay later"—contributed directly to this spending spree. Until World War II, credit was used sparingly, principally in making major purchases such as a home, but after 1945 short-term credit plans mushroomed, increasing 400-fold between 1946 and 1958 and became commonplace in the purchase of automobiles. Credit cards, created by oil

HERBLOCK'S EDITORIAL CARTOON

"Careful You Don't Get Yourself Down"

In the view of Herblock, easy postwar credit was a mixed blessing to eager consumers.

companies to take advantage of national advertising and customers away from home, proliferated into "all-purpose" cards such as Diner's Club, American Express, and Carte Blanche. Again, local retailers benefited from coast-to-coast advertising, got paid promptly, and, in turn, handed over a small service charge (2 percent to 5 percent) on each purchase to the card-issuing companies.

Like credit cards, the rise of franchise outlets such as Dairy Queen, Midas Muffler, and Holiday Inn exerted a homogenizing force throughout the nation as American towns and cities began to look more and more alike. A local citizen with a bit of capital could acquire a franchise, learn how to operate the business or hire a manager, and repay the parent company with a percentage of his annual profits. At the same time, the franchise holder benefited from national advertising and consumer recognition of products "just like they had at home."

By 1950, much of the nation's discretionary spending power was going for pleasure and leisure activities such as travel, gardening, and sports. Automobiles, used for both business and pleasure, were a key ingredient in the emergence of postwar America. Throughout the 1950s consumers spent about 4.7 percent of their disposable income on autos, a product that dovetailed well with the needs of a status-conscious suburbia. The monsters turned out by Detroit's assembly lines had shining chrome, size, and planned obsolesence. Standing proudly in a ranch house driveway of that era, one of these creations, more than anything else, typified personal success and upward (as well as horizontal) mobility.

The auto industry, well-developed long before World War II, was fully prepared to take advantage of the demand of suburbia's two-car families. In the peak year of 1955, Detroit turned out eight million passenger cars and a million and a quarter trucks and buses, but by that date shortages created by the war years and suburban sprawl largely had been taken care of. After that time small economy cars from abroad, especially Volkswagens, began to provide stiff competition both in America and overseas. The 1950s saw the demise of several major producers as General Motors, Ford, and Chrysler waxed fat. At the same time, customers, seemingly interested more in cost than the luxury of having 352 models to choose from, were becoming wary. Even now the auto industry has not achieved the economic importance of a public utility; yet, by virtue of its economic clout, its actions were becoming increasingly a matter of public concern.

More autos, whether foreign or domestic, meant that more roads had to be provided for more drivers. In 1940 the nation built about 40,000 miles of highways, one-fourth of these completed with federal aid, the rest by states themselves. Throughout the 1950s, some 70,000 miles to 80,000 miles of highways were constructed each year, with the ratio of federal assistance increasing somewhat in the latter part of that decade.

Another highly visible symbol of affluence was the television antenna which, in the late 1940s at least, did not always mean that a household actually had a receiving set. Detroit stores, for example did a good business in "false" TV antennas in 1948. However, nearly all of them, sooner or later, were tied into the new medium

New York Daily News Photo.

Suburban sprawl invited Americans to move farther and farther from their places of work. As a result, use of the automobile greatly increased, for both work and leisure purposes, and traffic jams worsened, despite rapid road construction. Here, weekend tourists queue up at Jones Beach, New York, in 1953.

which would have such profound effects upon U.S. life. In 1946 only 8,000 U.S. households could boast of TV sets, while 33,998,000 had radios. In 1947 there were only sixty-six commercial TV stations and manufacturers were producing fewer than 200,000 sets a year. During the next decade, studios, sets, and money spent on TV advertising grew by leaps and bounds. Throughout the 1950s manufacturers produced six to seven million sets per year, 500 broadcasting stations appeared, annual advertising budgets passed the billion-dollar mark, and by 1960 almost as many families had TV as radio: 45,750,000 to 50,193,000. Despite the dramatic growth of television, it should be noted that the use of radio nearly doubled during the same years.

Status, as these symbols indicate, was a very vital commodity in the new America, especially among members of the broad middle class that was striving upward. Since all status symbols were quickly recognized—whether based on homes, automobiles, clothes, church attendance, shopping patterns, or vacation and recreation habits—they created, at least within a given community, a type of conformity. Conformity, an eagerness "to keep up with the Joneses" and yet not to appear too much unlike them, long has been a recognizable trait in American society; however, it is true that after World War II more people than ever before had the discretionary income with which "to keep up." The search was for the most acceptable model of everything. As a result, especially in middle and upper middle class communities, appearance, symbols, and obvious consumption became, in some households, a passion born of wartime shortages often preceded by Depression poverty and perhaps even hunger.

Of course, mass production keyed to mass consumption would have produced conformity of sorts anyway, and this process was only quickened by certain postwar innovations. These included television, the most obvious universalizer, which gave millions of Americans, regardless of class, income, and place of residence, a continuing and common core of experiences. The rise of paperback books provided a similar, if less pervasive phenomenon as all who were eager to read new books could acquire them with relative ease at drugstores, supermarkets, and newsstands. Franchises for fastfood outlets, motels-hotels, and a variety of services as well as the mass construction of homes and automobiles were other universalizing factors. In many ways, then, at least one large segment of the American public—the expanding, affluent middle class—was shaping itself into a culturally unified mass, even if this did not contribute to the formation of a truly unified society.

Urbs and Suburbs

"Urbanization," broadly defined, continued as a central

demographic fact in the postwar years. In 1950, the United States was statistically 64 percent urban, in 1960, 70 percent. Growing cities and towns enhanced their role as marketing and service centers, and some industries clustered along new freeways; and beltways began to create important commercial centers of their own. In addition, growth of radio and television gave certain communities—New York, Chicago, and Los Angeles—even greater regional and national importance.

Yet growth statistics and a cursory survey of this sort are somewhat misleading. Much of this population explosion was metropolitan, covering huge areas; and, within those areas two other trends were evident: the spread of suburbia coupled with (frequently but not always) a deterioration of the "center city." Also, census takers added to the confusion by altering their definition of urban to include not only communities of 2,500 or more, but villages and towns of any size (incorporated or not) contiguous to a city or cities with a total population of 50,000 or more. Any such grouping of city, county, town, village, and farmland was called a Standard Metropolitan Statistical Area (SMSA).

This metropolitan dispersal consisted largely of suburbanization, actually not a new trend. For nearly a century railroads and streetcars had been creating commuter-bedroom satellites, and the automobile proved to be an even more effective catalyst for urban sprawl. Some of the inducements that fueled the move to outlying areas were better highways, more babies, and cheaper, less-crowded housing. Also, as some businesses left the inner city for suburbia, the job base moved with them. Shopping centers or malls, often virtually new towns in themselves, sprang up out of potato and wheat fields. By mid-century these unique emporiums, the first of which had appeared in Kansas City in the 1920s, accounted for 33 percent of all retail sales in the nation and their popularity was on the rise.

This urban diaspora was both cause and effect of massive outlays for road construction. The 1956 Federal Aid Highway Act, undertaken by a Republican administration which relied more upon suburbia than the inner city for votes, was the ultimate recognition of the new motorized America. This act proposed to build 41,000 miles of interstate highways, 5,500 of them urban freeways. For the first time federal road construction funds were not being earmarked for farm to market communication. In all, $25 billion was to be spent over a thirteen-year period. To gain enactment, Eisenhower stressed increased road safety, an end to massive congestion as automobile use increased, and quick evacuation "in case of an atomic attack on our key cities."

The postwar period saw the emergence of hundreds of planned and unplanned suburban communities. Critics have tended to lump all of suburbia together and blast the resultant culture as bland, standardized, and dehumanized. They claim, usually with one of three Levittowns built in the New York-Philadelphia area in mind, that mass suburbs disrupted and broke down traditional community patterns; however, the reverse seems to be true. Despite the fact that homeowners often possessed similar backgrounds (white, hard working, lower middle class with plans to move upward socially and economically), suburbia quickly coalesced into distinctive little neighborhoods based upon jobs, age, schools, number of children, recreation, shopping preferences, and religion.

The exodus to metropolitan suburbs from cities—and from small towns, too, since the drift of population away from rural areas continued—contrasted sharply with deteriorating urban cores and pockets of poverty hidden throughout rural America. The most visible result was a great increase in segregation. New York City lost 50,000 whites per year while gaining 30,000 Puerto Ricans and 10,000 blacks. At the same time, Cleveland, Ohio's largest city, watched as 6,500 blacks moved in and 3,000 whites left each year. This exchange was not accidental, for many new, white suburbanites were leaving precisely because of the influx of nonwhites.

During the period 1945–1960 the federal government passed legislation designed to help inner cities, but the results were not impressive. Under Eisenhower more housing was torn down than re-created, and much that appeared was built by private developers (as opposed to low-cost public housing) and was too expensive for all but the well-to-do. More importantly, attitudes toward race, the construction of freeways, and tax programs calculated to encourage home ownership in the suburbs frustrated most attempts to stem the outward flow of humanity, if indeed the federal government actually wanted to do that.

Nevertheless, housing legislation passed in 1949 and 1954 laid the foundation for programs dedicated, in theory at least, to slum clearance and urban rehabilitation by local, state, and federal agencies. The Housing Act of 1954, for example, reorganized the Federal National Mortgage Association (otherwise known as "Fannie Mae") as a corporation designed to continue as a second-

Shel Hershorn/Black Star.

Much maligned by social critics, the new planned suburban communities with their curvilinear streets and identical houses offered a new and different sense of community to postwar American families.

ary market for federally underwritten mortgages and to provide special assistance for Federal Home Loan (FHA) and veterans' housing.

The results of all these trends were ominous, complex, and contradictory. Inner city and suburb were becoming two hostile, separate worlds, one black and poor, the other white and relatively affluent. At the same time, metropolitan America was developing a sameness that was obliterating regional differences. Suburban New York, Chicago, Cleveland, Atlanta, Dallas, St. Louis, and Los Angeles looked much alike: mile after mile of homes ringed by freeways, motels, shopping centers, and fast-food outlets. And their inner centers tended to present similar symptoms of decay: abandoned stores and busi-

Standard Metropolitan Areas, 1950

ness establishments, ill-kept housing with black tenants, and an air of seedy disarray. Many small towns and villages, often disproportionately populated by older people, exhibited much the same seediness as they lost population to both parts of the metropolis—suburbia and inner city.

Just as blacks, Puerto Ricans, and Mexican-Americans began to feel they were being "left out" of the New America, many rural dwellers began to sense that they were being left behind. Ironically, radio, the press, and especially television told both groups that they were right. The gaps between inner city and suburbia and smalltown America and the SMSAs were huge and growing wider with each passing year.

The Land of the Young

The sharp increases in live births that began during World War II and continued throughout these years guaranteed, in a real sense, that postwar America would be "the land of the young." In 1942 there were about three million births compared to half as many deaths. During the next fifteen years the number of deaths rose slightly, while the total births swelled past four million per year. From 1940 to 1960 the birth rate for the third child in a family doubled, that for the fourth child tripled.

These numbers were accompanied by two phenomena that helped make the child all-important in American culture: new emphasis upon the woman's role as wife and homemaker and popularization of a style of childrearing that created "child-centered" homes and families. In part, as a reaction to the prominence of women in the work force, magazines such as *McCall's* and *Ladies Home Journal,* advertisers, and the media began to popularize the large family. These households, of course, would need larger, more powerful cars (such as station wagons), bigger homes and more consumer goods, and, in turn, would buy more of what U.S. industry was producing. Suburban living also increased the mother's role as all-round homemaker, chauffeur, gardener, den mother, planner, coordinator, and so on, especially if father spent long hours at his city job or traveled extensively on business for his employer.

Both mothers and fathers were cautioned by psychologists to give offspring the opportunity to develop their own personalities. Leaders in this field were Arnold L. Gesell (1880–1961) and Frances Ilg (1902–   ), authors of *Infant and Child in The Culture of Today* (1943). These Yale professors introduced the concept of behavioral "norms" for children, emphasizing that "considerate regard" for an individual's emerging character was the first essential in childrearing. Dr. Benjamin Spock (1903–   ) put this theory into cookbook practice in his *Common Sense Book of Baby and Child Care* (1949), which went through thirty printings in its first decade and became the "bible" of millions of households.

Just why postwar parents felt impelled to abandon center stage to their progeny is not entirely clear, but there are several plausible explanations. A generation buffeted by depression and war was determined its children would be spared such scars and enjoy a better life. Children and their playmates may have been the only tendrils holding otherwise rootless parents in suburbia; thus they logically became the focus of day-to-day life. And, the conditioning by the media, the proclamations of their peers (such as Dr. Spock), and the habits and attitudes of the folks next door—all had a cumulative effect. In fact, it might be noted that, for the first time, thousands of families had someone living "next door," not merely down the hall in some apartment building or a mile or so away on an adjoining farm. As a result, thou-

Some of America's "war babies" participate in a Diaper Derby in New Jersey.

Jay Leviton/Black Star.

Teen-age Idol Elvis Presley goes through some of his theatrical gyrations and brings a predictable frenzied reaction from his young fans.

sands could see at firsthand how other households much like their own really functioned.

From this cult of the adolescent there arose a powerful group of consumers—young, white, affluent—which by 1960, if one looks merely at the high school college crowd, was spending about $10 billion per year. By another yardstick, at the close of the 1950s, young people between twelve and twenty were spending an average of $555 each year on nonessential items. This included those from both well-to-do and poor homes. Not surprisingly, merchants began to extend credit to these individuals, often at very exorbitant rates of interest, as high as 80 percent. Armed with parental acquiescence, easy credit, and a teen-age compulsion to conform, they became fashion pace setters as they donned jeans, stenciled tee shirts, and unconventional footgear—or none at all. The young no longer modeled themselves after their elders—in either clothing or behavior.

Central to this youth culture and representative of its grip on the cultural and economic life of America was the new musical sensation: rock 'n' roll. In 1951, a white Cleveland disc jockey named Allen Freed pioneered with a rhythm-and-blues show that really caught on when he moved to New York City. "Shake, Rattle, and Roll" by Bill Haley and the Comets was the first rock song to break into the so-called Top Ten. In 1955, Elvis Presley and Chuck Berry adapted Haley's country and western rockabilly style to their own needs, Presley adding physical and overt sexual expression to his music. His appearance on nationwide TV a year later caused a storm of protest, fame, and instant success.

Thereafter it was clear that rock was a statement of rebellion which belonged almost exclusively to the young. The record industry began selling up to 25 percent of its output to preteens (ages 9-14) who raised Presley and several of his contemporaries to godlike status. Among these folk figures, were Frankie Avalon, Bobby Vee, Fabian, and Pat Boone.

Rock, more than anything else, spoke for the "young" world of the 1950s, and it talked a language that older generations could not help but hear. Many parents were uneasy, distrusting, and disapproving of an element in youth culture which they could not fully comprehend. Nevertheless, while deploring the end result, they sometimes pushed their children relentlessly into this maelstrom, eager that they become part of their peer culture.

The Organization Age

A basic ingredient of mass consumption, very obviously, is mass production. The latter requires considerable private investment and the expenditure of vast sums on the development of new products and new techniques. Much of the research leading to new products and better ways of making old ones comes from university laboratories, cementing ties between the industrial and university worlds. And the link between all of these loose threads—research, experimentation, production, advertising, distribution, sales—is something loosely called "organization," a term that gained special meaning in the

Leviton-Atlanta/Black Star.

Elvis Presley
(1935–1977)

In 1954, Elvis Aaron Presley, a lanky, loose-jointed, sullenly handsome youngster who was 6 feet 1 inch tall and one year out of high school, was driving a truck in Memphis, Tennessee, and studying at night to become an electrician. Two years later he earned an estimated $1 million; and by 1959 twenty-one of his records had each sold over one million copies. He also was on television and in movies, a major cult hero for thousands of youngsters.

Born in Tupelo, Mississippi, in 1935, he was the only child (a twin brother died at birth) of Vernon and Gladys Presley. He learned music by singing in church choirs and at twelve taught himself to play the guitar. In the summer of 1953 he paid $4 to record a song as a surprise gift for his mother. An executive of Sun Records happened to hear the recording and Elvis was on his way. Aided by a very shrewd promoter, Colonel Thomas Parker, Presley was launched in 1955 as the "Hillbilly Cat." While on tour he developed his distinctive rock 'n' roll style—a mix of hillbilly, blues, and gospel—which got him a contract with RCA. During that same year he produced "Blue Suede Shoes," "Heartbreak Hotel," and "Hound Dog," three of his best-known numbers.

Presley's appeal to the youth of the 1950s went far beyond his music. His blatantly sexual performances—one critic called it a "striptease with clothes on"—aroused the consternation of older Americans but made him a symbol of "revolt" to the young. Presley himself claimed he never did anything "dirty," he simply "moved as the spirit moved him." Although an expression of revolt, Elvis never was a critic of the establishment. He played no role in politics and served in the U.S. Army (1958–1959) without incident. His actions reflect, therefore, a keen difference between the outlook of young people in the 1950s and in the 1960s.

Although Britain's famed musical group, the Beatles, stole some of his thunder in the 1960s, Elvis continued to sell millions of records annually, appeared in highly successful movies, and still could draw sellout crowds to concerts held in the 1970s. He died suddenly of heart failure in 1977. As the greatest exponent of rock 'n' roll, Presley had a very dramatic impact upon popular music, which never was quite the same after he appeared, twisting, turning, and twanging on national television. ■

business-economic realm in the decade or so after World War II.

During these years as technological research grew rapidly, among its important products were automation and machine records that enabled consumers to buy more readily through prearranged credit and kept track of their purchases. Automation also, it should be noted, put thousands out of work, thereby limiting their consumer role, at least temporarily. The epitome of this automation revolution was the computer, first built at Harvard University and the University of Pennsylvania during World War II, but not marketed commercially until the early 1950s. During these years, scientists in both England and America developed electronic (as opposed to merely mechanical) computers. These electronic models had the distinct advantage of being able to store vast amounts of data, and much of the experimentation (1945–1953) concerned what method was best for such storage. By 1950 the U.S. Bureau of Standards was using a stored-program computer called "Edvac," and a year later the Bureau of the Census had Univac I, the first model to be reproduced and sold commercially.

International Business Machines (IBM), headed by Thomas J. Watson (1874–1956), was at the cutting edge of this blitzkreig of data processing by computer. And, although production increased dramatically (20 computers by 1954, 1,250 three years later), it was impossible to keep up with demand. By 1960 data-processing sales totaled $1 billion and most businesses had adapted much of their accounting, billing, and recordkeeping to the new technology.

One of the computer's achievements was its role in the launching of America's first artificial satellite in 1958, some time after the U.S.S.R. had sent up its rival Sputnik. Side effects of this tidal wave of automation included great expansion of the white-collar, college-educated ranks of the industrial-business sector and much job insecurity among the laboring classes. Many strikes of the 1950s had their genesis in one simple fact: human fear of being replaced by machines.

Between 1950 and 1960, nonfarm employment rose from 45.2 million to 54.2 million. Although about one-third of these workers were in manufacturing at the outset of that decade, the greatest gains were posted by the wholesale-retail trade, government at all levels, and service-related enterprises. By 1960 nearly half of all nonagricultural employees were engaged in those three areas. After a brief decline in the immediate postwar years, the number of women in the total labor force increased from 18.4 million in 1950 to 23.2 million ten years later.

Mass production and technological changes altered not only the way business operated but also its structure. Most notable was the increasing size of leading corporations, which grew unmolested; for both the Truman and Eisenhower administrations were more interested in maintaining prosperity than in questioning too closely the nature of mergers and takeovers. Large corporations were "safe" in this environment; "trustbusting" was not in vogue. During the 1950s, 147 of the 1,001 largest manufacturing companies disappeared, all but nine as a result of mergers. By 1960 the 500 largest corporations were making half of the sales in America and reaping 70 percent of the profits, which means the sales of many hard-pressed competitors must have been less than profitable.

The corporation became such a pervasive force in American life that in 1956 William H. Whyte, Jr. (1917–   ) saw, as he reported in his *Organization Man,* a new Social Ethic—dictated by the corporate structure and its concerns—replacing the well-known Protestant Ethic. Those employed by a large concern such as IBM or Time-Life, more than ever before, seemed to *belong* to it, body, heart, and soul. They dressed, acted, socialized, and thought as their associates did. In Whyte's view, corporation executives were reshaping all of society with a type of "collectivization" similar to that found in their own companies. Whyte and others undoubtedly exaggerated the degree of corporate influence and conformity evident in the 1950s, but it is true that business executives loomed large in some of the educational, community, and political functions of nonbusiness realms during that era.

Companies gave money to colleges and universities that turned out the research and the white-collar workers they needed. Community involvement, often orchestrated by expanding public relations departments, usually meant money for playgrounds, the arts, and the annual community-chest drive, yet such involvement could take bizarre turns at times. Sears, Roebuck in 1947, for example, gave strawberry plants to Kentucky farmers so as to promote development of a cash crop, the returns from which might, in time, promote department store sales. Several very large companies (Ford, General Electric,

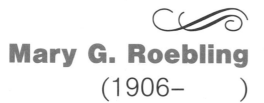

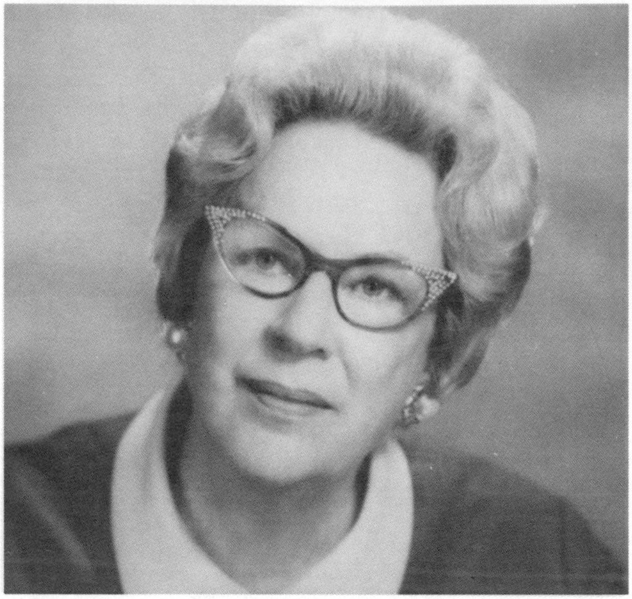

Courtesy Bradford Bachrach.

Mary G. Roebling (1906–)

One of America's richest women, Mary G. Roebling was born in modest circumstances and worked very hard to achieve her prominence in the world of banking and finance. Head of the Trenton Trust Company of New Jersey since 1937 and the first woman to serve as a governor of the American Stock Exchange, she lives with great flair and a zest for life reflected in her innovative business procedures and practices. In 1959 she built a luxurious townhouse not far from her office—"perhaps the only two-bedroom house in the country which cost upwards of $500,000"—complete with indoor pool and a dining room seating thirty-six. At that time her fortune was estimated at between $125 and $200 million. That same year a TV interview so impressed three burglars that they broke into her home and stole jewels and furs valued at $375,000. (They were caught the next day.)

Roebling was educated at Moorestown High School in New Jersey and while still a teen-ager, married a nephew of Victor Herbert, who died a short time later. To support herself and a young child she became a secretary with a Philadelphia brokerage firm, at the same time taking night classes in finance at the University of Pennsylvania. Her second husband, Siegfried Roebling, great-grandson of the man who built the Brooklyn Bridge and a successful banker-industrialist, also died within thirty-six months of their marriage, leaving her with yet another child but by no means penniless.

Twice widowed in eight years, Roebling now held a controlling interest in the Trenton Trust Company. Determined to rescue this rather shaky institution, she took over as president (1937) and as chairman of the board (1941), meanwhile studying banking and finance at New York University and taking private lessons in law in order to understand better her new responsibilities.

Within a decade, her hard work began to pay dividends. Roebling, who believes banking can be glamorous and that money can be sold like any other product, sponsored "financial teas" to explain trust funds to well-to-do women, held art shows and club meetings in her bank, hired professional window dressers and a personal public relations agent, and distributed 50,000 pots of shamrocks to customers on St. Patrick's Day.

An ardent feminist and inveterate joiner, she has been honored by many associations and numerous colleges and universities. A glamorous widow known for dressing and entertaining with great style and elegance, Mary G. Roebling is thoroughly wedded to her bank. "My job is my boss," she once remarked. "I would honestly rather curl up with the *Wall Street Journal* or a good financial statement than any novel." ■

and Gulf among them) operated "nonpartisan" schools in "practical politics" which utilized professional educators and probably tax writeoffs as well. The true intent of such seminars, obviously, was to activate and bolster conservative forces that favored corporations in both major parties at the local level, not to spread general knowledge. In franker moments, businessmen conceded this was an attempt to counter the work of labor unions.

Corporate America rolled on with a heavy beat just like a rock 'n' roll hit, but as the 1950s unfolded several questions had to be answered. What sort of world was the organization man creating? Did his "rock" son want to become part of it and follow his father's footsteps? And, more importantly, what of those who had no place in the suburban-corporate world of the 1950s? Could it expand to encompass them, and what would happen if they chose not to enter, even if invited to do so?

The Equilibrium of the 1950s

The forces of the 1950s such as mass production and mass consumption, a national focus upon suburbia and suburban wants and needs, a yen for conformity and domestic tranquility after the hurly-burly of depression, war, and reconversion to peacetime pursuits helped to produce an equilibrium that tended to dominate the 1950s. To make certain no one upset the applecart, voters usually played the White House off against Capitol Hill, thus giving neither liberals nor conservatives free rein to work their will.

Eisenhower and Reaffirming Republicanism

When Truman won in 1948, Republicans were shocked and midwestern nationalists, led by Senator Robert A. Taft of Ohio, were especially bitter. They believed, with firm conviction, that only a return to traditional, anti-New Deal values could rid the nation of its perplexing postwar problems (which, after June 1950, included Korea). This strong, inwardly looking wing of the party, never comfortable with Willkie, Dewey, and their Manhattan-based internationalist allies, began to find hope and encouragement in 1952. By that time Truman and the Democrats were extremely vulnerable. Their party was split, the President's personal popularity had sunk to new lows, and, after a poor showing in the New Hampshire primary, he gave up any idea of reelection. At their convention, with Truman's backing, the party nominated Adlai E. Stevenson (1900–1965), the very eloquent, urbane governor of Illinois. But urbanity, wit, and presidential endorsement were not enough. After a twenty-year drought, 1952 proved to be a Republican year.

Despite their bright opportunity the Republicans were deeply split as their convention approached. The well-defined, internationalist wing, opposed to the nomination of Taft, turned to Dwight D. Eisenhower. The general, who had served briefly as president of Columbia University (a move orchestrated by IBM's Thomas J. Watson, an influential trustee), narrowly defeated Taft for the nomination. This victory was the result of extremely effective convention management and the defection from Taft of several Deep South delegations, Georgia and Texas among them, whose members thought Eisenhower, an independent and a fresh face, could attract Democrats restless because of Truman's civil rights proposals. So, out of self-interest they voted for Ike. He chose as his running mate a young Californian, a senator who had distinguished himself by his anti-Red crusade: Richard M. Nixon (1913–   ).

To see Eisenhower as the "liberal" and Taft as the "conservative" in this struggle is an oversimplification. Both were anti-New Deal, and Taft, a flexible man and a proven liberal on some important issues, might also have become more international in outlook had he achieved his dream. Eisenhower's tantalizing appeal, as those southern Republicans realized, was that he was an unknown political quantity, free of the scars of the party's internal fray. The nomination of Senator Taft, a man who had taken stands on many key matters, could only complicate the campaign for the Republicans and drive wavering Democrats back into the fold.

Eisenhower won handily, capturing 442 electoral votes to 89 for Stevenson; the popular margin was 34 million to 27.3 million. The Republicans also carried Congress; however, the meaning of this sweep was not entirely clear. It appears, in retrospect, that this was a negative decision by an electorate that wanted no more of Korea, Communism, or corruption, all of these evils associated in one way or another in the public mind with Harry S Truman and his administration. And, before long, it became obvious voters did not want any dismantling of the New Deal either. As political analyst Samuel Lubell has observed, to become permanent Roo-

Dwight D. Eisenhower Library/Republican National Committee.

Eisenhower with Senator Robert A. Taft (right).

sevelt's reforms needed to weather at least one solidly Republican administration. As a minority party, its most extreme rightwing spokesman could promise to sweep away every law written since 1933; as the majority, the Republican party would discover the electorate would not permit it. They had the task of administering the New Deal programs and living with them: the welfare state was here to stay.

Once in office, and especially while enjoying the support of a Republican Congress (the only one, other than the Eightieth, between Hoover and the present), Eisenhower revealed his traditional Republican orientation. The President tried hard to balance the federal budget and four times succeeded. He also produced a few measures reminiscent of the New Deal, which utilized and expanded government power. These included creation in 1953 of the Department of Health, Education and Welfare (HEW)—headed up by ex-WAC chief Oveta Culp Hobby, the second woman ever to hold Cabinet rank; extension of social security programs; construction of the St. Lawrence Seaway; and the Federal Aid Highway Act of 1956.

Eisenhower frequently engineered these moves, however, to forestall passage of more drastic bills and throughout his eight years remained dedicated to frugality. He beat Stevenson again in 1956 by a slightly larger margin, even though his campaign stressed an increasing swing to conservatism and balanced budgets. In his last years Ike began to cut back on federal spending, wielding the veto with ever greater vigor. He worked hard to keep government out of the private sector, vetoing public housing, public works, and antipollution bills. The continued dominance of a conservative coalition of Republicans and southern Democrats—an informal bipartisanship of sorts at the domestic level—enabled Eisenhower to have his way, at least until 1958.

An unbiased view of the wartime leader as chief executive is only now emerging. The myth that Eisenhower was a nonpolitical, middle-of-the-road President is beginning to be questioned with more and more frequency. He apparently worked very closely and sometimes vigorously with Republicans in Congress. During the two years his party controlled Capitol Hill, Eisenhower managed to swing most members over to the internationalist foreign policy of Truman, which continued largely unaltered. On the domestic scene, the President proclaimed a "New Republicanism," but this was more rhetoric than reality. Conservative forces, strong in Republican circles since the days of Warren G. Harding, remained potent, and that was the way he wanted it. This is not to say that Eisenhower was overtly probusiness; in fact, in his eagerness not to use the leftover machinery of

New Deal days, he often backed away from the exercise of federal power in its behalf. In fact he headed up an administration perhaps more nearly laissez-faire than even those of Harding and Coolidge who actively *helped* businessmen.

In essence, Eisenhower was too orthodox a Republican to effect any great change in his party's outlook other than gathering support for a foreign policy sanctioned by the logic of events and his own military experience. Instead of ushering in a new political era, Dwight Eisenhower's leadership, especially during 1953–1954 when he had Congress on his side, merely signaled the return and reaffirmation of inherent, traditional Republicanism. The two-party system, it appeared at the close of the 1950s, would survive after all, and so would the New Deal. By the 1960s the Democrats were in control once again.

Seeds of the Civil Rights Revolution

Obscured beneath the surface of postwar American society were situations and forces full of potential trouble: the pressure-packed life of the young, the unhampered growth of supercorporations and oligopolies, the exodus of tax money and leadership from the cities, and a racial awareness that would provide the roots for a civil rights revolution. Throughout the 1940s and much of the 1950s race relations were viewed by liberals outside of Dixie as a southern problem. Consequently, all federal initiatives to ease segregation and race discrimination were targeted on that region, which merely increased southern hostility against northern "do-gooders" and Washington bureaucrats. What was happening in cities, schools, and industry in the rest of the nation was not a matter of immediate concern, even for liberals. It was there for all to see, but few cared to look.

Between 1940 and 1950, 1.6 million blacks left the rural South. About 300,000 of them went to southern urban centers, but over 500,000 settled in the upper Midwest, slightly fewer in the Northeast, and still fewer (293,000) in the West. During the 1950s the flow of blacks from cotton and tobacco fields, hastened by mechanization, continued unabated. In these ten years nearly 1.5 million blacks departed, spreading out much as in the previous decade—almost a million choosing cities of the upper Midwest and Northeast, 289,000 going to the metropolitan South, and 249,000 to the urban West. Interestingly, during the 1950s the only rural area where the number of blacks increased was in the West.

Truman's ambitious civil rights program on behalf of blacks (wherever they lived) got nowhere, hampered perhaps by his halfhearted commitment, but certainly by the Korean War and other more pressing problems the President had to deal with. (He did, however, end segregation in the armed forces by Executive Order 9981 in July 1948.) Yet several Supreme Court decisions during Truman's last years in office weakened Jim Crow somewhat. In a series of unrelated cases the justices ruled against an Alabama law requiring voters to understand and explain part of that state's constitution (*Schnell* v. *Davis,* 1949), segregation in higher education (*McLaurin* v. *Oklahoma State Regents,* 1950), and the all-white primary as being staged by Texas Democrats (*Terry* v. *Adams,* 1953). The effectiveness of such pronouncements depended upon popular support and/or federal enforcement; since neither was much in evidence, little happened. Black voter registration in the South (only 100,000 in 1932) surged past one million in 1952, but fewer than 30 percent of eligible blacks were on the rolls of any southern state.

Neither party took an advanced civil rights stand in 1952, and there was little reason to expect much progress in an era of apparent conformity and stability. But in May 1954, in *Brown* v. *Topeka Board of Education,* the Supreme Court, speaking with one voice, said "separate but equal" public education (segregation on the basis of race), which was widespread throughout the South, was inherently wrong and must cease. This ruling specifically exempted northern schools that were segregated as a result of residential patterns.

The result was a mixture of shock, disbelief, and some violence south of the Mason-Dixon Line. Several states engineered "massive resistance" campaigns, while the Court's "with all deliberate speed" ruling seemed to invite endless delays. "Massive resistance" (which turned out not to be very massive when the chips were down) included new state laws assigning students to specific schools and forbidding transfers to other schools in the same district without the approval of special boards, elimination of state funds to integrated schools, and, as a last resort, closing schools whenever a federal court ordered that integration be carried out. The Eisenhower administration watched passively, reluctant to interfere lest action might harm emerging state Republican parties in the South, but also because the President sincerely

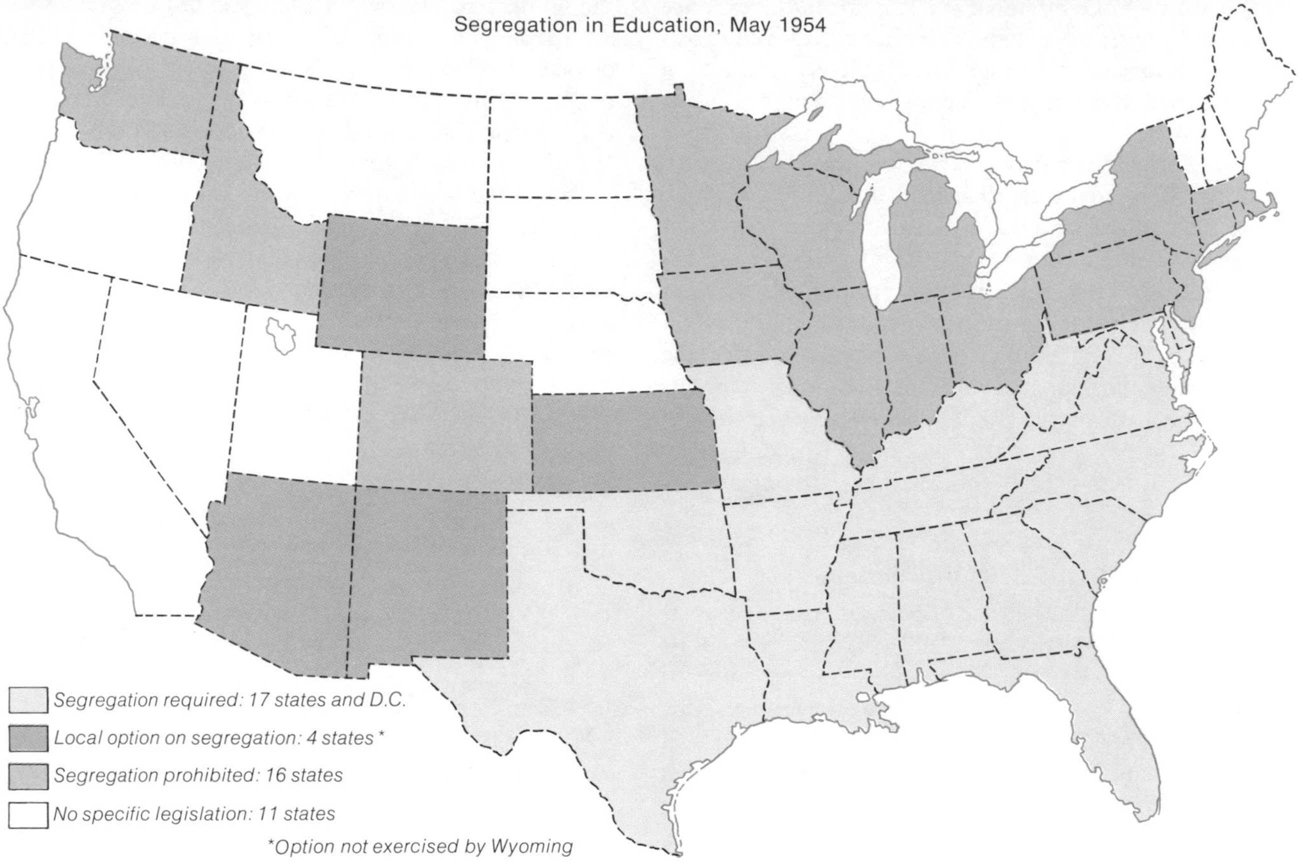

believed that the Constitution did not permit aggressive federal action in such matters. "You cannot change people's hearts by laws," the President said. Finally, when a crisis erupted in Little Rock in September 1957 Eisenhower sent federal troops into that city to back up the Supreme Court decision, and for over a year students at the city's Central High School attended classes under the watchful eyes of national guardsmen. By 1959 massive resistance had collapsed everywhere, notably in Virginia where it had been most strident, and border states and much of the urban South were dismantling their segregated systems, although racial hostility continued unabated and desegregation often was more technical than real.

Several powerful socioeconomic forces helped bring about the end of public school segregation. Perhaps the most important was the business community in almost every town and city in the South. Bankers, real estate salesmen, developers of all sorts, eager to lure outside industry that would create jobs, were not about to let a dispute over public education wreck their dreams and endanger their livelihood. White parents, many of them unable to bear the cost of private schools, were reluctant to see turmoil shut down public classrooms. Of less importance, but of some consequence, were the nationalizing trends evident in postwar society. Segregation on the basis of color simply did not fit in; it set the South apart and made it different from the rest of America. Some Southerners admittedly took great pride in this fact and waved the stars and bars with defiant pride, but many—in an age of seeming conformity—were willing to conform to new ways, especially if they had moved to the South since 1945.

There were certain realms—music, entertainment, sports, air travel, to name a few—where segregation never worked very well, if at all, and an urban America

Burt Glinn/Magnum.

Violence surrounding efforts to desegregate Little Rock Central High School in 1957 caused the federal government to send in troops.

that was busy building the same Holiday Inn East, South, North, and West, would not tolerate such regional differences for long. Segregation was simply too complicated and, above all else, bad for business.

Except for acting at Little Rock when local authorities virtually dared him to do so, Eisenhower did little else to encourage civil rights. His administration put forth a mild voting rights bill in 1956 (an election year), which passed a year later and saw passage of another in 1960 (also an election year). The 1957 measure set up an investigative commission and gave federal district courts the power to issue injunctions to protect the civil rights of citizens. The second, passed largely at the insistence of Democrats in Congress led by Senator Lyndon B. Johnson (1908–1973), empowered the federal government to appoint polling place "referees" *from the locality involved* to see that proper voting procedures were followed. It also enabled federal courts to issue orders clearing the way for blacks to register and vote and made it a federal crime to transport dynamite across state lines for the purpose of blowing up buildings. The last regulation was a clear reaction to widespread violence and terror tactics that had greeted the civil rights movement in many parts of the nation. Neither bill invited vigorous enforcement, but they were the first civil rights laws since Reconstruction and thus, taken together, they did have some symbolic significance. At the same time, 100 southern congressmen, led by North Carolina's Senator Samuel J. Ervin, Jr. (1896-   ), in March 1956 issued a "Southern Manifesto" attacking recent Supreme Court decisions, decrying unwarranted interference in local affairs and pledging to use "all lawful means" to reverse the trend of events.

By the mid-1950s, however, the future of civil rights and race relations was no longer being shaped by the

"Tsk Tsk — Somebody Should Do Something About That"

Herblock © 1956 The Washington Post.

This 1956 cartoon by Herblock captures the liberal view of Eisenhower's conservatism.

Bob Adelman/Magnum.

Martin Luther King, Jr.
(1929–1968)

Born Michael Luther King, Jr., in Atlanta, Georgia, in 1929, at the age of six he took his more familiar name. King came from a long line of distinguished black clergymen but, embarrassed by the emotionalism of their sermons, at first he did not plan to follow in their footsteps. However, after graduating from Morehouse College he went to Crozier Theological Seminary in Chester, Pennsylvania, and in 1955 received a doctorate in systematic theology from Boston University. Meanwhile, he married an Alabama girl whom he met in Boston, Coretta Scott. Together they went to Montgomery, Alabama, where King became pastor of the Dexter Avenue Baptist Church.

The next decade or so of his life was a crowded, exciting time as this young black man achieved both national and international fame. The catalyst was a woman named Rosa Parks, who on December 1, 1955, tired after a day's work, refused to move to the black section of a public bus in Montgomery. Her arrest sparked a 381-day boycott that, under King's leadership, finally broke down segregated seating on that city's transit system.

In 1957, King became president of the newly formed Southern Christian Leadership Conference and soon was much in demand as a speaker and organizer. In that year alone he traveled 780,000 miles and made 208 speeches. In 1959 he moved to Atlanta where he became copastor (with his father) of the Ebenezer Baptist Church. King figured prominently in all of the more important civil rights drives of the early 1960s, and in August of 1963 he mounted a march on Washington that culminated in a mass assembly at the Lincoln Memorial where over 250,000 people heard his eloquent "I have a dream" speech. The following year, to the astonishment and consternation of many white Americans, King was awarded the Nobel Peace Prize. At 35, he was the youngest man ever to be so honored.

A somewhat detached, elusive man, Martin Luther King—5 feet 7 inches with a stocky frame—was no ascetic. He enjoyed sports, opera, and eating. He once described himself as "an ambivert—half introvert and half extrovert." Because of his abilities as a leader and above all else his adherence to massive, but nonviolent, direct action, King fitted perfectly the needs of most civil rights activists from 1955 to 1965.

During the last years of his short life, however, he came under increasing fire from militant young blacks. King remained "Mr. Civil Rights" to most white liberals, the white press, and the black establishment, but younger and more radical groups began to chalk up successes in voting drives in the South and to undermine his support in other parts of the nation as well. A flexible, intelligent man, he moved in 1967–1968 towards a less passive position. He became an outspoken foe of the Vietnam war (thereby earning public denunciation as "a liar" by J. Edgar Hoover) and began to turn his attention to the needs of the urban poor. On April 4, 1968, he went to Memphis to support a strike by black sanitation workers, and in the midst of his new activism, was assassinated. ■

White House, Congress, or the courts but by blacks themselves. Beginning with a boycott in Montgomery, Alabama, in December 1955, against segregated seating on city buses—led by Dr. Martin Luther King, Jr., a local pastor—a new spirit arose bordering on militancy. This movement inspired the formation of new groups such as the Southern Christian Leadership Conference and the revitalization of old ones such as CORE. Unlike earlier decades, now blacks, not whites, were making decisions and directing marches, sit-ins, and protests. The NAACP and the Urban League stirred themselves in an attempt to keep pace, and radical groups such as the Black Muslims also picked up strength. By 1960 the Muslims alone had about 100,000 members.

Although tangible advances for blacks were few in number in the immediate postwar years (hence the growing militancy and the demand for action), some did occur. During the 1940s and 1950s more and more blacks, both males and females, were becoming office-workers, a reflection of accumulated gains in education and the flow from farm to city. Yet at the close of this era, after nearly a century of freedom, many blacks still had little but promises.

Between 1939 and 1958 the average wage received by blacks rose from 41 percent to 58 percent of that paid whites. Most blacks continued working in the worst, dirtiest, and lowest-paying jobs, with about one-third of them still clinging to near-poverty status somewhere in the rural South. On the other hand, by 1960, 6.7 percent of black employees (according to a Labor Department survey) were "professional, technical, and kindred" workers, compared to 25.9 percent of all white workers. Although the majority of blacks still were at the bottom of the economic ladder—in 1960 over one-third of all black women who worked outside their homes were domestics—this professional growth represented a distinct step forward in only two decades.

Nearly every other indicator also pointed to change. Desegregation of countless public facilities throughout the nation and in the armed forces, new sympathy and understanding in the courts, increasing political clout arising from black migration to areas outside of the South, proliferation of black job skills as a result of better educational opportunities and experiences in World War II and Korea, a nationalizing mood fostered by advertising and the media, and a new militancy demanding action, not words—all of these factors were on the side of blacks as Jim Crow's arsenal of excuses was growing weaker with each passing day. Unfortunately, the tendency of some whites of every region to resist change meant that the struggle for equality still would be marked by pain, turmoil, and bloodshed.

A new Ku Klux Klan (a pale and rather feeble replica of its nineteenth century and early twentieth century counterparts), White Citizens Councils, and dedicated conservatives from respectable elements throughout the South prepared to defend their way of life with rhetoric, legal maneuverings, and illegal means, too. In 1951 bomb blasts killed two NAACP leaders in Florida, and the Southern Regional Council said near the year's end that forty bombing incidents had occurred in the previous twelve months. A year later Tuskegee Institute announced that 1952 was the first year in nearly three-quarters of a century during which no lynchings had been reported, but soon such tragedies were making headlines once more—among them, both in Mississippi, Emmet Till (age 14) in 1955 and Mack Parker in 1959. Yet the civil rights-related violence of the 1950s was sporadic compared with what was to come. The determination of blacks and liberals to deal discrimination a mortal blow as they organized sit-ins, marches, "freedom rides," and voter registration drives ignited a backlash that gave the 1960s a quality all of their own.

Liberal Revival

Dwight Eisenhower, by his own admission, became more conservative during his White House years. Although he suffered some criticism from the far right, the most damaging and most frequent thrusts came from the left. Liberal intellectuals, like-minded politicians, and groups such as Americans for Democratic Action (to whom he was nothing more than "a sunburnt Coolidge") kept up the barrage for eight years. At times, Democratic liberals even worked against their own moderate congressional leadership, typified by men such as Senator Lyndon B. Johnson and House Speaker Sam Rayburn (1882–1961). This is not surprising since the party out of power usually speaks with many voices; and, although many Democrats were liberal, the Democratic party's spokesmen on Capitol Hill often were rural conservatives, comfortable and secure in the one-party politics of the South.

For much of the 1950s, American voters were content to divide national leadership and the job of governing the country between the two major parties, giving the

The Lyndon Baines Johnson Library, Photo by Art Kowert.

Sam Rayburn, Lyndon B. Johnson, and Adlai Stevenson during a get-together at Johnson's LBJ Ranch in September 1955. These Democratic leaders, eager to try their hand at the presidential helm, could not hope for much success against the ever-popular Eisenhower.

White House to Republicans and the Congress (except in 1953–1954) to the Democrats. Public opinion polls showed that throughout that decade 51 percent to 56 percent of the electorate considered themselves to be Democrats; only about 35 percent thought of themselves as true Republicans. However, the public did not view any issue as being of sufficient importance to break this deadlock, and a conservative coalition of Republicans and southern Democrats who thought the same way usually gave the President much that he wanted, at least until 1958. The task facing the Democrats was to activate the majority that was theirs and translate their true power into votes on election day.

During the 1950s, the Democratic party, badly split by defeat, personality clashes, and conservative-liberal warfare, gradually put together a program designed to stir interest and win widespread approval. It included federal aid to education and health insurance—old ideas dating back to the 1930s—and specific measures to combat unemployment, protect the environment, and provide help for the elderly when ill. One key dilemma facing the party was that, so long as its conservative wing was strong in Congress, enactment of such measures was all but impossible. Nevertheless, activist forces in both houses went to work, convinced that, win or lose, they would develop issues that the voter could understand and appreciate. The road was a hard one, for they were a distinct minority representing diverse states such as Minnesota, Wisconsin, Michigan, Illinois, Washington, Oregon, Montana, West Virginia, and Rhode Island.

The economic recession of 1957–1958 and Russia's spectacular achievements with Sputnik provided these

John Kenneth Galbraith (1908–)

Born in Ontario, John Kenneth Galbriath studied at the University of Toronto and Berkeley in the early 1930s and for five years (1934–1939) was a tutor and instructor in economics at Harvard. After a brief term as an assistant professor at Princeton, he became deputy administrator of the wartime Office of Price Administration in Washington. In 1943, however, he was forced to resign. Galbraith said the reason for his ouster was simple: "I reached the point that all price fixers reach—my enemies outnumbered my friends."

During 1945–1946 he served as director of the U.S. Strategic Bombing Survey and also headed up the Office of Economic Security Policy, which involved him in the postwar economies of both Germany and Japan. Since 1948 (with the exception of 1961–1963 when he was Kennedy's ambassador to India), Galbraith has taught economics at Harvard.

No ivory-tower type, this man has helped edit *Fortune* and written both technical and nontechnical books, many of which reflect his keen sense of humor. He is perhaps best known for *The Affluent Society* (1958), a critique of economic policy during the Eisenhower years. This volume argued that increased production does not now satisfy genuine needs in America; it merely gratifies the wants of the affluent that advertising stimulated. Galbraith called for a shift of priorities to aid the less well-to-do: more housing, better education, expansion of mass transit, such expenditures to be financed by a national sales tax. Some have credited (or blamed) this book for an alteration by later Democratic administrations from traditional New Deal policy to massive federal spending on behalf of middle class as well as poor Americans.

In another major work, *The New Industrial State* (1967), Galbraith proclaimed that a relatively few giant corporations were coming to dominate the United States, making the traditional free marketplace a thing of the past. Although he did not specifically say that mere bigness was bad, Galbraith criticized these huge corporations for their lack of concern for higher values and the public welfare.

Since the late 1940s Professor Galbraith has been extremely prominent as an activist liberal force in the Democratic party. He was a key aide to Stevenson, a confidant of Kennedy, and a backer of Eugene McCarthy for the presidency in 1968. He served as chairman of the Americans for Democratic Action (1967–1970), at which time he was a firm foe of the war in Vietnam. A challenging thinker, John Kenneth Galbraith has had considerable influence through his role in politics and as lecturer and writer. ■

Wide World.

The 1960 election saw the most important use yet for television in the political process, as Senator John F. Kennedy and Vice President Richard Nixon took the historic step of squaring off in four nationally televised debates. There was no follow-up to this precedent until the Carter-Ford contest of 1976.

Democratic activists with more campaign ammunition. In the congressional election of 1958 they gained enough House seats to give that body a distinctly liberal tinge for the first time in a decade; nevertheless, the hidebound seniority system frustrated their attempts at reform. In September 1959 they established the Democratic Study Group, which was nothing less than a "party within a party" in the House of Representatives. Meanwhile, a similar body called the Democratic Advisory Council was functioning at the national level, with both groups endeavoring to develop issues that would capture the voter's attention in 1960.

In that year all of the potential Democratic nominees except Lyndon Johnson came from the activist wing of the party. John F. Kennedy (1917-1963), a young senator from Massachusetts who had nearly become Stevenson's running mate in 1956, had a well-oiled machine and the cash to run it. When he defeated Hubert Humphrey the other leading liberal contender, in the West Virginia primary, the prize was his. Johnson's last-minute efforts to round up delegates failed but helped him gain the vice-presidential slot. Kennedy's opponent was Richard M. Nixon, Eisenhower's Vice President for two terms.

Kennedy won by about 120,000 votes out of nearly 69 million cast. His Catholicism may have hurt him nationwide, but probably helped him in populous northern cities with large electoral votes where black votes tipped the balance in his favor. In a general way, voters viewed the Democrats as the party of prosperity and the Republicans as the party of peace, and economic issues seemed to weigh heavily on their minds in November of 1960. Also, they seem to have been influenced by Kennedy's poise and his aggressive stance during highly publicized TV debates with his better-known opponent. With his call to "get this country moving again," JFK reactivated the New Deal coalition (with the exception of an anti-Catholic defection, largely in the South); and, by electing both a Democratic President and a Democratic Congress, the voters seemed to be choosing to break a decade of deadlock. The 1960 Democratic platform and Kennedy's campaign oratory had rekindled earlier hopes, and it appeared that the program initiated by FDR in the 1930s—and only tinkered with a bit in the 1950s—would resume in the 1960s. What no one could foresee, of course, was that the demise of equilibrium in the political realm might soon be duplicated in other sectors of American life as well.

The Presidential Election of 1960

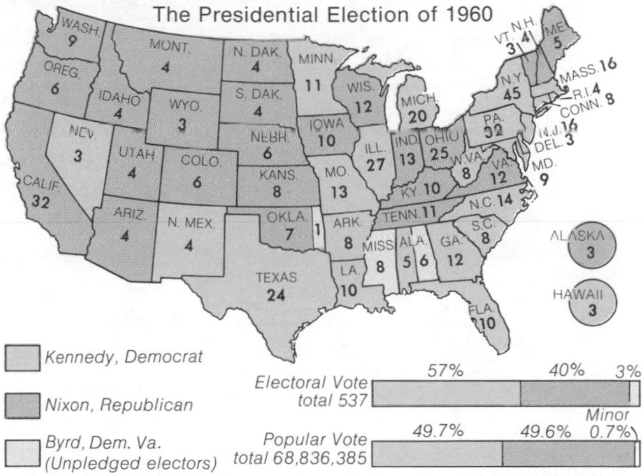

Essay

Babbage, Watson, and IBM

"Calculating machines comprise various pieces of mechanism for assisting the human mind in executing the operations of arithmetic." So wrote Charles Babbage (1792–1871), a brilliant English mathematician who pursued many interests, in his *Passages from the Life of a Philosopher.* Babbage, generally recognized today as the grandfather of the computer, at age thirty wrote a widely acclaimed paper on computations and even constructed a small working computer. Babbage soon got financial backing to build a larger one, but instead he began work on "an engine," as he called it, that utilized a complicated punch card process adapted from the weaving industry. Lord Byron's daughter was one of the few people who understood what Babbage was trying to do; but, whatever it was, he never finished the project.

Instead, this gregarious chatty man wandered off into various fields of research often unrelated to computers. His fascinating *Passages* tells of work on submarines, diving bells, and time signals. The volume also contains hints for travelers, notes on picking locks and deciphering codes, explanations of the operation of railways, and, for good measure, a few pages on glaciers, parcel-post systems, and games of skill. At his death he was best known for his one-man campaign against street musicians and organ grinders, both of which, he claimed, interrupted his research.

Despite a helter-skelter work pattern, Charles Babbage achieved some fundamental mathematical discoveries. His ideas, based on the writings of Blaise Pascal, a French mathematician of the 1640s, enunciated the fundamental principles upon which all present-day computers are based. He also was a true pioneer in operational research, the study of all kinds of scientific manufacturing processes. In addition, Babbage called for government subsidies to aid scientific research.

Despite this pioneer work of Babbage, only in this century, and especially since World War II, have computers become an important element in daily life. The man most responsible for this development that has wrought great changes in recordkeeping, payroll distribution, and storage of knowledge of all sorts was Thomas J. Watson, founder of International Business Machines, better known simply as IBM.

Watson, born in Campbell, New York, reminds one in many ways of George Eastman, the man who made Kodak a

New York Public Library, Picture Collection.

Charles Babbage, eccentric genius and grandfather of the computer.

household word. Neither was an inventor in the true sense of the word, but each had vision and skill in business management; each thought in international terms from the outset, overwhelmed or bought out his competition, and marketed superior products for which there was great demand.

After a brief career as a traveling salesman and peddler of stocks, Tom Watson joined up with the National Cash Register Company in Buffalo. A dedicated worker who always believed that sales were the key to success, he rose rapidly and soon held managerial posts in Rochester and Dayton, Ohio.

Shortly before World War I, at about the time Watson was thinking of marriage, he and several other National Cash Register executives were indicted and convicted by the U.S. government for monopolistic practices. Although this antitrust action eventually was withdrawn, similar suits would plague Watson for the remainder of his life.

Courtesy I.B.M.

Thomas J. Watson, reverentially known as "Our Founder" at IBM.

At the age of forty, while this antitrust indictment was still pending, Watson suddenly found himself unemployed as a result of a top-level management shuffle at National Cash Register. However, he did emerge with a hefty $50,000 as severance pay. Because of his keen business acumen and impressive sales record, Watson had numerous offers, but finally decided to become the business manager of a holding group known as the Computing-Tabulating-Recording Company. This firm, based in Endicott, New York, produced a variety of business machines; however, it was not doing particularly well.

For a decade (1914–1924) Watson worked in relative obscurity as he tried to improve the fortunes of both Computer-Tabulating-Recording and its business manager. In the mid-1920s he became president, and very shortly thereafter C-T-R became IBM. Meanwhile, Watson built carefully, insisting upon an aggressive sales force of white Protestant males who were carefully groomed at all times (only white shirts, no stripes or colors), knew the product line down to the last wire and screw, and conformed to a strict moral code. Herein lies at least one key to the astounding success of IBM: superb, highly trained salesmen who also were highly rewarded for their efforts. In addition, of course, these people were selling products that businessmen throughout the world really wanted, and they were working under near-monopolistic conditions.

By 1930, Thomas J. Watson was emerging as a figure of some national consequence as an executive of the U.S. Chamber of Commerce and one of the highest paid men in the country. In the depths of the Depression (1934) he received the largest salary of any American citizen, $364,432, which was about $40,000 more than his friend, movie star Will Rogers, made that same year. When this income became known two years later, Watson was very defensive, stressing how much he paid out in taxes and how that huge figure actually consisted of a fixed annual income and a percentage of profits after dividends were paid. But this executive had other public relations problems that caused him much more trouble, notably a private audience with Adolf Hitler in 1937 during which he accepted a high Nazi decoration.

Yet despite the bad publicity from his huge personal income in the midst of very hard times and his consorting with dictators, just before the outbreak of a world war, Watson's company continued to grow. In 1939, IBM had sales totaling $41 million (a net income of $12 million), and between 1941 and 1945 sales jumped from $63 million to $142 million. World War II clearly provided impetus for tremendous expansion, many IBM machines quickly being adapted to combat purposes such as calculating gunfire range.

During the first decade of peace IBM's gross income increased almost five times to $700 million. For it was in these years that large, functioning computers, aided by research at the University of Pennsylvania, Columbia University, and Massachusetts Institute of Technology, came into their own. Some of these monsters housed "stored programs" for the first time, an innovation giving them the ability to proceed with computations independent of external controls. IBM did not market its first computer—the 701—until 1953, two years after UNIVAC I, the first modern commercial digital computer, was installed in the Bureau of the Census. In 1955 the IBM 650 was introduced and became the most widely used of all first-generation computers. IBM continued to pour money into research and development and in 1959 with the introduction of its 7094 and 7040 became the established leader in the young computer industry. This so-called second generation of computers employed transistors (invented in 1948) instead of vacuum tubes and a magnetized core storage system for its primary memory. On April 7, 1964, IBM announced its System 360, which contained so many innovations that it was acknowledged as the advent of third-generation computers.

The enormous expenditures in research and development of computer technology along with aggressive marketing made IBM the unquestioned leader in the computer industry. By 1967 IBM sales reached $5,345,290,993; and, with 250,000 employees in 105 countries, Watson's dynamic empire had become the third largest American corporation in terms of earnings. But the "great man" was no longer guiding growth and expansion. He died in June 1956 at the age of eighty-two.

Patriarch, autocrat, man of vision, sentimentalist, supersalesman, advocate of world peace, multimillionaire

Courtesy I.B.M.

A "central control office," a result of the computer revolution.

monopolist, friend of heads of states, and himself the head of an international empire, Watson lived all of his roles ot the full. His competitors might laugh at his salesmen dressed in identical dark suits, white shirts, and proper hats, at the songs they sang praising Thomas J. Watson and IBM, and at the collegelike cheers punctuating the morning sales rallies. And competitors knew that no IBM salesman drank during business hours, cashed his paycheck in a bar, or asked questions when money was deducted from his paycheck (without permission) to buy gifts for Mr. and Mrs. Watson. (Certainly not if he wished to remain in the IBM family.) But competitors failed to be amused by the outstanding sales records these automatons posted with unceasing regularity.

Computers have a pervasive effect on the entire American economy and way of life, an effect that can only intensify in coming years. Medicine, education, national defense, banking and retail sales, postal and other communications, and research and analysis are areas in which the computer revolution is taking place. The electronic transfer of funds (checkless banking) and the electronic transfer of mail along with rapid facsimile-image reproduction represent only the tip of a computer technology iceberg. While the virtual overnight advances in computer technology make it difficult to predict the full impact upon our life and institutions, it seems safe to say that it has started a revolution the end of which is not in sight.

Charles Babbage, that amiable gadfly of London's organ grinders who had much to do with all this, once said in the mid-1800s that he would gladly give up the rest of his life if only he could return for seventy-two hours 500 years hence and be provided with a guide to all of the scientific discoveries made since his death. It seems quite possible that enough has happened in the last fifty years in computerization alone to keep Babbage totally fascinated during a three-day sojourn should he return after only a century. And, it seems equally possible that IBM could provide him with his desired "scientific guide," rolls of computer sheets spewed out by some gigantic, squat behemoth, a direct descendant of the little engine Babbage tinkered with throughout much of his life but never finished.

The Truman Presidency

Alonzo L. Hamby, *Beyond the New Deal: Harry S Truman and American Liberalism* (1973)

Barton Bernstein and Allen J. Matusow, eds., *The Truman Administration: A Documentary History* (1966)

Cabell Phillips, *The Truman Presidency: The History of a Triumphant Succession* (1966)

The Eisenhower Presidency

Charles C. Alexander, *Holding the Line: The Eisenhower Era, 1952–1961* (1975)

Herbert S. Parmet, *Eisenhower and the American Crusades* (1972)

Emmet J. Hughes, *Ordeal of Power: The Eisenhower Years* (1963)

Social Trends in Postwar America

Eric F. Goldman, *The Crucial Decade—and After; America, 1945–1960* (1960)

Douglas T. Miller and Marion Nowak, *The Fifties: The Way We Really Were* (1977)

John W. Aldridge, *In the Country of the Young* (1970)

William H. Chafe, *The American Woman* (1972)

Vance Packard, *The Status Seekers* (1959)

Grace Hechinger and Fred M. Hechinger, *Teen-Age Tyranny* (1963)

David Riesman, et al., *The Lonely Crowd: A Study of the Changing American Character* (1950)

William H. Whyte, Jr., *The Organization Man* (1956)

Robert C. Wood, *Suburbia: Its People and Their Politics* (1958)

Erik Barnouw, *Tube of Plenty: The Evolution of American Television* (1975)

Civil Rights Revolution

William C. Berman, *The Politics of Civil Rights in the Truman Administration* (1970)

Anthony Lewis, *Portrait of a Decade: The Second American Revolution* (1964)

Numan V. Bartley, *The Rise of Massive Resistance: Race and Politics in the South During the 1950s* (1969)

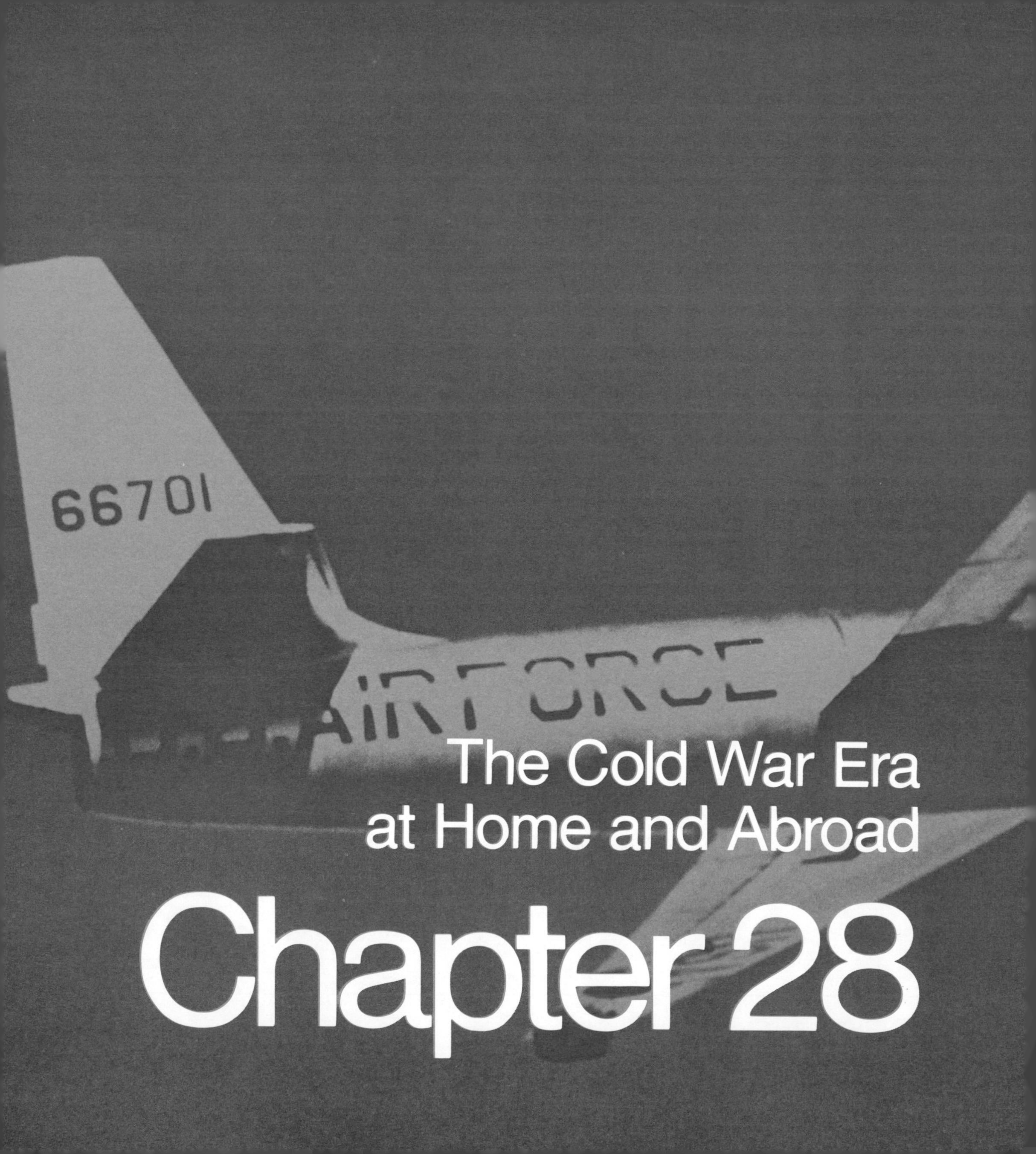

The Cold War Era at Home and Abroad

Chapter 28

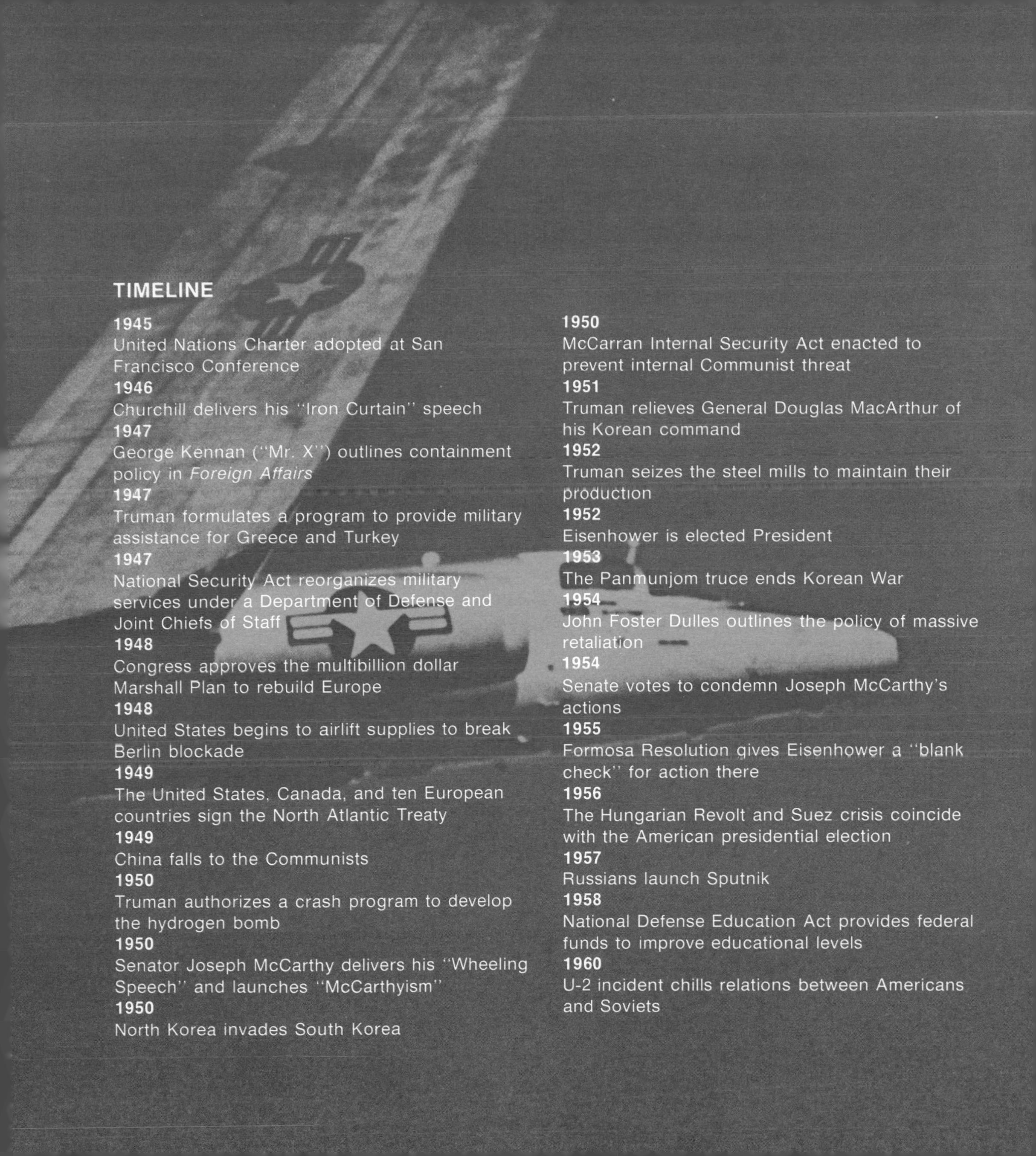

TIMELINE

1945
United Nations Charter adopted at San Francisco Conference

1946
Churchill delivers his "Iron Curtain" speech

1947
George Kennan ("Mr. X") outlines containment policy in *Foreign Affairs*

1947
Truman formulates a program to provide military assistance for Greece and Turkey

1947
National Security Act reorganizes military services under a Department of Defense and Joint Chiefs of Staff

1948
Congress approves the multibillion dollar Marshall Plan to rebuild Europe

1948
United States begins to airlift supplies to break Berlin blockade

1949
The United States, Canada, and ten European countries sign the North Atlantic Treaty

1949
China falls to the Communists

1950
Truman authorizes a crash program to develop the hydrogen bomb

1950
Senator Joseph McCarthy delivers his "Wheeling Speech" and launches "McCarthyism"

1950
North Korea invades South Korea

1950
McCarran Internal Security Act enacted to prevent internal Communist threat

1951
Truman relieves General Douglas MacArthur of his Korean command

1952
Truman seizes the steel mills to maintain their production

1952
Eisenhower is elected President

1953
The Panmunjom truce ends Korean War

1954
John Foster Dulles outlines the policy of massive retaliation

1954
Senate votes to condemn Joseph McCarthy's actions

1955
Formosa Resolution gives Eisenhower a "blank check" for action there

1956
The Hungarian Revolt and Suez crisis coincide with the American presidential election

1957
Russians launch Sputnik

1958
National Defense Education Act provides federal funds to improve educational levels

1960
U-2 incident chills relations between Americans and Soviets

CHAPTER OUTLINE

Despite the determination of many Americans to establish a conflict-free society at the end of World War II, the evolving East-West confrontation known as the Cold War would not permit them to enjoy such luxury. It would also exert a lasting impact upon U.S. life and institutions. Efforts at containment of the Communist threat abroad exacted a high price at home and shaped postwar America fully as much as the simultaneous suburban explosion and consumer-oriented economic growth. The new bipolar competition that was carried on throughout the world reinforced certain assumptions and elements that were long evident. And it also spawned attitudes and social forces of its own.

By mid-1946 the Cold War was a recognizable reality. Despite the claims of contemporary leftist politicians—and of revisionist historians later on—Harry Truman did not create it. He moved only slowly and haltingly from Roosevelt's policies as he formalized his anti-Soviet stance into what became "containment" by 1947. The Truman Doctrine represented its negative and defensive side; the Marshall Plan and NATO, its positive and offensive side.

By early 1950 the Truman administration clearly had accepted the task of defining the "Free World," and the Korean conflict was fought in this context. That Asian peninsula, divided by Russia and the U.S. at the end of World War II in an effort to evacuate Japanese forces and erase a half-century of occupation, had become split into two parts; and, when the North Koreans moved south in June 1950, Truman responded decisively, if a bit imprudently, since he did not consult Congress. Then, three months later when he permitted U.S. troops to cross the thirty-eighth parallel and invade the north, containment, with whatever justification, became "liberation." Reverses suffered at the hands of the Chinese Communists, however, soon forced a return to the policy of containment. This war ushered in a new era that increased permanently the level of U.S. military spending (and preparedness) and provided a significant precedent of war by executive action.

Eisenhower and Secretary of State John Foster Dulles (1888–1959), for all their differences from Truman in outlook and tactics, continued his containment strategy. Their policy included a "New Look" in defense and reliance upon indigenous forces (protected by the American nuclear umbrella) through multilateral security pacts. It stirred up much partisan Democratic criticism but in practice was much like the foreign policy of Truman and Dean Acheson (Secretary of State, 1949–1953). The U.S. tended to put somewhat more emphasis upon air power in the 1950s; but, although formal commitment abroad increased, the nation was neither more nor less willing to intervene in particular situations than before.

Eisenhower's personal interest in summit conferences and his restraint in crisis may seem in retrospect admirable features of his approach to foreign affairs. But he also failed to lead the American people in any sense toward a general detente, let alone toward acceptance of deescalation of the arms race. And many of the crises he confronted were, to some degree, a natural result of U.S. policy and rhetoric. Like Truman, Eisenhower believed in a bipolar world. It was America's mission to contain the Communist menace. His seemingly more temperate approach to that problem owed more to his greater self-assurance and wartime experiences than any pacific tendencies on his part. Also, he was able to profit and learn from what his predecessor had done and had not done.

Domestically, the Cold War had much impact. It spawned several new institutions such as the Defense Department, Central Intelligence Agency, and National Security Council and strengthened immeasurably the military-industrial complex of World War II days. American economic vitality came more and more to depend upon defense expenditures, so much so that one cannot help but wonder what might have happened to the postwar business-industrial realm in the United States if this confrontation had not developed. Cold War crises stirred interest in civil defense and education generally. They also fueled the short-lived excesses of McCarthyism in the early 1950s.

In politics, the vaunted and much exaggerated bipartisanship of the immediate postwar years did not endure; foreign policy and national security matters became heatedly partisan by the late 1950s. One effect of the Cold War was to spur many politicians to strike a more aggressive stance. Kennedy, for example, as a campaigner in 1960 said much that contradicted his own foreign policy views of the previous decade.

The Cold War, despite its prominence and great effect upon American life from 1945 to 1960, failed to develop an active, articulate consensus among voters. To meet the challenge of the Cold War some institutions, which seemed to be permanent, were reshaped; Truman and Eisenhower were given a greater voice in foreign policy; some limitations were imposed on civil liberties; and a defense-dependent economy was created. All of these were vital, far-reaching developments, but the Cold War never made foreign policy the most crucial matter to be considered when voters cast ballots: America, which was sprawling, suburban, contented, found its first concerns elsewhere much of the time. Only when an extreme crisis occurred did anyone actually build a bomb shelter or take much interest in civil defense. Perhaps the word "containment" itself contributed to this mood. It conjured up images of one great force effectively restraining and bottling up another opposing force somewhere several thousand miles away. For much of this period, so long as the bottling process took place in eastern Europe or Asia, the mass of Americans were largely oblivious to what was going on.

America Enters the Cold War

The Cold War had no clear starting point, but the reasons for American-Soviet distrust were rooted in different systems of government, different economies, quite different cultural backgrounds, and frequent disputes in the 1920s and 1930s. Only the crisis of World War II and common enemies created what proved to be a temporary friendship. The collapse of Europe and the weakening of the British Empire meant that the United States and Russia would emerge from that conflict as the two great powers in the world. All of these factors—historic, economic, and cultural—pointed to disagreement, but that in itself did not have to mean outright confrontation.

From Hot War to Cold

Russia had agreed to the Atlantic Charter of August 1941 only with the ominous qualification that "the practical application of these principles will necessarily adapt itself to the circumstances, needs, and historic peculiarities of particular countries." Those principles, drawn up by Roosevelt and Churchill when they met in the North Atlantic, sketched the broad outlines of their ideas for the postwar world. They pledged to seek no territory by conquest or sanction any boundary changes not in accord with the freely expressed wishes of those involved, to respect the right of self-government, to assure economic opportunity for both victor and vanquished, to strive for economic cooperation so as to improve living standards, and to establish a lasting peace through general disarmament. Although not official policy, all of the Allies endorsed these provisions in January 1942. They also were used effectively as propaganda throughout the war and incorporated (in part) in the United Nations Charter in 1945.

Nevertheless, Stalin made his nation's territorial aims clear to the British as early as December 1941. In general, he thought Nazi-occupied countries should resume their prewar frontiers when peace came; however, the Russian dictator pressed for incorporation of the Baltic states of Estonia, Latvia, and Lithuania into the U.S.S.R., as well as parts of Finland, Poland, and Rumania so as to provide added protection against future invasions from the west. Meanwhile, American commitment to an "open world"—so diametrically opposed to this view—was being voiced by U.S. spokesmen. Controversy with Soviet leaders over a second front in Europe and especially concerning postwar Poland and Germany itself proved especially divisive. The meetings at Teheran and Yalta merely "papered over" these issues: a Russian-backed government in Poland was to incorporate additional "representative elements" and Germany would be occupied jointly by the major Allied powers, although Russia would get unspecified reparations from that nation.

Yet these were not the only nations of eastern and central Europe facing an uncertain future. All of the peoples from Estonia, Latvia, and Lithuania in the north to Bulgaria, Rumania, and Yugoslavia in the south were at the mercy of Soviet legions as World War II drew to a close. And each of them (except Germany) had governments in exile eager to press their claims and several also enjoyed the support of very vocal ethnic lobbies in the United States. The eventual fate of these nations differed somewhat. The three Baltic states, all part of Russia until 1918 and again briefly in 1940–1941, became, as Stalin wished, states within the U.S.S.R. Much of the rest of eastern Europe, in time, adopted some form of Communist government, retaining only a semblance of national sovereignty and bowing to the will of Moscow. The lone exception in the immediate postwar era was Yugoslavia, which, although Communist, embarked under the leadership of Marshall Josep Tito (1892-) on an independent foreign policy that soon angered Stalin and led to an open break.

Roosevelt, flexible in his wartime dealings with Moscow, was confident he could broker a solution to these incipient conflicts, *not* because he was sympathetic to Russian aims, but because he and aides such as Harry Hopkins truly felt that "the dawn of a new day" in international relations was at hand. In this instance, FDR's confidence in his ability to manipulate others was unrealistic; in any case, his death in April 1945 ended whatever personal leverage he and his administration may have had in Soviet-American affairs. Officially at least, Truman continued Roosevelt's policies for a time, feeling his way on the foreign scene much as he did at home. Yet he talked very bluntly to Foreign Minister Vyacheslav M. Molotov when the two men met at the White House shortly after Roosevelt's death, and a week or so later Washington-Moscow differences flared up at an organizational meeting of the United Nations held in San Francisco.

Although Truman learned of a successful atomic bomb during the Potsdam Conference in July 1945 and that news made him somewhat less dependent upon Stalin for help against Japan, he certainly had not adopted a rigidly anti-Russian attitude by the time the meetings ended. After all, Japan still had five million men under arms, a formidable force indeed, and no one was certain just what effect the atomic bomb might have even if used against that nation. There always was the possibility it might prove less powerful than supposed or perhaps not even explode properly. In short, the United States still might need considerable Russian assistance in the Far East. At the same time, the President was being pulled this way and that by aides who wanted to tell him how to deal with the Russians. For one, Averell Harriman

Wide World.

President Truman introduces former Prime Minister Winston Churchill at Westminster College (Mo.), March 5, 1946. In his speech, Churchill warned of an "iron curtain" descending on Europe.

(1891–   ), the U.S. ambassador to Moscow, was urging Truman to take a hard line, and he seems to have had considerable influence.

The basic problem, simply put, was that Russia, ravaged twice by German troops in a quarter-century, was committed to a weak, divided Germany; the United States, believing that depression and chaos reparation payments had resulted from economic problems arising out of World War I, did not want to see the same pattern repeated. Stalin wanted a strong Russia and a weak Germany; the United States, by prediliction and because its postwar prosperity depended upon a reintegrated Europe, did not agree. By the winter of 1945–1946 it was clear that no compromise was possible, and in mid-1946 the East-West split known as the Cold War was becoming more obvious. Confrontation between Russia and the United States in Iran, Stalin's announcement of a new five-year plan and his withdrawal of a request for American aid, Winston Churchill's widely publicized "Iron Curtain" speech, and the standoff in Germany all bore witness to this fact. In the spring of 1946, polls showed that over 70 percent of the American public disapproved of Soviet policy, and 60 percent thought the U.S. was "soft" on this issue. The Cold War now had become a political football—potentially both a liability and an asset—and all politicians would have to play the game.

Churchill's words spoken at Fulton, Missouri, on March 5, 1946, undoubtedly marked a turning point in this drama: "From Stettin in the Baltic to Trieste in the Adriatic, an iron curtain has descended across the continent. From what I have seen of our Russian friends and allies during the war, I am convinced that there is nothing they admire so much as strength and there is nothing for which they have less respect than for military weakness." If nothing else, Churchill gave to the postwar period the phrase "Iron Curtain."

Truman, somewhat irked by Churchill's outspoken stance, nevertheless introduced the former prime minister to his Missouri audience and applauded his words. At the time, however, the President did not believe this utterance constituted an open break with Moscow (since Churchill spoke as a private citizen, not a government official), and he subsequently invited Stalin to come to the U.S. and present his views on various differences that seemed to pose a threat to postwar cooperation. The Soviet leader did not accept.

Who was to blame? With the advantage of hindsight it is apparent that both sides were at fault, although this is not to imply that the confrontation could have been avoided. Given the clashing objectives—a weak Germany or an integrated, prosperous Europe—no easy resolution was possible. Washington assumed Moscow's overt expansionism to mean a spread of Communism itself, which, at the outset, may not have been Stalin's intent. But he did not make his aims clear; and, having just defeated one dictator, Americans could only view the growing power of another with misgiving.

America had the atomic bomb and unimpaired industrial might, but also a rapidly dwindling army and a public not about to fight another war so soon. Yet, as the most powerful nation to come out of World War II, Americans thought they held all the cards and the U.S.S.R. would have to agree with their postwar plans. Efforts to extract Russian concessions in return for a loan failed when Moscow began stripping German factories to meet its reconstruction needs in mid-1946. Using the atomic bomb was out of the question, so, in effect, that advantage was no advantage at all.

Unable to break the international deadlock and with criticism mounting at home, between January and May 1947 the Truman administration embarked on a firm new policy: no more compromise without concessions from Moscow. Now, reacting to the Soviet challenge, Truman stepped up his counterattack.

The Cold War remains a complicated phenomenon. It is enough of a task to weigh the arguments of the West and evaluate the motives of its principal actors: Truman, Harriman, Churchill, and others. Even less clear are internal influences at work within the U.S.S.R. The craving for security and the need to rebuild Russian industry are obvious, but it is impossible to know what role ideology, the personality of Joseph Stalin, and pressures being exerted upon an aging dictator may have played in this drama.

The United Nations

Ironically, the United Nations, created in San Francisco in April 1945 as World War II was drawing to a close, provided a focus for growing East-West disenchantment and the machinery to ameliorate some of these differences. As constituted, the UN retained many features of the old League of Nations: a large deliberative body in which all members had a voice (the General Assembly)

Wide World.

With President Truman looking on, Secretary of State Edward R. Stettinius signs the United Nation security charter in San Francisco in June 1946.

and a smaller Security Council on which the five major wartime allies—Britain, Russia, U.S., China, and France—had permanent seats. Unlike the League, which required members to give unanimous approval to any measure before action could be taken, both UN bodies operated on the majority principle, with the five powers holding permanent veto power in the Council. The work of the UN was directed by a secretary-general, an administrator appointed by the Assembly upon the recommendation of the Council.

Despite what Americans soon regarded as delaying tactics on the part of the Russians and their satellite supporters, the Truman administration remained optimistic concerning the UN's future and firmly committed to the ideals of the fifty-nation organization, which set up housekeeping on Manhattan's East Side. In his first State of the Union message (January 1946), the President repeated the hopes his predecessor had expressed for lasting peace:

> "The United Nations Organization now being established represents a minimum essential beginning. It must be developed rapidly and steadily. Its work must be amplified to fill in the whole pattern that has been outlined. Economic collaboration, for example, already charted, now must be carried on as carefully and as comprehensively as the political and security measures.
>
> It is important that the nations come together as states in the Assembly and in the Security Council and in the other specialized assemblies and councils that have been and will be arranged. But this is not enough. Our ultimate security requires more than a process of consultation and compromise."

Truman then stressed the need for "world collaboration," adding that "many concessions and adjustments will be required." But, within a year, as each side tried to use the UN to project its own programs and policies, it became an arena for heated debate, not a forum for true reconciliation or compromise.

Containment and Commitment

The term most closely identified with America's early Cold War policy is "containment," generally meaning an effort to stem the flow of Communist expansion. Containment was first explained in an article published in *Foreign Affairs* in July 1947 by George Kennan (1904–), a veteran diplomat and then chief of the State Department's Policy Planning Staff. Although Kennan used a pseudonym ("X"), his authorship was soon established and the statement widely accepted as administration policy. This was true only in a general sense, for Kennan eventually left government service because his position was somewhat more restrained than that of Truman and others. Nevertheless, the concept enunciated by Kennan fitted well with the President's own ideas.

Four months earlier, on March 12, 1947, Truman had appeared before a special session of Congress and directed attention to Greece and Turkey. In stern and somber tones he requested $400 million in emergency aid to help those two countries combat Communist threats, assistance which that body soon granted. The President's appeal, now known as the "Truman Doctrine," concluded with these words:

> "The seeds of totalitarian regimes are nurtured by misery and want. They spread and grow in the evil soil of poverty and strife. They reach their full growth when the hope of a people for a better life has died.
>
> We must keep that hope alive.
>
> The free peoples of the world look to us for support in maintaining their freedoms.
>
> If we falter in our leadership, we may endanger the peace of the world—and we shall surely endanger the welfare of this Nation."

Truman clearly was beginning to side with the realists in his administration, men who endorsed Churchill's Iron Curtain views and believed the U.S. had to take a stern line against Russian expansion. The rise of Dean Acheson, Secretary of State during Truman's second term, provides a barometer of the President's hardening attitude toward the Soviets. Yet Kennan was unhappy with the universal tone of the President's approach.

Momentous events surrounded the shaping of the Truman Doctrine and this new departure in U.S. foreign policy. Two weeks earlier British representatives in Washington had quietly informed State Department officials that their country no longer could underwrite military aid to the eastern Mediterranean. As one American diplomat remarked later, without flourishes or drum rolls, Great Britain simply handed over the job of world leadership, "with all of its burdens and all of its glories," to the United States. A few days later, Secretary of State George C. Marshall (1880–1959), Acheson (then Under Secretary of State), and a group of key congressional leaders met at the White House. Once Acheson got the floor he launched into a vigorous, almost passionate analysis of America's mission in a bipolar world. The defense of Western civilization, as he saw it, now lay in U.S. hands. If the Russians gained a foothold in the Mediterranean basin, they could then penetrate deep into Asia and Africa and the psychological impact upon western Europe would be devastating. Writing in the *New York Times* (March 2, 1947), Hanson Baldwin picked up Acheson's theme: the United States held the key to the world's future, and it alone could "avert a decline in Western civilization and a reversion to nihilism and the Dark Ages."

At the same time that ideological and economic responses to the Soviet challenge were emerging, American activity in the military realm increased, at least at an organizational level. The National Security Act of July 26, 1947 (amended somewhat two years later) provided for the creation of a separate air force and the administration of the army, navy, and air force under a single Secretary of Defense. These acts also established the Joint Chiefs of Staff (really a continuation of wartime procedures), the National Security Council, the Central Intelligence Agency, and the National Security Resources Board. Nevertheless, throughout 1947 rearmament actually progressed rather slowly. In general, these efforts were plagued by interservice feuds, budgetary limitations, congressional bickering over manpower needs, and public conviction (despite warnings to the contrary from leading scientists) that America's atomic monopoly would keep the Communists at bay.

Having seen wartime waste in government contracts as a result of interservice rivalry and a lack of coordination, Truman wanted a strong, centralized Defense Department. The army and air force favored strong centralization, but the navy, fearing loss of prestige and influence, dragged its feet. The first man to head that department was James V. Forrestal, a dedicated cold warrior, who served from 1944 to 1947 as Secretary of the Navy. He had a rough, two-year reign and actually presided over a body that existed largely on paper until 1949.

The National Security Council grew out of the desire of Truman and others for an interdepartment War Cabinet that could shape and coordinate America's foreign-military policies. It consisted of the Secretaries of State and Defense, as well as others named by the President; however, the NSC had only an advisory function. Truman, fearing it might erode his own powers, used it sparingly until 1950, when the pressures of the Korean War led him to turn to it with greater frequency.

The third new institution, the CIA, resulted from need for an ongoing intelligence-gathering body. Truman, who disliked "cloak-and-dagger" hanky-panky, disbanded the wartime OSS in October 1945, but within three months he had set up an interim agency known as the Central Intelligence Group; and, in 1947, that organization became a statutory entity, reporting directly to the NSC. Within two years the CIA had increased greatly its rights of secrecy and autonomy, especially surrounding its use of money. And, in succeeding decades the CIA grew in size, technology, scope, power, and importance, largely unquestioned until the 1960s when serious mistakes for the first time invited congressional scrutiny.

That agency's first director was Rear Admiral Roscoe H. Hillenkocter, but Allen Dulles (1893–1969), the man who headed the OSS in Switzerland during World War II, soon emerged as the organization's most powerful voice. Dulles, a lawyer, and a brother of John Foster Dulles, who served as Eisenhower's Secretary of State, had helped formulate plans for the CIA and subsequently became deputy director (1951–1953) and then director (1953–1961).

In 1950 another security-related agency came into existence; The National Science Foundation. It had the responsibility to "promote the progress of science, to advance the national health, prosperity and welfare; and to secure the national defense." To carry out these broad objectives, this body began supporting research through grants and fellowships and encouraging exchange of information among scientists throughout the world. It began with a modest $500,000 allocation, but within fifteen years its annual budget—aided immeasurably by the demands of the Cold War—had swelled to $420 million.

The Marshall Plan

If the Truman Doctrine and renewed activity in military-scientific realms can be viewed as a defensive response to the emerging Cold War, this new American activism also had its positive side. Exactly one year after the President issued his call for emergency military aid for Greece and Turkey, Congress on March 12, 1948, approved the Marshall Plan, which provided $5 billion to begin rehabilitation of Europe's troubled economy. At that time, Truman projected $17 billion in loans and grants over a four-year period "to bridge the temporary gap between minimum European needs and war-dimin-

Wide World.

The Pentagon, constructed on the Virginia side of the Potomac River in 1943, houses the Department of Defense, symbolizing the unification of the defense establishment and the growth of national security concerns in the early Cold War years.

Walter Sanders/Life Magazine © 1948 Time, Inc.

West Berliners await a drop from an American cargo plane on one of hundreds of mercy flights flown during the Berlin Airlift.

ished European resources." This far-reaching measure, outlined by Secretary of State Marshall in an address at Harvard University in June 1947 (just before Kennan's "X" article appeared in print), encouraged Europe's leaders to formulate plans for their own recovery and to present them to the United States. Several features of the European Recovery Program (its official name) are worth noting. First, the offer was open, in theory, to *all* European states, but Russia and her Soviet-dominated satellites chose not to participate. Second, most of the funds were earmarked for the purchase of U.S. goods, which, in turn, aided the American economy as well. And, third, the Marshall Plan opened the door to widespread foreign aid to other countries in various parts of the world as economic assistance in many forms became a key feature of America's avowed policy to contain Communism.

Along with providing economic aid, the Truman administration also moved to implement collective security in a more tangible form than the United Nations, where Russia could veto such action. By late 1948 the U.S. had entered into a tentative pact with several European nations, and the dramatic airlift of supplies to Allied sectors of Berlin, made necessary by a Soviet blockade of land traffic, paved the way for still more cooperation.

That blockade, begun in June 1948, was the Soviet response to European economic aid and British-American plans to strengthen (and perhaps rearm) West Germany. This altercation ended four-power rule in the city, setting up Communist and non-Communist zones instead. By the spring of 1949, British and U.S. aircraft, landing every three minutes around the clock, were carrying 10,000 tons of goods into Berlin every twenty-four hours. After 324 days the Russians gave up and on May 12, 1949, abandoned the blockade.

Alarmed by this interference with land traffic, a Communist takeover in Czechoslovakia in February 1948 (the last of the so-called satellites to enter the Russian orbit), and Communist strength in the Italian elections, Republican Senator Arthur H. Vandenberg (1884-1951) proposed a resolution that soon took on considerable significance. It reaffirmed America's faith in the UN but stressed this nation's determination to defend itself through collective security if necessary. This resolution, passed by the Senate in June 1948 (64 to 4), had no legal force, yet it enabled the administration to begin formulating concrete plans for the defense of western Europe. The result was the North Atlantic Treaty Organization (NATO), organized in April 1949. The twelve original members—Britain, France, Belgium, Netherlands, Luxembourg, Canada, Norway, Denmark, Iceland, Italy, Portugal, and the United States—agreed to "unite their efforts for collective defense and for the preservation of peace and security."

This was, significantly, the first "entangling alliance" ratified by Congress since George Washington's famous farewell warning of 1796. Both the Marshall Plan and NATO comported well with containment, and Truman's anti-Communist commitment was clarified with his call for a Military Assistance Program under the direction of NATO. Explosion of an atomic bomb by the U.S.S.R. induced Congress to support such a measure, and by late 1950 NATO had its own military command, headed up by General Dwight D. Eisenhower, called back to duty by Truman from the presidency of Columbia University.

In the years 1946–1949, Harry Truman had moved from vacillation to a firm, even aggressive foreign policy based upon the assumption of a bipolar world divided between Communist and free nations. Bold Russian moves such as the coup in Prague and the Berlin blockade helped shape the President's response, as did public opinion at home. At the same time, the expansive rhetoric of the Truman Doctrine helped both to escalate tensions and to improve the administration's credibility with the electorate (hence, to some degree, its success in the 1948 campaign); it also encouraged other politicians to do likewise, regardless of party affiliation. Just as steps taken by the Soviets produced the Marshall Plan and NATO, those organizations, in turn, gave birth to Russian countermoves; in short, Truman's concept of a bipolar world proved to be a self-fulfilling prophecy.

U.P.I.

George C. Marshall (left) with his successor as Secretary of State, Dean G. Acheson.

As American policy stiffened, the role of Dean Acheson within the administration was extremely important. As Under Secretary of State and after 1948 as head of the State Department, Acheson waged a stern, no compromise battle against Soviet interests everywhere. To him, like Woodrow Wilson, evil was evil, no matter what form it might take. It was a case of Athens against Sparta and Rome against the Vandals; the United States of America stood as the last hope of Western civilization. To Acheson, the basic problem was one of economics; if vast areas of the world—the Mediterranean basin, western Europe, and Asia—went Communist, then American trade, American business, and soon American culture as well would suffer.

This emerging Truman-Acheson stance drew hard, fast ideological lines around the world, alerting everyone to the fact that the United States, not the United Nations, would decide when changes on the international scene violated the UN charter. And, as Washington did much to create an East-West frontier, Russia and various European nations joined in the act. Coalition cabinets in France and Italy were reshuffled in mid-1947 to exclude leftist groups, especially Communists. Czechoslovakia, caught in the middle, eventually toppled toward the East. In time, Acheson even saw the Truman Doctrine as a natural outgrowth of the Monroe Doctrine and hinted that the U.S. might adopt a more active role in eastern Europe, upsetting "little groups supported by foreign power" just as Maximilian and the French once had been driven out of Mexico. To him, the U.S.S.R. was the "evil force" responsible for turmoil and revolution everywhere, and no effort was made by American leaders to distinguish between Soviet-style Communism and that of other nations in eastern Europe. As far as the Truman administration was concerned, Communism was a monolithic threat boasting great military power. And Eisenhower, Dulles, and those in command after 1952 agreed without reservation.

Dennis Brack/Black Star.

Dean Acheson

(1893–1971)

Dean Gooderham Acheson, the fiftieth American to head up the State Department and principal architect of U.S. Cold War strategy, was born in Middletown, Connecticut, in 1893, son of a former British army officer turned Episcopalian bishop. His mother was the daughter of a wealthy Canadian distiller. Acheson attended Groton where he was thought to be "a lone wolf and a rebel," then went on to Yale where he did extremely well in his studies, graduating in 1915. His Harvard Law School career was interrupted briefly by a term as a naval ensign in World War I.

After obtaining his L.L.B. in 1918, Acheson served as private secretary to Supreme Court Justice Louis Brandeis for two years, an experience that broadened his views. From 1921 to 1933 he was associated with a prominent Washington law firm (Covington, Burling & Rublee) and then briefly was FDR's Undersecretary of the Treasury. Disagreement with Roosevelt's gold purchase plan sent him back into private practice, but by 1940 Acheson was very active in behalf of all-out aid to Britain. In 1941 he became Assistant Secretary of State and helped push the Lend-Lease Act through Congress. In his new government capacity Acheson participated in numerous wartime decisions, but almost quit in 1946 because he said he and his family could not live on $9,000 a year. Truman raised his salary to $10,000, but in 1947 Acheson returned to his law practice once more.

Two years later he became Secretary of State. Generally he accepted "containment," although his implementation tended to be more ideological and military-oriented than what George Kennan had proposed. During the McCarthy era, despite a stern anti-Communist record, Acheson became a prime target of administration critics. In part, his pseudo-British ways—bristling reddish moustache and Bond Street garb—invited this assault. Lean, over 6 feet tall, witty, amiable, but ever frank, he epitomized much that midwestern Republicans found irritating about Ivy Leaguers who dominated State Department affairs.

During the Eisenhower years, Acheson led a hard-line faction in the Democratic party, once more clashing publicly with Kennan. He later served as foreign policy adviser to Kennedy and Johnson, again advocating all-out use of force in both Cuba and Vietnam. Only in 1968 did Dean Acheson finally conclude that the cost of the Southeast Asian adventure was becoming excessive. He died three years later in Silver Spring, Maryland.

A man involved in many crucial decisions during the genesis of the Cold War, Acheson had both admirers and critics. His zealous anti-Communism may, in fact, have helped to ignite the McCarthy holocaust that later enveloped Acheson himself. Certainly his stern interpretation of containment allowed little room in which to maneuver or compromise and, as such, assured the continuation of the Cold War. ■

Late in January 1950, President Truman took the momentous step of authorizing a crash program to develop the hydrogen bomb; at the same time he put the National Security Council to work on a comprehensive study of defense and foreign policy. The result, National Security Council Policy Paper Number 68 (NSC-68) was the natural outgrowth of events since World War II as seen by Washington. It accepted the split between the United States and the Soviet Union as "a permanent and fundamental alteration in the shape of international relations." Ironically, although this may not have been true at that time, by 1957 and the launching of the Russian satellite Sputnik it was, and in the intervening years Soviet military might had grown to fulfill American expectations. More important, perhaps, NSC-68 established a rationale for huge defense expenditures, recommending annual appropriations "not much below the former wartime levels." Although not a blueprint for action, the paper set forth basic assumptions about the new world order and America's role in it. Paramount among these was a huge arms buildup based upon the realization, in the paper's words, that "Stalin respects the reality of force a great deal more than he does the abstraction of peace."

Containment as sternly practiced by the Truman administration has raised serious questions that are difficult to answer. To what extent did America's definition of free and unfree foster just such a division? Did Acheson, Truman, and others about them find it easier—especially when talking to Congress and the public—to speak in black-white terms? Did they perhaps even prefer a divided, bipolar world to one with grey areas? And, to what extent did the Communist bloc, although this may not have been the original plan, simply flesh out the picture sketched for it by leaders of the free world during the immediate postwar years?

The Cold War and the Political System

In the political realm the Cold War had widespread repercussions. "Isolationism" in the traditional sense was virtually a dead issue after World War II. Both parties accepted the reality that America could no longer ignore the rest of the world. The GOP formally pledged itself to postwar international cooperation in 1943, and that party's 1944 platform contained foreign policy planks consistent with Roosevelt's policies. Congressional leaders of both parties also endorsed resolutions supporting the idea of a United Nations in the postwar era. Thomas E. Dewey and his key foreign policy advisor, John Foster Dulles, kept international questions (especially organization of the U.N.) out of the campaign that year.

Learning from Woodrow Wilson's mistakes after World War I, the Truman administration enlisted Republican support for its foreign policy, notably in the person of Senator Arthur H. Vandenberg, senior Republican on the Foreign Relations Committee. This former Michigan newspaper publisher was an isolationist who before December 1941 had opposed FDR's foreign policy. However, in January 1945 he stunned his Senate colleagues by embracing internationalism, a move perhaps prompted by personal experience with V-2 rockets while visiting London. In any case, Vandenberg, more than anyone else, made bipartisanship in foreign policy possible in the immediate postwar period. As a UN delegate he was a firm supporter of Truman's emerging plans to stem the spread of Communism; whenever the President vacillated, opposition leaders such as Vandenberg began to speak out. These pressures undoubtedly convinced Truman to adopt a tougher line, especially in view of Republican victories in November 1946. And, as noted, Vandenberg's resolution, which was passed two years later, helped lay the foundations for NATO.

During these same years, the Cold War and the administration's new approach to it became hot political issues and inevitably played major roles in the 1948 presidential election. Growing differences with Moscow also created tensions within the Cabinet Truman had inherited from Roosevelt. In mid-July 1946, Secretary of Commerce Henry Wallace (and onetime Vice President) wrote privately to Truman asking how other nations might view U.S. actions since V-J day? "I mean by actions," he said, "concrete things like $13 billion for the War and Navy departments, the Bikini tests of the atomic bomb and continued production of bombs, the plan to arm Latin America with our weapons, production of B-29s and planned production of B-36s, and the effort to secure air bases spread over half the globe from which the other half can be bombed." To Wallace the answer was all too obvious. These measures seemed more aggressive than defensive, and American efforts to torpedo Russia's plans to create its own security system of "friendly" neighbors, in his words, "clinch the case."

Truman, not sympathetic to these views, later would claim that Wallace had proposed "surrendering" to Russia. In September, while Secretary of State Byrnes was in Paris negotiating treaties for the Balkan region with Russia and other powers, Wallace spoke out publicly against a get-tough policy: "The tougher we get the tougher the Russians will get. . . We have no more business in the *political* affairs of Eastern Europe than Russia has in the *political* affairs of Latin America, Western Europe, and the United States." Strange as it may seem, the man heading the U.S. Department of Commerce apparently thought that economics and politics could easily be separated. He also appears to have been convinced that Truman actually was an unwitting captive of Byrnes and other get-tough spokesmen. So, after waging a behind-the-scenes battle for several months, Wallace decided to go public. Eight days later the President fired him for his outspoken criticism of the administration's foreign policy, and with the departure of Wallace the Cabinet lost its last voice opposed to a hard line against Moscow. Wallace subsequently formed a new Progressive party and in 1948 campaigned vigorously (but unsuccessfully) for Truman's job.

The coup in Prague and the crisis of the Berlin blockade and airlift seemed to vindicate Truman's get-tough policies, demonstrating the need for a determined stand. From the point of view of Republican hopes, his Republican opponent in 1948, Thomas Dewey, probably erred when he agreed to a bipartisan moratorium on foreign policy matters. In fact, several historians see Truman's handling of the Berlin affair as one of his greatest assets in 1948. However, not to have had a freewheeling debate on international affairs was a grave mistake for the nation. The end result was a general and passive consensus. Meaningful inquiry into the assumptions and results of foreign policy was stifled until the endless war in Vietnam two decades later broke the long silence.

Embittered by defeat in 1948, some Republicans became less cooperative in foreign policy matters, calling for a still stronger reaction to Soviet threats. The majority of Republicans in the Senate supported NATO when it came to a vote in July 1949, but a hard core of eleven senators (led by Ohio's Robert A. Taft) dissented. A short time later, speaking on Drew Pearson's radio program, Taft explained his opposition to NATO. "I wanted to vote for it—at least to vote to let Russia know that if she attacked western Europe, the United States would be in the war. . . But the Atlantic Pact . . . obligates us to go to war if at any time during the next 20 years anyone makes an armed attack on any 12 nations. Under the Monroe Doctrine we could change our policy at any time. Under the new pact the President can take us into war without Congress." His principal objection, Taft stressed, was that NATO was merely a small part of a huge arms buildup, which could only stimulate similar action by Russia. NATO was, he added, both an offensive and defensive alliance: "I believe our foreign policy should be aimed primarily at security and peace, and I believe such an alliance is more likely to produce war than peace."

At the same time, Republicans were increasingly critical of the administration's policy in Asia, where the Communists seemed to be making great gains. Condemnation of Truman's "Europe First" orientation grew apace after the President suppressed a report critical of the relations between the United States and China. General Albert C. Wedemeyer (1897-   ), a wartime commander in that region, went back to survey the area and informed Truman that large-scale support should go to Nationalist China if Chiang Kai-Shek agreed to substantial economic and political reforms. The China Lobby, a mixed group of business and missionary interests eager to aid the Nationalist cause, immediately stepped up its demands for U.S. action, as did their GOP allies and

China-born Henry R. Luce (1898–1967), head of the *Time-Life* empire. After China fell to the Communists late in 1949, this chorus of criticism increased markedly. However, in retrospect, it appears that nothing short of a major U.S. expeditionary force (which might have invited World War III) could have saved Chiang, who had become, in fact, just another warlord without popular support.

The fall of China and the outbreak of war in Korea indicated to many Republicans that containment was not working well; the Red menace actually was spreading and gaining millions of new adherents. To make matters worse for the Democrats (and bipartisanship as well), many Republicans concluded that the reasons for failure in Asia lay in Washington itself, for they were certain there were Communists or Communist sympathizers within Truman's administration. Cooperation in foreign affairs, such as it was, was at an end, and the scene was set, in Dean Acheson's words, for "the attack of the primitives."

The Experience of Limited War: Korea

To some, Harry Truman's prompt decision to send U.S. troops to Korea when North Koreans invaded the southern half of the peninsula in June 1950 was idealistic and noble, but national and political concerns were evident, too. The method of involvement through the United Nations, rather than a conventional declaration of war, was questionable; and, in some ways, the Korean confrontation was the beginning of a grim transformation of the Cold War. Unfortunately, its lessons went unlearned: the impossibility of fighting limited war to a definitive conclusion and the folly of a democracy waging undeclared war.

"Mr. Truman's War"

Truman's response to the North Korean invasion of June 25, 1950, was conditioned by the strategy outlined in NSC-68, the recent success of Mao's forces in China, and the mounting attacks on the administration's foreign policy by political adversaries. The President saw Korea as "the Greece of the Far East" which could be used to shore up U.S. prestige in Asia and to blunt overt criticism at home. Truman was able to act quickly because intelligence reports warned him that an invasion was imminent. United States naval and air units were in the area and were diverted to support the South Koreans. After June 27 this technically became a UN operation, but General Douglas MacArthur, the military leader in charge, reported only to Truman. MacArthur's UN troops were almost exclusively of American and South Korean origin, and the general later said he had no "direct" connection with the United Nations.

In retrospect, Truman probably acted unwisely in Korea when he did not consult with congressional leaders before making key decisions and failed to obtain any resolution of support, which certainly would have been granted readily enough. Republicans favored intervention but questioned the President's methods. Robert A. Taft, for one, feared Truman was establishing a precedent that would take the act of declaring war out of the hands of Congress forever. Also, in September 1950 when UN forces went north of the thirty-eighth parallel, the border between North and South Korea, they violated the UN resolution of June 27, 1950, which clearly limited that body's role to repelling an invasion. In short, Truman erred tactically; the Congress and the American people generally supported what he was doing but later questioned his methods. Although few realized it at the time, the President had established an executive precedent that opened the door to still more "presidential wars."

Waging Containment: The Military Experience

At the outset, the tides of war changed rapidly and often. North Korea dominated the early fighting. Then in September 1950, MacArthur's brilliant Inchon landings behind enemy lines launched a counteroffensive that took the war north of the thirty-eighth parallel. What had begun as an exercise in containment, temporarily at least (September to November 1950) became aggression as forces under MacArthur overran the northern half of the peninsula. By October 26 these UN troops had reached the Yalu River on Manchuria's border and captured more than 100,000 North Korean soldiers. A month later, operating under orders from the Joint Chiefs of Staff to destroy enemy forces but not to cross into Manchuria or send planes over Chinese territory, MacArthur launched a drive that, he said, "should for all practical purposes end the war."

Instead, it was the Red Chinese who unleashed the real offensive, something MacArthur had insisted would never happen. Alarmed by the presence of U.N. forces on their borders, they dispatched an estimated 200,000 "volunteers" (with perhaps twice as many men in reserve behind the Yalu) to the aid of the beleagured North Koreans. Within eight weeks—as MacArthur called for a blockade of China, air strikes against its industrial centers, and even use of the atomic bomb—the Red Chinese pushed relentlessly southward. As UN troops fled southward below the thirty-eighth parallel once more (one of the longest retreats in U.S. military history), Truman declared a state of national emergency and stepped up mobilization. By January 1951 the fighting had stabilized close to the thirty-eighth parallel and, in time, became a stalemate that dragged on for two more years.

During this hectic, seesaw affair, the UN on October 7, 1950 formally abandoned (as victory loomed) its limited goal of merely resisting aggression from the north and agreed to create a united and democratic Korea; then, on December 14, staggered by the Chinese assault, the world body voted to resume its original objectives.

Although President Truman hinted shortly after the Chinese entered the fray that atomic weapons might be used, he soon reversed himself. In this turnabout of armies and of decision making lay the seeds of a fateful conflict between MacArthur and Truman and between the President and his most partisan GOP critics. Not surprisingly, the famous general who wanted to fight an all-out, not a limited, war became the idol of those who thought as he did. After January 1951 the struggle in Korea was merely an effort to arrive at an acceptable truce as soon as possible.

When MacArthur persisted in a public campaign to thwart efforts to achieve an armistice, the President fired him, an unusual step filled with considerable drama. From the outset Truman had been wary of MacArthur's imperial personality but backed him to the hilt at the time of the Inchon landings. In October 1950, as warnings filtered back from the Far East that China might indeed enter the war, Truman flew to Wake Island to confer with the general, taking with him as a goodwill gesture ten pounds of chocolates for Mrs. MacArthur. The two men met for several hours, and Truman departed amid assurances that the Chinese would not attack and that the fighting would be over by the end of the year.

When neither prediction proved to be true, friction between Truman and MacArthur mounted, especially as the general continued his efforts to change U.S. policy:

U.P.I.

This ticker-tape parade in New York for General Douglas MacArthur represented, as one critic said, the noisiest "fading away" that any old soldier ever achieved.

"There is no substitute for victory," he said. The final straw was a letter MacArthur sent to House Minority Leader Joseph W. Martin, Jr., embodying his views. When it was read on the House floor on April 5, the President decided to act. Six days later he relieved MacArthur of his command and that evening spoke to the American people concerning his decision. After a lengthy review of the war and U.S. policy, Truman said that "with the deepest personal regret" he had been compelled to act: ". . . the cause of world peace is more important than any individual."

The public reaction was tumultuous and largely pro-MacArthur. Within a fortnight the general returned home to a huge ovation (his first visit to America since before Pearl Harbor) and made a stirring address to a joint session of Congress. Despite an outpouring of conservative fervor, subsequent hearings by two combined Senate committees upheld the right of Harry Truman, commander-in-chief of the United States armed forces, to do what he had done.

MacArthur's dismissal was one of several moves by the President that intensified GOP criticism early in 1951. Frustrated by the Korean situation, Truman's adversaries also focused on a simultaneous buildup of American forces in Europe, precipitating a lengthy debate over whether the chief executive in peacetime could dispatch troops overseas without first obtaining the consent of Congress. This technical issue grew into a general reevaluation of administration policy encompassing the dismissal of MacArthur and similar issues. Nothing actually was resolved, but this discussion helped rekindle dormant isolationist spirit somewhat among responsible conservatives such as Taft and turn-the-clock-back inflexibles to whom MacArthur was now a great hero. By mid-1951, however, negotiations which would ultimately lead to a Korean truce were underway, and Truman and Acheson were busy constructing a series of mutual defense agreements in Asia, moves that bolstered sagging U.S. prestige in that part of the world. These agreements included a peace treaty with Japan and pacts with Japan, Australia, and New Zealand.

The long impasse in the Korean negotiations, frustrating to all Americans, caused Truman's stock to decline so that he eventually quit the 1952 presidential race. Republican candidate Eisenhower's pledge to "go to Korea" carried special weight (since he was an experienced, respected military man tending to military business), and his visit in December 1952 probably helped both troop morale and that of the public back home, though it did little to alter U.S. policy. Talks with the North Koreans were resumed in April 1953 and, at length, an implied threat by the United States to resort to nuclear weapons broke the stalemate. An armistice was signed at Panmunjom three months later on July 27, 1953. The Korean War was over, but the boundary between the two Koreas continued to be the scene of friction, dispute, hostility, and bitterness.

This experience in limited warfare was a very costly adventure for the United States: 5.7 million men in uniform (over one-third the number under arms in World War II), 54,246 deaths (33,629 of them in battle), and 103,284 other casualties. Institutional and financial costs were also great. The precedent of a presidential war was established, although most voters seemed disturbed only because there was not a clear-cut victory. The Korean affair increased U.S. military strength and military spending substantially, apparently saddling the nation with a permanent arms establishment. The Defense **budget more than tripled, rising from 13.4 billion in fiscal 1950 to $44.0 billion three years later. More importantly, in the short run the war increased American support for Chiang Kai-Shek's beleaguered forces on Taiwan and for the French fighting Ho Chi Minh in Indochina, both groups seeming to be enemies of a common foe: the Communists in Asia.**

Korea at Home

Truman did not exhibit the same decisiveness in domestic life as he did in foreign affairs during the Korean crisis. The Republican opposition, which began sniping at him in 1949, quickly pounced upon strains produced by war as weapons to be used against the

Dwight D. Eisenhower Library/U.S. Army Signal Corps.

Having promised the voters during the 1952 campaign that he would "go to Korea" to get a first-hand understanding of the war, President-elect Eisenhower fulfilled that pledge within a month of his election.

administration. The phenomenon known as "McCarthyism," a search for Communist sympathizers, was a major byproduct of the Korean era. Still, this war—for all of its temporary dislocations of American life—had little lasting impact on the domestic scene. The economy never experienced the grave inflationary bulge predicted by many, the President's domestic authority remained limited, and civil liberties—severely scarred by the excesses of McCarthyism—soon recovered, although in the process numerous careers were thwarted or lay in ruins.

President Truman, perhaps fearful of the political consequences of full-scale mobilization, acted slowly in harnessing the economy to wage war halfway around the globe. In effect, he had to shelve his wide-ranging plans for social reform (the Fair Deal), a program that most certainly would have encountered stiff opposition in Congress and weakened support for his foreign policy.

But in the wake of Chinese entry into the Korean conflict, the President had to act. In the grim days of mid-December 1950 he proclaimed a state of national emergency, noting that "events in Korea and elsewhere constitute a grave threat to the peace of the world and imperil the efforts of this country and those of the United Nations to prevent aggression and armed conflict." At the same time he set up an Office of Defense Mobilization (ODM) "to direct, control, and coordinate all mobilization activities." Charles E. Wilson (1888–1972), president of General Electric, was named to head up this new agency and given sweeping powers, much like those wielded by James Byrnes as director of the Office of War Mobilization during World War II. The first order to go forth from Washington was a "roll back" of a projected increase in auto prices and a general price freeze; however, this new organization never actually functioned very well. Wilson quickly surrounded himself with business tycoons and both labor and farm groups soon repudiated ODM and its subsidiary boards and commissions. By the time these disputes were ironed out in mid-1951, to nearly everyone's surprise inflation—which price regulations were designed to combat—no longer was a problem. The round of scare buying inspired by the outbreak of war and Red Chinese intervention had subsided, and higher taxes and restraints on consumer credit were beginning to have effect. Meanwhile, wholesale prices began a slow but steady drop that extended into 1953; the consumer price index continued to rise, although the rate of advance was slow. As a result, Truman's design for stringent controls was superfluous, and

Congress responded by watering down his requests considerably.

Truman's greatest error with respect to mobilization was his intemperate seizure of the steel industry in April 1952. The steel workers' wage contract expired at the end of 1951, and despite much talk and bargaining efforts, no agreement between labor and management seemed possible. From the outset, the sympathies of the White House lay with the strikers. On April 8, refusing to invoke the Taft-Hartley Act (which perhaps would have been preferable) and citing the danger a continued stalemate posed for U.S. troops in Korea, Truman ordered his Secretary of Commerce "to take possession of the steel mills, and to keep them operating." Although some administration aides cited the President's "inherent powers" to support his action, the courts disagreed. By a 6 to 3 vote, the Supreme Court held in *Youngstown Sheet and Tube Company* v. *Sawyer* (1952) that this was an unconstitutional usurpation of legislative power. In short, this was a victory for business and steel management, and a defeat for labor and the administration.

If the federal government intruded little into the economic affairs of private citizens, its record in the realm of civil liberties in a time of undeclared warfare was poor indeed. Tensions created by the Korean crisis accentuated longstanding tendencies toward suppression of dissent and Communist activity, giving Truman's conservative foes an excellent opportunity to institute repressive measures and launch a crusade against "subversives" in high places. Unhappily, even libertarian groups such as the American Civil Liberties Union wavered, liberal politicians acquiesced in questionable legislation, and the Supreme Court chose to define its protective role very narrowly.

Before examining this aspect of the Truman era, however, a backward glance is necessary. In the early 1930s the capitalist world was in chaos, while the U.S.S.R. claimed to have no unemployment or hunger whatsoever, This was a powerful message, and many college or university students certainly attended a few Communist-inspired meetings, perhaps some even flirting with party organizers for a time. If Communism was "the wave of the future," if it actually could solve problems that capitalism could not, then it was worth looking into. FDR's New Deal ended this brief flirtation, but some of the bright young men who studied Communism in the darkest days of the Depression found their way into government service. By 1950—and one should remember also that the U.S. and the U.S.S.R. were allies in World War II, thus giving Communism momentary respectability in the eyes of millions of Americans—they had risen in the ranks, sometimes to positions of prominence. The problem for them and many of their fellow citizens was that the Cold War altered the political climate, releasing new and emotionally charged concerns.

This climate inspired conservative businessmen, veterans' organizations, patriotic societies, and other zealous anti-Communists to join in a grand crusade that embraced much more than Communism. It became, in fact, an indictment of the New Deal, a movement that arch-reactionaries had said all along was leading the country to both hell and Communism. Senator Joseph R. McCarthy became their patron saint under the banner of driving Communists and their sympathizers from government. This holy war, the domestic analogue of containing Communism abroad, aided the Republicans in the 1952 election campaign.

At the same time, other forces were at work to encourage repression and brutal investigatory methods. The House Un-American Activities Committee (HUAC), organized in 1938 under the leadership of Texan Martin Dies, presumably was set up to ferret out all enemies of the American way of life, but throughout the years its targets seemed to be those on the radical left, not the conservative right. In 1948, against a background of growing concern over Communist infiltration of the federal government, the House passed the Mundt-Nixon Communist Registration Bill (the first legislative proposal ever framed by the HUAC), a forerunner of the McCarran Internal Security Act of 1950. This bill failed in the Senate; however, the HUAC then probed deeply into the affairs of several former government officials, the Alger Hiss case being their most celebrated foray. Unfortunately, Truman characterized this investigation as a "red herring," a remark that would haunt the Democrats for years. Ironically, Truman himself had fueled the fire with his Executive Order 9835 (March 1947) establishing a Loyalty Review Board to consider charges against any civilian employee of the executive branch. Needless to point out, this effort to head off any HUAC probe of his administration and its employees failed.

This climate of suspicion quickly found its way into state and local politics, the Communist issue apparently inducing some urban Catholics to help the Republicans on their way to victory in 1946. Truman, with his Loyalty Program and a strong stand against Russia, was able to turn the issue to his own temporary advantage in 1948—especially with Henry Wallace's candidacy serving as a lightning-rod for strong "anti-Red" criticisms. Groups such as the Chamber of Commerce and the American Legion stirred interest in the Communist threat as they held state and regional seminars. Catholic organizations and the Hearst press also kept the issue alive, as did many state legislators. What is remarkable about the laws passed by various states in the late 1940s regarding subversion is their similarity. One enacted in Maryland in 1949, which incorporated federal legislation with little or no change was copied in turn by Mississippi, New Hampshire, Washington, and Pennsylvania. In all, nearly thirty states enacted provisions designed to bar from public payrolls those advocating violent overthrow of the government or belonging to groups favoring such action. In only one instance did state action precede Truman's loyalty order, and that order itself soon was adopted by states, municipalities, and even private employers, among them the Columbia Broadcasting Company. Thus, state and local anti-Communist zeal, though widespread, appears to have been initiated in Washington. The rock was dropped through the surface there and the ripples spread outward. This was not a grassroots phenomenon like Populism of the 1890s, which began on farms, moved on to state capitals, and picked up steam.

Stimulated by the Cold War and especially by its "hot" phase in Korea, frustrated Republicans and conservative Democrats worked hand-in-hand in Congress to produce laws limiting civil liberties. The McCarran Internal Security Act of 1950 was a massive, complex conglomeration designed to go far beyond the administration's own loyalty program, accelerate security investigations in all phases of U.S. life, and shift the burden of security to Congress. The most severe measure of this sort passed since the Smith Act of 1940, which had outlawed the advocacy of violent overthrow of the U.S. government, it contained two parts known as the Subversive Activities Control Title and the Emergency Detention Title. The former required all Communist groups to register with the Attorney General and furnish membership lists and financial records. Although membership technically was not a crime, this measure made it illegal to "substantially contribute" in any way to the establishment of a totalitarian dictatorship in the United States. It also prohibited employing Communists in defense plants and granting passports to Communists. The second title authorized the Attorney General to round up subversives in a time of emergency and intern them "in such places of detention as may be prescribed by the Attorney General." All this, of course, sounded remarkably like the uprooting and corralling of Japanese-Americans a decade or so earlier. Truman vetoed the bill on September 22, but the next day Congress overrode his veto, which one congressman said was written by Supreme Court Justice Felix Frankfurter (allegedly one of the President's "subversive accomplices") and was clearly nothing but "Communist propaganda." Two years later, brushing aside yet another presidential veto, Congress passed the McCarran-Walter Immigration and Nationality Act, which allowed exclusion of possible subversives and expulsion of "dangerous" aliens.

Although the most notorious congressional infringements on civil liberties in this era grew out of investigative powers enjoyed by the Senate, both houses (and sometimes both parties) seemed determined during a four-year period from 1950 to 1954 to outdo each other in their display of anti-Communist zeal. The crest of these legislative efforts was the Communist Control Act of 1954, a patchwork, last-minute merger of several bills, which in the view of some critics was "cooked up over the weekend." It included an amendment to the 1950 McCarran Act expanding coverage to "Communist-infiltrated" organizations (meant to apply to labor unions) and denied to the Communist party all "rights, privileges, and immunities attendant upon legal bodies" under U.S. law. This legislation made it illegal for any party member to hold union office or to represent an employer before the National Labor Relations Board (NLRB), denied access to the NLRB to "Communist-infiltrated" groups, and set up a control board to determine if various organizations had indeed been infiltrated.

One man, more than any other, led this anti-Communist campaign and in fact gave his name to an era. On February 9, 1950, Senator Joseph R. McCarthy, a Republican from Wisconsin, told a Wheeling, West Virginia, audience that he held in his hand a list containing the names of 205 Communists currently employed by the State Department. A short time later he read a copy of that speech into the *Congressional Record,* reducing the number of allegedly disloyal Americans to only 57.

Wide World.

Joseph R. McCarthy
(1908–1957)

Born on a Wisconsin farm in 1908, one of seven children, Joseph R. McCarthy grew up in relative poverty. He quit school at the age of fourteen to become a chicken farmer; but, when disease decimated his flock, he returned to the classroom. In 1935 he graduated from Marquette University Law School and the following year ran unsuccessfully as a Democratic candidate for county attorney; in 1939, as a Republican, he was elected to the post of circuit court judge, the youngest in Wisconsin history.

Three years later McCarthy enlisted in the U.S. Marines and rose to the rank of captain in the South Pacific. While still in uniform, he mounted an unsuccessful challenge to Senator Alexander Wiley; then in 1945 he was reelected to his old circuit court post. In 1946, to the surprise of nearly everyone, McCarthy defeated Senator Robert La Follette, Jr., in the Republican primary and in that "good" Republican year went on to victory. Part of this success may have been a result of a proclivity to join almost anything: Veterans of Foreign Wars, American Legion, Elks, Eagles, Knights of Columbus, even honorary membership in Boys Town.

His career on Capitol Hill was rather mundane at first. He earned the nickname "the Pepsi-Cola Kid" for his strenuous efforts on behalf of that corporation as it fought sugar rationing and other postwar controls; he also became the darling of the real estate lobby. McCarthy's noted anti-Communist campaign, launched early in 1950, was in the beginning little more than an effort to win reelection two years later. However, it soon became much more than that, and for four years (1950–1954) "McCarthyism" dominated the American political scene.

This war to ferret out ostensible traitors played heavily upon popular resentment against "Establishment WASPs" such as Dean Acheson, George Marshall, Alger Hiss, and Adlai Stevenson. McCarthy's charges never resulted in the arrest of a single Communist, but his innuendos and outright lies ruined many careers and inspired imitators to use similar techniques. To a great extent, public frustration with Korea and the Cold War—abetted by an uprising of reactionaries who thought FDR's New Deal (or perhaps Roosevelt himself) was responsible for postwar unrest—fueled this witch hunt.

Eisenhower's election in 1952 marked the beginning of the end for McCarthyism, since the Communists-in-government charge no longer made much sense. For at that time, like all politicians, the President was reluctant to challenge the high-riding senator; but, when McCarthy tried to portray the United States Army as a hotbed of Reds, Eisenhower—a man who had spent most of his life in uniform—encouraged the Army to strike back. A series of televised hearings, disclosing McCarthy's methods to millions, led directly to his downfall in 1954. A short time later he was censured by the Senate. He died three years later, still a member of that body but virtually unnoticed and powerless. ■

A few weeks before McCarthy spoke out, Alger Hiss (1904–), a onetime State Department employee who had been present at Yalta and had helped to organize the San Francisco conference that established the UN, was convicted of perjury in connection with testimony before the House Un-American Activities Committee in 1948. Secretary of State Acheson angered McCarthy and others by announcing that "whatever the outcome" of an appeal filed by Hiss, "I do not intend to turn my back" on him. The outbreak of the Korean War in June 1950 aroused more interest in subversive activities within the United States, and that fall, voters, irritated by pressures of the war, revealed the popularity of the Communist issue in politics. This issue seemed to consume their attention in direct proportion to their ire at being prevented from enjoying the benefits of a conflict-free peace. Republican Harold Stassen, for example, attacked "the blinded, blundering, bewildering" foreign policy of the "spy-riddled" Truman administration. Stassen and others implied that the President was directly responsible for American casualties in Korea. Richard M. Nixon, a key HUAC member since 1947 and chief investigator of Alger Hiss, defeated Democrat Helen Gahagan Douglas for a Senate seat, largely by "associating" her House voting record with that of other members thought to be "soft" on Communism. Senator Millard Tydings of Maryland was beaten by an obscure Republican, John Marshall Butler, who had considerable help from McCarthy. The Wisconsin senator, furious because a committee headed by Tydings largely ignored his charges concerning Communists in the State Department, allegedly circulated a doctored photograph showing Tydings with U.S. Communist leader Earl Browder. In that same election, Ohio's Taft survived an attempt by organized labor to oust him because of his coauthorship of the Taft-Hartley Act, and Democrat Scott Lucas (1892–1968) of Illinois, Senate majority leader, was beaten by Republican Everett McKinley Dirksen (1896–1969), a conservative with neo-isolationist leanings.

As a result of this election the "soft-on-Communism" issue assumed greater importance, and many politicians began to perceive McCarthy as a powerful new entity, though, in fact, at the time he was merely searching for a means to win reelection in 1952. One of the few political figures to speak out consistently against McCarthy was Harry Truman. In late 1953, after he had left the White House, Truman publicly described McCarthyism as meaning "the corruption of the truth, the abandonment of our historical devotion to fair play . . . the abandonment of 'due process' of law . . . the use of the big lie and the unfounded accusation against any citizen in the name of Americanism and security."

In essence, as McCarthy and his band went forth to win public support for their views, they did three things. They capitalized upon a liberal-conservative split within the Republican party, exploited the frustrations of the Cold War being experienced by a public eager for an end to confrontation, and stirred up latent resentment against the New Deal, especially its social programs which challenged the status of certain individuals. McCarthy's attacks upon striped-pants diplomats and State Department intellectuals whom he characterized as Harvard, Yale, and Princeton products with pseudo-British accents, delighted many Midwest Republicans wary of eastern "liberalism." His onslaughts, demogogic in tone, also won the approval of many traditionally Democratic ethnic and social groups, among them, urban Irish and Italian Catholics, as well as Poles and other minorities with ties to eastern Europe. Various polls of the early 1950s indicated professionals and labor union members tended to be anti-McCarthy, but small businessmen and unskilled workers were among his most enthusiastic supporters.

McCarthy's unique advantage was coming to prominence at precisely the right time with the right issue; his basic weakness was that he was an unprincipled man with only one issue, nothing more. The election of Eisenhower, who was determined to heal the split in Republican ranks, and the resolution of the Korean fracas, which eased Cold War tensions to a degree, eliminated much of McCarthy's support. Yet for the first sixteen months of Eisenhower's administration, McCarthy continued his relentless crusade. Despite considerable criticism, the President had endorsed the Wisconsin senator for reelection in 1952 and subsequently tried to meet him halfway by revising Truman's loyalty program so that government employees could be dismissed not only for disloyalty, but for drug addiction, alcoholism, and immorality. Among those subject to review was Dr. Robert J. Oppenheimer, the scientist who directed development of the first atomic bomb. Although Oppenheimer had left government service in 1952, removal of his security clearance because of association with Communists and ex-Communists before and during World War II led to

New York Public Library, Picture Collection.

Helen Gahagan Douglas
(1900–   )

The first woman ever to address a national Democratic party convention (1944) and a glamorous actress and opera singer married to a famous actor (Melvyn Douglas), Helen Gahagan Douglas is perhaps best known as the woman who lost out in a hard-fought Senate race to Richard M. Nixon in 1950. That victory propelled Nixon into national politics, giving him the vice presidency and ultimately the White House.

Helen Gahagan was born in New Jersey in 1900. Her father, a well-to-do contractor, sent her to the best schools and tried hard to thwart an interest in the theater, but in 1922 she quit New York's Barnard College to go on the stage. The result was a meteoric rise to stardom and six extremely successful seasons. Slim, beautiful, vivacious, in the late 20s she was considered one of America's ten most beautiful women, although one wit said, "Helen Gahagan is the ten most beautiful women in the world."

To everyone's surprise, in 1928 she quit Broadway to study opera and then made a successful two-year tour of Europe, appearing at various houses in Czechoslovakia, Austria, Germany, and Italy. Gahagan returned to the New York stage in 1930, although she continued to sing light opera in both America and Europe from time to time. In 1931 she married Georgia-born Melvyn Douglas, her leading man in a Broadway production. During the succeeding decade, as they teamed up for various theatrical and screen ventures—Douglas sometimes producing or managing rather than starring—two experiences stirred their interest in politics. In 1932 this handsome couple drove cross-country to Arizona and en route saw migrant poverty and the decay of the Depression; then, three years later Gahagan appeared at the Salzburg Music Festival and toured Germany, returning home alarmed at the excesses of Nazism.

By the late 1930s both were very active in the Democratic party and occasionally visited the White House as guests of the Roosevelts. Melvyn Douglas was the first well-known actor ever to become a delegate to a national convention, and Gahagan was a national committee woman from California, from 1940 to 1944. In 1944 she was elected to Congress where she served three terms before making her unsuccessful bid for the Senate. During these congressional years she was inevitably compared with Republican Clare Boothe Luce whose attributes were so similar—a theatrical personality endowed with good looks and married to a famous man. In fact, in 1944 she was introduced to the party faithful as "the Democrats' answer to Clare Boothe Luce."

In 1946 Gahagan also served as a delegate to the United Nations. Since leaving Congress, Helen Gahagan Douglas has continued her involvement in Democratic party affairs and encouraged the participation of women in government. ■

Library of Congress.

J. Robert Oppenheimer (1904–1967)

Oppenheimer, born to well-to-do Jewish parents in New York City in 1904, was educated at Harvard, Cambridge University, and George-August University of Göttingen, Germany (Ph.D. 1927), where he studied physics with Max Born. He returned to the United States in 1929 and joined the faculties of both the University of California at Berkeley and California Institute of Technology. An excellent teacher, he helped to build up Berkeley's graduate department in theoretical physics and in 1935 shared in development of the Oppenheimer-Phillips process to break deuterons from the atom. With this distinguished background, he joined the atomic bomb project in 1942, acting as director at the Los Alamos installation until the bomb's completion in 1945. He served as consultant to the government thereafter, helping write the Acheson-Lilienthal Report (1946) urging international control of atomic weapons, and in 1947 he became head of the Princeton Institute for Advanced Study.

Ironically, Oppenheimer has become known primarily for the unhappy situation growing out of his opposition to expansion of nuclear warfare rather than for his role in its inception. As chairman of a committee of the Atomic Energy Commission to advise on development of the H-bomb in 1949, Oppenheimer argued that a weapon of such massive power had no defensive purpose. Though Oppenheimer withdrew from government in 1952, a year later the Eisenhower administration revoked his security clearance. After further review, the Personnel Security Board declared him loyal, but a "security risk" and sustained the revocation of clearance. Senator Joseph McCarthy and others claimed that Oppenheimer's opposition to the H-bomb had caused delay in its development, but in fact he was a victim of the frustration Americans felt when the Russians began to narrow the nuclear weapons gap with their own bomb detonated in 1949.

Oppenheimer returned to the Institute at Princeton after the public furor and was finally "cleared" in 1963 when the Atomic Energy Commission bestowed upon him its highest honor, the Fermi Award (for his work in theoretical physics). He died in Princeton, February 18, 1967. ■

charges and countercharges. Testimony before a review board revealed that, though opposed to development of the hydrogen bomb, he did nothing to hinder research once the President ordered a crash program to commence. This argument concerning construction of a superbomb, an answer to Russia's atomic blast of September 1949, had gone on behind closed doors, and only the Oppenheimer case finally revealed what had occurred.

A three-man review board eventually decided the scientist was a "loyal" citizen, but by a 2 to 1 vote declined to reinstate his clearance.

This was, of course, more grist for McCarthy's mill and he immediately accused Oppenheimer of delaying work on the H-bomb. It was when the controversial senator decided to do battle with institutions that conservatives revered—the United States Army, the Republican party, and even the Senate itself—that he got into trouble and his support melted away. McCarthy's battle with the military consisted of a series of running skirmishes going back to mid-1952 when the senator tried to probe Communist infiltration of the armed forces. By the spring of 1954 he was at war with high Pentagon officials and much of the Eisenhower administration, and in April of that year televised hearings conducted by his subcommittee (totaling 187 hours) sometimes had audiences of twenty million or more. The immediate issues were mistreatment of witnesses, the activities of subcommittee staff, refusal of some Army officers to testify upon orders from their superiors, and whether or not McCarthy used his influence to get preferrential treatment for an army private. Although none of these matters had much to do with actual subversion, American TV viewers were treated to drama such as few of them had ever seen. McCarthy's bully tactics and blatant disregard for fair play—"Mr. Chairman, point of order . . . I object"—revealed the true nature of his vindictive assaults.

A Gallup Poll taken shortly after the hearings revealed that 52 percent of those questioned thought McCarthy and his immediate staff were guilty of improper conduct; 24 percent said they were not. Thirty-eight percent believed the Army had used "improper means" to stop McCarthy's probe of the military; 32 percent thought it had not. McCarthy, however, had to answer to yet another court of opinion: that of his fellow senators. As early as March 9, 1954, Republican Ralph Flanders of Vermont had accused McCarthy of "shattering" their party and diverting attention from the Cold War. Speaking on the Senate floor on June 1, he compared McCarthy to Hitler. Ten days later he introduced a resolution seeking to remove the Wisconsin senator from his committee and subcommittee posts, but later withdrew it in favor of a censure motion backed by several other Republicans. On August 2, by a vote of 75 to 12, the Senate agreed to set up a special committee (3 Republicans, 3 Democrats) to consider charges of misconduct. Seven weeks later, following open but not televised hearings, the committee issued a 40,000-word report unanimously condemning McCarthy.

Debate on this report (begun after the congressional elections, it might be noted) led to more wrangling, with McCarthy calling the special committee "the unwitting handmaiden" of the Communist party. On December 2 by a vote of 67 to 22 (Democrats voting 44-0, Republicans 22-22, and the lone Independent voting yea) the

Robert Phillips/Black Star.

In the "Army-McCarthy hearings" of spring 1954, Senator Joseph McCarthy met his match in the able counsel for the Department of the Army, Joseph Welch of Boston (at left).

Senate condemned the Wisconsin senator, the third man in history ever to be so treated by that body. (Asked by newsmen what this action meant, McCarthy replied, "Well, I wouldn't call it a vote of confidence.") His power shattered, Joseph R. McCarthy faded from public view, dying of a liver ailment three years later.

Today, most historians see McCarthyism as a vendetta among the elite which attracted momentary mass interest (perhaps thanks much to the novelty of television) but not genuine mass support. After McCarthy apparently contributed to the defeat of several senators in 1950 and 1952, none of his colleagues dared stand up to him; and, for a time, this demagogue hogged front pages with startling charges and sinister innuendo, his associates doing nothing to halt his misuse of the Senate's investigatory powers. To that extent, the United States Senate was this man's main source of strength since it gave him a stage upon which to perform. But Joseph McCarthy's act could win applause only so long as his party was not in the White House. At the same time, Korea afforded conservatives and nationalists, long out of power, an opportunity to strike back (by means of the Communists-in-government issue) at their high-riding adversaries. Sadly, civil liberties suffered mightily as a result. But Eisenhower's succession to the presidency in January 1953 and McCarthy's clumsy excesses helped dampen this anti-Communist crusade, and after 1954 the intensely repressive spirit that marred the end of the Truman era and the beginning of a new Republican administration ebbed considerably.

The United States and the Cold War in the 1950s

For all of the publicity and talk of liberating "captive" nations, the Eisenhower administration continued to practice containment. There were different nuances, but any Rip Van Winkle who dozed off in 1950 and awoke eight or ten years later would have been hard pressed to describe actual changes. It is true that during that decade the focus of Cold War activity shifted somewhat to the so-called "developing" nations and tactics changed somewhat, or at least went under different names. The Eisenhower administration stressed a New Look in military posture (more emphasis on air power, a cut in defense expenditures, but "more bang for the buck") and signed several multilateral agreements. Yet the underlying premise of a divided, bipolar, Washington-Moscow world remained intact. The continuity of containment was ironic, in light of public expectations for a dramatic shift after the 1952 campaign in which the Republicans talked of the "liberation" of oppressed peoples as an alternative to containment. But within six months such an idea was little more than a sham.

"Massive Retaliation"

While holding firmly to the Democrats' policy of containing Communism, President Eisenhower and Secretary of State John Foster Dulles relied more upon strategic airpower, rather than conventional forces, a new approach the latter explained in January 1954. "Massive retaliation," he noted, would permit the U.S. "to respond vigorously at places and with means of its own choosing." It turned out that, at least in theory, the "means" often would be nuclear weaponry. Two years later Dulles emphasized that the administration was willing to go to the "brink of war" if necessary to maintain peace. This spirit of derring-do, suggested by "brinkmanship" and a seeming reliance upon dreaded new devices, alarmed many and awakened keen partisan criticism of such policies. On the other hand, in view of widespread dissatisfaction with what many thought was "wasteful" spending by the Truman administration, the public generally supported Eisenhower's New Look which presumably would reduce military outlays. Not surprisingly, the President soon replaced a Pentagon command held over from the Truman years, which the Republicans thought tilted toward a Europe-first policy, by naming a new Joint Chiefs of Staff more in tune with their interests in Asia.

As a policy, "massive retaliation," which basically meant big planes carrying big bombs, had limitations. The threat to use such weapons may have produced an armistice in Korea, but talk of such destruction tended to scare America's friends even more than its enemies. Also, some who were supposed to be influenced by such a challenge often did not take it seriously, secure in the belief that the U.S. would not actually use its nuclear strike force. So, as a law partner of John Foster Dulles commented, the United States was caught in the middle between those who were afraid that "massive retaliation" might actually be carried out and those who did not believe it would be.

Another drawback was that, even if a serious proposal, such action could be an inappropriate response,

Secretary of State John Foster Dulles (left) confers with Ngo Dinh Diem (center), the Premier of (South) Vietnam, in 1955.

rather like killing a fly with a cannon. For example, the French in Spring 1954 sought U.S. aid against insurgents in Indochina. Although Eisenhower believed in the "domino theory"—if one country fell to Communism its neighbor might do the same—he rejected pleas by Dulles, Nixon, and others to employ massive retaliation and to send outright military assistance. This may have been because Congress and the leaders of Great Britain were lukewarm to intervention, but it was also because the United States—now more reliant upon airborne nuclear striking power—did not have conventional forces to send to Southeast Asia.

While the U.S. did not sign the Geneva Accords of July 1954, which tried to settle the war there, it tacitly extended protection to the area. Through the Southeast Asia Treaty Organization (SEATO)—pieced together shortly after the Geneva meeting which initiated a withdrawal of French forces—and through direct assistance sent to the Diem regime in Saigon (300 military advisers and some aid), the Eisenhower administration made it clear that containment still was a viable policy, even if massive retaliation was not. Perhaps more indicative of American aims in Indochina (Vietnam) was the dispatching of Colonel Edward Lansdale and some CIA operatives to sabotage the operations of Diem's enemy, Ho Chi Minh, thought to be supported by Chinese and Russian Communists.

In October 1956, late in Eisenhower's successful campaign for reelection, twin crises suddenly shook the diplomatic world: revolt in Hungary against Communist rule and an Anglo-French-Israeli assault upon Egypt in an effort to secure control of the Suez Canal. Again, massive retaliation seemed both inappropriate and impractical. Nevertheless, President Eisenhower retained his commitment to the New Look defense scheme but switched to a goal of mere nuclear "sufficiency" rather than "superiority," and the American saber began to rattle less frequently.

Deemphasis upon U.S. ground troops led to increased dependence upon indigenous forces. Theoretically at least, they cost American taxpayers less and were more readily available in local crises not requiring massive retaliation. To foster such arrangements Eisenhower and Dulles entered into a number of pacts around the globe—one commentator called this phenomenon "pactomania"—which ended up enmeshing the U.S. in some rather complex local rivalries and regional disputes. In an attempt to solve these dilemmas, Eisenhower gave the CIA a very free hand to do what it could to help America's friends—the definition of friend and enemy largely being left up to the operatives themselves. The end result was increasing involvement in the internal affairs of Iran (1953), Guatemala (1954), and Indonesia (1958)—to name but a few random locations—in addition to on-

Erich Lessing/Magnum.

The early optimism during the short-lived rebellion by Hungarian anti-Communists faded when the Hungarians received no aid from the Eisenhower administration or anyone else and the Russians reasserted control by brute force.

going activities of various kinds in French Indochina. In other words, despite an avowed intent to reduce military expenditures and to cut direct U.S. involvement overseas, American presence throughout the world—thanks to the CIA and a multitude of treaty agreements—actually increased during the 1950s.

Eisenhower: Warrior of Peace?

Much has been made of the contrast between Eisenhower—a quiet and restrained military man who was eager and willing to engage in summitry and nuclear disarmament talks—and the much more bellicose Dulles, a Wall Street lawyer. True, as a humane man with a West Point background, Eisenhower knew war ought to be an instrument of last resort, but it is an exaggeration to view him as an antimilitarist. He was more sympathetic to peace and disarmament proposals than Truman, yet such a comparison is a bit unfair, since the two leaders presided in different times and faced different circumstances. To Dulles, Cold War foreign policy was much like the intricate and cunning maneuvering of two opposing courtroom attorneys. Since one always had to be on guard against the devious ways of his adversary, this approach allowed little room for talk of disarmament. For this reason, Eisenhower kept that subject away from his Secretary of State, assigning it instead to various aides such as Nelson Rockefeller (1908–1979) and Harold Stassen.

The President's interest in disarmament or arms limitation led him in July 1955 to make his dramatic

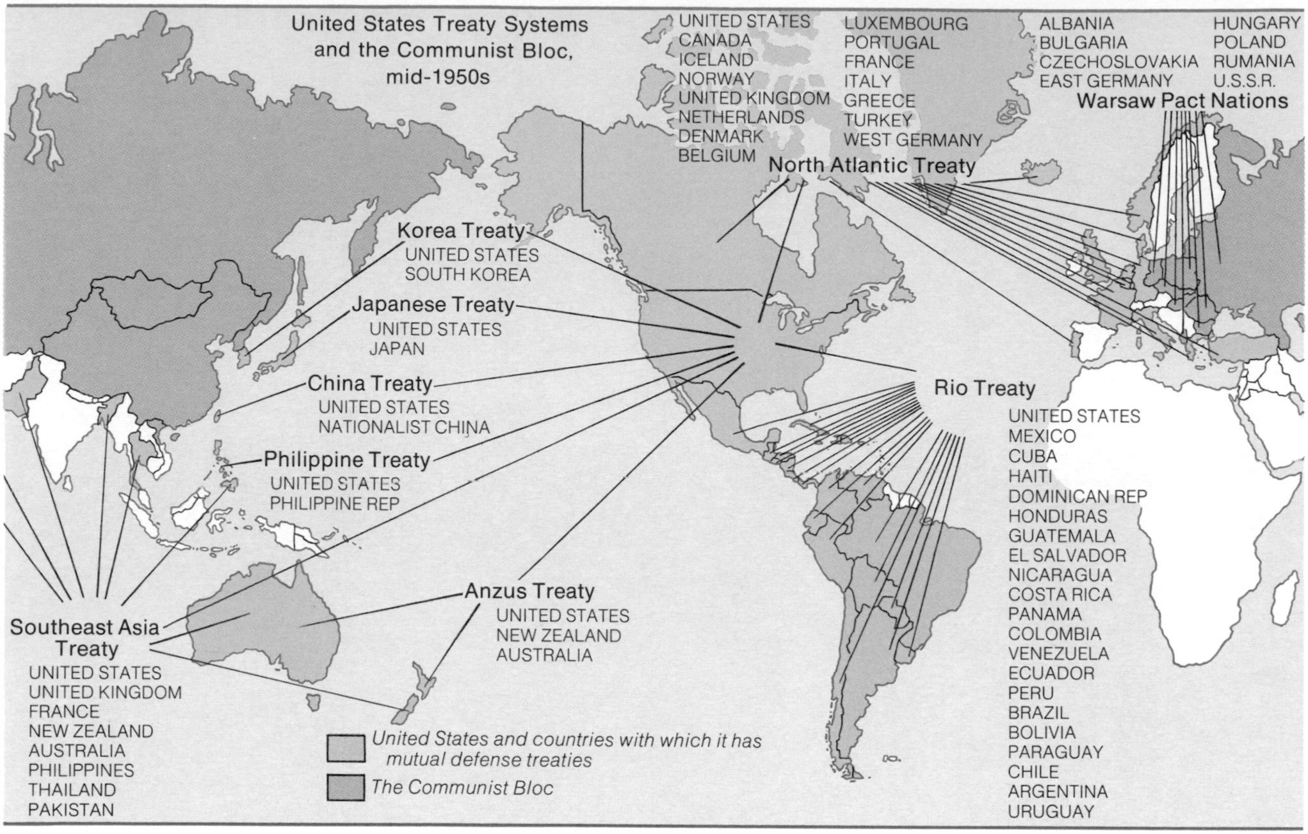

"Open Skies" proposal, the suggestion that Russia and the U.S. exchange plans of their military bases and permit aerial photography of each other's defense establishment. Nevertheless, like his Russian counterpart—Nikita A. Khrushchev (1894–1971), successor to Stalin upon the latter's death in March 1953—Eisenhower actually approached this matter with caution when discussion got underway. When Khrushchev scored a propaganda victory in 1958 by suggesting a ban on aboveground nuclear testing, Eisenhower (and the British as well) completed scheduled tests and then agreed to a de facto moratorium that lasted from late 1958 until 1961.

Cold War tensions did ease somewhat in the late 1950s, perhaps because Khrushchev was busy solidifying his position at home. The Russian leader's extensive coast-to-coast tour of the United States sparked hopes for real improvement in relations between Washington and Moscow, but, in May 1960 the capture of an American U-2 spy-pilot over Russia (and subsequent U.S. confusion and deceit concerning this incident) dashed these hopes. Alarmed by Russia's atomic bomb blast of 1949 and that nation's progress in the so-called "space race," the CIA had begun in 1955 biweekly espionage flights over the heart of the U.S.S.R. with Lockheed U-2 reconnaissance planes equipped with telescopic cameras and similar surveillance equipment. These aircraft flew slowly at a height of 70,000 feet and were said to be conducting "weather research." Then, after four years and repeated attempts to shoot down a U-2 plane, the Russians succeeded, capturing pilot Francis Gary Powers alive. Khrushchev, who had been alternating bluster and threats to blockade Berlin, once more, with smiles and amiability, used this event to cancel a summit conference with Eisenhower—and also an invitation that had been extended to the President to visit Russia. (Powers, convicted of spying by a Soviet court, received a ten-year sentence, but in 1962 he was exchanged for a Russian agent held by the U.S.) In addition to this dramatic incident, the 1960 political campaign injected new spirit into partisan disputes over which political party could best wage the holy war against godless Communism.

Eisenhower, who in 1956 won an easy reelection victory again over Stevenson—despite a serious heart attack in September 1955 and intestinal surgery nine months later, had eight years in which to try his hand at improving the climate of international relations. During his second administration especially, the President clearly had an excellent opportunity to take definite steps leading toward general detente. If he had used his tremendous prestige to mold public opinion, he might have made a true contribution to peace; instead, he fostered and sustained a Cold War mentality in American society. Although not a belligerent leader, he actually did very little to reduce Soviet-American friction during his years in the White House.

Eisenhower and Presidential Power

Dwight D. Eisenhower often is characterized as a President in the Whig tradition, that is, deferential to Congress, opposed to the use of presidential power, and

Erich Lessing/Magnum.

Bob Henriques/Magnum.

One of Eisenhower's signal achievements in foreign policy was to establish personal diplomacy through "summit" meetings with successive Soviet leaders who followed Stalin: Nikolai Bulganin (top) and Nikita Khrushchev (bottom).

somewhat reluctant to use it. Considerable evidence, however, indicates that he felt fully capable of directing foreign affairs and, while seeming to acquiesce to Congress in tone, contributed significantly to the expansion and growth of executive authority in foreign policymaking, a trend that became noticeable a decade later. Eisenhower's accumulation of presidential power in foreign affairs was almost sequential. Beginning with his victory in 1954 over supporters of the Bricker Amendment, a measure designed to limit the President's freedom to make treaties and conclude executive agreements, Eisenhower requested and received nearly a blank-check authorization from the Congress in the form of the Formosa (1955) and the Middle East (1957) Resolutions.

At the heart of the proposed Bricker Amendment to the Constitution was a phrase stating that "a treaty shall become effective as internal law in the United States only through legislation which would be valid in the absence of a treaty." There was little agreement as to what these words actually meant, but they clearly were designed to subordinate the President's treaty-making powers to congressional and state authority. After intense debate, considerable lobbying, and various substitute motions, a much revised version of Bricker's proposal failed by one vote to win the necessary two-thirds margin. Bricker, for whom the archenemy was the UN, obviously intended to fight on, but subsequent events revealed the tide of public opinion had turned against him.

Attacks on offshore islands near Chiang's Formosa by the Communist Chinese in January 1955 led Eisenhower to request a joint resolution authorizing him to "employ the armed forces of the United States as he deems necessary" in defense of Nationalist Chinese territory. The vote was 410 to 3 in the House, 85 to 3 in the Senate. The Middle East Resolution was passed early in 1957, and with much less enthusiasm. It unveiled the so-called "Eisenhower Doctrine," that is, the providing of economic and military aid to regions which, in the view of White House advisors (notably Dulles), suffered a power vacuum as a result of the Suez Crisis of 1956. Enacted with much skepticism, this resolution specifically identified Communism as the enemy to be stopped and gave the President the right to extend assistance if it were requested. This was done three times in succeeding months. In April Eisenhower dispatched the Sixth Fleet to the eastern Mediterranean to discourage an attack by Communist-oriented Syria on Jordan and in September airlifted arms to Jordan; then, in mid-1958, responding to an appeal from Lebanon, U.S. Marines landed in that nation. Within three months they were replaced by a UN peacekeeping force.

To gain these victories on Capitol Hill, the President played upon the strongly anti-Communist views of many congressmen (especially Republicans) who otherwise feared and mistrusted executive power. His personal prestige as a military and foreign policy expert was a trump card in this game between White House and Capitol Hill. Also, it is perhaps significant that Eisenhower's approach toward overseas activity became more assertive after Democrats gained the upper hand in Congress and thus could exert substantial influence on the homefront.

In the case of the Middle East Resolution there was some significant congressional opposition to Eisenhower's plans. Senator J. William Fulbright noted that passage of the resolution gave "consent without advice." The upper house gave the President only the right to undertake "military assistance programs" in that area and refused to authorize in advance the outright use of force. But Eisenhower got what he wanted in principle. In fact, his popularity and the very lack of public suspicion of his motives allowed him to take steps that would have been impossible under Truman.

The new preeminence of the executive branch in foreign affairs gave the White House an imperial grandeur as presidents, prime ministers, and even dictators made pilgrimages to Washington, the "new Rome." The ritual of parades, flags, and bands—the protocol of handshakes, speeches, banquets, and toasts—became almost daily routines. Being the chief policeman and protector of the Free World evidently meant that leaders from every quarter had to be met and entertained; and the spotlight fell naturally more and more upon the man in the White House, the embodiment of American prestige and greatness. He still was addressed as "Mr. President," but the trappings were unlike anything Washington, Jefferson, or Lincoln had ever seen.

The Cold War and American Society in the 1950s

The impact of the Cold War on American life was as dramatic as that of any previous war, exerting special impact upon the economy, education, and political institutions. As Eisenhower left office in January 1961, he warned the nation of the rising "military-industrial complex."

"In the councils of government, we must fight against the acquisition of unwarranted influence, whether sought or unsought, by the military-industrial complex. The potential for the disastrous rise of misplaced power exists and will persist.

We must never let the weight of this combination endanger our liberties or democratic processes. We should take nothing for granted. Only an alert and knowledgeable citizenry can compel the proper meshing of the huge industrial and military machinery of defense with our peaceful methods and goals, so that security and liberty may prosper together."

The network that Eisenhower referred to had existed since World War II, but few had paid much attention to it or criticized activities that actually were merely a continuation of practices inaugurated during that conflict. These included substantial growth of federal defense expenditures, interlocking political-military and industrial directorates, and the negotiated, cost-plus contract. The cost-plus incentive assured a contractor a fixed fee, which would be increased if he performed his task for less than the projected cost. Contracts also sometimes included a fixed-price feature that put a firm ceiling on costs, with all savings below estimated outlays being shared by the government and the contractor. Most of these contracts, not surprisingly, went to a few large companies. In 1958, for example, the 100 largest contractholders received 74 percent of all defense contract dollars. In practice, the cost-plus features encouraged both delay and waste and were a problem quite apart from the size of the complex itself.

The Korean War, naturally enough, swelled defense spending considerably. Eisenhower's New Look brought slight reductions for a time, but by the late 1950s defense outlays returned close to Korean levels. Much of this spending was for the purpose of building up stockpiles of strategic material and thus it helped to sustain entire industries. To put all of this in some perspective, between 1942 and 1946, military spending ate up 68 percent to 84 percent of the federal budget. During the next five years it averaged about 35 percent, then shot up to 60 percent, and only in 1958–1960 eased below 50 percent once more. Before Korea, for example, in the late 1940s national defense spending totaled about $12 billion annually. By 1953 it had risen to $50 billion, easing back to $40 billion two years later and then starting a slow, upward climb to $45 billion at the close of the decade.

Military-industrial needs had involved universities in research and development (R&D) for the federal government during World War II, and this relationship continued to flourish when peace came. Throughout the early postwar years, several prominent educators urged the national government to augment these trends by investing directly in pure research, and in 1950 the National Science Foundation was established to encourage research and dispense federal funds to support it. Thus, at last the laboratory scientist had found a permanent role as a cooperative force in the national quest to improve the general welfare of the United States. By 1960, defense and national security agencies accounted for more than 90 percent of the $8 billion the government was spending on research and development, with most of these efforts being conducted at industrial plants and on university campuses, not in government facilities. This new complex, drawing together elements of the military-industrial-educational worlds, was institutionalized in 1953 with the establishment of an Assistant Secretary of Defense for Research and Development and further confirmed three years later by the appointment of a Special Assistant for Guided Missiles in the Defense Department.

The Cold War also created momentary interest in what was known as civil defense. At first the emphasis was upon evacuation to safe and secure areas; but, when the Soviets got nuclear power, public attention shifted to survival alone. The Federal Civil Defense Administration (FCDA), set up by Truman in the Korean era, in 1956 urged a $32 billion shelterbuilding program, but Eisenhower refused to back it. Throughout that decade both the President and Congress showed much greater interest in deterrence; between 1951 and 1957 the Defense Department got over 90 percent of the $300 billion requested; the FCDA, just over 20 percent of $1.9 billion sought during the same time.

In mid-June 1955, for example, the FCDA staged Operation Alert, a mock drill during which the President and much of the executive branch took shelter in various relocation centers outside of Washington. In theory, "the enemy" attacked fifty-three U.S. cities with imaginary

U.P.I.

The nuclear presence was brought home even to American school children, who routinely underwent air raid drills in which they scurried under their desks to protect against the effects of "Russian attack."

bombs that killed or wounded an estimated 14.7 million people. The legislative branch "escaped" unscathed since Congress ignored the drill and took no part in it, as did Peoria, Illinois, whose civil defense director said it was more important for volunteers to stick to their jobs than to "run around with arm bands on." New York's Governor Averell Harriman complained during the drill that the FCDA had yet to tell him "what is expected of a Governor." The only true casualty was the District of Columbia's deputy director of civil defense, fired because he called the whole affair ridiculous—"not a drill but a show." Three years later the FCDA was merged with the Office of Defense Mobilization amid comments on Capitol Hill that "civil defense is in so low a state that nothing could make it worse and something could make it better."

Two key problems were (1) the public was interested in stopping the enemy before he got to America, not in hiding from him when he did; and (2) building shelters would not give much of an economic boost to the economy. And it certainly did not arouse much interest in the board rooms of General Motors and other big defense contractors. Thus the FCDA was reduced to constructing prototype shelters and producing pamphlets and radio-TV messages. Public school children held air raid drills and took various survival bulletins home to their families, but the impact was not great. Civil defense obviously did not enjoy federal backing; and, without it, the average citizen felt he could do little to augment any such program.

Despite a general sense of resignation, the Cold War was not without its critics. Both academics and pacifists spoke out strongly against U.S. policies that seemed designed to rivet a permanent war economy upon the nation. Although the 1950s marked the nadir of the peace movement, an easing of Soviet-American tensions (the so-called "thaw" in mid-decade) caused a revival of hope. Formation of the National Committee for a Sane Nuclear Policy (SANE) in 1957 was an important symbol of this resurgence. The nuclear pacifist movement reached its peak membership in the early 1960s, yet its impact upon public policy was slight indeed.

Two prime exponents of conflicting views on the Cold War and U.S. foreign policy were Senators Barry Goldwater of Arizona and J. William Fulbright of Arkansas. Goldwater, whose stern outlook would win him a presidential bid in 1964, urged total victory and official acts that would demonstrate to the nation and the world that "we mean business." Fulbright, on the other hand, rejected total victory as a goal that exceeded both American capabilities and the requirements of the world situation. He also reminded his fellow citizens that *total* military success would simply burden the U.S. with the task of rehabilitating millions of Russians and Chinese.

During the 1950s, as noted earlier, partisan dispute over foreign policy and defense increased. Although critics of Dulles, Eisenhower, and the Pentagon offered nonspecific and frequently conflicting alternatives, this did not keep them from speaking out. Presidential hopefuls such as Lyndon Johnson, John Kennedy, Stuart Symington, and Henry Jackson often turned their ire against both the New Look and brinkmanship; however, it actually was Sputnik (October 1957) that provided sound basis and clear context for Democratic charges.

The small satellite launched by the U.S.S.R. had profound implications for American life. Public faith in Eisenhower, U.S. defense systems, and American education was severly shaken. Important results were passage of the 1958 National Defense Education Act (NDEA), reorganization of the Defense Department, and establishment of the National Aeronautical and Space Administration (NASA).

The NDEA was a $1 billion commitment by the federal government to improve instruction in science, mathematics, and foreign languages at all levels. It consisted of loans to college students (canceled if the recipient later taught in public schools), matching grants to states and ten-year loans to private institutions for the purchase of instructional equipment, graduate fellowships for those interested in college teaching careers, and various other forms of assistance to schools, colleges, universities, state departments of education, and private agencies interested in raising the nation's educational standards.

The Defense Department overhaul was not so comprehensive as Eisenhower wanted. In view of his wartime experiences and the increasing complexities of defense planning, the President proposed considerable unification; Congress, however, disagreed. The compromise result gave the Secretary of Defense far-reaching powers to allocate the development of weapons systems among the services, although any "substantial" shift or reassignment was subject to congressional approval. The new law gave legal recognition to the Naval Air Force, Marine Corps, and National Guard (thus protecting their status) and authorized the service secretaries and members of the Joint Chiefs to make proposals to Congress directly, after informing the Defense Secretary of their intention to do so.

Wide World.

Though never a large number, some Americans protested against nuclear tests. In this 1958 photograph, anti-bomb demonstrators in Honolulu protest the arrest of the captain of the *Golden Rule* for defiantly sailing his ship toward a U.S. nuclear test site in the Marshall Islands.

Library of Congress.

At a 1959 Moscow exhibition, Vice President Nixon enhanced his anti-communist image by publicly wagging his finger at Soviet Premier Khrushchev and supposedly insisting on the superiority of the American system. Whatever the substance of the conversation (Khrushchev later disputed Nixon's version), it made a great hit with many American voters.

The act creating NASA, the third major piece of "fallout" from Sputnik, declared that "activities in space should be devoted to peaceful purposes for the benefit of all mankind," and made the President responsible for developing a comprehensive space program. The original $80 million appropriation set up a nine-member council on space activities and research (headed by the President) to assign military and nonmilitary projects to various agencies and departments. Two years later the space program was receiving over five times as much money, despite obvious organizational problems caused largely by inadequate coordination between NASA and the Defense Department and unclear definition of the roles of the U.S. Army, Navy, and Air Force in space research.

Failure and frustration in rocket development led Eisenhower in 1959 to transfer Dr. Wernher von Braun and his team from an Army ballistics agency to NASA in an effort to speed up work on huge missiles capable of trips to the moon and beyond. Yet the President still faced considerable criticism, and Democratic cries of "missile gap" grew louder as it became apparent he had disregarded warnings to increase federal spending for nuclear research in order to keep pace with the Soviet challenge. Nevertheless, despite congressional clamor, Eisenhower refused to act. In part this resulted from his continuing insistence upon fiscal conservatism, but he also knew from U-2 reconnaissance overflights that virtually no "gap" existed, if any at all.

Although it was obvious that the repercussions of Sputnik would play a major role in the 1960 elections, the most astonishing thing about debates on foreign policy between Democrat Kennedy and Republican Nixon was how very little difference existed between their views. In fact, Kennedy blurred somewhat his rather sophisticated understanding of the distinction between "Communism" and "nationalism" in various parts of the world. He kept up a general criticism of the Eisenhower administration's foreign policy, but his charges were nonspecific, and he consciously played down the foreign policy issue as election day approached.

In a jocular reference to Nixon's so-called "kitchen debate" with Khrushchev at a Moscow trade fair, Kennedy said his opponent shook his finger at the dictator and said, "You may be ahead of us in rocket thrust, but we are ahead of you in color television." "I will take my television in black and white," Kennedy added. "I want to be ahead in rocket thrust. . . Mr. Nixon may be very experienced in kitchen debates, but so are a great many married men I know."

This tendency to submerge foreign affairs in wit or generalities was without doubt a wise move on Kennedy's part: a poll taken in October 1960 revealed that only about 30 percent of Americans thought the Democrats were the more likely to keep the U.S. out of World War III, compared to 46 percent for the Republicans.

The 1960 election clearly turned more on domestic issues than on foreign policy. In the end JFK managed to reconstruct the New Deal coalition minus some religious defections because of his Catholicism. Yet Democratic charges of a missile gap and a general lack of preparedness took their toll among wavering voters. Kennedy's emphasis upon declining U.S. prestige served to reinforce the tendency among the electorate to search for security through national leadership. Once more in 1960 the opportunity to reshape American thinking on a divided, bipolar, East-West world was lost amid bunting, banter, and political interplay, just as it had been lost so often in the years since World War II.

Essay

The CIA and Secrecy in a Democracy

The Central Intelligence Agency (CIA), an arm of the federal government created in 1947 to give the executive branch and Congress a comprehensive picture of what was happening outside of the United States of America, had its roots in Pearl Harbor, wartime cloak-and-dagger operations, and tensions arising from the Cold War. Some observers claim that if intelligence reports concerning Japanese activity in November-December 1941 had been better coordinated (or *centralized*), our nation might have had more warning. Instead, various State Department functionaries, the Army, and the Navy were collecting the pieces of the puzzle, but no one was putting them together properly.

Events from 1941 to 1945 obviously dictated the need for all-out intelligence warfare and the Office of Strategic Services (OSS) did the job. This agency, created by executive order on June 13, 1942, was headed by Major General William J. Donovan. Until disbanded in October 1945, the OSS collected and analyzed strategic information and maintained contacts behind enemy lines and in enemy-occupied countries. How well OSS actually performed is still being debated—Winston Churchill preferred its maps to those produced by his own nation but, from all indications, OSS depended heavily upon the British spy network for much of its information. In any case, when the Defense Department took shape in 1947 (combining the Army, Navy, and Air Force), so did the CIA.

Nearly every government in history has carried on espionage in one form or another, often hiding its operatives in embassy and consulate staffs. During war and times of crisis, spying becomes a quite legitimate arm of statecraft. Nathan Hale, the Connecticut school teacher who was hanged by the British in 1776, the Pinkerton detectives who helped Abraham Lincoln during the Civil War, and U.S. Army officers who scouted the Panama jungles for Theodore Roosevelt at the turn of the century all operated in this tradition. Yet the OSS and its stepchild were somewhat different. For the first time, they tended to "institutionalize" within American society the often rather sordid occupation known as spying.

There is, of course, one fundamental problem with the creation of what became very shortly a huge agency: its activities are secret. And that secrecy can hide success and failure, brilliant maneuvering and woeful ineptitude, nepotism and

J. P. Laffont/Sygma.

CIA Headquarters, Langley, Virginia (1975).

old-school-tie benevolence, and the scope and nature of what is going on, even what all this is costing the American taxpayer.

No one can deny that a world power needs a foreign intelligence-gathering body and that its work must be protected by secrecy. Spying, by the very nature of the art, is not done in the open. Yet a growing feeling remains that something is wrong in such an arrangement. It is all too reminiscent of Britain's Star Chamber, the Spanish Inquisition, Hitler's Gestapo, and present-day Communist secret police.

For a dozen years or so, until the United States was caught redfaced telling an obvious lie when the U-2 spy plane carrying Gary Powers was shot down over the U.S.S.R. and John F. Kennedy had to face up to the Bay of Pigs fiasco, the CIA was permitted to do virtually whatever it wished. But after those two disasters things were never quite the same. The life of the CIA became more and more troubled; in fact, by the mid-1970s it was

Stanley Tretick/Sygma.

A "Burn Basket" for information too secret to keep.

obvious that a major housecleaning was in order. The Nixon administration's attempt to use that organization in an effort to hide the Watergate break-in only increased the CIA's difficulties. (Ironically, the Watergate office-hotel complex stands where that agency once had its temporary home.)

During its career the CIA has intrigued to overthrow established governments in Iran, Guatemala, Greece, Chile, and perhaps a half dozen other countries. Sometimes it has been successful, sometimes it has not. It is a simple enough matter to understand why agents of the United States want to work with regimes friendly to their own country: it makes their job easier, to point out one very obvious truth, and it also facilitates all aspects of America's relations with that nation and its citizens. But all too often a CIA agent's idea of a "friendly" government was rooted in concepts of the 1950s and could favor a very undemocratic dictatorship. So long as its leaders were stridently anti-Communist, few other questions were asked.

The CIA's most tragic attempt to play at statecraft was, of course, Vietnam. When Lyndon B. Johnson succeeded to the presidency in 1963, there were 16,000 U.S. troops there. Uncertain of what was actually going on in Southeast Asia, he sent his Secretary of Defense, Robert McNamara, on a personal fact finding tour. From all indications, that visit was stage managed by the CIA from Washington. McNamara was fed lies and half-truths, shown phony cables and false reports, all in an effort to buttress the fiction that the war in Vietnam was a clear-cut struggle between Communists and non-Communists. By the early 1970s, American troop strength in that ravaged country had soared to 550,000, some 43,000 U.S. soldiers had died, and the Vietcong enemy was stronger than ever.

At the same time, to support its Vietnamese policy, the CIA became very deeply involved in *domestic* hanky-panky. Foundations, guilds, federations, institutes, universities, student groups, even professors funded and paid by the CIA became active allies in a gigantic campaign to silence criticism of the government's Vietnam policy. In February 1967, *Ramparts* magazine blew the whistle on such operations and other leaks soon disclosed a widespread network of activity that most Americans thought was barred by the CIA's original charter.

Sometime later a German publisher produced a *Who's Who in the CIA* listing 6,000 agents in 120 countries. Although this exposed operatives to real dangers, to some extent, it was fair. The CIA has printed scores of directories of foreign officials and lists of personal names in Rumanian, Czech, Arabic, Armenian, and Amharic, to name a few of its compendiums.

Overseas CIA agents usually are hidden on the rosters of embassies and consulates, a procedure that can create antagonisms with State Department personnel since they too are supposed to be engaged in intelligence gathering. Yet perhaps State really has no one to blame but itself for this turn of events. If it had been doing a better job before 1941, then the CIA might never have to come into existence.

Although it is impossible to get a tally sheet on how successful or unsuccessful these operatives have been, the veil of secrecy has slipped several times. In the late 1960s and early 1970s, it became apparent that the fascinating world of foreign intrigue, dark glasses, code words, dart guns, and deadly poisons exists, but CIA agents apparently muddle through it in a clumsy, flatfooted fashion much of the time. Critics point out that, if the CIA's main purpose is to prevent another Pearl Harbor, its 16,500 employees with a budget in excess of $750

Dennis Brack/Black Star.

In its early years, the CIA's headquarters were camouflaged, being located in a building supposedly used by another agency. By the 1970s even the highway leading to the agency was marked.

million may or may not be able to do the job. For example, the agency failed to foresee the disastrous 1968 Tet offensive in Vietnam (a turning point in that war's tragic history) and, having misplaced one or two Russian armies for several weeks, did not know about the U.S.S.R.'s invasion of Czechoslovakia until after it took place that same year; in fact, it was the Russian ambassador in Washington who informed President Johnson of that rather important international development.

Some of the CIA's problems stem from the atmosphere in which it was born. It started life in the depths of the Cold War, manned largely by OSS veterans trained to do much more than merely collect intelligence. They had gone out and killed the enemy, parachuted behind his lines to aid partisan groups, and helped set up new governments when victory came in 1945. To them the CIA was merely another name for OSS, and the war was on again—only this time the enemy was Communism. At times, sadly, liberalism or any view not strictly in tune with that of Uncle Sam (as interpreted by aging operatives from World War II days) seems to have been equated with "the Red Menace."

Involvement of the CIA in the American domestic scene has few defenders, and many citizens are disturbed by that organization's attempts to destabilize established foreign governments. For a democracy to use its power to thwart democracy in someone else's country creates, to say the very least, a sense of deep disquietude.

From all indications, the CIA's analysis of foreign military data is of very high quality, a superb job in which those involved can take considerable pride, but its reports on politics, social trends, and other relevant aspects of overseas life sometimes leave much to be desired. Since much of what agents say undoubtedly is couched in words that support firmly established policies well-known to them, these results are indeed predictable.

Intelligence gathering certainly is necessary, and it must be done in secrecy. Few debate these two points. But when intelligence gathering becomes active subversion and murder by secret operatives both at home and abroad, one cannot help but ask who is watching the watch dog?

Selected Readings

Origins and Early Years of the Cold War

John L. Gaddis, *The United States and the Origins of the Cold War, 1941–1947* (1972)

Walter LaFeber, *America, Russia, and the Cold War, 1945–1975* (1976)

Lloyd C. Gardner, *Architects of Illusion: Men and Ideas in American Foreign Policy, 1941–1949* (1970)

Daniel Yergin, *Shattered Peace: The Origins of the Cold War and the National Security State* (1977)

John C. Donovan, *The Cold Warriors: A Policy-Making Elite* (1974)

Anti-Communism at Home

Robert Griffith, *The Politics of Fear: Joseph R. McCarthy and the Senate* (1970)

Robert Griffith and Athan Theoharis, eds. *The Specter: Original Essays on the Cold War and the Origins of McCarthyism* (1974)

Michael P. Rogin, *The Intellectuals and McCarthy: The Radical Specter* (1967)

The Korean War

David Rees, *Korea: The Limited War* (1964)

John W. Spanier, *The Truman-MacArthur Controversy and the Korean War* (1965)

Ronald J. Caridi, *The Korean War and American Politics: The Republican Party as a Case Study* (1968)

Eisenhower, Dulles, and the Cold War

Herbert S. Parmet, *Eisenhower and the American Crusades* (1972)

Townsend Hoopes, *The Devil and John Foster Dulles* (1972)

Cold War and American Society, 1945–1960

Robert A. Divine, *Foreign Policy and U.S. Presidential Elections, 1940–1960* (1974)

Harry H. Ransom, *The Intelligence Establishment* (1970)

Carroll W. Pursell, ed., *The Military-Industrial Complex* (1972)

Arthur M. Schlesinger, Jr., *The Imperial Presidency* (1973)

Lawrence S. Wittner, *Rebels Against War* (1969)

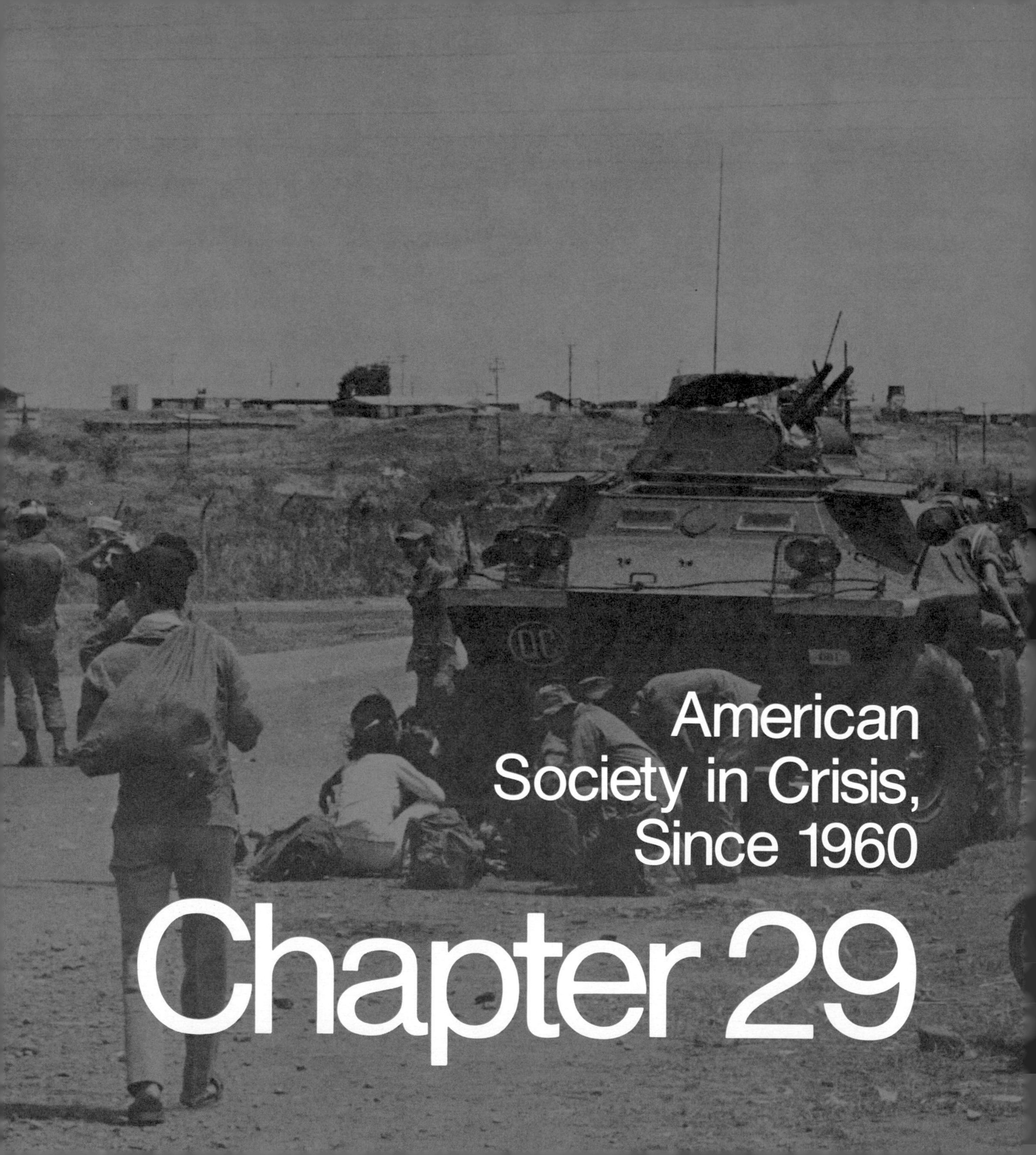

Chapter 29

American Society in Crisis, Since 1960

TIMELINE

1961
Kennedy approves the Bay of Pigs invasion of Cuba
1961
Kennedy commits American soldiers to Vietnam
1961
Khruschev's threats at Vienna produce a limited American mobilization to protect West Berlin
1962
Kennedy's hard line in the Cuban Missile Crisis forces withdrawal of missiles from Cuba
1962
Port Huron Statement by Students for a Democratic Society marks the beginning of the "youth revolt"
1963
The United States joins in a Nuclear Test Ban Treaty with over 100 other nations
1963
President Kennedy assassinated
1964
President Lyndon Johnson proposes a Great Society Program
1964
Congress approves a comprehensive Civil Rights Act
1965
Voting Rights Act ensures the right to vote for blacks in the South
1965
LBJ orders Operation Rolling Thunder—massive bombing raids on Vietnam.
1965
Watts Riot in Los Angeles leaves 34 dead and 856 injured
1966
Stokeley Carmichael coins phrase "black power"
1968
Johnson announces he will not seek reelection
1968
Martin Luther King assassinated; Robert Kennedy assassinated
1968
Richard Nixon narrowly wins Presidential election over Humphrey and Wallace.
1970
Campus unrest climaxes after the invasion of Cambodia and closes 448 colleges and universities
1971
President Nixon outlines a conservative domestic program called the "New American Revolution"
1972
Nixon visits Peking and opens communications between the United States and Communist China
1972
Nixon wins a landslide victory over George McGovern
1973
Armistice ends active American involvement in Vietnam War
1974
Nixon resigns and is succeeded by Gerald Ford
1975
South Vietnam falls to Communist military forces
1976
Jimmy Carter wins presidential election over President Ford

CHAPTER OUTLINE

It is always very difficult to view one's own time as history. The period since 1960, however, emerges as a period when the United States has been searching for a new equilibrium. This form of stability, if it is to last, must deal successfully with several obvious realities: the pressures for equality by various economic, racial, and sexual groups; the seeming permanence of America's dominant (but not unchallenged) world role; and the growing realization that all national resources are limited. In no relevant area such as social welfare, foreign policy, or economic programs has the United States solved its problems. Indeed, attempts to do so—while sometimes showing much promise and kindling great hopes—frequently have had disastrous repercussions. The other side of the coin is that, despite race violence, antiwar protest, loss of government credibility, and changing moral values, the nation and its people have survived and the search for stability has continued.

For a decade and a half following World War II, Americans were immobilized by two overriding considerations: the Cold War conflict with Russia and an overwhelming desire for a conflict-free society at home. In such an atmosphere continuation of social reform was barely possible and innovation out of the question. By the late 1950s, however, several disadvantaged groups eager to share the economic pie could no longer be nudged aside with excuses and soft words. At the same time, many Cold War arguments based on maintaining the preeminence of the U.S. in the Soviet-American monopoly of power began to sound hollow and fatuous as other countries made themselves active members in the nuclear club. No longer would all aspects of America's domestic life take second place to arguments based on America's responsibility to lead the free world at every turn, especially when that leadership proved so unproductive of tangible results. True, for the most part, Americans were ready to accept the international pressures of world leadership; but at the same time they were now ready to be more assertive at home.

As is often the American way, a shift in outlook or attention led to overreaction, and at home the decade of the 1960s was one of unusual unrest and considerable tension. The originally defensive theory of "containment," carried to illogical lengths in Southeast Asia, now seemed to be the central source of contamination for what was ailing America. In the end, Vietnam brought down a President, eroded public faith in the words and actions of U.S. leaders, and convinced nearly everyone that limits exist to what any nation can do: some tasks cost too much; some demand too great a sacrifice. It is in this context—the contrast between the faith of 1960 that federal money and federal policy can do almost anything and the sober realization eight or ten years later that it cannot—that one must view these tumultuous years.

Toward the Great Society: The Early Sixties

The underlying theme of John F. Kennedy's three years as president was the belief that his very narrow margin of victory in November 1960 was no mandate for change

Cornell Capa/Magnum.

The forty-three year old Kennedy found the tasks of fighting the Cold War and "getting the country moving again" on domestic policy to be formidable. Crises abroad and the conservative coalition at home limited his tangible achievements.

and, at the same time, limited effort to effect change anyway. During his third year in office, either because he was preparing for reelection or because he was perhaps more secure in his role as chief executive, Kennedy was clearly gearing up for action on various fronts and one could discern the outlines of what would become his successor's "Great Society."

The New Frontier

As a good politician, Kennedy, conscious of conservative strength in Congress, rode along with the Cold War rhetoric he inherited from Eisenhower and, for a year or so, kept his vaunted "New Frontier" more or less under wraps. His election in 1960 was marked most of all by its narrowness: a 114,673 vote margin out of 68 million ballots cast even though Kennedy caused a surge of normally Democratic voters to go to the polls. Kennedy gained 8 million more votes than Stevenson did in 1956, but Republican Nixon fell 1 million votes short of Eisenhower's total in 1956. Republicans did rebound somewhat, however, from the disastrous Democratic sweep of 1958 by picking up 20 seats in the House and 2 in the Senate. The Democrats still enjoyed huge majorities (64–36 in the Senate, 263–174 in the House), although the results strengthened the conservative coalition. The result was that Kennedy, heir to the New Deal, could deliver little that he had promised.

This position, difficult as it was, did not end planning for the future or stymie action on all fronts. Some two dozen task force groups, organized by Kennedy during his election campaign of 1960, were soon hard at work. To combat a six-month long economic slump, the President pushed immediately for minimum wage legislation, extended temporary employment benefits, improvements in social security, and aid to dependent children of the unemployed. These were largely stopgap measures, and for a year he clung steadfastly to the idea of a balanced budget. His larger goals, reminiscent of Truman's Fair Deal, had little success initially. Congress passed a $5 billion Housing Act (urban renewal) and an Area Redevelopment Act, designed to reduce unemployment and develop economic resources in a chronically depressed ten-state region of Appalachia, but little more. Not surprisingly, Kennedy reacted by becoming both more partisan and more frustrated and after 1962 went on the offensive in an effort to win support for his liberal program.

Despite this shift, the President also sought to create a "consensus" among all Americans, an elusive, nearly impossible goal. This effort, more than anything else, has earned Kennedy widespread criticism. His detractors note that any chief executive with a dynamic policy must, perforce, create division, not agreement. Nevertheless, Kennedy was instrumental in pushing several planks of his social welfare plan somewhat closer toward eventual enactment, and his attitude toward civil rights in mid-1963 was especially significant. Like Truman before him, Kennedy was unwilling to endanger congressional support in foreign affairs by moving ahead on the domestic front. But by late 1963 he had fostered a long period of sustained prosperity, cut unemployment by 2 percent, and was beginning to show signs of breaking up the legislative logjam.

Still, foreign policy dominated JFK's three years. The bold words of his inaugural speech and events in Cuba have given him a reputation as the consummate Cold Warrior; however, he was not necessarily devoted to these Cold War ideas even though he often tried to capitalize on the American voter's propensity to believe the worst of the Soviet Union and talked of a "missile gap" during his campaign. Kennedy's proclaimed resolve to restore "initiative" to American foreign policy was, after all, a natural development not unlike the cry of the Republicans eight years earlier.

Three dramatic events actually did much to create his Cold Warrior image: the Bay of Pigs fiasco (planned under Eisenhower but launched during the opening months of 1961); the confrontation during that same year with Khrushchev in Vienna and the subsequent Berlin Wall episode, which subsided without conflict; and the Cuban missile crisis of 1962. Some critics see Kennedy's actions as sheer bravado, but it is more likely that, certain America's course was correct, he held a genuine personal conviction (especially in the missile crisis) that the U.S. had no other choice but to act as it did.

On April 17, 1961, a force of 1,400 Cuban refugees who had been organized, trained, and equipped by the CIA, landed at the Bay of Pigs 90 miles south of Havana. Their goal was to overthrow a Communist-oriented regime established by Fidel Castro (1926-   ) early in 1959, but within seventy-two hours the invasion had been crushed. Just what went wrong is not entirely clear. Some sources indicate Kennedy withdrew air support at the last minute, although this was later denied. The result was, however, a severe blow to U.S. prestige, to a new President, and to the CIA. Kennedy assumed full responsibility for what happened, but five months later he named John A. McCone (1902-   ) to succeed Allen Dulles as head of the CIA.

In June 1961, Kennedy met Khrushchev for two days of summit talks in Vienna. The Russian dictator took a tough stance (perhaps because he thought his adversary "weak" after the Bay of Pigs defeat), reaffirming his 1958 vow to sign a separate peace treaty with East Germany, a decision interpreted as part of a general effort to push the Western powers out of Berlin. Kennedy returned home convinced that the U.S. had to bolster both its own forces and those of NATO as quickly as possible. With congressional approval he quickly increased defense appropriations for 1962 to $47.6 billion, the largest sum voted since 1951. Khrushchev's answer was a threat to mobilize and boasts of new nuclear weapons. Much more damaging was the Russian leader's swift and unexpected decision to seal off the border between East and West Berlin with a huge wall. The West replied with formal protests and the U.S. sent 1,500 more troops to West Berlin, but even visits to the beleaguered city by Kennedy and Vice President Johnson could not negate the fact that the Russian move had weakened the morale of West Berlin and dealt the Kennedy administration yet another blow.

Nevertheless, Cuba remained the new government's chief problem in foreign affairs. During mid-1962 Kennedy and his advisers dismissed complaints from Capitol Hill concerning the flow of Soviet arms to that island, claiming they were "defensive." Then, on October 22, following several days of intense, behind-the-scenes maneuvering, the President announced a huge missile buildup was underway only 90 miles from U.S. shores. He proclaimed a quarantine on all further shipments to Cuba, set up a naval blockade to check incoming cargos, and asked Khrushchev to withdraw all offensive weapons at once. After several very tense days as nuclear war loomed ominously, the Russian leader countered with a proposal to remove the weapons under UN supervision in return for an end to the quarantine and an American pledge not to invade Cuba. In the end, neither side got precisely what it wanted. Castro blocked UN inspection, the U.S. never formally agreed to refrain from invasion, and thousands of Russian personnel and considerable heavy weaponry remained in Cuba. Yet, the largest missile bases were quickly dismantled and the crisis atmosphere in East-West relations subsided somewhat.

These experiences undoubtedly caused President

Kennedy to seek ways to reduce Cold War tensions. Having "proved" himself as a Cold Warrior (both to friends and enemies), Kennedy felt he could proceed with a ban on nuclear testing under discussion for four years. The stumbling block had been American insistence upon on site inspection of nuclear facilities, which the Russian rejected. Late in 1962, however, the USSR seemed to be relaxing its stand and the talks resumed. Although agreement on inspection was not forthcoming, American, Russian, and British representatives turned their attention to the broader question of general disarmament and in July produced a draft proposal banning all tests above ground. In September, after prolonged debate, the Senate gave its approval 80–19. The Soviet Union ratified the pact the following day and 100 other nations soon agreed to abide by its provisions, the most notable exceptions being France and China.

During talks leading to this agreement, Soviet and U.S. spokesmen arranged for the establishment of a direct telegraphic "hot line" between the Kremlin and the White House, clear evidence that both nations were eager to avoid misunderstandings that might lead to yet another missile crisis. This treaty, the discussions surrounding it, and especially the Moscow-Washington hot line indicated that the nuclear powers, shaken by events of October 1962, had stepped back from the abyss of total war and were making a sincere effort to stabilize the arms race.

Leonard Freed/Magnum.

Two months after meeting Kennedy in Vienna, Khrushchev demanded that the U.S. presence in Berlin be ended, and the Russians constructed the Berlin Wall, dividing the eastern and western halves of the city. Tension ran high for several months, but the six-month deadline for U.S. withdrawal passed without incident.

Appreciating problems faced by developing nations, the President stressed that U.S. economic aid should be tied to objective economic need, *not* political alignment in the East-West struggle. His most far-reaching scheme was the Alliance for Progress to aid Latin America, but this plan never realized its brave goals. This ten-point proposal announced on March 13, 1961, a few weeks before the Bay of Pigs, actually was an expansion of some of Eisenhower's programs, largely in the form of loans. Despite efforts to change U.S. posture in the Middle East and various parts of Asia, Kennedy was unable to do so. He may have wanted to act in a less partisan manner, but his administration continued to aid regimes irrespective of reforms as a counter to possible Soviet expansion. In short, the name of the game still was "containment."

Considerable evidence exists that Kennedy had somewhat greater appreciation for subtle nuances of the Soviet-American confrontation than his predecessors; nevertheless, he was gripped by a compulsion for "action," which resulted in higher levels of military spending. One observer noted that this propensity to act and to be seen doing something swiftly and with apparent purpose was the "geological fault" of the action-prone Kennedy family. Both a general military buildup and creation of new "special forces" known as Green Berets to combat guerrillas reinforced the feeling that the U.S. might take new initiatives abroad to combat insurgency within developing nations. This counterinsurgency overseas, perhaps more than anything else, reflected Kennedy's drive and imagination, and it was, of course, Vietnam that provided the opportunity to act.

That Kennedy chose to assert American influence in Vietnam may stem in part from three developments in 1961: the Bay of Pigs debacle, his acceptance of a neutralist regime in nearby Laos, and his quiet acquiescence to the Berlin Wall. Meanwhile, in May of that year, shortly after the disappointing defeat in Cuba, he dispatched 400 Special Forces and 100 military advisors to Saigon. At the urging of various close advisors, including Vice President Lyndon Johnson, he applied the "domino theory" to Vietnam in November; by late 1962 he had increased the U.S. commitment to 10,000 troops, then to 15,000 a year later. Much of this was done in secret since introduction of foreign troops violated the Geneva Accord agreements. Yet what had been merely a "limited risk gamble" under Eisenhower grew into a broad campaign by Kennedy to prevent Communist domination of South Vietnam.

René Burri/Magnum.

Secretary of Defense Robert McNamara on a visit to South Vietnam in 1963. McNamara, an influential policy-maker in the Kennedy and Johnson administrations, became more cautious in his predictions of victory by the mid-1960s, and was disillusioned with the war by 1967.

The assassination of that nation's President Diem (with the apparent acquiescence of the CIA) only a few weeks before Kennedy was struck down in Dallas represented a possible watershed in U.S. policy. Whether John Kennedy would have continued his growing involvement in Vietnam after that shakeup is anyone's guess; but, considering the men about him who, under Johnson, exploded a brushfire into a major war, one is forced to conclude that Kennedy would have found it extremely difficult to extricate himself from Southeast Asia.

Few events have so stirred Americans as the assassination of John Fitzgerald Kennedy at the age of forty-six as he rode through the streets of Dallas on November 22,

1963. In full view of hundreds of spectators lining a parade route, he was struck by several bullets, dying almost instantly. His suspected assailant, Lee Harvey Oswald, a twenty-four-year-old Marxist and ex-U.S. Marine who had spent some years in the U.S.S.R. and had a Russian wife, was presumably the assassin who fired from a nearby building. Arrested that same day, Oswald was, in turn, shot and killed by Jack Ruby, a local nightclub operator, forty-eight hours later as he was being transferred from city to county authorities. A commission headed by Chief Justice Earl Warren subsequently decided that both Oswald and Ruby acted alone and that neither was part of "any conspiracy, domestic or foreign." Yet the *Warren Report* has failed to end the controversy that has surrounded these events. Scores of Americans remain convinced that Oswald actually was involved in some form of intrigue, a view strengthened in succeeding decades as they learned more concerning the secret operations of their own government.

The young President's legacy is a mix of pluses and minuses that some describe with high-blown praise, others with caution. For a time after his tragic death, the young Cold Warrior was a superhero, a near saint. Millions who had not voted for him in 1960 and were quick to find fault with his programs suddenly became his greatest and most vociferous admirers. In truth, John F. Kennedy increased the moral leadership of the presidency, but he registered few solid achievements; nor is it clear that he ever could have made his New Frontier a reality. No consensus on domestic social reform had developed by November 1963, and the President remained committed to the possible, not to the dream. Kennedy must receive another mixed verdict in foreign affairs. He demonstrated greater tolerance than Eisenhower and Dulles for nations that chose to be neutral in the Washington-Moscow competition and achieved a limited nuclear test ban treaty; yet his words and his actions helped to create the dilemmas faced by his successor, Lyndon Baines Johnson.

It is unfair, of course, to compare Kennedy's abbreviated White House tenure with those who served longer terms as chief executive. Nearly every President spends his first two years learning the new job and its ramifications. Highly intelligent, eager to learn and do well, Kennedy seemed to be growing in stature during his third year. He was able to stir a strong response among his fellow Americans—some hated him, but many more developed great affection for this engaging, witty leader. Nevertheless, we can only conjecture as to his place in history if he had been forced to deal with Vietnam, urban riots, the youth protest, and other disruptive forces that burst forth in what could have been his second four years in the White House.

Culmination of the Civil Rights Revolution

One area in which the legacy of John Fitzgerald Kennedy is less ambiguous is civil rights. The years from 1954 to 1964 comprise a decade of considerable and far-reaching change for millions of Americans. Although desegregation proceeded rather slowly in the mid-1950s, by 1960 both political parties were espousing advanced civil rights positions. The Democrats, for example, abandoned their attempts of 1952 and 1956 to accommodate to the views of Southern conservatives, and revived instead many of Truman's liberal proposals of 1949. They used nearly 800 words in their platform to promise the "full use" of legal and moral powers to end racial discrimination in voting, education, jobs, housing, and the administration of justice. The Republicans nearly equalled their adversaries in promises, if not in spirit.

Nixon hoped to build on Eisenhower's gains among blacks in 1956, but his opponent proved to be a better campaigner, capturing 68 percent of the black vote in 1960. During the campaign Kennedy criticized Eisenhower for not ending discrimination in some areas by issuing an executive order. It could be done, he noted, "with the stroke of a pen." (It might also be noted that, as President, Kennedy did not choose to use his pen in this fashion until November 1962, two years after his election.) More dramatic were the actions of both John and Robert Kennedy when Martin Luther King, Jr., was arrested for sitting-in at the Magnolia Room of Rich's Department Store in Atlanta on October 19, 1960. When King was sentenced to four months of hard labor, JFK immediately called King's wife to express sympathy, and his brother (also his campaign manager) telephoned the Georgia judge who had sentenced King and pleaded for his release. The next day the judge complied with this request, although it is not clear what effect, if any, the younger Kennedy may have had. News of these events swept through hundreds of black communities and the point was not lost on those who went to the polls a week or so later: the Kennedys had acted in their behalf, while Eisenhower and Nixon had done nothing.

King's Atlanta sit-in was only one of many during 1960–1961, as civil rights activists became more hopeful, organizing the new Student Nonviolent Coordinating Committee (SNCC) and setting forth on "freedom rides" throughout the South to challenge established customs. During his first two years Kennedy helped these protesters realize some of their goals, largely through action in the executive branch of the federal government. In November 1961 the Interstate Commerce Commission banned the segregation of interstate travel facilities, and the Justice Department (headed by Robert Kennedy) initiated suits designed to end voter discrimination. A year later, by executive order, the President ended discrimination in housing built with federal assistance (except FHA loans). Meanwhile, he was appointing more and more blacks to lower level federal jobs, and the Justice Department was aiding voter registration drives in the South. SNCC, however, was critical of this effort, noting that promises of physical protection by the administration often failed to prevent violence and even death. Yet, when mob action stirred by admission of a black man, James Meredith, to the University of Mississippi led to riots on that campus in October 1962, Kennedy intervened with federal troops, promptly and with much less public reluctance than displayed by Eisenhower at Little Rock a few years earlier.

The year 1963 proved to be a turning point in the civil rights struggle. On one hand, southern resistance stiffened; on the other, black resolve increased and JFK began to move on the legislative front. George Wallace, the dynamic, outspoken new governor of Alabama, threw down the gauntlet, proclaiming "segregation now, segregation tomorrow, segregation forever." In February 1963 the administration began to draw up legislation that, at the outset, was a mild extension of voting rights laws passed in 1957 and 1960. However, brutality and violence, especially in Alabama and Mississippi, ultimately converted this proposal into a much stronger measure.

Those outbreaks included, in addition to the bloody affair at the University of Mississippi and sporadic violence directed against "freedom riders," the use of dogs and fire hoses to disperse Birmingham school children demonstrating in behalf of civil rights in May 1963 and numerous bombings in the same city. The murders of a white Baltimore postman marching through northern Alabama carrying a sign "Equal Rights for All—Mississippi or Bust" and of Medgar Evers, state chairman of the Mississippi NAACP, inflamed racial tensions.

Charles Moore/Black Star.

In May 1963 black protesters in Birmingham, Alabama, suffered brutality at the hands of local police led by Commissioner of Public Safety Eugene "Bull" Connor. Scenes like this and others showing the use of high-pressure hoses on blacks, broadcast on nightly television news programs, helped to move much of the public—and President Kennedy—to favor civil rights legislation.

New York Daily News Photo.

Robert F. Kennedy
(1925–1968)

Energetic, athletic, boyish with an unruly shock of hair hanging over his forehead, Robert Francis Kennedy was born in Brookline, Massachusetts, on November 20, 1925, the third and smallest of four brothers in a large, competitive, and very wealthy family. He served in the U.S. Navy (1944–1946), graduated from Harvard in 1948, spent a year as the correspondent of the *Boston Post* in Palestine, and then earned a law degree from the University of Virginia in 1951. That same year he began working as a federal attorney, but in 1952 he quit to manage the successful senatorial campaign of his brother, John.

Returning to government service once more, Kennedy rose to prominence as counsel for various congressional committees. In this capacity he became known to the public through his work as the Democratic counsel to Senator Joseph McCarthy's famous subcommittee as well as through his thorough investigations of teamster bosses James R. Hoffa and David Beck, for another Senate Committee.

In 1960, Robert Kennedy once more became his brother's campaign manager, and after the election, was named Attorney General, one of the youngest men ever to hold that prestigious post. A zealous crusader for civil rights, he also continued his fight against labor racketeering and eventually won a conviction against Hoffa for jury tampering in 1964.

As heir apparent after his brother's assassination, Robert Kennedy was feared by Lyndon Johnson who eliminated him from consideration as a vice presidential candidate in 1964 by barring all of his Cabinet from the nomination. Kennedy then resigned from the Justice Department and won election to the Senate from New York state. Four years later, after Eugene McCarthy had demonstrated the strength of antiwar sentiment, Kennedy announced his candidacy for the presidency. A critic of American involvement in Vietnam since 1965, Kennedy won several important contests. On June 5, 1968, shortly after winning the California primary, he was assassinated in a Los Angeles hotel.

As the only candidate who appealed to both antiwar and antipoverty forces, and benefiting from Kennedy money and glamor, this dynamic young man might have won the nomination in 1968 and perhaps even gone on to the White House. His tragic death at the hands of Sirhan Sirhan on the night of his narrow victory in the California primary ensured a divisive, bitter political battle within Democratic ranks and aided immeasurably the Republican nominee. ■

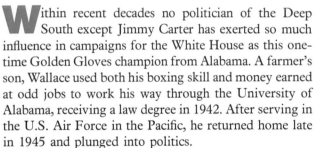

U.P.I.

George C. Wallace (1919–)

Within recent decades no politician of the Deep South except Jimmy Carter has exerted so much influence in campaigns for the White House as this one-time Golden Gloves champion from Alabama. A farmer's son, Wallace used both his boxing skill and money earned at odd jobs to work his way through the University of Alabama, receiving a law degree in 1942. After serving in the U.S. Air Force in the Pacific, he returned home late in 1945 and plunged into politics.

An eloquent and persuasive debater, Wallace was an outstanding member of the state legislature for two terms and then from 1953 to 1959 served as a circuit judge. From the bench he breathed defiance at federal civil rights laws and, although defeated in a bid to become governor in 1958, roared to victory four years later. As chief executive, Wallace cut government expenses, slashing his office budget by $100,000, but more important, as he had promised to do, "stood in the school house door" and personally turned away federal officials bent upon integrating the University of Alabama. Four hours later President Kennedy federalized the Alabama National Guard and Wallace stepped aside, having made his point.

Since the young governor was then barred by law from succeeding himself, he engineered in 1966 the election of his first wife, Lurleen, the third woman in history to head up a state government. She succumbed to cancer in May 1968 and her husband easily won back his old job in 1970 and, thanks to new ground rules, once more in 1974.

Meanwhile, Wallace used his Alabama constituency and a staunch segregationist stance to make a bid for the presidency in every election from 1964 to 1976. Only once, however—in 1968—was he a serious contender. He withdrew in 1964 after the Republicans nominated conservative Goldwater, was eliminated in 1972 by an assassin's bullet, which left him partially paralyzed, and quit in 1976 as soon as his native South decided to back Democrat Carter. In May of 1978 he announced, to the surprise of many, that he would not seek the Democratic nomination for a U.S. Senate seat from Alabama, claiming that he needed a rest from politics.

But in 1968 George Wallace bolted the Democratic Party to head up the new American Independent party. Running with General Curtis Lemay as his vice presidential candidate, he got on the ballot in fifty states and in November of that year captured nearly 10 million votes (46 in the Electoral College) in a three-way battle with Nixon and Humphrey. Only a concerted drive by organized labor checked his appeal in many blue-collar neighborhoods.

A dynamic, forthright speaker, Wallace is also a pragmatic politican capable of adapting to change. No longer the voice of segregation, he now brags about how much his native Alabama is doing for its black citizens.

His decision in 1978 not to seek a Senate seat was coupled with his claim that his efforts had contributed to a resurgence of the interests of middle class voters who had been ignored by liberal Democratic politicians. This suggests that his political career—despite many disappointments—may yet extend beyond the borders of Alabama. ■

Violence also broke out in Cambridge, Maryland, in mid-June when blacks demanded access to public accommodations. The governor called out the National Guard to restore order, and Attorney General Kennedy eventually negotiated a truce of sorts. That same month, over the strenuous objections of Governor George Wallace, two black students enrolled at the University of Alabama; and, when public schools opened three months later, all of the southern states (except Mississippi) either had blacks in their elementary and secondary classrooms or were about to admit them under court orders.

Meanwhile, on June 19, 1963, following several forceful statements on civil rights, Kennedy unveiled plans to end discrimination in employment and in all public accommodations. "The fires of frustration and discord are burning in every city, North and South, where legal remedies are not at hand," he emphasized. "Redress is sought in the streets, in demonstrations, parades, and protests which create tensions and threaten violence—and threaten lives." The heart of the President's proposals was a public accommodations provision assuring blacks of admittance to lunch counters, restaurants, amusement parks, theaters, hotels, and similar facilities open to the general public. His bill also included added protection for those exercising their voting rights, federal assistance to areas where schools were desegregated and a cutoff of funds where discrimination continued, and stronger machinery to prevent discrimination by employers fulfilling government contracts. Kennedy did not specifically seek new legislation on fair employment practices, pledging support instead for similar measures already before Congress.

As one might expect, his bill got bogged down in the House Rules Committee, and only the tumultuous events of the next six months finally pried it loose. These developments included the famous "March on Washington" on August 26, 1963, in which over 200,000 people took part (among them some 80,000 whites and 150 members of Congress), a succession of bombings throughout the South, and especially, the assassination of President Kennedy. The Washington demonstration, an unprecedented show of solidarity in support of Kennedy's civil rights legislation, featured the stirring words of Martin Luther King, Jr.: "I say to you today, my friends, even though we face the difficulties of today and tomorrow, I still have a dream. It is a dream deeply rooted in the American dream. I have a dream that one day this nation will rise up and live out the true meaning of its creed: 'We hold these truths to be self-evident that all men are created equal'. . . . I have a dream. . . ."

Kennedy's successor, Lyndon Johnson, called for "the earliest possible passage" of the civil rights bill as a tribute to Kennedy, an ironic twist since Johnson was put on the 1960 ticket to win over southern whites. Early in 1964 the Twenty-Fourth Amendment banning poll taxes won ratification, but the civil rights measure remained stalled in the Senate until July 2 when it at last was passed and signed into law. Much of the credit for final action must go to Johnson, who directed a drive for passage from the White House, and the Senate's Republican minority leader, Everett Dirksen, who, through compromise and negotiation, ended an attempted filibuster.

This measure, the most far-reaching civil rights legislation since Reconstruction days, guaranteed blacks the right to vote in federal elections. It also provided blacks with access to public places, authorized federal officials to sue to desegregate public facilities and schools, enhanced the ability of the federal government to enforce equality of opportunity for all citizens, set up a new Community Relations Service to resolve "disputes relating to discriminatory practices based on race, color, or national origin," and gave the Justice Department an active role in the desegregation of public education at all levels. In general, however, the Civil Rights Act of 1964

Fred Ward/Black Star.

The culmination of the March on Washington, August 1963.

urged local agencies to work out their differences before federal authorities had to intervene. One section of the Act—Title VII relating to Equal Employment Opportunity—outlawed discriminatory practices based not only upon race, color, or national origin, but also upon religion and sex.

Even before passage was assured, civil rights activists led by SNCC, which dominated a federated group of organizations, had launched "Freedom Summer" in Mississippi, a drive designed to register black voters, conduct "Freedom Schools," and organize a new political force (the Mississippi Freedom Democratic Party) at the local level. The results included some success and a violent white blacklash: over one thousand arrests, thirty-five shooting incidents, thirty bombings, thirty-five church burnings, eighty beatings, and at least six murders occurred. At Atlantic City the 1964 National Democratic convention turned a deaf ear to the new party, offering it only two nonvoting seats, a "compromise" that was rejected. Despite this rebuff and news of almost daily outrages from Mississippi the Democrats did not suffer. Lyndon Johnson received the bulk of black votes as he overwhelmed Republican Barry Goldwater. This reflected in part the 1964 Civil Rights Act and the Economic Opportunity Act, which set up Community Action Programs, the Neighborhood Youth Corps, and Head Start. Generally known as the President's antipoverty program, the Economic Opportunity Act proposed expenditure of $900 million in 1965 to combat the causes of conditions that kept nearly one-fifth of all Americans at the bottom of the economic ladder. Its passage in August 1964 assured Johnson of additional black support at the polls three months later.

After his landslide victory, Johnson, assisted by

violence in Alabama, carried the civil rights battle forward. The administration-sponsored Voting Rights Act of 1965 strengthened the power of blacks at the polls by substituting direct federal action to promote registration and balloting for often prolonged individual court suits. It suspended literacy tests and gave the Attorney General power to appoint federal examiners in regions where such qualifying devices were in effect in November 1964 and where, at that time, fewer than 50 percent of those qualified to vote either were registered or actually cast ballots. During the 1960s the number of eligible black voters who were registered in the South grew from 29.1 percent to 62 percent while white registration rose from 61.1 percent to 69.2 percent. The most dramatic gain for blacks was in Mississippi where the figure rose from 5.2 percent to 71 percent. In 1970, by percentage of potential voters actually registered, blacks surpassed whites in Arkansas and Virginia. Other measures passed in 1965 which helped blacks included housing legislation and an Elementary and Secondary School Act designed to aid less affluent students. The Housing and Urban Development Act setting up a new Cabinet-level Department of Housing and Urban Development (HUD) was accompanied by an omnibus housing bill designed to provide $7.8 billion in federal assistance for new housing and urban renewal, with special emphasis upon the needs of the poor. The education measure, which President Johnson considered to be of crucial importance, directed federal funds to school districts on the basis of the number of children from low-income households in an area. That

Bruce Davidson/Magnum.

Civil rights demonstrations captured public attention in the mid-1960s. In February 1965 the fifty-two mile "March for Freedom" from Selma, Alabama, to the state capital of Montgomery, and especially the violent response of Alabama state officials, helped to build support for passage of the 1965 Voting Rights Act.

Act also provided aid for college libraries, scholarships for needy students, and a teacher corps to help out in overburdened classrooms.

At this juncture the Supreme Court played a major role in the ongoing struggle for civil rights. In a variety of cases relating to public schools, the justices said there had been "entirely too much deliberation and not enough speed," a clear reference to the controversial 1954 decision ending "separate but equal" classrooms. The most notable of these decisions concerned the community of Farmville, Virginia, where all schools had been closed since 1959 to avoid integration. In 1964 the Court said (*Griffin* v. *Prince Edward County Schools*) that such discrimination against blacks violated the equal protection clause of the Constitution. It also prohibited tuition grants or tax credits to families using private white schools so long as public classrooms were closed to blacks. In December 1965 the Court, in *Rogers* v. *Paul*, ordered the school system of Fort Smith, Arkansas, to permit the immediate transfer of qualified blacks to an all-white high school, again stressing that such delays were "no longer tolerable."

A similar mood was evident in decisions relating to voting and the use of public accommodations. In 1964, the Court found unconstitutional a Louisiana requirement that a candidate's race be cited on local election ballots (*Anderson* v. *Martin*). Two years later in *South Carolina* v. *Katzenbach* the justices by a unanimous vote dismissed a challenge to the major provisions of the 1965 Voting Rights Act and in *Harper* v. *Virginia State Board of Elections* struck down the poll tax in state elections. In 1964 the Supreme Court overruled several sit-in convictions in Maryland, South Carolina, and Florida; in the same year the Court upheld access of blacks to public accommodations (*Heart of Atlanta Motel, Inc.* v. *U.S.; Katzenbach* v. *McClung*), stressing that Congress had acted within its powers to regulate interstate commerce when it opened motels, hotels, restaurants, parks, and lunch counters to all races.

All of these steps—increased voter rights, better housing, better education, more jobs—were part of what Lyndon Johnson called his "Great Society" program. To round out this very ambitious surge of social reform, the President proposed in 1966 an Open Housing Bill, which, unlike earlier measures, threatened racial patterns and customs outside of the South by opening up neighborhood real estate to black homebuyers. This measure, part of a general civil rights bill, eventually won House approval, but was beaten in the Senate. This defeat revealed the absence of a true national consensus on civil rights, and the movement, which seemed on the verge of complete success, became mired down in debate, dispute, and discord. Angry voices rose in both white and black communities throughout all parts of the nation: the civil rights coalition of blacks and white liberals—unable to find the path of compromise outside of Dixie—was beginning to unravel.

LBJ and the Great Society

Within five days of Kennedy's death, Lyndon Johnson had called for national unity and action by Congress to pass a variety of bills, the remainder of JFK's program: "So let us here highly resolve that John Fitzgerald Kennedy did not live—or die—in vain." Symbolically, this first major address by the new President was written by his predecessor's aides and then revised by Johnson's staff. Johnson's first moves were calculated to restore public confidence shaken by the horrifying events in Dallas. He immediately named a blue ribbon commission headed by Chief Justice Earl Warren to investigate the assassination of Kennedy and engineered a generally successful transition in all phases of government during the winter of 1963–1964. The legislation that Johnson got in 1964—an election year—probably would have passed if Kennedy had lived, but perhaps more slowly. Antipoverty programs, for example, were being planned late in 1963. Too-quick passage in 1964 may, in fact, have created some of the problems that later plagued the "war on poverty."

Johnson officially launched his Great Society in a commencement address in Ann Arbor, Michigan, in May 1964. The war on poverty, and the resulting Office of Economic Opportunity, was headed by Sargent Shriver, Kennedy's brother-in-law. The President pressed Congress hard, twisted arms, and got enactment of his Economic Opportunity Act in August, too soon to allow for meaningful debate and discussion. Firmly in control of his party, he helped draft the 1964 platform, orchestrated nearly every move when the Democrats met at Atlantic City, and then went forth to campaign on the Great Society theme. After eliminating Robert Kennedy as a possible running mate, he selected a liberal with impeccable credentials, Minnesota's Hubert Humphrey, although he did not reveal his choice until the last possible

This Native American may seem to be a stereotype, yet he fit well into the zany political atmosphere at Miami in 1972.

wen Franken/Stock, Boston.

Graffiti often reveal a need for attention, especially among groups who feel excluded from mainstream America, as do many young Puerto Ricans.

© Costa Manos/Magnum.

wen Franken/Stock, Boston.

Strong ethnic ties are maintained by imbuing children with a positive sense of their heritage. A young boy proudly watches a St. Patrick's Day Parade in Boston.

Jan Lukas/Rapho-Photo Researchers.

Ethnic groups concentrated in neighborhoods have a long history of involvement in American politics. Polish-American political clubs at the district and ward level have often formed the nucleus of urban party organizations.

Ethnic America

Owen Franken/Stock, Boston

Ethnic Americans seek equal access to American institutions. Some succeed, as this Harvard graduation suggests.

© Ted Horowitz / Image Bank

Interesting and colorful ethnic enclaves are great tourist attractions in most large American cities. Perhaps most famous and magnetic of all is San Francisco's Chinatown.

© Katrina Thomas / Photo Researchers

The presence of diverse ethnic groups is nowhere more evident than in the religious structures that dot the American landscape. Pictured here is a Russian Orthodox Church in Lakewood, New Jersey.

© Katrina Thomas / Photo Researchers

© Charles Harbutt / Magnum

Even among the most thoroughly assimilated groups, parades and festivals provide occasions for enthusiastic group expression. Marchers in New York don Bavarian dress for the Steuben Day Parade (left) and Italian-Americans celebrate the Feast of San Gennaro.

© Hanna W. Schreiber/Rapho-Photo Researchers.

Although many American Jews have departed from Orthodox religious customs, most still hold the traditional Seder in celebration of Passover.

Craighead/de Wys, Inc.

Scandinavians did not customarily remain in coastal cities, instead settling on farmlands in the American interior. Even today, whole communities in some Midwestern states are populated predominantly by Swedish- or Norwegian-Americans.

© Charles Harbutt/Magnum.

Buttons, literature, and other political paraphernalia reflect the rising group consciousness and activism of Mexican-Americans.

Steve Niedorf/Image Bank.

A strong sense of unity is characteristic of black families. Here a mother and children enjoy an outing in Philadelphia.

Library Collection.

Symbolizing the continuity of the Great Society with the agenda of the New and Fair Deals, President Johnson flew to Independence, Missouri, to sign the Medicare bill on July 30, 1965, with former President Truman present. Nearly twenty years earlier, Truman had urged adoption of national health insurance program.

moment. Other than the battle over seating rival Mississippi delegations, the choice of Humphrey was perhaps the only bit of drama at that carefully staged (and rather dull) affair.

Since the Great Society presumably had something in it for everyone, Johnson ran a broad "consensus" campaign against Barry Goldwater's narrow, sectional appeal. It may be significant that the President ended his search for votes at a tumultuous extravaganza held in New York's Madison Square Garden; that same evening his Republican opponent appeared before some 3,000 people in Columbia, South Carolina. Johnson, having worked hard to paper over traditional GOP-Democratic differences and isolate Goldwater as an "extremist," lost only the Deep South. Armed with this mandate, he went forth to achieve his Great Society goals. Yet the President had made a fatal error; he had received no such blank check. Big business, professional workers, and white-collar voters certainly rejected Goldwater in unprecedented numbers (in part perhaps because Johnson then appeared to be more reasonable in his foreign policy pronouncements), but their votes were no endorsement of the Great Society. Their votes represented merely a choice between two candidates for the highest office in the land.

Lyndon Johnson clearly hoped to preside over "an era of good feelings", and, aided by an overwhelmingly Democratic Congress, he secured easy passage of what one observer has termed "almost the entire agenda of twentieth century progressivism." In addition to education and housing bills already mentioned, these measures included Medicare/Medicaid, the Appalachian Regional Development Act, and a Higher Education Act. Medicare provided supplemental health care for the elderly under the Social Security System, while Medicaid was designed to pay the medical costs of younger needy persons. The Appalachian Regional Development Act appropriated $1 billion to assist residents of a twelve-state area stretching from southern New York state to Alabama, traditionally one of the nation's poorest regions. The Higher Education Act, passed with substantial bipartisan backing, was a revolutionary scheme to grant scholarship aid to college and university students. Congress in 1965 also established a National Foundation on the Arts and Humanities (counterpart of the National Science Foundation) for artists, musicians, and writers. In October 1965, Johnson presented fifty pens and a plaque to the Washington press corps. The plaque read: "With these fifty pens President Lyndon B. Johnson signed into law the foundations of the Great Society, which was passed by the historic and fabulous first session of the Eighty-Ninth Congress."

There was considerable irony in this presentation, for the President already was in deep trouble with both the press and the public. Poll after poll revealed he actually was not liked and suffered from what Madison Avenue describes as "an image problem," despite astonishing success at the ballot box and on Capitol Hill. In part, this resulted from his penchant for secrecy and surprise in dealing with reporters, politicians, rank-and-file citizens, and even high officials in his own administration. Johnson's insistence upon a unified front before the public ("consensus" again) and a tendency to push bills through Congress without responsible debate also created uneasiness. Perhaps a key to Johnson's dilemma was that, despite great power, he trusted virtually no one and thus hardly could inspire trust in return. His method of governing by persuasion was indeed impressive, but his secret ways troubled many Americans in all levels of society.

Underlying the President's difficulties were several diverse factors: secrecy that led to a "credibility gap," insistence upon rule by "consensus" (one should remember he came to power in one-party Texas and saw the Democrats run Congress and the nation much as they wished for over a quarter of a century), and decisions in foreign affairs which began to alienate many liberals. The dispatching of several thousand marines to the Dominican Republic in 1965 to thwart an alleged Communist coup alarmed liberals, but even more distressing was America's growing involvement in Vietnam. The President's very private, wheeling-and-dealing type of leadership which obscured issues and smothered debate in an effort to give an aura of general agreement won him a congressional license to construct his Great Society. That same brand of secretive, personal direction made it highly unlikely that the structure could ever be built; for, when the chips were down, his mythical "consensus" contained far too many interest groups with opposing views: black-white, labor-management, big business-small business, liberal-conservative, young-old, even Democrat-Republican. Legislation, after all, is not the same as social change. Arm-twisting and cajoling might work on a one-to-one basis, but Lyndon Johnson could not control events or reactions in America's ghettos, its all-white suburbs, or especially overseas.

The Rout of Reform: The Late Sixties

Nowhere was the lack of consensus more evident—or most costly—than in civil rights. Efforts to carry reform forward created a white backlash that soon became a crucial factor in U.S. politics at almost every level.

Backlash and Racial Explosions

The failure of LBJ to get a meaningful Open Housing Bill in 1966 and 1967 testified to mounting white resistance to civil rights legislation on behalf of minority groups. This backlash first surfaced in the 1964 Democratic primaries when Alabama's George Wallace got as high as 43 percent of the vote in the state of Maryland. According to some estimates, at that time only about 30 percent of all voters actually favored desegregation, with half of all northern residents conceding they had "mixed feelings" concerning civil rights programs in general. In the South fewer than 20 percent of the voters were willing to accept more desegregation.

Although Barry Goldwater's decisive defeat and election of a strongly Democratic Congress paved the way for the 1965 Voting Rights Act, the civil rights question—or the "race problem" as it was often called—was becoming increasingly nonsectional in nature. The percentage of blacks living in the South dropped to 60 percent in 1960 and to 53 percent by 1970. This meant that about twelve million blacks were living in northern communities, often crowded into cities of the upper Midwest and the Northeast—poor, highly visible, a new and disturbing presence that stiffened nonsouthern resistance to future civil rights legislation. In 1966, the Republicans, using as their battle cry "law and order" (a euphemism for "backlash"), rebounded from disaster and won an additional 47 seats in the House and 3 in the Senate.

A Harris Poll taken that year to measure alienation and white attitudes toward blacks revealed that low-income whites, more so than blacks, felt they were apart from and rarely considered by the rich and powerful. Over 50 percent of the less affluent whites questioned thought those in power did not care about their views, that their opinions were of no consequence, and that as "the rich get richer, the poor get poorer." Also, low-income whites as a group tended to demonstrate considerable hostility toward blacks throughout the nation. Fewer than 50 percent thought blacks actually were being discriminated against or lived in housing worse than that of whites. Over 50 percent said blacks had "lower morals" than whites, tried to live off handouts, should not live next door to them, and had children who would not be welcome at supper. Perhaps the most revealing statistic of all was that only 24 percent of low-income whites sympathized with the black protest for equal treatment, compared to 57 percent of affluent whites and 46 percent of all white Americans. These emotional reactions had keen political significance because (1) these feelings could be readily translated into votes and (2) less affluent whites were very numerous and certainly outnumbered blacks throughout the nation. Also, fewer than half of all white Americans by 1966 favored the protest movement, a statistic that boded ill for such efforts in the immediate future.

This backlash mood intensified an already developing hostility and militancy in black communities between 1964 and 1967. During those years some twenty-five cities experienced violent unrest, rioting, and looting. The toll was devastating: approximately 130 civilians (most of them blacks) and 12 civil personnel (mainly whites) killed, 4,700 people injured, over 20,000 arrested, and property damage mounting into the millions. These largely unplanned and unorganized outbursts, as a presidential commission later determined, were the actions of poor and dispossessed individuals crushed into huge slum ghettos. Rising up in protest against a society committed to democratic ideals, they were a mix of class antagonism, resentment against race prejudice, anger at nearby affluence, and an overwhelming sense of frustration which spilled over on a hot, steamy summer night, ignited by an explosive incident. In terms of death, violence, and destruction, a six-day rampage in the Watts section of Los Angeles in August of that same year was the worst of early outbursts. Touched off by a white policeman's attempt to give a black driver a sobriety test, it resulted in 34 dead, 856 injured, and property losses totaling nearly $200 million. Two years later, Detroit and Newark experienced nearly simultaneous explosions of even greater magnitude.

A report issued in March 1965 by Daniel P. Moynihan, then Assistant Secretary of Labor, focused attention upon the breakdown of the black family as a social unit. Within a short time, however, that argument came under sharp attack, especially when newsmen covering these urban riots tried to use family disorganization as a prime cause for violence.

Special targets of rioters everywhere were police who represented the establishment and white businessmen who exploited black customers with high and hidden interest rates, shoddy goods, high prices, and questionable service. Although whites usually blamed federal "coddling" for the destruction that swept through Watts, Harlem, Newark, Detroit, Boston, and Chicago (and even lesser centers such as Americus, Georgia, and Grenada,

Bob Clark/Black Star.

In 1967, the worst yet of the "long hot summers," Newark and Detroit exploded into racial violence in July. In Detroit 4700 paratroopers had to assist the National Guard in quelling the riot; in the end, forty-three persons died, hundreds were injured, and property worth hundreds of millions of dollars was destroyed. This picture gives a small glimpse of the damage.

Mississippi), the President's Commission on Civil Disorders (also known as the Kerner Commission), appointed in 1967, pointed to more deep-seated causes that included economic deprivation, institutional racism, repression, and a general sense of futility and hopelessness.

These urban riots led to eventual passage of the long-sought Open Housing Act in April 1968, although enactment was aided substantially by the assassination in Memphis of Dr. Martin Luther King, Jr. King was gunned down on April 4 while in the Tennessee city to assist striking garbage workers. His death touched off rioting, looting, and burning in many communities, notably Washington, D.C. A white suspect, James Earl Ray, was arrested in London two months later and subsequently convicted of the crime. As a means of collective atonement for the death of the famed Nobel Prize winner, long the voice of peaceful protest among black Americans, Congress rushed through a bill banning discrimination in the sale or rental of homes. But the bill was a strange amalgamation indeed. It did not include single-family dwellings sold privately and dragged in its wake a handful of repressive amendments that had nothing whatsoever to do with housing and revealed the changing nature of "civil rights" legislation. The Lausche-Thurmond amendment made it a federal crime to travel interstate or use interstate facilities such as telephones or the mails for the purpose of inciting, organizing, or participating in a riot. A riot, the lawmakers said, was any public disturbance involving three or more persons. Another amendment made it a federal crime to manufacture, transport across state lines, or teach/demonstrate the use of firearms, bombs, or other explosives intended for use in any form of civil disorder. A third rider protected firemen and policemen from obstruction in carrying out their duties.

The mid-1960s riots both dramatized and gave support to more militant leadership among blacks. Spokesmen such as Stokely Carmichael (1941-) and Floyd McKissick (1922-), "black power" advocates, joined their voices with those of separatist-minded blacks represented by followers of Malcolm X (1925-1965), who had recently been assassinated. Carmichael, speaking at a Greenwood, Mississippi, rally in June 1966 coined the phrase "black power," a term with various shades of meaning in economics, politics, and culture. To some it implied an end to job discrimination; to others, strength at the ballot box; and, to still others, new pride in race and in the achievements of black people. To Carmichael, however, it apparently meant the use of dormant forces in all parts of black community to make new federal legislation work. "The only way we're going to stop the white man from whuppin' us is to take over. We've been saying 'freedom' for six years and we ain't got nothin'. What we've got to start saying is 'black power'. . . . What we need is black power."

Disregarding some intellectual inconsistencies and bits of erratic logic as well, this new appeal launched a true, black-led movement, not a federation of groups influenced either directly or indirectly by well-meaning white liberals. Moderates such as King had only two choices: become more aggressive and move to the left or risk losing mass support and considerable prestige. His assassination, coupled with that of Malcolm X, gave this new militancy added fury, urgency, and frustration. The emergence of the Third World of African and Asian nations also influenced the growth of separatist, power-oriented activism in black America. For the first time—whether watching foreign statesmen on TV or listening to the arguments of those advocating separatism of one sort or another—American blacks in substantial numbers began to develop a sense of "black pride," one of the most positive byproducts of this highly emotional upheaval.

Although the almost aimless rioting of 1965-1967 ceased, the new ghetto mood was ominous. Typical of militants geared for action were the Black Panthers, a spinoff from SNCC. Espousing traditional goals of political action and economic self-help, the Panthers also demonstrated ready willingness to combat alleged police brutality with violence of their own. On the other hand, there is considerable evidence that the Panthers were a force for stability within some black communities. Despite much adverse publicity in the white press, a 1970 poll revealed that blacks living in six major cities felt that the NAACP and the SCLC had done the most for their race in the past; nevertheless, 62 percent of the respondents admired what the Panthers were doing and expected them to gain much more influence in the future, perhaps supplanting both the NAACP and the SCLS.

Clearly, their strict discipline, near religious fervor, political indoctrination, and community service projects were having an effect. State and national officials, especially high-ranking Nixon appointees, reacted violently to the Panthers and for obvious reasons; this was a

Doug Wilson/Black Star.

Stokely Carmichael

(1941–)

A lean, graceful man, Stokely Carmichael rose to prominence in the late 1960s as chairman of the Student Nonviolent Coordinating Committee (SNCC). For a brief time he engineered a cooperative effort with the militant Black Panthers, serving as their prime minister, and is generally credited with popularizing the cry "black power."

Carmichael was born in Port of Spain, Trinidad, in 1941 and as a small boy came to despise colonial ideals as put into practice by the British. At age eleven his family moved to Harlem, then to the Bronx where they lived in an all-white block. While his widowed mother worked as a maid, Stokely joined an auto-theft gang ("the Dukes") composed mostly of white, middle-class boys; yet, young Carmichael was able to attend the Bronx High School of Science (for gifted children) where he did well enough to win scholarship offers from several white universities. However, having had his fill of patronizing whites, he chose to attend Howard University in Washington, D.C.

In part, this decision came from an awakened black consciousness. He had participated in sit-ins at Woolworth's in New York City and during the early 1960s took part in freedom rides and other civil rights activities. After graduating from Howard in 1964, Carmichael began to work full-time for SNCC as a field secretary in Alabama. In 1965, he led SNCC's first voter drive with an all-black emphasis to create the Lowndes County (Alabama) Freedom Organization. This group, with a snarling black panther as its emblem, lost the 1966 election campaign for which it had been organized but its example soon spread to other communities throughout the South and beyond.

In May 1966, Carmichael replaced the more moderate John Lewis as chairman of SNCC and the following month gained considerable attention in a Mississippi march with his cry of black power. A year later he stepped down as chairman, but remained as a SNCC fieldworker. In 1968, SNCC and the Black Panther party briefly joined hands and Carmichael became a key figure among the Panthers. When the two groups split, he refused to give up his Panther post as prime minister and was ousted from SNCC. A feud then developed among the Panthers over whether to ally with sympathetic whites. Carmichael opposed formal association with white liberals and quit the Panthers in 1969.

A short time later, Carmichael and his wife, singer Miriam Makeba, who was born in South Africa and whom he married in 1968, went to live in Conakry, Guinea. After leaving America, this veteran of the civil rights movement became an outspoken Pan-Africanist, stressing unremitting opposition to the "white Western Empire" and studying the ideas of Kwame Nkrumah. His career—from Trinidad and the Bronx to Howard, SNCC, the Black Panthers, and Africa—can be viewed as a natural outgrowth of the rage and resentment of an able, astute, young black man. ■

U.P.I.

On occasion (as pictured here, in Sacramento) the Black Panthers took up arms. The Panthers were a particular target for FBI "counter-revolutionary" activities in the last years of J. Edgar Hoover's directorship of that agency.

group of dedicated revolutionaries with firm goals in mind who refused to take any instructions from even those whites who sympathized with them.

One example of much more moderate leadership was Jesse Jackson (1941–), a young North Carolina-born black who became associated with Martin Luther King, Jr., while still a seminary student. Jackson, a veteran of student sit-ins initiated at Greensboro, N.C. in the early 1960s, organized "Operation Breadbasket" in Chicago, an alliance designed to use threats of black economic boycotts to win concessions from white-owned businesses. This movement met with considerable success and by the end of the decade had expanded to sixteen other cities.

This struggle by blacks for a national solution to their problems aroused similar feelings and an increased self-consciousness among other underprivileged minorities such as Mexican-Americans, Indians, and Puerto Ricans, and even influenced youths of Asian-American communities. Although none faced the same widespread, institutionalized discrimination experienced by blacks, their complaints were real enough. Like blacks, they were often poor, crowded into ghettos or (in the case of Indians) reservations carved out of inhospitable and virtually useless land, and subject to unequal justice, poor educational facilities, and inadequate community services.

Some of the cries of these minorities also stirred a response among women. They, too, regardless of class, color, religion, or marital status, believed that the courts and the business world (perhaps society as a whole) viewed them as "second-class" citizens. Even their prominence in the civil rights movement was no assurance that their demands would be heeded, for all too often they found they were only "foot soldiers," not generals. The black protest had, in truth, revealed a deep flaw in American society: the nation's failure to cope with problems presented by minority status in a land governed and run largely by a male majority that was frequently both complacent and affluent.

Guns Over Butter: The High Costs of Vietnam

Along with pressure for domestic reform, Lyndon Johnson also inherited from his predecessor increasing involvement in South Vietnam. He accepted it with gusto, writing the commander of that nation's forces on January 1, 1964: "The United States will continue to furnish you and your people with the fullest measure of support in this bitter fight." While running as a "peace" candidate that year and charging Goldwater with irrational, warlike proposals, Johnson approved covert operations in Vietnam that included air reconnaissance and destroyer patrols by U.S. forces. An enemy attack upon American naval units in August led to quick congressional approval of the so-called Tonkin Gulf Resolution, a vague statement deploring this action by the North Vietnamese (in their own waters). It granted the President the power "to take all necessary measures to repel any armed attack against the forces of the United States and to prevent further aggression." Whatever those words meant, Johnson used them as the legal basis for a subsequent buildup of American forces in that part of the world.

By the end of 1964 American troop strength had increased from 16,000 to 23,300. Two months later the deaths of 8 American airmen during a raid by Vietcong (sympathizers with North Vietnamese communists who lived in South Vietnam) led to extensive bombing operations (Operation Rolling Thunder) and U.S. involvement grew enormously: 35,000 men in May of 1965, 130,000 in September, and 184,000 by the end of that year. Between July 1965 and September 1966, U.S. commanders in Southeast Asia pressed for more men and planes, and President Johnson (usually without telling the American public) readily gave them what they wanted. In June 1966, General William C. Westmoreland, promising complete victory within eighteen months, upped the total request to 542,000 men; and, by that time, U.S. bombers were making 1,500 sorties each week over enemy-held territory.

These developments, which had considerable influence upon U.S. foreign policy throughout the world, gave new prominence to the word "escalation," a term used to describe increasing American military presence in South Vietnam. This process of escalation dominated the remainder of Johnson's presidency, alienated some traditional allies, and aroused the ire of thousands of U.S. citizens who began to question the warlike policies of the administration. In mid-October an estimated 70,000 people marched and attended antiwar rallies in 60 cities, and on November 27 another 30,000 participated in a March on Washington for Peace in Vietnam.

The government's reaction was to send diplomats

Bob Fitch/Black Star.

The new militance among blacks fostered a like spirit among American Indians. Shown here are a group of Indians protesting local conditions and a series of murders in Farmington, New Mexico, in 1974.

Ralph Crane/Life Magazine © 1962 Time, Inc.

Joan Baez

(1941–   )

This young lady's dramatic rise to prominence as a folksinger and a strident voice against war and violence brought together two dominant threads of the 1960s: awakening interest in folk culture and the environment and concern over the effects of Vietnam upon U.S. life. Born in New York City to a Mexican-born physicist and his Scots-English wife, she and her two sisters moved frequently as their father's teaching and work as a UNESCO consultant took them to many parts of the world. In these travels, Joan, who inherited her father's dark skin, often felt the effects of discrimination.

In the late 1950s the family settled near Harvard University and Joan soon was singing at local coffee houses. Appearances at the Newport Jazz Festival (1959, 1960) and recordings of songs such as "Wildwood Flower," "Barbara Allen," and "All My Trials" soon brought national, even international, fame. Although she took lessons to master the guitar, her spectacular, three-octave-range voice is completely natural, untouched by professional training.

In the early 1960s Baez returned to California to live (she attended high school in Palo Alto) and quickly became involved in the emerging antiwar protest movement. Her refusal to pay federal taxes to support military expenditures and outspoken stance against the draft drew criticism from some quarters, praise from others. Meanwhile, she helped establish the Institute for the Study of Nonviolence. Her parents, by the way, are Quakers and her mother also joined Joan in civil disobedience protest.

These activities led to several arrests in 1967, some time behind bars, and romantic involvement with David Victor Harris, former president of the Stanford University student body. Their brief marriage (1968–1973) produced a son, Gabriel Earl. Harris was indicted for draft evasion in 1969 and subsequently spent twenty months in jail.

Baez, whose political interests have come to dominate her singing career, is author of two slim volumes: *Daybreak* (1968), an autobiography of sorts dedicated to all men locked up "for resisting the draft," and *Coming Out* (1971), coauthored with Harris and a salute to his release from prison. ■

---

scurrying to foreign capitals to "explain" the official position and to try to establish ties with the North Vietnamese so as to begin talks leading to a negotiated peace. Yet, as noted, 1966 witnessed a huge expansion of U.S. forces in South Vietnam, which Congress backed up with near universal enthusiasm and very little dissent. Johnson, who scoffed at critics such as Senator J. William Fulbright, even flew to wartorn Southeast Asia in February 1966 to demonstrate the strength of his commitment.

All of these steps that the President and his advisors were taking were based upon two colossal blunders: failure to appreciate the will and capability of the enemy and an overestimation of the effects of U.S. air strikes. Meanwhile, as frustration and stalemate increased, cracks in American resolve at home increased. Even before 1966 several liberal congressmen, many of them Democrats, came out against this tragic, undeclared war halfway around the world. Influential newspapers such as the *New York Post, Louisville Courier-Journal, San Francisco Chronicle,* and *New York Times* joined this mounting wave of protest. Dismayed by the lack of progress, even a few members of the administration began to express doubts, notably Under Secretary of State George Ball and (to some extent) Secretary of Defense Robert McNamara. Other officials, who may have begun to have private misgivings, remained publicly steadfast. Vice President Hubert Humphrey in April 1966 tried to stem the tide with the pragmatic observation: "Many people feel today...we should not be there in Vietnam. Well, whether we should be or not, we are....So I am not going to argue about whether we should have been there. That is ancient history." The problem was, of course, that the Vietnam crisis was not "ancient history;" it was "current events."

As criticism grew, President Johnson responded in two ways. He attacked the "nervous nellies" who wanted to cut and run as nothing but fair-weather patriots, and he increased his own and his nation's commitment. In October 1966, McNamara had had enough and privately recommended against granting Westmoreland's request for still more manpower. Then, nine months later, the general's plea for 200,000 men (which would have increased U.S. forces to 671,616) precipitated a stormy debate within the Johnson administration. McNamara argued for a much smaller increase and an end to the air war as a lever for peace talks. He eventually prevailed but soon left the Pentagon in late 1967 (perhaps under presidential pressure) to become head of the World Bank. His successor was Clark Clifford, a well-known Washington lawyer, former Truman advisor, and a man thought to be "hawkish" on Vietnam; however, faced with facts, Clifford quickly became a leading force for disengagement.

During sixty hectic days (January 31 to March 31, 1968), for Americans at home at least, this tragic story reached its climax. On the Vietnamese Tet holiday, the enemy launched a devastating and very successful offensive that ravaged most of the major cities in the south and even laid siege to the U.S. embassy in Saigon. Westmoreland immediately asked for 206,756 more men but got only 30,000. Even this increase, once it became public knowledge, set off a furious debate. On March 12, Senator Eugene J. McCarthy, stern opponent of U.S. involvement in Vietnam, won a "moral" victory in the New Hampshire presidential primary, capturing 42 percent of the Democratic vote, compared to Johnson's 49 percent. Four days later Robert Kennedy jumped into the Democratic race for the White House. The following week the President recalled Westmoreland and subsequently conferred with a group of key aides who strongly recommended deescalation in Vietnam. On March 31, Johnson went on national television to announce a bombing halt, his intentions to negotiate with the North Vietnamese, and his withdrawal from the presidential race. Much like Harry Truman in 1952, Johnson discovered that a foreign campaign was not the route to reelection at home.

By this time, the true costs of Vietnam—long hidden or obscured by government duplicity—were becoming apparent to everyone. During 1968, 14,589 Americans were killed in the war and 46,797 wounded. Johnson's public approval rating had been below 50 percent for over two years and his Great Society lay in shambles, destroyed by rising defense costs. The President insisted the nation could afford both guns and butter, but critics of the war on poverty soon began to cut appropriations for that program, making it the first homefront casualty. These reductions only increased bitterness and resentment among those whose hopes had been stirred by Johnson's rhetoric, a group also inclined to oppose the Vietnam adventure since their sons (unable to get college deferments) were meeting the enemy face to face. Meanwhile, the President rejected all efforts to raise taxes to pay war costs. As a result the national debt soared from $239.8 billion to $301.1 billion during the 1960s, and prices lunged upward, buoyed by inflation. In dollars alone, the Vietnam War (1965–1975) cost about $140 billion, rising from only $103 million in 1965 to a peak of over $28 billion in 1969.

This overseas entanglement, the first war ever watched live on TV sets in homefront living rooms,

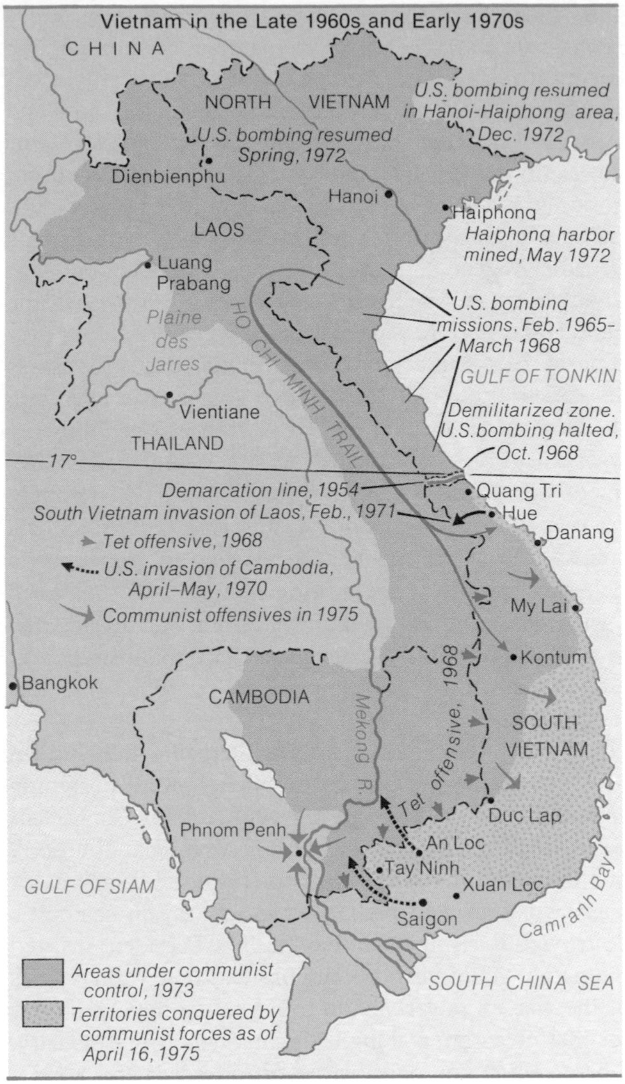

spawned a rash of violence, much of it rooted in frustration created by government secrecy. In the wake of the urban riots of 1964–1967 and the assassinations of King and presidential aspirant Robert F. Kennedy in 1968, Johnson appointed two prestigious investigating bodies to study the causes of such widespread violence. The National Advisory Commission on Civil Disorders, headed up by Illinois Governor Otto Kerner, said in March 1968 that "white racism" was the underlying cause of the urban riots. It noted that between 1963 and 1968, 2 million Americans engaged in demonstrations, riots, and terrorism that resulted in some 9,000 casualties. Discrimination, segregation, and an absence of white concern for how blacks lived and worked had created a truly explosive situation. "Our nation," the eleven-member group concluded, "is moving toward two societies, one black, one white—separate and unequal." It recommended action on various fronts such as education, housing, law enforcement, and welfare that would produce quick and highly visible results. The involvement of the poor and disadvantaged in all such programs, the commission stressed, was an absolute necessity.

The second group, the National Commission on the Causes and Prevention of Violence, held extensive hearings in 1968 that explored the history and the nature of violence in American life. Vietnam, "domestic turmoil," and brutality on television all were cited as contributing factors. The incidence of political assassination—John and Robert Kennedy, Malcolm X, and Martin Luther King—was found especially disturbing. And apparently many Americans agreed, frightened by the chaos that seemed to be threatening their way of life. Seen at one 1967 demonstration was the twisted slogan, "Where is Oswald now that we need him?" As Senator William Fulbright observed at the height of the war protest phenomenon, "The 'Great Society' has become the sick society."

Revolt of the Young

Almost inevitably, because of a huge baby boom and numerous child-centered attitudes and habits of the post-1945 years, youth tended to dominate many aspects of U.S. life in the 1960s. Although that decade's "revolt of the young" enjoyed the active support of only a distinct minority, it helped to focus the attention of all age groups upon the Vietnam war issue and thus had a profound impact upon both society and politics as a whole. This revolt had its roots in both the unrelated "beat generation" of the 1950s and in socialist and pacifist activities after World War II. Actually, two revolts were going on in the 1960s—one cultural, the other activist/political—and only briefly at the height of the antiwar protest did they meld into a single, semiunified outpouring of discontent. By the close of that decade, militant youth radicalism had spent its force and the so-called counterculture was in decline. Nevertheless, before this movement faded from view, it had significant impact on several aspects of life: marijuana use, pornography, sexual permissiveness, and dress codes. Again, although only a minority of young people joined this upsurge, millions of them (and their elders, too) felt its effects. Hardly a community in the nation was free from discussion and debate concerning drugs, long hair, and various aspects of sexual expression.

This political-activist youth rebellion began with the Students for a Democratic Society (SDS), which reflected a philosophical commitment to socialism. In 1962 the group issued the Port Huron Statement, a direct call for a "New Left." Its members participated in various civil rights protests such as sit-ins and worked in slum areas in an attempt to stir activism among others. In general, these young radicals, most of them from liberal, upper middle-class households, first concentrated their fire upon local issues easily found at huge, impersonal universities. A key factor, noted by Tom Hayden (1940-   ), onetime national president of SDS, was that his was the first generation to grow up in homes where parents encouraged their offspring to ask questions, make judgments, and think independently. The Port Huron Statement, which he helped draft, contained these words: "We are people of this generation, bred in at least modest comfort, housed in universities, looking uncomfortably at the world we inherit." Hayden, a social activist who was born in Michigan and attended a Catholic school in Father Coughlin's parish, was one of the New Left's most ubiquitous figures, seeming to be almost everywhere in the turbulent 1960s.

By 1968, however, the SDS was breaking up, in part because of competition from similar organizations, but also because women members discovered they had little to say concerning policy and leadership. Instead, they were relegated to tasks such as stuffing envelopes by day and performing as bed partners at night.

Yet in the spring of that year, twenty-year-old Mark Rudd led a loose confederation composed of SDS and similar New Left groups that shut down Columbia University for several weeks. Without the help of President Grayson Kirk and city police, however, they probably would not have had much success. Without consulting neighborhood groups, Kirk began to exercise the right to erect a new university gymnasium on nearby parkland. When student demonstrators appeared, Manhattan police overreacted, creating sympathy for the protest. In the end, the university capitulated to several student demands and halted work on the gym. Kirk subsequently quit as president and several dozen prominent protesters (including Rudd) were suspended. This was, however, not the final flurry of unrest at New York City's oldest institution of higher learning.

For a time, the University of California's "Free Speech" movement set the pace for other radicals. This protest movement, ignited late in 1964 when authorities at Berkeley tried to ban political discussion on campus, was led by Mario Savio. Savio, a twenty-two-year-old philosophy major who had spent the previous summer as a civil rights worker in Mississippi, aroused passions and issues that soon spread to other universities and colleges and ultimately challenged Lyndon Johnson's escalating war in Vietnam. By 1967, this antiwar movement, now a powerful voice against government policy, was able to mount huge rallies against the draft and the Pentagon. College students and others burned their Selective Service cards and sometimes fled to Canada or overseas to avoid fighting in an undeclared war they considered unjust and immoral. Efforts at unity among protest organizations usually ended in chaos, stymied by disagreement over whether to work within the current political "system" or make efforts to change it; one factor in the demise of the SDS was the withdrawal of blacks who became disenchanted with that group's policies and programs. Many young radicals backed Robert Kennedy and Eugene McCarthy in 1968, but the turmoil evident at the Chicago Democratic convention ended any cohesion achieved up to that time and also strengthened the Republican "law and order" bid for voter support.

The heat of the 1968 election campaign and frustration engendered by Nixon's close victory in the election created a wave of campus unrest, often aimed at departments of huge universities engaged in research for the Pentagon. Equally inspiring to many college protesters, however, were issues like the rights of black students and the insensitivity of administrators, even university housing, food, and curriculum policies. During the first half of 1968, over 100 campuses were the scene of protests; during the same months in 1969 over 230 outbursts occurred at various colleges and universities. This unrest reached unprecedented heights in the spring of 1970 when President Nixon expanded the Vietnam conflict by sending U.S. forces into nearby Cambodia. On May 4 an antiwar protest at Ohio's Kent State University ended in

Stephen Shames/Photon West/Black Star.

At the University of California, Berkeley, in 1969, students protesting the war meet a violent reaction from the forces of law and order.

tragedy as National Guardsmen fired into a band of demonstrators, killing four young people. This development swelled the numbers of a previously planned march held in Washington five days later to 100,000. Although the demonstration turned out to be peaceful, at that time 448 colleges and universities were on strike or closed down by antiwar furor. Yet, most of the nation's 2,200 institutions remained untouched by parades and meetings. For their students, riots, placards, smoke bombs, angry words, and confrontation were things that happened "somewhere else."

The youth protest of the 1960s actually flowed in two separate streams. Unlike politically motivated radicals, the cultural radicals were essentially alienated from society as they knew it and devoted to inner experiences. Spurning many aspects of contemporary American life, they tended to emphasize mysticism, communal living, sexual liberation, and drugs. Except for a brief merger typified by the "Yippie" movement, the two groups—one rejecting society, the other determined to change it—never really cooperated. By the end of the decade both had felt the wrath of the adult community and were rapidly losing influence. Yet out of their general rebellion came a new, more militant feminist revolt and increasing sympathy (or at least a measure of understanding) for those unwilling to conform to widely accepted sexual mores and customs.

Throughout this time of turmoil most Americans remained quiescent. Even the young often exhibited contempt for this sometimes disturbing social upheaval. In 1969, 50 percent of noncollege youth considered themselves "moderate" in their views and 21 percent "conservative"; only 10 percent of the nation's college students classified themselves as "radical dissidents" and 3 percent as "revolutionaries." With the winding down of the Vietnam fiasco, this general protest lost much of its reason for existence; then, at last the majority could assert its power and make its voice heard above the tumult.

The Search for Stability: The Seventies

The election of Richard M. Nixon in 1968, only four years after Lyndon Johnson had successfully fashioned his great liberal consensus, indeed seems ironic. What it represented, more than anything else, was a social reaction, not political change. In fact, influenced by John Kennedy's assassination and similar unsettling events of the early 1960s, the mood of America (at Lyndon Johnson's urging) had moved to the left. When Johnson's policies fell into disrepute and his party seemed unable to handle current problems—war, youth revolt, urban riots—it swayed back toward the right.

The Comeback of Middle America

The presidential campaign of 1968 was filled with unexpected twists and turns, perhaps a reflection of the uncertain mood of the nation. The withdrawal of Lyndon Johnson after his poor showing in the New Hampshire primary made the Democratic race a three-way affair among Senator Eugene McCarthy, Robert Kennedy, and Vice President Hubert Humphrey. Running well as an independent candidate calculated to harm the Democrats was Alabama's Governor George Wallace. The death of Kennedy made possible the nomination of Humphrey, earlier a very popular liberal, despite considerable hostility directed at the Johnson administration by many members of his own party. Humphrey, who selected Maine's Senator Edmund Muskie as his running mate, won the right to carry the Democratic banner at a convention held in Chicago under siegelike conditions. War protesters, youth groups, and disgruntled McCarthy followers battled police, federal agents, and eventually National Guardsmen; even the convention floor itself was a scene of rancor and tumult. The result was a broken, divided national organization, largely because of Johnson's Vietnam policy, which candidate Humphrey and the Democrats had been forced to endorse in their campaign platform.

Burt Glinn/Magnum.

American participation in Vietnam was not without support, especially in "Middle America." Above, a group of disgruntled "hard hats" wave flags and placards in support of the war.

Richard Nixon, the defeated Republican candidate of 1960, easily swept most of the preconvention primaries of 1968 after two moderate contenders, both of them governors—George Romney of Michigan and Nelson Rockefeller of New York—decided not to oppose the former Vice President. Nixon was nominated at Miami Beach early in August at a carefully staged affair that contrasted sharply with the chaos at Chicago (although riots were occurring in black ghettos only a few miles away). He selected as his running mate the 49-year-old governor of Maryland, Spiro T. Agnew, a border state politician who gained power as a moderate on race issues and then took a sharp turn to the right.

The third candidate, George Wallace, headed up the new American Independent party. Proclaiming he stood for the "little man" who was tired of the failure of Republicans and Democrats to maintain law and order throughout the land, he drew large crowds and talked of winning a balance of power in the Electoral College. Although the race issue had been Wallace's steppingstone to national prominence and played some implied role in nearly all of his speeches, he denied that he was a racist, saying: "What we now propose is in the interest of every citizen regardless of race or color."

The chaos of Chicago and Johnson's Vietnam policy proved to be heavy burdens, and the Democratic ticket faced a stiff, uphill fight. However, both Humphrey and Muskie were skillfull campaigners; and, once the Vice President separated himself somewhat from Johnson and Vietnam in late September, he began to pick up support. In the end he lost by a whisker: 31.7 to 31.2 million ballots. (Wallace got nearly 10 million.) Nixon received only 43.4 percent of the total votes cast, the lowest percentage for a winning presidential candidate since the three-way race of 1912.

The most striking shift was in the once strongly Democratic South. Humphrey carried only Texas, Wallace capturing five states in that region and Nixon, seven.

Henry Wilhelm/Black Star.

The 1968 Democratic convention brought to Chicago thousands of demonstrators with more or less interest in the party nominee, but united in their fervent opposition to war. Their tempers frayed, Mayor Richard Daley's police force overreacted to the protesters and the result was, in the words of a later investigating commission, a "police riot." Here, demonstrators gather outside the convention hall, as the police warily look on.

Outside of this traditional thirteen-state area, however, the Democratic urban-labor ties held fast. The Republicans gained only five seats in both the House and Senate, leaving the Democrats with comfortable margins: 58–42 in the upper chamber, 243–192 in the lower. Despite an outpouring of conservative-sponsored surveys, 1968 did not endanger the old New Deal coalition. Sometime in the mid-1960s, crime, race, civil rights, and lawlessness, issues that were only tangentially related to the Vietnam war, became the most pressing concerns in America. Yet much of mainstream America still favored an expanded and updated New Deal (Great Society) package—Medicare, aid to education, tax reform, consumer protection. The millions who had supported Johnson's Great Society in 1964 but shifted to Nixon four years later were not actually changing their party allegiance. The 1968 vote was a momentary protest stirred up by immediate social concerns. In addition, voters did not like the way new federal programs were being carried out or resented what they saw as an overemphasis upon minority rights.

Fred Ward/Black Star.

Third-party candidate George C. Wallace and his vice presidential candidate, General Curtis LeMay evoked emotional reactions from both supporters and opponents in 1968.

Tony Korody/Sygma.

Spiro T. Agnew

(1918–)

A tall, impressive figure of a man (6 feet 2 inches, 194 pounds, a natty dresser), Spiro T. Agnew was the epitome of the successful, Middle-American suburbanite when Richard Nixon tapped him as his running mate in 1968. Born in Baltimore, Maryland, in 1918, the son of a Greek immigrant, Agnew was attending law school night classes on the eve of World War II while working for insurance companies and managing a supermarket. He then served as commander of an armored division in France and Germany (winning a Bronze Star), returned to Baltimore, received his law degree, and set up practice in suburban Towson.

Originally a Democrat, "Ted" Agnew soon began to move in Republican circles, joining the Kiwanis and VFW, and serving as president of the Towson PTA. In 1957 he was named to the local zoning board of appeals. Four years later, when Democrats blocked his reappointment, Agnew shrewdly used the publicity to become the first Republican county executive (suburban mayor) of Baltimore County since 1895. In 1966 he ran for governor against an overtly racist campaigner, Democrat George Mahoney, and won handily with the support of blacks and liberals, as well as conservative Republicans.

For a year or so Agnew proposed and encouraged moderate to liberal programs; then, riding a popular tide, he turned to the law-and-order issue and fiscal conservatism, especially where welfare appropriations were involved. In the wake of rioting stirred by the death of Martin Luther King, Jr. in April 1968, he confronted moderate black leaders in Baltimore and personally chastised them for not "keeping the lid on things." Having established himself as a liberal conservative and coming from a border state, Agnew was an acceptable (if virtually unknown) vice presidential nominee in 1968.

After the election, at Nixon's direction, Agnew became an outspoken pressbaiter and guardian of public morality against anti-war protesters whom he called "an effete corps of impudent snobs" and "radical liberals." Reelected with Nixon in 1972, Agnew escaped Watergate only to be caught up in an investigation of Maryland corruption which revealed he had received payoffs from engineering firms in return for government contracts in Baltimore County. And, even more to his discredit, he continued to accept money after becoming Vice President. Agnew pleaded nolo contendere (no contest) to income tax evasion charges, was fined heavily, and put on three-year probation. He resigned as Vice President on October 10, 1973, and six months later was disbarred from the practice of law.

During the 1968 campaign, Spiro T. Agnew said, "The disease of our times is an artificial and masochistic sophistication—the vague uneasiness that our values are false, that there is something wrong with being patriotic, honest, moral, and hardworking." Five years later as he stood in a Baltimore courtroom awaiting sentence, these words, if he remembered them, must have had a hollow ring. ■

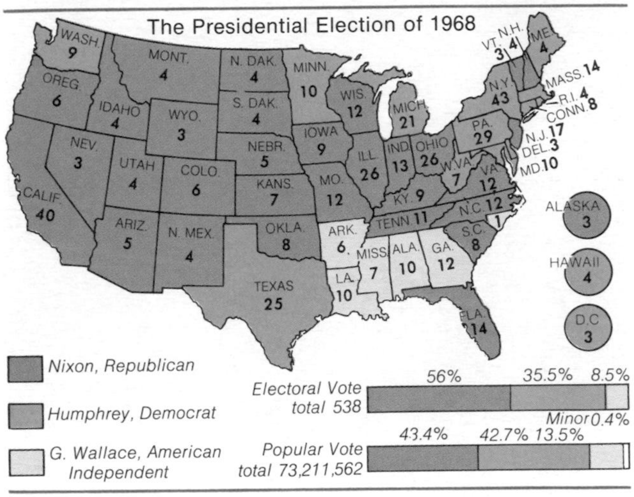

Who, they asked, will speak up for the average white worker, the "forgotten American" getting by on $5,000 to $15,000 a year? The answer was, at least in November 1968, Nixon and Agnew.

The task facing the Republicans after the election was how to meld these troubled Americans with their normal base of party support—merchants, businessmen, and lawyers, most of them quite well-to-do. For many reasons this would be a difficult undertaking, for the two groups were longtime rivals, frequently employee and employer. Elimination of irritants that put less affluent citizens in the Republican column might well send them scurrying back to the Democratic fold; yet, if their complaints were not heard, the same result could be anticipated.

The victorious Republicans portrayed the 1968 decision as a political revolution, the maturing of "Middle America." But this analysis was too facile. One problem is the fact that "Middle America" and "middle class" are vague, misleading concepts. The latter was far from homogeneous and in terms of actual income was not growing; rather the gap between its upper and lower reaches was widening. The truth is, no political party has stumbled upon a formula for bringing all Americans to a level of moderate subsistence, and members of the nearly mythical "middle class" are often, in some very important respects, not much better off than the poor. Thus, while "Middle America" and "middle class" are attractive campaign terms, they have little meaning. Those thought to qualify for membership may have primary goals and interests counter to those of others whom politicians and sociologists would like to group with them in a single mass.

"Bringing Us Together": Conservatism as Reform

In the 1968 campaign, Richard Nixon spotted a thirteen-year-old girl in an Ohio audience holding up a sign saying "Bring Us Together Again," which he then made his campaign theme. But in addition to his pragmatic (and political) wish to unify, Nixon was motivated by deep antagonism toward the disruptiveness of the 1960s. An early memo from Daniel Moynihan (resident "liberal" on the early White House staff and specialist in urban affairs) summarized the job the President faced: "Your task . . . is clear: To restore the authority of American institutions." Despite his own conservatism, Nixon pursued flexible, middle-of-the-road policies throughout 1969 and part of 1970. This moderation drew fire from both right and left, and Nixon's continuation of the Vietnam war and his efforts to aid an emerging Republican party in the South (his so-called southern strategy) began to alienate many liberal Democrats in Congress. By the time of the 1970 elections and certainly from 1971 on, the President dropped his middle-road approach and embraced instead increasingly conservative domestic programs. The Nixon administration enjoyed the brief

J. P. Laffont/Sygma.

The victors: the Republican ticket in 1968, Richard M. Nixon and his chosen running mate, Governor Spiro T. Agnew of Maryland.

"honeymoon" granted any new regime, but it did not, as promised, "bring us together again"; in fact, during Nixon's second term, those divisions actually were increased by the turmoil of Watergate.

Nixon's first major proposal in 1969 was a Family Assistance Program (FAP) with a minimum annual guaranteed income beginning at $1,600 for a family of four and increasing to a maximum of $3,920 in combined assistance and earnings. Although it was in some ways revolutionary, Nixon boasted that this plan, which included a "workfare" requirement, would do away with some of the welfare bureaucracy. Workfare, in effect, would make able-bodied family heads ineligible for welfare and require them to accept federally guaranteed jobs. Liberal suspicions, conservative opposition, and lack of strong White House backing, however, combined to doom FAP to defeat, as it was twice shelved by Senate committees. Nevertheless, a hard-line workfare requirement—the Talmadge amendment—was added to an appropriation for Aid to Families with Dependent Children late in 1971.

In general, Nixon's moderate approach in 1969–1970 amounted to a kind of drift. Although it was the proclaimed policy, conservatives always had substantial influence in Nixon circles. HEW Secretary Robert Finch's efforts to speed up school desegregation and treat student protest with tolerance got nowhere. By Spring 1970 he was replaced by the more cooperative Elliot Richardson, a gentleman of aristocratic mien from Massachusetts who had held a variety of government jobs. Nor did HUD Secretary George Romney get assistance when he urged construction of desegregated housing in white suburbs and, in the process, lost whatever credibility he had enjoyed within the Cabinet. Nixon's efforts to cool the rampant inflation of 1969 had the appearance more of indecision than moderation and achieved only slight results. For a time he tried to avoid price controls, but when evidence mounted that inflation would be a key issue in the 1972 elections, he acted. In December 1970 he named a flamboyant Texas Democrat, John Connally, as his Secretary of the Treasury and in succeeding months turned to price controls as a means of curbing inflation.

This program, developed in a series of phases during 1971–1972, set limits to increases in wages and prices charged for goods. By the end of 1972 the annual inflation rate had been cut to 3.5 percent, an important factor in Nixon's successful bid for reelection. However, once the campaign ended, so did Nixon's interest in controls and inflation roared ahead full steam once more.

One reason for the administration's shift from middle-of-the-road policies was clear evidence in the 1970 returns that the cry of law and order alone could not build a new majority; other appeals had to be found. Despite an unprecedented off-year campaign effort, the Republicans had little to cheer about. They picked up 2 Senate seats and lost 11 in the House. Even more striking was what happened at the state level where the Democrats gained substantial strength, ousting eleven Republican governors and reversing the margin of state house control from 32–18 in favor of the Republicans to 29–21 in favor of the Democrats.

In his 1971 State of the Union message, Nixon launched a dramatic but basically conservative campaign that he boldly labeled the "New American Revolution." It included functional reorganization of the Cabinet, revival of the FAP idea, national health insurance, several environmental initiatives, measures designed to achieve full employment, and revenue sharing between federal, state, and local governments. Only revenue sharing—in some ways a direct repudiation of Lyndon Johnson's Great Society—won congressional approval. This measure, the State and Local Fiscal Assistance Act of 1972, proposed to return federal revenues totaling $30.2 billion to localities over a five-year period. Critics called it a cruel hoax, fearing future cutbacks in federal spending would cause local authorities to drop long-range social welfare programs or render them meaningless. Senator Edmund Muskie of Maine, Humphrey's very effective running mate in 1968, declared, "If federal authorities no longer honor our national social responsibilities, no one will." Muskie was right; the cutbacks soon followed. New revenues at lower levels were more than offset by declining federal spending in other areas, especially social welfare.

Nixon's innate conservatism, despite his campaign promises, showed up in other ways during his first term. In 1971 and 1972 he used his veto power more and more frequently to curb spending for public works, regional development, child care, and antiwater pollution measures. During these same years he carried on a running battle with the Office of Economic Opportunity (OEO), vetoing appropriations and curtailing various programs. As a result, funds earmarked for OEO projects dropped from $1.9 billion in 1970 to $790 million in 1973. Nixon also faced considerable difficulty with Supreme Court nominations when the Senate refused to confirm two southern judges named to the high court. Rejection of Clement F. Haynsworth, Jr. and G. Harrold Carswell, largely because labor and civil rights leaders feared their conservative views (and in Carswell's case because of a mediocre record on the bench), marked the first time since 1894 that the Senate had turned down two Supreme Court nominees in quick order. The White House said these were partisan attempts to embarrass Nixon; but, in fact, only 23 of 43 Republican senators voted for or announced support for both men. Long before the ordeal of Watergate, Richard Nixon and the Congress were deadlocked.

Still, the seeming confrontation between the White House and Capitol Hill should not overshadow some important political innovations of Nixon's first term. Efforts to protect consumers as well as resources and the environment came into their own during the period. An act passed in 1970 set up an agency designed to guard the rights of consumers, and a year later, by executive order, Nixon established the Environmental Protection Agency. In effect, the federal government was now involved in totally new areas of concern; significantly, these were matters that obviously could enjoy support among conservatives as well as liberals.

By 1972, Nixon, a former Redbaiting senator, Vice President, and defeated gubernatorial and White House candidate who had made an astounding political comeback, was rapidly putting his imprint upon a whole era much as Lyndon Johnson had done. And his overwhelming victory at the polls in November of that year greatly enhanced his prestige.

Nixon won reelection with a minimum of campaigning, relying instead upon the work of Vice President Agnew and various prominent Republicans. The campaign was highly efficient, very well organized, and extremely expensive. By contrast, the Democratic ticket floundered and seemed incapable of developing clear-cut issues. South Dakota's Senator George McGovern (1922–) won the nomination over objections of middle-of-the-road Democrats and after bruising primary confrontations with Humphrey. McGovern first selected a fellow senator, Thomas F. Eagleton of Missouri, as his running mate, but disclosure of Eagleton's psychiatric history forced McGovern to replace him with Sargent Shriver, first director of the Peace Corps and later head of OEO. McGovern's initial proposal for tax and welfare reform created dissension in traditional Democratic strongholds, and White House predictions of a negotiated peace in Vietnam blunted his attacks on the war. A crucial factor in this election was the absence from the ballot of Alabama's George Wallace, crippled by an assassin's bullet while campaigning in the Maryland primary in May 1972. As a result, the South and much of the conservative support Wallace might have attracted went to Nixon. He also carried the rest of the nation except for Massachusetts and the District of Columbia. With his popular vote of 60.0 percent, Nixon entered an exclusive club: only three other Presidents had rolled up such impressive popular votes—Harding in 1920 (60.3 percent), Roosevelt in 1936 (60.7 percent), and Johnson in 1964 (61.0 percent).

A key ingredient in the lopsided result was the defection of normally Democratic voters, among them, Jews, Catholics, and blue-collar workers. Nixon even did well among young people and the unemployed groups McGovern thought were in his camp. Yet this landslide did little for Republicans in Congress. The Democrats picked up two seats in the Senate to gain a 57–43 margin there and lost only thirteen seats in the lower chamber where they still had a comfortable edge, 243–192.

Nevertheless, after such an impressive personal victory, an Age of Nixon might have developed, but that possibility began to evaporate rapidly. Using the same secretive methods as his predecessor, he failed to engage the public in his proposals, and thus no responsible consensus on crucial matters emerged. Voters seemed to respect Richard Nixon, but there was little warmth or humor in this relationship. A cool, pragmatic operator, he did not exhibit the same gregariousness as the two Kennedys or Lyndon Johnson. Watergate, of course, cost Nixon whatever chance he may have had to shape his age, although it is possible that inflation, reaction to his increasingly conservative policies, and a growing deadlock with Congress would have produced similar results: that is, a drifting, lame-duck presidency out of touch with current realities and unable to put its stamp upon an era in any meaningful manner.

Disengagement and Detente

Despite Nixon's reputation as a rigid Cold Warrior, he did effect sweeping changes in foreign policy. Disengagement from Vietnam and detente with Communist China and the Soviet Union were major accomplishments, however gradual the first and fragile the latter. In these innovative steps, Nixon had certain advantages. No one could accuse him of being "soft" on Communism and, as a Republican president, he could count on the support of numerous congressmen and millions of Americans who would have scorned similar foreign policy initiatives by a Democratic administration. Two other factors in this equation are worth noting. Stymied by deadlock with Congress, Nixon could accomplish little on the domestic front, and it is possible that his primary interests always lay in the foreign realm anyway. His bold moves did little to solve deep-seated Cold War issues, and the possibility of future U.S. intervention by force certainly did remain, but Richard Nixon gained for the nation considerable flexibility and independence in its conduct of foreign relations. On the other hand, so much was done in secret away from the public view that the American people still remained isolated from foreign affairs, unaware of what actually was going on and convinced they could do little to influence policies.

In 1968, Nixon was able to benefit from the Vietnam issue without revealing precisely how he would end the war. Hubert Humphrey, on the other hand, was saddled with Johnson's policies. After the election, Nixon's promised "plan" for peace turned out to be only a vague hope that the Russians might induce the North Vietnamese to negotiate as America began to limit its involvement. From early 1969 on, Nixon combined two approaches. He gradually reduced U.S. forces in Vietnam in an attempt to placate antiwar protesters at home, a plan that worked reasonably well until the spring of 1970 when he launched an invasion of Cambodia. At the same time, to demonstrate U.S. resolve, he used sporadic force in Southeast Asia in order to gain concessions there. Meanwhile, formal negotiations designed to end the fighting began in earnest in Paris during the spring of 1969.

Even while gradually pulling out U.S. troops, Nixon made the Vietnamese fiasco "his" war with the Cambodian offensive; and a year later the fighting had spread to Laos. Both of these steps Lyndon Johnson had declined to take. The announced purpose was to cut off supply routes and to deny sanctuary to enemy forces. At the same time, U.S. troop levels declined from 541,000 early in 1969 to 415,000 at the end of 1970; a year later they stood at 239,000, and by the close of 1972 at only 48,000.

This tug and pull of renewed force, intensified negotiations, and periods of relaxation was Nixon's mode of operation throughout his first term. The Paris peace talks, it turned out later, were mostly window dressing; the real work was done in secret by Le Duc Tho, the

North Vietnamese negotiator at Paris, and Henry Kissinger (1923-   ), Nixon's National Security Adviser. Left out of the deliberations were such men as Secretary of State William Rogers and Secretary of Defense Melvin Laird, who objected to the Cambodian adventure and did not share the Nixon-Kissinger enthusiasm for a balance-of-power approach to world affairs.

By June 1971, as a result of the secret Kissinger-Tho discussions, some sort of breakthrough seemed imminent. Hanoi presented a nine-point plan, while the United States wanted to discuss only military matters, leaving political problems to be dealt with by the Vietnamese themselves. When nothing happened, Nixon (through Kissinger) moved to reduce the threat of Chinese and Soviet pressure on the U.S. by negotiating detente with both nations. These steps, in effect, would tend to isolate North Vietnam, limiting whatever support the Chinese and Russians were willing to grant. On July 15, 1971, the President announced plans to visit Peking early in 1972. That much-publicized visit produced public agreement in principle between the Washington and Peking governments and ended two decades of hostile relations marked by confrontation and bitterness in Korea and Southeast Asia. Although the Chinese did not choose to exert direct pressure on the North Vietnamese, Nixon had widened his options considerably. As he surmised, neither China nor Russia was willing to risk actual involvement or endanger improving relations with America, despite stepped-up military activity in Vietnam. In effect, since Moscow and Peking did not trust each other and Chinese power was growing, the theory of a bipolar world no longer had much validity. Proof that neither Communist nation would interfere in Vietnam came when, despite extensive bombing of the Hanoi–Haiphong area and the mining of North Vietnamese harbors, the Chinese made no overt moves and the Russians proceeded to sign the first SALT agreement when Nixon visited Moscow in May 1972. That pact was an initial and vital step toward the limitation and restricted use of both offensive and defensive weaponry.

Nixon promised that Vietnam would not be an issue in the 1972 campaign, but on October 26, Kissinger suddenly emerged from four days of secret talks with the North Vietnamese and announced that "peace is at hand." Nixon's unsuccessful Democratic opponent, Senator George McGovern, denounced this as nothing more than an election-eve trick, which it may well have been. In December 1972, Nixon once more unleashed U.S. air power over Hanoi–Haiphong for twelve days of round-the-clock bombing raids. Finally, late in January

Sygma/Paris.

Richard Nixon and Mao Tse-Tung shaking hands during the President's visit in February, 1972. Reversing his staunchly anti-Communist position of more than twenty years' standing, President Nixon took the initiative in establishing contact with Mao's government.

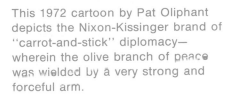

". . . AND ONE FOR MY FRIEND, HERE!"

This 1972 cartoon by Pat Oliphant depicts the Nixon-Kissinger brand of "carrot-and-stick" diplomacy—wherein the olive branch of peace was wielded by a very strong and forceful arm.

1973, Vietnamese and American representatives signed an armistice in Paris. By that time, the United States counted over 46,000 dead and 153,000 wounded. South Vietnamese combat casualties alone totaled some 200,000 dead and about 600,000 wounded. Enemy battlefield losses were estimated at close to one million.

Nixon's hot-cold display of bombs and the olive branch, despite what such maneuvers cost in terms of American domestic turmoil, in truth helped to convince the North Vietnamese to agree to a compromise. That agreement, although it did not immediately doom South Vietnam, opened the way for the North eventually to take over through elections or force, whichever method it preferred. Within a few weeks after the ceasefire, Henry Kissinger remarked during a television interview that if one side in Vietnam proved to be superior to the other "that is not an American concern." After years of the domino theory, much blood and death, millions of angry words, and the virtual destruction of three small Asian nations, the United States simply washed its hands of Southeast Asia. Whether involvement was necessary or had any constructive results, it is impossible to say. Perhaps lessons were learned, perhaps they were not.

The end of this American adventure did not mean the end of the war in Vietnam. Finally, late in April 1975, Communist troops overran Saigon, and in the final hours the American flag was hauled down at the U.S. embassy as 900 Americans and thousands of their Vietnamese allies were evacuated to safety aboard U.S. naval vessels, many of them flown out by helicopter in what seems to have been an unnecessarily dramatic last-minute showdown. This struggle, which ended in defeat, had cost the United States 46,370 dead, an estimated $140 billion in arms and supplies, and untold social and human chaos at home. Before the eventual outcome was known—though everyone knew what it would be—Nixon had Vietnamized that conflict on his own terms—that is, he had extricated U.S. troops and handed the fighting over to the Vietnamese themselves. In effect, things were about where they had been twenty years earlier.

Retreat from Southeast Asia was only the most dramatic part of Nixon's general policy of disengaging the U.S. from its role as the policeman of the free world. Following the balance-of-power approach, the President succeeded in reducing the rigidity of the American-Japanese versus Chinese-Russian alignment in Asia and also worked to defuse the Middle East crisis. His partner in these moves was Henry Kissinger who became Secretary of State in 1973. Born in Germany and a resident of the United States since 1938, and a highly respected Harvard University professor, Kissinger had been a foreign policy consultant to the Kennedy and Johnson administrations. During Nixon's first term he wielded considerable influence, actually overshadowing the man who then headed up the State Department, William Rogers. Kissinger's so-called shuttle diplomacy, characterized by his scurrying from one Middle East capital to another by plane, altered the traditional American-Israeli versus Russian-

Arab standoff in that part of the world with the adoption of more tolerance for Arab views. To some extent, the U.S. move away from Israel (roundly criticized by America's very vocal and influential Jewish minority) was the result of growing American dependence upon Arab oil and pressures resulting from new unity among those oil-rich nations. Problems inherent in an Israeli–Arab struggle certainly remained, but the potential for outright U.S.–Russian involvement was diminished by the mid-1970s.

This new American independence and the Nixon administration's insistence that the United States not carry all of the burdens of world leadership were underscored in late 1971 by the President's decision to devaluate the dollar. This decision and increasing concern for national interests in trade matters signified that the U.S. would not automatically continue all of its post-1945 commitments to be guardian of one-half of a bipolar world. Such steps were motivated by realization of the overwhelming cost of Vietnam and of worldwide defense in general, evidence of stable economies in Europe no longer dependent upon U.S. aid, emergence of third and even fourth world states not willing to play the U.S.–Russian game by the old rules, and considerable disenchantment at home with a foreign policy that had somehow never succeeded in achieving announced goals.

Buffon-Darquenne/Sygma.

At Tang Son Nhut in 1975, two South Vietnamese paratroopers survey the symbolic remnants of the long U.S. involvement in their country: war-shattered buildings and the ever-present Coca-Cola sign.

Nixon's moves in regard to Russia and China were not total reversals of form. Suspicion of all Communist states remained high, as did the U.S. commitment to internationalism and stability in world trade and monetary affairs. Nixon made it clear—as did his successors—that the U.S. was not backing away from its far-flung treaty obligations and would intervene whenever it perceived a threat to the balance of world power. Thus, by returning to an obvious balance-of-power approach, relatively untarnished by ideological crusading phrases, Richard M. Nixon moved the nation toward a more practical view of world affairs than it had embraced since 1945. In the future neither Washington nor Moscow could speak with the same authority as they had in the 1950s and 1960s. Changing conditions, new leaders, and new forces were challenging the right of either to speak for one-half of the world; bipolarism, if not discredited as a policy, was at least in deep trouble.

The Rip Tide of Watergate

Despite Nixon's new departures in foreign affairs and his landslide victory in November 1972, twenty-one months later he was a private citizen once more, the first President ever to resign from office. The nub of the matter which forced him out of the White House in disgrace was a minor burglary in June 1972 at the national headquarters of the Democratic party in an office-hotel complex on the north banks of the Potomac. The dramatic events that ensued as a special Senate committee probed this affair in 1973 (discussed in detail in Chapter 30) led to impeachment proceedings against Nixon in July 1974 and his resignation on August 9th of that year.

Ten months earlier, Vice President Agnew also had been forced to quit because of personal ties to corrupt practices in his home state of Maryland. Agnew subsequently was replaced by a veteran Michigan congressman, Gerald R. Ford. This was the first time that the Twenty-fifth Amendment to the Constitution had been used. That measure, ratified in 1967, provided the machinery to fill such a vacancy created by the death or resignation of a President. It also gave the Vice President the power to act for the President if he was temporarily incapacitated.

Ford, born in Omaha, Nebraska, in 1913, was a quiet, hard-working congressman who had been Minority Leader in the House of Representatives since 1965. And, until nominated by Nixon and confirmed by the Congress as Vice President, he seemed destined to round out his career there. Ford's first words to the nation as President were a message of healing: "My fellow Americans, our long national nightmare is over." He promised openness and candor and had the assistance of a very able wife and four outspoken children. Ford's decision to name Nelson W. Rockefeller to the vice presidency enjoyed widespread approval. Yet the new President's honeymoon was brief indeed. In September the full pardon he granted to Nixon "for all offenses against the United States" sent shock waves throughout the nation. Many thought this act contrasted strangely with Ford's offer of limited clemency for Vietnam draft evaders and deserters. Some even speculated that the pardon actually was part of a "deal" between Nixon and Ford, although the latter made an unprecedented appearance on Capitol Hill to deny such charges. Nevertheless, in the minds of many voters the pardon linked Ford to Watergate for the first time, a fact of considerable importance as he campaigned for the presidency two years later.

The pardon uproar ushered in several very rocky months for the new chief executive. During the remainder of 1974 he vetoed eighteen bills (four of his vetoes were overridden) and was widely criticized for campaigning extensively in the congressional elections instead of confronting economic problems in Washington. As anticipated, Watergate, the pardon, and twin problems of inflation and recession gave the Democrats a resounding victory at the polls. They increased their House strength to 291, gaining 43 seats, picked up 3 seats in the Senate (for a total of 61), and captured four more governorships. Among the winners at the state level were Edmund (Jerry) Brown, Jr., a dynamic young Californian, and Ella Grasso of Connecticut, the first woman ever to become head of a state government without having succeeded her husband to power.

The most momentous event in foreign affairs in 1975 was the fall of South Vietnam to Communist forces from North Vietnam on April 30. (During that same month, neighboring Cambodia also experienced a Communist takeover.) Three weeks earlier Ford had made one last effort to give nearly $1 billion in aid to the tottering Saigon regime, but Congress said no. The following month Ford, using a strike force of 250 marines and eleven helicopters, won the release of the merchant crew of the *Mayagüez*, a U.S. vessel seized by a Cambodian gunboat. This daring exploit gave the President's sagging popularity a shot in the arm, although later revelations that a number of marines were killed or missing and many were wounded as a result of this assault stifled some of the cheering.

On the homefront Congress extended the Voting Rights Act of 1965 for seven years and expanded coverage to linguistic minorities in Alaska, Texas, and parts of twelve other states. It also appropriated $455 million to aid in the rehabilitation of Cambodian and Vietnamese refugees, many of whom came to live in America. In November, President Ford affected a major shakeup of his administrative team, apparently with an eye on the 1976 election campaign. The most important of these changes were in the Defense Department and the CIA, an organization still troubled by ties to Watergate and ongoing revelations concerning its past activities. By the end of the year, only three Cabinet members were holdovers from the Nixon era: Henry Kissinger (State), William E. Simon (Treasury), and Earl Butz (Agriculture). Meanwhile, Rockefeller, the bane of many conservative Republicans, announced that he would not seek election as Vice President in 1976.

The political wars of the Bicentennial Year revealed that the Watergate tide still was running strong. The Republicans, who expected to make a comeback after the Democratic landslide of 1974, lost two House seats and just held their own in the Senate where the party margin (62–38) remained unchanged. The big political news was, however, the election of Jimmy Carter (1924–), a virtual unknown and the first Southerner to win the White House in his own right and not by succession in over a century. Carter, a former governor of Georgia, climaxed a nineteen-month campaign as an "outsider" untainted by Washington when he captured the Democratic nomination in New York City in July 1976. He prevailed by entering thirty primaries and gaining substantial national attention. Although Carter did not win all of these races, he scored some victories and, even if not the front-runner, always picked up delegate strength. By June his nomination was assured. At New York he chose as his running mate Walter F. Mondale, a liberal senator from Minnesota.

Meanwhile, Gerald Ford scored some primary victories but was unable to force his conservative challenger, former Governor Ronald Reagan of California, out of the race. Nevertheless, the President eventually won a first-ballot nomination when the Republicans held their convention in Kansas City. To strengthen his appeal in the Midwest farm belt, he selected Senator Robert Dole of Kansas to complete the party ticket. In a hard-hitting speech to the delegates, one of the best of his career, Ford challenged Carter to a series of televised debates. This was, of course, the tactic of a politician who realized he trailed badly in public opinion polls.

In the ensuing months both men made serious blunders, yet Ford was able to narrow the gap between them. He had the advantage of incumbency and a well-oiled campaign organization but was hampered by a record of indecision, the Nixon pardon, and a seeming inability to deal effectively with a Democratic Congress. The debates probably helped Carter since he showed himself to be at least as presidential as Ford; also, Mondale demonstrated he was a more effective campaigner than his Republican counterpart. Yet the vote was relatively close, Carter winning by about 2 million votes out of 79 million cast. He succeeded by taking all of the traditional South except Virginia and getting impressive support from blacks and labor. The West (except for Hawaii) and much of the midwestern farm belt went to Ford who actually captured 27 states to 23 for Carter (who also carried the District of Columbia). The electoral margin, however, was Carter 297, Ford 240.

Yet the Carter administration, for all of its promise and hope, also was subject to the ebb and flow of Watergate. As an outsider not associated with the federal structure and lacking personal ties to Capitol Hill, the ex-governor of Georgia seemed to be a near-perfect candidate for the presidency, apparently well-equipped to make that office less imperial. Nevertheless, the openness and candor that the American public demanded after the horrors of the early 1970s exacted a heavy political price. At the same time that the chief executive was asked to appear less regal (i.e., less powerful), Congress, in the aftermath of impeachment and what amounted to a lame-duck regime, was riding high after several decades of White House supremacy. This test of power made Capitol Hill, without regard to party, feisty and uncooperative with a President who was not "one of its own." Also, various Democrats representing marginal House districts often found it expedient to depart from administration policy on specific issues in order to strengthen support back home.

After two years in office the Carter administration seemed adrift. It had committed no great mistakes, but had scored few legislative triumphs, and had initiated few sweeping changes. Indeed, Jimmy Carter and his associates were reaping a bitter harvest. Many of the gigantic spending schemes of the Kennedy-Johnson years had failed to achieve avowed goals. Nixon and Ford, in turn, had set out to curb or scuttle liberal programs they viewed as wasteful and paid only fleeting attention to problems such as inflation, tax reform, and energy development. Thus an "outsider" without Capitol Hill experience was asked to wrestle with very complex issues, the residue of a decade or more of executive overreaction and inaction, at a time when Congress was in a truculent mood and the White House was supposed to keep a low profile.

In the short run, the rip tide of Watergate seemed to pose contradictory and almost impossible demands: a quiet, unassuming administration that wanted to deal efficiently with a Congress made somewhat unruly by a new sense of strength. Yet both branches of government were grappling simultaneously with far-reaching issues that tended only to increase the distance and exacerbate differences between the White House and Capitol Hill. Carter's widely hailed energy program, for example, languished for over a year as various special interests and innumerable committees tugged it this way and that.

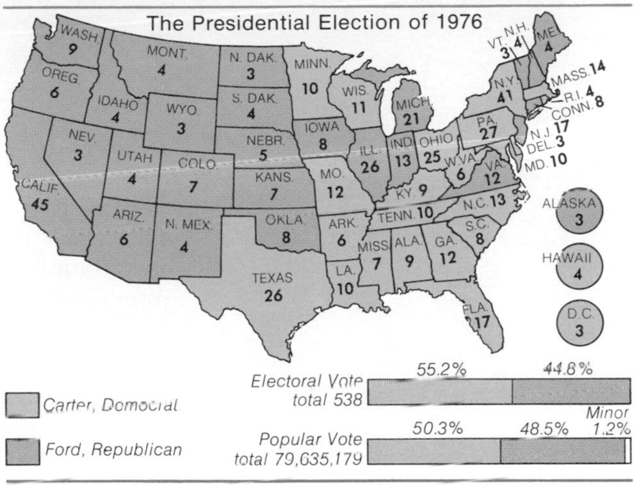

A sign of the times was the return in 1978 of the familiar flourishes of "Hail to the Chief" at occasional presidential appearances. The tune had been banished during the first year of the Carter administration, but apparently some advisors concluded that a minimum of imperial pomp was in fact necessary. Perhaps the rip tide of Watergate finally was beginning to run its course.

Essay

Bunnies, Bosoms, and Changing Sexual Mores

From earliest times the subject of sex has exuded a strange fascination, and succeeding civilizations have dealt with it in many different ways. A few have allowed relatively free public expression, but most have kept sexual activitity securely under wraps or at least out of sight, hidden in back alleys and so-called red light districts. Of course, the European, African, and Asiatic peoples who came to the New World brought their sexual attitudes and practices along with the rest of their baggage. Yet two general moral codes, Puritan in the eighteenth century and Victorian in the nineteenth, tended to dominate attitudes toward sex in America; but, since much of what went on behind closed doors did not get into history books, no one is quite certain how complete that dominance really was. Perhaps the sexual revolution of the late twentieth century is something new, then again perhaps it is not. In any case, few doubt that there has been a distinct change recently in attitudes towards sex.

A turning point in this tale of changing attitudes toward sex was publication in 1948 of Alfred C. Kinsey's *Sexual Behavior in the Human Male,* a very thorough study that forced a reexamination of long accepted assumptions. Based upon thousands of interviews, this work by an entomologist turned human biologist was planned as the first of several volumes. By questioning people from all parts of the nation on every socioeconomic level, Kinsey concluded that (1) notable differences in sexual patterns existed from group to group and (2) those patterns often deviated completely from the laws and conventions of society.

When this book appeared, Hugh Marston Hefner, an undergraduate at the University of Illinois, underscored these facts in a review written for a campus publication. He stressed that Kinsey's work clearly showed the "lack of understanding and realistic thinking that have gone into the formation of our sex standards and laws. Our moral pretense, our hypocrisy on matters of sex have led to incalculable frustration, delinquency, and unhappiness."

Hefner, born into a strict Methodist household in Chicago in 1926, went on to get his bachelor's degree in 1949 with a major in psychology. He attended graduate school briefly at Northwestern University, worked at a variety of jobs, married, and had two children. He and his wife later separated, then were

Wide World.

One of the least positive aspects of the freeing of sexual mores in the seventies was the explosion in pornography. Characteristic of the new freedom is this old-time Hollywood theater, converted to an "adult" film show.

divorced. In 1952, his employer, *Esquire* magazine, decided to consolidate its activities in New York City. *Esquire* offered Hefner an increase in weekly salary from $60 to $80 if he would move to Manhattan. Hefner asked for $85, *Esquire* said no, and Hefner quit. The magazine's refusal to pay this young man another $5 per week was an extremely costly decision. (In his luxurious home Hefner now has a single share of *Esquire* stock framed under glass with this attached message: "In case of emergency, break glass.") This action by the editors of *Esquire,* like the publication of the Kinsey book, was yet another turning point in the story of changing attitudes toward sex and sexual customs in America.

Hefner left his former employers firmly convinced that the time was ripe for a new, fresh magazine for men, one that would reflect trends evident in the national social milieu. Within a year he raised $10,000 through stock sold to friends, pooled that money with $600 he had in his savings account, and in December 1953 published 70,000 copies of the first issue of

Playboy. Thanks to a colorful nude picture of Marilyn Monroe which cost Hefner $200, some 54,000 copies (a phenomenal number for the first issue of any publication) soon were sold at fifty cents each.

That initial issue, complete with the now familiar bunny motif, opened with these words: "If you're a man between the ages of 18 and 80, PLAYBOY is meant for you. If you like your entertainment served up with humor, sophistication, and spice, PLAYBOY will become a very special favorite." *Playboy* was not, warned its creator (who disclosed only his initials, not his name) a family magazine; instead it would emphasize entertainment and humor, and become "a pleasure-primer styled to the masculine taste." The forty-pages that followed contained shots of nudes, sports articles, and reprints of stories by Arthur Conan Doyle, Ambrose Bierce, and Boccaccio.

By February 1954 *Playboy* felt secure enough to announce annual subscription rates and two months later produced its first full-color cover. Throughout the first year the magazine existed on sales alone, but by the second it began to attract local and then national advertising. During the third year the nude centerfold added a third panel as the publication swelled to ninety pages of high-grade, coated paper. By December 1956 the format known to millions was firmly established.

Since that time the *Playboy* empire has produced numerous 300-page issues, a myriad of assorted reprints (joke books; readers; anniversary editions; guides to eating, drinking, and sex customs; games; and so on), and grown to include its own publishing house, clubs, restaurants, and hotels. By 1967 the magazine alone had sales in excess of $50 million, and a year later circulation increased to over five million. In 1971 Hefner and his operations had a total corporate income of $131 million, a creditable showing for a personal investment of $600.

In no small way, *Playboy* was aided by several Supreme Court decisions which, although the justices were often sharply divided and dissent strong, tended to define obscenity in such a way as to permit greater license. In June 1957, four split rulings upheld lower court convictions concerning the publication or distribution of materials thought to be offensive. The majority said, in essence, that the First Amendment does not permit obscenity in the guise of free speech. Yet in *Roth* v. *U.S.,* a case involving a New York dealer of books and magazines and the use of the mails to solicit business, the justices ruled that to be obscene a publication must (1) have a dominant sexual theme, (2) be "patently offensive because it affronts contemporary community standards relating to the description or representation of sexual matters," and (3) be "utterly without redeeming social value."

Teri Leigh

Hugh Hefner's *Playboy* was only one—even if the most successful—among a growing number of 'girlie' magazines to appear on newsstands in the 1950s and 1960s.

During that same year the Court in *Butler* v. *Michigan* struck down the conviction of a bookshop operator who sold an allegedly obscene book to a police officer. The Michigan statute in question (relating only to young people) would have the effect, if properly enforced, the justices noted, of reducing "the adult population of Michigan to reading only fit for children." And, in 1966, referring specifically to guidelines established in the Roth case, the Court in "*John Cleland's Memoirs*" v. *Massachusetts* reversed a ruling concerning a bawdy eighteenth-century book, *Fanny Hill,* a volume sold in many other states without incident.

Hefner has told interviewers that he thinks he began at precisely the right moment, just as a sexual insurrection was getting underway, and that *Playboy* was something like waving a banner of freedom or revolution. Perhaps this is true; but, despite obvious success, Hefner has not been without critics.

Some observers believe that Editor Hefner, a strange recluse who drinks gallons of Pepsi-Cola and lives and works in a vast, fifty-four room mansion, has never left the 1950s. One secret of his phenomenal good fortune, they agree, was linking sex with the upward mobility of American society. But the generation to which he tied his dreams now is older and may want more out of life than sexual fantasies and an unending fraternity party atmosphere. Its offspring, a far different breed, are involved in politics, ecology, mountain climbing, and sexual experimentation—thanks to the pill and changing mores that Hefner nudged along—which often make *Playboy* seem a superfluous relic of an earlier time.

Although it has set extremely high literary standards and pays top dollar for fine articles, *Playboy* only belatedly developed any interest in race relations, the environment, the feminist movement, and other issues that now seem really to matter. A former *Playboy* executive says Hugh Hefner had no social consciousness whatsoever until "whacked on the ass" by a policeman during the riots that marred the 1968 Democratic convention held in Chicago. Eight years later a *Playboy* interview in which candidate Jimmy Carter spoke of sexual lust became a fleeting issue in the 1976 presidential campaign.

Not everything that Hugh Hefner has touched has turned to gold. Entertainment and humor magazines were flops; two television ventures produced huge yawns; and his restaurants, resorts, and hotels reportedly are not real moneymakers.

The changing nature of Hefner's reader audience, a hard fact any successful magazine must grapple with, is only one of his problems. By the late 1970s, competition in the form of a revived and rejuvenated *Esquire* and less inhibited imitators such as *Penthouse* and *Hustler* were making things warm for *Playboy.*

Nevertheless, like the Godey print, Gibson girl, and World

U.P.I.

Hugh Hefner and assorted bunnies at one of his plush Playboy clubs in 1961.

War II pinups, "The Playmate of the Month," a huge foldout of skin, pulchritude, and bosomy charms, remains the symbol of an age. In the 1950s she was daring and so were *Playboy* and its readers. As time raced by, she has remained about twenty years of age and always part of a warm sexual fantasy, but seems increasingly less daring.

For Hefner and *Playboy,* merely waving a banner that says freedom or one that displays naked female charms in living color may no longer be enough. In any case, it certainly is not very risqué by current standards. Hefner's opening statement in that first issue—"if you like your entertainment served up with humor, sophistication, and spice"—provides a clue to the dilemma his empire faces. New sexual codes have little time for such a passive attitude; they demand action. And, as for "sophistication," it suffered a heavy body blow in the turbulent 1960s.

Hugh Marston Hefner clearly touched a vibrant nerve in a large segment of the American male population shortly after mid-century. He rode the sexual revolution to wealth and fame.

But riding a revolution is a very dangerous game, especially a social revolution. Changing mores and changing customs create everchanging demands.

Selected Readings

John F. Kennedy and the New Frontier

Arthur M. Schlesinger, Jr., *A Thousand Days: John F. Kennedy in the White House* (1965)
Henry Fairlie, *The Kennedy Promise: The Politics of Expectation* (1973)
Jim F. Heath, *Decade of Disillusionment: The Kennedy-Johnson Years* (1975)

Lyndon B. Johnson and the Great Society

Doris Kearns, *Lyndon Johnson and the American Dream* (1976)
Lyndon B. Johnson, *The Vantage Point* (1971)
John C. Donovan, *The Politics of Poverty* (1973)

The Vietnam War

Neil Sheehan, et al., *The Pentagon Papers as Published by* The New York Times (1971)
David Halberstam, *The Best and the Brightest* (1972)
Townsend Hoopes, *The Limits of Intervention* (1969)
Robert W. Stevens, *Vain Hopes, Grim Realities: The Economic Consequences of the Vietnam War* (1976)

Civil Rights: Culmination and Backlash

Stokely Carmichael and Charles V. Hamilton, *Black Power: The Politics of Liberation* (1967)
Cleveland Sellers with Robert Terrell, *The River of No Return: The Autobiography of a Black Militant and the Life and Death of SNCC* (1973)
Carl M. Brauer, *John F. Kennedy and the Second Reconstruction* (1977)

American Society During the 1960s

William L. O'Neill, *Coming Apart: An Informal History of America in the 1960s* (1971)
Irwin Unger, *The Movement: A History of the American New Left, 1959–1972* (1974)
Archibald Cox, *The Warren Court: Constitutional Decision as an Instrument of Reform* (1968)

The Nixon Administration: Early Policies

Rowland Evans and Robert Novak, *Nixon in the White House: The Frustration of Power* (1972)
Dan Rather and Gary P. Gates, *The Palace Guard* (1974)
Henry Brandon, *The Retreat of American Power* (1973)
Garry Wills, *Nixon Agonistes* (1970)

Chapter 30

American Institutions in Transition, Since 1960

TIMELINE

1962
In *Baker* v. *Carr* the Supreme Court requires reapportionment of rural-dominated state legislatures

1963
Kennedy issues order barring discrimination against women in federal employment

1966
In *Miranda* case Supreme Court orders due process for those under arrest

1969
Indians assert treaty rights and seize Alcatraz Island in San Francisco Bay

1970
Cooper-Church Amendment limits use of American combat troops in Cambodia

1971
Daniel Ellsberg releases "The Pentagon Papers" to *The New York Times*

1972
An attempted assassination eliminates George Wallace from the presidential contest

1972
Nixon wins a landslide victory over George McGovern

February 1973
Judge John Sirica sentences Watergate burglars and suggests a Congressional investigation

February 1973
American Indian Movement seizes Wounded Knee, South Dakota

October 1973
Vice-President Spiro Agnew resigns from office and pleads no contest to tax evasion charges

October 1973
Nixon removes Special Prosecutor in "Saturday Night Massacre"

November 1973
War Powers Act limits presidential authority to use American troops

April 1974
Nixon releases transcripts of some of the White House tapes

July 1974
House Judiciary Committee votes articles of impeachment against Nixon

August 1974
Nixon resigns the Presidency

September 1974
President Ford pardons former President Nixon

May 1975
Mayaguez incident brings Ford temporary praise

November 1976
Jimmy Carter defeats Ford in presidential contest

CHAPTER OUTLINE

Marc Bloch, the famous French medieval historian who was shot by the Nazis during World War II for resistance activity, once observed that, when examined closely, every period in history represents "a time of transition." A corollary of this truth is that almost any era is crowded with crises that, as decades pass, are often forgotten or somehow lose their importance. The closer one is to events, the more difficult it may be to see them in perspective. No one can say precisely what is important and unimportant in his own time or how various trends and developments may affect the future. Historians are not soothsayers. Their function is to study the past in the hope that the body of knowledge they produce may be instructive and help both present and future generations avoid mistakes of the past. The problem is, of course, that crises and confrontations rarely happen in the same context or even under similar circumstances.

Since 1960, America has passed through a difficult time. One President was assassinated and another was forced to resign in disgrace. The struggle for minority and individual rights has continued, often taking unexpected twists that have affected nearly every community throughout the nation. Antiwar protest, drug use, and changing sexual attitudes have caused widespread unrest. Yet little in this total picture is new, and the governmental apparatus set up in the late 1780s seems to have dealt with these crises in a reasonable (if sometimes tardy) manner. This does not mean that all problems have been solved. Judges, congressmen, and government officials—often with public approbation—have skirted around issues or swept them under the rug for the moment in the hope that they would go away or at least remain dormant and become the problem of some future generation. However, such matters as government secrecy, defense costs, the Pentagon-corporate network, structural problems of capitalism (among them chronic unemployment), and the search for sources of energy for an expanding economy are ongoing crises. And, through it all, two paramount facts are evident: the three branches of the federal government continue their constant and indeed proper warfare, and the public at large still pursues its quest for a "lost" equilibrium that probably, in truth, never actually existed. Most of those concerned shun sudden, radical change, preferring instead to adapt to current realities; meanwhile, the triangular federal tug of war goes on, as does the search for social stability.

Political Crisis and Resolution

The fortunes of the three men who have headed up the executive branch during the past decade—Richard Nixon, Gerald Ford, and Jimmy Carter—are tied closely to the Watergate affair. That convoluted political scandal forced Nixon to resign the presidency in mid-1974, posed great problems for Ford, his appointed successor, and created the opportunity that Carter exploited in his successful campaign for the White House two years later. It also weakened, perhaps decisively, the hold of the presidency over the American public and Congress.

Watergate: The Ultimate Confrontation

Watergate, a pleasant stretch of the Potomac's northern shoreline not far from the Lincoln Memorial, takes its name from canal developments of the nineteenth century. During the 1930s, a bandstand shell appeared there on a barge, and on warm summer evenings Washington residents could sit on the riverbank and enjoy concerts; also, not far away the country-styled Watergate Inn became famous for good food and its legendary popovers. In the 1960s, however, that eatery was replaced by a vast, rambling complex of offices, hotels, apartments, and shops, soon one of the most prestigious addresses in the nation's capital.

As the result of a bizarre break-in at the national headquarters of the Democratic party in a Watergate office building in June 1972—a crime as yet not entirely explained—the word "Watergate" has taken on special meaning unrelated to canals, band concerts, good food, and gracious living. The outcome was an unfolding institutional and constitutional crisis that culminated in the resignation of Richard M. Nixon, the first U.S. President ever to step down as chief executive before completing his term. In light of his overwhelming reelection victory in November 1972 and the original assumption by most Americans that the break-in was a minor burglary, this is indeed an ironic tale. Democrat George McGovern tried to make something of Watergate during the campaign of that year but got nowhere. Then, in February 1973, Judge John Sirica (a Republican who had earlier campaigned for both Eisenhower and Nixon) sentenced the seven burglars to prison. Disturbed because some of these men had obvious White House ties and sensing there was much more to the story, Sirica suggested that Congress pursue the matter further. As a result, the

J. P. Laffont/Sygma.

The exclusive Watergate apartment-office complex, the site of the break-in at Democratic National Committee headquarters in 1972.

Katharine Meyer Graham

(1917–)

A "working publisher" who gives her editors both responsibility and money to recruit talent and then encourages competition among them ("It makes for journalism of a high calibre," she says), Katharine Graham is a formidable figure in the media world. The center of her empire is the *Washington Post,* but she also controls *Newsweek* and Washington area radio and TV stations. Largely because of her drive for excellence, the *Post* has become a major force in American journalism, read and consulted each day by thousands of U.S. government officials both at home and abroad.

Born in New York City in 1917 and educated at Vassar and the University of Chicago, she worked at the *Post* in the late 1930s, an ailing newspaper her banker father bought in 1933. In 1940 she married Philip Graham, law clerk to Supreme Court Justice Felix Frankfurter. After serving in World War II, her husband became publisher of the *Post,* and in 1948 Katharine Graham's father sold the young couple all voting rights in the paper's operations for $1.

During the next fifteen years Philip Graham bought up other daily papers, as well as *Newsweek,* and linked up with the *Los Angeles Times* to form a highly respected international news service. Following his suicide in 1963, his widow took over as president of the *Post* company, becoming publisher in 1969. During these years she carefully analyzed operations, and recruited new talent. By 1966 the *Post* was third in the nation in advertising lineage, topped only by the *New York Times* and *Los Angeles Times.* She also invested $25 million in a new plant and soon was recording annual sales of $125 million ($10 million in profits). The *Post's* relentless probing of the Watergate affair boosted those sales and profits figures even higher in the early 1970s.

Leading that inquiry, almost from the moment the burglary was discovered, were two young investigative reporters, Robert Woodward and Carl Bernstein. Working with the complete backing and wholehearted cooperation of Publisher Graham (reportedly the object of a 1973 White House campaign of harassment), this youthful pair unleashed one bombshell after another in dynamic prose that won them top journalistic honors and the respect of millions.

As a manager, she gives staff a free hand and backs up editors. Although Graham may question their policy on specific issues, she refuses to dictate what they write. "You want intelligent, large-scale thinkers and writers," she once remarked, "and nobody for whom you have any respect would take an edict from on high."

Katharine Graham is a hard-working woman who usually spends two days each week in New York with *Newsweek,* the remainder of her time in Washington where she maintains a busy schedule. Mother of four and once described as "a lonely widow," Graham remarked, "I have to *fight* to get two hours to myself. I wish I were lonelier." ■

Senate by a vote of 70–0 established a committee of four Democrats and three Republicans to investigate Watergate and other alleged 1972 campaign abuses. In May that committee, headed by Sam Ervin (D–North Carolina) and Howard Baker (R–Tennessee), began fifty-three days of televised hearings. With each passing week the question of presidential involvement became more crucial; then, on July 16, 1973, a White House aide, Alexander Butterfield, revealed that the Oval Office had an intricate tape-recording system, a turning point in the investigation.

For the next thirteen months the nation staggered from one constitutional confrontation to another. Eventually, Nixon, his administration in disarray and riddled by rumor and resignation, accepted full responsibility for Watergate, at the same time protesting he was innocent of any wrongdoing. He adamantly refused to release White House tapes to Archibald Cox, a Harvard professor named in May as special prosecutor of the Watergate matter by Elliot Richardson, the new Attorney General. To do so, the President claimed, would violate "executive privilege."

October and November of 1973 turned out to be especially dramatic months. On October 10, Spiro Agnew (who was not involved in Watergate) resigned as Vice President and pleaded no contest to income tax evasion charges. Two days later, Nixon nominated House Minority Leader Gerald R. Ford of Michigan to replace Agnew. On October 20, Cox went on television to announce he would not compromise on the tapes issue and would not quit as special prosecutor. A few hours later the President fired Cox, abolished the special prosecutor's office, and accepted the resignation of both Attorney General Richardson and his deputy, William Ruckelshaus, because they refused to carry out his orders to fire Cox. (The third man at the Justice Department eventually did the President's bidding.)

This brutal chain of events, which the media dubbed the "Saturday Night Massacre," greatly complicated Nixon's tangled web. The following day hundreds of noisy cars drove by the White House with placards reading "Honk if you think he's guilty" and both the press and the public roared their disapproval. Within seventy-two hours the White House agreed to release the tapes Cox had sought, but it soon developed that some were missing and one had a vital 18.5-minute erasure. On October 30, the House Judiciary Committee began consideration of impeachment procedures. Two days later, William R. Saxbe, Nixon's fourth Attorney General in as many years, named a Houston lawyer, Leon Jaworski, as Cox's successor. On November 3, a Gallup Poll revealed that only 27 percent of Americans approved of Nixon's

Fred Ward/Black Star.

Before the special Senate committee investigating the Watergate break-in and related incidents, former White House counsel John Dean (back to camera) testifies, while committee chairman Senator Sam Ervin third from right) and vice-chairman Senator Howard Baker (left of Ervin) listen.

J. P. Laffont/Sygma.

J. P. Laffont/Sygma.

The President's (former) men: John Ehrlichman (left) and H. R. Haldeman (right) along with John Dean, were the highest-ranking former officials of the Nixon administration to be brought before the Senate Watergate committee. They eventually received prison terms for their roles in the abuse of executive power surrounding the Watergate incident.

conduct as President, an alltime low for him; a year earlier (almost to the day) the Nixon-Agnew ticket had received 61 percent of the popular vote, sweeping every state except Massachusetts and the District of Columbia.

In mid-November the President toured friendly sections of the South in an effort to drum up support, at one stop stating bluntly: "People have got to know whether or not their President is a crook. Well, I'm no crook." Early the following month Nixon was forced to disclose that he had become a millionaire in the White House but had paid less than $1,000 in income taxes in both 1970 and 1971. Four months later the Internal Revenue Service disallowed a huge deduction taken for donation of his vice presidential papers to the National Archives and said he owed $432,787 in back taxes and $33,000 in interest. The President agreed to pay.

On April 30, 1974, facing an impeachment inquiry, Nixon released 1,239 pages of transcripts taken from the White House tapes, vowing that nothing more would be handed over to Jaworski or to the House Judiciary Committee. These materials, although riddled with omissions, revealed brutally frank top-level discussions of Watergate and related problems and of administration and political personalities. On July 24, 1974, the Supreme Court ruled unanimously in a landmark decision (*U.S.* v. *Richard Nixon*) that the President had no right to withhold evidence required in various criminal proceedings arising from Watergate and would thus have to relinquish all tapes the courts might request. Nixon agreed to comply.

The following day the House Judiciary Committee began televised debate on articles of impeachment and within six days passed three such articles, charging the President of the United States with covering up and obstructing an investigation of the Watergate break-in, misuse of his powers so as to violate the constitutional rights of American citizens, and defiance of subpoenas. During the period 1973–1974, as impeachment became likely, numerous White House aides and several key members of Nixon's administration were sentenced to prison as a result of Watergate and other secret (and illegal) operations. On August 5, three new transcripts disclosed that Richard Nixon had personally ordered a coverup of the facts of Watergate within six days of the break-in, completely demolishing months of carefully constructed denial. With his support in Congress and the nation almost gone and conviction on impeachment charges a virtual certainty, the President appeared on television on the evening of August 8 to announce that he would resign, effective at noon the following day.

Most Americans, saturated with crises, were relieved that the federal structure "had worked," but some were not so sure that it had. The nation had reeled this way and that, virtually leaderless for a year or so, the Supreme Court's narrow ruling on the tapes actually upheld the principle of "executive privilege," and numerous members of the executive branch of government had used their great power to subvert laws they had sworn to administer and uphold. President Ford's pardon of Nixon in September 1974 heightened this sense of frustration and bewilderment; also, whether or not his decision was just, by his actions, the new President tied himself to Watergate, a fact that later had political importance during the 1976 election campaign.

The residue of Watergate was a nation sobered, and scores of reputations ruined. Various departments and agencies such as Justice, FBI, and CIA were in disarray and the morale of their employees at an alltime low. But the most disturbing result of all was the erosion of public faith in the political process. With so many domestic problems jostling for attention and crying out for solutions, it was a poor time indeed for American citizens to lose respect for their elected officials and to doubt the effectiveness of the only mechanism designed to deal with such serious issues.

J. P. Laffont/Sygma.

In a deeply emotional—if not fully penitent—speech, President Nixon became the first American Chief Executive to resign his office, on August 9, 1974.

Politics as Usual

Most analyses of American politics since 1960 concentrate on the themes of disruption and transformation prompted by antiwar protest and Watergate. Observers tend to comment on social changes that have threatened—or actually destroyed—the New Deal coalition born in the 1930s. Divisive issues such as race, Vietnam, and "law and order" are seen as the precursors of a realignment; and the shocks of Watergate and the subsequent decline of public faith in government are viewed as threats to the party system as a whole.

Yet through it all, not only has the system endured, but so has the Democratic party majority. In 1976, the Democratic candidate won with strong support from much the same coalition that elected four Democratic Presidents during the preceding four decades. Democrats, meanwhile, continued to control the Congress, as they have (with only two exceptions) since the onset of the Depression. It is difficult to conclude, then, that the "Democratic era" has ended. Whatever its prospect for future success, and however tenuous its hold on the electorate may be, the party of the New Deal, Fair Deal, New Frontier, and Great Society was still dominant in the late 1970s.

The 1968 presidential election comported well with theories of party breakdown. The majority Democratic party was so split by Vietnam and "law and order" that, for a time, George Wallace's ultraconservative third party threatened to deadlock the Electoral College; yet, in the end, Richard Nixon got no less than 30 percent of Johnson's 1964 Democratic support. The combination of Wallace's 13 percent and Nixon's 43 percent of the total vote was hailed by some as the harbinger of a new conservative majority. The problem was, this "conservatism" was little more than an emotional reaction to a handful of specific issues and in no way endangered the cumulative work of Roosevelt, Truman, Kennedy, and Johnson. When the Republicans later tried to translate this transient mood into party strength, the results were (for them) discouraging, and Nixon's New American Revolution served only to reactivate dormant elements of the New Deal coalition to oppose him.

As a result of internal party reform, the most liberal wing controlled the Democratic Party in 1972 and nominated Senator George McGovern. He proceeded (mistakenly) to run a heavily ideological campaign that alienated many traditional Democrats. Nixon was able to secure 80 percent of the Wallace vote (the Alabama governor having been eliminated from the race in May by a cruel assassination attempt which left him crippled) and gained a sweeping re-election victory over McGovern.

Institutions in Conflict

In a sense, America always has been on trial, first as colonies trying to demonstrate their worth, then as a republican experiment in an age of monarchies, and more recently as a nation with worldwide responsibilities. How the United States handles its current dilemmas in an age of mass communication, Cold War detente, and an emerging Third World cannot help but have great repercussions.

Wars and War Powers

One of the most significant byproducts of the Vietnam War was conflict between Congress and the White House over war powers, a debate that had been developing since Harry Truman sent U.S. forces to Korea in 1950. Congress, distressed by trends evident under Truman, Eisenhower, and Kennedy and emboldened by antiwar sentiment, eventually began to challenge the maneuverings of Johnson and Nixon in Southeast Asia. This politically inspired attempt to assert historic legislative rights (the Constitution declares that "The Congress shall have the Power . . . To declare War . . . To raise and support Armies") culminated in the War Powers Act of 1973. Its limitations, however, soon became evident, for political realities apparently continued to set the real limit on presidential action in foreign affairs.

Lyndon Johnson, learning from the experiences of his predecessors, on the basis of an alleged attack on U.S. naval units off the coast of North Vietnam, secured the so-called Gulf of Tonkin Resolution in August 1964. Later, when the administration came under congressional fire, Johnson stated that this action, while politically desirable, had not actually been necessary. "We thought," he observed, "if we were going to ask them [Congress] to stay the whole route, and if we expected them to be there at the landing, we ought to ask them to be there on the

Dirck Halstead/Contact Press.

In 1976, for the first time in sixteen years, the two major presidential candidates met in a series of live televised debates. Unlike 1960, neither President Ford nor challenger Jimmy Carter gained decisively by his showing in the debates.

J. William Fulbright
(1905–   )

Alfred Eisenstaedt/Life Magazine © 1964 Time, Inc.

A gentle, quiet, modest man nearly 6 feet tall, James William Fulbright was born in Sumner, Missouri, in 1905, grew up in Fayetteville, Arkansas, and graduated from the University of Arkansas in 1925. A Rhodes Scholar, he earned two degrees at Oxford and then returned to George Washington University to study law. After teaching law for three years at the University of Arkansas (1936–1939), he became president of that institution. During his two-year tenure he fought hard to raise academic standards and earned the enmity of the governor's office because of his methods.

Elected to the House of Representatives in 1942 on a "no more war" platform, Fulbright quickly became a spokesman for international cooperation. In the U.S. Senate from 1944 to 1975, he gave his name to an international educational exchange program for graduate students—a sort of expanded Rhodes plan—which has provided financial support for thousands of scholars since World War II.

Democrat Fulbright, not one to avoid controversy, suggested in 1946 (following Republican victories) that Harry Truman appoint a Republican Secretary of State as his successor and then resign. Eight years later he cosponsored the resolution censuring Senator Joseph R. McCarthy. It was Vietnam, however, that turned out to be Fulbright's most important battleground. At first he supported Lyndon Johnson's Southeast Asia adventure, even serving as floor leader when Johnson wanted quick approval of his Tonkin Gulf Resolution. Then, becoming disillusioned, the Arkansas senator (chairman of the Senate Foreign Relations Committee after 1959) began to conduct televised hearings that provided a forum for criticism of Vietnam policies.

Articulate in foreign affairs, despite his conservatism on civil rights, Fulbright emerged nonetheless as the darling of radicals and liberals in the late 1960s and early 1970s and the bane of both Johnson and Nixon. Defeated in the 1974 Democratic primary, largely because he had apparently lost touch with Arkansas voters in his quest for statesmanship, J. William Fulbright in retirement remains a respected voice and an accomplished writer and speaker in foreign policy matters. ■

take-off." At the same time that Johnson asked for cooperation of sorts in foreign policy, he also moved to stifle all internal opposition to the Vietnam adventure within his administration, thereby isolating the presidency.

The upsurge in congressional antiwar sentiment after Nixon's victory in 1968—in part because Democrats now felt more free to criticize White House policy—made clear the essentially political motivation behind arguments concerning warmaking powers of the chief executive. Nixon, even while slowly defusing the Vietnam issue, extended presidential war action by his "incursion" into Cambodia (April 1970) and similar operations in Laos. In each instance, he justified such moves as "protection" for American troops already in Vietnam and ignored the original legality or constitutionality of the war itself.

Meanwhile, congressional opposition mounted. Senators John Sherman Cooper (R—Kentucky) and Frank Church (D—Idaho), especially disturbed by the Cambodian offensive in 1970, sponsored an amendment to a foreign aid bill barring the introduction of American combat troops into that country. Although substantially weakened before it was passed later that same year, the Cooper-Church measure represented a turning point since it inspired other lawmakers to delve more deeply into secret foreign commitments and to consider the full scope of presidential activity overseas. Within a year the Senate was making deep cuts in foreign aid proposals, which the White House found difficult to restore. For a generation or more the American public had been told that such expenditures were necessary in a bipolar world divided between Washington and Moscow. The switch to a balance-of-power detente indicated that some of this spending might no longer be necessary—or at least that it was increasingly hard to justify in the light of changing conditions.

It was in this context, a mood of disenchantment with warfare in Southeast Asia, a lessening of Cold War tensions, and the reassertion of congressional initiative, that a War Powers Bill designed to limit presidential action was introduced in late 1971. Sponsored by both liberal and conservative senators, the resolution in altered form was passed over Nixon's veto on November 7, 1973. In essence, it gave the President the right to move promptly without a declaration of war if such action seemed necessary, provided he immediately consulted with Congress and submitted a report to that body within forty-eight hours. Unless Congress subsequently declared war or specifically approved this action, it had to be brought to a halt within sixty days. Some senators felt the bill merely legitimized the chief executive's usurpation of congressional authority and amounted to little more than an undated declaration of war. And the *Mayagüez* incident in May of 1975 revealed that such fears were well founded. Gerald Ford, Nixon's successor, acted without reference either to this measure or to legislation that cut off funds for all military operations in Indochina. When Cambodian forces boarded and seized the *Mayagüez,* a U.S. vessel, Ford mounted a secret operation that quickly freed the ship and its crew. He subsequently complied with the War Powers Act by submitting a written report to Congress within the required forty-eight hours, by which time the incident was closed anyway. Instead of raising legal objections, most Americans applauded this staunch bit of late nineteenth-century jingoism, at least until they discovered how many lives it cost.

It would appear, then, that in a real sense little has changed. Any chief executive probably can make military moves overseas on his own if that action is successful and of short duration. Nevertheless, Capitol Hill has issued definite signals that it wants no more Koreas or Vietnams, a sentiment firmly grounded in public opinion polls and mail from constituents.

Buses, Bills, and the Federal System

Although Americans at large usually could view the war powers issue philosophically and at a safe distance, they could not so view issues much closer to home: civil rights and urban/welfare policies. Few other matters have produced more heated clashes between the branches of government and between federal and local authorities. Federal solutions have often been incomplete or illusory, and the strength of localism will probably force some readjustment in twentieth-century liberal formulas included in the New Frontier and the Great Society, and will cause even liberals to abandon some of their once-cherished goals.

Desegregation efforts produced numerous institutional and local-federal conflicts before 1968, yet the power of federal (and especially executive) forces seemed destined to prevail. Then, as the Nixon administration relaxed executive commitment to civil rights, the seemingly permanent constitutional crisis appeared to be

Ellis Herwig/Stock, Boston.

In Boston in 1974, as in many cities, busing provoked sharp public opposition and even required protection by law-enforcement officials.

heading for a different resolution, with local forces gaining the upper hand. Eager to develop a strong Republican party in the South, Nixon made clear overtures to conservatives of that region opposed to desegregation. As the "southern strategy" unfolded, Nixon appointees fought HEW guidelines requiring school desegregation in Mississippi in 1969, and the President tried unsuccessfully to name two southern judges to the Supreme Court. He also announced his personal opposition to busing, a scheme designed to achieve racial balance in local school systems by transporting students to facilities at some distance from their homes—in short, to a school other than a neighborhood school.

Throughout the early 1970s this issue festered, especially in the North. In April 1971, the Supreme Court declared busing to be constitutional (*Swann* v. *Charlotte-Mecklenberg Board of Education*); but, the following year, in the wake of a Florida referendum showing 80 percent of the voters in that state in favor of a constitutional amendment banning busing, Nixon called for a congressional moratorium on all new busing and for legislation to end it for all time. Meanwhile, the Justice Department intervened to block imposition of busing in several cities, and Congress limited the ways in which federal funds could be used for busing purposes.

The administration of Gerald Ford continued this opposition and conservative lawmakers used various pressures designed to discourage use of HEW appropriations for busing. Yet, in light of the Supreme Court ruling, only a constitutional amendment could bar lower courts from continuing to order busing to promote racial balance. The source of disagreement was not the dual (racially separate) school systems outlawed in 1954, but de facto segregation of schools created by segregated housing patterns, especially in northern cities. Local opposition to busing erupted in widely scattered cities such as Boston, Detroit, and Louisville. This was by no means a clear-cut choice between good and evil since the question of neighborhood identity was also involved. Nevertheless, the preeminence of the law was recognized and by the mid-1970s school desegregation was proceeding very slowly, even though no permanent solution to

'I'VE SOLVED THE BUSING-FOR-INTEGRATION PROBLEM—I'M BUSING ALL THE FEDERAL JUDGES TO PODUNK, IOWA.'

President Ford's policy on busing, according to a 1975 cartoon by Oliphant.

segregation was apparent. The American commitment to local control of schools clashed head on in this instance with the basic American tenet of equality of opportunity. It remained to be seen whether a revival of sympathy for busing in the executive or legislative branches, or in both, might enable court decisions concerning this complex matter to be carried out.

Although busing played no central role in the 1976 election (and indeed Democratic candidate Jimmy Carter attempted to come across as the defender of local autonomy and private morality), it was generally apparent that the Democrats were more likely than the Republicans to support continuing efforts to achieve desegregation in the schools, by whatever means necessary. This assumption was reinforced when President and Mrs. Carter, immediately upon moving into the White House, enrolled their young daughter in an integrated inner-city elementary school in the District of Columbia.

Yet the knotty busing issue could not be resolved by presidential good intentions and appeals to individual morality. In the Congress strong forces continued to try to ban the HEW Department from insisting on the clustering or merging of school systems to achieve racial balance. As 1977 ended, opponents of such a ban—especially in the Senate—fought successfully to insure that no legislative enactment would interfere with court enforcement of the Fifth or Fourteenth Amendments to the Constitution.

Outside the halls of Congress, a similar stalemate prevailed, as court-ordered busing served in numerous northern cities to help bring about defeat for proposed school-levy increases, and the existence of traditional locally funded public education itself came to be threatened. Clearly, as the 1970s waned, no answer was yet in sight as to how that landmark 1954 desegregation decision might finally and totally be put into effect throughout the United States.

Great Society schemes to deal with urban problems (including poverty) also sparked local-federal disagreement. Despite high hopes that a federal-urban "synthesis" had been forged in the 1960s, the war on poverty encountered considerable trouble routing federal money through Community Action Programs. The resentment of local power structures and middle-class whites who had fled to suburbia eventually helped to torpedo federally controlled urban policies. These failures and various pressures led Richard Nixon to seek greater local control over spending, producing his revenue-sharing State and Local Fiscal Assistance Act of October 1972. This scheme replaced some seventy categorical grant programs with five broad, block-grant programs, authorizing $30.2 billion over five years (two-thirds going to local governments, one-third to states). The local officials receiving the federal dollars fulfilled the fears of opponents of revenue sharing by reacting cautiously and used the money for one-shot capital outlays such as sewers and fire trucks, rather than for the funding of long-range, people-oriented programs. By late 1974, only 3 percent of these funds were going to the poor. Gerald Ford continued and even increased Nixon's revenue-sharing program, and the plan appeared well entrenched by the end of his term. The new Carter administration, owing more politically to the nation's urban centers, appeared to be inclined to help cities. Yet urban policy initiatives were not forthcoming from either the administration or the Democratic Congress in 1977; like school desegregation, the means for financing and solving the problems of urban America remained a perplexing issue.

Local authorities, however, paid a price for the money they received under revenue sharing. With local control of funds went local responsibility. When New York City faced financial disaster in 1975, President Ford proved basically unwilling to make any extensive federal commitment to help bail the city out of its troubles. Although he eventually backed an emergency "pay-as-you-go" credit arrangement patched together by Congress, his administration's assault on "profligate" Manhattan threatened to open up old rural-urban wounds and to undo the spirit as well as the limited results of the 1960s when Washington seemed aware of and eager to solve metropolitan problems.

By the late 1970s urban dilemmas were no closer to solution than they had been a decade earlier. It was increasingly clear to all that neighborhoods, cities, suburbs, and even metropolitan regions and states could not cope with some of these matters; only the federal government could act effectively. Yet something had to give. Either bureaucratic solutions out of Washington must demonstrate more respect for the strong attachment of Americans to the value of local control, or the spirit of "localism" must be diluted somewhat for the good of all concerned. Actually, the key to the problem lies buried in a hazy, romantic view of a rural, smalltown, or compact neighborhood—a past (rather than a present) cherished by congressmen, editors, and even the public at large. Yet the metropolitan dilemma has its roots in a quite different

J. P. Laffont/Sygma.

In the late 1970s black ghettos in most large American cities were little improved over their deplorable condition a decade earlier. Here, storefronts in the Bedford-Stuyvesant section in New York reflect the decay resulting from official inattention.

milieu: great migrations, overcrowded and unsafe tenements, bureaucratic nightmares, and racial and ethnic antagonisms—all alien and very disturbing to those dreaming the American Dream. Unless and until those experiencing the dilemma firsthand rise to positions of power or demonstrate clout at the ballot box, the "dreaming" probably will continue and so will incomplete solutions to very complex issues.

Rights in Recent America

The diverse federal programs and group activism of the 1960s seemed to promise diminishing inequality on the basis of race and sex, but by the late 1970s it was clear much remained to be done. Although blacks, Spanish-speaking Americans, and women made some economic gains, those institutions sympathetic to minority demands in the 1960s now seemed less so.

The Struggle for Equal Rights: Racial Minorities

Blacks, major beneficiaries of the civil rights revolution of the Kennedy-Johnson years, ceased to make significant advances under Presidents Nixon and Ford. "Blacks and their special problems have gone out of fashion in government, in politics and in civil concern, "*Newsweek* observed in 1973. Under Nixon all three branches of the federal government seemed to shun direct advocacy of the black cause, and the U.S. Civil Rights Commission complained in 1973 that civil rights enforcement was "not adequate or even close to it." Although the registration of black voters in the South increased by about ten times within the decade following passage of the 1965 Voting Rights Act, enforcement of its provisions was spotty throughout the region, and black turnout remained low. On the other hand, the Omnibus Crime Bill of 1970 carried forward the repressive side of the schizoid 1968 Civil Rights Act by beefing up police forces and stressing "law and order," so beloved by Nixon and Agnew.

Black economic progress slowed to a crawl in the 1970s, unemployment among blacks remained disproportionately high, and even their educational gains were threatened by continued inferior schooling. Nixon's vaunted efforts to aid "Black Capitalism" in the early part of the decade amounted to little; and, in fact, by executive order, he even abolished quotas for black employment under federal contracts. Neither the courts nor the Congress seemed inclined to counter this drift to the right, which apparently was condoned by the mass of American voters. Not surprisingly, Nixon got only about 13 percent of the black vote in 1972, nearly all of their ballots going instead to Democrat McGovern.

In view of these new realities, blacks applied various countertactics. Some continued lobbying or dickering with the white power structure and others, such as Chicago's Jesse Jackson, tried direct economic boycotts of companies that were doing business in black neighborhoods and refused to hire black employees. Political action, however, emerged as the most important vehicle for black advancement. "Politics," said Maynard Jackson (1938-   ), Atlanta's black mayor, "is the civil rights movement of the '70s." In essence, mass violence had been tried and found wanting; the only reasonable alternative in a time of federal hostility or disinterest was to build a political structure capable of effecting change at all levels of government. This meant direct involvement by blacks as mayors and state and national legislators, not just as protesters and members of pressure groups. It also meant using their votes to secure needed changes. After playing a major part (decisive, according to many analysts) in the election of Jimmy Carter in 1976, black leaders aggressively pressed their claims on the new Democratic administration. But since the President seemed to prefer addressing civil rights questions through legislative programs aimed at unemployment and welfare reform, blacks' goals remained largely unrealized in the late 1970s as the Carter legislative program spun its wheels.

The second largest minority—labeled the "Spanish-surnamed" by the 1950 Census and totaling nine millions by 1970—suffered a different plight, but the general outline of their experience is similar. Spanish-Americans, largely of Mexican, Puerto Rican, and Cuban origin and located primarily in the Southwest but also scattered in sizable concentrations in urban areas such as Chicago, New York, and Miami, were far less well organized than blacks. By the latter part of the 1960s, however, various groups were beginning to take shape among Chicanos (Mexican-Americans). The most notable advance was achieved by Cesar Chavez and his largely Spanish-speaking United Farmworkers. For the first time migrants in California and nearby states had found a means to express their grievances and be heard. Never-

Bob Fitch/Black Star.

The drive for Mexican-American rights in the late 1960s and early 1970s was tied closely to efforts to organize migrant farm workers in the Southwest. Shown here outside their headquarters in Delano, California, are staff members who helped the movement's leader, Cesar Chavez, to organize strikes and boycotts of such products as grapes and lettuce.

theless, continued Mexican immigration made full integration into American society an elusive goal; moreover, militant Chicano organizations—like black nationalists—did not always desire it, preferring to remain apart and culturally distinct.

Another champion of Spanish-speaking peoples was Reies Lopez Tijerina (1926-), a man whose aggressive scheme to reassert pre-1848 land claims in New Mexico led to frequent clashes with authorities in that state. Tijerina, who formed a series of alliances designed to achieve immediate land reform, took part in the Poor People's Campaign in Washington in 1968 and also has cooperated at times with Chavez and Rudulfo (Corky) Gonzales, another fighter for the rights of Spanish-speaking Americans who headed up the Denver-based Crusade for Justice. In 1967 Gonzales wrote the epic poem "I am Joaquin," an influential history of the Chicano experience that ends with the ringing phrase "I will endure."

Since World War II the movement of Puerto Ricans to the United States has ebbed and flowed, depending upon economic conditions. By 1970, 1.5 million Puerto Ricans had departed for the mainland, 900,000 of them living in New York City alone, almost twice as many people as reside in Puerto Rico's capital city of San Juan. At the same time, that commonwealth ruled by the U.S. has become home to thousands who have fled from Cuba and the Dominican Republic because of political unrest. Cubans, of course, have also migrated in large numbers to Florida, especially Miami. Aside from the politically inspired exodus from Cuba, these movements of Spanish-speaking peoples can be viewed part of a worldwide trend toward urbanization.

In general, American institutions have not been especially sympathetic to the stirrings of the Chicano and other Spanish-oriented movements; and, as several perceptive observers have noted, unlike blacks, Spanish-speaking Americans cannot draw upon any special reservoir of white guilt.

But a group that can make a strong and direct appeal to the white American conscience, though admittedly much smaller in numbers than either blacks or Mexican-Americans, is the American Indian. Pushed around for generations and finally tucked out of sight on reservations or forgotten in towns and cities, Indians have begun to assert their rights as a result of the protests of other minorities. The problem is, their grievances often have a territorial basis that can endanger the landholdings of millions of Americans and numerous giant corporations as well. Ineptly drawn or fraudulent treaties are returning to haunt residents of Maine, Massachusetts, and the Pacific Northwest. As a result, although whites may have a keen sense of guilt concerning how their forefathers mistreated native Americans, they are far from agreement on how to erase that stain on their collective past with compensation in the form of land and money.

Indian protest has its roots firmly planted in centu-

Stephen Shames/Black Star.

Cesar Chavez
(1927–)

Cesar Chavez, a somewhat unlikely leader of an unlikely cause, was born in 1927 to Mexican-American migrant parents living near Yuma, Arizona. During the Depression his farmworker family moved to California where from early childhood Chavez worked in fields and orchards. He received little formal education, served in the U.S. Navy (1944–1945), and then returned to the cottonfields, orchards, and vineyards once more.

In 1952 Chavez became a paid staff member of a local self-help movement based in Delano, California. By 1958 he was general director of this group designed to increase voter registration and coordinate community-wide activities. Four years later, however, unhappy with such middle-class goals and lack of concern for migrant labor, he quit and established his National Farm Workers Association (NFWA) with the aim of aiding those unprotected by federal regulations and thus at the mercy of seasonal employers. By the mid-1960s the Association represented 1,700 families.

Under the leadership of Chavez, the NFWA joined with others to form the United Farm Workers Organizing Committee of the AFL-CIO. And, adopting techniques used by the civil rights movement—nonviolence, boycotts, church meetings, marches—the UFW in 1970 forced table grape growers to listen to their demands. With somewhat less success, members then tried a lettuce boycott and organization of citrus workers in both California and Florida.

Throughout these campaigns, Chavez—a short, stocky, dedicated man with jet black hair, father of eight children—has kept his salary low. He works out of a Mexican-American barrio in Delano, a sunbaked town of 13,000 located 140 miles north of Los Angeles; and, although less than ten percent of all migrant workers now are organized, Chavez fights on, a symbol of the rising strength of the Spanish-speaking "voice" of the Southwest. "If you're outraged at conditions," he once remarked, "then you can't possibly be free or happy until you devote all your time to changing them . . . . we can't change anything if we want to hold on to a good job, a good way of life, and avoid sacrifice." ■

ries of broken promises, the example of the black civil rights movement, and the rapidly expanding numbers of red Americans; by growing much faster than the population as a whole, Indians have nearly doubled their numbers in the two decades since 1950. By 1970 there were 800,000, about evenly divided between reservation and city life. At the same time, their situation was much worse than that of any other identifiable group since the annual income of an Indian family was $1,000 less than that of blacks and Indians had an unemployment rate ten times the national average.

In 1953, after decades of vacillation, the federal government actively embraced a program designed to make Indians full, participating citizens and to end their status "as wards of the United States." This meant the expansion of state laws over reservations and the demise of tribes, some of whom, such as the Menominees of Wisconsin and the Klamaths of Oregon, held title to rich timberlands. Many of these and similar areas soon were in the hands of lumbermen and developers. Within five years federal officials began to have second thoughts once more, and the Kennedy administration reverted to New Deal-like programs designed to protect Indian lands and foster cultural heritage.

These steps produced some results, including a national Indian conference in 1961, and an end to passive acceptance of "things as they are." In the mid-1960s Indians in Washington state (with federal help) overcame local opposition and enforced ancient fishing rights. In November 1969 eighty young Indians seized Alcatraz Island in San Francisco Bay (an obsolete penal institution) and, citing a Sioux treaty giving them title to unused federal land, began a nineteen-month sit-in. Although this effort ended in failure, the publicity engendered stirred widespread interest, prompting Nixon to name Louis R. Bruce, Jr., a Mohawk-Ogala Sioux who was a Manhattan advertising executive, to be Commissioner of Indian Affairs.

This new mood of action inspired Lehman Brightman, a Sioux-Creek and head of the San Francisco-based United Native Americans, to speak out forcefully against OEO programs, the Bureau of Indian Affairs, and especially what he viewed as a "white colonial" education policy. In 1969, Vine Deloria, Jr., a Colorado-educated Sioux, published the first of three stern appeals to permit Indians to develop their own way at their own pace: *Custer Died for Your Sins: An Indian Manifesto.*

Indian protest in the 1970s was much more violent, culminating in seizure of the Bureau of Indian Affairs in Washington (which cost Commissioner Bruce his job) and startling confrontations in South Dakota led by the American Indian Movement (AIM). First organized in Minneapolis, AIM dispensed with picket lines and printed appeals and set up patrols to protect Indians living in Minneapolis–St. Paul from alleged police harassment and illegal arrest. In February 1973, leaders Dennis Banks and Russell Means expanded AIM's influence to Custer and Rapid City, South Dakota, where local law enforcement appeared to be discriminatory. Both communities witnessed outbreaks of violence and arrests as a result of this drive for equal justice, but nothing compared to the confrontation that developed a short time later at nearby Wounded Knee. Seizing this symbolic bit of ground, AIM issued sweeping demands for reform, even taking its appeal to the United Nations, initiating a prolonged siege, more bloodshed, and months of courtroom debate.

Although it is too soon to evaluate the full impact of these outbursts, several facts are apparent. The quiet, placid, blanket-encased Indian who once petitioned for an audience with the Great White Father is no more. Even "traditionalists" among Indians have endorsed AIM's goals, and it is obvious that activism now is an acceptable mode of behavior among both rural and urban Indians.

The Struggle for Equal Rights: Women

American women, no minority by numerical standards and often called "the largest minority," nevertheless share with various racial groups a history of social, educational, and economic discrimination. They, too, developed a new consciousness in the militant, reform-oriented 1960s. Like minorities, women experienced rough going in the 1970s and, despite tangible gains, seemed to reach an impasse of sorts as their demands stirred less and less response.

Several diverse factors fed female activism after 1960. These included demographic changes (a decreasing birthrate, especially for second and third children, which resulted in smaller families and fewer home responsibilities and more women with college degrees entering the work force), efforts by some politicians to interest women in government as an occupation, publication of Betty Friedan's *The Feminine Mystique* (1963) and similar

Michael Abramson/Black Star.

The high point of militance among American Indians in the 1970s came at Wounded Knee, South Dakota, scene of a massacre of Indians nearly a century earlier.

works examining women's role in America, and the increasing momentum and example of the civil rights movement.

The Feminine Mystique by Friedan was a brilliant analysis of the post-World War II back-to-the-home-and-kitchen movement. In her opinion, society conned American women into believing housework, babies, and suburban living were the only paths to female fulfillment, a development she thought had produced considerable frustration, tension, and tragedy.

Two women, Kate Millett (1934-) and Germaine Greer (1939-) have added their voices to this movement as it embraced a great variety of goals other than simply total equality for women and an end to "male chauvinism." These include legalized abortion, use of terms such as "spokesperson" (instead of the male-oriented "spokesman"), acceptance of the abbreviation "Ms." rather than "Miss" or "Mrs." and, of course, advocacy of the Equal Rights Amendment to the Constitution. Millet, sometimes called "the high priestess of woman's lib," published her Columbia University doctoral dissertation in late 1970 entitled *Sexual Politics.* Born into a Catholic family and raised in Minnesota, she claimed that relations between the sexes are little more than broadly defined "politics." By means of history, conditioning, and attitudes, the male of the species has developed and maintained an undeserved dominance. A year later, Australian Greer turned out a racy, acerbic work entitled *The Female Eunuch.* Taking a somewhat different tack, she maintained that society had castrated women by assigning them passive, insipid roles. She proposed not rebellion but a revolutionary change in spirit that would enable

Bettye Lane.

Betty Friedan

(1921–   )

"Mother of the current feminist movement," Betty Naomi Goldstein was born in Peoria, Illinois, in 1921 and educated at Smith College and Berkeley. In 1947 she married Carl Friedan and during the next decade raised three children in a New York suburb while doing occasional free-lance writing. In 1957 she conducted a poll of Smith College classmates and uncovered what she called "the problem that has no name." An article Betty Friedan subsequently published in *Good Housekeeping* ("Women are People, Too!") aroused considerable interest, leading to her best-known book, *The Feminine Mystique* (1963). In it she argued that educators, outdated Freudian psychology, and mass media promote an image of women that stifles their creativity and intellect, wasting very valuable human potential.

The fame of this nonstop talker described as "a combination of Hermione Gingold and Bette Davis" was immediate. *The Feminine Mystique* sold over 1.5 million copies in a decade and was translated into thirteen languages. Ms. Friedan soon was on the lecture circuit, and in 1966 became a cofounder of the National Organization of Women (NOW) and served as its president until 1970. NOW, a middle- and upper-middle class, educated group, has remained basically oriented toward legal reforms: equal pay, legalization of abortion, child-care centers for working mothers, and nondiscriminatory hiring practices. In the early 1970s, however, members joined with other organizations more political in nature.

In essence, Ms. Friedan is a moderate reformer who, until 1963, led an ordinary, upwardly mobile suburban life. Since becoming a national (even international) figure, she has faced considerable criticism. Her 1969 divorce provided ammunition for antifeminists who charge that she and her followers are merely women who cannot "make it" in traditional roles, while leftist feminists heap scorn upon both her views and her tactics. ■

---

women to direct their energies free of repression. Less anti male in her approach, Greer attracted widespread attention, even winning the approval of many who rejected more strident aspects of woman's liberation.

Throughout the 1960s women mounted a drive to knock down barriers to equal employment. The 1963 report of Kennedy's Commission on the Status of Women, entitled simply *American Woman,* provided a blueprint for government activity by and on behalf of women. And, on July 24th of that year, the President

Sidney Harris.

S. Harris
"I'D LIKE TO BE A TRUCKDRIVER LIKE MS FROBISHER."

The women's movement of the late 1960s & 1970s led to significant changes in women's expectations and roles, and in the ways they were perceived in American society.

issued a memorandum barring discrimination against women in federal government, emphasizing that future appointments and promotions had to be made "without regard to sex except in unusual cases." This reversed a 1934 opinion of the Attorney General that government agencies and departments could limit certain jobs to one sex or the other.

Women enjoyed limited gains even before their movement became a widely recognized force. These included a federal Equal Pay Act in 1963 and addition of the word "sex" to the 1964 Civil Rights Act's Title VII, "Equal Employment Opportunity." However, these gains were more symbolic than actual, and in 1966 Betty Friedan and twenty-six other female activitists organized the National Organization of Women (NOW). Thus, after a long period of dormancy, there was once again a militant women's movement. In 1968, NOW attempted to pressure the major political parties to endorse a "Bill of Rights" for women; simultaneously, a feminist movement appeared within the ranks of more militant radical minority groups as more and more women became fed up with their position as subordinate ("prone," Stokely Carmichael termed it). Not always in agreement, at times these two diverse forces—women seeking female rights per se and their sisters marching under other radical banners—could cooperate to achieve short-term gains.

By 1972, feminists had made some progress, although institutional safeguards often were halfhearted and uneven. Many state "protective" laws on behalf of women, actually discriminatory in nature, were removed, and the Ninety-second Congress produced a bumper crop of legislation in 1971-1972, some of which Nixon vetoed. But most important of all, lawmakers such as Bella Abzug (D-New York) and Martha Griffiths (R-Michigan) secured passage of an Equal Rights Amendment to the Constitution (ERA), first introduced in Congress in 1923. Approved by votes of 84-8 in the Senate and 354-24 in the House, it said, "Equality of rights under the law shall not be denied or abridged by the United States or by any state on account of sex." The most vociferous opponent was North Carolina's Sam Ervin who thought the measure unnecessary because protection was already granted by the Fourteenth Amendment. Shortly before the Senate gave its approval, thereby setting off demonstrations by ERA supporters crowding the galleries, Ervin said women were being crucified "upon a cross of dubious equality and specious uniformity." After a fast start that saw ERA win approval in 28 state legislatures, momentum ceased, and in January 1973 a national "Stop ERA" movement appeared, apparently backed in part by funds from conservative groups. By the late 1970s, with success in sight, ERA proponents mounted a convention boycott against several states that had refused to approve the Amendment, an economic weapon that cut off millions in convention spending in several major centers such as Chicago, Miami, and Las Vegas. Still, with ratification necessary within seven years of its proposal to the states (by March 1979), ERA was in deep trouble; by 1978 thirty-five (of a needed thirty-eight) states had ratified, but two of those had rescinded their action. Legal and constitutional questions abounded: Could Congress extend the seven-year period allowed for ratification? Could states reverse their ratifying actions? Nevertheless, despite disappointments, discussion concerning ERA created a new climate of opinion and demonstrated—in spite of superficial arguments about drafting women in wartime and banning separate washrooms for men and women—that serious interest in the fundamental rights of women existed among voters from all walks of life.

The fight to legalize abortion was one of the most dramatic and important of feminist successes in the 1970s, although problems remained late in the decade. In 1973 the Supreme Court in *Roe* v. *Wade* declared existing state antiabortion laws unconstitutional. By 1974 about 900,000 legal and 300,000 illegal abortions were being performed throughout the nation, reversing a pre-1970 ratio of 100 illegal abortions for every one performed legally. Some groups, especially those associated with the Catholic Church, continued to press Congress for an antiabortion Amendment to the Constitution; even though public opinion appeared to be evenly divided on this issue, Congress, demonstrating its usual reluctance to pioneer in any direction that might gain as many votes as it lost, approved a prohibition against the use of federal funds for abortions. The question of the use of other public funds for abortions was left to the states to decide. Other basic questions remained: What was the responsibility of a doctor for the aborted fetus? In the case of legally married persons, must the husband consent to an abortion?

In general, in the late 1970s the woman's rights movement seemed to have greater vitality than any other major protest movement and a more substantial political base, thanks especially to female members of Congress such as Shirley Chisholm (D-New York). Yet the cause faced opposition from traditionalists symbolized by the Stop ERA forces and movements such as Fascinating Womanhood and Total Woman. Without any doubt, something vital and important was occurring among American women which was altering their basic attitudes. Referring to *Ms.*, a slick and influential publication born of the movement, one feminist shrewdly observed, "There is a female mind-set on those glossy pages slipping into American homes concealed in bags of groceries like tarantulas on banana boats. . . . Curious girl children will accidentally discover feminism in *Ms.* the way we stumbled onto sex in *Ladies Home Journal.*" It is a giant step from *Ladies Home Journal* to *Ms.* and tarantulas might be an inappropriate symbol of feminist values, yet no one could deny that American women, like other minority groups, were displaying new toughness and new assurance and voicing new demands.

Courts, Laws, and Individual Rights

The 1960s witnessed a virtual revolution in American justice. The activist Warren Court staunchly upheld the primacy of individual rights; ironically, at the same time the executive branch and the Congress were busily sketching out new dimensions of federal power and authority. Following the election of Nixon on a law-and-order platform in 1968, reaction set in to some extent. Yet, even though federal legislation and Supreme Court decisions of the 1970s altered prevailing trends of the previous decade somewhat, no reversal occurred. And

Owen Franken/Sygma.

By the late 1970s, the woman's movement—like the earlier civil rights movement—evidenced a diversity of leadership and objectives. Pictured here at the National Women's Conference in Houston (November 1977) are Bella Abzug (left) and Gloria Steinem, women of differing style and beliefs. The Conference, held five years after congressional passage of ERA (but with the amendment still unratified), adopted a twenty-six point program that echoed many unfulfilled objectives of the early movement.

although evil men in high places obviously could "bend" the Constitution to comport with their immediate needs and could find justification for illegal action ("national security," for example), individual freedom under law remained basically secure.

The Warren Court worked hard for the rights of the individual citizens in three vital areas: desegregation and antidiscrimination, free speech and due process, and equal rights for all. During the 1960s several landmark decisions strengthened protections against self-incrimination and state wiretapping. An especially noteworthy case was *Miranda* v. *Arizona* (1966) in which the justices held that before police interrogated a suspect they had to advise him that anything he said could be used against him in court and that he had the right (1) to remain silent, (2) to obtain a lawyer of his own choice, and (3) to have an attorney appointed to assist him if he were indigent. If such procedures were not followed, the Court warned, an individual's Fifth Amendment rights concerning self-incrimination could be violated.

Among the most important of the cases opening up the door to equal political rights was *Baker* v. *Carr* (1962)—the "one man, one vote case"—which, in time, forced redistricting in scores of states; in effect, rural-dominated legislatures were forced to catch up with migration trends and make county and city votes as nearly equal as possible.

The election results of 1968 were as much a reaction to the Warren Court and its decisions as they were to Lyndon Johnson's policies. After a decade during which "Impeach Earl Warren" billboards appeared throughout the South, candidate Nixon promised to restore "basic values" to American life by means of conservative appointments to the Supreme Court. Four years later a Nixon fundraiser boasted to potential contributors that the four men Nixon already had named to the Supreme Court (Chief Justice Warren E. Burger and Associate Justices Harry A. Blackmun, Lewis F. Powell, Jr., and William H. Rehnquist) could be expected to render a "strict" interpretation of the Constitution and protect the interests of "the average law-abiding citizen." He added that their collective influence "had shifted the balance away from protection of the criminal."

Yet, in essence, the Burger Court proved to be more middle-of-the-road than strict constructionist. In contrast, the Congress enacted certain repressive law-and-order bills such as the pretrial detention provision found in the District of Columbia's Court Reform and Criminal Procedure Act of 1970. This measure, hotly debated in the Senate, drew fire from many liberals, and another section of the Act allowing juveniles to be found delinquent "by the preponderence of the evidence" was invalidated by the Supreme Court only a few days after enactment. Yet for the most part, the judicial branch did not match the law-and-order spirit of the legislative. True, the justices reduced somewhat the safeguards thrown around individual rights by Earl Warren and his associates, but they did not remove them. Interestingly, while the Nixon administration engaged in a virtual orgy of wiretapping and of the use of agent provocateurs, crime statistics in general—and especially those for violent crime—continued to rise. Law-and-order legislation advocated by those busy subverting its provisions somehow failed to deter others for whom it was primarily designed; in short, both white- and blue-collar crime continued apace.

Even before Watergate began to dominate American life, the Burger Court acted in behalf of civil liberties. Particularly notable were its June 1972 decisions against the death penalty and wiretapping without a court order in domestic security cases. In three capital punishment cases (*Furman* v. *Georgia, Jackson* v. *Georgia,* and *Branch* v. *Texas*) by a 5-4 vote the justices declared, in effect, that the death penalty as then imposed in each of the fifty states was unconstitutional. The majority's reasoning varied in these three cases but included observations that execution was "cruel and inhuman punishment," that it was "unusually severe and degrading punishment" sometimes inflicted arbitrarily and in an unconstitutional manner, and that laws relating to the death penalty allowed both judges and juries to exert discretion and discrimination. In *U.S.* v. *U.S. District Court of Eastern Michigan* the justices rejected Justice Department claims that it did not have to get court approval to conduct electronic surveillance of persons or groups thought to be subversive. "If the threat is too subtle or complex for our senior law enforcement officers to convey its significance to a court," said Justice Powell, "one may question whether there is probable cause for surveillance." And in two other cases (*Gelbard* v. *U.S., U.S.* v. *Egan*) the Supreme Court ruled that a grand jury witness did not risk contempt if he refused to testify until the federal government proved that evidence in question had not been obtained by means of illegal electronic surveillance.

Even when ruling on busing and abortion, the justices left loopholes wide enough to permit lawmakers to "re-define" those issues if they chose to do so. The Court clearly was no pliant tool of law-and-order forces nor was it (as Richard Nixon learned in July 1974) fearful of ruling against the President of the United States.

The 1970s were not without serious efforts to circumscribe individual rights. The Justice Department in the Nixon administration, for example, routinely used the device of grand jury investigations to disrupt legitimate political activities of American citizens seen as administration "enemies." While the practice seemed to fall into abeyance after Nixon's resignation, no corrective legislation was offered to make it impossible in the future.

Proposals to reform the nation's criminal justice code, long overdue, aroused acrimonious debate in the middle years of the decade. Liberals were especially concerned by new definitions of espionage, sabotage, and insanity and by provisions for the death penalty for those convicted of certain crimes. At the same time, new militancy was evident among groups determined to assert their legitimate rights (as they interpreted them) under the Constitution. No longer did the defense of individual liberty rest solely upon the shoulders of a handful of liberal-minded attorneys and organizations such as the American Civil Liberties Union. Men and women from all walks of life were speaking out and demanding their individual rights as guaranteed by the law of the land; perhaps that, after all, was the best protection for the rights of others and for those of future generations, a bright, encouraging sign at a time when basic trends were both unclear and indistinct.

The State of American Democracy

The United States of America is now beginning, if one is willing to count the years of revolution and confederation before 1789, its third century. Nearly all the problems faced at the onset of this new era are related directly to the Cold War and to responsibilities and pressures created by world leadership. These include secrecy in government, the burdens of national defense, the role of the federal government in the economy, as well as strains placed upon the traditional political structure by this new internationalism. One should remember, perhaps, that the last dilemma is quite new: only since 1945 has America played at the world power game in any real sense—and the same may be said of her most stalwart adversary, the U.S.S.R.

Secrecy and Democracy

Diplomacy is, of course, largely a matter of secrets and, as America's overseas involvement has increased, so have both diplomacy and secrecy. This is a trend that frightens those who believe a democracy, unlike a dictatorship, should be open and above board in all its dealings, proud that it has nothing to hide. Yet, in a sense, how a foe in any contest operates sets some of the ground rules for all those who choose to participate. In 1947, because of the critical nature of the Cold War, the Truman administration reverted to some of the operational techniques of World War II days and established the Central Intelligence Agency (CIA) and a National Security Council, thus removing many top-level matters from the scrutiny of all but a few members of Congress.

For a decade or so no one asked questions. The CIA grew in power and influence but Americans generally feared Communism more than they feared the secrecy that the experts of the executive branch presumably had well in hand. The first jarring note was the Bay of Pigs (planned under Eisenhower and executed with singular ineptness under Kennedy), which turned out to be the CIA'a first public disaster. Within the next few years books appeared warning that the CIA had become the nucleus of "an invisible government" with 200,000 employees spending billions each year (largely wherever and however they wished) and with secret ties to various universities and foundations. Although key spokesmen in both the Eisenhower and Kennedy administrations obviously lied to the American public during the late 1950s and early 1960s concerning the U-2 incident, Bay of Pigs, and U.S. activities in Indonesia and Guatemala, these warnings went unheeded until Lyndon Johnson got mired down in Southeast Asia. When both LBJ and Nixon overreacted to what they viewed as "radical" protest, the idea of "an invisible government" aided by a cadre of domestic "secret police" suddenly became all too believable. Rumors of illegal wiretaps, complaints concerning the highhandedness of the FBI's aging director, J. Edgar Hoover, and growing unease about the insulation of American security policy formulation helped awaken widespread opposition to "covert" official operations.

In June 1971, Daniel Ellsberg, an analyst for the Rand Corporation, provided the *New York Times* with what became known as the *Pentagon Papers.* This "top secret" study of U.S. activity in Southeast Asia from 1945 to 1967 had been prepared by a special task force created by then Secretary of Defense Robert McNamara. These materials were a dual threat to the federal government because they revealed pre-1964 involvement in Vietnam in great detail as well as numerous official deceptions as the fighting escalated after that date. The Justice Department tried successively to muzzle the *New York Times, Washington Post,* and *Boston Globe* in order to prevent publication, but the Burger Court ruled against such restraints. By a 6–3 vote (*New York Times Company* v. *U.S., U.S.* v. *The Washington Post*), the justices said the federal government had failed to show sufficient cause for its request for various court orders. Justice Black, joined by Douglas, wrote that the purpose of the press was to serve the governed, not the governors. "The government's power to censure the press was abolished so that the press would remain forever free to censure the government." Burger, who dissented along with Harlan and Blackmun, noted that a newspaper, like any citizen, had a specific duty with respect to stolen property or secret documents: "That duty, I had thought—perhaps naively—was to report forthwith, to responsible public officers. This duty rests on taxi drivers, justices, and the *New York Times.*"

Although publication went forward (no doubt gaining thousands of converts for the antiwar cause), the federal government prosecuted Ellsberg and a *Times* reporter, Neil Russo, for conspiracy, misappropriation of government property, and violations of the Espionage Act. The trial itself, however, became a symbol of covert government activity, the whole affair ending in a mistrial because White House hirelings broke into the office of Ellsberg's psychiatrist to get "evidence" against Ellsberg and the government illegally tapped his phone. Also, the *Pentagon Papers* break-in became hopelessly entangled with the Watergate scandal since a number of individuals had leading roles in both dramas.

Covert FBI and CIA operations disclosed during the Watergate hearings and trials fueled further investigations, as did press reports late in 1974 of CIA involvement in both illegal and domestic surveillance and attempts to assassinate foreign leaders. In 1975 President Ford set up a task force under the direction of Vice President Nelson Rockefeller to study these matters. At the same time, Senate and House select committees began a belated inquiry into just what the CIA and FBI actually had been doing for a quarter of a century. The results tended to confirm more rumors and charges than they exploded, although testimony often stretched one's imagination to the breaking point. There apparently were, for example, at least eight CIA plots between 1960 and 1965 to assassinate Cuba's Fidel Castro. These schemes included, among other things, poison pens, deadly pills, and poison cigars. One plan in 1960 involved dusting the Cuban leader's shoes with a powder that would cause his beard to fall out. If beardless, the CIA reasoned, Castro would lose forever his charismatic image. (Who would play the role of Delilah was not clear.) Congressmen also uncovered a concentrated and incredibly cruel effort by J. Edgar Hoover to discredit Martin Luther King, Jr., a campaign that once tried to provoke the noted black leader to take his own life. Other FBI "counterintelligence" (COINTELPRO) operations were directed against such targets as the New Left, the Ku Klux Klan, the Communist party, and civil rights and antiwar organizations.

The upshot of these disclosures was demand for greater control by Congress of the CIA and the FBI—although Capitol Hill was partly to blame for these excesses, having "looked the other way" for years on end—and still more investigations of some of the more traumatic events of the 1960s. The assassination of John F. Kennedy was an especially fruitful area for controversy as scores of theories were propounded. Competing interpretations were many and diverse (possible CIA-Mafia connections, the existence of "two Oswalds," possible Cuban retribution for plots against Castro), and contained enough plausibility to keep alive public suspicions that the Warren Commission had itself engaged in a monumental coverup. Such suspicion appeared likely to continue until some sort of reinvestigation was launched by Congress.

These inquiries and widespread public doubts of the 1970s revealed that Vietnam and Watergate had taken a very heavy toll. No longer could any government spokesman (even a President) be certain that all who heard his voice would believe his words. Official "truths" were dissected and examined much more carefully than before. The traumas of assassination, antiwar protest, and White House corruption were unnerving, but as a result,

Wide World.

J. Edgar Hoover
(1895–1972)

Few individuals have cast such a long, controversial, and elusive shadow upon American life as J. Edgar Hoover, a tenacious bulldog of a man. Born in Washington, D.C., he was known as "Speed" while in high school. Although he weighed only 110 pounds, he headed the school cadet corps and was valedictorian of his class when he graduated in 1913. During the next four years Hoover was a messenger at the Library of Congress, studied law at George Washington University (A.B. 1916, M.A. 1917), and began working for the Justice Department.

When war broke out, he shunned active service and turned his attention to an extensive survey of German population centers throughout the nation. The findings of his research (the first of many such efforts) came to the attention of Hoover's superiors, and he was soon on his way to greater heights. In 1919 he was named director of a new antiradical unit named the General Intelligence Division. Two years later Hoover became assistant director of the Bureau of Investigation (a body established in 1908), and in 1924 when that unit took the more familiar name of the Federal Bureau of Investigation (FBI), he became its chief.

For the next forty-eight years, one president after another dutifully reappointed J. Edgar Hoover, some out of habit, others out of fear, as the man's power grew. Hoover's happiest days were those before World War II when he built up a truly professional agent corps, elevating so-called G-men to national hero status as they thwarted crime and blasted away at dastardly public enemies. However, Hoover's penchant for publicity, nightclub life, and absolute secrecy—and his innate ability to see criminals and saboteurs almost anywhere—also won him critics and detractors. Liberals were especially distressed by his extralegal swashbuckling stance and disregard for the rights of those accused of wrongdoing.

Hoover's suspicious nature and his firm grip on the FBI comported well with the McCarthy era that followed World War II but ill-fitted him for events that unfolded in succeeding decades. Determined to remain at the FBI helm at any price, he compiled dossiers on congressmen, senators—anyone who might challenge his authority—and he began to use illegal means to subvert anything that in his opinion was subversive.

After this bachelor recluse died suddenly in May 1972, the facade he had created began to crumble, aided immeasurably by FBI involvement in the Watergate affair. Although the organization that was Hoover's lifework experienced very difficult days, its fortresslike headquarters in Washington stands as a memorial to his dedication and zeal and a constant reminder that even a democracy must use secrecy to protect itself from both external and internal enemies. The lofty walls of the J. Edgar Hoover Building also should alert Americans to the fact that watchdogs, especially old and wily ones, must be watched with considerable care. ■

American democracy was revitalized. For the first time since the birth of the "secret government" in the early days of the Cold War, proposals for its control gained strong popular support. Members of Congress and the public alike began to recognize the need to bring intelligence budgets out into the open, to legislate the boundaries of authority for such agencies, and to set up institutional safeguards for the rights of private citizens against possible misuse of power by the FBI, the IRS, and other arms of the federal government. Even if such reforms might be difficult to frame and slow in coming, these pressures showed that Americans were increasingly insisting on their constitutional rights, a demonstration that the democratic process was not likely to be subverted in the United States.

The Problems of National Defense

Like government secrecy, the burdens of national defense also troubled many Americans in the 1960s and 1970s. In terms of dollar outlays alone, the increase in cost was staggering: $43.9 billion in 1960, $50.7 billion in 1965, $78 billion in 1970. For much of the defense buildup, the Vietnam War was, of course, directly responsible. Estimates of the total cost of that conflict ranged widely, but direct costs alone may have come to approximately $171 billion between 1965 and 1974; depending on how indirect costs are defined, the total long-range cost could be five times that figure.

The end of the Vietnam War brought some relief but did not seem to check the growth of defense spending. With inflation continuing apace, defense costs in 1975 soared to $93 billion. Moreover, for all the talk in the Carter administration about reducing federal spending, defense was the area least likely to suffer cuts. The pessimistic estimate of the *New York Times* that defense costs would mount to $150 billion by 1980 seemed unlikely to come true, but the costs of continuing the nation's Cold War defense posture were truly enormous. The only prospect for limiting those costs was the rather dim hope that the successive SALT agreements might result in reductions in the American and Russian nuclear arsenals and thus might reduce the dollars needed to maintain those arsenals.

Defense—specifically the Vietnam War—also exacted a tremendous toll in human terms during the 1960s and 1970s. Some of those who resisted and interfered with the draft in the late 1960s were indicted, convicted, and sent to prison; others fled overseas to live. Within the armed forces, opposition to the war sometimes led to desertion, and by 1970 nearly 100,000 men in uniform had quit the struggle. Many more expressed their displeasure by merely going absent without leave (AWOL), but returned or were apprehended within thirty days, thus escaping the much more serious charge of desertion. In all, more than 450,000 servicemen of the Vietnam era received less-than-honorable discharges, a status that could deny them GI benefits and cause them considerable difficulty later when seeking employment.

Some of these individuals took to the streets and actively crusaded against government policies. On one occasion, a thousand ex-servicemen, representing Vietnam Veterans Against the War, marched in Washington, returned their service decorations to Congress, and knelt, fists clenched and upraised in a symbol of protest, at Arlington Cemetery. Most of the 2.6 million veterans (except perhaps a small number of POWs whose dramatic return was televised in January-February 1973) received no hero's welcome from American society. GI benefits proved inadequate in an inflationary economy, and a disturbed, guilt-ridden society often viewed them as "hired killers" from an immoral war. The irony was that those who first refused to become "hired killers" bore the greatest stigma: that of draft dodger or deserter.

President Ford's amnesty-clemency program of September 1974 aimed at permitting reentry into American life for some of these men by means of an oath of allegiance and up to twenty-four months of alternative service. Some 15,000 young men eventually sought pardons, but over 100,000 of those eligible spurned this olive branch as essentially meaningless because the offer contained so many restrictions and qualifications. Amnesty became an issue once again during the 1976 presidential campaign. Candidate Jimmy Carter, speaking at an American Legion convention, aroused intense feelings by promising that, if elected, he would grant a blanket pardon to draft evaders. In January 1977, he made good on the promise, issuing such a pardon as his first executive order. Those who had engaged in violence and military desertion were excluded, but their cases could be individually reviewed. After some initial furor, the opposition subsided, and what had been a divisive issue receded from public view.

As a result of unprecedented defense costs, structural problems appeared in American life, notably the

Michael Abramson/Black Star.

This April 1971 demonstration in Washington, D.C. typified the many antiwar demonstrations led by those who had fought in Vietnam and become disillusioned. This was the first war in U.S. history to produce such visible opposition among its veterans.

New York Daily News Photo.

In contrast to the masses of disillusioned veterans were those, like the returning troops pictured above, who tended to view the Vietnam War as similar to earlier U.S. wars—winnable, and perhaps even won.

military-industrial complex that Eisenhower had deplored so eloquently in his final address to the nation early in 1961. The space program of the 1960s, combined with ongoing weapon expenditures, created an enormous defense-dependent sector within the American economy. The practices of this complex, many of them inherited from World War II days, were as disturbing as its size: cost-plus and negotiated contracts leading to many overruns, substantial waste, and contract favoritism all played into the hands of the nation's largest corporations. By the early 1970s the military-industrial complex—waxing fat and complacent as a result of the Cold War and the Vietnam War—was eating up $40 billion a year, roughly half of the annual defense budget. At the same time, one witnessed the strange spectacle of some conglomerates offering millions to foreign officials in order to get business and—if endangered by inept management—running to Congress for salvation, arguing that their collapse would be a heavier blow than the U.S. economy could sustain. This vast spending created, of course, a natural and very influential voter constituency—and consequently a momentum of its own. In 1970, for example, California's defense plant workers wore buttons bearing the warning "Don't knock the war that feeds you"; and, in a jocular way, several senators were known not by their states but by the industries located in the states they represented—for example, Henry Jackson (D-Washington) became known as the "Senator from Boeing" (the aircraft company is located in Seattle).

Yet the complex had its critics, typified by Democratic Senator William Proxmire, a gadfly from Wisconsin, who in 1969 commissioned and publicized a report showing that 2,072 high-ranking officers drawing substantial pensions were employed by the top 100 contract-holding corporations doing business with their old friends at the Pentagon. Although Congress remained basically reluctant throughout the 1960s to criticize either such cozy relationships or defense spending in general, in the 1970s military spenders could no longer count upon automatic approval from either Capitol Hill or the White House. When President Carter scrapped plans in 1977 to build the huge and very costly B-1 bomber, Congress, by a narrow margin, backed him up.

Other changes in attitudes and practices emerged from the Southeast Asian experience. In 1973 a transitional draft lottery which had been set up by Richard Nixon in late 1969 gave way to a new all-volunteer Army. A step forward in some ways, this new military arrangement presented problems since many young men in the service thought of themselves primarily as civilians who were temporarily in uniform, not as career soldiers. Some Americans (almost always much too old to be affected by their own proposals) continued to demand universal national service, scorning both a draft lottery and a volunteer army. To some extent, these arguments were based in racial and class attitudes, and those who supported such arguments frequently feared that army ranks would be filled largely by minority, poor, and ill-educated youth; such groups had always joined up in time of peace.

Also, by the late 1970s the Pentagon's word no longer had as much impact as in previous decades. The reasons were obvious. Nothing succeeds like success and in Vietnam the United States Army had not succeeded. This led to internal bickering and efforts to find scapegoats, not cures. At the same time, the detente, balance-of-power approach advocated successively by the Nixon, Ford, and Carter administrations, together with U.S. disengagement from some overseas commitments, dictated a diminishing role for Pentagon generals. In this situation, of course, lay the danger of potential military weakness and ineffectiveness should a real emergency occur.

For all of its trauma and discord, the Vietnam experience and its excesses seem to have provided an opportunity for sober, rational analysis of military expenditures and activity by both Congress and the public. The burdens of national defense, approaching surrealistic levels in the quarter-century after Korea and threatening to damage American institutions and the lives of American citizens, perhaps could now be alleviated somewhat.

The foreign policy of the Carter administration began in very much this spirit. While the President did considerable traveling in his first year in office and attempted to play a role in the search for peace in the Middle East, other administration actions indicated its commitment to a low international profile. In pursuing a second SALT accord and successfully negotiating a Panama Canal treaty that gave control of the canal to Panama by the year 2000, Carter gave evidence of wanting to lessen the post-World War II tendency to American interventionism. Yet in pressing such policies, even a President had to be careful, so powerful had the defense establishment become in American society.

Transformation and Crises in the Capitalist Order

The basic "soundness" of the American economic system is attested by continued economic growth and expansion since 1960, resulting in a Gross National Product (GNP) of $1.15 trillion by the early 1970s. Yet there are also obvious structural problems: increasing inequalities among both corporations and individuals, dangers to the environment, limitations on resources, declining public control over private engines for profit, and seeming government irresolution in the face of changing economic conditions. Finally, the "moral relativism" of Watergate era politics—"everybody cheats and lies a bit now and then, you know, it's part of the American way of doing things"—both reflected and fostered excesses in the private sector.

A central feature of national economic growth continued to be increasing government purchase of goods and services, mostly for defense purposes. Even in the face of rapid overall economic expansion, such buying increased slightly as a percentage of the GNP from the mid-1960s to the early 1970s. On the other hand, in part because of close military-industrial relations, the federal government remained reluctant to interfere with the operations of private business. However, hearing antitrust rumblings from the Johnson White House in the late 1960s, several huge corporations became "conglomerates" (a collection of unrelated operations), shedding their trustlike skins.

This path was blazed by companies such as Litton and Textron, which in the 1950s began acquiring a variety of concerns. Litton, with sales growing from $3 million in 1954 to $1 billion in 1966, entered numerous fields but always as a challenger, thus avoiding the danger of antitrust action. Textron, on the other hand, tended to pick up stagnating firms almost anywhere and transform them into profitable operations. More established names such as Studebaker, W. R. Grace, and Gillette also joined in the fun, launching into realms remote to transportation and razor blades. Despite this trend, the government's definition of "trust" (monopoly tendencies in a single area) remained unchanged, and conglomerates, because of their diffuse and diverse nature, grew unhindered and unhampered. The result has been precious little regulation of corporate growth during the years since 1960.

This does not mean, however, that conglomerates proliferated free of criticism. All too often they were prime examples of personal empire building by aggressive manipulators indifferent to inefficiencies inherent in large-scale operations. Several very thorough economic studies have concluded that there is no demonstrable relationship between conglomeration and efficiency. By the 1970s congressional committees were taking a closer look at this business phenomenon.

Another major shift in the economic realm was the tendency of American corporations to become major exporters of both goods and capital, often setting up far-flung plants in all parts of the world. Private investment of this sort increased from $49.3 billion in 1960 to $120.2 billion in 1970. This was only one of many factors undermining the U.S. balance of trade during the 1960s and 1970s. Many goods once manufactured in the domestic market and shipped abroad were now being made overseas and, in some instances, even appearing in the United States as imports. A handful of American corporations became in a sense multinational powers answerable only to themselves and occasionally working with the CIA (as in Chile) to undo legitimate governments they did not like.

Watergate-related investigations of corporate influence in politics at home also caused some alarm. Approximately twenty-five companies, including American Airlines, Braniff International, Gulf Oil, Minnesota Mining and Manufacturing, and Goodyear, were convicted of illegal campaign-spending practices in the mid-1970s. Congressmen and administration officials began looking closely at alleged kickbacks and bribes paid by U.S. companies to foreign governments since their tax reports might well contain fraudulent statements. But, while corporations sometimes were being fined relatively small sums and getting a bad press, those actually guilty of misdeeds usually remained at the helm. The "moral relativism" spawned by Watergate seemed to wink at such activity, and efforts to control corporate lobbying practices on Capitol Hill only stirred highly paid lobbyists to apply new (and usually successful) pressures.

Perhaps the greatest danger to corporate dominance of U.S. life in the 1970s lay in publicity engendered by extremely high profits, especially those enjoyed by oil companies and public utilities. The average citizen, battling inflation and rising living costs, had little sympathy for such totals, as corporate accountants attempted to hide true earnings by means of detailed balance sheets, tax writeoffs, and other financial legerdemain. Nevertheless, any massive restructuring of federal tax laws to end such sleight of hand seemed unlikely; given corporate influence and often entangling alliances with Congress, the odds were against it.

In one area of public concern, voter protest did bring action in the 1960s and 1970s: environmental protection. Here again, strong corporate influence negated some of the impact of legislation and regulation. Four separate clean air acts from 1963 through 1970 and a like number of clean water acts from 1965 through 1972 (the last one over Richard Nixon's veto) aimed at policing the actions of industry in general. Several measures hit hard at Detroit's automakers, creators of considerable pollution throughout the land. In July 1971, Nixon set up the Environmental Protection Agency (EPA) which, while it augured well for the future, soon lost impact within his troubled administration and had only limited effectiveness. Nevertheless, attention of this sort induced more and more corporations to "clean up their act" or at least to make strenuous public relations efforts to convince a wary public that, next to their product, the environment was their greatest concern. Countless millions watched TV ads, for example, indicating how giant oil companies

Paolo Koch/Photo Researchers.

By the late 1970s American technological developments had produced pollution of every sort, everywhere. Clean air and clean water acts seemed inadequate to control the spreading blight.

such as Texaco, Mobil, Exxon, and Gulf were building and operating oil wells without disturbing native bird life or movie production on Hollywood sets—all in the interests, it would appear, of a better and stronger America, not profits.

Nevertheless, the 1970s saw heightened public concern over energy costs and availability. Made aware by the 1973–1974 Arab oil embargo that American oil reserves were inadequate to sustain current consumption patterns, the nation's population was forced to realize in the bitter cold winter of 1976–1977 that its natural gas supply, too, was overburdened and perhaps inadequate. Despite great alarm expressed by the public, the media, and politicians, little was done to remedy the situation. President Carter, inaugurated during the coldest point of a recordbreaking cold season, attempted without success to rally Congress and the public to action. Dressed in a cardigan sweater, Carter pleaded with Americans in a televised "fireside chat" to cut back their energy consumption and promised a comprehensive legislative program to conserve major sources of energy. Yet like so many of the new President's comprehensive approaches, his energy program met with frustration. Congress quickly adopted the administration bill to establish a new Department of Energy, but Carter's package (taxes on domestic oil and gas-guzzling automobiles, penalty taxes on utility and industrial use of natural gas, establishment of federal guidelines for electric utility rates, and incentives for industries to convert to the use of coal) ran into strong opposition in the Senate and was still stalled during his second year in office.

The persistent inflation and unemployment of the 1970s added to a general sense of uneasiness. Although Jimmy Carter came to the presidency promising to solve both problems, in fact, there was little improvement in 1977, and the following year inflation seemed to be getting much worse. A lengthy coal strike which threatened the nation's economy early in 1978 finally was settled, but it left a residue of bitterness. Carter's critics said he was indecisive during that impasse and the settlement ignited yet another round of wage-price increases. Meanwhile, the administration and Congress engaged in a standoff over the issue of tax reform and public spending to aid unemployment, while the lower and middle classes—and especially unemployed minority youths—suffered the consequences of inaction.

This malaise did not represent overt criticism of capitalism: most Americans seemed simply to want the system to work better—and specifically for their benefit. Yet the long absence of governmental action in the face of constant economic crisis proved once again that it was very difficult to translate public outcry into public policy.

Carter, Congress, and the Voter

Almost halfway through his term, Jimmy Carter faced not only mounting inflationary pressures but a declining popularity among voters as well. Although his blunders as chief executive were few in number, so (said his detractors) were his legislative victories. To some degree, the President still was plagued by his assault upon Washington as an "outsider," Nixon's preoccupation with Watergate and foreign travel, and Ford's resistance to change in any guise. Eight years of Republican control of the White House and Democratic dominance on Capitol Hill had taken a severe toll. (Most Democratic lawmakers won in 1976 without Carter's help and thus owed him little. In fact, his legislative proposals might have fared somewhat better if his party's representatives enjoyed less power in Congress and were forced to cooperate more.) In essence, President Carter found gigantic problems on his desk in the Oval Office when he moved into the White House in January 1977, many of which should have been handled by the executive and legislative branches during the previous decade.

Carter's decision to "de-imperialize" the presidency—certainly a natural and welcome post-Watergate reform—may have weakened that office at precisely the wrong moment, for the Congress, profiting from Watergate, seemingly emerged more powerful than ever. Its members now had the assistance of personal and committee staffs that continued to proliferate at an alarming rate, and access to tax monies to achieve both laudatory and questionable goals. One of the most profound changes on the Washington scene during the 1960s and 1970s, in fact, was the rapid growth of this congressional bureaucracy. Ironically, among its staunchest backers were conservatives who opposed federal programs in general and the growth of the U.S. government work force in particular.

Yet staff aides and press functionaries have been unable to shield their bosses from public criticism and the penetrating eyes of investigative reporters, their appetites whetted by Watergate. Inquiries into the personal affairs of Congressmen, especially those who took bribes from South Korean officials in recent years (an episode newsmen dubbed "Koreagate"), have done little to bolster the generally poor rating most Americans give Congress as a body. At the same time, strangely, these individuals often bestow praise upon their own Representative or Senator, usually because he and his associates have performed a favor for them or for their friends and relatives.

The lesson which Presidents and Congressmen constantly must relearn is that Washington is not America. Despite the growth of federal power and influence, nearly half of all eligible citizens do not even bother to vote in presidential election years, and far more stay away in other elections. Politics is the lifeblood of the nation's capital and those who work and live there; but, except for momentary spasms of interest, it does not enjoy top billing in the minds of most Americans. Here one confronts an obvious dilemma: voters can exercise some voice over problems they want solved, but not over the process of putting into office those capable of providing solutions.

There is a self-serving saying among politicians that it is not how much they have done for constituents in the past that counts, but whatever they did yesterday. This inference that voters have short memories actually has only limited application. The assassinations of the 1960s, the horrors of Vietnam, the turmoil of Watergate, and the hopes that spring up every time a newcomer such as Jimmy Carter enters the White House remain vivid and real—and so does the American dream.

America: Ever-Changing

In the broad sweep, as the United States faced 1976, a presidential campaign, and a bicentennial celebration which stressed the continuity of American life, it appeared to some that little had changed in the recent past, yet everyone knew a great deal had changed. In that year the Democratic party continued to enjoy the nominal loyalty of about 45 percent of the voters, a figure which has varied little over the past quarter of a century. The South that backed native son Jimmy Carter now had well-developed Republican strongholds, blacks were voting in truly substantial numbers in all parts of the nation, and an ambitious, determined candidate had shrewdly used state primaries, new campaign spending provisions, and momentary public disenchantment with the "old hands" to take over first his party, then the White House. Herein lay an obvious secret to America's success: adaptability and change. These factors obviously add much to the zest of everyday life. They make interpretation of the past difficult, analysis of the present troublesome and subject to endless qualification, and prediction of the future foolhardy.

Nevertheless, going forward without a sense of history or some appreciation for what has happened in the past is like starting out on a long journey without a map. And the only map Americans have for their third century is what has taken place in the previous two. In much that occurred they can take pride, and from all of it they may learn.

Essay

Looking Back . . . and Ahead

In the midst of campaign rhetoric and the bitter memories of Vietnam and Watergate, the United States paused in 1976 to celebrate its bicentennial. This actually was a year-long extravaganza marked by parades, concerts, fireworks, speeches, art exhibitions, and similar commemorative events. The most spectacular was Operation Sail, the massing of fifty-three warships from twenty-two countries and sixteen huge square-rigged sailing vessels in New York harbor. On July 4 they passed in review, watched by an estimated six million people. Two days later Queen Elizabeth II arrived in Philadelphia to present a bell, cast in the same foundry as the Liberty Bell, to the United States as a bicentennial gift from the British people. In her remarks she noted that the American Revolution had taught Britain a valuable lesson: "To know the right time and manner of yielding what it is impossible to keep."

What struck many who participated in bicentennial celebrations, especially those held on July 4, 1976, was the spontaneous quality evident everywhere. Thousands sang, waved flags, and jostled goodnaturedly on the very soil where antiwar protesters and police had met in pitched battle only a few years before. America's age of crises perhaps was not at an end, but the mood of the nation was changing. The rancor and bitterness of the 1960s and early 1970s was much less evident. Former SDS leader Tom Hayden, for example, was making a serious (though unsuccessful) bid for a seat in the U.S. Senate. Like Great Britain, millions of Americans had learned through confrontation enflamed by protest and war that there is a right time to "yield," as well as a time to take a stand.

Yet an altered mood and momentary birthday euphoria can not conceal problems that America faces in the future. It is obvious, for example, that certain factors will become increasingly important as America's third century unfolds: the changing nature of our society, the search for different sources of energy, efforts to protect the environment, and both competition and cooperation in outer space. To some degree, other industrialized nations—in fact, perhaps *all* nations—must grapple with these same issues. To this extent, therefore, the United States has ceased to be exceptional and has become part of the multinational world.

In the foreseeable future, the percentage of America's elderly will increase at a time when family ties that once provided

Ray Ellis/Photo Researchers.

Operation Sail, 1976.

comfort in old age are declining. This throws the burden of their care upon local, state, and federal authorities. In the mid-1970s, the average life expectancy of American males was about sixty-eight years, and that of American females, seventy-six years. The elderly in some nations—Israel, Japan, Iceland, Canada, and several western European countries—tend to live slightly longer.

At the same time, the American birthrate (which had been declining rapidly) seems to have leveled off at about 14.8 births per 1,000 population. This translates into a natural increase (excess of births over deaths per 1,000) of about 5.8 percent each year. Yet the breakup of families by divorce and the great number of children born out of wedlock, as well as the tendency of mothers to seek out nonhomemaking careers, means that governments also must often provide day-care centers for the young. This preoccupation with those just out of the cradle and others bound for the grave—a phenomenon common to many nations—cannot help but shape and even transform vital social institutions. It may mean longer working careers and later retirement or the growth of forms of communal living designed to cut the costs of caring for the young, old, and disabled.

Energy—until a few hundred years ago supplied by man, animal, wind, and water—has recently become a very complex issue. In 1964, the leading industrial nations, with one-fourth of the world's inhabitants, consumed 75 percent of the world's coal production, 80 percent of its oil and electric power, and 95 percent of its natural gas. To put it another way, in 1964 the most fortunate citizens living in developed nations used up more than fifty times as much industrial energy as their counterparts in underdeveloped areas. The United States, with 6 percent of the world's population, accounted for one-third of the world's industrial production, utilizing 32 percent of the minerals and 39 percent of the oil produced that year. Ironically, many of these precious materials came from so-called poor nations.

Until 1950, the United States, as producer, consumer, and exporter, set crude oil prices throughout the world, but development of new sources in the Middle East and the Caribbean soon ended this monopoly. Production in Arab lands, for example, rose from 26.5 tons in 1945 to nearly 700 tons in 1970, conferring upon the nations of that area—especially Saudi Arabia—considerable economic and political clout. Despite new wells in Alaska, the North Sea, and various other offshore fields, the Middle East now controls about 95 percent of the Western world's oil production.

This "energy crisis" has both long- and short-range implications. Consuming nations cannot go on burning up fossil fuels at the 1964 rate much longer because known reserves of coal, oil, and natural gas are limited. Coal supplies may last three or four more centuries, but oil and natural gas could become scarce within a generation. Yet hard facts are difficult to come by since the seven companies that control two-thirds of the world's petroleum-mineral resources rarely divulge much information, even to their own governments. Solutions to this dilemma seem to lie in a search for still more oil fields, the use of atomic power, a crash program to develop solar energy, and expansion of geothermal power utilizing underground steam and hot water.

The short-range aspects of this problem were highlighted in the early 1970s by dislocations resulting from open warfare in the Middle East and a brief embargo on oil from that region to America. In 1960, led by Saudi Arabia, major producers formed the Organization of Petroleum Exporting Countries (OPEC). At that time, their goal was to stabilize prices in the face of a momentary oversupply; but, alarmed by continued outside support for Israel and conflict between Jews and Arabs (as well as being fed up with what they viewed as "exploitation" by industrialized nations supplying them with manufactured goods), OPEC members decided to use oil as a political-economic tool. During 1973 the price of Middle East oil quadrupled and in the

Georg Gerster/Rapho-Photo Researchers.

ensuing winter shipments to the United States and the Netherlands were temporarily suspended.

The decision of oil-rich Arabs to use their major product in this fashion produced consternation, fear, and widespread inflation as millions of dollars, pounds, marks, lire, and yen flowed outward to buy the lifeblood that highly developed industries must have. It also forced many of those same powers to reappraise and even reshape their foreign policies in regard to the Middle East.

Linked closely to any discussion of energy is the debate concerning the environment. Increasing industrialization (yet another reason for the oil shortage) and a world population that may rise from 3.7 billion to 6.4 billion between 1970 and 2000 have prompted widespread fears regarding hunger, poverty, and the effects of nearly twice as many people jammed into sprawling urban areas. Even if scientists and bureaucrats find the technical means to keep such a bloated society muddling along, the cultural impact could be staggering.

Added to these considerations are the impact of exhaust fumes from more and more vehicles, smoke created by new industrial plants, and pollution fostered by often thoughtless and ill-conceived use of natural waterways as outlets for waste material of various kinds. In almost any part of the U.S., fathers and grandfathers can show teen-agers ponds and streams where they once fished which now are little more than eyesores. Yet some of the answers proposed as solutions to the energy question—hunting for still more oil and proliferation of nuclear power plants, for example—stir fears of greater and even more deadly, uncontrolled pollution of the environment.

However, if all this sounds rather dreary—conglomerates,

Productive Arab oilfields, such as this one in Libya, altered the balance of power among nations in the 1970s as "modernized" western nations realized their true dependence on the oil-rich "underdeveloped" nations.

Courtesy NASA.

American astronauts aboard Apollo XI landed on the moon on July 19, 1969, culminating a major stage in the "space race" between the U.S. and the Soviet Union. While competition continued, it became increasingly likely in the 1970s that the two powers and other nations might ultimately share information and techniques in the effort to conquer outer space.

neighbors living cheek to jowl with each other, not enough electricity and no hot water—outer space presents a unique challenge, a sense of vibrant excitement, and the potential for solving some of the dilemmas of "inner" space. Simultaneously, however, it may increase friction between the superpowers, the United States and Russia.

During the late 1950s and throughout the 1960s the "space race" heated up to a fever pitch as those two nations vied with each other. By the mid-1970s, however, it seemed that competition had become less spectacular even if perhaps more frightening. Both Americans and Russians now were experimenting with space shuttles, interplanetary probes to Mars and Venus, unmanned craft, killer satellites, and newer and deadlier forms of rocket warfare. Yet despite the tremendous advances of recent decades, outer space remains the great unknown. The striving to get to the moon and beyond has had dramatic impact as various machines and techniques for the astronauts have been adapted to the needs of people here on Earth. Nevertheless, the outer atmosphere remains a hostile, cruel, and—in fact—unconquered realm that may or may not live up to its advance billing.

There is, of course, a consistent thread running through this glimpse into the future: the growth of a global society with a consequent lessening of importance of national borders. Population trends, the search for material resources, environmental concerns, and air and space travel—much like epidemics and popular songs—tend to ignore such artificial creations. Furthermore, most twentieth-century wars have treated victor and vanquished with surprising equanimity—a fact that may deter those contemplating outright confrontation.

Allen Green/Photo Researchers.

American-based fast-food chains became worldwide phenomena by the 1970s. The McDonald's Hamburger franchise on the Ginza, one of Tokyo's main streets, is one of that company's busiest anywhere.

The truth is, Americans now share a multinational, planetary culture linked together by radio, movies, TV, advertising, commerce, and, above all else, common needs and common desires created by a technical milieu dominated by industrialized urban centers. The computer, teletype, telephone, and transistor work the same way in Baltimore and Bangkok, and airplanes—easily recognized by young Eskimos and their counterparts in steaming jungles halfway around the world—land and take off with little or no regard to national entities. In much the same way, Volkswagen, Volvo, Datsun, British rock groups, and American fastfood outlets such as McDonald's and Colonel Sanders have spread to far-flung corners of the world.

Just how Americans of future generations will adapt to this multinational existence is a matter of considerable concern. If they try to run roughshod in a manner reminiscent of late nineteenth century swashbuckling or to juggle facts to fit preconceived goals (as in Vietnam), the decades ahead may be stormy. If, on the other hand, they "yield" at the proper moment and use a little common sense, their third century may be fully as rewarding and equally productive for all mankind as the first 200 years of American civilization have been.

Selected Readings

The Nixon Administration and American Institutions

Jonathan Schell, *The Time of Illusion: An Historical and Reflective Account of the Nixon Era* (1975)

Richard P. Nathan, *The Plot That Failed: Nixon and the Administrative Presidency* (1975)

Leonard W. Levy, *Against the Law: The Nixon Court and Criminal Justice* (1974)

James F. Simon, *In His Own Image: The Supreme Court in Richard Nixon's America* (1973)

Arthur M. Schlesinger, *The Imperial Presidency* (1974)

Watergate

U.S. Senate, Select Committee on Presidential Campaign Activities, *Senate Watergate Report* (1974)

Philip B. Kurland, *Watergate and the Constitution* (1978)

Carl Bernstein and Bob Woodward, *All the President's Men* (1974)

Defense Establishment and Intelligence Gathering

David Wise and Thomas B. Ross, *The Invisible Government* (1964)

Nelson Blackstock, *Cointelpro: The FBI's Secret War on Political Freedom* (1975)

Norman Dorsen and Stephen Gillers, eds., *None of Your Business: Government Secrecy in America* (1974)

Adam Yarmolinsky, *The Military Establishment: Its Impact on American Society* (1971)

The Struggle for Equal Rights

Sar A. Levitan, et al., *Still a Dream: The Changing Status of Blacks Since 1960* (1975)

Jo Freeman, *The Politics of Women's Liberation* (1975)

Barbara S. Deckard, *The Woman's Movement: Political, Socioeconomic, and Psychological Issues* (1975)

Gayle Graham Yates, *What Women Want: The Ideas of the Movement* (1975)

James C. Mohr, *Abortion in America: The Origins and Evolution of National Policy* (1978)

Politics in the Mid-Seventies

Jules Witcover, *Marathon: The Pursuit of the Presidency; 1972–1976* (1977)

Appendixes

The Declaration of Independence

When in the Course of human events, it becomes necessary for one people to dissolve the political bands which have connected them with another, and to assume among the Powers of the earth, the separate and equal station to which the Laws of Nature and of Nature's God entitle them, a decent respect to the opinions of mankind requires that they should declare the causes which impel them to the separation.

We hold these truths to be self-evident, that all men are created equal, that they are endowed by their Creator with certain unalienable Rights, that among these are Life, Liberty and the pursuit of Happiness. That to secure these rights, Governments are instituted among Men, deriving their just powers from the consent of the governed, That whenever any Form of Government becomes destructive of these ends, it is the Right of the People to alter or to abolish it, and to institute new Government, laying its foundation on such principles and organizing its powers in such form, as to them shall seem most likely to effect their Safety and Happiness. Prudence, indeed, will dictate that Governments long established should not be changed for light and transient causes; and accordingly all experience hath shown, that mankind are more disposed to suffer, while evils are sufferable, than to right themselves by abolishing the forms to which they are accustomed. When a long train of abuses and usurpations, pursuing invariably the same Object evinces a design to reduce them under absolute Despotism, it is their right, it is their duty, to throw off such Government, and to provide new Guards for their future security.—Such has been the patient sufferance of these Colonies; and such is now the necessity which constrains them to alter their former Systems of Government. The history of the present King of Great Britain is a history of repeated injuries and usurpations, all having in direct object the establishment of an absolute Tyranny over these States. To prove this, let Facts be submitted to a candid world.

He has refused his Assent to Laws, the most wholesome and necessary for the public good.

He has forbidden his Governors to pass Laws of immediate and pressing importance, unless suspended in their operation till his Assent should be obtained; and when so suspended, he has utterly neglected to attend to them.

He has refused to pass other Laws for the accommodation of large districts of people, unless those people would relinquish the right of Representation in the Legislature, a right inestimable to them and formidable to tyrants only.

He has called together legislative bodies at places unusual, uncomfortable, and distant from the depository of their Public Records, for the sole purpose of fatiguing them into compliance with his measures.

He has dissolved Representative Houses repeatedly, for opposing with manly firmness his invasions on the rights of the people.

He has refused for a long time, after such dissolutions, to cause others to be elected; whereby the Legislative Powers, incapable of Annihilation, have returned to the People at large for their exercise; the State remaining in the mean time exposed to all the dangers of invasion from without, and convulsions within.

He has endeavoured to prevent the population of these States; for that purpose obstructing the Laws of Naturalization of Foreigners; refusing to pass others to encourage their migration hither, and raising the conditions of new Appropriations of Lands.

He has obstructed the Administration of Justice, by refusing his Assent to Laws for establishing Judiciary Powers.

He has made Judges dependent on his Will alone, for the tenure of their offices, and the amount and payment of their salaries.

He has erected a multitude of New Offices, and sent hither swarms of Officers to harass our People, and eat out their substance.

He has kept among us, in times of peace, Standing Armies without the Consent of our legislature.

He has affected to render the Military independent of and superior to the Civil Power.

He has combined with others to subject us to a jurisdiction foreign to our constitution, and unacknowledged by our laws; giving his Assent to their acts of pretended legislation:

For quartering large bodies of armed troops among us:

For protecting them, by a mock Trial, from Punishment for any Murders which they should commit on the Inhabitants of these States:

For cutting off our Trade with all parts of the world:

For imposing taxes on us without our Consent:

For depriving us in many cases, of the benefits of Trial by Jury:

For transporting us beyond Seas to be tried for pretended offences:

For abolishing the free System of English Laws in a neighbouring Province, establishing therein an Arbitrary government, and enlarging its Boundaries so as to render it at once an example and fit instrument for introducing the same absolute rule into these Colonies:

For taking away our Charters, abolishing our most valuable Laws, and altering fundamentally the Forms of our Governments:

For suspending our own Legislature, and declaring themselves invested with Power to legislate for us in all cases whatsoever.

He has abdicated Government here, by declaring us out of his Protection and waging War against us.

He has plundered our seas, ravaged our Coasts, burnt our towns, and destroyed the lives of our people.

He is at this time transporting large armies of foreign mercenaries to compleat the works of death, desolation and tyranny, already begun with circumstances of Cruelty & perfidy scarcely paralleled in the most barbarous ages, and totally unworthy the Head of a civilized nation.

He has constrained our fellow Citizens taken Captive on the high Seas to bear Arms against their Country, to become the executioners of their friends and Brethren, or to fall themselves by their Hands.

He has excited domestic insurrections amongst us, and has endeavoured to bring on the inhabitants of our frontiers, the merciless Indian Savages, whose known rule of warfare, is an undistinguished destruction of all ages, sexes and conditions.

In every stage of these Oppressions We have Petitioned for Redress in the most humble terms: Our repeated Petitions have been answered only by repeated injury. A Prince, whose character is thus marked by every act which may define a Tyrant, is unfit to be the ruler of a free People.

Nor have We been wanting in attention to our British brethren. We have warned them from time to time of attempts by their legislature to extend an unwarrantable jurisdiction over us. We have reminded them of the circumstances of our emigration and settlement here. We have appealed to their native justice and magnanimity, and we have conjured them by the ties of our common kindred to disavow these usurpations, which, would inevitably interrupt our connections and correspondence. They too have been deaf to the voice of justice and of consanguinity. We must, therefore, acquiesce in the necessity, which denounces our Separation, and hold them, as we hold the rest of mankind, Enemies in War, in Peace Friends.

We, therefore, the Representatives of the United States of America, in General Congress, Assembled, appealing to the Supreme Judge of the world for the rectitude of our intentions, do, in the Name, and by Authority of the good People of these Colonies, solemnly publish and declare, That these United Colonies are, and of Right ought to be Free and Independent States; that they are Absolved from all Allegiance to the British Crown, and that all political connection between them and the State of Great Britain, is and ought to be totally dissolved; and that as Free and Independent States, they have full Power to levy War, conclude Peace, contract Alliances, establish Commerce, and to do all other Acts and Things which Independent States may of right do. And for the support of this Declaration, with a firm reliance on the Protection of Divine Providence, we mutually pledge to each other our Lives, our Fortunes and our sacred Honor.

The Constitution of the United States

We the people of the United States, in Order to form a more perfect Union, establish Justice, insure domestic Tranquility, provide for the common defence, promote the general Welfare, and secure the Blessings of Liberty to ourselves and our Posterity, do ordain and establish this CONSTITUTION for the United States of America.

ARTICLE I

Section 1. All legislative Powers herein granted shall be vested in a Congress of the United States which shall consist of a Senate and House of Representatives.

Section 2. The House of Representatives shall be composed of Members chosen every second Year by the People of the several States, and the Electors in each State shall have the Qualifications requisite for Electors of the most numerous Branch of the State Legislature.

No Person shall be a Representative who shall not have attained to the Age of twenty-five Years, and been seven Years a Citizen of the United States, and who shall not, when elected, be an inhabitant of that State in which he shall be chosen.

Representatives and direct Taxes shall be apportioned among the several States which may be included within this Union, according to their respective Numbers, which shall be determined by adding to the whole Number of free Persons, including those bound to Service for a Term of Years and excluding Indians not taxed, three fifths of all other Persons. The actual Enumeration shall be made within three Years after the first Meeting of the Congress of the United States, and within every subsequent Term of ten Years, in such Manner as they shall be Law direct. The Number of Representatives shall not exceed one for every thirty Thousand, but each State shall have at Least one Representative; and until such enumeration shall be made, the State of New Hampshire shall be entitled to chuse three, Massachusetts eight, Rhode-Island and Providence Plantations one, Connecticut five, New-York six, New Jersey four, Pennsylvania eight, Delaware one, Maryland six, Virginia ten, North Carolina five, South Carolina five, and Georgia three.

When vacancies happen in the Representation from any State, the Executive Authority thereof shall issue Writs of Election to fill such Vacancies.

The House of Representatives shall chuse their Speaker and other Officers; and shall have the sole Power of Impeachment.

Section 3. The Senate of the United States shall be composed of two Senators from each State, chosen by the Legislature thereof, for six Years; and each Senator shall have one Vote.

Immediately after they shall be assembled in Consequence of the first Election, they shall be divided as equally as may be into three Classes. The Seats of the Senators of the first Class shall be vacated at the Expiration of the second Year, of the second Class at the Expiration of the fourth Year, and of the third Class at the Expiration of the sixth Year, so that one-third may be chosen every second Year; and if Vacancies happen by Resignation, or otherwise, during the Recess of the Legislature of any State, the Executive thereof may make temporary Appointments until the next Meeting of the Legislature, which shall then fill such Vacancies.

No Person shall be a Senator who shall not have attained to the Age of thirty Years, and been nine Years a Citizen of the United States, and who shall not, when elected, be an Inhabitant of that State in which he shall be chosen.

The Vice President of the United States shall be President of the Senate, but shall have no vote, unless they be equally divided.

The Senate shall chuse their other Officers, and also a President pro tempore, in the absence of the Vice President, or when he shall exercise the Office of the President of the United States.

The Senate shall have the sole Power to try all Impeachments. When sitting for that purpose, they shall be on Oath or Affirmation. When the President of the United States is tried, the Chief Justice shall preside: And no person shall be convicted without the Concurrence of two thirds of the Members present.

Judgment in Cases of Impeachment shall not extend further than to removal from Office, and disqualification to hold and enjoy any Office of honor, Trust, or Profit under the United States: but the Party convicted shall nevertheless be liable and subject to Indictment, Trial, Judgment, and Punishment, according to Law.

Section 4. The Times, Places and Manner of holding Elections for Senators and Representatives, shall be prescribed in each state by the Legislature thereof; but the Congress may at any time by Law make or alter such Regulations, except as to the Places of Chusing Senators.

The Congress shall assemble at least once in every Year, and such Meeting shall be on the first Monday in December, unless they shall by Law appoint a different Day.

Section 5. Each House shall be the Judge of the Elections, Returns and Qualifications of its own Members, and a Majority of each shall constitute a Quorum to do Business; but a smaller number may adjourn from day to day, and may be authorized to compel the Attendance of absent Members, in such Manner, and under such Penalties, as each House may provide.

Each House may determine the Rules of its Proceedings, punish its Members for disorderly Behavior, and, with the Concurrence of two thirds, expel a Member.

Each House shall keep a Journal of its Proceedings, and from time to time publish the same, excepting such Parts as may in their Judgment require Secrecy; and the Yeas and Nays of the Members of either House on any question shall, at the Desire of one fifth of those Present, be entered on the Journal.

Neither House, during the Session of Congress, shall, without the Consent of the other, adjourn for more than three days, nor to any other Place than that in which the two Houses shall be sitting.

Section 6. The Senators and Representatives shall receive a Compensation for their Services, to be ascertained by Law, and paid out of the Treasury of the United States. They shall in all Cases, except Treason, Felony, and Breach of the Peace, be privileged from Arrest during their Attendance at the Session of their respective Houses, and in going to and returning from the same; and for any Speech or Debate in either House, they shall not be questioned in any other Place.

No Senator or Representative shall, during the Time for which he was elected, be appointed to any civil Office under the Authority of the United States, which shall have been created, or the Emoluments whereof shall have been increased, during such time; and no Person holding any Office under the United States shall be a Member of either House during his continuance in Office.

Section 7. All Bills for raising Revenue shall originate in the House of Representatives; but the Senate may propose or concur with Amendments as on other bills.

Every Bill which shall have passed the House of Representatives and the Senate, shall, before it become a Law, be presented to the President of the United States; If he approve he shall sign it, but if not he shall return it, with his Objections, to that House in which it shall have originated, who shall enter the Objections at large on their Journal, and proceed to reconsider it. If after such Reconsideration two thirds of that House shall agree to pass the bill, it shall be sent, together with the objections, to the other House, by which it shall likewise be reconsidered, and if approved by two thirds of that House, it shall become a Law. But in all such Cases the Votes of both Houses shall be determined by Yeas and Nays, and the Names of the Persons voting for and against the Bill shall be entered on the Journal of each House respectively. If any Bill shall not be returned by the President within ten Days (Sundays excepted) after it shall have been presented to him, the Same shall be a Law, in like Manner as if he had signed it, unless the Congress by their Adjournment prevent its Return, in which Case it shall not be a Law.

Every Order, Resolution, or Vote to which the Concurrence of the Senate and House of Representatives may be necessary (except on a question of Adjournment) shall be presented to the President of the United States; and before the Same shall take Effect, shall be approved by him, or being disapproved by him, shall be repassed by two thirds of the Senate and House of Representatives, according to the Rules and Limitations prescribed in the Case of a Bill.

Section 8. The Congress shall have Power To lay and collect Taxes, Duties, Imposts and Excises, to pay the Debts and provide for the common Defence and general Welfare of the United States; but all Duties, Imposts and Excises shall be uniform throughout the United States;

To borrow money on the credit of the United States;

To regulate Commerce with foreign Nations, and among the several States, and with the Indian Tribes;

To establish an uniform Rule of Naturalization, and uniform Laws on the subject of Bankruptcies throughout the United States;

To coin Money, regulate the Value thereof, and of foreign Coin, and fix the Standard of Weights and Measures;

To provide for the Punishment of counterfeiting the Securities and current Coin of the United States;

To establish Post Offices and post Roads;

To promote the Progress of Science and useful Arts, by securing for limited Times to Authors and Inventors the exclusive Right to their respective Writings and Discoveries;

To constitute Tribunals inferior to the Supreme Court;

To define and punish Piracies and Felonies committed on the high Seas, and Offences against the Law of Nations;

To declare War, grant Letters of Marque and Reprisal, and make Rules concerning Captures on Land and Water;

To raise and support Armies, but no Appropriation of Money to that Use shall be for a longer Term than two Years;

To provide and maintain a Navy;

To make Rules for the Government and Regulation of the land and naval forces;

To provide for calling forth the Militia to execute the Laws of the Union, suppress Insurrections and repel Invasions;

To provide for organizing, arming, and disciplining the Militia, and for governing such Part of them as may be employed in the Service of the United States, reserving to the States respectively, the Appointment of the Officers, and the Authority of training the Militia according to the discipline prescribed by Congress;

To exercise exclusive Legislation in all Cases whatsoever, over such District (not exceeding ten Miles square) as may, be Cession of particular States, and the acceptance of Congress, become the Seat of Government of the United States, and to exercise like Authority over all Places purchased by the Consent of the Legislature of the States in which the Same shall be, for the Erection of Forts, Magazines, Arsenals, dock-Yards, and other needful Buildings;—And

To make all Laws which shall be necessary and proper for carrying into Execution the foregoing Powers, and all other Powers vested by this Constitution in the Government of the United States, or in any Department or Officer thereof.

Section 9. The Migration or Importation of such Persons as any of the States now existing shall think proper to admit, shall not be prohibited by the Congress prior to the Year one thousand eight hundred and eight, but a tax or duty may be imposed on such Importation, not exceeding ten dollars for each Person.

The privilege of the Writ of Habeas Corpus shall not be suspended, unless when in Cases of Rebellion or Invasion the public Safety may require it.

No Bill of Attainder or ex post facto Law shall be passed.

No capitation, or other direct, Tax shall be laid unless in Proportion to the Census or Enumeration herein before directed to be taken.

No Tax or Duty shall be laid on Articles exported from any State.

No Preference shall be given by any Regulation of Revenue to the Ports of one State over those of another: nor shall Vessels bound to, or from, one State, be obliged to enter, clear, or pay Duties in another.

No Money shall be drawn from the Treasury, but in Consequence of Appropriations made by Law; and a regular Statement and Account of the Receipts and Expenditures of all public Money shall be published from time to time.

No Title of Nobility shall be granted by the United States: And no Person holding any Office of Profit or Trust under them, shall, without the Consent of the Congress, accept of any present, Emolument, Office, or Title, of any kind whatever, from any King, Prince, or foreign State.

Section 10. No State shall enter any Treaty, Alliance, or Confederation; grant Letters of Marque and Reprisal; coin Money; emit Bills of Credit; make any Thing but gold and silver Coin a Tender in Payment of Debts; pass any Bill of Attainder, ex post facto Law, or Law impairing the Obligation of Contracts, or grant any Title of Nobility.

No State shall, without the Consent of the Congress, lay any Imposts or Duties on Imports or Exports, except what may be absolutely necessary for executing its inspection Laws: and the net Produce of all Duties and Imposts, laid by any State on Imports or Exports, shall be for the Use of the Treasury of the United States; and all such Laws shall be subject to the Revision and Control of the Congress.

No State shall, without the Consent of Congress, lay any duty of Tonnage, keep Troops, or Ships of War in time of Peace, enter into any Agreement or Compact with another State, or with a foreign Power, or engage in War, unless actually invaded, or in such imminent Danger as will not admit of delay.

ARTICLE II

Section 1. The executive Power shall be vested in a President of the United States of America. He shall hold his Office during the Term of four years, and, together with the Vice-President, chosen for the same Term, be elected, as follows:

Each State shall appoint, in such Manner as the Legislature thereof may direct, a Number of Electors, equal to the whole Number of Senators and Representatives to which the State may be entitled in the Congress; but no Senator or Representative, or Person holding an Office of Trust or Profit under the United States, shall be appointed an Elector.

The Electors shall meet in their respective States, and vote by Ballot for two persons, of whom one at least shall not be an Inhabitant of the same State with themselves. And they shall make a List of all the Persons voted for, and of the Number of Votes for each; which List they shall sign and certify, and transmit sealed to the Seat of the Government of the United States, directed to the President of the Senate. The President of the Senate shall, in the Presence of the Senate and Houe of Representatives, open all the Certificates, and the Votes shall then be counted. The Person having the greatest Number of Votes shall be the President, if such Number be a Majority of the whole Number of Electors appointed; and if there be more than one who have such Majority, and have an equal Number of Votes, then the House of Representatives shall immediately chuse by Ballot one of them for President; and if no Person have a Majority, then from the five highest on the List the said House shall in like Manner chuse the President. But in chusing the President, the Votes shall be taken by States, the Representation from each State having one Vote; a quorum for this Purpose shall consist of a Member or Members from two-thirds of the States, and a Majority of all the States shall be necessary to a Choice. In every Case, after the Choice of the President, the Person having the greatest Number of Votes of the Electors shall be the Vice President. But if there should remain two or more who have equal votes, the Senate shall chuse from them by Ballot the Vice-President.

The Congress may determine the Time of chusing the Electors, and the Day on which they shall give their Votes; which Day shall be the same throughout the United States.

No person except a natural-born Citizen, or a Citizen of the United States, at the time of the Adoption of this Constitution, shall be eligible to the Office of President; neither shall any Person be eligible to that Office who shall not have attained to the Age of thirty-five years, and been fourteen Years a Resident within the United States.

In Case of the Removal of the President from Office, or of his Death, Resignation, or Inability to discharge the Powers and Duties of the said Office, the same shall devolve on the Vice President, and the Congress may by Law provide for the Case of Removal, Death, Resignation, or Inability, both of the President and Vice President, declaring what Officer shall then act as President, and such Officer shall act accordingly, until the disability be removed, or a President shall be elected.

The President shall, at stated Times, receive for his Services a Compensation, which shall neither be increased nor diminished during the Period for which he shall have been elected, and he shall not receive within that Period any other Emolument from the United States, or any of them.

Before he enter on the execution of his Office, he shall take the following Oath or Affirmation:—"I do solemnly swear (or affirm) that I will faithfully execute the Office of President of the United States, and will, to the best of my Ability, preserve, protect, and defend the Constitution of the United States."

Section 2. The President shall be Commander in Chief of the Army and Navy of the United States, and of the Militia of the several States, when called into the actual Service of the United States; he may require the Opinion, in writing, of the principal Officer in each of the executive Departments, upon any subject relating to the Duties of their respective Offices, and he shall have Power to Grant Reprieves and Pardons for Offences against the United States, except in Cases of Impeachment.

He shall have Power, by and with the Advice and Consent of the Senate, to make Treaties, provided two thirds of the Senators present concur; and he shall nominate, and by and with the Advice and Consent of the Senate, shall appoint Ambassadors, other public Ministers and Consuls, Judges of the supreme Court, and all other Officers of the United States, whose Appointments are not herein otherwise provided for, and which shall be established by Law: but the Congress may by Law vest the Appointments of such inferior Officers, as they think proper, in the President alone, in the Courts of Law, or in the Heads of Departments.

The President shall have Power to fill up all Vacancies that may happen during the Recess of the Senate, by granting Commissions which shall expire at the End of their next Session.

Section 3. He shall from time to time give to the Congress Information of the State of the Union, and recommend to their Consideration such Measures as he shall judge necessary and expedient; he may, on extraordinary occasions, convene both Houses, or either of them, and in Case of Disagreement between them, with respect to the Time of Adjournment, he may adjourn them to such Time as he shall think proper; he shall receive Ambassadors and other public Ministers; he shall take Care that the Laws be faithfully executed, and shall Commission all the Officers of the United States.

Section 4. The President, Vice President and all civil Officers of the United States, shall be removed from Office on Impeachment for, and Conviction of, Treason, Bribery, or other high Crimes and Misdemeanors.

ARTICLE III

Section 1. The judicial Power of the United States, shall be vested in one supreme Court, and in such inferior Courts as the Congress may from time to time ordain and establish. The Judges, both of the supreme and inferior Courts, shall hold their Offices during good Behaviour, and shall, at stated Times, receive for their Services, a Compensation, which shall not be diminished during their Continuance in Office.

Section 2. The judicial Power shall extend to all Cases, in Law and Equity, arising under this Constitution, the Laws of the United States, and treaties made, or which shall be made, under their Authority;—to all Cases affecting ambassadors, other public ministers and consuls;—to all cases of admiralty and maritime Jurisdiction;—to Controversies to which the United States shall be a Party;—to Controversies between two or more States;—between a State and Citizens of another State;—between Citizens of different States,—between Citizens of the same State claiming Lands under Grants of different States, and between a State, or the Citizens thereof, and foreign States, Citizens or Subjects.

In all Cases affecting Ambassadors, other public Ministers and Consuls, and those in which a State shall be Party, the supreme Court shall have original Jurisdiction. In all the other Cases before mentioned, the supreme Court shall have appellate Jurisdiction, both as to Law and Fact, with such Exceptions, and under such Regulations as the Congress shall make.

The trial of all Crimes, except in Cases of Impeachment, shall be by Jury; and such Trial shall be held in the State where the said Crimes shall have been committed; but when not committed within any State, the Trial shall be at such Place or Places as the Congress may by Law have directed.

Section 3. Treason against the United States, shall consist only in levying War against them, or in adhering to their Enemies, giving them Aid and Comfort. No Person shall be convicted of Treason unless on the Testimony of two Witnesses to the same overt Act, or on Confession in open Court.

The Congress shall have power to declare the Punishment of Treason, but no Attainder of Treason shall work Corruption of Blood, or Forfeiture except during the Life of the Person attainted.

ARTICLE IV

Section 1. Full Faith and Credit shall be given in each State to the public Acts, Records, and judicial Proceedings of every other State. And the Congress may by general Laws prescribe the Manner in which such Acts, Records and Proceedings shall be proved, and the Effect thereof.

Section 2. The Citizens of each State shall be entitled to all Privileges and Immunities of Citizens in the several States.

A Person charged in any State with Treason, Felony, or other Crime, who shall flee from Justice, and be found in another State, shall on demand of the executive Authority of the State from which he fled, be delivered up, to be removed to the State having Jurisdiction of the crime.

No Person held to Service or Labour in one State, under the Laws thereof, escaping into another, shall, in Consequence of any Law or Regulation therein, be discharged from such Service or Labour, but shall be delivered up on Claim of the Party to whom such Service or Labour may be due.

Section 3. New States may be admitted by the Congress into this Union; but no new State shall be formed or erected within the Jurisdiction of any other State; nor any State be formed by the Junction of two or more States, or parts of States, without the Consent of the Legislatures of the States concerned as well as of the Congress.

The Congress shall have Power to dispose of and make all needful Rules and Regulations respecting the Territory or other Property belonging to the United States; and nothing in this Constitution shall be so construed as to Prejudice any Claims of the United States, or of any particular State.

Section 4. The United States shall guarantee to every State in this Union a Republican Form of Government, and shall protect each of them against Invasion; and on Application of the Legislature, or the Executive (when the Legislature cannot be convened) against domestic Violence.

ARTICLE V

The Congress, whenever two-thirds of both Houses shall deem it necessary, shall propose Amendments to this Constitution, or, on the Application of the Legislatures of two-thirds of the several States, shall call a Convention for proposing Amendments, which, in either Case, shall be valid to all Intents and Purposes, as part of this Constitution, when ratified by the Legislatures of three-fourths of the several States, or by Conventions in three-fourths thereof, as the one or the other Mode of Ratification may be proposed by the Congress; Provided that no Amendment which may be made prior to the Year One thousand eight hundred and eight shall in any Manner affect the first and fourth Clauses in the Ninth Section of the first Article; and that no State, without its Consent, shall be deprived of its equal Suffrage in the Senate.

ARTICLE VI

All Debts contracted and Engagements entered into, before the Adoption of this Constitution, shall be as valid against the United States under this Constitution, as under the Confederation.

This Constitution, and the Laws of the United States which shall be made in Pursuance thereof; and all Treaties made, or which shall be made, under the Authority of the United States, shall be the supreme Law of the Land; and the Judges in every State shall be bound thereby, any Thing in the Constitution or Laws of any State to the Contrary notwithstanding.

The Senators and Representatives before mentioned, and the Members of the several State Legislatures, and all executive and judicial Officers, both of the United States and of the several States, shall be bound by Oath or Affirmation to support this Constitution; but no religious Test shall every be required as a qualification to any Office or public Trust under the United States.

ARTICLE VII

The Ratification of the Conventions of nine States shall be sufficient for the Establishment of this Constitution between the States so ratifying the same.

Done in Convention by the Unanimous Consent of the States present the Seventeenth Day of September in the Year of our Lord one thousand seven hundred and Eighty seven, and of the Independence of the United States of America the Twelfth. In Witness whereof We have hereunto subscribed our names.

Articles in Addition to, and Amendment of, the Constitution of the United States of America. Proposed by Congress, and Ratified by the Legislatures of the Several States, Pursuant to the Fifth Article of the Original Constitution.

AMENDMENT I [1791]

Congress shall make no law respecting an establishment of religion, or prohibiting the free exercise thereof; or abridging the freedom of speech, or of the press; or the right of the people peaceably to assemble, and to petition the Government for a redress of grievances.

AMENDMENT II [1791]

A well regulated Militia, being necessary to the security of a free State, the right of the people to keep and bear Arms shall not be infringed.

AMENDMENT III [1791]

No Soldier shall, in time of peace, be quartered in any house, without the consent of the Owner, nor in time of war, but in a manner to be prescribed by law.

AMENDMENT IV [1791]

The right of the people to be secure in their persons, houses, papers, and effects, against unreasonable searches and seizures, shall not be violated, and no Warrants shall issue, but upon probable cause, supported by Oath or affirmation, and particularly describing the place to be searched, and the persons or things to be seized.

AMENDMENT V [1791]

No person shall be held to answer for a capital or otherwise infamous crime, unless on a presentment or indictment of a Grand Jury, except in cases arising in the land or naval forces, or in the Militia, when in actual service in time of War or public danger; nor shall any person be subject for the same offence to be twice put in jeopardy of life or limb; nor shall be compelled in any criminal case to be a witness against himself, nor be deprived of life, liberty, or property, without due process of law; nor shall private property be taken for public use, without just compensation.

AMENDMENT VI [1791]

In all criminal prosecutions, the accused shall enjoy the right to a speedy and public trial, by an impartial jury of the State and district wherein the crime shall have been committed, which district shall have been previously ascertained by law, and to be informed of the nature and cause of the accusation; to be confronted with the witnesses against him; to have compulsory process for obtaining witnesses in his favor, and to have the Assistance of Counsel for his defence.

AMENDMENT VII [1791]

In suits at common law, where the value in controversy shall exceed twenty dollars, the right of trial by jury shall be preserved, and no fact tried by a jury, shall be otherwise reexamined in any Court of the United States, than according to the rules of the common law.

AMENDMENT VIII [1791]

Excessive bail shall not be required, nor excessive fines imposed, nor cruel and unusual punishments inflicted.

AMENDMENT IX [1791]

The enumeration in the Constitution, of certain rights, shall not be construed to deny or disparage others retained by the people.

AMENDMENT X [1791]

The powers not delegated to the United States by the Constitution, nor prohibited by it to the States, are reserved to the States respectively, or to the people.

AMENDMENT XI [1798]

The Judicial power of the United States shall not be construed to extend to any suit in law or equity, commenced or prosecuted against one of the United States by Citizens of another State, or by Citizens or Subjects of any Foreign State.

AMENDMENT XII [1804]

The Electors shall meet in their respective States and vote by ballot for President and Vice-President, one of whom, at least, shall not be an inhabitant of the same State with themselves; they shall name in their ballots the person voted for as President, and in distinct ballots the person voted for as Vice-President, and they shall make distinct lists of all persons voted for as President, and of all persons voted for as Vice-President, and of the number of votes for each, which lists they shall sign and certify, and transmit sealed to the seat of the government of the United States, directed to the President of the Senate;—The President of the Senate shall, in the presence of the Senate and House of Representatives, open all the certificates and the votes shall then be counted;—The person having the greatest number of votes for President, shall be the President, if such number be a majority of the whole number of Electors appointed; and if no person have such majority, then from the persons having the highest numbers not exceeding three on the list of those voted for as President, the House of Representatives shall choose immediately, by ballot, the President. But in choosing the President, the votes shall be taken by states, the representation from each state having one vote; a quorum for this purpose shall consist of a member or members from two-thirds of the states, and a majority of all the states shall be necessary to a choice. And if the House of Representatives shall not choose a President whenever the right of choice shall devolve upon them, before the fourth day of March next following, then the Vice-President shall act as President, as in the case of the death or other constitutional disability of the President.—The person having the greatest number of votes as Vice-President, shall be the Vice-President, if such number be a majority of the whole number of Electors appointed, and if no person have a majority, then from the two highest numbers on the list, the Senate shall choose the Vice-President; a quorum for the purpose shall consist of two-thirds of the whole number of Senators, and a majority of the whole number shall be necessary to a choice. But no person constitutionally ineligible to the office of President shall be eligible to that of Vice-President of the United States.

AMENDMENT XIII [1865]

Section 1. Neither slavery nor involuntary servitude, except as a punishment for crime whereof the party shall have been duly convicted, shall exist within the United States, or any place subject to their jurisdiction.

Section 2. Congress shall have power to enforce this article by appropriate legislation.

AMENDMENT XIV [1868]

Section 1. All persons born or naturalized

in the United States, and subject to the jurisdiction thereof, are citizens of the United States and of the State wherein they reside. No State shall make or enforce any law which shall abridge the privileges or immunities of citizens of the United States; nor shall any State deprive any person of life, liberty, or property, without due process of law; nor deny to any person within its jurisdiction the equal protection of the laws.

Section 2. Representatives shall be apportioned among the several States according to their respective numbers, counting the whole number of persons in each State, excluding Indians not taxed. But when the right to vote at any election for the choice of electors for President and Vice-President of the United States, Representatives in Congress, the Executive and Judicial officers of a State, or the members of the Legislature thereof, is denied to any of the male inhabitants of such State, being twenty-one years of age, and citizens of the United States, or in any way abridged, except for participation in rebellion, or other crime, the basis of representation therein shall be reduced in the proportion which the number of such male citizens shall bear to the whole number of male citizens twenty-one years of age in such State.

Section 3. No person shall be a Senator or Representative in Congress, or elector of President and Vice-President, or hold any office, civil or military, under the United States, or under any State, who, having previously taken an oath, as a member of Congress, or as an officer of the United States, or as a member of any State legislature, or as an executive or judicial officer of any State, to support the Constitution of the United States, shall have engaged in insurrection or rebellion against the same, or given aid or comfort to the enemies thereof. But Congress may by a vote of two-thirds of each House, remove such disability.

Section 4. The validity of the public debt of the United States, authorized by law, including debts incurred for payment of pensions and bounties for services in suppressing insurrection or rebellion, shall not be questioned. But neither the United States nor any State shall assume or pay any debt or obligation incurred in aid of insurrection or rebellion against the United States or any claim for the loss or emancipation of any slave; but all such debts, obligations, and claims shall be held illegal and void.

Section 5. The Congress shall have the power to enforce, by appropriate legislation, the provisions of this article.

AMENDMENT XV [1870]

Section 1. The right of citizens of the United States to vote shall not be denied or abridged by the United States or by any State on account of race, color, or previous condition of servitude—

Section 2. The Congress shall have power to enforce this article by appropriate legislation.

AMENDMENT XVI [1913]

The Congress shall have power to lay and collect taxes on incomes, from whatever source derived, without apportionment among the several States, and without regard to any census or enumeration.

AMENDMENT XVII [1913]

The Senate of the United States shall be composed of two Senators from each State, elected by the people thereof, for six years; and each Senator shall have one vote. The electors in each State shall have the qualifications requisite for electors of the most numerous branch of the State legislatures.

When vacancies happen in the representation of any State in the Senate, the executive authority of such State shall issue writs of election to fill such vacancies: *Provided,* That the legislature of any State may empower the executive thereof to make temporary appointments until the people fill the vacancies by election as the legislature may direct.

This amendment shall not be so construed as to affect the election or term of any Senator chosen before it becomes valid as part of the Constitution.

AMENDMENT XVIII [1919]

Section 1. After one year from the ratificatin of this article the manufacture, sale, or transportation of intoxicating liquors within, the importation thereof into, or the exportation thereof from the United States and all territory subject to the jurisdiction thereof for beverage purposes is hereby prohibited.

Section 2. The Congress and the several States shall have concurrent power to enforce this article by appropriate legislation.

Section 3. This article shall be inoperative unless it shall have been ratified as an amendment to the Constitution by the legislatures of the several States, as provided in the Constitution, within seven years from the date of the submission hereof to the States by the Congress.

AMENDMENT XIX [1920]

The right of citizens of the United States to vote shall not be denied or abridged by the United States or by any State on account of sex.

Congress shall have power to enforce this article by appropriate legislation.

AMENDMENT XX [1933]

Section 1. The terms of the President and Vice-President shall end at noon on the 20th day of January, and the terms of Senators and Representatives at noon on the 3d day of January, of the years in which such terms would have ended if this article had not been ratified; and the terms of their successors shall then begin.

Section 2. The Congress shall assemble at least once in every year, and such meeting shall begin at noon on the 3d day of January, unless they shall by law appoint a different day.

Section 3. If, at the time fixed for the beginning of the term of the President, the President elect shall have died, the Vice-President elect shall become President. If a President shall not have been chosen before the time fixed for the beginning of his term, or if the President elect shall have failed to qualify, then the Vice-President elect shall act as President until a President shall have qualified; and the Congress may by law provide for the case wherein neither a President elect nor a Vice-President elect shall have qualified, declaring who shall then act as President, or the manner in which one who is to act shall be selected, and such person shall act accordingly until a President or Vice-President shall have qualified.

Section 4. The Congress may by law provide for the case of the death of any of the persons from whom the House of Representatives may choose a President whenever the right of choice shall have devolved upon them, and for the case of the death of any of the persons from whom the Senate may choose a Vice-President whenever the right of choice shall have devolved upon them.

Section 5. Sections 1 and 2 shall take effect on the 15th day of October following the ratification of this article.

Section 6. This article shall be inoperative unless it shall have been ratified as an amendment to the Constitution by the legislatures of three-fourths of the several States within seven years from the date of its submission.

AMENDMENT XXI [1933]

Section 1. The eighteenth article of amendment to the Constitution of the United States is hereby repealed.

Section 2. The transportation or importation into any State, Territory, or possession of the United States for delivery or use therein of intoxicating liquors, in violation of the laws thereof, is hereby prohibited.

Section 3. This article shall be inoperative unless it shall have been ratified as an amendment to the Constitution by conventions in the several States, as provided in the Constitution, within seven years from the date of the submission hereof to the States by the Congress.

AMENDMENT XXII [1951]

No person shall be elected to the office of the President more than twice, and no person who has held the office of President, or acted as President, for more than two years of a term to which some other person was elected President shall be elected to the office of the President more than once.

But this Article shall not apply to any person holding the office of President when this Article was proposed by the Congress, and shall not prevent any person who may be holding the office of President, or acting as President, during the term within which this Article becomes operative from holding the office of President or acting as President during the remainder of such term.

AMENDMENT XXIII [1961]

Section 1. The District constituting the seat of Government of the United States shall appoint in such manner as the Congress may direct:

A number of electors of President and Vice President equal to the whole number of Senators and Representatives in Congress to which the District would be entitled if it were a State, but in no event more than the least populous State; they shall be in addition to those appointed by the States, but they shall be considered, for the purposes of the election of President and Vice President, to be electors appointed by a State; and they shall meet in the District and perform such duties as provided by the twelfth article of amendment.

Section 2. The Congress shall have power to enforce this article by appropriate legislation.

AMENDMENT XXIV [1964]

Section 1. The right of citizens of the United States to vote in any primary or other election for President or Vice President, for electors for President or Vice President, or for Senator or Representative in Congress, shall not be denied or abridged by the United States or any State by reason of failure to pay any poll tax or other tax.

Section 2. The Congress shall have the power to enforce this article by appropriate legislation.

AMENDMENT XXV [1967]

Section 1. In case of the removal of the President from office or his death or resignation, the Vice President shall become President.

Section 2. Whenever there is a vacancy in the office of the Vice President, the President shall nominate a Vice President who shall take the office upon confirmation by a majority vote of both houses of Congress.

Section 3. Whenever the President transmits to the President pro tempore of the Senate and the Speaker of the House of Representatives his written declaration that he is unable to discharge the powers and duties of his office, and until he transmits to them a written declaration to the contrary, such powers and duties shall be discharged by the Vice President as Acting President.

Section 4. Whenever the Vice President and a majority of either the principal officers of the executive departments, or of such other body as Congress may by law provide, transmit to the President pro tempore of the Senate and the Speaker of the House of Representatives their written declaration that the President is unable to discharge the powers and duties of his office, the Vice President shall immediately assume the powers and duties of the office as Acting President.

Thereafter, when the President transmits to the President pro tempore of the Senate and the Speaker of the House of Representatives his written declaration that no inability exists, he shall resume the powers and duties of his office unless the Vice President and a majority of either the principal officers of the executive departments, or of such other body as Congress may by law provide, transmit within four days to the President pro tempore of the Senate and the Speaker of the House of Representatives their written declaration that the President is unable to discharge the powers and duties of his office. Thereupon Congress shall decide the issue, assembling within 48 hours for that purpose if not in session. If the Congress, within 21 days after receipt of the latter written declaration, or, if Congress is not in session, within 21 days after Congress is required to assemble, determines by two-thirds vote of both houses that the President is unable to discharge the powers and duties of his office, the Vice President shall continue to discharge the same as Acting President; otherwise, the President shall resume the powers and duties of his office.

Admission of States to the Union

1	Delaware	*Dec. 7, 1787*
2	Pennsylvania	*Dec. 12, 1787*
3	New Jersey	*Dec. 18, 1787*
4	Georgia	*Jan. 2, 1788*
5	Connecticut	*Jan. 9, 1788*
6	Massachusetts	*Feb. 6, 1788*
7	Maryland	*Apr. 28, 1788*
8	South Carolina	*May 23, 1788*
9	New Hampshire	*June 21, 1788*
10	Virginia	*June 25, 1788*
11	New York	*July 26, 1788*
12	North Carolina	*Nov. 21, 1789*
13	Rhode Island	*May 29, 1790*
14	Vermont	*Mar. 4, 1791*
15	Kentucky	*June 1, 1792*
16	Tennessee	*June 1, 1796*
17	Ohio	*Mar. 1, 1803*
18	Louisiana	*Apr. 30, 1812*
19	Indiana	*Dec. 11, 1816*
20	Mississippi	*Dec. 10, 1817*
21	Illinois	*Dec. 3, 1818*
22	Alabama	*Dec. 14, 1819*
23	Maine	*Mar. 15, 1820*
24	Missouri	*Aug. 10, 1821*
25	Arkansas	*June 15, 1836*
26	Michigan	*Jan. 26, 1837*
27	Florida	*Mar. 3, 1845*
28	Texas	*Dec. 29, 1845*
29	Iowa	*Dec. 28, 1846*
30	Wisconsin	*May 29, 1848*
31	California	*Sept. 9, 1850*
32	Minnesota	*May 11, 1858*
33	Oregon	*Feb. 14, 1859*
34	Kansas	*Jan. 29, 1861*
35	West Virginia	*June 19, 1863*
36	Nevada	*Oct. 31, 1864*
37	Nebraska	*Mar. 1, 1867*
38	Colorado	*Aug. 1, 1876*
39	North Dakota	*Nov. 2, 1889*
40	South Dakota	*Nov. 2, 1889*
41	Montana	*Nov. 8, 1889*
42	Washington	*Nov. 11, 1889*
43	Idaho	*July 3, 1890*
44	Wyoming	*July 10, 1890*
45	Utah	*Jan. 4, 1896*
46	Oklahoma	*Nov. 16, 1907*
47	New Mexico	*Jan. 6, 1912*
48	Arizona	*Feb. 14, 1912*
49	Alaska	*Jan. 3, 1959*
50	Hawaii	*Aug. 21, 1959*

Population of the United States, 1790–1978

Year	Total population (in thousands)	Number per square mile of land area (continental United States)	Year	Total population (in thousands)	Number per square mile of land area (continental United States)
1790	3,929	4.5	1837	15,843	
1791	4,056		1838	16,264	
1792	4,194		1839	16,684	
1793	4,332		1840	17,120	9.8
1794	4,469		1841	17,733	
1795	4,607		1842	18,345	
1796	4,745		1843	18,957	
1797	4,883		1844	19,569	
1798	5,021		1845	20,182	
1799	5,159		1846	20,794	
1800	5,297	6.1	1847	21,406	
1801	5,486		1848	22,018	
1802	5,679		1849	22,631	
1803	5,872		1850	23,261	7.9
1804	5,065		1851	24,086	
1805	6,258		1852	24,911	
1806	6,451		1853	25,736	
1807	6,644		1854	26,561	
1808	6,838		1855	27,386	
1809	7,031		1856	28,212	
1810	7,224	4.3	1857	29,037	
1811	7,460		1858	29,862	
1812	7,700		1859	30,687	
1813	7,939		1860	31,513	10.6
1814	8,179		1861	32,351	
1815	8,419		1862	33,188	
1816	8,659		1863	34,026	
1817	8,899		1864	34,863	
1818	9,139		1865	35,701	
1819	9,379		1866	36,538	
1820	9,618	5.6	1867	37,376	
1821	9,939		1868	38,213	
1822	10,268		1869	39,051	
1823	10,596		1870	39,905	13.4
1824	10,924		1871	40,938	
1825	11,252		1872	41,972	
1826	11,580		1873	43,006	
1827	11,909		1874	44,040	
1828	12,237		1875	45,073	
1829	12,565		1876	46,107	
1830	12,901	7.4	1877	47,141	
1831	13,321		1878	48,174	
1832	13,742		1879	49,208	
1833	14,162		1880	50,262	16.9
1834	14,582		1881	51,542	
1835	15,003		1882	52,821	
1836	15,423		1883	54,100	

Figures are from pp. 7, 8; *Statistical Abstract of the United States: 1974,* p. 5; Census Bureau for 1974 through 1978.

Year	Total population (in thousands)	Number per square mile of land area (continental United States)
1884	55,379	
1885	56,658	
1886	57,938	
1887	59,217	
1888	60,496	
1889	61,775	
1890	63,056	21.2
1891	64,361	
1892	65,666	
1893	66,970	
1894	68,275	
1895	69,580	
1896	70,885	
1897	72,189	
1898	73,494	
1899	74,799	
1900	76,094	25.6
1901	77,585	
1902	79,160	
1903	80,632	
1904	82,165	
1905	83,820	
1906	85,437	
1907	87,000	
1908	88,709	
1909	90,492	
1910	92,407	31.0
1911	93,868	
1912	95,331	
1913	97,227	
1914	99,118	
1915	100,549	
1916	101,966	
1917	103,414	
1918	104,550	
1919	105,063	
1920	106,466	35.6
1921	108,541	
1922	110,055	
1923	111,950	
1924	114,113	
1925	115,832	
1926	117,399	
1927	119,038	
1928	120,501	
1929	121,770	
1930	122,775	41.2
1931	124,040	

Year	Total population (in thousands)*	Number per square mile of land area (continental United States)
1932	124,840	
1933	125,579	
1934	126,374	
1935	127,250	
1936	128,053	
1937	128,825	
1938	129,825	
1939	130,880	
1940	131,669	44.2
1941	133,894	
1942	135,361	
1943	137,250	
1944	138,916	
1945	140,468	
1946	141,936	
1947	144,698	
1948	147,208	
1949	149,767	
1950	150,697	
1951	154,878	
1952	157,553	
1953	160,184	
1954	163,026	
1955	165,931	
1956	168,903	
1957	171,984	
1958	174,882	
1959	177,830	
1960	178,464	60.1
1961	183,672	
1962	186,504	
1963	189,197	
1964	191,833	
1965	194,237	
1966	196,485	
1967	198,629	
1968	200,619	
1969	202,599	
1970	203,875	57.5†
1971	207,045	
1972	208,842	
1973	210,396	
1974	211,894	
1975	213,631	
1976	215,142††	
1977	216,817††	
1978	218,931††	

*Figures after 1940 reprent total population including Armed Forces abroad, except in official census years.
†Figure includes Alaska and Hawaii.
††As of July 1.

Presidential Elections, 1789–1976

Year	Candidates	Party	Popular Vote	Electoral Vote
1789	**George Washington**			69
	John Adams			34
	Others			35
1792	**George Washington**			132
	John Adams			77
	George Clinton			50
	Others			5
1796	**John Adams**	Federalist		71
	Thomas Jefferson	Democrat-Republican		68
	Thomas Pinckney	Federalist		59
	Aaron Burr	Democrat-Republican		30
	Others			48
1800	**Thomas Jefferson**	Democrat-Republican		73
	Aaron Burr	Democrat-Republican		73
	John Adams	Federalist		65
	Charles C. Pinckney	Federalist		64
1804	**Thomas Jefferson**	Democrat-Republican		162
	Charles C. Pinckney	Federalist		14
1808	**James Madison**	Democrat-Republican		122
	Charles C. Pinckney	Federalist		47
	George Clinton	Independent-Republican		6
1812	**James Madison**	Democrat-Republican		128
	DeWitt Clinton	Federalist		89
1816	**James Monroe**	Democrat-Republican		183
	Rufus King	Federalist		34
1820	**James Monroe**	Democrat-Republican		231
	John Quincy Adams	Independent-Republican		1
1824	**John Quincy Adams**	Democrat-Republican	113,122 (30.9%)	84
	Andrew Jackson	Democrat-Republican	151,271 (41.3%)	99
	Henry Clay	Democrat-Republican	47,531 (12.9%)	37
	William H. Crawford	Democrat-Republican	40,856 (11.1%)	41
1828	**Andrew Jackson**	Democrat	642,553 (55.9%)	178
	John Quincy Adams	National Republican	500,897 (43.6%)	83
1832	**Andrew Jackson**	Democrat	701,780 (54.2%)	219
	Henry Clay	National Republican	484,205 (37.4%)	49
	William Wirt	Anti-Masonic	100,715 (7.7%)	7

Year	Candidates	Party	Popular Vote	Electoral Vote
1836	**Martin Van Buren**	Democrat	764,176 (50.8%)	170
	William H. Harrison	Whig	550,816 (36.6%)	73
	Hugh L. White	Whig	146,107 (9.7%)	26
	Daniel Webster	Whig	41,201 (2.7%)	14
1840	**William H. Harrison**	Whig	1,275,390 (52.8%)	234
	(**John Tyler,** 1841)			
	Martin Van Buren	Democrat	1,128,854 (46.8%)	60
1844	**James K. Polk**	Democrat	1,339,494 (49.5%)	170
	Henry Clay	Whig	1,300,004 (48.0%)	105
	James G. Birney	Liberty	62,103 (2.3%)	
1848	**Zachary Taylor**	Whig	1,361,393 (47.2%)	163
	(**Millard Fillmore,** 1850)			
	Lewis Cass	Democrat	1,223,460 (42.4%)	127
	Martin Van Buren	Free Soil	291,501 (10.1%)	
1852	**Franklin Pierce**	Democrat	1,607,510 (50.8%)	254
	Winfield Scott	Whig	1,386,942 (43.8%)	42
1856	**James Buchanan**	Democrat	1,836,072 (45.2%)	174
	John C. Frémont	Republican	1,342,345 (33.1%)	114
	Millard Fillmore	American	873,053 (21.5%)	8
1860	**Abraham Lincoln**	Republican	1,865,908 (39.8%)	180
	Stephen A. Douglas	Democrat	1,382,202 (29.4%)	12
	John C. Breckinridge	Democrat	848,019 (18.0%)	72
	John Bell	Constitutional Union	591,901 (12.6%)	39
1864	**Abraham Lincoln**	Republican	2,218,388 (55.0%)	212
	(**Andrew Johnson,** 1865)			
	George B. McClellan	Democrat	1,812,807 (44.9%)	21
1868	**Ulysses S. Grant**	Republican	3,013,650 (52.6%)	214
	Horatio Seymour	Democrat	2,708,744 (47.3%)	80
1872	**Ulysses S. Grant**	Republican	3,598,235 (55.6%)	286
	Horace Greeley	Democrat	2,834,761 (43.8%)	66
1876	**Rutherford B. Hayes**	Republican	4,034,311 (47.9%)	185
	Samuel J. Tilden	Democrat	4,288,546 (50.9%)	184
1880	**James A. Garfield**	Republican	4,446,158 (48.2%)	214
	(**Chester A. Arthur,** 1881)			
	Winfield S. Hancock	Democrat	4,444,260 (48.2%)	155
	James B. Weaver	Greenback-Labor	305,997 (3.3%)	
1884	**Grover Cleveland**	Democrat	4,874,621 (48.5%)	219
	James G. Blaine	Republican	4,848,936 (48.2%)	182
	Benjamin F. Butler	Greenback-Labor	175,096 (1.7%)	
1888	**Benjamin Harrison**	Republican	5,443,892 (47.8%)	233
	Grover Cleveland	Democrat	5,534,488 (48.6%)	168

Year	Candidates	Party	Popular Vote	Electoral Vote
1892	**Grover Cleveland**	Democrat	5,551.883 (46.0%)	277
	Benjamin Harrison	Republican	5,179,244 (42.9%)	145
	James B. Weaver	People's	1,024,280 (8.5%)	22
1896	**William McKinley**	Republican	7,108,480 (51.0%)	271
	William J. Bryan	Democrat; Populist	6,511,495 (46.7%)	176
1900	**William McKinley**	Republican	7,218,039 (51.6%)	292
	(**Theodore Roosevelt,** 1901)			
	William J. Bryan	Democrat; Populist	6,358,345 (45.5%)	155
1904	**Theodore Roosevelt**	Republican	7,626,593 (56.4%)	336
	Alton B. Parker	Democrat	5,082,898 (37.6%)	140
	Eugene V. Debs	Socialist	402,489 (2.9%)	
1908	**William H. Taft**	Republican	7,676,258 (51.5%)	321
	William J. Bryan	Democrat	6,406,801 (43.0%)	162
	Eugene V. Debs	Socialist	420,380 (2.8%)	
1912	**Woodrow Wilson**	Democrat	6,293,152 (41.8%)	435
	Theodore Roosevelt	Progressive	4,119,207 (27.3%)	88
	William H. Taft	Republican	3,486,383 (23.1%)	8
	Eugene V. Debs	Socialist	900,369 (5.9%)	
1916	**Woodrow Wilson**	Democrat	9,126,300 (49.2%)	277
	Charles E. Hughes	Republican	8,546,789 (46.1%)	254
1920	**Warren G. Harding**	Republican	16,133,314 (60.3%)	404
	(**Calvin Coolidge,** 1923)			
	James M. Cox	Democrat	9,140,884 (34.1%)	127
	Eugene V. Debs	Socialist	913,664 (3.4%)	
1924	**Calvin Coolidge**	Republican	15,717,553 (54.0%)	382
	John W. Davis	Democrat	8,386,169 (28.8%)	136
	Robert M. La Follette	Progressive	4,814,050 (16.5%)	13
1928	**Herbert C. Hoover**	Republican	21,411,991 (58.2%)	444
	Alfred E. Smith	Democrat	15,000,185 (40.7%)	87
1932	**Franklin D. Roosevelt**	Democrat	22,825,016 (57.4%)	472
	Herbert C. Hoover	Republican	15,758,397 (39.6%)	59
	Norman Thomas	Socialist	883,990 (2.2%)	
1936	**Franklin D. Roosevelt**	Democrat	27,747,636 (60.7%)	523
	Alfred M. Landon	Republican	16,679,543 (36.5%)	8
	William Lemke	Union	892,492 (1.9%)	
1940	**Franklin D. Roosevelt**	Democrat	27,263,448 (54.7%)	449
	Wendell L. Wilkie	Republican	22,336,260 (44.8%)	82
1944	**Franklin D. Roosevelt**	Democrat	25,611,936 (53.3%)	432
	(**Harry S Truman,** 1945)			
	Thomas E. Dewey	Republican	22,013,372 (45.8%)	99

Year	Candidates	Party	Popular Vote	Electoral Vote
1948	**Harry S Truman**	Democrat	24,105,587 (49.5%)	303
	Thomas E. Dewey	Republican	21,970,017 (45.1%)	189
	J. Strom Thurmond	States' Rights	1,169,134 (2.4%)	39
	Henry A. Wallace	Progressive	1,157,057 (2.3%)	
1952	**Dwight D. Eisenhower**	Republican	33,936,137 (55.1%)	442
	Adlai E. Stevenson	Democrat	27,314,649 (44.3%)	89
1956	**Dwight D. Eisenhower**	Republican	35,585,245 (57.3%)	457
	Adlai E. Stevenson	Democrat	26,030,172 (41.9%)	73
1960	**John F. Kennedy** (**Lyndon B. Johnson,** 1963)	Democrat	34,221,344 (49.7%)	303
	Richard M. Nixon	Republican	34,106,671 (49.5%)	219
1964	**Lyndon B. Johnson**	Democrat	43,126,584 (61.0%)	486
	Barry M. Goldwater	Republican	27,177,838 (38.4%)	52
1968	**Richard M. Nixon**	Republican	31,783,148 (43.4%)	301
	Hubert H. Humphrey	Democrat	31,274,503 (42.7%)	191
	George C. Wallace	Amer. Independent	9,901,151 (13.5%)	46
1972	**Richard M. Nixon**	Republican	47,170,179 (60.6%)	520
	George S. McGovern	Democrat	29,171,791 (37.5%)	17
1974	**Gerald R. Ford**	Republican	Appointed on August 9, 1974 as President after the resignation of Richard M. Nixon. No election was held.	
1976	**Jimmy Carter**	Democrat	40,828,587 (50.1%)	297
	Gerald R. Ford	Republican	39,147,613 (48.0%)	240

Because only the leading candidates are listed, popular vote percentages do not always total 100. The elections of 1800 and 1824, in which no candidate received an electoral-vote majority, were decided in the House of Representatives.

Election Returns are from *Congressional Quarterly, Presidential Elections, Since 1789* (1975) and *Congressional Quarterly Weekly Reports* (March 19, 1977).

The Vice Presidency and the Cabinet, 1789–1978

VICE PRESIDENT

John Adams	1789-97
Thomas Jefferson	1797-1801
Aaron Burr	1801-05
George Clinton	1805-13
Elbridge Gerry	1813-17
Daniel D. Tompkins	1817-25
John C. Calhoun	1825-33
Martin Van Buren	1833-37
Richard M. Johnson	1837-41
John Tyler	1841
George M. Dallas	1845-49
Millard Fillmore	1849-50
William R. King	1853-57
John C. Breckinridge	1857-61
Hannibal Hamlin	1861-65
Andrew Johnson	1865
Schuyler Colfax	1869-73
Henry Wilson	1873-77
William A. Wheeler	1877-81
Chester A. Arthur	1881
Thomas A. Hendricks	1885-89
Levi P. Morton	1889-93
Adlai E. Stevenson	1893-97
Garret A. Hobart	1897-1901
Theodore Roosevelt	1901
Charles W. Fairbanks	1905-09
James S. Sherman	1909-13
Thomas R. Marshall	1913-21
Calvin Coolidge	1921-23
Charles G. Dawes	1925-29
Charles Curtis	1929-33
John Nance Garner	1933-41
Henry A. Wallace	1941-45
Harry S. Truman	1945
Alben W. Barkley	1949-53
Richard M. Nixon	1953-61
Lyndon B. Johnson	1961-63
Hubert H. Humphrey	1965-69
Spiro T. Agnew	1969-73
Gerald R. Ford	1973-74
Nelson A. Rockefeller	1974-76
Walter F. Mondale	1977

SECRETARY OF STATE (1789–)

Thomas Jefferson	1789
Edmund Randolph	1794
Timothy Pickering	1795
John Marshall	1800
James Madison	1801
Robert Smith	1809
James Monroe	1811
John Q. Adams	1817
Henry Clay	1825
Martin Van Buren	1829
Edward Livingston	1831
Louis McLane	1833
John Forsyth	1834
Daniel Webster	1841
Hugh S. Legaré	1843
Abel P. Upshur	1843
John C. Calhoun	1844
James Buchanan	1845
John M. Clayton	1849
Daniel Webster	1850
Edward Everett	1852
William L. Marcy	1853
Lewis Cass	1857
Jeremiah S. Black	1860
William H. Seward	1861
E. B. Washburne	1869
Hamilton Fish	1869
William M. Evarts	1877
James G. Blaine	1881
F. T. Frelinghuysen	1881
Thomas F. Bayard	1885
James G. Blaine	1889
John W. Foster	1892
Walter Q. Gresham	1893
Richard Olney	1895
John Sherman	1897
William R. Day	1897
John Hay	1898
Elihu Root	1905
Robert Bacon	1909
Philander C. Knox	1909
William J. Bryan	1913
Robert Lansing	1915
Bainbridge Colby	1920
Charles E. Hughes	1921
Frank B. Kellogg	1925
Henry L. Stimson	1929
Cordell Hull	1933
E. R. Stettinius, Jr.	1944
James F. Byrnes	1945
George C. Marshall	1947
Dean Acheson	1949
John Foster Dulles	1953
Christian A. Herter	1959
Dean Rusk	1961
William P. Rogers	1969

Henry A. Kissinger	1973
Cyrus Vance	1977

SECRETARY OF THE TREASURY (1789–   )

Alexander Hamilton	1789
Oliver Wolcott	1795
Samuel Dexter	1801
Albert Gallatin	1801
G. W. Campbell	1814
A. J. Dallas	1814
William H. Crawford	1816
Richard Rush	1825
Samuel D. Ingham	1829
Louis McLane	1831
William J. Duane	1833
Roger B. Taney	1833
Levi Woodbury	1834
Thomas Ewing	1841
Walter Forward	1841
John C. Spencer	1843
George M. Bibb	1844
Robert J. Walker	1845
William M. Meredith	1849
Thomas Corwin	1850
James Guthrie	1853
Howell Cobb	1857
Philip F. Thomas	1860
John A. Dix	1861
Salmon P. Chase	1861
Wm. P. Fessenden	1864
Hugh McCulloch	1865
George S. Boutwell	1869
William A. Richardson	1873
Benjamin H. Bristow	1874
Lot M. Morrill	1876
John Sherman	1877
William Windom	1881
Charles J. Folger	1881
Walter Q. Gresham	1884
Hugh McCulloch	1884
Daniel Manning	1885
Charles S. Fairchild	1887
William Windom	1889
Charles Foster	1891
John G. Carlisle	1893
Lyman J. Gage	1897
Leslie M. Shaw	1902
George B. Cortelyou	1907
Franklin MacVeagh	1909
William G. McAdoo	1913
Carter Glass	1919
David F. Houston	1919
Andrew W. Mellon	1921
Ogden L. Mills	1932
William H. Woodin	1933
Henry Morgenthau, Jr.	1934
Fred M. Vinson	1945
John W. Snyder	1946
George M. Humphrey	1953
Robert B. Anderson	1957
C. Douglas Dillon	1961
Henry H. Fowler	1965
David M. Kennedy	1969
John B. Connally	1970
George P. Shultz	1972
William E. Simon	1974
Michael W. Blumenthal	1977

SECRETARY OF WAR (1789–1947)

Henry Knox	1789
Timothy Pickering	1795
James McHenry	1796
John Marshall	1800
Samuel Dexter	1800
Roger Griswold	1801
Henry Dearborn	1801
William Eustis	1809
John Armstrong	1813
James Monroe	1814
William H. Crawford	1815
Isaac Shelby	1817
George Graham	1817
John C. Calhoun	1817
James Barbour	1825
Peter B. Porter	1828
John H. Eaton	1829
Lewis Cass	1831
Benjamin F. Butler	1837
Joel R. Poinsett	1837
John Bell	1841
John McLean	1841
John C. Spencer	1841
James M. Porter	1843
William Wilkins	1844
William L. Marcy	1845
George W. Crawford	1849
Charles M. Conrad	1850
Jefferson Davis	1853
John B. Floyd	1857
Joseph Holt	1861
Simon Cameron	1861
Edwin M. Stanton	1862
Ulysses S. Grant	1867
Lorenzo Thomas	1868
John M. Schofield	1868
John A. Rawlins	1869
William T. Sherman	1869
William W. Belknap	1869
Alphonso Taft	1876
James D. Cameron	1876
George W. McCrary	1877
Alexander Ramsey	1879
Robert T. Lincoln	1881
William C. Endicott	1885
Redfield Proctor	1889
Stephen B. Elkins	1891
Daniel S. Lamont	1893
Russell A. Alger	1897
Elihu Root	1899
William H. Taft	1904
Luke E. Wright	1908
J. M. Dickinson	1909
Henry L. Stimson	1911
L. M. Garrison	1913
Newton D. Baker	1916
John W. Weeks	1921
Dwight F. Davis	1925
James W. Good	1929
Patrick J. Hurley	1929
George H. Dern	1933
H. A. Woodring	1936
Henry L. Stimson	1940
Robert P. Patterson	1945
Kenneth C. Royall	1947

SECRETARY OF THE NAVY (1798–1947)

Benjamin Stoddert	1798
Robert Smith	1801
Paul Hamilton	1809
William Jones	1813
B. W. Crowninshield	1814
Smith Thompson	1818
S. L. Southard	1823
John Branch	1829
Levi Woodbury	1831
Mahlon Dickerson	1834
James K. Paulding	1838
George E. Badger	1841
Abel P. Upshur	1841
David Henshaw	1843

Thomas W. Gilmer	1844
John Y. Mason	1844
George Bancroft	1845
John Y. Mason	1846
William B. Preston	1849
William A. Graham	1850
John P. Kennedy	1852
James C. Dobbin	1853
Isaac Toucey	1857
Gideon Welles	1861
Adolph E. Borie	1869
George M. Robeson	1869
R. W. Thompson	1877
Nathan Goff, Jr.	1881
William H. Hunt	1881
William E. Chandler	1881
William C. Whitney	1885
Benjamin F. Tracy	1889
Hilary A. Herbert	1893
John D. Long	1897
William H. Moody	1902
Paul Morton	1904
Charles J. Bonaparte	1905
Victor H. Metcalf	1907
T. H. Newberry	1908
George von L. Meyer	1909
Josephus Daniels	1913
Edwin Denby	1921
Curtis D. Wilbur	1924
Charles F. Adams	1929
Claude A. Swanson	1933
Charles Edison	1940
Frank Knox	1940
James V. Forrestal	1945

SECRETARY OF DEFENSE (1947–)

James V. Forrestal	1947
Louis A. Johnson	1949
George C. Marshall	1950
Robert A. Lovett	1951
Charles E. Wilson	1953
Neil H. McElroy	1957
Thomas S. Gates, Jr.	1959
Robert S. McNamara	1961
Clark M. Clifford	1968
Melvin R. Laird	1969
Elliot L. Richardson	1973
James R. Schlesinger	1973
Donald Rumsfield	1974
Harold Brown	1977

POSTMASTER GENERAL (1789–1970)

Samuel Osgood	1789
Timothy Pickering	1791
Joseph Habersham	1795
Gideon Granger	1801
Return J. Meigs, Jr.	1814
John McLean	1823
William T. Barry	1829
Amos Kendall	1835
John M. Niles	1840
Francis Granger	1841
Charles A. Wickliffe	1841
Cave Johnson	1845
Jacob Collamer	1849
Nathan K. Hall	1850
Samuel D. Hubbard	1852
James Campbell	1853
Aaron V. Brown	1857
Joseph Holt	1859
Horatio King	1861
Montgomery Blair	1861
William Dennison	1864
Alexander W. Randall	1866
John A. J. Creswell	1869
James W. Marshall	1874
Marshall Jewell	1874
James N. Tyner	1876
David M. Key	1877
Horace Maynard	1880
Thomas L. James	1881
Timothy O. Howe	1881
Walter Q. Gresham	1883
Frank Hatton	1884
William F. Vilas	1885
Don M. Dickinson	1888
John Wanamaker	1889
Wilson S. Bissel	1893
William L. Wilson	1895
James A. Gary	1897
Charles E. Smith	1898
Henry C. Payne	1902
Robert J. Wynne	1904
George B. Cortelyou	1905
George von L. Meyer	1907
F. H. Hitchcock	1909
Albert S. Burleson	1913
Will H. Hays	1921
Hubert Work	1922
Harry S. New	1923
Walter F. Brown	1929
James A. Farley	1933
Frank C. Walker	1940
Robert E. Hannegan	1945
J. M. Donaldson	1947
A. E. Summerfield	1953
J. Edward Day	1961
John A. Gronouski	1963
Lawrence F. O'Brien	1965
W. Marvin Watson	1968
Winton M. Blount	1969

ATTORNEY GENERAL (1789–)

Edmund Randolph	1789
William Bradford	1794
Charles Lee	1795
Theophilus Parsons	1801
Levi Lincoln	1801
Robert Smith	1805
John Breckinridge	1805
Caesar A. Rodney	1807
William Pinkney	1811
Richard Rush	1814
William Wirt	1817
John M. Berrien	1829
Roger B. Taney	1831
Benjamin F. Butler	1833
Felix Grundy	1838
Henry D. Gilpin	1840
John J. Crittenden	1841
Hugh S. Legaré	1841
John Nelson	1843
John Y. Mason	1845
Nathan Clifford	1846
Isaac Toucey	1848
Reverdy Johnson	1849
John J. Crittenden	1850
Caleb Cushing	1853
Jeremiah S. Black	1857
Edwin M. Stanton	1860
Edward Bates	1861
Titian J. Coffey	1863
James Speed	1864
Henry Stanbery	1866
William M. Evarts	1868
Ebenezer R. Hoar	1869
Amos T. Ackerman	1870
George H. Williams	1871
Edward Pierrepont	1875
Alphonso Taft	1876
Charles Devens	1877

Wayne MacVeagh	1881
Benjamin H. Brewster	1881
A. H. Garland	1885
William H. H. Miller	1889
Richard Olney	1893
Judson Harmon	1895
Joseph McKenna	1897
John W. Griggs	1897
Philander C. Knox	1901
William H. Moody	1904
Charles J. Bonaparte	1907
G. W. Wickersham	1909
J. C. McReynolds	1913
Thomas W. Gregory	1914
A. Mitchell Palmer	1919
H. M. Daugherty	1921
Harlan F. Stone	1924
John G. Sargent	1925
William D. Mitchell	1929
H. S. Cummings	1933
Frank Murphy	1939
Robert H. Jackson	1940
Francis Biddle	1941
Tom C. Clark	1945
J. H. McGrath	1949
J. P. McGranery	1952
H. Brownell, Jr.	1953
William P. Rogers	1957
Robert F. Kennedy	1961
Nicholas Katzenbach	1964
Ramsey Clark	1967
John N. Mitchell	1969
Richard G. Kleindienst	1972
Elliot L. Richardson	1973
William Saxbe	1974
Edward H. Levi	1974
Griffin B. Bell	1977

SECRETARY OF THE INTERIOR (1849–)

Thomas Ewing	1849
T. M. T. McKennan	1850
Alexander H. H. Stuart	1850
Robert McClelland	1853
Jacob Thompson	1857
Caleb B. Smith	1861
John P. Usher	1863
James Harlan	1865
O. H. Browning	1866
Jacob D. Cox	1869
Columbus Delano	1870
Zachariah Chandler	1875
Carl Schurz	1877
Samuel J. Kirkwood	1881
Henry M. Teller	1881
L. Q. C. Lamar	1885
William F. Vilas	1888
John W. Noble	1889
Hoke Smith	1893
David R. Francis	1896
Cornelius N. Bliss	1897
E. A. Hitchcock	1899
James R. Garfield	1907
R. A. Ballinger	1909
Walter L. Fisher	1911
Franklin K. Lane	1913
John B. Payne	1920
Albert B. Fall	1921
Hubert Work	1923
Roy O. West	1928
Ray L. Wilbur	1929
Harold L. Ickes	1933
Julius A. Krug	1946
Oscar L. Chapman	1949
Douglas McKay	1953
Fred A. Seaton	1956
Stewart L. Udall	1961
Walter J. Hickel	1969
Rogers C. B. Morton	1971
Thomas S. Kleppe	1975
Cecil D. Andrus	1977

SECRETARY OF AGRICULTURE (1889–)

Norman J. Colman	1889
Jeremiah M. Rusk	1889
J. Sterling Morton	1893
James Wilson	1897
David F. Houston	1913
Edward T. Meredith	1920
Henry C. Wallace	1921
Howard M. Gore	1924
William M. Jardine	1925
Arthur M. Hyde	1929
Henry A. Wallace	1933
Claude R. Wickard	1940
Clinton P. Anderson	1945
Charles F. Brannan	1948
Ezra Taft Benson	1953
Orville L. Freeman	1961
Clifford M. Hardin	1969
Earl L. Butz	1971
John A. Knebel	1976
Bob Bergland	1977

SECRETARY OF COMMERCE AND LABOR (1903–1913)

George B. Cortelyou	1903
Victor H. Metcalf	1904
Oscar S. Straus	1906
Charles Nagel	1909

SECRETARY OF COMMERCE (1913–)

William C. Redfield	1913
Joshua W. Alexander	1919
Herbert Hoover	1921
William F. Whiting	1928
Robert P. Lamont	1929
Roy D. Chapin	1932
Daniel C. Roper	1933
Harry L. Hopkins	1939
Jesse Jones	1940
Henry A. Wallace	1945
W. A. Harriman	1946
Charles Sawyer	1948
Sinclair Weeks	1953
Lewis L. Strauss	1958
F. H. Mueller	1959
Luther Hodges	1961
John T. Connor	1965
A. B. Trowbridge	1967
C. R. Smith	1968
Maurice H. Stans	1969
Peter G. Peterson	1972
Frederick B. Dent	1973
Elliot L. Richardson	1974
Juanita M. Kreps	1977

SECRETARY OF LABOR (1913–)

William B. Wilson	1913
James J. Davis	1921
William N. Doak	1930
Frances Perkins	1933
L. B. Schwellenbach	1945
Maurice J. Tobin	1948
Martin P. Durkin	1953
James P. Mitchell	1953
Arthur J. Goldberg	1961
W. Willard Wirtz	1962
George P. Shultz	1969
James D. Hodgson	1970

Peter J. Brennan	1973
W. J. Usery, Jr.	1974
Ray Marshall	1977

SECRETARY OF HEALTH, EDUCATION, AND WELFARE (1953–)

Oveta Culp Hobby	1953
Marion B. Folsom	1955
Arthur S. Flemming	1958
Abraham A. Ribicoff	1961
Anthony J. Celebrezze	1962
John W. Gardner	1965
Wilbur J. Cohen	1968
Robert H. Finch	1969
Elliot L. Richardson	1970
Caspar W. Weinberger	1973
David Matthews	1974
Joseph A. Califano, Jr.	1977

SECRETARY OF HOUSING AND URBAN DEVELOPMENT (1966–)

Robert C. Weaver	1966
George W. Romney	1969
James T. Lynn	1973
Carla Anderson Hills	1974
Patricia Harris	1977

SECRETARY OF TRANSPORTATION (1967–)

Alan S. Boyd	1967
John A. Volpe	1969
Claude S. Brinegar	1973
William T. Coleman	1974
Brock Adams	1977

SECRETARY OF ENERGY (1977–)

James R. Schlesinger	1977

Index

K

L

O

Q

R

X

Y

Z